ESSENTIALS
OF
MERCANTILE LAW

ESSENTIALS
OF
MERCANTILE LAW

BY

KENNETH SMITH

M.Sc.(Econ.), B.Com., Ph.D., A.C.C.S., F.S.S.

of Lincoln's Inn, Barrister-at-Law,
Late Head of the Department of Commerce and Management,
Mid-Essex Technical College and School of Art

AND

DENIS J. KEENAN

LL.B.(Hons.), F.C.I.S., D.M.A., Cert. E., M.B.I.M.

of the Middle Temple, Barrister-at-Law,
Formerly Head of Department of Business Studies and Law,
Mid-Essex Technical College and School of Art,
Visiting Lecturer, City of London Polytechnic

PITMAN PUBLISHING

First published 1965
First paperback edition 1967
Reprinted 1967
Second edition 1969
Reprinted 1970
Reprinted 1972
Third edition 1973

SIR ISAAC PITMAN AND SONS LTD
Pitman House, Parker Street, Kingsway, London WC2B 5PB
Pitman House, 158 Bouverie Street, Carlton, Victoria 3053, Australia
P.O. Box 11231, Johannesburg, South Africa
P.O. Box 46038, Portal Street, Nairobi, Kenya

THE CARSWELL COMPANY LTD, CANADA

ISBN: 0 273 36046 9

Text set in 10/11 pt Monotype Baskerville, printed by letterpress, and
bound in Great Britain at The Pitman Press, Bath
L.869:44

PREFACE TO THIRD EDITION

COMMERCIAL law continues to develop rapidly and I have tried in this edition to keep pace with that development even though the book has in consequence increased in length yet again. There are three main approaches to this problem:

(*a*) to retain the subject areas formerly covered but to cut down the content of each;

(*b*) to reduce the number of subject areas covered and retain a reasonable depth of treatment in each;

(*c*) to retain the subject areas formerly covered and the level of treatment, relying on the teacher to make an appropriate selection from the available material.

In my view the approach outlined in (*c*) above is to be preferred. In the last analysis a student's understanding of the subject and the benefit which he derives from it in his subsequent career depend upon the ability of his teacher to decide, on the basis of his information with regard to the related studies in a course (of which law is often only a part), which topics ought to be covered and in what depth.

I believe it is wrong for the author of a general work of this kind to reach definitive conclusions as to the academic needs of the generality of students following business studies and other courses. In doing so he is tending to impose his views upon those whose task it is to teach the subject. This I would not wish to do. Obviously the commercial viability of a book has to be taken into account, but I have been fortunate in my choice of publishers who have never adopted a wholly rigid attitude in this matter. This explains at least in part the success which the book has achieved.

The matter of the suitability of the book for a particular course is also something which I am glad to leave to the teacher concerned, and in the case of external examinations, to the examining body concerned. It is my hope that both those who teach and those who examine will continue to find the book useful.

The ever-increasing volume of case law has led in this edition to a different approach to certain of the summaries of cases. Where a recent case illustrates only the application of existing law to a new fact situation, the summary of that case has been reduced in size and given the same main number as the leading case, being distinguished from it by the addition of the letters 'a', 'b', 'c' and so on.

I have tried my best to ensure that the book is free from error but it is unlikely that I have entirely succeeded. In this connection I would like to say how much I value the comments of teachers, students and reviewers who have been kind enough to draw my attention to mistakes in previous editions.

October, 1972
D.J.K.

PREFACE TO FIRST EDITION

THIS book has been written for students preparing for professional examinations and the writers have borne in mind particularly the needs of students in technical and commercial colleges.

Mercantile law is a difficult subject—indeed it is a collection of subjects—and examiners year by year demand an ever wider and more comprehensive knowledge of the various topics which normally fall under this heading. We have deliberately made certain omissions—partly to keep down the bulk of the book, but mainly on educational grounds, since a superficial knowledge of a large variety of subjects is, in our opinion, useless. We have, therefore, while giving a coverage wide enough for students preparing for external examinations, aimed at a depth of treatment of the major topics that will enable examiners setting internal assessed papers to improve their standards in those subjects we believe to be important and fundamental. For the benefit of those who have not preceded their study of Mercantile Law with a course in General Principles of English Law, we have included at the beginning of the book a comprehensive chapter on the Law of Contract.

This book covers the following syllabuses in Mercantile Law—The Final Examinations of the Chartered Institute of Secretaries and the Corporation of Secretaries; the Intermediate Examination of the Association of Certified and Corporate Accountants and, with the inclusion of a chapter on Registered Companies, the relevant sections of the subject in the Part II Examination of the Institute of Bankers. It will also be of great help to students preparing for a variety of other professional examinations even where the coverage is not quite complete, e.g. those of the Institute of Cost and Works Accountants, and also to students in a variety of management courses which include the subject of Business Law.

We believe the book will prove particularly appropriate for courses for National and Higher National Certificates and Diplomas in Business Studies, where the lecturer has a greater freedom of treatment due to a greater control of his syllabuses, and where the lavish use of cases can add variety to the course and depth to the understanding.

As to the form of the book, we have adopted the same approach as in our earlier work, *English Law*. The cases are segregated at the end of the book, a practice which we feel gives the following advantages—

1. There is less interruption in the text, which makes it more readable.

2. The text can be read independently of the cases, which may be advisable on first reading so as to get a general grasp of a whole topic.

3. The cases can be studied independently of the text.

4. Examination students will find this lay-out eminently suitable for quick revision, since the reading of the text, which contains the names of the cases, will act as a check on the ability to recall the facts of the

cases. If this cannot be done, there is an easy numerical reference to the appendix.

5. Some cases illustrate more than one point of law, and printing them at the back and numbering them has enabled us to refer to them in several parts of the book without cumbrous cross-references or repetition.

6. The case summaries can be made long enough to include the relevant facts and the essential points of the judgment with, where appropriate, the gist of dissenting judgments.

Lack of time is the chief enemy of the technical college lecturer trying to cover an extensive syllabus, and the inclusion of so many cases will save time in dictating notes or preparing duplicated material.

In conclusion we would add that, while this book has been written with the needs of the examination student in mind, we feel that the treatment and coverage are such as to make it of considerable value to anyone engaged in the commercial world.

January, 1965.

K.S.
D.J.K.

CONTENTS

PAGE

Preface to Third Edition . . . . **v**

Preface to First Edition . . . . **vi**

CHAPTER I. THE LAW OF CONTRACT **1**

The essentials of a valid contract—Classification of contracts—The
formation of contracts—Offer and acceptance—Intention to create
legal relations—Formalities—Consideration—Capacity to contract
—Reality of consent—Mistake—Misrepresentation—Remedies—
Terms of the contract—Express terms—Implied terms—Contracts
uberrimae fidei—Duress and undue influence—Illegal contracts—
Contracts in restraint of trade—The Restrictive Trade Practices Acts,
1956 and 1968—The Resale Prices Act, 1964—Other relevant statutes
—Discharge of a contract—Remedies for Breach of contract—Quasi-
contractual rights and duties.

CHAPTER II. SOME FUNDAMENTAL CONCEPTS . . . **98**

Assignment of contractual rights—Bailment—Securities—Lien—
Mortgages of land—Mortgages of personal chattels—Bills of Sale—
Pawns and pledges—Pawnbrokers—Mortgages of choses in action.

CHAPTER III. THE SALE OF GOODS **121**

Goods—The existence of goods—Contracts of sale and similar transactions—The contract of sale—Conditions and warranties—Terms
implied by the Act—Liability of the manufacturer—Exclusion of
seller's liability—Treating a breach of condition as a breach of
warranty—Transfer of the property in the goods—Transfer of title
by non-owners—Performance of the contract—The remedies of the
seller—Remedies of the buyer—Special sales—Trade Descriptions
Acts 1968/72—Export sales.

CHAPTER IV. HIRE PURCHASE AND CREDIT SALES . . **168**

The nature of the agreement—Liability of the owner at common
law—Liability of the dealer at common law—Obligations of the
hirer at common law—The Hire Purchase Act, 1965—General
requirements—The right of cancellation—Right of determination—
Supply of documents and information—Legibility of documents—
Dealer's liability—Terms implied in hire-purchase agreements—
Owner's right to recover possession—Guarantees and indemnities—
Execution, distress and bankruptcy—Conditional sale agreements—
Credit sales—Motor vehicles on hire purchase or conditional sale—
Advertisements—The Crowther Report.

CHAPTER V. AGENCY . . . .
PAGE
191

Capacity—Creation of agency—The agency of a wife—The duties of an agent—Rights of the agent against his principal—Termination of agency—Limitation on principal's power to terminate the agency—Rights of third parties against principal and agent—Particular agents.

CHAPTER VI. PARTNERSHIPS 214

Nature of partnership—The partnership agreement—Relations of partners to one another—Relations of partners to persons dealing with them—Dissolution of partnership—Powers on dissolution—Treatment of assets on dissolution—Bankruptcy of partners—Limited partnerships.

CHAPTER VII. REGISTERED COMPANIES 236

The memorandum of association—Articles of association—Membership of a company—Nominee holdings—Directors—Share capital—The prospectus—Underwriting—Incorporation—Promoters—Share certificates—Meetings and resolutions—Company accounts—Dividends and profits—Alteration of share capital—Borrowing powers—Public and private companies—Statutory books and returns—Auditors—Winding up—Creditors—Secured creditors—The costs of winding up—Preferential creditors—Unsecured creditors—Judgment creditors—Rights of contributories.

CHAPTER VIII. NEGOTIABLE INSTRUMENTS . . . 286

The nature of a bill of exchange—The advantages of a bill of exchange—The life cycle of a bill of exchange—The Bills of Exchange Act, 1882—The holder of a bill—Order in writing—Acceptance—Payment—Time of payment—Negotiability—Holders—Discharge of a bill—Liability of the parties—Bills in a set—Lost instruments—Conflict of laws—Promissory notes—Cheques—Relationship of banker and customer—Crossed cheques—Banker's protection.

CHAPTER IX. BANKRUPTCY 337

Acts of bankruptcy—The petition—Capacity in bankruptcy—The receiving order—Statement of affairs—Meetings of creditors—The public examination of the debtor—The adjudication order—The Official Receiver—The special manager—Committee of inspection—The trustee—The doctrine of relation back—Creditors—Composition and schemes of arrangement—The debtor's property—Disclaimer—Discharge of bankrupt.

CHAPTER X. INSURANCE 369

The contract of insurance—Types of policy—Duration of policy—The risk (1) Non-marine insurance; (2) Marine insurance—The premium—Claims—Insurable interest—Wagering policies—Double insurance—Average—Re-insurance—Subrogation—Assignment—Bankruptcy or liquidation of insured.

CHAPTER XI. CARRIAGE OF GOODS 406

Carriage by road—The Carriers Act, 1830—International carriage of goods by road—Carriage by rail—Carriage by inland waterways—Pipe-lines—Carriage by sea—Common law position—Carriage of Goods by Sea Act, 1924—Merchant Shipping Act—Affreightment—The Carriage of Goods by Sea Act, 1971—Carriage by Air—The original Warsaw Convention of 1929—The Amended Convention of 1955—Rules of non-international carriage—Carriage by Air (Supplementary Provisions) Act, 1962.

CHAPTER XII. SURETYSHIP AND GUARANTEE . . . 439

Surety's liability—Surety's rights against the creditor—Surety's rights against the principal debtor—The rights and liability of co-sureties—Discharge of guarantee.

CHAPTER XIII. ARBITRATION 449

The arbitration agreement—Arbitrators—Conduct of arbitration—The award—Common law submissions—Statutory arbitrations.

APPENDIX 461

Index to Statutes 709

Index to Cases 719

General Index 729

CHAPTER I

THE LAW OF CONTRACT

A CONTRACT may be defined as an *agreement*, enforceable by the law, between two or more persons to do or abstain from doing some act or acts, their intention being to create *legal relations* and not merely to exchange mutual promises.

The definition can be criticised in that some contracts turn out to be unenforceable and in addition not all legally binding agreements are true contracts. For example, a transaction by deed under seal derives its legally binding quality from the special way in which it is made rather than from the operation of the laws of contract. In consequence transactions under seal are not true contracts at all. Nevertheless the definition at least emphasises the fact that the basic elements of contracts are (i) an agreement; and (ii) an intention to create legal relations.

THE ESSENTIALS OF A VALID CONTRACT

The essential elements of the formation of a valid and enforceable contract can be summarised under the following headings—

(i) There must be offer and acceptance, which is in effect the agreement.

(ii) There must be an intention to create legal relations.

(iii) There is a requirement of written formalities in some cases.

(iv) There must be consideration (unless the agreement is under seal).

(v) The parties must have capacity to contract.

(vi) There must be genuineness of consent by the parties to the terms of the contract.

(vii) The contract must be legal and possible.

In the absence of one or more of these essentials, the contract may be void, voidable, or unenforceable.

CLASSIFICATION OF CONTRACTS

Before proceeding to examine the meaning and significance of the points enumerated above the following distinctions should be noted.

Void, Voidable and Unenforceable contracts. A *void* contract has no binding effect at all and in reality the expression is a contradiction in terms. However, it has been used by lawyers for a long time in order to describe particular situations in the law of contract and its use is now a matter of convenience. A *voidable* contract is binding on one of the parties but the other has the right, at his option, to set it aside.

An *unenforceable* contract is valid in all respects except that it cannot be enforced in a court of law by one or sometimes both of the parties should the other refuse to carry out his obligations under it.

We shall consider examples of contracts falling within the above categories in the law relating to *mistake* (void contracts), *misrepresentation* (voidable contracts) and *formalities* (unenforceable contracts).

Executed and Executory Contracts. A contract is said to be executed when one or both of the parties have done all that the contract requires. A contract is said to be *executory* when the obligations of one or both of the parties remain to be carried out. For example, if A and B agree to exchange A's scooter for B's motor cycle and do it immediately, the *possession* of the goods and the *right* to the goods are transferred *together* and the contract is *executed*. If they agree to exchange the following week the *right* to the goods is transferred but not the *possession* and the contract is *executory*. Thus an *executed* contract conveys a *chose in possession*, while an *executory* contract conveys a *chose in action*.

Speciality and Simple Contracts and Contracts of Record.

Speciality contracts are also called contracts under seal, or deeds. All the terms of such contracts are reduced to writing and then the contract is signed, sealed and delivered. The signature is usually attested, i.e. witnessed. A deed operates from the date of delivery, though a deed is presumed to have been delivered on the day of the date of the deed, unless this can be rebutted by evidence to the contrary. Delivery may be (*a*) *actual*, where the deed is handed over to the other party, or (*b*) *constructive*, where the party delivering the deed touches the seal with his finger and says: "I deliver this my act and deed!" This is then construed as delivery and the deed becomes operative. In many cases, however, there is no delivery, actual or constructive, and once a deed has been signed by the parties, it will be extremely difficult for either of them to show that the deed was not delivered. (*Per* Danckwerts, J., in *Stromdale and Ball Ltd.* v. *Burden*, [1952] 1 All E.R. 59.)

The general law of contract *requires* a deed in only one case, i.e. a lease of more than three years which must be under seal if it is to create a legal estate.

Sometimes a deed is delivered subject to a condition, e.g. that it is not effective until the purchase money has been paid; or is delivered now, but is not to become operative until some future time. In these cases the deed is not operative until the condition is carried out or the stipulated time has elapsed and such a deed has the special name of "escrow." (*Vincent* v. *Premo Enterprises* (*Voucher Sales*) *Ltd.*, 1969.)[1]

There are two forms of escrow—

  (i) Where the deed is delivered to a third party who delivers to the other party when the condition is fulfilled.
  (ii) Where the deed is delivered to the other party directly, but is not operative until the condition is fulfilled.

An escrow is useful where a person is selling property but will be abroad before completion. He may sign and deliver an escrow before leaving the country so that the deal can be completed if the conditions are carried out.

A deed has certain characteristics which serve to distinguish it from a simple contract—

(*a*) *Merger.* If a simple contract is afterwards embodied in a deed made between the same parties, the simple contract merges into, or is swallowed up by the deed, for the deed is the superior document. But if the deed is only intended to cover part of the terms of the previous simple contract, there is no merger of that part of the simple contract not covered by the deed.

(*b*) *Limitation of actions.* The right of action under a specialty contract is barred unless it is brought within twelve years from the date when the cause of action arises on it, i.e. when the deed could first have been sued upon. Time does not run from the date of making the deed. A similar right of action is barred under a simple contract after only six years. (Limitation Act, 1939.)

(*c*) *Consideration is not essential* to support a deed, though specific performance will not be granted if the promise is gratuitous. (See p. 93.) Simple contracts must be supported by consideration.

(*d*) *Estoppel.* Statements in a deed tend to be conclusive against the party making them, and although he might be able to prove they were not true, the rule of evidence called "estoppel" will prevent this by excluding the very evidence which would be needed. In modern law, however, a deed does not operate as an estoppel where one of the parties wishes to bring evidence to show fraud, duress, mistake, lack of capacity, illegality, or that the deed is an escrow. In addition where a deed is rectifiable (see p. 38) the doctrine of estoppel by deed does not bind the parties to it. (*Wilson* v. *Wilson*, 1969.)[2]

SIMPLE CONTRACTS form the great majority of contracts, and are sometimes referred to as parol contracts. This class includes all contracts not under seal, and for their enforcement they require consideration. Simple contracts may be made orally or in writing, or they may be inferred from the conduct of the parties; but no simple contract can exist which does not arise from a valid offer and a valid acceptance supported by some consideration. When these elements exist, the contract is valid in the absence of some vitiating element such as lack of capacity of one of the parties, lack of reality of consent, or illegality or impossibility of performance.

A CONTRACT OF RECORD consists of obligations imposed upon a person by the Crown in its judicial capacity. Examples are a recognisance binding a person over to be of good behaviour and arising from criminal proceedings, or a recognisance to appear as a witness in a Crown Court after giving a deposition before the magistrates. Such contracts are formed by an entry on the Court Records and the signing of a form by the individual concerned. There is no need for the Crown to sue on a recognisance. On failure to observe its terms, an extract of it is copied from the court's record and sent to the clerk of the peace, who directs the sheriff immediately to levy execution of the goods of the person giving the recognisance. There is a sense in which such contracts are not true contracts because of the absence of agreement of the person against whom the judgment is entered.

THE FORMATION OF CONTRACT

In order to decide whether a contract has come into being it is necessary to establish that there has been an *agreement* between the parties. In consequence it must be shown that an *offer* was made by one party (called the offeror) which was *accepted* by the other party (called the offeree), and that *legal relations* were intended.

OFFER AND ACCEPTANCE

A contract is an agreement and comes into existence when one party makes an offer which the other accepts. The person making the offer is called the offeror, and the person to whom it is made is called the offeree. An offer may be express or implied. Suppose X says to Y— "I will sell you this watch for £5," and Y says——"I agree." An express offer and acceptance have been made; X is the offeror and Y the offeree. Alternatively Y may say to X—"I will give you £5 for that watch." If X says—"I agree," then another express offer has been made, but Y is the offeror and X is the offeree. In both cases the acceptance brings a contract into being. In order to find out who makes the offer and who the acceptance, it is necessary to examine the way in which the contract is negotiated. Often it matters little, if at all; in some cases it is crucial.

Offer. An offer may be made to a specific person or to any member of a group of persons, or to the world at large (*Carlill* v. *Carbolic Smoke Ball Co.*, 1893),[3] though sometimes what looks like an offer may be no more than an invitation to make an offer, or as it is sometimes called an *invitation to treat*. If I expose in my shop window a coat priced £15, this is not an offer to sell. It is not possible for a person to enter the shop and say: "I accept your offer; here is the £15." It is the would-be buyer who makes the offer when tendering the money. (*Pharmaceutical Society of Great Britain* v. *Boots Cash Chemists Ltd.*, 1953.)[4] If by chance the coat has been wrongly priced, I shall be entitled to say: "I am sorry; the price is £50," and refuse to sell.

The same principles have been applied to prices set out in price lists, catalogues and circulars and advertisements. (*Spencer* v. *Harding*, 1870,[5] and *Partridge* v. *Crittenden*, 1968.)[6] In other cases, such as automatic vending machines, the position is doubtful, and it has not been decided whether such machines are invitations to treat or represent an implied offer which is accepted when a coin is put into the machine. However, it does seem that if a bus travels along a certain route, there is an *implied offer* on the part of its owners to carry passengers at the published fares for the various stages, and it would appear that when a passenger boards the bus, he makes an *implied acceptance* of the offer, agreeing to be bound by the company's conditions and to pay the appropriate fare. (*Wilkie* v. *London Passenger Transport Board*, [1947] 1 All E.R. 258.) With regard to negotiations for the sale of land the same principles are again applied with perhaps this difference that in the case of a sale of land the Court is likely to regard a communication as an invitation to treat unless the intention to contract is very clear. (*Harvey* v. *Facey*, 1893,[7] *Clifton* v. *Palumbo*, 1944,[8] and *Bigg* v. *Boyd Gibbins Ltd.*, 1971.)[9]

Problems relating to contractual offers have arisen in the case of *auction sales* but the position is now largely resolved. An advertisement of an auction is not an offer to hold it. (*Harris* v. *Nickerson*, 1873.)[10] At an auction the bid is the offer; the auctioneer's request for bids is merely an invitation to treat. The sale is complete when the hammer falls, and until that time any bid may be withdrawn. (*Payne* v. *Cave* (1789), 3 Term Rep. 148.)

The position when the auction is without reserve is not absolutely certain because it has never been clearly decided whether an advertisement to sell articles by auction without any reserve price constitutes an offer to sell to the highest bidder. If it does constitute such an offer, the article is purchased and the contract is made when the highest bidder is ascertained by the cessation of bids, and there is no need for the auctioneer to accept by fall of the hammer. The matter was considered *obiter* in *Warlow* v. *Harrison* (1859), 1 E & E 309, and it was said that once bidding commences in an auction without reserve, the auctioneer must sell to the highest bidder.

Acceptance. Once the existence of an offer has been proved, the Court must be satisfied that the offeree has accepted the offer, otherwise there is no contract. An agreement may nevertheless be inferred from the conduct of the parties. (*Brogden* v. *Metropolitan Railway*, 1877.)[11]

The person who accepts an offer must be aware that the offer has been made. Thus if B has found A's lost dog and, not having seen an advertisement by A offering a reward for its return, returns it out of goodness of heart, B will not be able to claim the reward. He cannot be held to accept an offer of which he is unaware. However, as long as the acceptor *is aware* of the making of the offer, his motive in accepting it is immaterial. (*Williams* v. *Carwardine*, 1833.)[12]

CONDITIONAL ASSENT. An acceptance must be absolute and unconditional. One form of conditional assent is an acceptance "subject to contract." The law has placed a special significance on these words, and they are always construed as meaning that the parties do not intend to be bound until a formal contract is prepared. (*Winn* v. *Bull*, 1877.)[13] However, if the statement is qualified and the terms of a proposed contract can be identified, the court will enforce it. (*Filby* v. *Hounsell*,

1896.)[14] A potential purchaser can generally recover any deposit paid if he does not continue with a "subject to contract" purchase. (*Chillingworth* v. *Esch*, 1923.)[15] Where the deposit had been paid to an estate agent it was thought that he received it as agent for the vendor so that the latter was liable to return the money even though he had not received it. (*Goding* v. *Frazer*, 1966,[16] *Burt* v. *Claude Cousins & Co. Ltd.*, 1971,[16a] but see now *Barrington* v. *Lee*, 1971.)[16b]

In other cases of conditional assent the attitude of the court is not so predictable, but it would seem that if the court decides that the further agreement of the parties is not a condition precedent to the formation of the contract, but is merely part of the performance of an already binding agreement, the court will enforce the contract. (*Branca* v. *Cobarro*, 1947.)[17] The effect of the use of the words "without prejudice" in letters forming the basis of negotiations between parties to a contract was considered by the court in *Tomlin* v. *Standard Telephone and Cables Ltd.*, 1969.[18] It was decided that the words meant "without prejudice to the position of the writer of it if the terms which he proposed therein were not accepted." If the terms were accepted a binding contract was established.

CONTRACTUAL TERMS. While considering the matter of conditional assent it is convenient to deal briefly with an additional problem which may face a court in certain of these cases.

A contract will not be enforced unless the parties have expressed themselves with reasonable clarity on the matter of essential terms. A situation may therefore exist in which there is sufficient assent to satisfy the basic requirements of offer and acceptance yet the contract is incomplete (or inchoate) as to certain of its terms.

In such a case it may be possible for the court to complete the contract by reference to a *trade practice* or *course of dealing* between the parties. (*Hillas* v. *Arcos*, 1932.)[19] Sometimes the contract itself may contain a method of completion by providing a formula, under which the particular term might be agreed, either with or without effective machinery (e.g. arbitration) for resolving disputes as to the application of the formula. However, provided a formula exists the Court will be prepared to apply it in a manner reasonable to the interests of the parties and enforce the contract. (*Foley* v. *Classique Coaches Ltd.*, 1934,[20] and *Brown* v. *Gould*, 1971.)[20a] If the Court cannot obtain assistance from the contract or other sources it will not usually complete the agreement for the parties, and the contract, being *inchoate*, cannot be enforced. (*Scammell* v. *Ouston*, 1941.)[21] However, a covenant in a conveyance that the purchaser should be given "the first option of purchasing . . . at a price to be agreed upon" certain adjoining land imposes an obligation on the vendor at least to offer the land at a price at which he is willing to sell. (*Smith* v. *Morgan*, *The Times*, March 26th, 1971.)

It should be noted that the court may *imply a term* into a contract in order to give "business efficacy" to it. Such an implied term is based upon the presumption that both parties would have agreed to include it in the contract if they had thought about it, and that the term is essential in order to achieve the *clear* intentions of the parties. (*The Moorcock*, 1889.)[22]

Furthermore, it is necessary to distinguish between a term which has yet to be agreed by the parties and a term on which they have agreed but is in the event meaningless or ambiguous. In the first case no contract exists unless the deficiency can be made good by the methods outlined above. In the second case it may be possible to ignore the term and enforce the contract without it. (*Nicolene* v. *Simmonds*, 1953.)[23] However, the court cannot ignore a term unless it represents the final agreement of the parties. If, as in *Scammell* v. *Ouston*, 1941,[21] the term is still being negotiated, the contract will be *inchoate* and unenforceable. In addition the term must be *clearly* severable from the rest of the contract, i.e. it must be possible to enforce the contract without it, which was not the case in *Scammell* v. *Ouston*, 1941.[21]

COUNTER-OFFER. A counter-offer is a rejection of the original offer and in some cases has the effect of cancelling it. Where the counter-offer *introduces a new term*, the original offer is cancelled (*Hyde* v. *Wrench*, 1840,[24] *Neale* v. *Merrett*, 1930,[24a] and *Northland Airlines Ltd.* v. *Dennis Ferranti Meters Ltd.*, 1971);[24b] but a simple request for information where the offeree merely *tries to induce a new term* may not amount to an actual counter-offer. (*Stevenson* v. *McLean*, 1880.)[25]

RETROSPECTIVE ACCEPTANCE. Acceptance may be retrospective, i.e. the parties may carry out certain acts on the assumption that a contract will eventually be made. When the acceptance is eventually made, it is capable of operating retrospectively, thus giving legal effect to everything that has been done before. That the contract is to operate retrospectively may be provided for by an express term in the contract or may be inferred from conduct. (*Trollope and Colls Ltd.* v. *Atomic Power Constructions Ltd.*, 1962.)[26]

TENDERS. It is common enough in business for companies wishing to buy goods to invite suppliers to submit tenders giving details of the price for which the goods may be bought. It is essential to understand precisely what is meant by "accepting" a tender, since different legal results are obtained according to the wording of the invitation to tender. If the invitation by its wording implies that the potential buyer *will* require the goods, acceptance of a tender sent in response to such an invitation results in a binding contract under which the buyer undertakes to buy all the goods specified in the tender from the person who has submitted it. On the other hand if the invitation by its wording suggests that the potential buyer *may* require the goods, acceptance of a tender results in a standing offer by the supplier to supply the goods set out in the tender as and when required by the person accepting it. Each time the buyer orders a quantity, there is a contract confined to that quantity; but if the buyer does not order any of the goods set out in the tender, or a smaller number than the supplier quoted for, there is no breach of contract. Conversely, if the person submitting the tender wishes to revoke his standing offer, he may do so, except in so far as the buyer has already ordered goods under the tender. These must be supplied or the tenderer is in breach of contract. (*Great Northern Railway* v. *Witham*, 1873.)[27]

Methods of Acceptance. An acceptance may be made in various ways. It may be made in writing or orally, but it must in general be communicated and communication must be made by a person authorised to make it. (*Powell* v. *Lee*, 1908.)[28] Silence cannot amount to acceptance, except perhaps in the case of prior consent by the offeree. Thus if P says to Q: "If I do not hear from you before noon tomorrow, I shall assume you accept my offer," he will find he is unable, at least without Q's consent, to bind Q in this way, and Q need take no action at all. (*Felthouse* v. *Bindley*, 1862.)[29] This rule of the common law goes some way towards preventing inertia selling, though protection is now provided by the Unsolicited Goods and Services Act, 1971 (see p. 101).

However, there are some cases in which the offeror is deemed to have waived communication of the acceptance. This most often occurs in the case of *unilateral contracts* such as a promise to pay money in return for some act to be carried out by the offeree. Performance of the act operates as an acceptance, and no communication is required. (*Carlill* v. *Carbolic Smoke Ball Co.*, 1893.)[3]

The offeror may stipulate a method of acceptance (*Eliason* v. *Henshaw*, 1819),[30] and where this is done it would seem that, if the offeror makes it clear that one method only will suffice, then there is no contract unless the offeree accepts by the method prescribed. Nevertheless in such a case the offeror could waive his right to have the acceptance communicated in a given way and agree to the substituted method. If the offeror has stipulated a method of acceptance *but does not make it clear that only one method will suffice*, then a quicker or equally expeditious method will be effective, since there is no prejudice to the offeror if he learns that the offer has been accepted sooner than, or at the same time as he would have known had the offeree used the prescribed method. (*Manchester Diocesan Council for Education* v. *Commercial and General Investments Ltd.*, 1969.)[31] Certainly an offer by telegram is good evidence of the offeror's desire for a quick reply so that a reply by letter would probably be ineffective.

If the offeror has not stipulated a method of acceptance, the offeree may choose his own method though where acceptance is by word of mouth, it is not enough that it be spoken, it must actually be heard by the offeror. In this connection an interesting development occurs with the use of the telephone and teleprinter. Since these are methods of instantaneous communication, it is held that the contract is not complete unless the apparent communication takes place. (*Entores Ltd.* v. *Miles Far East Corporation*, 1955.)[32]

Use of Post. The general rule is that acceptance must be communicated to the offeror and that the contract is made *when* and *where* the acceptance is received by the offeror. (*Entores Ltd.* v. *Miles Far East Corporation,* 1955.)[32]

However, if the post is the proper method of communication between the parties then acceptance is deemed complete immediately the letter of acceptance is posted, even if it is delayed or is lost or destroyed in the post so that it never reaches the offeror. (*Household Fire Insurance Co.* v. *Grant,* 1879.)[33] Nevertheless the letter of acceptance must be properly addressed and properly posted (*Re London and Northern Bank, ex parte Jones,* 1900)[34] and the court must be satisfied that it was within the contemplation of the parties that the post might be used as a method of communicating acceptance. It is not certain whether the exchange of contracts for the sale of land falls within the post rule and whether posting or delivery is the vital time. However, where the sale is governed by the Law Society's Conditions posting is regarded as the time of exchange.

Where there is a misdirection of the letter containing the offer, then the offer is made when it actually reaches the offeree, and not when it would have reached him in the ordinary course of post. (*Adams* v. *Lindsell,* 1818.)[35] In contrast with the rule regarding acceptance by post, a letter of revocation is not effective until it actually reaches the offeree, whereas a letter of acceptance is effective when it is posted. (*Byrne* v. *Van Tienhoven,* 1880.)[36] A telegram is effective as an acceptance when it is handed in at the post-office.

The better view is that, in English law, an acceptance cannot be recalled once it has been posted even though it has not reached the offeror. Thus, if X posted a letter accepting Y's offer to sell goods, X could not withdraw the acceptance by telephoning Y and asking him to ignore the letter of acceptance when it arrived, and Y could hold X bound by the contract if he wished to do so. This is obvious, the rules being what they are, since otherwise Y would be bound when the letter was posted, and X would be reserving the right to withdraw his acceptance during the transit of the letter even though Y was still bound. However, by Scots law the affect of an acceptance can be altered after posting. (*Dunmore (Countess)* v. *Alexander,* 1830.)[37]

There is some controversy as to whether agreement can result from *cross-offers.* For example, suppose X by letter offers to sell his scooter to Y for £50, and Y by means of a second letter, which crosses X's letter in the post, offers to buy X's scooter for £50. Can there be a contract? The matter was discussed by an English court in *Tinn* v. *Hoffman* (1873), 29 L.T. 271, and the court's conclusion was that no contract could arise. However, the matter is still at large and it is possible to hold the view that a contract would come into being where it appears that the parties have intended to create a legally binding agreement on the same footing.

Revocation of Offer. The general rule is that *an offer may be revoked at any time before acceptance* though sometimes there is what is known as an option attached to the offer, and time is given in which to make the decision whether to accept or not. If the offeror agrees to give seven days, then the offeree may accept the offer at any time within seven days, or he need not accept at all. However, the offeror need not keep the offer open for seven days but can revoke it, unless the offeree has given some consideration for the option. The option is really a separate contract to allow time to decide whether to accept the original offer or not. It was thought at one time that, where the option to buy property was not supported by consideration, the offer could be revoked by its sale to another, but in modern law it is necessary for the offeror to communicate the revocation to the offeree either himself, or by means of some reliable person. (*Stevenson* v. *McLean*, 1880.)[25]

Revocation to be effective must be communicated to the offeree before he has accepted the offer. The word "communication" merely implies that the revocation must have come to the knowledge of the offeree. (*Byrne* v. *Van Tienhoven*, 1880.)[36] Communication may be made directly by the offeror or may reach the offeree through some other reliable source. Suppose X offers to sell a car to Y and gives Y a few days to think the matter over without actually giving him a valid option. If, before Y has accepted, X sells the car to Z and Y hears from P that X has in fact sold the car, it will be of no avail for Y to purport to accept and try to enforce the contract against X. (*Dickinson* v. *Dodds*, 1876.)[38]

Where the offer consists of a promise in return for an act, as where a reward is offered for the return of lost property, the offer, although made to the whole world, can be revoked as any other offer can. It is thought to be enough that the same publicity be given to the revocation as was given to the offer, even though the revocation may not be seen by all the persons who saw the offer.

A more difficult problem arises when an offer which requires a certain act to be carried out is revoked after some person has begun to perform the act but before he has completed it. If, for example, X offers £1,000 to anyone who can successfully swim the Channel, and Y, deciding he will try to obtain the money, starts his swim from Dover, can X revoke his offer when Y is half way across the Channel? The better view is that he cannot on the grounds that an offer of the kind made by X is two offers in one, namely (i) to pay £1,000 to a successful swimmer and (ii) something in the nature of an option to hold the offer open for a reasonable time once performance has been embarked upon, so that the person trying to complete the task has a reasonable time in which to do so.

Lapse of Time. If a time for acceptance has been stipulated, then the offer lapses when the time has expired. If no time has been stipulated, then the acceptance must be within a reasonable time. What is reasonable is determined by the court from the circumstances of the case. (*Ramsgate Victoria Hotel Co.* v. *Montefiore*, 1866,[39] and *Manchester Diocesan Council or Education* v. *Commercial and General Investments Ltd.*,

1969.)[31] Where the offer is made by telegram, it is likely to lapse very quickly.

Conditional Offers. An offer may terminate on the happening of a given event if it is made subject to a condition that it will do so, e.g. that the offer is to terminate if the goods offered for sale are damaged before acceptance. Such a condition may be made expressly, but may also be implied from the circumstances. (*Financings Ltd.* v. *Stimson*, 1962.)[40]

Effect of Death of a Party. The effect of death would appear to vary according to the type of contract in question, whether the death is that of the offeror or offeree, and whether death takes place before or after acceptance.

(*a*) DEATH OF OFFEROR BEFORE ACCEPTANCE. It would seem that if the contract envisaged by the offer is not one involving the personality of the offeror, the death of the offeror will not, until notified to the offeree, prevent acceptance. (*Bradbury* v. *Morgan*, 1862.)[41] If the contract envisaged by the offer does involve a personal relationship, such as an offer to act as agent, then the death of the offeror prevents acceptance.

(*b*) DEATH OF OFFEREE BEFORE ACCEPTANCE. Once the offeree is dead, there is no offer which can be accepted. His executors cannot, therefore, accept the offer in his stead. The offer being made to a living person can only be accepted by that person and assumes his continued existence. The rule would seem to apply *whether the proposed contract involves a personal relationship or not.* (*Re Cheshire Banking Co., Duff's Executors' Case*, 1886.)[42]

(*c*) DEATH OF PARTIES AFTER ACCEPTANCE. Death after acceptance has normally no effect unless the contract is for personal services, when the liability under the contract ceases. Thus, if X sells his car to Y and before the car is delivered X dies, it would be possible for Y to sue X's personal representatives for breach of contract if they were to refuse to deliver the car. But if X agrees to play the piano at a concert and dies two days before the performance one could hardly expect his personal representatives to play the piano in his stead.

INTENTION TO CREATE LEGAL RELATIONS

The law will not necessarily recognise the existence of a contract simply because of the presence of mutual promises. Some agreements are not intended to be the subject of legal actions, and if the parties expressly declare, or clearly indicate in their agreement, that they do not intend to assume contractual obligations, then the law accepts and implements their intention. There are many promises made which are of such a nature that no reasonable person could imagine that there was any intention to create legal relations. If P invites Q to dinner, he does not also invite an action for damages if he fails to keep the appointment.

In deciding the question of intention the courts use an objective, not a subjective test, and what the parties had in mind is not conclusive. The court considers what inferences reasonable people would draw from the words or conduct of the parties. If reasonable people would assume that there was no intention to create a binding agreement, the courts will not enforce it.

The subject can be considered under two headings—

(i) **Cases where the parties have not expressly denied their intention to create legal relations.**

(*a*) *Advertisements*. It is a commonplace in business to advertise goods by making extravagant claims as to their efficacy, often supported by promises or guarantees of a vague character if the goods do not live up to expectations. The construction placed by the courts on such statements depends on the circumstances, but where a company deposits money in the bank against possible claims, then the court is likely to hold that legal relations were contemplated. (*Carlill* v. *Carbolic Smoke Ball Co.*, 1893.)[3] But not all advertisements are treated as serious offers, and advertising "puffs" are often treated as mere sales talk; otherwise the courts would be perpetually passing judgment on the merits or demerits of a host of products.

(*b*) *Family Agreements*. Many of these cannot be imagined to be the subject of litigation, but some may be. The question is basically one of construction, and the court looks at the words used and the surrounding circumstances. With regard to agreements between husband and wife it is difficult to draw precise conclusions from the decided cases. However, it seems that the courts will not enforce these agreements where—

(i) The husband and wife were living together when the agreement was made—on the ground perhaps that in the view of the court it would be unseemly and distressing to use legal proceedings for settling marital differences. (*Balfour* v. *Balfour*, 1919,[43] and *Spellman* v. *Spellman*, 1961.)[44] However, where husband and wife were not living together in amity when the agreement was made the court may enforce it. (*Merritt* v. *Merritt*, 1970.)[45]

(ii) The words used by the parties were uncertain—on the ground perhaps that uncertainty in deciding upon important terms of the agreement leads to the conclusion that there was no intention to create legal relations. (*Gould* v. *Gould*, 1969.)[46]

An agreement between husband and wife is much more likely to be enforced if it is clear and unequivocal. This might be achieved if the parties made an agreement supported by a simple note or memorandum setting out the terms and preferably prepared by a solicitor.

It should be noted that agreements of a non-domestic nature made between husband and wife may be enforceable, e.g. a husband may be his wife's tenant.

In family agreements other than those between husband and wife the court may reach the conclusion that legal relations can be inferred and the injured party may be given a remedy. (*Simpkins* v. *Pays*, 1955.)[47] This is particularly true where one of the parties has altered his position to his detriment in reliance on the promises of the other (*Parker* v. *Clark*, 1960),[48] though uncertainty as to terms normally leads to the conclusion that there was no contractual intent. (*Jones* v. *Padavatton*, 1969.)[49]

(c) *Other Cases.* In other situations whether there is an intention to create legal relations must be deduced by the Court from the circumstances of the case. (*Buckpitt* v. *Oates*, 1968.)[50] However in the case of clubs and societies, many of the relationships which exist and promises which are made are enforceable only as moral obligations. Thus, if a man competes for a prize in a golf competition and is the winner, he may not be able to sue for the prize he has won if it is not otherwise forthcoming.

(ii) Cases where the parties expressly deny any intention to create legal relations. Some types of agreement, which would normally be the subject of a contract, are expressly taken outside the scope of the law by the parties' agreeing to rely on each other's honour. (*Jones* v. *Vernon's Pools Ltd.*, 1938.)[51] In such cases there is a standardised agreement and the advantage of excluding legal action appears to be predominantly in favour of one of the parties, although it is difficult to see how pools could run if they had the prospect of weekly legal actions from disgruntled investors. It has been pleaded, but without success, that standardised agreements which exclude the possibility of legal redress are against public policy, and clearly if such procedures become widespread Parliament may have to intervene. There is no such objection where business men reach agreements at arm's length, and if the parties expressly declare or clearly indicate that they do not wish to assume contractual obligations, then the law accepts and implements their decision. (*Rose and Frank Co.* v. *Crompton and Brothers Ltd.*, 1925.)[52]

FORMALITIES

We have already discussed the main differences between contracts under seal and simple or "parol" contracts. In most cases it does not matter which of the various forms of simple contract is used and a contract made orally or by conduct will usually be just as effective as a written one. Exceptionally, however, written formalities are required.

Contracts which must be in writing. The following simple contracts are required by statute to be in writing otherwise they are *void*—

    (a) bills of exchange and promissory notes (see pp. 287 and 321);
    (b) hire-purchase contracts (see p. 172);
    (c) contracts of marine insurance (see p. 370);
    (d) acknowledgments of statute-barred debts (see p. 86).

Contracts which must be evidenced in writing. In two cases writing, though not essential to the formation of a contract, is needed for evidential purposes, and in its absence the courts will not enforce the agreement. These two special cases are—

    (i) contracts of guarantee, and
    (ii) contracts for the sale or other disposition of land or any interest in land.

The Statute of Frauds, 1677, originally set out six classes of contracts which required this evidential writing. The provision concerning land was embodied in Sect. 40 of the Law of Property Act, 1925, as part of the consolidation of the law of property. The provision regarding guarantees remained after the Statute of Frauds was largely repealed by the Law Reform (Enforcement of Contracts) Act, 1954.

Even in these cases the writing need not be in the form of a contract, but may be the exchange of letters or other memoranda; and where one party has partly performed his side of the contract, the courts may dispense with the need for written evidence. Further, the absence of a memorandum must be specially pleaded by the party seeking to rely on its absence, otherwise the court will hear oral evidence to prove the contract.

These rules apply to contracts of guarantee but they do not apply to contracts of indemnity. It is necessary, therefore, to distinguish between these two. In a contract of indemnity, the person giving the indemnity makes himself primarily liable by using such words as, "I will see that you are paid." In a contract of guarantee, the guarantor expects the person he has guaranteed to carry out his obligations, and the substance of the wording would be, "If he does not pay you, I will." An indemnity does not require writing because it did not come within the Statute of Frauds; a guarantee requires a memorandum. (*Mountstephen* v. *Lakeman,* 1871.)[53]

In this connection it should be noted that it is an essential feature of a guarantee that the person giving it is totally unconnected with the contract he guarantees except by reason of his promise to pay the debt. Thus a *del credere* agent who for an extra commission promises to make good losses incurred by his principal in respect of the unpaid debts of third parties introduced by the agent, gives an indemnity and not a guarantee because his undertaking to reimburse his principal is part of a wider transaction, i.e. agency.

Difficulties have arisen in the application of the provisions concerning land in cases dealing with the sale of crops. A distinction must be made between *fructus naturales* (natural products of the soil, or the products of things which do not have to be sown each year) and *fructus industriales* (crops produced annually by man). Thus, an agreement to sell growing timber or grass must be evidenced in writing but an agreement to sell growing potatoes need not be. (*Parker* v. *Staniland* (1809), 11 East, 362.) However, if the *fructus naturales* are to be cut at once by either party and therefore *no further benefit is to be derived from the soil* the contract is regarded as one for the sale of goods and no memorandum is required. (*Marshall* v. *Green* (1875), 1 C.P.D., 35.)

THE MEMORANDUM. The memorandum in writing, to satisfy the courts in the two cases where it is now required, need not be made when the contract is made, but must exist before the action is brought. There are four requirements—

(i) *It must contain the names or a sufficient description of the parties.* To be a memorandum within the Act a document need not contain the names of the parties. It is sufficient if they are described so as to be capable of identification even if this involves the giving of some oral evidence. (*Carr* v. *Lynch*, 1900.)[54]

The fact that one of the parties is misnamed will not prevent the contract being enforced if he can be identified by reference to characteristics other than his name. (*F. Goldsmith (Sicklesmere) Ltd.* v. *Baxter*, 1969.)[55]

(ii) *The subject matter of the contract must be described so that it can be identified, and all the material terms of the contract must be stated.* However, the subject matter may be sufficiently described without going into great detail, e.g. a memorandum recording the sale of "24 acres of land at Totmanslow," was held sufficient on proof that the seller had no other land there. (*Plant* v. *Bourne*, [1897] 2 Ch. 281.) The absence of a material term may be fatal to the memorandum, though not if it is beneficial to one party and the other party agrees to carry it out or the party to benefit agrees to waive it. (*Hawkins* v. *Price*, 1947,[56] and *Scott* v. *Bradley*, 1971.)[56a]

(iii) *The consideration must appear*, except in contracts of guarantee. In the latter case Sect. 3 of the Mercantile Law Amendment Act, 1856, dispenses with the necessity for setting out the consideration, but it must exist. The consideration for a guarantee is usually the extension of credit. It follows that the guarantee must be given before the credit was extended, otherwise it is for past consideration, and is unenforceable unless made under seal.

(iv) *The memorandum must contain the signature of the party to be charged or his agent properly authorised to sign.* This means in effect that there may be cases where one party has a sufficient memorandum to found an action, whereas the other may lack the necessary signature. The rule is made less rigid by a somewhat free interpretation of the word signature, and it may take any form so long as it was intended to be a signature. (*Caton* v. *Caton*, 1867.)[57] It may be printed, typed, or stamped, and mere initials or an identifying mark will suffice. It need not be at the end of the document, but may be in the middle or at the beginning. In the case of an auction sale, the auctioneer or his clerk signs for both buyer and seller.

The rigidity of these rules is further mitigated by the fact that the memorandum need not be a single document, but may consist of a number of connected documents. Oral evidence will be admitted to connect them if (*a*) one refers to the other; or (*b*) the documents are *prima facie* connected, since in the latter case proof of connection is not entirely oral. (*Pearce* v. *Gardner*, 1897,[58] and *Timmins* v. *Moreland Street Property Ltd.*, 1958.)[59] In addition a memorandum is not defective merely because it contains the words "subject to contract" provided that there is evidence to show that the parties have waived the provision. (*Griffiths* v. *Young*, 1970.)[60]

In the absence of a memorandum the contract is not void at common law but is unenforceable, although it may sometimes be relied upon as a defence. Thus, if X orally agrees to let Y dig for gravel on X's land, Y would not commit a trespass if he entered on the land to dig. If, however, X asks him to leave and Y refuses, then he may become a trespasser in spite of the contract, since it was at best a licence which has now been withdrawn. It follows that, if the contract is not void, money paid or property transferred under it cannot be recovered, unless there is a total lack of consideration. (*Monnickendam* v. *Leanse*, 1923.)[61]

Although the common law requires a written memorandum, there may still be equitable remedies, and equity will grant specific performance in suitable cases where the plaintiff has partly performed his agreement. This remedy is particularly appropriate in contracts for the sale or other disposition of land. The basis of this equitable jurisdiction probably stems from the maxim: "Equity will not allow a statute to be used as an engine of fraud."

The following conditions must exist before the doctrine can operate—

(*a*) *The contract must be one of which specific performance will be granted.* Specific performance is a discretionary remedy and it follows that: "He who comes to Equity must come with clean hands." It will not be granted where the court thinks damages are an adequate remedy, and never in the case of contracts with minors (see p. 94). This seems to confine the remedy to contracts concerning land, because Equity will not specifically enforce a guarantee.

(*b*) *Relationship of the act(s) of part performance to the alleged contract.* In *Chaproniere* v. *Lambert*, [1917] 2 Ch. 356, Washington, L. J., laid down in the Court of Appeal the doctrine that the act(s) of part performance relied on must be not only referable to a contract such as that alleged but referable to no other, and this rule was applied in some subsequent cases. Thus in *Rawlinson* v. *Ames*, 1925,[62] and *Broughton* v. *Snook*, 1938,[63] we find the court requiring acts of part performance which are unequivocal to a high degree. However strict adherence to this doctrine could produce hardship and in some circumstances run contrary to the over-riding principle that a Court of Equity will not allow a statute to be used as an engine of fraud, i.e. if the party seeking to enforce the contract can show that on the faith of that contract and in performance of his obligations under it he has so altered his position that unless the other party is bound by it there will be injustice of a kind which the statute cannot be thought to have had in contemplation. (*Daniels* v. *Trefusis*, 1914.)[64]

Accordingly in *Kingswood Estate Co. Ltd.* v. *Anderson*, [1962] 3 All E.R. 593, the Court of Appeal refused to follow *Chaproniere* v. *Lambert* and stated that the plaintiff's part performance need not be unequivocally exclusively referable to the contract alleged. It was sufficient if it proved the existence of some contract and was consistent with the contract which the plaintiff claimed existed. This principle was applied by Stamp, J., in *Wakeham* v. *Mackenzie*, 1968.[65]

However, acts of part performance may still be ineffective if they are explainable on grounds other than the existence of a contract. (*Maddison* v. *Alderson*, 1883.)[66]

(*c*) *There must be adequate oral evidence of the terms of the contract, and the act of part performance must be the act of the plaintiff.*

A mere payment of money is not by itself a sufficient act of part performance for this purpose, because money has no exclusive nature; such a payment raises no equity except the right to recover the money. Occupation of property is usually considered a sufficient act of part performance.

The Moneylenders Act, 1927. Under Sect. 6 of the Moneylenders Act, 1927, no contract for the repayment by a borrower of money lent by a moneylender (as defined in Sect. 6), and no security given by the borrower, is enforceable unless a memorandum is drawn up in accordance with this section. The memorandum must contain all the terms of the contract, and in particular must state the amount of the loan and the rate of interest and the date on which the loan was made. (*Congresbury Motors Ltd.* v. *Anglo-Belge Finance Co. Ltd.*, 1969.)[67]

It differs from the Statute of Frauds as follows—

(*a*) These provisions only operate against the lender though they can affect third parties. (*Spector* v. *Ageda*, 1971.)[68]

(*b*) The memorandum must be signed by the borrower personally; it need not be signed by the lender

(*c*) The memorandum must be signed or the security (if any) given, before the money is actually lent and a copy must be sent to the borrower within seven days of making the contract

(*d*) The memorandum must be drawn up expressly to record the transaction.

(*e*) Securities and guarantees are unenforceable.

A point of similarity between this statute and the Statute of Frauds is that money actually paid under oral contracts is in all cases irrecoverable, as the contracts are only unenforceable, not void so that a title to the money has passed.

CONSIDERATION

Consideration, which is essential to the formation of any contract not made under seal, was defined in *Currie* v. *Misa* (1875), L.R. 10 Ex. 153, as—

> Some right, interest, profit or benefit accruing to one party, or some forbearance, detriment, loss or responsibility given, suffered or undertaken by the other.

The payment of money is a common form of consideration.

Consideration may be *executory*, where the parties exchange promises to perform acts in the future, e.g. C promises to deliver goods to D and D promises to pay for the goods; or it may be *executed*, where one party promises to do something in return for the act of another, rather than for the mere promise of future performance of an act. Here the performance of the act is required before there is any liability on the promise. Where X offers a reward for the return of his lost dog, X is buying the act of the finder, and will not be liable until the dog is found and returned.

The definition in *Currie* v. *Misa* suggests that consideration always refers to the type called executed consideration, since it talks of "benefit" and "detriment," whereas in modern law executory contracts are enforceable. Perhaps the definition given by Sir Frederick Pollock is to be preferred—

> An act or forbearance of one party, *or the promise thereof*, is the price for which *the promise* of the other is bought, and the promise thus given for value is enforceable.

This definition, which was adopted by the House of Lords in *Dunlop* v. *Selfridge*, 1915,[69] fits executory contracts.

There are a number of general rules governing consideration—

(*a*) *Simple contracts must be supported by consideration.* This has a long history, and we can note only the following points.

Towards the end of the eighteenth century, Lord Mansfield attacked the doctrine of consideration in two ways. In *Pillans* v. *Van Mierop* (1765), 3 Burr. 1663, he said that where a contract was reduced to writing no consideration was necessary, thus reducing consideration to an aspect of evidence. It may be that this is why consideration is not necessary in a deed, for a deed is good evidence, being written and sealed, and entered into with due solemnity. In France and Scotland, gratuitous promises are enforced, but the court normally requires some good evidence, and often asks for writing. However, Lord Mansfield's attempt to dispense with consideration was short-lived, and his ruling was rejected in *Rann* v. *Hughes* (1778), 7 Term Rep. 350 n. Lord Mansfield also desired the recognition of pre-existing moral obligations as consideration, e.g. a promise to pay a statute-barred debt, or a promise after attaining majority to pay a debt contracted during minority, but this view was finally rejected in *Eastwood* v. *Kenyon* (1840), & El. 11 Ad. 438. Some of these matters are now dealt with by statute, e.g. a written acknowledgment of a statute-barred debt is binding, even though not supported by consideration. (Limitation Act 1939, Sect. 23.) Nevertheless, a promise to pay a debt incurred during minority is not enforceable. (Infants' Relief Act, 1874, Sect. 2.)

(*b*) *Consideration need not be adequate, but must have some value, however slight.* The courts do not exist to repair bad bargains, and though consideration must be present, the parties themselves must attend to its value. (*Haigh* v. *Brooks*, 1839.)[70] However, where the consideration embodied in a deal is woefully inadequate, it may raise a suspicion of fraud, duress, or undue influence on the part of the person gaining the advantage. The value must be of an economic character, and mere natural affection of itself is not enough. (*White* v. *Bluett*, 1853.)[71] Nevertheless acts or omissions even of a trivial nature may be sufficient to support a contract. (*Chappell* v. *Nestlé*, 1959.)[72] A self-seeking act in itself may not suffice, and in the case of *Carlill* v. *Carbolic Smoke Ball Co.*, 1893,[3] the consideration was provided not by using the smoke ball to cure influenza, but by the unpleasant method of its use. A gift promised conditionally may be binding, if the performance of the condition causes the promisee trouble or inconvenience, e.g. "I will give you my old car if you will tow it away." So too may a gift of property with onerous obligations attached to it, e.g. a promise to give away a lease would be binding, if the donee promised to perform the covenants to repair and pay rent. A promise to give away shares which were partly paid up would be good, if the donee promised to pay the outstanding calls.

The concept of *bailment* gives rise to problems because a person may be held liable for negligent damage to or loss of goods in his care, although he received no money or other consideration for looking after them. (*Coggs* v. *Bernard*, 1703,[73] and *Gilchrist Watt and Sanderson Pty.* v. *York Products Pty.*, 1970.)[73a] However, confusion can best be avoided by regarding bailment as an independent transaction, which has characteristics of contract and tort but is neither. It seems that when X hands his goods to Y under a bailment Y has certain duties in regard to the care of the goods, whether the bailment is accompanied by a contract or not.

(*c*) *Consideration must be sufficient.* Sufficiency of consideration is not the same thing as adequacy of consideration. The concept of sufficiency arises in the course of deciding whether the acts in question *amount to consideration at all*. This situation arises where the consideration offered by the promiser is an act which he is already bound to carry out. Thus the discharge of a *public duty* imposed by law is not consideration (*Collins* v. *Godefroy*, 1831);[74] nor is the performance of a *contractual duty* already owed to the defendant. (*Vanbergen* v. *St. Edmund's Properties Ltd.*, 1933;[75] *Stilk* v. *Myrick*, 1809.)[76] However, where the contractual duty is not precisely coincident with the public duty but is in excess of it, performance of the contractual duty may provide consideration (*Ward* v. *Byham*, 1956)[77] and the actual performance of an outstanding contractual obligation may be sufficient to support a promise of a further payment by a third party. (*Shadwell v. Shadwell*, 1860.)[78]

(*d*) *Consideration must be legal.* An illegal consideration makes the whole contract invalid.

(*e*) *Consideration must not be past.* Sometimes the act which one party to a contract puts forward as consideration was performed before any promise of reward was made by the other. Where this is so the act in question may be regarded as past *consideration* and will not support a contractual claim. This somewhat technical rule seems to be based on the idea that the act of one party to an alleged contract can only be regarded as consideration if it was carried out in response to some promise of the other. Where this is not so the act is regarded as gratuitous, being carried out before any promise of reward was made. (*Roscorla* v. *Thomas*, 1842,[79] and *Re McArdle*, 1951.)[80]

However there are exceptions to this rule—

(i) Where services are rendered at the express or implied request of the promisor in circumstances which raise an implication of a promise to pay. (*Re Casey's Patents, Stewart* v. *Casey*, 1892.)[81] This exception is not entirely a genuine one since the promisor is assumed to have given an implied undertaking to pay at the time of the request, his subsequent promise being regarded as deciding merely *the actual amount to be paid*. In this situation the act, which follows the request but precedes the settling of the reward, is more in the nature of *executed consideration* which, as we have seen, will support a contract.

(ii) Where a debt is barred by the Limitation Act, 1939, since this can be revived by a subsequent acknowledgment in writing. Such an acknowledgment is effective if it indicates that a debt is due even if it does not state the amount. (*Dungate* v. *Dungate*, 1965.)[82] Again this exception is not wholly genuine since the Limitation Act, 1939, does not provide that past-consideration will support the subsequent acknowledgment of a debt. The Act simply states that *no consideration of any kind need be sought*.

(iii) Sect. 27 of the Bills of Exchange Act, 1882, provides that past consideration will support a bill of exchange. This exception was probably based on a pre-existing commercial custom.

(*f*) *Consideration must move from the promisee,* i.e. the person to whom the promise is made must give some consideration for it. This arises from the doctrine of privity of contract.

Privity of Contract. This means that in general third parties cannot sue for the carrying out of promises made by the parties to a contract. (*Tweddle* v. *Atkinson*, 1861,[83] *Dunlop* v. *Selfridge*, 1915,[69] *Dunlop* v. *New Garage and Motor Co. Ltd.*, 1915.)[84]

However, there are cases in which a person is allowed to sue upon a contract to which he is not a party—

(*a*) A principal, even if undisclosed, may sue on a contract made by an agent. This exception is perhaps more apparent than real, because in fact the principal is the contracting party who has merely acted through the instrumentality of the agent.

(*b*) Attempts have been made to modify the rule of privity by invoking the equitable doctrine of the constructive trust. Thus, if A and B agree to confer a benefit on C, it may be possible to regard B as a constructive trustee for C of the benefit of the contract. C would then have an action against B if the latter had received the benefit and would not pass it on to C, or against A. However, if A were sued, B would be joined in the action. The application of this principle has always been uncertain and limited, and the courts do not seem eager to extend it. However, one aspect of this equitable doctrine has been established in the commercial world, and was recognised by the House of Lords in *Les Affréteurs Réunis Société Anonyme* v. *Walford*, 1919.[85]

(*c*) In other cases, where a fund is created in the hands of one of the contracting parties in favour of a third party, it may be possible to give the latter a remedy in quasi-contract (see p. 96), on the grounds that to allow the contracting party to keep the fund would be to allow unjust enrichment. (*Shamia* v. *Joory,* 1958.)[86]

(*d*) The assignee of a debt or chose in action may, if the assignment is a legal assignment, sue the original debtor (see p. 98).

(*e*) The holder for value of a bill of exchange can sue prior parties and the acceptor (see p. 291).

(*f*) Under the Restrictive Trade Practices Act, 1956, Sect. 25, the supplier of goods is given a statutory cause of action, so that he may enforce against a person not a party to the contract of sale a condition as to re-sale price. However, the re-sale price agreement must have been approved under the provisions of the Resale Prices Act, 1964, otherwise there can be no enforcement of it (see p. 71).

(*g*) Certain other exceptions are to be found in statute, e.g. Sect. 11 of the Married Women's Property Act, 1882, provides that if a man insures his life for the benefit of his wife and/or children, or a woman insures her life for the benefit of her husband and/or children, a trust is created in favour of the objects of the policy, and the policy moneys are not liable for the deceased's debts, other than Estate duty (Finance Act, 1968, Sects. 35–38).

(*h*) The position in land law is that benefits and liabilities attached to or imposed on land may in certain circumstances follow the land into the hands of other owners. (*Smith and Snipes Hall Farm Ltd.* v. *River Douglas Catchment Board*, 1949,[87] and *Tulk* v. *Moxhay*, 1848.)[88]

(*i*) Bankers' Commercial Credits also present problems in the field of privity. It is common commercial practice for an exporter, E, to ask the buyer of the goods, B, to open, with his banker, a credit in favour of E, the credit to remain irrevocable for a specified time. B agrees with his banker that the credit should be opened and, in return, promises to repay the banker, and usually gives him a lien over the shipping documents. The banker will also require a commission for his services. B's banker then notifies E that a credit has been opened in his favour, and E can draw upon it on presentation of the shipping documents.

However, if B's banker refuses to pay E on presentation of the documents, E could sue B on the original contract of sale, but would be unable to sue B's banker if the rule of privity were applied. The credit arises out of an agreement between B and his banker, and E is a stranger to it. It is unfortunate that this convenient commercial practice should be of doubtful legal validity though it is likely that if an exporter had to sue the buyer's banker on a commercial credit the court would allow the action as an exception to the rule of privity on the grounds that a commercial practice in favour of third party rights exists. (See *Hanzeh etc.* v. *British Imex etc.*, [1958] 2 Q.B. 127).

(*j*) Attempts have also been made to modify the rule of privity by an *appropriate interpretation of Sect.* 56 (1) *of the Law of Property Act*, 1925. The subsection provides that "a person may take an immediate or other interest in land or other property, or the benefit of any condition, right of entry, covenant or agreement over or respecting land or other property, although he may not be named as a party to the conveyance or other instrument."

Sect. 205 (1) of the 1925 Act provides that "unless the context otherwise requires, the following expressions have the meanings hereby assigned to them . . . (xx) 'property' includes any thing in action and any interest in real or personal property."

Sect. 56 (1) certainly applies to provisions in covenants concerning land. Thus, if X derives his title to real property under a conveyance of, say, 1971, he can enforce a restrictive covenant regarding the use of the land made in an earlier conveyance between other parties. However, some Judges, including Lord Denning, have been of the opinion that the word 'property' in Sect. 56 (1) should be interpreted as covering all things in action, even contractual rights in a contract not concerned with land.

This interpretation would open the door to claims formerly barred by the rule of privity, and would do away with the rule in *Tweddle* v. *Atkinson*, 1861,[83] and similar cases.

The matter came before the House of Lords in *Beswick* v. *Beswick*, 1967,[89] and their Lordships could not accept the wider interpretation of Section 56 (1) advocated by Lord Denning and others in previous cases, but regarded the subsection as being limited to cases concerning real property. Before leaving the subject of privity it is perhaps worth noting that the fact that an insurance company has agreed to indemnify one of the contracting parties does not rule out the existence of a contract between those parties. (*Charnock* v. *Liverpool Corporation*, 1968.)[90] See also *Snelling* v. *John G. Snelling Ltd.*, 1972.[691]

Accord and Satisfaction. Where X has performed his part of a contract, but Y has not, X may release Y from his obligations under the contract, but only if the release is under seal or if X receives valuable consideration for forgoing his rights. Such an agreement, where there is the necessary consideration, is called *accord and satisfaction*. The accord is the agreement by which the obligation is discharged; the satisfaction is the consideration which makes the agreement operative.

The doctrine may be illustrated by the following example. Payment of a smaller sum of money is not satisfaction of an agreement to pay a larger sum, even though the creditor agrees to take it in full discharge. If Y owes X £100, and X agrees to take £75, X can subsequently sue Y for the balance of £25 since there is no consideration for his forgiveness. There is accord but no satisfaction. The rule is an ancient one and an early example of it is to be found in the judgment of Brian, C. J., in *Pinnel's Case* (1602), 5 Co. Rep., 117a. Pinnel sued Cole in Debt for £8 10s which was due on a bond on 11th November, 1600. Cole's defence was that, at Pinnel's request, he had paid him £5 2s 6d on 1st October, and that Pinnel had accepted this payment in full satisfaction of the original debt. Although the court found for Pinnel on a technical point of pleading, it was said that—

(*a*) Payment of a lesser sum on the due day in satisfaction of a greater sum cannot be any satisfaction for the whole; but that

(*b*) Payment of a smaller sum at the creditor's request before the due day is good consideration for a promise to forgo the balance, for it is a benefit to the creditor to be paid before he was entitled to payment, and a corresponding detriment to the debtor to pay early.

The first branch of the rule in *Pinnel's* case was much criticised, but was approved by the House of Lords in *Foakes* v. *Beer*, 1884,[91] and the doctrine then hardened because of the system of binding precedent.

However, the practical effect of the rule is considerably reduced by the following—

(i) Where there is a dispute as to the sum owed, if the creditor accepts less than he thinks is owed to him, the debt will be discharged.

(ii) Where the creditor agrees to take something different in kind, e.g. a chattel, the debt is discharged by *substituted performance*. A cheque for a smaller sum *no longer* constitutes substituted performance (*D. & C. Builders Ltd.* v. *Rees*, 1965),[92] except perhaps where the creditor has asked for payment by cheque or appears to have accepted a cheque or other negotiable instrument as a substitution for the debt and not merely as a conditional payment. (*per* Lord Denning, M. R. *D. & C. Builders Ltd.* v. *Rees*, [1965] 3 All E.R. 837 at p. 840.)

(iii) The payment of a smaller sum before the larger is due gives the debtor a good discharge. This is the second branch of the rule in *Pinnel's* case.

(iv) If a debtor makes an arrangement with his creditors to compound his debts, e.g. by paying them 87½p in the £, he is satisfying a debt for a larger sum by the payment of a smaller sum. Nevertheless it is a good discharge, the consideration being the agreement by the creditors with each other and with the debtor not to insist on their full rights. (*Good* v. *Cheeseman*, 1831.)[93]

(v) Payment of a smaller sum by a third party operates as a good discharge. (*Welby* v. *Drake*, 1825.)[94]

(vi) Forbearance to sue may be valuable consideration. It is important that there should be some evidence that the debtor requested the forbearance, either expressly or by implication (*Combe* v. *Combe*, 1951),[95] and, if a person forbears to sue on a claim which is clearly invalid, and the plaintiff knows this to be so, there is no consideration. Thus a promise by a bookmaker not to sue his client for the amount of lost bets is no consideration for a promise made in return by the client, but a promise to abandon a claim that is doubtful is sufficient consideration, for the claim may turn out to be good. (*Haigh* v. *Brooks*, 1839.)[70]

(vii) The equitable rule of *promissory estoppel*, derived from the judgment of Lord Cairns in *Hughes* v. *Metropolitan Railway* (1877), 2 App. Cas. 439, and again enunciated in the *High Trees* case[96] may apply. When a promise is made which is intended to create legal relations, which is likely to be acted upon, and which is acted upon by the person to whom it is made, the law does not give a cause of action if the promise is broken, but it will require the promise to be honoured to the extent of refusing the promisor the right to act inconsistently with it, even though the promise is not supported by consideration. Thus if a landlord agrees to remit a portion of the rent of a property, and the tenant pays the reduced rent for a certain period, the landlord will not be able to claim as arrears the rent which he has voluntarily remitted, since the tenant may have altered his position in reliance upon the remission of rent. (*Central London Property Trust Ltd.* v. *High Trees House Ltd.*, 1947.)[96]

The doctrine of equitable or promissory estoppel seems most often to operate when the terms of one contract are modified or varied by a later promise. However, in *Durham Fancy Goods Ltd.* v. *Michael Jackson (Fancy Goods) Ltd.*, 1968,[97] Donaldson, J., was of the opinion that a pre-existing *contractual* relationship (assumed by Lord Cairns in *Hughes* v. *Metropolitan Railway* (1877) 2 App. Cas. 439) was not essential "provided that there is a pre-existing *legal* relationship which could in certain circumstances give rise to liabilities and penalties."

Nevertheless the doctrine cannot be used by a plaintiff who alleges that a simple contract has been formed without consideration. As Birkett, L.J., said in *Combe* v. *Combe*, 1951,[95] "The principle must be used as a shield not a sword." The doctrine which gives a defence against a claim and is not sufficient to found an action may be summed up in the words of Lord Cohen in *Tool Metal Manufacturing Co. Ltd.* v. *Tungsten Electric Co. Ltd.*, [1955] 2 All E.R. 657.

It is not thought right that a man who has indicated that he is not going to insist on his strict legal rights as a result of which the other party has altered his position should be able at a minute's notice to insist upon his rights however inconvenient it may be to the other party.

The doctrine was further considered in *Ajayi* v. *Briscoe*, 1964,[98] where it was held that the promisor may resile from the promise to discharge the promisee until the promisee has acted in reliance on it and has altered his position. Further it was held in *D. & C. Builders* v. *Rees*, 1965,[92] that if the promisee has extorted the promise, as in that case by threatening a breach of contract, the promise will not bind the promisor and the original contract will apply.

CAPACITY TO CONTRACT

Adult citizens have full capacity to enter into any kind of contract, but certain groups of persons, and corporations or unincorporated groups, have certain disabilities in this connection.

Aliens. They normally have full capacity to contract, but they cannot acquire property in a British ship (Merchant Shipping Act, 1894, Sect. 1), save as a member of a limited liability company if the company itself is British. However, contracts with *enemy aliens* during the period of hostilities are illegal and void. The term "enemy alien" includes not only aliens but also British subjects voluntarily resident or carrying on business in the enemy's country or in a country occupied or controlled by the enemy. The test is not nationality but the place where the person resides or carries on business.

An enemy alien who is in England during the period of hostilities *may be sued* in the English courts but he cannot himself *bring an action* in those courts. (*Porter* v. *Freudenberg*, [1915] 1 K.B. 857.) However, an enemy alien present in England by licence of the Crown, as where he is registered under relevant legislation, may sue and be sued in the English courts and may make valid contracts even during hostilities.

Contracts made during peace-time with persons who later become enemy aliens by reason of outbreak of war and which require continuous business relations or are prejudicial to this country, e.g. armaments contracts, are treated as follows—

(a) *The contract gives no rights to the parties after the outbreak of war.* It is thus cut short and enforcement of the contract will relate only to the part which was *executed* before the war, the *executory* rights and duties being cancelled. Thus, if A and B enter into a contract under which A charters a ship from B for ten years, then if after two years B becomes an enemy alien, the contract will be cut in effect to two years and the parties released from all obligations arising under the charter after the outbreak of war. This is so even though hostilities may cease before the eight years remaining under the charter have elapsed.

(b) *The rights and duties outstanding in respect of performance before the outbreak of war are not destroyed though they cannot be enforced until hostilities cease.* Thus a debt due under a contract before the outbreak of war would survive the hostilities and be enforceable on the return of peace. (*Arab Bank Ltd.* v. *Barclays Bank*, [1954] A.C. 495.) Where the contract does not involve commercial intercourse with the enemy alien or prejudice to this country, the rights and duties are merely suspended and not destroyed. Thus in a separation agreement made between husband and wife before the outbreak of hostilities, the husband would be liable after the war to pay to the wife sums falling due by way of maintenance during the period of hostilities even though the wife became an enemy alien for that period. (*Bevan* v. *Bevan*, [1955] 2 Q.B. 227.)

Foreign sovereigns and diplomats are in a privileged position, since they cannot be sued at civil law or prosecuted in this country unless they submit to the jurisdiction of our courts. (*Mighell* v. *Sultan of Johore*, 1894.)[99]

The law relating to the privileges and immunities of diplomatic representatives in the United Kingdom is now laid down by the Diplomatic Privileges Act, 1964.

The Act gives effect to most of the provisions of the Vienna Convention on Diplomatic Relations, 1961, and replaces the Diplomatic Privileges Act, 1708. The Act divides the members of a diplomatic mission into three classes—

(*a*) Members of the diplomatic staff, who have full personal immunity, civil and criminal, with three exceptions—

(i) a real action relating to private immovable property situated in the territory of the receiving State, unless the diplomatic agent holds it on behalf of the sending State for the purposes of the mission;

(ii) an action relating to succession in which the diplomatic agent is involved as an executor, administrator, heir or legatee as a private person and not on behalf of the sending State;

(iii) an action relating to any professional or commercial activity exercised by the diplomatic agent in the receiving state outside his official functions.

(*b*) Members of the administrative and technical staff, who enjoy full immunity for official acts, but who are liable civilly, though not criminally, for acts performed outside the course of their duties.

(*c*) Members of the Service Staff, who enjoy immunity for official acts, but are liable civilly and criminally for acts performed outside the course of their duties.

It follows from the above provisions of the Act that the courts will, for the first time, have power to determine whether an act committed by a member of a diplomatic mission was performed in the course of his duties.

Privileges and immunities may be withdrawn by Her Majesty by Order in Council from any State granting fewer privileges and immunities to British missions. The certificate of the Foreign Secretary is conclusive as to the entitlement of a person to any privilege or immunity, though, as we have seen, the courts have the power to decide whether the act was performed in the course of his duties.

The privileges and immunities set out in the Diplomatic Privileges Act, 1964, are extended to the following persons among others—

(i) The chief representatives of the Republic of Ireland and Commonwealth countries, e.g. High Commissioners, their staffs, families and servants. (Diplomatic Immunities (Commonwealth Countries and Republic of Ireland) Act, 1952.)

(ii) Persons connected with International Organisations of appropriate status, immunity being derived from the International Organisations Act, 1968. Such organisations are defined from time to time by Orders in Council made in pursuance of the Act, and include such bodies as the United Nations Organisation and the International Court of Justice.

Immunity is not normally conferred on persons of quasi-diplomatic character, such as consular officials, but an exception may be made where the diplomatic and consular functions are carried out by the same person. However, some immunities, e.g., in respect of rates and taxes, are given to consular officers by orders made under the Consular Relations Act, 1968, and by the Diplomatic Privileges Act, 1971, Sect. 4.

Diplomatic privilege may be waived, though in the case of an ambassador or other head of a mission, waiver must be with the consent of his Sovereign. In other cases waiver must be by the head of the mission.

It should be noted that a foreign state's unilateral action in appointing a diplomatic agent does not confer immunity on him. Until this country has accepted and received him, i.e. until he has been officially accredited to the Court of St. James, he is not immune from proceedings in the English Courts. (*R. v. Pentonville Prison Governor, Ex parte Teja*, [1971] 2 W.L.R. 816.) Foreign state corporations are also immune from suit in the English courts. (*Mellenger v. New Brunswick Development Corporation*, [1971] 1 W.L.R. 604.)

Minors. The Family Law Reform Act, 1969, Sect. 1 (1), reduces the age of majority from 21 to 18 years. This provision operates from 1st January, 1970, and if a person is over 18 and under 21 on 1st January, 1970, he is deemed to have attained his majority on that date. There is also a provision in the Act which states that a person attains a particular age, i.e. not merely the age of majority, at the first moment of the relevant birthday, though this rule is subject to any contrary provision in any instrument (i.e. a deed) or statute. (Sect. 9.) However, the common law rule that the age is attained at the first moment of the day preceding the birthday is repealed.

Sect. 1 (2) provides that the age of 18 is to be substituted for 21 wherever there is a reference to "full age," "infant," "minor," "minority" in—

(a) any statutory provision made *before or after* 1st January, 1970;
(b) any deed, will or other instrument made *on or after* that date.

This subsection draws a distinction between *statutory provisions* and *private dispositions*. In the case of the former the new age of 18 is substituted. Thus, in the Infants' Relief Act, 1874, references to "infants" will be construed as applying to persons under 18 years of age. However, in the case of private dispositions such as deeds, wills and settlements the Act does not apply retrospectively. Accordingly if, in a deed made before 1st January, 1970, a person is to take property "on attaining his majority," he will take at age 21 years. If the deed was made on or after 1st January, 1970, he would take at 18 years. The reason for this rule is that where persons in the past have arranged their affairs in reliance on the law as it stood, it would be unjust to interfere.

With regard to procedure, a minor sues, as we have seen, through a "next friend," i.e. an adult who is liable for the costs (if any) awarded against the minor in the action, though the minor must indemnify him. A minor defends an action through a "guardian *ad litem*," who is not liable for costs.

A minor's contracts may be void, valid, voidable or unenforceable.

Void Contracts Include the Following—

　(*a*) *Those under the Infants' Relief Act*, 1874, *Sect.* 1—

　　(i) Contracts for the repayment of money lent or to be lent. (*Coutts & Co.* v. *Browne-Lecky*, 1947.)[100]

　　(ii) Contracts for goods supplied, or to be supplied, other than necessaries.

　　(iii) All accounts stated with infants, e.g. I.O.U.'s, and other statements of indebtedness.

　(*b*) *Those under the Betting and Loans (Infants) Act*, 1892. This Act renders void any agreement made by a person after he comes of age to pay a loan contracted during minority.

A minor cannot be held liable on a bill of exchange (e.g. a cheque) even though given in payment of a debt incurred for necessaries supplied and delivered. (Bills of Exchange Act, 1882, Sect. 22.) So far as the actual supplier is concerned there would be an action in quasi-contract on the consideration, i.e. for a reasonable price, not necessarily the contract price, but third parties, to whom the bill had been negotiated, would have no claim whatever on the minor.

It appears that despite the use of the words "absolutely void" in Sect. 1 of the Infants Relief Act, 1874, a minor can sue on the void contract, except as against another minor, because an adult party cannot use the other's minority as a defence to an action. Furthermore, it will be seen that the minor cannot recover money paid or goods transferred under a void contract unless there has been total failure of consideration. In addition, the minor seems to obtain property in the goods and can give a good title to third parties. However, in some cases the courts have held contracts with Sect. 1 to be without any legal effect. (*Coutts & Co.* v. *Browne-Lecky*, 1947;[100] *R.* v. *Wilson*, 1879.)[101]

Valid Contracts are of Two Types—

(*a*) *Executed contracts for necessaries.* These are defined in the Sale of Goods Act, 1893, Sect. 2, as "goods suitable to the condition in life of the minor and to his actual requirements at the time of sale and delivery."

If the goods are deemed necessaries, the minor may be compelled to pay a reasonable price which is not necessarily the contract price. The minor is not liable if the goods, though necessaries, have not been delivered. This illustrates that a minor's liability for necessaries is only quasi-contractual.

The general test of necessaries is that of utility, and in this connection the minor's condition in life, together with the supply of such goods which he already has, becomes relevant. (*Nash* v. *Inman*, 1908.)[102] Thus food, clothes, lodging and the like are obviously necessary; but educational books, medical attention, burial of the minor's wife or children, and legal advice, and in some cases even articles of apparent luxury are classed as necessaries. (*Elkington* v. *Amery*, 1936.)[103] Necessaries for a married minor's family are judged by the same standards as necessaries for himself. These considerations apply not merely to the purchase of goods but also to necessary services. Thus a contract to hire a car may be a necessary contract for a salesman who is a minor.

(*b*) *Contracts for the minor's benefit.* A minor may make valid contracts if they are for his benefit, but these have generally been contracts of apprenticeship, contracts of service, contracts for education, or something analogous thereto. (*Roberts* v. *Gray*, 1913.)[104] However, the concept of the beneficial contract may not be restricted to the above categories. (*Chaplin* v. *Leslie Frewin* (*Publishers*), 1965.)[105] A contract which is in general for the minor's benefit will not be enforced if its terms are onerous, although the court will look at the whole contract, not merely at isolated terms, and will arrive at its decision on the total effect of the agreement. (*De Francesco* v. *Barnum*, 1890,[106] and *Clements* v. *L. and N.W. Railway Co.*, 1894.)[107] Trading contracts of minors are not enforceable, no matter how beneficial they may be to the minor's trade or business. (*Mercantile Union Guarantee Corporation Ltd.* v. *Ball*, 1937.)[108]

Voidable Contracts. These are usually contracts by which the minor acquires an interest of a permanent nature in the subject matter of the contract, e.g. a lease of premises, a partnership contract, or the holding of shares in a company. Such contracts bind the minor unless he takes active steps to avoid them either during his minority (*Steinberg* v.

Scala, 1923),[109] or within a reasonable time thereafter. (*Davies* v. *Beynon-Harris,* 1931,[110] and *Goode* v. *Harrison,* 1821.)[111]

Contracts within the Infants' Relief Act, 1874, *Sect.* 2. This section is concerned with the effect of the minor's ratification after full age of a contract made during minority, and with fresh promises made by the minor after reaching full age in respect of transactions which took place during minority.

Before the effect of Sect. 2 can be appreciated it is necessary to look at the common law position before the Act of 1874 was passed. The common law classified minor's contracts as follows—

(i) *Contracts for necessaries,* where the seller had a quasi-contractual claim and there could be no ratification after full age.

(ii) *Contracts of a continuing nature,* e.g. leases and partnerships. Such contracts were voidable during minority or within a reasonable time thereafter, so that the minor could and still can ratify a contract of this nature.

(iii) *Loans.* These were void at common law and there could be no ratification by the minor after age, but a fresh promise plus new consideration, e.g. a fresh advance, might bind the minor.

(iv) *Contracts of a beneficial nature.* These were and are still binding on the minor.

All other contracts made by minors were voidable at common law, and consequently were capable of ratification after full age. The most important contracts in this residuary class were (*a*) the minor's contract of engagement, which was capable of ratification after full age; and (*b*) debts incurred under contracts for non-necessary goods, which debts could also be ratified after full age.

Sect. 2 provides—

No action shall be brought whereby to charge any person upon any promise made after full age to pay any debt contracted during infancy or upon any ratification made after full age of any promise or contract made during infancy whether there shall or shall not be any new consideration for such promise or ratification after full age.

The effect of this section is as follows—

(i) It prevents ratification of contracts of engagement and debts for non-necessaries (*Coxhead* v. *Mullis,* 1878);[112] but

(ii) A fresh promise binds in the case of engagements (*Northcote* v. *Doughty,* 1879),[113] but not in the case of a debt even if the fresh promise after age is supported by new consideration.

Sect. 2 of the Infants' Relief Act, 1874, was not entirely effective in the case of loans. It rendered certain promises unenforceable against the minor but, although the promise to repay the loan was unenforceable, the lender could sell any security the minor had used to secure the loan, because here he was pursuing a real remedy against the security and was not suing the minor on his promise.

The Betting and Loans (Infants) Act, 1892, was therefore passed rendering loans as distinct from debts void, so that any security taken is also void, and the lender can neither enforce the minor's promise, nor proceed against any security the minor may have given to secure the loan.

It is noteworthy that, since a minor's contracts cannot in general be enforced against him, Equity will not grant him the remedy of specific performance. He may, however, sue at common law for damages, since common law, unlike Equity, does not require mutuality of remedies.

When a minor has paid money under a void or voidable contract, he can repudiate the contract and disclaim all future liability, but cannot recover money paid unless he can prove a total failure of consideration, i.e. that he has received no benefit at all under the contract. It would seem that the court is reluctant to find that no benefit has been received (*Pearce* v. *Brain*, 1929,[114] and *Steinberg* v. *Scala*, 1923),[109] though if there has been no consideration at all the minor will be able to recover his money. (*Corpe* v. *Overton*, 1833.)[115]

Although the Infants' Relief Act, 1874, states that contracts for goods other than necessaries are absolutely void, yet the minor can give a good title to a third party who acquires goods which have been bought by the minor, provided the third party takes *bona fide* and for value. (*Stocks* v. *Wilson*, 1913)[116] The tradesman who sold the goods to the minor cannot recover them from the third party; whether he can recover money paid to the minor for the goods is doubtful. (*Stocks* v. *Wilson*, 1913,[116] and *Leslie* (*R.*) *Ltd.* v. *Sheill*, 1914.)[117]

Where a minor has committed a fraud, e.g. overstated his age, then the equitable doctrine of restitution of the goods is available to the tradesman, assuming the goods are non-necessaries and that no action for a reasonable price is available. The remedy of restitution exists so long as the minor still has the goods in his possession and they can be identified. It is well established that a tradesman cannot sue the minor on the tort of deceit, as this would amount to using the law of torts to circumvent the Infants' Relief Act (*Leslie* v. *Sheill*, 1914),[117] though, apart from circumstances such as this, a minor is fully liable in tort. (*Burnard* v. *Haggis*, 1863.)[118]

The doctrine of estoppel, which is a rule of evidence rather than a rule of law, means that a person is sometimes prevented from denying in court the truth of a statement which he has made where another person has relied on that statement to his detriment. This doctrine might have prevented a fraudulent minor from proving his real age when defending an action for the price of goods delivered to him, but the court is so concerned that the 1874 Act should not be circumvented that this doctrine has been held not to apply to a minor so as to prevent him from setting up his real age as a defence.

Married Women. Married women used to be under certain disabilities in regard to the making of contracts and the holding of property, but since the Law Reform (Married Women and Tortfeasors) Act, 1935, and the Married Women (Restraint upon Anticipation) Act, 1949, a married woman has had the same contractual capacity as an unmarried woman (*feme sole*) or a man. Although a husband is not in general liable for his wife's contracts a wife may, in certain circumstances, bind her husband in contract under the law of agency, though she can no longer be an agent of necessity in respect of domestic transactions (see p. 196).

Corporations. Corporations are another special case of capacity to contract. A corporation aggregate may be a body incorporated by Royal Charter, a corporation formed by a special Act of Parliament, or a company registered under the Companies Act, 1948, or previous Acts.

The contractual capacity of a corporation is limited—

(*a*) *By natural impossibility*, which arises from the fact that it is an *artificial* and not a *natural* person. Thus it can only make contracts through an agent and in consequence cannot fulfil contractual obligations of a *personal nature*. It is obviously impossible for a corporation to marry and it cannot act as a solicitor, doctor or accountant, nor can it act as the treasurer of a friendly society. (*Re West of England and South Wales District Bank* (1879), 11 Ch.D. 768.)

(*b*) *By legal impossibility*, since corporations are subject to what is called the *ultra vires* rule, which limits what they can legally do. A corporation can only act within its powers, and actions outside this scope are called *ultra vires*, or beyond its powers.

Charter corporations may contract as an ordinary person can, and even though the Charter may impose limitations on the corporation's contractual capacity, any contracts which it makes beyond those limitations are nevertheless good. (*Baroness Wenlock* v. *River Dee Co.* (1887), 36 Ch.D. 674.) The Crown may in such a case forfeit the Charter, or a member of the corporation may ask the court to restrain the corporation by injunction from doing acts which are *ultra vires*. (*Jenkin* v. *Pharmaceutical Society*, 1921.)[119]

Statutory corporations have powers contained in the statute setting them up, and these powers are sometimes increased by subsequent statutes or by delegated legislation. Any acts beyond these powers are *ultra vires* and void.

A registered company possesses powers which are determined by the Objects Clause of its Memorandum of Association, and an act in excess of the powers given in this Memorandum is *ultra vires* and void. (*Ashbury Railway Carriage and Iron Co.* v. *Riche*, 1875,[120] and *Re Jon Beauforte*, 1953.)[121] Corporations may carry out acts "fairly incidental" to the specified objects (*Deuchar* v. *Gas, Light and Coke Co.*, 1925),[122] though whether an activity was fairly incidental has hitherto been a matter for the Court to decide. However, the rule has been so uncertain in its operation that it has become customary for legal draftsmen to draft objects clauses which are extremely wide in scope and in addition include a provision that each specified object or power should be considered separate and distinct and in no way anciliary to, or dependent upon, any other object. (*Cotman* v. *Brougham*, 1918.)[123] In this way the severe limitations placed on a company's business by the *ultra vires* rule have been mitigated, provided that each paragraph of the objects clause can genuinely be regarded as separate and distinct. (*Introductions Ltd.* v. *National Provincial Bank Ltd.*, 1969.)[124] However, in a recent case the Court of Appeal made a decision which may, in effect, allow the directors of a company to usurp the Courts in deciding what is reasonably incidental to the company's stated objects, and furthermore allow them, through ignorance or mistaken intention, to bind the company to an activity which cannot conveniently be combined with the existing objects, and ought therefore to be regarded as *ultra vires*. (*Bell Houses Ltd.* v. *City Wall Properties Ltd.*, 1966.)[125]

At common law contracts made by corporations had to be under seal. The requirement of sealing would have been extremely onerous but for the exceptions allowed, e.g. contracts of trifling importance or daily necessity were not required to bear the company's seal.

The above rules have been amended by statute. The Companies Act, 1948, provides in Sect. 32 that a registered company need not contract under seal except where an ordinary person would have to do so, and the Corporate Bodies' Contracts Act, 1960, extends this privilege to all companies, no matter how formed, in respect of contracts made after 29th July, 1960.

Unincorporated Bodies. In addition to corporations there are certain types of unincorporated bodies, such as tennis clubs and other societies. These bodies contract through agents, and the persons authorising these agents are personally liable, since the association has no separate existence in law, being only an aggregate of its members, though the rules of the Supreme Court allow unincorporated groups of persons to sue or be sued collectively.

The contractual liability of the members of an unincorporated body rests on the principles of the law of agency. Thus a member who purports to make a contract on behalf of his club is usually personally liable. The other members will be liable as co-principals only if they have authorised the making of the contract. Often the rules of a club provide that the member shall be deemed to have authorised the making of contracts on its behalf. Alternatively the members may ratify a contract *after* it has been made. However, it appears that no member has authority to make a *purchase on credit* (*Flemyng* v. *Hector* (1836), 3 M & W 172) unless he is *specifically* authorised to do so. Membership of a club usually involves payment of an annual subscription and nothing more. Consequently it is expected that everything needed by the club will be paid for from existing funds. If more money is needed a meeting of members should be called so that subscriptions might be raised. A purchase other than for cash involves pledging the credit of the members without their consent.

Persons Suffering from Mental Disorder. Contracts made by a person of unsound mind are valid, but if the other party knew that he was contracting with a person who, by reason of the unsoundness of his mind, *could not understand the nature of the contract,* then the contract is voidable at the option of the insane party. The person of unsound mind must prove (*a*) the unsoundness of mind at the time of the contract, and (*b*) that the other party knew of it. (*Imperial Loan Co.* v. *Stone,* [1892] 1 Q.B. 599.) If necessaries are supplied to an insane person he, like a minor, is bound to pay a reasonable price under the Sale of Goods Act, 1893. A person of unsound mind can make a valid contract during a lucid interval, even though the other party knew that he was insane at times. Further, a contract made during insanity can be ratified during a lucid interval. There seems to be no reason why persons suffering from some forms of mental disorder should not make valid contracts for non-necessary goods and services even where the other party knows of the disorder. Provided the person concerned understands the *nature* of the transaction a contract resulting from it could be binding. For example, a person who suffers under an insane delusion that he is Napoleon may nevertheless understand the nature of a commercial transaction such as the purchase of a watch. Where this is so he may be bound by a contract to buy the watch even though the seller knew of the delusion. (*Birkin* v. *Wing* (1890), 63 L.T. 80.) Nevertheless, it is likely that the court would regard the contract as voidable if it was shown that the person suffering from the delusion had been overreached as where the price asked for the watch was extortionate.

The above rules of law relating to persons of unsound mind must be read in the context of the provisions of the Mental Health Act, 1959. This Act, which came into operation fully on 1st November, 1960, introduced a completely new code and system for the care, treatment, and detention, of persons suffering from mental disorder. "Mental disorder" is now a statutory term embracing all forms of unsoundness of mind and in particular a person of unsound mind whose property is subject to the control of the Court under Part VIII of the Act cannot personally make a valid contract. However, persons of unsound mind whose property is not subject to the control of the court are governed in contractual matters by the common law rules given above.

Drunkards. Similar rules apply to contracts made by drunkards. The contract is voidable at the option of the party who was drunk at the time it was made, if he can show (i) that he was drunk, and (ii) that the other party knew this. (*Gore* v. *Gibson* (1845), 14 L.J. Ex. 151.) A contract made by a person when drunk can be ratified by him if at the time of ratification he understands what he is doing as when he is sober. (*Matthews* v. *Baxter* (1873), L.R. 8 Ex. 132.) Both insane and drunken persons have a quasi-contractual liability to pay a reasonable price for necessaries supplied to them. (Sale of Goods Act, 1893, Sect. 2.)

REALITY OF CONSENT

A contract which is regular in all other respects may still fail because there is no real consent to it by one or both of the parties. There is no *consensus ad idem* or meeting of the minds. Consent may be rendered unreal by mistake, fraud, misrepresentation, duress and undue influence.

MISTAKE

Mistake rarely affects the validity of a contract, but mistake which has this effect is called an operative mistake, and must be one of fact and not of law. (*Sharp Bros. and Knight* v. *Chant*, 1917.)[126] An operative mistake renders the contract void.

The concept of mistake has a somewhat technical meaning, and what would be considered a mistake by the layman will not always amount to an operative mistake in law. For example, errors of judgment are not operative mistakes. So if A buys an article thinking it is worth £100 when in fact it is worth only £50, the contract is good and A must bear the loss if there has been no misrepresentation by the seller. A mistake by one party as to his power to perform the contract is not an operative mistake. Where X agrees to build a house by 1st July, and finds he cannot complete the job before 1st September, he will be liable to an action for damages unless there is a provision in the contract to excuse him.

OPERATIVE MISTAKE. Operative mistakes may be classified into the following categories—

    (1) Mistake as to the nature of the contract itself.

    (2) Unilateral mistake, i.e. a mistake made by one party only.

    (3) Bilateral mistake, i.e. where both parties make a mistake, and subdivided into (*a*) Common Mistake; (*b*) Mutual Mistake.

These categories are helpful, but students find considerable difficulty in distinguishing between common and mutual mistake because the words are frequently confused, or used synonymously, even in law reports. This can be illustrated by the case of *Solle* v. *Butcher*.[127] Bucknill, L.J., in the course of his judgment is reported in the *All England Reports*, [1949] 2 All E.R. at page 1116 as saying: "In my opinion, therefore, there was a *mutual* mistake of fact on a matter of fundamental importance."

In the *Law Reports*, [1950] 1 K.B. at page 686 this is rendered as: "In my opinion, therefore, there was a *common* mistake of fact on a matter of fundamental importance."

In *Cooper* v. *Phibbs*, 1867,[128] at page 170, Lord Westbury says: ". . . but if the parties contract under a *mutual* mistake and misapprehension as to their relative and respective rights, the result is that that agreement is liable to be set aside as having proceeded upon a *common* mistake."

We therefore propose to use words more self-identifying than common or mutual in order to assist the reader to understand and remember the categories. Common mistake occurs where *both* parties have made the *same* mistake and will be called, alternatively, *identical bilateral* mistake. Mutual mistake occurs where *both* parties make a *different* mistake and will be called *non-identical bilateral* mistake. These will then be clearly differentiated between themselves and contrasted with *unilateral* mistake.

1. **Mistake as to the Nature of the Contract Itself.** If a person signs a contract in the mistaken belief that he is signing a document of a different nature, there will be a mistake which avoids the contract. (*Foster* v. *Mackinnon*, 1869.)[129] He will be able to plead *non est factum*. The plea of mistake is available in such circumstances unless the document happens to be a negotiable instrument which has been taken by an innocent third party for value. In such a case the person signing under a mistake is liable to the third party unless he can show that he was not negligent in so doing. In the case of other contracts, the person signing was not liable even if he had been negligent. (*Carlisle and Cumberland Banking Co.* v. *Bragg*, 1911.)[130] This view of the state of the law came under considerable criticism by the Court of Appeal in *Gallie* v. *Lee*, 1969,[131] and when the case came to the House of Lords under the name of *Saunders* v. *Anglia Building Society*, 1970,[131a] *Bragg's* case was overruled and more logical principles established.

2. **Unilateral Mistake.** Unilateral mistake occurs when one of the parties to a contract is mistaken as to some fundamental fact concerning the contract and *the other party knows, or ought to know, this.* (*Legal and General Assurance Society Ltd.* v. *General Metal Agencies Ltd.*, 1969.)[132] This latter requirement is important because if Y does not know that X is mistaken the contract is good. (*Higgins* v. *Northampton Corporation*, 1927.)[133]

EFFECT OF UNILATERAL MISTAKE AT COMMON LAW. The cases are mainly concerned with mistake by one party as to the *identity* of the other party. Thus a contract may be void if X makes a contract with Y, thinking that Y is another person, Z, and if Y knows that X is under that misapprehension. Proof of Y's knowledge is essential, but since in most cases Y is a fraudulent person, the point does not present great difficulties. (*Cundy* v. *Lindsay*, 1878.)[134]

It is also essential that there should exist in the mind of the party who has been misled some other person (or entity) with whom the contract could have been made, as in *Cundy* v. *Lindsay*, 1878[134] If Jones contracts with Brown by leading Brown to believe that he (Jones) is Green, the contract *will not be void* for mistake if Brown has never heard before of either Jones or Green. It *may be voidable* for fraud but the difference may vitally affect the interests of third parties. (*King's Norton Metal Co. Ltd.* v. *Edridge, Merrett & Co. Ltd.*, 1897.)[135] However, even where there are two entities, the court may still find, *on the facts, of the case*, that the contract is not void for mistake. (*Phillips* v. *Brooks* 1919,[136] *Lewis* v. *Averay*, 1971,[136a] and *Ingram* v. *Little*, 1961.)[137]

EFFECT OF UNILATERAL MISTAKE IN EQUITY. Equity follows the law and regards a contract affected by unilateral mistake as void, and will rescind it or refuse specific performance of it. (*Webster* v. *Cecil*, 1861.)[138]

3. Bilateral Mistake. A bilateral mistake arises when both parties to a contract are mistaken. They may have made a *common* or *identical* mistake; or a *mutual* or *non-identical* mistake.

(*A*) *COMMON OR IDENTICAL MISTAKE.* This occurs when the two parties have reached agreement but both have made an identical mistake as to some fundamental fact concerning the contract. Suppose, for example, that X sells a particular drawing to Y for £5,000 and all the usual elements of agreement are present including offer and acceptance and consideration, and the agreement concerns an identified article. Nevertheless, if both X and Y think that the drawing is by Rembrandt, when it is in fact only a copy worth £25, then the agreement is rendered imperfect by the *identical* or *common* mistake.

EFFECT OF IDENTICAL BILATERAL MISTAKE AT COMMON LAW. At common law a mistake of the kind outlined above has no effect on the contract, and the parties would be bound in the absence of fraud or misrepresentation. There are only two cases in which the common law appears to regard an *identical bilateral* mistake as a vitiating element, and even these cases are probably examples of precedent impossibility rather than mistake. The two categories of case are—

(a) *Cases of Res Extincta*

(i) *Identical bilateral mistake as to the existence of the thing contracted for.* If X agrees to sell his car to Y, and unknown to them both the car had at the time of the sale been destroyed by fire, then the contract will be void because X has innocently undertaken an obligation which he cannot possibly fulfil. (*Couturier* v. *Hastie*, 1856.)[139] There are, however, cases in which the court may assume from the circumstances that the seller is warranting the existence of the goods. (*McRae* v. *Commonwealth Disposals Commission*, 1951.)[140]

If the goods are lost after the sale takes place then the contract is good, and the loss lies with the buyer if the property in the goods has passed to him; if not, the loss lies with the seller. The goods must also be specific or ascertained, otherwise the property will not normally pass, and the seller must supply similar goods or be liable in breach of contract.

(ii) *Identical bilateral mistake as to the existence of a state of affairs forming the basis of the contract* If A and B, believing themselves to be married, enter into a separation agreement and later learn that they are not validly married, the agreement is void.

(*b*) *Cases of Res Sua.* These occur where a person makes a contract to buy something which already belongs to him. Such a contract is void. (*Cochrane* v. *Willis*, 1865.)[141]

Apart from cases of *res extincta* and *res sua* the common law does not seem to recognise an *identical* bilateral mistake as having any effect on a contract. (*Bell* v. *Lever Bros. Ltd.*, 1932,[142] and *Leaf* v. *International Galleries*, 1950.)[143]

EFFECT OF IDENTICAL BILATERAL MISTAKE IN EQUITY. The position in Equity is as follows—

(*a*) *Cases of Res Extincta and Res Sua.* Equity treats these in the same way as the common law, regarding the agreement as void. Consequently Equity will not grant specific performance of such an agreement (*Jones* v. *Clifford*, 1876)[144] but will rescind it. (*Cooper* v. *Phibbs*, 1867.)[128]

(*b*) *Other cases.* Equity will apparently regard an agreement affected by *identical* bilateral mistake as *voidable*, even though the case is not one of *res extincta* or *res sua*. (*Solle* v. *Butcher*, 1950,[127] and *Magee* v. *Pennine Insurance Co. Ltd.*, 1969.)[145] This remedy is a discretionary one and the party seeking it may be put on terms. (*Solle* v. *Butcher*, 1950,[127] and *Grist* v. *Bailey*, 1966.)[146]

(*c*) *Rectification.* Equity has power to rectify *written* agreements affected by *identical bilateral* or common mistake.

If the parties are agreed on the terms of their contract, but by mistake write them down incorrectly, the court may order equitable rectification of the contract. In order to obtain rectification it must be proved—

(i) that there was complete agreement on all the terms of the contract or at least some outward expression of agreement between the parties *on the term in question* (*Joscelyne* v. *Nissen*, 1969);[147]

(ii) that the agreement continued unchanged until it was reduced into writing (for if the parties disputed the terms of the agreement, then the written contract will be taken to represent their final agreement); and

(iii) that the writing does not express what the parties had agreed. (*Rose* v. *Pim*, 1953.)[148]

The power of the court to rectify agreements is generally confined to identical bilateral and not to unilateral mistake. (*Higgins* (*W.*) *Ltd.* v. *Northampton Corporation*, 1927.)[133] In the case of unilateral mistake, rectification will only be granted in cases of fraud or misrepresentation.

(*B*) *MUTUAL OR NON-IDENTICAL MISTAKE.* This occurs where the parties are both mistaken as to a fundamental fact concerning the contract but each party has made a *different* mistake. Thus if X offers to sell car A, and Y agrees to buy thinking X means car B, there is a bilateral mistake which is *non-identical*. This may prevent a contract coming into being between the parties because of *defective offer and acceptance* and may result from the negligence of a third party. (*Henkel* v. *Pape*, 1870.)[149] It will be remembered that in the previous category the mistake was bilateral but both parties had made an *identical* mistake.

EFFECT OF NON-IDENTICAL BILATERAL MISTAKE AT COMMON LAW. The contract is not necessarily void, because the court will try to find the "sense of the promise," i.e. the sort of bargain which the reasonable man looking at the dealings of the parties would have thought had been made.

In many cases of *non-identical mistake* the court has been able to ascertain the "sense of the promise" and has decided that an enforceable contract has been made *on the terms understood by one of the parties*. (*Wood* v. *Scarth*, 1858.)[150] If the circumstances are such that the court cannot find the "sense of the promise," then the contract is void not so much because of mistake as because of uncertainty. (*Raffles* v. *Wichelhaus*, 1864,[151] and *Scriven Brothers & Co.* v. *Hindley & Co.*, 1913.)[152]

EFFECT OF NON-IDENTICAL BILATERAL MISTAKE IN EQUITY. Equity also tries to find the "sense of the promise," thus following the law in this respect. (*Tamplin* v. *James*, 1880.)[153] However, equitable remedies are discretionary, and even where the "sense of the promise" can be ascertained, Equity will not necessarily insist on performance, particularly if this would cause hardship to the defendant. (*Wood* v. *Scarth*, 1858.)[150]

MISREPRESENTATION

Representation—Meaning of. A representation is an inducement only and its effect is generally to lead the other party merely to make the contract. A representation must be a statement of some *specific, existing* and *verifiable fact* or *past event* and in consequence the following are excluded—

(*a*) STATEMENTS OF LAW.

(*b*) STATEMENTS AS TO FUTURE CONDUCT OR INTENTION. In some cases, however, a statement of intention may, in effect, be a representation of existing fact. (*Edgington* v. *Fitzmaurice*, 1885.)[154]

(*c*) STATEMENTS OF OPINION. However, if it can be shown that the person making the statement had no such opinion it may be considered in law to be a misstatement of existing fact. (*Smith* v. *Land and House Property Co.*, 1884.)[155]

(*d*) MERE "PUFFING," AS IN ADVERTISING OR SALES TALK. Not all statements amount to representations. Some of them are obviously of the nature of sales talk and cannot be relied upon. If a salesman says: "This polish is as good as Snook's Polish," this is a mere statement of opinion. If he says: "This is the finest polish in the world," this is mere sales talk. However, if he says: "This polish has as much wax in it as Snook's Wax Polish," he is making a statement of fact. The first two of these statements have no effect on the contract whether true or untrue; the third if untrue will amount to a misrepresentation.

(e) SILENCE. Silence or non-disclosure by one or both of the parties does not normally affect the contract. However, it may do so—

(i) *where the statement is a half-truth:* if the statement made is true but *partial* so that a false impression is created it may be regarded as an actionable misrepresentation (*Curtis* v. *Chemical Cleaning and Dyeing Co.,* 1951);[156]

(ii) *where the statement was true when made but became false before the contract was concluded:* where a statement is made in the course of negotiating a contract and that statement, though true when it was made, becomes false because of a change in circumstances, there is a duty on the party making the statement to disclose the change, otherwise the contract may be rescinded (*With* v. *O'Flanagan,* 1936);[157]

(iii) *where the contract is "uberrimae fidei"* (of utmost good faith): such as a contract of insurance (see p. 373);

(iv) *where there is a fiduciary or confidential relationship between the parties:* the equitable doctrine of *constructive fraud* may be applied whenever the relationship between the parties to a contract is such that one of them has a special influence over the other. In such a case the person having the special influence cannot hold the other to the contract unless he can satisfy the court that it was advantageous to the other and that there was full disclosure of all material facts. A situation of special influence occurs for example in family relationships such as parent and child (see p. 54), but the doctrine of constructive fraud may be applied—

Whenever two persons stand in such a relation that, while it continues, confidence is necessarily reposed by one, and the influence which naturally grows out of that confidence is possessed by the other, and this confidence is abused, or the influence is exerted to obtain an advantage at the expense of the confiding party, the person so availing himself of his position will not be permitted to retain the advantage, although the transaction could not have been impeached if no such confidential relation had existed.

per Lord Chelmsford in *Tate* v. *Williamson,* 1866.[158]

Inducement—Meaning of. In order to operate as an inducement the representation must—

(a) be made with the intention that it should be acted upon by the person misled (*Peek* v. *Gurney,* 1873,[159] and *Gross* v. *Lewis Hillman Ltd.,* 1969);[160]

(b) induce the contract so that the person making the claim to have been misled must not have relied on his own skill and judgment (*Redgrave* v. *Hurd,* 1881);[161]

(c) be material in the sense that it affected the plaintiff's judgment (*Smith* v. *Chadwick*, 1884);[162]

(d) be known to the plaintiff (*Horsfall* v. *Thomas*, 1862).[163]

Types of Actionable Misrepresentation. A *purely innocent misrepresentation* is a false statement made by a person *who had reasonable grounds* to believe that the statement was true not only when he made it but also at the time the contract was entered into.

A *negligent misrepresentation* is a false statement made by a person *who had no reasonable grounds* for believing the statement to be true. A *fraudulent misrepresentation* is a false representation of a material fact made knowing it to be false, or believing it to be false, or recklessly, not caring whether it be true or false. (*Derry* v. *Peek*, 1889.)[164]

In addition, under the law of agency, where an agent represents himself as having authority he does not possess the third party may sue the agent for breach of warranty of authority if he suffers loss by not obtaining a contract with the principal, the action being based on quasi-contract (see p. 209).

Furthermore, under Sect. 43 of the Companies Act, 1948, company promoters and directors are liable for negligent misstatements in prospectuses though they have certain defences (see p. 45). It should also be noted that the House of Lords has ruled in *Hedley Byrne* v. *Heller and Partners*, 1963,[165] that where there is a sufficient "special relationship" between the maker of the statement and the person who is to rely on it, the former owes the latter a duty of reasonable care in making the statement and may be liable in damages to the recipient if the statement contains false information given negligently rather than intentionally.

REMEDIES

There are the following possible remedies for misrepresentation—

(a) Rescission of the contract is a possible remedy in all cases of misrepresentation, whether fraudulent, negligent, or purely innocent.

(b) The refusal of the injured party to perform his part of the contract if he has not already done so. He can then raise the misrepresentation as a defence to an action for specific performance or damages.

(c) An action for damages in the case of fraud. In this case the plaintiff sues not on the contract but on the tort of deceit. The object of damages in fraud is to compensate the plaintiff for all the loss he has incurred as a result of the fraudulent inducement (*Doyle* v. *Olby* (*Ironmongers*) *Ltd.*, 1969)[166] although it has not been finally decided whether an award of exemplary damages may be made. (*Mafo* v. *Adams*, 1969.)[167]

(d) Where the misrepresentation is negligent the person making the false statement is liable in damages and the onus of proving that the statement was not made negligently, but that there were reasonable grounds for believing it to be true, is on the maker of the statement (Misrepresentation Act, 1967, Sect. 2 (1).) (*Gosling* v. *Anderson*, 1972.)[692]

(*e*) A purely innocent misrepresentation may be remedied by an award of damages but these cannot be claimed as such. The person seeking relief must ask for rescission of the contract and the court may, in its discretion, award damages instead. (Misrepresentation Act, 1967, Sect. 2 (2).)

Rescission. Rescission dates from the time when the party misled notifies his repudiation of the contract to the other party, or does any other act indicating repudiation. (*Car & Universal Finance Co.* v. *Caldwell*, 1963.)[168] A contract induced by fraud or misrepresentation (innocent or negligent) is voidable at the option of the party misled, but the injured party may lose the right of rescission in the following circumstances—

(*a*) *If the injured party affirms the contract, he cannot rescind.* He will affirm the contract if, with full knowledge of the misrepresentation, he *expressly* affirms it by stating that he intends to go on with it, or if he does some act from which an implied intention may properly be deduced. (*Long* v. *Lloyd*, 1958.)[169]

Lapse of time, or delay in asking for the remedy, is evidence of affirmation and can defeat an action for rescission. This is sometimes known as the doctrine of *laches,* and it is based on the maxim: "Delay defeats equities." (*Leaf* v. *International Galleries*, 1950.)[143] Lapse of time has no effect on rescission where fraud is alleged as long as the action is brought within six years of the time when the fraud was, or with reasonable diligence could have been, discovered. (Limitation Act, 1939, Sect. 26.)

(*b*) *Rescission is impossible if the parties cannot be restored to their original positions.* (*Clarke* v. *Dickson*, 1858.)[170]

(*c*) *It cannot be obtained where third party rights have accrued.* Rescission of a contract to take shares in a company cannot be obtained if the company has gone into liquidation, because creditors' rights are paramount. Further, if X obtains goods from Y by fraud and pawns them with Z, Y cannot rescind the contract on learning of the fraud in order to recover the goods from Z. (*Phillips* v. *Brooks Ltd.*, 1919.[136] See also *Lewis* v. *Averay*, 1971,[136a] and *Gross* v. *Lewis Hillman Ltd.*, 1969.)[160]

(*d*) There were two further rules which had a serious effect on the remedy—

(i) Where a representation had been sufficiently important to be incorporated in the contract, the party to whom it was made could not claim rescission of the contract in Equity but had to pursue the common law remedies for breach of a term. These remedies depended upon the status of the term. If a condition was broken the aggrieved party could repudiate the contract, but for breach of warranty the only remedy was a claim for damages.

Now the equitable right of rescission is preserved even where the representation has been incorporated in the contract. (Misrepresentation Act, 1967, Sect. 1 (*a*).) Although the Section says "where . . . the misrepresentation has become a *term* of the contract," it is not thought that there is a right to rescind for breach of a warranty but only for a representation *incorporated in* the contract. If this is so, the availability of a remedy as drastic as rescission for a misrepresentation of minor importance when mere damages are available for a more serious breach of warranty is anomalous. Possibly, if the court is asked to rescind a contract for misrepresentation of minor importance, it will exercise its discretion under Sect. 2 (2) of the 1967 Act to award damages in lieu of rescission.

(ii) Where the contract had been performed rescission could not be obtained if the misrepresentation was non-fraudulent. (*Seddon* v. *North Eastern Salt Co. Ltd.*, 1905,[171] and *Angel* v. *Jay*, 1911.)[172] Now a person is not prevented from asking for rescission merely because the contract has been performed. (Misrepresentation Act, 1967, Sect. 1 (*b*).)

Certain problems are raised by the provisions of these sections which are illustrated by the following example. A buys a drawing from B having been told by B, in innocence, that it is by Constable though it is in fact a fake. This assertion is then written in the subsequent contract as a condition of sale. If A wishes to reject the goods, he must do so within a reasonable time otherwise conditions become warranties for the purposes of remedies and A will have only an action for damages for the breach of condition. However, it seems that under Sects. 1 (*a*) and 1 (*b*) of the 1967 Act, A may ask for rescission for the innocent misrepresentation made by B. Thus a contract may be rescinded for innocent misrepresentation when the right to reject for breach of condition is barred. Presumably the court may regard performance of the contract as *evidence* of the plaintiff's intention to treat the contract as subsisting leaving him with an action for damages for the misrepresentation. Nevertheless, whenever a buyer wishes to reject goods for breach of a term of the contract and the seller contends that there is no right to reject, the buyer would be well advised to ask, in the alternative, for rescission for misrepresentation *provided the breach complained of is a misstatement of fact.* Failure *to perform* the contract properly is not a matter of misrepresentation and would not be covered by the Act of 1967.

Damages for Non-fraudulent Misrepresentation. Damages are obtainable for non-fraudulent misrepresentation in the following cases—

1. *Wholly Innocent Misrepresentation*

(*a*) Section 2 (2) of the Misrepresentation Act, 1967, provides that—

Where a person has entered into a contract after a misrepresentation has been made to him otherwise than fraudulently, and he would be *entitled*, by reason of the misrepresentation, to rescind the contract, then, if it is claimed, in any proceedings arising out of the contract, that the contract *ought to be* or has been rescinded, the court or arbitrator may declare the contract subsisting and award damages in lieu of rescission, if of opinion that it would be equitable to do so, having regard to the nature of the misrepresentation and the loss that would be caused by it if the contract were upheld, as well as to the loss that rescission would cause to the other party.

This subsection seems to be designed to give the court discretion to treat a contract as subsisting and award damages to the injured party in those cases where the misrepresentation is of a minor nature. However, damages cannot be awarded unless the party seeking them would have been *entitled* to rescind. Presumably therefore, if a bar to rescission exists, e.g. delay, then damages cannot be awarded either. However, the subsection also uses the words "ought to be . . . rescinded" and this may give the court a discretion to award damages even when a bar to rescission exists. For example, A sells a car to B, innocently representing that it is a 1948 model whereas it is a 1939 model. Six months later B discovers this fact and asks for rescission. Presumably B is not *entitled* to rescind on grounds of delay, but whether he can obtain damages or not will depend upon which of the two constructions outlined above is adopted by the court.

(*b*) *Agency.* Where an agent in good faith represents himself as having authority he does not possess, the third party may sue the agent for breach of warranty of authority if he suffers loss by not obtaining a contract with the principal, the action being based on quasi-contract.

2. *Negligent Misrepresentation*

(*a*) Section 2 (1) of the Misrepresentation Act, 1967, provides that—

Where a person has entered into a contract after a misrepresentation has been made to him by another party thereto and as a result thereof he has suffered loss, then, if the person making the misrepresentation would be liable to damages in respect thereof had the misrepresentation been made fraudulently, that person shall be so liable notwithstanding that the misrepresentation was not made fraudulently, unless he proves that he had reasonable ground to believe and did believe up to the time the contract was made that the facts represented were true.

Presumably the representor must have reasonable grounds for believing the statement to be true when he made it and right up to the time the contract was made. Thus if a person makes a representation honestly and reasonably believing it to be true, and before contract receives additional information, which makes his belief unreasonable, he may be liable for negligent misrepresentation if he does nothing to correct his statement.

(*b*) Under Sect. 43 of the Companies Act, 1948, where the directors publish a prospectus containing false statements made innocently, the directors will have to pay what is called compensation unless—

    (i) the directors had reasonable grounds for believing the statements to be true;

    (ii) the statements were made on the authority of an expert who was thought to be competent; or

    (iii) the statements were a copy of an official document.

(*c*) *Negligence at Common Law.* Where the parties concerned were not in a pre-contractual relationship when the statement was made Section 2 (1) of the Misrepresentation Act, 1967, will not apply. However, an action for damages for negligence will lie in tort provided the false statement is made negligently and a special relationship exists between the parties. (*Hedley Byrne and Co. Ltd.* v. *Heller and Partners Ltd.*, 1963.)[165]

3. *Misrepresentation may raise an estoppel.* If a person has relied on misstatement and has altered his previous position because of it, he may be able to base an action for damages on estoppel. (*Henderson* v. *Williams*, 1895)[173]

It is also possible to recover a monetary indemnity for some losses caused by misrepresentation. This remedy can be asked for along with rescission where the court decides it will not award damages. Sect. 2 (2) of the Misrepresentation Act, 1967, gives the court power to award damages instead of rescission but it cannot award both. Thus, if the court decides to grant rescission it is limited in its monetary award to that amount of loss for which equity would give an indemnity. (*Whittington* v. *Seale-Hayne*, 1900.)[174]

Criminal Penalties. In addition to the civil law remedies set out above the Trade Descriptions Act, 1968, makes it a criminal offence for a person to falsely or misleadingly describe goods (see p. 165).

TERMS OF THE CONTRACT

Up to this point we have been considering the principles relating to *the formation of a contract* by outlining the rules governing offer and acceptance, intention to create legal relations, consideration, capacity, and genuineness of consent. In consequence we have seen that failure to satisfy the requirements of the law in these areas can prevent *the formation of a valid contract.*

However, even where it is clear that a valid contract has been made it is still necessary to decide precisely what it is the parties have undertaken to do in order to be able to say whether each has performed, or not performed, his part of the agreement.

EXPRESS TERMS

The Statements of the Parties. In order to decide upon the *express terms* of the contract it is necessary to find out what was said or written by the parties.

Where the contract is wholly oral this is a matter of fact to be decided by the court from the evidence presented to it and may give rise to problems where the evidence is conflicting and difficult to substantiate.

In the case of a written contract it is usually obvious what the parties have written down, though problems of interpretation may arise, for example, from ambiguity, which the court may have to resolve. In addition it should be noted that where the terms of a contract have been written down the court may refuse to allow oral evidence to be admitted if it has the effect of adding to, varying or contradicting the written agreement. This rule is, however, subject to the following exceptions—

(*a*) *Oral evidence may be admitted to prove a trade custom or usage*, this will usually have the effect of adding a term or terms to the agreement;

(*b*) *oral evidence may be admitted to show that the contract has not yet become effective*, this is not truly an exception since the contract is not varied, added to or contradicted (*Pym* v. *Campbell*, 1856);[175]

(*c*) *oral evidence may be admitted where the court is of the opinion that the written document contains part only of the agreement*, this device is quite frequently used by the courts and represents a major exception to the rule relating to the admission of oral evidence (*Quickmaid Rental Services* v. *Reece*, 1970).[176]

Representation and Terms. Having ascertained what the parties said or wrote it is necessary to decide whether the statements are representations or terms. Representations are statements which merely induce a contract whereas terms are part of the contract itself and make up its contents. The distinction is, of course, less important than it was since before the Misrepresentation Act, 1967, there was often no remedy for a misrepresentation which was not fraudulent and in such a case the plaintiff's only hope of obtaining a remedy was to convince the court that the defendant's statement was not a mere inducement but a term of the contract of which the defendant was in breach. As we have seen the Misrepresentation Act, 1967, has broadened the scope of the remedies available for non-fraudulent misrepresentation.

Certain tests may be applied in order to decide whether a statement is a representation or a term of the contract—

(i) The court is always concerned to implement the *intentions of the parties* as they appear from statements made by them. Where, in a written contract, the parties have by their words indicated that a particular provision is to be considered as a term of the contract, then the court will normally follow that intention. Where the statement is an oral one, the court will decide the question by trying to ascertain the intentions of the parties and may come to the conclusion that the circumstances suggest that the statement was intended to be a term.

(ii) A statement is not likely to be a term if the person making the statement asks the other party to check or verify it, e.g. "The car is sound, but I should get an engineer's report on it."

(iii) A statement is likely to be a term if it is made with the intention of preventing the other party from finding any defects, and succeeds in doing this, e.g. "The horse is sound; you need not look him over."

(iv) If the statement is such that the aggrieved party would not have made the contract without it, then the statement will be a term of the contract. (*Bannerman* v. *White*, 1861.)[177]

(v) A statement made during *preliminary negotiations* tends to be pre-contractual. Where the interval between the making of the statement and the making of the contract is distinct, then the statement is almost certain to be a representation. However, the interval is not always so well marked, and in such cases there is difficulty in deciding whether the statement is a representation or a term.

If the statement was oral and the contract was afterwards reduced to writing then the terms of the contract tend to be contained in the writing, and all oral statements tend to be pre-contractual.

(vi) Where one of the parties has *special knowledge or skill* with regard to the subject-matter of the contract, then such a party can more easily give warranties to the other, and will find it difficult to convince the court that warranties have been given to him. (*Oscar Chess Ltd.* v. *Williams*, 1957.)[178]

The case of *D'Mello* v. *Loughborough College of Technology*, 1970,[179] is a good example of some of the problems which may face a court in deciding whether or not preliminary dealings are part of a contract.

Collateral Contracts. The courts have sometimes resorted to the concept of the "collateral contract" or "collateral warranty" in order to provide a remedy of damages for what was, in effect, non-fraudulent misrepresentation.

The concept proved useful where an important statement made by the defendant could not, under the rules outlined above, be regarded as a term of the main contract but might be construed as a separate and parallel contractual obligation for breach of which damages could be awarded.

The concept has been used in two sorts of case—

(*a*) *Cases where only two parties are involved.* Suppose that X is leasing a house to Y and the terms of the lease are written up in a document, but that Y is induced to sign the lease by an innocent misstatement by X that the drains are sound. If the court had treated this sort of statement as a mere innocent misrepresentation then Y would most probably have been left without a remedy, since, before the Misrepresentation Act, 1967, he could not have recovered damages in respect of the statement, and it was also likely that for one reason or another he had lost his right to rescind. Therefore, to provide a remedy in appropriate cases, the court would sometimes regard innocent misstatements as collateral contracts or warranties and award damages for their breach. (*De Lassalle* v. *Guildford*, 1901.)[180]

Now that damages may be awarded for innocent misrepresentation under Sect. 2 (2) of the Misrepresentation Act, 1967, and that the right to rescind is not lost by mere performance of the contract under Sect. 1 (*b*) of the same Act, the concept of the collateral contract may have become redundant where the only persons involved are the two parties to the contract. In the case of negligent misstatements, the court might, before the Misrepresentation Act, 1967, have had to resort to the concept of the collateral contract because although *Hedley Byrne* v. *Heller and Partners*, 1963,[165] had established a potential action for damages in respect of negligent misstatements resulting in monetary loss, the boundaries of the action were not, and still are not, clear.

However, the Misrepresentation Act, 1967, Sect. 2 (1) gives the court power to award damages for negligent misrepresentation and it should no longer be necessary to resort to the concept of the collateral contract or warranty in the case of negligent misrepresentation.

(*b*) *Cases in which three parties are involved.* The concept of the collateral contract or warranty has also been used in cases where the representation upon which the plaintiff claims has been made to him by a stranger to the main contract.

Suppose that X, a representative of A Brand paint, calls on Y, a householder, to try to sell him some paint. In the course of conversation X makes a statement that the paint will last for five years and Y is impressed but does not buy any paint from X. However, the next day, when contracting with a decorator, D, for the painting of his house, Y insists that D uses A Brand paint for the job. D buys the paint from the manufacturer, receiving no undertakings as to its lasting qualities, and uses it to paint Y's house. Twelve months later the paint is peeling badly and Y wishes to sue the firm. However, since X's misstatement did not induce a contract between Y and the paint manufacturer, there should, strictly speaking, be no action in contract against the manufacturer. Nevertheless, the court might use the concept of the collateral contract to give Y damages against the manufacturer. (*Shanklin Pier Ltd.* v. *Detel Products Ltd.*, 1951.)[181]

Since, in this three-party situation, there is still no contract between the plaintiff and the third party, the provisions of the Misrepresentation Act, 1967, will not help, but the decision in *Hedley Byrne and Co. Ltd.* v. *Heller and Partners Ltd.*, 1963,[165] may provide persons in the position of Y with an action for damages in pure tort, provided the statement is made negligently and the special relationship aspect of the decision is satisfied.

Conditions and Warranties. Not all of the obligations created by a contract are of equal importance and this is recognised by the law which has applied a special terminology to contractual terms in order to distinguish the vital or fundamental obligations from the less vital, the expression *condition* being applied to the former and the expression *warranty* to the latter.

A *condition* is a vital term which goes to the root of the contract. It is an obligation which goes directly to the substance of the contract, or is so essential to its very nature that its non-performance may be considered by the other party as a substantial failure to perform the contract at all.

A *warranty*, on the other hand, is subsidiary to the main purpose, and there is no right in the injured party to repudiate the contract; there is only an action for damages. A warranty has been variously defined, but it may be said to be an obligation which, though it must be performed, is not so vital that a failure to perform it goes to the substance of the contract.

Whether a stipulation is a condition or a warranty is a question of the intention of the parties, and this is deduced from the circumstances of the case. Furthermore, the words used by the parties, while not conclusive will often be followed. They may have called a particular term a condition or a warranty, or even have used less specific terms whose intention is clear. In some cases where the parties state the effect of a breach, it becomes clear whether a condition or warranty was intended. (*Harling* v. *Eddy*, 1951.)[182] If there is no such indication, the court may address itself to the commercial importance of the term. (*Behn* v. *Burness*, 1863.)[183] An interesting contrast is provided in *Poussard* v. *Spiers and Pond*, 1876,[184] and *Bettini* v. *Gye*, 1876.[185] Where there is a breach of condition, the injured party may elect either to repudiate the contract or claim damages. For a breach of warranty the only remedy is an action for damages.

Exception, Exemption or Exclusion Clauses. The parties may insert terms into their contract excluding or limiting liability in certain contingencies. Such terms are permissible and effective provided they are *communicated* to the other party. However, in the absence of fraud or misrepresentation, a person is not excused if he does not read a written contract. So if a contract contains exemption clauses, and the person concerned does not bother to read the document which manifestly purports to set out those terms, he will be bound by them in spite of his ignorance. There are circumstances in which the person accepting the offer is not aware of the conditions attaching to it, but is nevertheless bound by them. The situation often occurs where a ticket or other document, containing the terms of the contract or an indication as to where they may be found, is delivered to the acceptor but is not read by him.

In such cases it is essential that the ticket or other document should be an integral part of the contract and not, for example, a mere receipt evidencing payment. (*Chapelton* v. *Barry U.D.C.*, 1940.)[186] If it is such a document, much depends upon whether it was signed by the acceptor or not. Where an unsigned document sets out the terms of the contract, or says where they may be found, then the acceptor, may have constructive notice of the terms and conditions, so long as the ticket or other document adequately draws the attention of a reasonable person to the existence of such terms and conditions. (*Thompson* v. *L.M.S. Railway*, 1930,[187] and *Richardson Steamship Co. Ltd.* v. *Rowntree*, 1894.)[188] Where the document is signed by the acceptor, it will be difficult for him to avoid the terms and conditions (*L'Estrange* v. *Graucob Ltd.*, 1934),[189] though it may be possible for him to do so if he is misled as to the effect of the document by an oral representation. (*Curtis* v. *Chemical Cleaning and Dyeing Co.*, 1951,[156] see also *Mendelssohn* v. *Normand Ltd.*, 1969.)[156a]

Any conditions attaching to the offer must be notified at the time the offer is made, since a belated notice is valueless. (*Olley* v. *Marlborough Court Ltd.*, 1949,[190] and *Thornton* v. *Shoe Lane Parking Ltd.*, 1971.)[190a] It is true that where a ticket is used to communicate conditions, the notice may often be belated as in the case of a railway ticket which is not received until after the contract is made. It seems that, in this sort of case, the law assumes that members of the public must realise that certain conditions will be attached to such contracts. In any case they have a right to assume that the conditions when ascertained will be reasonable, and the court would presumably strike out an unreasonable clause which had been communicated solely by constructive notice. It should also be noted that a person cannot take advantage of an exemption clause in a contract to which he was not a party. (*Adler* v. *Dickson*, 1955.)[191]

In the absence of any contractual document, the principle of constructive notice implicit in the "ticket cases" has no application, and previous dealings between the parties are relevant only if they prove knowledge of the terms, actual or constructive, and also prove assent to them. (*McCutcheon* v. *David MacBrayne Ltd.*, 1964.)[192] Any ambiguities in an exclusion clause are construed against the party who inserted the clause. (*Akerib* v. *Booth*, 1961.)[193]

Effect of Misrepresentation Act, 1967. Section 3 of the Act provides as follows—

> If any agreement (whether made before or after the commencement of this Act) contains a provision which would exclude or restrict—
>
> > (*a*) any liability to which a party to a contract may be subject by reason of any misrepresentation made by him before the contract was made; or
> >
> > (*b*) any remedy available to another party to the contract by reason of such a misrepresentation;

that provision shall be of no effect except to the extent (if any), that, in any proceedings arising out of the contract, the court or arbitrator may allow reliance on it as being fair and reasonable in the circumstances of the case.

The section, although attacking exclusion clauses designed to exclude liability for misrepresentation, appears to allow a person to exclude his liability for breaches of conditions and warranties. Furthermore, the court is given a discretion and may allow an exemption clause to take effect in appropriate circumstances.

The Doctrine of Fundamental Breach. This doctrine was usually invoked when a plaintiff sought a remedy on a contract which contained exemption clauses which had been adequately communicated. It amounted to saying that where a person had committed a fundamental breach of his contract he could not rely on exemption clauses introduced into the contract for his benefit. (*Karsales (Harrow) Ltd.* v. *Wallis*, 1956,[194] and *Alexander* v. *Railway Executive*, 1951.)[195]

It also appeared that the person who alleged fundamental breach bore the burden of proving that this was so. (*Hunt and Winterbottom (West of England) Ltd.* v. *B.R.S. (Parcels) Ltd.*, 1962.)[196]

There has always been difficulty over the meaning of a fundamental breach and attempts have been made to distinguish it from a condition (or repudiatory breach) so that an exemption clause excluding liability for breach of condition would be ineffective to exclude liability for fundamental breach, but as a result of *Suisse Atlantique Société D'Armament Maritime S.A.* v. *N.V. Rotterdamsche Kolen Centrale*, 1966[197] (known as the *Suisse Case*), and *Harbutt's Plasticine Ltd.* v. *Wayne Tank & Pump Co. Ltd.*, 1970,[198] the position appears to be as follows—

(1) There is no breach of contract more fundamental than a breach of condition. In the *Suisse Case* the House of Lords defined a fundamental breach as a breach by one party entitling the other to treat the contract as terminated. This definition equates fundamental breach with repudiatory breach of condition.

(2) A fundamental breach will normally occur only where the method of performance is totally different from that contemplated by the contract (*Kenyon, Son & Craven Ltd.* v. *Baxter Hoare & Co. Ltd.*, 1971).[197a]

(3) The effect of a breach of condition on an exclusion clause would appear to be as follows—

(*a*) if a breach of condition is established and the innocent party has *elected* to treat the breach as a repudiation of the contract thus bringing it to an end, then the exclusion clause falls with the rest of the contract and cannot be used to exclude an action for loss arising from the breach of condition concerned—this point was made by Lord Reid in the *Suisse Case*;[197]

(*b*) the position is the same where the defendant's breach of condition brings the contract to an end automatically without the innocent party being in a position to *elect* (*per* Lord Denning in *Harbutt's Case*);[198]

(*c*) if a breach of condition is established but the innocent party with knowledge of the breach proceeds to treat the contract as continuing and then sues for damages, the exclusion clause may survive and be raised as a defence. Whether it will be effective to exclude or modify the defendant's liability will depend upon the relevant rules of construction of contracts (*per* Lord Denning in *Harbutt's Case*),[198] These are as follows—

(i) under the *contra proferentem rule* exclusion clauses are read strictly against those wishing to rely on them (*Alexander* v. *Railway Executive*, 1951;[195] *Akerib* v. *Booth*);[193]

(ii) a court will either strike out or modify an exemption clause which is repugnant to the *main purpose* of the contract (*Pollock and Co.* v. *Macrae*, 1922),[199] the application of this rule would be an alternative way of arriving at the decision in *Karsales (Harrow) Ltd.* v. *Wallis*, 1956;[194]

(iii) exemption clauses only protect a party when he is acting within *the four corners of the contract*, deviation from the contract is usually regarded as a fundamental breach (*Thomas National Transport (Melbourne) Pty. Ltd. and Pay* v. *May and Baker (Australia) Pty. Ltd.*, 1966[200] and *Mendelssohn* v. *Normand Ltd.*, 1969);[156a]

(iv) In addition the courts may reject, as a matter of construction, even the widest exemption clause if it: ". . . would lead to an absurdity, or because it would defeat the main object of the contract or perhaps for other reasons. And where some limit must be read into a clause, it is generally reasonable to draw the line at fundamental breaches." (*per* Lord Denning in *Harbutt's Case*.)[198]

This general rule of construction that normally an exception or exclusion clause or similar provision in a contract should be construed as not applying to a situation created by a fundamental breach of contract was approved by the House of Lords in the *Suisse Case*[197] and applied by the Court of Appeal in *Farnworth Finance Facilities* v. *Attryde*, 1970.[198a]

(*d*) In order to determine whether a breach is fundamental or not the court may look with hindsight at its *results* and not merely at its *quality*. (*per* Lord Denning in *Harbutt's Case*.)[198]

IMPLIED TERMS

In addition to the *express* terms inserted by the parties a contract may contain and be subject to *implied* terms. Such terms are derived from custom or statute. Furthermore a term may be implied by the court where it is necessary in order to achieve the result which the parties obviously intended the contract to have.

Customary implied Terms. A contract may be subject to customary terms not specifically mentioned by the parties. (*Hutton* v. *Warren*, 1836.)[201] However, customary terms will not be implied if the express terms of the contract reveal that the parties had a contrary intention.

Statutory implied Terms. In a contract for the sale of goods or hire purchase the Sale of Goods Act, 1893, and the Hire Purchase Act, 1965, respectively settle the matter of implied terms unless the relevant provisions have been specifically excluded. The terms implied by these Acts relate to title, description, fitness for the purpose and quality, and certain of them cannot be excluded (see pp. 178–80).

Judicial implied Terms. The court may imply a term into a contract whenever it is necessary to do so in order that the express terms decided upon by the parties shall have the effect which was presumably intended by them. This is often expressed as the giving of "business efficacy" to the contract, the judge regarding himself as doing merely what the parties themselves would have done in order to cover the situation if they had addressed themselves to it. The operation of the doctrine is illustrated by *The Moorcock*, 1889,[22] and *Lister* v. *Romford Ice and Cold Storage Co. Ltd.*, 1957.[202]

CONTRACTS *UBERRIMAE FIDEI*

A contract *uberrimae fidei* is a contract of the utmost good faith. There is generally no obligation on a contracting party to enlighten the other party even where he knows or suspects there is a misapprehension. For example, X offers to sell a watch to Y, and Y, thinking it is a gold watch, offers £30 for it. X, knowing the watch is not gold, accepts Y's offer without enlightening him. The contract is binding provided X made no representation in the matter. The essential maxim in such cases is *caveat emptor*! (Let the buyer beware!) This rather harsh rule is modified in certain circumstances, e.g. in the case of sales by dealers, the Sale of Goods Act, 1893, imports into the contract certain implied conditions and warranties, unless the parties exclude them.

There are certain contracts in which disclosure of material facts is required by law. They are called contracts *uberrimae fidei* or contracts of the utmost good faith. Here silence can amount to misrepresentation, in the sense that non-disclosure of some material fact by one of the parties to the contract will give rise to a remedy in the injured party. The following contracts are of this type—

(i) *Contracts of Insurance.* There is a duty on the person insured to disclose to the insurer all facts which might affect the premium. Failure to do so renders the contract voidable at the option of the insurer.

(ii) *Contracts to take shares in a company under a prospectus.* There is a duty on the company or its promoters to disclose the various matters set out in the Fourth Schedule to the Companies Act, 1948. Failure to do so may render those responsible liable in damages, and give the injured party the right to rescind his contract as against the company.

(iii) *Family Arrangements.* In contracts and dealings between members of a family, each member must disclose all material facts within his knowledge.

(iv) *Contracts for the sale of land.* The vendor is under a duty to disclose all defects in his title if they are known to him, and also the extent of any restrictive covenants affecting the land.

(v) *Suretyship and Partnership Contracts.* There is a duty on partners to disclose all matters within their knowledge which affect or may affect the business. However, this duty arises only when the partners *are partners* so that disclosure is not required during the negotiations leading to the partnership agreement. Similarly there is some duty of disclosure between a creditor and the person who guarantees the debt due from the principal debtor.

Probably contracts of insurance are the only true contracts *uberrimae fidei*. The others are analogous thereto, but are based more on the equitable concept of fiduciary relationship. The question of disclosure in the case of company prospectuses is, of course, statutory, the courts having consistently refused to declare that a contract to take shares from a company was of the class *uberrimae fidei*, though a rather higher duty of disclosure was placed on company promoters and directors. A contract of service does not give rise to duties of disclosure. (*Bell* v. *Lever Brothers Ltd.*, 1932.)[142]

DURESS AND UNDUE INFLUENCE

Contracts and gifts effected by duress or undue influence are voidable at the option of the party coerced or influenced. *Duress* is limited to actual violence or threats of violence to the person, or imprisonment or the threat of criminal proceedings to the person coerced or to those near and dear to him. (*Cumming* v. *Ince*, 1847.)[203] Threats to property are not enough.

The doctrine of *undue influence* was developed by Equity. Where no special relationship exists between the parties, the party seeking to avoid the contract must prove that he was subjected to influences which excluded free consent. (*Williams* v. *Bayley*, 1866.)[204] But where a confidential or *fiduciary* relationship exists between the parties, the party in whom the confidence was reposed must show that undue influence was not used; i.e. that the contract was the act of a free and independent mind. It is desirable, though not essential, that independent advice should have been given.

There are several confidential relationships known to the law, viz. parent and child, solicitor and client, trustee and *cestui que trust* (or beneficiary), guardian and ward; but there is no presumption of such relationship between husband and wife. The fiduciary relationship between parent and child continues until the child is emancipated which is usually, but not necessarily, on reaching eighteen or on getting married. (*Lancashire Loans Ltd.* v. *Black*, 1934.)[205]

It should be noted, however, that there may be a presumption of undue influence even though the relationship between the parties is not in the established categories outlined above. *In re Craig dec'd*, [1970] 2 W.L.R. 1221, Ungoed Thomas, J., held that a presumption of undue influence arose on proof—

(*a*) of a gift so substantial or of such a nature that it could not on the face of it be accounted for on the grounds of the ordinary motives on which ordinary men acted; and

(*b*) of a relationship of trust and confidence such that the recipient of the gift was in a position to exercise undue influence over the person making it. (*Hodgson* v. *Marks*, 1970.)[206]

A claim to set aside a contract for undue influence must be made within a reasonable time after the contract was made or the influence ceased to have effect. Delay in claiming relief may bar the claim since delay is possible evidence of affirmation. (*Allcard* v. *Skinner*, 1887.)[207]

A contract procured by undue influence cannot be avoided by rescission after affirmation, express or implied, nor against persons who acquire rights for value without notice of the facts; but it may be avoided against third parties for value who had notice of the undue influence, and also against volunteers (i.e. persons who have given no consideration) even though they were unaware of the facts.

ILLEGAL CONTRACTS

When the word "illegal" is used of a contract it does not mean that a criminal offence is necessarily involved. It does mean, however, that the courts will not enforce the contract because it is in some way injurious to society.

According to the decision in *Goodinson* v. *Goodinson*, 1954,[208] illegal contracts can be divided into two classes.

(i) Illegal contracts strictly so called because although not necessarily criminal they involve a degree of moral wrong; and

(ii) Illegal contracts traditionally so called by the courts but which do not involve a degree of moral wrong.

Illegal Contracts Strictly so called.

CONTRACTS WHICH INVOLVE THE COMMISSION OF A CRIME OR CIVIL WRONG. Obviously contracts to commit crimes are rarely brought before the courts for enforcement, but such cases have occurred. (*Dann* v. *Curzon*, 1911.)[209] The following are examples of agreements to commit a civil wrong—

(i) Agreements to procure a breach of contract, e.g. where X contracts with Y that Y will break his contract with Z, the agreement between X and Y is illegal.

(ii) Agreements between a principal debtor and the creditor which are prejudicial to the surety, e.g. in the case of a fidelity bond for an officer of a company, the contract is avoided by a material change in the duties of the office, if the change increases the risk of misconduct in the officer.

(iii) Contracts under which agents take double or secret commissions, since the interest and duty of the agent are then in conflict.

Contracts prohibited by Statute

(*a*) *Contracts which incidentally infringe the provisions of a statute.* A contract may be restricted or controlled by the provisions of a statute, but it does follow that every contract which infringes the statutory provisions will necessarily be void. It seems that—

(i) The contract will be void if it appears from the wording of the statute that the legislature intended the statute to preserve public order, to maintain or improve public safety, or to protect the public, and the contract tends to endanger this objective: (*Anderson* v. *Daniel,* 1924,[210] but see *Shaw* v. *Groom,* 1970.)[211]

(ii) The contract will be valid if it appears that the statutory provision was imposed for some administrative purpose only, and one which is not directly connected with the making of the contract itself. (*Smith* v. *Mawhood,* 1845.)[212]

(*b*) *Cases where a statute definitely prohibits a certain type of contract.* Two of the more important examples of these are (i) Contracts infringing the Restrictive Trade Practices Act, 1956 (these will be dealt with along with contracts in restraint of trade), and (ii) Gaming and Wagering Contracts.

Wagering contracts are defined by Hawkins, J., in *Carlill* v. *Carbolic Smoke Ball Co. Ltd.,* 1892,[3] as those "by which two persons professing to hold opposite views touching the issue of a future uncertain event mutually agree that dependent upon the determination of that event one shall win from the other and that other shall pay or hand over to him a sum of money or other stake; neither of the contracting parties having any other interest in that contract than the sum or stake he will so win or lose, there being no other real consideration for the making of such contract by either of the parties."

For a wager to exist it must be possible for one party to win and one party to lose, and there must be two persons or two groups opposed to each other. Thus, where X, Y, and Z each put £5 into a fund to be given to the party whose selected horse wins a given race, there is no wager. A contract is not a wager if the person to whom the money is promised on the occurrence of the event has an interest in the non-occurrence of that event, e.g. where a man pays a premium to insure his house against destruction by fire. Such an interest is called an *insurable interest.* To insure someone else's property would be a wager.

In order to ascertain whether a contract is or is not a wager in doubtful cases, the court will go to the substance of the contract and will not concern itself solely with external appearances. So what looks like a contract of sale may in fact be a wager. (*Brogden* v. *Marriott*, 1836,[213] and *Rourke* v. *Short*, 1856.)[214]

Gaming means the playing of a game of chance for winnings in money or money's worth. A gaming contract is not necessarily a wager since there may be more than two parties to it. In general such transactions are lawful if all the players have an equal chance of winning. A bet on the outcome of a game is, of course, a wager.

IMMORAL CONTRACTS. These may be considered under two headings—

(*a*) *Sexual immorality.* It seems that the court has no general power to declare transactions immoral but is restricted to contracts involving sexual immorality. Agreements for illicit cohabitation are therefore void. But the rule applies only to a contract in which men and women agree to live in sin in the future. A contract in which a man promises to pay a woman money in return for past cohabitation is not illegal, because it does not necessarily encourage future immorality between the parties. Such a contract will, however, be unenforceable unless made under seal because it is for a past consideration. Contracts the purpose of which is *prima facie* good will be unenforceable if they are knowingly made to further an immoral purpose. (*Pearce* v. *Brooks*, 1866.)[215]

(*b*) *Immoral publications.* No enforceable contract can arise out of a blasphemous, seditious or indecent publication. Here again the courts do not seem to have a general power to declare publications immoral. It would seem that, unless the publication is one which infringes the present rules of the criminal law and is punishable as a crime, the Civil courts have no power to declare a contract made in connection with the publication illegal.

CONTRACTS CONTRARY TO PUBLIC POLICY. Such contracts do not necessarily involve the commission of a legal wrong, but are disapproved of by the law because—

(i) they tend to be prejudicial to the State in its relations with other States; or

(ii) they affect adversely the internal relations of the State, i.e. good rule and government and the proper administration of justice; or

(iii) they are in derogation of marriage; or

(iv) they involve unreasonable and excessive interference with the lawful activities and duties of individual citizens.

It was at one time thought that the judiciary had wide powers of discretion in the matter of creating new categories of public policy, but this view is now unacceptable. In *Fender* v. *Mildmay*, [1938] A.C. 1, the House of Lords declared against the extension of the heads of public policy, at least by the judiciary. There is a suggestion in the case that the categories of public policy are closed, and it is thought to be difficult and unusual for the judiciary to discover a new one.

The major categories of Public Policy are—

(*a*) *Contracts affecting the State in external relations.*

(i) Trading contracts with the enemy. At common law all contracts made with a person (regardless of nationality) living in enemy territory in time of war are illegal, unless made with licence of the Crown (see p. 25). During the wars of 1914–18 and 1939–45, the common law on the subject was reinforced by emergency legislation.

(ii) Contracts to carry out acts which are illegal by the law of a foreign and friendly country. Examples of such contracts are found in *Foster* v. *Driscoll*, 1929,[216] and *Regazzoni* v. *K. C. Sethia*, 1958.[217]

(*b*) *Contracts prejudicial to the Administration of Justice.*

(i) Contracts stifling a prosecution for a criminal offence, and contracts tending to defeat the bankruptcy laws. (*John* v. *Mendoza*, 1939.)[218]

(ii) Collusive divorce which occurs where the parties to a marriage make an agreement which concerns the commencement of a suit for divorce, or provides for its conduct, e.g. an agreement to commit adultery to provide grounds for a petition.

(iii) Contracts of Champerty and Maintenance were considered illegal as tending to upset the proper administration of justice. A person who encouraged another to bring a civil action committed the tort and crime of maintenance. If he agreed to take a share in the proceeds of the action he was guilty of the further offence of champerty. The Criminal Law Act, 1967, in Sections 13 and 14, abolishes champerty and maintenance as crimes and as torts, but contracts involving these former offences are, by Sect. 14, rendered unenforceable.

(*c*) *Contracts tending to corruption in public life*, e.g. the sale of public offices, the assignment of the salaries of public officials, or contracts to procure titles. (*Parkinson* v. *College of Ambulance*, 1925.)[219]

(*d*) *Contracts to defraud the revenue*, whether national or local. (*Napier* v. *National Business Agency Ltd.*, 1951;[220] *Alexander* v. *Rayson*, 1936.)[221]

Illegal contracts strictly so called may be illegal as formed, that is, agreements which cannot be lawfully performed, such as an agreement to commit a crime. Thus in *Dann* v. *Curzon*, 1911,[209] the contract was illegal as formed.

Such a contract is void and neither party can claim any right or redress under it, for the maxim is *ex turpi causa non oritur actio* (no right of action arises from a base cause). Thus in *Napier* v. *National Business Agency Ltd.*, 1957,[220] the servant could not recover arrears of salary. Money paid or property transferred under the contract are not usually recoverable for in *pari delicto potior est conditio defendentis* (or *possidentis*) (where both parties are equally in the wrong, the position of the defendant (or possessor) is the stronger). Thus in *Parkinson* v. *College of Ambulance*, 1925,[219] the plaintiff was unable to recover money paid under an illegal contract to procure a title.

However recovery is possible in the following situations—

(i) Where ownership has not been transferred under the contract the plaintiff may be able to recover his property without pleading the illegal contract. Thus if A leases property to B for 5 years and A knows that B intends to use the property as a brothel, then A cannot recover rent or require any covenant to be performed without pleading the illegal lease. However, at the end of the term A can bring an action for the return of his property as *owner* and not as a landlord under an illegal lease. However, if the action is to redress a wrong which, although in a sense connected with the contract, can really be considered independent of it, the law will allow the action. (*Edler* v. *Auerbach*, 1950.)[222] It is this basic principle which allows a party to an illegal transaction to recover property transferred under it if he can do so without relying on the illegal contract as by proving his ownership of the goods. (*Bowmakers Ltd.* v. *Barnet Instruments Ltd.*, 1944.)[223]

The rule is restricted to the recovery of property other than money for there cannot be a bailment of money, and when a person hands over money he hands over the entire title. To recover he must proceed on the contract and if it is illegal there can be no recovery.

(ii) The plaintiff will recover in spite of a defence of illegality unless the defendant can show that the plaintiff had *knowledge* of the illegality and *actively participated* in it. (*Fielding and Platt Ltd.* v. *Najjar*, 1969.)[224] However, where the parties have both participated in the illegal transaction but are not in *pari delicto* (equal wrong) the less guilty party may be allowed to recover. However, in order to rebut the presumption of equal guilt it must be shown that the defendant was guilty of fraud or oppression, or abused a fiduciary position. (*Atkinson* v. *Denby*, 1862;[225] *Hughes* v. *Liverpool Victoria Friendly Society*, 1916.)[226]

In the case of statutory illegality, it may be that the object of the statute is to protect a class of persons and the plaintiff is within that class. If so, the plaintiff may be able to recover money or property transferred under the contract, for he is not deemed to be in *pari delicto*. (*Kiriri Cotton Co. Ltd.* v. *Dawani*, 1960.)[227]

(iii) Where the illegal purpose has not been fully performed because of the plaintiff's repentance, he may be allowed to recover. Problems have arisen in deciding what constitutes full performance and it would seem that a person may repent after *partial* performance (*Taylor* v. *Bowers*, 1876)[228] but not after *substantial* performance (*Kearley* v. *Thomson*, 1890.)[229] However, in spite of the two cases mentioned the better view is that the plaintiff must also show that his repentance is *voluntary*, and not that he has merely been thwarted in an illegal scheme. (*Bigos* v. *Bousted*, 1951.)[230]

It should be noted that collateral transactions *between the same parties* are void (*Fisher* v. *Bridges*, 1854).[231] Where a *third party* enters into a collateral contract with one or both of the parties to the original transaction his rights will depend upon whether he knew or not that the original transaction was illegal. (*Southern Industrial Trust* v. *Brooke House Motors*, 1968[232] and *Spector* v. *Ageda*, 1971.)[68]

In all actions brought in England the contract is subject to English rules of public policy even though the proper law of the contract is not English Law. (*Kaufman* v. *Gerson*, 1904.)[233]

Illegal as performed means that the contract is in respect of a prima facie innocent transaction but one party performs part of the agreement in an illegal manner. (*Cowan* v. *Milbourn*, 1867.)[234]

Where the contract is of this type the guilty party cannot sue on the contract for damages (*Cowan* v. *Milbourn*, 1867,)[234] nor can he recover property delivered to the other party under the contract. (*Berg* v. *Sadler and Moore*, 1937.)[235] However, the position of the innocent party is strong for he can—

(i) Sue on a *quantum meruit* (as much as he has earned) (see p. 92) for work done (*Clay* v. *Yates*, 1856),[236] or *quantum valebant* (as much as they are worth) for goods supplied;

(ii) sue on a separate promise, if one was given, that the work would be legally performed (*Strongman* v. *Sincock*, 1955);[237]

(iii) recover money paid or property transferred, because he is not in *pari delicto*;

(iv) recover damages for breach of contract. (*Marles* v. *Trant (Philip) and Sons Ltd.*, 1954.)[238]

Illegal Contracts Traditionally so called

Some writers do not apply the word "illegal" to the following contracts because they do not regard it as appropriate. Instead they refer to the contracts as "void at common law on grounds of public policy."

CONTRACTS TO OUST THE JURISDICTION OF THE COURTS. A contract which has the effect of taking away the right of one or both of the parties to bring an action before a court of law is illegal. (*Re Davstone Estates Ltd.*, 1969.)[239] This rule does not render illegal contracts where the parties do not intend to create legal relationships (see pp. 11–13). In such cases the parties *do not intend to be bound by the contract at all*. If, however, the contract is to be binding, then the parties cannot exclude it from the jurisdiction of the courts.

Many commercial contracts contain an arbitration clause, the usual object being to provide a cheaper or more convenient remedy than a court action. An arbitration clause in a contract is not illegal if the effect of it is that the parties are to go to arbitration *first* before going to court. An arbitration clause which denies the parties access to the courts completely is invalid.

CONTRACTS IN DEROGATION OF MARRIAGE. A contract in absolute restraint of marriage (i.e. one in which a person promises not to marry at all) is void. Partial restraints, if reasonable, are valid, e.g. a contract not to marry a person of a certain religious faith. Marriage brokage contracts (i.e. contracts to introduce men and women with a view to their subsequent marriage) are also void.

Contracts by persons already married to marry a third party are void as being in derogation of marriage and also because they tend to immorality. Thus, if X, a married man, promises to marry Y, a spinster, the contract cannot be enforced by X; nor in damages by Y if she was aware of X's marital state. Agreements between spouses for future separation are void if made before marriage or during cohabitation. Separation agreements are valid where they set out the rights of persons already separated, or are part of a reconciliation agreement.

CONTRACTS IN RESTRAINT OF TRADE. These are so important that they will receive separate treatment (see p. 62).

CONTRACTS RESTRAINING THE LIBERTY OF THE INDIVIDUAL ARE ILLEGAL (*Horwood* v. *Millar's Timber and Trading Co. Ltd.*, 1917),[240] though such restriction may be valid for certain purposes. (*Denny's Trustee* v. *Denny*, 1919.)[241] Contracts which seek to stifle comment on public affairs are also void either under this heading or as in restraint of trade. (*Neville* v. *Dominion of Canada News Co. Ltd.*, 1915.)[242]

EFFECT OF ILLEGALITY WHERE CONTRACT IS TRADITIONALLY CALLED ILLEGAL. Such contracts are void only in so far as they conflict with the rules of public policy. (*Wallis* v. *Day*, 1837.)[243] Money paid and property transferred is recoverable. (*Hermann* v. *Charlesworth*, 1905.)[244] The doctrine of severance applies so that, where the contract is legal in part only, it may be possible to obtain the assistance of the court in enforcing the good part of the agreement. It was held in *Goodinson* v. *Goodinson*, 1954,[208] that—

(*a*) there can be no severance of contracts which are illegal in the strict sense;

(*b*) there may be severance where the contract is illegal only in the traditional sense.

If the illegal part is a substantial part of the contract as a whole, severance may prove impossible; but if the illegal part is subsidiary, the legal part may be enforced. Thus, a servant, who has entered into a contract of service which contains a restraint which is too wide, can recover his wages or salary because the restraint is subsidiary, the substantial purpose of the contract being to obtain the services of the employee.

The court will not add to a contract or in any way redraft it, but will merely strike out the offending words. What is left must make sense without further additions, otherwise the court will not sever the illegal part in order to enforce the good part. It should be noted that, even where severance is possible, the court is not bound to sever, and the court will not sever a contract unless the provisions remaining leave the contract substantially what it was before. Severance will not be allowed if it alters the nature of the contract. (*Kenyon* v. *Darwin Cotton Manufacturing Co.*, 1936.)[245]

CONTRACTS IN RESTRAINT OF TRADE

Restraints of trade may appear in ordinary contracts, leases and mortgages. In *Nordenfelt* v. *Maxim Nordenfelt Guns and Ammunition Co.*, 1894,[246] the House of Lords laid down that all restraints of trade are void unless reasonable in the interests of the parties and the public. Later in *Morris* v. *Saxelby*, 1916,[247] the House decided that, to be reasonable between the parties, the restraint must be no wider than required to protect the covenantee's interests; mere competition not being an interest entitled to such protection.

However, special considerations seem to apply to transactions concerning land such as leases and mortgages. Thus a landlord being fully entitled to the property at the end of the lease (i.e. the reversion) or on forfeiture, can protect the amenities or structure of the property by restraints on the tenant's trade. Similarly, a mortgagee (the lender) may impose restraints on the trade of the mortgagor (the borrower) as in the case of a public house where the brewery, having lent money to the publican by mortgage, can insert a covenant binding the publican to sell no other beer but that of the lending brewery. Furthermore, when a landlord conveys his land or a part of it, he may reserve a proprietory right as to the use to be made of the land by the owner. (*Foley* v. *Classique Coaches Ltd.*, 1934.)[20] However, in *Esso Petroleum Co. Ltd.* v. *Harper's Garage (Stourport) Ltd.*, 1967[248] and *Cleveland Petroleum Co. Ltd.* v. *Dartstone*, 1969,[248a] it was decided that the rules against unreasonable restraints of trade can apply, even where restraint is confined to a particular piece of land and is in a mortgage or a lease. However, a covenant not to *let* premises for a particular purpose cannot be enlarged into a covenant not to *permit* the premises to be *used* for that purpose. (*Rother* v. *Colchester Corporation*, 1969.)[249] Contracts in restraint of trade may be divided into five classes: (*a*) agreements between the buyer and seller of a business; (*b*) agreements between employer and employee; (*c*) agreements between partners; (*d*) agreements between manufacturers, and between manufacturers and retailers, with regard to price maintenance and restrictive practices generally; (*e*) regulation of the conduct of members by professional associations.

1. Agreements between the Buyer and Seller of a Business. The restraining clauses which commonly appear in contracts made between the buyer and seller of a business are usually intended to protect a proprietary interest such as the sale of the goodwill of a business, or to protect trade secrets and special processes.

In these cases the court has to reconcile two conflicting principles, i.e. to uphold and honour business agreements freely entered into whilst at the same time recognising that restraints of trade create monopolies and that the public interest requires a man to be free to use his business talents or professional skill as he wishes. Accordingly, a restraint in a contract between the buyer and seller of a business will be enforced only if it is (*a*) no wider than is reasonably necessary to protect the party in whose interest it is imposed; (*b*) reasonable with reference to the party against whom it is made; and (*c*) reasonable with reference to the public as a whole.

What is reasonable depends very much on the circumstances. A world-wide restraint not to compete in the manufacture of certain goods for a period of twenty-five years has been held valid, whereas an agreement as part of the same contract not to compete in any way was held to be unreasonable and void. This shows that if the whole contract is unreasonable it cannot be enforced; but if certain clauses are reasonable, and are so arranged that they can be severed, the court will enforce the reasonable clauses. (*Nordenfelt* v. *Maxim Nordenfelt Guns and Ammunition Co.*, 1894.)[246]

2. Agreements between Employer and Employee. The restraining clauses which appear in contracts of service usually consist of agreements under which an employee covenants with his employer that on the termination of his contract he will not enter a rival firm or start a competing business. It is not unusual to find that, where a person is to be engaged on work of a confidential or secret nature, or where his employment brings him into personal contact with his employer's customers and business associates, his contract of employment includes a clause limiting his future activities in that particular field. However, it should be noted that since in a contract of service the parties are not on an equal bargaining footing, master and servant restraints are construed more strictly than business restraints, though in some cases the standard applied may be that between buyer and seller of a business. (*George Silverman Ltd.* v. *Silverman*, 1969.)[250]

Whether a restraint in a contract of service will be regarded as valid and enforceable must always depend upon the circumstances of each case, and no hard and fast rules can be laid down. However, a number of principles have emerged from decided cases and they are as follows.

THE PURPOSE OF THE RESTRAINT. The restraint must seek to protect the genuine trade interests of the party enforcing it, and not be an attempt to control the movements of employees, unless there is an underlying need for protection of a legally recognised interest. A classical statement of the law in this respect was made by Lord Parker of Waddington in *Herbert Morris* v. *Saxelby*, 1916,[247] where he said—

I cannot find any case in which a covenant against competition by a servant or apprentice has, as such, ever been upheld by the court. Wherever such covenants have been upheld it has been on the grounds, not that the servant or apprentice would, by reason of his employment or training, obtain the skill and knowledge necessary to equip him as a possible competitor in the trade, but that he might obtain such personal knowledge of, and influence over, the customers of his employer, or such acquaintance with his employer's trade secrets as would enable him, if competition were allowed, to take advantage of his employer's trade connections or utilise information confidentially obtained.

Thus in *Attwood* v. *Lamont*, 1920,[251] a covenant, which, in effect, restrained competition was held unenforceable.

CONSIDERATION. Consideration is necessary to support a contract in restraint of trade, even though the agreement is under seal. This factor will not normally present a problem in the case of a contract of service, because it is difficult to imagine such a contract existing without consideration, as the whole purpose of such agreements, from the employee's point of view, is remuneration.

THE STATUS OF THE EMPLOYEE. In considering whether a person ought to be restricted in his future business activities it is generally necessary to have regard to the position in which he was employed. It was suggested in *Morris* v. *Saxelby*, 1916[247] that apart from trade secrets, the master cannot restrict servants merely because they have contact with customers; they must also have some influence over them. Thus, it would be difficult to show the necessity to restrain the future activities of an office boy, but where the person restrained was in a managerial or other influential position, this difficulty would probably not arise. Thus in *M. & S. Drapers* v. *Reynolds*, [1956] 3 All E.R. 814, the Court of Appeal would not allow a restraint in respect of a person employed to canvass customers and solicit orders, because although it was limited as to time, there was no limit as to area. However, the Court of Appeal recognised that there could be reasons why a restraint unlimited as to area might be upheld. It depended on the kind of employee who was to be subject to the restraint. In *Gilford Motor Co. Ltd.* v. *Horne*, [1933] Ch. 935, where the employee was the managing director of a firm of car dealers, it was held that his position required that he be restrained from acting against the interests of his employer, though no area was specified.

THE DURATION OF THE RESTRAINT. The duration of the restraint must be reasonable and may be long or short depending upon the minimum period required for it to be effective, though in exceptional cases a restraint unlimited in time has been allowed. (*Fitch* v. *Dewes*, 1921.)[252] Where it is sought to establish a long restraint, the burden of proving its reasonableness will be a heavy one and will rest upon the party who seeks to enforce it, i.e. the master.

THE AREA OF THE RESTRAINT. This must be considered in the light of all the circumstances, and it may be necessary to allow a world wide restraint in order to protect the genuine trade interests of the plaintiff. (*Nordenfelt* v. *Maxim-Nordenfelt Guns & Ammunition Co.*, 1894.)[246] However, much depends on the influence over customers and clients which the servant may have acquired, and in *S. W. Strange Ltd.* v. *Mann*, [1965], 1 All E.R. 1069, Stamp, J., drew a distinction between a credit business and a cash business. In a cash business the names of customers are known only to the employees and are not recorded in the books of the firm. For this reason the employees in a cash business are more likely to have influence over the customers of the firm and the court may be more sympathetic towards a wider restraint in respect of them, provided it does not exceed the area of the employer's trade. Nevertheless, in *Empire Meat Co. Ltd.* v. *Patrick*, [1939] 2 All E.R. 85, a restraint concerning a retail butcher's business which was unlimited in time was held to be invalid because the area within which the employee agreed not to carry on or be employed in the business of butcher, although it was only five miles from the place where the employer carried on business, was too wide in view of the limited area of the employer's trade.

COVENANTS AGAINST SOLICITATION. In cases where it is felt that an area restraint not to enter a similar employment is inappropriate, it may be possible to use a covenant against *solicitation* of persons with whom the employer does business, though it may be necessary to restrict the restraint to persons with whom the servant has *actually dealt*. No problem of area arises in this type of covenant though its scope and duration must be reasonable. (*G. W. Plowman & Son Ltd.* v. *Ash*, 1964;[253] *Home Counties Dairies Ltd.* v. *Skilton*, 1970[253a] and *Gledhow Autoparts Ltd.* v. *Delaney*, 1965.)[254]

In order to enforce a covenant in restraint of solicitation it is normally necessary to show that the business has recurring customers. (*Scorer* v. *Seymour Jones*, 1966.)[255]

ESTABLISHED CUSTOMS. It is permissible for a party to attempt to establish the validity of a covenant by giving evidence that similar covenants are usually undertaken in employments of the same kind.

THE DUTY OF FIDELITY. It is also possible to prevent an employee from using trade secrets or business connections without any specific contract in restraint of trade. Certain activities by employees are regarded by the law as breaches of the duty of faithful service which an employee owes to his employer. Breaches of the duty of fidelity will sometimes be prevented by the court so a person who retains secret processes in his memory can be restrained from using them to his employer's disadvantage (*Printers & Finishers Ltd.* v. *Holloway*, 1964),[256] and a servant who copies names and addresses of his employer's customers for use after leaving his employment, can be restrained from using the lists without any express restriction in his contract. (*Robb* v. *Green*, 1895.)[257] Reliance on the duty of fidelity is to some extent unsatisfactory, because the master has usually no method of discovering whether a servant copied lists of customers, or if he has done so, what use has been made of it.

In connection with the duty of fidelity it should be noted that it does not matter who initiates the infidelity and, although in most cases the employee approaches the customers, the rule still applies even where the customers approach the employee. (*Sanders* v. *Parry*, 1967.)[258]

Furthermore, skilled men with access to their employers' secrets may not be able to work for a rival firm even in their spare time. (*Hivac Ltd.* v. *Park Royal Scientific Instruments Ltd.*, 1946.)[259]

AREA COVENANTS. In the protection of trade secrets as distinct from trade connections, employers have relied on area covenants and the implied duty of fidelity.

Area *covenants* must be aimed at the protection of true trade secrets and must not be concerned to prevent the employee's use of his general skill and his knowledge of his employer's general organisation and business methods. The duration of the restraint must be reasonable, and in this connection it seems that a longer restraint is possible where a trade is static than in cases where there is rapid development as, for example, in the plastics industry. The area must be reasonable and the restraint must be restricted to the sphere of activity in which the employee has been engaged. (*Commerical Plastics Ltd.* v. *Vincent*, 1965.)[260]

The operation of the implied duty of fidelity in connection with trade secrets is illustrated by *Printers & Finishers Ltd.* v. *Holloway*, 1964.[256]

GENERALLY. It should be noted that the principles outlined above still apply if the restraint is contained in a contract between two employers with respect to their employees. (*Kores Manufacturing Co. Ltd.* v. *Kolok Manufacturing Co. Ltd.*, 1959.)[261]

It must also be remembered that a covenant in restraint of trade is merely part of a larger contract of employment, so that if the master unjustifiably terminates the contract, as by wrongfully dismissing his servant, or the servant is, in the circumstances, justified in terminating his employment, the restraint will be unenforceable. (*General Billposting Co.* v. *Atkinson*, 1909.)[262]

Furthermore, an employer cannot enforce a covenant restraining his employee from entering a particular field of business activity on the ground that the employer *may* at a *later date* wish to set up business in that field. (*Bromley* v. *Smith*, 1909.)[263] It should also be noted that a restraint may be applied even where an employee forms a limited company to carry on a business in defiance of a restraint. Corporate status cannot generally be used for such a purpose.

In addition, where entry into a pension scheme is a term of a contract of service, a term in the scheme that the pension is to be forfeited if the employee works for a competitor is void as an unreasonable restraint of trade. (*Bull* v. *Pitney-Bowes*, 1966.)[264]

Finally a servant is under no implied obligation not to disclose information concerning his employer's misconduct if it ought in the public interest to be disclosed to a person having a proper interest to receive it. (*Initial Services* v *Putterill*, 1967.)[265]

3. **Agreements between Partners.** Clauses restricting an outgoing or retiring partner from practising within a defined area are frequently found in partnership agreements between professional men. Such clauses will not be enforceable if they are wider than is reasonably necessary for the protection of the practice. However, protection *against competition* as such is to some extent allowed and this distinguishes professional practice restraint from master and servant re-

straint, though the test of reasonableness still applies. (*Lyne-Pirkis* v. *Jones*, 1969.)[266]

4. Agreements between Manufacturers, and between Manufacturers and Retailers with regard to Restrictive Practices Generally. This branch of the law is now largely regulated by statute, i.e. the Restrictive Trade Practices Act, 1956. Nevertheless it is necessary to consider the common law position because not all restrictive agreements are necessarily covered by the Act, and in cases where the Act does not apply the common law on the topic may be invoked. For example, the restrictive agreement which was at the root of *Kores Manufacturing Co. Ltd.* v. *Kolok Manufacturing Co. Ltd.*, 1959,[261] was not covered by the Act and was decided on common law principles.

At common law an agreement between a group of manufacturers or persons engaged in a particular industry, regulating the conditions of that industry and the price of its products, is binding although it is in restraint of trade, provided that it does not impose a restraint which is unreasonable in the interests of the parties themselves, or one which is disadvantageous to the public. As far as the parties themselves are concerned the court usually regards them as the best judges of their own interests and is loth to interfere. The court will, however, interfere on behalf of the public, though once it has been decided that a contract in restraint of trade is reasonable as between the parties, then the burden of showing that it is unreasonable in the public interest is a heavy one. The burden could be discharged by showing that the agreement created a monopoly calculated to enhance prices to an unreasonable extent, though the courts did not support free and unrestrained competition. The attitude of the common law may be found in the remarks of Lord Haldane in *North Western Salt Co. Ltd.* v. *Electrolytic Alkali Co. Ltd.*, [1914] A.C. 461.

> An ill-regulated supply and unremunerative prices may in point of fact be disadvantageous to the public. Such a state of affairs may, if not controlled, drive manufacturers out of business or lower wages, and so cause labour disturbance and unemployment. It must always be a question of circumstances whether a combination of manufacturers in a particular trade is an evil from the public point of view.

5. Regulation of the Conduct of Members by Professional Associations. A resolution by a professional association regulating the conduct of its members will be void if it is in unreasonable restraint of trade. (*Pharmaceutical Society of Great Britain* v. *Dickson*, 1968.)[267]

THE RESTRICTIVE TRADE PRACTICES ACTS, 1956 & 1968

This legislation was introduced because of the failure of the courts to accept responsibility as guardian of the public interest. The main provisions of the Act are as follows—

1. Registration and Investigation of Restrictive Agreements. The rules and procedure for registration are set out in Sects. 1 and

6–19 of Part I of the Act. Sect. 1 creates the post of Registrar of Restrictive Practices and states that he shall be in charge of a public register in which all restrictive agreements are to be registered, though provision is made for some agreements to be kept in a secret section of the Register. (Sect. 11 (3).)

Sect. 6 is concerned with the important though difficult task of defining the types of restrictive agreements to which the Act applies. Broadly speaking all agreements between two or more people are registrable if they lead to a restriction in—

(*a*) the prices to be charged, quoted or paid for goods; or
(*b*) the terms or conditions of supply of goods; or
(*c*) the quantities or descriptions of goods to be produced; or
(*d*) the process of manufacture to be applied to any goods; or
(*e*) the classes of buyers and sellers.

Recent attempts to circumvent the Act by setting up joint marketing companies seem doomed to failure. Thus if A company and B company set up C company in order that C company shall control the distribution of the products of A and B so as to achieve a competition-less situation between them, the series of agreements leading to the setting up of the marketing company are registrable and their validity is subject to a decision of the Restrictive Practices Court. This is so even though the restrictive practices involved take place within a "group", the marketing company being a subsidiary of the supplying company or companies. Nevertheless this cannot be regarded as an activity by a "single person" and is covered by the Act of 1956. (*Re Schweppes Ltd.'s Agreement (No. 2)*, [1971] 2 All E.R. 1473.)

Sect. 6 (3) defines "*agreement*" in rather loose terms as including "any agreement or arrangement, whether or not it is intended to be enforceable . . . by legal proceedings", and "*restriction*" as including "any negative obligation, whether express or implied and whether absolute or not". It was hoped that this wide definition would bring most trade association agreements within the scope of the Act.

In this connection the case of *Re Electrical Installations at Exeter Hospital Agreement*, [1970] 1 All E.R. 1391, is of interest. The Restrictive Practices Court decided that an agreement between contractors to delay submitting tenders until they had a meeting to discuss each others' tenders was a restrictive trading agreement requiring registration under Sect. 6 of the 1956 Act.

Sect. 7 provides for various exceptions to the general rule of registration. These exceptions relate, for example, to trade union agreements, patent and some trademark restrictions, export agreements and information agreements.

Failure to require registration of agreements for the exchange of information lead to a major loophole in the registration provisions in relation to open price agreements. Under such an agreement each of the firms involved notifies a central agency, such as a trade association, of the prices it is charging for its goods, a full list of such prices being made available to all the members of the trade association. Since there is no restriction of any kind but merely an exchange of information, the agreement did not come within the scope of the 1956 Act. Nevertheless it will be seen that such agreements provided ample scope for price leadership, collusion and even coercion.

Although Sect. 14 gives the Registrar certain powers to enable him to obtain information regarding restrictive agreements, these can only be used if "he has reasonable cause to believe" that they exist. Furthermore, the Act did not provide for the setting up of an organisation and staff to discover unregistered agreements. In consequence the Registrar has had to rely largely on the co-operation of businessmen in providing details of restrictive agreements and fortunately this co-operation has been forthcoming. Nevertheless some unregistered but registrable agreements have been discovered as a result of investigations by the Registrar.

Sect. 12 of the 1956 Act gives a power to remove agreements "of no substantial economic significance" from the register. This provision shows the economic character of the legislation which is not concerned merely with restrictive agreements generally but mainly with those which are of substantial economic importance.

Agreements remaining on the register may have to be justified as being in the public interest by the firms concerned before a specially formed tribunal consisting of High Court Judges and laymen with experience in business, and entitled the Restrictive Practices Court.

Possible grounds for justification are set out in the Act and are as follows—

(a) to protect the public from danger or injury;
(b) that "other benefits" would suffer by removal;
(c) to counteract similar practices abroad;
(d) to apply "countervailing power" against a monopoly or monopsony;
(e) maintenance of employment in a concentrated area;
(f) maintenance of export trade;
(g) maintenance of another restrictive agreement already approved.

The jurisdiction of the court is invoked by the Registrar, and ability to prove justification for a restrictive agreement on one or other of the above grounds would not of itself give sufficient grounds for approval. The court would consider whether the public interest was being harmed, taking all the circumstances into account. It is obvious from the agreements reviewed to date that the court is not taking a lenient attitude towards restrictive practices, and most of the agreements put forward have been rejected by the court. The court has power to issue injunctions if its rulings are not carried out, but in most cases the firms concerned do not attempt to operate the agreement if it has been rejected by the court.

However, in *Re Galvanized Tank Manufacturers' Association's Agreement*, [1965] 1 W.L.R. 1074, the court imposed fines amounting to £102,000 on eight members of the Association for contempt of court in breaking their undertakings to the court that they would not enforce or give effect to the restrictions in a price-fixing agreement which the court had declared to be contrary to the public interest six years before.

The 1956 Act is not entirely effective to protect the public from restrictive practices in trade for the following reasons—

(i) Business men are not prevented from exchanging information about prices without an actual agreement. (See now Sect. 5 of 1968 Act.) Nor are they prevented from following the prices of a member of their branch of trade whom they acknowledge as a price leader.

(ii) The fact that the law will not allow different companies to agree to trade in a restrictive manner has probably led some of them to merge in order to trade restrictively.

The Restrictive Trade Practices Act, 1968, came into force on 25th November, 1968. It is intended to amend Part I of the Restrictive Trade Practices Act, 1956, and to make further provisions as to agreement conflicting with Free Trade agreements.

Under Sect. 1 the Department of Trade and Industry may exempt from registration for a specific period under the 1956 Act any agreement which it considers necessary to promote the carrying out of a project or scheme of national importance and the aim of which is to promote efficiency in a trade or industry.

Sect. 2 gives certain government departments power to exempt from registration agreements relating exclusively to prices and designed to prevent or restrict price increases or to secure reductions in prices.

Sect. 4 extends the scope of existing provisions to allow exemption from registration of agreements relating to standards of design, quality or dimension.

Sect. 5 gives the Department of Trade and Industry power to bring certain classes of agreements for exchange of information within Part I of the Act of 1956. This power has now been exercised by the Restrictive Trade Practices (Information Agreements) Order, 1969 (S.I. 1969/1842). Under the Order Part I of the Act of 1956 is applied to information agreements which provide for the furnishing of information about prices and the terms and conditions of sale of goods or the application of any manufacturing process to goods. However, by Part I of the Schedule to the Order certain categories of information agreements are exempted from registration and judicial investigation, e.g. agreements relating to exports.

The principal change under Sect. 6 is that particulars of new restrictive agreements must be given to the Registrar before the restrictions take effect or before the expiration of three months from the making of the agreement, whichever is the earlier. Sect. 6 also provided that agreements which were in existence before the commencement of the 1968 Act but had not been registered had to be registered within three months of the commencement of the Act. During this amnesty period about 100 such agreements were disclosed.

Sect. 7 proposes that any restrictive agreement which is not registered is, for that reason, void and it is unlawful to enforce it or carry it out.

Sect. 10 provides that parties to restrictive agreements should have a new defence in proceedings before the Restrictive Practices Court, *viz.* that a restriction does not directly or indirectly restrict or discourage competition to any material degree.

This defence was in issue in *Brekkes Ltd.* v. *Cattel*, [1971] 2 W.L.R. 647. A ruling by the Birmingham Fish Association that fish landed at Hull should be transported by only one company was held to be unlawful interference with the Hull fish merchants' trade. Pennycuick, V.C., J., granted an interim injunction to prevent operation of the rule although it had been submitted to the Restrictive Practices Court under Sect. 10 of the 1968 Act. The injunction was granted on the basis that the defence would not apply and that the Restrictive Practices Court would declare the rule void.

2. Resale Price Conditions. The 1956 Act made collective determination of prices and the enforcement of penalties for breach by means of stop lists or less favourable terms illegal unless sanctioned, although Sect. 25 allowed individual suppliers to enforce resale price maintenance agreements even against a person not a party to the first sale, providing prior notice of the conditions had been given.

The purpose of Sect. 25 was to allow a manufacturer to bring a cut-price retailer before an ordinary court of law, which was not possible before 1956 unless the retailer had bought the goods direct from the manufacturer. Consequently manufacturers, not having access to the ordinary courts of law, often brought the retailer before a secret and possibly unjust trade association tribunal which might put the retailer quite unreasonably on a stop list so that he was denied supplies.

The section still exists, but before a manufacturer can have recourse to it to enforce a resale price condition, the agreement imposing the minimum resale price must comply with the Resale Prices Act, 1964.

THE RESALE PRICES ACT, 1964

The enforcement of resale price conditions is now governed by the Resale Prices Act, 1964.

1. Terms and Conditions in Contracts. Any term or condition of a contract for the sale of goods by a supplier to a dealer, i.e. a wholesaler or retailer, or any agreement between a supplier and a dealer, shall be void so far as it purports to establish or provide for the establishment of minimum prices to be charged on the resale of goods in the United Kingdom, whether the goods are patented or not. (Sect. 1 (1).)

In is unlawful for suppliers to include such a term or condition in their contracts, or to require an undertaking as to resale price as a condition of supplying goods to a dealer, or to send to dealers notification of minimum resale prices. However, suppliers or trade associations or their agents are not precluded from notifying dealers or otherwise publishing prices at which it would be *appropriate* to sell the goods. (Sect. 1 (4).)

A contract of sale or other agreement containing a term regarding resale price maintenance is not wholly void, but remains enforceable except for the term relating to the resale price. (Sect. 1 (3).)

In the case of *patented goods*, where the proprietor of the patent has granted a licence to another person to make the patented article provided he does not sell below a certain price, the terms of the licence are not affected by Sect. 1 (1) and remain enforceable; similarly where a patent has been assigned subject to a provision regarding the resale price of the patented article. Thus the proprietor of the patent can sue the licensee or the assignee for infringing a provision relating to the resale price of the article. (Sect. 1 (2).)

2. Withholding Supplies from Dealers. Sect. 2 (1) provides that it shall be unlawful for any supplier to withhold supplies of any goods, or procure another supplier to withhold goods from a dealer seeking to obtain them for resale in the United Kingdom on the grounds that the dealer—

(i) has sold or advertised for sale (*Comet Radiovision Services* v. *Farnell-Tandberg*, [1971] 1 W.L.R. 1287) in the United Kingdom at a price below the resale price goods obtained either directly or indirectly from that supplier, or has supplied goods either directly or indirectly to a third party who has done so; or

(ii) is likely, if the goods are supplied to him, to sell them in the United Kingdom at a price below that price, or supply them directly or indirectly to a third party who would be likely to do so.

For the purposes of the 1964 Act a supplier of goods is to be treated as withholding supplies from the dealer—

(*a*) If he refuses or fails to supply those goods to the order of the dealer;

(*b*) If he refuses to supply those goods to the dealer except at prices or on terms or conditions as to credit, discount or other matters, which are significantly less favourable than those at or on which he normally supplies those goods to other dealers carrying on business in similar circumstances; or

(*c*) If, although he contracts to supply the goods to the dealer, he treats him in a manner significantly less favourable than that in which he normally treats other such dealers in respect of times or methods of delivery or other matters arising in the execution of the contracts. (Sect. 2 (3).)

If, of course, the supplier has other reasons for withholding supplies, as where the dealer owes him money, then the supplier will not be treated as withholding supplies of goods for the purposes of the Act. (Sect. 2 (4).) In *Oxford Printing Ltd.* v. *Letraset Ltd.*, [1970] 2 All E.R. 815, when Letraset were sued by the plaintiffs for an injunction to prevent withholding of supplies, it was held by Plowman, J., that the defendants had a good defence when they showed that their reason for withholding supplies was that the plaintiffs were, in addition to cutting the price, also using the defendants' products to promote the sales of the goods of a rival firm. An injunction was refused.

3. Loss Leaders. A supplier may withhold supplies from a dealer, or procure other suppliers to do so, if within the previous twelve months the dealer, or any other dealer supplied by him, has been using the goods withheld or similar goods as loss leaders. (Sect. 3 (1).)

Goods are used as *loss leaders* when they are sold cheaply in order to attract to the establishment customers likely to purchase other goods, or merely to advertise the business of the dealer. (Sect. 3 (2).)

The provisions of the above subsection do not apply where—

(i) The goods are sold by the dealer as part of a *genuine* seasonal or clearance sale;
(ii) The consent of the manufacturer has been obtained; or
(iii) The consent of the supplier has been obtained where the goods were made to the design of the supplier, or where they are made to his order and bear his trade mark.

4. Remedies for Breach of Restrictions. No criminal proceedings shall arise out of any contravention of the Act. (Sect. 4 (1).) However, any person who is affected by a contravention of the Act may bring a civil action against the supplier for damages or an injunction. The provisions of the Act are also enforceable by the Crown by injunction. (Sect. 4 (2) and (3).)

Where the dealer to the knowledge of the supplier has within six months prior to the withholding of the goods sold goods below resale price, and the supplier was down to the time of withholding the goods doing business with the dealer or supplying goods of similar description to other dealers, there is a presumption that the supplier is unlawfully withholding supplies. (Sect. 4 (4).) The presumption does not apply if the restrictions placed on the dealer by the supplier consist only of time or method of payment for the goods. (Sect. 4 (4).)

5. Power of Court to make Exemption Orders. The Restrictive Practices Court may, on a reference made by the Registrar of Restrictive Trading Agreements, order that goods of any class specified in the order shall be *exempted goods* for the purposes of the Act. Particulars of such goods must be entered in the Register kept for this purpose. (Sect. 5 (1).)

Sect. 5 (2) lays down the *circumstances under which an exemption order may be made*. The Restrictive Practices Court may make an order directing that goods shall be exempted goods if it appears to the court that unless a system of maintained minimum resale prices is allowed then—

(*a*) The quality of the goods available for sale, or the varieties of the goods so available, would be substantially reduced to the detriment of the public as consumers or users of such goods; *or*

(*b*) The number of establishments in which the goods are sold by retail would be substantially reduced to the detriment of the public as consumers or users; *or*

(*c*) The prices at which the goods are sold by retail would in general and in the long run be increased to the detriment of the public as consumers or users; *or*

(*d*) The goods would be sold by retail under conditions likely to cause danger to health in consequence of their misuse by the public as consumers or users; *or*

(*e*) Any necessary services actually provided in connection with or after the sale of goods by retail would cease to be provided or would be substantially reduced.

In *re Medicaments Reference (No. 2)*, [1970] 1 W.L.R. 1339, the Restrictive Practices Court held, on an application by the Association of the British Pharmaceutical Industry, that drugs were exempt under Sect. 5 (2) of the 1964 Act. Although when medicines were prescribed under the Health Service they were not "sold" within the meaning of Sect. 5 (2) they were nevertheless available for sale. In addition, without resale price maintenance distributors would emerge who would only stock fast-moving drugs. Furthermore, as the majority of chemists made only small profits and would be likely to make less if supermarkets could undercut them, a declaration that drugs be exempted should be made.

6. Registration of Goods for Exemption. Sect. 6 (2) provides that any supplier who supplies goods under arrangements for maintaining minimum prices on resale, or any Trade Association whose members consist of or include such suppliers, may give notice to the Registrar claiming registration in respect of the goods. This notice had to be given within three months of the section coming into force, i.e. three months from 16th August, 1964.

The Registrar has a duty to prepare, compile and maintain a register of goods in respect of which notices are given to him under Sect. 6. He must also make reference to the court under Sect. 5 in respect of all goods of which particulars are for the time being entered in the Register.

On receipt of a notice under Sect. 6 (2) the Registrar must enter on the Register particulars of the goods and of the person giving notice and also particulars of the minimum resale price arrangements. Once such a notice is entered on the Register, the resale price arrangements may continue until the court makes or refuses to make an order under Sect. 5 in respect of the goods registered. (Sect. 6 (3).)

The Registrar is required by Sect. 6 (4) to *publish the following* lists from time to time—

(i) *A list of the classes of goods which are entered on the Register.* In any legal proceedings resulting from a resale price maintenance agreement the fact that the goods are included in a list published by the Registrar shall be *conclusive evidence* that they are goods of which particulars are entered on the Register. Where goods are not included in the list it shall be *prima facie* evidence that they are not goods of which particulars are so entered.

(ii) *Lists of the classes of goods in respect of which the court has made or refused to make or has discharged orders under the Act.*

The above lists may be combined and the Registrar may combine or divide the goods into such classes as appear to him to be appropriate (Sect. 6 (6).)

7. Late Application to and Review of Decisions by the Court. If a supplier has not given notice to the Registrar under Sect. 6 (1) within the time laid down in that subsection, the court may at any time thereafter make an order exempting or refusing to exempt the goods. (Sect. 7 (1).)

The court is also given power under Sect. 7 (2) to review its previous decisions, and upon application being made to the court for review, the court may—

(*a*) discharge any order previously made by the court directing that goods of any class shall be exempted goods;

(*b*) make an order exempting goods where an order was previously refused or has been discharged.

Application under Sect. 7 (1) or (2) may be made by the Registrar, by any supplier of goods of the class in question, or by any trade association whose members consist of or include suppliers of such goods. (Sect. 7 (3).)

No application to the court can be made under Sect. 7 (1) or (2) unless the court gives leave. (Sect. 7 (4).) *Leave will not be granted unless—*

(i) in the case of an application to exempt goods under Sect. 7 (1) there is *prima facie* evidence of facts suggesting that the goods ought to be exempted; and

(ii) in the case of an application to review a previous decision under Sect. 7 (2) there is *prima facie* evidence of material changes in the relevant circumstances since the last decision of the court in respect of the goods in question.

Some suppliers and trade associations applied to the Restrictive Practices Court under the Restrictive Trade Practices Act, 1956, and were successful in establishing a resale price maintenance agreement. It would not be fair to ask such suppliers and associations to apply under the 1964 Act and prove their case all over again, so Sect. 13 of the Resale Prices Act, 1964, provides that such approved schemes are to continue in force and are not affected by the Act.

In re Chocolate and Sugar Confectionary Reference, 1967,[268] was the first case to be contested under the Resale Prices Act and is illustrative of the attitude of the Restrictive Practices Court to what is in effect a general ban on resale price maintenance.

OTHER RELEVANT STATUTES

Before leaving the topic of restrictive trade practices it is worth noting the broad provisions of two other important statutes as follows—

(*a*) THE MONOPOLIES AND RESTRICTIVE PRACTICES ACT, 1948. This Act makes provision for inquiry into mischief resulting from monopoly or restriction. It set up the Monopolies Commission with power to obtain information. The Department of Trade and Industry may refer cases involving monopoly situations to the Commission. A monopoly is defined as control of one-third of the sales in a market and the basis of investigation is the public interest. Under this Act the Commission could make recommendations only and had no sanctions. In addition there was a wide range of exempted activities, notably professional and other bodies.

(*b*) MONOPOLIES AND MERGERS ACT, 1965. This act extends the range of the 1948 Act. In particular it gives the Monopolies Commission power to investigate the supply of services. The Department of Trade and Industry is empowered to make orders enforcing the anti-monopoly recommendations of the Commission. Mergers involving monopolies of more than £5m can be referred to the Commission by the Department of Trade and Industry for recommendations as to the likely effect on the public interest.

DISCHARGE OF A CONTRACT

A contract is discharged when the obligation created by it ceases to be binding on the promisor, who is then no longer under a duty to perform his part of the agreement. Discharge may take place in various ways.

1. **Discharge by Agreement.** A contract is made by agreement and it is also possible to end it by a subsequent agreement if there is new consideration for the discharge, or if it is under seal. Where the contract is executory, i.e. a promise for a promise, and there has been no performance, the mutual release of the parties provides the consideration and is called bilateral discharge. But where the contract is executed, i.e. where it has been performed or partly performed by one party, then the party to be released must provide consideration, unless

the agreement to abandon the contract is under seal. In other words there must be *accord and satisfaction*, the agreement to discharge being the accord and the new consideration being the satisfaction. This method of discharge is called unilateral discharge. Where the discharge by agreement takes the form of the substitution of a new contract, the substitution is called a novation.

Sometimes a contract makes provision for its own discharge. It may make the completion of the contract subject to the fulfilment of a *condition precedent or warranty*. Thus, if I say I will buy your car if you fit new tyres to it, I shall incur no liability unless the tyres are so fitted. Similarly a contract to purchase land subject to planning permission being obtained can be rescinded if planning permission is refused. (*Hargreaves Transport Ltd.* v. *Lynch*, [1969] 1 All E.R. 455.)

A contract may provide that it shall be discharged by a *condition subsequent*, i.e. upon the occurrence of a certain subsequent event. An example of this is found in pre-incorporation contracts which company promoters make on behalf of a company in process of formation. The law does not allow them to act as agents for the company which, until incorporation, is a non-existent principal. Further, the company is not allowed to ratify the contract after incorporation, but must enter into a new contract or novation if it is to become liable. The promoters are, therefore, likely to incur personal liability. In order to avoid this, promoters' contracts may provide that they shall be discharged if the company is not incorporated at all, or within a reasonable time, or if the company when formed does not accept the contract by novation.

Some contracts may provide for the withdrawal of either party on terms, e.g. one month's notice. Contracts of employment usually provide for their own discharge in this way, but it should be noted that the Contracts of Employment Act, 1972 (which consolidates all the previous legislation on the subject) provides for certain minimum periods of notice to be given by and to employees whose contracts are terminable by notice. These periods are as follows—

Period of Employee's Continuous Service	Minimum Notice By employer	By employee
13 weeks–2 years	1 week	1 week
2 years–5 years	2 weeks	1 week
5 years–10 years	4 weeks	1 week
10 years–15 years	6 weeks	1 week
More than 15 years	8 weeks	1 week

Longer periods of notice can, of course, be provided for expressly in particular contracts.

With regard to the form of discharge, a contract which is made in writing may be rescinded or varied by an oral agreement. A contract under seal may be rescinded or varied by a simple contract. However, while a contract required by statute to be evidenced in writing can be rescinded, i.e. totally discharged, by an oral agreement, if an oral attempt is made to vary it, the contract can be enforced in its original form, the oral variation being disregarded.

It is also possible to discharge a contract by release. At any time before a contract is due to be performed, or after a breach of contract has taken place, a release of the obligations under the contract may be granted by deed. Such a deed dissolves the contract and is binding, whether or not it is based on consideration. No new contract is made; the old obligations are simply released.

2. Discharge by Performance. A contract may be discharged by performance, the discharge taking place when both parties have performed the obligations which the contract places upon them. The general rule is that the manner of performance must comply exactly with the terms of the contract (*Moore & Co.* v. *Landauer & Co.*, 1921)[269] and the strict application of this rule would mean that all contracts would be entire so that no payment could be obtained for partial performance. The law assumes a contract between X and Y to be entire when it appears on construction of the contract that X has undertaken his obligations on the express or implied condition that he will not be obliged to perform those obligations unless Y completes or is willing to complete his obligations fully and exactly. (*Cutter* v. *Powell*, 1795.)[270]

However, there are *certain exceptions* to the rule of precise performance—

(i) *Where the contract is divisible.* Although there is a presumption in favour of entire contracts, the court may sometimes find that a contract is a divisible one, a usual instance being the contract between landlord and tenant. This means that the tenant cannot refuse to pay the rent even though the landlord is not carrying out the covenants of the lease, e.g. a covenant to repair. The tenant can sue the landlord for breach of covenant but must continue to pay.

(ii) *Where a partial performance has been accepted.* Where one of the parties to the contract has only partially carried out his obligations under the contract but the other party appears from his conduct to have accepted the benefit of the partial performance, the court may infer a promise to pay for the benefit received, and allow an action on a *quantum meruit* to the party who has partly performed the contract. If, for example, S agrees to deliver 3 dozen bottles of brandy to B and delivers 2 dozen bottles only, then B may exercise his right to reject the whole consignment. But if he has accepted delivery of the 2 dozen bottles, he must pay a reasonable price for the bottles retained, and S's *quantum meruit* will normally be the agreed contract price per bottle.

However, the mere conferring of a benefit on one party by another is not enough; there must be evidence of the acceptance of that benefit by the party upon whom it was conferred. (*Sumpter* v. *Hedges*, 1898.)[271]

(iii) *Where the performance is prevented by one party.* Here the party who cannot further perform his part of the contract may bring an action on a *quantum meruit* against the party in default for the value of work done up to the time when further performance was prevented. (*De Barnardy* v. *Harding*, 1853.)[272]

(iv) *Where there has been substantial performance.* The doctrine of substantial performance is based on the notion that precise performance of every term of the contract by one party is not required in order to make the other party liable to some extent on it. If the court, as a matter of construction, decides that there has been substantial performance, the plaintiff may recover for work done under the contract, though the defendant can, of course, counter-claim for any defects in performance. (*Hoenig* v. *Isaacs*, 1952.)[273]

In this connection it should be noted that where a contractor is employed under the Royal Institution of British Architects' standard form of contract, an architect's final certificate that the work has been carried out properly is conclusive evidence in any proceedings. (*P. & M. Kaye Ltd.* v. *Hosier & Dickinson Ltd.*, [1972] 1 All E.R. 121.)

In construing a contract to see whether a particular term must be fully performed or whether substantial performance is enough, the court must refer to the difference between conditions and warranties. A condition must be wholly performed, whereas substantial performance of a warranty is enough. (*Poussard* v. *Spiers & Pond*, 1876,[184] and *Bettini* v. *Gye*, 1876.)[185]

A contract may provide for optional methods of performance. (*Narbeth* v. *James. The Lady Tahilla*, 1967.)[274]

The time for performance may in some cases be *of the essence of the contract* and in others it may not. At common law, where the parties have fixed a time for performance, time is the essence of the contract, even though the parties have not expressly said so in the contract. The rule may be applied even where performance is earlier than the contract specifies. (*Bowes* v. *Shand*, 1877.)[275]

However, Equity took a different view, and where the plaintiff was asking for an equitable remedy, e.g. for specific performance of a contract to sell land, the failure of either the vendor or the purchaser to complete exactly to time did not prevent a claim for specific performance so long as no injustice was done to either party. *Time was of the essence even in Equity* (a) where the parties had stipulated a time for performance in the contract and had in addition indicated that this time was in the nature of a condition; or (b) where time was not originally of the essence but had been made so by the aggrieved party giving notice to this effect (*Rickards (Charles) Ltd.* v. *Oppenheim*, 1950);[276] or (c) where from the circumstances of the case it appeared that the contract should be performed at the agreed time.

The sale of a reversionary interest would come into this last category. Suppose property is left by will to X for life with remainder to Y, then if Y sells his remainder, as he may do, it is obvious that the contract of sale should be completed at the agreed date, for delay will mean that the life tenant T is growing older and the value of the reversion is therefore increasing. Similarly in the sale of a business, Equity will generally take the view that the contract should be completed on time so that uncertainties regarding a change of owner should not be so prolonged as to affect adversely the goodwill of the business. Further, it was held in *Hare* v. *Nichol*, [1966] 1 All E.R. 285, that time is the essence of the contract where the property concerned is shares of a highly speculative nature. In addition there is a presumption that time is of the essence of all mercantile contracts unless the circumstances show otherwise. (*Elmdore Ltd.* v. *Keech*, 1969.)[277]

Where the contract is capable of specific performance, the equitable rule still applies, even though the plaintiff may in fact be asking for damages. In other cases the common law rule that time is of the essence of the contract prevails. (Sect. 41, Law of Property Act, 1925.)

With regard to the manner of performance, the question of what is good tender arises. *Tender is an offer of performance which complies with the terms of the contract.* If goods are tendered by the seller and refused by the buyer, the seller is freed from liability, given that the goods are in accordance with the contract as to quantity and quality. A tender of money which is refused does not discharge the tenderer, but if he pays the money into court without delay, he will have a good defence to an action brought against him, and the debt will not bear interest. In a tender of money, the exact amount must be tendered without request for change. In England and Wales the notes of the Bank of England are legal tender. From 15th February, 1971, the decimal bronze coins are legal tender for amounts up to 20p. Silver or cupro-nickel coins up to and including the 10p piece are legal tender for amounts up to £5. The 50p coin is legal tender up to £10. The old 10/- note ceased to be legal tender after 20th November, 1970. The old penny and the old threepenny piece have been withdrawn. Tender by cheque or other negotiable instrument is not good tender unless the creditor does not object; and the debt is discharged when the instrument is honoured, not when it is received. If the instrument is dishonoured, the creditor may sue for his money either under the contract or on the instrument. The tender must be unconditional, and must comply with the terms of the contract as to time, place and mode of performance. A payment of the amount due under a contract is a discharge, but the payment of a smaller sum is no discharge unless made earlier than it is due or by a third party.

It is customary to give *receipts* on payment, but a receipt is only *prima facie* and not conclusive evidence of payment. A payment may be proved by parol in cases where a receipt is lost or no receipt is given. At common law there is no right to demand a receipt, but under the

Stamp Act, 1891, a receipt for £2 and upwards had to be stamped with a twopenny stamp, and if a creditor for such an amount refused to give a receipt when asked or did not stamp a receipt, he was liable to a penalty of £10. There were certain exceptions to this rule, e.g. a receipt for the payment of wages need not be stamped.

The Finance Act, 1970, abolished the old 2d. duty on bills of exchange and receipts as from 1st February, 1971.

If money is sent by post it is not good payment if the letter is lost in the post unless the creditor requested payment in this way. Even a request to pay through the post does not absolve the debtor from paying in a reasonable manner and according to business practice, e.g. by registered cash. Where there is such a request, payment is established by proof of posting, even though the letter is lost in transit, and delay in the post excuses late payment.

It is important to consider the *rules governing appropriation of payments*. Certain debts are barred by the Limitation Act, and money which has been owed for six years under simple contracts or twelve years under specialty contracts, without acknowledgment, may not be recoverable by an action in the courts. Where a debtor owes several debts to the same creditor and makes a payment which does not cover them all, there are rules governing how the money should be appropriated—

(*a*) The debtor can appropriate the payment expressly or by implication. If he owes two debts, one of £50 and one of £25, and he sends a cheque for £25, there is an implied appropriation to the second debt.

(*b*) If there is no appropriation by the debtor, the creditor can appropriate the payment to any of the debts at any time, even to a statute-barred debt, since such a debt has not been extinguished; only the right of action in court has been lost.

(*c*) Where there is what is called a current account, appropriation follows the rule in *Clayton's* case (1816), 1 Mer. 572. Bank current accounts provide a good example of accounts to which this rule applies. *Clayton's* case says that, in the absence of contrary intention, the money first paid in is to be regarded as the money which is first withdrawn. (*Deeley* v. *Lloyds Bank Ltd.*, 1912.)[278]

3. Discharge by Breach. A breach does not of itself discharge a contract, but it may in some circumstances give the innocent party the right to treat it as discharged if he so wishes.

There are several forms of breach of contract—

(*a*) Failure to perform the contract is the most usual form, as where a seller fails to deliver goods by the appointed time, or where they are not up to standard as to quality or quantity.

(*b*) Express repudiation arises where one party states that he will not perform his part of the contract. (*Hochster* v. *De La Tour*, 1853,[279] see also *Gorse* v. *Durham County Council*, 1971.)[279a]

(*c*) Some action by one party may make performance impossible, as where A agrees to marry B in June but in fact marries C in April. (*Omnium D'Entreprises* v. *Sutherland*, 1919.)[280]

Any breach which takes place before the time for performance has arrived is called an anticipatory breach.

The remedies where a contract has been discharged by breach are an action for damages if any have been suffered, or, if the parties have stipulated the damages to be payable on breach, an action for that sum which is called liquidated damages. Not every breach entitles the innocent party to treat the contract as discharged. It must be shown that the breach affects a vital part of the contract, i.e. that it is a breach of condition rather than a breach of warranty, or that the other party has no intention of performing his part of the contract. Thus in *Decro-Wall International S.A.* v. *Practitioners in Marketing*, [1971] 1 W.L.R. 361, the Court of Appeal held that the defendants' failure to pay for goods at the time stipulated in the agreement, i.e. within 90 days of invoice, was not a breach which went to the root of the contract and the plaintiffs had no right to repudiate it. Payments had been on average between two and twenty days' late and the plaintiffs had never had any reason to doubt the defendants' ability to pay. In the case of anticipatory breach, the innocent party may treat the contract as discharged at once and sue for damages, though the Court may have regard to whether the contract could have been carried out by the plaintiff at the time scheduled for performance. (*The Mihalis Angelos*, 1969.)[281] Alternatively the innocent party may ignore the breach and wait until the time for performance arrives. It may be dangerous to wait since the contract may later become impossible of performance, so providing the party who was in breach with a good defence to an action. (*Avery* v. *Bowden*, 1855.)[282]

Where one party to a contract wrongfully repudiates it and the other party refuses to accept the repudiation, it seems that the contract survives and the rights of the innocent party are preserved. He may, if it is within his power, perform his part of the contract and recover on that basis, for there is no duty on him to vary the contract at the request of the other party so as to deprive himself of its benefit. (*White and Carter (Councils) Ltd.* v. *McGregor*, 1961.)[283]

It should also be noted that where a person is entitled to repudiate his liability under a contract by reason of the other party's breach, his delay in so doing will not operate against him unless other parties are prejudiced or the delay is so long as to indicate to the court that he has accepted liability. (*Allen* v. *Robles* (*Compagnie Parisienne de Garantie, Third Party*), 1969.)[284]

Regarding leases it appears that since a lease conveys an estate in land it does not necessarily come to an end by repudiation and acceptance of repudiation as an ordinary contract would. (*Total Oil Great Britain Ltd.* v. *Thompson Garages (Biggin Hill) Ltd.*, 1971.)[285]

4. Discharge by Subsequent Impossibility (or Frustration)

If an agreement is impossible of performance from the outset it is no contract; but sometimes it is possible to enter into a contract which subsequently becomes impossible to carry out in full or in part. The view of the early common law judges was that such eventualities should be provided for in the contract, and if this was not done the party liable for the performance of an impossible undertaking would be obliged to pay damages to the other party for such non-performance.

This rule was gradually modified and made less rigorous, but even now the courts are not anxious to give remedies for eventualities which could have been foreseen, e.g. if a strike prevents performance this could have been provided for in the contract. (*Davis Contractors Ltd.* v. *Fareham U.D.C.*, 1956.)[286]

The present doctrine is that, if performance was possible when the contract was made, subsequent impossibility may discharge it in the following cases—

(*a*) If the impossibility is due to changes in law or operation of law, the contract is discharged. (*Re Shipton, Anderson & Co. and Harrison Brothers' Arbitration*, 1915.)[287]

(*b*) If the contract is for personal services, it becomes discharged by the death or incapacity of the person who has to perform it. Temporary illness will not, in most cases, discharge a contract (*Storey* v. *Fulham Steel Works*, 1907),[288] but if the illness goes right to the root of the contract, it will. (*Poussard* v. *Spiers and Pond*, 1876.)[184]

(*c*) If the performance depends upon the existence of a certain thing, or a state of affairs which ceases to exist, the contract is discharged. (*Taylor* v. *Caldwell*, 1863,[289] and *Krell* v. *Henry*, 1903.)[290] But it must be shown that the contract will be substantially affected by the new circumstances. (*Herne Bay Steam Boat Co.* v. *Hutton*, 1903.)[291]

(*d*) A contract is also discharged when its commercial purpose is frustrated, often because its completion would be so delayed as to make the performance, when it occurred, of little or no value. (*Joseph Constantine Steamship Line Ltd.* v. *Imperial Smelting Corporation Ltd.*, 1942,[292] and *Jackson* v. *Union Marine Insurance Co. Ltd.*, 1874.)[293]

The doctrine will not apply—

(i) where the parties have made express provision for the event which has occurred—in such a case the provisions inserted into the contract by the parties will apply;

(ii) where the frustrating event is self-induced (*Maritime National Fish Ltd.* v. *Ocean Trawlers Ltd.*, 1935);[294]

(iii) probably to a lease, because a lease creates an estate not a mere contract. The same rule may also apply to an agreement for a lease and a contract for the sale of land. (*Cricklewood Property and Investment Trust Ltd.* v. *Leightons Investment Trust Ltd.*, 1945;[295] *Hillingdon Estates Co.* v. *Stonefields Estates Ltd.*, 1952[296] and see also

Total Oil Great Britain Ltd. v. *Thompson Garages (Biggin Hill) Ltd.*, 1971.[285]

An important modern statute has laid down the conditions which will govern the rights and duties of the parties when certain contracts are frustrated. This measure is the Law Reform (Frustrated Contracts) Act, 1943. Before this Act it was the law that when subsequent impossibility discharged a contract, it did not discharge it *ab initio* (from the beginning), but only from the time when the event making the contract impossible of performance actually occurred. Thus any loss lay where it fell. Money not due at the time could not be claimed. Money due and not paid could be claimed. Money paid under the contract before it became impossible could not be recovered. (*Chandler* v. *Webster*, 1904.)[297] However money paid was recoverable if there was a total failure of consideration. (*The Fibrosa Case*, 1943.)[298]

The statute has amended the common law and provides what shall happen if the contract becomes discharged by frustration—

(i) All money paid before discharge is recoverable.

(ii) Money which was payable ceases to be payable.

(iii) The court will allow the parties to recover sums of money paid out on expenses incurred in connection with the contract, or to retain such sums from money already received under the contract.

(iv) It is also possible to recover, on a *quantum meruit*, a reasonable sum of money as compensation where one of the parties has carried out acts of part performance before frustration, i.e. where one party has received a benefit under the contract other than a money payment.

The Act does not apply to contracts for the carriage of goods by sea or to contracts of insurance. If X insures against sickness on 1st January, and dies on 1st February, his executors cannot recover eleven-twelfths of the premium paid, even though the contract is now impossible of performance.

The Act also excepts from its provisions certain *sales* of *specific* goods which have *perished*, the effect of which is, broadly speaking, as follows—

(*a*) *The goods must be specific and not unascertained.* Sect. 62 of the Sale of Goods Act, 1893, states that specific goods are goods identified and agreed upon at the time the contract of sale is made. Thus a contract to sell "my 1969 Morris Minor" is a contract to sell specific goods, whereas a contract to sell "one of my two cars" would be a contract for the sale of unascertained goods since it is not certain which of the two cars will be sold.

(*b*) *The goods must have perished.* Goods are regarded as having perished—

(i) where they have been physically destroyed, say by fire, or

(ii) where although they physically exist they are so damaged that they cannot reasonably be regarded as the goods actually purchased, e.g. apples contaminated by sewage.

(*c*) *The contract must be a sale and not an agreement to sell.* A *contract of sale* is one in which the property (normally ownership) in the goods is transferred to the buyer at the time when the contract is made. In an *agreement to sell* ownership is transferred to the buyer at a future date after the making of the contract. It should be noted that in English law the transfer of ownership does not depend upon *delivery* of the goods. Where the goods are specific, and in the absence of any contrary intention, the property in the goods passes to the buyer when he accepts the seller's offer, even though the seller physically retains the goods.

The application of these concepts may be illustrated by the following examples—

(1) If A offers to sell the only car he has, which is at his home, to B for £100 and B accepts the offer, the contract will be for the sale of specific goods and ownership (and normally risk) will pass to B when he accepts A's offer regardless of actual delivery of the vehicle. Ordinarily A will deliver the car to B and all will be well, but let us suppose that the car is destroyed by fire before delivery so that A cannot perform the contract. In such circumstances the legal position would appear to be as follows—

(*a*) if the car was destroyed *before* B accepted A's offer the contract is rendered *void* by Sect. 6 of the Sale of Goods Act, 1893. Thus A need not pay damages for non-performance nor is B obliged to pay for the car. Furthermore, if B had made a payment to A it could be recovered.

(*b*) If the car was destroyed *after* B accepted A's offer B would have become owner of the car and would have to pay A £100 for it even though the car could never be delivered.

(*c*) If in the course of selling the car to B it was agreed that ownership should not pass for one week, then if the car was destroyed before the week had elapsed the position would be as follows—

(i) A would have to bear the loss of the car.

(ii) The contract would be avoided by Sect. 7 of the Sale of Goods Act, 1893, so that A would not be liable in damages for failure to perform the contract. B would not be required to pay for it and could recover any money paid to A.

(2) If the goods were *unascertained* as where A sold to B "one of my two cars" then if one or both of the cars were destroyed before ascertainment the Act of 1943 would apply and the rules laid down therein would come into force, though B could of course accept the remaining car (if any) if he wished. B would probably not be compelled to accept the remaining car unless perhaps it was in all respects the

same as the one destroyed. This is unlikely in the case of a car but might apply where the goods were, say, sugar or wheat.

(3) If the goods were *specific* but had not *perished* as where A's only car was requisitioned by the Crown in an emergency, then the Act of 1943 and the rules thereunder would also apply.

Before leaving the topic of frustration it should be noted that the Act of 1943 does not apply to contracts governed by foreign law.

5. Discharge by Lapse of Time. Contracts entered into for a specified time are discharged when that period of time has elapsed. In other cases time is of no effect as regards discharge, but lapse of time may render contracts unenforceable in a court of law.

The Limitation Act, 1939, provides that actions on simple contracts are barred after six years from the date upon which the plaintiff could first have brought his action. Actions on specialty contracts are barred after twelve years from the cause of action. The Act does not truly discharge a contract, it merely makes it unenforceable in a court of law. It can, therefore be made actionable again by a subsequent payment of money not appropriated by the debtor, or by the debtor, or his duly authorised agent, making a written acknowledgment of the debt to the creditor or his agent. Such an acknowledgment need not have been written for the purpose and is effective if it indicates that a debt is due even if it does not state the amount. (*Dungate* v. *Dungate*, 1965.)[82] Thus a statement of liabilities to "sundry creditors" in a company balance sheet was held to be enough. (*Jones* v. *Bellgrove Properties Ltd.*, [1949] 2 K.B. 700.) A person cannot, however, be forced to acknowledge a statute barred debt. (*Lovell* v. *Lovell*, 1970.)[299]

Where the plaintiff is a minor or person of unsound mind, the period of limitation does not run against him until his contractual disability ends, i.e. at eighteen (or twenty-one if the cause of action arose before 1st January, 1970 (Family Law Reform Act, 1969, Sch. 3)) or on becoming sane. But once time has started to run, any subsequent incapacity will not stop it running. The defendant's fraud may also prevent his pleading the Statutes of Limitation. (*Lynn* v. *Bamber*, 1930.)[300]

6. Discharge by Operation of Law. This may occur in certain cases—

(*a*) MERGER. A simple contract is swallowed up, or merged into, a subsequent deed covering the same subject matter, and in such circumstances an action lies only on the deed. Similarly a judgment, which is a contract of record, merges the contract debt on which the action was brought, so that all future actions are based on the judgment.

(*b*) MATERIAL ALTERATION. An alteration of a material part of a deed or written contract, made by one party intentionally and without the consent of the other party, will discharge the contract. The alteration must alter the legal effect of the contract, and the mere alteration of a misdescription of one of the parties, or the insertion of the true date, will not operate as a discharge.

(c) DEATH. Death will discharge a contract for personal services. Other contractual rights and liabilities survive for the benefit, or otherwise, of the estate.

(d) BANKRUPTCY. A right of action for breach of contract possessed by a debtor, which relates to his property and which if brought will increase his assets, will pass to his trustee in bankruptcy, e.g. a contract with a third party to deliver goods or to pay money to the debtor. The right to sue for injury to the debtor's character or reputation does not pass to the trustee, even though it arises from breach of contract. (*Wilson* v. *United Counties Bank*, 1920.)[301]

With regard to contracts for personal services, it depends upon the date of the breach whether the debtor's right to sue remains with him or passes to his trustee. If the breach occurs before the commencement of the bankruptcy, the right of action passes to the trustee; if it occurs after this date, the debtor may sue, but the trustee may intervene and deduct from the sum recovered such sums as are not required for the reasonable maintenance of the bankrupt and his family. A trustee cannot force the debtor to carry out contracts involving personal service by him.

REMEDIES FOR BREACH OF CONTRACT

When there is a breach of contract the following remedies may be available—

(i) A right of action for damages at common law (the most common remedy).

(ii) A right of action on a *quantum meruit*.

(iii) A right to sue for specific performance or for an injunction.

(iv) A right to ask for rescission of the contract.

(v) A refusal of any further performance by the injured party.

It will be convenient to consider also in this section those cases where similar remedies are available in non-contractual actions, e.g. tort.

1. Damages. Damages are a common law remedy consisting of a payment of money, and are intended as compensation for the plaintiff's loss and not as a punishment for the defendant. The aim is to put the injured party in the same financial position as he would have been if the contract had been performed according to its terms. (*B. Sunley & Co. Ltd.* v. *Cunard White Star Ltd.*, 1940.)[302] Expenses incurred prior to the date on which the contract was made may be recoverable provided they are within the contemplation of the parties as likely to result from the breach. (*Anglia Television Ltd.* v. *Reed*, *The Times*, August 2nd, 1971.) On rare occasions punitive damages were awarded, i.e. damages in excess of the actual loss, and these might be appropriate in cases of breach of promise of marriage, particularly if there had been a seduction. Under the Law Reform (Miscellaneous Provisions) Act, 1970, Sect. 1, engagements to marry are not enforceable at law. Compensation for pregnancy where this has occurred must now be pursued in affiliation proceedings in a Magistrates' Court. Generally, however, the aim of damages is one of simple compensation for actual loss, though much depends upon the nature of the property forming the subject matter of the claim. (*Harbutt's Plasticine* v. *Wayne Tank & Pump Co. Ltd.*, 1969.)[198] Difficulty in assessing damages is not necessarily a bar to a claim. (*Chaplin* v. *Hicks*, 1911.)[303]

The plaintiff's liability to taxation is taken into account. (*Beach* v. *Reed Corrugated Cases Ltd.*, 1956.)[304]

Apart from the question of assessment, the question of *remoteness of damage* arises. The consequences of a breach of contract may be far-reaching, and the law must draw the line somewhere and say that damages incurred beyond a certain limit are too remote to be recovered. Damages in contrast must therefore be proximate. The modern law regarding remoteness of damage in contract is founded upon the case of *Hadley* v. *Baxendale*, 1854.[305] The case is authority for the statement that damages in contract will be too remote to be recovered unless they are such that the defendant, as a reasonable man, would have foreseen them as likely to result, according to the usual course of things or because of special facts made known to him. Where damages do not arise naturally from the breach, they may be recovered only if the defendant was made aware of the possibility of such damage (*Horne* v. *Midland Railway Co.*, 1873),[306] though notice of possible loss can be constructive as well as actual. (*Pinnock Bros.* v. *Lewis and Peat Ltd.*, 1923.)[307]

Regarding changes in the relative value of currencies, these are irrelevant in assessing damages and in the payment of debts if—

(*a*) they occur *after* the date on which the damages are assessed or the debt became due. Thus a revaluation of sterling after a case has been decided and the judge has awarded damages, or after the date on which a debt should have been paid, must be ignored and the defendant will pay at the rate of exchange prevailing when the award of damages was made or the debt became due;

(*b*) they occur *on or before* the date on which damages were assessed or the debt became due *unless* the loss caused by revaluation can be shown to have been within the assumed contemplation of the parties or the contract expressly provides for variations in price if prevailing rates of exchange vary. Otherwise the Court will not increase the sterling value of the damages or the debt in order to give the plaintiff the same amount of money under the new rate of exchange as he would have received under the old. (*Aruna Mills* v. *Dhanrajmal Gobindram*, [1968] 1 All E.R. 113 and *The Teh Hu*, [1969] 3 All E.R. 1200.)

It must be understood that, when a breach occurs, the party suffering from the breach must do all he can to reduce his loss, and he cannot recover damages which have resulted from his failure to do so. If a person cancels a hotel booking, the hotel proprietor must try to relet the rooms. If a seller refuses to deliver goods, the buyer must attempt to obtain supplies elsewhere. In the latter case, where there is an available market, the damages might amount to no more than the difference between the contract price and the market price on the day appointed for delivery, together with incidental expenses. These principles can be seen in the context of contract in *Charter* v. *Sullivan*, 1957,[308] and *Thompson (W.L.) Ltd.* v. *Robinson (Gunmakers) Ltd.*, 1955.[309] The concept of mitigation is not confined to actions for breach of contract but applies also to actions in tort. (*Luker* v. *Chapman*, 1970.)[310]

It should also be noted that the general requirement is that a plaintiff who suffers loss as a result of a tort or breach of contract must act reasonably to mitigate loss. In this connection a course of action will not necessarily be judged unreasonable merely because there was another course which would have been cheaper and less burdensome to the defendants. Thus in *Moore* v. *D.E.R. Ltd.*, *The Times*, June 19, 1971, a dentist who ordered a new Rover 2000 to replace one which became a total loss in an accident instead of buying a second-hand car was held by the Court of Appeal to have acted reasonably. He had a busy practice and needed to be certain that his car was reliable. He was also entitled to the cost of hiring alternative transport for the time it took to obtain the new car even though he could have acquired a secondhand car much sooner.

It is possible to classify damages under a number of headings, and this classification applies to both contract and tort.

(*a*) ORDINARY DAMAGES. These are damages assessed by the court for losses arising naturally from the breach of contract; and in tort for losses which cannot be positively proved or ascertained, and depend upon the court's view of the nature of the plaintiff's injury. For example, the court may have to decide what to award for the loss of an eye, there being no scale of payments; and this is so whether the action be in tort or for breach of contract.

(*b*) SPECIAL DAMAGES. These are awarded in tort for losses which can be positively proved or ascertained, e.g. damage to clothing; garage bills, where a vehicle has been damaged; doctor's fees; and so on. However, where it is difficult to determine the exact proportions of a claim for special damages, the court must do its best to arrive at a fair valuation. *Dixons Ltd.* v. *J. L. Cooper Ltd.* (1970), 114 S.J. 319. In contract the term covers losses which do not arise naturally from the breach, so that they will not be recoverable unless within the contemplation of the parties as described above.

(*c*) EXEMPLARY AND AGGRAVATED DAMAGES. The usual object of damages both in contract and tort is to compensate the plaintiff for loss which he has incurred arising from the defendant's conduct. The object of *exemplary damages* is to punish the defendant, and to deter him and others from similar conduct in the future. Thus it was at one time thought that, if the court had arrived at a sum of money which would sufficiently compensate the plaintiff, it could award a further sum, not as compensation for the plaintiff, but as a punishment to the defendant, the exemplary damages being in the nature of a fine. An award of exemplary damages had always confused the functions of the civil and criminal law, and it would appear that since the judgment of Lord Devlin in *Rookes* v. *Barnard*, [1964], 1 All E.R. 367, an award of exemplary damages should only be made in certain special cases (see below).

Aggravated damages on the other hand can be awarded (generally only in tort) where the defendant's conduct is such that the plaintiff requires more than the usual amount of damages to *compensate* him for the unpleasant method in which the tort was committed against him. However, an award of aggravated damages is still *compensatory*.

The state of the law after *Rookes* v. *Barnard*, [1964] 1 All E.R. 367, may perhaps be illustrated by taking a hypothetical case. Suppose a tenant T is evicted from his flat by the landlord L before T's term has expired, and that in order to evict T the landlord uses excessive violence. The court may decide that in an ordinary case of trespass and assault T would be adequately compensated by an award of damages of (say) £500. However, if the court considers that L used particularly violent and unpleasant methods to achieve this eviction, it may award a further sum (say) £100 as aggravated damages because, on the facts of the case, this is necessary to compensate T. It would appear that the court cannot now go on and make a further award to T in order to punish and deter L.

Exemplary or punitive damages were sometimes awarded in contract for breach of promise of marriage, particularly where a female plaintiff has allowed the defendant to have sexual intercourse with her on the promise of marriage. This action is now abolished by the Law Reform (Miscellaneous Provisions) Act, 1970, Sect. 1 and examples of exemplary damages would seem in the main to be confined to actions in tort. However, an action may lie where a promise to marry is made by a man *who is already married* on the grounds of breach by the man of an implied warranty that he is in a position to marry. That such an implied warranty exists in such circumstances was decided by the Court of Appeal in *Shaw* v. *Shaw*, [1954] 2 Q.B. 424. Damages for breach of such a warranty could be and possibly still can be exemplary.

Subject to what has been said above and as a result of Lord Devlin's judgment in *Rookes* v. *Barnard*, [1964] 1 All E.R. 367, exemplary damages can be awarded only—

(i) *Where there is arbitrary or unconstitutional action by servants of the State*, e.g. an unreasonable false imprisonment or detention by State Authorities.

(ii) *Where the defendant's conduct has been calculated by him to make a profit for himself which may well exceed the compensation payable to the plaintiff.* Thus a newspaper may decide that the increased sales of the paper containing a libel will more than compensate for any damages which may have to be paid to the person libelled. In such a case exemplary damages may be awarded to the plaintiff, though the intention to profit must be proved. It is not enough that the newspaper has been sold and some profit necessarily made.

(iii) *Where exemplary damages are expressly authorised by statute.*

It is perhaps worth noting that having apparently restricted the number of situations in which exemplary damages might be awarded, Lord Devlin said at one point in his judgment (see *Rookes* v. *Barnard*, [1964] 1 All E.R. 367 at p. 411) "Exemplary damages can properly be awarded whenever it is necessary to teach a wrongdoer that tort does not pay." The ramifications of this statement were considered in regard to the tort of deceit in *Mafo* v. *Adams*, 1969.[167]

In addition the House of Lords in *Cassells & Co. Ltd.* v. *Broome*, [1972] 1 All E.R. 801, were unanimously of the opinion that *Rookes* v. *Barnard* was properly decided in this respect and that the pre-1964 common law relating to exemplary damages no longer applied.

(d) NOMINAL DAMAGES. Sometimes a small sum (say £2) is awarded where the plaintiff proves a breach of contract, or the infringement of a right, but has suffered no actual loss.

(e) CONTEMPTUOUS DAMAGES. A farthing was sometimes awarded to mark the court's disapproval of the plaintiff's conduct in bringing the action. Such damages have been awarded to male plaintiffs in breach of promise of marriage actions, and where the plaintiff has sued for defamation of character in spite of the fact that he has engaged in defamatory activities against the defendant. Since farthings are no longer legal tender, the new decimal halfpenny will be used in future.

(f) LIQUIDATED DAMAGES. These are damages agreed upon by the parties to the contract, and only a breach of contract need be proved; no proof of loss is required. Damages in tort are not liquidated.

(g) UNLIQUIDATED DAMAGES. Where no damages are fixed by the contract it is left to the court to decide their amount. In such a case the plaintiff must produce evidence of the loss he has suffered, as is normal in the case of tort.

Liquidated damages must appear to be a genuine pre-estimate of loss, not a *penalty* inserted to make it an ill bargain for the defendant not to carry out his part of the contract. The court will not enforce a penalty, but will award damages on normal principles. It will be seen, therefore, that the term "penalty clause" is a misnomer in that a clause which is truly penal will not be enforced. Nevertheless this terminology is often used in commercial contracts but such a clause is unenforceable unless it defines a method of calculating liquidated damages.

Certain tests are applied in order to decide whether or not the provision is a penalty. Obviously extravagant sums are generally in the nature of penalties. Where the contractual obligation lying on the defendant is to pay money, then any provision in the contract which requires the payment of a larger sum on default of payment is a penalty, because the damage can be accurately assessed. Where the sum provided for in the contract is payable on the occurrence of any one of several events, it is probably a penalty; for it is unlikely that each event can produce the same loss (*Ford Motor Co. (England) Ltd.* v. *Armstrong*, 1915),[311] though this rule is not always applied. (*Dunlop* v. *New Garage and Motor Co. Ltd.*, 1915.)[84] If a sum is agreed by the parties as liquidated damages, it will be enforced as agreed, even though the actual loss is greater or smaller. (*Cellulose Acetate Silk Co. Ltd.* v. *Widnes Foundry Ltd.*, 1933.)[312]

2. Quantum meruit. This remedy means that the plaintiff will be awarded as much as is earned or deserved. In the event of a breach of contract, the injured party may have a claim other than one for damages. He may have carried out work or performed services and for such he may be entitled to claim on a *quantum meruit*. He will be awarded what the court thinks the work or services are worth. This action is quite distinct from an action for breach of contract and is in the nature of restitution for work done. The remedy can be used contractually or quasi-contractually, and, although the topic cannot be treated fully, examples of the use of the remedy are given below—

(*a*) CONTRACTUALLY. Here it may be used to recover a reasonable price or remuneration where there is a contract for the supply of goods or services, but the contract does not fix any precise sum to be paid. It may also be used where the original contract has been replaced by a new one, and a payment is required under the new agreement, e.g. X orders 20 bottles of brandy from Y at a certain price, and Y sends 18 bottles of brandy and 2 bottles of whisky. X is not, of course, bound to take delivery, but if he does he must pay a reasonable price for the whisky on a *quantum meruit*.

(*b*) QUASI-CONTRACTUALLY. Here the remedy may be used to recover a sum of money for work done under a contract discharged by the defendant's breach. This is really an alternative to a claim for damages for breach of contract, but it does enable the court to award whatever it thinks the plaintiff has earned by his work, and this may be greater than the contract price. The remedy is also available when a contract is void, since for breach of a void contract no damages can be awarded (*Craven-Ellis* v. *Canons Ltd.*, 1936);[313] and sometimes where the contract is frustrated. (*Davis Contractors Ltd.* v. *Fareham U.D.C.*, 1956.)[286] The remedy is also available where there never was a contract. However, where A continues to pay B an agreed fee in respect of certain work and later B agrees to do further work, without a further fee being mentioned, B cannot claim payment in respect of the further work on a *quantum meruit* while the original contract subsists and has not been discharged. (*Gilbert and Partners* v. *Knight*, 1968.)[314]

3. Specific Performance and Injunction. These are equitable remedies and are available not as of right, as is the case with damages, but at the discretion of the court. Formerly these remedies would have had to be sought in the courts of equity, but since the Judicature Acts, 1873-75, these remedies, as well as damages, are available in any court.

A degree of *specific performance* is an order of the court, and constitutes an express instruction to a party to a contract to perform the actual obligation which he undertook under its terms. It is often granted in contracts connected with land, and under the Companies Act, 1948, a contract to take debentures in a company can be specifically enforced, though normally specific performance of a loan would not be granted. In the case of contracts for the sale of goods, specific performance is not usually given, unless the goods are unique and cannot be purchased easily in the market, or where their value is difficult to assess.

An *injunction* is an order of the court whereby an individual is required to refrain from the further doing of the act complained of. It may be used to prevent many wrongful acts, e.g. torts, but in the context of contract the remedy will be granted to enforce a negative stipulation in a contract in a case where damages would not be an adequate remedy. Its application may be extended to contracts where there is no actual negative stipulation but where one may be *inferred*. (*Metropolitan Electric Supply Co.* v. *Ginder*, 1901.)[315] In a proper case an injunction may be used as an indirect method of enforcing a contract for personal services, but in that case a *clear* negative stipulation is required. (*Whitwood Chemical Co.* v. *Hardman*, 1891,[316] and *Warner Bros. Pictures Incorporated* v. *Nelson*, 1937.)[317]

Injunctions may be (*a*) Interlocutory, (*b*) Perpetual, (*c*) Prohibitory, (*d*) Mandatory. An *interlocutory injunction* is granted before the hearing of the action, the plaintiff undertaking to be responsible for any damage caused to the defendant if in the subsequent action the plaintiff does not succeed. There is a form of interlocutory injunction called *quia timet* (because he fears). This may be granted, though rarely, even though the injury has not taken place but is merely threatened. A *perpetual injunction* is granted after a trial, and when the point at issue has been finally determined. A *prohibitory injunction* orders that a certain act shall not be done; a *mandatory injunction* orders that a certain positive act shall be done, e.g. an order to pull down a wall erected in breach of covenant.

Since specific performance is an equitable remedy, it will be granted only when certain conditions apply—

(i) CONSIDERATION MUST EXIST, since "Equity will not assist a volunteer."

(ii) THE COURT MUST BE ABLE TO SUPERVISE THE PERFORMANCE. Specific performance will not be granted if constant supervision is necessary to ensure that the defendant complies with the decree. (*Ryan* v. *Mutual Tontine Westminster Chambers Association*, 1893.)[318]

(iii) It must be just and equitable that the remedy be granted. If the court considers that damages are an adequate remedy, it will not grant an equitable one.

(iv) Both parties must be able to obtain the remedy. The courts will not grant equitable remedies to a minor because his contracts cannot be enforced against him, and Equity requires equality or mutuality.

(v) The plaintiff must show that he was in a position to carry out his part of the bargain at the time fixed for performance.

(vi) The plaintiff's own conduct in the matter must be above reproach; for it is said that "He who comes into Equity must come with clean hands."

A contract for personal services will not be specifically enforced because—

(*a*) it would be undesirable to force persons to work together if they did not wish to do so; and

(*b*) it would be impossible to ensure that the contract was properly carried out unless the defendant were under the constant supervision of the court. (But see now *Hill* v. *Parsons*, 1971.)[693]

However, as we have seen, the court may *encourage* but not *compel* performance of a contract of personal service by means of an injunction. (*Whitworth Chemical Co.* v. *Hardman*, 1891[316] and *Warner Bros. Pictures Incorporated* v. *Nelson*, 1937.)[317]

If the effect of an injunction would be to *compel* performance it will not be granted. (*Page One Records Ltd.* v. *Britton*, 1967.)[319]

Defiance of the court's order granting an equitable remedy constitutes contempt of court, which is punishable by fine or imprisonment. The court's order is, therefore, likely to be obeyed. Some equitable remedies must be asked for within a given time by statute, but otherwise they must be asked for within a reasonable time, since "Delay defeats equities." What is a reasonable time is determined by the court from the circumstances.

4. Rescission. This is a further equitable remedy for breach of contract. The rule is the same when the remedy is used for breach as it is when it is used for misrepresentation. If the contract cannot be completely rescinded, it cannot be rescinded at all; it must be possible to restore the *status quo*. All part payments must be returned on rescission and cannot be retained as security against future damages, but there are circumstances where part payment is regarded as a guarantee for the due performance of the payer's obligations, and, if this is so, it will be forfeited if he does not go on with the contract, although Equity will sometimes grant relief against forfeiture of deposits.

5. Refusal of Further Performance. If the person suffering from the breach desires merely to be quit of his obligations under the contract, he may refuse any further performance on his own part and set up the breach as a defence if the party who has committed the breach attempts to enforce the contract against him. Even so he may, if he wishes, reinforce his position by bringing an action for rescission.

The Recovery of Interest. The rules governing the recovery of interest are as follows—

(*a*) It is payable where the parties have so agreed in the contract.

(*b*) The dealings between the parties may show that an agreement to pay interest may be implied.

(*c*) Overdue bills of exchange and promissory notes bear interest.

(*d*) Under the Law Reform (Miscellaneous Provisions) Act, 1934, the court may at its discretion allow interest at such a rate as it thinks fit on all claims for debt or special damages from the date when the claim arose to judgment.

It should be noted, however, that under Sect. 22 of the Administration of Justice Act, 1969, as from 1st January, 1970, judges are directed in personal injuries cases to award interest on damages, though the rate of interest, the portion of the judgment on which it is to be calculated, and the particular period during which interest is to be paid is left to the discretion of the court.

QUASI-CONTRACTUAL RIGHTS AND DUTIES

Quasi-contract is based on the idea that a person should not obtain a benefit or an unjust enrichment as against another merely because there is no obligation in contract or another established branch of law which will operate to make him account for it. The law may in these circumstances provide a remedy by implying *a fictitious promise* to account for the benefit or enrichment. This promise can then form the basis of an action in quasi-contract. The main areas in which quasi-contractual remedies have been used are as follows—

Actions for Money paid. Where A has a secondary and B has a primary *legal liability* to a third person and A has paid over money which B was in the ultimate liable to pay, an action will lie in quasi-contract to enable A to recover from B. (*Brook's Wharf and Bull Wharf Ltd.* v. *Goodman Bros.*, 1936.)[320]

It is essential to the claim that B should have been under a *common and legal obligation* to pay. (*Metropolitan Police District Receiver* v. *Croydon Corporation*, 1957.)[321]

Actions for Money had and received. An action for money had and received by the defendant to the use of the plaintiff lies in the following circumstances—

(*a*) TOTAL FAILURE OF CONSIDERATION. The plaintiff must prove that there has been a *total* and not a *partial* failure of consideration. A *partial* failure of consideration may result in an action for damages. A *total* failure will result in recovery of all that was paid. A common reason for total failure of consideration arises where A, who has no title, sells goods to B and B has to give up the goods to the true owner. (*Rowland* v. *Divall*, 1923.)[322]

In addition the action is based on *failure* of consideration, not its *absence*. Thus money paid by way of a gift cannot be recovered in quasi-contract.

(*b*) MISTAKE OF FACT. Where there is a fundamental and material mistake of fact which results in a payment of money, there may be an action in quasi-contract to recover the sums so paid either in whole or in part according to the effect of the mistake. (*Cox* v. *Prentice*, 1815.)[323]

(*c*) MISTAKE OF LAW. Money paid as a result of a mistake of law cannot generally be recovered since ignorance of the law is no excuse. However, as we have seen, it is not easy to distinguish a mistake of law from a mistake of fact, and legislation relating to rents and security of tenure has produced some interesting cases showing the different results obtainable according to the category into which the mistake is put. (*Sharp Bros. and Knight* v. *Chant*, 1917,[126] *Solle* v. *Butcher*, 1950[127] and *Grist* v. *Bailey*, 1966.)[146] It appears that a mistake as to a person's legal rights can be construed, at least in equity, as a mistake of fact thus giving rise to a remedy. (*Cooper* v. *Phibbs*, 1876.)[128] There may be another ground for recovering money paid in circumstances of mistake of law, e.g. as in the case of an oppressed party to an illegal contract not *in pari delicto* with the other. Where this is so the plaintiff will not be prevented from succeeding simply because he has made a mistake of law. (*Kiriri Cotton Co.* v. *Dawani*, 1960.)[227]

(*d*) DURESS AND EXTORTION. Money paid under threats of physical violence or undue influence, i.e. moral duress, is not paid voluntarily and may be recovered in quasi-contract.

(*e*) MONEY RECEIVED FROM A THIRD PERSON. An application of this aspect of quasi-contract is to be found in insurance. If an insurance company pays out a sum of money to A (the insured) in respect of loss or damage to himself or his property and A later recovers additional money in respect of that loss from another, e.g. the person causing the loss, the insurance company may sue A in quasi-contract to recover the sums received from the third person. (*Darrell* v. *Tibbitts*, 1880.)[646]

In addition where A has received money from B with instructions to pay it to C then C may sue A in quasi-contract if A refuses to pay the money over. (*Shamia* v. *Joory*, 1958.)[86]

(*f*) WAIVER OF TORT. If A steals B's car which is valued at £500 and sells it to a dealer C for £550, then B may sue A or C for the tort of conversion but can if he wishes waive his right to sue in tort and recover the money in quasi-contract. The action in quasi-contract has some advantages over the action in tort, e.g. B may prove in a winding-up or bankruptcy for the sum of £550 which he cannot do if his claim is in tort and has not reached judgment.

Claims on a quantum meruit. Where a plaintiff has done work for the defendant but no specific sum is owing, the plaintiff can recover a reasonable sum of money on a *quantum meruit*. This aspect of quasi-contract is dealt with on pages 92–93.

Accounts stated. If A gives B an I.O.U. for £10 the I.O.U. operates as an admission of the debt and gives a separate cause of action in quasi-contract. An I.O.U. is not conclusive and A can prove that the debt is void for want of consideration or illegality or that he gave the I.O.U. under circumstances of mistake. Nevertheless A has the burden of proving these matters and if he cannot B will succeed on the I.O.U.

Furthermore, if A (a debtor) and B (a creditor) have an account recording a number of transactions and agree to strike a balance at an agreed figure, this operates as an account stated and B can sue in quasi-contract for the amount. This is a separate course of action and would enable B to recover even in respect of debts which were formerly statute barred.

CHAPTER II

SOME FUNDAMENTAL CONCEPTS

BEFORE proceeding to consider in detail some of the major branches of Mercantile Law it is necessary to examine briefly certain frequently recurring concepts of mercantile significance. The applications will be studied in detail in the appropriate connections.

ASSIGNMENT OF CONTRACTUAL RIGHTS

It has been mentioned that the rule of the common law is that only the actual parties to a contract can acquire rights under it, i.e. the doctrine of privity of contract applies. If, therefore, X has sold goods to the value of £10 to Y, can X assign the right to receive the £10 to Z?

Rights under a contract are called *choses in action* which is a legal expression used to denote all personal rights in property which can only be claimed or enforced by an action at law, e.g. contract debts, shares in companies and negotiable instruments. They may be contrasted with *choses in possession* which are things capable of actual physical assignment, e.g. a watch, a piece of furniture and so on.

The common law does not recognise assignments of *choses in action*, but Equity does and so does statute.

1. Assignment by Act of Parties. There are four possible categories—

(*a*) A LEGAL ASSIGNMENT OF A LEGAL CHOSE UNDER SECT. 136 OF THE LAW OF PROPERTY ACT, 1925. (This provision was originally contained in the Judicature Act, 1873.) To be effective such an assignment must be absolute and not partial or by way of charge (*Durham Bros.* v. *Robertson*, 1898,[324] and see *Hughes* v. *Pump House Hotel Co.*, 1902);[324a] must be in writing signed by the assignor; and must be notified in writing to the debtor, generally by the assignee. If the above requirements are complied with, the assignee can sue the debtor without making the assignor a party to the action. Failure to give notice to the debtor means that there is no legal assignment; the debtor can validly pay the assignor, and the assignee is liable to be postponed to a later assignee for value who notifies the debtor. However, it is not necessary for the date of the assignment to be given in the notice of assignment as long as the letter, or other form of written notice, states clearly that there has been an assignment and identifies the assignee. (*Van Lynn Developments* v. *Pelias Construction Co.*, [1968] 3 All E.R. 824.)

(*b*) EQUITABLE ASSIGNMENTS OF LEGAL CHOSES.

(*c*) EQUITABLE ASSIGNMENTS OF EQUITABLE CHOSES.

The difference between a legal and an equitable chose is historical in that an equitable chose is a right which, before 1875, could only be enforced in the Court of Chancery, e.g. the interest of a beneficiary under a trust fund. A debt, a bill of exchange and a claim on a policy of insurance are legal choses in action. However, a legacy is an equitable chose because the common law courts would not consider an action on a legacy. A share in a partnership is an equitable chose but a share in a company is a legal chose though its assignment is provided for by statute.

In equitable assignments of legal choses the assignor must be made a party in any action against the debtor, but if the chose is equitable this is not necessary. No particular form is required; all that is necessary is evidence of intention to assign. Notice should be given to the debtor or the trustees, as the case may be, in order to preserve priority as outlined above. Thus the transfer of a debt by word of mouth although invalid under statute may nevertheless be good and enforceable in equity.

(*d*) Equitable Assignments of Mere Expectancies. These are mere hopes of future entitlement, e.g. a legacy under the will of a living testator. The rules regarding such assignments are the same as those set out in (*b*) and (*c*) above, but no notice to the debtor can be given because there is none. Value is not needed for assignments within Sect. 136 of the Law of Property Act, 1925, or for equitable assignments of equitable choses in action. It is probably not needed for an equitable assignment of a legal chose, though the position is not clear. Value is needed for the assignment of mere expectancies; a document under seal is not enough. Value is also needed to support an agreement to assign an equitable chose, but if the assignee lawfully takes delivery of the property assigned, the assignor cannot recover it.

Assignments are said to be "subject to equities"; the person to whom the right is assigned takes it subject to any right of set off which was available against the original assignor. So if X assigns to Z a debt of £10 due from Y, and X also owes Y £5, then in any action brought by Z for the money, Y can set off the debt of £5. But the assignee is not subject to purely personal claims which would have been available against the assignor, e.g. damages for fraud, though the remedy of rescission is available against the assignee where the assignor obtained the contract by fraud.

Assignments of certain choses in action are governed by special statutes so that the rules outlined above do not apply. In such cases the special statute must be complied with. Examples are—

(*a*) Bills of Exchange and Promissory Notes—Bills of Exchange Act, 1882.

(*b*) Shares in companies registered under the Companies Act, 1967, and previous Acts—The Companies Act, 1948, and the Stock Transfer Act, 1963.

(*c*) Policies of Life Assurance—Policies of Assurance Act, 1867.

Rights of a personal nature under a contract cannot be assigned. If X contracts to write newspaper articles for a certain newspaper, it cannot assign its rights under the contract to another. The right to recover damages in litigation cannot be assigned, for this would amount to a breach of the law of maintenance. Liabilities under a contract cannot be assigned; the party to benefit cannot be compelled by mere notice to accept the performance of another, though a liability can be transferred by a novation, if the party to benefit agrees.

2. Assignment by Operation of Law. The involuntary assignment of rights and liabilities arises in the case of death and bankruptcy.

(i) DEATH. The personal representatives of the deceased acquire his rights and liabilities, the latter to the extent of the estate. Contracts of personal service are discharged.

(ii) BANKRUPTCY. The trustee in bankruptcy has vested in him all the rights of the bankrupt, except for actions of a purely personal nature which in no way affect the value of the estate, e.g. actions for defamation. The trustee is liable to the extent of the estate for the bankrupt's liabilities, though the trustee has a right to disclaim onerous or unprofitable contracts.

BAILMENT

A bailment arises when one person (the bailor) hands over his property to the care of another (the bailee). The reasons for such a situation are many. The bailee may have the custody of the property by way of loan or for carriage. The article may be pledged, or left with another to be repaired or altered. Sometimes the bailee has the mere custody of the goods; sometimes he may use the property, as when he "purchases" a radio set under a hire-purchase agreement or borrows a lawn mower. In all cases of bailment, the property or ownership remains with the bailor; the possession with the bailee.

Bailments are concerned with pure personality and not with real property.

The bailment may or may not originate in a contract and an infant may be a bailee of goods even though he obtained them under a void contract. (*Ballett* v. *Mingay*, 1943.)[325]

Possession. As essential feature of a bailment is the transfer of possession to the bailee. There is no precise definition of possession but the basic features are *control* and *an intention to exclude others*. However, a person can have possession of chattels which he does not know exist. (*South Staffordshire Water Co.* v. *Sharman*, 1896.)[326] A servant who receives goods from his master to take to a third party has mere *custody*; possession remains with the master and the servant is not a bailee. If a third party hands goods to a servant for his master the servant obtains possession and is the bailee.

In a bailment for a *fixed term* the bailee has possession to the exclusion of the bailor, and is, therefore, the only person who can sue a third party for trespass or conversion if there is interference with possession. In a bailment at will, i.e. one which the bailor can terminate at will, the bailor retains either possession or an immediate right to possess and the actions of trespass and conversion are available to him as well as to the bailee. A bailee can sue a third party in tort for loss of or damage to the goods even though the bailee is not liable to the bailor for the loss or damage. (*The Winkfield*, 1902.)[327]

Bailment and Licence. The problem of distinguishing between bailment and licence has arisen mainly in connection with the parking of vehicles. If a vehicle is parked on land, either gratuitously or even on payment of a charge, the transaction may amount to a mere licence and not a bailment which gives rise to duties of care. (*Ashby* v. *Tolhurst*, 1937.)[328] The decisions in *Ultzen* v. *Nicols*, 1894,[329] and *Deyong* v. *Shenburn*, 1946,[330] are illustrative of the problems involved in distinguishing bailment and licence.

Finders and Involuntary Recipients. To constitute a bailment the person who is given possession of goods must be entrusted with them for a particular purpose, e.g. to use and return as in the case of loan or hire, or to take from one place to another as in carriage. A banker is not a bailee of money paid into a customer's account, for his obligation is to return an equivalent sum and not the identical notes and coins. However, a banker is a bailee of property deposited with him for safe custody.

A finder is not a true bailee because he is not entrusted with the goods for a particular purpose. However, if he takes them into his possession he will be liable for loss or damage resulting from his negligence. (*Newman* v. *Bourne and Hollingsworth*, 1915.)[331]

A person cannot be made a bailee against his will. (*Neuwirth* v. *Over Darwin Industrial Co-operative Society*, 1894.)[332] Where the receipt of the goods is involuntary it is unlikely that the recipient is under any higher duty than to refrain from intentional damage. However, he must not convert the goods but although liability for conversion is usually strict, an involuntary recipient will only be liable if he acts intentionally or negligently. (*Elvin and Powell Ltd.* v. *Plummer Roddis Ltd.*, 1933.)[333]

The Unsolicited Goods and Services Act, 1971, is relevant in this connection. The Act is designed to deal with selling techniques involving the sending of unsolicited goods thus rendering the recipient an involuntary bailee. The Act provides for fines to be made on persons making demands for payment for goods which they know are unsolicited. If the demand is accompanied by threats a higher scale of fines applies. Furthermore, unsolicited goods may be kept by the recipient without payment *after a period of 30 days* provided the recipient gives notice to the sender asking that they be collected, or *after six months* even it no such notice has been given.

Obligations of the Bailor. Where the bailment is gratuitous it has been said that the limit of the liability of the bailor is to communicate to the bailee defects in the article lent *of which he is aware*. However, the principle in *Donoghue* v. *Stevenson*, 1932,[334] may apply to gratuitous bailments so that the bailor would be liable if he had not taken reasonable care to ensure that the goods bailed were not dangerous, even though he had no actual knowledge of a defect in the chattels lent.

When the bailment is for reward there is an implied warranty on the part of the bailor that he has a title to the goods so that the bailee's possession will not be disturbed, and that the goods are fit and suitable for the bailee's purpose. This does not mean that the bailee is liable for all defects but only for those which skill and care can guard against. (*Hyman* v. *Nye*, 1881;[335] *Reed* v. *Dean*, 1949.)[336] However, the warranty as to fitness and suitability does not apply where the defect is apparent to the bailee and he does not rely on the skill or judgment of the bailor.

Obligations of the Bailee. When Lord Holt, in *Coggs* v. *Bernard*, 1703,[73] established the liability of the bailee in negligence he laid down different duties of care for different kinds of bailments. Thus, in a bailment for the sole benefit of the bailee such as a gratuitous loan, the bailee's duty of care was much higher than in a bailment for the benefit of both parties such as a hiring. However, in recent times there has been disapproval of Lord Holt's different standards of care (*Houghland* v. *R. Low* (*Luxury Coaches*), *Ltd.*, 1962),[337] and it is now the better view that the standard of care required of a bailee is to take reasonable care in all the circumstances of the case, which equates his duty with that owed by any person in the law relating to negligence, though the burden of disproving negligence is on the bailee. (*Global Dress Co.* v. *Boase & Co.*, 1966.)[338]

The *main* circumstances which the court is likely to consider when deciding the question of negligence in a bailee are—

(a) *The type of bailment.* Although some current legal opinion is against a doctrinal distinction between bailment for reward and gratuitous bailment, reward or lack of reward will continue to be an *important circumstance* in the matter of the bailee's negligence. A gratuitous bailee must take the same care of the property bailed as a reasonable man would take of his own property. It is no defence for a bailee to show that he kept the goods with as much care as his own because the test of reasonableness is objective. (*Doorman* v. *Jenkins*, 1834.)[339] In a bailment for reward the duty of care tends to be somewhat higher. (*Brabant* v. *King*, 1895.)[340]

(b) *The expertise of the bailee.* If the bailee's profession or situation implies a certain expertise he will be liable if he fails to show it. (*Wilson* v. *Brett*, 1843.)[341]

(c) *The property bailed.* If the goods bailed are, to the knowledge of the bailee, fragile or valuable, a high standard of care will be expected. (*Sanders* (*Mayfair*) *Furs* v. *Davies*, 1965.)[342]

A bailee may be liable in negligence if he does not give notice to the bailor of a loss or try to recover lost or stolen property. (*Coldman v. Hill*, 1919.)[343]

A bailee is vicariously liable for the torts of his servants, but a servant who became a thief was not regarded as acting within the scope of his employment. (*Cheshire v. Bailey*, 1905.)[344] However, in *Morris v. C. W. Martin & Sons Ltd.*, 1965,[345] it was held that a bailee for reward cannot always escape liability for loss of goods stolen by his servant because theft is not necessarily beyond the scope of employment.

A bailee may attempt to exclude his liability by an exemption clause in the contract of bailment. This matter must now be considered in the light of the *Suisse Case*[197] and subsequent decisions and the rules of construction of contracts (pp. 51–52).

Delegation by bailee. Whether a bailee can delegate performance of the contract to another depends upon the nature of the bailment and the particular contract which may authorise delegation. Contracts involving the carriage, storage, repair or cleaning of goods often assume personal performance by the bailee. (*Davies v. Collins*, 1945;[346] *Edwards v. Newland*, 1950.)[347] Where there is a delegation, even though unknown to the bailor, the delegate is a bailee and owes a duty of care directly to the bailor. (*Learoyd Bros. v. Pope*, 1966.)[348]

Estoppel and Interpleader. A bailee is estopped at common law from denying the title of his bailor and if the bailor demands the return of the goods it is no defence for the bailee to plead that the bailor is not the owner. However, a bailee may defend an action for non-delivery of the goods—

(*a*) by showing that he has delivered them under an authorisation by the bailor;

(*b*) by showing that he has not got the goods because he has been dispossessed by a person with a better title, as in a bailment of stolen goods which are reclaimed by the owner;

(*c*) if he still retains possession he may allege that a third party has a better title but he must defend the action on behalf of, and with the authority of, the true owner. (*Rogers, Sons & Co. v. Lambert & Co.*, 1891.)[349]

Where adverse claims are made against the bailee by the bailor and a third party, the bailee should take interpleader proceedings under the Rules of the Supreme Court. The effect of this will be to bring the bailor and the third party together in an action which will decide the validity of their claims. The bailee can then hand over the goods to whichever party has established his claim and will not risk liability in detinue or conversion.

Lien. A bailee may, in certain circumstances, have a lien on the goods and the general nature of a lien is described below.

Bailment is a very common aspect of a variety of commercial transactions and its incidents will be considered in detail in the various chapters which follow.

SECURITIES

A security is some right or interest in a property given to a creditor so that, if the debt is not paid, the creditor can obtain the amount of the debt by exercising certain remedies against the property, rather than by suing the debtor by means of a personal action on his promise to pay. Securities, therefore, create rights over the property of another, and here we shall discuss liens, mortgages of land, chattels and choses in action.

LIEN

A lien is a right over the property of another which arises by operation of law and independently of any agreement. It gives a creditor the right (*a*) to retain possession of the debtor's property until he has paid or settled the debt, or (*b*) to sell the property in satisfaction of the debt in those cases where the lien is not possessory. Where the parties agree that a lien shall be created, such agreement will effectively create one.

1. Possessory or Common Law Lien. To exercise this type of lien the creditor must have actual possession of the debtor's property, in which case he can retain it until the debt is paid or settled. It should be noted that a creditor cannot ask for possession of the debtor's goods in order to exercise a lien.

A common law lien may be particular or general—

(*a*) PARTICULAR LIEN. This gives the possessor the right to retain goods until a debt arising in connection with these goods is paid.

(*b*) GENERAL LIEN. This gives the possessor the right to retain goods not only for debts specifically connected with them, but also for all debts due from the owner of the goods however arising.

The law favours particular rather than general liens.

If X sends a clock to R to be repaired at a cost of 50p R may retain the clock under a particular lien until the 50p is paid. If, however, X owed R 75p for the earlier repair of a watch, R cannot retain the clock to enforce the payment of £1·25 unless, as is unlikely, he can claim a general lien.

The following are cases of *particular lien*—

(i) A carrier can retain goods entrusted to him for carriage until his charges are paid. This will be dealt with in the chapter on Carriage.

(ii) An innkeeper has a lien over the property brought into the inn by a guest and also over property sent to him while there, even if it does not belong to him (*Robins* v. *Gray*, 1895.)[350] The lien does not extend to motor cars or other vehicles, or to horses or other animals.

(iii) A shipowner has a lien on the cargo for freight due.

(iv) In a sale of goods, the unpaid seller has a lien on the goods, if still in his possession, to recover the price. This will be dealt with in the chapter on Sale of Goods.

(v) Where a chattel is bailed in order that work may be done on it or labour and skill expended in connection with it, it may be retained until the charge is paid. Such liens may arise in favour of a car repairer over the car repaired; by an arbitrator on the award; by an architect over plans he has prepared; by a miller over corn for the cost of grinding; and innumerable other instances of this character.

A *general lien* may arise out of contract or custom, and the following classes of persons may have a general lien over the property of their customers or clients—factors, bankers, solicitors, stockbrokers, and in some cases insurance brokers. (*Caldwell* v. *Sumpters*, 1972.)[351]

Although a common law lien normally gives no power of sale, there are some exceptional cases in which a right of sale is given by statute. Such a right is given to innkeepers (Innkeepers Act, 1878), unpaid sellers of goods (Sale of Goods Act, 1893,) and bailees who accept goods for repair or other treatment for reward (Disposal of Uncollected Goods Act, 1952). Briefly, the latter Act provides for the sale of goods accepted for repair or other treatment which are ready for delivery if the bailee has given the bailor twelve months' notice that they are ready, and the bailor at the end of twelve months takes no action to collect the goods. The bailee may then sell the goods by public auction, provided that he gives the bailor fourteen days' notice of his intention to do so, and accounts to the bailor for the balance of the proceeds of sale *after* deduction of charges and expenses.

It should also be noted that the High Court has a discretion to order the sale of goods if it is just to do so, e.g. where the goods are perishable. (*Larner* v. *Fawcett*, 1950.)[352]

A common law lien is discharged—

(*a*) By payment of the sum owing;

(*b*) By parting with the possession of the goods or other property upon which the lien is being exercised; but see *Caldwell* v. *Sumpters*, 1972;[351]

(*c*) By an agreement to give credit for the amount due;

(*d*) By accepting an alternative security for the debt owing.

2. Maritime Lien. A maritime lien does not depend on possession. It is a right which attaches to a ship in connection with a maritime liability. It travels with the ship and may be enforced by the arrest and the sale of the ship through the medium of a court having Admiralty jurisdiction. Examples of such liens are—

(*a*) Liens of salvors.

(*b*) The lien of seamen for their wages.

(*c*) The lien of a master for his outgoings.

(*d*) Liens which arise from damage due to collision.

(*e*) Liens of bottomry bond holders.

The order of attachment is important and depends on circumstances. Successive salvage liens attach in inverse order, later ones being preferred to earlier ones, since the earlier lien would be useless if the later salvage had not preserved the ship from loss. Claims for collision damage are treated as of equal rank. Liens for wages, in the absence of salvage liens, have priority over other liens; however, liens for wages earned before a salvage operation are postponed to the lien for salvage, since the value of such a lien has been preserved by the salvage operation.

If a ship which is subject to lien is sold, the purchaser takes it subject to the lien and is responsible for discharging it.

3. Equitable Lien. An equitable lien is an equitable right, conferred by law, whereby one man acquires a charge on the property of another until certain claims have been met. It differs from a common law lien which is founded on possession and does not confer a power of sale. An equitable lien is independent of possession and may be enforced by a judicial sale.

An equitable lien may arise out of an express provision in a contract or from the relationship between parties. Thus a partner has an equitable lien on the partnership assets for the purpose of ensuring that they are applied, on dissolution, to paying partnership debts. Furthermore, an *unpaid* vendor of land has an equitable lien on the property after conveyance of ownership to the purchaser, or a third party who has taken it with notice of the lien, under which he may ask the court for an order to sell the property so that he may obtain the purchase money owing to him.

An equitable lien can, like all equitable rights, be extinguished by the owner selling the property to a *bona fide* purchaser for value who has no notice of the lien.

An equitable lien differs from a mortgage. A mortgage as we shall see is always created by the act of parties, an equitable lien may arise by operation of law.

4. Banker's Lien. At common law a banker has a general possessory lien on all securities, such as bills of exchange, promissory notes and bonds, deposited with him by customers in the ordinary course of business unless there is an agreement, express or implied, to the contrary. The lien does not extend to property or securities deposited for safe custody. However, a customer may deposit a security as collateral for a loan, in which case the banker has rights over it, but the transaction is an equitable mortgage rather than a lien.

A banker's lien gives a right of sale, at least of negotiable securities subject to the lien, because Sect. 27 of the Bills of Exchange Act, 1882, provides that a person having a possessory lien over a bill is deemed a holder for value to the extent of the lien, and can, therefore, sell and transfer the bill.

MORTGAGES OF LAND

Legal Mortgage of Freeholds. Under the 1925 legislation the mortgagor (the borrower) does not divest himself of his legal estate, but grants to the mortgagee (the lender) a demise for a term of years absolute. Thus, if X owns Blackacre and borrows money on mortgage from Y, he will grant Y a term of usually three thousand years in Blackacre, both agreeing that the term of years will end when the loan is repaid. X will also agree to pay interest on the loan at a stipulated rate.

Alternatively, under the provisions of Sect. 87 of the Law of Property Act, 1925, it is possible to create a legal mortgage of freeholds by means of a short deed stating that a charge on the land is created. Such a charge does not give a term of years, but the mortgagee has the same rights and powers as if he had received a term of years under a mortgage by demise.

Before 1926 mortgages were created by conveying the freehold to the mortgagee. Since 1925 an attempt to create a mortgage by this method operates as a grant of a mortgage lease of 3,000 years, subject to cesser on redemption, Sect. 85 Law of Property Act, 1925.

Legal Mortgages of Leaseholds. If X, the owner of a ninety-nine years lease of Blackacre, borrows money on mortgage from Y, he may grant Y a sub-lease of (say) ninety-nine years less ten days, both agreeing that when the loan is repaid the term shall cease. X also agrees to pay interest. Such a term is known as a *mortgage by demise*.

Alternatively a legal mortgage of leaseholds may be created by a charge by way of legal mortgage under Sect. 87 of the Law of Property Act, 1925, if made by deed. No sub-lease is created but the remedies of the mortgagee are the same as if it had been.

When a person has borrowed money by mortgaging property, he may still be able to borrow further sums, if the amount of the charge is not equal to the full value of the property and there seems to be adequate security for further loans. The owner of freehold land may grant a term of three thousand years plus one day to another mortgagee, whilst the owner of a lease may grant a second sub-lease of (say) ninety-nine years less nine days. Alternatively, a second charge by way of legal mortgage may be created by a further deed.

The only limit to further borrowing on second and subsequent mortgages is that of finding a lender who is prepared to become a second, third, or fourth mortgagee.

Equitable Mortgages. A mortgagee who receives a mere equitable interest in the land is said to have an equitable mortgage. Thus if the borrower's interest is equitable, e.g. a life interest, then any mortgage of it is necessarily equitable. Such an interest may be mortgaged by lease or charge, as in legal mortgages, or by a deposit of title deeds with the lender, usually accompanied by a memorandum explaining the transaction. Such mortgages must be in writing and signed by the borrower or his agent. (Sect. 53 Law of Property Act, 1925.)

An informal mortgage of a legal estate or interest creates an equitable mortgage, e.g. an attempt to create a legal mortgage otherwise than by deed.

Where there is a binding agreement to create a legal mortgage, but the formalities necessary to do so have not been carried out, Equity regards the agreement as an equitable mortgage. The agreement can be enforced by specific performance so that the mortgagee can obtain a legal mortgage from the borrower under the Rule in *Walsh* v. *Lonsdale,* 1882.[353] Before there is a binding agreement there must be either written evidence of the agreement, signed by the borrower or his agent, or a sufficient act of part performance by the lender.

Rights of the Mortgagor or Borrower. The main right of the mortgagor is the right to redeem (or recover) the land. Originally at common law the land became the property of the lender as soon as the date decided upon for repayment had passed, unless during that time the loan had been repaid. However, Equity regarded a mortgage as essentially a security, and gave the mortgagor the right to redeem the land at any time on payment of the principal sum, plus interest due to the date of payment. What is more important, this rule applied even though the common law date for repayment had passed. This right, which still exists, is called the *Equity of Redemption,* and there are two important rules connected with it—

(*a*) Once a Mortgage Always a Mortgage. This means that Equity looks at the real purpose of the transaction and does not always have regard to its form. If Equity considers that the transaction is a mortgage, the rules appertaining to mortgages will apply, particularly the right to redeem the property even though the contractual date for repayment has passed, or has not yet arrived. In the latter case, however, the mortgagor must generally give six months' notice of his intention to redeem, or pay six months' interest in lieu, so that the mortgagee may find another investment. However, if the parties contract at arm's length, and there is no evidence of oppression by the mortgagee, the court will endeavour to uphold the principle of sanctity of contract and will enforce any reasonable restriction on the right to redeem. (*Knightsbridge Estates Trust Ltd.* v. *Byrne,* 1939.)[354]

(*b*) There Must Be No Clog on the Equity of Redemption. This means—

(i) that the court will not allow postponement of the repayment period for an unreasonable time; and

(ii) the property mortgaged must, when the loan is repaid, be returned to the borrower in the same condition as when it was pledged. (*Noakes* v. *Rice,* 1902.)[355]

Nevertheless, particularly in modern times, so long as the parties are at arm's length when the loan is negotiated, Equity will allow a collateral transaction. (*Kreglinger* v. *New Patagonia Meat and Cold Storage Co.,* 1914;[356] *Cityland and Property (Holdings) Ltd.* v. *Dabrah,* 1967.)[357]

It is worth noting that the mortgagor may, where he is in possession of the land, grant leases to third parties subject to any special agreement to the contrary.

Powers and Remedies of the Legal Mortgagee. A legal mortgagee (the lender) has the following concurrent powers and remedies—

(a) To TAKE POSSESSION. This right does not depend upon default by the mortgagor, but the mortgagee will normally only enter into possession of the property under the term of years granted to him, or under the charge by way of legal mortgage, when he is not being paid the sum due, and when he wishes to pay himself from the proceeds of the property. This is not a desirable remedy, however, because when the mortgagee takes possession, he is strictly accountable to the mortgagor not only for what he has received, but for what he might have received with the exercise of due diligence and proper management. (*White* v. *City of London Brewery Co.*, 1889.)[358]

Most mortgagees who ask for a possession order do so in order to sell with vacant possession. However, if the mortgagee is simply concerned to intercept rents, where the mortgaged property is let and the mortgagor is a landlord, he will do better to appoint a receiver under the Law of Property Act, 1925, Sect. 109. The Administration of Justice Act, 1970, which is concerned, among other things, with mortgage possession actions, reinstates the old practice of the Chancery masters by allowing the Court to make an order adjourning the proceedings, or suspending or postponing a possession order, provided it appears that the mortgagor is likely to be able to pay within a reasonable time any sums due under the mortgage (Sect. 36). The Act applies wherever a mortgage includes a dwelling house even though part may be used for business purposes. Sect. 36 does not apply to a foreclosure action in which a claim for possession is also made.

(b) FORECLOSURE. The mortgagee may obtain an order from the court if the mortgagor fails to pay for an unreasonable time. The first order is a *foreclosure order nisi* providing that the debt must be paid within a stated time. If it is not so paid, the order is made *absolute* and the property becomes that of the mortgagee, the mortgagor's equity of redemption being barred, and the property vesting in the mortgagee, free from any right of redemption either in law or equity. Such orders are seldom used, for it is still open to the court to re-open the foreclosure, i.e. to give the mortgagor a further opportunity to redeem.

(c) RIGHT OF SALE. Normally this is the most valuable right of the mortgagee. Subject to certain conditions he can, on the default of the mortgagor, sell and convey to a purchaser the whole of the mortgaged property, and recoup himself out of the proceeds. Unless the mortgagee is a building society (Building Societies Act, 1962, Sect. 36) he is not a trustee of the power of sale for the benefit of the mortgagor. However, he must not fraudulently, wilfully or recklessly sacrifice the property of the mortgagor (*Kennedy* v. *De Trafford*, [1897]

A.C. 180), and in addition owes a duty to the mortgagor to take reasonable care to obtain the best price that can be had in the circumstances. (*Cuckmere Brick Co.* v. *Mutual Finance*, 1971.)[359] A mortgagee cannot sell to himself or to his nominee.

(*d*) To Sue for the Money Owing. The mortgage is a pledge for the repayment of the money, but mortgagors almost invariably give a personal covenant to repay. This is of value should the property be destroyed or lose its value. When the date fixed for redemption is passed, the mortgage money is due and the mortgagee can sue for it. He will rarely do so, for in most cases the other remedies will be more satisfactory.

(*e*) The Right to Appoint a Receiver. The Law of Property Act, 1925, Sect. 109, gives the mortgagee the right to appoint a receiver to receive the rents and profits on the mortgagee's behalf in order to pay the money due. The receiver is deemed to be the agent of the mortgagor, who is liable for his acts and defaults unless otherwise provided by the mortgage. The mortgagee thus avoids the disadvantage of strict accountability to which he would be subject if he entered himself.

Remedies of Equitable Mortgagees. Where the mortgage is equitable and is created by deed, then the mortgagee has virtually the same remedies as have been set out above. Otherwise, if the mortgage is by a mere deposit of title deeds, then the mortgagee must ask the court—

(*a*) for an order to sell, or
(*b*) for an order appointing a receiver.

Other Rights of Mortgagees. A mortgagee has other rights and he may, where the mortgage is created by deed, insure the mortgaged property against loss by fire up to two-thirds of its value, and charge the premiums on the property in the same way as the mortgage money.

A mortgagee has a right to the title deeds of the property, and if the mortgage is redeemed by the mortgagor, the mortgagee must return the deeds to him in the absence of notice of a second or subsequent mortgage, in which case the deeds should be handed to the next mortgagee.

There are two other important rights which a mortgagee may exercise in appropriate circumstances—the right to consolidate and the right to tack.

Consolidation. Where a person has two or more mortgages, he may refuse to allow one mortgage to be redeemed unless the other or others are also redeemed. This right is particularly valuable where property might fluctuate in value, and where a mortgagor might redeem one mortgage where the security was more than adequate, leaving the mortgagee with a debt on the other property not properly secured.

Consolidation is only possible if the right to consolidate was reserved in one of the mortgage deeds, or if the mortgage was contracted prior to 1882. The contractual date for redemption must have passed on all mortgages and they must have been created by the same mortgagor, though not necessarily in favour of the same mortgagee. Nevertheless in such cases, where it is proposed to consolidate two mortgages, both the mortgages must have been vested in one person at the same time as both the equities of redemption were vested in another.

TACKING. The right to tack may bring about a modification of the priority of mortgages. It is now confined to the tacking of further advances. Thus, where a man has lent money on a first mortgage and there are second and third mortgages, if the first mortgagee agrees to advance a further sum, he may tack this to his first mortgage and thus get priority over the second and third, which would normally rank before the tacked mortgage. This can now only be done if the intervening mortgagees agree, or if the further advance is made without notice of an intervening mortgage, or if the prior mortgage imposed an obligation to make further advances.

ATTORNMENT CLAUSE. Many mortgages contain an attornment clause by which the borrower attorns or acknowledges himself as a tenant at will, or from year to year, of the lender at a nominal rent such as a peppercorn. The advantage of such a clause was that it entitled the lender to evict the borrower for failure to pay the mortgage instalments and so obtain possession more speedily. However, changes in the rules of court from 1933–37 made a speedy procedure available to mortgagees as such, and there is now no substantial advantage in an attornment clause.

Priority of Mortgages. The Land Charges Act, 1925, introduced the principle of registering charges on land. The object of searching the Land Charges Register is to discover the rights, if any, of third parties which are enforceable against the land. It is a general principle that a purchaser or mortgagee of land is deemed to have actual notice of all third party rights capable of registration and actually registered, whereas he acquires his interest in the land free from third party rights capable of registration and not registered. There are five separate registers kept at the Land Charges Department of the Land Registry in London. Search may be made in person, but is usually done by filling in an appropriate form and sending it to the Land Charges Superintendent in London. This results in an *official search certificate*.

Where there is a mortgage of a legal estate with deposit of title deeds, the mortgage ranks from the date of its creation and such a mortgage cannot be registered.

Where there is a mortgage of a legal estate without deposit of title deeds, the mortgage ranks from its date of registration as a land charge.

Regarding mortgages of equitable interests, the question of priority is based on the rule in *Dearle* v. *Hall* (1828), 3 Russ. 1, and such mortgages rank from the date on which the mortgagee gave notice of his mortgage to the trustees of the equitable interest, though such notice will not postpone a previous mortgage of which the mortgagee giving notice was aware. It should be noted that an equitable mortgagee who subsequently obtains a legal interest does not thereby obtain priority over an equitable interest *prior to his own of which he had constructive notice* when entering into his own equitable mortgage. (*McCarthy & Stone Ltd.* v. *Julian S. Hodge & Co. Ltd.*, 1971.)[360]

MORTGAGES OF PERSONAL CHATTELS

Just as land can be used as a means of securing debts, so also can personal chattels. There are two principal ways in which this can be done—

(*a*) *by mortgage*: in this case the borrower retains possession of his goods but transfers their ownership to the lender to secure the loan. If the transaction is carried out by means of a written document it is known as a conditional bill of sale and must be registered at the Central Office at the Royal Courts of Justice in London.

The purpose of registration is to give public notice of the transaction and so prevent the borrower from dealing with the goods as his own.

(*b*) *By pledge*, or "*pawn*": in this case the lender obtains possession of the goods, the borrower retaining ownership. Thus there is no danger that the borrower will obtain credit on the strength of his possession of the chattels, and the law relating to pledges is mainly concerned to protect the interests of the borrower (or pledger) against dishonest pawnbrokers.

BILLS OF SALE

Bills of Sale are now regulated by the Bills of Sale Act, 1878, called the principal act, and the Bills of Sale Act (1878) Amendment Act, 1882, normally cited together as the Bills of Sale Acts, 1878–1882.

The Bills of Sale Act, 1878, was *designed to protect creditors* from being deceived by the fact that a man might retain possession of goods, apparently his, the ownership of which he had surrendered.

The amending Act of 1882 *aimed at preventing needy persons from being oppressed* by their creditors by the provisions of complicated documents imperfectly understood. In order to achieve this the Act prescribed a particular form of words expressing clearly the precise nature of the contract and the security given for the loan.

Two classes of bills of sale have thus been created—

(1) *Absolute Bills of Sale*, to which the principal Act continues to apply, and

(2) *Bills of Sale to secure the payment of money* (often called Conditional Bills). The 1882 Act applies only to this class, although the amending

Act and the principal Act are to be construed as one so far as this is consistently possible.

Definition. A bill of sale is a mortgage of personal chattels by means of an instrument in writing in which the grantor transfers to the grantee the property he has in goods or chattels, even though he intends to remain in possession of them. A bill of sale is defined in the Act of 1878 so as to include any agreement by which a right in equity to any personal chattels, or to any charge or security thereon, is conferred, e.g. assignments, transfers, declarations of trust without transfer, and inventories of goods with receipts attached.

The Following are not Bills of Sale: assignments for the benefit of creditors, marriage settlements, transfers or assignments of ships, bills of lading, warehouse-keepers' certificates, or any other documents used in the ordinary course of business (*a*) as proof of the possession or control of goods; or (*b*) as authorising the possessor of such document to transfer or receive the goods thereby represented. In deciding whether a document comes within the Act, the court looks at the substance rather than the form of the transaction.

The operation of both Acts is restricted to bills of sale whereby the holder or grantee has power, with or without notice, and either immediately or at any future time, to seize or take possession of any personal chattels comprised in or made subject to such bill of sale. An oral agreement to give a bill of sale is not covered by the Acts.

Personal Chattels. The Acts refer only to personal chattels and the principal Act regards as personal chattels—

(1) Goods, furniture and other articles capable of complete transfer by delivery;

(2) Fixtures and growing crops, assigned or charged separately from the land;

(3) Trade machinery, which includes machines used in a factory or workshop, exclusive of fixed motive-powers, shafting, or steam, gas or water pipes.

The Acts do not apply to choses in action, e.g. shares or interests in government stock or securities, or capital or property of incorporated or joint stock companies.

An absolute bill of sale does not require a schedule of the chattels charged, but the amending Act requires that *every conditional bill,* i.e. a bill of sale given by way of security for the payment of money, *must have a schedule* containing an inventory of the personal chattels comprised in the bill of sale. A conditional bill of sale is void, except as against the grantor, in respect of any personal chattels not specifically described in the schedule, which must be attached to the bill of sale before or at the time it is executed.

If the bill is in correct form but has a schedule which specifically describes some but not all of the chattels assigned, it is not wholly void; but it is *of no effect* in respect of the chattels not specifically described, *except as against the grantor.*

A bill of sale, given by way of security for the payment of money, without a schedule, or comprising chattels not capable of specific description, is void. The description must be adequate to identify the chattels assigned, but where a bill of sale covers all the chattels in a particular house, it may not be necessary to describe each article in detail; a more general description may suffice, e.g. twelve oil paintings in gold frames. However, a description by number will not be enough if there may be other similar articles on the same premises. A person who asserts that the description is inadequate must show that the articles cannot be identified.

The grantor must be the true owner of the goods assigned under a conditional bill of sale or the bill will be void, except where the real owner is estopped from denying its validity by having represented that the grantor was the true owner.

Statutory Requirements. The Acts lay down the following requirements—

(1) CONSIDERATION. A bill of sale *by way of security* made or given in consideration of a sum under £30 is void, and *every bill of sale* must set forth the consideration for which it was given.

(2) FORM. (*a*) An absolute bill of sale need not be in any particular form.

(*b*) A conditional bill of sale is void unless made in accordance with the form prescribed by the amending Act. (Below.)

SCHEDULE

FORM OF BILL OF SALE

This Indenture made the   day of   , between *A.B.* of   of the one part, and *C.D.* of   of the other part, witnesseth that in consideration of the sum of £   now paid to *A.B.* by *C.D.*, the receipt of which the said *A.B.* hereby acknowledges [*or whatever else the consideration may be*], he the said *A.B.* doth hereby assign unto *C.D.*, his executors, administrators, and assigns, all and singular the several chattels and things specifically described in the schedule hereto annexed by way of security for the payment of the sum of £   , and interest thereon at the rate of per cent per annum [*or whatever else may be the rate*]. And the said *A.B.* doth further agree and declare that he will duly pay to the said *C.D.* the principal sum aforesaid, together with the interest then due, by equal   payments of £   on the   day of [*or whatever else may be the stipulated times or time of payment*]. And the said *A.B.* doth also agree with the said *C.D.* that he will [*here insert terms as to insurance, payment of rent, or otherwise, which the parties may agree to for the maintenance or defeasance of the security*].

Provided always, that the chattels hereby assigned shall not be liable to seizure or to be taken possession of by the said *C.D.* for any cause other than those specified in section seven of the Bills of Sale Act (1878) Amendment Act, 1882.

In witness, etc.

Signed and sealed by the said *A.B.* in the presence of me *E.F.* [*add witness's name, address, and description*].

(3) ATTESTATION. (*a*) An absolute bill of sale must be attested by a solicitor, and the attestation must state that, before the bill was executed, its effect had been explained by the solicitor to the grantor. An *affidavit* proving the attestation must be filed when the bill is registered.

(*b*) In the case of a bill of sale given by way of security (a conditional bill), its execution must be attested by one or more credible witnesses who are not parties to the bill.

(4) REGISTRATION. Both absolute and conditional bills of sale must be registered within seven clear days of their making or execution. The bill of sale with every schedule or inventory thereto annexed or therein referred to, also a *true copy* of such bill, schedule or inventory, and of every *attestation* of the execution of such bill of sale, together with an *affidavit* containing the particulars set out below, must be presented to the registrar and the copies must be filed with him. The office of Registrar is carried out by the Masters of the Supreme Court (Queen's Bench Division) and the place of registration is the Bills of Sale Department of the Central Office at the Royal Courts of Justice in London.

The *affidavit* just mentioned must prove (*a*) the time that the bill of sale was made or given; (*b*) its due attestation; (*c*) the residence and occupation of the person making or giving the bill and of every attesting witness.

The registration must be renewed once at least every five years, and if not so renewed, the registration becomes void. Renewal is effected by filing an affidavit stating the date of the bill and its last registration, and the names, residences and occupations of the parties to it, and that the bill of sale is still a subsisting security.

A transfer or assignment of a registered bill of sale need not be registered, nor is a renewal of registration necessary on such transfer or assignment. Nevertheless, if the transferee allows the period of renewal to elapse without re-registration, the original registration becomes void despite the transfer.

An absolute bill of sale will not be void for want of registration unless the chattels remain in the sole possession, or apparent possession, of the transferor (or grantor) of the bill. (*Koppel* v. *Koppel*, 1966.)[361]

Void Bills. A bill of sale by way of security for the payment of money is void altogether if it is not made in the statutory form and the agreement for the repayment of the loan and interest contained in it is unenforceable. (*Davies* v. *Rees*, 1886.)[362]

Where it is made for a consideration of less than £30, it is void, but the money lent, with interest, may be recovered as money had and received.

Where a bill is void in respect of the personal chattels in it because it is not attested or registered or does not contain the consideration, it is void only as regards the personal chattels but may be used for enforcing the repayment of principal with interest.

Rights and Liabilities of the Parties. A bill of sale by way of security, if made in the statutory form, vests the chattels in the grantee and leaves the right to possession in the grantor unless and until an event giving a right to seizure occurs.

On such seizure, *the grantor* loses his interest in the chattels and cannot sue for trespass but may (*a*) within five days of the seizure apply for relief to the High Court or a judge in chambers; or (*b*) after five days have elapsed, take proceedings for redemption. If the grantor tenders the principal, interest and expenses, he may recover the goods together with the bill of sale thereon. A grantor cannot normally redeem a bill of sale before the time fixed for payment.

On the execution of an *absolute* bill of sale, both the property in the chattels and the right of possession pass to the *grantee*. In the case of a *conditional* bill (given by way of security) the grantor retains the right of possession and the grantee can only seize or take possession of the chattels for a cause set out in the Act of 1882.

Statutory Causes of Seizure. Five causes and five only justify the grantee in seizing the goods—

(1) *If the grantor makes default in the payment* of the sum or sums secured at the time provided for payment, *or in the performance of any covenant* or agreement contained in the bill of sale and necessary to maintain the security.

(2) *If the grantor becomes bankrupt, or suffers the goods to be distrained* for rent, rates, or taxes.

(3) *If the grantor fraudulently removes or allows the goods to be removed* from the premises.

(4) *If the grantor refuses*, without reasonable excuse, *to produce*, if the grantee demands them, his last *receipts* for rent, rates, and taxes.

(5) *If execution is levied* against the goods of the grantor under any judgment at law.

No power of seizure arises outside these causes and substantial damages may be awarded to the grantor for wrongful seizure.

The Act of 1882 provides that all personal chattels seized, or of which possession is taken under or by virtue of a bill of sale, shall remain on the premises where they were so seized or taken possession of, and shall not be moved or sold until the expiration of five clear days from the date of such seizure or possession. During this period the grantor may apply for relief or he may permit the grantee to remove the property.

A bill of sale does not protect the grantee against a distress for rent or for the recovery of taxes or local authority rates, and the grantee who fears distraint by the landlord may remove the goods before five clear days have elapsed and before distress is levied, and even if this removal is with the grantor's consent, it is not a fraud on the landlord.

Where the amount secured by the bill is paid off or discharged, the registrar may direct that a memorandum of satisfaction be written upon the registered copy of the bill, and the grantee may be ordered to surrender the bill of sale.

The registrar's books may be inspected, and any person may have an office copy or extract of any registered bill of sale on paying the prescribed fee. Any person may search the register at reasonable times on payment of a small fee, or may ask for a search or the issue of a certificate for a higher fee.

PAWNS AND PLEDGES

Nature of Pledge or Pawn. A pawn or pledge arises when there is a bailment of personal property as a security for a debt. The property in the pledge vests in the pledgee so far as is necessary to secure the debt. The common law applies to all pawns except those falling within the Pawnbrokers Act, 1872 and 1960, i.e. those made with a pawnbroker for sums not exceeding £50; and even in these cases the common law applies unless the Acts expressly exclude it.

A pawn differs from a mortgage in that the property pledged must be delivered to the pawnee, either actually or constructively. Also the pawnee only acquires a special property in the pledge, the general property remaining in the pawner and reverting to him when the debt is paid. A pawn differs from a lien because a lien cannot be transferred to a third party, and a person's right of lien does not give him a special property but only a right to detain the subject matter until the debt is paid.

A person may pawn any goods or chattels capable of actual or constructive delivery, or any personal property capable of identification, e.g. a bill of exchange.

A contract to pawn *is not enough—the chattel* pawned *must be delivered* to the pawnee, though the loan and delivery need not be simultaneous *if they are part of the same contract.* Delivery may be *actual or constructive.* Actual delivery occurs when the chattel is handed over; constructive delivery occurs when the chattel is legally delivered but does not in fact change hands, and may be achieved by a symbolic act such as the delivery of the key of a room or warehouse in which the goods are kept.

On paying off the debt, the property pledged is re-delivered to the pawner. The pawner gives an implied undertaking that the property pledged is his, or that he has been authorised by the owner to pledge it. In the absence of such authority, the pawnee must return the goods pledged to the real owner unless, by his conduct, the owner is estopped from denying the pawner's authority. The pawner does not, however, warrant the quality of the thing pledged, although he must not make a false representation concerning it.

The Pawner. The general property in the thing pledged is retained by the pawner who has at common law an absolute right to redeem it on paying off the debt. If no time for payment is stipulated, the pawner may redeem it at any time and, if the pawnee dies, the pawner may still redeem it from the personal representatives. If the pawner sells the pledge before redemption, the purchaser acquires the same interest as the pawner had. However, once the pawnee has lawfully sold the article pledged, the right to redeem is gone.

The Pawnee. Although the pawner retains the general property in the pledge, the pawnee has a right to possession giving him a *special property or interest*, which arises on delivery and which is more than a mere right of retention. The pawnee may assign or pledge this special property or interest, or sell the goods in due course.

The pawnee need only take ordinary care of the thing pawned, and if he loses it without default, the loss falls on the pawner and the pawnee may still obtain payment of the debt. If, however, the price of redemption has been offered and the pawnee still retains the goods pledged, they are thereafter at the pawnee's risk and he is liable to the pawner for loss.

The pawnee may, at his own risk, use the thing pledged if it will not suffer by use, e.g. he may use jewellery but not clothes. Indeed, if reasonable use of the pledge is beneficial or is necessary to preserve it, the pawnee should use it, e.g. a horse *may* be ridden and a cow *must* be milked. If the custody of the pledge involves him in expense, the pawnee may recover this amount.

Since the security is available to satisfy the debt, the pawnee has a power of sale if payment is not made by the time stipulated. If no time has been fixed for payment and the pawnee has demanded payment, has not been paid, and has given notice of his intention to sell the pledge, the pawnee may then proceed to sell it, although the pawner may still redeem at any time before the sale takes place. Any surplus after paying the debt belongs to the pawner, and the pawnee must sell at a reasonable price. If a quantity of goods is pawned, e.g. twelve silver spoons, he must not sell more than are required to satisfy the debt, e.g. six.

The pawnee may sue for his debt independent of the pledge, and if a sale does not realise enough to clear the debt, the pawnee has an action for the balance.

PAWNBROKERS

Pawnbrokers are regulated by the Pawnbrokers Act, 1872 and 1960. A pawnbroker is a person who carries on the business of taking goods and chattels in pawn and who makes loans not exceeding £50 on them. He must take out a yearly excise licence and keep and use the specified books and documents, e.g. pledge books, sale books, pawn tickets, receipts and forms of special contracts, and declarations of claim and loss.

When a pawnbroker takes a pledge, he must insist on the pawner taking a pawn ticket. For loans over £5 the pawnbroker may make a special contract with the pawner by giving him a special contract pawn ticket, signed by the pawnee, the pawner himself signing a duplicate.

There are *limits set on the profits and charges* of the pawnbroker. Where a loan exceeds £5 but does not exceed £50, the statutory provisions relating to profit and charges apply (unless they are excluded by special contract). The pawnbroker is allowed, for example, in the case of a loan of £5 or under, one half-pence for every month or part of a month, for each 10p. or fraction of 10p. lent, or on loans over £5, the same rate for each 12½p. He may also charge 1p. for a pawn ticket and may make charges for valuing goods or inspecting entries in the sale book.

A pledge may be redeemed within six months of the day of pawning, and a further seven days of grace are allowed within which the pledge continues to be redeemable. Where a pledge is pawned for £2 or less and is not redeemed within the above period, it becomes the absolute property of the pawnee at the end of the days of grace. A pledge pawned for more than £2 remains redeemable until disposed of by sale or otherwise. The assignees and personal representatives of the pawner have the same right to redeem as the pawner himself.

When a pawnbroker disposes of a pledge on which he has lent more than £2, he must sell it by public auction. Where the proceeds exceed the amount of the loan and profit due at the time of the sale, the pawnbroker must, on demand, pay the surplus to the holder of the pawn ticket with a deduction for the costs of the sale, but after three years the surplus belongs to the pawnbroker and cannot be reclaimed. However, if the sale of one pledge yields a surplus and, within twelve months before or after, another sale of a pledge by the same person has produced or does produce a deficit, the deficit may be set off against the surplus, and the pawnbroker is only liable for the balance. The pawnbroker may bid when a pledge is sold, and if he purchases it, it becomes his absolute property.

When a person produces a pawn ticket and offers payment of loan and profit, the pawnbroker must deliver the pledge to him. If a person claims to be the owner of a pledge but does not hold the pawn ticket, he is entitled to obtain the printed form of declaration from the pawnbroker. On completing this and handing it over to the pawnbroker, he recovers the rights attaching to the pawn ticket, and the pawnbroker will be indemnified for any loss arising from the handing over of the pledge, unless he has notice that the declaration is fraudulent or false in a material particular.

If a pledge is destroyed by fire and application to redeem is made during the period allowed for redemption, the pawnbroker is liable for the difference between the value of the pledge and the amount of loan and profit, and he may insure to this extent. If the pawner can prove that the pledge has been damaged by the default or neglect of the pawnbroker, the pawner can claim reasonable compensation on redemption.

MORTGAGES OF CHOSES IN ACTION

It is possible to use a chose in action as security for a loan, and mortgagees frequently take life assurance policies as security, e.g. a bank in the case of an overdraft. However, shares in companies are perhaps the commonest chose in action to be used as security.

Shares may be made subject to a legal mortgage, but here the shares must actually be transferred to the mortgagee so that his name may appear on the company's share register. An agreement is made out in which the mortgagee agrees to re-transfer the shares to the mortgagor when the loan is repaid.

It is also possible to have an equitable mortgage of company shares, and this is in fact the usual method adopted. The share certificate is deposited with the mortgagee, together with a blank transfer signed by the registered holder, the name of the transferee being left blank. The shares are not actually transferred, but the agreement accompanying the transaction allows the mortgagee to sell the shares by completing the form of transfer and registering himself as the legal owner if the mortgagor fails to repay the loan.

CHAPTER III

THE SALE OF GOODS

THE law relating to the sale of goods is to be found—

    (i) in the Sale of Goods Act, 1893 as amended by later Acts;

    (ii) in the Factors Act, 1889;

    (iii) in the rules of the common law which are not dealt with by either of the above Acts.

Definition. A contract of sale of goods is a contract whereby the seller transfers or agrees to transfer the property in goods to the buyer for a money consideration called the price. (Sect. 1 (1).) The definition covers—

    (i) A CONTRACT OF SALE in which the property in goods is transferred from seller to buyer; and

    (ii) AN AGREEMENT TO SELL in which the transfer of property takes place at a future time or on fulfilment of certain conditions. (Sect. 1 (3).) A contract for the sale of goods yet to be manufactured is an agreement to sell because the property in the goods cannot pass until they are manufactured and ascertained.

Unless the contract otherwise provides, the property in goods which are the subject of a contract of sale passes to the buyer when the contract is made. English law does not require actual delivery of the goods, and the contract of sale operates as the conveyance.

Property is defined as the general property in goods and not merely a special property (Sect. 62), and to say that the property passes to the buyer presumably means that he gets ownership and not mere possession. *Delivery* is the voluntary transfer of possession from one person to another, and whether the property in the goods passes on delivery is a question to be decided from the contract or, where the contract is silent, from the circumstances.

GOODS

Sect. 62 provides that *goods* includes all personal chattels but excludes all choses in action (e.g. share certificates) and money, although a coin which is a curio piece may be goods for the purposes of a contract of sale. The term also includes *emblements*, i.e. crops to be severed before sale or under the contract of sale. Products of the soil are always sold with a view to severance and though they may sometimes be of the nature of land for the purposes of Sect. 40 of the Law of Property Act, 1925 (see p. 14), they are always goods within the meaning of the Act of 1893. The Act does not apply to the *sale of an interest in the land itself*. The sale of gravel *in situ* under land would not be covered by the Act.

Goods may be—

(i) EXISTING GOODS, i.e. goods actually in existence when the contract is made, though they need not be specific and may yet have to be appropriated to the contract.

(ii) FUTURE GOODS, i.e. goods yet to be acquired or manufactured by the seller.

(iii) SPECIFIC GOODS, i.e. goods identified and agreed upon at the time the contract of sale is made.

(iv) UNASCERTAINED GOODS which consist of the following—

(*a*) Goods to be made or grown by the seller, which are, of course, future goods;

(*b*) Goods defined by description only; and

(*c*) An unidentified part of a specified whole.

If X sells to Y two hundred bags of flour from a stock of two thousand lying in X's warehouse, the flour is existing goods, but so far as the contract is concerned, the goods are not specific until a selection of bags has been made by Y. Generally, future goods are not specific, but if they can be sufficiently identified, they may be, and their destruction will frustrate the contract. (*Howell* v. *Coupland*, 1876.)[363] Where X agrees to sell to Y 100 bags of coal, these are identified by description only and are unascertained, and X would perform his contract by delivering any hundred bags of coal he chose. Since such goods are not appropriated to the contract, they are also future goods.

THE EXISTENCE OF GOODS

There is no provision in the Act that the seller warrants the existence of the goods, but Sect. 6 provides that where there is a contract for the sale of *specific* goods and the goods without the knowledge of the seller have perished at the time when the contract is made, the contract is void.

Thus, if X sells his car to Y, and unknown to X the car has caught fire and burnt out an hour before the sale, the contract would be void and there would be no liabilities on either side. The goods must be specific before Sect. 6 can operate, and if X agrees to sell Y "100 tons of coal," X is still liable to supply the coal or pay damages, even though he had a particular 100 tons in mind which have in fact perished.

Difficulties may arise where the goods are to some extent ascertained. For example, suppose X agrees to sell to Y "Six dozen bottles of Grandiosa Port from the stock at present in my warehouse." If, unknown to X, the stock is wholly destroyed before the sale, the contract would be void under Sect. 6. But if ten dozen bottles were left, i.e. if performance of the contract were still possible, presumably the seller X would be required to carry out his obligations. If there were only two dozen bottles left the contract would presumably be avoided.

Where, although the goods are specific, they exist only in part, the parties are released from their liabilities. (*Barrow, Lane & Ballard*

Ltd. v. *Phillip Phillips & Co.*, 1929),[364] unless the contract is severable, when Sect. 6 would avoid the contract only in respect of the goods which had perished.

Sect. 6 does not apply at all if the goods have never existed. In such a case it seems that either (i) Common law principles apply and the seller impliedly warrants the existence of the goods; or (ii) the court may regard the existence of the goods as a condition precedent to liability in either party. (*McRae* v. *Commonwealth Disposals Commission*, 1951.)[140] This will depend upon the contract itself and the circumstances.

Sect. 7 provides that where there is an agreement to sell specific, goods which have perished, without any fault on the part of the seller or buyer, *before the risk passes to the buyer*, the agreement is thereby avoided. In other words, the contract is frustrated and the buyer is not liable for the price, and the seller is not liable to deliver the goods and consequently cannot be sued for non-delivery.

The application of the section is limited for the goods must be *specific* and the *risk must not have passed*, and in a contract for the sale of specific goods, property and risk usually pass when the contract is made. The section will apply to contracts of sale where the goods are not in a deliverable state, since in such a case the property will not have passed.

It seems that if only some, but not all, of the goods have perished the parties are released from their liabilities. (*Barrow, Lane & Ballard Ltd.* v. *Phillip Phillips & Co.*, 1929.)[364] But if the contract is severable, presumably it is valid with regard to the goods which have not perished. (On the issue of frustration see also p. 84.)

CONTRACTS OF SALE AND SIMILAR TRANSACTIONS

Before the repeal of Sect. 4 of the Sale of Goods Act, 1893, it was necessary to distinguish a sale from other contracts of a similar nature. If the contract was one for the sale of goods of £10 or over, a memorandum in writing would normally be required; but if the contract was (say) for skill and labour, it could be enforced, even though not evidenced in writing.

Sect. 4 of the Sale of Goods Act was repealed by the Law Reform (Enforcement of Contracts) Act, 1954, and contracts of sale can now be made orally regardless of the value of the goods sold. A reason for distinguishing still survives in that the Sale of Goods Act implies certain terms into a contract of sale, while in other cases, e.g. contracts for skill and labour, there are no statutory implied terms, and the parties must rely on express terms regarding the fitness and quality of articles supplied under such contracts. Nevertheless the courts are inclined to imply into contracts not covered by the Act terms which are very similar to those of the Act itself. (*Myers & Co. Ltd.* v. *Brent Cross Service Co.*, 1934.)[365]

1. Contracts for Sale and Contracts for Work and Materials. In *Lee* v. *Griffin*, [1861] 1 B. & S. 272, where the contract was for the manufacture of false teeth, Blackburn, J., ruled that, if the contract results in the transfer of the property in a chattel from one person to another, it is a contract of sale. This statement was considered too sweeping and was not followed in *Robinson* v. *Graves*, [1935] 1 K.B. 579, where it was held that a contract to paint a portrait was a contract for work and materials and not a sale of goods, even though the property in the chattel, i.e. the portrait, was eventually to be transferred. However, much depends upon the circumstances, and a contract for the construction of two ship's propellers was held to be a contract of sale of goods (*Cammell Laird & Co. Ltd.* v. *Manganese Bronze & Brass Co. Ltd.*, [1934] A.C. 402); so too was a contract for the making of a fur coat from selected skins (*Marcel (Furriers) Ltd.* v. *Tapper*, [1953] 1 All E.R. 15).

2. Contracts for Sale and Barter or Exchange. Sect. 1 (1) requires that the consideration be money, and contracts of pure exchange are not within the Act. Difficulties arise where a seller takes goods in part-exchange, as where a car dealer takes in part-exchange the car of the purchaser in reduction of the purchase price of another car. Certainly the contract will be a sale of goods so long as money is a substantial part of the consideration, and even if it is not the court may regard the transaction as a sale if the parties appear to have done so. Thus where the difference in price between the car which is "traded in" and the one which is purchased is marginal, there would most probably be a sale since that is what the parties envisaged.

3. Sale and Hire Purchase. A sale of goods differs from a hire-purchase transaction because a hire-purchase contract gives the hirer a mere bailment of the goods, with an option to purchase them, an option which the hirer may or may not exercise after payment of the agreed instalments. There is a contract of sale when the hirer exercises his option to purchase, which he will normally do, since the purchase price is then nominal and the eventual sale of the goods is the object of the contract.

A further distinction is that, while a contract of sale normally involves two parties only, a hire-purchase contract generally involves three. The owner of the goods selected by the hirer sells them to a finance company which in turn hires them to the hirer. The Sale of Goods Act does not apply to the hiring contract, but certain terms are implied into that contract by the Hire-Purchase Act, 1965, and are available against the finance company.

The distinction between a contract of sale and hire purchase is also important in the matter of title. If the contract is one of hire purchase it does not come within the provisions of Sect. 25 (2) of the Sale of Goods Act because the hirer is not a person who has bought or agreed to buy the goods. He is hiring with an option to purchase and is under no obligation to buy. The hirer, therefore, cannot give a good title to a third party and, on the bankruptcy of the hirer, the owner of the goods can recover them subject to the doctrine of reputed ownership.

Where the contract is one of sale, but payment is to be made by instalments, the contract may pass the property, in which case there is an unconditional contract of sale, and the buyer, having ownership, can give a good title to a third party. On the bankruptcy of the buyer, his trustee takes the goods, and the seller must prove in the bankruptcy for the instalments.

If, although the goods have been delivered, the passing of the property is postponed until all instalments are paid, then there is a conditional contract of sale; such a contract is within Sect. 25 (2) and the buyer can give a good title to a third party if the total purchase price exceeds £2,000. If the total purchase price is £2,000 or under, the contract is governed by the Hire-Purchase Act, 1965, and the conditions and warranties implied will be those under the Hire-Purchase Act and not those under the Sale of Goods Act, and the buyer cannot give a good title to third parties, though there are exceptions in the case of motor cars (see p. 184). In both cases, however, the seller can claim the goods on the bankruptcy of the buyer subject to the doctrine of reputed ownership. (Hire purchase contracts are considered further on pages 168–190.)

4. Sale and Agency. Brief mention should be made of certain problems arising in agency. If the person who is selling the goods is an agent there will be privity of contract between the buyer and the supplier. (*Dunlop* v. *New Garage and Motor Co. Ltd.*, 1915.)[84] If the seller is not an agent no action can be brought against the supplier in respect of the condition and quality of the goods. (*Dunlop* v. *Selfridge*, 1915.)[69]

Problems may arise in relation to title. If the seller is an agent he cannot pass a title in the goods to a buyer unless the sale is within the agent's actual or apparent authority (see p. 192), or he has the goods on "sale or return" terms (*London Jewellers Ltd.* v. *Attenborough*, 1934)[366] (see p. 144).

5. Sale of a mere Possessory Title. It appears to be an essential ingredient of a *sale* of goods that the *property* in them is transferred. Property seems to mean an *absolute* title and not a mere *possessory* one. (*Rowland* v. *Divell*, 1923.)[322]

Thus a contract under which F (a finder) transfers goods to a purchaser is not a contract of sale to which the Act applies.

6. Sale and Loans on Security. If A, who is the owner of goods, borrows money by using the goods as a security and gives a charge or mortgage over them but retains possession, the transaction resembles a sale in the sense that the lender has a right to take the goods if A does not repay the loan or interest. This is not, however, a sale, but in view of the fact that A retains the goods so that third parties

might give him credit on the strength of his apparent absolute ownership of them, the transaction must be committed to writing as a bill of
sale which must be registered under the Bills of Sale Acts, 1879 and
1882 (see p. 112).

THE CONTRACT OF SALE

Capacity of the Parties. Capacity to buy and sell is regulated by
the general law concerning capacity to contract and to transfer and
acquire property. Where necessaries are sold and delivered to a
minor, or to a person who by reason of mental incapacity or drunken-
ness is incompetent to contract, he must pay a reasonable price for
them. "Necessaries" means goods suitable to the condition in life of
the minor or other person, and to his actual requirements at the time
of sale and delivery. (Sect. 2.) The problems relating to capacity
have already been dealt with in the chapter on the law of contract
and no further comment is necessary.

The Price. The price may be—

   (i) fixed by the contract; or
   (ii) left to be fixed in a manner provided by the contract, e.g. by
a valuation or an arbitration; or
   (iii) determined by the course of dealing between the parties, e.g.
previous transactions between them, or any relevant custom of the
trade or profession. If the price is not so fixed, there is a presumption
that the buyer will pay a reasonable price. (Sect. 8.) Thus a contract of sale of goods should not be regarded as *inchoate* simply
because the parties have not agreed a price. (For inchoate agreements see p. 6.)

Where the price is to be determined by the valuation of a third
party, and no such valuation is made, then the contract is avoided,
but—

   (i) If the goods or part thereof have been delivered to the buyer
and he has appropriated them to his use, the buyer must pay a
reasonable price for them.
   (ii) If the valuation is prevented by either party to the contract,
the non-defaulting party may sue for damages against the party in
default. (Sect. 9.)

It is difficult to see how the buyer would be able to prevent valuation but presumably the Act is concerned to cover all possibilities.
Sect. 9 applies only if the agreement *names* a valuer. Thus a sale of
"stock at valuation" is an agreement to sell at a reasonable price,
and Sect. 8 will apply if the parties do not appoint a valuer or otherwise agree a price.

The Consideration. It has already been mentioned that the
consideration for a sale must consist wholly or in part of money;
otherwise the transaction is an exchange or barter. Where goods are

conveyed without consideration there is a gift, and any agreement to be enforceable must be under seal, though actual delivery of the goods will give the recipient or donee a good title.

Formalities of the Contract. Contracts for the sale of goods can now be made orally regardless of the value of the goods sold, and, by virtue of Sect. 32 of the Companies Act, 1948, registered companies need not now contract under seal, except where an ordinary person would have to do so. The Corporate Bodies Contracts Act, 1960 extends this privilege to all companies no matter how formed in respect of contracts made since 29th July, 1960.

Nevertheless provisions in other statutes may affect a sale. For example, Sect. 24 of the Merchant Shipping Act, 1894, provides that the sale of a ship or a share in a ship must be in writing. Furthermore, since Sect. 62 of the Sale of Goods Act defines goods as including *emblements*, e.g. growing crops, it may be that before severance such crops are *goods* under the Sale of Goods Act and also *land* under the Law of Property Act, 1925, in which case the contract if made before severance may require a memorandum in writing under Sect. 40 of the Law of Property Act, 1925 (see also p. 121).

In addition certain formalities are prescribed for *credit sale agreements* covered by the Hire Purchase Act, 1965 (see p. 14).

The provisions of the Bills of Sale Acts (see p. 112) may also affect the position regarding formalities. It is necessary to distinguish two situations—

(*a*) *a straight sale—the seller retaining possession*
(i) if the sale is and remains *oral* the Acts do not apply and the buyer takes the risk (subject to an action for breach of contract or non-delivery) that the seller may dispose of the goods either voluntarily (by subsequent sale) or involuntarily (by e.g. execution of a judgment or on bankruptcy);

(ii) if, as is usual, the buyer takes written evidence by means of a bill of sale this must be registered, though it need not be in any special form. If this is not done, the contract of sale is void in respect of *involuntary dispositions*, e.g. to a trustee in bankruptcy or a sheriff levying execution; but if the seller, while still in possession of the goods already sold, *voluntarily transfers* the property by way of sale to a third party, the latter may obtain a good title under Sect. 25 (1) of the Sale of Goods Act or under Sect. 8 of the Factors Act, 1889.

(*b*) *A sale operating as a security—the seller retaining possession.*
(i) The Sale of Goods Act does not apply (see Sect. 61 (4) of that Act);

(ii) Sect. 8 of the Bills of Sale Act, 1882, covers the transaction and unless there is a registered bill of sale made out in the form required by the Act of 1882 the transaction is *void altogether*, even as between the parties, though money advanced on an unregistered bill may be recovered in quasi-contract (see p. 95) as money had and received. (*North Central Wagon Finance Co. Ltd.* v. *Brailsford*, [1962] 1 All E.R. 502.) Thus *involuntary* and *voluntary* dispositions by the seller are effective to give title.

CONDITIONS AND WARRANTIES

In the chapter on the law of contract (pp. 39–45) we have discussed the problems relating to statements made in the course of negotiating an agreement, and we have seen that such statements may be—

(*a*) *Pre-contractual*, i.e. representations; or

(*b*) *Contractual*, i.e. terms of the contract which may be either conditions or warranties.

The importance of the distinction lies in the remedies which are available.

(i) WHOLLY INNOCENT MISREPRESENTATION. The party misled may ask for rescission of the contract, though under Sect. 2 (2) of the Misrepresentation Act, 1967, the court has power to award damages instead of rescission but not both. If the court decides to grant rescission it is limited in its monetary award to that amount of loss for which equity would give an indemnity. (*Whittington* v. *Seale-Hayne*, 1900.)[174]

(ii) NEGLIGENT MISREPRESENTATION. The party misled may rescind the contract and/or sue for damages under Sect. 2 (1) of the Misrepresentation Act, 1967.

(iii) FRAUDULENT MISREPRESENTATION. The party defrauded may *rescind* the contract and/or *sue for damages* on the tort of deceit.

(iv) BREACH OF CONDITION. The aggrieved party may *elect either*—

(*a*) *To repudiate the contract* by rejecting the goods with no liability to pay the price, or, if the price has been paid, it may be recovered; *or*

(*b*) *To treat the contract as subsisting* but to *claim damages*.

(v) BREACH OF WARRANTY. The aggrieved party has *no right to repudiate* the contract, but *may sue for damages*.

In the chapter on the law of contract we were concerned with express statements made by the parties; here we are concerned with the conditions and warranties *implied* into contracts for the sale of goods by the Sale of Goods Act, 1893, and with how those conditions and warranties are defined by the Act.

The Act does not define a condition, but a condition may be said to be a material term or provision which, while going to the root of the contract, falls short of non-performance. A condition is a contractual term of a major description.

A warranty is defined by Sect. 62 of the Sale of Goods Act as an agreement with reference to goods which are the subject of a contract of sale, but collateral to the main purpose of the contract, the breach of which gives rise to a claim for damages, but not the right to reject the goods and treat the contract as repudiated. Although Sect. 62 uses the word "collateral" which gives the impression that a warranty is a term outside of the contract (see p. 47 and *De Lassalle* v. *Guildford*, 1901),[180] a warranty in the intention of Sect. 62 is a term inside the contract but of a minor description which does not go to the root of the contract.

The Act does not say how we are to distinguish between conditions and warranties, and, although the words used by the parties are relevant, a stipulation may nevertheless be a condition though called a warranty in the contract. (Sect. 11 (1) (*b*).) When in doubt as to the nature of a stipulation, the court will look at the contract and the surrounding circumstances, and decide what the intentions of the parties were, and whether those intentions can best be carried out by treating the statement as a condition or as a warranty. (*Wallis, Son & Wells* v. *Pratt & Haynes*, 1911.)[367]

With regard to the possible effect of the Misrepresentation Act, 1967 the following matters should be noted—

(*a*) it is probable that claims based on negligent misrepresentation under Sect. 2 (1) of the 1967 Act will be joined with claims for damages for breach of condition or warranty. This is especially likely where the action is based on a misdescription of the goods under Sect. 13 of the 1893 Act (see p. 132);

(*b*) under the 1967 Act the burden of disproving that the misrepresentation was negligent is on the representor which is helpful to the plaintiff. Nevertheless the best remedy for misdescription is still one based on the Act of 1893 because liability under that Act is *strict* and cannot be avoided by the seller showing he was not negligent;

(*c*) a further advantage of an action for negligent misrepresentation is that Sect. 3 of the 1967 Act provides that exclusion clauses in respect of misrepresentation can be declared void by the court if it is reasonable to do so. Such a power is not as yet available in respect of actions under the 1893 Act though the cases indicate that it is difficult to exclude liability for misdescription (see p. 133).

It should also be noted that in addition to the various remedies for loss arising out of false pre-contractual representations and breaches of contractual terms an action for negligence may lie in tort provided the false statement is made negligently and a special relationship exists between the parties (*Hedley Byrne & Co. Ltd.* v. *Heller and Partners Ltd.*, 1963.)[165] This action is probably of little importance in the context of contract since Sect. 2 (1) of the Act of 1967 provides a statutory course of action in negligence specifically designed for the contractual situation.

TERMS IMPLIED BY THE ACT

We must now consider the question of implied terms.

1. Time. Where this has not been dealt with expressly the following rules apply—

(*a*) PAYMENT. The Act provides that, unless a different intention appears from the contract, stipulations as to the time of payment are not deemed to be of the essence of a contract of sale. Whether any other stipulation as to time is of the essence of the contract or not depends upon the terms of the contract. (Sect. 10 (1).)

The effect of this seems to be that failure to pay on time is a breach of warranty rather than a breach of condition, and the seller cannot repudiate the contract and re-sell the goods, but may sue the buyer for damages. However, where payment is delayed for an excessive time, the seller may treat the contract as abandoned and re-sell the goods. The seller can, of course, provide expressly for a right of re-sale in the absence of prompt payment, and this right is implied where the goods are perishable. (Sect. 48 (3).)

(*b*) DELIVERY. The Act does not lay down any rules regarding the time of delivery of the goods, but the decided cases show that, where the time of delivery is fixed by the contract, failure to deliver or allow collection on time is a breach of condition and the buyer can reject the goods even though they are not damaged or in any way affected by the delay. (*Bowes* v. *Shand*, 1877.)[275] Where the goods are unaffected the buyer will normally only reject if external circumstances such as a fall in the market price lead him to do so. Nevertheless his right to reject remains. Where the seller is bound to send the goods to the buyer but no time of delivery is fixed by the contract, the seller is bound to deliver the goods within a reasonable time. (Sect. 29 (2).) Failure to deliver within a reasonable time may amount to breach of condition. (*Borthwick* (*Thomas*) (*Glasgow*) *Ltd.* v. *Bunge & Co. Ltd.*, [1969] 1 Lloyd's Rep. 17.) It is assumed that this rule applies also where the seller's duty is to have the goods *ready for collection.*

The time of delivery may be waived by the buyer and such a waiver is binding even though the seller has given no consideration for it. The basis of this rule according to Denning, L.J., in *Rickards* (*Charles*) *Ltd.* v. *Oppenheim*, 1950,[276] was equitable estoppel (see p. 24), though in *Hartley* v. *Hymans*, [1920] 3 K.B. 475, McCardie, J., relied on Sect. 11 (1) (*a*) of the 1893 Act which provides that where a contract of sale is subject to any condition to be fulfilled by the seller, the buyer may waive the condition. Presumably both jurisdictions are acceptable.

Other rules relating to delivery will be considered when dealing with performance of the contract (see p. 152).

2. Title. The rules governing title are as follows—

(*a*) IMPLIED CONDITION AS TO TITLE. Sect. 12 (1) provides that, unless the circumstances show a different intention, there is an implied condition on the part of the seller that in the case of a sale he has the right to sell the goods, and that in the case of an agreement to sell, he will have the right to sell the goods at the time when the property is to pass. (*Rowland* v. *Divall*, 1923.)[322]

The decision in *Rowland*,[322] which has been applied in subsequent cases (see *Karflex Ltd.* v. *Poole*, [1933] 2 K.B. 251), produces an unfortunate result in that a person who buys goods to which the seller has no title is allowed to recover the whole of the purchase price even though he has had some use and enjoyment from the goods before he is dispossessed by the true owner. It is thus difficult to suggest that there has been total failure of consideration. The Law Reform Committee (see 1966 Cmnd 2958 para. 36) has recommended that, subject to further study of the law relating to restitution, an allowance in respect of use and enjoyment should be deducted from the purchase price and the balance returned to the plaintiff.

Section 12 (1) might be construed as meaning that the seller must have the power to give ownership of the goods to the buyer, but in *Niblett* v. *Confectioners' Materials Co. Ltd.*, 1921,[368] it was decided that, if the goods can only be sold by infringing a trade mark, the seller has no right to sell for the purposes of Sect. 12 (1).

(*b*) IMPLIED WARRANTIES AS TO TITLE. The Act implies certain warranties—

(i) *Quiet Possession.* Unless the circumstances of the contract are such as to show a different intention, there is an implied warranty that the buyer shall have and enjoy quiet possession of the goods. (Sect. 12 (2).) It is hard to see what rights are given by Sect. 12 (2) additional to those already given by Sect. 12 (1) which gives a condition as to title. There is, it would seem, one advantage with regard to limitation of actions, because time begins to run from the date of sale under Sect. 12 (1) but from the disturbance of possession under Sect. 12 (2).

(ii) *Encumbrances.* Sect. 12 (3) provides that, unless the circumstances of the contract are such as to show a different intention, there is an implied warranty that the goods shall be free from any charge or encumbrance in favour of any third party, not declared or known to the buyer before or at the time when the contract is made. (Sect. 12 (3).)

Again it is not easy to see what rights this subsection gives. The law does not recognise encumbrances over chattels unless the person trying to enforce them is in possession of the goods or in privity of contract with the person who is in possession. (*Dunlop* v. *Selfridge*, 1915.)[69] Thus if A uses his car as security for a loan from B then—

(i) if B takes the car into his possession the charge will be enforceable if necessary by a sale of the vehicle;

(ii) the charge is equally enforceable against the car while it is still in A's possession, though if A sells it to C then B will be prevented by lack of privity of contract from enforcing any remedies against the vehicle once it is in the possession of C.

Thus if situation (i) above applied the subsection is unnecessary since B could not deliver the vehicle even if he sold it and would therefore be liable in damage for non-delivery to C. If situation (ii) above applied then the encumbrances would not attach to the vehicle once C had taken possession. C would not, therefore, require a remedy.

However the subsection may be useful if, for example, B buys goods from S and the goods are in the warehouse of a carrier, C, who has a lien on them for his charges, then—

(i) S must inform B of the lien and B will allow for it in the price he is prepared to pay; or

(ii) If S does not inform B of the lien and B has to pay the carrier's charges to obtain the goods, then B has an action for damages against S under Sect. 12 (3).

Sect. 12 (1) would not apply because S has the right to sell the goods, though subject to the rights of C. Sect. 12 (2) seems to refer to a situation in which the buyer has been dispossessed of the goods after delivery and so may not apply.

3. Sale by Description. Sect. 13 provides that, where there is a contract for the sale of goods by description, there is an implied condition that the goods shall correspond with the description.

(*a*) A sale is by description where the purchaser is buying on a mere description having never seen the goods, e.g. a sale of future goods.

(*b*) A sale may still be by description even though the goods are seen or examined or even selected from the seller's stock by the purchaser, as in a sale over the counter, because most goods are described if only by the package in which they are contained. (*Beale* v. *Taylor*, 1967.)[369] Therefore a sale in a self-service store *could* be covered by Sect. 13 though no words were spoken by the seller. The courts appear to have expanded the situations in which goods are regarded as sold by description in order to provide a remedy under Sect. 14 (2) for delivery of unmerchantable goods. Sect. 14 (2) does not apply unless the sale was by description (see p. 134).

Sect. 13 is applied strictly, and if the sale is by description, every statement which forms part of that description is treated as a condition giving the buyer the right to reject the goods, even though the misdescription is of a trivial nature, and might more properly have been regarded as a misrepresentation or warranty not giving the right to reject. Thus buyers have been allowed to reject goods on seemingly trivial grounds, e.g. misdescriptions of how the goods are packed, and regardless of the fact that no damage has been suffered. (*Moore & Co. Ltd.* v. *Landauer & Co. Ltd.*, 1921.)[269] Although the Sale of Goods

Act applies in the main to sales by dealers, Sect. 13 applies even where the seller is not a dealer in the goods sold. (*Varley* v. *Whipp*, 1900.)[370]

It is doubtful whether the seller can contract out of a substantial breach of this section by means of an exemption clause (*Robert A. Munro & Co. Ltd.* v. *Meyer*, 1930),[371] though presumably liability for more trivial breaches can be excluded.

Provided the goods correspond to their description there is no action under Sect. 13 if they are of unmerchantable quality and/or unfit for the purpose, though Sect. 14 could then apply. (*Ashington Piggeries Ltd.* v. *Christopher Hill Ltd.*, 1971.)[372] Where the sale is by sample as well as by description, the section also provides that the bulk must correspond with both the sample and the description. (*Nichol* v. *Godts*, 1854.)[373]

4. Implied Conditions as to Quality and Fitness. There is no implied warranty or condition as to the quality or fitness for any particular purpose of goods supplied under a contract of sale except as provided by statute.

(*a*) FITNESS FOR PURPOSE. Sect. 14 (1) provides that, where the buyer, expressly or by implication, makes known to the seller the particular purpose for which the goods are required, so as to show that the buyer relies on the seller's skill and judgment, and the goods are of a description which it is in the course of the seller's business to supply (whether he be the manufacturer or not), there is an implied condition that the goods shall be reasonably fit for such purpose.

There is no need for the buyer to specify the particular purpose for which the goods are required when they have in the ordinary way only one purpose. (*Priest* v. *Last*, 1903.)[374] Although the Act uses the words "particular purpose" the Section has been applied where the goods were sold for a variety of uses and were unsuitable for a particular use to which a particular buyer put them. (*Ashington Piggeries Ltd.* v. *Christopher Hill Ltd.*, 1971,[372] and *Kendall* v. *Lillico*, 1969.)[372a] Reliance on the seller's skill and judgment will be readily implied even to the extent of saying that, at least in sales to the general public as consumers, the buyer has gone to the seller because he relies on the seller having selected his stock with skill and judgment (*per* Lord Wright in *Grant* v. *Australian Knitting Mills Ltd.*, 1936.)[375] However, where the buyer knows that the seller deals in only one brand of goods, e.g. where a public house sells only one brand of beer, there will not in general be any implication of such reliance. (*Wren* v. *Holt*, 1903,[376] but see *Manchester Liners Ltd.* v. *Rea*, 1922.)[376a] The section applies to non-manufactured goods (*Frost* v. *Aylesbury Dairy Co. Ltd.*, 1905),[377] and to the containers in which the goods are packed (*Geddling* v. *Marsh*, 1920),[378] but, where there are special circumstances of which the seller is unaware, it does not apply. (*Griffiths* v. *Peter Conway Ltd.*, 1939.)[379]

A majority of the Court of Appeal held, in *Hardwick Game Farm* v. *Suffolk Agricultural and Poultry Producers Association Ltd.*, [1966] 1 All

E.R. 309, that the fact that the seller and the buyer were dealers did not prevent a finding that the buyer relied on the seller's skill and judgment.

However, there is no ground for assuming reliance in this sort of case and proof of it must be forthcoming. (*Kendall* v. *Lillico*, [1969], 2 A.C. pp. 79–85 (Lord Reid).)

Sect. 14 (1) also provides that, in the case of a contract for the sale of a specified article under its patent or other trade name, there is no implied condition as to its fitness for any particular purpose. However if, when buying the article under its patent or other trade name, the buyer makes it clear to the seller that he is relying on the seller's skill and judgment to recommend an article, it must be reasonably fit for the purpose. (*Baldry* v. *Marshall*, 1925.)[380]

As a result of the judgment of Bankes, L.J., in *Baldry* the following situations can be distinguished—

> (i) B says to S "I want something for a leaky car radiator" and S sells him an article called "Sealup".
>
> (ii) B says to S "I have been recommended to buy 'Sealup'— will it deal effectively with my leaky car radiator?" S sells B a tin of 'Sealup' without any reservations as to its efficiency.
>
> (iii) B says to S "I have been told to buy 'Sealup' to cure my car radiator which is leaking. Please sell me a tin." S supplies the goods.

In (i) and (ii) above the proviso does not apply and the goods must be fit for the purpose. The proviso does apply in (iii) above and S is not liable if the goods are not fit for the purpose. However, (iii) above outlines such a rare situation that the proviso can almost be regarded as of no effect and the Law Commission has recommended its repeal. (Exemption Clauses, First Report, para. 33.)

Liability under Sect. 14 (1) is strict and extends to latent defects which the seller could not have discovered even by the use of proper care and diligence. (*Frost* v. *Aylesbury Dairy Co. Ltd.*, 1905.)[377]

(*b*) MERCHANTABLE QUALITY. Sect. 14 (2) provides that, where goods are bought by description from a seller who deals in goods of that description (whether he be manufacturer or not), there is an implied condition that the goods shall be of merchantable quality. (*Wilson* v. *Rickett, Cockerell & Co. Ltd.*, 1954.)[381]

If the seller does not normally deal in goods of the type in question, there is no condition as to fitness (nor as to merchantability unless the sale is by sample which is dealt with below). *The only condition in such a case is that the goods correspond with the description.* If, therefore, S (who is not a dealer) sells a car to B with no express terms as to quality and fitness, the court is prevented by Sect. 14 from implying conditions or warranties, even though S seems, from the circumstances, to have been warranting the car in good order.

A difficulty was presented when the sale was by a dealer who did not ordinarily sell goods of precisely the same description. Thus if B ordered an "X" brand motor scooter from S who had not formerly sold that make, it was not certain whether Sect. 14 applied if the scooter was unfit or unmerchantable. The position was clarified by the House of Lords in the *Ashington Piggeries* case[372] from which it appears that Sect. 14 applies provided *the seller is selling in the ordinary course of business or holds himself out as willing to supply the goods* even though he has not sold the particular goods before. The Law Commission has also recommended an amendment to the Act in the above terms. (Exemption Clauses, First Report, para. 31.)

There is no need under Sect. 14 (2) for the buyer to show that he relied on the seller's skill and judgment, and the seller is liable, in the absence of an exemption clause, for latent defects even though he is not the manufacturer and is merely marketing the goods as a wholesaler or retailer. Such a seller can, however, obtain an indemnity from the manufacturer if the buyer successfully sues him for defects in the goods.

If the buyer has examined the goods, there is no implied condition as regards defects which such an examination *ought* to have revealed. (*Thornett & Fehr* v. *Beers & Son*, 1919.)[382]

The word "quality" includes the state or condition of the goods (see Sect. 62 of the Act and *Niblett* v. *Confectioners' Materials Co. Ltd.*, 1921.)[368] Thus the state of the packing can affect the merchantable quality of the goods. This interpretation ought also to be applied to a sale by sample even though Sect. 15 (2) (*c*) uses the expression "defect" rather than "quality".

The interpretation of the word "merchantable" has often been discussed in the courts. The Law Commission has now recommended the enactment of the following definition which takes into account a number of judicial statements—

> "*Goods of any kind are of merchantable quality within the meaning of this Act if they are as fit for the purpose or purposes for which goods of that kind are commonly bought as it is reasonable to expect having regard to their price, any description applied to them and all the other circumstances.*"

The price paid by the buyer is therefore a factor to be taken into account. Goods (provided they are not defective) are not unmerchantable simply because their resale price is slightly less than that which the buyer paid, though they may be if the difference in purchase and resale price is substantial. (*B. S. Brown & Son Ltd.* v. *Craiks Ltd.*, 1970.)[383] Even where the goods are not purchased for resale the purchase price may be relevant. Thus the sale of a car with a defective clutch would be a sale of unmerchantable goods but if the seller makes an allowance in the price to cover the defect it may not be. (*Bartlett* v. *Sydney Marcus Ltd.*, [1965] 2 All E.R. 753.)

The rules as to fitness for purpose and merchantable quality do not

apply to private sales of secondhand goods and there is still a fairly
wide application of the maxim *caveat emptor* (Let the buyer beware!).
In practice only manufacturers, wholesalers, retailers and dealers in
new or secondhand goods will be caught by the implied conditions.
The courts cannot imply conditions and warranties into private contracts similar to those implied by the Act into sales by dealers, because
the introduction to the section implicitly forbids it.

5. Usage of Trade. Sect. 14 (3) provides that an implied warranty
or condition as to quality or fitness for a particular purpose may be
annexed by the usage of trade. (*Hutton* v. *Warren*, 1836.)[201] Where
the transaction is connected with a particular trade, the customs and
usages of that trade give the context in which the parties made their
contract and may give a guide as to their intentions. Thus in a sale
of canary seed in accordance with the customs of the trade it was held
that the buyer could not reject the seed delivered on the grounds that
there were impurities in it. A custom of the trade prevented this but
allowed instead a rebate on the price paid. (*Peter Darlington Partners
Ltd.* v. *Gosho Co. Ltd.*, [1964] 1 Lloyds Rep. 149.)

6. Sale by Sample. Sect. 15 (1) states that a contract of sale is a
contract of sale by sample where there is a term in the contract,
express or implied, to that effect. The mere fact that the seller provides a sample for the buyer's inspection is not enough; to be such a
sale there must be either an express provision in the contract to that
effect, or there must be evidence that the parties intended the sale to
be by sample.

There are *three implied conditions* in a sale by sample—

(*a*) The Bulk Must Correspond with the Sample in Quality
(Sect. 15 (2) (*a*)), and the seller cannot avoid this condition by an
exemption clause.

(*b*) The Buyer Shall Have a Reasonable Opportunity of
Comparing the Bulk with the Sample. (Sect. 15 (2) (*b*).) The
buyer will not be deemed to have accepted the goods until he has had
an opportunity to compare the bulk with the sample, and will be able,
therefore, to reject the goods, even though they have been delivered,
if the bulk does not correspond with the sample. He is not left with
the remedy of damages for breach of warranty.

(*c*) The Goods Shall be Free From Any Defect, Rendering them
Unmerchantable, Which Would Not Be Apparent on Reasonable
Examination of the Sample. (Sect. 15 (2) (*c*).) (*Godley* v. *Perry*,
1960.)[384] An exemption clause will only affect the condition of merchantability, if the sample would on reasonable inspection reveal the
defects (*Champanhac & Co. Ltd.* v. *Waller & Co. Ltd.*, 1948.)[385]

The effect of Sect. 15 (2) (*c*) is to exclude the implied condition of
merchantability if the defect could have been discovered by reasonable
examination of the sample *whether or not there has in fact been any examination of the sample*. This is presumably based upon the premise that
the seller is entitled to assume that the buyer will examine the sample.

The provision is in contrast with Sect. 14 (2) where the implied condition of merchantability is not excluded unless an examination has actually taken place. (See p. 135.)

Liability of Seller where Goods are in a Dangerous Condition. Quite apart from any question of implied conditions or warranties, there is a duty lying upon a seller who knows of the dangerous character of the goods he is supplying, to warn the buyer of the danger. (*Clarke* v. *Army & Navy Co-operative Society Ltd.*, 1903;[386] *Fisher* v. *Harrods*, 1966.)[387]

LIABILITY OF MANUFACTURER

The Tort of Negligence. Where the goods are purchased from a retailer, no action can be brought under the Sale of Goods Act by the purchaser against the manufacturer. The doctrine of privity of contract applies (see p. 20) with the result that there is no contract between them into which the warranties and conditions set out in the Act can be implied. However, the purchaser may have an action in negligence against the manufacturer in respect of *physical* injuries caused by defects in the goods. (*Donoghue* v. *Stevenson*, 1932.)[334]

The rule enunciated in *Donoghue* v. *Stevenson*[334] has been widened since 1932, and now applies to defective chattels generally which cause injuries to purchasers. (*Grant* v. *Australian Knitting Mills Ltd.*, 1936.)[375] though it still does not cover complaints relating to defects in the goods which have not caused physical injury. However, although the above cases show that the manufacturer has a duty to take care, evidence may show that he was not in breach of that duty because he took proper precautions. (*Daniels* v. *White & Sons*, 1938.)[388]

In the cases mentioned above the question of inspection of the goods was raised. It was an important fact in the decision in *Donoghue* v. *Stevenson*, 1932,[334] that the bottle was made of dark glass, so that the snail could not be seen on external inspection of the bottle, and that normally no inspection of the goods would take place until they reached the consumer. It is not thought that in the developing law of negligence, a manufacturer can rely on an inspection revealing the defects in his product, except perhaps in a special case where it is known that an expert inspection normally takes place. If such an inspection does not take place, or fails to find the defect which it should have found, the manufacturer may regard this as a *novus actus interveniens* (a new act intervening) breaking the chain of causation between his negligence and the injury.

Further, it may not be enough for a manufacturer to prove a safe system of manufacture as in *Daniels* v. *White & Sons*, 1938,[388] because the fact that the goods are dangerous postulates negligence. The maxim *res ipsa loquitur* (the thing speaks for itself) may apply so that the manufacturer bears the burden of explaining the matter on grounds other than his own negligence. Since in these cases there is often no evidence or explanation as to how the dangerous substance got into the goods the manufacturer will rarely be able to discharge his burden of explanation and will lose the action.

Third Party Proceedings. Strict liability under the Act of 1893 can, in effect, be imposed on a manufacturer by means of third (or fourth) party proceedings. Thus if the seller is sued by the buyer for breach of an implied condition under the Act, the seller may claim an indemnity from his own supplier which may be the manufacturer. If the retailer has purchased from a wholesaler the retailer may claim an indemnity from that wholesaler who may in turn claim an indemnity from the manufacturer who supplied the goods. In this way the manufacturer can be made to pay for defects affecting the quality or fitness of the goods.

Collateral Contracts. The manufacturer may also be liable for defects in quality or fitness under a collateral contract. (*Shanklin Pier Ltd.* v. *Detel Products Ltd.*, 1951.)[181] This applies however, only where a specific and express undertaking has been given by the manufacturer to the seller and it is doubtful whether such a claim could be based on statements made in a manufacturer's public advertisements.

The Law Commission has recognised the need to provide some general form of action against the manufacturer but has felt that this cannot be done by a simple amendment to the Sale of Goods Act, 1893. The Commission therefore recommends that a wider study of the problem be made before embarking upon legislative measures. (Exemption Clauses, First Report, para. 63.)

Manufacturers' Guarantees. A typical manufacturers' guarantee contains undertakings in regard to defects in the goods sold. Frequently the guarantee is stated to be given in substitution for the statutory implied conditions and warranties. Frequently also the manufacturer does not warrant the goods free from defects nor does he accept liability for consequential damage, e.g. physical injury, arising from using the goods. His guarantee normally amounts to a warranty to repair or replace during a specified time with the addition in the case of vehicles of a mileage limit.

There is little, if any, authority in English Law as to the legal effect of a manufacturers' guarantee. However, the position would appear to be as follows—

(a) *as between buyer and retailer*, the guarantee should not have any effect on the implied conditions and warranties which the buyer receives under the Act of 1893. Insofar as the guarantee is in the nature of an exemption clause it is presumably governed by cases such as *Adler* v. *Dickson*, 1955[191] which state that an exemption clause in a contract between A and B cannot by reason of privity of contract affect the legal rights and duties arising between A and C. It is likely that the Court would apply this rule so that the terms of the guarantee would not affect the contract of sale;

(b) *as between buyer and manufacturer* the effect is probably as follows—

(i) the guarantee cannot exclude statutory implied terms as between buyer and manufacturer since these do not exist being implied only into the contract of sale with the retailer;

(ii) the guarantee could effectively exclude liability for consequential loss, e.g. physical injury of the kind envisaged in *Donoghue* v. *Stevenson*, 1932,[334] though since this involves the buyer in giving up certain legal rights, he must have accepted the guarantee in the sense of signing and returning a card or form to the manufacturer;

(iii) The guarantee is probably enforceable by the buyer as a collateral contract (see *Shanklin Pier* v. *Detel Products Ltd.*, 1951),[181] the purchase of the goods from the retailer being sufficient consideration;

Other Statutory Duties. In addition to the Sale of Goods Act, 1893, Parliament has passed a number of statutes all of which seek to provide some form of consumer protection. There is Food and Drugs and Weights and Measures legislation and more recently the Trade Descriptions Acts, 1968–72 (see p. 165). These Acts, however, normally rely on criminal law for their enforcement and do not provide civil remedies. An exception is the Consumer Protection Act, 1961 (as amended by the Consumer Protection Act, 1971). This legislation gives the Home Secretary power to make regulations regarding standards of manufacture of goods, and regulations have been made, for example, in relation to oil heaters. The Acts give a civil remedy for damages to the consumer for injury arising out of defects in the goods. This action can be brought against the retailer or the manufacturer or importer and is also available to a person suffering injury who was not the purchaser, e.g. a child of the buyer. Exemption clauses are of no avail to the defendant because there is a general rule of law which provides that a person cannot contract out of a statutory duty.

Before leaving the topic of consumer protection it is worth noting that the remedies available to the consumer are in most cases restricted to an action in a court of law for damages. Since this postulates an involvement in the process of litigation, with all that that means in terms of consulting lawyers and paying fees, the remedy is not appropriate in the case of small claims. Other methods of enforcing the legal rights of the consumer should be found.

EXCLUSION OF SELLER'S LIABILITY

Sect. 55 of the Sale of Goods Act makes provision for the exclusion of the implied terms set out above. Thus if a contract of sale contains a clause which clearly excludes a term set out in the Act, the court should apply it. (*L'Estrange* v. *Graucob*, 1934.)[189] An implied term may also be negatived by the course of dealing, or by usage, if the usage is such as to bind both parties.

However, the courts are hostile to exception or exclusion clauses and have avoided them in the following ways—

(i) *By interpreting them strictly* so that they do not cover the circumstances of the case in question. (*Wallis, Son & Wells* v. *Pratt & Haynes*, 1911,[367] and *Baldry* v. *Marshall*, 1925.)[380]

(ii) *By searching for collateral express warranties.* An example of this is to be seen in *Andrews* v. *Hopkinson*, 1957.[389]

However, the decision in *Hedley Byrne & Co. Ltd.* v. *Heller and Partners Ltd.*, 1963,[165] and the relevant provisions of the Misrepresentation Act, 1967, may make it unnecessary to resort so frequently to the concept of the collateral warranty. (See pp. 39–45.)

(iii) *By ruling* that the agreement to the clause was obtained by *fraud or misrepresentation.* (*Curtis* v. *Chemical Cleaning & Dyeing Co. Ltd.*, 1951.)[156]

(iv) *By ruling that the exception clause was never incorporated* into the contract. (*Harling* v. *Eddy*, 1951.)[182]

(v) *By relying on the doctrine of fundamental breach of contract.* This doctrine means in effect that no exception clause can protect a person against a complete failure to perform the contract. (*Karsales (Harrow) Ltd.* v. *Wallis*, 1956.)[194]

This doctrine must now be considered in the light of the *Suisse Case*[197] and subsequent decisions though it is thought that the earlier decisions will stand if they are now regarded as decided on the rules of construction. (See pp. 49–52.)

An exception clause may also purport to exclude express terms as well as implied ones; thus there may be an express condition as to quality in the main body of the contract, and its exclusion by a later clause. The difficulty may be resolved by treating the express warranty as paramount, and rejecting the exception clause.

Sect. 3 of the Misrepresentation Act restricts the right to exclude liability for *pre-contractual misrepresentations* (see p. 50). Strictly speaking this section does not apply to exemption clauses seeking to exclude *contractual terms.* However, since an exemption clause will often seek to exclude the seller's liability for pre-contractual misrepresentations and contractual terms, Section 3 of the 1967 Act may apply to the whole clause and thus give the court power to decide upon the extent of its application. On the other hand, where an exemption clause is clearly severable as between exclusion of liability for pre-contractual misrepresentation and contractual terms, Sect. 3 would probably only operate on the part concerned to deal with pre-contractual statements.

Reform. In spite of the efforts made by the courts to circumvent exemption clauses, the consumers' position is a very vulnerable one, and two inquiries have been made into the situation. (Molony Committee on Consumer Protection, 1962, and more recently, the Law Commission.) Although the views expressed by the two bodies concerned were not entirely co-incident, it is thought that any resulting legislation is likely to be on the following lines—

(*a*) all exclusion of the implied terms in Sects. 12 to 15 (as amended) should be void provided the goods are normally bought for private use or consumption. It would still be possible for the seller to show under Sect. 14 (1) that the buyer did not rely on his skill and judgment and under Sect. 14 (2) that the goods were still merchantable despite defects which were drawn to the buyer's attention;

(*b*) the ability to exclude implied terms will probably remain where the goods sold are not normally purchased for private use, e.g. industrial machinery, so that complete freedom of contract will prevail in these cases.

TREATING A BREACH OF CONDITION AS A
BREACH OF WARRANTY

Sect. 11 (1) (*c*) provides that the buyer can waive a breach of condition altogether or may treat it as a breach of warranty. If he chooses to treat the breach of condition as a breach of warranty, then he may sue for damages but cannot reject the goods.

However, unless there is a contrary provision in the contract, a breach of a condition implied under the Sale of Goods Act *MUST* be treated as a breach of warranty in the following cases—

1. **Where the Contract is not severable and the Buyer has accepted the Goods or part thereof.** (Sect. 11(1)(*c*).) Problems of severability arise where the goods are delivered by instalments. Where the price is paid for the whole consignment and delivery is by instalments, the contract is probably not severable, and acceptance by the buyer of early instalments will prevent him from rejecting later instalments which are not in accordance with the contract.

However, if, under the terms of the contract, each instalment is to be paid for separately, the contract is probably severable (Sect. 31 (2)), and acceptance of earlier instalments will not prevent the buyer from rejecting later deliveries which are not in accordance with the contract.

A contract may, however, be regarded as severable in a number of other situations. Thus in *Longbottom & Co. Ltd.* v. *Bass Walker & Co. Ltd.*, [1922] W.N. 245, a contract for the sale of cloth was regarded as severable where delivery was by instalments but the price was paid as part of a monthly account and not separately for each delivery of cloth.

Section 11 (1) (*c*) does not come into force when the goods are merely delivered; there must be some act by the buyer indicating his acceptance of the goods. A buyer is deemed to have accepted the goods—

(*a*) When he informs the seller that he has accepted them; or

(*b*)) Where, after delivery, he acts in a manner inconsistent with the continued ownership of the seller, as where he uses or consumes the goods; or

(*c*) Where, after the lapse of a reasonable time, he still retains the goods, without giving notice of rejection. (Sect. 35.)

2. Where the Contract is for Specific goods the Property in which has passed to the Buyer. (Sect. 11 (1) (*c*).) Where the property in the goods has passed to the buyer there is no right, upon breach of condition, to return the articles to the seller and recover the price. Instead the buyer must retain the goods and sue for damages, unless there is a special provision in the contract that the goods may be returned, or the seller has, by taking the goods back, expressly or impliedly consented to rescind the contract.

The serious effect of this rule upon the right of the buyer emerges when Sect. 11 is read in conjunction with Sect. 18 of the Act which governs the passing of the property. Sect. 18, Rule 1 provides that, in the absence of a contrary intention, where there is an unconditional contract for the sale of specific goods in a deliverable state, the property in the goods passes to the buyer when the contract is made, and it is immaterial whether the time of payment or the time of delivery, or both, be postponed.

Therefore, in many of the cases in which a statutory condition was broken, the buyer was not able to reject the goods but was left with an action for damages.

However, Sect. 4 of the Misrepresentation Act, 1967, amends Sects. 11 and 35 of the Sale of Goods Act, 1893, so as to prevent a buyer losing his right to reject the goods or rescind the contract before he has a chance to examine them. Under Sect. 11 (1) (*c*), as amended, a breach of condition must be treated as a breach of warranty when the buyer has *accepted* the goods. However, Sect. 35 of the Sale of Goods Act, 1893, is amended so that a buyer is not deemed to have accepted goods which have been delivered to him, even where he has acted in a manner inconsistent with the continued ownership of the seller, unless he has had a reasonable opportunity to examine them. However, delay in rejection will still defeat a claim for repudiation for breach of condition but not a claim for damages for breach of warranty.

Rescission of a Contract of Sale. It is useful at this point to compare the rules set out in Sect. 11 of the Act of 1893 with the right to rescind a contract of sale for misrepresentation arising from a misstatement of fact. The rules relating to rescission are governed by separate principles (see p. 42). Since the Misrepresentation Act, 1967, rescission of a contract of sale is barred only where there is affirmation, lapse of time, inability to make restitution or acquisition of rights by an innocent third party for value. It seems that a buyer's right to rescind for misrepresentation and his right to reject for breach of condition are now much the same in principle, since an act which amounts to acceptance under Sect. 35 of the 1893 Act will almost always amount to affirmation so as to bar rescission. There may, however, be exceptional cases where rescission is available when rejection is not. For example, under Sect. 35 if a buyer does not intimate his rejection of the goods within a reasonable time he is automatically deemed to have accepted them and cannot reject. In equity lapse of time is not in itself sufficient to prevent rescission unless it amounts to affirmation, or the person making the representation (i.e. the seller) is prejudiced. Thus if in spite of lapse of time there is no prejudice to the seller, equity may allow rescission although the right to reject has been lost under Sect. 35.

TRANSFER OF THE PROPERTY IN GOODS

The provisions of the Act regarding the transfer of the property in the goods are important because the parties to contracts of sale do not usually express their intentions as to the passing of the property. In addition the *risk* normally passes when the property passes and the seller can in general terms only sue for the *price* as distinct from *damages* if the property has passed.

The following are the relevant statutory provisions—

1. Where the Goods are Specific. We will consider six cases.

(i) *Sect.* 17 *provides that, where there is a contract for the sale of specific or ascertained goods*, the property in them is transferred to the buyer at such time as the parties intend it to be transferred, and, for the purpose of ascertaining the intention of the parties, regard shall be had to the terms of the contract, the conduct of the parties, and the circumstances of the case. Thus, an obligation on one party to insure is an indication that he has the risk and, by inference, the property. (*Allison* v. *Bristol Marine Insurance Co. Ltd.* (1876), 1 App. Cas. 209.)

(ii) *Sect.* 18, *Rule* 1, *provides that, where there is an unconditional contract for the sale of specific goods, in a deliverable state*, the property in the goods passes to the buyer when the contract is made, and it is immaterial whether the time of payment or the time of delivery, or both, be postponed. (*Underwood Ltd.* v. *Burgh Castle Brick & Cement Syndicate*, 1922.[390] See also *Phillip Head & Sons Ltd.* v. *Showfronts Ltd.* 1969.)[390a]

However, since Sect. 18 provides that the statutory rules do not apply if a contrary intention appears, it may be that postponement of payment or delivery would indicate that the parties do not intend the property to pass.

Other factors may indicate that there is no intention to pass the property. Thus in *Ingram* v. *Little*, 1961,[137] it seems to have been assumed that no property was to pass until the method of payment, i.e. cash or cheque, had been agreed by the parties and in *Lacis* v. *Cashmarts*, [1969] 2 Q.B. 400, it was held that in a supermarket no contract was made until the price was actually paid.

(iii) *In the case of specific goods not in a deliverable state, Sect.* 18, *Rule* 2, *provides* that the property does not pass until the seller puts them into a deliverable state, and the buyer is notified thereof.

(iv) *In the case of conditional sales of specific goods, Sect.* 18, *Rule* 3, *provides* that, where there is a contract for the sale of specific goods in a deliverable state, but the seller is bound to weigh, measure, test, or do some other act or thing with reference to the goods for the purpose of ascertaining the price, the property does not pass until such act or thing is done, and the buyer has notice thereof.

Rules 2 and 3 (and Rule 4 below) are concerned with *certain types of conditional* contracts of sale, whereas Rule 1 deals with *all unconditional* contracts of sale. Some conditional sales would not be covered by Rule 2, e.g. the sale of a secondhand vacuum cleaner which works but which the seller has agreed to overhaul before delivery. Such a sale may be covered by Sect. 17 so that the circumstances will be regarded as showing that *the parties did not intend* the property to pass until the overhaul had been completed. Rule 3 applies only *to acts which must be done by the seller.* Thus where X sold a consignment of cocoa to Y at an agreed price for 60 lb, the arrangement being that Y would resell the cocoa and weigh it in order to ascertain the amount owed to X, it was held that the fact that Y had to weigh the cocoa did not make the contract conditional. The property passed to Y before the price was arrived at. (*Nanka Bruce* v. *Commonwealth Trust Ltd.*, [1926] A.C. 77.)

(v) *In the case of sales on approval, or on sale or return, or other similar terms*, Sect. 18, Rule 4, provides as follows—

(a) The property passes to the buyer when he signifies his approval or acceptance to the seller, or does any other act adopting the transaction, such as pledging the goods with a third party. (*London Jewellers Ltd.* v. *Attenborough*, 1934.)[366]

(b) If the buyer does not signify his approval or acceptance to the seller but *retains the goods without giving notice of rejection*, then the property passes on the expiration of the time, if any, fixed for the return of goods, or on the expiration of a reasonable time. What is a reasonable time is a question of fact. (*Poole* v. *Smith's Car Sales (Balham) Ltd.*, 1962.)[391] This part of the rule applies only if it is the buyer who retains the goods. Thus if goods on sale or return are seized and retained by the buyer's unpaid creditors, the property will not pass under 4 (*b*). (*In re Ferrier*, [1944] Ch. 295.)

Where the goods are on approval and the seller has expressly provided in the contract that the property is not to pass until they are paid for, then Rule 4 will not operate because the express provision indicates a contrary intention. But if the buyer sells or disposes of the goods, a third party may still get a good title under the doctrine of estoppel, or under Sect. 2 of the Factors Act, 1889. (*Weiner* v. *Harris*, 1910.)[392]

(vi) Sect. 19 (1) provides that, where there is a contract for the sale of specific goods or where goods are subsequently appropriated to the contract, *the seller may*, by the terms of the appropriation or contract, *reserve the right of disposal* of the goods until certain conditions are fulfilled. In such a case, even if the goods are delivered to the buyer, or to a carrier or other bailee for the purpose of transmission to the buyer, the property in the goods does not pass until the conditions imposed by the seller are fulfilled.

The section does not safeguard the seller as much as might appear because the buyer, being a person who has bought or agreed to buy the goods, can give a good title to a third party under Sect. 25 (2) of the Act.

Sect. 19 (3) provides that where the seller of goods draws a bill of exchange on the buyer for the price, and transmits the bill of exchange and bill of lading to the buyer together to secure acceptance or payment of the bill of exchange, the buyer is bound to return the bill of lading if he does not honour the bill of exchange, and if he wrongfully retains the bill of lading, the property in the goods does not pass to him.

Here again there is no complete safeguard for the seller. It is true that the passing of the property is conditional upon the bill of exchange being accepted and honoured, but a transfer of the bill of lading to a third party who takes it bona fide and for value gives the third party a good title under Sect. 25 (2) of the Sale of Goods Act, does prevent the seller from exercising his right of lien or stoppage *in transitu* against the third party under Sect. 47 of the Sale of Goods Act and Sect. 10 of the Factors Act, 1889.

2. Where the Goods are Unascertained. Sect. 16 provides that, where there is a contract for the sale of unascertained goods, no property in the goods is transferred to the buyer unless and until the goods are ascertained. Where an unidentified part of a bulk is sold there is no appropriation until there is severance of the goods sold from the rest. (*Laurie & Morewood* v. *John Dudin & Sons*, 1926,[393] *Gibraltar Packers Ltd.* v. *Basic Economy and Development Corporation Ltd.*, 1966.)[394]

Sect. 18, *Rule* 5 (1), *provides* that where there is a contract for the sale of unascertained or future goods by description, and goods of that description and in a deliverable state are unconditionally appropriated to the contract (but see *Wait and James* v. *Midland Bank*, 1926),[395] either by the seller with the assent of the buyer, or by the buyer with the assent of the seller, the property in the goods thereupon passes to the buyer. Such assent may be express or implied and may be given either before or after the appropriation is made. (*Pignataro* v. *Gilroy & Son*, 1919.)[396]

The necessity for the buyer's assent to appropriation gives rise to difficulties where a consumer orders goods by post. Where under a commercial contract the seller is required to ship the goods to the buyer the shipping is regarded as an unconditional appropriation and the assent of the buyer is *assumed*. (*James* v. *Commonwealth* (1939), 62 C.L.R. 339.) This rule seems inappropriate in the case of consumer sales by post. Though the law is not clear it is suggested that the posting of consumer goods should not pass the property otherwise the goods are, unknown to the buyer, at his risk during transit. There is no need to assume the consumer's consent to appropriation since in that sort of case he has agreed merely to dispatch of the goods and not to a particular appropriation.

An example of an unconditional appropriation, i.e. delivery to a carrier, is given in Sect. 18, Rule 5 (2) which provides that where, in pursuance of the contract, the seller delivers goods to the buyer or to a carrier or other bailee (whether named by the buyer or not) for the purpose of transmission to the buyer, and does not reserve the right of disposal, he is deemed to have unconditionally appropriated the goods to the contract. However, delivery to a carrier does not pass the property if identical goods destined for different owners are mixed (*Healey* v. *Howlett & Sons*, 1917),[397] nor if the seller is bound to weigh, measure or test the goods in order to ascertain the price. (*N.C.B.* v. *Gamble*, 1958.)[398]

The question of the transfer of property in goods is important, because risk generally passes with the property. The maxim is "*res perit domino.*" (A thing perishes to the disadvantage of its owner.)

Sect. 20 provides that, unless otherwise agreed, the goods remain at the seller's risk until the property therein is transferred to the buyer, but when the property in them is transferred to the buyer, the goods are at the buyer's risk whether delivery has been made or not. It seems that there may sometimes be a transfer of risk without transfer of the property (*Sterns Ltd.* v. *Vickers Ltd.*, 1923),[399] and a transfer of the property without risk. (*Head* v. *Tattersall*, 1870.)[400]

Of course, the goods may be despatched at the seller's risk, in which case Sect. 33 provides that, where the seller of goods agrees to deliver them at his own risk at a place other than that where they are when sold, the buyer must, nevertheless, unless otherwise agreed, take any risk of deterioration in the goods necessarily incident to the course of transit.

In connection with this it is necessary to note two further provisions of Sect. 20—

(*a*) Where delivery has been delayed through the fault of either buyer or seller, the goods are at the risk of the party in fault as regards any loss which might not have occurred but for such fault (*Demby Hamilton & Co. Ltd.* v. *Barden*, 1949);[401] and

(*b*) Nothing in Sect. 20 shall affect the duties and liabilities of either seller or buyer as a bailee of the goods of the other party. Thus a seller must still take proper care of the goods even though the buyer is late in taking delivery of them.

TRANSFER OF TITLE BY NON-OWNERS

The sections in the Sale of Goods Act which will be discussed here are concerned with the circumstances in which a person who is not the owner of goods can give a good title to those goods to a third party.

In most of the cases which we shall review the question for the court to decide is which of two innocent people shall suffer for the fraud of a third. The dilemma which faces the court in these cases is whether to uphold the rights of the owner on the one hand or whether to protect the interests of a person who had bought in good faith and for value from the fraudulent third party.

The general rule of common law is expressed in the maxim *Nemo dat quod non habet*. (No-one can give what he has not got.) It follows that, if the seller's title is defective, so is the buyer's. This rule of the common law is confirmed by Sect. 21 (1) which provides that, subject to certain other sections of the Act, where goods are sold by a person who is not the owner thereof, and who does not sell them under the authority or with the consent of the owner, the buyer acquires no better title to the goods than the seller had, unless the owner of the goods is by his conduct precluded from denying the seller's authority to sell.

There are, however, the following exceptions to the rule—

1. ENCUMBRANCES OVER CHATTELS. The law does not generally allow encumbrances to run with chattels. (*Dunlop Pneumatic Tyre Co. Ltd. v. Selfridge & Co. Ltd.*, 1915.)[69]

2. ESTOPPEL. Where the owner of goods, by his words or conduct, represents to the buyer that the seller is the true owner, the owner is precluded from denying the title of the buyer. (*Henderson & Co. v. Williams*, 1895.)[173] The doctrine of estoppel is preserved in the final words of Sect. 21 (1) of the Act.

Estoppel does not arise merely because the owner of goods allows another to have possession of them (*Mercantile Bank of India Ltd. v. Central Bank of India Ltd.*, [1938], A.C. 287) and attempts have been made to set up a doctrine of estoppel by negligence, the third party alleging that it is the negligence of the true owner which has given the non-owner the apparent authority to sell. However, in order to establish negligence, it is necessary to show the existence of a duty of care in the owner, and such a duty, which is a matter of law, does not seem to exist where the owner has even by negligence lost his property or facilitated its theft or other form of fraudulent disposition. (See for example *Cundy v. Lindsay*, 1878,[134] and *Ingram v. Little*, 1961.)[137] So, if X loses his watch, and Y finds it and sells it to Z, then X can still claim his property; and it is nothing to the point that X's negligence enabled Y to sell the watch to Z. For the doctrine of estoppel to operate there must be a more deliberate act holding out the non-owner as a person having authority to sell. (*Eastern Distributors v. Goldring*, 1957.)[402]

3. SALE BY A FACTOR. Sect. 21 (2) provides that nothing in the Sale of Goods Act shall affect the provisions of the Factors Acts, or any enactment enabling the apparent owner of goods to dispose of them as if he were the true owner thereof. The Sale of Goods Act thus preserves the power of disposition in such cases (see further p. 211).

4. SALE BY AN AGENT UNDER APPARENT OR USUAL AUTHORITY. Sect. 61 provides that the rules relating to the law of principal and agent are to be preserved, and so a sale by an agent without actual authority will give the purchaser a good title if the sale is within the agent's apparent authority or usual authority (see further p. 193).

5. Special Powers of Sale. Sect. 21 (2) provides that nothing in the Act shall affect the validity of any contract of sale under any special common law or statutory power of sale, or under the order of a court of competent jurisdiction.

Thus a *pledgee* has a power to sell the goods pledged at common law and may give a good title to the purchaser from him. However, if the pledgee is a pawnbroker, the sale will be governed by the Pawnbrokers Acts, 1872 and 1960, in cases where the pledge is over two pounds.

A *sheriff* has power by statute to sell goods taken in execution under a writ of *fieri facias*, and under Sect. 1 of the Innkeepers Act, 1878, an *innkeeper's lien* over the goods of his guests for his charges may be converted into a power of sale. A sale by a *bailee* who has carried out work on goods, e.g. a watch repairer, is possible under the provisions of the Disposal of Uncollected Goods Act, 1952.

The Rules of the Supreme Court give the court a jurisdiction to order the sale of goods which for any just and sufficient reason it may be desirable to have sold at once, e.g. where they are perishable. (*Larner* v. *Fawcett*, 1950.)[352] The purchaser of the goods sold will obtain a good title in spite of the owner's lack of consent.

6. Market Overt. Sect. 22 (1) provides that where goods are sold in *market overt*, according to the usage of the market, the buyer acquires a good title to the goods, provided he buys them in good faith and without notice of any defect or want of title on the part of the seller. The sale of horses is not covered by this section but certain ancient provisions relating to the sale of horses in market overt were preserved by Sect. 22 (2) of the 1893 Act. These provisions were repealed by the Criminal Law Act, 1967, so that the sale of horses is not now within the rules of market overt. Apart from this the Act preserves the ancient rule relating to sales in *open market*, and applies to markets throughout England so long as the market is open, public, and legally constituted either by grant, prescription, or statute, provided the goods are usually sold in the market. The person who wishes so to protect his title must prove that the place in which the sale took place was *market overt*. Every shop within the City of London is market overt in respect of goods usually sold in that shop. Thus a sale of a watch by a confectioner would not be a sale in market overt, even though the shop was within the market.

Market overt is held every day except Sunday and Bank Holidays in London, but elsewhere only on recognised market days. The rule does not apply to sales between traders in the same market; nor does it apply to dispositions other than sales, so that a pledge would not be covered by the rule.

To obtain the protection of market overt, the sale must commence and finish in open market in full view of the public between sunrise and sunset, and the buyer must act in good faith and give value. A sale in the back room of a shop to which the public can only gain access by invitation is not a sale in market overt. (*Clayton* v. *Le Roy*, 1911.)[403]

A purchaser in market overt obtains a good title against the whole world, even though the seller had no title, except—

(i) Where the purchaser is on actual notice that the seller has no title; or
(ii) Where the goods belong to the Crown.

In former times the title of a purchaser in market overt could be defeated if the person responsible for dispossessing the true owner was later convicted of false pretences or larceny. The Theft Act, 1968, repeals this rule and there is no longer any question of a title acquired in market overt revesting in the true owner. Under Sect. 28 of the Theft Act a criminal court can give a restitution order to a person who has been deprived of his property by theft but such an order does not lie against a *bona fide* purchaser of the goods.

7. SALE UNDER A VOIDABLE TITLE. Sect. 23 provides that, when the seller of goods has a *voidable title*, but his title has not been avoided at the time of the sale, the buyer acquires a good title to the goods, provided he buys them in good faith and without notice of the seller's defect of title. Thus, if B obtains goods from S by giving S a fictitious cheque, and B sells the goods to T, who takes them *bona fide* and for value, T obtains a good title, provided S has not avoided the contract with B before B sells to T. (*Car & Universal Finance Co. Ltd.* v. *Caldwell*, 1963.)[168] The section only applies to sales, but pledges are subject to the same rule by virtue of the common law. (*Phillips* v. *Brooks*, 1919.)[136] Where the fraud is such as to render the original contract of sale *void for mistake*, the fraudulent buyer cannot give a good title to a third party. (*Cundy* v. *Lindsay*, 1878.)[134]

8. SALE BY A SELLER IN POSSESSION OF THE GOODS AFTER SALE. Sect. 25 (1), which is similar to Sect. 8 of the Factors Act, 1889, provides that, where a person, *having sold goods*, without executing a bill of sale, continues in possession of the goods, or of the documents of title to the goods, the delivery or transfer by that person or by a mercantile agent acting for him, of the goods or documents of title under any sale, pledge, or other disposition thereof, to any person receiving the same in good faith and without notice of the previous sale, shall have the same effect as if the person making the delivery or transfer were expressly authorised by the owner of the goods to make the same.

The section applies where the property in the goods has passed but the seller still retains possession. If the property in the goods has not passed, the seller gives a good title by virtue of his ownership and not by virtue of the section.

There are a number of decisions which suggest that it is not enough to prove that the seller was still in possession but that the third party must show that the seller was in possession as a seller and that he had not changed his legal position by some subsequent transaction, e.g. as where he had become a bailee under a hire purchase agreement.

(See for example, *Eastern Distributors* v. *Goldring*, 1957.)[402] These decisions were put in doubt by the ruling of the Privy Council in *Pacific Motor Auctions* v. *Motor Credits Ltd.*, 1965[402a] which was followed by the Court of Appeal in *Worcester Finance* v. *Cooden Engineering Co.*, 1971.[402b]

The section only protects the title of third parties, and the original buyer can sue the seller either in conversion, or for breach of contract when he fails to deliver the goods, or may protect himself by means of a Bill of Sale.

9. SALE BY A BUYER IN POSSESSION. Sect. 25 (2) of the Sale of Goods Act, which is similar to Sect. 9 of the Factors Act, 1889, provides that, where a person, *having bought or agreed to buy goods*, obtains, with the consent of the seller, possession of the goods or the documents of title thereto, the delivery or transfer by that person, or by a mercantile agent acting for him, of the goods or documents of title, under any sale, pledge, or other disposition thereof, to any person receiving the same in good faith and without notice of any lien or other right of the original seller in respect of the goods, shall have the same effect as if the person making the delivery or transfer were a mercantile agent in possession of the goods or documents of title with the consent of the owner.

The section applies where the buyer has possession, but the property has not passed to him. If the buyer has the property in the goods, he can give a good title without the aid of the section.

The section does not apply to persons in possession under hire-purchase contracts, because a person who is hiring the goods is not a person who has agreed to buy them. A hire-purchase contract is a contract of *bailment only*, with an option to purchase. The section would apply to a person in possession under a credit sale agreement where the property had not passed, because such a person has bought or agreed to buy the goods. If, although the goods have been delivered, the passing of the property is postponed until all instalments of the purchase price are paid, then there is a conditional contract of sale; such a contract is within Sect. 25 (2) and the buyer can give a good title to a third party if the total purchase price exceeds £2,000, or if the buyer is a corporation. If the total purchase price is £2,000 or under, the contract is now governed by the Hire Purchase Act, 1965, and the buyer cannot give a good title to third parties (Sect. 54, Hire Purchase Act, 1965), though Part III of the Hire Purchase Act, 1964, protects a *bone fide* purchaser of a motor vehicle who has brought it from a person in possession under a hire purchase or conditional sale agreement (see p. 184).

A person who has goods *on approval* cannot pass a good title under this section because he has not bought or agreed to buy the goods; he has a mere option. However, he may pass a good title by virtue of his ownership if, by selling the goods, he indicates his approval. (*London Jewellers Ltd.* v. *Attenborough*, 1934.)[366]

It appears that the "consent" of the seller may be sufficient to protect the title of a purchaser from the original buyer even if the latter obtained the goods by criminal fraud, as where he paid for them by a cheque which he knew would not be met. (*Du Jardin* v. *Beadman Bros.*, [1952] 2 All E.R. 160.) Furthermore the fact that the seller withdraws his consent after he has given the buyer possession does not prevent Sect. 9 of the Factors Act, 1889, operating to protect the title of a purchaser from the buyer since Sect. 2 (2) of the 1889 Act specifically provides for this situation. Thus in *Car & Universal Finance Co. Ltd.* v. *Caldwell*, 1963,[168] the third party would have obtained a title by relying on Sect. 9 of the Factors Act, rather than Sect. 23 of the Sale of Goods Act.

It should be noted that where the buyer has possession of the documents of title but not of the goods complications can arise in respect to the seller's lien and right of *stoppage in transitu* (see p. 156).

Sect. 9 of the Factors Act states that the buyer is deemed to make delivery or transfer of the goods *as if he were a mercantile agent.* However, Sect. 2 (1) of the same Act provides, in effect, that the protection given to a person buying from a mercantile agent applies only where the agent is acting *in the ordinary course of business.* Thus where the buyer who re-sells is not in fact a mercantile agent, it is difficult to see how Sect. 9 can have effect. The better view, which was supported by the Law Reform Committee (12th Report Cmnd 2958, 1966) is that the Section should operate as if the buyer was a mercantile agent without the need to show that he acted like one.

Sect. 9 could also operate to validate the title of a purchaser from a thief because the purchaser could be regarded as in possession with the consent of the seller (i.e. the thief). This unfortunate result could be avoided if the court decided, as a matter of interpretation, that "seller" meant "owner" in this situation, though there is no authority on this point.

10. THE HIRE PURCHASE ACT, 1964, PART III. This Act protects the title of a *bona fide* purchaser of a motor vehicle from a seller in possession under a hire purchase or conditional sale agreement (see p. 184).

Reform. The Twelfth Report of the Law Reform Committee (Cmnd 2958, 1966) having rejected the idea that it should be possible for any bailee to pass a good title, went on to make the following proposals for reform—

(*a*) that there should be no distinction between void (*Cundy* v. *Lindsay*, 1878)[134] and voidable (*Phillips* v. *Brooks*, 1919)[136] contracts in regard to the title of a third party; in each case he would be protected;

(*b*) that the rule in *Caldwell*[168] be reversed so that rescission of a voidable contract would require actual communication;

(*c*) that Sect. 9 should be amended so as to apply more clearly to a sale by a private buyer in possession (see above);

(*d*) that the rule of market overt be extended by a wider provision covering sales at any retail premises.

PERFORMANCE OF THE CONTRACT

Delivery. Sect. 62 defines delivery as the voluntary transfer of possession from one person to another. There are various forms of delivery as follows—

(*a*) *by physical transfer* as where the goods are handed to the buyer with the intention of transferring possession;

(*b*) *by delivery of the means of control* as where the key of a warehouse or store is handed to the buyer;

(*c*) *by attornment* as where the goods are in the possession of a third party, e.g. a warehouseman who acknowledges to the buyer that he holds the goods on his behalf (Sect. 39 (3));

(*d*) *by delivery of documents of title* as where a *bill of lading* representing the goods is delivered (Sect. 29 (3)). Neither a delivery order nor a car log book are documents of title for this purpose;

(*e*) *by constructive delivery* as where the buyer already has possession of the goods as a bailee. Thus in a hire purchase contract the character of possession changes when the instalments have been paid and the hirer becomes owner by constructive delivery. This form of delivery also applies where a seller agrees to hold the goods as a bailee or agent of the buyer.

Place of Delivery. Sect. 27 provides that it is the duty of the seller to deliver the goods, and of the buyer to accept and pay for them, in accordance with the terms of sale. The seller's duty to deliver does not mean he must necessarily take or send them to the buyer. The place of delivery, in the absence of express agreement to the contrary, is the place of business of the seller or, if he has no place of business, his residence. (Sect. 29 (1).) If the contract is for the sale of specific goods which to the knowledge of the parties when the contract is made are in some other place, then that place is the place of delivery. (Sect. 29 (1).) Thus, in the absence of a contrary intention, the buyer is under a duty to collect the goods.

Where the seller is, under a special contract, bound to deliver the goods, he discharges the duty by delivering them to a person who, being at the buyer's premises, appears respectable and likely to be authorised to take delivery, even if in the event he is not. (*Galbraith & Grant Ltd.* v. *Block*, 1922.)[404]

Delivery of goods to the wrong address may amount to conversion by the carrier, thus providing the owner with a remedy in tort against him if the goods are not recovered.

Payment and Delivery are Concurrent Conditions. Sect. 28 provides that, unless otherwise agreed, e.g. where the seller gives credit to the buyer, delivery and payment of the price are concurrent conditions. The seller must be ready and willing to give possession of the goods to the buyer in exchange for the price, and the buyer must be ready and willing to pay the price in exchange for possession of the goods.

Thus, if the buyer is suing the seller for non-delivery, he need not give evidence that he has paid, but merely that he was ready and willing to pay. In an action for non-acceptance of the goods, the seller need not prove that he has tendered delivery, but merely that he was ready and willing to deliver.

Other Rules as to Delivery. Where under the contract of sale the seller is bound to send the goods to the buyer, but no time for sending them is fixed, the seller is bound to send them within a reasonable time (Sect. 29 (3)) and at a reasonable hour. (Sect. 29 (4).) What is reasonable in both cases is a matter of fact.

Quantity of Goods Delivered. Where the seller delivers to the buyer a quantity of goods *less* than he contracted to sell, the *buyer may reject them*, but if he accepts them, he must pay for them at the contract rate. (Sect. 30 (1).)

Where the seller delivers to the buyer a quantity of goods *larger* than he contracted to sell, the buyer may *accept the goods included in the contract* and reject the rest, *or* he may *reject the whole*. If the buyer accepts the whole of the goods so delivered, he must pay for them at the contract rate. (Sect. 30 (2).)

If the goods delivered are mixed with goods of a different description not included in the contract, the buyer may accept the goods which are in accordance with the contract and reject the rest, or he may reject the whole. (Sect. 30 (3).) (*Moore & Co.* v. *Landauer & Co.*, 1921.)[269]

The above provisions are subject to any usage of trade, special agreement, or course of dealing between the parties (Sect. 30 (4)), and the buyer's right to reject may not exist if the differences are microscopic. (*De minimus non curat lex*—The law does not concern itself with trifles.) (*Shipton Anderson & Co. Ltd.* v. *Weil Bros.*, 1912.)[405]

Delivery by Instalments. Unless otherwise agreed, the buyer of goods is not bound to accept delivery by instalments. (Sect. 31 (1).) Thus the seller cannot excuse short delivery by undertaking to deliver the balance in due course. Where there is a contract of sale of goods to be delivered by stated instalments, which are to be separately paid for, and the seller makes defective deliveries in respect of one or more instalments, or the buyer neglects or refuses to take delivery of or pay for one or more instalments, it is a question in each case depending on the terms of the contract and the circumstances of the case, whether the breach of contract is a repudiation of the whole contract, or whether it is a severable breach giving rise to a claim for compensation but not a right to treat the whole contract as repudiated. (Sect. 31 (2).) The main tests to be considered in applying Sect. 31 (2) are—

(*a*) the ratio quantitatively which the breach bears to the contract as a whole; and (*b*) the degree of probability or improbability that such a breach will be repeated. (*Maple Flock Co. Ltd.* v. *Universal Furniture Products (Wembley) Ltd.*, 1934[406] and *R. A. Munro & Co. Ltd.* v. *Meyer*, 1930.)[371]

Delivery to a Carrier. Where the seller is authorised or required to send the goods to the buyer, delivery by the seller to a carrier is, in the absence of any evidence to the contrary, deemed to be delivery to the buyer. (Sect. 32 (1).) In the absence of a contrary agreement the seller is required to make a contract with a carrier which is reasonable in terms of the goods to be carried. If he does not and the goods are lost or damaged the buyer may refuse to regard delivery to the carrier as delivery to himself and may sue the seller for damages. (Sect. 32 (2).) Where the carriage involves a sea voyage where it is usual to insure, the seller must make it possible for the buyer to insure otherwise the goods are at the seller's risk during sea transit. (Sect. 32 (3).)

Where the seller of goods agrees to deliver them at his own risk at a place other than that where they are when sold, the buyer must, unless otherwise agreed, take the risk of accidental destruction or deterioration, but not the risk of damage caused by the fault of the seller. (Sect. 33.) Where the goods are perishable, they are not considered merchantable unless they are sent off by the seller in time to reach their destination in saleable condition. (*Broome* v. *Pardess Co-operative Society*, 1939.)[407]

The Buyer's Right to Examine the Goods. A buyer is not deemed to have accepted goods delivered to him unless and until he has had a reasonable opportunity of examining them for the purpose of ascertaining whether they are in conformity with the contract. (Sect. 34 (1).) When the seller tenders delivery of goods to the buyer, he is bound, on request, to give the buyer a reasonable opportunity of examining the goods to see whether they are in conformity with the contract. (Sect. 34 (2).)

Acceptance of the Goods. The buyer is deemed to have accepted the goods—

(i) When he intimates to the seller that he has accepted them; or
(ii) When the goods have been delivered to him and he does any act in relation to them which is inconsistent with the ownership of the seller; or
(iii) When after the lapse of a reasonable time, he retains the goods without intimating to the seller that he has rejected them. (Sect. 35.)

Under the Act, Sect. 35 prevailed over Sect. 34, and if the buyer had not examined the goods, but informed the seller that he had accepted them, he was deemed to have waived his right of examination; and if he retained the goods for an unreasonable time, he was deemed to have accepted them. Acts inconsistent with ownership of the seller also amounted to acceptance as where the buyer resold the goods or part of them before examination.

This unfortunate result is now avoided by Sect. 4 of the Misrepresentation Act, 1967, which provides that Sect. 34 is always to prevail over Sect. 35 so that a buyer is not prevented from rejecting goods until he has examined them or at least has had a reasonable opportunity of examining them. It should be noted, however, that delay in rejection will still defeat a claim for repudiation for breach of condition, but not a claim for damages for breach of warranty.

The effect of Sect. 4 of the 1967 Act will be, therefore, that persons who buy goods such as refrigerators, washing machines and radios, will be able to examine and test them in their own homes. If the goods are faulty they will be able to repudiate the contract and return the goods demanding a refund of the purchase price. However, the goods must be returned within a reasonable time otherwise the buyer's only remedy will be an action for damages.

Where the buyer has the right to refuse to accept the goods and does so refuse he is not bound to return them but only to notify the seller of the refusal. (Sect. 36.) If the seller is able to deliver the goods and requests the buyer to take delivery the buyer must do so within a reasonable time. If he does not do so he is liable to the seller for any resulting loss and also for a reasonable charge for the care and custody of the goods. If the buyer's refusal amounts only to a request to postpone delivery for a short time, the seller is still bound to deliver. If, however, the refusal is absolute or involves a long postponement it may amount to a repudiation of the contract which discharges the seller from liability to deliver and gives him a right of action in damages against the buyer. (Sect. 37.)

THE REMEDIES OF THE SELLER

1. REAL REMEDIES AGAINST THE GOODS. The unpaid seller, in addition to his personal remedies, e.g. an action for damages, has, under Part IV of the Act, certain *real remedies* against the goods.

Sect. 39 (1) provides that, even if the property in the goods has passed to the buyer, the unpaid seller of goods, as such, has by implication of law—

    (i) A *lien* on the goods or the right to retain them for the price while he is still in possession of them;

    (ii) In the case of the insolvency of the buyer, a right of stopping the goods *in transitu* after he has parted with possession of them;

    (iii) A right of resale as limited by the Act.

Sect. 39 (2) provides that, *where the property in goods has not passed to the buyer*, the unpaid seller has, in addition to his other remedies, a right of withholding delivery similar to and co-extensive with his rights of lien and stoppage *in transitu* where the property has passed to the buyer.

The rights set out in Sect. 39 (1) may only be exercised by an *unpaid seller*, and Sect. 38 (1) provides that a seller of goods is deemed to be an *unpaid seller*—

(i) When the whole of the price has not been paid or tendered;
(ii) When a bill of exchange or other negotiable instrument has been received as conditional payment, and the condition on which it was received has not been fulfilled by reason of the dishonour of the instrument or otherwise.

The term *seller* includes in certain circumstances the agent of the seller. (Sect. 38 (2).) Thus where the goods are sold through an agent who has either paid the price to his principal, or has made himself liable to pay the price under the terms of his contract of agency, the agent can exercise any of the rights of the unpaid seller.

Lien. A lien is generally speaking the right of a creditor in possession of the goods of his debtor to retain possession of them until the price has been paid or tendered, or his debt has been secured or satisfied. *A lien does not normally carry with it a power of sale*, though the unpaid seller of goods has a statutory power, and will generally exercise his lien as a preliminary to resale.

The lien conferred by the Act is a particular lien, though a general lien may be conferred by an express contractual provision. This means that *the unpaid seller can retain only the goods which are not paid for*, and not other goods belonging to the buyer. However, where delivery is being made by instalments and an unpaid seller has made part delivery of the goods, he may exercise his lien on the remainder, unless such part delivery can, in the circumstances, be construed as a waiver of the right of lien by the seller. (Sect. 42.)

Where the goods have been sold *without any stipulation as to credit*, the unpaid seller who is in possession of them is entitled to retain possession until payment or tender of the price. (Sect. 41 (1) (*a*).) A lien can also be claimed, *even though credit has been given*—

(*a*) Where the goods have been sold on credit but the term of credit has expired. (Sect. 41 (1) (*b*).); and
(*b*) Where the buyer becomes insolvent. (Sect. 41 (1) (*c*).)

A person is deemed to be insolvent within the meaning of the Act if he has either ceased to pay his debts in the ordinary course of business, or cannot pay his debts as they become due, whether he has committed an act of bankruptcy or not. (Sect. 62 (3).)

The effect of the insolvency provision is that the seller cannot be compelled to deliver the goods to an insolvent person and to prove for a dividend in the bankruptcy. However, a trustee in bankruptcy can have the goods if he tenders the whole price.

The seller's lien is a possessory lien. The seller must be in possession of the goods, but he need not be in possession as a seller and may exercise his right of lien even if he is in possession of the goods as agent or bailee for the buyer. (Sect. 41 (2).) The seller's lien is for the price of the goods, and cannot be exercised in respect of other costs, e.g. storage charges and the like.

Loss of Lien. The right of lien is lost—

(i) If the price is paid or tendered;

(ii) If the right of lien has been waived by the seller;

(iii) If the buyer or his agent lawfully obtains possession of the goods;

(iv) If the unpaid seller delivers the goods to a carrier or bailee for the purpose of transmission to the buyer, without reserving the right of disposal of the goods. A right of *stoppage in transitu* may arise here, but *only if the buyer is insolvent.*

A waiver may be an express waiver under the contract between the parties, or may be implied from the conduct of the seller. For example, suppose B buys furniture on credit from S, and after the sale has taken place, S then asks B to lend him the furniture for a week until he can get more furniture to display in his shop. Here the conduct of S would imply that, although the property was B's, he held the furniture on a new contract of loan, and that his right of lien on the contract of sale was waived.

The exercise of a lien by the seller does not rescind the contract (Sect. 48 (1)) and the right of lien is not lost when the seller obtains a judgment from the court for the price of the goods. (Sect. 43 (2).)

Stoppage *in transitu*. When the buyer of goods becomes insolvent, the unpaid seller who has parted with the possession of the goods has the right of stopping them *in transitu*, i.e. he may resume possession of the goods as long as they are *in course of transit*, and may retain them until payment or tender of the price. (Sect. 44.)

The remedy is only available when the buyer is insolvent and, if exercised, means that the seller need not allow the goods to form part of an insolvent estate, leaving himself with a mere right to prove for a dividend for the price. Nevertheless, the exercise of stoppage *in transitu* does not rescind the contract of sale, and if the buyer's trustee in bankruptcy tenders the price, the seller must deliver the goods or be liable for breach of contract. *Three conditions must be satisfied* before the right can be exercised: (1) the seller must be unpaid; (2) the buyer must be insolvent; and (3) the goods must still be in transit.

Sect. 45 (1) provides that goods are deemed to be *in course of transit* from the time when they are delivered to a carrier by land or water, or other bailee for the purpose of transmission to the buyer, until the buyer, or his agent in that behalf, takes delivery of them from such carrier or other bailee.

We have seen that delivery to a carrier is *prima facie* deemed to be *constructive* delivery of the goods to the buyer, and where the carrier is the agent of the buyer this constitutes *actual* delivery and there can be no stoppage *in transitu*. Where, however, the carrier is an independent contractor, the remedy is available until the goods are *actually* delivered to the buyer.

If the buyer or his agent obtains delivery of the goods before their arrival at the appointed destination, the transit is at an end. (Sect. 45 (2).) If, after the arrival of the goods at the appointed destination, the carrier or other bailee acknowledges to the buyer, or his agent, that he holds the goods on his behalf and continues in possession of them as bailee for the buyer or his agent, the transit is at an end, and it is immaterial that a further destination for the goods may have been indicated by the buyer. (Sect. 45 (3).) (*Kendall* v. *Marshall Stevens & Co.*, 1883.)[408]

If, however, the goods are rejected by the buyer, and the carrier or other bailee continues in possession of them, the transit is not deemed to be at an end, even if the seller has refused to take them back. (Sect. 45 (4).) When goods are delivered to a ship chartered by the buyer, it is a question depending on the circumstances of the particular case, whether they are in the possession of the master as a carrier, or as an agent of the buyer. (Sect. 45 (5).) The ship's master will not normally be the agent of the buyer where the goods are shipped under a charter for one voyage. The master will be the buyer's agent where the ship belongs to the buyer, and may well be where the ship is chartered by the buyer for several voyages, as under a time charter.

Where the carrier or other bailee wrongfully refuses to deliver the goods to the buyer or his agent, the transit is deemed to be at an end. (Sect. 45 (6).)

Where part delivery of the goods has been made to the buyer or his agent, the remainder of the goods may be stopped in transit, unless such part delivery has been made under such circumstances as to show an agreement to give up possession of the whole of the goods. (Sect. 45 (7).)

The unpaid seller's right of lien or stoppage *in transitu* is not affected by any sale or other disposition of the goods which the buyer may have made unless the seller has agreed to it. However, where documents of title, e.g. bills of lading respecting the goods, have been lawfully transferred to the buyer, and he has transferred them to a third party, who takes them in good faith and for value *by way of sale*, the seller's right of lien or stoppage *in transitu* is defeated. (Sect. 47.) Where the transfer is *by way of pledge*, however, the seller can exercise a lien or stop the goods in transit, but only subject to the rights of the pledge. (*Leask* v. *Scott Bros.*, 1877.)[409]

The unpaid seller may exercise his right of stoppage *in transitu* either by taking actual possession of the goods, or by giving notice of his claim to the carrier or other bailee in whose possession the goods are. Such notice may be given either to the person in actual possession of the goods or to his principal. In the latter case the notice, to be effectual, must be given at such time and under such circumstances that the principal, by the exercise of reasonable diligence, may communicate it to his servant or agent in time to prevent delivery to the buyer. (Sect. 46 (1).)

When notice of stoppage in transitu is given by the seller to the carrier, or other bailee in possession of the goods, he must redeliver the goods to or according to the directions of the seller. The expenses of such redelivery must be borne by the seller. (Sect. 46 (2).) If the carrier delivers the goods after notice to the contrary, the unpaid seller has his remedy, for what it is worth, against the buyer, *or* may sue the carrier in tort for conversion.

The carrier can refuse to redeliver if his charges have not been paid, and his lien overrides the seller's right of stoppage *in transitu*. However, unless a general lien is conferred by the contract, a carrier's lien is normally a *particular lien* so that he can only refuse to redeliver the actual goods in respect of which charges are outstanding, and not other goods dispatched by the seller.

The Right of Resale. The unpaid seller of goods has a right to resell, without being in breach of contract, in the following circumstances—

(i) *Where the buyer repudiates the contract* either expressly or by conduct, the seller can resell the goods, retain any profit made, returning to the buyer any part payments.

(ii) *Where the contract of sale expressly provides for resale in case the buyer should make default,* and the seller resells the goods on default, the original contract of sale is rescinded, but without prejudice to any claim the seller may have for damages. (Sect. 48 (4).) Since the contract is rescinded, the property in the goods revests in the seller who is, therefore, selling his own goods again, and can retain any profit he makes on the resale. If the seller incurs a loss on resale, he can recover the loss from the original buyer but, as the section does not deal with part payments by the buyer, these are presumably irrecoverable.

(iii) *Where the goods are of a perishable nature, or where the unpaid seller gives notice to the buyer of his intention to resell,* and the buyer does not within a reasonable time pay or tender the price, the unpaid seller may resell the goods and recover from the original buyer damages for any loss occasioned by the breach of contract. (Sect. 48 (3).) The contract of sale is not rescinded by the seller's mere exercise of his right of lien or stoppage *in transitu*, but it is when the unpaid seller resells the goods or part of them. If the property in the goods has passed to the original buyer it reverts to the unpaid seller on resale and his proper claim is for damages for non-acceptance, whether or not the property has passed to the original buyer. Therefore, if the unpaid seller resells at a profit he need not account for it to the original buyer, and if he resells at less than the original purchase price he cannot recover his loss from the original buyer. (*R. V. Ward Ltd.* v. *Bignall*, 1967.)[410]

Title. A seller has power to give a title, whether he has the right to sell or not in the following circumstances—

(*a*) Where, although the goods are sold, *the property is still in the seller;*

(*b*) Under Sect. 25 (1) of the Sale of Goods Act, 1893, or Sect. 8 of the Factors Act, 1889, *if he is in possession;*

(*c*) Under Sect. 48 (2) of the Sale of Goods Act, 1893, which provides that *where an unpaid seller who has exercised his right of lien or stoppage* in transitu *resells the goods,* the buyer acquires a good title thereto as against the original buyer.

Unless the seller resells in accordance with the rules laid down in Sects. 48 (3) and 48 (4) he will usually be liable in breach of contract to the original buyer, though in most cases the second buyer will obtain a good title to the goods.

2. PERSONAL REMEDIES OF THE SELLER. In addition to the real remedies discussed above, the seller has a personal action against the buyer either—

(*a*) for the price under Sect. 49 (1); or
(*b*) for damages for non-acceptance under Sect. 50 (1).

The passing of the property and the conduct of the buyer will determine the sort of action which the seller will bring, and the property may, of course, have passed before delivery.

If the property has passed and the buyer has accepted the goods, the seller has an action for the price. If the property has not passed and the buyer will not accept the goods, the seller has an action for damages. Finally, if the property has passed and the buyer will not accept the goods, the seller has an action either for the price or for damages. If the seller sues for the price he may also include a claim for losses and expenses, e.g. in storing the goods because the buyer would not take them. (Sect. 37.) If the seller sues for damages, such losses will be taken into account.

Sect. 49 (2) provides that where, under a contract of sale, the price is payable on a day certain irrespective of delivery, and the buyer wrongfully neglects or refuses to pay such price, the seller may maintain an action for the price, although the property in the goods has not passed, and the goods have not been appropriated to the contract.

MEASUREMENT OF DAMAGES. In an action for damages the main problem is that of assessment. Sect. 50 (2) provides that the measure of damages is the estimated *loss directly and naturally resulting,* in the ordinary course of events, from the buyer's breach of contract.

Sect. 50 (3) further expands the concept by providing that, where there is an available market for the goods in question, the measure of damages is *prima facie* to be ascertained by the *difference between the contract price and the market or current price* at the time or times when the goods ought to have been accepted, or, if no time was fixed for acceptance, then at the time of the refusal to accept. The section is *a guide to the assessment of damages and does not exclude other methods of assessment in appropriate cases.* (*Thompson Ltd.* v. *Robinson* (*Gunmakers*) *Ltd.*, 1955[309] and *Charter* v. *Sullivan*, 1957.)[308] An available market exists when there are a number of buyers and sellers, and where it is possible to go into the market and buy and sell what one wants. It is not necessarily a place but there must be adequate possibilities of contract, and the person suffering the breach is not obliged to scour the earth in search of a market.

Where there is an available market and the seller has sold the goods at the market price, then—

(*a*) if that price is less than the contract price, the seller can recover the balance by way of damages;

(*b*) if the market price is the same as or even higher than the contract price, the seller will only be entitled to nominal damages;

(*c*) if the seller sells for less than the market price, then he cannot recover the difference between the contract price and the resale price. It is the seller's duty to mitigate or reduce the loss and not to aggravate it;

(*d*) even if the seller keeps the goods after the buyer's breach of contract, and later sells them for more than the market price was at the date of the breach, the seller can still recover the difference between the contract price and market price at the date of the breach, if the market price was then lower than the contract price.

Suppose the contract price was £100 and the market price at the time of the breach was £80, then the seller is entitled to £20 damages.

(*a*) If he sells on the day of the breach for £60, the damages will still only be £20.

(*b*) If, hoping the market will improve, he delays the sale, he will still have the right to £20 damages and can retain all the proceeds of the subsequent sale.

Where there is an anticipatory breach of contract, e.g. where the goods are to be delivered in May but the buyer tells the seller in February that he will not accept, then damages are assessed on the market price at the date when the goods were to be delivered and accepted, i.e. the May market price. Where the seller accepts an anticipatory breach and sues upon it, the date for delivery having not yet arrived when the case is tried, the court will have to estimate the market price at the date of delivery.

Where there is an anticipatory breach and the market is falling, there are two possible situations—

(i) *If the seller does not accept the repudiation*, he need not resell the goods at once but is entitled to wait until the delivery date. If the buyer refuses to take delivery, the seller may resell and may recover from the original buyer as damages the difference between contract and market price at that date. It should be noted that the seller cannot be required to accept an anticipatory breach. (*White and Carter* (*Councils*) *Ltd.* v. *McGregor*, 1961.)[283]

(ii) *If the seller accepts the repudiation*, he must sell immediately when the market is falling in order to mitigate loss. If he delays in selling the goods, he will only be able to recover as damages the difference between contract and market price at the date of repudiation.

Where there is no market for the goods, as where the goods were made or procured specially for the purposes of the contract and cannot be sold to another buyer (e.g. because they are highly specialised goods) then there are two possible situations—

(*a*) *Where the seller has actually made or procured the goods*, he can claim the whole contract price, that is to say the cost to him of procuring or making the goods plus his profit.

(*b*) *Where the seller has not made or procured the goods*, he can claim his profit only.

REMEDIES OF THE BUYER

1. Rejection of the Goods. The buyer may repudiate the contract and reject the goods where the seller is in breach of a condition. The effect of this is that the buyer may refuse to pay the price, or recover it if paid, or sue for damages, basing the latter claim on the seller's failure to deliver goods in accordance with the contract.

If the buyer rejects the goods, the property revests in the seller, and the buyer has no lien on the goods for the return of money paid by him under the contract. Sect. 36 provides that, unless otherwise agreed, where goods are delivered to the buyer, and he refuses to accept them, having the right to do so, he is not bound to return them to the seller, but it is sufficient if he intimates to the seller that he refuses to accept them.

Obviously the right to reject the goods will be lost where the property in them has passed to the buyer, or where they have been accepted by him. A breach of condition will have to be treated as a breach of warranty and rescission will not be possible. (The meaning of *acceptance* for the purpose of the Act has already been given.)

However, the buyer might ask for rescission of the contract on the grounds that the statements made regarding the goods were not conditions or warranties (i.e. terms) but were pre-contractual misrepresentations, and, if this is possible, *the remedy of rescission of contracts of sale of goods* has survived the Sale of Goods Act, 1893, and a remedy may be given *for a mere misrepresentation* which is superior to that available for breach of a term.

2. An Action for Damages. The buyer may be able to bring an action for damages for non-delivery of the goods; or for breach of condition or warranty; or, where the property has passed to the buyer, an action in tort for detinue or conversion.

(*a*) NON-DELIVERY. Where the seller wrongfully neglects or refuses to deliver the goods to the buyer, the buyer may maintain an action against the seller for damages for non-delivery. (Sect. 51 (1).) The measure of damages is the estimated loss directly and naturally resulting, in the ordinary course of events, from the seller's breach of contract. (Sect. 51 (2).)

The buyer will, therefore, recover the difference (if any) between the market price and the contract price (Sect. 51 (3)), and if he can buy similar goods cheaper in the market, the damages will be nominal. Where there is an anticipatory breach by the seller, the market price for the purpose of damages is that ruling when delivery ought to have been made, though if the buyer accepts the breach, he must buy quickly if the market price is rising for he has a duty to mitigate loss.

In addition where a buyer has lawfully rejected goods under a contract and makes a new agreement with the seller for the sale and purchase of the same goods at a reduced price, then although the buyer can sue under the original contract, the principle of mitigation of damages allows the court to take account of any profit made by the buyer on the subsequent contract provided that the subsequent contract is part of a continuous dealing between the parties. If, therefore, S delivers 100 tons of wheat at £30 per ton to B and B lawfully rejects the wheat because it is not up to standard, then according to Sect. 51 (3) B has an action for damages based on the difference between the contract price and the market price. If we suppose that the market price was £32 per ton B should recover damages of £200. If, however, at a later date B agrees to accept the same wheat at £28 per ton he has no loss which is claimable, Sect. 51 (3) being a mere guide to the assessment of damages which does not preclude other methods of assessment in appropriate cases. (*R. Pagnan & Fratelli* v. *Corbisa Industrial Agropacuaria*, [1971] 1 All E.R. 165.)

Loss of profit on resale by the buyer is generally ignored in assessing damages for non-delivery, but such loss may be brought in as special damage if the seller knew that the buyer had resold. (*R. H. Hall Ltd.* v. *W. H. Pim & Co. Ltd.*, 1928.)[411] It is probably not enough if the seller merely knows that the buyer is in trade and might, therefore, be likely to resell.

(*b*) BREACH OF CONDITION OR WARRANTY. Where there is a breach of warranty by the seller or where the buyer elects, or is compelled, to treat any breach of condition on the part of the seller as a breach of warranty, the buyer is not by reason only of such breach of warranty entitled to reject the goods. However, he may—

(*a*) Set up against the seller the breach of warranty in diminution or extinction of the price; or

(*b*) Maintain an action against the seller for damages for the breach of warranty. (Sect. 53 (1).)

When there is late delivery, damages will be assessed on the basis of the actual loss resulting from the breach. Thus, if X should have delivered goods to Y on January 1st when the market price was £3·50 a ton, and in fact delivers them on February 1st when the market price is £2·50 a ton, the measure of damages would appear to be £1 a ton. But if Y in fact resells the goods at £3·25 a ton, the damages will only be the difference between £3·25 and £3·50 i.e. 25p a ton.

In the case of breach of warranty of quality the loss resulting is *prima facie* the difference between the value of the goods at the time of delivery to the buyer, and the value they would have had if they had answered to the warranty. (Sect. 53 (3).)

Losses incurred or damages paid by the buyer on sub-contracts are disregarded (*Slater* v. *Hoyle and Smith*, 1920),[412] unless the buyer can show either—

(i) That the seller had actual notice of the sub-contracts; or
(ii) That from the circumstances the seller had constructive notice of the sub-contracts. (*Pinnock Bros.* v. *Lewis and Peat Ltd.*, 1923.)[307]

(*c*) DETINUE AND CONVERSION. Where the property in the goods has passed to the buyer, he may bring an action for detention of the goods if the seller refuses to deliver them, or an action in conversion against the seller or a third party who has dealt with the goods. If the buyer sues the seller in detinue, however, he will obtain damages only and not restitution of the goods, unless the goods are rare and unique, and the damages in both detinue and conversion will, as between buyer and seller, be assessed in the same way as if the buyer were suing for breach of contract. Thus the buyer gains no advantage by suing in tort.

3. Specific Performance. Where the goods are of peculiar value or great rarity the court may, if it thinks fit, grant a decree of specific performance. (Sect. 52.) The remedy is rarely available because similar goods are usually obtainable and an award of damages is adequate.

SPECIAL SALES

Auction Sales. Where goods are put up for sale by auction in lots, each lot is *prima facie* deemed to be the subject of a separate contract of sale. (Sect. 58 (1).) A sale by auction is complete when the auctioneer announces its completion by the fall of the hammer, or in other customary manner. Until such announcement is made, any bidder may retract his bid. (Sect. 58 (2).)

It seems also that, at an auction, each bid lapses when a new one is made. So, if X bids £10 for certain goods, and then Y bids £12, X's bid of £10 lapses. If Y withdraws his bid before the auctioneer has accepted it, the auctioneer cannot return to X's bid and accept that; X must be prepared to bid again.

A sale by auction may be notified to be subject to a reserve or upset price, and a right to bid may also be expressly reserved by or on behalf of the seller. Where a right to bid is expressly reserved, but not otherwise, the seller, or any person on his behalf, may bid at the auction. (Sect. 58 (4).)

(*a*) SELLER'S RIGHT TO BID. If in a sale by auction the seller does not specifically reserve the right to bid, it is not lawful for the seller to bid himself or to employ any person to do so, or for the auctioneer knowingly to take any bid from the seller or any such person. Any sale contravening this rule may be treated as fraudulent by the buyer. (Sect. 58 (3).)

If there is no express statement as to the seller's right to bid, but he does bid, the buyer may repudiate the contract or *sue for damages where he has paid a greater price* than he would have had to pay because the seller has been bidding against him.

The seller is not allowed to bid merely because the sale is advertised to be without a reserve price. There must be some express notification of the seller's right to bid. Where the sale is subject to a reserve price, and the seller bids without notification, the buyer may repudiate the contract or sue for damages, though, if the reserve price was not reached, the would-be buyer will not have suffered loss, since he would not have obtained the goods even if the seller had not made bids.

(*b*) SIGNIFICANCE OF RESERVE PRICE. Where a sale is expressly notified to be subject to a reserve, the auctioneer has no power to sell below that reserve. (*McManus* v. *Fortescue*, 1907.)[413] Where there is no express statement as to a reserve price, the auctioneer is still entitled to refuse to accept any bid. Where an auction is expressly advertised to be without reserve, it is clear that there is no sale of the goods if the auctioneer refuses to accept a bid. (Sect. 58 (2).) It is, however, possible that the auctioneer may be personally liable for breach of warranty of authority on the ground that he has contracted to sell to the highest bidder. (*Warlow* v. *Harrison* (1859), 1 E. & E. 309.)

The Auctions (Bidding Agreements) Act, 1927, as amended by the Auctions (Bidding Agreements) Act, 1969, provides for certain criminal penalties designed to prevent illegal auction rings which involve the giving of consideration to a person to abstain from bidding. Of interest as regards the civil law is Sect. 3 of the 1969 Act which provides that a seller at an auction to anyone party to an agreement with a dealer not to bid for the goods may avoid the contract. If the goods have been resold and cannot be handed back to the seller all the parties to the ring are liable to the seller to make good the loss he has suffered by selling at a lower price as a result of the activities of the ring.

TRADE DESCRIPTIONS ACTS, 1968/1972

Criminal sanctions for falsely or misleadingly describing goods have existed for some time under the Merchandise Marks Acts. They have now been replaced and extended by the 1968 Act which came into force on November 30th, 1968.

The details of the Act are not included since they are, strictly speaking, beyond the scope of this book which is concerned with the civil rather than the criminal law. The Act is very comprehensive and has to some extent prevented false or misleading statements or advertisements by retail sellers, though there are loopholes. Sect. 35 of the Act expressly provides that failure to comply with the provisions does not render any contract void or unenforceable; in consequence civil remedies are expressly disallowed by the Act. Under the Act of 1972 it is an offence not to give an indication of origin where goods bearing a U.K. name or make have been produced or made outside the U.K.

EXPORT SALES

Certain special clauses have been used over the years in sales where delivery has involved carriage by sea. These clauses have given rise to four main types of contract, the major terms of which have become largely standardised, though there are variations as regards detailed provisions. These four contracts and their major terms are dealt with briefly below.

F.O.B. Contracts. Under such a contract the seller must put the goods *free on board* a ship for despatch to the buyer. The buyer is generally responsible for selecting the port of shipment and the date of shipment of the goods. The seller pays all charges incurred prior to the goods being put on board, but the buyer is liable to pay the freight or insurance. Once the goods are over the ship's rail, they are normally at the buyer's risk.

It is a matter for the buyer to insure the goods and his risk if they are lost, damaged, delayed or uninsured *en route*. (*Frebold* v. *Circle Products Ltd.*, [1970] 1 Lloyd's Rep. 499.) The seller may under a particular contract be responsible for shipping the goods and where this is so it is important to know whether the seller ships on his own account as principal or as an agent for the buyer. If he ships as principal the property in the goods will not normally pass on shipment, though it will usually do so if he ships as agent. (*President of India* v. *Metcalfe Shipping Co.*, [1969] 1 All E.R. 861.)

Sect. 32 (3) provides that, unless otherwise agreed, where the goods are sent by the seller to the buyer by a route involving sea transit, under circumstances in which it is usual to insure, the seller must give such notice to the buyer as may enable him to insure them during their sea transit, and, if the seller fails to do so, the goods shall be deemed to be at his risk during such sea transit. Thus delivery to the carrier will not necessarily pass the risk in f.o.b. contracts.

Nowadays the seller often makes the contract of carriage. It must be reasonable in terms of the nature of the goods and other circumstances. If not and the goods are lost or damaged in the course of transit, the buyer may decline to treat the delivery to the carrier as a delivery to himself, or may hold the seller responsible in damages. (Sect. 32 (2).)

C.I.F. Contracts. In a contract of this sort the price of the goods includes *cost, insurance and freight*. The duties of the seller are—

(*a*) To ship goods of the description contained in the contract under a contract of affreightment which will ensure the delivery of the goods at the destination contemplated in the contract. Undertakings in the contract as to the time and place of shipment are nearly always treated as conditions. Thus the buyer may reject the goods if they are shipped too late. (*Aruna Mills Ltd.* v. *Dhanrajmal Gobindram*, 1968.)[414] or too soon. (*Bowes* v. *Shand*, 1877.)[275]

(*b*) To arrange for insurance which will be available to the buyer.

(*c*) To make out an invoice for the goods.

(*d*) To tender the documents to the buyer in exchange for the price, so that the buyer will know the amount of the freight he must pay, and so that he can obtain delivery of the goods if they arrive, or recover for their loss if they are lost on the voyage.

The risk passes in a c.i.f. contract when the goods are shipped, and the buyer will still have to pay for the goods if they are lost on the voyage, though he will have the insurance cover. The property in the goods does not pass until the seller transfers the documents to the buyer and the latter has paid for them. (*Mirabita* v. *Imperial Ottoman Bank* (1878), 3 Ex. D. 164.) If the goods have been shipped, but the documents have not been transferred, there is a conditional appropriation of the goods to the contract which will not become unconditional until the buyer takes up the documents and pays for them. It will be seen, therefore, that a c.i.f. contract is in essence a "sale of documents" the delivery of which transfers the property and the possession of the goods to the transferee. However, a c.i.f. contract is regarded as a sale of goods because it contemplates the transfer of goods in due course and for this reason the Act of 1893 applies.

Ex-Ship Contracts. Here the seller is required to deliver the goods to the buyer at a named port of discharge and the latter need not concern himself with the shipment of the goods. If the seller does not make delivery, the buyer cannot be made to pay the price, or, if the price has been paid, it can be recovered on the basis of total failure of consideration. The property and the risk in the goods pass when the goods are delivered, and the seller is under no obligation to insure them; if he does so it is entirely for his own benefit.

Ex-Works or Ex-Store Contracts. Here it is the duty of the buyer to take delivery of the goods at the works or store of the seller as the case may be. The property and risk usually pass when the buyer takes delivery. These sales are almost always of unascertained goods, the appropriation taking place when the goods are selected or handed over at the works or store. They are perhaps not ideally categorised as export sales because they consist of the mere collection of goods by the buyer who may then deal with them as he wishes. There need not in fact be any export involving carriage by sea.

CHAPTER IV

HIRE PURCHASE AND CREDIT SALES

THE NATURE OF THE AGREEMENT

A hire-purchase agreement is an agreement under which the owner of goods hires them to another person called the hirer, the agreement also providing that the hirer shall have the *option* to buy the goods if and when the number of instalments specified in the agreement have been paid. *There is no obligation on the hirer to pay all the instalments.*

A credit-sale agreement is an agreement under which goods are sold, the property in them passing to the buyer on sale but payment being by instalments.

There is also *a conditional sale agreement* where the goods are sold but the property is to remain in the seller until the last instalment has been paid. *In both these cases there is an obligation on the purchaser to pay the whole of the purchase price by instalments.*

Since the passing of the Factors Act, 1899, hire-purchase agreements have been used rather than conditional sale agreements because of the different effect of Sect. 9 of this Act in the two cases.

This section provides that a buyer who has agreed to buy and is in possession of goods can give a good title to the goods to an innocent purchaser, and this applied even though the seller had tried to retain the ownership as in the case of conditional sale agreements.

On the other hand, the hirer cannot generally give a good title to an innocent purchaser from him either under Sect. 9 of the Factors Act, 1889, or under Sect. 25 (2) of the Sale of Goods Act, 1893, which contains a similar provision. (*Helby* v. *Matthews,* 1895.)[415]

However, the Hire-Purchase Act, 1965, puts both types of agreement on a similar footing. Most of the provisions of the 1965 Act apply to conditional sales, but few apply to credit sales.

Parties. A hire-purchase transaction may have *two* parties, namely the dealer and his customer, and this will be so where the dealer finances the transaction. Very often, however, *three* parties are involved —the dealer, his customer, and a finance company. The goods to be hired are selected by the customer and the dealer then *sells* those goods to a finance company which *hires* the goods to the customer under a hire-purchase agreement. Thus the finance company becomes the *legal owner* of the goods. Finance companies could, of course, lend the money required to the customer, the security of the finance company being a mortgage over the chattels purchased with the loan, and a power in the finance company to sell if the borrower failed to repay the loan. However, this method has not been used in England because the Moneylenders Acts, 1900–27, greatly restrict money lending, and chattel mortgages are governed as to formalities by the Bills of Sale

Act, 1882. In order to avoid these restrictions the *contract of hiring was used.*

Two major drawbacks existed in the common law of hire purchase as established in *Helby* v. *Matthews,* 1895.[415] *In the first place* the owner of the goods could, by putting a special provision in the agreement, take back the goods if the hirer failed to pay an instalment. This was hard on the hirer who had paid, say, ten out of twelve instalments, since this would represent almost the purchase price, and much more than the charge for pure hire. *Secondly,* the owner could, by a clause in the agreement, exclude liability for defects in the goods. These drawbacks, and others which emerged later, have largely been overcome by hire-purchase legislation.

LIABILITY OF THE OWNER AT COMMON LAW

The common law obligations of the owner of goods bailed under a hire-purchase agreement are as follows—

(*a*) he must deliver the goods to the hirer and can be sued for damages for non-delivery if he fails to do so;

(*b*) a condition as to title is implied into the contract and operates on delivery of the goods. (*Karflex* v. *Poole,* [1933] 2 K.B. 251.) Breach of this condition will allow the hirer to recover money paid under the contract on the ground of total failure of consideration, if, e.g. the goods are taken from him by the true owner either during hire or subsequently;

(*c*) a term that the goods shall correspond with their description is implied. This is a condition which, if broken, will bring into operation the doctrine of fundamental breach; (*Astley Industrial Trust Ltd.* v. *Grimley,* [1963] 2 All E.R. 33.)

(*d*) a term that the goods are fit for the purpose or at least as fit as reasonable skill and care can make them is implied. This term is in the nature of a warranty giving a remedy in damages, though a serious breach could give a right to repudiate the contract;

(*e*) a term relating to merchantability is probably implied though there is no direct authority on this matter.

The owner can exclude or modify his liability by means of an exemption clause, though in practice no attempt is made to exclude the condition as to title.

LIABILITY OF THE DEALER AT COMMON LAW

The dealer will usually sell the goods to a finance company and the company will hire them out to the hirer. Thus, the dealer will not be a party to the contract of hiring and no other contract will exist between dealer and hirer. (*Drury* v. *Victor Buckland Ltd.,* [1941] 1 All E.R. 269.) However, where the dealer gives an express warranty regarding the goods he may be liable to the hirer under the doctrine of the collateral contract. (*Andrews* v. *Hopkinson*, 1957.)[389] It was suggested *obiter* by McNair, J. in *Andrews* v. *Hopkinson*, 1957,[389] that it might be possible to *imply* terms as to quality and fitness into the collateral contract.

Because there is no contract between dealer and hirer the provisions of the Misrepresentation Act, 1967, will not apply. However, the decision in *Hedley Byrne & Co. Ltd.* v. *Heller and Partners Ltd.*, 1963,[165] may provide the hirer with a remedy in tort against the dealer where the latter's negligent misstatements regarding the goods cause financial loss to the hirer by reason of their poor quality. Where the goods are not merely of poor quality but are dangerous, as in the case of a car with defective brakes, the dealer may be liable in negligence under *Donoghue* v. *Stevenson*, 1932,[334] if the defect has caused physical injury and could or ought to have been discovered by the exercise of reasonable diligence on his part. (*Andrews* v. *Hopkinson*, 1957.)[389]

OBLIGATIONS OF THE HIRER AT COMMON LAW

At common law the hirer must—

(*a*) take delivery of the goods;

(*b*) take reasonable care of them which in the case of motor vehicles normally involves taking out a comprehensive insurance. If he fails to do so he will be liable in damages if the contract is terminated and the damaged goods are returned to the owner;

(*c*) not convert the goods by dealing with them in a manner which is inconsistent with the title of the owner, e.g. by selling the goods;

(*d*) pay the instalments. The agreement usually provides that if the hirer defaults in payment the owner may repossess the goods. If the owner exercises his option to terminate the contract because instalments are in arrear the hirer will have to pay damages representing the instalments due but unpaid, compensation for unreasonable care of the goods (if appropriate) and the costs incurred by the owner in repossessing the goods.

However, if the hirer repudiates the contract, e.g. by informing the owner that he does not intend to pay further instalments, he will be liable to pay damages representing the difference between the total hire-purchase price (less instalments already paid), and the resale price of the goods, though the hirer would receive a discount because the award of damages results in early payment to the owner.

The above rules apply in the absence of an *express* provision in the contract. In fact hire-purchase agreements invariably contain express provisions relating to forfeiture of payments made and additional minimum payments by the hirer if the contract is terminated either voluntarily by the hirer himself or by the owner seizing the goods for non-payment of the rental. For example, a particular contract may provide—

(*a*) that all payments made up to the termination of the contract are to be forfeited (*a forfeiture clause*); and

(*b*) that the hirer is to bring his total payments up to a certain percentage (generally ranging between 50% and 75%) of the full price if his payments do not reach that figure (*a minimum payments clause*).

Forfeiture of payments can produce an inequitable result as where a contract involving the hire purchase of a car priced at £3,000 is terminated when the hirer has paid £2,500. Even so forfeiture clauses are permissable and no form of relief either in law or equity is available.

A minimum payments clause may, however, be avoided if it is not regarded by the court as a genuine pre-estimate of loss but in the nature of a penalty (see p. 91). Avoidance on this ground applies, however, only to a situation in which the hirer has broken the contract as where he is refusing to make the agreed payments. If the hirer *voluntarily* returns the goods he may be regarded as exercising a right to terminate given by the contract, the "fee" for this "privilege" being the minimum payment provided in the contract. The courts are, however, inclined to regard voluntary termination by the hirer as in effect a breach of contract except where the hirer was obviously fully aware of his rights and appears to have been exercising them. (*Bridge* v. *Campbell Discount & Co. Ltd.*, 1962.)[416]

THE HIRE-PURCHASE ACT, 1965

Scope of the Act. The Hire-Purchase Act, 1938, applied to all hire-purchase and credit-sale agreements where the hire-purchase price or total purchase price of the goods did not exceed £100. The Hire-Purchase Act, 1954, raised the limit to £300 in general, and £1,000 in the case of the purchase of livestock. Sect. 2 of the Hire-Purchase Act, 1965, extends to all hire-purchase and credit sale agreements under which the hire-purchase or total purchase price does not exceed £2,000. The Act does not apply to credit-sale agreements unless the total purchase price exceeds £30. (Hire-Purchase Act, 1965, Sect. 2 (3).) The limit specified in Sect. 2 of the 1965 Act can be raised by Order in Council. (Sect. 3.)

Where a *corporate body* is the hirer or buyer of the goods, the Hire-Purchase Acts do not apply. (Hire-Purchase Act, 1965, Sect. 4.) Thus corporations are left to make their own contractual arrangements when they are buying goods on hire purchase or credit sale, which is an indication that hire purchase legislation is primarily intended to protect the ordinary consumer.

GENERAL REQUIREMENTS

The owner of the goods cannot enforce a hire-purchase or credit-sale agreement, or any guarantee relating thereto, or recover the goods from the hirer, or enforce any security given by the hirer or buyer or guarantor unless the following rules are complied with—

(i) NOTIFICATION OF CASH PRICE. Before the agreement is made the owner must have stated in writing to the prospective hirer, otherwise than in the agreement, the *cash price of the goods*. (Hire-Purchase Act, 1965, Sect. 6 (3).) The subsection is, however, deemed to have been complied with if the hirer has—

(*a*) inspected the goods or like goods on which were price tickets clearly stating the cash price; *or*

(*b*) selected the goods by reference to a catalogue, price list or advertisement, which clearly stated the cash price.

(ii) FORM OF AGREEMENT. The agreement must be *in writing* and signed by the hirer *himself* and *by or on behalf of* all the other parties to the agreement. (Hire Purchase Act, 1965, Sect. 5 (1).) The 1938 Act did not require a wholly written agreement, but merely a note or memorandum in writing evidencing the agreement. A written agreement is now required by the 1965 Act. It seems clear from the wording of Sect. 5 (1) that the hirer cannot sign through an agent. Furthermore the Act is not complied with if the hirer signs blank forms for subsequent completion by the owner or dealer since the object of the legislation is that the hirer should know and understand what he is agreeing to (*per* Devlin, J., in *Eastern Distributors* v. *Goldring*, [1957] 2 Q.B. 600 at p. 612).

(iii) NOTICE. The agreement must contain a statement of the hire-purchase or total purchase price and of the cash price of the goods, the amount of each instalment and the date on which it is payable (Sect. 7 (1) (*a*). The agreement must also contain a list of the goods to which the agreement relates (Sect. 7 (1) (*b*)), and, in the case of a hire-purchase or a conditional sale agreement, a *notice* in the terms prescribed by a Schedule to the 1965 Act informing the buyer of his right to terminate the agreement and also the restrictions on the owner's right to recover the goods. Similar requirements are imposed by the Act on credit sales if the price is in excess of £30. The fact that the agreement contains the cash price does not satisfy Sect. 6 (1) and the cash price must be stated in writing *before* the agreement is *made*.

(iv) STATUTORY COPIES. A copy of the agreement must be delivered to the hirer when he makes the agreement, and Sects. 8 and 9 of the 1965 Act provide as follows—

(*a*) If the agreement was signed at a place other than the trade premises of the owner or seller, two statutory copies must be delivered to the hirer or buyer;

(*b*) he must be given the first statutory copy at once, though if the agreement is sent to him the first statutory copy must be enclosed;

(*c*) a second statutory copy must be sent to the hirer by post within seven days of the transaction (Sect. 9);

(*d*) if the agreement is signed at the trade premises of the owner or seller, it is only necessary for one copy to be given to the hirer or buyer (Sect. 8).

The copies of the agreement must be in accordance with the Department of Trade and Industry's regulations as to legibility. (See p. 177.)

If the court is satisfied in any action brought on a hire-purchase or credit-sale agreement that failure to comply with the matters set out in (i), (iii) and (iv) above has not prejudiced the hirer, it may dispense with the requirements on such terms as it thinks fit and enforce the contract. (Sect. 10.)

The court cannot, however, grant relief under Sect. 10 if there is no duly signed agreement, or if the statutory copy is not sent at all, or is not sent by post, or if either of the copies does not contain a statement regarding the hirer's right of cancellation.

(v) POSITION OF SIGNATURE. Where in a hire-purchase or credit-sale agreement the total purchase price exceeds £30, the Department has power to make regulations as to where the hirer's or buyer's signature shall appear on the agreement, and what words shall accompany the signature in the document. (Hire-Purchase Act, 1965, Sect. 7 (2).) The words used at present are: "This document contains the terms of a hire-purchase agreement. Sign it only if you want to be legally bound by them." This provision is designed to enable the Department to ensure that matters important to the hirer are near to his signature so that he is likely to see and note them, but Sect. 10 (1) provides that an agreement is not invalidated *merely* because it does not comply with any regulation made under Sect. 7 (2).

THE RIGHT OF CANCELLATION

Where a prospective hirer or buyer signs at a place other than "appropriate trade premises" a hire-purchase or credit-sale agreement, or a document in which he *offers* to hire or buy the goods and which would become an agreement if signed by the owner or his agent, then he has certain rights of cancellation. (Sect. 11 (1).)

(1) At any time after he has signed the relevant document and before the end of four days beginning with the day on which he receives the *second* statutory copy of the agreement or document, the prospective hirer or buyer may serve a "notice of cancellation" on the owner or seller, or on any person who is the agent of the owner or seller for the purpose of receiving such notice. (Hire-Purchase Act, 1965, Sect. 11 (2).)

A notice of cancellation shall have effect if, however expressed, it indicates the intentions of the prospective hirer or buyer to withdraw from the transaction.

(2) The effect of service of notice is as follows—

(*a*) If the document signed by the prospective hirer or buyer constituted an agreement, that agreement is rescinded;

(*b*) If the document constituted an offer express or implied to enter into an agreement, that offer is withdrawn. (Sect. 11 (4).)

(3) The "cooling off" period given by the above provisions is designed to prevent high pressure salesmanship carried out on the hirer's doorstep or in his home, and not to affect transactions in shops. Therefore the provisions do not apply where the transaction takes place on "appropriate trade premises." This means premises at which goods of the description to which the document relates, or goods of a similar description, are normally offered or exposed for sale in the course of the business carried on at those premises. (Sect. 58 (1).)

(4) The cancellation provisions apply only to hire-purchase and credit-sale transactions which come within the price limits of the Hire-Purchase Acts.

Information as to Right of Cancellation. Each copy of the agreement delivered or sent to the hirer must contain a *statement* relating to the hirer's or buyer's right of cancellation. The Department of Trade may make regulations regarding the position of the statement, its type size, colour or disposition of lettering, etc. (Hire-Purchase Act, 1965, Sect. 9 (4).) The statement must specify the name of the person to whom, and the address to which, the notice of cancellation may be sent. (Sect. 9 (5).) The court has no power to dispense with the requirements set out in the sub-sects. (4) and (5) above.

Service of Notice of Cancellation. A notice of cancellation shall be deemed to be served on the owner or seller if it is sent by post to a person specified in the statement as being a person to whom such notice may be sent. (Sect. 12 (1) (*a*).) The notice is deemed to be served when it is posted. (Sect. 12 (1) (*b*).) However, the above method is not the only way of serving notice on the owner or seller, and Sect. 12 (2) provides that service in other ways is to be valid, e.g. service in person.

Redelivery and Care of Goods. Where the transaction is cancelled and any of the goods to which it relates are in the possession of the prospective hirer or buyer, he shall not be under any obligation (whether arising by contract or otherwise) to redeliver the goods to the person entitled to them except (*a*) at the hirer's or buyer's own premises; and (*b*) after a request in writing signed by or on behalf of the person entitled. (Sect. 13 (2).)

The prospective hirer or buyer is not obliged to deliver up the goods if he is exercising a lien for money paid under the cancelled agreement, or for goods given in part-exchange. (Hire-Purchase Act, 1965, Sect. 14 (2).)

The prospective hirer or buyer may have difficulty in finding out who the true owner of the goods is. He may have entered into the transaction through a door-to-door salesman who is employed by a dealer, and yet it may well be that the dealer is not the owner of the goods. If on cancellation the hirer or buyer delivered the goods to someone other than the true owner, he might face an action in conversion by the owner if for some reason the goods did not reach him. The prospective hirer or buyer is protected against this sort of action by the provisions of Sect. 13 (3) of the Hire-Purchase Act, 1965.

The prospective hirer or buyer must deliver the goods to "*an authorised person*" either by making them available for collection from his premises or by sending them to an authorised person, or a person designated for the purpose by an authorised person. If he does this the hirer or buyer cannot be sued should the person to whom he delivers the goods not be entitled to them. Sect. 13 (9) states that an "authorised person" is—

(*a*) the person who conducted any antecedent negotiations in pursuance of which the prospective hirer or buyer signed the hire-purchase or credit-sale document; or

(*b*) the owner or seller; or

(*c*) any person specified in either of the statutory copies as the person to whom notice of cancellation may be sent; or

(*d*) the person for the time being entitled to possession of the goods, whoever that may be.

The prospective hirer or buyer is under a *statutory duty* to take reasonable care of the goods until (i) he delivers them to an authorised person; or (ii) a period of 21 days has elapsed beginning with the date of service of the notice of cancellation. If within that time the hirer or buyer has received a request to deliver up the goods which he has refused to comply with, the duty to take reasonable care continues until the goods are delivered.

Where the goods are sent to an authorised person, the hirer or buyer must take reasonable care to see that they are received by that person and are not damaged in transit. (Hire-Purchase Act, 1965, Sect. 13 (5).)

Further Consequences of Cancellation. Where a hire-purchase or credit-sale agreement has actually come into being, the notice of cancellation operates to rescind it. The agreement, and any contract of guarantee relating to it, shall be deemed never to have had effect, and any security given by the hirer or buyer, or by a guarantor, in respect of money payable under the agreement shall be deemed never to have been enforceable. (Hire-Purchase Act, 1965, Sect. 14 (1).)

Regarding sums of money already paid under the agreement or before it was made, Sect. 14 (2) and (3) provides that, on service of notice of cancellation, such sums shall be *recoverable*, and any obligation to pay money shall be deemed *extinguished*, and the hirer or buyer shall have a *lien* on the goods in his possession for any sum repayable under the section.

Where the dealer has taken the prospective hirer's or buyer's goods in *part-exchange*, he must return the goods within a period of ten days beginning with the date of service of the notice of cancellation, and unless they are so returned in a condition substantially as good as when they were delivered to the dealer, the hirer or buyer shall be entitled to recover from the dealer a sum equal to the part-exchange allowance. Once the prospective hirer or buyer has recovered from the dealer a sum equal to the part-exchange allowance, then the title to the goods agreed to be taken in part-exchange vests in the dealer if it had not done so before. The part-exchange allowance is the sum agreed by the parties in the antecedent negotiations or, if no sum was agreed, a reasonable sum. The hirer is also given a lien on goods in his possession for the goods or the part-exchange allowance mentioned above. (Hire-Purchase Act, 1965, Sect. 15.)

RIGHT OF DETERMINATION

The hirer is entitled at any time before the final payment falls due to determine a hire-purchase agreement by giving notice in writing to the person entitled or authorised to receive the sums payable under it. (Sect. 27 (1).) On terminating the agreement the hirer must pay all sums then due under the contract, plus, where necessary, a sum to make up the amount paid under the contract to one-half of the hire-purchase price. (Hire-Purchase Act, 1965, Sect. 28.)

Suppose H hires goods from F, a finance company, the hire-purchase price being £120 and the instalments £10 per month. If H terminates the agreement after paying two instalments and before the third is due, he must pay F £40. If, however, H terminates the agreement after paying 7 instalments and before the eighth is due, he need not pay anything. If the eighth instalment is due and unpaid, he will have to pay that one instalment.

However, Sect. 28 (2) of the 1965 Act provides that if the court is satisfied in any case before it that *a sum less than the amount* by which *one-half of the hire-purchase price* exceeds the total of the sums paid and the sums due in respect of the hire-purchase price would *sufficiently compensate the owner* for his loss, the court may make an order for the payment of that sum in lieu of a sum sufficient to make up half the hire-purchase price.

So, in the above example, the court might decide that F would be sufficiently compensated by a payment of £10 and would make an order requiring H to pay that sum instead of £40. The agreement may also specify a lesser amount.

If the hirer has failed to take reasonable care of the goods he is liable to pay damages to the owner of the goods. (Hire-Purchase Act, 1965, Sect. 28 (3).) On ending the agreement the hirer must give up possession of the goods, and if he does not do so, the owner may recover them, though the court may, if it thinks the circumstances warrant it, give the hirer the option to pay the value of the goods. (Hire-Purchase Act, 1965, Sect. 28 (4).)

SUPPLY OF DOCUMENTS AND INFORMATION

Duty of Owner or Seller. At any time before a final payment has been made under a hire-purchase or credit-sale agreement, the hirer or buyer may by a request in writing, and on payment of 12½p for expenses, require the other party to the contract to supply him with a copy of the agreement. The copy of the agreement must be sent within four days after the receipt of the request, and must be accompanied by a statement, signed by the other party to the contract or his agent, showing—

    (i) The amount paid by or on behalf of the hirer or buyer;

    (ii) The amount which has become due under the agreement but remains unpaid, the date upon which each unpaid instalment became due, and the amount of each such instalment;

    (iii) The amount which is to become payable under the agreement and the date or mode of determining the date upon which each future instalment is to become payable and the amount of each such instalment. (Hire-Purchase Act, 1965, Sect. 21 (1).)

If a copy of the agreement and the statement are not sent, the contract cannot be enforced against the hirer or buyer while the default continues; guarantees and securities are unenforceable and the goods cannot be recovered. If the default continues for *one month*, the defaulter is liable on summary conviction to a fine not exceeding £25. (Hire-Purchase Act, 1965, Sect. 21 (2).)

Duty of Hirer. The hirer must, on receipt of a request in writing from the owner, inform the owner where the goods are at the time when the information is given, or if it is sent by post at the time of posting. (Hire-Purchase Act, 1965, Sect. 24 (1).) If the hirer fails without reasonable cause to give the said information within 14 days of the receipt of the notice, he shall be liable on summary conviction to a fine not exceeding £25. (Hire-Purchase Act, 1965, Sect. 24 (2).)

LEGIBILITY OF DOCUMENTS

Sect. 32 of the Hire-Purchase Act, 1965, provides that the Department of Trade and Industry may make regulations to secure the legibility of documents used in hire-purchase and credit-sale agreements, e.g. as to type, size, colour, and distribution of lettering, quality or colour of paper or otherwise.

DEALER'S LIABILITY

If the dealer gives express undertakings about the goods which are false, the hirer may sue him for damages on a collateral warranty. This is so even though there is no contract between the dealer and the hirer, as where the goods have been sold to a finance company which has made the hiring contract with the hirer. Thus the dealer may be liable to pay damages even though his statement is not fraudulent. (*Brown* v. *Sheen and Richmond Car Sales Ltd.*, 1950.)[417] In addition it was suggested *obiter* by McNair, J., in *Andrews* v. *Hopkinson*, 1957,[389] that it might be possible to *imply* terms as to quality and fitness into the collateral contract. The dealer may also be liable where the hirer suffers *physical* injury as a result of the dealer's negligence, e.g. in preparing a car for sale. (*Herschtal* v. *Stewart and Ardern Ltd.*, 1940.)[418] In some cases the dealer may be liable for breach of warranty and negligence. (*Andrews* v. *Hopkinson*, 1956.)[389]

The provisions of the Misrepresentation Act, 1967, do not apply as between dealer and hirer because although the statements of the dealer may induce the contract of hiring from the finance company, the dealer is not a party to it. However, the decision in *Hedley Byrne & Co. Ltd.* v. *Heller and Partners Ltd.*, 1963,[165] may provide the hirer with a remedy in tort against the dealer where the latter's negligent misstatements regarding the goods cause *financial* loss to the hirer by reason of their poor quality.

Before the 1964 Act, finance companies were not liable for statements made by dealers, the courts having held that the dealer was not the agent of the finance company for the purpose of giving express warranties regarding the goods. Sect. 10 (1) and (3) of the 1964 Act provided that the dealer was to be the agent of the owner or seller in respect of such representations, conditions and warranties, and the finance company can now be sued. Sect. 10 (2) of the 1964 Act preserved the liability of the dealer should the hirer wish to sue him. These provisions are now contained in the Hire Purchase Act, 1965, Sect. 16.

If the dealer conducted the antecedent negotiations, he is also the agent for the purpose of receiving any notice of cancellation served by the prospective hirer or buyer, which either rescinds a complete agreement or withdraws an offer. (Hire-Purchase Act, 1965, Sect. 12 (3).)

TERMS IMPLIED IN HIRE-PURCHASE AGREEMENTS

In every hire-purchase agreement to which the Act applies there shall be—

    (*a*) An implied condition on the part of the owner that he shall have a *right to sell* the goods at the time when the property is to pass (Sect. 17 (1));

    (*b*) An implied warranty that the hirer shall have and enjoy *quiet possession* of the goods (Sect. 17 (1));

    (*c*) An implied warranty that the goods shall be *free from any charge or encumbrance* in favour of any third party at the time when the property is to pass. (Sect. 17 (1).)

It should be noted that this warranty is not restricted to cases of undisclosed encumbrances (cf. Sect. 12 (3) of the Sale of Goods Act, 1893, *ante*, p. 131);

The wording of Sect. 17 (1) para. (*a*) suggests that the Act is complied with if the finance company can pass a good title when the hirer acquires ownership, i.e. at the conclusion of the hiring period. This interpretation would modify *Karflex* v. *Poole,* [1933] 2 K.B. 251 (see p. 169) where it was said, in effect, that the hirer must acquire a good title *on delivery* of the goods otherwise he may recover all the payments made during the hiring period and before he has exercised his option to purchase. However, Sect. 17 (5) of the Act preserves, in effect, conditions and warranties implied under "any other enactment or rule of law" so that *Karflex* would appear to apply notwithstanding the wording of Sect. 17 (1) para. (*a*), so that the hirer must obtain a good title *on delivery.*

(*d*) An implied condition that the goods shall be of *merchantable quality,* but if the buyer has examined the goods or a sample thereof, there is no such condition as regards defects which the examination ought to have revealed. (Sect. 17 (2) and (3).) The condition is excluded only if the sample *has been examined.* The corresponding provision in the Sale of Goods Act (see p. 136) excludes the condition where the sample would (or ought) to have revealed the defect whether there was *examination or not.*

The warranties and conditions set out above are to be implied notwithstanding any agreement to the contrary.

Where the goods are let as second-hand goods and the agreement contains a statement to that effect and also to the effect that the condition as to merchantable quality is excluded, it shall be deemed excluded. However, it must be shown that the above exclusion provision was brought to the notice of the hirer and its effect made clear to him. (Sect. 18.)

Where goods are let subject to defects specified in the agreement, the condition as to merchantable quality may be excluded if the agreement contains a provision excluding it, and if it is proved that before the agreement was made these defects and the provision excluding the condition were brought to the notice of the hirer and the effects made clear. (Sect. 18.)

Where the hirer expressly or by implication makes known to the owner, or to a servant or agent of the owner, or to the person who conducted the antecedent negotiations or his servant or agent, the particular purpose for which the goods are required, there shall be an implied condition that the goods shall be reasonably fit for the purpose. (Sect. 17 (4).) This condition may be excluded by an express provision which was brought to the notice of the hirer and the effect made clear to him. (Sect. 18 (4).)

In addition the proviso to Sect. 14 (1) of the Sale of Goods Act (see p. 134) does not appear in Sect. 17 (4). Thus the owner is liable whether or not the goods were bought under a patent or trade name. Furthermore, the section is worded so as to operate where the dealer conducts the negotiations and is the person to whom the hirer communicated the purpose for which the goods were required.

(*e*) Where goods are let under a hire-purchase agreement and the goods are so *let by reference to a sample,* there shall be an implied condition (i) that the bulk will correspond with the sample in quality; and

(ii) that the hirer will have a reasonable opportunity of comparing the bulk with the sample. (Sect. 19 (1).)

(*f*) Where goods are let under a hire-purchase agreement and are so *let by description*, there is an implied condition that the goods will correspond with the description; and where the goods are let by sample as well as description, the goods must correspond both with the sample and the description. (Sect. 19 (2).)

The provisions set out in (*e*) and (*f*) above may not be excluded or modified. (Sect. 18 (3).)

Exclusion Clauses. It will be noted that the Act allows certain of the implied terms to be excluded by a provision in the contract to that effect, provided the clause and its effect are brought to the notice of the hirer. Where this is not done, the exclusion clause is not effective. (*Lowe* v. *Lombank Ltd.*, 1960.)[419] Even where the clause and its effect are brought to the notice of the hirer, the court may still provide a remedy by invoking the doctrine of *fundamental breach of contract* (*Karsales (Harrow) Ltd.* v. *Wallis*, 1956),[194] though the doctrine does not seem to apply unless the defects are extreme. (*Handley* v. *Marston*, 1962.)[420] This doctrine must now be considered in the light of the *Suisse Case*.[197] and other more recent decisions (see pp. 51–52). It is thought that the older decisions will stand if they are now regarded as decided on the rules of construction of contracts which are based upon the presumed intentions of the parties and not upon independent rules of law.

OWNER'S RIGHT TO RECOVER POSSESSION

By Court Order. Where goods have been let under a hire-purchase agreement, and *one-third* of the hire purchase price has been paid or tendered by or on behalf of the hirer or any guarantor, the owner can only recover the goods from the hirer by bringing an action in the county court. (Hire-Purchase Act, 1965, Sect. 33.)

Before bringing an action for possession the owner must show a previous demand (*Smart Bros.* v. *Pratt*, [1940] 2 K.B. 499) and that a notice of default under Sect. 25 has been served (see p. 181). Under Sect. 58 (2) *a deposit* paid under the agreement to a dealer is regarded as part of the hire purchase price as is a *credit* given by the dealer as where the hirer trades in a car in part-exchange.

If the owner does repossess in the above circumstances without a court order, the hire-purchase agreement is terminated and the hirer is released from all liability and may recover sums paid under the contract or by virtue of any security given by the hirer. Guarantors can also recover money paid to the owner under the contract of guarantee, or under any security given by the guarantor. (Hire-Purchase Act, 1965, Sect. 34 (2).)

If, however, the owner repossesses the goods with the free and informed consent of the hirer there is no breach of Sect. 34. (*Mercantile Credit Co. Ltd.* v. *Cross*, [1965] 1 All E.R. 577.)

The court may under Sect. 35 make a reasonable order regardless of the terms of the contract. Such an order could provide for—

(*a*) immediate delivery of the goods to the owner;

(*b*) delivery of the goods to the owner with a period of postponement to give the hirer a chance to pay the money owed;

(*c*) an apportionment of the goods where possible as between owner and hirer.

By reason of Sect. 41 an owner cannot sue independently for instalments owing once he has commenced an action for possession. Both matters must then be determined in the court's discretion as part of the action for possession.

Without Court Order. Sect. 25 of the Hire-Purchase Act, 1965, provides that if the hirer defaults in the performance of his obligations to pay the instalments or any other sum payable under the agreement, the bailment terminates if a provision that it shall so terminate is contained in the agreement. The owner then has a right to recover the goods without a court order provided *less* than *one-third* of the hire purchase price has been paid or tendered by or on behalf of the hirer.

However, before the contract is deemed terminated, a notice of default must be served on the hirer telling him how much he owes and giving him at least seven days to pay. The contract terminates at the end of the seven days or such longer time as may be specified in the notice. During the time elapsing between service of the notice and the expiration of the precribed period the goods are not deemed in the possession of the hirer with the consent of the owner, or to be in the hirer's possession, order or disposition for the purposes of distress or reputed ownership in bankruptcy.

A notice of default must not be misleading as it will be if it refers merely to the non-payment of one or two instalments as constituting a repudiation of the contract, does not state the consequences of default and the provision of the agreement which is relied upon to enforce possession, and does not specify the time within which the amount owing must be paid. (*Eshun* v. *Moorgate Mercantile Co.* [1971], 2 All E.R. 402.)

In conclusion it should be noted that any repossession of the goods without the express or implied consent of the hirer will be regarded as an enforcement of the owner's right to recover possession, the lawfulness of which will be governed by the provisions described above. Thus the owner is regarded as exercising his right to repossess if the goods are taken not from the hirer himself but from a third party to whom they have been delivered for repair (*F. C. Finance Ltd.* v. *Francis* (1970), 114 S.J. 568), though the owner is entitled to repossess goods without the consent of the hirer if the hirer has abandoned them. (*Bentinck Ltd.* v. *Cromwell Engineering Co.*, [1971] 1 Q.B. 324.)

7

GUARANTEES AND INDEMNITIES

A guarantee or indemnity relating to a hire-purchase or credit-sale agreement to which the Act applies, and any security given by the guarantor, shall not be enforceable unless within seven days of the making of the agreement there is delivered or sent to the guarantor: (i) a copy of the agreement; and (ii) a copy of a note or memorandum of the contract of guarantee which was signed by the guarantor or a person authorised to sign for him. (Hire-Purchase Act, 1965, Sect. 22.) The court may dispense with the above requirements if it feels that failure to comply with them has not prejudiced the guarantor.

While the agreement is in force the person entitled to enforce the guarantee must within four days of receiving a request in writing from the guarantor along with $12\frac{1}{2}$p for expenses, supply the guarantor with the documents specified below—

(i) A copy of the hire-purchase or credit-sale agreement;

(ii) A copy of the note or memorandum of the contract of guarantee;

(iii) A signed statement showing the amount paid under the contract; the amount unpaid and when the payments became due; the amount which will become payable under the agreement and when each instalment falls due, together with the amount of each instalment. (Hire-Purchase Act, 1964, Sect. 20 (3) and (4).)

If the above requirements are not complied with, then, while the default continues, the guarantee is unenforceable and so also are securities given by the guarantor. If the default continues for a period of one month, the defaulter shall be liable on summary conviction to a fine not exceeding £25. (Sect. 23.) The same provisions apply in the case of an indemnity. (Sect. 58 (1).)

EXECUTION, DISTRESS AND BANKRUPTCY

It should be noted that the owner of goods may lose his property to the creditors of the hirer as a result of execution, distress or bankruptcy. A hire purchase agreement will usually provide for termination on the happening of these events but such a provision is not always effective to enable the owner to retain his rights of ownership over the goods. These matters are dealt with as appropriate in other chapters, particularly Chapter IX which is concerned with bankruptcy.

CONDITIONAL SALE AGREEMENTS

A conditional sale agreement is one in which the purchase price is to be paid by instalments and the property remains in the seller though the buyer has possession. (Hire-Purchase Act, 1965, Sect. 1.) Sect. 4 provides that the Hire-Purchase Act, 1965, shall apply almost entirely to such agreements if the total purchase price does not exceed £2,000, except where a corporate body is the buyer of the goods.

However, there are two cases in which the 1965 Act does not apply—

(*a*) a buyer under a conditional sale agreement cannot terminate the contract under Sect. 27 if the property in the goods has passed to him, and he has transferred it to a third party, who has purchased the goods outright (Sect. 27 (2));

(*b*) where the seller sues to recover goods on which one-third of the price has been paid or tendered (protected goods), and the court postpones recovery, the buyer is deemed to be in possession of the goods on the terms of the agreement, but any term giving him ownership before he has paid the total purchase price is of no effect. (Sect. 45 (3).)

The Sale of Goods Act, 1893, applies to conditional sales with three exceptions—

(*a*) the conditions and warranties implied by the Sale of Goods Act are excluded (Sect. 20 (3)) and the buyer takes the largely non-excludable terms set out in Sects. 17–19 of the 1965 Act;

(*b*) Sect. 11 (1) (*c*) of the Sale of Goods Act, as amended by the Misrepresentation Act, 1967, does not apply: whether a breach of condition must be treated as a warranty depends upon the provisions of the 1965 Act regarding hire-purchase agreements (Sect. 20 (1) and 20 (2));

(*c*) Sect. 25 (2) of the Sale of Goods Act and the similar provision in Sect. 9 of the Factors Act do not apply (Sect. 54), the buyer is not regarded as a person who has agreed to buy and this is fair because he can terminate the agreement.

CREDIT SALES

A credit sale is an agreement for the sale of goods under which the purchase price is payable by five or more instalments, not being a conditional-sale agreement. (Sect. 1.) In such a sale the property must pass at once to the buyer. The 1965 Act applies some of its provisions to credit-sale agreements under which the total purchase price exceeds £30 but does not exceed £2,000 except where a corporate body is the buyer of the goods. These are as follows—

(*a*) the formality provisions (Sects. 5–10);

(*b*) Sects. 11–15 (Cancellation);

(*c*) Sect. 22 (provisions regarding guarantees).

Two provisions only apply where the total purchase price does not exceed £30—

(*d*) Sects. 21 and 23 (rights of buyer and guarantor to receive information and additional copies);

(*e*) Sects. 16, 29 (3) and 31 (provisions relating to agency).

The whole of the Sale of Goods Act, 1893, applies to credit sales.

MOTOR VEHICLES ON HIRE-PURCHASE OR
CONDITIONAL SALE

Formerly, if the hirer of a motor vehicle sold the vehicle whilst it was bailed to him under a hire-purchase or conditional sale agreement, the purchaser did not get a good title and the true owner of the vehicle, usually a finance company, could recover the vehicle from the purchaser or sue him in conversion. This was so even though the hirer had all the indicia of title including the registration book. Part III of the Hire-Purchase Act, 1964, which has not been affected by the consolidating Act of 1965, is designed to protect *bona fide* purchasers for value of motor vehicles where the seller is a mere bailee under a hire-purchase or conditional sale agreement and where he disposes of the vehicle before the property is vested in him. The Act does not apply unless the vehicle has been let under a hire purchase agreement or there is an agreement to sell under a conditional sale agreement. Thus if as in *Central Newbury Car Auctions Ltd.* v. *Unity Finance Ltd.*, [1957] 1 Q.B. 371, a dealer allows a fraudulent person to take possession of a vehicle after he has signed hire purchase forms which are then rejected by the finance company, a purchaser from the fraudulent person will not be protected because the vehicle is not let under a hire purchase agreement.

(*a*) *Private Purchasers.* A private purchaser means a purchaser who at the time of the disposition is not a motor vehicle dealer or a person engaged in financing motor vehicle deals. (Sect. 29 (2).)

Where the disposition is to a *private purchaser* who takes the vehicle in good faith and without notice of the hire-purchase or conditional sale agreement, that disposition shall have effect as if the title of the owner or seller of the vehicle had been vested in the hirer or buyer *immediately before that disposition.* (Sect. 27 (2).) (*Barker* v. *Bell*, 1971.)[421] Thus a private purchaser gets a good title and the owner or seller must pursue his remedies against the hirer or buyer.

(*b*) *Trade or Finance Purchasers.* Where the disposition is made to a *trade or finance purchaser*, i.e. a person who deals in motor vehicles or finances such transactions, then the trade or finance purchaser does not get a good title.

However, if a private purchaser buys the vehicle from the trade or finance purchaser, either by paying cash for it or as a result of paying up all the instalments under a hire-purchase or conditional sale agreement, then the trade or finance purchaser is deemed to have had a good title in order that the private purchaser shall obtain one. (Sect. 27 (3) and (4).)

(*c*) *Factors.* The provisions of Sect. 27 are to have effect in spite of the provisions of Sect. 21 of the Sale of Goods Act, 1893 (which relates to the sale of goods by a person who is not the owner). However, the provisions of Sect. 27 operate without prejudice to the provisions of the Factors Acts or of any other Act enabling the apparent owner of goods to dispose of them as if he were the true owner. Thus a person may still claim a title because the person from whom he bought the goods was a factor.

However, the provisions of the 1964 Act are wider than those of Sect. 9 of the Factors Act in that they protect a purchaser even though the goods have not been *delivered* to him. Under the Factors Act delivery is an essential part of the protection of title.

(*d*) *Liabilities after Unlawful Disposal.* The liability of the hirer who has unlawfully disposed of the vehicle is not affected by Sect. 27. Thus he may still be guilty of theft at criminal law and liable in *conversion* at civil law. The liability of any trade or finance purchaser to whom the hirer disposes of the vehicle is also unchanged, and such a purchaser could be sued in *conversion*. The first private purchaser is not liable in conversion, and subsequent purchasers from him are not liable even though they may be trade or finance purchasers. (Sect. 27 (6).)

(*e*) *Presumptions.* In order to assist a purchaser to establish his title in any action, Sect. 28 of the 1964 Act provides that certain presumptions shall be made which will apply unless evidence is brought to the contrary.

(i) If the purchaser who seeks to establish his title can show that the vehicle he has acquired was let to someone under a hire-purchase or conditional sale agreement, and that a private purchaser acquired the vehicle in good faith and without notice of the letting agreement, it is presumed that the *hirer or buyer* made the original disposition and that Sect. 27 applies to perfect the present purchaser's title.

(ii) If it is proved that the hirer or buyer did not in fact make the disposition, but that a purchaser from him did so, then it is presumed that the said purchaser was a private purchaser in good faith and without notice, so that the present purchaser's title is again perfected under Sect. 27.

(iii) If it is proved that the purchaser from the hirer or buyer was not a private purchaser but a trade or finance purchaser, then it is presumed that the purchaser from the trade or finance purchasers was a private purchaser in good faith and without notice, and that the present purchaser's title is again perfected under Sect. 27.

A *disposition* for the purposes of Sect. 27 includes any sale or contract of sale, including a conditional sale agreement, any letting under a hire-purchase agreement, or the transfer of the property to the hirer on payment of agreed instalments. (Sect. 29 (1).)

ADVERTISEMENTS

The Advertisements (Hire-Purchase) Act, 1957, as amended and extended by the unrepealed parts of the Hire-Purchase Act, 1964, ensures that when goods are advertised for sale on hire-purchase or credit-sale, the advertisement shall contain the information required by the Act.

Advertisements to which the Act applies. The Act applies to advertisements which include one or more of the following elements—

(i) An indication that a deposit of some kind is payable;

(ii) Words indicating that no deposit is payable;

(iii) An indication of the amount of any instalments payable;

(iv) A fraction represented as being the rate of interest, or a rate of charge to be borne by the hirer or buyer in hiring or purchasing goods in accordance with the advertisement;

(v) A sum stated as the hire-purchase price or total purchase price of the goods. (Advertisements (Hire-Purchase) Act, 1957, Sect. 1 (1) and (2) as amended by the 1964 Act, Sect. 30.)

Information to be Included. An advertisement to which the Act applies shall not be displayed or issued unless it includes the following information clearly displayed—

(1) WHERE AN ADVERTISEMENT CONTAINS DETAILS OF PAYMENTS in respect of goods, the advertisement must state—

Regarding the Deposit—

(a) The amount of the deposit directly expressed; or

(b) A statement that the amount of the deposit is a fraction, specified in the advertisement, of a sum the amount of which is directly expressed therein; or

(c) A statement that no deposit is payable.

Regarding the Instalments—

(d) The amount of each instalment directly expressed;

(e) The total number of instalments payable;

(f) The length of the period in respect of which each instalment is payable;

(g) If any instalments are payable before delivery of the goods, the number of instalments so payable.

The advertisement must also state the cash price of the goods, and the hire-purchase or total price of the goods.

(2) WHERE AN ADVERTISEMENT DOES NOT CONTAIN DETAILS OF PAYMENTS, the information required is—

(a) *With regard to the deposit* either—

(i) A statement that the amount of the deposit is a fraction specified in the advertisement of a price or sum the nature of which is clearly indicated in the advertisement; or

(ii) A statement that no deposit is payable;

(b) *With regard to the instalments—*

(iii) The total number of instalments payable;

(iv) The length of the period in respect of which each instalment is payable;

(v) If any instalments are payable before delivery of the goods, the number of instalments so payable.

It is not necessary to give the amount of each instalment, the cash price of the goods, or the hire-purchase or total purchase price. (Advertisements (Hire-Purchase) Act, 1957, Sect. 2 as amended by the 1964 Act, Sect. 31.)

The Hire-Purchase Act, 1964, in Sect. 32 also requires that the advertisements to which the 1957 Act applies must give information as to the *rate of interest* being charged.

Penalties. Any person who displays or issues an advertisement in contravention of the provisions of the 1957 Act as amended is guilty of an offence punishable on summary conviction by a fine, not exceeding £50 for a first offence, and not exceeding £100 for subsequent offences.

THE CROWTHER REPORT

The Report of the Crowther Committee on Consumer Credit was published in March, 1971 (Cmnd 4596). The proposals and recommendations contained in the Report would, if implemented by the Government, have considerable effect upon the structure, law and control of consumer and business credit. Certain aspects of the Report are also concerned with the law of sale. The Committee acknowledges the considerable influence on its recommendations of the American Uniform Commercial Code which has also had a bearing on the legal aspects of consumer credit in Canada, Australia and New Zealand.

Existing Law. The Committee recommends the repeal of all existing legislation relating to credit in favour of a complete new code of credit law. The new law would be based upon the recognition that the giving of credit in a sale or hire purchase transaction is in fact a loan and that reservation of title by the owner until the instalments are paid is in fact a chattel mortgage securing the loan.

The Proposed Lending and Security Act. This Act would cover the loan and security aspects of all credit transactions except house mortgages. In particular the provisions of the Sale of Goods Act, 1893, relating to the rights of an unpaid seller would be repealed and new remedies provided for default in payment and in respect of the security interest in the goods.

RIGHTS AND DUTIES OF THE PARTIES TO A CREDIT TRANSACTION.

(*a*) The lender would not be able, in any circumstances, to recover from the debtor more than the amount of the loan plus interest and charges, so that there could be no arrangements similar to those outlined on page 171 in connection with *minimum payment clauses*.

(*b*) the debtor would be free to complete repayment of the loan before the due date except where the creditor had stipulated a time before which full repayment could not be made.

(*c*) As regards the security position the parties would be regarded as mortgagee and mortgagor, the debtor being the beneficial owner of the property forming the security, subject to the creditor's security interest.

(*d*) The debtor would have an absolute right to dispose of the property subject only to the right of the creditor to be paid off.

(*e*) If the debtor failed to pay, the creditor would be allowed to sell the security and could take possession without a court order after giving the debtor thirty days' notice of his intention to foreclose. On sale of the security the creditor would be required to hand over any surplus money to the debtor. Where the creditor did not sell the security in a reasonably commercial manner so that the money he received was less than it should be, the debtor would not be liable to make up the balance, if any, required to pay off the loan, and could recover from the creditor the surplus which he would have received if the creditor had obtained a proper price.

THIRD PARTIES.

(*a*) In order to enable the secured creditor to protect his interest in the security and also to give third parties notice of the existence of that interest, the Report recommends the abolition of present forms of registration, e.g. those relating to bills of sale (see p. 112) in favour of a computerised filing system under which one simple document called a *financing statement* would be filed. The main security agreement would not be filed. Minor errors in the financing statement would not affect its validity, though where a statement was filed later than 21 days after the execution of the main security agreement, the security would be void as against a trustee in bankruptcy or liquidator of the debtor provided the bankruptcy or liquidation took place within three months of the actual date of filing.

(*b*) The filing of a financing statement would protect the interest of the creditor for five years from filing, the statement being then removed from the file and destroyed unless a renewal notice had been filed. The financing statement would also be removed from the file if the debtor filed a *termination statement* obtainable from the creditor once there was no obligation outstanding in respect of the security.

(*c*) Securities on transactions other than motor vehicle deals would be excluded from the system of filing where the sum secured did not exceed £300. The filing system would, however, apply to securities given by companies over their personal property though these would also require registration under the Companies Act, 1948 (see p. 272).

In summary, the recommendations set out above would, if enacted, allow all forms of personal property to be used as security for a loan without the difficulties which now face non-corporate borrowers in terms, for example, of the Bills of Sale Acts (which would be repealed).

The Proposed Consumer Sale and Loan Act. The purpose of this Act would be to give legal protection to consumers who have entered into credit transactions relating to straightforward loans, sales of goods on credit, and rental agreements. For this purpose a *consumer loan* is defined as any loan (which includes any form of credit) other than a loan which—

(*a*) exceeds £2,000; or
(*b*) is made by a corporate body; or

(*c*) is made at an effective annual rate not exceeding $2\frac{1}{2}\%$ over bank rate; or

(*d*) is not a loan made in connection with a *financed consumer sale* (see below).

A "financed consumer sale" would be covered by the Act if—

(*a*) the whole or part of the price of the goods or services purchased was advanced by the seller or a connected lender, e.g. a finance company; and

(*b*) the sum advanced did not exceed £2,000 and was repayable by three or more instalments; and

(*c*) the buyer is not a corporate body.

Rental agreements would be covered except where the total sum payable exceeded £2,000 or the agreement was for a period not exceeding three months with no provision for renewal, or the hirer was a corporate body.

ADVERTISING. All persons providing credit to the consumer are made subject to certain restrictions on advertising, though these are less inhibiting than the existing provisions of the Moneylenders' Acts. In general terms advertisements relating to the provision of consumer credit must not be false or misleading and the Act is likely to follow the lines of the Advertisements (Hire Purchase) Act, 1957 (see p. 185). Doorstep canvassing of loans is prohibited but postal canvassing is permitted.

DISCLOSURE. In large measure the Crowther Committee adopts the provisions of the Hire Purchase Act, 1965, in regard to the form and content of loan agreements and copies thereof (see p. 172) though there are additional requirements designed to show the precise cost of the credit. These recommendations would not apply to an unsecured *connected loan* not exceeding £30. A connected loan is one made by a lender in the course of a regular business transaction with one or more sellers, the loan being used to buy goods or services from one such seller. This would apply, for example, to check traders.

INTEREST CHARGED. No maximum limit is imposed, though the current provision of the Moneylenders' Acts that a rate in excess of 48% is harsh and unconscionable would continue to operate. The licensing system and the Credit Commissioner (see below) would be the means of controlling the persistent charging of excessive interest.

CONDITIONS AND WARRANTIES. The Committee recommends that the provisions of the Hire Purchase Act, 1965, in connection with implied conditions and warranties should apply to all consumer credit sales. They would, however, regard these as in the nature of warranties so that neither party to a consumer credit sale agreement would be able to reject the goods unless the other party had a reasonable opportunity to remedy the breach (provided this is possible) after being notified of it in writing.

Connected lenders (see above) would be liable along with the seller for misrepresentation or defects in title, fitness or quality of the goods, though an indemnity against the seller would be given to a connected lender if he had to pay damages to the consumer.

Clauses in consumer sale agreements seeking to exclude the rights of the borrower or increase his liability would be invalid and the use of negotiable instruments as a means of payment would be prohibited. A person taking such an instrument *with notice* that it had been used in a consumer credit sale transaction would not be a holder in due course (see p. 291). However, an instrument, e.g. a cheque, which was not negotiable could be used.

RIGHT OF CANCELLATION. The Committee recommends that a right of cancellation where the agreement is signed other than on appropriate trade premises should continue and be extended to all "off-trade premises" transactions where the amount of the loan is not less than £30.

The existing rules relating to termination of an agreement under the Hire Purchase Act, 1965, including the limitation of the hirer's liability of 50% of the purchase price in the event of termination, would disappear from the law. The owner's right to repossess and sell or dispose of the goods would, however, remain substantially as at present.

CONTRACTS FOR SERVICES. The Committee recommends that the Consumer Sale and Loan Act should give the same protection to persons entering into contract *to buy services*, e.g. installation of double-glazing, as is given to persons buying goods. Contracts for *the hire of services*, e.g. education, would be treated in the same way as would agreements for goods, though insurance services would be excluded.

ADMINISTRATION OF THE LAW. The law will be administered by the Consumer Credit Commissioner who would control the system of licensing and the register of security interests. He would also make detailed regulations and amendments to regulations under the Consumer Sale and Loan Act to ensure that the law was complied with. In addition he would be required to inform and educate the public on matters of consumer credit and act as an ombudsman in regard to complaints.

Licensing. Every person carrying on the business of granting consumer credit would require a licence from the Commissioner and door-to-door salesmen and canvassers would require an additional and special licence. Licences would be renewable every three years, the Commissioner having power to refuse renewal or suspend or revoke a licence subject to a right to appeal to an Appeal Tribunal. There are no exemptions for banks so that a bank would require a licence where it carried on the business of making loans within the Act, e.g. personal loans which may be made at more than $2\frac{1}{2}\%$ over bank rate.

CHAPTER V

AGENCY

AGENCY is a relationship existing between two parties, called principal and agent, the function of the agent being to create a contractual relationship between the principal and third parties.

There is a similarity between agents and servants. An agent is, generally speaking, a person who is employed or appointed to make contracts, whereas many servants are not agents because they do not make contracts for their employers. Nevertheless one person may occupy both roles, e.g. an usherette in a theatre is a servant when she is showing patrons to their seats, but becomes an agent when she sells them programmes. Moreover an agent may be a servant or an independent contractor, i.e. an agent may be employed or self-employed. Thus an estate agent, engaged to sell a house, is both an agent and an independent contractor.

CAPACITY

The ordinary rules of contract apply to the contract of agency. It follows that—

(i) The third party must have capacity to contract in order that the contract which the agent makes with him on behalf of the principal may be enforceable.

(ii) The agent must have capacity to contract if his contract with the principal is to be enforceable; otherwise agent and principal may not be able to enforce the rights and duties arising under the contract of agency.

(iii) However, a person does not require contractual capacity merely to *act* as an agent, and a minor may so act. So also may a bankrupt unless his insolvency makes him unfit for the position of agent. Thus a company director who is a bankrupt cannot continue to act as such without the permission of the court which adjudicated him bankrupt. The appointment of an insane person as agent would be invalid, and if an agent becomes insane, the appointment will be terminated. Nevertheless, if the agent lacks capacity, this will affect an action for breach of warranty of authority.

(iv) The principal must have capacity in order that the contracts made between principal and third party and principal and agent shall be enforceable. *A minor or person of unsound mind* is bound by a contract made on his behalf by his authorised agent where the circumstances are such that he would be bound if he had made the contract himself. In *Shephard* v. *Cartwright*, [1953] 2 All E.R. 608 at p. 618 Denning, L.J., as he then was, said " . . . the appointment by an infant of an agent . . . has always been void." This view was not absolutely in line with earlier cases and in *G.* v. *G.*, [1970] 3 W.L.R. 132, Lord Denning, M.R., retracted the statement and held that a minor could appoint an agent to pay maintenance to support his illegitimate child, the payment being lawful and something he could be compelled to do.

Thus it is too sweeping to say that a minor can never appoint an agent. The Infants' Relief Act, 1874, will invalidate contracts made on behalf of a minor unless they are for his benefit or for necessaries, but it does not follow from this that a minor cannot appoint an agent. It may simply be that, if the minor does appoint an agent who makes a contract which is not for the minor's benefit or for necessaries, the agent has merely exceeded his authority and that is why the minor is not bound.

CREATION OF AGENCY

The agent may bind his principal in contract by virtue of *actual* authority, or *apparent* authority, or because of *necessity*. The agent may also bind his principal where there is *subsequent* authority (i.e. where the principal *ratifies* the acts of the agent). We propose to deal separately with the *agency of the wife*.

1. Actual Authority. This may arise as follows—

(i) ACTUAL AUTHORITY BY EXPRESS AGREEMENT. The agent is entitled to exercise the powers actually given to him under the contract of agency and will bind the principal by the exercise of those powers. No particular form of agreement is required, though the following special cases are worth noting—

(*a*) Where the agent is to contract under seal he must be appointed by deed, i.e. a power of attorney. Thus an agent appointed to grant leases of more than three years must be appointed under seal. It should be noted, however, that an agent not appointed by power of attorney can validly execute a deed if he does so in the presence and by the authority of his principal.

(*b*) Under Sect. 181 (1) of the Companies Act, 1948, an agent who signs the prospectus of a company on behalf of a person named therein as a director, must be appointed in writing.

(*c*) An agent who is appointed orally may bind his principal by a written contract or a contract which requires a memorandum in writing, e.g. an agreement concerning land.

(ii) ACTUAL AUTHORITY BY IMPLICATION. While the court may be prepared to imply an authority not *expressly* contained in the contract of agency, it is, in general, reluctant to imply powers where the contract of agency is under seal. Where the contract is not sealed, there is greater latitude and the court may more easily construe a discretion. (*Comber* v. *Anderson*, 1808;[422] *Australia and New Zealand Bank* v. *Ateliers de Constructions Electriques de Charleroi*, 1966.)[423]

(iii) ACTUAL AUTHORITY DERIVED FROM USUAL OR CUSTOMARY AUTHORITY. Where the agent is one of a class of agents, e.g. an auctioneer, estate agent, factor, solicitor, or partner, his actual authority may be extended to cover the powers which an agent of his class normally possesses. Thus in *Panorama Developments (Guildford)* v. *Fidelis Furnishing Fabrics*, [1971] 3 All E.R. 16, the Court of Appeal held that a modern company secretary was not a mere clerk and must be regarded as having authority to sign contracts connected with the administrative side of the company's affairs. Unless the third party knows that the usual powers have been withdrawn, the agent will bind the principal so long as the contract is one which an agent of the class has *usual* authority to make, even though the agent has exceeded his express authority. (*Watteau* v. *Fenwick*, 1893.)[424]

Where the agent has actual authority the third party will obtain a contract with the principal; the agent will be able to enforce the contract of agency against the principal and recover his remuneration or claim indemnity for any losses incurred, and the principal cannot sue the agent for breach of the contract of agency and the third party cannot sue the agent for breach of warranty of authority, *except in the case of usual authority.*

Where the principal has expressly withdrawn the usual powers of the agent, as in *Watteau* v. *Fenwick*, 1893,[424] the third party obtains a contract with the principal by virtue of the *usual authority* of the agent, but the principal can sue the agent for breach of the contract of agency, and the agent cannot claim either remuneration or indemnity.

2. Apparent Authority. This arises where the principal holds out a person as his agent for the purpose of making a contract with a third party, and the third party relies on that fact. The third party will obtain a contract with the principal, but the principal can sue the agent for damages and the agent cannot recover remuneration or indemnity if he had in fact no authority. Such apparent authority often arises from the course of dealing between the parties. (*Dodsley* v. *Varley*, 1840;[425] *Povey* v. *Taylor*, 1966.)[426]

3. Agency of Necessity. An agent of necessity is a person who, in an emergency, acquires, by operation of law, presumed authority to act as an agent. The topic may be considered under the following headings—

(*a*) Ships' Masters. A ship's master may mortgage the ship or the cargo in order to pay for repairs necessary to successfully complete the voyage. Where the ship's master mortgages the ship, he is an agent of necessity for the ship owner and, in the case of cargo, for the cargo owner. If the cargo is perishable, the ship's master can presumably sell it if it is going bad.

The authority of the ship's master is said to depend upon inability to communicate with the owner, and, if this is a basic requirement, then modern systems of communication make the situation less likely to occur today.

(*b*) Salvors. A person who aids a ship in distress at sea and saves life or property may claim a reward which is generally at the discretion of the court.

(*c*) ACCEPTANCE OF A BILL OF EXCHANGE FOR THE HONOUR OF THE DRAWER. Where the drawee of a bill dishonours it by non-acceptance, a person not already liable on the bill may, with the holder's consent, accept the bill for the honour of the drawer. If the person so accepting has to pay on his acceptance, he becomes entitled to the rights of the holder to sue the drawer on the bill. (Bills of Exchange Act, 1882, Sects. 65–68.)

(*d*) CARRIERS AND OTHER BAILEES. Carriers and other bailees may do acts intended to preserve the things in their custody. (*Great Northern Railway* v. *Swaffild*, 1874.)[427] However, they cannot sell the things entrusted to them without facing an action for conversion unless there is (i) *some emergency*, e.g. where the goods are perishing; or where the agent's premises are destroyed and the goods are exposed to weather or thieves; *and* (ii) *it is impossible to communicate with the owner in time to save the goods.* (*Springer* v. *Great Western Railway*, 1921.)[428]

The doctrine of agency of necessity is rarely applied where the goods are not perishable (*Prager* v. *Blatspiel Stamp and Heacock Ltd.*, 1924),[429] or where the goods are sold merely because they are an inconvenience to the bailee. (*Sachs* v. *Miklos*, 1948.)[430] This is a harsh rule for bailees who are left with goods and are unable to find the owner, although as we have seen, where the bailees are repairers of the goods, the Disposal of Uncollected Goods Act, 1952 (see p. 105), provides a power of sale in appropriate circumstances. In the case of other bailees, it may be possible to obtain an order for sale from the court. (*Larner* v. *Fawcett*, 1950.)[352]

It is doubtful whether the cases in which carriers and other bailees have been able to sell or dispose of the goods in their care are really true examples of agency of necessity, and it is perhaps better to regard their powers of disposition as an example of an implied term in the pre-existing contract of carriage or bailment.

Where a complete stranger deals with the goods of another, agency of necessity does not arise. (*Binstead* v. *Buck*, 1777[431] and *Nicholson* v. *Chapman*, 1793.)[432] This rule seems to be based upon the fact that liabilities are not to be forced upon persons behind their backs.

4. Subsequent Authority or Ratification. Where an agent makes an unauthorised contract on behalf of his principal, though purporting to act for him, the principal may afterwards ratify or adopt the contract.

The principal may, alternatively, make an *implied* ratification by his conduct. For example, if the agent makes an unauthorised contract to buy goods, and his principal receives the goods and fails to return them or uses them, he has ratified by implication of law. No formal ratification is required. Again where an agent makes a contract for the supply of goods to be delivered in the future, then, if the principal delays unduly in repudiating it after he has notice that the agent has made it, he will be regarded as having ratified by his acquiescence.

The following rules govern whether ratification can take place.

(i) *The agent must contract expressly as an agent for a principal*, who must be named or so described as to make it possible for the third party to identify him. (*Keighley, Maxsted v. Durant*, 1901.)[433]

(ii) *The principal must be in existence when the agent makes the contract.* Thus a prospective agent cannot enter into a contract on behalf of a company before incorporation, and the company cannot ratify the contract after its incorporation. In such a case the prospective agent is considered to have contracted as a principal, and is liable to the other party *on the contract*, and not merely for *breach of warranty of authority*; and this is so even though the prospective agent contracted expressly as an agent. (*Kelner v. Baxter*, 1866.)[434] However, where the prospective agent signs the company's name on the pre-incorporation contract, adding his own as a mere authorisation, the contract is a nullity. (*Newborne v. Sensolid (Great Britain) Ltd.*, 1954.)[435]

(iii) *A void contract cannot be ratified.* Thus a company cannot ratify *ultra vires* contracts made by its agents on its behalf. (*Ashbury Railway Carriage Co. v. Riche*, 1875.)[120] A *voidable* contract can be ratified but the principal becomes liable for the fraud or misrepresentation of the agent. For example, if an agent, acting without authority, sells P's house and represents that the drains are in good order when they are not, and P later ratifies the contract, P becomes liable along with the agent for *fraud*, if the agent knew that the drains were not in good order. If the agent's statement is made innocently, the third party can rescind the contract with P.

(iv) *A forgery cannot be ratified.* If X forges Y's signature on a document, Y cannot ratify the signature so as to make the document good. However, if the person whose signature is forged knows of the forgery and acts in such a way as to induce a third party to believe that the signature is genuine, he will be estopped from denying that it is his signature in any action between him and the third party who has acted upon it. (*Greenwood v. Martins Bank Ltd.*, 1933.)[436]

(v) *Ratification must be based on full knowledge of the material facts.* If the agent tells his principal: "I have sold your house for £6,000," when he has only sold for £5,000, the principal can cancel the ratification.

(vi) *Ratification must be of the whole contract.* The court will not allow ratification of the beneficial parts only To do so would be to impose on the third party a contract he did not make.

(vii) *Ratification can only be retrospective.* A principal cannot say to his agent in advance, "I will ratify all your future contracts."

(viii) *Where ratification of a contract is validly effected, it is retrospective in its operation*, i.e. the parties are put in the position they would have occupied if the professed agent had, when the contract was made, the authority he purported to possess. (*Bolton Partners v. Lambert*, 1889.)[437]

The rule of retrospective ratification is subject to certain exceptions—

(a) The rule does not apply to insurance other than marine insurance. (*Grover and Grover v. Mathews*, 1910.)[438]

(*b*) The rule does not apply where it would cause excessive hardship to the third party. (*Walter* v. *James*, 1871.)[439]

(*c*) Negotiations between the agent and the third party must have produced a contractual relationship. (*Watson* v. *Davies*, 1931,[440] and *Warehousing and Forwarding Co. of East Africa* v. *Jafferali & Sons*, 1963.)[441]

(*d*) Ratification must be within a reasonable time, and before the time fixed for performance has expired.

Where the contract between the agent and the third party has been made under seal, the ratification must be under seal. Otherwise ratification may be made informally even where the contract between the agent and the third party is in writing or requires a memorandum in writing.

The principal must have capacity both when he ratifies and when the agent made the unauthorised contract, e.g. he must not be a minor or a person of unsound mind at either time. So if the principal was insane when his agent made the contract, he cannot ratify it when he regains his sanity. The Infants' Relief Act, 1874, Sect. 2, provides that, if an agent makes a contract for a minor, then the minor cannot ratify it after reaching his majority, unless the contract was for necessaries or beneficial services, or was a voidable contract, e.g. a contract to take shares in a company.

THE AGENCY OF A WIFE

The subject may be considered under the following headings.

Real Authority. This arises where the husband actually authorises his wife to buy the goods needed by the family.

Apparent Authority. This arises where, for example, a husband pays the debts his wife incurs with tradesmen. Having established in the mind of the tradesmen the fact that the wife has authority to pledge his credit, the husband must continue to pay the debts his wife incurs until he has informed each tradesman with whom she has had dealings that she has no further authority. The real and apparent authority of the wife in the above circumstances have no necessary connection with her marital status, and could just as well arise in the case of a mistress, housekeeper, or servant.

Agency of Necessity. Sect. 41 of the Matrimonial Proceedings and Property Act, 1970, *abolishes* the concept of a wife's agency of necessity but has no effect on the ordinary law of agency. Thus if a wife acts on the real or apparent authority of her husband she will still be his agent as she would be even if she were a stranger. A wife cannot, however, pledge her husband's credit for necessary goods either during co-habitation or while deserted and the section should remove the need for advertisements by husbands renouncing liability. These were in any case of dubious legal effect.

It is worth noting that there is no agency of necessity in a child to pledge its father's credit; there must be some evidence of assent by the father.

THE DUTIES OF AN AGENT

1. As a general rule the agent must perform his duties in person. The maxim is *delegatus non potest delegare.* (A delegate cannot delegate.) The rule arises out of the personal trust and confidence which must be reposed in an agent by his principal. The principal may, of course, give his agent authority to delegate, or may ratify the agent's act of delegation either expressly or by his conduct, and the maxim does not rule out the employment of clerks and assistants, i.e. persons who carry out mere ministerial acts. Clearly anyone can type letters for an agent so long as he dictates them.

Delegation is allowed in certain cases—

(*a*) Where delegation of authority is authorised by custom. It is the practice of country solicitors to employ town agents in the matter of litigation.

(*b*) Delegation by implication may arise from the circumstances. Where the agent is a company, the company must obviously act through agents, and where the agent is a partnership, each partner may bind the firm.

(*c*) Delegation may be permitted in a sudden emergency, as where the agent is ill.

(*d*) Delegation may be permitted, even though it has not been expressly authorised, where the work of the agency is such that it does not require the discretion or particular skill of the agent.

Where delegation is authorised expressly or by implication, or where the agent's conduct in delegating is known to the principal and is acquiesced in, or where the delegation is in the nature of a mere ministerial act, the principal is liable to the third party.

The legal relationship of the principal and the sub-agent depends upon whether there is privity of contract between them.

(i) Where the sub-agent completely replaces the agent, there is privity of contract between the principal and the sub-agent. (*De Bussche* v. *Alt*, 1878.)[442]

(ii) Where the sub-agent merely assists in the carrying out of the agency, but does not entirely replace the agent, there is no privity of contract between the principal and the sub-agent, and only the agent can be sued by the principal in respect of the sub-agent's breaches of agreement. However, the sub-agent is under a fiduciary duty to the principal to disclose secret profits, and probably also for negligence resulting in loss or damage to the principal's goods while in the sub-agent's possession. This liability arises from the law of bailment and is based upon cases concerning the liability of sub-bailees. (*Learoyd Bros.* v. *Pope*, 1966.)[348] In a proper case of delegation where the agent exercises care in selecting the sub-agent, the agent is not liable to the principal for the sub-agent's fraud.

2. The agent must carry out his work with ordinary skill and diligence. Both gratuitous agents and paid agents are responsible to the principal for the negligent performance of their duties. A gratuitous agency arises where the agent renders the principal some friendly service for which there is no payment. In such cases there is no question of the principal suing the agent for breach of an agency contract because, without consideration, there is no contract to enforce. Nevertheless the fiduciary duties of principal and agent exist, so that a gratuitous agent must not make secret profits, and must act throughout with the same good faith as a paid one. A gratuitous agent will be held liable for negligent acts in the course of his work, but not for neglecting to act at all, i.e. for *misfeasance* but *not* for *nonfeasance*. Where he damages the principal's goods by negligent handling of them, he will be liable. Where he agrees to sell the principal's house for him without reward and makes no attempt to sell it, thus losing a favourable market, he will not be liable. *A paid agent will be liable* in both cases, i.e. *for either misfeasance or nonfeasance.*

3. The agent has a fiduciary duty towards his principal. The agent must acquaint his principal immediately with everything relating to the agency, and must obtain the best possible price on sale. The fiduciary duty which the agent owes to his principal is a high one. (*Keppel* v. *Wheeler*, 1927.)[443]

The agent must not use his position for his personal benefit to the detriment of his principal, and he must not become a principal as against his employer. In other words there must be no conflict of interest between principal and agent. Therefore unless full disclosure exists between them, the agent cannot buy the principal's property, and it is immaterial that the contract is in all respects fair (*McPherson* v. *Watt*, 1877),[444] nor may he act for the two principals in the same transaction unless both agree. (*Anglo-African Merchants Ltd.* v. *Bayley*, 1969.)[445] The fiduciary duty may continue to rest on an ex-agent (*Reiger* v. *Campbell-Stuart*, 1939)[446] though only where the agency is confidential in its subject matter or concerned with trade secrets. However, as a general rule the continued duty to observe the principal's interest can only be achieved by a contract in restraint of trade which is not against public policy or excessively wide.

4. The agent must keep proper accounts of all transactions connected with the agency and render them to the principal on request. This duty is very useful where the agent is a general agent carrying out a series of transactions for the principal, and enables the principal to see what profits have been made, what charges the agent has incurred, and whether the expenditure is legitimate. An agent must pay over to his principal all money received on the principal's behalf. This applies even though the transaction under which the money was received was void or illegal. Thus if an agent is employed to make bets he must pay over any winnings he received as a result. (*De Mattos* v. *Benjamin* (1894), 63 L.J.Q.B. 248.)

5. The agent must hand over all profits resulting directly or indirectly from the agency.

6. The agent is under a duty to obey the lawful instructions of his principal. In the absence of instructions, and where matters are left to his discretion, the agent must act in good faith and to the best of his judgment for the benefit of the principal. If he does not do so, he is liable to his principal for loss incurred. Where he has specific instructions he must follow them (*Bertram, Armstrong & Co.* v. *Godfrey,* 1830),[447] unless they are unlawful. (*Bexwell* v. *Christie,* 1776.)[448]

7. The agent has a duty to keep the principal's property separate. The agent must keep his principal's property and money separate from his own. If he fails to do so, everything which he cannot prove to be his own will be presumed to belong to the principal, and there is a presumption that everything in a mixed account is the principal's, the onus of proving otherwise being on the agent. The principal has a common law right to follow his property into the hands of others so long as the property can be identified, e.g. where the proceeds of its sale are ascertainable in a specific fund. Where the proceeds have been used to buy another chattel, that chattel can be claimed in lieu. If the property or fund cannot be identified as the principal's, the equitable remedy *in rem* of a *charging order* is available against the property or fund, and persons claiming on the fund or property do so in the ratio in which they originally contributed to it.

For example, suppose that the agent has mixed his principal's property with that of two other persons X and Y. Let us suppose that the mixed fund stands at £8,000 and P's property was worth £5,000, X's property was worth £2,500 and Y's was worth £2,500. P will claim half the fund, i.e. £4,000, X and Y will each claim a quarter, or £2,000 each.

8. Secret Profits and Bribes. If the agent takes any secret profit or bribe the principal has all the following rights—

(*a*) To dismiss the agent without notice; and

(*b*) To refuse the agent his remuneration or commission, or to recover it if paid (*Andrews* v. *Ramsay & Co.,* 1903);[449]

(*c*) To recover the bribe—

    (i) From the agent if he has received it (*Andrews* v. *Ramsay & Co.,* 1903);[449] or

    (ii) From the third party if it has not been paid but only promised; and

(*d*) To sue the third party for damages. These are awarded without deduction of the amount of any bribe recovered by the principal. (*Salford Corporation* v. *Lever,* 1891.)[450]

(*e*) The principal may repudiate the contract with the third party whether or not the secret payment had any effect on the agent. (*Shipway* v. *Broadwood,* 1889.)[451]

(*f*) The principal may prosecute the agent and the third party under the Prevention of Corruption Act, 1906, with the consent of the Attorney-General or Solicitor-General. (See also the Public Bodies

Corrupt Practices Act, 1889, which operates where the agency occurs in a public service situation, e.g. local government.)

The rules relating to secret profits and bribes apply even to an agent who is not receiving payment. (*Turnbull* v. *Garden*, 1869.)[452]

It should be noted that an agent may keep a profit if the principal knows of it and consents to the arrangement. If the secret profit was obtained without a fraud being practised on the principal the agent will retain his rights under the agency but cannot keep the profit. (*Hippisley* v. *Knee*, 1905.)[453]

9. An agent is estopped from denying his principal's title to money or goods on the ground that he or others have superior rights. If there are competing demands for property in the agent's possession, the agent must not deliver it to a third party who may be claiming for example that the principal has sold him the goods. This would constitute a denial of the principal's title. What the agent may do is to institute interpleader proceedings whereby the principal and the third party are brought into an action together to decide who has the right to the property. The agent can then hand over the property to the person entitled and will not be liable in conversion.

An agent may deny the principal's title to *property* where—

(*a*) at the time of taking possession the agent had no knowledge of other claims; and

(*b*) the agent is defending the third party's title with the latter's authority against the principal.

Thus if P (a landlord) takes T's (a tenant's) goods for non-payment of rent and gives them to A his agent to sell, then if in fact T had paid his rent so that P's taking of the goods was unlawful, A could refuse to sell them and defend T's title against P. (*Biddle* v. *Bond* (1865), 6 B. & S. 225.) A could not take this action if he was aware of the unlawful taking when he received the goods for he is then virtually a party to the illegality himself and cannot stand aside from it. T could sue P for unlawful distraint.

As regards the receipt of *money* unlawfully obtained, the agent is not accountable to the third party unless he is involved in the wrongful act. Thus if P (a trustee) wrongfully takes trust money and gives it to A (his agent) to buy goods, then T (a beneficiary) cannot sue A unless A was involved in and had knowledge of the unlawful act of P. T could sue P for breach of trust. (*Carl-Zeiss Stiftung* v. *Herbert Smith & Co.* (No. 2), [1969] 2 All E.R. 367.)

RIGHTS OF THE AGENT AGAINST HIS PRINCIPAL

1. The Agent's Lien. This is a special right under which the agent may retain the principal's goods which are in the agent's lawful possession where the principal has not satisfied his liabilities to the agent. The power is to retain in the hope of a settlement; there is not in general a power to sell.

Lien may be of two kinds—

(*a*) A GENERAL LIEN. Under a general lien the agent may retain goods of the principal even though the principal does not owe the agent money in respect of those goods, but in respect of other goods the agent has dealt with. Such a lien may be possessed by a general agent, i.e. an agent who carries out a series of transactions for the principal. However, the law does not favour general liens, and such a lien will only arise—

(i) By express agreement of the principal and agent; or
(ii) By judicially recognised custom, e.g. a customary general lien is possessed by solicitors, bankers and factors.

(*b*) A PARTICULAR LIEN. Under such a lien the agent is only entitled to retain a particular article until the principal pays him what he owes in respect of it. Such a lien arises where the agent is a particular agent, i.e. one who is appointed to carry out a single transaction for the principal. A particular lien is favoured by the law and a lien, where it exists, is likely to be particular rather than general.

2. The Agent's Right to Remuneration. The remuneration is generally specified in the agreement and may take the form of salary or commission or both. If no remuneration is specified, the court will imply a reasonable remuneration where the relationship is a commercial one and payment is usual. If the agent wishes to sue for remuneration under the contract, then it must comply with the general law of contract. Thus it must not be illegal, as where the agent is employed to make bets or wagers. (See also *Crouch and Lees* v. *Haridas*, 1971.)[454] The agent loses his right to remuneration if he is in breach of a fiduciary duty or acts without authority. The agent must also substantially perform his part of the contract before he is entitled to remuneration. (*Rimmer* v. *Knowles*, 1874.)[455]

Where the agent buys or sells goods on behalf of the principal he can generally ensure that a contract binding on the principal is made. The main difficulties with regard to remuneration have arisen in connection with commission agents, e.g. estate agents. Such an agent, being paid by commission, is not really paid for the work he does, but for the contracts he procures. If he does not procure a contract, he does not seem to be entitled to any payment, unless he has made some provision regarding this in his agreement with the principal. Such agents have less control over the making of the contract than other agents. Estate agents merely introduce a possible purchaser to the principal and hope that a contract will be made between them.

The agent's right to commission can be considered under the following headings—

(*a*) WHERE THE TRANSACTION GOES THROUGH, i.e. where the third party and the principal actually make a contract. To obtain his commission the agent must show that the sale really and substantially proceeded from his acts. (*Coles* v. *Enoch*, 1939[456] and *Rolfe & Co.* v. *George*, 1968.)[456a]

(*b*) WHERE THE TRANSACTION DOES NOT GO THROUGH. Here the rule seems to be that the agent gets all or nothing according to whether the principal and the third party make a contract or not. The courts are not anxious to imply terms into the contract of agency in order to secure the agent's commission. (*Luxor (Eastbourne) Ltd.* v. *Cooper*, 1941.)[457]

In this case the House of Lords held that it was not possible to imply a term into the agency contract compelling the vendor to sell when once a purchaser had been introduced who was willing and able to go through with the deal. The difficulty was that the agency contract provided expressly that the commission was to be payable "on completion." After this decision it was obvious that some alternative formula would be required and this has not proved easy to find.

Estate agents tried to make commission payable on "introducing a purchaser." This failed because it was construed by the courts as a "willing purchaser," and a purchaser is not "willing" if he accepts "subject to contract." (*Christie, Owen and Davies Ltd.* v. *Stockton*, 1953.)[458]

It is also worth noting that a potential purchaser can generally recover any deposit paid if he does not continue with a "subject to contract" purchase. (*Chillingworth* v. *Esche*, 1923.)[15] Where a deposit has been paid to an estate agent it has been held that he receives it as agent of the vendor, unless there is an agreement to the contrary, and the vendor remains liable for returning the deposit even though he never had the money. (*Goding* v. *Frazer*, 1966[16] and *Burt* v. *Cousins & Co.*, 1971.)[16a] However, Lord Denning, M.R., in *Barrington* v. *Lee*, 1971,[16b] took the view that in the absence of agreement to the contrary an estate agent should be regarded as receiving the deposit in the capacity of a "stakeholder" and not on behalf of the purchaser. Thus the vendor who had not received the deposit would not be liable to repay it on default of the agent.

The agent can find some answer to his dilemma by providing in his contract that he is appointed sole agent, and that he has the sole and exclusive right to sell. This protects him against sales by other agents and the owner. He may further provide that commission is payable when the prospective purchaser signs the agent's purchaser's agreement and the vendor signs the agent's vendor's agreement. In such a case it seems that commission is payable whether the sale takes place or not, depending as it does merely on the signing of the two agreements. (*Drewery & Drewery* v. *Ware Lane*, 1960.)[459]

There is no right of action on a *quantum meruit* in these cases for the nature of the contract is such that the agent gets the whole commission or nothing.

Where the agent misleads the purchaser so that the contract is voidable, commission will not be payable, since its payment depends upon the agent introducing a purchaser "ready, willing and able" to enter into a *binding* contract, and a voidable contract is not binding. (*Peter Long and Partners* v. *Burns*, 1956[460] and *Blake & Co.* v. *Sohn*, 1969.)[460a] However, *Scheggia* v. *Gradwell*, 1963[461] suggests that the third party need not be able to purchase so long as he is willing to sign the contract, though in *Wilkinson* v. *Brown*, 1966,[462] it was said that the scope of this decision should not be extended and that normally the third party must be able to *complete* the purchase if he wishes to do so.

3. Agent's Right to an Indemnity. The agent may in the course of his duty incur liabilities or make payments of money for the principal, and he has a right to be indemnified against such liabilities and to recover any money paid. (*Christoforides* v. *Terry*, 1924.)[463] He can enforce this right by action, by exercise of lien, or, if he is sued by the principal, by set-off.

The agent has no right to an indemnity if he acts without or against authority, nor can he recover if, although obeying instructions, he commits a breach of a fiduciary duty or does not use skill and care. (*Davison* v. *Fernandes*, 1889.)[464]

TERMINATION OF AGENCY

The contract between the agent and the principal may be terminated in many ways—

(i) By MUTUAL AGREEMENT on terms acceptable to both parties;

(ii) By CUSTOM (*Dickinson* v. *Lilwal*, 1815);[465]

(iii) By COMPLETE PERFORMANCE of the contract, i.e. the completion of the business for which the agency was created. Thus an agent who is employed to sell a house determines his agency on selling it.

(iv) By EXPIRATION OF TIME, where the agency is entered into for a definite period;

(v) By FRUSTRATION, which may arise—

(*a*) By impossibility of performance, as where the subject matter of the agency is destroyed. Thus, if an agent is employed to sell a house, the agency terminates if the house is destroyed by fire.

(*b*) By illegality, as where the agency involves dealings with enemy aliens. (*Stevenson & Sons Ltd.* v. *A. G. für Cartonnagen Industrie*, 1917.)[466]

(vi) By THE DEATH OF EITHER PARTY. Obviously the death of the agent will terminate the contract, since it is one of personal service. The agent's personal representatives could not be required to carry on the agency and the agent, being dead, cannot execute it. Similarly the agent's authority is terminated by the death of the principal, and this is so whether the agent or third party knows of the principal's death or not. Where the agent purports to contract on behalf of his principal after the principal's death, there is no contract with the principal's estate, and the agent can be sued for breach of warranty of authority. However, it should be noted that Brett, L.J., in *Drew* v. *Nunn*, 1879,[467] considered that, on the death of the principal, his estate would be liable to third parties who dealt with the agent in ignorance of the principal's death.

(vii) By Insanity. When the principal has become insane the agency itself is automatically terminated; and the same is true where the agent becomes insane, so long as the insanity is such as to render the principal or agent incapable of making a contract for himself. (*Yonge* v. *Toynbee*, 1910.)[468] However, where the principal is insane it seems that, if the agent purports to contract with persons who are ignorant of the fact of the principal's insanity and to whom the principal, when sane, had held out the agent as having authority, the principal cannot deny to those persons the continuation of the agent's authority. Thus it seems that, although actual authority is lost, apparent authority continues. (*Drew* v. *Nunn*, 1879.)[467]

The cases cited above are difficult to reconcile. The goods in *Drew* v. *Nunn*[467] may have been necessaries but the report does not say, and the court did not make its decision on that ground. If the liability of the principal is based on the ground of holding out the agent to the third party as having authority, the principal can only prevent liability from arising by giving notice to the third party, and, since the principal is insane, it seems somewhat unjust to expect him to do this. On the other hand *Drew* v. *Nunn*[467] may be an aspect of the agency of necessity of a wife, and may have more to do with family law as it then was than with the law of agency as such. However, it can be said that the question whether the third party must have notice or not of the death or insanity of the principal is not finally settled.

(viii) By Bankruptcy. The principal's bankruptcy terminates the authority of the agent but the agent's bankruptcy does not of itself give the principal the right to dismiss him unless the insolvency affects the agent's fitness to act.

(ix) Revocation of the Agent's Authority by the Principal. The principal may terminate the agent's real or actual authority at any time. No special formalities are required and even an appointment by deed is revocable by parol notice. However, this may not terminate the contract of employment and the agent will have an action for damages for wrongful dismissal if the principal does not give him the period of notice specified in the contract, or, if none is specified, such notice as is customary and reasonable. Nevertheless the agent's apparent authority continues until third parties with whom he has had dealings are notified of the agent's lack of authority.

Sometimes the continuation of apparent authority causes no difficulty, e.g. managers of shops or clerks, when they are dismissed, normally disappear from the shop or office. The more difficult case is the agent who is an independent contractor, such as a broker, who may well continue to act as a broker even though a particular principal has terminated his authority. If the agent does contract on behalf of the principal in circumstances where he has apparent authority but after his actual authority is terminated, the principal will be bound by the contract but will have an action against his agent.

(x) By Renunciation. The agent may renounce his authority and thus terminate the agency, but again the contract of employment cannot be arbitrarily broken. The agent must give his principal the specified, or customary or reasonable notice, and, if he does not do so, the principal may sue the agent for breach of contract. The agent's apparent authority continues until third parties with whom he has had dealings are on notice of the agent's renunciation and, if the agent does make a contract on behalf of his principal after renouncing his authority, the principal will be bound to the third party, but will have an action against the former agent.

LIMITATIONS ON PRINCIPAL'S POWER TO TERMINATE THE AGENCY

The power of the principal to terminate the agent's authority is limited in certain circumstances.

(i) The principal cannot revoke the agent's authority *where the agent has carried out, or is in process of carrying out, his instructions*. Similarly the principal cannot terminate the agent's authority after a third party has started to act in reliance on the contract negotiated with the agent. (*Chappell* v. *Bray*, 1860.)[469]

(ii) The principal cannot revoke *where the agency is coupled with an interest*. The interest of the agent must be more than a mere right to salary or commission and must amount to a form of security, as where P gives his creditor a power of attorney to collect P's debts and pay himself out of the proceeds, or where X gives Y a power to sell certain land and discharge his debt to Y out of the purchase money. Such an agency is not terminated by revocation, death or other incapacity of principal or agent.

(iii) *Irrevocable powers of attorney*. The Powers of Attorney Act, 1971, provides for a type of irrevocable agency. For example, under the Act a power of attorney which states that it is irrevocable and is given as a security for a proprietory interest of the person to whom it is given (the donee) or anyone deriving title to it from him, is not capable of being revoked so long as the interest remains unsatisfied—

(*a*) by the person giving it (the donor)—unless the donee consents; or

(*b*) by the death, unsoundness of mind, or bankruptcy of the donor including, where the donor is a corporation, winding-up or dissolution.

Thus if P owes A £1,000 and gives A a power of attorney expressed to be irrevocable so that A can collect rents from properties owned by P for a period sufficient to enable A to recoup the debt, the power of attorney will be irrevocable as outlined above until A has paid himself from the rents.

Powers of attorney which are not given as security may be revoked at any time by the donor and will be revoked automatically by his death, unsoundness of mind, or bankruptcy.

However, the donee and persons dealing with him after the power
has been revoked and whether given for security or not, will be protected as follows—

    (*a*) where the donee acts under the power at a time when it has
been revoked he will not be liable to the donor or any other party
if at the material time the donee was unaware of the revocation. A
donee for security will normally only be in that position when his
interest has been satisfied, since he should know that this has
happened;

    (*b*) where a power has been revoked and a person not knowing
of the revocation deals with the donee, the transaction will be as
valid as if the power had still been in being, though the donee may be
liable to the donor if the donee knows of the revocation.

The Act abolishes the need to file copies of powers of attorney in
the Central Office of the Supreme Court and at the Land Registry
where appropriate. Copies filed before the Act may still be inspected.
In this connection it was always difficult to see what real purpose
filing served as the fact of a power being on file was not evidence that
it was in force.

A power of attorney need not be by deed except where the agent is to
contract by deed as in the case of land deals but there must be an instrument in writing properly signed and witnessed as in the case of a will.

RIGHTS OF THIRD PARTIES AGAINST PRINCIPAL AND AGENT

Once there is a contract between the principal and the third party the
agent normally drops out of the transaction and is no longer liable on it.

Liability of Agent to Third Parties. In exceptional cases the
agent retains liability independently of or concurrently with the
principal.

    (i) BILLS OF EXCHANGE. The general rule is that an agent is liable
on a bill of exchange if he signs it without making it clear that he is
signing on behalf of a named principal. The rule may be modified
where the agent signs as acceptor, since a bill cannot be accepted by
anyone other than the person on whom it is drawn, and an agent's
signature is more likely to be considered as made in a representative
capacity when the drawee is his principal who alone can accept the
bill. (Bills of Exchange Act, 1882, Sect. 26 (2).)

    (ii) CONTRACTS UNDER SEAL. Where the agent enters into a deed
on behalf of the principal, it is the agent who must sue and be sued.
Thus where a chartered accountant entered into an agreement under
seal as liquidator of a company it was held that because the agreement
was in the form of a deed the defendant was personally liable on it.
(*Plant Engineers (Sales)* v. *Davies* (1969), 113 S.J. 484.)

    (iii) CUSTOM. The agent may retain liability by virtue of custom
and an example of this can be seen in *Davison* v. *Fernandes*, 1889.[464]

(iv) THIRD PARTY INSISTENCE. There may be cases where the third party has insisted that the agent also accepts liability before he will make the contract. If the agent has agreed to do this, he will be liable along with the principal. In other cases the agent may have agreed to be the principal's guarantor.

(v) FOREIGN PRINCIPALS. A foreign principal is one who does not reside in England and Wales and does not carry on business there. There was a presumption of law in earlier times that the agent was liable, the rule being based on the jurisdictional problems involved in suing the principal. This presumption of law no longer applies and it seems that the agent's liability is a matter of the intentions of the parties in each case.

The problem of suing foreign principals is to some extent solved by the use of *confirmatory agents* who act as sureties. A *confirmatory agent* takes the order from the foreign buyer and guarantees to the seller that the order will be accepted and paid for.

Another course open to an English seller is to require the foreign buyer to open an *irrevocable credit* with an English bank, the bank becoming liable to pay the seller when he tenders the shipping documents to it. However, since the seller and the bank are not in direct contractual relationship, problems of privity of contract may arise, (but see p. 22) and in any case banks are not usually prepared to accept liability for the buyer's non-acceptance or cancellation.

(vi) UNDISCLOSED PRINCIPAL. Suppose an agent contracts with a third party on behalf of his principal but does not inform the third party that he is an agent and appears to be himself a principal, then *the doctrine of the undisclosed principal* applies. The rights and liabilities of the parties are as follows—

(1) The third party can, at his election, sue either the principal or the agent.

(2) Election must be made within a reasonable time, otherwise only the agent can be sued.

(3) Having made his election, the third party cannot return to the other party and sue him.

(4) The undisclosed principal can sue the third party on the contract, subject to certain qualifications which will be discussed later. This includes an undisclosed foreign principal who can sue and be sued on a contract except where the contract limits rights of action to the English agent and excludes the foreign principal. (*Teheran-Europe Co.* v. *S. T. Belton (Tractors)*, [1968] 2 All E.R. 886.)

(5) Since the agent is the contracting party, he too can sue.

(6) If the undisclosed principal intervenes and brings an action against the third party, then the agent cannot sue, or must discontinue any action he has begun.

(7) The doctrine does not apply where the agent has expressly described himself as a principal.

If the third party sues the agent, this is not an irrevocable election unless he knows of the existence and identity of the principal. *It is an election* to prove or petition in the bankruptcy of the agent or the principal, but not merely to ask one or the other for payment. The question of election is one of fact and the institution of proceedings against either agent or principal does not amount, as a matter of law, to a binding election so as to bar proceedings against the other. In order to constitute an election the decision to initiate proceedings must have been taken with full knowledge of all the relevant facts and must be an unequivocal act (*Clarkson Booker Ltd.* v. *Andjel*, 1964).[470] However, if the third party elects to sue and actually obtains judgment against the agent or principal, he cannot sue the other even if the judgment is unsatisfied. If the third party has a claim against the agent before he discovers the existence of the principal, the principal's right to sue is subject to the third party's right to set off the debt due from the agent.

There are certain limitations on the right of the principal to intervene.

(*a*) The principal cannot ratify unless the authority of the agent to act for him existed at the time the contract was made.

(*b*) Since the undisclosed principal is not identified, he can never ratify the *unauthorised* acts of his agent. (*Keighley Maxsted* v. *Durant*, 1901.)[435]

(*c*) If the personality of the agent is a matter of importance to the third party, the undisclosed principal is not allowed to intervene. (*Said* v. *Butt*, 1920.)[471] As Lord Denman said in *Humble* v. *Hunter*, (1848) 12 Q.B. 310: "You have a right to the benefit you contemplate from the character, credit and substance of the party with whom you contract."

Thus a promise by the third party to lend money to the agent cannot be enforced by a principal who was unknown, and contracts of personal service cannot be performed by an undisclosed principal. A landlord has an obvious interest in the substance and reputation of his tenant, and if a lease is granted to an agent, the undisclosed principal cannot normally intervene.

(*d*) Where there is actual misrepresentation by the agent, the undisclosed principal will not be able to intervene. If the third party says to the agent, "Are you selling for a principal?" and the agent replies that he is not, the contract with the agent can be rescinded and the undisclosed principal cannot intervene.

(vii) WHERE THE AGENT PURPORTS TO CONTRACT FOR A PRINCIPAL WHO HAS NOT YET COME INTO EXISTENCE. In the case of a company prior to incorporation, the "agent" or promoter is not merely liable for breach of warranty of authority, but is personally liable on the contract unless the company, when incorporated, enters into a new contract, called a *novation*, with the third party. The company cannot ratify the acts of its "agent" expressly or by conduct after its formation. (*Kelner* v. *Baxter*, 1866.)[434]

(viii) PRINCIPAL'S LACK OF CAPACITY. Where company directors make a contract with a third party which is *ultra vires* the company, the contract will be void and the company cannot ratify it even if all the members agree to do so. (*Ashbury Railway Carriage Co.* v. *Riche*, 1875.)[120] The directors may be liable in damages to the third party for breach of warranty of authority, though much depends upon whether the company is formed by special statute or registered under the Companies Acts.

If the company's powers are contained in a special Act of Parliament, a misrepresentation as to their extent is probably a matter of law and the third party cannot claim to have been misled. (Ignorance of the law is no excuse.)

Where the company is a registered company, misrepresentation of the contents of the objects clause is a matter of fact and unless the doctrine of constructive notice of the contents of the clause binds a third party, he may be able to sue the directors.

(ix) AGENT'S LACK OF AUTHORITY. Where an agent exceeds his authority he is liable to the third party for breach of warranty of authority—

(a) if the third party does not know of the lack of authority; and
(b) if the third party suffers loss as a result of this lack.

The agent's liability is strict and does not depend upon his fraud or misrepresentation. (*Starkey* v. *Bank of England*, 1903.)[472] Thus, where the agent enters into a contract and acts in all respects *bona fide*, without notice that his authority has been terminated (e.g. by the death or insanity of his principal or the dissolution of the company he represents), he will nevertheless be liable for impliedly warranting that his authority still exists. (*Yonge* v. *Toynbee*, 1910.)[468]

The action seems to be based on *quasi-contract*, for the agent is not liable on the contract as such and cannot be required to carry it out. However, the *measure of damages* awarded against the agent will include compensation for the loss of the bargain with the principal, and damages will be awarded in the same way as if the third party had been suing the principal for breach of contract.

Liability of the Principal for the Agent's Warranties. Where the principal is a dealer, his agent will generally be able to give warranties as to the quality of the principal's goods even though he is not authorised to do so. Where the principal is not a dealer in the goods in question, the agent is unlikely to be able to give warranties because he is probably a *particular agent relying on a specific authority*. (*Brady* v. *Todd*, 1861.)[473] Much also depends upon the type of agent appointed, i.e. whether or not he is the sort of agent who can give warranties, e.g. a factor.

However, an estate agent has no implied or ostensible authority to give a warranty that premises can be used for any particular purpose. (*Hill* v. *Harris*, 1965.)[474]

Liability of the Principal for the Agent's Frauds and Misrepresentations. In general a principal is liable only for the fraud of his agent where the agent has committed the fraud in order to sell the principal's property. For example, if the agent, in selling the principal's house, states that the drains are sound when he knows they are not, principal and agent will be liable as joint tortfeasors.

Where, however, the agent's fraud is not committed in order to sell the principal's property, but in order that the agent may gain an advantage for himself, the principal will only be liable if the act which forms the basis of the fraud is within the agent's apparent authority. (*Lloyd* v. *Grace Smith & Co.*, 1912.)[475]

Where the agent makes an innocent misrepresentation in the course of selling the principal's property, the contract with the principal can be rescinded by the third party. A more difficult situation arises where the agent makes a representation which he believes to be true but which the principal knows to be false. Suppose the principal knows that the drains of a house are faulty but has not told his agent and the agent, who is selling it, states that the drains are sound, believing this to be true. It might be thought that, in this sort of situation, the untrue statement of the agent could be added to the knowledge of the principal so as to make the principal liable in deceit. But in *Armstrong* v. *Strain*, 1952,[476] the Court of Appeal rejected this idea and, as the law now stands, the principal will not be liable in deceit unless it can be established that he kept his agent in ignorance of the truth in the *expectation* and *hope* that he would make some false statement as to the quality of the article he was employed to sell. It is uncertain what effect *Hedley Byrne* v. *Heller*, 1963,[165] might have on this situation. If the agent could be regarded as having made negligent misstatements because he might be regarded as under a duty to check their validity, he could be liable in negligence and his principal could be liable vicariously in the absence of an effective exemption clause. P. could also be liable vicariously for A's negligent statements under the Misrepresentation Act, 1967.

Authority of the Agent to Receive Payment. Suppose that the third party pays money to the agent and the agent has no authority to collect it, must the third party pay again? It seems that, unless the agent has written authority allowing him to receive payment on the principal's behalf, the third party will get a good discharge only if the agent has apparent authority to receive payment, as where the agent is a cashier in a bank or a salesman in a shop or a rent collector. It should be noted that authority to sell is not necessarily an authority to receive payment.

Notice to Agent. It is a matter of importance as to how far notice given to the agent operates as notice to the principal. The general rule is that notice to the agent is imputed to the principal in all matters which the agent is employed to carry out. If the agent is buying property for the principal and discovers an incumbrance, e.g. a mortgage, but does not inform the principal, the principal cannot refuse to complete the transaction as the agent's knowledge is imputed to him. Notice will not be imputed where the agent acts contrary to the principal's interests and the third party knows this. (*Wells* v. *Smith,* 1914.)[477]

It is important that the agent received the notice while acting for the principal, and the principal is not generally affected by matters coming to the agent's notice in other agencies and employments. This applies more particularly to confidential relationships, e.g. solicitor and client, but in commercial situations it seems that the principal may sometimes be affected by the knowledge of the agent gained in another capacity. (*Dresser* v. *Norwood,* 1864.)[478]

PARTICULAR AGENTS

The Factor. The Factors Act, 1889, using the term *mercantile agent* for what is commonly known as a *factor,* defines him as follows: "A mercantile agent having in the customary course of his business as such agent authority either to sell goods, or to consign goods for the purpose of sale, or to buy goods, or to raise money on the security of goods." (Sect. 1 (1).)

The following points arise from this definition—

(i) MERCANTILE AGENT. An agent is a factor if, and only if, it is in the customary course of his business as such agent—

    (*a*) to sell goods; or
    (*b*) to consign goods for sale; or
    (*c*) to buy goods; or
    (*d*) to raise money on the security of goods.

A person who is not normally a factor may become one if he satisfies one of these four requirements, and a person may be a factor even though he acts for one principal only, or where he acts as a factor for the first time. (*Lowther* v. *Harris,* 1927.)[479] Conversely a person who is normally in business as a factor will not be one for any transaction outside the scope of these four categories. (*Staffs. Motor Guarantee Co.* v. *British Wagon Co.,* 1934.)[480] The term factor does not, however, include carriers, wharfingers, warehousemen or other mere bailees (*Kendrick* v. *Sotheby & Co.,* 1967),[481] nor does it include a person who is selling goods on behalf of himself and not for another, or a mercantile agent who is in possession of goods as a result of an illegal hire purchase agreement as where statutory regulations as to deposit or period of payment have been infringed. (*Belvoir Finance* v. *Cole,* [1969] 2 All E.R. 904.)

(ii) CUSTOMARY COURSE OF BUSINESS. An agent may be a factor although he is not normally in business as a factor, nor a known kind of commercial agent. For example, a man who normally sells second-hand furniture which he has previously bought on his own account, becomes a factor if he undertakes to sell a bedroom suite for a principal.

(iii) GOODS. This term includes all forms of merchandise, but does not include stocks and shares and negotiable instruments.

Title. The Factors Act, 1889, Sect. 2 (1) makes an important amendment to the common law rule *nemo dat quod non habet* (no-one can give what he has not got) as regards agents who may properly be called factors. The section provides that "where a mercantile agent is, with the consent of the owner, in possession of goods or of the documents of title to goods, any sale, pledge, or other disposition of the goods, made by him when acting in the ordinary course of business of a mercantile agent, shall, subject to the provisions of this Act, be as valid as if he were expressly authorised by the owner of the goods to make the same; provided that the person taking under the disposition acts in good faith, and has not at the time of the disposition notice that the person making the disposition has not authority to make the same."

The main points of interest in the section are as follows—

(i) THE CONSENT OF THE OWNER. Consent is presumed in the absence of evidence to the contrary. (Sect. 2 (4).) Even where the mercantile agent obtains the goods by *false pretences* or fraud he has usually obtained them with the consent, however mistaken, of the owner, and will give a good title to a purchaser from him. Where, however, the agent had obtained the goods by the old offence known as *larceny by a trick* he was not normally regarded as having the real consent of the owner, but the better view was that he could still give a good title. (*Pearson* v. *Rose & Young Ltd.*, 1951.)[482] Many modern cases on consent have arisen in connection with the sale of motor vehicles by fraudulent agents. From these cases it seems clear that the owner must consent not only to the agent's possession of the vehicle but also to his possession of the registration book and ignition key, because the sale of a vehicle without these items is not a sale in the ordinary course of business. (*Pearson* v. *Rose & Young Ltd.*, 1951;[482] *Stadium Finance* v. *Robbins*, 1962;[483] *George* v. *Revis*, 1966.)[484] Since the passing of the Theft Act, 1968, the offence of larceny by trick has disappeared from English law and it is likely that deceptions of the kind practised in *Pearson* and similar cases will no longer be regarded as preventing the consent of the owner, the new offence of obtaining property by deception being more akin to false pretences. Thus it may be easier to obtain a good title from the deceiver.

(ii) REGARDING PLEDGE. The factor's power to pledge goods is statutory; there was no such power prior to the Factors Act. In order to obtain the protection of the section, the pledge must be for valuable consideration.

The principal can, of course, redeem the goods pledged by paying to the pledgee the amount of any loan or other consideration, e.g. goods given to the agent under the pledge. Where the consideration is goods and not money, the principal cannot be required to pay more than their value at the time of the pledge, even if the goods which formed the consideration have since appreciated in value. Whatever the principal has to pay to redeem the goods pledged he may recover from the agent, subject to an offset by the agent for any rights he had over the goods pledged, e.g. for a lien he may have had over the goods for his charges when he pledged the goods.

(iii) ACTING IN THE ORDINARY COURSE OF BUSINESS. The factor must make the sale, pledge or other disposition, within business hours and at some place of business, and generally in circumstances which do not give rise to suspicion.

A sale or pledge by a mercantile agent through a clerk or other person, authorised in the ordinary course of business to make contracts of sale or pledge on behalf of the mercantile agent, is considered to be an agreement with the mercantile agent. (Sect. 6.)

(iv) REGARDING NOTICE. The person taking from the factor must prove that he did so in good faith and without notice of lack of authority. This probably means actual knowledge, though there may be circumstances where the third party is put on inquiry, as where a car is sold without a registration book. If in such circumstances the third party fails to make further inquiries he may be fixed with notice of the factor's lack of authority.

Del Credere Agents. In return for an extra commission, called a *del credere* commission, a *del credere agent* promises to indemnify the principal if the third party introduced by the agent fails to pay for the goods delivered to him, or if the third party becomes insolvent. As the contract with the *del credere agent*, is one of indemnity, no memorandum is required. This derives from the fact that a *del credere* agent is not totally unconnected in an economic sense with the transaction he is underwriting, as a guarantor must be. He receives some benefit from it by reason of the commission. *The del credere agent* is not liable for any other breach by the third party, e.g. where the third party refuses to take delivery of the goods; his liability, therefore, is not so extensive as that of the confirmatory agent mentioned earlier in the chapter.

CHAPTER VI

PARTNERSHIPS

The Partnership Act, 1890, provides the basic rules which govern the relationship between the partners, unless varied by the partnership agreement. Other provisions of the Act govern the relationship between the firm and third parties and these cannot be varied. All section references are to the Act of 1890 unless otherwise stated.

NATURE OF PARTNERSHIP

A partnership is the relation which subsists between persons carrying on a business in common with a view of profit. (Sect. 1 (1).) Thus, if an association of persons is to be considered a partnership, it must exist for some professional or commercial purpose, though the association may be for one transaction only. (*Reid* v. *Hollingshead*, 1825.)[485] Persons working together to form a company, although they may intend to become members of the company after its formation, are not partners if this is the only relation between them. (*Keith Spicer* v. *Mansell*, 1970.)[486]

The partners, or one or some of them as agents for them all, must manage the business, and the profits must be owned by the partners. It is not enough that they have a financial interest in the association or a mere charge on its profits. (*Cox* v. *Hickman*, 1860.)[487] However, it is possible to have *dormant or sleeping partners* who take a share in the profits but have no power to take part in the management of the firm.

There is no partnership where the association is a company incorporated under the Companies Acts, or by statute or letters patent or Royal Charter. (Sect. 1 (2).) Such associations are governed by separate rules.

Partnerships and Other Associations. The normal test of the existence of a partnership is the sharing of profits, but while a person in receipt of such a share is *prima facie* a partner, the test is not conclusive. Nor is a payment contingent on or varying with such profits. (*Holme* v. *Hammond*, 1871.)[488]

The following facts or relationships do not of themselves create a partnership or give rise to the obligations of partners—

(*a*) Ownership of property under a joint tenancy or tenancy in common, whether the owners do or do not share any profits made by the use of the property. (Sect. 2 (1).)

(*b*) The sharing of gross returns of a business, whether the persons sharing such returns are co-owners of the property from which or from the use of which the returns are derived. (Sect. 2 (2).) (*Cox* v. *Coulson*, 1916.)[489]

(*c*) The payment by a person of a debt or other liquidated amount by instalments or otherwise out of the accruing profits of the business.

(*d*) The payment of a servant or agent by a share of the profits of a business. (*Walker* v. *Hirsch*, 1884.)[490]

(*e*) The payment to a widow or a child of a deceased partner of an annuity by way of a portion of the profits made in the business in which the deceased was a partner.

(*f*) The advance of money by way of loan to a person engaged, or about to engage, in any business, the contract of loan providing that the lender shall receive a rate of interest varying with the profits, or shall receive a share of the profits arising from carrying on the business, provided that the contract is in writing and signed by or on behalf of all the parties thereto.

(*g*) The receipt by a person by way of annuity or otherwise of a portion of the profits of a business in consideration of the sale by him of the goodwill of the business. (Sect. 2 (3).)

The provision in (*f*) above only applies where the contract is truly a personal loan to the proprietor, and he is personally liable to repay it. If the assets of the business are charged with its repayment, the lender will be a partner. The lender will also be a partner if he can claim a share in the surplus assets of the business on its termination.

The recipients of money under the headings (*f*) and (*g*) above are deferred creditors where the proprietor of the business is adjudged bankrupt, or enters into an agreement to compound with his creditors, or dies insolvent. In such circumstances the lender of the loan will not be entitled to recover anything in respect of his loan and the seller of the goodwill cannot recover anything in respect of the share of profit until the claims of the other creditors of the borrower or buyer, as the case may be, have been satisfied. (Sect. 3.)

Salaried Partners. The Act of 1890 does not deal with a person who does not receive a share of the profits or a payment contingent on or varying with such profits but a salary in any event. However, a salaried partner may be liable for the debts and other liabilities of the business by reason of "holding out" under Sect. 14 of the Act (see p. 226). He should, therefore, agree with the full partners that they will indemnify him if, for example, he has to pay the firm's debts.

As between the partners themselves there seems no reason why a salaried partner's contract should not give rise to rights and liabilities with the full partners in regard to the business. Although a salaried partner may appear to be a servant the particular contract must be considered and interpreted.

Number of Partners. Under the Companies Act, 1948, Sect. 429 and 434, no partnership could consist of more than twenty persons (ten if the business was banking) if it had as its object the acquisition of gain, and if the partnership exceeded this number of members it was void. However, the partners retain a right to ask each other to account for the assets of the firm, and third parties who contract with the firm without notice of the excess of members have an action against the partners.

This provision has now been amended by the Companies Act, 1967. Under the provisions of Sect. 119 of that Act banking partnerships may now consist of not more than twenty persons each of whom is authorised by the Department of Trade and Industry to be a member of a banking partnership. Sect. 120 provides that partnerships of more than twenty persons may be created in the case of solicitors, members of a body of accountants recognised by the Department under Sect. 161 of the 1948 Act, or members of a recognised stock exchange.

The Department of Trade and Industry may by regulation exempt other professions or trades from the restriction on the number of partners. This power has been exercised in order to exempt certain partnerships of patent agents, surveyors, auctioneers, valuers and estate agents.

THE PARTNERSHIP AGREEMENT

Form. There are no legal requirements regarding form, and a partnership agreement may be made by deed, in writing or orally.

Illegality. The partnership agreement is void if the partners intend—

(a) *To carry on an illegal business (Foster v. Driscoll, 1929),*[216] though a partnership between bookmakers is not illegal in spite of the fact that wagers made by clients with the firm are illegal at civil law. (*Dungate v. Lee, 1967.*)[491]

(b) *To carry on a lawful business but in an unlawful way.* If X and Y are in partnership as doctors, and one of them is not qualified, the partnership agreement will be void.

Capacity. The general rules of the law of contract apply and, although a minor may be a partner, the partnership is voidable by him during his minority and for a reasonable time after reaching majority. If, however, he chooses to avoid the agreement, he will not be able to recover money paid by way of capital or premium unless he has had no benefit whatsoever out of the partnership. The court is reluctant to accept the fact of total failure of consideration except where the partnership never materialises.

With regard to contracts made by the firm with third parties the position is as follows—

(a) CONTRACTS MADE WITH THE FIRM WHILST THE PARTNER CONCERNED IS STILL A MINOR. Such contracts are void so far as the minor is concerned, though they will be enforceable against the adult partners. Since the contracts are void, the minor need not take any active steps to repudiate them, but the minor's fellow partners are able to apply the assets of the firm in carrying out such contracts, and the minor's capital and/or share of the firm's profits may be used to satisfy his share of the debts.

(b) CONTRACTS MADE BY THE FIRM AFTER THE PARTNER CONCERNED

REACHES MAJORITY. Such contracts bind the person who was formerly a minor unless he has repudiated the partnership before the contract in question was made, and, if the contract is made with a third party who dealt with the firm during the partner's minority and he was not informed of the repudiation before the contract was made, he can hold the person who was formerly a minor liable on it by way of *estoppel*.

The Firm and the Firm Name. Persons who have entered into a partnership with one another are called collectively a firm and the name under which their business is carried on is called the firm-name. (Sect. 4.)

The firm is not a *persona at law* i.e. the firm is not a legal entity separate and distinct from the partners, though it is possible for the partners to sue and be sued in the firm name.

Registration. Generally speaking partners may choose any name they wish as the firm name, but under the provisions of the Registration of Business Names Act, 1916, it may be necessary to register the following particulars with the Registrar of Business Names within fourteen days of commencing trading—

(i) the business name;
(ii) certain other particulars designed to show who the proprietors of the business are and what the nature of the business is.

Registration is required where the name is a name other than

(*a*) in the case of a sole trader, the true surname of the sole trader;
(*b*) in the case of a firm, the true surnames of each partner; and
(*c*) in the case of a company, the corporate name of the company.

Registration is also required in the case of a sole trader or a partnership where the sole trader or one or more of the partners has changed his name at any time during the twenty years prior to commencing in business, unless the change took place before the age of eighteen years or, in the case of a woman, on marriage.

On registration the Registrar, who is also the Registrar of Companies, will issue a *certificate of registration* which must be displayed in a prominent place at the principal place of business. Any changes in the particulars registered must be notified to the Registrar.

Failure to register as required by the Act has the following consequences to the proprietors of the unregistered business—

(i) A penalty of £5 for every day during which default continues, and
(ii) The loss of the right to enforce the business contracts made during default.

The court may grant relief where the other party to the contract is not prejudiced by the failure to register the true identity of the proprietors, but if he sues the proprietors on it, the proprietors can set up as a defence any counterclaim or set-off arising out of the contract. Thus if P, the proprietor of a firm which is not registered as required by the Act, delivers goods to X, then in the ordinary way P has no action for the price of the goods. However, if X sues P for damages for (say) breach of warranty in connection with the goods supplied, P could set up the price of the goods as a defence.

The Registrar can refuse to register a name if he thinks it is undesirable. It is then an offence to use the name, but contracts are not affected.

Passing Off. The firm name must not be one which is so like that of an existing concern that the public will confuse the two businesses. Similarity of name is not enough; the two concerns must also carry on similar businesses. Where the name chosen raises the possibility of such confusion, the rival concern may ask the court for an injunction to restrain the use of the name and, if there is evidence that the name was used knowingly to cause confusion, there may be an action for damages.

Nevertheless a firm may use a name consisting of the proper names of one or more of the partners even though there is the possibility of confusion, provided it does not advertise or mark its goods with the firm name in such a way as to confuse its products with those of an existing concern. Where one or more of the partners has previously traded in an assumed name, the firm may use that name also. (*Jay's Ltd.* v. *Jacobi*, 1933.)[492]

Objects. In the absence of special agreement no change may be made in the nature of the partnership business without the consent of all existing partners. (Sect. 24 (8).) The partnership agreement usually states the objects or business which the firm will carry on, but if the firm contracts outside the stated objects, there is no question of the contract being *ultra vires* and void, as would be the case with a company.

RELATIONS OF PARTNERS TO ONE ANOTHER

1. Variation of the Partnership Agreement. The mutual rights and duties of the partners, whether expressed in the partnership agreement or implied under the Partnership Act, 1890, may be varied by the consent of all the partners, and such consent may be either express or inferred from the course of dealing. (Sect. 19.) (*Pilling* v. *Pilling*, 1865.)[493] The partnership agreement, even if under seal, can be varied by an informal agreement of the partners.

2. Partnership Property. Partnership property, whether originally brought in or subsequently acquired by purchase or otherwise on account of the firm, must be held and applied by the partners exclusively for the purposes of the partnership, and in accordance with the partnership agreement. (Sect. 20 (1).) Although partnership property is normally in the joint ownership of the partners, a partner can be guilty of theft of such property under the Theft Act, 1968. Although he is the owner of it he is in effect dishonestly appropriating his co-owners share. (*R.* v. *Bonner,* [1970] 2 All E.R. 97.)

The persons in whom *partnership land* is vested hold the land *on trust* for those beneficially interested under the partnership agreement e.g. the partners themselves or retired partners who have annuities. (Sect. 20 (2).) The exact nature of the trust is doubtful and, to avoid difficulties, the partners should ensure that when land is conveyed either to themselves or other trustees for the firm, it is conveyed so as to be held *on trust for sale.* Thereafter, if the land is sold, the purchaser can take conveyance of the land without concerning himself with the interests of the partners in it. The interests of those beneficially interested in partnership land are interests in personalty, not realty (Sect. 22), and on the death of a partner, his interest in the partnership land goes to those entitled to his personalty.

(*a*) PROPERTY ORIGINALLY BROUGHT IN. In most cases the partnership agreement will give details of the property brought in by each partner and, of course, credit will be given in respect of its value in the partner's capital account. A partner may bring an asset into the firm—

    (i) By transferring the property to all the partners, including himself;

    (ii) By transferring it to trustees to hold on trust for the firm;

    (iii) By retaining the title in the property himself but holding it on trust for the firm.

If the partnership agreement does not concern itself with property brought in by the partners but property belonging to the partners has been used in the business, the court will generally not regard it as partnership property (*Miles* v. *Clark,* 1953)[494] unless in the circumstances it is essential to do so. (*Waterer* v. *Waterer,* 1873.)[495] In addition it was held in *Eardley* v. *Brood, The Times,* 28th April, 1970, that where a partnership deed between father and son did not specifically refer to a farm lease held by the father, the lease did not become partnership property even though it had been used in the business.

(*b*) PROPERTY SUBSEQUENTLY ACQUIRED. Property bought with money belonging to the firm is deemed to have been bought on account of the firm unless a contrary intention appears. (Sect. 21.)

Where partners make profits out of the use of land which is not partnership land but of which the partners are co-owners, and the profits are used to improve the land or to buy additional land, then the additional value arising from the improvements or the additional land, as the case may be, will belong to the partners as co-owners for the same interests and in the same shares as the original land was held. (*Davis* v. *Davis,* 1894.)[496] This rule does not apply where the partners agree to the contrary, or where the property is chattels.

(*c*) WITHDRAWAL OF ASSETS. If the partners agree, one partner may withdraw an asset from the firm either by buying it or taking a reduction in his capital. If the property is withdrawn at a time when the firm is insolvent, the withdrawal is void as against the creditors, who may require the return of the property to the firm.

(*d*) PARTNER'S SEPARATE JUDGMENT DEBT. Sect. 23 of the Partnership Act provides that, where the creditor of a partner has obtained a judgment against that partner in respect of a private debt, the creditor cannot execute judgment against the partnership property, but he may apply to the court for an order *charging* the partner's share with payment of the debt. The court has power to appoint a receiver of the partner's share of the profits and, should the firm be dissolved, of the assets.

The other partners may redeem the charge at any time by paying off the judgment creditor, in which case the charge becomes vested in them. The court may order a sale of the partner's share and, if it does, the other partners may purchase the share.

A separate creditor who obtains a charging order becomes a secured creditor and can demand payment out of the property charged before the partner's other *separate* creditors, but he has *no priority over the creditors of the firm.*

3. Capital. Unless the partnership agreement otherwise provides, partners are entitled to capital in equal shares, regardless of the value of assets brought in. (Sect. 24 (1).) However, the partnership agreement usually makes some provision regarding the amount of capital to be credited to each partner, the basis being the value of assets brought in or the value of services to be rendered in the future. When the partnership agreement is under seal, it is enforceable by a partner who has not supplied consideration.

(*a*) LOANS. A partner may advance money to the firm over and above the amount of his capital, by lending money to the firm or by paying certain of its debts from his own funds. Such advances or payments are not deemed to have increased his capital unless the partners have so agreed, and he is entitled to interest at 5 per cent per annum from the date of the payment or advance if the partners do not come to some other arrangement. (Sect. 24 (3).) The interest is payable whether profits are made or not.

(*b*) INTEREST ON CAPITAL. This is only payable if the partnership agreement expressly provides for it and sufficient profits are earned to pay it. (Sect. 24 (4).)

(*c*) REDUCTION OF CAPITAL. A reduction of capital may be effected, if the partners agree—

(i) *By the repayment of money* to the partner concerned (though if the firm is insolvent such a payment may be set aside as a fraud on creditors); or

(ii) *Where the firm has incurred losses*, by writing down the capital accounts of the partners to correspond with the reduced value of the assets.

4. Profits. The partnership agreement will usually provide for the sharing of profits in certain proportions. In the absence of such agreement the Act provides that all partners are entitled to share equally in the profits of the business and must contribute equally towards the losses. (Sect. 24 (1).) The Act does not require partners to keep books or to draw up a profit and loss account and balance sheet, but the partnership agreement usually does so.

5. Indemnity. The firm must indemnify each partner in respect of payments made and personal liabilities incurred by him in the ordinary and proper conduct of its business, or in doing anything necessary to preserve the business or property of the firm. (Sect. 24 (2).)

Thus if a partner pays the firm's debts or pays a premium to insure the firm's property, he can look to the firm for re-imbursement or, if the firm is insolvent, to his fellow partners for a contribution.

6. Management. The partnership agreement usually outlines the powers of the partners in the matter of management; otherwise every partner may take part in the management of the partnership business. (Sect. 24 (5).) A partner may also inspect and copy the firm's books, which must be kept at the principal place of business. (Sect. 24 (9).) He can, however, be restrained from doing this if he intends to take the names of the firm's customers in order to solicit them for his own business. The Act provides that no partner shall be entitled to remuneration for acting in the partnership business (Sect. 24 (6)), but where a firm consists of active and non-active partners, the partnership agreement often provides that the active or managing partners shall have a salary in addition to their share of profit.

No person may be introduced as a partner, nor may any change be made in the nature of the partnership business, without the consent of *all* existing partners. However differences between the partners in other matters connected with the ordinary business of the firm may be settled by a majority in number of the partners, regardless of the capital introduced by each. (Sect. 24 (7) & (8).) Such majority decisions must be made after consultation with the other partners and in good faith, and no majority of the partners can expel any partner unless a power to do so has been conferred by express agreement between the partners. (Sect. 25.)

7. Duties of Partners. The partners have the following duties—

(a) DUTY TO RENDER ACCOUNTS AND DISCLOSE INFORMATION. Partners are bound to render true accounts and full information of all things affecting the partnership to any partner or his legal representative. (Sect. 28.)

The duty arises out of the *fiduciary relationship* of partners and a partner must disclose full information regarding the firm whether it is asked for or not. (*Law* v. *Law*, 1905.)[497] No such duty is owed to incoming partners, but an incoming partner can rescind the contract if the existing partners have been guilty of misrepresenting the prospects and worth of the firm.

(*b*) Duty to Account for Private Profits. Every partner must account to the firm for any benefit derived by him without the consent of the other partners from any transaction concerning the partnership, or from any use by him of the partnership property, name or business connection. (Sect. 29 (1).) (*Bentley* v. *Craven*, 1853;[498] *Pathirana* v. *Pathirana*, 1966.)[499] There is no need to account if the transaction could not possibly have affected the partnership business. (*Aas* v. *Benham*, 1891.)[500]

This duty to account applies also to transactions undertaken after the partnership has been dissolved by the death of a partner and before the affairs of the partnership have been completely wound up. (Sect. 29 (2).) A potential partner is accountable to the firm when it comes into being for profits made during the negotiations leading up to the formation of the firm, if the transaction out of which he made the profit would have affected the firm had it been in existence. (*Fawcett* v. *Whitehouse*, 1829.)[501]

(*c*) Duty of Partners not to Compete with the Firm. If a partner, without the consent of the other partners, carries on any business of the same nature as and competing with that of the firm, he must account for and pay over to the firm all profits made by him in that business. (Sect. 30.) The business must be a competing business. Thus, if X and Y were partners in a firm of Savile Row tailors, Y would not have to account to the Savile Row firm if he set up a cheap clothing store in another area.

Sect. 30 merely provides for an account of profits and does not prohibit the carrying on of a competing business. However, the partnership agreement may do so, in which case the competing partner could be restrained by injunction from carrying on the competing business. Even where there is no specific prohibition in the agreement, the court may be prepared to dissolve the partnership where one partner persists in competition.

8. Assignment of a Share in a Partnership. An assignment by any partner of his share in the partnership, either absolutely or by way of mortgage or redeemable charge, does not make the assignee a partner. The assignee is not entitled to interfere in the management or administration of the firm or to require accounts or to inspect the firm's books. He is entitled only to receive the share of profits to which the assigning partner would otherwise be entitled, and he must accept the account of profits agreed to by the partners. (Sect. 31 (1).) However the partners cannot alter their shares of profit and/or capital so as to reduce the share to which the assignee is entitled.

If the partnership is dissolved, the assignee is entitled to receive the share of the assets to which the assigning partner is entitled, and in order to ascertain that share the assignee is entitled to an account from the date of dissolution. (Sect. 31 (2).) The assignee is not personally liable for the debts of the firm though, *where the assignment is absolute* and not by way of mortgage, *he must indemnify* the assigning partner against the latter's liability to pay the firm's debts whether incurred before or after the assignment.

The assignee may become a partner if the other partners agree, but as a mere assignee he has no control over the way in which the partners manage the firm. (*Re Garwood's Trusts, Garwood* v. *Paynter*, 1903.)[502]

9. Transmission of a Share in the Partnership. When a partner dies or becomes bankrupt, his property vests by operation of law in his personal representatives or trustee in bankruptcy as the case may be. A partner's property includes his interest in the assets of the firm. The personal representatives or trustee do not become partners in the firm; indeed the firm will have been dissolved by the death or bankruptcy unless the partnership agreement otherwise provides. The personal representatives or trustee are entitled to receive the deceased or bankrupt's share of the assets on dissolution, unless the partnership agreement gives the other partners an option, which they exercise, to buy a deceased or bankrupt partner's share. In the latter case, the personal representatives or the trustee are only entitled to the price payable under the option which may be less valuable than a share of the assets.

10. Remedies for Breach of the Partnership Agreement. The usual remedies for breach of contract are available, and one partner may bring an action for *damages* against another partner who is in breach of the partnership agreement, or may ask for an *injunction* to enforce a negative stipulation in it. Thus, where a partner agrees not to compete with the firm, he may be restrained by injunction from doing so.

Specific performance will rarely be available to enforce the partnership agreement, since a partnership is a contract for personal services and such contracts are not enforceable by specific performance. However, where two persons agree informally to form a partnership, and one later refuses to sign the agreement, then specific performance will lie to make him do so, but only if the plaintiff has partially performed the partnership contract.

RELATIONS OF PARTNERS TO PERSONS DEALING WITH THEM

1. Partner's Powers. Every partner is an agent of the firm and his other partners for the purpose of the business of the partnership; and the acts of every partner done for carrying on the business in the usual way will bind the firm and his partners. (*Mann* v. *D'Arcy*, 1968.)[503] However, the firm and co-partners will not be bound where the partner who acts has in fact *no authority* to bind the firm in the particular matter and the *person who deals with him knows* that he has no authority or does not believe him to be a partner. (Sects. 5 and 8.)

(i) EXTENT OF POWER. Decided cases indicate that the implied authority of a partner envisaged by Sect. 5 is as follows—

A. *All Partnerships.* Partners have implied authority to—

(*a*) Buy and sell goods of the type in which the firm deals;
(*b*) Give valid receipts;
(*c*) Sign cheques;
(*d*) Engage and dismiss employees;
(*e*) Sue on behalf of the firm or defend an action against it, and consent to judgment being entered against the firm;
(*f*) Compromise or release the claims of the firm against others. The compromise or release must be genuine and not designed to defraud the other partners.

B. Trading Partnerships, i.e. partnerships whose business consists in the buying and selling of goods. Here the partners have the following additional powers—

(*g*) To borrow money and give security over the firm's land or chattels;
(*h*) To draw, accept or indorse bills of exchange and promissory notes.

The reference of a dispute to arbitration requires the signature of all the partners unless all have agreed to give one partner the authority to sign the agreement. Similarly one partner cannot bind the firm by giving a guarantee of a third party's obligations unless the firm gives guarantees in the ordinary course of its business. The other partners may, of course, ratify the unauthorised acts of a fellow partner and thus become bound by the transaction.

(ii) FORM. Sect. 6 of the Partnership Act provides that an act or instrument relating to the business of the firm and done or executed in the firm's name, or in any other way showing an intention to bind the firm, by an authorised agent, whether a partner or not, is binding on the firm and all the partners, but this does not affect the law relating to the execution of deeds and negotiable instruments.

Thus the firm will not be bound by deed unless—

(*a*) all the partners sign it; or
(*b*) if one partner or other agent signs it, he must be appointed by and act within the scope of a power of attorney given by all the partners.

But if a deed has been used in circumstances where the law does not require one, the firm will be bound if the deed is signed by one partner. Bills of exchange, cheques and promissory notes will bind the partners only if the agent signs for and on behalf of the firm (Bills of Exchange Act, 1882, Sect. 23 (2)) or puts the names of all the partners on the bill. (Sect. 91 (1).)

(iii) PARTNER USING CREDIT OF FIRM FOR PRIVATE PURPOSES. Where one partner pledges the credit of the firm for a purpose apparently not connected with the firm's ordinary course of business, the firm is not bound unless he is in fact specially authorised by the other partners. (Partnership Act, Sect. 7.) Thus if a partner gives a negotiable instrument in the name of the firm to obtain money for his private purposes, and the person taking the bill knows of this, the firm will not be bound.

2. **Partner's Liabilities.** The Act lays down the liabilities of the partners in several important respects—

(i) LIABILITY FOR DEBTS AND CONTRACTS. Every partner in a firm is liable *jointly* with the other partners for all the debts and obligations of the firm incurred while he is a partner; and after his death his estate is also severally liable for such debts and obligations so far as they remain unsatisfied, subject to prior payment of his separate debts. (Sect. 9.)

Thus the liability of partners for debts and contracts is *joint* and not *joint and several*, and where a creditor has only one cause of action against the firm and sues one partner to judgment, he cannot sue the other partners even if the judgment is unsatisfied. The same rule applies if the creditor releases one partner from liability, unless in the release he expressly reserves his right to sue the other partners. Where a creditor has two causes of action, signing judgment against one partner on the one cause will not prevent the creditor from suing the partners on the other. (*Wegg-Prosser* v. *Evans*, 1895.)[504]

A deceased partner's estate can be sued by creditors in respect of debts incurred by the firm prior to death, even though judgment has been entered against one or more of the surviving partners on the same cause of action. The rule of joint liability applies only as between the partners and the firm's creditors and not as between the partners themselves. Thus if a partner has paid a debt of the firm, he can turn to his fellow partners for a contribution. (Sect. 24 (2).)

(ii) LIABILITY FOR TORTS GENERALLY. Sect. 10 provides that the firm is liable for the torts of partners committed in the ordinary course of the firm's business (*Hamlyn* v. *Houston & Co.*, 1903),[505] but this does not extend to a partner's acts outside the scope of the firm's usual activities. (*Arbuckle* v. *Taylor*, 1815.)[506]

The firm is also liable *vicariously* for the torts of its servants committed within the scope of their employment. If the firm's van driver negligently injures a pedestrian while delivering the firm's goods, the firm will be liable along with the driver.

(iii) MISAPPLICATION OF MONEY OR PROPERTY. Sect. 11 provides that the firm is liable to make good the loss incurred if a partner has tortiously misapplied the money or property of a third person—

(*a*) Where the partner in question was acting within the scope of his apparent authority when he received the money or property (*Plumer* v. *Gregory*, 1874);[507] or

(*b*) Where the firm in the course of its business received the money or property, and it was misapplied by one or more of the partners while it was in the custody of the firm. (*Cleather* v. *Twisden*, 1884.)[508]

(iv) NATURE OF PARTNER'S LIABILITY FOR TORTS. Every partner is liable *jointly with his co-partners* and also *severally* for torts for which the firm becomes liable whilst he is a partner. (Sect. 12.) Thus a judgment against one partner is no bar to an action against the other or others. In the case of a deceased partner his estate remains liable for the firm's torts committed during his lifetime though certain claims, e.g. for defamation, cannot be made against his estate. (Law Reform (Miscellaneous Provisions) Act, 1934, Sect. 1.) If one partner is sued and pays damages in respect of a tort for which the firm is liable, he may obtain a contribution from his co-partners. (Law Reform (Married Women and Tortfeasors) Act, 1935.)

(v) IMPROPER EMPLOYMENT OF TRUST PROPERTY. If a partner, being a trustee, improperly employs trust property in the business or on its account, no other partner is liable for the breach of trust; the trustee-partner is personally liable. However, the trustee-partner's co-partners will be liable if they have notice of the breach of trust, as where they know that trust property is being used in the firm's business, and in any case *the beneficiaries can trace the property* into the firm's hands. (Partnership Act, Sect. 13.)

(vi) PARTNERSHIP BY ESTOPPEL. Every one who *by words spoken or written* or *by conduct* represents himself, or knowingly allows himself to be represented, as a partner in a particular firm, is liable as a partner to any one who has on the faith of any such representation given credit to the firm. (Sect. 14 (1).)

He may be sued by the third party as if he were a partner. It is not enough that a person knows he is being held out as a partner; there must also be evidence of consent. Carelessness or negligence is not enough. (*Tower Cabinet Co. Ltd.*, v. *Ingram*, 1949.)[509]

Sect. 14 (2) provides that where after a partner's death the business is continued in the old firm name, the continued use of that name, or of the deceased partner's name as part of it, shall not of itself render his personal representatives or his estate liable for partnership debts contracted after his death.

As regards internal relations between the partners, the fact that A holds out B as his partner will not necessarily by itself create the rights, duties and liabilities of partners between them. (*Floydd* v. *Cheney*, 1970.)[510]

3. Liabilities of Incoming and Outgoing Partners. A person who is admitted as a partner into an existing firm does not thereby become liable to the firm's creditors for debts incurred before he became a partner (Sect. 17 (1).), and a partner who retires from a firm does not thereby cease to be liable for partnership debts or obligations incurred before his retirement. (Sect. 17 (2).)

The date when the contract was made decides the question of liability. Thus in a contract for the sale of goods a partner is liable if he was a partner when a contract was made, even though the goods were delivered after he ceased to be a partner.

Sect. 17 (3) provides that a retiring partner may be discharged from any existing liabilities by an agreement to that effect between himself, the members of the firm as newly constituted, and the creditors. This agreement, which is called a *novation*, may be either express or inferred from the course of dealing between the creditors and the firm as newly constituted. (*Thompson* v. *Percival*, 1834.)[511]

The creditors cannot be made to accept a novation, and if a particular creditor refuses to enter into such an arrangement, he may still hold the retired partner liable for liabilities existing at his retirement. However, the new or continuing partners may agree to indemnify him.

A partnership may take part in a *continuing guarantee* either as guarantor, creditor or principal debtor. If the firm which is the creditor or principal debtor changes its composition, the guarantee is, in the absence of contrary agreement revoked, but a change in the composition of the guarantor firm has no such effect and a retiring partner remains liable in the absence of a novation or indemnity from the remaining partners (Sect. 18.)

4. Effect of Changes in Constitution. Where a person deals with a firm after a change in its constitution, he is entitled to treat all apparent members of the old firm as still being members of the firm until he has notice of the change. (Sect. 36 (1).) If X, who was a partner in F and Co., leaves the firm, and the firm contracts with Y, who knew that X was a member of the firm but does not know that he has left it, X will be liable to Y under this section. Individual notices must be sent to all persons who were customers of the firm when the former partner left it. Where the firm's principal place of business is in England and Wales, an advertisement in the *London Gazette* by the former partner constitutes notice to all persons who did not have dealings with the firm while he was a member of it. (Sect. 36 (2).)

The estate of a *partner who dies or becomes bankrupt, or* of a partner who, not having been known to the person dealing with the firm to be a partner, *retires* from the firm, is not liable for partnership debts contracted after the date of death, bankruptcy or retirement respectively. (Sect. 36 (3).)

DISSOLUTION OF PARTNERSHIP

A partnership may be terminated in a number of ways.

1. Without a Court Order

(i) BY EXPIRATION OR NOTICE. The partnership agreement often stipulates the duration of the partnership, e.g.

(*a*) It shall last for a certain number of years and continue thereafter until one partner gives a certain length of notice to the other or others;

(*b*) It shall last for the life or lives of one or more partners;

(*c*) It shall be terminated by mutual agreement, in which case all must agree, although the death of one also terminates it.

Such partnerships are not determinable by notice but only in accordance with the terms of the agreement.

Subject to such agreement, the Partnership Act, 1890 provides that a partnership is dissolved—

(*a*) if entered into for a fixed term, by the expiration of the term;

(*b*) if entered into for a single adventure or undertaking by its completion;

(*c*) if entered into for an undefined time, by any partner giving notice to the other or others of his intention to dissolve the partnership, such notice operating from the date (if any) mentioned in the notice, or, if no date is mentioned, from the date of the notice. (Sect. 32.)

Where no fixed period has been agreed for the duration of the partnership, or where the partners carry on the business after the expiration of a fixed term of partnership without any express new agreement, the partnership is a *partnership at will. In both cases* it can be terminated by any partner at any time. (*Firth* v. *Armslake*, 1964.)[512] *In the second case*, while it continues, it is governed by the provisions of the former partnership agreement, except in so far as that agreement is inconsistent with a partnership at will. (Sect. 27.) A notice of dissolution in such circumstances cannot be withdrawn by the partner giving it.

(ii) DISSOLUTION BY BANKRUPTCY, DEATH OR CHARGE. Subject to any agreement between the partners, every partnership is dissolved as regards all the partners by the death or bankruptcy of any partner. (Sect. 33 (1).) Dissolution operates from the date of death or the commencement of bankruptcy. A partnership may, if the other partners wish it, be dissolved if any partner's share is charged to secure a separate judgment debt. (Sect. 33 (2).)

(iii) DISSOLUTION BY ILLEGALITY. A partnership is in every case dissolved by the happening of any event which makes it unlawful for the business of the firm to be carried on, or for the members of the firm to carry it on in partnership. (Sect. 34.) (*Stevenson* v. *A.G. für Cartonnagen Industrie*, 1918.)[466]

2. Dissolution by the Court. On application by a partner the court may decree a dissolution of the partnership in any of the following cases—

(*a*) *Where a partner is suffering from mental disorder;*

(*b*) *Where a partner, other than the partner suing,*—

(i) *Becomes permanently incapable*, other than by mental disorder, of performing his part of the partnership contract; or

(ii) *Has been guilty of misconduct* in his business or private life likely to be harmful to the carrying on of the business; or

(iii) Wilfully or persistently *commits a breach of the partnership agreement* or makes it impracticable for the others to carry on the business in partnership with him;

(*c*) *Where the business of the partnership can only be carried on at a loss;*
(*d*) *Where circumstances have arisen which,* in the opinion of the court, render it *just and equitable that the partnership be dissolved* (Sect. 35.), e.g. where there is hostility between the partners. (*Re Yenidji Tobacco Co. Ltd.,* 1916.)[513]

Dissolution generally takes effect from the date of the court order.

POWERS ON DISSOLUTION

The partners possess certain rights and may exercise authority in certain respects for the purpose of winding up the firm.

(*a*) **Notification.** On the dissolution of a partnership or the retirement of a partner, any partner may publicly notify the same, and may require the other partner or partners to concur in all necessary or proper acts to achieve that purpose. (Sect. 37.) (*Troughton v. Hunter,* 1854.)[514]

(*b*) **Authority of Partners after Winding Up.** After the dissolution of the partnership the authority of each partner to bind the firm continues so far as may be necessary to wind up the affairs of the partnership and to complete transactions begun but unfinished at the date of dissolution. Partners will not bind the firm if they enter into new transactions after dissolution. (Sect. 38.) (*Re Bourne,* 1906.)[515] However, the firm is in no case bound by the acts of a partner who has become bankrupt unless the partners (*a*) have represented themselves, or (*b*) have knowingly allowed themselves to be represented, as still the partners of the bankrupt. (Sect. 38.)

(*c*) **Partner's Lien for Proper Administration.** On the dissolution of a partnership every partner is entitled, as against his co-partners and all persons claiming through them (e.g. personal representatives or trustees in bankruptcy), to have the property of the partnership applied in payment of the debts and liabilities of the firm, and to have the surplus assets, after such payment, applied in payment of what may be due to the partners, after deducting any sums which the partners may owe the firm. In order to achieve this purpose, any partner or his representative may on the termination of the partnership apply to the court to wind up the business and affairs of the firm. (Sect. 39.)

The section creates a lien which is in the nature of a personal right against co-partners and their representatives. The lien assists a partner in getting proper administration of the winding up, and prevents the assets from being used to pay the separate debts of the partners before the firm's debts. The lien created by Sect. 39 does not allow a partner to sell the assets to third parties in the course of the winding up; it is merely a personal right against co-partners and their representatives to assist in obtaining proper administration.

(*d*) **Apportionment of Premiums.** Where one partner has paid a premium to another on entering into a partnership for a fixed term, and the partnership is dissolved before the expiration of that term, the court may order the repayment of the premium or such part of it as it thinks just, having regard to the partnership agreement, the length of time the partnership has lasted and how long it had to run.

However, the court cannot order the return of any part of the premium if—

(*a*) The dissolution is, in the judgment of the court, wholly or chiefly due to the misconduct of the partner who paid the premium; or

(*b*) The partnership has been dissolved by an agreement containing no provision for the return of any part of the premium; or

(*c*) The dissolution is due to the death of a partner. (Sect. 40.)

TREATMENT OF ASSETS ON DISSOLUTION

In addition to the physical assets of the firm most partnerships have an asset called goodwill, i.e. a number of customers or clients who will probably continue to resort to the firm even if it changes hands. On dissolution these assets may be disposed of in the following ways—

(1) **The Firm may be Sold as a Going Concern.** The firm may be sold either to an outsider or to one of the partners who may acquire, or may by the agreement have the right to acquire, the shares of the other partners. In these cases goodwill forms part of the assets sold and must be paid for, and the purchaser of the business may then use the firm's name and restrain the outgoing partners from continuing to use it as well as from trying to attract former customers to any new business they may form. The goodwill is valued in these circumstances and is allocated to the various retiring partners. If an outsider buys the business he pays the whole; if one of the partners buys it he must compensate the other partners.

(2) **The Assets may be divided among the Partners in specie.** In this case the goodwill of the business disappears and the partners take the assets forming their own particular share in accordance with their agreement, subject to cash adjustments if the values of the assets taken do not correspond precisely with the shares due to each partner. Where the assets are divided in this way there is no goodwill left, and any partner may use the firm name so long as he does not involve his former partners in liability for the debts of the new business.

If the partners agree on a division *in specie* in general terms but ultimately cannot agree on the precise disposition of the physical assets, the court will order the business to be sold and if it is sold as an entity, goodwill will once again form one of the assets.

Application of Assets on Dissolution. Unless there is a contrary agreement between the partners, the assets are applied as follows—

(i) In paying the debts and liabilities of the firm to persons who are not partners therein;

(ii) In paying to each partner rateably what is due from the firm to him for advances as distinct from capital;

(iii) In paying each partner what is due to him in respect of capital;

(iv) The ultimate residue, if any, to be divided among the partners in the proportion in which profits were divisible. (Sect. 44 (*b*).)

If the assets are not sufficient to satisfy the creditors, partners' advances and repayment of capital, the deficiency is to be made up—

(*a*) out of profits (if any) brought forward from previous years;
(*b*) out of partners' capital;
(*c*) by the partners individually in the proportion in which they were entitled to share profits. (Sect. 44 (*a*).)

Partner's Insolvency on Dissolution. Where a partner is insolvent and the firm's assets are not sufficient to repay the creditors and partners' advances, this deficiency must be borne by the solvent co-partners in the ratio in which they were entitled to share profits.

Where the assets of the firm are more than sufficient to pay the firm's creditors and partners' advances, but are not sufficient to repay the partners' capitals, then each partner must contribute to this deficiency in the proportion in which he shares profits and losses. However, where a partner is insolvent and cannot pay in his share of the deficiency, the other partners need only pay in their own share. (*Garner* v. *Murray*, 1904.)[516] The effect of the Rule in *Garner* v. *Murray* is that the insolvent partner's portion of the deficiency falls on the solvent partners not in proportion to their share of profits and losses but in the ratio of their last agreed capitals.

Suppose A, B and C are partners whose last agreed capitals were £6,000, £4,000 and £700 respectively and who agreed to share profits and losses equally. After the creditors had been paid off there was a fund left of £8,000, leaving a deficiency of £2,700 on capital. Each partner must, therefore, contribute £900. However, if C is insolvent and can pay nothing, he will lose his right to a repayment of his capital of £700 but the fund will be £200 short and this loss will fall on A and B in the proportion to their capitals, and not equally. A will emerge £120 short and B £80 short.

If A and B actually paid in the £900 each, the capital fund would stand at £9,800 and would be shared as follows—A £5,880; B £3,920; C Nil.

Since the adjustment would normally be carried out by book entries, the partners would actually receive £900 each less, namely—A £4,980; B £3,020; C Nil.

It should be noted that if the assets only realise sufficient money to repay or partly repay partners' advances, then the *loss will fall upon the solvent partners in the proportion of their advances* because the money obtained from the assets does not go far enough to pay off capital.

Profits made after Winding Up. Sometimes, after the dissolution of the firm or the retirement of one of the partners, the surviving or continuing partners carry on the business of the firm with its capital or assets without any final settlement of accounts as between the firm and the outgoing partner or his estate. In the absence of any agreement to the contrary, the outgoing partner or his estate is entitled at the option of himself or his representatives—

(*a*) to such share of the profits made since the dissolution as the court may find to be attributable to the use of his share of the partnership assets, or

(*b*) to interest at 5 per cent per annum on the amount of his share of the partnership assets. (Sect. 42 (1).) (*Pathirana* v. *Pathirana*, 1966.)[499]

Thus the outgoing partner is not entitled to the same proportion of the profits as he was when the firm existed, and the court has discretion as to the amount to be awarded. If the post-dissolution profits have, in the opinion of the court, been earned mainly by the skilful management of the continuing partners and not from the use of the outgoing partner's capital, the court will exclude such profits when ascertaining what is due to the outgoing partner. (*Manley* v. *Sartori*, 1927.)[517]

However, where by the partnership agreement an option is given to surviving or continuing partners to purchase the interest of a deceased or outgoing partner, and that option is duly exercised, the estate of the deceased partner, or the outgoing partner or his estate, as the case may be, is not entitled to any further share of the profits. But if the person exercising the option does not comply with its material terms, or does not exercise it within the time allowed, he is liable to account for a proportion of the post-dissolution profits. (Sect. 42 (2).)

Rescission of Partnership Agreement. Where a partnership agreement is rescinded on the grounds of the fraud or misrepresentation of one of the parties to it, the person entitled to rescind is entitled under Sect. 41—

(*a*) *to a lien* on the surplus assets of the firm after the firm's liabilities have been paid for any sum of money paid by him for the purchase of a share in the partnership and for any surplus capital contributed by him;

(*b*) *to be subrogated* to the rights of the creditors of the firm for any payment made by him in respect of the firm's liabilities;

(*c*) *to be indemnified* by the person guilty of the fraud or making the misrepresentation against all the debts and liabilities of the firm.

The object of this section is to reconcile the right to rescind in the general law of contract with the partnership situation in which creditors are involved. The reconciliation is achieved by treating the rescission rather like a dissolution.

BANKRUPTCY OF PARTNERS

The following effects flow from a partner's bankruptcy.

(a) **Bankruptcy of One Partner.** This will, in the absence of any agreement to the contrary, dissolve the partnership leaving the administration of the dissolution in the hands of the other partners. (Sect. 38.)

(b) **Bankruptcy of All Partners.** A receiving order may be made against the firm but it acts as a receiving order against each partner. The firm must present a statement of affairs and each partner must also submit a statement regarding his separate estate. The adjudication order is made against the partners individually and not against the firm. The first meeting of creditors consists of the joint creditors and of each partner's private creditors. Each estate is entitled to appoint a committee of inspection but the joint creditors appoint the trustee.

Application of the Partnership Estate. The firm's property is called the *joint estate* and the separate property of each partner is called the *separate estate*. The principle applied is that the joint estate is used to pay the debts of the firm and each partner's separate estate is applied in payment of his private debts. If there is a surplus on a separate estate, it is transferred to the joint estate should that estate be insufficient. Suppose P and Q are partners and the firm has debts of £1,000 and assets totalling £800. P has private means of £300 and debts of £600; Q has £500 and has debts of £400. P's creditors will get 50p. in the £ and there will be no surplus for the creditors of the firm. Q can pay off his debts in full, and the surplus of £100 will be available for the firm's creditors.

If there is a surplus on the joint estate, it is transferred to the separate estates of the partners in ratio based on each partner's interest in the firm.

The following special cases are worthy of note—

(a) If a partner has fraudulently used partnership property for private purposes, the joint estate may prove against the fraudulent partner's separate estate in *equal competition* with the separate creditors.

(b) A firm creditor whose debt was the result of a fraud by a partner or partners has an *election*. He may prove *either* against the firm *or* against the separate estates of the partner or partners guilty of the fraud.

(c) It is also possible for one estate to prove against another where a partner also carries on an independent business and debts have been incurred in the course of trading between that business and the partnership.

(d) If there is no joint estate and no solvent partner, the firm creditors can prove against the separate estates equally with the separate creditors, but partners cannot compete with the firm's creditors against either the joint or separate estates.

A partner can, however, prove in the separate estate of another partner—

(i) where the firm's creditors have been paid off; or
(ii) where the separate estate of a partner is not enough to pay his separate debts in full. Here the firm's creditors are not prejudiced because there would have been no surplus to come to them in any event.

X and Y are partners and Y is insolvent having creditors amounting to £900 as well as owing £100 to X on a private matter. If Y's assets are £500 there is no reason why X should not prove for the £100, since if he abstains the creditors of the partnership will get nothing, X will lose £50 and Y's separate creditors would get a slightly larger dividend.

Secured Creditors. The position is as follows—

(*a*) A creditor of the firm with a security on the separate property of a partner may prove against the joint estate and need not give up the security against the separate estate.

(*b*) A partner's separate creditor who has a security on the partnership property may prove against the separate estate and need not give up the security on the joint estate.

In neither case may the creditor, by the exercise of both rights, receive more than the full amount of his debt.

LIMITED PARTNERSHIPS

The Limited Partnerships Act, 1907, provides for the formation of limited partnerships in which one or more of the partners has only limited liability for the firm's debts. Such partnerships are not common because in most cases the objective desired may be better achieved by incorporation as a private company, though Corporation Tax may make them more popular.

A limited partnership is not a *persona at law* or *legal entity* and must not have more than twenty members (ten if the business is banking), though this provision does not apply to limited partnerships of solicitors, accountants or stockbrokers among others. (Companies Act, 1967, Sect. 121, see page 216). There must also be one general partner whose liability for the debts of the firm is unlimited. A body corporate may nevertheless be a limited partner.

Registration. Every limited partnership must be registered with the Registrar of Joint Stock Companies. The following particulars must be registered by means of a statement signed by the partners—

(*a*) The firm name;
(*b*) The general nature of the business;
(*c*) The principal place of business;

(*d*) The full name of each partner;

(*e*) The date of commencement and the term of the partnership, if any;

(*f*) A statement that it is a limited partnership;

(*g*) Particulars of each limited partner and the amount contributed by him whether in cash or otherwise.

Any change in the above particulars, or the fact that a general partner becomes a limited partner, must be notified to the Registrar within seven days. Failure to register means that the limited partner is fully liable as a general partner. When a general partner becomes a limited partner, or an assignment of a limited partner's share is made to another person, the fact must be advertised in the *London Gazette* if the transactions are to be effective in law.

The Register of Limited Partnerships is open to inspection by the public who may also obtain certified copies of, or extracts from, any registered statement.

Rights and Duties of Limited Partners. A limited partner is not liable for the debts of the firm beyond his capital, but he may not withdraw any part of his capital and, even if he were to do so, he would still be liable to the firm's creditors for the amount of capital he originally subscribed.

A limited partner has no power to bind the firm and may not take part in its management. If he does manage the firm he becomes liable for all the liabilities incurred by the firm during that period. Nevertheless he may give advice on management to the other partners and he may also inspect the books.

The death, bankruptcy or mental disorder of a limited partner does not dissolve the partnership, and a limited partner cannot dissolve the partnership by notice.

CHAPTER VII

REGISTERED COMPANIES

A REGISTERED company is a species of corporation and is an association of persons formed for the purpose of some business or undertaking carried on in the name of the association, each member having the right to transfer his shares to any person, subject to the regulations of the company. The relevant legislation is contained in the Companies Acts, 1948 and 1967, and section references are to the 1948 Act unless otherwise stated.

Classification of Registered Companies. Registered companies may be *limited by shares*, in which case the members are liable only to the extent of the amount, if any, unpaid on their shares; or *limited by guarantee*, in which case the members are liable only to the extent to which they have agreed by the Memorandum of Association to contribute to the assets on a winding up. Companies of the latter type may be registered with or without a share capital.

Companies may also be registered in which the liability of members is *unlimited*. Such companies are more acceptable in certain circles, e.g. the turf and stockbroking.

Each of the above companies may be a public or a private company, and private companies were further sub-divided into exempt and non-exempt private companies. However, the Companies Act, 1967, Sect. 2 abolishes the status of exempt private company.

Registered Companies and Partnerships Compared. A company has a legal personality distinct from that of its members and is a *persona* at law. (*Salomon* v. *Salomon & Co.*, 1897.)[518] A partnership firm is not a *persona* at law but is made up of the several persons who compose it.

Thus, a company continues to exist in spite of the death or bankruptcy of any of its members, whereas these events will bring about the dissolution of a partnership.

In a company the shares of the members are freely transferable whereas no partner can transfer his share without the consent of the other partners.

A public company must have at least seven members, though no upper limit is laid down. A private company must have at least two members and there is an upper limit of fifty (excluding employees and ex-employees). A partnership may not consist of more than twenty persons, though under Sect. 120 of the Companies Act, 1967, this maximum does not apply to all partnerships (see p. 215).

A shareholder is not an agent for the company, but each partner is an agent of the firm to make contracts which will bind the firm.

The members of the company as such have no power to manage its affairs whereas, unless the partnership agreement otherwise provides, all partners have a right to take part in the management of the firm.

The liability of each shareholder may be limited either by shares or by guarantee, but the liability of partners for the debts of the firm is unlimited, except in the case of a limited partner.

The affairs of a registered company are closely controlled by the Companies Acts, 1948 and 1967, and it must trade within the objects as set out in the objects clause of the Memorandum. Partners may enter into any business they please and may make any arrangements they choose regarding the running of the firm.

THE MEMORANDUM OF ASSOCIATION

This is one of the two major documents which govern the formation of a company.

The memorandum is required by statute to state—

(*a*) The name of the company with "Limited" as the last word;

(*b*) Whether the Registered Office is in England or Scotland;

(*c*) The company's objects;

(*d*) That the liability of members is limited, unless the company is an unlimited one;

(*e*) The amount of the company's nominal or authorised capital, and its division into shares of a certain nominal or par value.

The memorandum must be signed by seven persons called subscribers (two in the case of a private company) and they must state opposite their names the number of shares they take, and each must take at least one share. The signatures of the subscribers must be witnessed, though one witness will do for all.

The Company's Name. There are the following restrictions on the choice of a company's name.

(*a*) *At common law* a company can be restrained by injunction from using the name of an existing firm where this would lead to confusion in the mind of the public. (*Ewing* v. *Buttercup Margarine Co. Ltd.,* 1917.)[519]

(*b*) *The Companies Act* provides that no name shall be registered which in the opinion of the Department of Trade and Industry is undesirable, e.g. names which misrepresent the size of the firm or suggest connection with the Royal Family or Government. (Sect. 17.) If a company is registered with a name similar to that of another company, the Department of Trade and Industry may direct that it be changed up to six months after registration. The company must then change its name within six weeks of the Department's direction. (Sect. 18.)

Sect. 46 of the Companies Act, 1967, gives the Department of Trade and Industry power to direct a company to change its name if it gives so misleading an indication of its activities as to be likely to cause harm to the public. This power is exercisable at any time and is not restricted to within six months of registration as is the power in the principal Act. A direction made under Sect. 46 must be complied with by the company concerned within six weeks from the date of the direction or such longer period as the Department of Trade and Industry may allow. The company may, however, ask the Court to set aside the direction within three weeks of its being made. The Court may set it aside or confirm it and if it confirms it, it must specify a period within which it must be complied with.

(*c*) If a company carries on business under a name which does not consist of its corporate name without addition, it must register the business name and certain other particulars under the Registration of Business Names Act, 1916.

A company can change its name by special resolution together with the written approval of the Department of Trade and Industry.

Registered Office. The Memorandum states whether the registered office is situated in England or Scotland. The actual address is not set out but must be filed with the Registrar on or before the day of commencement of business, or within 14 days of incorporation, whichever is earlier. (Sect. 107 (2).) The address cannot be changed to a place outside the country of registration, but otherwise can be changed by an ordinary resolution of members or by the directors to whom the power is usually delegated.

Objects Clause. This clause sets out the activities which the company is formed to pursue. Any transaction not authorised by the clause, or fairly incidental to it, is *ultra vires* and void. (*Ashbury Railway Carriage Co.* v. *Riche*, 1875[120] and *Re Jon Beauforte (London) Ltd.*, 1953,[121] and *Deuchar* v. *Gas, Light and Coke Co.*, 1925.)[122] It is usual to include a large number of objects, and to stipulate that each object is an independent main object which can be pursued separately if need be. (*Cotman* v. *Brougham*, 1918.)[123] In this way the limitations placed on a company's business activities by the *ultra vires* rule have been mitigated, though inevitably control over the activities of the directors has been reduced. In this connection a recent decision of the Court of Appeal suggests that an objects clause can be drafted in such a way as to allow the company to carry on any business the directors choose. (*Bell Houses Ltd.* v. *City Wall Properties Ltd.*, 1966.)[125]

The clause may be altered by a special resolution for the purposes set out in Sect. 5 of the Act, namely—

(i) To carry on its business more economically or efficiently;

(ii) To attain its main purpose by new and improved means;

(iii) To enlarge or change the local area of its operations;

(iv) To carry on some business which under existing circumstances may conveniently or advantageously be combined with the business of the company (It seems that this provision gives scope for quite sweeping changes—*Re Parent Tyre Co. Ltd.*, 1923);[520]

(v) To restrict or abandon any of the objects specified in the Memorandum;

(vi) To sell or dispose of the whole or any part of the undertaking of the company;

(vii) To amalgamate with any other company or body of persons.

Once a special resolution has been passed, it stands unless within 21 days an application for its cancellation is made by (*a*) the holders of 15 per cent of the company's issued capital, or any class thereof; or (*b*) the holders of 15 per cent of the company's issued debentures, if secured by a floating charge and if they were issued before 1st December, 1947, or form part of a series the first of which was issued before that date. The applicants must not have consented to, or voted for, the alteration.

Limitation of Liability. This clause simply states: "The liability of the members is limited,"—unless the company is unlimited. It is not possible to alter this clause so as to make the company an unlimited one, though the company may be re-registered under Sect. 43 of the 1967 Act. An unlimited company may re-register as a limited company under Sect. 44 of the 1967 Act.

Capital Clause. This clause must state the amount of the company's authorised capital and its division into shares of a fixed nominal or par value, e.g. "The share capital of the company is £100,000 divided into 100,000 shares of one pound each."

Association Clause. This clause states that the subscribers wish to be formed into a company and that they agree to take the shares opposite their names.

ARTICLES OF ASSOCIATION

The second major document governing the company is the Articles of Association. The articles regulate the rights of the members of the company among themselves, and the manner in which the business of the company shall be conducted. They contain rules relating to the issue of shares, the rights of different classes and methods of altering class rights, the issue of share certificates, calls on shares and forfeitures, transfer and transmission of shares, audits and accounts, notice and procedure at general meetings, appointment and duties of directors and the secretary. A company may adopt the model set of articles set out in *Table A* of the Companies Act, or may register its own articles. The articles must be printed and signed by each subscriber to the Memorandum in the presence of at least one witness.

Legal Effect of the Memorandum and Articles. The memorandum and articles when registered form a contract which binds the company and the members as if signed by each member. Thus—

(*a*) *The members are bound to the company to conform to the articles* (*Hickman* v. *Kent or Romney Marsh Sheepbreeders Association,* 1915);[521]

(*b*) *Each member is bound to the other members* (*Rayfield* v. *Hands*, 1958);[522]

(*c*) *Neither the company nor the members are bound to outsiders* (*Eley* v. *Positive Life Assurance Co.*, 1876).[523]

Alteration of Articles. A company may alter or add to its articles by a special resolution (Sect. 10) subject to the following restrictions—

(i) *An alteration will be set aside by the court if it is not for the benefit of the members as a whole*, as where the company takes a power of expulsion. (*Dafen Tinplate Co.* v. *Llanelly Steel Co. Ltd.*, 1920.)[524] However, expulsion is allowed where it would benefit the members as a whole, as where the member expelled is competing with the company. (*Sidebottom* v. *Kershaw, Leese & Co. Ltd.*, 1920.)[525]

(ii) *A company cannot justify a breach of contract by showing that the breach results from an alteration of the articles.* (*Baily* v. *British Equitable Assurance Co.*, 1904;[526] *Southern Foundries* v. *Shirlaw*, 1940.)[527]

(iii) No alteration may be made requiring a member at the date of the alteration to subscribe for additional shares of the company, or in any other way to increase his liability. (Sect. 22.)

Constructive Notice of Memorandum and Articles. Since both documents have to be registered and are open to the inspection of the public, any person dealing with the company is deemed to know their contents. (*Re Jon Beauforte Ltd.*, 1953.)[121] However, if the transaction appears to be a proper one when compared with the memorandum and articles, an outsider is not affected by internal irregularities, unless he actually knew of them. (*Royal British Bank* v. *Turquand*, 1855.)[528] Thus, a transaction will be good even though the directors who carried it out were not properly appointed, or had exceeded the authority conferred upon them as in *Turquand's* case itself. The rule also validates a transaction not authorised by a proper board meeting, as where there was no quorum.

MEMBERSHIP OF A COMPANY

Membership of a company is achieved by subscribing the Memorandum; by applying for and being allotted shares; or by taking a transfer from a member. Entry on the Register of Members is a basic requirement of membership. The following special cases may be noted.

A minor may be a member unless the articles forbid it. A minor can repudiate the contract in respect of money due on the shares, but cannot recover money paid for them if the shares ever had any value. (*Steinberg* v. *Scala*, 1923.)[109]

Personal Representatives of a deceased member do not become members unless they ask for and obtain registration, but Sect. 64 gives them the right to transfer the shares.

A Bankrupt may be a member unless the articles forbid it, though the beneficial interest in his shares will be vested in his trustee in bankruptcy.

A company may, if authorised by its memorandum, own shares in another company.

Shareholders' Rights and Liabilities. A shareholder has the right to apply for rectification of the Register of Members so as to complete his membership. He is also given the right to transfer his shares, subject to the restrictions required by the Act in the case of private companies, and subject to any right given by the articles of a private company to directors to refuse registration.

There is a right under various provisions of the Act to convene meetings, to receive notice of meetings, and to attend and vote at meetings.

A shareholder's right to dividend depends upon sufficient profits having been made to pay it, and upon the declaration of a dividend by the directors. He has also a right to receive a copy of the company's balance sheet not less than 21 days prior to the Annual General Meeting.

A shareholder is under a statutory liability to pay for his shares when called upon to do so, but is not liable for the company's debts beyond the amount (if any) outstanding on his shares except where, to his knowledge, the membership of the company falls below seven (or two in the case of a private company), and the company carries on business with that reduced number for more than six months. In such a case the liability of the existing member or members for debts incurred after the expiration of the six months is unlimited.

NOMINEE HOLDINGS

Sects. 33–34 of the Companies Act, 1967, are concerned with the prevention of some of the problems created by nominee holdings, and provide that a quoted company must keep a register giving particulars of persons having an interest in a holding of 10 per cent or more of shares carrying unrestricted voting rights. The interests concerned include rights to subscribe, joint interests, interests under trusts or via companies in which the member concerned has control of one third of the voting rights or control of the board. Bare trustee holdings are excluded, as are interests in remainder, but additionally, particulars need not be given if the interest is a life interest in shares created by an irrevocable settlement under which the settlor has no interest in any income or property comprised in the settlement. It is not necessary to give particulars of shares held as security for money lent in the ordinary course of business.

The Act makes provision for notice to be given to the company by members in the event of their coming within the 10 per cent holding provision, and also if subsequently they become interested in more or fewer shares so that the register may be kept up to date. The register is to be open for inspection by any person and copies may be requested, although the necessary information given in respect of companies able to claim the benefit of Sects. 3 (3) or 4 (3) (oversea companies) may be withheld from the public register.

The entries made in this register do not affect the company with notice of the rights of any person in relation to the shares. This is a similar provision to the one contained in Section 117 of the principal Act.

DIRECTORS

The directors manage the company and the shareholders' main control lies in their power to appoint the directors.

Every public company must have at least two directors and every private company must have at least one director. (Sect. 176.) Every company must have a secretary and a sole director cannot also be the secretary. (Sect. 177.)

Appointment. The first directors are usually named in the articles but such an appointment is not valid unless the director named has delivered to the Registrar a written consent to act, and a written undertaking to take his qualification shares, unless he has subscribed the memorandum for a sufficient number. If no appointment is made in the articles, the subscribers of the memorandum, or a majority of them, may appoint.

Subsequently directors are usually appointed by the members of the company in general meeting by ordinary resolution. The Board of Directors is normally empowered to fill casual vacancies, and to appoint additional directors up to the permitted maximum. Persons so appointed usually hold office until the next annual general meeting when the members decide whether they are to continue in office.

Generally one or more of the full-time directors is appointed *managing director* and is given powers exercisable without reference to the Board. The articles must provide for the appointment, and articles usually enable the Board to confer on the managing director any of the powers exercisable by the Board, and to vary his powers.

Share Qualification. The articles may require directors to hold a certain minimum number of shares in the company. The number of shares is often specified in the articles, but may be fixed by the company by ordinary resolution in general meeting, and until so fixed none is required.

A director need not obtain his qualification shares before he is appointed unless the articles require this, but unless he obtains them within two months of his appointment, or such shorter time as may be fixed by the articles, he ceases to be a director, and cannot be re-appointed until he gets his share qualification. A director is not qualified merely by holding share warrants.

Articles often require a director to hold his qualification shares "in his own right," but this does not mean that he must be the unencumbered owner so long as the company can safely deal with him as a member. Thus a director has been held qualified even though he had created an equitable mortgage of his shares.

The modern trend is for articles of association not to require a share qualification for directors. It is now a generally held view that no useful purpose is served by the requirement. The small number of shares normally required as a qualification are insignificant as a stake in the business, which was formerly a major reason for qualification shares.

Remuneration. If a director is to receive remuneration his contract of service or the articles must expressly provide for it, and in the absence of such provision, no remuneration is payable even if the members resolve in general meeting that it shall be. If a director has a service contract with the company, Sect. 26 of the Companies Act, 1967, requires the company to keep a copy of it which is to be open to inspection by members. Under the provisions of Sect. 6 of the 1967 Act the accounts of the company must disclose the emoluments of the directors and the chairman.

Removal. Under the provisions of Sect. 184 every company has power to remove any director before the expiration of his period of office, regardless of anything in the articles or in his service contract. The removal is effected by an ordinary resolution at a general meeting. Special notice of 28 days must be given to the company that the resolution will be moved. The removal of a director under Sect. 184 does not prejudice any right he has for compensation for loss of office or for damages for wrongful dismissal.

Retirement. The company's articles generally provide that a given number of directors shall retire at the Annual General Meeting. *Table A* provides that one-third shall so retire, though they may be re-elected. This is called retirement by rotation.

Resignation. The articles usually provide that a director vacates office when he notifies his resignation to the company. The articles may require the notice to be in writing. Notice is effective as soon as it is communicated, and there can be no withdrawal except with the consent of the persons entitled to appoint directors.

Disqualification. If a director becomes disqualified, by law or by the articles, from continuing to be a director, he automatically vacates office. The following are grounds for disqualification—

(i) BANKRUPTCY, unless the court gives leave to act (Sect. 187).

(ii) AGE LIMIT. A director of a public company (or a private company which is a subsidiary to a public company) who is already in office and attains the age of 70 years, vacates office at the annual general meeting next after his 70th birthday. He may be re-elected by an ordinary resolution of members in general meeting of which special notice has been given.

(iii) LOSS OF SHARE QUALIFICATION.

(iv) UNDER A PROVISION IN THE ARTICLES. A company's articles usually state several grounds on which directors will vacate office. *Table A* provides that a director ceases to hold office if he becomes bankrupt; or arranges or compounds with his creditors; becomes of unsound mind; or is absent for more than six months from meetings of the Board without the Board's permission.

Powers of Directors. The Board and the members in general meeting can exercise all of the company's powers. The Act requires certain powers to be exercised by the members, e.g. alteration of Memorandum, but apart from this, the distribution of powers between Board and members depends entirely on the articles.

Quorum. A Board meeting cannot validly transact business unless a quorum of directors is present. The quorum is usually fixed by the articles, and *Table A* fixes it at *two* or as many as the directors may decide. A director who has an interest of a personal nature in the matter before the Board may be disabled by the articles from voting, in which case he does not count towards a quorum.

Duties of Directors. The relationship between a company and its directors is that of principal and agent and as agents the directors stand in a fiduciary relationship to their principal, the company. In addition directors owe a duty of care at common law not to act negligently in managing the company's affairs.

FIDUCIARY DUTIES.

(*a*) *duty to act bona fide.* This duty requires directors to act in what they honestly believe to be the best interests of the company;

(*b*) *duty to act intra vires and within the law.* This duty requires directors to exercise their powers for the purpose for which they were given. The acts concerned are not only those which are beyond their own or the company's powers or are illegal. It is enough if the act is one which, although within their power, is not contemplated as an ordinary or proper use of it; (*Piercy* v. *Mills*, 1920.)[529]

(*c*) *duty to retain freedom of action.* This duty requires that directors shall not restrict their right to freely and fully exercise their duties and powers. Thus directors cannot validly contract with one another or with third parties on the way in which they will vote at board meetings;

(*d*) *duty to avoid conflict of interest.* This duty manifests itself in regard to directors' contracts with the company and the making of secret profits. Sect. 199 provides that every director who has an interest, whether direct or indirect, in a contract or proposed contract must disclose his interest to the company at the first possible board meeting. A director must account to the company for any personal profit made in the course of his dealings with the company's property. Thus if he receives gifts of money or shares from the company's promoters he must account for these sums to the company but may keep a personal profit if the members in general meeting consent.

COMMON LAW DUTY OF SKILL AND CARE. A director also owes a duty of care to the company at common law not to act negligently in managing its affairs. The decided cases show that the duty is not a high one. (*Overend & Gurney* v. *Gibb*, 1872.)[530]

However, in modern times when the directors of companies are often experts in particular fields, e.g. accounting and engineering, a higher standard of competence may be expected of them, particularly in their own sphere.

It should be noted that directors do not owe any contractual or fiduciary duties to the members. (*Percival* v. *Wright*, 1902.)[531]

Publicity in respect of Directors. Every company must keep at its registered office a Register of Directors and Secretaries, showing in respect of each director his Christian name and surname, his residential address, nationality, business occupation and other directorships held, his date of birth and, in the case of a corporate member, the address of the registered office. The name and address of the Secretary is also included.

A return must be made to the Registrar within 14 days after any new appointment or change in the particulars. The register is open to inspection of the members free of charge and to the public on payment of a fee. The names of the directors must also appear on letters and trade publications, though the Department of Trade and Industry can grant exemption.

Directors' Contracts and Dealings in Shares. Sect. 25 of the 1967 Act makes it illegal for directors, their spouses and minor children (Sect. 30), to deal in options to buy or sell shares in or debentures of their companies or associated companies (holding, subsidiary or fellow-subsidiary), except where the shares or debentures are not quoted on any Stock Exchange.

The penalty for an infringement is, on summary conviction, imprisonment for a term not exceeding three months or a fine not exceeding £200 or both. On conviction on indictment the penalties are imprisonment for a term not exceeding two years or a fine or both.

Under Sect. 26 a company must keep at its registered office a copy of each director's service contract where this is in writing, and if it is not in writing there must be kept a written memorandum setting out the terms of the contract. These documents are to be open to inspection by members without charge and failure to keep the necessary particulars or refusal to allow inspection renders the company and every officer in default liable to a fine not exceeding £500 and also to a default fine. The section does not apply to contracts which have less than twelve months to run, or to those which can be terminated by the company within the next ensuing twelve months without payment of compensation. Further, it does not apply to contracts under which a director is required to work wholly or mainly outside the United Kingdom.

Sects. 27 to 29 of the 1967 Act replace the provisions of Sect. 195 of the principal Act relating to the register of directors' shareholdings.

The effect is to strengthen the provisions and to require much greater disclosure to members of the company of the interests of directors in the securities of the company and associated companies.

The former register of directors' holdings of shares and debentures in the company or its group is replaced by a register showing directors' (and by Sect. 31 their spouses' and infant children's) interests in such shares and debentures. Under Sect. 28 directors' interests include rights to subscribe, joint interests, interests under trusts, or via companies in which the director concerned controls one-third of the voting rights or whose directors are accustomed to act in accordance with his directions or instructions.

Bare trustee holdings are excluded as are interests in remainder where some other person receives the income for his lifetime or that of someone else. Thus if shares are left to X for life and after X's death to Y, then during the lifetime of X, Y has no interest in the shares for the purposes of the Act.

A director must notify the company of his interests on 27th October, 1967, or on his appointment if later, and of any change in the details given. The information required for entry includes purchase and sale prices and the register is to be kept in chronological order for each director.

Sect. 32 provides that if it appears to the Board of Trade that there are circumstances suggesting that the requisite disclosures regarding share or debenture dealings have not been made, the Board may appoint one or more competent inspectors to carry out such investigations as may be necessary to establish whether or not contraventions have occurred, and to report the result of their investigations to the Board.

Directors' Report. This is annexed to the balance sheet and circularised and published with it. Before the Act of 1967 the reports of directors were often formal and of little value. Now, however, the 1967 Act makes them a source of annual information which could not conveniently be given in the accounts. Sects. 16 to 23 of the 1967 Act require additional information to be disclosed in the directors' report and Sect. 15 defines "directors' report" for the purposes of Sects. 16 to 23 as "the report by the directors of a company which by Sect. 157 (1) of the principal Act is required to be attached to every balance sheet of the company laid before it in general meeting."

ADDITIONAL MATTERS OF A GENERAL NATURE. (i) Under Sect. 16 (1) a company must give the names of the persons who, at the end of the financial year, were directors of the company and details of the principal activities of the company and of its subsidiaries in the course of that year and of any significant changes therein.

(ii) SECT. 16 (1) (*a*) states that if significant changes in the *fixed assets* of the company or any of its subsidiaries have occurred during the year under review, particulars of the changes must be given, and if the market value of such of those assets as consist in *interests in land* differs substantially from the value as shown in the balance sheet, particulars of the difference should be given if, in the opinion of the directors, it is of such significance that the attention of members and debenture holders should be drawn to it.

(iii) Under Sect. 16 (1) (*b*) details must be given of any issue of stock, shares or debentures and the consideration received by the company, together with reasons for making the issue.

(iv) Sect. 16 (1) (c) requires particulars of contracts of significance made during the year in question in which any director has a material interest whether direct or indirect. In this respect the directors' report should include—

(a) a statement of the fact that the contract exists or has existed during the year;

(b) the names of the parties to the contract (other than the company);

(c) the name of the director concerned if he is not a party to the contract (because a director may have an interest in a contract without being a party to it);

(d) an indication of the nature of the contract; and

(e) the nature of the director's interest in the contract.

This subsection is not concerned with a director's contract of service or a contract between the company and another body corporate, being a contract in which a director of the company has or had an interest merely as a director of that other body.

(v) Under Sect. 16 (1) (d) a statement must be given explaining any arrangement to which the company is a party which enables directors to obtain benefits by acquiring securities of the company or of any other body corporate. The statement must give the names of the persons who at any time during the year in question were directors of the company and held or whose nominees held shares or debentures acquired under such an arrangement.

(vi) By Sect. 16 (1) (e) disclosure is also required of directors who at the end of the year had an interest in securities of the company or any other body corporate being—

(a) a subsidiary of the company, or

(b) the company's holding company, or

(c) a subsidiary of the company's holding company,

and the extent of his interest and whether he was interested at the beginning of the year or, if he was not a director at the beginning of the year, the date on which he became a director.

(vii) Finally, under Sect. 16 (1) (f) there must be disclosed "any matter material for the appreciation of the state of the company's affairs by its members." However, disclosure is not required if in the opinion of the directors it would be harmful to the business of the company or its subsidiaries.

DETAILS OF TURNOVER AND PROFITABILITY. Sect. 17 states that if, in the course of a financial year, a company or group of companies has carried on business of two or more classes (with certain exceptions, e.g. banking or discounting) the directors' report must state the proportions in which the turnover for the year is divided amongst the different classes, and the extent (expressed in monetary terms) to which in the opinion of the directors the business of each class contributed to or restricted the profit or loss for that year (before taxation) of the company, and, as the case may be, the subsidiaries dealt with by the accounts.

AVERAGE NUMBER OF EMPLOYEES AND THE AMOUNT OF THEIR WAGES. Sect. 18 requires that the directors' report shall state the *average* number of persons employed by the company and its subsidiaries (if any) in each week of the financial year, and the aggregate *gross* remuneration (including contractual or other bonuses) paid or payable to them.

The average number of persons employed is to be ascertained by adding together the number of persons who are working in each week of the financial year taken week by week, and dividing the figure obtained by fifty-two or fifty-three according to the number of weeks in the financial year.

The Section does not apply if the *average* number of persons employed is less than 100, nor does it apply to a company which is a wholly owned subsidiary of a company incorporated in Great Britain.

The report is not to include employees who worked wholly or mainly outside the United Kingdom.

PARTICULARS OF CONTRIBUTIONS FOR POLITICAL AND CHARITABLE PURPOSES. Sect. 19 requires that the directors' report must give the following details of any contribution (if it exceeded £50) made by the company for political or charitable purposes—

(*a*) the name of each person to whom it has been given or if given for charitable purposes and received by some person on behalf of the charity, the purposes for which it was given and the amount of money given;

(*b*) in the case of money given for political purposes by way of donation or subscription to a political party, the identity of the party and the amount of money given.

The above provisions apply to money given to a political party of the United Kingdom or of any part thereof, or to a person who is known to be carrying on activities reasonably likely to affect public support for such a party.

VALUE OF GOODS EXPORTED. Sect. 20 states that if the business of a company or its subsidiaries consists in or includes the supplying of goods, the report must state the total value of goods exported, or, as the case may be, that no goods have been exported.

If the turnover of the company, or the group if there are subsidiaries, does not exceed £250,000 disclosure of the value of goods exported is not required. For the purposes of Sect. 20 goods exported by a company as the agent of another person are to be disregarded, and disclosure is not required if the directors can satisfy the Department of Trade and Industry that it would not be in the national interest.

Sect. 21 provides that Sects. 16 to 19 of the Act shall not apply to a report attached to the balance sheet of a company laid before it in general meeting which relates to a financial year ending before the Act became law.

Sect. 22 states that where a company takes advantage of Sect. 163 of the principal Act which allows the disclosures required by Sect. 196 of the principal Act and Sects. 6, 7 and 8 of the 1967 Act to be made in the directors' report and not in the accounts or in a statement annexed thereto, the directors' report shall also show the corresponding amount for the immediately preceding financial year for each item.

Penalties of imprisonment for a term not exceeding six months or a fine not exceeding £200 are provided for by Sect. 23 in respect of a director who fails to take all reasonable steps to comply with the provisions regarding the directors' report. However, it is a defence for him to prove that he had reasonable grounds to believe that a competent and reliable person was charged with the duty of securing compliance. There shall be no sentence of imprisonment unless in the opinion of the court dealing with the case the offence was committed wilfully.

Sect. 24 confers upon members of the company, debenture holders and persons entitled to receive notices of general meetings of the company, the right to receive copies of the directors' report.

SHARE CAPITAL

A company may, if given power by its Memorandum or Articles, issue shares of different classes carrying different rights. The capital of a company is usually divided into Preference and Ordinary Shares.

Preference Shares. These are shares which have the right to payment of a fixed dividend, e.g. 6 per cent of the nominal value, before any dividend is paid on the other shares. There is no right to such dividend unless it is declared in general meeting and the company has made sufficient profits to pay it.

Once the Preference Dividend has been paid in full, there is no right to a share in the surplus profits, unless the shares are *participating preference shares*. Preference shares are assumed to be *cumulative*, so if, in any one year, the preference dividend cannot be paid, it is carried forward and added to the dividend for the following year and so on. It is possible to have *non-cumulative* preference shares if the terms of the issue so provide.

Preference shares have no right to claim repayment of capital before the ordinary shares on a winding up unless the terms of issue expressly so provide. In the absence of such provision the preference shares and ordinary shares take the assets on an equal footing. If the preference shares are in fact preferential as to capital, they can only be paid the actual value of their share capital, even if this means that the ordinary shares receive more than the value of the share capital out of the surplus assets.

A company may, if authorised by its articles, issue *redeemable preference shares* which may be redeemed by the company at a future date. The shares cannot be redeemed unless they are fully paid, and the fund to redeem them must be provided (i) out of the proceeds of a new issue of shares; or (ii) out of profits. In the latter case an amount equal to the nominal value of the shares redeemed must be transferred from the company's revenue reserves to an account called the *Capital Redemption Reserve Fund*. This fund can then only be used to issue fully-paid bonus shares to members of the company.

Ordinary Shares. These rank for dividend and often for capital repayment after the preference shares and therefore carry most of the risk. Generally they have most of the voting rights in general meetings. They receive a fluctuating dividend which depends on the profits left after preference dividend has been paid.

Deferred Shares. There were sometimes called Founders' Shares and were usually held by the founders of a business which had grown and which had attracted a large volume of capital from subsequent investors. They rank last for payment of dividend after the claims of other types of share have been satisfied, but where a company was very successful, these shares were extremely valuable and earned very large dividends indeed. However, since these shares were often used to perpetrate frauds, companies with such shares became unpopular with investors. Consequently these shares are not issued today, and most public companies which had deferred shares have converted them into Ordinary Shares.

Stock. Shares and stock are distinguishable in that shares are units transferable only as such, whereas stock is expressed in terms of money and is transferable in fractions. For example, £1 shares are transferable only as units, and a shareholder cannot transfer a half- or quarter-share, but where the company has converted its shares into stock it is possible to transfer odd amounts, e.g. £15·17 worth. It is usual, however, for the articles to prohibit the transfer of stock except in round sums. A company cannot convert its shares into stock unless the shares are fully paid.

Issue of Shares. When a company wishes to issue shares, it issues a prospectus which is an invitation to treat. A would-be investor makes application to the company and this is the contractual offer. The investor will also send the application money, which must not be less than 5 per cent of the nominal value of the shares offered. The applications are considered by the Board, and letters of allotment are sent to applicants who are to receive shares. The contract to take shares is complete when the letter of allotment is posted. (*Household Fire Insurance Co.* v. *Grant*, 1878.)[33] Eventually a share certificate will be issued under the company's seal.

If the prospectus is the first which the company has issued, the company may not allot any shares under it unless the minimum subscription has been subscribed. (Sect. 47.) If the minimum subscription has not been subscribed within 40 days after the prospectus was first issued, all money received must be returned; and if it is not returned within eight days, the directors are personally liable to repay it with interest at 5 per cent per annum.

If the shares are allotted before the minimum subscription has been subscribed, any allottee may rescind the allotment within one month after the allotment, or one month after the statutory meeting whichever is the later. This is so even if the company is being wound up. Allottees may also, within the next two years, sue the directors who allotted the shares for damage suffered, if any.

Issue of Shares at a Discount. If certain provisions of the Companies Act, 1948, are complied with a company may issue shares at a discount. These conditions are contained in Sect. 57—

(*a*) The shares must belong to a class of shares some of which have already been issued;

(*b*) The issue must be authorised by an ordinary resolution in general meeting of the company, and must be sanctioned by the court;

(*c*) The resolution must specify the maximum rate of discount at which the shares are to be issued;

(*d*) At least a year must have elapsed since the date on which the company was entitled to commence business;

(*e*) The shares must be issued within one month after the date on which the issue is sanctioned by the court, but the court may extend the time.

THE PROSPECTUS

This is a document issued by a company in order to induce the public to subscribe for its shares. A prospectus is defined by Sect. 455 (1) as "any prospectus, notice, circular, advertisement, or other invitation, offering to the public for subscription or purchase any shares or debentures of the company."

The company will want to make the prospectus as attractive as possible, and to prevent the public from being misled, Sect. 38 and the Fourth Schedule require certain disclosures to be made, the most important of which are—

(i) **The Minimum Subscription.** This is an estimate of the amount required to be raised by the issue to pay the purchase price of any property to be acquired by the company; to meet preliminary expenses; to repay any money borrowed for these purposes; and to provide the company with working capital.

(ii) **Persons concerned in Property Transactions.** If the proceeds of the issue are to be applied in purchasing property or a business, a statement must be made giving the purchase price (goodwill being stated separately), and particulars of the vendors and details of any transaction within the previous two years in which any vendor, promoter or director was interested.

(iii) **Material Contracts.** Particulars of all material contracts entered into by the company within the last two years, copies of such contracts being filed with the Registrar. Material contracts are those which are not made in the ordinary course of the company's business and which are likely to influence investors in deciding whether to buy the securities offered or not.

(iv) **Auditor's Report.** This must show the state of the company's assets and liabilities, and the profits and losses made and the dividends paid during the last five years.

(v) **Profit of Issuing House.** Where the prospectus is issued by an issuing house, i.e. where it is an offer for sale, it must disclose how much of the money received from the public will be paid to the company, thus revealing how much money is retained by the issuing house.

Liability for Misstatements in the Prospectus. A person who is induced to subscribe for shares by false statements of fact made by the company, or its officers or agents, has certain remedies.

(*a*) He may rescind the allotment of shares and reclaim any money paid to the company for them.

(*b*) He may sue the persons responsible for the false statement—

    (i) *in damages* for deceit where the statement is fraudulent;
    (ii) *for compensation*, under Sect. 43 of the Act.

In a claim under Sect. 43, the subscriber need not prove deceit or even negligence, and since this lightens the burden of proof, the statutory claim under Sect. 43 is to be preferred even where there is fraud. However, the *liability* of the defendant under Sect. 43 is *not an absolute one* because he may plead any of the following defences—

(1) That he had reasonable grounds for believing the statement to be true;

(2) That the statement was contained in the report of an expert whom he had reasonable grounds for believing to be competent;

(3) That the statement was taken from a public official statement or document;

(4) That he withdrew his consent to become a director before the prospectus was issued;

(5) That he did not consent to the issue of the prospectus, and gave public notice of the fact;

(6) That he believed the statement to be true when the prospectus was issued, and on subsequently discovering it to be false, he withdrew his consent to it, and gave reasonable public notice that he had done so *before shares were allotted* to the plaintiff.

An action is also available under Sect. 2 (1) of the Misrepresentation Act, 1967. Sect. 2 (1) is similar in conception to Sect. 43 of the Companies Act, 1948, but the two sections do not entirely overlap in that an action for damages under Sect. 43 can be brought only against *individuals* responsible for the prospectus, whereas under Sect. 2 (1) of the 1967 Act it is possible that the company may also be sued.

Individuals responsible for the prospectus may possibly be sued for damages under the principle in *Hedley Byrne*[165] where they are persons possessed of special skill who have *negligently* prepared a prospectus.

UNDERWRITING

Before an issue of shares is made to the public it is usual to insure the success of the issue by having it underwritten. The underwriter agrees with the company to subscribe for any shares which the public do not take and the consideration paid to the underwriter is called underwriting commission. Since the payment of this commission operates as an issue of shares at a discount, it cannot be paid unless—

(*a*) It is authorised by the articles;

(*b*) It does not exceed either 10 per cent of the price at which the shares are issued, or the rate authorised by the articles whichever is the less;

(*c*) The amount or rate per cent is disclosed in the prospectus or statement in lieu;

(*d*) The number of shares which the underwriters have agreed to subscribe for is disclosed in the prospectus or statement in lieu. (Sect. 53.)

It is common practice for underwriters to relieve themselves of some of the risk by entering into sub-underwriting contracts, the difference between the commission paid by the company to the principal underwriters and the commission paid by the latter to the sub-underwriters being called "overriding commission."

Brokerage. This differs from underwriting in that it is a payment made to a broker for placing shares or debentures with his clients without involving him in any risk of having to take them up. The payment of brokerage is not controlled by the Act, but it must not be excessive. The rate is a matter for negotiation according to the degree of risk. The amount of brokerage payable must be disclosed in the prospectus or statement in lieu. Underwriting commission and brokerage can be paid on an issue of debentures and there is no statutory control as to the amount payable.

INCORPORATION

A company is incorporated by applying for registration which is effected by the promoters filing the following documents with the Registrar of Companies—

(i) The Memorandum of Association;

(ii) The Articles of Association;

(iii) A Statutory Declaration of compliance with the requirements of the Act regarding the company's formation, made by a solicitor or the secretary or a director of the company;

(iv) A Statement of Nominal Capital for the purpose of calculating the duty payable on the registered capital of the company.

If the company is a private company the above documents suffice, but *a public company must also file—*

(v) A list of persons who have consented to act as directors;
(vi) The written consent of each such person to act;
(vii) A written undertaking by each person to take and pay for his qualification shares (if any) unless he has already taken and paid for them or has signed the Memorandum for a sufficient number.

If the Registrar is satisfied with the contents of the above documents he will issue a certificate of incorporation.

PROMOTERS

Cockburn, C.J. in *Twycross* v. *Grant* (1877), 2 C.P.D. 469, described a promoter as "one who undertakes to form a company with reference to a given project, and to set it going, and who takes the necessary steps to accomplish that purpose." However, Sect. 43 of the 1948 Act gives special protection to persons who merely assist the promoters in the formation of the company, e.g. a solicitor who advised on the requirements of registration would not be regarded as a promoter.

A promoter stands in a fiduciary relationship towards the company he is promoting but is not a trustee. He is not forbidden to make a profit out of the promotion so long as he has disclosed his interests in the transaction out of which the profit arose and the company consents to the retention of the profit. Any profits which he makes on the promotion and fails to disclose must be surrendered to the company. (*Gluckstein* v. *Barnes*, 1900.)[532]

Under the rules of the law of agency promoters incur personal liability on pre-incorporation contracts, and the company cannot ratify the transaction so as to accept liability itself. (*Kelner* v. *Baxter*, 1866.)[434] A company may become bound by making, after incorporation, an *express contract* on the same terms as the pre-incorporation contract and so release the promoter from liability. Such a contract may also be *implied* from the way in which the company acts after its incorporation. Therefore, pre-incorporation contracts usually contain a clause stating that if the company fails to make an express contract or novation within a given time the promoter or the other party may terminate the contract. It should be noted that contracts made by a public company after incorporation but before issue of a trading certificate are *provisional* only. However, when the trading certificate is issued they immediately and automatically become binding.

Promoters have no inherent right to payment for their services, but the company may pay them if it chooses to do so, often by granting them fully paid shares.

SHARE CERTIFICATES

A company is required to have a share certificate ready for delivery within two months after allotment or transfer. A share certificate is issued usually under the company's seal.

Effect of Certificate. A company may be estopped from denying the truth of statements made in its share certificates where innocent third parties have acted on such statements. Thus, if a share certificate states that the shares are fully paid when they are not, or that a certain person is the owner when he is not, then if the company recognises the validity of the certificate by registering or certifying a transfer, the transferee may have an action against the company in respect of loss arising from the false certificate.

Share Warrants. Public companies may issue share warrants provided there is authority in the articles. Warrants are issued under the company's seal and the shares represented by the warrant must be fully paid. Three times the normal transfer duty is payable when the shares are exchanged for a warrant, but thereafter they are transferable by mere delivery and do not attract transfer duty. The holders' names are not entered on the company's register of members. Since warrants are negotiable instruments, and dividend is payable by the holder producing a coupon, several of which are attached to the warrant, the holder of a share warrant cannot use it to qualify as a director.

Calls. The normal practice today is for the issue price to be payable by instalments over a period of time, rarely more than six months from allotment. However, a fraction of the issue price may be left outstanding for an indefinite period, and such money is said to be *at call*. Calls on shares are generally made by the Board of Directors and the company generally has a lien on the shares of its members for unpaid calls. The lien includes the power to sell the shares and recoup the money owing for calls out of the proceeds.

Forfeiture and Surrender. Shares may be forfeited or surrendered for non-payment of calls. The procedure is laid down in the articles. *Table A* provides that the directors may forfeit by a resolution of the Board any shares on which a call has been made but not paid if—

(i) notice is served on the shareholder stating that if payment is not made within 14 days the shares will be liable to forfeiture; and
(ii) payment is not so made.

When the shares have been forfeited the shareholder is informed and asked to return his share certificate. The company may re-sell the shares, though the original shareholder remains liable to pay until the company has actually received the called-up value of the shares from a purchaser. A shareholder may surrender his shares, if the articles give the directors power to accept a surrender. The circumstances must be such as would warrant a forfeiture or the surrender is invalid, e.g. where it is done merely to relieve shareholders of liability to pay future calls.

Transfer and Transmission of Shares. Under the provisions of the Stock Transfer Act, 1963, the method of transferring fully-paid shares or stock is as follows.

The shareholder executes a form, termed a *stock transfer form*, in favour of the purchaser, and hands it to the purchaser, or the purchaser's broker or agent, together with the share or stock certificate. The purchaser, or his broker or agent, sends the stock transfer form along with the certificate to the company for registration. The purchaser need not sign the stock transfer form, nor need the form be under seal. The selling broker has the stock transfer form stamped by the Inland Revenue.

A shareholder may wish to sell part of his holding. Thus he may have a certificate representing 300 shares or £300 worth of stock, and may wish to transfer 100 shares or £100 worth of stock.

(*a*) The selling broker will obtain a stock transfer form signed by the seller, containing details of the stock being transferred. The broker will add the consideration, and stamp the form with his identifying rubber stamp and have the form stamped by the Inland Revenue.

(*b*) The *stock transfer form* and the *certificate* and an *Advice of Certification* completed by the seller's broker are taken by the broker to the Stock Exchange for certification where the stock transfer from is certified to the effect that a certificate has been lodged.

(*c*) The Stock Exchange will send the certificate and the *Advice of Certification* to the company's Registrar who will then await the lodgment of the stock transfer form for registration.

(*d*) The transaction is completed by the selling broker handing the certified stock transfer form to the buying broker who then sends it to the company for registration, having stamped the form with his identifying rubber stamp.

(*e*) Eventually the purchaser gets a certificate for 100 shares or £100 worth of stock, and the seller gets a certificate for the balance.

Where the holding is being divided among several transferees the selling broker gets a stock transfer form signed by his client and prepares a *broker's transfer form* for each separate block of shares or stock being transferred. He enters on each *broker's transfer form* details of the transferor and the stock being transferred in each sale plus the consideration, and adds his identifying rubber stamp. He cancels the *transferee section* of the *stock transfer form*, and lists the individual *broker's transfer forms* on the back of it. The total of this list with any balance retained by the transferor should equal the amount of the shares or stock on the stock transfer form. The broker's transfer forms and not the stock transfer form attract Inland Revenue Stamp Duty.

The procedure is then as follows—

(i) The stock transfer form and the broker's transfer forms and certificates are lodged with the Stock Exchange.

(ii) The broker's transfer forms are certified and returned to the selling broker.

(iii) The selling broker sends the broker's transfer forms to the buying brokers who enter details of the transferees and add their identifying rubber stamps.

(iv) The certificates and the stock transfer form are sent to the company which retains them until the relative broker's transfer forms are lodged for registration by the buying brokers.

(v) Eventually the company will issue the necessary certificates to the persons entitled to them.

Transmission takes place when persons become entitled to deal with shares by operation of law, e.g. on the death or brankruptcy of the shareholder. Generally persons taking by transmission have all the rights attaching to the shares except those relating to attendance and voting at meetings.

Forged Transfers. Where a forged transfer is registered, the company may incur liability to a person who acts upon it and suffers loss. However, there is no liability to the actual transferee but only to purchasers from him. When the forgery is discovered, the original member is put back on the register. To prevent loss arising out of forged transfers, the company may, on receipt of a transfer, notify the transferor and give some time in which to object. However, he does not lose his right to be restored to the register if he ignores the notice.

Mortgages of Shares. Such mortgages may be legal or equitable.

A *legal mortgage* involves the transfer of the shares to the lender, such transfer being registered with the company and the lender's name being put on the register. A separate instrument records the terms of the loan and provides for re-transfer when the loan is repaid. If the borrower defaults the lender can, as a member, sell the shares to recoup his loan.

An *equitable mortgage* may be effected—

(*a*) By depositing the share certificates with the lender. If this method is used, the lender will have to apply to the court for an order for sale or transfer to himself.

(*b*) There may be a deposit of certificates together with a blank transfer form, signed by the borrower but with the transferee's name left blank. If the borrower defaults the lender can insert his own name as transferee, and become a member or sell the shares.

The lender under an equitable mortgage is not absolutely safe because the borrower may obtain a new certificate from the company by saying that he has lost the original, and may then transfer the shares to a purchaser, thus displacing the lender. It is not possible for the lender to give the company a general notice of his interest because, by

Sect. 117, a company may not recognise a trust or any other equity affecting its shares.

The lender can achieve some protection by serving on the company what is called a *notice in lieu of distringas*. Once such a notice has been served, the company must give the lender eight days' notice if any attempt is made to transfer or deal in the shares. Thereafter the company can register the transfer unless the lender has obtained during that time a court order preventing transfer.

MEETINGS AND RESOLUTIONS

Shareholders' Meetings. There are three kinds of company general meetings: (i) The Statutory Meeting; (ii) The Annual General Meeting; (iii) An Extraordinary General Meeting.

THE STATUTORY MEETING. Only one such meeting is held during the company's life. It must be held not less than one month nor more than three months from the date at which the company is entitled to commence business, and the Statutory Report must be sent to each member at least 14 clear days before the date on which the meeting is to be held.

The *Statutory Report* is required by Sect. 130 to contain the following information—

 (i) The number of shares allotted, the amount paid up on them and, if allotted for a consideration other than cash, details of the consideration;

 (ii) The cash received for the shares allotted;

 (iii) An abstract of the receipts and payments up to a date within 7 days of the report together with an estimate of the preliminary expenses;

 (iv) The names, addresses, and descriptions of the directors, auditors, managers and secretary;

 (v) Particulars of any contract which it is desired to modify at the meeting.

A copy of the Report must be filed at the Companies Registry at the time when it is sent to the members. It must be certified by two directors and by the auditors in so far as it relates to shares allotted, cash received, and payments made. The business of the Statutory Meeting is to consider any matters relating to the formation of the company or arising out of the Statutory Report. Private companies need not hold a statutory meeting nor file a Statutory Report.

ANNUAL GENERAL MEETING. Sect. 131 requires that an Annual General Meeting be held every calendar year, and not more than 15 months after the previous meeting. The meeting must be specified as the Annual General Meeting in the notice calling it. However, if a company intends to hold its first Annual General Meeting within 18 months of its incorporation, it need not hold one in its year of incorporation or in the following year. Thus, if a company was incorporated on 1st November, 1972, it has until 30th April, 1974, to hold its first Annual General Meeting.

EXTRAORDINARY MEETINGS. All general meetings other than the Annual General Meeting are Extraordinary Meetings. They may be called by the directors at any time. Sect. 132 gives holders of not less than one-tenth of the paid-up share capital on which all calls due have been paid the right to requisition such a meeting. The requisition must state the objects of the meeting, be signed by the requisitionists, and deposited at the registered office of the company. If the directors do not cause a meeting to be held within 21 days of the date of lodging of the requisition, the requisitionists, or a majority in value of them, may call the meeting within 3 months from the date of the deposit.

NOTICE OF MEETINGS. This must be given in accordance with the provisions of the Articles. *Table A* requires 21 clear days' notice of the Annual General Meeting and for a meeting called to pass a special resolution, and 14 clear days in other cases. The articles usually provide that the meeting shall not be invalidated because a particular member does not receive notice.

QUORUM AT GENERAL MEETINGS. No business may be transacted at a general meeting unless a quorum of members is present, and Sect. 134 (c) provides that three members present in person shall be a quorum in the case of a public company and *two* in the case of a private company.

Directors' Meetings. Unless the articles otherwise provide, directors can only exercise their powers *collectively* at Board Meetings, although *Table A* provides that a *unanimous* resolution of the directors, even if informal, binds the company if put into writing and signed by all the directors.

Notice of Board meetings must be given to all directors early enough to enable them to attend. This may mean notice of days, hours, or minutes, depending upon what is reasonable in the circumstances. Unless the articles otherwise provide, any director can call a Board meeting.

QUORUM. Table A provides that the quorum necessary for the transaction of the business of directors may be fixed by the directors, and unless so fixed shall be two.

VOTING. Unless the articles otherwise provide, each director has one vote and resolutions of the Board require a majority of at least one. If there is equality, the resolution is lost, unless the chairman has and exercises a casting vote.

MINUTES. A company must keep minutes of the proceedings at its general meetings and Board meetings. When signed by the chairman of the meeting or the next succeeding one, they are *prima facie* evidence that the meeting was duly convened and the resolutions duly passed. (Sect. 145.) Minutes of directors' meetings are open to inspection by the directors, but members have no general right of inspection as they have of the minutes of general meetings.

Resolutions. There are three kinds of resolutions: Ordinary, Extraordinary and Special.

(i) AN ORDINARY RESOLUTION may be defined as "a resolution passed by a majority of persons present, or voting by their representatives or by their proxies, at a general meeting."

Any business may be validly transacted by this type of resolution unless the Act or the company's Articles provide that a special or extraordinary resolution is required for that particular business.

(ii) AN EXTRAORDINARY RESOLUTION is one which has been passed by a majority of not less than three-quarters of the members who, being entitled to vote, do so, whether present in person or by proxy, at a general meeting of which notice specifying the intention to propose the resolution as an extraordinary resolution has been duly given. (Sect. 141.) The company may resolve to wind up by an extraordinary resolution if it cannot by reason of liabilities continue in business.

(iii) A SPECIAL RESOLUTION is one which has been passed by the same majority as is required for an extraordinary resolution, at a general meeting of which at least 21 days' notice has been given specifying the intention to propose the resolution as a special resolution. (Sect. 141.)

Special resolutions are required, for example, to alter the objects clause, to change the company's name or the Articles, and to effect a reduction of capital.

Sect. 143 provides that, within 15 days of the passing of an extraordinary or special resolution, a copy of the resolution must be forwarded to the Registrar.

Sect. 51 of the Companies Act, 1967, provides that the copy may be in any form approved by the Registrar, e.g. typewritten.

Voting. This may be by show of hands, in which case each member has one vote regardless of the number of shares or proxies he holds. However, the articles usually lay down that the chairman or a certain number of persons may demand a poll. If a poll is successfully demanded, each member has one vote per share, and proxies can be used. The provision in the articles regarding a poll applies only to ordinary resolutions.

In the case of extraordinary and special resolutions, Sect. 137 provides that a poll may be demanded by—

(i) The number of persons specified in the articles but not exceeding five; or

(ii) Any one or more members holding 15 per cent of the paid-up capital.

Proxies. If the articles so provide, voting may be by proxy. A proxy is a written authority given to another to vote at a given meeting. Proxy papers may be deposited at the company's office in advance. However, the articles cannot require their deposit more than 48 hours before the meeting. (Sect. 136.)

COMPANY ACCOUNTS

Books of Account. Every company must keep proper books of account with respect to—

(a) all sums of money received and expended by the company, and the matters in respect of which the receipts and expenditure take place;

(b) all sales and purchases of goods by the company;

(c) the assets and liabilities of the company. (Sect. 147 (1).)

Proper books of account shall not be deemed to be kept unless they give a true and fair view of the state of the company's affairs and explain its transactions. (Sect. 147 (2).) The books of account are to be kept at the Registered Office of the company or at such other place as the directors think fit, and must at all times be open to inspection by the directors. (Sect. 147 (3).)

Profit and Loss Account. The directors of every company must at some date, not later than eighteen months after the incorporation of the company and subsequently once at least in every calendar year, lay before the company in general meeting a profit and loss account or, in the case of a company not trading for profit, an income and expenditure account.

The profit and loss account must be made up at a date not earlier than *nine months* before the date of the meeting at which it is presented, or, in the case of a company carrying on business or having interests abroad, at a date not earlier than *twelve months* before the date of the relevant meeting. However, the Department of Trade may, for any special reason, extend the period of eighteen months, and the periods of nine and twelve months mentioned above (Sect. 148 (1).)

Balance Sheet. The directors must ensure that in every calendar year a balance sheet is made out and laid before the company in general meeting. The date of the balance sheet must be the same as that to which the profit and loss account or the income and expenditure account is made up. (Sect. 148 (2).)

Every balance sheet and profit and loss account of a company must give a true and fair view of the state of affairs of the company and its profit or loss at the end of its financial year. (Sect. 149 (1).)

Group Accounts. If a company has subsidiaries, group accounts showing the state of affairs and profit or loss of the company and the subsidiaries must be laid before the company at the general meeting at which the company's own balance sheet and profit and loss account is laid. (Sect. 150 (1).)

However *group accounts are not required* if the company is, at the end of its financial year, the wholly owned subsidiary of another body corporate incorporated in Great Britain. (Sect. 150 (2).) Group accounts need not deal with a subsidiary of the company if the company's directors are of opinion that—

(*a*) it is *impracticable*, or would be of *no real value* to members of the company, in view of the insignificant amounts involved, or would involve *expense or delay* out of proportion to the value to members of the company; or

(*b*) the result would be *misleading*, or *harmful* to the business of the company or any of its subsidiaries; or

(*c*) it is *unreasonable* because the business of the holding company and subsidiary are so different that they cannot reasonably be treated as a single undertaking.

The permission of the Department of Trade is required before a subsidiary can be omitted from the group accounts on the grounds of *unreasonableness* and where the directors allege that *harm* would accrue by the inclusion of the subsidiary. (Sect. 150 (2).)

Any director who fails to take all reasonable steps to secure compliance with the statutory requirements regarding the accounts, is liable on summary conviction to a term of imprisonment not exceeding six months or to a fine not exceeding two hundred pounds. However, it is a defence for a director to prove that he had reasonable ground to believe, and did believe, that a competent and reliable person was charged with the duty of seeing that the relevant statutory provisions were complied with, and was in a position to discharge that duty. However, a director must not be sentenced to imprisonment unless, in the opinion of the court, the offence was committed wilfully. (Sects. 147–150.)

The items to be included in the accounts of companies are set out in Schedule 2 of the Companies Act, 1967, which reprints Schedule 8 of the Companies Act, 1948, with amendments. In particular Sects. 3 to 9 and *Schedule I* of the 1967 Act require additional information to be given in the accounts of companies as follows—

Identity of Subsidiaries and Other Companies in which Shares are Held. Sect. 3 (1) requires a statement to be made in the accounts of a holding company showing the name of each subsidiary, the country (if other than Great Britain) in which it was incorporated, the identity of the class of shares held and the proportion of the nominal value of the issued shares of the class which the company holds. If the holding company is registered in England and the subsidiary is registered in Scotland or vice versa, the statement must also show the country of registration of the subsidiary.

Under Sect. 3 (3) the above information regarding subsidiaries need not be given if the subsidiary is incorporated outside the United Kingdom, or, if incorporated in the United Kingdom, it carries on business abroad, and the information required would, in the opinion of the directors of the holding company, be harmful to the business of the holding company or its subsidiaries, and the Department of Trade and Industry consents to non-disclosure.

Sect. 3 (4) provides that if, in the opinion of the directors of a company having, at the end of its financial year, subsidiaries and the number of such subsidiaries is so great that compliance with Sect. 3 (3) would result in particulars of excessive length being given, full compliance will be excused. However, Sect. 3 (1) must still be complied with in respect of subsidiaries the business of which, in the opinion of the directors, principally contributed to the amount of profit or loss of the group or to the amount of its assets.

Sect. 3 (5) states that if advantage is taken of Sect. 3 (4), the statement made at the end of the financial year shall say that it deals only with subsidiaries principally contributing to the profit or loss, or assets of the group and full compliance with Sect. 3 (1) is later required in a statement to be sent with the Annual Return first made by the company *after* its accounts have been laid before it in general meeting.

Under Sect. 3 (6) failure to annex the above particulars to the appropriate Annual Return will result in a fine on the company and any officer in default.

Sect. 4 (1) provides that where a company A holds shares of any class comprised in the equity share capital of another company B which is not its subsidiary and the holding exceeds one-tenth of the nominal value of such shares, the following information must be stated in the accounts of company A or in a note or statement annexed thereto—

(*a*) the name of company B;

(*b*) the country (if other than Great Britain) in which it is incorporated;

(*c*) the country of registration of company B if company A is registered in England and company B is registered in Scotland or vice versa;

(*d*) the identity of the class of shares held by company A; and

(*e*) the proportion of the nominal value of the issued shares of that class held.

Particulars are also required of company A's holdings in other shares of company B, even though these holdings are less than 10 per cent of the nominal value of the class concerned and whether or not the shares held are part of the equity share capital of company B. Sect. 4 (8) provides that "equity share capital" has the meaning assigned to it by Sect. 154 (5) of the principal Act and is the issued share capital of a company excluding any part thereof which, neither as respects dividends nor as respects capital, carries any right to participate beyond a specified amount in a distribution. As a general rule therefore, the equity share capital consists of the company's ordinary shares.

Under Sect. 4 (2) similar disclosures are required where company A's holdings of the shares of another company B (company B not being a subsidiary) exceeds one-tenth of the assets of company A.

Under Sect. 4 (3) the information required under Sect. 4 (1) and (2) need not be given if company B is incorporated outside the United Kingdom, or, if incorporated in the United Kingdom, it carries on business abroad and the information required would in the opinion of the directors of company A be harmful to the business of company A or B, and the Department of Trade and Industry consents to non-disclosure.

Where the disclosing company holds shares in a large number of companies and particulars of excessive length would have to be given, Sect. 4 (4) and 4 (5) provide for non-compliance in the same terms as Sect. 3 (4) and 3 (5) above.

Ultimate Holding Company. Sect. 5 (1) states that where at the end of its financial year a company is a subsidiary of another company, the accounts of the subsidiary must state the name of the company regarded by the directors of the subsidiary as its ultimate holding company and, if known to them, the country in which it is incorporated.

Under Sect. 5 (2) the above disclosure is not required by a company which carries on business outside the United Kingdom if, in the opinion of the directors of the subsidiary, it would be harmful to the interests of the subsidiary, the ultimate holding company, or any other companies in the group.

Emoluments of Directors and Chairmen. Under Sect. 6 (1) the emoluments of the company's chairman, or if in the financial year more persons than one have been chairman, the emoluments of each of them, so far as attributable to the period during which each was chairman, must be disclosed in the accounts.

With regard to directors disclosure is required—

(a) of the number of directors who did not receive emoluments;
(b) of directors whose emoluments did not exceed £2,500; and
(c) by reference to each pair of adjacent points on a scale whereon the lowest point is £2,500 and the succeeding ones are successive integral multiples of £2,500, the number (if any) whose several emoluments exceeded the lower point but did not exceed the higher. The statement could appear in the following form—

Emoluments of Chairman £10,000

Number of Directors receiving emoluments—6

Emoluments range	*Number of Directors within range*
£	
0	0
0– 2,500	2
2,500– 5,000	3
5,000– 7,500	1
7,500–10,000	0

Disclosure is not required if the person's duties as chairman or director were wholly or mainly discharged outside the United Kingdom.

Sect. 6 (2) provides that the emoluments of any one director receiving more than the chairman must also be disclosed. If two or more directors are receiving more than the chairman then the emoluments paid to them (in the case of equality) must be disclosed. Where their emoluments are not equal the emoluments of the director receiving the greater or, as the case may be, the greatest must be disclosed.

Under Sect. 6 (3) "emoluments" for this purpose are as defined in Sect. 196 of the principal Act.

Sect. 6 (7) states that "chairman" for the purposes of Sect. 6 means the person elected by the directors of the company to be chairman of their meetings and includes a person who, though not so elected, holds any office (however designated) which, in accordance with the constitution of the company, carries with it functions substantially similar to those discharged by a person so elected.

Sect. 6 (6) states that a company which is neither a holding company nor a subsidiary of another body corporate is not subject to the requirements of Sect. 6 if the emoluments of all the directors in the year in question do not exceed £15,000.

Under Sect. 7 disclosure is also required of the number of directors who have waived rights to receive emoluments and the aggregate amount of those emoluments.

Employees' Emoluments. For the first time in company legislation disclosure is required of the emoluments of highly paid employees who are not directors, and who are not working wholly or mainly outside the United Kingdom. The relevant provision, which is in Sect. 8, states that "there shall be shown by reference to each pair of adjacent points on a scale whereon the lowest point is £10,000 and the succeeding ones are successive integral multiples of £2,500 beginning with that in which the multiplier is five, the number (if any) of persons in the company's employment (other than directors of the company and employees working wholly or mainly outside the United Kingdom) whose several emoluments exceeded the lower point but did not exceed the higher."

Such a statement could be set out as follows—

Number of employees whose emoluments exceed £10,000—6

Emoluments range	Employees within range
£	
10,000–12,500	3
12,500–15,000	2
15,000–17,500	1

Under Sects. 6 (4), 7 (3) and 8 (4), if a company's accounts do not comply with the requirements of Sects. 6, 7 and 8, the auditors are required to include in their report so far as they reasonably can do so a statement giving the required information.

Miscellaneous Amendments to Contents of Accounts. Sect. 9 provides that Schedule 8 of the principal Act shall be amended in accordance with the provisions of *Schedule* 1 of the Companies Act, 1967, and shall have effect as set out in *Schedule* 2 of that Act.

Schedule 2 reprints Schedule 8 of the Companies Act, 1948, with the amendments required by the Companies Act, 1967.

Under Sect. 10 the additional information which the Act requires in company accounts need not be given if the accounts relate to a period ending before the Act came into force even though the accounts are laid before the company in a general meeting held after the Act came into force.

Sect. 11 (1) states that when a company makes in its accounts the disclosures regarding directors' and employers' emoluments required by Sects. 6, 7 and 8 of the Act, and particulars of directors' salaries, pensions, etc., required by Sect. 196 of the principal Act, it must also give the corresponding amount for the immediately preceding financial year.

Under Sect. 11 (2) a director who fails to take reasonable steps to see that Sect. 11 (1) is complied with shall be liable to imprisonment for a term not exceeding six months or to a fine not exceeding £200. However, it shall be a defence for a director to show that he had reasonable ground to believe and did believe that a competent person was charged with the duty of seeing that the provisions were complied with and was in a position to discharge that duty. Furthermore, no person shall be sentenced to imprisonment unless, in the opinion of the court, there is wilful default.

Sect. 12 provides that the Department of Trade and Industry may by regulations made by statutory instrument under Sect. 454 (1) of the principal Act alter or add to the matters to be stated in the accounts of a company and may abolish the exceptions at present possessed by some banking and discount companies from certain provisions of Schedule 8 of the principal Act regarding disclosure in accounts. However, the Department of Trade and Industry's power to make regulations extends to all companies and whether a company is within a class of companies being dealt with by any such regulations shall be decided by the Department of Trade and Industry, whose decision is to be final.

DIVIDENDS AND PROFIT

Dividends are the amounts authorised to be paid out of the profits, and are paid to members of the company in proportion to their shareholdings. The fact that profits have been made does not in itself give the shareholders a right to dividend. No dividend is payable unless the directors declare one, and the directors' recommendation is voted upon at the annual general meeting, no amendment to increase the dividend being allowed. Directors are not forced to recommend a dividend, and could, for example, transfer all profits to reserve. The articles usually give the directors power to declare *interim* dividends between general meetings based on an estimate of profits. The shareholders approve the interim and final dividend at the next general meeting.

Table A provides that the dividends shall be reckoned on the amounts paid, or credited as paid on the shares, and not on their nominal value. Dividends when declared become a specialty debt, and an action against the company for dividends declared is not barred for twelve years.

Dividends must be paid only out of profits and not out of capital and profits were defined in *Re Spanish Prospecting Co. Ltd.*, [1911], 1 Ch. 92 as "the gain made by a business during a given period, this being ascertained only by a comparison of the assets of the business at the two dates." Considerable difficulty has been experienced in arriving at "divisible profits" and the Act gives no real assistance. However, certain rules emerge from the case law on the subject, though it should be noted that they do not necessarily represent good accounting practice.

(*a*) **Dividends may be paid out of profits without making good losses of fixed assets.** Thus it is not necessary to provide for depreciation of fixed assets. (*Lee* v. *Neuchatel Asphalte Co. Ltd.*, 1889[533] and *Verner* v. *General and Commercial Investment Trust*, 1894.)[534]

(*b*) **Losses of circulating assets in the accounting period must be made good.** Thus if insufficient provision is made for bad and doubtful debts, there may be a payment of dividend out of capital. The following definitions were given by Swinfen-Eady, L.J., in *Ammonia Soda Co.* v. *Chamberlain*, 1918[535]—

(i) *Fixed Capital* is capital which is fixed in the sense of being invested in assets intended to be retained by the company more or less permanently and used in producing income.

(ii) *Circulating Capital* is a portion of the subscribed capital of the company intended to be used by being temporarily parted with and circulated in the business in the form of money, goods or other assets, and which, or the proceeds of which, are intended to return to the company with an increment, and are intended to be used again and again and always to return with some accretion.

Thus cash is used to buy goods; goods when sold produce debtors; debtors pay cash and the cash is used to buy more goods and so on.

(*c*) **Unless the articles otherwise provide a company cannot pay dividends out of the appreciation of its capital assets.** However, the whole concern must be looked at. An increase in the value of one capital asset may not by itself justify the payment of a dividend. (*Foster* v. *New Trinidad Lake Asphalte Co. Ltd.* 1901[536] and

Ammonia Soda Co. v. *Chamberlain*, 1918.)[535] If on a revaluation of assets there is an unrealised capital profit it can be distributed by way of dividend or used to pay a bonus issue. (*Dimbula Valley (Ceylon) Tea Co. Ltd.* v. *Laurie*, 1961.)[537]

(*d*) **A company may pay dividend out of the profits made in one year without making good losses made in previous years.** (*Ammonia Soda Co.* v. *Chamberlain*, 1918.)[535]

(*e*) **Profits carried to a reserve fund remain available for the payment of dividend,** and there may be a Dividend Equalisation Reserve into which a proportion of the profits in good years is placed to provide dividend in bad years. A reserve fund representing share premiums or the Capital Redemption Reserve Fund is not so available.

(*f*) **Profits applied to the Reduction of Assets in the past may be brought back into the Profit and Loss Account and paid as dividend if in fact the depreciation has not taken place.** (*Sapley* v. *Read Bros.*, 1924.)[538]

Directors who knowingly pay dividend out of capital are jointly and severally liable to replace the amount paid out with interest, but they can claim an indemnity from the shareholders who received the dividend knowing it to have been paid out of capital.

Payment of Dividend. Dividend is paid by means of dividend warrants which are in two parts. One part shows the dividend declared and the amount due to the shareholder, together with the amount deducted for tax. This part can be used to claim tax rebate, if any. The other part is like a cheque, and is made out for the sum arrived at on the first part. It can be paid into the shareholder's bank account. Dividend warrants in respect of share warrants are made out when the holder sends the coupon to the company's office.

Capitalising Profits. When a revenue reserve has reached the limit of the company's needs it may be capitalised. The reserve is capitalised by the passing of a resolution in general meeting, capitalising the reserve or part of it, and declaring that out of that sum a bonus shall be paid to the shareholders, to be satisfied by the distribution of unissued shares or debentures in the company.

Payment of Interest out of Capital. Sect. 65 provides that where shares are issued for raising money to be spent on the construction of works which cannot be made profitable for some time, the company may pay interest on the capital so raised, even though no profit is made, if the payment is authorised by the articles. The payment must be sanctioned by the Department of Trade and Industry and must not exceed 4 per cent or such other rate as may be prescribed from time to time by the Treasury.

ALTERATION OF SHARE CAPITAL

If a company's articles authorise it, the company may, under Sect. 61, by an ordinary resolution in general meeting, make the following alterations to its capital—

(*a*) Increase its *Authorised Capital* by any amount;

(*b*) Consolidate its present shares into shares of larger nominal value, e.g. four 25p shares into one share of £1;

(*c*) Convert any paid-up shares into stock;

(*d*) Subdivide all or any of its shares into shares of smaller nominal value, e.g. a £1 share may be subdivided into four 25p shares, but the proportion paid and unpaid on each share must remain unaltered;

(*e*) Cancel unissued capital, thus reducing the authorised capital.

Notice of the above alterations must be given to the Registrar within one month, except in the case of increases of Authorised Capital, where notice must be given within 15 days together with a printed copy of the resolution authorising the increase. Capital duty is payable on the increase.

Reduction of Capital. A company may, if authorised by its articles, reduce its share capital by a special resolution confirmed by the court. Sect. 66 (1) provides that the reduction may be effected in three ways—

(i) By extinguishing or reducing the liability of the shareholders to contribute unpaid capital in respect of their shares, e.g. a company which has 50,000 £1 shares on which 50p per share has been paid, may reduce its capital to 50,000 shares of 50p each fully-paid, cancelling the liability to pay the other 50p per share.

(ii) By returning to the shareholders any paid-up capital in excess of its wants, e.g. a company which has issued 50,000 £1 shares fully-paid, may reduce its capital to 50,000 50p shares fully-paid, by repaying 50p per share.

(iii) By cancelling any paid-up capital which is not represented by available assets, e.g. a company which has issued 50,000 £1 shares fully paid, and has suffered losses so that its assets are worth only £25,000 may reduce its capital to 50,000 50p shares fully-paid.

In methods (i) and (ii) the creditors are deprived of funds which would have been available to them in a winding up and so, as a general rule, the company's petition for a confirmation of the reduction will not be heard until the company has filed a list of its creditors, and advertised for claims against it. All persons claiming must be paid in full or consent to the reduction, or the company must give security to the court's satisfaction where the claim is disputed. The reduction must be advertised and the court may also require the company to publish the reasons for reducing.

BORROWING POWERS

Trading companies have implied power to borrow and charge their assets as security. However, the Memorandum usually gives express power to borrow together with details of the extent to which the company can charge its assets as security. Where a company borrows money in excess of the powers so given, the loan is *ultra vires* and void.

Nevertheless if the loan is within the company's powers, but in excess of the directors' powers, the lender may be protected by the rule in *Turquand's case*, or alternatively the company may ratify the acts of the directors, thus making the loan good. Where the loan is *ultra vires the company*, the lender may have an action against the directors for breach of warranty of authority. (*Weeks* v. *Propert*, 1873.)[539]

Debentures. A company usually borrows money by issuing transferable debentures. These may be unsecured; or they may be mortgage debentures, secured on some specific assets of the company, or secured by a floating charge on all the assets. In the case of a floating charge, if the company defaults in payment of interest or principal, the charge is said to crystallise, and a receiver may be appointed to realise the assets for the debenture holders.

REGISTERED DEBENTURES. Companies usually issue registered debentures which are like shares in the matter of registration and transfer. Such debentures are numbered, and the conditions of issue are set out in the debenture certificate. The most important condition is that the debentures are to rank *pari passu*, which means that there is no priority for the first of the series to be issued. Where a further series of debentures is subsequently issued, this series will not normally rank *pari passu* with the earlier series, unless the terms of issue of the earlier issue expressly provide for this.

BEARER DEBENTURES. A company may issue bearer debentures which are negotiable instruments. They are transferable by mere delivery, and interest is paid on production of interest coupons which are attached to the debenture certificate. Notice of matters affecting holders is given by advertisement, and there is often a right to exchange bearer debentures for registered ones.

ISSUE AT A DISCOUNT. Debentures may be issued at any price, i.e. at par, at a premium, or at a discount, unless the articles expressly forbid it.

FURTHER SERIES. The terms of issue of debentures usually give the company power to issue further series of debentures, but a special power must be taken if the new series is to be secured on the same property and to rank *pari passu*. If no such special power is taken, and the new series is secured on the same property, the security of the new series is good but they cannot claim the assets until the first series have been paid in full.

Agreements to lend money are not in general enforceable by specific performance, but a contract to take debentures or give debentures is. (Sect. 92.)

REDEEMABLE DEBENTURES. Debentures are usually of the redeemable type, the date of repayment by the company being stated in the certificate. The company may redeem them by purchasing them in the market on or after a specified time. Alternatively they may be redeemed by instalments, the debenture numbers to be redeemed on each occasion being determined by drawing lots.

Debentures may be irredeemable or perpetual and in this case there is no date for redemption. Such debentures are repayable on a winding up, or when the company is in breach of the terms of issue, as where it fails to pay interest or where a receiver of the company's property is appointed.

REMEDIES OF DEBENTURE HOLDERS. These remedies differ according as the debentures are secured or unsecured.

(i) *Where debentures are secured* the debenture holders may sue the company if it defaults in payment of interest or principal; or petition for a winding up; or sell the assets forming the security; or appoint a receiver; or apply to the court for a foreclosure order. A sale of assets or appointment of a receiver is only possible if express powers are given in the terms of issue. Any action taken by one debenture holder must be on behalf of them all, but since there is usually a trust deed, it is normally the trustees who take the necessary action on behalf of all the debenture holders. An order of foreclosure would make the debenture holders the actual owners of the assets involved, but since *every* debenture holder must be present in court at the same time to bring the action, it is often not a possible remedy.

(ii) *Where debentures are unsecured* the debenture holders may sue the company if it defaults in payment of interest or principal, or may petition for a winding up and prove therein.

TRUST DEED. When debentures are issued for public subscription, it is common to execute a trust deed in favour of the debenture holders. The trustees are usually appointed from finance or insurance companies, and are paid by the company to look after the interests of the debenture holders. The trust deed usually contains the following items—

(*a*) Particulars of the property forming the security and the nature of the charge, either specific or floating or both;

(*b*) The powers, if any, of the company to create other mortgages having priority to the one set up by the deed;

(*c*) The price payable on redemption, and the date and method of redemption;

(*d*) Whether the debentures are registered or bearer stock, and if the latter, what is the smallest amount transferable.

(*e*) The powers of the trustees over the property if the company defaults in payment of interest or capital, or on winding up. Trustees are usually given power to sell the assets charged without need to resort to the court.

REGISTERS TO BE KEPT BY THE COMPANY. The company must keep a register of Mortgages and Charges affecting its property. (Sect. 104.) The Register must contain the amount of the charge, the identity of the mortgagees, and a description of the property charged. Creditors may inspect the Register. The company must also keep a Register of Debenture Holders if the terms of the issue require it. The Register of Directors' Shareholdings required by Sects. 27–29 and 31 of the Act of 1967 must show their debenture holdings also.

REGISTRATION OF CHARGES. Under the provisions of Sect. 95 the following charges must be registered with the Registrar of Companies—

    (i) A charge for the purpose of securing an issue of debentures;

    (ii) A charge on uncalled share capital;

    (iii) A charge created by an instrument which, if executed by an individual, would require registration as a bill of sale, e.g. a mortgage of chattels;

    (iv) A charge on land or any interest therein;

    (v) A charge on the book debts of the company;

    (vi) A floating charge on the property of the company;

    (vii) A charge on calls made but not paid;

    (viii) A charge on a ship, or any share in a ship;

    (ix) A charge on goodwill, patents, trade marks, copyrights, or any licence under a copyright.

The object of registration is to show creditors what other charges there are affecting their funds. Copies of mortgages or charges registered with the Registrar must be kept at the company's registered office, and must be available for the inspection of members and creditors free of charge. Failure to register one of the above charges with the Registrar within 21 days of its creation means that the charge is void as against the liquidator or creditors of the company. It is because the security may be lost that the law allows a secured creditor to register the charge himself, if the company does not seem to be doing so, and to claim the cost from the company.

PUBLIC AND PRIVATE COMPANIES

A minimum of seven persons is required to form a Public Company; a Private Company can be formed with as few as two.

A private company is defined by Sect. 28 of the Act as one which by its Articles—

    (*a*) Restricts the right to transfer its shares;

    (*b*) Limits the number of its members to fifty (excluding present employees and past employees who obtained their shares whilst working for the company and have retained them since that time); and

    (*c*) Prohibits any invitation to the public to subscribe for any shares or debentures of the company.

It must send with the annual return a certificate to the effect that the company has not invited the public to subscribe for its shares or debentures, and if the membership exceeds fifty, it must certify that the excess consists of employees or past employees.

A private company has the following privileges—

(i) The company is not required to hold a statutory meeting.

(ii) The directors need not file a consent to act or sign the Memorandum or a separate contract for qualification shares.

(iii) The company need not file a statement in lieu of prospectus, before it allots its shares or debentures.

(iv) It may allot its shares without obtaining the "minimum subscription."

(v) It can commence business on receipt of the certificate of incorporation.

(vi) A private company may have one director only, and need not have two as is the case with a public company.

(vii) In a private company two or more directors may be appointed by a single resolution.

(viii) The age limit placed upon directors does not apply to a private company unless it is a subsidiary of a public company.

STATUTORY BOOKS AND RETURNS

1. The Register of Members. Sect. 110 requires every company to keep a Register of its members containing their names and addresses; a statement of the shares held by each, distinguishing each share by its number if it has one; and the amount paid, or agreed to be considered as paid, on the shares. The Register must also show the date at which each person was entered in the Register, and the date at which any person ceased to be a member. Sect. 111 provides that a company with more than 50 members must keep an index of its members, unless the Register is kept in the form of an index.

2. Register of Debenture Holders. This Register need not be kept in any particular form but is generally kept on the same lines as the Register of Members. It must be open to inspection by any member or registered debenture holder without charge, and to any other person on payment of a fee not exceeding 5p. (Sect. 87.)

3. Register of Charges. A company must keep a Register of Mortgages and Charges specifically affecting its property, and of all floating charges. (Sect. 104.) The register must give a description of the property charged, the amount of the charge, and details of the persons entitled to the charge.

A company must also keep a Register of Directors and Secretaries, and this has already been dealt with in the section on Directors.

4. Minute Books. By the provisions of Sect. 145, every company must keep minute books of general and directors' meetings. It is necessary to separate the two sets of minutes because the shareholders may inspect the minutes of general meetings (Sect. 146), but have no general right to inspect the minutes of Board meetings.

5. Books of Account. The 1948 Act requires a company to keep proper books of account with respect to cash receipts and expenditure, sales and purchases, assets and liabilities, in order to give a true and fair view of the company's affairs and to explain its transactions.

6. An Indexed Register of Directors' Interests in shares in, or debentures of, the company or associated companies. This register must show the interest of the directors (including those of spouse or infant children) in group debentures or shares, changes in which are to be notified in writing to the company by the directors. (Companies Act, 1967, Sects. 27–29 and 31.)

This register is also to contain details of rights granted to directors to subscribe for shares or debentures and details of rights exercised (Companies Act, 1967, Sect. 29 (2)); details of directors' contracts to sell group shares or debentures or the assignment of rights granted by the company to subscribe for shares or debentures. These details are to be notified in writing to the company by the directors concerned. (Companies Act, 1967, Sect. 27 (1) (b).) These matters are more fully explained on p. 245.

7. Directors' Service Contracts. Under Sect. 26 of the Companies Act, 1967, copies must be kept of directors' service contracts or variations thereof that have more than twelve months' unexpired life and are not in respect of employment wholly or mainly outside the United Kingdom. If the said contracts are not in writing a memorandum must be kept. (See p. 245.)

8. An Indexed Register of Shareholders' Interests in ten per cent or more of the nominal value of any class of issued share capital which is quoted and has unrestricted voting rights. Shareholders are required to notify the company in writing of these details and any changes therein. (Companies Act, 1967, Sects. 33–4) Further details of the register are given on pp. 241–242.

Certain of the above books are open to inspection by the public during business hours with a minimum of two hours per day. However, 3, 4, 5 and the Register of Directors and Secretaries are not open to inspection; minute books of general meetings and directors' service contracts are open to inspection by members of the company only; the information made available by 8 above may be restricted where the company is within Sects. 3 (3) or 4 (3) of the 1967 Act. (See pp. 262 and 263.)

All the statutory books are to be kept at the company's Registered Office except—

(*a*) *The Register of Members and the Register of Debenture Holders.* In certain circumstances these need not be kept at the Registered Office though the Registrar of Companies must then be informed of their whereabouts. (Companies Act 1948, Sects. 86 and 110.)

(*b*) *The Register of Directors' Interests in Group Debentures or Shares.* This is to be kept with the Register of Members or at the company's Registered Office. The Registrar of Companies must be told where it is if it is not at the Registered Office. (Companies Act, 1967, Sect. 29.)

(*c*) *Directors' Service Contracts and Memoranda.* These may be kept at the Registered Office, or where the Register of Members is kept, or at the company's principal place of business if this is situated in the country in which the company is registered. The Registrar of Companies must be told where the above documents are if they are not at the Registered Office. (Companies Act, 1967, Sect. 26.)

(*d*) *Register of shareholders' interests.* This is to be kept where the Register of Directors' Interests in Group Debentures or Shares is kept. (Companies Act, 1967, Sect. 34.)

Annual Return. By Sect. 124, every company having a share capital must once in every year make a return called the Annual Return to the Registrar of Companies. The return must contain the particulars set out in Part I of the Sixth Schedule and be in the form set out in Part II of that Schedule. The particulars to be set out are as follows—

(*a*) The address of the registered office together with the address at which the Register of Members and the Register of Debentures Holders are kept, if not at the Registered Office.

(*b*) A summary distinguishing between shares issued for cash and shares issued as fully-paid or partly-paid up otherwise than for cash, and specifying calls made, the amounts received and the amounts unpaid, commissions paid or discount allowed on shares or debentures, shares forfeited, and share warrants issued or surrendered.

(*c*) The amount of the indebtedness of the company in respect of all mortgages and charges which are required to be registered with the Registrar.

(*d*) A List (i) containing the names and addresses of all persons who on the fourteenth day after the Annual General Meeting are members, and of persons who have ceased to be members since the date of the last return; and (ii) stating the number of shares held by each member at the date of the return, specifying shares transferred since the date of the last return and the dates of registration of the transfers.

If the members' names are not arranged in alphabetical order, an index is required.

Sect. 124 provides that a complete list of members and their holdings need only be made every third year, and in the intervening two years only a list of changes of membership need be given. If any shares have been converted into stock, the same particulars of the stock must be given. The company must also at the date of the return give the same particulars of the directors and secretary as are required to be in the Register of Directors and Secretaries.

Documents to be Annexed to the Annual Return. There must be annexed to the Annual Return—

(i) A copy of every balance sheet laid before the company in general meeting during the period to which the return relates, together with a profit and loss account, and group accounts, if any. The above documents must be certified by a director and the secretary.

(ii) A copy of the Auditors' Report and of the Directors' Report accompanying the balance sheet.

The Annual Return must be completed within 42 days of the Annual

General Meeting and a copy, signed by a director and the secretary, must then be sent *forthwith* to the Registrar. (Sect. 126.)

A private company must send with the Annual Return a certificate, signed by a director and the secretary, that the company has not since the date of the last return issued any invitation to the public to subscribe for shares or debentures of the company, and if the membership exceeds 50, that the excess consists of employees or ex-employees. (Sect. 128.)

Sect. 47 of the 1967 Act provides that certain unlimited companies shall be exempted from the provisions of Sect. 127 of the principal Act and will therefore not be required to file copies of their accounts, and directors' and auditors' reports with their Annual Returns. However, no exemption from Sect. 127 of the principal Act is to be given unless the unlimited company has—

(*a*) at no time during the period to which the Annual Return relates been the subsidiary of a company that was then limited and at no time to its knowledge have there been held or exercisable by or on behalf of two or more companies that were then limited (say the A Co. Ltd., and the B Co. Ltd.) shares or powers which, had they been held or exercisable by one of them (say A Co. Ltd.), would have made the unlimited company a subsidiary of the A Co. Ltd.

(*b*) at no such time been the holding company of a company that was then limited;

(*c*) at no such time been carrying on business as the promoter of a trading-stamp scheme within the meaning of the Trading Stamps Act, 1964.

AUDITORS

Appointment. Sect. 159 requires that the company shall at each Annual General Meeting appoint and fix the remuneration of an auditor or auditors to hold office until the next Annual General Meeting. If no such appointment is made, the Board of Trade may appoint an auditor. Where there is a retiring auditor and no appointment is made, he will continue in office unless—

(*a*) he is not qualified for reappointment; or

(*b*) a resolution has been passed providing expressly that he shall not be reappointed; or

(*c*) he has given the company written notice that he is unwilling to be reappointed; or

(*d*) notice has been given of an intended resolution to appoint someone other than the existing auditor and by reason of death, incapacity or disqualification of that person the resolution cannot be proceeded with.

The directors have power to fill any casual vacancy in the office of auditor. The first auditors of a company may be appointed by the directors before the first Annual General Meeting, and auditors so appointed hold office until the conclusion of that meeting. The company in general meeting may remove any such auditors and appoint in their place any other persons who have been nominated for appointment by any member of the company and of whose nomination notice has been given to the members of the company not less than fourteen days before the date of the meeting.

Duties. The auditor is required to report to the members on the accounts and balance sheets laid before the company in general meeting during his tenure of office. (Companies Act, 1967, Sect. 14.) In his report the auditor must specifically state—

(*a*) whether the company's balance sheet and profit and loss account group accounts, if any, have been properly prepared and represent a true and fair view of the company's financial position;

(*b*) whether he has received all the necessary information and explanations, and that proper books of account have not been kept or that adequate returns have not been made by branches if this is so;

(*c*) that the balance sheet and accounts do not agree with the books and returns if this is so.

An auditor is also required to obtain a knowledge of the Articles. The auditor's duty is to the company and the members and there was formerly no duty to third parties in respect of the accounts. However, in view of the decision in *Hedley Byrne*, 1963,[165] there is now a duty to third parties who are likely to rely on the audited accounts unless there is a disclaimer.

Rights. The auditor has a right of access at all times to the books, accounts, and vouchers of the company, and may require from the directors and other officers such information and explanations as are necessary for the proper performance of his duties. The auditor is also entitled to receive notice of and attend any general meetings of the company.

The auditor is required by law to carry out a *careful* audit, and can be sued for damages if he fails to do so. The auditor is not under a duty to take stock and may accept the certificate of a responsible officer unless his suspicions are aroused. (*Re Kingston Cotton Mill Co.*, 1896.)[540] Certainly he does not guarantee that the books of account show the true state of the company's affairs.

It should be noted, however, that professional standards have risen in recent times. Thus, it is now generally accepted that an auditor should not rely on the accuracy and honesty of other persons even in the matter of stocktaking, and that he should carry out a check on at least one or more sample items. The standard of care required of an auditor at the present time was probably more accurately expressed by Lord Denning in *Fomento (Sterling Area) Ltd.* v. *Selsdon Fountain Pen Co. Ltd.*, [1958] W.L.R. at p. 61, where he said—

"An auditor is not confined to the mechanics of checking vouchers and making arithmetical computations. He is not to be written off as a professional "adder-upper and subtracter." His vital task is to take care to see that errors are not made, be they errors of computation, or errors of omission or commission, or downright untruths. To perform this task properly he must come to it with an enquiring mind—not suspicious of dishonesty . . . —but suspecting that someone may have made a mistake somewhere and that a check must be made to ensure that there has been none."

This higher duty of care was to some extent applied in *Re Thomas Gerrard & Sons Ltd.*, 1968.[541]

Sect. 161 prohibits the following persons from being auditors—

(*a*) Officers and servants of the company;
(*b*) A partner of, or a person employed by officers of the company;
(*c*) A corporation;
(*d*) A person not qualified or authorised by the Department of Trade and Industry.

The qualification requirement means that the auditor must be a member of The Institute of Chartered Accountants in England and Wales; or The Association of Certified Accountants; or The Institute of Chartered Accountants in Scotland or Ireland.

However, in certain circumstances, a person may be authorised by the Department of Trade and Industry to be appointed as auditor of a company because of appropriate experience, or similar qualifications obtained abroad.

Remuneration. Sect. 159 provides that the remuneration of the auditors of the company must be fixed either by the company in general meeting, or in such manner as may be determined by the company in general meeting. For example, auditors may be appointed by the annual general meeting "at a remuneration to be fixed by the directors." Where an auditor is appointed by the Department of Trade, his remuneration is fixed by the Department and paid by the company.

WINDING UP

There are three methods of winding up—

(i) A compulsory winding up by the court;
(ii) A voluntary winding up which may be a members' or creditors' winding up;
(iii) A winding up under the supervision of the court.

1. Compulsory Winding Up. A company may be wound up by the court when one of the following situations occurs—

(*a*) The company has not commenced business within a year from incorporation, or has suspended business for one year.

(*b*) The number of members of the company has fallen below the statutory minimum.

(*c*) The company is unable to pay its debts.

(*d*) The company resolves to wind up by special resolution. Any ground will suffice, but it is rather unusual to use this method because if the company is in a position to obtain a special resolution to this effect, it will be cheaper and more convenient to wind up voluntarily.

(*e*) The company fails to file the Statutory Report or hold the Statutory Meeting. This ground is not likely to be used since the Registrar will normally require the company to comply, and in any case the petition to wind up in this case can only be made by a shareholder.

(*f*) The court is of the opinion that it is just and equitable that the company be wound up. (Sect. 222.) This is a wide ground and might be used where the company's objects are illegal, or where the shareholders are divided into opposing groups and there is deadlock.

A company is deemed to be unable to pay its debts when—

(i) A creditor to whom the company owes £50 or more has served on it, at its registered office, a written demand for payment and the debt is not paid within three weeks;

(ii) A judgment creditor of the company has not been able to satisfy his debt by execution on the company's property;

(iii) The court is satisfied that the company cannot pay its debts.

A petition for winding up may be presented by a *contributory* or a *creditor*. In the case of a contributory, he must have held his shares for at least six months during the preceding 18 months, unless he is an original allottee; or he has taken the shares as a result of the death of the former holder; or the number of members has fallen below the statutory minimum.

CONTRIBUTORIES. For the purposes of a winding up, owners of fully-paid shares, as well as owners of partly-paid shares, are included in the term contributory. Two lists of contributories are made out—(i) *The A List*, which contains present members; and (ii) *The B List*, which includes all persons who were members during the preceding 12 months. No contribution is required from those members on the A or B Lists whose shares are fully paid. Where shares are not fully paid, the liquidator calls first on the members on the A List, and if they cannot pay, he has recourse to ex-members on the B List.

A contributory on the B List cannot be required to contribute in respect of debts which were incurred by the company after he ceased to be a member.

When there is a petition for winding up, the court is not forced to make an order, but if it does, it will appoint the liquidator, who realises the assets and pays the creditors, handing over the surplus (if any) to the shareholders. When the company's affairs are fully wound up, the court will make an order dissolving the company. The order is registered with the Registrar of Companies by the liquidator, and the Registrar makes an entry on the Register dissolving the company from the date of the court order.

2. Voluntary Winding Up. A company may be voluntarily wound up under Sect. 278—

(*a*) At the end of the period (if any) fixed for its duration by the articles; or

(*b*) When the articles provide that the company is to be dissolved on the occurrence of an event, and the event occurs and the company in general meeting has passed an ordinary resolution requiring that the company be wound up;

(*c*) If the company resolves by special resolution that the company be wound up voluntarily;

(*d*) If the company resolves by extraordinary resolution to the effect that it cannot by reason of its liabilities continue in business and that it is advisable to wind up.

(i) MEMBERS' VOLUNTARY WINDING UP. Whether the members are left in control of the winding up or not depends upon the directors giving a declaration of solvency, i.e. a statutory declaration, filed with the Registrar, to the effect that the company will be able to pay its debts in full within 12 months.

As soon as the affairs of the company are fully wound up, the liquidator makes up an account of the winding up, showing how it has been conducted and how the company's property has been disposed of. He then calls a general meeting and lays the account before it and explains it. Within one week after the meeting, the liquidator sends to the Registrar of Companies a copy of the account, and a return as to the holding of the meeting. Both are registered, and three months from registration the company is deemed dissolved.

(ii) CREDITORS' VOLUNTARY WINDING UP. If no declaration of solvency is given, the directors call a company meeting at which the resolution for voluntary winding up is to be proposed, and they must also call a meeting of the creditors to be held either on the same day or on the day after.

The creditors and the members at their respective meetings may nominate a liquidator, and if they nominate different persons, the creditors' nominee becomes the liquidator.

However, if different persons are nominated, any director, member, or creditor of the company, may apply to the court for an order *either* directing that the person nominated by the company shall be the liquidator instead of, or jointly with, the creditors' choice; *or* appointing some other person to be liquidator instead of the creditors' nominee. (Sect. 294.)

In the event of the winding up continuing for more than one year, the liquidator must summon a general meeting of the company and a meeting of the creditors at the end of the first year, and also each succeeding year, and must lay before the meetings an account of his acts and dealings, and of the conduct of the winding up during the preceding year. (Sect. 299.)

As soon as the affairs of the company are fully wound up, the liquidator must make up an account of the winding up, showing how the winding up has been conducted and how the property of the company has been disposed of, and must call a general meeting of the company and a meeting of the creditors and lay the account of the winding up before each meeting, giving suitable explanations. (Sect. 340.)

Within one week after the date of the meetings or, if the meetings are not held on the same date, after the date of the later meeting, the liquidator must send to the Registrar a copy of the account and a return as to the holding of the meetings and of their dates. (Sect. 300.) The account and return are registered, and three months after registration, the company is deemed dissolved.

3. Winding Up under the Supervision of the Court. When a company has passed a resolution for voluntary winding up, the court may make an order that the voluntary winding up shall continue, subject to the supervision of the court. (Sect. 311.) The voluntary liquidator carries on, but is subject to the court's power to make orders in connection with the winding up. A winding up under supervision may result from a creditor's petition for the compulsory winding up of a company already in voluntary liquidation.

When the affairs of the company have been fully wound up, the court on the application of the liquidator makes an order that the company be dissolved from the date of the order. A copy of the order must within 14 days from the date of the order be forwarded by the liquidator to the Registrar, who makes in his books a minute of the dissolution of the company.

Defunct Companies. Where a company has ceased to carry on business and no longer appears to be in active existence, it may be struck off the register as a *defunct company*.

CREDITORS

When the company is solvent, the debts and liabilities may be settled in any order because all will in due course be paid before the balance is distributed among the members.

If the company is insolvent, the bankruptcy rules apply; and we shall have to consider separately the claims of the liquidator for his costs, expenses and remuneration, preferential creditors, secured creditors, unsecured creditors and judgment creditors. The assets available to the liquidator are applied in the following order—

(1) Secured creditors out of the proceeds of their securities, but excluding debenture holders secured by a floating charge.

(2) The costs of the liquidation.

(3) The preferential debts.

(4) Debenture holders secured by a floating charge.
(5) Unsecured creditors.
(6) Balance returned to the contributories.

SECURED CREDITORS

These are creditors who hold some security for debts due to them from the company, e.g. they may be mortgagees of some of the company's assets. A secured creditor has certain optional courses of action—

(1) He may sell his security and not prove in the liquidation, handing over any balance over and above what is needed to satisfy his debt to the liquidator. He is not bound to get the best price possible (except in the case of a building society) but he must not sell at a ridiculously low price.

(2) He may sell his security and prove for the balance (if any) and he may deduct the cost of realisation from the amount he receives from the sale of his security.

(3) He may surrender his security and prove for the whole debt.

(4) He may state in his proof the particulars of the security, the date when it was given, and its value. In that case the value so stated will be deducted from the amount of the debt, and he will be entitled to receive dividends on the balance.

If the secured creditor adopts the last course, the liquidator has the following alternatives—

(i) he may redeem the security within twenty-eight days by paying to the creditor its estimated value; or

(ii) he may require it to be sold on such terms and conditions and at such time as the liquidator and the creditor shall agree, or in default of such agreement, as the court may direct.

The secured creditor, therefore, having valued the security, may write to the liquidator, asking him to elect whether he will redeem it or require it to be sold, and if the liquidator does not elect within six months of such notice, his rights are lost, the security is vested in the creditor, and his debt is reduced by the amount of the security's valuation.

As we have seen, where the security is a floating charge in favour of debenture holders, it is postponed to the costs of the liquidation and the preferential debts, but ranks before the claims of unsecured creditors.

THE COSTS OF WINDING UP

In the case of a winding up by the court, the expenses of winding up are payable in the following order—

(1) The fees and expenses incurred in realising and getting in the company's assets.

(2) The costs of the petitioner and of any person who appeared on the hearing of the petition so far as the court directs them to be paid.

(3) The remuneration of the special manager (if there is one).

(4) Costs and expenses incurred in preparing the statement of affairs.

(5) The taxed charges of shorthand writers appointed to take notes at any examination.

(6) The liquidator's necessary disbursements (other than those in (1) above).

(7) The costs of any person properly employed by the liquidator.

(8) The remuneration of the liquidator.

(9) The actual out-of-pocket expenses necessarily incurred by the committee of inspection as approved by the Department of Trade and Industry.

PREFERENTIAL CREDITORS

These are creditors whose debts are to be paid in priority to other debts The most important of them are—

(1) Local rates due from the company and payable within the preceding twelve months.

(2) Land tax, income tax or other assessed taxes up to the preceding fifth day of April, not exceeding one year's assessment. The Inland Revenue may select any year's assessment where more than one year's tax is due.

(3) Purchase tax due, and having become due, within the previous twelve months.

(4) Wages or salaries of any clerk or servant in respect of any services rendered to the company during the four months preceding and all wages of any workmen or labourer (whether payable for time or piece work) for services so rendered. The sum to which priority is given must not exceed £200 in the case of any one claimant. It was decided in *Re C. W. & A. L. Hughes*, [1966] 2 All E.R. 702, that wages payable under "labour only" sub-contracts are not preferential debts under Sect. 319 (4) of the Companies Act, 1948.

(5) Accrued holiday remuneration becoming payable to any clerk, servant, workmen or labourer on the termination of his employment before or resulting from the winding-up order or resolution.

(6) Contributions payable by the company under various National Insurance Acts, unless the company is being wound up voluntarily for the purposes of reconstruction or amalgamation with another company.

(7) Where payments have been made in advance of wages and salary or on account of holiday remuneration out of money advanced by some person for that purpose, he shall have the same priority in respect of those advances as the recipient would have had. Thus it was held in *Re Rampgill Mill Ltd.*, [1967] 1 All E.R. 56, that where money was lent

to a company and it was arranged that part of it should be used to pay employees' wages the debt was preferential under Sect. 319 (4) to the extent that the advances were used for that purpose.

These debts rank equally among themselves and are to be paid in full unless the assets are inadequate, when they abate in equal proportions. In the case of a company registered in England, they have priority over the claims of holders of debentures under a floating charge and also over the claims of a landlord or other person over goods which have been distrained on within three months next before the winding-up order, but not over the claims of other secured creditors.

The relevant date for the purposes of the above calculations is, in the case of a company being wound up compulsorily, the date of the first appointment of a provisional liquidator, or, if there is no such appointment, the date of the winding-up order, or in the case of the voluntary liquidation, the date of the resolution for winding up. (Sect. 319.)

UNSECURED CREDITORS

When the preferential debts have been paid in full, the liquidator must pay the remaining debts, and, if the assets are not sufficient, these debts abate in equal proportions. However, debts due to a member of the company, *in his character of member*, are deferred until the ordinary creditors have been paid in full, though such debts must be taken into account when the final adjustment is made among the contributories themselves. (Sect. 212 (1) (g).) Nevertheless, even if the creditor is a member, he may claim along with the other creditors *if the debt is an ordinary trade debt or loan*. Debts due to the Crown are not preferential debts except as listed in the Act.

JUDGMENT CREDITORS

Where a judgment creditor has levied execution and completed it by sale before the winding up, he may keep the proceeds. If the execution is incomplete or the sale has not been carried out, the property must be given to the liquidator, but the judgment creditor is entitled to receive the costs of the execution and prove for the debt in the winding up.

RIGHTS OF CONTRIBUTORIES

If the debts are insufficient to satisfy the creditors, then the contributories must bring in the sums due from them in accordance with the principles we have already examined. If, however, when all the debts have been paid there are suplus assets, then these are available for the repayment of capital to the contributories, and in certain cases the residue may exceed the nominal capital of the company and there may be even larger sums to distribute.

The way in which the balance is distributed among the contributories will depend upon the rights attaching to the particular shares.

(i) It was held in *Re Roberts and Cooper Ltd.*, [1929] 2 Ch. 383 that if preference shares are preferred as to capital on winding up, they will be paid in full before the ordinary shares receive anything.

(ii) If they are not so preferred, they will rank equally with the ordinary shares and, if the assets are not sufficient to repay the whole of the capital, both classes will be paid out in equal proportions.

(iii) If, when the original capital subscribed has been repaid, there are still assets remaining, these may go to the ordinary shareholders entirely if the preference shareholders were preferential as to repayment of capital. If the preference shares ranked equally if the capital were in deficit, then they will probably rank equally in their share of the surplus.

It must be stressed that the rights of the various classes of shares should be clearly laid down in the Memorandum or Articles, or in the terms of the issue, since it is from an interpretation of these documents that the rights will be ascertained.

CHAPTER VIII

NEGOTIABLE INSTRUMENTS

THE major characteristics of a negotiable instrument are as follows—

(a) The rights represented by the instrument are transferable merely by delivering it to another, though bills made payable to order require indorsement.

(b) Unlike the assignee of an ordinary contractual right, the transferee of a negotiable instrument does not take subject to equities, and he is not affected by defects in the title of his predecessor provided he is what is known as a *holder in due course.*

(c) The acceptor of a bill of exchange, or the banker in the case of a cheque, is under a duty to pay the *holder for the time being* of the instrument. So, upon transfer of the instrument, there is no need to notify the acceptor or the banker of a change of ownership, as there is on a legal assignment of other choses in action under the Law of Property Act, 1925.

(d) The holder of a bill of exchange can sue upon it in his own name. This can be done with a legal assignment, but not with an equitable one.

To rank as a negotiable instrument, a document must be recognised as such either by statute, or by the custom of merchants (*Goodwin* v. *Robarts*, 1875)[542] arising out of the Law Merchant (*Crouch* v. *Credit Foncier of England*, 1873),[543] and accepted as valid by the courts.

Types of Instrument. The most important negotiable instruments are bills of exchange, promissory notes and cheques, and these three types are the subject-matter of the Bills of Exchange Act, 1882. Nevertheless, certain other instruments are negotiable namely—

(1) TREASURY BILLS, i.e. bills issued by the British Government subject to the provisions of the Treasury Bills Act, 1877, amended by the National Debt Act, 1972, and by subsequent regulations.

(2) SHARE WARRANTS, if they are to bearer but not otherwise.

(3) DIVIDEND WARRANTS.

(4) BONDS issued by English companies are negotiable if payable to *bearer*, and bonds issued by a foreign government, or indeed by a foreign corporation, may be negotiable if they are negotiable in the country of issue and also negotiable by custom in England.

(5) DEBENTURES payable to bearer.

(6) BEARER SCRIP, e.g. where debentures or debenture stock are alloted under terms that they shall be paid for by instalments provisional bearer scrip certificates may be issued to subscribers to be exchanged for proper debentures or stock certificates when all instalments have been paid.

Postal orders, money orders, I.O.U.s, Share Certificates and Share Transfers are not negotiable instruments, nor is a bill of lading. (See pp. 428–9.)

THE NATURE OF A BILL OF EXCHANGE

A bill of exchange is an unconditional order in writing, addressed by one person to another, signed by the person giving it, requiring the person to whom it is addressed to pay on demand, or at a fixed or determinable future time, a sum certain in money to, or to the order of, a specified person, or to bearer. (Bills of Exchange Act, 1882, Sect. 3.)

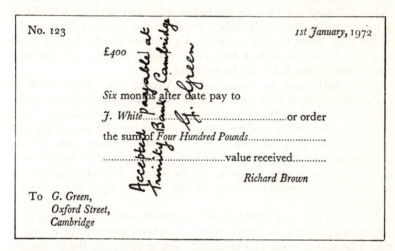

The example given is a bill of exchange which is addressed by Richard Brown to G. Green, and requires him to pay £400 to J. White, or his order, six months after the date of the bill which is 1st January, 1972. Richard Brown is called the *drawer*, G. Green is called the *drawee*, and J. White is called the *payee*.

THE ADVANTAGES OF A BILL OF EXCHANGE

Before proceeding to discuss in detail the law relating to Bills of Exchange it is worth examining why they are used at all.

(1) **A bill of exchange provides a creditor with a better remedy.** Once a bill of exchange has been accepted, it settles the amount of the debt owing, and makes a legal remedy easier to obtain than would be the case under an ordinary contract. If Green owes Brown the £400 for building work done to his premises, and an action were brought on the contract, Green might be able to defend the action by alleging poor workmanship, or proving some other way in which Brown had fallen short of his contractual obligations. If, however, he accepts the liability on the bill of exchange, then he agrees that the

sum of £400 is owing, and there is no need to prove in detail the terms of the contract giving rise to the debt.

(2) **Bills of exchange may be discounted.** Thus anybody who holds the bill, and is entitled to claim the money on the due date, can discount the bill by taking it to a bank or discounting house. The bank will, in many cases, be willing to take the bill off the holder's hands, pay the holder the present value of the bill and collect the money when due. If, for instance, White is in possession of the bill and he holds it for two months and then takes it to the bank for discounting, the bank will deduct from the £400 four months' interest, since the money is still not due for a further four months. If the bank rate is 6 per cent per annum, discount will be deducted at the rate of £2 per hundred. White will thus get £392 for the bill at once, and the bank will obtain £8 for granting the facility when it collects the £400 on the maturity of the bill. Since the bill is the bank's security for the loan, the bill will only be discountable if the bank is satisfied as to the creditworthiness of the parties liable for its payment.

(3) **A bill may be negotiated.** Anyone who holds a bill of exchange can transfer it to a creditor in payment and White could, if he chose, use the bill in this manner to settle a debt with Gray. In the past bills were freely used in settlement of debts and passed through many hands. They are still common in foreign trade, although the development of modern monetary and banking facilities has reduced their importance and the scope of their use. Nevertheless the use of cheques, a specialised form of bill of exchange, has extended rapidly.

It is thus clear that a bill has advantages all round. Green may have purchased goods from Brown which he wishes to resell, or materials which he wishes to use in a manufacturing process, and the six months allowed for payment give him time to sell the goods or have them manufactured before payment is due. The bill allows Brown to settle his indebtedness to White, and allows White, also, if he chooses, to negotiate the bill in settlement of his own debts, or to discount it and obtain ready cash, subject to the deduction of the bank's charge for discounting. Such a bill may, therefore, be a great convenience to the parties.

THE LIFE CYCLE OF A BILL OF EXCHANGE

Let us now see what happens to this bill in the simplest possible case. Brown sends the bill to Green and, if Green agrees that the amount is owing and is willing to pay this amount on the due date of the bill, he *accepts* the bill by writing across its face the word *Accepted* and his signature. The bill is then sent to White who may in fact retain the bill until its due date. The due date in this case is July 1st. On July 1st, therefore, White, if he still retains the bill, will present it for payment to Green, and in the normal course of events Green will pay the £400 and that is the end of the matter. Green has paid his bill, Brown has settled his indebtedness to White and White has now received the £400 which was owed him.

If, however, Green does not pay the bill when it is presented, the bill is said to be *dishonoured*. White will not get his money from Green, but he will have redress by being able to recover the £400 from Brown, which is fair enough since Brown owed White the sum in the first place and cannot rid himself of his obligations by offering White a bill which turns out to be worthless.

More rarely the bill is dishonoured by non-acceptance. In this case, if Brown sent the bill to Green, and Green refused to accept it, although Green was the *drawee* he would never become the *acceptor* of the bill and it would not have any effective existence. However, a bill may get into circulation after it has been drawn and before it has been accepted. For instance, Brown might send the bill to White without presenting it to Green and if White at a later date submitted the bill to Green for acceptance, and Green did not agree that the money was owing or did not agree to pay according to the terms of the bill, it would be dishonoured by non-acceptance. This would mean that White could not get the money from Green but would have to have recourse to Brown.

This is, of course, a very simple case and a bill, being a negotiable instrument, often passes through a number of hands before maturity. If Brown had wished merely to get the money quickly for himself, he could have made the bill payable to his own order and not to White, in which case Brown himself could have discounted the bill with the bank immediately. Thus Green would obtain six months' credit, while Brown would be able to put his hands immediately on the cash owing, less of course the bank's discount which presumably he would have covered in the price he originally charged Green. Such a procedure would be an alternative to what is now a more common method of raising money, namely an overdraft.

Negotiation. In many cases, however, a bill of exchange is negotiated and, to return to our example, White on January 15th might pass the bill on to Gray to whom he in turn owed £400. In order to do this White would *indorse* the bill, that is he would write his name on the back before handing it over. Such an indorsement, together with the transfer, would effectively negotiate the bill to Gray who would then have all the rights which formerly belonged to White and also, if the bill were dishonoured, the right to call on White to pay the £400. Gray in turn might pass on the bill to Black, Gray indorsing the bill and undertaking the same sort of responsibilities by making this indorsement. By the time the bill had run its course and was due for payment it might have passed through the hands of a number of holders, all of whom would have indorsed the bill in succession in order to negotiate it and pass on the title. If, on July 1st, the bill were in the hands of Martin, Martin would then present the bill for payment and, assuming Green met his obligations, all the intervening transactions would have been satisfactorily cleared up.

If, however, Green failed to pay then Martin would be able to claim the money from Brown, the drawer, or indeed from any of the intervening indorsers. He might decide to claim it from Black and, if he did so, Black would be able to claim from Gray, Gray from White, and White from Brown. The advantage accruing from the liability assumed by intervening indorsers to subsequent holders is that, provided there is on the bill the signature of a man of substance whose credit is beyond question, all subsequent holders and all subsequent indorsers realise that they run little risk of losing money by taking the bill.

Noting and Protesting. It is convenient at this point to mention that, when a bill is dishonoured, it is sometimes obligatory and often desirable to *note* and *protest* the bill for non-acceptance or non-payment. Many solicitors carry out the office of *notary public*, and this office is universally recognised throughout the world.

In order to *note* the bill, the notary makes a formal demand upon the drawee for acceptance, or upon the acceptor for payment, as the case may be, and if the demand is refused, he writes a minute on the face of the bill consisting of the date, the noting charges, a reference to his register, and his initials. He also attaches to the bill a ticket giving the answer received to the request for acceptance or payment. To evidence these transactions the notary makes in his register a full copy of the bill, and a note of the answer, if any, received to his request.

The *protest* is against any loss sustained by the non-acceptance or non-payment of the bill, and is embodied in a solemn declaration made on behalf of the holder by a *notary public* who signs it. Where it is necessary to protest a bill and no notary is available, the function can be performed by a householder or substantial resident who gives a certificate of dishonour attested by two witnesses. The form of protest is described on p. 318 (*post*).

It is important to note the distinction between an *inland bill* and a *foreign bill*. An *inland bill* is one which is or on the face of it purports to be (a) both drawn and payable within the British Islands, or (b) drawn within the British Islands upon some person resident therein. *Any other bill is a foreign bill*, and foreign bills must be protested.

For the purposes of the Act "British Islands" means any part of the United Kingdom of Great Britain and Ireland (not Eire), the Islands of Man, Guernsey, Jersey, Alderney, Sark and the islands adjacent to any of them being part of the dominions of Her Majesty. (Sect. 4 (1).)

It is not necessary to note or protest inland bills, but there are certain advantages derived from noting a bill, and the costs of noting are recoverable as damages. The notary knows clearly what measures must be taken when a bill is dishonoured; he is the best witness at a trial that proper steps were taken; and his minute on the bill is the best record of dishonour for the purpose of notifying parties to the bill that they have acquired liability.

THE BILLS OF EXCHANGE ACT, 1882

Most of the law relating to bills of exchange has been codified in the Bills of Exchange Act, 1882, and *all section references in this chapter are to this Act unless otherwise indicated.*

THE HOLDER OF A BILL

Holders of bills of exchange fall into three categories.

1. Holder. The term *holder* means the payee or indorsee of a bill who is in possession of it, or the person in possession of a bill which is payable to bearer. (Sect. 2.)

2. Holder for Value. Where value has at any time been given for a bill the holder is deemed to be a holder for value as regards the acceptor and all parties to the bill who became parties prior to such time. (Sect. 27 (2).)

The effect of this section is that consideration need not move from the promisee. (See pp. 20–22.) Suppose that X draws a cheque payable to Y or order as a gift and that Y endorses it to Z, a dealer, as payment for a radio. If Z tries to cash the cheque and it is dishonoured, Z, having given value, can sue X or Y because they became parties before value was given. If instead of trying to cash the cheque, Z endorses it to his niece N as a birthday present then, if N seeks payment and the cheque is dishonoured, she would be a holder for value as regards X and Y because they became parties before value was given. N could not, however, sue Z because absence of consideration is always a defence as between immediate parties.

Where the holder of a bill has a lien on it arising either from contract or by implication of law, he is deemed to be a holder for value to the extent of the sum for which he has a lien. (Sect. 27 (3).)

Thus, if H, the holder of a bill for £100, deposits the bill with his bank as security for an overdraft of £50, the bank is a holder for value as to £50 and could recover this sum in an action against H or other parties. Further a banker has by implication of law, and in the absence of an agreement to the contrary, a lien on all bills received from customers. (*Barclays Bank Ltd.* v. *Astley Industrial Trust Ltd.*, 1970.)[544] However, a banker's lien is not a true lien but a rather special application of the general law of lien. In consequence it does not take precedence over the statutory rules relating to set-off in Sect. 31 of the Bankruptcy Act, 1914 and Sect. 317 of the Companies Act, 1948. (*Halesowen Presswork* v. *Westminster Bank Ltd.*, 1970.)[545]

A holder for value cannot obtain a better title than the person who transfers the bill to him and if the transferor's title is defective, as where, for example, a signature was obtained by fraud, the holder for value will be affected by that fraud.

3. Holder in Due Course. A holder in due course is a holder who has taken a bill, complete and regular on the face of it (*Arab Bank Ltd.* v. *Ross*, 1952),[546] under the following conditions; namely—

(*a*) that he became a holder of it before it was overdue, and without notice that it had been previously dishonoured, if such was the fact;

(*b*) that he took the bill in good faith and for value, and that at the time the bill was negotiated to him he had no notice of any defect in the title of the person who negotiated it. (Sect. 29 (1).)

A holder in due course takes the bill free from any defects in the title of previous holders, thus providing an exception to the general *nemo dat* rule (pp. 146–152).

Normally a drawer of a bill of exchange has given valuable consideration to the drawee, and valuable consideration may be (i) any consideration sufficient to support a simple contract; or (ii) an antecedent debt or liability. (Sect. 27.) (*Barclays Bank Ltd.* v. *Astley Industrial Trust Ltd.*, 1970.)[544] Though past consideration would not be sufficient to support a simple contract in the ordinary way, the consideration for a bill of exchange may be past if the bill is drawn by the original debtor. (*Oliver* v. *Davis and Another*, 1949.)[547] The reason for departing from the general rule of the law of contract is that very many cheques are drawn in respect of past debts.

ORDER IN WRITING

A bill of exchange is an unconditional order in writing addressed by one person to another. We will now consider these elements.

The Drawer. A bill of exchange is a written document and in this context writing includes print. (Sect. 2.) The person who originates it is called the *drawer*, and he must have capacity to incur liability and this is co-extensive with capacity to contract. (Sect. 22.) A trading company has implied power to draw, accept or indorse bills of exchange, the power being incidental to the carrying out of its objects. If it is not a trading company, it must have either express or implied authority under its memorandum or other constitution. However, it is likely that, regardless of any constitutional provisions, a power would now be implied since the drawing of cheques is so common. It is essential that the payment being made by the bill relates to an *intra vires* transaction otherwise the corporation is without capacity.

Where a bill is drawn or indorsed by a minor, or a corporation without capacity, the drawing or indorsement entitles the holder to receive payment of the bill, and to enforce it against any other party to it, but gives no recourse against the minor or the corporation.

Suppose John, a minor, buys necessary goods from Jones and uses a cheque to pay for them, and that Jones indorses the cheque to a wholesaler Brown, who on presenting the cheque for payment finds that it is dishonoured. Brown cannot sue John because he is not liable on the bill as such, but he can sue Jones on his indorsement. Jones cannot sue John on the cheque but would have a quasi-contractual action for a reasonable price under Sect. 2 of the Sale of Goods Act, 1893 (p. 29).

The drawer of a bill (or any indorser) may insert in it an express stipulation negativing or limiting his own liability to the holder, or waiving as regards himself some or all of the holder's duties, e.g. notice of dishonour. (Sect. 16.)

Thus bills are sometimes drawn or indorsed "*sans recours*" or "*sans frais*" or "without recourse." These words tell the holder that in the event of dishonour he cannot go to the drawer or indorser for payment. Such an indorsement would probably not be accepted, but if it were, the immediate indorsee may have some legal redress for he, but not a later holder, may recover the value given to the indorser "without recourse" not by an action on the bill but upon the underlying contract for total failure of consideration if—

(i) the indorser's title was defective; or

(ii) the indorser knew at the time of indorsement that for some reason the bill would not be paid; or

(iii) the bill was a forgery.

The Order. There must be an order to pay and not a mere request. Thus the word "Pay" or the words "Please pay" will suffice but probably not words such as "I hope you will kindly pay" for such words are not imperative.

Further the order must be unconditional as between drawer and drawee, and an instrument which orders any act to be done in addition to the payment of money is not a Bill of Exchange. (Sect. 3 (2).) (*Bavins v. London & S. W. Bank*, 1900;[548] and *Nathan* v. *Ogdens Ltd.*, 1905.)[549]

An order to pay out of a particular fund is not unconditional e.g. "pay X £100 out of the money due to me from Y when this is received." Sect. 3 (3).

However, an unqualified order to pay, coupled with an indication of a particular fund out of which the drawee is to re-imburse himself, or a particular account to be debited with the amount, is regarded as unconditional, e.g., a cheque drawn "pay X £50 and debit my No. 2 A/C." Here the wording indicates that X is to be paid in any case out of the drawer's funds even if No. 2 A/C is insufficient. Similarly an unqualified order to pay, coupled with a statement of the transaction which gives rise to the bill is unconditional e.g. "Pay X £5,000 being the purchase price of Greenacre." Provided a bill is initially unconditional it remains valid even though there is subsequently a conditional delivery acceptance or indorsement.

Signature. A bill of exchange must be signed, and no person is liable as drawer, indorser or acceptor of a bill who has not signed it as such. Thus, a bank on whom a cheque has been drawn is not liable to the holder in the event of dishonour and an undisclosed principal is not liable on a bill signed by his agent in the agent's own name.

The following cases should also be noted—

(1) Where a person signs a bill in a trade or assumed name, he is liable on it as if he had signed in his own name.

(2) The signature of the name of a firm is equivalent to the signature by the person so signing of the names of all the persons liable as partners in that firm. (Sect. 23.) In the case of a trading firm, the partner is *prima facie* entitled to bind the other partners, and the presumption is conclusive in favour of a holder in due course. In the case of a non-trading firm, the person who wishes to enforce the bill must show that the partner signing had authority to bind the other partners.

(3) A corporation must, by its nature, sign through the agency of its officers, though a bill drawn by a corporation is valid if it bears the corporate seal. Further, Sect. 108 (4) of the Companies Act, 1948, provides that if officers of the company have signed or authorised the signature of the company on a bill, cheque or note, on which the company's name does not appear, the officers are personally liable to the holder of the instrument if it is not paid by the company. Thus, the omission of the word "limited" on the bill might render an officer personally liable (*Penrose* v. *Martyr*, 1858),[550] though the abbreviation "Ltd." can be used. (*Stacey* v. *Wallis*, 1912.)[551] In addition an officer of a company may be liable if the company is described by the wrong name though the doctrine of equitable estoppel may prevent a person from enforcing his claim where he has himself written the words containing the misdescription. (*Durham Fancy Goods Ltd.* v. *Michael Jackson (Fancy Goods) Ltd.*, 1968.)[97]

(4) A signature by procuration (e.g. per pro B. Brown, J. Jones), operates as notice that the agent has a limited authority to sign, and the principal is only bound by such signature if the agent so signing was acting within the actual limits of his authority. (Sect. 25.)

Where a person signs a bill as a drawer, indorser, or acceptor, and adds words to his signature indicating that he signs for or on behalf of a principal or in a representative character, he is not personally liable thereon; but the mere addition to his signature of words describing him as an agent, or as filling a representative character, does not exempt him from personal liability. (*Childs* v. *Monins and Bowles*, 1821.)[552]

(5) In determining whether a signature on a bill is that of a principal, or that of an agent by whose hand it is written, the construction most favourable to the validity of the bill is adopted. (Sect. 26.)

(6) If a person signs a bill in the mistaken belief that he is signing a document of a different nature, he will not be liable unless he was negligent. (*Foster* v. *MacKinnon*, 1869.)[129]

(7) A recognised personal mark may be used where a person is illiterate.

Forged or Unauthorised Signature. Where a signature on a bill is forged or unauthorised, it is wholly inoperative and no rights can be acquired through or under that signature, unless the party against whom it is sought to retain or enforce payment of the bill is precluded from setting up the forgery or want of authority.

Forged signatures. Here, the person signing the instrument, A, intends to pass the signature off as that of some other person B and it is not essential that it should be an attempted copy of B's signature.

Unauthorised signatures. Here the signature is genuine but the person signing has no authority to sign the bill as where an office boy signs a bill on behalf of his employers.

Ratification. An authorised signature can be ratified if the rules relating to ratification are complied with. (See p. 194.) A forged signature cannot usually be ratified, because the forger does not purport to act as agent for the person whose signature he forges. However, a forgery may be adopted if the person whose signature was forged acknowledges the signature as his own and another person has acted to his detriment upon the faith of that acknowledgement.

Apart from the possibility of ratification, an unauthorised signature has the same effect as a forgery. E.g., X draws a bill on Y payable to Z and Y accepts. A then steals the bill and forges Z's indorsement and negotiates the bill to B. B has no title to the bill and it is still the property of Z. If Y pays the bill to B he does not obtain a good discharge and remains liable to pay Z.

Estoppel. If a signature on a bill has been forged and the party whose signature it purports to be gets to know of the forgery, he may, if he does not inform the holder within a reasonable time, be stopped from asserting it. (*Greenwood* v. *Martins Bank Ltd.*, 1933.)[436] There are also two statutory estoppels which can affect other parties. Thus, estoppel is not confined to the person whose signature was forged.

(1) *The acceptor of a bill*, by accepting it, is precluded from denying to a holder in due course the existence of the drawer, the genuineness of his signature, and his capacity and authority to draw the bill (Sect. 54 (2)). E.g., an instrument supposedly drawn by X on Y, payable to Z, is accepted by Y. Suppose that Z has forged X's signature on the instrument and that Z negotiates it to A who is a holder in due course. A can sue Y, because Y is estopped from setting up the forgery and this is so even though the instrument is not really a bill at all, since it was not signed by the person who gave it.

(2) *The indorser of a bill*, by indorsing it, is precluded from denying to a holder in due course the genuineness and regularity in all respects of the drawer's signature and all previous indorsements (Sect. 55 (2)).

Thus, if in the example given above, A had indorsed the instrument to B who was a holder in due course, then B would be able to sue Y under Sect. 54 (2) and A under Sect. 55 (2).

The Drawee. The drawee must be named or otherwise indicated in the bill with reasonable certainty. A bill may be addressed to two or more drawees, whether they are partners or not, but an order addressed to two or more drawees *in the alternative* or *in succession* is not a bill of exchange (Sect. 6). The reason for this provision is that alternative or successive drawees would give rise to difficulties regarding liability in the case of dishonour.

ACCEPTANCE

Section 17 provides that by accepting a bill the drawee signifies his assent to the order of the drawer and becomes liable on the bill in the capacity of acceptor.

An acceptance must not express that the drawee will perform his promise by any other means than the payment of money, and it must be written on the bill and signed by the drawee. The drawee's signature without additional words is sufficient, although frequently the word "Accepted" and the date is added, and he need not sign with his own hand; the signature may be written by some other person by or under his authority.

(1) *A bill may be accepted after it is overdue,* or after it has been dishonoured by a previous refusal to accept or by non-payment. (Sect. 18 (2).)

(2) *A bill may be accepted before it has been signed by the drawer or while otherwise incomplete.* (Sect. 18 (1).) Incompleteness does not invalidate a bill and a bill is not invalid by reason (*a*) that it is not dated; (*b*) that it does not specify the value given, or that any value has been given therefor; (*c*) that it does not specify the place where it is drawn or the place where it is payable. (Sect. 3 (4).)

Although the bill may contain a statement of value or the words "value received" this is not essential because there is a *prima facie* presumption of consideration. However, where bills are used in export sales, the bank or discount house concerned will generally prefer a bill to contain a short description of the nature of the transaction.

Inchoate Instruments. When a bill lacks a material particular, the person in possession of it has *prima facie* authority to fill up the omission in any way he thinks fit. Where a simple signature on a blank stamped paper is delivered to the signer in order that it may be converted into a bill, it operates as a *prima facie* authority to fill it up within a reasonable time, and strictly in accordance with the authority given; but if such an instrument is negotiated to a holder in due course, his rights are fully protected, even if the person completing the bill exceeded his authority, e.g. by inserting an excessive amount. (Sect. 20.)

If therefore X owes Y £50 and writes an acceptance for that sum on an otherwise blank stamped paper and hands it to Y, then Y can write in his own name as drawer and payee, and can then sue X. However, the stamped paper must be *delivered*, and so if in the above example X had put the blank acceptance in his desk and Z had stolen it, and then filled in his name as drawer and payee, he would not be entitled to sue X upon it, nor would a holder in due course.

However, if the paper is properly delivered, then Sect. 20 will protect a holder in due course, e.g. X gives Y a blank cheque so that Y can purchase for X a lawn mower up to, but not in excess of, £40 in value. If Y fills in the cheque for £50 and inserts his own name as payee, then he cannot sue X, but if after completion, Y negotiates the cheque to Z, a holder in due course, Z is not affected by Y's lack of authority and can sue X for £50 if the cheque is dishonoured.

Types of Acceptance. An acceptance may be either general or qualified. A *general acceptance* assents without qualification to the order of the drawer. A *qualified acceptance* varies the effect of the bill as drawn.

The following are examples of qualified acceptances—

(*a*) *Conditional.* The acceptor undertakes to pay on the fulfilment of a condition stated, e.g. Payable on delivery of bills of lading.

(*b*) *Partial.* The acceptor undertakes to pay part only of the amount of the bill, e.g. a bill drawn on X for £200. X accepts it as to £100.

(*c*) *Local.* An acceptance to pay *only at a particular specified place*. An acceptance to pay at a particular place is a general acceptance, unless it expressly states that the bill is to be paid there only and not elsewhere, e.g. a bill accepted payable at the Barchester Bank, Sudbury only, is a qualified acceptance, whereas a bill payable at the Barchester Bank Sudbury is a general acceptance.

(*d*) *Qualified as to Time.* Accepted payable in six months instead of three.

(*e*) *The acceptance of some one or more of the drawees but not all.* (Sect. 19 (2).)

Wherever possible an acceptance will be construed as a general and not as a qualified acceptance.

EFFECT OF QUALIFIED ACCEPTANCE. A holder may either refuse to take a qualified acceptance and treat the bill as dishonoured by the non-acceptance, or take it. If he takes a qualified acceptance, any drawer or indorser is discharged from liability on the bill unless it appears from the circumstances that he has expressly or impliedly authorised the holder to take a qualified acceptance or subsequently gives his express consent to it. (Sect. 44 (2).) The holder may serve notice on him in order to ascertain whether there is such assent, and if having received such a notice a drawer or any indorser does not give notice to the holder of his dissent within a reasonable time, he will be deemed to have assented. (Sect. 44 (3).)

However, these provisions *do not apply to a partial acceptance* of which due notice has been given, although, where a foreign bill has been accepted as to part, it must be protested as to the balance (Sect. 44 (2)), e.g., A draws an inland bill on B for £100 payable to C six months after date, and C indorses it to D. D presents the bill to B for acceptance and B accepts "as to £50 only." D can refuse to take this qualified acceptance and can serve notice of dishonour and proceed against the drawer A and the indorser C. However, D may take the partial acceptance, and if he does, and gives notice to A and C, he can hold them *liable at once* for the £50 for which the bill has, in effect, been dishonoured and they will also remain liable for the balance of £50 should B not pay on maturity.

ACCOMMODATION BILLS. Sometimes a bill is what is called an *accommodation bill*, and an accommodation party to such a bill is one who has signed it as drawer, acceptor, or indorser, without receiving value for it. His object is to lend his name and credit to some other person. (Sect. 28 (1).)

An accommodation party is liable on the bill to a holder for value; and it is immaterial whether, when such a holder took the bill, he knew the party to be an accommodation party or not (Sect. 28 (2).), e.g. A is in business and requires capital to purchase a new van but will not be able to pay for it out of the profits of the business for three months. He asks a prosperous friend B to accept a bill drawn by A on B for £800 payable "three months after date." B accepts the bill but receives no value for it. A can now discount the bill at his bank and because the bill bears B's signature, the bank will probably give a good price for it. Where a person accepts a bill for the accommodation of the drawer, it is understood that the drawer will make available funds to meet the bill on maturity, and, if he does not do so, and the acceptor has to pay the bill, the drawer must indemnify the acceptor. This is, however, of no concern to the banker, who can sue B on his acceptance even though he knew that B was an accommodation party. However, B is not liable to A because no consideration was given by A to B.

Presentment for Acceptance. This is required only where a holder receives a bill which has not been accepted. Where this is so, the holder will normally present the bill twice, once for acceptance, and again for payment on maturity. Where a bill is payable on demand there is no need to present for acceptance and in such a case the holder need only present the bill for payment. *Thus the rules relating to presentment for acceptance apply only to time bills.*

By virtue of Sect. 39 presentment for acceptance is essential in only three cases—

(i) Where a bill is payable after sight presentment is clearly necessary in order to fix the maturity of the instrument.

(ii) Where a bill is drawn payable elsewhere than at the residence or place of business of the drawee, it must be presented for acceptance before it can be presented for payment. Where the holder of a bill drawn payable elsewhere than at the place of business or residence of the drawee, has not time with the exercise of reasonable diligence to present the bill for acceptance before presenting it for payment on the day it falls due, the delay caused by presenting the bill for acceptance before presenting it for payment is excused, and does not discharge the drawer or indorsers. This situation might arise where the holder of a foreign bill only received it on the day it matured.

(iii) Where a bill expressly stipulates that it shall be presented for acceptance, it must also be presented for acceptance before it can be presented for payment.

However, it is always wise to present a bill for acceptance even if it does not come within (i) to (iii) above because the drawee is not liable until he has accepted the bill and if he refuses to accept it the holder can seek immediate reimbursement from the drawer and any prior indorsers without waiting for the bill to mature.

When a bill payable after sight is negotiated, the holder must either present it for acceptance or negotiate it within a reasonable time. If he does not do so, the drawer and all indorsers prior to the holder are discharged. (Sect. 40.)

Rules for Presentment. The presentment must be made *by or on behalf of the holder to the drawee, or to some person authorised to accept or refuse acceptance on his behalf*, at a reasonable hour on a business day and before the bill is overdue. As the banks now close on Saturday, the Banking and Financial Dealings Act, 1971, defines Saturday as a "non-business day".

(*a*) METHOD OF PRESENTMENT. The following rules apply—

(i) When a bill is addressed to two or more drawees who are not partners, it must be presented to them all, unless one has authority to accept for all, when it may be presented to him only.

(ii) Where the drawee is dead, presentment *may* be made to his personal representative.

(iii) Where the drawee is bankrupt, presentment *may* be made either to him or to his trustee.

(iv) Where authorised by agreement or usage, a presentment through the post office is sufficient. (Sect. 41 (1).)

(*b*) PRESENTMENT EXCUSED. Presentment in accordance with these rules is excused, and *the bill may be treated as dishonoured by non-acceptance*—

(i) where the drawee is dead or bankrupt, or is a fictitious person, or a person not having capacity to contract by bill;

(ii) where, after the exercise of reasonable diligence, such presentment cannot be effected;

(iii) where, although the presentment has been irregular, acceptance has been refused on some other ground. (Sect. 41 (2).)

The fact that the holder has reason to believe that the bill, on presentment, will be dishonoured does not excuse presentment. (Sect. 41 (3).)

Non-acceptance. When presentment is excused or when a bill is duly presented for acceptance and is not accepted within the customary time (usually twenty-four hours), the person presenting it must treat it as dishonoured by non-acceptance.

In case of such dishonour, the holder has an immediate right of recourse against the drawer and indorsers, and no presentment for payment is necessary. He must, however, give them notice of dishonour without delay otherwise they are discharged not only from liability on the bill but also on the consideration given for it.

Acceptance for Honour. Where an unaccepted bill has been negotiated many times and is then dishonoured, the holder has an immediate right to sue the drawer and prior indorsers for the amount of the bill. If the holder claims against his prior indorser and each transaction is performed in reverse, the original payee will eventually claim from the drawer not only the amount of the bill but also the cumulative costs incurred by each indorsee claiming from his respective indorser. To avoid this inconvenience Sect. 65 provides that where a bill has been protested for dishonour by non-acceptance, or protested for better security, and is not overdue, any person who is not already a party may, with the consent of the holder, intervene and accept the bill *supra protest* for the honour of *any party* liable on it for all or part of the sum drawn.

The acceptor for honour engages to pay the bill according to the tenor of his acceptance if it is not paid by the drawee, provided that it has been duly presented for payment and protested for non-payment, and that he receives notice of these facts. The acceptor for honour is liable to the holder, and to all parties to the bill subsequent to the party for whose honour he has accepted. (Sect. 66.)

The holder is not bound to take an acceptance for honour and his rights on the bill are not prejudiced if he refuses it.

PAYMENT

The Payee. Where a bill is not payable to bearer, the payee must be named or otherwise indicated therein with reasonable certainty. A bill may be made payable to two or more payees, jointly or in the alternative, to one of two, or to one or some of several payees. Thus it is possible to have alternative payees (Pay A or B) though not alternative drawees. A bill may also be made payable to the holder of an office for the time being. Thus a cheque payable to trustees is quite valid. Where the payee is a fictitious or non-existent person, the bill may be treated as payable to bearer. (Sect. 7 (3).)

The payee is considered *existing* where the drawer knows of his existence and intends him to benefit. (*Vinden* v. *Hughes*, 1905.)[553] The payee is considered *fictitious* when his name is inserted by the drawer by way of a pretence and without any intention that the named payee should obtain payment. (*Bank of England* v. *Vagliano Bros.*, 1891.)[554] The payee is considered *non-existent* where the drawer does not know of the payee's existence, though there is an existing person with that name. (*Clutton* v. *Attenborough*, 1879.)[555]

A bill or cheque which directs payment to be made to an *impersonal payee*, e.g., "Cash" or "Wages" is not a valid bill because it is not payable to a specified person. However, if such an instrument is issued by a customer of a bank it may be a document which is intended to enable a person to obtain payment from a banker within the meaning of Sect. 4 (2) of the Cheques Act, 1957. Therefore, a banker who pays or collects the instrument without negligence may claim statutory protection if there have been wrongful dealings in respect of it. (*Orbit Mining and Trading Co. Ltd.*, v. *Westminster Bank*, 1962.)[556]

The Sum Certain. The sum payable by a bill is a sum certain although it is required to be paid—

(*a*) With interest;

(*b*) By stated instalments;

(*c*) By stated instalments, with a provision that on default in payment of any instalment the whole sum shall become due;

(*d*) According to an indicated rate of exchange to be ascertained as directed by the bill. (Sect. 9 (1).)

The amount must be capable of being exactly calculated, e.g. the rate of interest must generally be stated, or the rate of exchange indicated or its method of ascertainment specified. However, if a rate of interest is not actually agreed, it will probably be taken as five per cent.

Where the sum payable is expressed in words and also in figures, and there is a discrepancy between the two, the sum denoted by the words is the amount payable. (Sect. 9 (2).) However, in the case of a cheque, the banker will in practice return it unpaid marked "words and figures differ."

Where a bill is expressed to be payable with interest, unless the bill otherwise provides, interest runs from the date of the bill, and, if the bill is undated, from its issue. (Sect. 9 (3).)

Presentment for Payment. A bill must be duly presented for payment, otherwise the drawer and indorsers are discharged from liability. (Sect. 45.) (*Hamilton Finance Co. Ltd.* v. *Coverley and Others*, 1969.)[557] The acceptor is not, however, discharged. (Sect. 52.)

1. TIME OF PRESENTMENT. The following rules apply—

(*a*) Where the bill is not payable on demand, presentment must be made on the day it falls due. (Sect. 45 (1).) (*Hamilton Finance Co. Ltd.* v. *Coverley and Others*, 1969.)[557]

(*b*) Where the bill is payable on demand, presentment must be made within a reasonable time after its issue in order to render the drawer liable, and within a reasonable time after its indorsement to render the indorser liable. (Sect. 45 (2).) However, Section 74 modifies this provision in the case of a drawer of a cheque. (See p. 326.)

2. METHOD OF PRESENTMENT. The bill must be presented by the holder or by some person authorised to receive payment on his behalf, at a reasonable hour on a business day, at the proper place, either to the person designated by the bill as the payer, or to some person authorised to pay or refuse payment on his behalf, if with the exercise of

reasonable diligence such person can there be found. Where it is authorised by agreement or usage, a presentment through the post office is sufficient. (Sect. 45 (3) and (8).)

3. PLACE. The proper place to present a bill is—

(*a*) The place specified in the bill, if any;

(*b*) Where no place of payment is specified, at the address of the drawee or acceptor if given in the bill;

(*c*) In the absence of these, at the drawee's or acceptor's place of business (if known) or at his ordinary residence (if known);

(*d*) Failing these, to the drawee or acceptor wherever he may be found, or at his last known place of business or residence. (Sect. 45 (4).)

Where a bill is presented at the proper place, and after the exercise of reasonable diligence no person authorised to pay or refuse payment can be found there, no further presentment is required. (Sect. 45 (5).)

4. SPECIAL CASES. The following special rules apply—

(*a*) Where a bill is drawn upon, or accepted by two or more persons who are not partners, and no place of payment is specified, presentment must be made to them all. (Sect. 45 (6).) Though if one pays, or refuses payment as agent of the others, no further presentment is required.

(*b*) Where the drawee or acceptor of a bill is dead, and no place of payment is specified, the bill must be presented to his personal representative, if there is one and he can be found with the exercise of reasonable diligence. It should be noted that, while *presentment for acceptance is excused in the case of death or bankruptcy of the drawee, this is not the case with presentment for payment.*

5. EXCUSES FOR NON-PRESENTMENT. Delay in presenting the bill for payment is excused when the delay is caused by circumstances beyond the control of the holder, and not imputable to his default, misconduct or negligence. When the cause of the delay ceases to operate, presentment must then be made with reasonable diligence. (Sect. 46 (1).) (*Hamilton Finance Co. Ltd.* v. *Coverley and Others*, 1969)[557]

6. PRESENTMENT UNNECESSARY. Presentment for payment is dispensed with under Sect. 46 (2)—

(*a*) Where, after the exercise of reasonable diligence, it cannot be effected; (*Cornelius* v. *Banque Franco-Serbe*, 1942.)[558]

(*b*) Where the drawee is a fictitious person;

(*c*) As regards the drawer where the drawee or acceptor is not bound, as between himself and the drawer, to accept or pay the bill, and the drawer has no reason to believe that the bill would be paid if presented, e.g. where the acceptor is an accommodation party who would not be liable to the drawer.

(*d*) As regards an indorser, where the bill was accepted or made for the accommodation of that indorser, and he has no reason to believe that the bill would be paid if presented;

(*e*) By waiver of presentment, express or implied.

In general, the fact that the holder has reason to believe that the bill will, on presentment be dishonoured, does not dispense with the need to present it.

7. PAYMENT FOR HONOUR. Where a bill has been presented for non-payment, any person may intervene and pay it (*supra protest* as it is called) for the honour of any party liable thereon, or for the honour of the person for whose account the bill is drawn. (Sect. 68 (1).) Payment for honour *supra protest*, in order to operate as such and not as a mere voluntary payment, must be attested by a notarial act of honour which is a document prepared by a notary public. (Sect. 68 (3).) Where a bill has been paid for honour, all parties subsequent to the party for whose honour it is paid are discharged, but the payer for honour takes over the rights of the party for whose honour he pays against prior parties. (Sect. 68 (5).) Where the holder of a bill refuses payment *supra protest* he loses his right of recourse against all persons who would have been discharged by such payment. (Sect. 68 (7).)

TIME OF PAYMENT

Demand. A bill is payable on demand (*a*) which is expressed to be payable on demand, or at sight, or on presentation; or (*b*) in which no time for payment is expressed. (Sect. 10.)

Where a bill is accepted or indorsed when it is overdue, it is, as regards the acceptor who so accepts, or any indorser who indorses it, deemed to be a bill payable on demand. (Sect. 10.)

Where a bill is payable on demand the holder can ask for payment immediately. The most important type of bill payable on demand is a cheque.

Fixed or Determinable Future Time. A bill is payable at a determinable future time when it is expressed to be payable (i) at a fixed period after date or sight; (ii) on or at a fixed period after the occurrence of a specified event which is certain to happen, though the time of happening may be uncertain, e.g., 3 months after A's death. An instrument expressed to be payable on a contingency is not a bill, and the happening of the event does not cure the defect. (Sect. 11.) Suppose a bill runs "Pay B Brown or Order Five Hundred Pounds on the marriage of his daughter Jane to William Smith." This would not be a valid bill, even though the wedding took place shortly afterwards. The words "on or before" a given date imports an element of contingency and an instrument ordering payment in this form is not a valid bill. (*Williamson* v. *Rider*, 1962.)[559]

A bill is not invalid by reason only of the fact that it is ante-dated, post-dated, or dated on a Sunday. (Sect. 13 (2).)

Where a bill expressed to be payable at a fixed period after date is issued undated, or where the acceptance of a bill payable at a fixed period after sight is undated, any holder may insert therein the true date of issue or acceptance, and the bill will be payable accordingly.

(1) Where the holder in good faith and by mistake inserts the wrong date; and

(2) In every case where a wrong date is inserted and the bill comes into the hands of a holder in due course, the bill is valid and the date so inserted is deemed to be the true one. (Sect. 12.)

Finally, there is a presumption that where a bill, acceptance or indorsement is dated, that date is the true date unless the contrary can be proved. (Sect. 13 (1).)

Ascertainment of Due Date. Where a bill is not payable on demand, the day on which it falls due is determined as follows—

1. AFTER DATE. Where a bill is payable at a *fixed period after date*, after sight, or after the happening of a specified event, the time of payment is determined by excluding the day from which the time is to begin to run, and by including the day of payment. (Sect. 14 (2).)

2. AFTER SIGHT. Where a bill is payable at a *fixed period after sight*, the term begins to run from the date of acceptance if the bill be accepted, and from the date of noting or protest if the bill be noted or protested for non-acceptance or non-delivery. (Sect. 14 (3).)

3. DAYS OF GRACE. The normal period of the bill was calculated as above and then three days, called *days of grace*, were added to the time of payment as fixed by the bill, and the bill was due and payable on the last day of grace. (Sect. 14 (1).) However, a bill of exchange could specifically exclude days of grace by the insertion of such words as "without grace." The Banking and Financial Dealings Act, 1971, which came into force on 16th December, 1971, abolishes the three days of grace which Sect. 14 (1) allowed to be added to the time of payment of all bills not payable on demand. This is designed to bring the United Kingdom into line with general international practice.

4. CALENDAR MONTHS. The term "month" in a bill means "calendar month." (Sect. 14 (4).) A bill payable three months after date, and dated January 15th would be payable on April 15th. Difficulties might arise when a bill is drawn at the end of a month which is longer than the month in which payment is to be made. Thus a bill drawn payable one month after date on January 28th would be payable on February 28th. But so too would bills drawn on January 29th, January 30th, and January 31st, except in a leap year when they would be payable on February 29th. In a normal year, therefore, such bills drawn on January 28th to 31st inclusive would all fall due on February 28th.

5. NON-BUSINESS DAYS. All bills whose payment falls due on non-business days, i.e. Saturdays, Sundays, and bank holidays, are payable on the succeeding business day. (Banking and Financial Dealings Act, 1971.)

When the due date has passed the bill is overdue and if it is not presented on that date the drawer and indorsers are discharged unless the holder can claim exemption under Sect. 46. Further, an overdue bill cannot be negotiated to a holder in due course.

NEGOTIABILITY

Order of a Specified Person. Where a bill of exchange is made payable to a payee or order, this means that the payee may indorse the bill and pass it on to any person according to his own order. If the payee indorses the bill as follows: "Pay J. Jones or Order," signing his own name underneath, the bill then becomes payable to J. Jones on delivery to him, and he in turn may repeat the process by a further indorsement. If, on the other hand, the payee simply indorses the bill with his own signature, without addition, the bill on delivery becomes payable to bearer.

A bill is payable to order which is expressed to be so payable, or which is expressed to be payable to a particular person, and does not contain words prohibiting transfer or indicating an intention that it should not be transferable, as "Pay J. Jones only." A bill drawn "Pay X" is an order bill because the words "or order" are implied. Thus the striking out of the words "or order" on a cheque will have no effect because the words will be implied. An instrument payable "to the order of X" has the same meaning and effect as one payable "to X or order." (Sect. 8 (5).)

Delivery. A contract on a bill, whether it be the drawer's, the acceptor's, or an indorser's, must be completed by delivery of the instrument, and is revocable until delivered. (*Baxendale* v. *Bennett*, (1878), 3 Q.B.D. 525.) However, where an acceptance is written on a bill, and the drawee gives notice of his acceptance to the person entitled to the bill, the acceptance becomes complete and irrevocable even before delivery. (Sect. 21 (1).)

Delivery may be made by post and in England, once the bill is posted, the delivery is irrevocable. Elsewhere, if the letter can be reclaimed from the post office before actual delivery to the addressee, delivery can be revoked.

The delivery, in order to be effectual, must be made either by or under the authority of the party drawing, accepting, or indorsing, as the case may be, but where a bill is no longer in the possession of such party, a valid and unconditional delivery by him is presumed until the contrary is proved. It may, however, be shown to have been conditional or for a special purpose only, and not for the purpose of transferring the property in the bill. Nevertheless, *if the bill be in the hands of a holder in due course, a valid delivery of the bill by all parties prior to him so as to make them liable to him is conclusively presumed.* (Sect. 21.)

For example, X draws a cheque in favour of Y or order, and Y indorses it in blank thus converting it into a bearer cheque. It is then stolen by T. T has no title because the cheque was not delivered to him, but if T negotiates the cheque to H, a holder in due course, H can sue all prior parties because in his case delivery from Y to T is conclusively presumed.

Regarding the delivery of incomplete or inchoate instruments, Sect. 20 (1) provides that where a simple signature on a blank paper is delivered by the signer in order that it may be converted into a bill, it operates as a *prima facie* authority to fill it up as a complete bill for any amount, using the signature for that of the drawer, or the acceptor, or an indorser. Further, when a bill is wanting in any material particular, the person in possession of it has a *prima facie* authority to fill up the omission in any way he thinks fit. Thus if X owes Y £100, and writes an acceptance for that sum on a piece of paper and hands it to Y, then Y can write in his own name as drawer and payee and sue X on the bill.

Section 20 (2) dealing with wrongly completed instruments states that if an incomplete instrument is, when completed, to be enforceable against any person who became a party to it prior to completion, it must be filled up within a reasonable time and strictly in accordance with the authority given; provided that if such an instrument is *negotiated* to a holder in due course his rights are fully protected even if the person completing the bill exceeded his authority, e.g., by inserting an excessive amount.

By way of example let us suppose that P asks A to buy a lawn-mower for him and gives A a blank cheque with authority to complete it for up to £50. If A writes up the cheque for £100 with his own name as payee he cannot sue P. However, if he negotiates the cheque to T, a holder in due course, T can sue P for the full £100 by virtue of Sect. 20 (2). If T's name is inserted as payee the proviso to Section 20 (2) will not apply because the payee of an instrument cannot be a holder in due course because it is not negotiated to him. (*Jones* v. *Waring and Gillow*, 1926.)[560] However, T, even as payee, may be able to sue P by virtue of common law estoppel if he has changed his position in reliance on P's signature as where he has lent money to A. (*Lloyds Bank* v. *Cooke*, 1907.)[561] Nevertheless P cannot be liable beyond the amount authorised either under Section 20, or at common law if the blank instrument is crossed "not negotiable." (*Wilson and Meeson* v. *Pickering*, 1946.)[562]

Negotiation. When a bill contains words prohibiting transfer, or indicating an intention that it should not be transferable, it is valid as between the parties thereto, but is not negotiable. (Sect. 8 (1).) An example of this would be a bill made payable to *G. Green only*, or one marked "Not Transferable" or crossed "Not Negotiable." The meaning generally given to the word "negotiable" is "transferable free from Equities" but in Section 8 (1) the draftsman has used it to mean "transferable" and therefore a bill of exchange payable to "G. Green only" or marked "not negotiable" is not even transferable. Thus if A draws a bill on B payable to "C only" or the bill is marked "not negotiable" it is valid as between A, B and C but C cannot transfer it. (*Hibernian Bank* v. *Gysin and Hanson*, 1939.)[563] The position in regard to cheques is different for a cheque crossed "not negotiable" is at least transferable but the transferee takes it subject to Equities.

Where a bill is negotiable, it may be payable either to order or to bearer, and a bill is payable to bearer which is expressed to be so payable, or on which the only or last indorsement is an indorsement in blank.

A bill is negotiated when it is transferred from one person to another in such a manner as to constitute the transferee the holder of the bill. *A bill payable to bearer is negotiated by delivery; a bill payable to order is negotiated by the indorsement of the holder completed by delivery.* Where the holder of a bill payable to his order transfers it for value without indorsing it, the transferee gets such title as the transferor had in the bill, together with the right to have the indorsement of the transferor. If the transferor refuses to indorse, the court has power under the Judicature Act, 1925, Sect. 47, to order some other person to sign on his behalf. However, any person who is under an obligation to indorse the bill in a representative capacity may indorse the bill in such terms as to negative his personal liability. (Sect. 31.)

Where a bill is negotiable in its origin, it continues to be negotiable until it has been (*a*) restrictively indorsed; or (*b*) discharged by payment or otherwise. *Where an overdue bill is negotiated*, it can only be negotiated subject to any defects of title affecting it at maturity, and thenceforward no person who takes it can acquire or give a better title than that which the person from whom he took it had. *Future holders cannot be holders in due course.*

A bill payable on demand is deemed to be overdue when it appears on the face of it to have been in circulation for an unreasonable length of time, and this is a question of fact. Except where an indorsement bears date after the maturity of the bill, every negotiation is *prima facie* deemed to have been effected before the bill was overdue. When a bill which was not overdue has been dishonoured, any person who takes it with notice of the dishonour, takes it subject to any defects of title attaching to it at the time of dishonour, but not so as to affect the rights of a holder in due course. (Sect. 36.)

Valid Indorsement. An indorsement, in order to operate as a negotiation, must comply with the following conditions, namely—

(1) *It must be written on the bill itself* and be signed by the indorser. The simple signature of the indorser on the bill, without additional words, is sufficient. Where there is no more room on the bill for indorsements, a slip of paper called an "allonge" is attached to the bill, and indorsements written on the allonge are valid, but the first should be written partly on the bill and partly on the allonge to avoid fraud. An indorsement on a copy of the bill, in countries where copies are recognised, is valid.

(2) *It must be an indorsement of the entire bill.* A partial indorsement

which purports to transfer to an indorsee a part only of the amount payable, or which purports to transfer the bill to two or more indorsees severally, does not operate as a negotiation of the bill.

(3) Where a bill is payable to the order of *two or more payees* or indorsees who are not partners, *all must indorse* unless the one indorsing has authority to indorse for the others.

(4) Where, in a bill payable to order, the *payee or indorsee is wrongly designated*, or his name is mis-spelt, he may indorse the bill as therein described adding, if he wishes, his proper signature.

(5) *Where there are two or more indorsements* on the bill, each indorsement is deemed to have been made in the order in which it appears on the bill until the contrary is proved.

(6) *An indorsement may be made in blank or special.* It may also contain terms making it restrictive. (Sect. 32.)

(a) CONDITIONAL INDORSEMENT. Where a bill purports to be indorsed conditionally, e.g., "Pay X when he delivers the bill of lading", the condition may be disregarded by the payer, and a payment made to the indorsee is valid whether the condition has been fulfilled or not. (Sect. 33.) Nevertheless the indorsee is bound by the condition and holds the money in trust for the indorser until the condition is fulfilled.

(b) SPECIAL INDORSEMENT. An indorsement in blank specifies no indorsee, and a bill so indorsed becomes payable to bearer. *A special indorsement* specifies the person to whom, or to whose order, the bill is to be payable. When a bill has been indorsed in blank, any holder may convert the blank indorsement into a special indorsement, by writing above the indorser's signature a direction to pay the bill to, or to the order of, himself or some other person. (Sect. 34.)

(c) RESTRICTIVE INDORSEMENT. An indorsement is restrictive which prohibits the further negotiation of the bill, or which expresses that it is a mere authority to deal with the bill as thereby directed and not a transfer of the ownership thereof, e.g. "Pay D only." or "Pay D for the Account of Y." or "Pay D or order for collection."

A restrictive indorsement gives the indorsee the right to receive payment of the bill and to sue any party thereto that the indorser could have sued, but gives him no power to transfer his rights as indorsee unless it expressly authorises him to do so. Where a restrictive indorsement authorises further transfer, all subsequent indorsees take the bill with the same rights and subject to the same liabilities as the first indorsee under the restrictive indorsement. (Sect. 35.) Examples of the use of restrictive indorsements are as follows—

(i) X the payee of a cheque owes a debt to an overseas supplier P and he wishes to indorse the cheque over to P's agent A who is in England but wishes to make it clear that A is not the beneficial owner of the cheque. X can indorse "Pay A for the account of P." A can now obtain payment and must then account to P, though A cannot transfer the bill.

(ii) Suppose X is the payee of a cheque drawn on a German bank and wishes A his German agent to collect payment for him. X can indorse "Pay A for collection" or "Pay A or order for collection."

A can obtain payment but must then account to the person who authorised him to collect. Where the words "on order" are used A can transfer his rights (and liabilities) to another person but such person cannot obtain a better title than A because A's ownership is restricted and this passes with the bill.

A holder may strike out indorsements on a bill. If the parties are D, the drawer; A, the acceptor; P, the payee; I_1, I_2, I_3, I_4, the indorsers; and H, the holder; and H strikes out I_2's indorsement, he frees I_2, I_3, and I_4 from liability, but preserves the right of recourse against I_1, P, A and D.

Irregular indorsements. An indorsement is irregular if it gives rise to doubt whether it is the indorsement of the person entitled to indorse. If, for example, William Brown is in business as "William Brown & Co." and he indorses a cheque made out in favour of the business by signing "Brown" there is a valid but irregular indorsement. If Brown delivers the cheque to Green a good title will pass if Brown's title is good. If Brown's title is defective then Green cannot obtain a better one by claiming to be a holder in due course, because the bill is not "complete and regular on the face of it."

Transferor by Delivery. Where the holder of a bill payable to bearer negotiates it by delivery without indorsing it, he is called a *transferor by delivery*. A transferor by delivery is not liable on the instrument. If he negotiates the bill, he warrants to his immediate transferee, being a holder for value, that the bill is what it purports to be, that he has a right to transfer it, and that at the time of the transfer he is not aware of any fact which renders it valueless. (Sect. 58.)

HOLDERS

The term "holder" means the payee or indorsee of a bill or note who is in possession of it, or the person in possession of a bill or note which is payable to bearer. (Sect. 2.)

Holder in Due Course. A holder in due course is a holder who has taken the bill complete and regular on the face of it (*Arab Bank Ltd.* v. *Ross*, 1952),[546] provided that he became a holder before it was overdue, and without notice that it had been previously dishonoured, if such was the fact; and that he took the bill in good faith and for value and at the time the bill was negotiated to him he had no notice of any defect in title of the person who negotiated it. (Sect. 29 (1).) Notice means actual and not constructive knowledge. (*Raphael* v. *Bank of England*, 1885.)[564]

The title of a person who negotiates a bill is defective when he obtained the bill, or the acceptance thereof, by fraud, duress, or other unlawful means, or for an illegal consideration, or when he negotiates it in breach of faith, or under such circumstances as to amount to fraud. (Sect. 29 (2).)

A holder (whether for value or not), who derives his title to a bill through a holder in due course, and who is himself not a party to any fraud or illegality affecting it, has all the rights of that holder in due course as regards the acceptor and all parties to the bill *prior to* that holder. (Sect. 29 (3).)

Thus P, who was a partner, fraudulently indorsed one of the firm's bills to I_1 in order to settle a private debt. I_1 indorsed the bill to I_2 who took for value and without notice, thus becoming a holder in due course. I_2 indorsed the bill to I_3, who knew of the fraud but was not a party to it. I_3 can sue all parties to the bill if he gave value for it, and all parties prior to I_2 if he did not.

Sect. 29 (3) creates a kind of holder in due course. Such a person is prevented from being a *true* holder in due course because he knows of the fraud, but is not a party to it. However, he has the rights of a holder in due course because he has derived his title from one. If he wishes to sue the holder in due course from whom he derived his title he must have given that holder value, but in any case he can sue parties prior to that holder so long as value has at some time been given for the bill.

Every party whose signature appears on a bill is *prima facie* deemed to have become a party thereto for value. Every holder of a bill is *prima facie* deemed to be a holder in due course; but if in an action on a bill it is admitted or proved that the acceptance, issue, or subsequent negotiation of the bill is affected with fraud, duress, or illegality, the burden of proof is shifted unless and until the holder proves that, subsequent to the alleged fraud or illegality, value has in good faith been given for the bill. (Sect. 30.) Suppose X pays a gaming debt by giving a cheque to Y and that Y negotiates the cheque to Z. If the cheque is dishonoured when Z presents it for payment Z can only sue X if he has a good title to the cheque. The presumption is that Z has a good title but if X pleads that the transaction between himself and Y is illegal under the Gaming Acts the burden of proof shifts to Z and he must show that he gave value for the bill without notice of its illegality, i.e., that he is a holder in due course.

Duties of the Holder. Sections 39–52 impose certain duties on the holder of a bill.

Duty to present for acceptance. This arises only where the holder receives a bill (not a cheque) which has not been accepted. The rules relating to presentment for acceptance are set out on p. 299.

Duty to present for payment. Presentment for payment is essential for all bills, including cheques, unless excused. The rules relating to presentment for payment are set out on pp. 301–3.

Duty to give notice of dishonour. When a bill has been dishonoured by non-acceptance or by non-payment, notice of dishonour must be given to the drawer and each indorser otherwise they may be discharged from liability on the bill. The rules relating to notice of dishonour are set out on pp. 314–16.

Duty to note and protest. The object of noting and protesting is to obtain formal and universally recognised evidence of dishonour. In English law noting and protesting is necessary in some cases, the most important being the dishonour of a foreign bill. The rules relating to noting and protesting are set out on pp. 316–18.

Rights and Powers of the Holder. The holder of a bill has the following rights and powers—

(1) He may sue on the bill in his own name. (Sect. 38 (1).)

(2) Where he is a holder in due course, he holds the bill free from any defect of title of prior parties as well as from mere personal defences available to prior parties among themselves, and may enforce payment against all parties liable on the bill. (Sect. 38 (2).) (*Re Keever,* 1966.)[565]

(3) Where his title is defective (*a*) if he negotiates the bill to a holder in due course, that holder obtains a good and complete title to the bill; and (*b*) if he obtains payment of the bill, the person who pays him in due course gets a valid discharge for the bill. (Sect. 38 (3).)

DISCHARGE OF A BILL

A bill is said to be discharged when all rights of action on it are extinguished.

1. Discharge by Payment. A bill is discharged by payment as follows—

(*a*) By payment in due course by or on behalf of the drawee or acceptor; (Sect. 59 (1).)

(*b*) Where an accommodation bill is paid in due course by the party accommodated. (Sect. 59 (3).)

Payment in due course means payment made at or after the maturity of the bill to the holder thereof in good faith and without notice that his title to the bill is defective. Payment by the accommodation acceptor does not discharge the bill for he still retains the right to claim an indemnity from the party accommodated. Where a bill is paid by the drawer or an indorser it is not discharged but—

(*a*) *Where a bill payable to, or to the order of a third party is paid by the drawer,* all subsequent parties are relieved of liability, and the drawer may enforce payment of the bill against the acceptor, but *he may not reissue it* as this would amount to materially altering the bill by substituting himself as the payee, and would discharge the acceptor

(*b*) *Where a bill is paid by an indorser, or where a bill payable to the drawer's order is paid by the drawer,* the indorser or drawer, as the case may be, is remitted to his former rights as regards the acceptor and antecedent parties. He may, therefore, if he thinks fit, strike out his own and subsequent indorsements and re-negotiate the bill. (Sect. 59 (2).) (*Callow* v. *Lawrence,* 1814.)[566]

The bill must paid to a person who can properly be described as the holder. For example, suppose A draws an order bill payable to B and accepted by C. If the bill is stolen from B by T and transferred to D by a forged indorsement a payment by C to D will not discharge the bill for D is not the holder. The real owner B could sue T and D in conversion and enforce the bill against C. If he acts quickly he may be able to recover the money from D as money paid under a mistake of fact. In *London and River Plate Bank* v. *Bank of Liverpool*, [1896] 1 Q.B. 7, a delay of six weeks was held to prevent the acceptor from recovering money paid to the wrong person.

If in the above example the bill had been payable to bearer a payment by C to T would have discharged the bill for T would be a holder. If T had transferred the bearer bill to D a payment to D would discharge it, for D would also be a holder.

2. Circuity. When the acceptor of a bill is or becomes the holder of it at or after its maturity in his own right, the bill is discharged. (Sect. 61.) Suppose A has accepted a bill for £100 and has sold goods worth £100 to H. If a subsequent indorser I_4 negotiates the bill to H, and H negotiates it back to A in settlement, the bill is discharged. The Section cannot apply to cheques because they are never accepted, and apart from the Section there is a rule of common law that when the acceptor becomes the executor of the holder the debt is discharged. (*Jenkins* v. *Jenkins*, 1928.)[567]

3. Express Waiver. When the holder of a bill at or after its maturity absolutely and unconditionally renounces his rights against the acceptor, the bill is discharged. The renunciation must be in writing unless the bill is delivered up to the acceptor. Similarly the liabilities of any party to a bill may be renounced by the holder before, at, or after maturity, but these actions shall not affect the rights of a holder in due course without notice of the renunciation. (Sect. 62.)

Thus a holder in due course can enforce the bill against all parties if he took the bill without notice of the renunciation. If a renunciation of rights is to be effective at common law it must be under seal or supported by consideration or the debtor must have altered his position in reliance on it. This is unnecessary in many foreign systems of law and, because bills of exchange are widely used in international trade, Section 62 brings English law into line with foreign jurisdictions.

4. Cancellation. Where a bill is intentionally cancelled by the holder or his agent, and the cancellation is apparent thereon, the bill is discharged. (Sect. 63 (1).)

In like manner any party liable on a bill may be discharged by the intentional cancellation of his signature by the holder or his agent, but in such a case any indorser who would not have had a right of recourse against the party whose signature is cancelled is also discharged. (Sect. 63 (2).) The existence of this subsection prevents a party to a bill of exchange having rights taken away from him without his consent. Thus if H cancels I_1's indorsement I_2, I_3, and I_4 are also discharged.

A cancellation made unintentionally, or under a mistake, or without the authority of the holder, is inoperative, but the burden of proof lies on the party who alleges this to be the case. (Sect. 63 (3).)

5. Alteration of a Bill. Where a bill or acceptance is materially altered without the assent of all parties liable on the bill, the bill is discharged except as against (i) the party who has himself made, authorised, or assented to the alteration; and (ii) subsequent indorsers. The alteration must be intentional and not accidental. Where a bill has been materially altered, but the alteration is not apparent, and the bill is in the hands of a holder in due course, such holder may avail himself of the bill as if it had not been altered, and may enforce payment of it according to its original tenor. (Sect. 64 (1).) For example A draws a bill on B for £100, the payee being C, and B accepts. Suppose that C fraudulently alters the sum payable to £1,000, and although the alteration is apparent C obtains £1,000 for the bill from D, to whom he indorses the bill. D then indorses the bill to E. The position would then be that E would have no rights against A and B but he could sue C (who made the alteration) and D (a subsequent indorser).

If the alteration had not been apparent and E had been a holder in due course then he could have enforced the bill against C and D for £1,000 and *additionally* he could have enforced it against A and B for £100. This additional right would be useful to E if C and D were insolvent. The acceptor need not take precautions against subsequent alteration. (*Scholfield* v. *Earl of Londesborough*, 1896.)[568]

With regard to cheques the position is similar in that no party to a cheque owes a duty of care in respect of negligent drawing or indorsing to the holder. However, the drawer owes a contractual duty of care to the bank in respect of negligent drawing. (*London Joint Stock Bank* v. *Macmillan and Arthur*, 1918.)[569]

The following alterations are material, namely (i) any alteration of the date, the sum payable, the time of payment, the place of payment; and (ii) the addition of a place of payment without the acceptor's assent, where a bill has been accepted generally. (Sect. 64(2).) An alteration may be material even if the change is beneficial. (*Gardner* v. *Walsh*, 1855.)[570]

Examples of immaterial alterations are (a) changing a bill payable to *Jones or Bearer* into *Jones or Order*; (b) striking out of the words *or Order*; (c) the alteration of the drawee's name, when it is wrong, to agree with a name correctly signed by way of acceptance.

DISHONOUR

A bill is dishonoured by non-payment—

(a) When it is duly presented for payment and payment is refused or cannot be obtained; and

(b) When presentment is excused and the bill is overdue and

unpaid. When a bill is dishonoured by non-payment, an immediate right of recourse against the drawer and indorsers accrues to the holder. (Sect. 47.)

Notice of Dishonour. When a bill has been dishonoured by non-acceptance or by non-payment, notice of dishonour must be given to the drawer and each indorser, and any drawer or indorser to whom such notice is not given is discharged. Provided that—

(i) Where a bill is dishonoured by non-acceptance and notice of dishonour is not given, the rights of a holder in due course subsequent to the omission shall not be prejudiced by the omission;

(ii) Where a bill is dishonoured by non-acceptance, and due notice of dishonour is given, it shall not be necessary to give notice of a subsequent dishonour by non-payment, unless the bill has been accepted in the meantime. (Sect. 48.)

If A draws a bill on B payable to C and indorsed to D which is dishonoured by non-acceptance, D must give notice of dishonour to A and C before he can enforce his rights against them. However, if D negotiates the bill to a holder in due course (E) then E will be able to sue A and C regardless of D's failure to give them notice.

E must, however, be unaware of the dishonour when he takes the bill, and where dishonour is due to non-payment there cannot be a holder in due course since the bill must be overdue at the time of negotiation.

Notice of dishonour in order to be valid and effectual must be given in accordance with the following rules—

1. FORM. (*a*) The notice may be given in writing or by personal communication.

(*b*) The return of a dishonoured bill to the drawer or an indorser is deemed a sufficient notice of dishonour.

(*c*) A written notice need not be signed, and an insufficient written notice may be supplemented and validated by verbal communication. A misdescription of the bill does not vitiate the notice unless the party to whom the notice is given is in fact misled by it.

(*d*) Where a notice of dishonour is duly addressed and posted, the sender is deemed to have given due notice of dishonour, notwithstanding any miscarriage by the post office.

2. THE GIVER. (*a*) The notice must be given by or on behalf of the holder, or by or on behalf of an indorser who, at the time of giving it, is himself liable on the bill.

(*b*) Notice of dishonour may be given by an agent, either in his own name or in the name of the party entitled to give notice, whether that party be his principal or not, e.g. a bill indorsed by A and held by B is dishonoured. C, who was at one time employed by B but is not in any sense now acting for B, informs A that the bill has been dishonoured. This is not enough and A is discharged. However, if

C had been B's agent, e.g. his solicitor and had given notice to the drawer but by mistake in A's name such notice would be sufficient provided A was liable to B and had a right of recourse against the drawer.

3. THE RECIPIENT. (*a*) Where notice of dishonour is required to be given to any person, it may be given either to him or to his agent.

(*b*) Where the drawer or indorser is dead, and the party giving notice knows it, the notice must be given to a personal representative if there is one, and if he can be found by exercising reasonable diligence.

(*c*) Where the drawer or indorser is bankrupt, notice may be given either to the party himself or to his trustee.

(*d*) Where there are two or more drawers or indorsers who are not partners, notice must be given to each of them, unless one has authority to receive notice for the others.

4. TIME LIMITS. (*a*) The notice may be given when the bill is dishonoured (not before, *Eagleshill* v. *Needham*, 1972)[571] and must be given within a reasonable time thereafter. In the absence of special circumstances notice is not given within a reasonable time unless—

(i) where the person giving and the person to receive notice reside in the same place, the notice is given or sent off in time to reach the latter on the day after dishonour of the bill; or

(ii) where they reside in different places, the notice is sent off on the day of dishonour of the bill, if there is a convenient post that day, and if there is no such post then by the next post thereafter. (Sect. 49 (12).)

There is no legal decision on the meaning of the word "place" but it probably means "postal district." The time limits laid down in Sect. 49 (12) must be strictly adhered to. A slight delay (even one day) may cause the holder to lose his rights against the drawer and indorsers.

(*b*) Where a bill when dishonoured is in the hands of an agent, he may either himself give notice to the parties liable on the bill, or he may give notice to his principal. In the latter event, he must do so within the same time as if he were the holder, and the principal upon receipt of such notice has himself the same time for giving notice as if the agent had been an independent holder.

(*c*) Where a party to a bill receives due notice of dishonour, he has after the receipt of such notice the same period of time for giving notice to antecedent parties that the holder has after dishonour. Suppose that A draws a bill on B payable to C who indorses it to D and that all the parties live in the same district. If B refuses to accept it on, say, 2nd June and D serves notice on C which he receives on 3rd June then C has a further twenty-four hours to give notice to A.

Delay in giving notice of dishonour is excused where it is caused by circumstances beyond the control of the party giving notice, and is not imputable to his default, misconduct or negligence. When the cause of the delay ceases to operate the notice must be given with reasonable diligence. A number of interesting points relating to notice of dishonour were raised in *Hamilton Finance Co. Ltd.* v. *Coverley and Others*, 1969.[557]

5. EFFECT. (*a*) Where the notice is given on behalf of the holder it enures for the benefit of subsequent holders, and all prior indorsers who have a right of recourse against the party to whom it is given.

If D is the drawer, P the payee, I_1, I_2, I_3, subsequent indorsers and H the holder, then if H gives notice to P, this would retain the liability of P, not only to H and subsequent holders, but also to I_1, I_2, and I_3, *although these latter three would not be liable to H.*

(*b*) Where notice is given by or on behalf of an indorser entitled to give notice, it enures for the benefit of the holder, and all indorsers subsequent to the party to whom notice is given.

If I_2 gives notice to P, then P is liable to I_1, I_2, I_3, H and subsequent holders.

(*c*) Actually if H gives notice to I_3, the chances are that I_3 will give notice to I_2, I_2 to I_1, I_1 to P, and P to D, since otherwise the person breaking the chain would lose his right of recourse though remaining liable himself. However, since one of these might fail to give notice and lose the right of recourse both for himself and for subsequent parties, the safest way is for H to notify all prior parties.

6. NOTICE EXCUSED. Notice of dishonour is dispensed with—

(*a*) *When*, after the exercise of reasonable diligence, *notice as required by the Act cannot be given* to, or does not reach the drawer or indorser sought to be charged.

(*b*) *By waiver, express or implied.* Notice of dishonour may be waived before the time of notice has arrived, or after the omission to give due notice.

(*c*) *As regards the drawer* in the following cases: (i) where drawer and drawee are the same person; (ii) where the drawee is a fictitious person or a person having no capacity to contract; (iii) where the drawer is the person to whom the bill is presented for payment; (iv) where the drawee or acceptor is as between himself and the drawer under no obligation to accept or pay the bill, e.g. where the bill is an accommodation bill or a cheque drawn on a banker in excess of the deposit or agreed overdraft; (v) where the drawer has countermanded payment.

(*d*) *As regards the indorser* in the following cases: (i) where the drawee is a fictitious person or a person not having capacity to contract, and the indorser was aware of the fact at the time he indorsed the bill; (ii) where the indorser is the person to whom the bill is presented for payment; (iii) where the bill was accepted or made for his accommodation. (Sect. 50.)

Noting or Protest of a Bill. Sect. 51 lays down the following rules—

A. CIRCUMSTANCES. (1) Where an *inland bill* has been dishonoured it may, if the holder thinks fit, be noted for non-acceptance or non-payment as the case may be.

(2) Where a *foreign bill*, appearing on the face of it to be such, has

been dishonoured by non-acceptance, it *must be duly protested for non-acceptance*, and where such a bill, which has not previously been dishonoured by non-acceptance, is dishonoured by non-payment, it must be duly protested for non-payment, otherwise the drawer and indorsers are discharged.

(3) A bill which has been protested for non-acceptance may be subsequently protested for non-payment, e.g. to charge a drawer or indorser in a foreign country whose law requires it.

(4) *Where the acceptor of a bill becomes bankrupt* or insolvent or suspends payment *before it matures*, the holder may cause the bill to be *protested for better security* against the drawer and indorsers. This enables the bill to be accepted for honour, as well as placing on record the circumstances of dishonour.

(5) Before a bill can be accepted or paid for honour it must be noted and protested. (See p. 303.)

(6) Noting and protesting is essential before resorting to a referee in case of need.

A referee in case of need is not really a party to the bill because, although his name appears on it, he does not sign it. The drawer of a bill and any indorser may insert therein the name of a person to whom the holder may resort in case of need, that is to say, in case the bill is dishonoured by non-acceptance or non-payment. It is in the option of the holder to resort to the referee in case of need or not as he may think fit.

For example A ships goods from London to B in Bombay, the bill of lading to be released to B when he accepts a bill of exchange for the price of the goods. Where an export is being financed in this way problems arise if B refuses to accept the bill. The goods cannot be released except to a person holding the bill of lading and so they must be shipped back to the seller. However, this may be avoided if A inserts into the bill the name of a referee in case of need, e.g. A's own agent in Bombay. If B dishonours the bill the referee in case of need can accept or pay it, obtain the shipping documents himself and sell the goods in Bombay.

(7) Protest is dispensed with by any circumstances which would dispense with notice of dishonour.

B. Time and Place. A bill must be protested at the place where it is dishonoured, but—

(*a*) When a bill is presented by post and is returned by post dishonoured, it may be protested at the place to which it is returned (i) on the day of return, if received during business hours; or (ii) if not so received, then on the next business day. Delay in noting or protesting is excused in circumstances beyond the control of the holder, and not imputable to his default, misconduct or negligence. When the cause of the delay ceases to operate, the bill must be noted or protested with reasonable diligence.

(*b*) When a bill drawn payable at the place of business or residence of some person other than the drawee is dishonoured by non-acceptance, it *must be protested for non-payment at the place where it is expressed to be payable*, and no further presentment for payment to, or demand on, the drawee is necessary.

C. FORM. (1) A protest must contain a copy of the bill, and must be signed by the notary making it, and must specify—(a) the person at whose request the bill is protested; (b) the place and date of protest, the reason for protesting the bill, the demand made, and the answer given, if any, or the fact that the drawee or acceptor could not be found.

(2) Where a bill is lost or destroyed, or is wrongly detained from the person entitled to hold it, protest may be made on a copy or written particulars thereof.

LIABILITIES OF THE PARTIES

The Acceptor. The acceptor of a bill by accepting it engages that he will pay it according to the tenor of his acceptance. (Sect. 54 (1).) He is also precluded from denying to a holder in due course—

(a) the existence of the drawer, the genuineness of his signature, and his capacity and authority to draw the bill;

(b) in the case of a bill payable to drawer's order the then capacity of the drawer to indorse, but not the genuineness or validity of his indorsement;

(c) in the case of a bill payable to the order of a third person, the existence of the payee and his then capacity to indorse, but not the genuineness or validity of his indorsement. (Sect. 54 (2).)

A bill supposedly drawn by A on B payable to C is accepted by B. C has, in fact, forged A's signature. If C negotiates the bill to D, who is a holder in due course, D can sue B because B is prevented from setting up the forgery by Sect. 54 (2).

When a bill is accepted generally, presentment for payment is not necessary in order to render the acceptor liable, and when by the terms of a qualified acceptance presentment for payment is required, the acceptor, in the absence of express stipulation to that effect, is not discharged by the omission to present the bill for payment on the day that it matures. Nor is it necessary in order to render the acceptor liable to protest the bill, or to give him notice of dishonour. (Sect. 52.) Thus the acceptor cannot escape liability by any mere irregularity in presentment for payment, for it is his duty to seek out his creditor and pay him.

The Drawer. The drawer of a bill by drawing it engages that on due presentment it shall be accepted and paid according to its tenor, and that if it is dishonoured, he will compensate the holder or any indorser who is compelled to pay it, provided that the requisite proceedings on dishonour are duly taken. The drawer is also precluded from denying to a holder in due course the existence of the payee and his then capacity to indorse. (Sect. 55 (1).)

The Indorser. The indorser of a bill by indorsing it engages that on due presentment it shall be accepted and paid according to its tenor, and that if it is dishonoured, he will compensate the holder or a subsequent indorser who is compelled to pay it, provided that the requisite proceedings on dishonour are duly taken. He is precluded from denying to a holder in due course the genuineness and regularity in all respects of the drawer's signature and all previous indorsements.

He is precluded from denying to his immediate or a subsequent indorsee that the bill was at the time of his indorsement a valid and subsisting bill, and that he had a good title thereto. (Sect. 55 (2).)

If, in the example given above, D had indorsed the bill to E (a holder in due course) E could have brought an action against B under Section 54 (2) and against D under Section 55 (2).

If an indorser has to pay the bill he has an action against prior parties, e.g. A draws a bill on B for £200 payable to C or order and the bill is indorsed to D who indorses to E who indorses to F. If B fails to accept the bill F can sue E who in turn can sue D who in turn can sue C who in turn can sue A. However, F is not bound to pass the liability down the line in this way because he can sue A, C, D, and E, all of whom are liable to him.

Where a person signs a bill otherwise than as drawer or acceptor, he thereby incurs the liabilities of an indorser to a holder in due course. (Sect. 56.) (*McDonald & Co.* v. *Nash & Co.*, 1924.)[572]

Damages on Dishonour. Where a bill is dishonoured damages are recoverable. These are deemed to be liquidated damages and are as follows—

(i) *In the case of inland bills*—the amount of the bill with interest thereon from the time of presentment for payment, if the bill is payable on demand, and from the maturity of the bill in any other case; together with the expenses of noting or protest, when necessary.

(ii) *In the case of a bill which has been dishonoured abroad*, the amount of re-exchange with interest thereon until the time of payment.

Interest may, if justice requires it, be withheld fully or in part, and where a bill is expressed to be payable with interest at a given rate, interest as damages may or may not be given at the same rate as interest proper. (Sect. 57.)

Where no interest is specified the court may make an award and generally gives four or five per cent until judgment. However, failure to pay must involve a breach of duty. (*N. V. Ledebeter* v. *Hibbert*, 1947.)[573]

BILLS IN A SET

These bills are used mainly in foreign trade, and the law relating to them is to be found in Sect. 71. Sets of three are common and three copies of the bill are prepared and the wording on each part indicates that it is part of a set. The copies are called respectively the First of Exchange, the Second of Exchange and the Third of Exchange. The individual parts form one bill, but under certain circumstances they may acquire an independent existence. The advantage of such bills is that copies can be sent separately by mail, and, if one copy is lost, one of the other parts can be submitted to the drawee for acceptance and used for subsequent negotiation. *The drawee should, therefore, accept only one part* since, if he accepts two parts, he may have to pay twice in the event of the two parts being negotiated to different holders.

Where two or more parts of a set are negotiated to different holders in due course, the holder whose title first accrues is, as between such holders, deemed to be the true owner of the bill. Nevertheless where the acceptor pays the holder of the accepted part of the bill, he will be exempt from liability on the unaccepted part. If he is sufficiently unwise to pay the part which has not been accepted, then, if the accepted part is subsequently presented to him, he will have to pay that also.

Suppose P is in possession of all three parts of a set and P indorses and transfers each part to different individuals, Q, R, and S.

Q now indorses his part to Q_1 who in turn indorses it to Q_2.

R indorses his part to R_1 who in turn indorses it to R_2.

S indorses his part to S_1 who in turn indorses it to S_2.

If the bill was drawn by D and the part negotiated by Q contains A's acceptance, the rights and liabilities of the parties are as follows.

(*a*) Q_2 will have a right of recourse against Q_1, Q, P, D and A.
(*b*) R_2 will have a right of recourse against R_1, R and P only.
(*c*) S_2 will have a right of recourse against S_1, S and P only.

It is assumed that all the transfers were transfers for value.

LOST INSTRUMENTS

Where a bill has been lost before it is overdue, the person who was the holder of it may apply to the drawer to give him another bill of the same tenor, giving security to the drawer, if required, to indemnify him against all persons whatever in case the bill alleged to have been lost shall be found again. And if the drawer refuses to give such a duplicate bill on these terms, he may be compelled to do so. (Sect. 69.)

In any action or proceeding upon a bill, the court or a judge may order that the loss of the instrument shall not be set up, provided an indemnity be given to the satisfaction of the judge against the claim of any other person upon the instrument in question. (Sect. 70.) No indemnity is required if the bill is accidentally destroyed.

It should be noted that Sect. 69 gives the holder a mere right to a new bill with the drawer's signature on it but not the signatures of other parties to the lost bill (if any). Sect. 70 is a better provision for the holder because it is available to him in an action against *any* person who was a party to the lost bill. Loss of a bill does not excuse the holder from giving notice of dishonour.

CONFLICT OF LAWS

Where a bill drawn in one country is negotiated, accepted or payable in another, the following rules apply.

1. Form. The validity of a bill as regards requisites in form is determined by the law of the place of issue, and the validity as regards requisites in form of supervening contracts, e.g. acceptance, indorsement, or acceptance *supra protest* is determined by the law of the place where they were made.

However, where a bill is issued out of the United Kingdom it is not invalid by reason only that it is not stamped in accordance with the law of the place of issue; and, where a bill, issued out of the United Kingdom, conforms, as regards requisites in form, to the law of the United Kingdom, it may, for the purpose of enforcing payment thereof, be treated as valid as between all persons who negotiate it, hold it, or become parties to it in the United Kingdom. (Sect. 72 (1).)

2. Interpretation. Subject to the provisions of the Act, the interpretation of the drawing, indorsement, acceptance, or acceptance *supra protest* of a bill, is determined by the law of the place where such contract is made.

Provided that where an inland bill is indorsed in a foreign country the indorsement shall as regards the payer be interpreted according to the law of the United Kingdom. (Sect. 72 (2).)

3. Duties of the Holder. The duties of the holder with respect to presentment for acceptance or payment and the necessity for or sufficiency of a protest or notice of dishonour, or otherwise, are determined by the law of the place where the act is done or the bill is dishonoured. (Sect. 72 (3).)

4. Amount Expressed in Foreign Currency. Where a bill is drawn out of, but payable in, the United Kingdom and the sum payable is not expressed in the currency of the United Kingdom, the amount shall, in the absence of some express stipulation, be calculated according to the rate of exchange for sight drafts at the place of payment on the day the bill is payable. (Sect. 72 (4).)

5. Due Date. Where a bill is drawn in one country and is payable in another, the due date thereof is determined according to the law of the place where it is payable. (Sect. 72 (5).)

PROMISSORY NOTES

Generally. A promissory note is an unconditional promise in writing, made by one person to another, signed by the maker, engaging to pay, on demand or at a fixed or determinable future time, a sum certain in money to, or to the order of, a specified person or to bearer. (Sect. 83 (1).)

An instrument in the form of a note payable to the maker's order is not a note within the meaning of the Act unless and until it is indorsed by the maker. (Sect. 83 (2).)

Sometimes a promissory note made by a person borrowing money is accompanied by some additional security such as the title deeds of property and Sect. 83 (3) provides that a note is not invalid by reason only that it contains also a pledge of collateral security with authority to sell or dispose thereof.

A promissory note may also be used as collateral security where, for example, a mortgage has been negotiated. It gives the lender a quick method of enforcing repayment of the loan. The ordinary form of I.O.U. is not a promissory note because it is a statement of indebtedness, not a promise to pay. If, however, additional words amounting to a promise to pay are included then it may be one.

Where a note on the face of it purports to be both made and payable within the British Isles it is an inland note. Any other note is a foreign note. (Sect. 83 (4).)

Sect. 89 (4) provides that a dishonoured foreign note need not be protested but many foreign systems of law require protest. Protest should therefore be made when an action on the note is to be brought in a foreign court.

A promissory note is inchoate and incomplete until delivery is made to the payee or to bearer.

Joint and Several Notes. A promissory note may be made by two or more makers, and they may be liable jointly, or jointly and severally according to its tenor. Where a note runs "I promise to pay," and is signed by two or more persons, it is deemed to be their joint and several note. (Sect. 85.) Where the note reads "we promise" and is signed by two or more makers their liability is joint only.

In the case of a joint and several note, the holder can either sue all the parties together, or can sue each one in turn, and if he does not get satisfaction from the first party, he may bring a further action against a second or a third. If, however, the note is a joint note, the holder has only one right of action, and he can sue one party alone, or two or more or all of the parties, but he has only one option. If in the action of his first choice he fails to recover the full amount of the note, he will be unable to sue any of the makers of the note who were not joined in the first action. In no case may the holder recover the sum due from more than one party, and if one party is compelled to pay, he has a right of contribution from the other or others. Whether liability is joint or joint and several each person who signs the note as maker is liable to the holder for the full amount of the note and not merely for his share.

Notes Payable on Demand. Where a note payable on demand has been indorsed, it must be presented for payment within a reasonable time of the indorsement or *the indorser is discharged*. Where a note payable on demand is negotiated, it is not, for the purpose of affecting the holder with defects of title of which he had no notice, deemed to be overdue by reason that it appears that a reasonable time for presenting it for payment has elapsed since its issue. (Sect. 86.)

It appears, therefore, from this section that *a holder of a note payable on demand is in a better position than the holder of a bill payable on demand*, since a holder in due course must take a bill before it is overdue, whereas a holder may be a holder in due course of a promissory note payable on demand even where it appears to be overdue when it is negotiated to him. It is worth noting that it is *only the indorser who is discharged for delay*; the maker of the note remains liable, as on any other contract, for six years in accordance with the Limitation Act, 1939.

Presentment of Note for Payment. Presentment for payment is necessary in order to render the indorser of a note liable. Where a promissory note is in the body of it made payable at a particular place, it must be presented for payment at that place in order *to render the maker and indorser liable*. In any other case, presentment for payment is not necessary in order to render the maker, but is necessary in order to render the indorser, liable.

When a place of payment is indicated by way of memorandum only, while presentment there will render the indorser liable, a presentment to the maker elsewhere, if sufficient in other respects, will suffice. (Sect. 87.)

Liability of Maker. The maker of a promissory note by making it—

    (1) Engages that he will pay it according to its tenor;

    (2) Is precluded from denying to a holder in due course the existence of the payee and his then capacity to indorse. (Sect. 88.)

A person transferring a bearer note without indorsement will incur the usual liability of a transferor by delivery under Sect. 58. (See p. 309.)

Application of General Provisions to Notes. The provisions of the Act relating to Bills of Exchange apply, with the necessary modifications, to promissory notes. *In applying these provisions the maker of the note is deemed to correspond with the acceptor of a bill, and the first indorser of a note is deemed to correspond with the drawer of an accepted bill payable to the drawer's order.*

The following provisions as to bills do not apply to notes, namely, provisions relating to—

    (*a*) Presentment for acceptance;

    (*b*) Acceptance;

    (*c*) Acceptance *supra protest*;

    (*d*) Bills in a set.

CHEQUES

A cheque is defined in Sect. 73 of the Bills of Exchange Act, 1882, as "A bill of exchange drawn on a banker payable on demand." The relevant provisions of the Act applicable to bills of exchange payable on demand apply also to cheques. However, the provisions regarding acceptance have no application to cheques and the rules relating to crossings on cheques do not apply to other bills. Further, a delay in presenting a cheque for payment will not, in itself, discharge the drawer, although it may do if he can prove actual loss. (Sect. 74, see p. 326.) If a banker pays a cheque bearing a forged or unauthorised indorsement he is nevertheless discharged, although in a similar case the acceptor of a bill would not be. (See pp. 294–5.) There are also certain special obligations which arise in the case of cheques because of the contract between banker and customer.

The words "on demand" are not usually printed on cheques but under the provisions of Section 10 (1)(b) they are implied. (See p. 303.)

A cheque need not take any particular form unless there is a contrary agreement between banker and customer. A mere printed statement on the cheque-book cover is not enough. (*Burnett* v. *Westminster Bank*, 1966.)[574]

RELATIONSHIP OF BANKER AND CUSTOMER

The relationship between a banker and a customer is that of *debtor and creditor* and is not fiduciary. Where a customer deposits money in a bank, this money is under the control of the banker and is not held by the banker in the form of a trust although he has obligations in connection with it.

Banker's Obligation to Repay. The banker can invest the money and deal with it as he pleases, but he is answerable for the amount deposited by the customer, and is under an obligation to pay it on demand, or to pay it to third parties on the order of the customer. The banker is not an agent or a factor, he is a debtor who promises to repay the money or any part of it at the branch of the bank where the account is kept, during banking hours, against the written order of the customer presented at, or addressed to, the bank at that branch. The bank must honour a customer's cheques up to the amount of the customer's deposit or up to the amount of an agreed overdraft but not without enquiry in unusual cases (*Karak* etc. v. *Burden*, 1972.)[694]

The banker is under *no obligation to pay cheques in part*, and if a customer with a deposit or agreed overdraft of £400 draws against it a cheque for £500, the bank is not empowered to pay it as to £400, but should either pay it in full or refuse payment altogether.

Banker's Obligation not to Disclose. The bank has a further contractual obligation not to disclose information concerning the customer's affairs (*Tournier* v. *National Provincial and Union Bank of England*, 1924).[575] The obligation extends to all facts discovered by the banker while acting in that capacity and is not confined merely to the state of the account. Failure to comply with this obligation will render the banker liable to damages which will, however, be nominal unless actual loss can be proved.

The duty of non-disclosure is not absolute but qualified. On principle disclosure is excusable:

(*a*) *Under compulsion of law*, for example, under Sect. 7 of the Bankers' Books Evidence Act, 1879, the court may by order authorise a party to an action to inspect and copy entries in a banker's books, although the power is exercised with caution.

(*b*) *Where there is a duty to the public to disclose*, as where the account concerned is that of a person suspected of being a spy and receiving payments from a foreign government.

(*c*) *Where the interests of the bank require disclosure*, as where the bank is in the process of enforcing an overdraft.

(*d*) Where the disclosure is made with the express or implied consent of the customer. (*Sunderland* v. *Barclays Bank Ltd.*, 1939.)[576]

There is a growing practice of making credit enquiries, and banker's references are commonly given and asked for. If the customer gives the bank's name as a reference, the position is clear enough, but in the absence of the customer's express or implied consent the general practice may not be justifiable merely on the ground that it is an existing usage to supply such information to another bank. A misleading and negligent reference may render the banker liable in damages. (*Hedley Byrne & Co. Ltd.* v. *Heller and Partners Ltd.*, 1964.)[165]

Customer's Obligation of Care. The customer on his part undertakes to exercise reasonable care in drawing up his written orders so as not to mislead the bank or facilitate forgery. (*London Joint Stock Bank Ltd.* v. *Macmillan and Arthur*, 1918;[569] *C. H. Slingsby* v. *District Bank*, 1931.)[577]

Although a customer receives from time to time a bank statement he is not under a duty to check it and is not bound by any errors in it which he does not find. However, a bank may, by reason of estoppel, have to pay a cheque drawn by a customer who has relied upon an incorrect credit balance on his bank statement.

Wrongful Dishonour. A banker has a duty to honour a customer's cheques up to the amount of his credit balance or agreed overdraft. This duty is owed to the customer only and not to any other party. If a banker wrongfully dishonours the cheque of a customer, and if the customer is a man of business, the harm to his credit might lead to the award of substantial sums in an action for damages. Where, however, the customer is not in business, he will only receive nominal damages unless he can prove special damage. (*Gibbons* v. *Westminster Bank Ltd.*, 1940.)[578] In certain cases there may indeed be a possible action for libel against the bank. (*Davidson* v. *Barclays Bank Ltd.*, 1940.)[579]

Presentment of Cheque for Payment. Since a cheque is payable on demand against funds which are already provided, presentment for acceptance it quite unnecessary and would indeed have no significance. The cheque must, however, be presented for payment, and if not so presented within a reasonable time of its issue, and if the drawer or the person on whose account it is drawn had the right at the time of such presentment as between him and the banker to have the cheque paid and suffers actual damage through the delay, he is discharged to the extent of such damage. In determining what is a reasonable time regard is had to the nature of the instrument, the usage of trade and of bankers, and the facts of the particular case.

The holder of such cheque as to which such drawer or person is discharged shall be a creditor, in lieu of such drawer or person, of such banker to the extent of such discharge, and entitled to recover the amount from him. (Sect. 74.)

The effect of Sect. 74 is that the drawer of a cheque is liable on it for the usual limitation period of six years, but he will be discharged before then if the holder does not present it for payment within a reasonable time and the drawer suffers actual damage because of the delay.

For example, if D has £500 in his banking account and draws a cheque in favour of P for £300, and P is dilatory in presenting it so that before he does so D's bank goes into liquidation and is only able to pay ten shillings in the pound, D will be regarded as a creditor of the bank for £200 and P for £300. Thus D will receive £100 and P £150 in the liquidation. It is obviously, therefore, in the interest of payees to present cheques for payment without undue delay. Quite apart from the question of loss on liquidation a cheque may go *stale*. In some banks a cheque goes stale after six months; in others it is as long as twelve months, and a bank might be reluctant to pay a stale cheque since such a payment would not be in the usual course of business.

Revocation of Banker's Authority. The duty and authority of a banker to pay a cheque drawn on him by his customer are determined by—

    (1) Countermand of payment;
    (2) Notice of the customer's death. (Sect. 75.)

Countermand of payment must be brought to the notice of the banker in unambiguous terms if it is to be effective. (*Curtice* v. *London, City and Midland Bank Ltd.*, 1908.)[580] Moreover, it must be clear to the bank that the order for taking such a serious step comes from the person entitled to give the order. In this sense a telegram countermanding payment of a cheque might be acted upon by the bank to the extent of postponing honouring the cheque until further enquiries could be made. To countermand a cheque by an unauthenticated telegram would involve the bank in a certain amount of risk.

If a bank were to cash a cheque within a few minutes after the usual closing time, and were to receive a countermand of payment before the opening of business next day, the payment would nevertheless be in order from the bank's point of view. The bank would not be able to dishonour a cheque after closing hours, but is entitled, within a reasonable business margin of its advertised time of closing, to deal with a cheque, not to dishonour it, but to do what it is asked to do, namely, to pay it. If the bank closes its doors at the usual closing time there may still be customers in the bank whose wishes have not yet been attended to.

It should be noted that a countermand notice sent to one branch of a bank does not operate as notice to another branch. (*Burnett* v. *Westminster Bank*, 1966.)[574]

A banker's authority to pay a cheque is determined by notice of the customer's death, and to this may be added notice of the customer's mental disorder, notice of an act of bankruptcy on which a bankruptcy petition could be presented against him, or that a receiving order has been made, or that he is an undischarged bankrupt, or on service of a garnishee order nisi. Garnishee proceedings may be taken by a judgment creditor where the judgment debtor (in this case the customer) is himself owed money by a third party (in this case the bank). The order nisi binds the debt in the hands of the bank and cheques drawn by the customer cannot be paid. The bank will usually open a new account for subsequent receipts and payments. Where the customer is a limited company, notice of a petition for compulsory winding up or a resolution for voluntary winding up (see pp. 278–85), will terminate the banker's duty to honour cheques. The banker need not, as we have seen, pay cheques where a customer has an insufficient balance to cover the cheque, or has not previously arranged an adequate overdraft, and the banker should not pay if he has notice of any defect in the title of the person presenting the cheque.

Payment without Authority. A banker is liable for wrongfully dishonouring the cheques of his customers but may also be liable if he pays a cheque when he should not have done so. Thus, a banker will not be able to debit the customer's account if he pays a countermanded cheque, a cheque void for material alteration, or a cheque on which the drawer's signature is forged.

However, where the customer has been *negligent* in drawing up his cheque so as to mislead the bank or facilitate forgery, the bank may debit his account. (*London Joint Stock Bank* v. *Macmillan and Arthur*, 1918)[569] Further, if the drawer's signature has been forged and he gets to know of the forgery, he may, if he does not inform the bank promptly and the bank is put to loss, be *estopped* for asserting the forgery. (*Greenwood* v. *Martins Bank*, 1933.)[436]

Where the wrongful payment by the bank actually satisfies a debt due from a customer to his creditor, the customer would make a profit by reason of the restoration rule. For example, if the bank paid a countermanded cheque which A, a customer, had drawn in favour of B, to whom A owed money, the result of the restoration rule would be that A's debt to B would be satisfied and A's balance at the bank would have to be restored. To prevent this profit being made the bank, on restoring A's account, is *subrogated* to B's rights against A, and can recover from A by this means.

Limitation. The six-year limitation period applicable to simple contract debts does not run against the customer of a bank from the date of payment in, for there is no cause of action until the customer demands the money and the demand is not met. For example, if A deposited £100 with his bank in 1965 and did not draw cheques against the account until 1972, there would be no question of the bank pleading the Limitation Act as an excuse for not paying it. However, if the cheque was not paid by the bank time would then begin to run against A and he would have to sue the bank in respect of their failure to pay within six years.

Joint Accounts. In *Brewer* v. *Westminster Bank*, 1952,[581] McNair, J., decided that in the case of a joint account, the bank's duties were owed to the account holders *jointly* and not *severally*. The result of this decision was that where one account-holder forged the other's signature on cheques drawn on the account and then added his own signature, the innocent account-holder had no action against the bank.

However, in *Jackson* v. *White and Midland Bank Ltd.*, [1967] 2 Lloyd's Rep. 68, where one joint-account-holder forged the signature of the other, Park, J., declined to follow *Brewer's* case, holding that where there was a joint account with, say, A and B, the bank in effect agreed with A and B *jointly* that it would honour cheques signed by them both and with A *separately* that it would not honour cheques unless signed by him, and with B *separately* that it would not honour cheques unless signed by him. Thus, where the bank honours a cheque on which B has forged A's signature, A should be able to sue the bank because it is in breach of the separate agreement with him.

It should be noted that *Jackson's* case cannot overrule *Brewer's* case because both are decisions at first instance. However, the decision in *Brewer's* case has received much criticism and it is likely that the reasoning in *Jackson's* case will be applied in future.

Generally. Banks often accept valuable property for safe custody and are liable as ordinary bailees in this respect, i.e. they must take reasonable care for the safety of the property. Should the banker misdeliver the goods to the wrong person, then he is liable in conversion even though there was no negligence on his part.

Bankers nowadays often give advice on investment to customers and potential customers and, if the giving of such advice forms part of the banker's business, he will be liable in damages if his advice is negligent. (*Woods* v. *Martins Bank*, 1959.)[582] If such advice is not part of the business of a particular banker, the person who gave the advice might be personally liable for negligence. (*Hedley Byrne & Co. Ltd.* v. *Heller & Partners Ltd.*, 1963.)[165]

It should be noted, however, that in the absence of an express instruction it is not a banker's duty to consider a customer's tax liability when crediting an account with a dividend. (*Schioler* v. *Westminster Bank*, 1970.)[583]

CROSSED CHEQUES

Nature of Crossing. The Act provides—

(1) Where a cheque bears across its face an addition of—

(*a*) The words "and company" or any abbreviation thereof between two parallel transverse lines, either with or without the words "not negotiable"; or

(*b*) Two parallel transverse lines simply, either with or without the words "not negotiable," *that addition constitutes a crossing and the cheque is crossed generally.* (Sect. 76 (1).)

Where there is a general crossing the banker must pay the cheque to another banker and must not cash the cheque across the counter.

(2) Where a cheque bears across its face an addition of the name of a banker, either with or without the words "not negotiable," that addition constitutes a crossing, and *the cheque is crossed specially and to that banker.* (Sect. 76 (2).) Where there is a special crossing the cheque must be paid to the banker named in the crossing.

General and special crossings give additional protection to holders in the case of theft, for the thief may not have a bank account and, even if he has, the extra time involved in clearing the crossed cheque may enable the drawer or holder to stop payment.

In addition to the crossings specified in the Act, it is not uncommon for the drawer to add the words "Account payee", and this is regarded as an instruction to the collecting banker to collect only for the account of that payee, an instruction which he neglects at his peril.

Crossing Procedure. Sect. 77 of the Act lays down the following rules—

(1) A cheque may be crossed generally or specially by the drawer.

(2) Where a cheque is uncrossed, the holder may cross it generally or specially.

(3) Where a cheque is crossed generally, the holder may cross it specially.

EXAMPLES OF CROSSINGS ON CHEQUES

(4) Where a cheque is crossed generally or specially, the holder may add the words "not negotiable."

(5) Where a cheque is crossed specially, the banker to whom it is crossed, may again cross it specially to another banker for collection.

(6) Where an uncrossed cheque, or a cheque crossed generally, is sent to a banker for collection, he may cross it specially to himself. (Sect. 77.)

There is no reason why the payee cannot also add "Account payee."

A crossing authorised by the Act is a material part of the cheque and it is not lawful for any person to obliterate or, except as authorised by the Act, to add to or alter the crossing. (Sect. 78.)

Duties of Banker as to Crossed Cheques. Sect. 79 provides that if a paying banker receives a cheque—

(i) crossed specially to more than one banker he must not pay it; however, if one of the bankers named is acting as an agent for collection for the other, the cheque may be paid to the agent bank; collection through an agent is rare today, but was more frequent when there were a number of small banks using a major London bank as agents for collection;

(ii) crossed specially to a named banker, he must pay only the named banker (or the named banker's agent for collection, if any);

(iii) crossed generally, it cannot be paid except through a banker, though payment through any banker will suffice.

If a banker fails to observe the above rules he is liable to the true owner for loss incurred because the cheque was not paid as directed by the crossing. There are two possible sets of circumstances to consider.

(a) *The banker may, in fact, have paid the true owner* in which case there can be no claim against him. However, Lord Cairns once said of such a cheque ". . . the drawers might refuse to be debited with it as having been paid contrary to their mandate." (*Smith* v. *Union Bank of London* (1875), 1 Q.B.D. 31 at p. 36)

(b) *Payment may have been made to a person who is not the true owner.* In the case of an uncrossed cheque, the banker may be protected by Sect. 59 of the Act if the person he pays is the holder, and by Sect. 60 if the person to whom payment was made was in possession under a forged or unauthorised indorsement.

Thus, if a bearer cheque is stolen from its owner by T, and the drawee bank pays him, it has no liability to the true owner because T is the holder and Sect. 59 applies. Furthermore, if A draws a cheque on his bank payable to C and it is stolen by T who forges C's indorsement and negotiates it to E, who is paid by the bank in good faith and in the ordinary course of business, Sect. 60 will apply and the bank will not be liable to the true owner, C.

However, if, in the examples given above, the cheque had been crossed and the banker had not observed the instructions on the crossing, he would be liable to the true owner in each case and could not derive protection from Sects. 59 and 60.

Protection against Alterations and Obliterations. Where a cheque is presented for payment which does not at the time of presentment *appear to be crossed,* or to have had a crossing which has been obliterated, or to have been added to or altered otherwise than as authorised by the Act, *the banker paying the cheque in good faith and without negligence shall not be responsible or incur any liability.* Nor shall the payment be questioned *even if the cheque had been crossed,* or if the crossing had been obliterated or been added to or altered otherwise than as authorised by the Act, or if payment had been made otherwise than to a banker or to the banker to whom the cheque was crossed, or to his agent for collection being a banker, as the case may be. (Sect. 79.)

Effect of Crossing "Not Negotiable". Where a person takes a crossed cheque which bears on it the words "not negotiable," he shall not have and shall not be capable of giving a better title to the cheque than that which the person from whom he took it had. (Sect. 81.)

While the words "not negotiable" do not prevent the cheque from being transferred, they do have a serious effect on the title of subsequent holders.

(1) ORDER CHEQUES. To negotiate an order cheque, an appropriate indorsement must be made. If such a cheque were lost or stolen, then any such indorsement would be forged and no subsequent holder could obtain a title. The addition of the words "not negotiable" does not affect the position.

(2) BEARER CHEQUES. A bearer cheque is negotiable by transfer without indorsement and a person taking such a cheque might have a title as a holder in due course even if a previous holder had none. The addition of the words "not negotiable" to a bearer cheque protects the rights of the true holder against a subsequent holder, and if such a cheque were stolen and transferred to an innocent third party who obtained payment, the true owner could demand restitution within the limitation period of six years.

The words "not negotiable" can be written on a crossed cheque when making the crossing or subsequently. A cheque crossed "not negotiable" is still transferable subject to defects in title. A bill of exchange so crossed is not even transferable. (See p. 306.) If the words "not negotiable" appear on a cheque otherwise than as part of the crossing, the better view is that they are of no effect.

Account Payee. We have seen that, although such a crossing is not authorised by the Act, it is not uncommon for the drawer of a cheque to include in the crossing the words "A/c payee" or "A/c payee only." This is an *instruction to the collecting banker and not to the paying banker.* It will be in order for the paying banker to pay the amount of the cheque to the collecting banker, leaving it to the latter to ensure that this instruction on the cheque is carried out. It would, no doubt, be negligence in the banker if he collected the money for some other account, but the point is rather academic for bankers do not normally collect for any account except that of the payee. The words "Account payee" or "Account payee only" do not prevent a cheque from being negotiated. The holder of such a cheque, not being the payee, might find it difficult to persuade a bank to collect the cheque for him, but he could collect the money himself from the drawer who would certainly be liable on such a cheque to a holder in due course.

Application of Crossings Rules. The crossings rules apply not only to cheques but also—

(i) to the instruments other than cheques specified in Sect. 4 of the Cheques Act, 1957 (see below p. 334), and

(ii) to dividend warrants. (Sect. 95, Bills of Exchange Act, 1882.)

BANKER'S PROTECTION

Paying Bankers. If a banker pays one of his customer's cheques to the wrong person then he is liable to the true owner in conversion for the face value of the cheque and he cannot debit the customer's account. However, the following statutory provisions may provide the banker with a defence—

(*a*) *Under Sect.* 59 payment by the banker to the holder at or after maturity in good faith and without notice of any defect in his title discharges the bill, frees the banker from all liability and enables him to debit the customer's account. However, the person paid *must be the holder*, and a person holding an order bill by means of a forged or unauthorised indorsement is not a holder. Therefore payment to him would not discharge the bill or free the banker from liability. The Section would provide a defence where a banker paid the bearer of a bearer cheque.

(*b*) *Under Sect.* 60 if a banker on whom a cheque is drawn pays it, in good faith and in the ordinary course of business, he is deemed to have paid it in due course and is not prejudiced by the fact that the *indorsement* was forged or made without authority. The Section applies only to indorsements on cheques and does not apply where the drawer's signature has been forged, nor where the cheque is void for material alteration.

(*c*) *Where cheque is crossed.* Where the banker, on whom a crossed cheque is drawn, in good faith and without negligence pays it, if crossed generally, to a banker, and if crossed specially, to the banker to whom it is crossed (or his agent for collection being a banker), *the banker* paying the cheque, *and*, if the cheque has come into the hands of the payee, *the drawer shall* respectively be entitled to the same rights and *be placed in the same position as if payment of the cheque had been made to the true owner* thereof. (Sect. 80.)

For example, A draws a cheque on the B Bank payable to C. C, on receipt of the cheque, crosses it generally. The cheque is then stolen by T who opens an account at the Z Bank in the name of C. The Z Bank presents the cheque to the B bank which pays in good faith and without negligence. The B Bank is protected by Sect. 80 from liability to C, and C cannot sue A.

(*d*) *Cheques Act*, 1957, *Sect.* 1. Although cheques are bills of exchange, most of them have a very short life, being sent by the drawers to the payees who promptly pay them straight into their banking accounts. Prior to the Act, although there was no transfer by the payee to an indorsee, such cheques required indorsement, a laborious and rather useless process.

Sect. 1 of the Cheques Act, 1957, provides—

Where a *paying banker* in good faith and in the ordinary course of business pays a cheque drawn on him which is not indorsed or is irregularly indorsed, he does not, in doing so, incur any liability by reason only of the absence of, or irregularity in, indorsement, and he is deemed to have paid it in due course.

The same protection is extended to him if he pays—

(i) A document issued by a customer of the bank which, though not a bill of exchange, is intended to enable a person to obtain from the bank the sum mentioned in the document; or

(ii) A draft payable on demand drawn by him on himself, whether payable at the head office or some other office of the bank.

The Committee of London Clearing Bankers announced, shortly after the Act was passed, that they would still require indorsement of cheques other than those paid into a banking account for the credit of the payee. Accordingly, if the payee pays a cheque into his own account there is no need for him to indorse it. However, if a payee or indorsee presents a cheque for payment over the counter (the cheque being uncrossed), the person receiving payment will have to indorse it. Where a crossed cheque is negotiated and paid into a bank by the last indorsee, the banker will require the indorsement of all indorsers but not that of the last indorsee who is paying in.

Whilst the decisions of the Committee of London Clearing Bankers are not law, it is thought that a banker who pays a cheque without obtaining an indorsement where the Committee says he should would not be acting in the ordinary course of business and would not, therefore, be protected by Sect. 1 of the Cheques Act, 1967, nor by Sect. 60 of the Bills of Exchange Act, 1882. He would probably also be negligent and be unable to claim the protection of Sect. 80.

Further, it is assumed that where the Committee requires an indorsement it must be a regular indorsement, and payment of a cheque with an irregular indorsement would be negligent and not in the ordinary course of business, so that there could be no statutory protection if there was a wrongful payment.

Bankers Collecting Cheques. The Cheques Act, 1957, Sect. 4, extends protection to *bankers who collect payment* on the following instruments—

(i) Cheques.

(ii) Any document issued by a customer of a banker which, though not a bill of exchange, is intended to enable a person to obtain payment from that banker of the sum mentioned in the document.

(iii) Any document issued by a public officer which is intended to enable a person to obtain payment from the Paymaster General or the Queen's and Lord Treasurer's Remembrancer of the sum mentioned in the document but which is not a bill of exchange.

(iv) Any draft payable on demand drawn by a banker upon himself, whether payable at the head office or some other office of the bank. (Sect. 4 (2).)

Where a banker, *in good faith and without negligence*—

(*a*) receives payment for a customer of one of the above instruments; or

(*b*) having credited a customer's account with the amount of such an instrument receives payment thereof for himself;

and the customer has no title, or a defective title, to the instrument, the banker does not incur any liability to the true owner of the instrument by reason only of having received payment thereof. (Sect. 4 (1).)

A banker is not to be treated for the purposes of the section as having been negligent by reason only of his failure to concern himself with absence of, or irregularity in, indorsement of an instrument. (Sect. 4 (3).)

This section repeals, replaces and extends Sect. 82 of the Bills of Exchange Act, 1882, and provides *protection for the collecting banker against an action for conversion* if he collects for someone with no or a defective title.

Sect. 4 applies to all cheques, whether crossed or not, and also extends to a range of other instruments. However, an instrument on which the drawer's signature is forged is not a cheque nor is an instrument which has become void for material alteration, and no protection is given in respect of the collection of such instruments.

The Section applies only where the banker collects payment for a *customer* and acts without negligence, and in the matter of negligence the onus of proof is on him. Thus there must be an account, but it seems to be enough that the customer has opened it with the cheque which is in dispute.

A banker may be negligent on many counts, for example where he has failed to obtain or follow up the references of a customer opening an account, if this failure was to some extent responsible for the wrongful collection. Failure to inquire as to a new customer's employer is negligence if the banker knows that the customer is in a position which might enable him to misappropriate his employer's cheques, as where he is a cashier. A banker should not collect, without inquiry, cheques for employees or partners or officials which are drawn on their firm or company, nor should he collect a cheque marked "Account Payee" for another account. Finally, a banker will be held to have been negligent in any case where it appears to the court that inquiries should have been made. (*Lloyds Bank Ltd.* v. *E. B. Savory & Co.*, 1933[584] and see *Lumsden & Co.* v. *London Trustee Savings Bank*, 1971.)[585]

It should be noted, however, that the above decision represents the high-water mark of judicial severity in the matter of bankers' negligence and in two recent cases, *Orbit Mining and Trading Co.* v. *Westminster Bank*, 1963,[556] and *Marfani & Co.* v. *Midland Bank*, 1967,[586] the judiciary seems to have accepted that bank employees cannot be highly inquisitive if they are to deal promptly with the large number of cheques which are cleared every day and the standard of care required has been lowered, possibly too far.

Collecting Banker as Holder in Due Course. Where a banker collects payment of a cheque for a person who is not the true owner, he may be liable in conversion although, as we have seen, he may derive protection from Sect. 4 of the Cheques Act, 1957. However, he may also escape liability if he can prove that he has become a holder in due course of the cheque. Where this is so the banker will obtain a good title to the cheque even if the title of the transferee was non-existent or defective, and in spite of his own negligence, if any.

A banker, like any other person, must give *value* before he can become a holder in due course, and this may happen in *three* ways—

    (i) where the customer pays in a cheque to reduce his overdraft, if the banker forgoes interest;

    (ii) where there is an express or implied agreement between banker and customer under which the customer can and does draw against the cheque before it has been cleared: where there is no prior agreement it seems that the banker does not give value; and

    (iii) where the banker cashes a cheque for a person who is not a customer and therefore *buys* it from that person rather than *collecting* it for him.

A banker cannot become a holder in due course if an *essential* indorsement is forged but he can, by virtue of Sect. 2 of the Cheques Act, 1957, become the holder in due course of an order cheque, even though it is not indorsed to him. The banker will, therefore, have the right to sue the drawer if the cheque is dishonoured.

The Section provides that a *collecting banker* who gives value for, or has a lien on, a cheque payable to order which the holder delivers to him for collection without indorsing it, has such (if any) rights as he would have had if, upon delivery, the holder had indorsed in blank.

The Section provides an exception to Sect. 31 of the Bills of Exchange Act, 1882, in that it allows an order cheque to be negotiated without indorsement. It should also be noted that the Section applies only to cheques and not to analogous instruments, as do Sects. 1 and 4, and that it does not deal with the case in which an indorsement exists and is irregular. Presumably, where this is so the cheque is not complete and regular on the face of it and the banker will not be a holder in due course. The cases of *Westminster Bank Ltd.* v. *Zang*, 1965[587] and *Barclays Bank* v. *Astley Industrial Trust Ltd.*, 1970[544] are illustrative of some of the problems arising out of the operation of Sect. 2.

Unindorsed Cheques as Evidence of Payment. Sect. 3 of the Cheques Act provides that an unindorsed cheque which appears to have been paid by the banker on whom it is drawn is evidence of the receipt by the payee of the sum payable by the cheque. Prior to the Act such an indorsed cheque was *prima facie* but not conclusive evidence that the payee had received the sum payable; the Act merely confirms that in future an unindorsed cheque can fulfil the same function. Nevertheless, by drawing attention to this virtue of a cheque, it has led to a widespread practice among business men of dispensing with the issue of receipts where payment is by cheque, with a consequent saving in effort, time and money.

CHAPTER IX

BANKRUPTCY

BANKRUPTCY is a proceeding in which the property of a debtor is taken over by an officer of the State, and is then realised and distributed according to certain priorities amongst the persons to whom the debtor owes money or is in some way under a liability.

The law of bankruptcy is to be found in the Bankruptcy Acts, 1914 and 1926, and these Acts are supplemented by the Bankruptcy Rules which govern procedure in bankruptcy matters. All references in this chapter are to the Act of 1914 unless otherwise stated.

ACTS OF BANKRUPTCY

Before bankruptcy proceedings can be taken the debtor must—

(i) be under the jurisdiction of the court; and
(ii) be indebted to the extent of £50 to one creditor, or to several who are jointly taking proceedings; and
(iii) have committed within three months of the petition an act of bankruptcy, i.e. an act which indicates that he is unable to pay his debts.

The term *act of bankruptcy* is perhaps not an appropriate one, because such an act does not make a person bankrupt; it is simply an act on which a bankruptcy petition may be founded.

Sect. 1 of the Bankruptcy Act, 1914, lays down eight courses of conduct by a debtor which are deemed to be acts of bankruptcy.

(i) **If in England or elsewhere he makes a conveyance or assignment of his property to a trustee or trustees for the benefit of his creditors generally.** The conveyance or assignment must be of the whole, or substantially the whole, of the debtor's property and it must be for the benefit of his creditors generally. Thus an assignment for the benefit of one or more particular creditors, e.g. trade creditors, is not in itself an act of bankruptcy, though it may be a fraudulent preference. (*In re Phillips, ex parte Barton*, 1900.)[588] It is not necessary to prove an intention to defeat or delay creditors and it is immaterial whether the assignment is made in England or elsewhere. A creditor who has assented to the assignment cannot regard the assignment as an act of bankruptcy. If the conveyance of the debtor's property is effected by a written instrument, whether under seal or not, it will fall within the Deeds of Arrangement Act, 1914 (see p. 357). The arrangement is available as an act of bankruptcy to a non-assenting creditor, though few arrangements are so used since creditors tend to receive more money under an arrangement than a bankruptcy. However, notice can be served on a non-assenting creditor requiring him to petition in bankruptcy, if at all, within one month of the notice.

(ii) If in England or elsewhere he makes a fraudulent conveyance, gift, delivery or transfer of his property or any part thereof. A fraudulent conveyance of this kind is very often a transfer to a member of the debtor's family with the intention of defeating or delaying creditors. However, if the property has been conveyed for a reasonable consideration, then the transfer will not be fraudulent and will not be an act of bankruptcy. It is necessary to show an intention to defeat or delay creditors generally or an intention to give a creditor some advantage which he would not have obtained if the estate had been distributed under the rules of bankruptcy. A conveyance or assignment of this nature is void and the transferee must give up the property to the trustee in bankruptcy (Sect. 42). The conveyance may also be void under Sect. 172 of the Law of Property Act, 1925, if made with an intention to defraud creditors.

A transfer is fraudulent under Sect. 172 of the Law of Property Act, 1925, if it is designed to put certain or all of the debtor's assets beyond the reach of creditors generally. A transfer is fraudulent under the Bankruptcy Act, 1914, if it gives a creditor(s) an advantage over others in respect of the assets available which he would not have had under the bankruptcy laws.

(iii) If in England or elsewhere he makes a conveyance or transfer of his property or any part thereof or creates any charge thereon which amounts to a fraudulent preference. The essence of a fraudulent preference is the intention to prefer one creditor before the others. The debtor must really intend to prefer, and, if a particular creditor is pressing the debtor for payment and the debtor pays him, there is no fraudulent preference. (*Sharp* v. *Jackson*, 1899.)[589] The onus of proof of fraudulent preference is on the trustee in bankruptcy.

A transaction which amounts to a fraudulent preference, if performed within the six months prior to the presentation of the petition upon which the debtor is adjudicated bankrupt, may be avoided by the trustee in bankruptcy if it does not prejudice persons who have taken the property in good faith and for value from the creditor preferred. Thus, if A prefers B by conveying property to him four months before the presentation of a bankruptcy petition, and B sells the property to C, who buys in good faith, A's trustee cannot claim the property from C, though he can claim its value from B.

A petition is rarely based on a fraudulent preference because such preferences are not normally discovered until the bankruptcy proceedings reach the stage of an examination into the debtor's affairs.

(iv) Leaving England, or remaining out of it, or departing from his dwelling house, or keeping house with intent to delay creditors. A debtor *keeps house* if he withdraws to a remote part of his dwelling house so that the creditors cannot see him or speak to him.

Evidence must be brought to show that this was a studied course of conduct on the part of the debtor and that creditors were denied access to him at reasonable hours. The intention to defeat or delay must be proved by the creditors but such intent can be *presumed* without proof in appropriate circumstances. Thus, where a person with an English domicil leaves the country, and his creditors are in fact delayed or defeated no further proof of intent is required. This is a rare act of bankruptcy but may sometimes be a useful one. It is the better view that there can be no "keeping house" unless there is a house. Thus keeping a tent would not suffice, nor probably would a caravan, at least if it was mobile.

(v) **If the debtor's goods which have been seized by the sheriff are sold by the sheriff or the sheriff remains in possession of them for 21 days.** It should be noted that a sheriff remains in possession even if he takes "walking possession" giving the debtor permission to sell the goods. (*Re Dalton*, 1962.)[590]

(vi) **By the debtor filing in court a declaration of inability to pay his debts or presenting a bankruptcy petition against himself.** The declaration of inability to pay debts must be dated and signed and witnessed by a solicitor or justice of the peace or the Official Receiver or the Registrar of the Bankruptcy Court concerned. The act of bankruptcy takes place on delivery of the declaration to the proper court.

(vii) **By the debtor failing to comply with a bankruptcy notice.** A bankruptcy notice is a notice served by a judgment creditor who has obtained final judgment against the debtor, requiring the debtor to pay or secure the judgment debt. This notice is not an act of bankruptcy, but if the debtor has not complied with the notice within seven days of its service, such failure is an act of bankruptcy upon which a petition may be presented.

The procedure is to ask the bankruptcy court to issue a bankruptcy notice which is then served on the debtor in much the same way as a writ. The judgment debt may be for any amount, although the petition, if any, which is later presented on the ground of failure to comply with a bankruptcy notice, must allege a debt of £50 or more. The majority of bankruptcy petitions are founded on a bankruptcy notice which has not been complied with. A debtor may resist a bankruptcy notice by showing that he has a set-off or counterclaim against the debt, which was not available to him in the action under which the judgment was obtained.

(viii) **If the debtor gives notice that he has suspended, or is about to suspend payment of his debts.** The notice need not be in writing or in any particular form, and a temporary suspension is enough. An intention to suspend may be inferred. (*Crook* v. *Morley*, 1891).[591]

In addition, Sect. 21 of the Administration of Justice Act, 1965, provides that an application to the county court for an order for the administration of the debtor's estate shall be an act of bankruptcy. A county court has power to make such an order where—

(*a*) a debtor is unable to pay forthwith the amount of a judgment obtained against him in the county court, and alleges that his whole indebtedness amounts to a sum not exceeding £300 inclusive of the debt for which the judgment was obtained; or

(*b*) an application is made to the county court to have the debtor committed and his liabilities do not exceed £300. Under the Administration of Justice Act, 1965, Sect. 20, the sum of £300 can be increased by Order in Council.

Once an administration order is made the court will administer the assets of the debtor for the benefit of his creditors.

Finally, where on an application to a County Court for an attachment of earnings to secure the payment of a judgment debt it appears that the debtor has other debts and therefore that his liabilities should be looked at as a whole in order to be fair to his creditors, the Court may order the debtor to furnish a list of his creditors under Sect. 29 of the Administration of Justice Act, 1970. This order operates as an act of bankruptcy by the debtor.

THE PETITION

A petition requests the court to make a receiving order. If the debtor presents his own petition he need only allege inability to pay his debts.

A creditor who presents a petition must prove that—

(*a*) The debt due to him or others joining in the petition is at least £50;

(*b*) The debt is a liquidated sum payable either immediately or at some certain future time;

(*c*) The act of bankruptcy on which the petition is founded has been committed within the previous three months;

(*d*) The debtor is subject to the bankruptcy laws of England.

(*e*) The act of bankruptcy is not one to which he was a party, e.g. a creditor who has consented to a deed of arrangement cannot petition on it.

A petition that a receiving order be made may be presented by the debtor himself or by his creditors. The number of debtors' petitions is usually considerably higher than creditors' petitions, at least in County Courts.

A secured creditor cannot present a petition unless in it he states that he is willing to give up his security. Alternatively he may value his security and petition as to the balance, if any.

If the debtor lives in London or carries on business there or if his residence is unknown, the petition should be presented in the High Court. In other cases it should be presented in the County Court having bankruptcy jurisdiction where the debtor resides or carries on business.

CAPACITY IN BANKRUPTCY

As a general rule any person who has capacity to contract may be made bankrupt, but the position of persons having imperfect contractual capacity must be noted.

Minors. The Infants' Relief Act, 1874, does not protect a minor against bankruptcy proceedings as such if the debt on which the bankruptcy is based is an enforceable one, i.e. a debt contracted for necessaries or upon a judgment arising out of an action in tort or more commonly for some liability created by statute such as taxes. (*Re A Debtor, Ex parte Customs and Excise Commissioners* v. *The Debtor*, 1950.)[592] Before a minor can be made bankrupt on a contract for necessaries, a court must have pronounced that the goods are necessaries and what is a reasonable price.

Although a minor may present a bankruptcy petition against another person, that person may require an adult to be joined with the minor so that there will be security for costs if the minor does not succeed with his petition.

Persons of Unsound Mind. Such persons may be made bankrupt so long as the debts they owe are enforceable under the general law, though the consent of the Patients' Committee (if any) or of the Court of Protection is required before they can be adjudicated bankrupt. A person of unsound mind is incapable of committing an act of bankruptcy which requires intent on his part, e.g. fraudulent preference, unless it can be shown that the act was committed during a lucid interval.

Aliens. An alien may be subject to the bankruptcy laws and may also petition. To be subject to the jurisdiction of an English court, he or his agent must carry on business here or he must be a member of a firm carrying on business here or he must ordinarily reside here. Foreign Sovereigns, Ambassadors, and the representatives of certain international organisations can claim diplomatic immunity.

Corporations. A corporation cannot be made bankrupt but must be wound up under other enactments, e.g. liquidation under the Companies Act, 1948 (see p. 278).

Partnerships. A partnership can be made bankrupt and the separate estate of each partner may be brought into the bankruptcy.

Deceased Persons. A deceased person cannot be made bankrupt but his estate may be administered in bankruptcy. Petition may be made by a creditor or the legal personal representatives.

Married Women. By virtue of the Law Reform (Married Women and Tortfeasors) Act, 1935, a married woman can now be made bankrupt whether she engages in trade or not.

Undischarged Bankrupts. An undischarged bankrupt may have a second or subsequent adjudication order made against him in respect of debts incurred after the date of the receiving order in the prior bankruptcy.

THE RECEIVING ORDER

When the Court is satisfied that the facts alleged in the petition are correct and that the debtor has no substantial defence, it will make a receiving order against the debtor. This order is served on the debtor and is advertised in the *London Gazette* and a local newspaper.

Effect of Receiving Order. The Official Receiver, who is a public officer appointed by the Department of Trade, becomes the receiver of the property of the debtor and the Receiving Order stays any legal process against the debtor in respect of matters provable in the bankruptcy. No creditor can commence an action or any other legal proceeding without leave of the court. (Sect. 7.)

The Receiving Order does not divest the debtor of his property. This is effected by the subsequent Adjudication Order, if any. The receiving order is protective not divestive.

The receiving order does not affect the right of a secured creditor to deal with the secured property as he chooses, subject to the right of the trustee or Official Receiver to inspect and possibly redeem it. Moreover, a landlord is not precluded from distraining for rent.

Interim Receiver. The Official Receiver may be appointed by the court as interim receiver of the debtor's property. This can be done at any time *after* presentation of the petition and *before* the receiving order is made. However, it must be shown that such an appointment is necessary for the protection of the estate. Application to make such an appointment may be made by a creditor, or even by the debtor himself if he feels that he cannot handle his affairs until a receiving order is made.

Procedure. The receiving order is made out in triplicate, one copy being filed in court, and the other two sent to the Official Receiver who serves one copy on the debtor. If land is an asset in the debtor's hands, the Official Receiver informs the Chief Land Registrar so that the Receiving Order can be entered on the Land Register.

The Official Receiver organises the advertisement of the receiving order as guardian of the public interest, but it need not be advertised if the debtor is appealing against the making of the order. The receiving order is deemed to have been made on the day when it was pronounced by the judge and not the day on which it was drawn up.

Rescission of Receiving Order.

(i) The receiving order may be discharged or rescinded when a composition or scheme of arrangement is approved by the court under Sect. 16 of the Bankruptcy Act, but not until after the public examination of the debtor has taken place.

(ii) The court may, on application by the Official Receiver or a creditor, rescind the receiving order if most of the debtor's property is in Scotland or Northern Ireland, or most of the debtor's creditors are there. The proceedings will then be taken in the appropriate country. (Sect. 12.)

(iii) The court has, under Sect. 108 of the Bankruptcy Act, 1914, a general jurisdiction to rescind the receiving order. The power is discretionary and the court will not usually exercise it before holding the Public Examination of the debtor. A receiving order might be rescinded under Sect. 108 where it was clear that there were no assets and the bankruptcy proceedings were not likely to produce any. However, the Court of Appeal has decided that a court in exercising its discretion to rescind a receiving order under Sect. 108 must take into account the interests of future and present creditors and of the public at large. The considerations involved are analogous to those applying to an application for annulment of an adjudication order under Sect. 29 of the 1914 Act. (See p. 347.) (*Re A Debtor*, (No. 12 of 1970), [1971] 1 W.L.R. 1212.)

STATEMENT OF AFFAIRS

A debtor is called upon to make a statement of his affairs. (Sect. 14.) It must be made within *three days* after the receiving order if the petition was presented by the debtor, and within *seven days* of the receiving order if the petition was presented by a creditor. If a debtor fails to submit a statement of affairs within the time allowed, the court may adjudge him bankrupt on the application of the Official Receiver or any creditor, but the court may allow an extension of time in special circumstances.

The statement, which must be submitted to the Official Receiver, must be verified by affidavit, and must show—

(*a*) Particulars of the debtor's assets and liabilities;
(*b*) The names, residences and occupations of his creditors;
(*c*) The securities, if any, held by them;
(*d*) The dates on which such securities were given;
(*e*) Any further information which the Official Receiver may require.

Procedure. Immediately after the service of the receiving order, the debtor is required to attend upon the Official Receiver for a preliminary examination, and there is a notice to this effect at the foot of the debtor's copy of the receiving order. At the preliminary examination the Official Receiver gives the debtor or his advisers instructions for the preparation of the Statement of Affairs. If, for some reason, the debtor cannot prepare his Statement of Affairs the Official Receiver may do so and charge the expenses to the estate. (Sect. 74.)

Inspection. After having been filed with the Official Receiver, the Statement of Affairs can be inspected by any person who states in writing that he is a creditor of the debtor's estate, and a copy or extracts therefrom may be taken. A creditor can appoint an agent to do this for him. If the debtor intends to put before the meeting of his creditors any proposals for the payment of his debts he must submit them to the Official Receiver within four days after the submission of the Statement of Affairs. (Sect. 16.) Any such composition or scheme must be approved by a majority in number and three-quarters in value of the proving creditors and has also to be approved by the court. If such approval is given all creditors are bound by the composition or scheme of arrangement.

MEETINGS OF CREDITORS

The question whether or not an adjudication order is to be made against the debtor will be decided at a meeting of the creditors. In many cases there will be only one meeting and this, or the first of the series if there are several, must be held within 14 days after the date of the receiving order, though this time may be extended by the court. The meeting is called by the Official Receiver and six days' notice of the first meeting must be given in the *London Gazette*, in a local newspaper, and to each creditor named in the statement of affairs, though the proceedings are not invalidated by failure to send a notice, or if a notice is sent but not received. Where there are three or more creditors, three constitute a quorum. If there are only two, both must be present.

The Official Receiver, or a person nominated by him, acts as chairman at the first meeting. Three days' notice at least must be given of any meeting after the first, and at such meetings the creditors may choose their own chairman. A creditor can only vote if he has lodged proof of his debt within the time specified by the Official Receiver in the notice convening the meeting. If he has not proved and the meeting is adjourned, he may still prove not later than 24 hours before the adjourned meeting is held.

The principal matter for discussion at the meeting of creditors will be the Statement of Affairs presented by the debtor. A summary of this, together with any observations upon it made by the Official Receiver, will have previously been supplied to the creditors. The debtor must be present at the first meeting unless good cause is shown for his absence.

The courses which are open to the creditors at the first or any subsequent meeting are as follows—

(*a*) *To agree to a composition*, e.g. 85p in the £1. This is often the best course to adopt if the offer is reasonable and the debtor appears genuine, since it saves the cost of bankruptcy proceedings.

(*b*) *To agree to a scheme of arrangement*, i.e. a transfer of the debtor's property to trustees for the benefit of the creditors.

The basic difference between a composition and a scheme is that, *in a composition* the debtor keeps the assets and pays from them a certain sum to his creditors, whereas *in a scheme* the debtor transfers his assets to a trustee or trustees who then make payments to the creditors. A scheme will avoid bankruptcy though it must be operated in a similar manner to a bankruptcy.

(*c*) *To agree to ask the court to adjudicate the debtor bankrupt.*

As we have seen a composition or scheme of arrangement must be accepted by a majority in number and three-quarters in value of the creditors and approved by the court.

THE PUBLIC EXAMINATION OF THE DEBTOR

Every debtor must undergo a public examination as to his conduct, dealings and property, though the court may in a special case rescind the receiving order before the public examination where the debtor has reached an arrangement with his creditors. The debtor is not publicly examined where he is of unsound mind, or is so physically disabled as to be in the opinion of the court unfit to attend. In such a case the examination may be in private or there may be no examination at all. In addition the court may make an order under Sect. 25 of the 1914 Act for the examination of the executors of a deceased bankrupt, even though he may have obtained his discharge before death. (*Re A Debtor*, (No. 12 of 1968), [1968] 2 All E.R. 425.)

The public examination is held as soon as possible after the debtor has submitted his statement of affairs. The Official Receiver applies to the court, and the court by order appoints a day and hour for the public examination. A copy of the order is served on the debtor by the Official Receiver and he also gives the creditors notice of the order. The date and time are also advertised in a local newspaper. (Sect. 15 (2).)

At the public examination the debtor is first questioned by the Official Receiver and then by the trustee, if one has been appointed. The creditors who have tendered proofs may also question the debtor, as may members of the court itself. Questions relating to the debtor's property and affairs must be answered even if the answer incriminates the debtor and the answers given by the debtor may be used afterwards in criminal proceedings.

When satisfied that the debtor's affairs have been sufficiently investigated, the court declares the examination closed, but not until after the day appointed for the first meeting of the creditors. On an adjournment *sine die*, as where the debtor is not attending or not co-operating, the court may make such order as it thinks fit, including an adjudication order.

THE ADJUDICATION ORDER

When the receiving order has been made, or at any time thereafter, the court may, *on the application of the debtor*, adjudge him bankrupt. Such application may be made orally and without notice.

On the application of the Official Receiver or a creditor, the court may adjudge the debtor bankrupt forthwith as follows—

(i) If the creditors' meeting passes an ordinary resolution (i.e. by a simple majority *in value*) in favour of adjudging him bankrupt;

(ii) If it has not been possible to obtain any kind of resolution from the creditors;

(iii) If it has not been possible to get a meeting of the creditors;

(iv) If a scheme or composition which has been put forward by the debtor is not approved by the court under Sect. 16 within 14 days after the conclusion of the Public Examination, unless the court extends the time;

(v) If there is no quorum at the first meeting of creditors or any adjournment thereof;

(vi) Where the Official Receiver satisfies the court that the debtor has absconded or does not intend to propose a scheme or composition;

(vii) Where a composition or scheme is not accepted by the creditors at their first meeting or at any adjournment;

(viii) Where the public examination has been adjourned *sine die*;

(ix) If the debtor fails to file his statement of affairs without reasonable excuse;

(x) Where the debtor fails to pay an instalment under a composition or scheme or the court considers that the scheme or composition cannot continue without injustice or delay to the creditors. This may happen where the debtor is having difficulty in getting property in, or where the court's approval of the scheme was obtained by fraud as where there is no property available for the composition or scheme.

Effect of the Adjudication Order. When an adjudication order is made, the debtor's property passes to his trustee in bankruptcy, and until a trustee is appointed the Official Receiver acts as trustee. In the case of registered land the trustee must be registered as proprietor before he can deal with it. The remedies of the creditors against the debtor are extinguished; they may prove in the bankruptcy and that is all.

The debtor now incurs the disqualifications of a bankrupt.

(i) He cannot sit or vote in the House of Lords and cannot be elected to sit, or if he is elected, continue to sit or vote in the House of Commons.

(ii) He is similarly disqualified from being elected to, or being a member of, a local authority. Neither can he be appointed or continue to act as a Justice of the Peace. (Sect. 32.)

The above disqualifications are removed if (*a*) the adjudication order is annulled; or (*b*) if the bankrupt is discharged, the court giving him a "Certificate of Misfortune"; or (*c*) if five years have elapsed from the date of his discharge. A Certificate of Misfortune is given where the bankruptcy was, for example, due to a business failure which the bankrupt could not have been expected to prevent.

(iii) An undischarged bankrupt may not act as a director of, or take part in the management of any company registered or unregistered except with the leave of the court by which he was adjudicated bankrupt. (Companies Act, 1948, Sect. 187.)

(iv) An undischarged bankrupt may not obtain credit beyond £10 without disclosing that he is an undischarged bankrupt. Failure to make this disclosure is an offence for which the maximum sentence is one year's imprisonment, and the offence is committed even where the bankrupt obtains credit jointly with another. The crime is an absolute offence, and it is not necessary to prove fraud. Credits under £10 can be added together to make the offence (*R.* v. *Hartley* [1972] 1 All E.R. 599.)

(v) The bankrupt may also be liable to criminal penalties under the Debtors Act, 1869, Sect. 11, if he trades under another name without disclosing the name under which he was made bankrupt.

Annulment of Adjudication Order. The bankruptcy may be annulled on approval of a composition or scheme of arrangement under Sect. 21 of the Bankruptcy Act, 1914.

The court may also annul an adjudication order where—

(*a*) In the opinion of the court it ought not to have been made (Sect. 29), e.g. where an order has been made against a minor, no debt being enforceable against him (*Re A. and M.* (*Debtors*), 1926);[593]

(*b*) It is proved to the satisfaction of the court that the debts of the bankrupt are paid in full (Sect. 29.) Even so the power is discretionary, and annulment may be refused, even where all debts have been paid in full, if the debtor has committed serious offences.

The effect of an annulment is that the assets re-vest in the former bankrupt who is also restored to his former position so far as debts and liabilities are concerned. He may then be sued for outstanding claims. The annulment order must be published in the London Gazette and a local newspaper.

THE OFFICIAL RECEIVER

The Official Receiver is appointed by the Department of Trade and Industry and acts as the receiver of the debtor's property until a trustee is appointed. Separate appointments are not made for each bankruptcy as there is, attached to each bankruptcy court, an officer called the *official receiver for the district.*

The Official Receiver has the following duties—

(i) To report to the court on the conduct of the debtor during his bankruptcy and to take part in the public examination and in criminal prosecutions should these arise;

(ii) To ensure that the statement of affairs is properly prepared;

(iii) To act as trustee should there be a vacancy in that office;

(iv) To call the first meeting of creditors and act as chairman;

(v) To make the proper advertisements as required by bank-ruptcy law;

(vi) To appoint, and if necessary remove, a special manager of the debtor's business.

THE SPECIAL MANAGER

The Official Receiver may, on application by a creditor, appoint a *special manager* to carry on the debtor's business if such a course would be for the benefit of the creditors.

A special manager is answerable to the Official Receiver and can only take office on giving security to the satisfaction of the Department of Trade and Industry. His remuneration is payable out of the estate and is fixed either by the Department of Trade and Industry or by the creditors on the recommendation of the Official Receiver. The appointment cannot operate after the appointment of a trustee.

COMMITTEE OF INSPECTION

It is often necessary for a small number of creditors to work with and assist the trustee if the bankruptcy is one of difficulty and complexity. The members of the committee are appointed by the creditors from among their number at their first or any subsequent meeting.

The committee consists of three, four, or five persons, and must meet at least once a month though the trustee or any member may call a meeting at any time. The trustee must submit his accounts periodically to the committee for examination.

If there is no committee of inspection, the trustee obtains the requisite permissions from the general body of creditors or from the Department of Trade and Industry. Members of the committee are not entitled to remuneration but *expenses are payable*.

Members of the committee cease holding office—

(i) By resigning after written notice to the trustee; or

(ii) By becoming bankrupt; or

(iii) By being absent from five consecutive meetings; or

(iv) By removal at a meeting of creditors, of which seven days notice has been given specifying the object of the meeting

THE TRUSTEE

The office of trustee is filled by the appointment of a person, who may or may not be a creditor, either—

(*a*) By an ordinary resolution in value of the creditors;

(*b*) By the committee of inspection, if the main body of creditors decides to leave the matter to the committee;

(*c*) By the Department of Trade and Industry.

If the creditors fail to make an appointment (i) within four weeks of the making of the adjudication order; or (ii) within seven days after failure to get a scheme or composition approved; or (iii) within three weeks of a vacancy, the Department of Trade and Industry will appoint a fit person who may still be removed by the creditors if they then appoint their own trustee.

The Official Receiver can act as trustee where the value of the estate is not likely to exceed £300, where there is a casual vacancy in the office of trustee, or in the case of a deceased insolvent. He may also be directed to act by the Department of Trade and Industry.

A trustee cannot act as such unless and until he receives from the Department of Trade and Industry a Certificate of Appointment. In order to obtain this certificate, the trustee must give security for the proper administration of the estate as directed by the Department of Trade and Industry. The appointment dates from the granting of the certificate and must be advertised in the *London Gazette* and a local newspaper.

Duties of the Trustee. The trustee is under a duty not to make any profit for himself and to take only his agreed remuneration; nor must he purchase the estate or part of it. He is obliged to collect the debts and realise the estate as quickly as he can and make a proper distribution of it. He must also have regard to the wishes and resolutions of the creditors and to the orders of the Department of Trade and Industry and keep proper accounts.

Powers of the Trustee. A trustee can *without permission*—

(i) sell all or any part of the bankrupt's property;

(ii) give good receipts for money paid to him;

(iii) prove debts due to the bankrupt in any other bankruptcy;

(iv) exercise any power given to him by the bankruptcy legislation;

(v) take out letters of administration to a deceased debtor of the bankrupt;

(vi) deal with property to which the debtor is tenant in tail. The trustee can, on selling such property, give a freehold interest to the purchaser, thus increasing the value of the land.

A trustee can *with the permission of the creditors, Committee of Inspection or the Department of Trade and Industry* exercise the following additional powers—

(*a*) carry on the debtor's business for more beneficial winding up of the estate;

(*b*) bring or defend legal proceedings for the benefit of the estate; compromise claims by or against the estate; refer disputes to arbitration;

(*c*) employ a solicitor or other agents to do particular acts;

(*d*) raise money on the security of the debtor's property;

(*e*) divide the debtor's property in its existing form, where realisation would prove a disadvantage;

(*f*) appoint the debtor to carry on the business or to assist therein;

(*g*) make a reasonable allowance to the bankrupt as consideration for his services or otherwise.

Trustee's Books. The trustee must keep what is known as a *Record Book* which contains a record of the administration of the estate, e.g. the various resolutions of the creditors. He is also required to keep a *cash book* for receipts and payments and, if he is carrying on a business, he must keep a *trading account book* showing a weekly account of the trading position. The trading account book should be verified once a month by affidavit, and certified by the committee of inspection or one of their number appointed by the committee for this purpose.

Audit. The trustee's accounts are audited by the committee of inspection at least once every three months, and by the Department of Trade and Industry every six months.

Remuneration of Trustee. This is fixed either by the creditors or by the committee of inspection if the creditors by resolution depute the committee to do it. The remuneration will, however, be fixed by the Department of Trade and Industry where at least one-fourth in value or number of the creditors do not agree to the amount fixed by the others, or the bankrupt convinces the Department of Trade and Industry that the remuneration is too great. Where the trustee is appointed by the Department of Trade and Industry, the Department will fix his remuneration.

The payment is made in the form of a percentage based on the value of the assets realised by the trustee and the amount paid out in dividend, together with an additional allowance for expenses.

Termination of Appointment. If the trustee wishes to *resign* he must call a meeting of the creditors to obtain their approval. The creditors are not bound to accept the resignation but, if they do, the trustee must give at least seven days notice of his resignation to the Official Receiver.

The trustee may be *removed* at a creditors' meeting. An ordinary resolution will suffice.

The Department of Trade and Industry can remove a trustee—

(*a*) If he is guilty of misconduct or fails to carry out his duties;

(*b*) If he is unduly slow in winding up the estate;

(*c*) If he is of unsound mind, or by reason of illness or absence cannot carry out his duties;

(*d*) If his relationship with the bankrupt, or a creditor or creditors, is such that he can no longer be regarded as impartial;

(*e*) If he has been removed for misconduct in some other matter with which he is also concerned, e.g. another bankruptcy or receivership.

The creditors can object to the removal of the trustee, and if they pass a resolution in his favour, they may appeal to the High Court. The trustee can also appeal.

The trustee's appointment is terminated when a scheme is adopted, or the estate is fully wound up, or if a receiving order is made against him.

Department of Trade and Industry Release. When a trustee has resigned or been removed, or the estate has been fully wound up, he may apply to the Department of Trade and Industry for his release. (Sect. 93.) This will be granted after the Department has made full investigation into his accounts and has informed the debtor and the creditors. When granted it frees the trustee from liability in respect of the period of his trusteeship, but can be revoked if fraud or concealment is shown. If the Department of Trade and Industry refuse to grant his release the trustee may apply to the court.

THE DOCTRINE OF RELATION BACK

Sect. 37 of the Bankruptcy Act, 1914, provides that the title of the trustee in bankruptcy dates back to the time of the act of bankruptcy on which a receiving order was made, or the first of such acts within the period of three months preceding the date of the presentation of the bankruptcy petition. As from that moment the debtor is not entitled to deal with his estate.

Debtors rarely consider this provision and continue to deal with what they consider to be their property, and much hardship would be caused to persons dealing with the debtor if all such transactions were invalid. The Bankruptcy Act provides some protection.

Protected Transactions. The following transactions are protected under Sect. 45 of the Bankruptcy Act, 1914—

(*a*) Payments by the debtor to any of his creditors, but not if they are fraudulent preferences;

(*b*) Payments or deliveries of money or goods to the bankrupt;

(*c*) Contracts or dealings by or with the bankrupt for valuable consideration;

(*d*) Conveyances or assignments by the bankrupt for valuable consideration;

provided the transaction takes place before the date of the receiving order *and* the third party had not at the time of the transaction notice of any available act of bankruptcy committed by the debtor. (*Re Keever*, 1966.)[565]

The burden of proving that he had no notice is on the third party who is seeking to protect the transaction. If the original transferee from the debtor is protected by Sect. 45, then others who take the property from him are protected. If not, no title passes.

Further protection is given by Sect. 46 which provides that a payment of money or delivery of property to a debtor subsequently adjudged bankrupt is good even if the person making the payment or delivery has notice of an available act of bankruptcy provided it is made before the receiving order is made, and without notice of the presentation of a bankruptcy petition, in good faith, and in the ordinary course of business. Without this protection a deed of arrangement would not be viable since the deed is an act of bankruptcy and a debtor would not pay his debt to the trustee of the deed. In addition, without the protection of Sect. 46, a bank, with notice of an act of bankruptcy, could not pay its customers with safety. However, payment by cheque is not effective until the cheque has been paid or credited. If a receiving order is made against the drawer of a cheque before payment in and collection, the person entitled to the money is not protected.

Sects. 45 and 46 operate independently and the fact that a person is not able to use one section will not bar him from using the other. (*Re Dalton*, 1962.)[590]

The Bankruptcy Act of 1914 *gives no protection* to persons dealing with the bankrupt between the date of the receiving order and the adjudication order. (*Re Wigzell, Ex parte Hart*, 1921.)[594]

However, Sect. 4 *of the Bankruptcy (Amendment) Act*, 1926, *gives some relief* to bona fide third parties, e.g. banks who pay out the debtor's funds after the receiving order, provided that—

(i) The Receiving Order has not been advertised in the *London Gazette*; and

(ii) The person making the payment has not had other notice of the receiving order.

Even where the third party satisfies the above requirements, the trustee can still recover from him by showing that it is not practicable to recover the money from the person to whom it was paid.

Nevertheless, the rule in *Ex parte James*, which was first enunciated in *Re Condon, Ex parte James*, 1874,[595] is that a court in bankruptcy will not allow its officer, the trustee in bankruptcy, to retain or claim money for distribution among the creditors where it would be inconsistent with natural justice to do so. (*In Re Thellusson, Ex parte Abdy*, 1919.)[596] The application of the rule is discretionary and is only applied where the court thinks fit. It was not applied, for instance, in *Re Wigzell, Ex parte Hart*, 1921.)[594]

Executions and Attachments. Sect. 40 provides that an execution creditor is not entitled to retain the benefit of the execution or attachment against the trustee in bankruptcy unless he has completed the execution or attachment *before* the date of the receiving order, and *before notice of* the presentation of any bankruptcy petition or of the commission of any available act of bankruptcy.

For the purposes of the Act, execution against goods is completed by seizure and sale; attachment of a debt by receipt of the debt; execution against land by seizure, or in the case of an equitable interest by the appointment of a receiver. An execution is not invalid merely because it is an act of bankruptcy.

CREDITORS

Creditors are of two kinds—*unsecured* and *secured*.

Unsecured creditors are either—

(a) *Ordinary trade creditors* who prove in the usual way, or

(b) *Preferential creditors* who rank before the ordinary creditors, or

(c) *Deferred creditors* who are paid only when the other creditors have received 100p in the pound on their debts.

Secured creditors are those who hold a mortgage, charge or lien upon any property of the debtor.

The rights of a secured creditor in a bankruptcy are as follows—

(i) HE MAY SELL HIS SECURITY AND NOT PROVE IN THE BANKRUPTCY AT ALL. The secured creditor is not bound to get the best price possible, except in the case of a building society, which is a trustee of the power of sale and must obtain the market price or be liable for the balance to the trustee in bankruptcy. The secured creditor will also be liable to the trustee in bankruptcy if he sells at a ridiculously low price so that the sale is clearly fraudulent.

(ii) HE MAY SELL HIS SECURITY AND PROVE FOR THE BALANCE (if any) and he may deduct the cost of realisation from the amount he receives from the sale of the security. "Property of a debtor" within Sect. 167 of the Act of 1914 includes property held under a joint tenancy. Thus a creditor secured on property jointly owned by the bankrupt and another is a secured creditor to the extent of one-half of that property. Therefore if property owned jointly by A and B is charged to secure a debt of, say, £10,000, then if A *only* goes bankrupt and the secured creditor sells the property for £7,000 he must return £2,000 to the trustee and can only prove in A's bankruptcy for £5,000 and not £10,000. Thus if a dividend of 50p in the £1 is paid, the secured creditor will receive £5,000 from the security and £2,500 from the bankruptcy, making £7,500 in all. (*Re A Debtor* (No. 5 of 1967) *ex parte National Westminster Bank* v. *Official Receiver*, [1971] 2 All E.R. 938.)

(iii) HE MAY SURRENDER HIS SECURITY AND PROVE FOR THE WHOLE DEBT.

(iv) HE MAY STATE IN HIS PROOF THE PARTICULARS OF THE SECURITY, THE DATE WHEN IT WAS GIVEN AND ITS VALUE. In that case the value so stated will be deducted from the amount of his debt and he will be entitled to receive dividends on the balance.

If the secured creditor adopts this course, *the trustee has the following powers*—

(a) He may at any time redeem the security on payment to the creditor of the assessed value;

(b) If he is dissatisfied with the value at which the security is assessed, he may require that the property comprised in any security so valued be offered for sale, at such times and on such terms and conditions as may be agreed between the creditor and the trustee, or in default of such agreement as the court may direct. If the sale is by public auction the creditor or the trustee on behalf of the estate may bid or purchase.

The secured creditor also has certain rights in these circumstances. After valuation the creditor is entitled to write to the trustee requiring him to elect whether he will or will not exercise his power of redeeming the security or requiring it to be sold. The trustee has six months after receipt of such notice within which to declare his election. If he fails to do so, his right of election is lost, and the interest in the security is wholly vested in the creditor whose debt is reduced by the amount at which the security has been valued.

Proof of Debts. Provable debts are all debts and liabilities, present or future, certain or contingent, e.g. possible liability as an indorser of a bill of exchange. They include all debts to which the debtor is subject at the date of the receiving order, or to which he may become subject by reason of an obligation incurred before the date of the receiving order. Contract debts of uncertain value may be valued by the trustee, with an appeal to the court if necessary. Demands in the nature of *unliquidated damages*, not arising out of breach of contract or breach of trust, are not provable.

A debt contracted by the debtor with a person who had previous knowledge of an act of bankruptcy is not provable; nor is a debt which the court decides cannot be valued, e.g. future sums payable under a court maintenance order. However, where there is a separation deed between husband and wife, the debt is contractual and the capital value of the payments under the deed can be ascertained and then proved. Illegal and statute-barred debts cannot be proved.

Mutual Dealings. If C owes D £100 and D owes C £150, D could settle his debt to C by paying £50 and "setting off" the £100. If D were bankrupt, then the *right of set-off remains*, and C, instead of paying £100 into the estate and receiving a mere dividend on the £150, need only prove for £50, setting-off the £100.

A creditor cannot set-off if at the time of giving the debtor credit he had notice of the debtor's act of bankruptcy, and where there is an account between the parties, the date of the receiving order is the relevant date in ascertaining what can be set-off.

The debts must be due between the same parties and in the same right. For this reason a debt owed jointly by a partnership firm cannot be set-off against a separate debt owed to one of the partners in his private capacity. Further, it was held in *Rolls Razor* v. *Cox* (1966), 110 S.J. 943, that parties cannot contract out of the right of set-off given by Sect. 31 of the Bankruptcy Act, 1914. However, it may be possible for parties to agree that their dealings shall not be regarded as mutual. (*Halesowen Presswork Ltd.* v. *Westminster Bank Ltd.*, 1970.)[545]

Preferential Creditors. The following are the chief preferential payments—

1. THE EXPENSES OF THE BANKRUPTCY PROCEEDINGS. These must be paid in full if the assets are sufficient to meet them. They include the expenses of the Official Receiver, the costs of the petitioning creditor, the expenses of the trustee, his remuneration, and the expenses of the committee of inspection.

2. WHERE THE BANKRUPT WAS AN OFFICER OF A FRIENDLY SOCIETY OR A SAVINGS BANK, any liability for money or property of the society or bank, received or not accounted for, must be discharged prior to ALL the creditors of the Officer concerned. (Sect. 33.)

3. WHERE THE BANKRUPT HAS BEEN THE PRINCIPAL OF AN ARTICLED CLERK OR APPRENTICE. The trustee *may* refund to the clerk or apprentice a portion of any premium received by the bankrupt. However, the trustee is not obliged to make a refund. (Sect. 34.)

4. THE FOLLOWING CLAIMS ARE THEN PAYABLE and must be paid before any other debts are paid. If the debtor's assets are insufficient to pay them in full, they abate equally.

(*a*) All wages and salaries, not exceeding £200, of any clerk or servant or of any workman or labourer in respect of services rendered during the *four* months next before the making of the receiving order.

It was decided in *Re C. W. & A. L. Hughes*, [1966] 2 All E.R. 702, that money payable under "labour only" sub-contracts was not in the nature of a preferential debt. Thus, if the bankrupt has been hiring a gang of workmen on a labour-only basis, the gang leader receiving payment without deductions for P.A.Y.E. or Insurance, then any sums of money owed to the gang leader in respect of the hiring will not be preferential. As regards contractors in the construction industry, the matter of tax deduction is now dealt with by Sect. 29 of the Finance Act, 1971, which requires 30 per cent to be deducted from payments to sub-contractors, the person making the payment accounting to the Revenue for it. The sum deducted is a preferential payment so far as the Revenue is concerned but the balance payable to the contractor is still not preferential in the way that salaries and wages are.

(*b*) Rates and Taxes for one year's assessment. The Crown, but not the local authority, can choose any year before the receiving order, and can thus choose the one in which most money is owed.

(*c*) National Health Contributions for the twelve months next before the making of the receiving order.

(*d*) Accrued holiday pay due to employees.

(*e*) P.A.Y.E. deductions made during the twelve months next before the making of the receiving order, and due from the bankrupt employer to the Crown.

Special Position of the Landlord. A landlord has a special right in law to distrain for rent, i.e. to move in on the debtor's personal property and remove it for sale to satisfy the amount owing. His position in a bankruptcy is governed by Sects. 33 and 35 of the Bankruptcy Act, 1914, and is as follows.

The landlord may distrain despite the making of the receiving order, but if distress is levied after the commencement of the bankruptcy, the rent recoverable is limited to six months. The landlord may prove in the bankruptcy along with the unsecured creditors for any surplus.

The landlord may not, however, be able to keep the six months' rent obtained from distraining on the debtor's property because, if he distrains (*a*) within three months next before the receiving order; or (*b*) after the receiving order, the preferential debts must be paid out of the money received from the distraint. Thereafter the landlord becomes a preferential creditor in respect of sums so paid with the same rights of priority on the remaining assets as the persons to whom payment was made. (Sect. 33 (4).)

Under the provisions of the Landlord and Tenant Act, 1709, where an execution creditor wishes to levy execution on a debtor's goods, he must pay the landlord the rent due, if any, up to a maximum of one year's arrears. The sheriff therefore levies on the debtor's goods, if sufficient, for the amount of rent due in addition to the execution monies.

Since, under Sect. 35 (2) of the Bankruptcy Act, the landlord may retain a maximum of six months' rent only, and must account to the trustee for any excess he may have received from an execution creditor, he must prove in the bankruptcy for this latter amount and any other rent outstanding as an unsecured creditor.

A landlord who distrains before the commencement of the bankruptcy, can keep whatever he has obtained in order to satisfy the amount owing.

General Debts. These are debts which are not preferential or deferred, e.g. those due to trade creditors. They are paid after the preferential debts and rank pari-passu (on an equal footing).

Deferred Debts. Payment of these is postponed until all the other creditors have received 100p in the pound.

(*a*) THOSE UNDER SECT. 36 OF THE BANKRUPTCY ACT, 1914. Where a married woman is adjudged bankrupt, her husband cannot claim any dividend in respect of any loan by him to her for the purposes of her trade or business until the claims of the other creditors have been satisfied. A married woman is similarly a deferred creditor in respect of trade loans she has made to her husband. The section does not apply to a loan made to a firm of which the spouse is a partner, nor to a loan to a spouse for private purposes not connected with trade or business.

(*b*) THOSE UNDER SECT. 66 OF THE BANKRUPTCY ACT, 1914. Interest due by contract under a debt which has been proved is, for the purposes of dividend, calculated at a rate not exceeding 5 per cent per annum, and any greater sum charged by way of interest is a deferred debt.

(*c*) THOSE UNDER SECT. 3 OF THE PARTNERSHIP ACT, 1890.

(i) Where a loan is made under a written contract to a person engaged or about to engage in any business, on terms that the lender is to receive a rate of interest varying with the profits, or a share of the profits of the business, this loan is a deferred debt.

(ii) A transaction whereby a person is to receive a share of the profits in payment of the sale of the goodwill of the business also produces a deferred debt.

(*d*) THOSE UNDER THE BANKRUPTCY ACT, SECT. 42. Claims by the trustees of any settlement avoided in the bankruptcy are deferred.

COMPOSITION AND SCHEMES OF ARRANGEMENT

1. Those under the Deeds of Arrangement Act, 1914. An arrangement made under the above provisions does not necessarily involve the debtor in bankruptcy, provided the creditors agree to it and there is no secret preference to one creditor; otherwise the other creditors are not bound. A creditor whose assent has been obtained by mistake or misrepresentation may avoid the arrangement and take proceedings on the debt. However, a creditor cannot withdraw his assent to a deed of assignment, even though induced by misrepresentation, if third party rights have accrued. (*Re Clarke*, 1966.)[597] The essential provisions regarding such an arrangement are as follows—

(i) Any instrument, *whether made under seal or not*, which is an arrangement by a debtor for the benefit of his creditors generally, or is made by an *insolvent* debtor for the benefit of three or more creditors, must within seven days be registered as a *deed of arrangement* with the Department of Trade and Industry.

(ii) It must receive the assent of the majority in number and value of the creditors within twenty-one days of its execution or it is void, and any creditor can base a petition on it, even though he assented to it.

(iii) If the arrangement affects real property, it must be registered as a land charge under the Land Charges Act, 1925; otherwise it will not affect a purchaser for value of the land in question.

(iv) Creditors who have not assented to the arrangement are not bound by it, and if it is for the benefit of creditors generally, they can treat it as an act of bankruptcy and may petition on it. However, this right is limited to a period of one month if the trustee of the arrangement gives notice to the creditors of the execution of the arrangement, and files the assents of the creditors who have agreed. (Deeds of Arrangement Act, Sect. 24.)

2. Those under the Bankruptcy Act, 1914. These may be either compositions or schemes and we shall use the word *scheme* to cover either type of arrangement.

A. SCHEME BEFORE ADJUDICATION ORDER BUT AFTER RECEIVING ORDER. Under the provisions of Sect. 16 the debtor settles the terms of his proposal which must be accepted by the required majority of his creditors and approved by the court. Although the court has, in general, complete discretion with regard to approval, there are cases in which the court *must refuse* approval—

(i) If the debts given priority by the Bankruptcy Act are not given similar priority in the scheme;

(ii) If the scheme does not provide for the payment of at least 25p in the pound on all unsecured debts provable against the debtor's estate;

(iii) If the scheme is not calculated to benefit the general body of creditors. It seems that it will not benefit them unless it gives them some advantages that they would not have in an ordinary bankruptcy.

Except in the cases outlined above the court is reluctant to deny approval to a scheme which the creditors have approved.

Procedure. The following procedure must be adopted—

(*a*) Within four days of submitting his Statement of Affairs (the time may be extended by the Official Receiver), the debtor must lodge his proposals with the Official Receiver. The proposals must be in writing and signed by the debtor, and must set out the terms of the scheme and give particulars of any security proposed.

(*b*) The Official Receiver calls a meeting of the creditors which must be held before the Public Examination of the debtor is concluded. Each creditor receives from the Official Receiver before the meeting copies of the debtor's proposals, together with the Official Receiver's report thereon. If a majority in number and three-quarters in value of all the creditors who have proved accept the proposals, they are deemed accepted.

(*c*) After the proposal has been accepted by the creditors, the debtor or the Official Receiver will apply to the court for approval. The court will not hear the application until after the Public Examination.

(*d*) Creditors who have proved may oppose the application, even though they voted for acceptance at the meeting of creditors. If the scheme is approved, the receiving order is discharged. The Official Receiver will then put the trustee of the scheme (or the debtor in the case of a composition) into possession of the debtor's property.

(*e*) A scheme when approved is binding on all creditors so far as it relates to any debts due to them from the debtor and provable in the bankruptcy.

(*f*) A scheme does not attach to after-acquired property unless there is an express stipulation to that effect. (*Re Croom, England* v. *Provincial Assets Co.*, 1891.)[598]

Annulment of Scheme. The court may adjudge the debtor bankrupt and annul the scheme on application by the Official Receiver or the trustee or any creditor—

(i) If the debtor defaults in payment of any instalment under the scheme; or

(ii) If the scheme cannot proceed without injustice or undue delay to the creditors or to the debtor, e.g. where there is difficulty in getting in some fund which is the basis of the scheme; or

(iii) Where approval of the scheme was obtained by the debtor's fraud.

On annulment the property is handed back to the Official Receiver, but acts done prior to the annulment are good.

B. SCHEME AFTER ADJUDICATION ORDER. Sect. 21 provides that a bankrupt may put forward a scheme after adjudication. Acceptance of the scheme must be by a majority in number and three-quarters in value of all the creditors who have proved. Approval by the court is also required.

If approval is obtained the bankruptcy may be annulled, in which case the court makes the order revesting the property in some appropriate person, e.g. the trustee under the scheme. If no order is made, the property revests in the debtor. A scheme after adjudication may be annulled in the same way as a scheme under Sect. 16 above.

THE DEBTOR'S PROPERTY

Property available to pay the debts of the bankrupt is as follows—

(i) That owned by him when his bankruptcy commenced;

(ii) That acquired by him between the commencement of the bankruptcy and his discharge;

(iii) Goods of which the bankrupt was reputed owner at the commencement of the bankruptcy;

(iv) Invalid assignments.

1. Property in Ownership. Sect. 38 provides that all property in ownership of the debtor at the commencement of his bankruptcy is divisible among his creditors *except*—

(i) Property of which the debtor is trustee for others;

(ii) Tools of trade, necessary wearing apparel and bedding of himself, his wife and children to a total value of £20; and

(iii) Property in which the debtor's interest is terminated by his bankruptcy, as where property is settled upon the debtor with a gift over to another person should the debtor become bankrupt, unless the debtor has so settled the property on himself.

(iv) Where the bankrupt has entered into a contract to buy goods, but the goods are subject to the *unpaid seller's rights of lien and stoppage in transitu,* the trustee cannot obtain the goods unless he pays the price. The principle applies even though the property in the goods has passed to the bankrupt.

In addition, a statutory tenancy under the Rent Act does not vest in the trustee because it is not property.

2. After-Acquired Property. The personal earnings of the bankrupt do not pass to his trustee, but he may retain only so much of his earnings as are necessary to support himself and his family. Profits of a business, even though earned mainly as a result of the personal skill of the bankrupt, do pass to the trustee, though the trustee may employ the bankrupt in the business and pay him an allowance. A life interest in a trust fund is not a salary and vests in the trustee. (*Re Cohen*, [1961] Ch 246.)

Actions in contract or tort in respect of injury to person or reputation do not pass to the trustee, unless the tort or breach of contract causes loss to the estate, in which case the damages are apportioned between the debtor and the trustee.

Old age pensions and other state benefits under the National Insurance Acts do not pass to the trustee.

The rule in *Cohen* v. *Mitchell* (1890)[599] states that all transactions by a bankrupt after his bankruptcy, with any person dealing with him bona fide and for value, in respect of his after-acquired property, whether with or without knowledge of his bankruptcy, are valid as against the trustee, unless the trustee has intervened. (*Hill* v. *Settle*, 1917.)[600]

Sect. 47 (1) of the Bankruptcy Act, 1914, merely puts the rule into statutory form with certain additions, the most important of which is to extend the rule to real property. The burden of proving *bona fides* and value is on the person who dealt with the bankrupt.

Where money, securities or negotiable instruments acquired by the bankrupt after adjudication are received or paid out by a banker, the transaction is valid against the customer's trustee and the banker is not liable to account for the funds. (Sect. 47.) However, if the banker discovers that his customer is an undischarged bankrupt he must inform the trustee or the Department of Trade and Industry and must not make further payments from the account without leave of the court. If, one month after notifying the trustee or the Department, no instructions are received the banker may make payments from the account. (Sect. 47.)

3. Reputed Ownership. Sect. 38 of the Act enables the trustee to claim, on behalf of the general body of creditors, property which does not belong to the bankrupt, if the property is in the bankrupt's possession order or disposition at the commencement of the bankruptcy. However, the following five conditions must be fulfilled—

(i) Only goods can be claimed, i.e. movable chattels.

(ii) The property must be in the bankrupt's possession order or disposition in the way of trade or business. Household furniture held under a hire-purchase agreement cannot, therefore, be claimed. (*Re Ginger*, 1897.)[601]

(iii) The bankrupt must be the reputed owner of the goods. If it is well-known that the bankrupt does not own his trade stock, as where it is the custom of the bankrupt's trade to hold stock on sale or return terms, the section will not apply.

(iv) The true owner must have consented to the bankrupt's possession and to the use of the goods in his trade. (*Lamb* v. *Wright & Co.*, 1924.)[602]

(v) The possession of the bankrupt must be sole not joint possession.

If the true owner, without notice of an available act of bankruptcy, can take possession of the goods before the date of the receiving order, his title will prevail against the trustee. If in similar circumstances the true owner demands the goods, and dissents from their remaining in the bankrupt's possession, his title prevails even though he does not get possession. Where the goods are on hire purchase, the matter is now covered by the Hire-Purchase Act, 1965, Sect. 53 (1).

Chattels comprised in an absolute Bill of Sale, if registered under the Bills of Sale Act, 1878, are protected from the operation of the reputed ownership clause. Chattels comprised in a conditional (or security) bill are subject to the operation of the reputed ownership clause. (*Re Ginger*, 1897.)[601]

The true owner who loses his goods as a result of the operation of the doctrine may prove in the bankruptcy for their value.

4. Invalid Assignments. In certain circumstances, where the bankrupt has made assignments of property within a period which renders such assignments void as against the trustee, the trustee may be able to claim it.

A. Fraudulent Preferences. Under Sect. 44 of the Bankruptcy Act, 1914, such preferential payments, if made within six months of the presentation of the bankruptcy petition, are void against the trustee. This means that the trustee may recover from the preferred creditor any money or property transferred to him even though the preferred creditor was not aware of the preference. However, if the creditor has sold the property to an innocent third party, the purchaser cannot be made to surrender it to the trustee. In these circumstances the preferred creditor may be required to reimburse the estate.

In order to set aside a *fraudulent preference* it is necessary to show—

(*a*) That when he made the payment the debtor was unable to pay his debts as they fell due;

(*b*) That the object was to prefer one creditor over the others;

(*c*) That the debtor making the preference was adjudicated bankrupt on a petition presented within six months of making the preference.

No payment will be deemed to be a fraudulent preference unless it is made with the free will of the bankrupt and with the intention to prefer a creditor. (*Sharp* v. *Jackson*, 1899.)[589]

The act can be a fraudulent preference only if done before the petition is presented. Thus, a payment by the debtor between presentation of the petition and issue of the receiving order cannot be avoided under the Act, and it would seem that a debtor can prefer his creditors during this period. (*Re Seymour*, 1937.)[603]

A payment of money or other preference will fall within Sect. 44 if made with the intention of preferring a person who has guaranteed the insolvent payer's debt (i.e. a surety) as distinct from the creditor himself.

B. FRAUDULENT CONVEYANCES. *Sect.* 172 *of the Law of Property Act,* 1925, provides that every conveyance of property made with the intent to defraud creditors is voidable at any time at the instance of any person thereby prejudiced.

The section does not extend to property acquired for consideration and *bona fide* by a person not having at the time of the conveyance notice of the intention to defraud.

The transfer must be of the whole or substantially the whole of the debtor's property and must be made with intent to defraud creditors, as where the transferee has notice of the intention or the consideration is inadequate.

Where marriage is the consideration it may not be possible to avoid the settlement as against the children of the marriage, but the wife may lose her interest if she is aware of her husband's fraudulent intention. (*Columbine* v. *Penhall*, 1853.)[604]

The existence of fraud where the settlement is voluntary may be proved in several ways, e.g. by the fact that the settlor remains in possession of the property settled; or that he reserves a power of revocation in the settlement to allow him to reclaim the property in the future. The insolvency of the settlor at the time of making the voluntary settlement is also relevant to the question of fraud.

The mere fact that the settlor was solvent at the time of the settlement will not necessarily prevent the settlement being fraudulent as against creditors. (*Re Butterworth*, 1882.)[605]

Under Sect. 1 (*b*) *of the Bankruptcy Act*, 1914, a fraudulent conveyance, gift, delivery or transfer of property is an act of bankruptcy and if made within three months next before presentation of the petition it will be void against the trustee under the doctrine of relation back though the transaction may be protected by Sect. 45.

Every conveyance voidable under Sect. 172 of the Law of Property Act, 1925, is also of necessity an act of Bankruptcy, but not every conveyance, gift, delivery or transfer under Sect. 1 (*b*) of the Bankruptcy Act is voidable under Sect. 172 of the Law of Property Act, 1925.

The distinction is important because conveyances voidable under Sect. 172 of the Law of Property Act, 1925, may be avoided by the trustee even though they were made more than three months before the presentation of the petition. However, conveyances under Sect. 1 (*b*) of the Bankruptcy Act, 1914, which are not also covered by Sect. 172 of the Law of Property Act, 1925, will not be void against the trustee unless made within the three months next before the presentation of the petition. The distinction between the two statutory jurisdications is a matter of the debtor's intention. No conveyance is voidable under Sect. 172 of the Law of Property Act, 1925, unless it is made with dishonest intent to prefer a creditor, whereas a conveyance is an act of bankruptcy under Sect. 1 (*b*) of the Bankruptcy Act, 1914, even where there is no dishonest intention, but a creditor in fact obtains an advantage he would not have obtained under the rules of bankruptcy.

C. Trusts Void under the Bankruptcy Laws. Sect. 42 of the Bankruptcy Act, 1914 provides that—

(*a*) *A voluntary settlement within two years prior to the commencement of the bankruptcy* is void as against the trustee; and *a voluntary settlement made more than two but less than ten years prior to the bankruptcy* is also void unless the persons claiming under the settlement can prove that the settlor was solvent at the date of the disposition and that the whole interest of the settlor passed to the trustees of the settlement.

These provisions do not apply to marriage settlements because these are for consideration, nor do they apply to a *bona fide* purchaser of property for value. Although the section states that such settlements are void, the judicial interpretation is that they are voidable, and it follows that, if the settled property is transferred for value before the bankruptcy, the title of the transferee cannot be disturbed.

(*b*) *A covenant to settle after-acquired property* is void in so far as the covenant has not been executed at the commencement of the bankruptcy, but the disappointed beneficiaries may prove as deferred creditors, i.e. after 100p in the pound has been paid to the other creditors.

Even where property has actually been transferred to the trustees of the settlement under such a covenant, the transfer can be avoided unless the beneficiaries can prove—

(1) that the transfer was made more than two years before the bankruptcy; or

(2) that the transferor was solvent at the time without the aid of the property transferred; or

(3) that the covenant was to settle property expected to come from or on the death of *some specified person*, and that the property was transferred within three months from the date when it came under the settlor's control.

Suppose that by a property settlement Henry agrees to transfer to the trustees of the settlement property which is expected to come to him on the death of his brother George, and any other property received on the death of any of Henry's other relatives. George dies in January, 1971, and Henry receives £2,000 from his estate in August, 1971, which he transfers into the settlement in December, 1971. Henry also receives in February, 1972, £3,000 from the estate of his uncle John which he transfers into the settlement in March, 1972. If we suppose that Henry was adjudicated bankrupt in July, 1972, it will be seen—

(i) Since the property was not transferred more than two years before the bankruptcy there can be no help from Provision 1 above.

(ii) It may be possible to prove that Henry was solvent without the property transferred.

(iii) The property received from George is from a named person but has not been transferred into the settlement within three months of Henry receiving it. The sum received from his uncle John was transferred within three months but does not come from the estate of a specified person. (Provision 3.) Thus both transfers could be avoided by Henry's trustee in bankruptcy.

Under Sect. 4 of the Matrimonial Proceedings and Property Act, 1970, the court may on granting a decree of divorce, nullity, or judicial separation, order certain transfers of property or vary ante-nuptial or post-nuptial settlements. Sect. 23 however, provides that settlements or transfers made in compliance with an order of the court under Sect. 4 are to be regarded as dispositions avoidable by a trustee in bankruptcy under Sect. 42 of the 1914 Act.

D. Assignment of Book Debts. Sect. 43 provides that an assignment of book debts or any class of book debts by a debtor is void as against the trustee as regards any book debts not paid at the commencement of the bankruptcy unless the assignment was by an absolute Bill of Sale, and the said bill was duly registered and the provisions of the Bills of Sale Act, 1878, complied with. *This section does not render void—*

(a) Assignments of the debts of specified debtors if due at the date of assignment;

(b) An assignment of debts growing due under specified contracts;

(c) An assignment of book debts as part of the transfer of a business *bona fide* and for value;

(d) An assignment for the benefit of creditors generally, e.g. as part of a scheme.

Assignment under Sect. 43 includes assignment by way of security or charge.

DISCLAIMER

Some of the property of the debtor may be saddled with considerable burdens, and the retention of it by the trustee would diminish rather than increase the total amount of money available for distribution among the creditors. In such a case the trustee is entitled, within certain limits, to disclaim the property. (Sect. 54.)

Property Capable of being Disclaimed.

(i) Land burdened with onerous covenants, e.g. a lease with covenants to repair and insure.

(ii) Stocks and shares in companies.

(iii) Unprofitable contracts.

(iv) Any other property which is unsaleable.

Effecting Disclaimer. The trustee may disclaim the property in writing signed by him at any time within twelve months after the first appointment of a trustee. If the existence of the property has not come to the notice of the trustee within one month after his appointment, he may disclaim the property at any time within twelve months after he first became aware of its existence.

Effect of Disclaimer. Disclaimer terminates any *personal* liability which might arise out of the fact that the trustee has taken over the debtor's property, e.g. the trustee may become personally liable for carrying out onerous covenants attaching to a property when he takes possession of it. Disclaimer also terminates the liability of the estate.

After disclaimer any party interested may ask the court to make an order *vesting* the property in him. Any person injured by the disclaimer can ask the court to assess the damage suffered and prove for this as a debt in the bankruptcy. The court will award such damages as are just and equitable. (*Re Hooley, Ex parte United Ordnance & Engineering Co.*, 1899.)[606]

Disclaimer of a Lease. The general rule is that a lease cannot be disclaimed without leave of the court. Before granting leave the court may require notices to be served on all persons interested, e.g. where a lease or the landlord's freehold is charged to secure a loan, or where there are sub-leases. The court may also impose terms and make orders as to fixtures, covenants to repair, and any other matters.

Any person claiming under the bankruptcy in respect of the lease, e.g. an underlessee or a mortgagee, may apply to the court for an order vesting the property in him. The order will only be made—

(i) subject to the same liabilities and obligations as the bankrupt had under the lease at the date of filing the bankruptcy petition;

or

(ii) if the court thinks fit, subject to the same liabilities and obligations as if the lease had been *assigned* at the date of the order to the person applying.

If the court makes an order of the former type, the *doctrine of subrogation applies*, and the person taking the property will do so subject to all the debtor's breaches of covenant or other defaults.

An order of the latter kind is often made to vest leases in mortgagees, and enables them to get rid of liability for the debtor's breaches of covenant before the date of assignment. This was not possible before the Bankruptcy Act, 1914.

A trustee may disclaim a lease without leave of court where the bankrupt has not sub-let or charged it and (*a*) the estate is being administered as a small bankruptcy; or (*b*) the gross annual value for tax purposes is less than £20 per annum; or (*c*) the trustee has served the lessor with notice of his intention to disclaim, and the lessor has not within seven days given notice requiring the matter to be brought before the court.

The trustee may also disclaim without leave of court where the bankrupt *has* sub-let or charged the lease, if the trustee has served the parties interested with notice of his intention to disclaim and none of them have written within 14 days requiring the matter to be brought before the court.

In all cases of disclaimer, the trustee cannot disclaim any property (*a*) if notice in writing is served on him by a person interested requiring him to decide whether he will disclaim or not within 28 days; *and* (*b*) if he does not disclaim within that time. In the case of a contract, if the trustee does not disclaim within the time allowed, he is deemed to have adopted it.

A disclaimer of leaseholds must be filed in court, and until so filed it is inoperative.

Rescission of a Contract. The other party to a contract with the bankrupt may ask the court to rescind it on such terms as to payment of damages as the court thinks equitable. The damages are then provable in the bankruptcy.

DISCHARGE OF BANKRUPT

Application. At any time after adjudication the bankrupt may apply to the court for an order of discharge, but not until after the close of the Public Examination. The application is heard in open court, unless it is unopposed and the court directs it to be heard in chambers. The court has before it the Official Receiver's report made for the court, and the creditors may appear and oppose the discharge.

The Order. The court may either—

    (i) Grant an absolute order of discharge; or
    (ii) Suspend discharge for a specified time; or
    (iii) Grant discharge subject to conditions with respect to any earnings or income which may afterwards become due to the bankrupt, or with respect to his after-acquired property; or
    (iv) Refuse discharge.

Where the bankrupt has committed a criminal offence in connection with his bankruptcy, e.g. criminal fraud, *the court's discretion is limited* to one or more of the following—

    (*a*) Refusal of the Order; or
    (*b*) Suspension of discharge until a dividend of not less than 50p in the pound has been paid to the creditors; or
    (*c*) Suspension for such period as the court thinks fit; or
    (*d*) The making of an order requiring the bankrupt, as a condition of his discharge, to consent to judgment being entered against him by the Official Receiver or trustee for any balance of the debts provable but not satisfied at the date of discharge. (Sect. 26 (2).)

It was held in *Re Mills*, [1966] 1 All E.R. 516, that a court may impose more than one condition under Sect. 26 (2) and a discharge, suspended for three years and conditional on the bankrupt consenting to judgment being entered for £400, was upheld.

After the expiration of two years from the date of any order made under Sect. 26 (2), the bankrupt may apply to the court for a modification, but he must show that there is no reasonable possibility of his being in a position to comply with the terms of the order.

The court's discretion is similarly limited when certain "special facts" set out in Sect. 26 (3) exist, e.g. where the debtor has failed to keep usual and proper books during the three years preceding his bankruptcy; or has failed to account for his assets; or has deliberately continued in trade after knowledge of his insolvency, and when he knew he could not pay his debts; or where the cause of his bankruptcy is extravagance in living or gambling or the like.

Procedure. The Order for Discharge is prepared by the debtor or his solicitor and is submitted to the Official Receiver for approval. An appointment is made by the solicitor with the court to settle the order and the solicitor must give reasonable notice to persons likely to be affected by it. The order takes effect from the date when it is signed by the Registrar of the court, and there may be an appeal to the Court of Appeal by the bankrupt or any person interested.

The following debts are not released by an order of discharge—

(i) A debt on a recognisance, a debt for any offence against a public revenue statute, or a debt on a bail bond, unless the Treasury certifies in writing its consent;

(ii) A debt incurred by fraud or by a fraudulent breach of trust, or a debt whereof the bankrupt obtained forbearance by fraud;

(iii) Liability under an affiliation order, unless the court so orders.

All other debts are discharged, but not unliquidated sums which were not provable in the bankruptcy. An order of discharge does not release a partner, co-trustee, co-debtor or surety.

Small Bankruptcies. The court may make an order for the summary administration of the debtor's estate where the Official Receiver has reported or where the court is satisfied by affidavit or otherwise that the property of the debtor is not likely to exceed £300. (Sect. 129.) The provisions of the Act apply subject to certain modifications prescribed by Rule 298 of the Bankruptcy Rules. This rule is designed to save expenses and simplify procedure. For example, the Official Receiver is always the trustee and there is no committee of inspection, the Department of Trade and Industry giving sanction for acts normally requiring that of the committee.

The creditors may by a special resolution remove the Official Receiver and put in another trustee. The bankruptcy then proceeds as if no order for summary administration had been made.

Subsequent Bankruptcies. Sometimes an undischarged bankrupt becomes bankrupt again at the petition of new creditors before discharge. Sect. 3 of the Bankruptcy (Amendment) Act, 1926, states that, when a second receiving order is made, the trustee in the first bankruptcy is deemed a creditor for the unsatisfied balance of debts provable in the first bankruptcy, and the second bankruptcy proceeds.

Any property acquired by the bankrupt since he was last adjudged a bankrupt, and which has not been distributed among creditors at the date of the new petition, vests in the trustee in the new bankruptcy.

CHAPTER X

INSURANCE

THE first form of insurance concerned marine risks, i.e. the insurance of ships and their cargoes, but other forms of insurance have since developed, notably at first fire insurance and life assurance. More recently the range of insurance has been enormously extended and now includes motor vehicle insurance, personal accident insurance, fidelity insurance and many other types; indeed there is hardly any limit to the scope of insurance contracts.

The law of marine insurance was codified in the Marine Insurance Act, 1906, and unless otherwise stipulated all section references in this chapter refer to this Act. However, the Act does not cover all the rules relating to marine insurance, and reference has still to be made to earlier cases as well as, of course, to more recent ones for interpretation and expansion. With regard to life and fire insurance and types of insurance more recently developed, the law must be sought in the same sources, with due allowance for the circumstances which are peculiar to marine insurance. However, it should be noted that the Marine Insurance Act, 1906, does not apply to classes of insurance other than marine although many of the rules are similar, having been applied by analogy. Moreover, although life and fire insurance have a long history, most early policies stipulated for arbitration in the settlement of disputes and consequently legal precedent is comparatively scarce.

The Nature of Insurance. A contract of insurance is one in which one party (called the insurer) agrees in consideration of a single or periodical payment (called the premium) to accept a risk to which the assured is subject, and to compensate or indemnify the assured for or against any loss which may occur if the risk insured against happens.

There is a practical difference between the terms *insurance* and *assurance*, although there is an increasing tendency to treat them as synonymous.

Insurance implies that the contract is designed to indemnify the insured against unforeseeable loss or damage which may or may not occur, e.g. damage to property by fire. A contract of *assurance* is one in which the assured or his representatives are to receive a sum of money on the occurrence of an event which is bound to happen at some time, although the time of happening is uncertain, e.g. the death of the assured.

It is a requirement in a contract of insurance that the insured has an *insurable interest*, which means that the happening against which he insures must be one adverse to him, and likely to cause him loss or to saddle him with a liabilty.

THE CONTRACT OF INSURANCE

A contract of insurance comes into being when one party makes an offer and the other party makes a valid acceptance. Sometimes, as where baggage is insured, it is the insurer who makes the offer, and the insured, by signing a standardised form or even by merely paying a premium, acquires the rights of insurance set out in the form. In most cases, however, the would-be insured fills in a proposal form inviting the insurer to cover him for certain risks, and when the insurer accepts this proposal, the contract of insurance comes into being. Although acceptance may have taken place earlier, it is normally conclusive once a policy has been issued in accordance with the proposal.

While *writing is essential in the case of marine insurance* (Sect. 22 Marine Insurance Act, 1906) *and Fidelity Guarantees* (Statute of Frauds, 1677), there is no legal necessity in other cases, and if the insurer accepted the proposal and a premium without qualification, he would probably be held bound after a reasonable time had elapsed. However, in view of the practical difficulties which would arise in ascertaining the precise terms of the contract if it was wholly oral, most insurance contracts are evidenced in writing.

A marine policy must be signed by or on behalf of the insurer but, in the case of a corporation, the corporate seal is sufficient but not essential. Individual underwriters at Lloyd's used to sign their names at the foot of the policy, writing opposite their names the sum insured by each. These underwriters do not now sign policies; instead, they are signed on behalf of all the underwriters concerned by Lloyd's Policy Signing Office. (See p. 372.) Unless the contrary is expressed, each underwriter makes a distinct contract with the insured for the amount opposite his name. (Sect. 24 (2).) The liability of the underwriters is several and not joint, and the insured has a right of action against each one separately and not against them all jointly.

The Proposal. In non-marine insurance a standard form, called a proposal form, is usually handed by the insurer to the proposed insured and contains details of the risk the insured wishes to be covered. It asks him to answer a number of questions on the basis of which the insurer will decide whether to accept the risk and complete the contract.

When an insurer issues a blank proposal form he is not making an offer of insurance even if premium rates are quoted on the form. The blank proposal form is an invitation to treat. If, however, an insurer, on receipt of a completed proposal form, indicates that he will accept the insurance on the basis of, say, an increased premium, this would operate as an offer which could be accepted by the proposer.

The proposal asks for the name, address and occupation of the insured, and where a man has several occupations it might be relevant to declare them all. The form then goes on to describe the scope of the risk to be covered and to elicit the former experience of the proposer in connection with such a risk. For instance, if it is insurance against fire, has he had previous fires, or if it is against motor accidents, has he had previous accidents? Clearly this information is of value to the insurer in estimating the degree of risk, and may in fact induce him to charge a higher premium. It is also quite common to ask the insured whether he has previously been refused insurance by other insurers, or whether they have refused to renew insurances formerly held.

The duty of the proposer to make *full disclosure of all material facts* means that he must scrutinise the proposal form with great care. Where the specific questions to be answered appear to be exhaustive, the matter is comparatively simple, but in other cases the proposer may be in doubt as to what additional information he ought to supply, and the line between what is material and what is immaterial is not always easy to draw. He should, therefore, in his own interests, amplify the information specifically requested if he feels that there are other material facts which he ought to disclose. (*London Assurance* v. *Mansel*, 1879.)[607] Neglect to do this may mean that, if the insurer accepts the proposal and the loss actually occurs, the insured may find that the insurer can avoid the contract and have no liability beyond the return of the premiums paid. (*Roselodge Ltd.* v. *Castle*, 1966.)[608]

Proposal forms seldom if ever ask for disclosures relating to the integrity or morality of the insured, and yet these matters can affect the risk and lead to avoidance of the insurance by the insurer. For example, a history of heavy drinking or drug dependence is likely to be material to most risks and yet would seldom be disclosed voluntarily. It would seem more satisfactory, therefore, to ask a question dealing broadly with integrity in order to minimise the risk that a particular policy which the insured is relying on is not in fact voidable.

Most proposals require the proposer to sign a declaration in which he warrants that the statements he has made are true, and agrees that they be incorporated into the contract. (*Dawsons Ltd.* v. *Bonnin*, 1922.)[609] Thus the proposal and the policy of insurance issued by the insurer must be read together.

It is quite common for the insurance to be effected by an *employee* of the insurer, who often fills in, or assists in filling in, the proposal form. In doing this the agent is not regarded as the agent of the insurer but of the insured, (*Anglo-African Merchants Ltd.* v. *Bayley*, 1969)[445] and when the latter signs the form, he should read it carefully, since he will be bound by the answers as if he had filled them in himself. (*Newsholme Brothers* v. *Road Transport and General Insurance Co.*, 1929,[610] and *O'Connor* v. *Kirby*, 1971.[610a] but see *Stone etc.* (1972). ([695] This is not so in the case of industrial assurance (life policies for small amounts), where the agent has authority to fill in the form on behalf of his employers.

Cover Notes. It is not unusual for some time to elapse between the completion of the proposal form and the acceptance of the contract by the insurer and the issue of a policy. In these circumstances it is common for the agent to hand over to the person who has made the proposal a *cover note* which stipulates a number of days, e.g. 14, during which the insurers will accept the risk of the insurance. This cover note gives the assured the benefit of cover while the insurers are deciding whether to accept the proposal or not, and expires at the end of the number of days specified, although it may be terminated earlier by the insurers giving notice to the assured that they do not propose to issue a policy. In the case of insurances effected at Lloyd's, a *slip* is issued and not a cover note, the difference being that a slip, once initialled, constitutes an acceptance of the proposal and is binding on the insurers.

Effecting Marine Insurance. Much marine and other insurance is effected through Lloyd's. Lloyd's began in the seventeenth century when marine insurers gathered together along with shipowners and merchants in a coffee house for the convenient transacting of insurance business. In 1871 Lloyd's was incorporated by Act of Parliament and Lloyd's underwriters now handle both marine and non-marine risks and are subject to stringent rules and have to make deposits by way of security. While a large number of marine risks are handled by Lloyd's underwriters, marine insurance is also carried out by other associations and corporations.

In marine insurance, an insurance broker acts as the agent of the insured, and his business is to take instructions from the insured as to the risk to be insured against, and to effect a policy with underwriters on the best possible terms. He pays the premium to the underwriters and receives from them monies due under the policy in the event of loss.

In order to place an insurance risk at Lloyd's the broker prepares a *slip* which is literally a slip of paper containing brief details of the risk to be placed. He then takes the slip round to underwriters. An underwriter willing to accept the risk initials the *slip* for the amount he is willing to cover. When the total sum assured has been covered, the broker prepares a policy and submits it to Lloyd's Policy Signing Office for checking and signing. The policy is also impressed with the formal seal.

The insurance slip is, in practice, a complete contract of insurance, and Sect. 21 of the Marine Insurance Act, 1906, states that a contract of marine insurance is deemed to be concluded when the proposal of the assured is accepted by the insurer, whether the policy be then issued or not; and for the purpose of showing when the proposal was accepted, reference may be made to the slip or covering note or other customary memorandum of the contract.

Unless otherwise agreed, where a marine policy is effected on behalf of the insured by a broker, the broker is directly responsible to the underwriter for the premium and the underwriter is directly responsible to the insured for the amount which may be payable in respect of losses, or in respect of returnable premium. (Sect. 53 (1).)

Uberrimae Fidei. We have already seen that the insured must disclose all material facts and a contract of insurance is *uberrimae fidei*, i.e. a contract based on the utmost good faith. Thus either party may avoid a contract of insurance if he can establish that the other party failed to disclose a material fact or made a misrepresentation, even if innocent, of such a fact. Although the duty lies heaviest on the insured, there is nevertheless a similar duty on the insurer. Thus, if an insurer in a prospectus, misrepresents the effects of an insurance, the insured can obtain rectification of his policy, and claim on the basis of the actual representations.

The insured must disclose every material circumstance which is known to him, and he is deemed to know every circumstance which, in the ordinary course of business, ought to be known to him. (Sect. 18 (1).) A circumstance is material which would influence the judgment of a prudent insurer in fixing the premium, or determining whether he will take the risk. (Sect. 18 (2).) (*Mutual Life Insurance Company of New York v. Ontario Metal Products Co. Ltd.*, 1925.)[611] Where a proposer answers specific questions, his answers will be taken to be representations. If the questions indicate a limited field of inquiry, he may or may not have to go outside this with his disclosures according to the form of the wording. (*London Assurance v. Mansel*, 1879.)[607] However, in the absence of inquiry, the insured need not disclose any circumstance—

(*a*) which diminishes the risk, e.g. the existence of a sprinkler system in premises proposed for fire insurance;

(*b*) which is known or presumed to be known to the insurer, e.g. the existence of a state of war;

(*c*) regarding matters of law, e.g. the contents of the Factories Act, which are particularly relevant to employer's liability insurance;

(*d*) which it is superfluous to disclose because it is already covered by an express or implied warranty, (Sect. 18 (3)) e.g. a particular policy for burglary insurance may be subject to a warranty that a certain form of lock be fitted. It is thus superfluous to disclose whether they are or are not fitted since the policy operates only if they are;

(*e*) which the insurer's representative fails to notice on a survey, e.g. hazardous features in premises proposed for fire insurance, provided there is no concealment by the proposer. (*Re Universal Non-Tariff Fire Insurance Co., Forbes & Co.'s Claim*, 1875.)[612]

It is a question of fact whether a circumstance which is not disclosed is material or not. (*Ionides v. Pender*, 1874;[613] *Roselodge Ltd. v. Castle*, 1966.)[608]

The duty of disclosure continues throughout the negotiations, and where circumstances alter, previous statements should be corrected. (*Looker v. Law Union and Rock Insurance Co. Ltd.*, 1928.)[614] Thus, if between submitting a proposal for life assurance and receiving the actual acceptance the insured learns that he has a serious disease, he must disclose this fact to the insurer, and even the fact that the insurer has compelled him to undergo a medical examination does not relieve him of this duty. Nevertheless the duty of disclosure ceases when the contract is completed.

If a statement is substantially true but is incorrect in minor details which, if they had been correct, would not have affected the insurer, then the inaccuracy does not affect the contract. (*Dawson's Ltd.* v. *Bonnin*, 1922.)[609] Nor can the insurer take advantage of a mis-statement if he is really aware of the true facts of the case. (*Re Universal Non-Tariff Fire Insurance Co., Forbes & Co.'s Claim*, 1875.)[612]

Even if a mis-statement is honest, it may still invalidate the contract. Thus, in contracting for life assurance, proposers have to make statements concerning their state of health and, while they are here expressing their opinions, which is all they can express, they may find that, if the proposal is made the basis of the assurance by a *basis clause*, they will be held to have warranted the truth of the statements made. If the statements turn out to be false, the insurer can avoid the contract without having to prove that the facts were or were not material. (*Dawson's Ltd.* v. *Bonnin*, 1922.)[609] In special cases the court may prevent the operation of a warranty by regarding a statement as a mere description of the risk. (*Farr* v. *Motor Traders' Mutual Insurance Society*, 1920.)[615]

The duties of disclosure cannot be escaped by appointing an agent, and the insured is bound to disclose to his agent every material circumstance unless it has come to his knowledge too late to communicate it. The agent must disclose to the insurer every material circumstance which is known to himself, and he is deemed to know every circumstance which, in the ordinary course of business, ought to be known by, or to have been communicated to, him. (Sect. 19.)

However, there are certain cases, e.g. in fire insurance, where an agent of the company makes inspection of premises on behalf of his employers, and any such knowledge he ought to have acquired is imputed to the insurer, and non-disclosure of such facts by the insured would not invalidate the policy. (*Re Universal Non-Tariff Fire Insurance Co., Forbes & Co's. Claim*, 1875.)[612] In addition to his duty of full disclosure the insured has a duty to see that material representations made while the contract is being negotiated are true. The insurer may avoid the contract if any material representation is untrue. (Sect. 20.)

The Policy. Normally, before the expiry of the cover note, the insurer delivers to the insured a contractual document called the policy, which contains the undertaking of the insurer to pay to the policy holder the sum assured on the happening of the specified event. The policy is not the contract but merely written evidence of it. Nevertheless a court will regard it as containing the expressed intentions of the parties in the absence of proof to the contrary. It contains all the terms necessary for the contract, including the name, address and occupation of the insured, the subject matter of the insurance and the scope of the risk, the period of the insurance, the premium, and the amount for which the risk is insured. The policy contains the general conditions governing the insurance, commonly endorsed on the back, and, where a policy continues from year to year, variations may be incorporated by means of endorsement slips which are stuck on the back of the policy.

The general conditions include such matters as the giving of notice of an event leading to a claim, the information which must be given in support of a claim, and many others. Most policies also contain a clause which incorporates the relevant parts of the proposal, and makes the truth of its contents a condition precedent to the liability of the insurer to pay claims under the policy.

TYPES OF POLICY

Life Assurance. The characteristics of life assurance are that the person insured pays specified premiums at regular intervals and the amount for which he is covered is payable on his death. There may, however, be modifications of such insurance, the commonest being that of endowment insurance. In this case the insured pays regular premiums for a specified term of years, and an agreed sum is payable either at the end of the period to the insured himself, or on his earlier death to his personal representatives. Another widespread form of life assurance which needs only a mention is that of Industrial Assurance, where the premiums are payable at intervals of less than two months and are collected by agents of the insurance company from the insured. While there are a large number of these policies, a discussion of them lies outside the scope of a book on mercantile law.

Personal Accident Insurance. An insured sometimes insures himself against the possibility of accidental injury which may result in disablement or death, and the loss of income occasioned thereby. Such an insurance may be a continuing contract like life assurance, or may be for a year or for a shorter period, and it is not a contract of indemnity since the loss suffered may not be capable of accurate estimation.

Fire Insurance. This is a very common form of insurance and is intended to indemnify the insured against loss of property by fire, including lightning and explosion. In the ordinary way it does not matter what caused the fire, and a claim can be made even where the fire is due to the negligence of the insured or the wilful act of a third party. (*Harris* v. *Poland*, 1941.)[616] But the insured is not entitled to recover for loss which is due to his *wilful misconduct*, and he cannot recover if he intentionally sets fire to his own property. In order to constitute a loss by fire there must be actual ignition. Loss by heating or fermentation is not enough.

Most policies contain excepted perils and these include fires caused by riot, civil commotion and war. The connection between an explosion and a fire is of interest, since an explosion may cause damage by blast or by fire. Where the property is consumed by fire then a claim can clearly be made, but where the damage is due to the blast of the explosion only, there will be no claim under a fire policy unless the explosion was actually caused by a fire and not by some other means. Actually, explosions are usually dealt with by specific clauses in the policy, and the wording of these clauses covers the situation. In general, the policy provides that, where there is an explosion, any damage due to fire is covered and any damage due to blast or concussion is excluded.

Liability Insurance. Every man runs the risk of becoming liable to pay damages to some other person as a result of committing a tort or in some other way. Cover for such liability is frequently part of other types of insurance, e.g. the insurance of houses, or of motor vehicles, but the scope of third party liability is much wider and can be separately insured against. *The object of such an insurance is to be indemnified against legal liabilities,* and the legal liability must come within the categories of the policy.

A policy covering liability for negligence is valid but an insured person cannot recover for an intentional criminal act, nor presumably for a tort intentionally committed such as defamation. However, acts of criminal negligence, such as reckless driving, or the committing of statutory offences, such as speeding, do not prevent the insured recovering under a liability insurance.

Employers must insure themselves against claims which may be made upon them by their workmen for personal injury. (Employers' Liability (Compulsory Insurance) Act, 1969.) Clearly in such cases the risk run by insurers depends on such factors as the number of persons employed or, in the case of equipment, the extent and range of its use. It is, therefore, customary to charge at the outset of the insurance a provisional premium which is adjusted at the end of the year when the degree of risk borne can be calculated from the figures of the number of persons employed or the amount of wages paid or the extent to which equipment was used. Insurers usually reserve to themselves the power to take over and defend any proceedings which may be taken against the assured.

The extent of the indemnity may be limited in various ways. The policy may provide for a full indemnity, or it may fix a maximum indemnity which will be exhausted when a sufficient number of smaller claims reach such an aggregate. A policy may provide for a maximum sum in respect of any one incident, or it may provide that the insured bears the first proportion of each claim up to a specified amount so that he only makes claims of a substantial character. The policy normally provides for an indemnity to the insured for costs of any proceedings against him in connection with any claims made under the policy.

The insurer is not liable to pay unless the insured is legally liable in respect of the damage and in this connection the Law Reform (Husband & Wife) Act, 1962, enables a husband and wife to sue each other in tort. Thus, if a husband negligently injures his wife he will be legally liable and could claim an indemnity under a liability policy.

Motor Vehicle Insurance. Although a motorist will often take out a comprehensive policy covering a variety of risks, the Road Traffic Act, 1972, Sect. 143, places a legal duty on the motorist to insure in respect of injury to third parties. Failure to take out this compulsory insurance is a criminal offence and both owner and driver, where these are different persons, are liable to prosecution. A voidable policy does not operate as an infringement of the Act, though compulsory insurance is still required even when the car is immobilised. (*Elliott* v. *Grey*, 1959.)[617] This section also imposes a statutory duty for the purposes of a civil action in negligence and this is useful to a plaintiff in circumstances where it would be difficult to establish a duty in the defendant on general principles. (*Monk* v. *Warbey*, 1904.)[618]

In order to comply with the provisions of the Act the assured must receive a *certificate of insurance* from the insurer, or, if the vehicle is driven under his own control, he must have deposited the sum of £15,000 with the Accountant-General of the Supreme Court, in which case the Act will not apply. Some very large organisations with a large fleet of vehicles do take advantage of this provision.

It is possible to insure a motor vehicle to cover both driving by the owner and by other persons who may from time to time use the vehicle, and Sect. 148 (4) of the Road Traffic Act, 1972, provides that the insurers must indemnify any person driving the vehicle with the owner's consent, thus providing a *statutory exception to the doctrine of privity of contract*.

It is interesting to note that the House of Lords held, in *Kelly* v. *Cornhill Insurance Co.*, [1964] 1 All E.R. 321, that permission given by the insured before his death can continue afterwards thus rendering the policy effective even though the insured is dead. The subsection applies to all risks covered by the policy and is not restricted to cases of compulsory insurance. (*Digby* v. *General Accident Fire and Life Assurance Corporation*, 1943.)[619]

In the case of compulsory insurance, Sect. 149 of the Road Traffic Act, 1972, requires the insurer to pay a third party who has obtained judgment against the insured. However, the judgment must be in respect of a compulsory risk; the liability must be covered by the policy, so that the section would not apply if, when the accident happened, the car was being used for business purposes when it was insured for private purposes only; a certificate of insurance must have been issued to the insured; notice of the action in which the judgment was obtained must have been given to the insurer not later than seven days after it began. The insurer need not meet the judgment if—

(*a*) an appeal is pending; or
(*b*) the policy was cancelled before the accident, though the certificate of insurance must have been surrendered, or the insured

must have made a statutory declaration that it was lost or destroyed, or the insurer must commence proceedings to recover it not later than fourteen days after cancelling; or

(c) the insurer obtains a declaration from the court that the policy is void for non-disclosure or misrepresentation, provided that the action for the declaration was commenced within three months from the commencement of the proceedings in which the third party obtained his judgment.

Sect. 149 will not assist a third party whose injury or damage is non-compulsory though if the insured is bankrupt or has compounded with his creditors or, in the case of a company, goes into liquidation the Third Party (Rights against Insurers) Act, 1930, may apply. Policies of motor insurance may, in addition to covering a specified vehicle, extend cover to the insured while driving some other vehicle not owned by him. However, the policy becomes ineffective if the insured ceases to have an interest in the specified vehicle. This principle applies to comprehensive policies (*Tattersall* v *Drysdale*, 1935,[620] and to third party policies. (*Boss* v. *Kingston*, 1963.)[621] The seller of a vehicle cannot transfer the policy of insurance to the buyer unless the insurer consents.

The policy must cover the persons insured against liability as a result of the death of, or bodily injury to, any person arising out of the vehicle's use on the road. *The policy need not cover* (1) liability to an employee of the person insured in respect of death or bodily injury arising out of and in the course of employment; (2) liability arising under a contract.

The Road Traffic Act, 1972, which came into force on 1st July, 1972, has the effect of requiring users of motor vehicles to be covered against any liability which they might incur in respect of the death or personal injuries to their passengers arising out of the use of their motor vehicles on the roads. The Act also renders ineffective "own risk" agreements under which a passenger agrees to accept the risk of injury without compensation from the owner of the vehicle.

A person injured is not prejudiced in his claim by restrictive conditions in the policy, and if a judgment is obtained against the assured, the insurers must pay, although they may have a claim on the assured for violating the conditions. Nor shall third parties be prejudiced by the fact that the assured does some act, or fails to do some act, required by the policy after the accident, e.g. if the assured fails to give proper notice of the accident within the time specified by the policy.

Where, however, a policy covering compulsory risks provides that it shall only apply when the vehicle is being used "for social, domestic and pleasure purposes", then the insurers are under no liability if the insured incurs liability for the death or injury of a third party while driving the vehicle for business purposes. The third party is also prejudiced by such a restriction and cannot recover.

Most motorists take out insurance policies of a much more comprehensive character than the law requires, of which the following are examples—

(1) Third Party Liability Policies, covering not only death or bodily injury but also damage to third parties' property.

(2) Third Party Cover with the addition of cover for losses by fire and theft.

(3) Comprehensive Cover, including third party claims and damage to the vehicle however caused.

There are many modifications to these policies, e.g. where a policy applies to one named driver only, where the assured agrees to bear the first £x of any claim, where the policy provides for some personal accident insurance, or for compensation for loss of use if the vehicle is out of action.

A motor insurance policy will almost invariably specify the user in respect of which the insurer takes risk, e.g. a vehicle may only be covered for "social, domestic and pleasure purposes." (*D. H. R. Moody (Chemists)* v. *Iron Trades Mutual Insurance Co.*, 1970.)[622] Policies often exclude liability where the vehicle is used for hiring or reward and where the vehicle is in an unroadworthy state.

Marine Insurance. The Marine Insurance Act, 1906, defines a contract of marine insurance as one whereby the insurer undertakes to indemnify the insured, in the manner and to the extent agreed, against marine losses, that is to say losses incidental to a marine adventure. (Sect. 1.) Every lawful marine adventure may be the subject of a contract of marine insurance, and a marine policy may cover the loss of ship or goods, loss of freight, passage money, commission, profit, or other pecuniary benefit, or liabilities to third parties by reason of maritime perils. (Sect. 3.) It may also be its express terms, or by usage of trade, be extended to protect the insured against losses on inland waters, or a land risk incidental to a sea voyage. (Sect. 2.)

Marine policies may be of many kinds—

(1) *For a voyage*, i.e. where the contract is to insure the subject-matter "at and from" or "from" one place to another or others.

(2) *For time*, i.e. where the contract is to insure the subject-matter for a definite period of time, usually not exceeding twelve months.

(3) *For a voyage and for time.* In this case the loss is covered only on a particular voyage and the loss must also occur within the time specified.

(4) *A floating policy.* This describes the insurance in general terms, but leaves the name of the ship or ships and other particulars to be specified later.

(5) *A valued policy.* This specifies the agreed value of the subject-matter, and the value so fixed is, as between the insurer and insured conclusive of the value of the subject-matter insured, though not in the case of constructive total loss. (Sect. 27.)

(6) *An unvalued or open policy.* This does not specify the value of the subject-matter but, subject to the limit of the sum insured, leaves it to be subsequently determined.

There are many forms of marine policy but the Lloyd's policy is the basis of most of them, and the Lloyd's policy is recognised by, and forms a schedule to, the Marine Insurance Act, 1906.

The name of the ship in which the insured voyage is to be performed *is usually specified in the policy* but, since this is only needed for identification, an error in the name is not material if it can be shown that the underwriter intended to insure the ship on which the loss in fact occurred. Often the insured does not know the ship on which the insured goods will travel and so he effects a floating policy, leaving the name of the ship or ships and other particulars to be defined by subsequent declaration. (Sect. 29 (1).) The ship named in the policy must not, after the commencement of the risk, be changed without the consent of the underwriters, or in case of necessity.

The subject-matter insured must be designated in a marine policy with reasonable certainty, though the nature and extent of the interest of the assured in the subject-matter need not be specified in the policy. (Sect. 26.) Where the policy designates the subject-matter in general terms, it is construed to apply to the interest intended by the insured to be covered, and regard must be had to any usage regulating the designation of the subject-matter insured. (Sect. 26.)

The term "ship" includes the hull, materials and outfit, stores and provisions for the officers and crew, and, in the case of vessels engaged in a special trade, the ordinary fittings requisite for the trade, and also, in the case of a steamship, the machinery, boiler, and coals and engine stores, if owned by the insured. (Marine Insurance Act, 1906, Schedule 1, Rule 15.)

The term "goods" means goods in the nature of merchandise, and does not include personal effects, or provisions and stores for use on board. In the absence of any usage to the contrary, deck cargo and living animals must be insured specifically, and not under the general denomination of goods. (Schedule 1, Rule 17.) In addition, freight, expected profits and commissions to be made, must be specifically insured.

DURATION OF POLICY

Non-Marine Insurance. The policy should stipulate the period for which the insurance is to continue and, although a common term is twelve months, any period may be fixed by mutual agreement. In some cases, e.g. fire insurance, the duration of the policy is specified to the precise day and hour, but where no such specification occurs, the policy runs from the first moment of the day next after issue to the last moment of the day specified for the termination of the policy. However, since an insurance policy is not effective until it is issued, the person insured will have no claim for losses occurring between the proposal and the issue of the policy unless the policy so provides, as it may do if it replaces a cover note previously issued. In other cases it is stipulated that the policy does not operate until the premium has been paid.

Termination of Policy. A policy may expire with the *effluxion of time*. It may also come to an end when the risk which is covered occurs and the insurer pays out an indemnity on the basis of total loss. Thus, where a house is insured for a period of twelve months and it is totally destroyed after a month, the insurance company ends its liability on payment of the value of the loss. Nevertheless, if there are in the same house a number of fires during the course of one year's insurance and not one of them causes total loss, the insurer is liable successively for each fire as it occurs, but only if in the aggregate the losses do not exceed the sum insured.

A policy may also be ended *by either the insured or the insurer under the provisions contained in it*. For instance, many life insurance policies provide for the insured to surrender his rights under the policy at any time instead of paying renewal premiums and, on such surrender, he usually receives a sum calculated in relation to the premiums paid and the amount of cover he has enjoyed. Similarly policies often stipulate the terms upon which the insurer may bring them to an end.

(i) POLICIES OF A CONTINUING CHARACTER. It is clear that certain types of insurance, such as life assurance, are of a continuing character, and it is expected that the insurance will remain valid until the death of the insured. It would be inequitable for the insurers to continue to take premiums while a man was young and, as he grew older, refuse to renew the insurance when the risk of death became greater. Such contracts, therefore, are treated as *continuing contracts for the life of the insured*, and the insurers are bound to accept the periodic premiums if they are offered on the due date, or within the period of grace allowed for each successive payment. (*Stuart* v. *Freeman*, 1903.)[623] Only if the premium is not paid when due may the insurers terminate the policy.

(ii) POLICIES NOT OF A CONTINUING CHARACTER. Other forms of insurance, e.g. fire insurance, are not of a continuing character and the policy is *renewable with the consent of the parties* at the expiration of each specific period. The renewal depends on mutual consent but, since it is expected that the policy may be renewed time after time, provision is often made for renewal. In practice, the insurers normally send out a renewal notice specifying the renewal premium, and a period of grace is allowed for payment. The payment of the premium so requested renews the insurance for a further period.

(iii) RENEWAL. It should be noted that *each renewal is a fresh contract*. In the case of indemnity insurance the same duty of disclosure attaches on renewal as on making the original proposal, so that any changes of circumstances which would affect the insurers must be brought to their notice. This is not the case, however, with life assurance because the insurance policy, being continuous, is governed by the proposal originally made. It is obvious that the risk to the insurers will increase as the insured grows older, but this must have been within the contemplation of the parties when the contract was originally made.

(iv) PERIOD OF GRACE. It is common in insurance policies to make provision for a period of grace during which a renewal premium may be paid, and this is often thirty days in the case of life assurance, and fifteen days in other forms. This period is in the nature of an option to renew on payment of a specific premium, and the insured can accept the offer by making such a payment. If the insured avails himself of the days of grace and a loss occurs after the renewal date but before the expiration of the period of grace, the question arises as to whether the insurers must indemnify him for the loss so suffered. This situation will normally be covered by the terms of the policy which lay down the conditions under which grace for payment is allowed. However, in the case of life assurance, where the premium is paid during the period of grace it is regarded as having been paid on the due date and, if a person so insured dies after the due date of the premium but before the expiry of the days of grace, his representatives can pay the premium and claim the benefit of the policy.

Marine Insurance. The duration of marine insurance varies with the type of policy.

1. TIME POLICIES. While the two limits set out in a time policy determine the insured period, a time policy may nevertheless be effected retrospectively by inserting the clause "lost or not lost." Thus a policy effected on 10th April to commence on 5th April will cover any losses on or after the latter date. Unless otherwise provided, a time policy covers the ship on any voyage during the insured period, although voyages in certain geographical areas may be excluded.

2. MIXED POLICIES. A policy may specify not only the time for which the risk is insured but also the voyage in contemplation (Sect. 25), e.g. the insurance may be "At and from London to New York for three months," or "From 1st January, 1972 to 1st April, 1972, at and from London to New York." This is a *mixed policy* and the underwriter is only liable for a loss which occurs within the insured period and then only if (i) the ship originally sailed on the voyage described; and (ii) it was, at the time of the loss, sailing on the prescribed course.

Where goods or other moveables are insured "from the loading thereof," the risk does not attach until they are actually on board, and the insurer is not liable for them while in transit from shore to ship, unless the insurer's liability is expressly extended by a clause in the policy.

(a) *Duration of Risk on Ship.* Where the insurance is "from" a particular place, the risk commences when the ship begins the voyage insured. When a ship is insured "at and from" a particular place, and she is at that place in good safety when the contract is concluded, the risk attaches immediately. If she is not there, the risk attaches as soon as she arrives there in good safety and, unless the policy otherwise provides, it is immaterial that she is covered by another policy for a specified time after arrival. A ship may be in good safety, even though damaged, if she can lie in port in reasonable safety until properly repaired and equipped for her voyage. In the case of a *voyage* policy *at and from* a particular place, it is not necessary that the ship should be at that place when the contract is concluded, but there is an implied condition that the adventure must be commenced within a reasonable time, and that if the adventure be not so commenced, the insurer may avoid the contract. (Sect. 42 (1).) The insurance continues "until she hath moored at Anchor Twenty-four Hours in good Safety," and this implies that she is in political safety, not in quarantine, and in such a state of physical safety that her cargo can be unloaded.

(*b*) *Duration of Risk on Freight.* Where chartered freight is insured "at and from" a particular place, and the ship is at that place in good safety when the contract is concluded, the risk attaches immediately. If she is not there when the contract is concluded, the risk attaches as soon as she does arrive there "in good safety." In the case of a voyage policy the insurance continues until the goods are discharged. In the case of a time policy, the rules are the same as for ships.

3. VOYAGE POLICIES. The place at which the voyage is to commence and the place at which it is to end are called respectively the *terminus a quo* and the *terminus ad quem*. These places sufficiently define the voyage, because the ship, in the absence of a contrary provision, is bound to follow the normal and customary course or, if there is more than one such course, one of them, and she must not trade at intermediate ports. A departure from the proper course of the insured voyage may constitute either a "change of voyage" or a "deviation," and these must be distinguished.

(*a*) *Change of Voyage.* Where, after the commencement of the risk, the destination of the ship is voluntarily changed from the destination contemplated by the policy, there is said to be a change of voyage. Unless the policy otherwise provides, where there is a change of voyage, *the insurer is discharged from liability*, as from the time of the change, that is to say, *as from the time when the determination to change it is manifested;* and it is immaterial that the ship may not in fact have left the course of the voyage contemplated by the policy when the loss occurs. (Sect. 45.) In this case *it is the intention to change which is important.*

(*b*) *Deviation.* There is a deviation from the voyage contemplated by the policy—(*a*) where the course of the voyage is specifically designated by the policy, and that course is departed from; or (*b*) where the course of the voyage is not specifically designated, but the usual and customary course is departed from. *The intention to deviate is immaterial; there must be deviation in fact to discharge the insurer from liability under the contract.* (*James Morrison and Co. Ltd.* v. *Shaw, Savill and Albion Co. Ltd.,* 1916.)[624] Where the ship, without lawful excuse, deviates from the voyage contemplated by the policy, the insurer is discharged from liability as from the time of deviation, and it is immaterial that the ship may have regained her route before any loss occurs. (Sect. 46.)

A deviation arises when there is an *actual* departure from the course of the insured voyage, and, whether the deviation increases the risk or not, the insurers are free from liability for all losses thereafter, while retaining their liability for earlier losses.

It is now common for underwriters to agree to cover the insured in case of deviation or change of voyage at an extra premium to be subsequently determined. Where an insurance is effected in the terms that an additional premium is to be arranged in a given event, and that event happens, but no arrangement is made, then a reasonable additional premium is payable. (Sect. 31 (2).)

(*c*) *Excuses for Deviation and Delay.* Deviation and delay in prosecuting the voyage contemplated in the policy is excused—

(i) Where authorised by any special term in the policy; or

(ii) Where caused by circumstances beyond the control of the master and his employer; or

(iii) Where reasonably necessary in order to comply with an express or implied warranty; or

(iv) Where reasonably necessary for the safety of the ship or subject-matter insured; or

(v) For the purpose of saving human life, or aiding a ship in distress where human life may be in danger, but not merely to save property, *Scaramanga* v. *Stamp* (1880), 5 C.P.D. 295; or

(vi) Where reasonably necessary for the purpose of obtaining medical or surgical aid for any person on board the ship; or

(vii) Where caused by the barratrous conduct of the master or crew, if barratry be one of the perils insured against. (See p. 387.)

Where a policy specifies several ports of discharge, the vessel must, if she goes to more than one, proceed in the order designated by the policy otherwise there will be a deviation. (Sect. 47.)

When the cause excusing the deviation or delay ceases to operate, the ship must resume her course, and prosecute her voyage with reasonable despatch. (Sect. 49.)

THE RISK

The policy should clearly set out the nature and precise extent of the peril which the insured wishes to be protected against. The subject-matter of the policy must be adequately identified and this may be done *either* by limiting the insurance to objects specifically described, *or* by taking out an insurance to cover all objects which fall within a particular class. A policy frequently includes details of the circumstances which affect the risk, e.g. details of the construction and use of buildings insured against fire, or of the nature of the insured's business, or the uses to which he proposes to put an insured motor vehicle. When an insurer has undertaken to insure against a specific risk, he will not be able to escape liability by virtue of the fact that the insured's conduct, e.g. his increased use of the property insured, has increased the likelihood of loss, unless specific clauses are inserted in the policy to achieve this. Insurance companies, however, do commonly include such clauses so as to restrict or remove their liability if the circumstances of the contemplated insurance are changed.

Even in an "all risks" policy there are certain types of loss which cannot be covered in the absence of an express provision. Thus, the insured cannot recover for losses resulting from his wilful acts, e.g. a deliberate destruction of property. An accident policy would not cover death from natural causes nor would such a policy cover depreciation of the goods insured. Further, it is not lawful to cover certain risks, e.g. a criminal cannot insure against imprisonment. The insured is required to prove that the loss comes within the risk covered, though where the insurers wish to repudiate the contract for fraud or arson the burden of proof is on them. (*Slattery* v. *Mance*, 1962.)[625]

1. NON-MARINE INSURANCE

Life Assurance. In the normal case the sum insured is payable on death however caused, but the payment of money due under an insurance policy may in certain circumstances be illegal as being contrary to public policy. So neither a person guilty of murder or manslaughter, nor persons claiming through him, e.g. personal representatives, can obtain a benefit under a policy on the life of the victim. (*Cleaver* v. *Mutual Reserve Fund Life Association*, 1892,[626] and *Gray* v. *Barr*, 1970,[626a] and *Re Giles*, 1971.)[626b]

The same was formerly true of *sane suicide* (*Beresford* v. *Royal Insurance Co. Ltd.*, 1938)[627] but, since the Suicide Act, 1961, suicide is no longer a crime and the question of public policy may not arise. However, the concept of risk does not include loss due to the wilful act of the insured, unless there is an express provision to this effect. Thus, insurers may still be able to reject a claim in the absence of an express provision to the contrary, and it is perhaps unlikely that a policy would be issued specifically covering suicide. If the insured commits suicide while insane his act will not be regarded as wilful and the insurers will be liable unless the policy provides to the contrary.

Some policies specifically state that the insurance shall be void on a sane suicide unless the policy has been assigned for value in which case the assignee can claim. In many policies restrictive clauses prohibit the assured from engaging in hazardous enterprises.

A proposal for life assurance requires the insured to give detailed information on his health, habits and medical history, and, of course, his age is of great importance, since different premiums are quoted to people of different ages. The questions on the form indicate the scope of the information the company requires, but if there is a clause that the insured warrants the truth of the information given, and if he has made general statements that he is in good health, he may find, if this proves not to be the case, that the insurance is invalidated. In the case of people who are getting on in years, or who wish to insure themselves for substantial amounts, it is common for insurance companies to insist on a medical examination.

Personal Accident Insurance. An accident has been defined as an unlooked for mishap or an untoward event which was not expected or designed, though even the murder of the victim may be regarded as accidental so far as he is concerned. (*Trim Joint District School Board of Management* v. *Kelly*, 1914.)[628] An injury, even if caused by another's negligence, is still accidental, as indeed may be hernias or injuries to the spine resulting from lifting or carrying heavy loads. *In the case of diseases*, where an occupational disease develops over a long period of time, this will probably not be regarded as accidental, but where a disease has a definite and specific cause, e.g. anthrax, then the disease may well come within the meaning of the word *accident*.

Types of benefit are (*a*) *lump sum benefits* in the case of death, or of specific injuries such as the loss of a limb or an eye; or (*b*) *periodical payments* made during disablement through accident, either for its duration or for a specified period named in the policy, e.g. thirteen weeks.

A policy will often exclude cover for certain risks, such as war risks, and may forbid the assured to expose himself to certain specified perils.

Most policies exclude disablement through disease, although, if the disease is not the proximate but only the remote cause of disablement or death, then the event may still be regarded as an accident. Thus death would be accidental (*a*) if a man walking along the pavement had a fit and, falling into the street, was killed by a passing bus; or (*b*) if the disease followed and resulted from the accident, as where a man bitten by a dog died of hydrophobia.

Fire Insurance. In estimating the loss caused by fire, consequential damage may be included. Thus where a wall is burnt it may cause the rest of the building to collapse without being consumed, and other property may be destroyed by those who are attempting to extinguish the fire or to stop it from spreading. However, the insured may not be able to claim for all the consequential loss he has suffered and if, as a result of premises being destroyed by fire, he has to take over others to carry on his business, he will not be able to claim for any loss of profits or additional expenses so incurred.

The sum insured is specified in the policy and this represents the maximum liability of the insurer. The insured, therefore, cannot recover more than the amount for which he has insured, even though the property insured and lost was worth more.

2. MARINE INSURANCE

Maritime perils mean the perils consequent on, or incidental to, the navigation of the sea, that is to say, perils of the seas, fire, war perils, pirates, rovers, thieves, captures, seizures, restraints, and detainments of princes and peoples, jettisons, barratry, and any other perils, either of the like kind or which may be designated by the policy. (Sect. 3.)

Perils of the Seas. Not every loss or damage of which the sea is the immediate cause is covered by these words. They do not protect against the natural and inevitable action of weather and sea which results in what may be described as wear and tear. The purpose of the policy is to secure an indemnity against accidents which may happen, not against events which must happen. Thus, if a vessel strikes a sunken rock in fair weather and sinks, this is a loss by perils of the sea, as also is a loss by foundering when one vessel comes into collision with another, even when the collision results from the negligence of that other vessel. The assured must prove in all cases that the loss was accidental. (*Slattery* v. *Mance*, 1962.)[625]

Fire. This includes fire caused by lightning, fire due to enemy action if not excluded by an F.C. and S. clause (see war risks below), and fire due to heating unless the goods were stored in an improper condition so as to make fire inevitable. Spontaneous combustion due to inherent vice is not covered, unless expressly provided by the policy.

Pirates. The term *pirates* includes passengers who mutiny, and rioters who attack the ship from the shore. The ordinary meaning of a pirate is a man who is plundering indiscriminately for his own ends and not a man who is operating against the property of a particular state for a public end. The existence of political bias rules out piracy. *Rovers* are synonymous with pirates.

Thieves. The term *thieves* does not cover clandestine theft, or a theft committed by anyone of the ship's company, whether crew or passengers.

Jettisons. To jettison means to throw overboard intentionally. It is done in time of peril for the common safety.

Arrests. The term *Arrests, Restraints, and Detainments of all Kings, Princes and People* refers to political or executive acts, and does not include loss by riot or by ordinary judicial process. The effect is not limited to acts of restraint in war time, and where cattle were prohibited from being landed by virtue of a local prohibition, there was a loss by *restraint of princes*. (*Miller* v. *Law Accident Insurance Co. Ltd.*, 1903.)[629]

Barratry. The term *barratry* includes every wrongful act wilfully committed by the master or crew to the prejudice of the owner, or, as the case may be, the charterer. Such an act would be barratry even if the intention was to benefit the ship owner. Negligence, even amounting to recklessness, does not constitute barratry; there must be an *intention* to injure the goods or the ship. Examples of barratry are sinking or deserting the ship, embezzling the cargo, or wilfully carrying her out of her proper course. A master of a ship who is also its owner cannot commit barratry.

War Risks. Since the time of the Napoleonic wars it has been customary to exclude certain war risks by a warranty known as the

F. C. and S. Clause. (Free of Capture and Seizure Clause.) The latest modification of the clause now runs—

> Warranted free of capture, seizure, arrest, restraint or detainment, and the consequences thereof or of any attempt thereat; also the consequences of hostilities or warlike operations, whether there be a declaration of war or not; but this warranty shall not exclude collision, contact with any fixed or floating object (other than a mine or torpedo), stranding, heavy weather or fire unless caused directly . . . by a hostile act by or against a belligerent power; and for the purpose of this warranty "power" includes any authority maintaining naval, military or air forces in association with a power.
>
> Further warranted free from the consequences of civil war, revolution, rebellion, insurrection, or civil strife arising therefrom or piracy.

Before the introduction of this modified clause, nearly all the casualties suffered by merchant vessels in war time had to be dealt with under a war risk policy, but the clause, as it now stands, throws back on to a marine policy the normal marine risks such as stranding, collision, heavy weather, and fire, unless they are obviously caused by hostile acts of a belligerent power.

Other Perils. The term *all other perils* includes only perils *similar in kind* to the perils specifically mentioned in the policy. It is, therefore, subject to the principle known as the *ejusdem generis* rule.

Inchmaree Clause. In order to offer a *wider cover* it is possible to include in the policy a clause, called the Inchmaree Clause after a ship of that name, which runs as follows—

> This insurance also specially to cover (subject to the free of average warranty) loss of or damage to the subject-matter insured directly caused by the following—
>> Accidents in loading, discharging or shifting cargo or fuel
>> Explosions on shipboard or elsewhere
>> Breakdown of or accident to nuclear installation or reactors on shipboard or elsewhere
>> Bursting of boilers, breakage of shafts or any latent defect in the machinery or hull
>> Contact with aircraft
>> Negligence of Master, Officers, Crew or Pilots, provided such loss or damage has not resulted from want of due diligence by the Assured, Owners or Managers.
>> Masters, Officers, Crew or Pilots not to be considered as part Owners within the meaning of this clause should they hold shares in the Vessel.

The effect of this clause is to give cover for a number of risks which are not marine perils as ordinarily understood. The words of the clause are strictly construed.

The Collision or Running Down Clause. Where there is a collision between two vessels and both are to blame, then the total damage of the two vessels is added together, and the amount so arrived at is divided in proportion to the blame attributable to each, if this can be established, or otherwise equally. This clause is designed to protect shipowners where a ship is in collision with another ship, but not with other objects such as a landing stage or a dock wall. Normally the protection afforded by the clause is limited to three-fourths of the damage sustained. The object of the clause is to indemnify the assured for liability for damage arising out of torts, but not for liability arising out of contract.

Included and Excluded Losses. Generally the insurer is liable for a loss *proximately* caused, but not for one which is *not proximately* caused, by a peril insured against. *Unless the policy otherwise provides*, he is *liable* for a loss proximately caused even though it would not have happened but for the misconduct or negligence of the master or crew: he is *not liable* for any loss attributable to the wilful misconduct of the insured himself; for any loss proximately caused by delay, even if the delay was caused by the peril insured against; or for ordinary wear and tear, ordinary leakage and breakage, inherent vice or nature of the subject matter insured, or for any loss proximately caused by rats or vermin, or for any injury to machinery not caused by maritime perils. (Sect. 55.)

Proximate Cause. Where a loss occurs, the insured has the onus of proving that it falls within the terms of the policy, but if he establishes a *prima facie* case, the onus shifts to the insurers to prove that the loss arose from an excepted peril. The question of *what is the proximate cause of loss* arises (*a*) where a number of causes act concurrently; or (*b*) where a number of successive causes inevitably follow a first originating cause; or (*c*) where there are a number of causes which follow one another, but where the chain of causation is broken by an intervening cause, i.e. a *novus actus interveniens*.

The proximate cause of loss is proximate not necessarily in time but in efficiency, but the rule must be applied with good sense so as to give effect to, and not to defeat, the intentions of the parties to the contract. (*Leyland Shipping Co. Ltd.* v. *Norwich Union Fire Insurance Society Ltd.*, 1918.)[630] The connection between the proximate cause and the loss must be by a direct and uninterrupted sequence, and a *novus actus interveniens* which is a predominant and efficient cause operates to exclude all preceding causes.

The position may be briefly summed up by saying that the underwriters will be liable (i) where the loss has been caused by a single peril which has been insured against; (ii) where two or more causes are in operation and either the final cause, or the dominant and paramount cause, is covered by the policy. (*Hamilton, Fraser and Co.* v. *Pandorf and Co.*, 1887.)[631]

It is possible that there may be more than one proximate cause of loss, and if one of these is covered by the policy and none of the others is expressly excluded, the assured will be able to recover. *If one of the causes is excluded* from the policy, the relative efficiency of the various causes must be estimated *and*, if, out of the dominant causes, *the most effective is the one excluded, the assured will fail in his claim.* If a ship sustains damage by an insured peril and, before the damage is repaired, is totally lost by an excepted peril, the insured will be unable to recover on either ground.

THE PREMIUM

In return for the acceptance by the insurer of the risk, the insured person pays a premium which may be either a single lump sum, or a series of payments made at appropriate intervals. The premium is calculated by the insurers, having regard to the frequency with which claims will have to be met and the amount of loss they will entail. These premiums are calculated on a statistical basis and it would normally be expected that the premiums collected from insured persons covered for a particular type of risk would be sufficient to pay all claims, and leave a margin for the costs of administration and residue of profit.

A contract of insurance cannot be completed until a premium is agreed but, where the precise degree of risk cannot be calculated in advance, it is possible to pay a provisional premium, and this can be adjusted in either direction at the expiry of the term of insurance when the precise cover has been ascertained. The premium may be paid either direct to the insurers or, if an agent has authority to receive payment, it may be paid to him and the insurers will then be bound. The person insured is liable for the premium immediately on completion of the contract, and it is common for insurance companies to make payment of the premium a condition precedent to the assumption of liability. If payment is made by cheque it is conditional only. Thus, if a policy provided for forfeiture on non-payment of premium by 1st March the giving of a cheque on that date would not prevent forfeiture if it was dishonoured. In most types of insurance, except life, the policy requires renewal and the insurers are not bound to accept a renewal premium. (See p. 381.) It is also common for policies to make provision for a period of grace during which a renewal premium may be paid. (See p. 382.)

The person insured may claim a return of premiums if there has been total failure of consideration, e.g. where a person whose life was insured had in fact died before the insurance contract was made.

We have seen that, where a proposal form contains misrepresentations, however innocent, the insurers may be able to refuse to indemnify the insured, but if they avoid the policy they will have to return any premiums paid.

If the insured obtained the policy by fraud he cannot claim return of premium, though if the insurer brings an action to rescind the contract the court may ask him to return the premium on the maxim "he who seeks equity must do equity."

Where there is no insurable interest the policy will be illegal and premiums cannot generally be recovered, though there are exceptions. (*Hughes* v. *Liverpool Victoria Friendly Society*, 1916.)[226]

Actually an insurance policy frequently lays down conditions governing the return of premiums, e.g. in the case of motor insurance it is often provided that a premature termination of the insurance by either party may give rights to some repayment of premium.

CLAIMS

When the insured suffers the loss insured, he is normally required to make a formal claim and to give the insurer speedy notice of the loss. The question of notice is governed by the terms of the policy which may be very strict, but normally notice must be given "within a reasonable time" or "as soon as possible." (*Verelst's Administratrix* v. *Motor Union Insurance Co. Ltd.*, 1925.)[632] It need not be in writing and may be given either by the insured in person or by someone acting on his behalf, and may be given either to the insurers themselves or to any of their authorised agents. If a clause regarding notice makes it a condition precedent of liability of the insurers, they are entitled to notice as soon as an accident or mishap occurs, even if there is no immediate damage. (*Cassel* v. *Lancashire and Yorkshire Accident Insurance Co. Ltd.*, 1885.)[633]

If the insured does not give notice in accordance with the policy the insurer may repudiate liability. Lapse of time in repudiating liability will not operate against the insurer unless there is prejudice to other parties or implied acceptance of liability. (*Allen* v. *Robles*, 1969.)[284]

An insurer sued directly by an employee under the Third Parties (Rights against Insurers) Act, 1930, can set up any defence available against the employer including failure to notify a claim on time. (*Farrell* v. *Federated Employers Insurance Association*, [1970] 1 W.L.R. 1400.)

Where a specific procedure is laid down, the claimant should adhere to it. The normal procedure is for the insured to fill in a claim form supplied to him by the insurance company or its agent, the object of the form being to supply the insurers with all the information they require in order to deal with the claim. Where there is a dispute arising as a result of a claim, it is common for the policy to contain an arbitration clause which may require various matters to be submitted to an arbitrator, e.g. the amount payable under the claim or even the question of liability under the policy. An arbitration clause does not necessarily stop the insured from bringing an action but it may restrict the scope of the action to the amount of the award, and require the question of liability to be settled by an arbitrator before an action can be brought.

Where it is possible to give more than one meaning to a clause in a policy or proposal form, the court will generally adopt the meaning most favourable to the insured, because the policy and proposal form are documents drafted by the insurers whose position is, therefore, stronger than that of the assured. This is called the *contra proferentem* rule, but it only applies where there is real ambiguity. (*Provincial Insurance Co.* v. *Morgan and Foxon*, 1933.)[634]

Claims are usually paid in cash, though the policy may provide for re-instatement. Payments must be made to the proper person but, where on the death of the insured there are conflicting claims to the money payable under the policy, the insurers may pay the money into court. In other cases they must interplead.

1. Life Assurance. The sum payable under the policy is often augmented by the addition of annual bonuses which are a share of the profits made by the insurance company. Moreover, even if the insured does not continue to pay premiums for the full period of the insurance, or until death as the case may be, he will not necessarily be without any claim on the company. He will usually have the choice of two alternatives—

(*a*) To surrender the policy and accept a sum of money called its surrender value;

(*b*) To accept a fully-paid policy which will provide that, on his death, a reduced amount may be payable based on the number of premiums already paid and his probable expectation of life.

2. Fire Insurance. In valuing the property in the case of total loss, the value is the intrinsic value of the property destroyed with no allowance for loss of possible profits or for sentimental value. It is the value at the place of the fire and at the time of the fire, irrespective of whether the property has increased or decreased in value since the taking out of the insurance, and subject only to the fact that no more can be recovered than the sum for which the property was insured.

Where the property is marketable, the value is its market value, but where the property is not strictly marketable, as for instance business premises which the assured would wish to have re-instated, the assured can recover the cost of re-instatement even if this would be in excess of the market value. Clearly in the case of specialised buildings, such as a church or an art gallery, the notion of market value has no particular significance. Where the loss is partial, the indemnity is the cost of repairing the damage caused by the fire.

The Fires Prevention (Metropolis) Act, 1774, which in spite of its name applies also outside London, creates a statutory obligation on insurance companies to re-instate a house or building damaged by fire if the insured requests this, but the cost of re-instatement must not exceed the sum insured. In addition to the insured owners, mortgagors, mortgagees, lessors and lessees, tenants for life and remaindermen may request re-instatement, since they have an interest in the continued existence of the property.

In other circumstances the insurers have an obligation to pay money compensation only and cannot insist on re-instatement without the consent of the assured, unless they have reserved the right in the policy. Most insurers find it in their interest to reserve the option of either paying the claim or re-instating the property. Where the policy is a *valued policy* the *agreed value* is paid on total loss, or a proportion of that value on partial loss, and nothing in excess of this is recoverable. (*Elcock* v. *Thomson*, 1949.)[635]

3. Marine Insurance. Losses under a marine insurance policy may be either General Average losses or Particular Average losses.

(*a*) A GENERAL AVERAGE LOSS is a loss caused by or directly consequential on a general average act. It includes a general average expenditure as well as a general average sacrifice. *There is a general average act* where any extraordinary sacrifice or expenditure is voluntarily and reasonably made or incurred in time of peril for the purpose of preserving the property imperilled by the common adventure. Where there is a general average loss, the party on whom the loss falls is entitled, subject to the conditions imposed by maritime law, to a rateable contribution from the other parties interested, and such contribution is called a general average contribution. (Sect. 66 (1–3).) Examples of general average occur when, in time of peril, cargo is jettisoned or a mast cut away to save a ship.

(*b*) A PARTICULAR AVERAGE LOSS is a partial loss of the subject-matter insured, caused by a peril insured against, and which is not a general average loss. It should be noted that a particular average loss is a partial loss not arising under conditions of general average. An example of particular average is damage by seawater which does not amount to total loss.

A general average loss is incurred voluntarily; a particular average loss is fortuitous. Since a general average loss is incurred voluntarily for the common safety, it has to be borne by a rateable contribution from all; a particular average loss must be borne by the party on whom it actually falls.

In the case of *general average expenditure* the insured may recover from the insurer only the proportion of the loss which falls on him, but in the case of *general average sacrifice*, he may recover the whole of the loss from the insurer without having to enforce his right of contribution from the other parties liable to contribute, though the insurer is subrogated to the rights of the assured in this respect. (Sect. 66 (4).) Salvage charges incurred in preventing a loss by perils insured against may be recovered as a loss by those perils. (Sect. 65 (1).)

MEASURE OF INDEMNITY. Subject to any express provision or valuation in the policy, the *insurable value* of the ship includes the ship, its outfit, provisions and stores, wages and disbursements, plus the charges for insurance. In the case of a steam ship it includes the machinery, boilers, coals and engine stores and, in ships engaged in special trade, the ordinary fittings requisite for that trade. (Sect. 16 (1).)

(*a*) *Total Loss.* Where there is total loss, if the policy is a valued policy, the measure of indemnity is the sum fixed by the policy; if the policy is an unvalued policy, the insurable value of the subject-matter insured. (Sect. 68.)

(*b*) *Partial Loss.* Where a ship is damaged, but is not totally lost, the measure of indemnity, subject to any express provision in the policy, is as follows—

(i) *Where the ship has been repaired* the insured is entitled to the reasonable cost of repairs, less the customary deductions, but not exceeding the sum insured in respect of any one casualty;

(ii) *Where the ship has been partially repaired,* the insured is entitled to the reasonable cost of such repairs, plus the reasonable depreciation, if any, arising from the unrepaired damage, provided that the aggregate amount shall not exceed the cost of repairing the whole damage computed as above;

(iii) *Where the ship has not been repaired,* and has not been sold in her damaged state during the risk, the insured is entitled to be indemnified for the reasonable depreciation arising from the unrepaired damage, but not exceeding the reasonable cost of repairing such damage as computed above. (Sect. 69.)

It is usual to deduct one-third of the total expenditure on repairs unless the ship is a new one, and this is called "Deducting one-third new for old." The deduction is made because an old ship so repaired will usually be worth more than she was before she was damaged, but such deductions are not made if the ship is damaged on her first voyage.

(*c*) *Successive Losses.* Unless the policy otherwise provides, and subject to the provisions of the Act, the insurer is liable for *successive losses*, even though the total amount of such losses may exceed the sum insured, but, where under the same policy a partial loss, which has not been repaired or otherwise made good, is followed by a total loss, the insured can only recover in respect of a total loss. (Sect. 77.)

(*d*) *Constructive Total Loss.* A total loss may be either an actual total loss or a constructive total loss, and, in the absence of a provision to the contrary, both of these are covered. (Sect. 56.)

Subject to any express provision in the policy, there is a constructive total loss where the subject-matter insured is reasonably abandoned because its actual total loss appears to be unavoidable, or because it cannot be preserved from actual total loss without an expenditure which would exceed its value when the expenditure had been incurred, e.g. where the cost of repairing a ship would exceed her value when repaired, or in the case of damaged goods where the cost of repairing them and forwarding them to their destination would exceed their value on arrival. (Sect. 60.) Where there is a constructive total loss the insured may either treat the loss as a partial loss, or abandon the subject-matter to the insurer and treat the loss as if it were an actual total loss. (Sect. 61.) (*Rodoconachi* v. *Elliott*, 1874.)[636]

(*e*) *Abandonment*. Where the insured elects to abandon the subject-matter to the insurer, he must give notice of abandonment and, if he fails to do so, the loss can only be treated as a partial loss. Notice may be either in writing or by word of mouth and must be given with reasonable diligence. Where notice of abandonment is properly given, the rights of the insured are not prejudiced by the fact that the insurer refuses to accept the abandonment.

Acceptance of abandonment may be express or implied, but the mere silence of the insurer after notice is not acceptance. Where notice of abandonment is accepted, the abandonment is irrevocable, and the insurer's acceptance of notice conclusively admits his liability for the loss and the sufficiency of the notice. Notice of abandonment is unnecessary where, at the time when the insured receives the information of the loss, there would be no possibility of benefit to the insurer if notice were given to him, and notice of abandonment may be waived by the insurer. Where an insurer has re-insured the risk, no notice of abandonment need be given to him. (Sect. 62.)

Where there is valid abandonment, the insurer is entitled to take over any interest of the insured in whatever remains of the subject-matter insured, and all proprietary rights incidental thereto. (Sect. 63 (1).)

Where a ship which has been insured is missing, an actual loss may be presumed after the lapse of a reasonable time without news, but there is no presumption that the loss occurred at any particular time, and the insured must show that it occurred, or must have occurred, within the insured period.

Warranties. A warranty may be express or implied and by it the insured undertakes that some particular thing shall or shall not be done, or that some condition shall be fulfilled, or affirms or negatives the existence of a particular state of facts. It is a condition which must be complied with, whether material to the risk or not. (*Overseas Commodities Ltd.* v. *G. W. Style*, 1958.)[637] Otherwise the insurer is discharged from liability as from the date of the breach, without prejudice to earlier liabilities. (Sect. 33.)

Non-compliance with a warranty may be excused when, by reason of a change in circumstances, it ceases to be applicable, and where it is broken, the insured cannot avail himself of the defence that the breach has been remedied, and the warranty complied with, before loss. Nevertheless a breach of warranty may be waived by the insurer.

An *express warranty* may be in any form of words from which the intention to warrant may be inferred. It must be included in or be referred to by the policy, and it does not exclude an implied warranty unless inconsistent with it. A ship or goods may be *warranted neutral* and this implies that the property was neutral at the beginning of the risk and so far as the insured can control the matter, shall remain so. A ship may be warranted *well* or *in good safety* on a particular day, and it is sufficient in this case if she be safe at any time during the day.

Implied Warranties. The Marine Insurance Act, 1906, sets out certain implied warranties, e.g. that the adventure insured is a lawful one or that, in a voyage policy, the ship was seaworthy at the commencement of the voyage.

SEAWORTHINESS. In a voyage policy the ship must be seaworthy for the purpose of the particular adventure insured. Where the policy attaches while the ship is in port, she must be reasonably fit to encounter the perils of the port. Where the policy relates to a voyage to be performed in stages during which the ship requires different preparation and equipment, there is an implied warranty that at each stage she shall be seaworthy in respect of such preparation and equipment.

A ship is deemed to be *seaworthy* when she is reasonably fit in all respects to encounter the ordinary perils of the seas on the adventure insured. Seaworthiness is a relative term and varies with the voyage: it may vary from season to season or with the type of cargo. (*Quebec Marine Insurance Co.* v. *Commercial Bank of Canada*, 1870.)[638] *Unseaworthiness is a question of fact* and the onus of proof is on the underwriter unless (say) a ship which has just sailed sinks in fair weather without apparent cause, in which case the onus of proof of seaworthiness would lie with the assured.

In a *time policy* there is no implied warranty of seaworthiness at any stage of the adventure, but if the insured knows she is putting to sea in an unseaworthy state, the insurer is not liable for losses due to unseaworthiness. (*Thomas* v. *Tyne and Wear Freight Insurance Association*, 1917.)[639]

There is no implied warranty that goods or moveables are seaworthy, but in a *voyage policy* on goods and moveables there is an implied warranty that, at the commencement of the voyage, the ship is seaworthy and is reasonably fit to carry the goods to the destination contemplated by the policy.

4. Motor Vehicle Insurance—Claims against Motor Insurers Bureau. A person may be injured by a motorist who does not carry the compulsory insurance required by the current Road Traffic legislation, or in circumstances where a vehicle insured is used outside the scope of its cover. In such a case, although the injured person may obtain a judgment against the motorist, he may not be able to enforce it because of the motorist's lack of funds.

He may, however, have a claim against the *Motor Insurers' Bureau*. By an agreement made in 1946 with the Ministry of Transport, the Motor Insurers' Bureau, an incorporated body kept in funds by the motor vehicle insurers under what is called the "Domestic Agreement" which was revised in 1971 and entitled Motor Insurers' Bureau (Compensation of Victims of Uninsured Drivers), will satisfy any judgment in respect of a compulsory insurable risk which is not satisfied within seven days against a motorist who is not covered by a policy as required by law. The risk involved must be one against which the motorist must insure (*Lees* v. *Motor Insurers' Bureau*, 1952)[640] and the agreement can only be enforced if the Bureau receives notice of the proceedings either before or within 21 days of their commencement. The claimant must take all reasonable steps, subject to full indemnity by the bureau as to costs, to enforce his legal rights if the bureau requires him to do so, and any judgment so obtained must be assigned to the bureau or its nominee.

Where, of course, the insured has a valid insurance the claims against him by third parties will be met in accordance with the terms of the policy, and he will be able to claim for damage to his vehicle up to the limit of the sum assured in the case of policies giving suitable cover.

INSURABLE INTEREST

Life Assurance. An insured person must have an insurable interest and the Life Assurance Act, 1774, Sect. 1, states that "No insurance is to be made on the life or lives of any person or persons, or on any other event or events whatsoever, wherein the person for whose use or benefit, or on whose account the policy is made, has no interest, or by way of gaming or wagering; every insurance made contrary to this provision is void." The names of the person or persons for whose benefit the policy is made must be stated in the policy, and the amount recoverable from the assurance is limited to the value of the insurable interest.

The Life Assurance Act, 1774, applies also to personal accident insurance, but does not apply to insurance on ships or goods (*Prudential Staff Union* v. *Hall*, 1947),[641] or to motor vehicle insurance. The act does not apply to insurances taken out by the insured on his own life and for his own benefit, or to insurances by husband and wife of each other's lives.

Insurable interest for the purposes of life assurance is the financial loss which will be suffered by the insured on the death of the person insured. An insurable interest is not presumed in the case of parents and children, or brothers and sisters, or more distant relatives, unless there may be a legal, not merely a moral obligation, to pay funeral expenses. However, creditors may insure the lives of their debtors, and masters and servants may insure each other's lives. Where the insured contracts for the benefit of another person, that person must be named in the policy.

While no more can be recovered under the policy than the value of the insurable interest, this value is determined at the commencement of the policy. It may well be, therefore, that, when death occurs, the loss may be less than the sum assured, but this sum will nevertheless be payable since a life assurance is not strictly one of indemnity. For example, a creditor who insures the life of his debtor may continue to maintain the insurance after the debt has been repaid. There is no need for the insurable interest to exist at the time of death, so long as there was such an interest at the time the contract was made.

Fire Insurance. In the case of an insurance of buildings, e.g. against fire, an interest must exist (*a*) when the contract is made (by virtue of the Life Assurance Act, 1774); and (*b*) when the loss occurs, because such a contract is in the nature of an indemnity. Whereas in life assurance the sum assured will normally be paid out in full on the death of the insured, in fire insurance the amount payable will be such sum as does not exceed the sum assured and is just sufficient to indemnify the assured against the loss which has occurred. (*Castellain* v. *Preston*, 1883.)[642]

Insurance of Goods. Contracts of insurance of goods are not within the Life Assurance Act, 1774, but are covered by the Gaming Act, 1845. Thus they require an insurable interest at the time of making the contract, or an expectation of such interest. Therefore a buyer may insure goods before purchase, and a warehouseman may take out a policy to cover all the goods in his warehouse at the time of loss up to a fixed amount. Nevertheless the goods must be ascertainable in some way or other.

It is not necessary to be the owner of the thing in question, and an insurable interest may be based on possession. A bailee has an insurable interest to cover his liability to the owner in the event of loss, or to cover any lien he may have on the goods for his charges. In some cases the court may take the view that on a proper interpretation of the policy the bailee has also assumed the interest of the bailor who is the owner of the goods. Where this is so the bailee is entitled to keep what is owing to him out of the insurance money and holds the rest in trust for the bailor in spite of the doctrine of privity of contract. (*A. Tomlinson* (*Hauliers*) *Ltd.* v. *Hepburn*, 1966.)[643] However, possession must be coupled with liability, and if the person in possession has no liability in respect of the goods, he has no insurable interest. (*Macaura* v. *Northern Assurance Co. Ltd.*, 1925.)[644]

Insurance on behalf of a person with an insurable interest may be effected by an agent, or by a person entrusted with the goods, even though the agent or person entrusted has no insurable interest in the property. There is no general requirement of ratification by the party with an interest, or that the person having the interest be mentioned in the policy. An agent can make a valid contract of insurance in respect of the principal's goods, and either the agent or the principal can sue on the contract.

The word "trustee" is often used of a person entrusted with goods, but the word is not used in its strict technical sense, for a trustee under a trust is the legal owner and has an insurable interest arising from that fact. Nevertheless a person without an insurable interest may insure so long as he does so as a *quasi-trustee* for those with an interest. (*Prudential*

Staff Union v. *Hall,* 1947.)[641] In such cases of trusteeship the intention to protect the interests of others must be clear from the terms of the policy or the circumstances.

Marine Insurance. The Marine Insurance Act, 1906, lays down the following—

(1) Subject to the provisions of the Act every person has an insurable interest who is interested in a marine adventure.

(2) In particular a person is interested in a marine adventure where he stands in any legal or equitable relation to the adventure, or to any insurable property at risk therein, in consequence of which he may benefit by the safety or due arrival of insurable property, or may be prejudiced by its loss, or by damage thereto, or by detention thereof, or may incur liability in respect thereof. (Sect. 5.) A partial interest of any nature is insurable. (Sect. 8.)

The insured must be interested in the subject-matter insured at the time of the loss, though he need not be interested when the insurance was effected: provided that where the subject-matter is insured "Lost or not lost," the insured may recover although he may not have acquired his interest until after the loss, unless at the time of effecting the insurance the insured was aware of the loss and the insurer was not. Where the insured has no interest at the time of the loss, he cannot acquire an interest by any act or election after he is aware of the loss. (Sect. 6.)

A defeasible interest is insurable, as also is a contingent interest. In particular, where the buyer of goods has insured them, he has an insurable interest, even though he might, at his election, have rejected the goods or have treated them as at seller's risk by reason of the latter's delay in making delivery or otherwise.

The master or any member of the crew of a ship has an insurable interest in respect of his wages, and the insurer under a contract of marine insurance has an insurable interest in respect of his risk so that he may re-insure in respect of it. The assured has an insurable interest in the charges of any insurance which he may effect.

Where the subject-matter insured is mortgaged, the mortgagor has an insurable interest in the full value thereof, and the mortgagee has an insurable interest in respect of any sum due or to become due under the mortgage. (Sect. 14(1).) This is right and proper since in the event of loss the mortgagor would lose the property and still be liable for the mortgage debt.

A mortgagee, consignee, or other person having an interest in the subject-matter insured may insure on behalf of and for the benefit of other persons interested as well as for his own benefit. (Sect. 14 (2).) If, however, a mortgagee recovers more than the amount of the mortgage debt, he will hold the balance in trust for the mortgagor.

The owner of insurable property has an insurable interest in respect of its full value, notwithstanding that some third person may have agreed or be liable to indemnify him in case of loss.

WAGERING POLICIES

We have seen that, where there is no insurable interest, a policy may well be a wagering policy, and it is laid down in Sect. 4 of the Marine Insurance Act, 1906, that every contract of marine insurance by way of gaming or wagering is void. A contract of marine insurance is deemed to be a gaming or wagering contract—

(*a*) Where the insured has not an insurable interest as defined by the Act, and the contract is entered into with no expectation of acquiring such an interest; or

(*b*) Where the policy is made "interest or no interest" or "without further proof of interest than the policy itself," or "without benefit of salvage to the insurer," or subject to any other like term:

Provided that, where there is no possibility of salvage, a policy may be effected without benefit of salvage to the insurer. (Sect. 4 (2).)

All insurances which are really wagers are null and void, regardless of whether they are in the form of P.P.I. policies (Policy proof of interest) or not. However, a P.P.I. policy need not be inconsistent with the existence of an insurable interest. It may merely be made in that form because the insured has an insurable interest but may find it difficult to prove.

Where a contract of marine insurance is in good faith effected by one person on behalf of another, the person on whose behalf it is effected may ratify the contract even after he is aware of the loss (Sect. 86), but only if it was the *bona fide* intention of the person effecting the policy to protect the other's interests. (*Grover and Grover* v. *Mathews*, 1910.)[438]

DOUBLE INSURANCE

It sometimes happens that a person takes out more than one policy in respect of the same risk of loss and, if each of the insurers were required to pay the full extent of the loss, the insured person would gain by this procedure. Provided a particular policy does not forbid it, the insured person may insure the same risk as often as he chooses but, in the case of indemnity insurance, he cannot recover more than the amount of his loss. He may either claim a rateable proportion from each insurer or, if there is no contribution clause in one of the policies, he may claim the full amount under that policy, leaving the various insurers to claim contribution among themselves.

As regards marine insurance, the matter is covered by Sect. 32 of the Marine Insurance Act, 1906—

(1) Where two or more policies are effected by or on behalf of the insured on the same adventure and interest or any part thereof, and the sums insured exceed the indemnity allowed by this Act, the assured is said to be *over-insured by double insurance*.

(2) Where the assured is over-insured by double insurance—

(*a*) The insured, unless the policy otherwise provides, may claim payment from the insurers in such order as he may think fit, provided that he is not entitled to receive any sum in excess of the indemnity allowed by the Act;

(*b*) Where the policy under which the insured claims is a *valued policy*, the insured must give credit *as against the valuation* for any sum received by him under any other policy without regard to the actual value of the subject-matter insured;

(*c*) Where the policy under which the insured claims is an *unvalued policy* he must give credit, *against the full insurable value*, for any sum received by him under any other policy;

(*d*) Where the insured receives any sum in excess of the indemnity allowed by the Act, he is deemed to hold such sum in trust for the insurers, according to their right of contribution among themselves.

Double insurance occurs when the policies cover the same adventure, the same risk and the *same interest in the same subject-matter*. Where the interests covered by the policies are different, there is no double insurance. (*North British and Mercantile Insurance Co.* v. *London, Liverpool and Globe Insurance Co.*, 1877.)[645] Such insurance is often effected unintentionally, as where both the consignor and the consignee insure to protect the consignee's interests. It may, however, be done intentionally as where the insured doubts the security of one of the insurers.

In marine insurance the insured may present his claim on the insurers successively in any order he pleases. Marine policies normally do not contain a contribution clause and although the underwriters do in fact claim contribution from each other towards the amount paid under the claim, this is a matter to be settled among themselves.

Fire policies commonly do contain a contribution clause and in this case the insured cannot claim the whole of the loss from any one insurer, but must claim from each the proportion each is liable for. Thus if a house worth £5,000 is totally destroyed and is insured for £4,000 with Company A and for £6,000 with Company B, and the policies contain contribution clauses, the insured must claim £2,000 from A and £3,000 from B. If, however, the policy with B did not contain a contribution clause, the insured could claim £5,000 from B, leaving B to assert his right of contribution against A in order to recover the contribution of £2,000.

In many cases where there has been double insurance and the claim is met in part by several insurers, they will make a proportionate return of premium for the risk they have escaped, but where a policy has for any length of time borne the whole of the risk, no return of premium will be made in respect of that policy. Where the insured claims and receives more than the indemnity to which he is entitled, the balance is held in trust and will be shared by the insurers in proportion to their liability to contribute.

AVERAGE

It may occur to the insured that the risk of total loss is very slight, and he may, therefore, underinsure, e.g. insure for £6,000 a house worth £8,000. This is quite permissible and, unless there is an *average clause* in the policy, he will be able to recover the total loss suffered subject to a maximum of £6,000. Thus, if the house suffers damage to the tune of £2,000, he will be able to recover £2,000.

Nevertheless there is a principle called *average* (not to be confused with general average in marine insurance) under which the insured is regarded as being *his own insurer* for any difference between the amount for which he has insured his property and the actual value. In the case we have mentioned, therefore, if the policy had an average clause in it and £2,000 damage were done to the property, the insured would only be able to claim £1,500, namely three-quarters of the loss, since he would be regarded as his own insurer for one-quarter of the property.

RE-INSURANCE

An insurer who has undertaken a risk on a marine or non-marine policy of insurance may wish to be relieved of his commitment and the Marine Insurance Act, 1906, specifically gives him an insurable interest in his risk and the right to re-insure. There may be many reasons why an underwriter might wish to re-insure. He may not wish to run a large risk on a single hazard. He may have accepted a comprehensive risk and wish to be rid of certain elements of it. He may even be able to re-insure at a cheaper premium, thus ridding himself of a liability and gaining the difference between the premium received and the premium paid. When a ship is missing or when news is heard that a loss is imminent, he may still find a market for re-insurance, and exchange a doubtful and possibly large contingent liability for a stiff but definite re-insurance premium.

Normally a policy of re-insurance contains a re-insurance clause which stipulates that the re-insurance is subject to the same clauses and conditions as the original policy and will be paid on the same terms. Unless the policy otherwise provides, the original insured has no right or interest in respect of the re-insurance. (Sect. 9 (2).) The two policies are quite distinct: the person who re-insures is solely liable to the original insured and has the sole right of claim against the re-insurer.

SUBROGATION

Where the loss under a contract is total and the insurer pays the full amount, the insurer is entitled to all the interest of the insured in what is left of the subject-matter of the contract. He is thereby subrogated to all the relevant rights and remedies of the insured. Where the insurer pays for a partial loss, he acquires no title to the subject-matter insured, or what remains of it, but he is subrogated to all the rights and remedies of the insured in, and in respect of, the subject-matter insured as from the time of the casualty causing the loss, in so far as the insured has been indemnified in respect of it.

Thus, if X's motor car collides with that of Y, and the collision is due to Y's negligence, X may sue Y and recover damages, in which case X's insurers will not need to indemnify him. Alternatively X may claim from his insurers who, when they have indemnified him, will be able to take over X's claim and recover from Y the amount so paid. X cannot claim both from the insurers and also from Y by means of an action. Indeed, as we have seen, it is a general principle of indemnity insurance that a person suffering loss under an insurance policy cannot claim to be indemnified by a sum of money greater than his actual loss. (*Darrell v. Tibbitts*, 1880.)[646]

The insurers, therefore, acquire a right as against third parties to all the rights which the insured person had, and this is particularly important in cases of tortious damage. (*Goole and Hull Steam Towing Co.* v. *Ocean Marine Insurance Co.*, 1928.)[647] However, it is not confined to tort, and where the insured has a remedy under a contract, the insurers can take over his rights and remedies. If the insurers recover more than the amount they have paid to the assured, they must hand over the excess to him. It follows from the right of subrogation that insured persons must not settle or compromise claims with third parties without the consent of the insurers. (*Phoenix Assurance Co.* v. *Spooner*, 1905.)[648]

The right of subrogation does not apply to life assurance, and if the insured were killed in a road accident, the full sum assured under the policy would be payable, and any rights of action in respect of the accident would remain with the legal representatives of the insured.

In the majority of cases of loss the insured will naturally claim against the insurance company, leaving them to their rights of subrogation. In the case of collisions between motor vehicles insured by different companies, the insurers may have a *knock for knock* agreement, each insurer compensating his own assured for the damage, without regard to which of the drivers was legally responsible. This saves much costly litigation and probably does rough justice in the long run as between insurers, although it may lead to both drivers losing their *no-claims bonus*, which is a reduction in premium for careful drivers. Nevertheless, it is still open to one of the drivers who thinks he has an action to refrain from claiming against his insurer and to pursue his legal remedy if he so chooses, and the fact that he has rights against his insurers is no bar to such an action. (*Morley* v. *Moore*, 1936.)[649]

ASSIGNMENT

The right to receive the proceeds of an insurance policy is a proprietary right known as a *chose in action* and may be assigned in the same way as other choses in action. Clearly this is a great convenience and is often essential where the property which is at risk passes through the hands of various owners, e.g. when cargoes are transported from buyer to seller and when goods and houses are bought and sold

1. Life Assurance. The insured benefit under a *life policy* may be assigned like any other chose in action, but may also be assigned under the rules of assignment set out in the Policies of Assurance Act, 1867. Under the Act assignment is effected by writing, either in the form of an endorsement on the policy or by a separate instrument. The assignment must be attested and stamped. The assignee must give the insurers written notice of the assignment and they must acknowledge it if requested to do so. If the proceeds of the policy are assigned more than once, the date of receipt of the notice governs the priority of the various assignees. The Act enables the assignee to sue the insurers in his own name, but his right is still subject to equities. Even where a policy forbids assignment, though this will prevent a legal assignment, it will not affect the equitable rights of an assignee.

2. Fire Insurance. In the case of *fire insurance* when the insured dies or becomes bankrupt, his insurable interest is assigned by operation of law to his personal representatives or his trustee respectively, and they can enforce the policy. Where the insured parts with his interest in the subject-matter he must, if he wishes the insurance to remain effective, assign the policy. This requires the consent of the insurers whose consent must take the form prescribed by the policy, and the assignment of both policy and interest must take place at the same time.

In the case of real property, once a contract of sale is signed, the purchaser acquires an equitable interest therein but does not acquire the legal estate until conveyance. He can insure his interest in the property and it is advisable for him to do so. If he does not do so, and the house is destroyed or damaged by fire between the time of the contract and the time of the conveyance, Sect. 47 of the Law of Property Act, 1925, obliges the vendor to hold any moneys received under a policy for the benefit of the purchaser to be paid to him on completion, though the purchaser may be able to require re-instatement under Sect. 83 of the Fires Prevention (Metropolis) Act, 1774. This procedure requires the consent of the insurers, and the purchaser must pay the proportionate part of the premium from the date of the contract.

3. Marine Insurance. A marine policy is assignable unless it contains terms expressly prohibiting assignment, and it may be assigned either before or after loss. Where a marine policy has been assigned so as to pass the beneficial interest in such a policy, the assignee of the policy is entitled to sue thereon in his own name; and the defendant is entitled to make any defence arising out of the contract which he would have been entitled to make if the action had been brought in the name of the person by or on behalf of whom the policy was effected. A marine policy may be assigned by indorsement thereon or in other customary manner. (Sect. 50.)

For assignment to be effective there must be continuity of insurable interest and where the insured has parted with or lost his interest in the subject-matter insured, and has not, before or at the time of so doing, expressly or impliedly agreed to assign the policy, any subsequent assignment of the policy is inoperative; but this does not affect the assignment of a policy after loss. (Sect. 51.)

What has been said above on the matter of assignment refers to the assignment of the policy moneys, and not to the transfer of the policy itself. A life policy cannot be transferred from the life of one person to another. In the case of indemnity policies a transfer is possible only with the consent of the insurer.

BANKRUPTCY OR LIQUIDATION OF INSURED

The insured may either before or after incurring liability to a third party become bankrupt, or in the case of a company go into liquidation. In such a case the injured party would have to obtain judgment and prove in the bankruptcy for the judgment debt but for the Third Party (Rights against Insurers) Act, 1930, which provides that on bankruptcy or liquidation of the insured, the right of the insured under *any* liability insurance vests in the injured third party for the full amount of the judgment. Moreover, he is not to be defeated by any provision in the policy purporting to exclude the Act, although he may be affected by the provisions of the policy short of exclusion, e.g. he may be required to submit to arbitration if the policy so provides. The insurance company cannot set-off any premiums due but must prove for this in the bankruptcy or liquidation. (*Murray* v. *Legal and General Assurance Society*, [1969] 3 All E.R. 794.) However, an insurer sued directly by an employee under the Act of 1930 can set up any defence, as distinct from a counterclaim, available against the employer including failure to notify a claim on time. (*Farrell* v. *Federated Employers Insurance Association*, [1970] 1 W.L.R. 1400.)

CHAPTER XI

CARRIAGE OF GOODS

CARRIAGE BY ROAD

A CARRIER of goods by road is either a common carrier or a private carrier.

1. Common Carriers. A common carrier is one who holds himself out as being ready to carry for reward the goods of any person, no matter who that person may be. If he retains the right to choose as among persons for whom he will carry goods, he is not a common carrier.

Nevertheless, a carrier is a common carrier only to the extent to which he holds himself out as such and no further, and—

(a) If he offers to carry only a particular kind of goods, he is a common carrier of that class of goods only; and

(b) If he offers to carry goods from one specified place to another, he is only a common carrier between those places and not to intermediate places or to anywhere else.

If a common carrier carries *both goods and passengers*, and allows *fare-paying* passengers to carry luggage free of charge, he is still deemed to be carrying such luggage for reward. The right of the passengers to carry the luggage free is part of the consideration given by the carrier in return for the fare and the carrier is a common carrier to the same extent as if the goods had been carried without passengers. A person may be a common carrier in appropriate circumstances for one particular journey. Indeed, whether a person is or is not a common carrier does not depend on how he *describes* his business; it is a question of fact based on how he *conducts* the business.

However, a carrier is not a common carrier if he holds himself out as ready to carry goods for the public at large *only in connection with another business*. Thus where the owner of a warehouse held himself out as prepared to carry goods from ships to his warehouse *for all persons agreeing to use it to store their goods*, he was not a common carrier of those goods. The carriage was merely ancillary to the warehouse business and restricted to those storing goods with him. (*Consolidated Tea and Lands Company* v. *Oliver's Wharf*, [1910] 2 K.B. 395.)

The liability of a common carrier for loss or damage is very high and he is regarded as the insurer of the goods carried in all but exceptional circumstances.

In early times the law relating to common carriers was important and even the railways had the status of common carriers. Today most road hauliers reserve the right to refuse loads and the railways are no longer common carriers (Sect. 43, Transport Act, 1962) and the subject has less practical importance.

A person may cease at any time to be a common carrier by giving public notice that he is no longer prepared to carry goods for the public at large. If the notice relates only to goods of a particular kind, he ceases to be a common carrier of those goods but remains a common carrier of all other goods of which he was formerly a common carrier.

2. **Private Carriers.** Where a man carries goods occasionally or by special agreement, he is called a private carrier. A private carrier for reward has the responsibility of a bailee, and negligence must be proved to make him liable for loss or damage, although loss or non-delivery is *prima facie* evidence of negligence and must be rebutted by him.

A private carrier may limit or exclude his liability for negligence by a term in the contract of carriage. A gratuitous carrier, i.e. a carrier who does not seek reward, is bound to take reasonable care of the goods. He is liable for negligence unless when he takes possession he makes it clear that he will not accept liability. The standard of care expected of a gratuitous bailee or carrier is generally less than that expected of a bailee or carrier for reward, but in both cases the standard required depends upon the circumstances. (*Houghland* v. *R. Low (Luxury Coaches) Ltd.*, 1962.)[337]

Common Carrier's Duties and Liabilities at Common Law. A common carrier must accept goods offered to him for carriage, and if he refuses without lawful excuse to carry such goods, he is liable in tort for damage suffered by the owner and resulting from such refusal. (*Jackson* v. *Rogers*, 1683.)[650]

PAYMENT OF CARRIAGE. A common carrier may demand the cost of carriage when the goods are delivered to him, and if this is not paid, he may lawfully refuse to accept them. If the carrier demands an unreasonably high freight or insists on unreasonable conditions of carriage, this amounts to a refusal to carry and the carrier will be liable for damages. Nevertheless, he is not obliged to charge all customers the same, and provided differential charges have a reasonable basis, he may charge one customer more than another. (*Baxendale* v. *Eastern Counties Railway Co.*, 1858.)[651]

EXCUSES FOR REFUSAL TO CARRY. A common carrier has the following lawful excuses for refusal to carry—

(i) That he does not carry the type of goods offered or operate to the prescribed destination;

(ii) That the goods are dangerous, are likely to cause damage, and cannot be carried safely;

(iii) That the country through which the goods are to be carried is in a disturbed and riotous state (*Edward* v. *Sherratt*, 1801);[652]

(iv) That his vehicle is full;

(v) That the goods are not properly packed;

(vi) That the consignor refuses to disclose the nature of the goods offered for carriage.

DEVIATION AND DELAY. A carrier must follow his customary route and must not deviate from it without cause. He need not carry by the shortest route, indeed to do so would be to deviate if it were not his usual route. (*Hales* v. *London & N.W. Railway Co.*, 1863.)[653]

A carrier who deviates is in breach of contract and the breach amounts to repudiation of the contract. This means that the carrier cannot rely on any of the terms of the contract by which he may have limited his liability, though he is entitled to a reasonable sum as freight, (*Hain Steamship Co.* v. *Tate and Lyle Ltd.*, [1936] 2 All E.R. 597) and may rely on the provisions of the Carriers' Act, 1830. The parties may agree by an express term in the contract that the carrier may deviate either generally or for agreed purposes. In these circumstances, the carrier incurs no liability for deviation within the express provisions of the contract.

The carrier must deliver the goods within the time expressed in the contract or within a reasonable time. He is liable for any delay caused by his negligence. If he deviates unnecessarily from his ordinary route, he is liable for damage caused by delay resulting from such deviation. Where the delay is caused by an accident arising from circumstances outside the carrier's control, he must take reasonable, but not extraordinary steps to mitigate the consequences of delay. He need not incur unreasonable expenses.

If the consignor has insufficiently addressed the goods, the carrier is not liable for loss or delay arising from this cause.

LIABILITY FOR LOSS OR DAMAGE. A common carrier is entirely responsible for the safety of the goods carried except when the loss or damage arises: (i) from Act of God; (ii) from Acts of the Queen's enemies; (iii) from the fault or fraud of the consignor; (iv) from inherent vice in the goods themselves.

There was a real possibility of carriers conspiring with robbers, and therefore a carrier has been held liable without excuse even when he is overwhelmed and robbed by an "irresistible number of people." He is regarded as the insurer of the safety of the goods against any external cause which may give rise to loss or injury, even where caused by the negligence of persons over whom he has no control, except acts of God or the Queen's Enemies. This responsibility arises out of the custom of the realm and not out of the contract between the carrier and the consignor, and even where there is a contract, the common law rules as to liability apply unless expressly limited by its terms. (*Harris* v. *Packwood*, 1810.)[654]

The scope of a common carrier's liability makes it unnecessary for him to warrant the roadworthiness or seaworthiness of his conveyance. If the goods are conveyed safely then such a warranty is irrelevant; and if they are lost or damaged, he is liable in any case, apart from excepted perils.

EXCEPTED PERILS. We have seen that there are four excepted perils, but even so, the common carrier must use *reasonable care* to avoid their consequences or he will remain liable. The onus of proof that the loss or damage was due to an excepted peril is on the carrier.

(i) *Act of God.* The carrier is not responsible for the consequences of an act of God, i.e. an operation of natural forces beyond the reasonable anticipation of human knowledge and foresight such as an abnormal fall of rain. (*Nugent* v. *Smith*, 1876.)[655] The carrier must take reasonable steps to avoid the consequences of such acts and must make reasonable efforts to protect the goods, but he is not bound to take precautions against quite abnormal contingencies.

(ii) *Acts of the Queen's Enemies.* In practice this is restricted to the acts of enemies in war-time or possibly to revolutionaries in a time of civil war. It does not include acts of rioters or strikers or bandits.

(iii) *Fault or Fraud of the Consignor.* If the consignor is guilty of fraud, e.g. by making an untrue statement as to the nature of the goods, the carrier is relieved of all liability for damage. Nor is he liable for loss or damage arising from acts or omissions of the consignor or his agents. There is an implied warranty on the part of the consignor that the goods offered for carriage are not dangerous or likely to cause delay.

The common carrier need not accept goods improperly packed. If, however, he does accept badly packed goods, he must take reasonable care of them according to the state they are in, and is *liable for damage not ascribable to faulty packing*.

No information need normally be given as to the contents of a package unless requested by the carrier, but if the carrier does ask questions, an untrue answer will relieve the carrier of his liabilities.

(iv) *Inherent Vice.* A common carrier's liability extends to harm from external causes, but not to loss from inherent vice, i.e. defects arising out of the nature of the goods themselves. Thus, animals carried in the normal way may attack each other or injure themselves in unusual ways, and soft fruit may rot in transit or be damaged by pressure resulting from its own weight.

Where the damage is confined to the goods inherently vicious, the carrier is absolved from liability. If, however, the inherent vice involves danger to other goods carried, the carrier will be liable to the consignors of those other goods if damage does arise, and may recover from the consignor of the dangerous goods. Even if the carrier has excluded his liability to the owners of the other goods, he may still recover the amount of the damage from the owner of the offending goods, but he holds any sums so recovered in trust for the owners of the damaged goods.

Delivery. The carrier's duties and liabilities begin when he accepts the goods for carriage, and he must not only carry them safely but also deliver them safely to their destination, which may be stipulated in the agreement or arise from the ordinary course of business. He has a duty to deliver them to the right person and is liable if he delivers them to another. Moreover, if a person D is entitled to demand the goods and does so, and the carrier, believing the goods to belong to another, refuses to deliver them, D has a right of action.

The carrier must deliver the goods to the consignee at a reasonable hour. He is safe in delivering them at the premises to which they are addressed, even if it turns out that the person taking delivery had no authority to do so; but if he delivers the goods elsewhere to any person other than the consignee, this probably amounts to a conversion. If the consignee cannot be found at the address given, or if the goods are presented at a reasonable hour and are refused, the carrier's liability as a carrier ends but his liability as a warehouseman begins. He is thereafter a bailee of the goods, and has the liabilities of a bailee for the degree of negligence attaching to such a bailment. (*Heugh* v. *London & North Western Railway Co.*, 1870.)[656]

Where the goods are to be delivered to the consignee at the carrier's office, the carrier must inform the consignee of the arrival of the goods, and if they are not collected within a reasonable time, the carriage is at an end and the carrier holds as a warehouseman.

A carrier may limit or exclude his liability for misdelivery by an express term in the contract of carriage. Such a term is seemingly not void as being repugnant to the main purpose of the contract, provided it covers the circumstances of the case. (*Alexander* v. *Railway Executive*, 1951.)[195]

Carrier's Lien. The carrier has a common law lien to retain the goods until his charges for the carriage are paid. (*Skinner* v. *Upshaw*, 1702.)[657] He is not entitled to sell the goods unless his contract gives him an *active lien* (see below), nor may he use them in any way while they are in his possession. A carrier's lien is a *particular and possessory lien* and may be exercised only in respect of freight charges for that particular consignment of goods, and not for other carriage charges or other debts owed by that particular consignor. The lien cannot be enforced if the carrier has agreed to give credit.

A carrier who lawfully exercises his lien over goods is in possession of them as a bailee and is liable as such.

In exceptional cases and by *express provision* in a contract, the carrier may have a *general lien* covering all freight charges and other debts due to him from the consignor, and if such a lien carries with it a right of sale, it becomes what is known as an *active lien*. Once a lien has been exercised the carrier may not charge warehousing costs to the consignor, but he may recover costs reasonably incurred in preserving the value of the goods, e.g. the cost of feed for animals.

Where an unpaid seller exercises his right of stoppage *in transitu* (see page 157) the carrier may exercise his common law lien against the seller and keep the goods until he has been paid the freight and costs of re-delivery. He cannot, however, exercise a *general* or *active* lien which may have been granted in the contract of carriage. Any general or active lien is usually regarded as applying only against the consignee unless the contractual provision states clearly that they may operate against a seller exercising his right of stoppage *in transitu.*

A common carrier may exercise his common law lien against the lawful owners of goods for freight incurred by a thief or other wrongful possessor who delivered the goods to the carrier.

Unlike a common carrier, a private carrier has no right of lien, unless his contract gives him one.

Measure of Damages. In cases of total loss, the measure of damages is the value of the property lost.

(*a*) Where there is a market for the type of goods lost, the damages are the market value of the goods at the place to which they were consigned at the time they should have been delivered.

(*b*) If there is no such market, the damages are the cost price of the goods, the cost of carriage, and *if the carrier knew that the goods were bought for resale,* the profit which might reasonably have been made in the ordinary course of business. However, the rule of remoteness of damage in *Hadley* v. *Baxendale*[305] applies, and loss of profits will not normally be recoverable unless the special circumstances are brought to the notice of the carrier at or before the time of the contract.

It is common for goods to deteriorate in value owing to delay, and the consignor can recover the loss in value between the projected and actual times of delivery, as well as any reasonable expenses incurred in looking for the goods during the period of delay. He is under a duty to mitigate the loss where this can reasonably be done and his conduct in this respect will be taken into account when assessing damages. If the value of the goods has been declared, no greater value can be received.

The contract may provide for a sum to be payable as liquidated damages for breach, though if the sum mentioned is a penalty it will be void (see p. 91).

Variation of Common Law Duties and Liabilities. A common carrier may restrict his liability by contract, but the court leans heavily against clauses whereby a carrier attempts to escape liability for the misconduct of his servants. Where the contract is made by a ticket or form handed to the consignor, he will not be bound by its terms unless he has agreed to them either expressly or by implication.

THE CARRIERS ACT, 1830

The Carriers Act, 1830, was passed to give some relief to common carriers in respect of liability for extremely valuable articles contained in small parcels.

The Act no longer applies to the carriage of mails nor to the carriage of goods by sea. Originally it applied to carriage by railway since the railway companies were common carriers. The Transport Act, 1962, provided that the Railways Board should not be regarded as a common carrier and consequently the Carriers Act no longer applies to carriage by railway.

Where certain specified goods *exceeding* £10 *in value* contained in a parcel or package are delivered to a carrier, either to be carried for reward or to accompany a passenger, the nature and value of the goods must be declared or the carrier will not be liable for their loss or damage, unless caused by the theft of his servants. The carrier may also charge an additional amount over and above the ordinary rate by way of insurance. The value of the goods is, it seems, to be taken as the value to the consignor at the time of the carriage. Although the Act refers to a "parcel or package" containing the valuables, Sect. 1 seems to apply where the valuables are placed without any wrapping in a truck. (*Whaite* v. *Lancashire and Yorkshire Rail. Company* (1874), L.R. 9 Ex. 67.)

Goods Specified. The goods specified include gold and silver, whether in coin or other form, precious stones and jewellery, watches and clocks, bills and bank notes, valuable documents and pictures, glass and china, furs and silks. (Sect. 1.) The value of the goods *must exceed* £10 and goods outside the specified categories are not included in the calculation if contained in mixed parcels. Thus a parcel containing £10 worth of jewellery and £10 worth of goods outside the definition need not be declared. The cost of the wrapping or container can be added to the value of the enclosed goods if they are all within the Act; but not otherwise unless the container itself were (say) of glass or china, in which case its value would be added to the value of the declarable contents.

Declaration. The declaration may be made in any form, either written or by word of mouth, and if such a declaration is not made, the carrier remains liable for delay but is relieved of all liability for loss, except in the case of his servants' theft.

The carrier will normally charge *an additional sum by way of insurance* on receiving the declaration, but provided that the consignor has made the required declaration, the carrier has his full common law liability regardless of whether he has made the additional charge or not.

The carrier must exhibit a conspicuous notice where the goods are received drawing attention to the need for a declaration and giving the scale of extra charges, and must give a receipt for the *extra charge by way of insurance* on demand. Failure to do these things deprives him of the protection of the Act and he must return any increased charge he has made. (Sect. 2.)

Where the goods have been stolen by one of the carrier's servants he is liable, declaration or no declaration (Sect. 8), but the onus of proving that the loss was by theft is on the consignor, although if he can prove that the goods must have been stolen by one of two or more servants, but the evidence is not strong enough to say which, the onus is discharged.

The Act also provides that the carrier may not by means of a public notice limit his common law liability (Sect. 4), although he may do so by means of a special contract specifically drawn to the consignor's attention. (Sect. 6.)

Where a parcel which has been duly declared and on which the increased charge has been paid suffers loss or damage, the consignor may recover not only the amount of the loss but also the increased charges paid. The owner cannot recover in respect of the contents more than the amount of the declared value, and in the event of loss this value is not assumed to be correct but the owner is required to prove it.

Private Carriers. The Carriers Act, 1830, does not apply to private carriers. The liability of such carriers is unlimited though they can, and frequently do, limit or exclude their liability by contract. The standard conditions of the Road Haulage Association contain a clause limiting the carrier's liability to a fixed sum, and in this connection the Court of Appeal held in *John Carter Ltd.* v. *H. Hanson Haulage (Leeds) Ltd.*, [1965] 1 All E.R. 113, that the clause was effective even though the goods were stolen by a servant who was employed without proper references.

INTERNATIONAL CARRIAGE OF GOODS BY ROAD

The Carriage of Goods by Road Act, 1965, which was brought into force on 5th June, 1967, provides that all cases of international carriage by road (other than carriage of postal packets, funeral consignments and furniture removal) shall be governed by the provisions of the Convention of Geneva of 1956. The provisions do not apply to carriage between Great Britain and Northern Ireland or between Great Britain and the Republic of Ireland.

International carriage by road is the carriage of goods by road from a place in one state to a place in another state if either of the two states is a party to the Convention of Geneva. If part of the journey is by sea, the whole journey is regarded as international carriage by road if the goods remain unloaded on the vehicle while they are on the ship. The following countries are parties to the Convention: United Kingdom, Austria, Belgium, Denmark, France, West Germany, Holland, Italy, Luxembourg, Poland and Yugoslavia.

Consignment Note. The person sending the goods and the carrier must make out a three-part consignment note, one being retained by the sender, one by the carrier, and the other accompanying the goods.

Under Art. 6 of the Convention, the consignment note must contain—

(*a*) the date of the consignment note and the place at which it is made out;

(*b*) the name and address of the sender;

(*c*) the name and address of the carrier;

(*d*) the place and the date of taking over of the goods and the place designated for delivery;

(*e*) the name and address of the consignee;

(*f*) the description in common use of the nature of the goods and the method of packing, and, in the case of dangerous goods, their generally recognised description;

(*g*) the number of packages and their special marks and numbers;

(*h*) the gross weight of the goods or their quantity otherwise expressed;

(*i*) charges relating to the carriage (carriage charges, supplementary charges, customs duties and other charges incurred from the making of the contract to the time of delivery);

(*j*) the requisite instructions for Customs and other formalities;

(*k*) a statement that the carriage is subject, notwithstanding any clause to the contrary, to the provisions of the Convention.

The consignment note shall also contain, "where applicable," these additional particulars—

(*a*) a statement that trans-shipment is not allowed;

(*b*) the charges which the sender undertakes to pay;

(*c*) the amount of "cash on delivery" charges;

(*d*) a declaration of the value of the goods and the amount representing agreed special value (if any);

(*e*) the sender's instructions to the carrier regarding insurance of the goods;

(*f*) the agreed time-limit within which the carriage is to be carried out (see page 415);

(*g*) a list of the documents handed to the carrier.

Other matters of useful information may be inserted by the parties if they wish.

Art. 7 of the Convention makes the sender responsible for expenses, loss and damage sustained by the carrier as a result of the inaccuracy or inadequacy of the instructions or particulars given or specified by the sender in the consignment note.

In order that the person entitled to the goods shall have the protection of the Convention, the consignment note must contain a statement required by Article 6 that the carriage is subject, notwithstanding any clause to the contrary, to the provisions of the Convention. If the consignment note does not contain this statement so that the Convention does not apply, the carrier is liable for all expenses, loss and damage sustained, by reason of the omission, to the person entitled to dispose of the goods.

Carrier's Liability. Art. 17 (2) makes the carrier liable for any loss or damage to the goods from the time he takes them over until delivery. The Article also provides that the carrier will be exempted from liability if he can prove that any loss, damage or delay was caused by the act of the claimant (or plaintiff), or the inherent vice of the goods or circumstances which he could not prevent. This would include an Act of God or the Queen's enemies and probably many other situations in which a common carrier would be liable. His position would seem, therefore, to be stronger than that of a common carrier but weaker than the private carrier by road. The carrier is given additional defences in Art. 17 (4) which provides that the carrier shall not be liable where loss or damage arises from the special risks involved in—

(*a*) use of open unsheeted vehicles, when their use has been expressly agreed and specified in the consignment note; or

(*b*) the lack of, or defective condition of packing in the case of goods which, by their nature, are liable to wastage or to be damaged when not packed or when not properly packed; or

(*c*) handling, loading, stowage or unloading of the goods by the sender, the consignee or persons acting on behalf of the sender or the consignee; or

(*d*) the nature of certain kinds of goods which particularly exposes them to total or partial loss or to damage, especially through breakage, rust, decay, desiccation, leakage, normal wastage, or the action of moth or vermin; or

(*e*) insufficiency or inadequacy of marks or numbers on the packages.

The defence under (*d*)above is not available to a carrier if his vehicle is specially equipped to protect the goods from damage by heat, cold, temperature variation, or humidity unless the carrier shows that he has taken reasonable steps to maintain the vehicle and complied with any special instructions given to him. (Art. 18 (4).)

Provided the carrier takes "all steps normally incumbent on him in the circumstances" he is not liable for loss or damage caused by the special risks involved in the carriage of livestock. (Art. 17 (4) (*f*) and and Art. 18 (5).)

Under Art. 17 (3) the carrier cannot escape liability by pleading the defective condition of the vehicle used for the carriage or the wrongful act or neglect of the person from whom it was hired or of that person's servants or agents.

Delay. The carrier is liable for delay if the goods are not delivered by the time agreed or within a reasonable time if no time limit is agreed. (Art. 19.) Agreed time limits must be stated in the consignment note, (Art. 6 (2) (*f*)) and the sender is made responsible for all expenses, loss or damage incurred by the carrier by reason of the inadequacy or inaccuracy of the information as to the agreed time limit given in the consignment note. (Art. 7 (1) (*b*).) The carrier is exempt where the delay is caused by the wrongful act or neglect of the claimant or his instructions or by inherent vice of the goods or through circumstances which the carrier could not prevent. (Art. 17 (2).)

Presumption of Loss. Under Art. 20, if the goods are not delivered within 30 days after the agreed time limit or, in the absence of an agreed time limit, within 60 days from the carrier taking over the goods, the position is as follows—

(*a*) there is a conclusive presumption that the goods are lost;

(*b*) the owner may claim compensation from the carrier;

(*c*) the owner may by a request in writing ask the carrier to notify him if the goods are found within a year;

(*d*) if they are so found the carrier must deliver them to the owner and the owner must repay any compensation received and the costs of carriage though without prejudice to his right to claim compensation for the delay.

In the absence of the request set out in (*c*) above the carrier may deal with any goods which are found and the consignee retains the compensation.

Deviation. The Convention does not contain any provision relating to deviation. In consequence a carrier is not deprived of the rights given to him by the Convention merely because he deviates from the route.

Dangerous Goods. Under Art. 22 the position is as follows—

(*a*) the sender must inform the carrier of the precise nature of dangerous goods delivered to him which must also be stated on the consignment note;

(*b*) where this is not so, the carrier may unload or destroy them or render them harmless without liability to pay compensation.

Limitation of Damages. Under the provisions of Art. 23 the position is as follows—

TOTAL OR PARTIAL LOSS

(*a*) damages are *based* on the value of the goods at the place and time at which they were accepted for carriage but are limited to 25 gold francs per kilogram of gross weight short, being a gold franc weighing 10/31 of a gramme and of millesimal fineness 900;

(*b*) the carrier must also refund all Customs duties, carriage and other charges;

(*c*) if the parties have agreed, that in consideration of a surcharge to be paid to the carrier, the goods shall have a stated and special value which is set out on the consignment note, the special value as stated is recoverable and not the 25 gold francs per kilogram.

DAMAGED GOODS. The reduction in value as a result of the damage is recoverable provided this does not exceed the maximum sum recoverable if the goods have been lost, i.e. 25 gold francs per kilogram.

DELAY. Damages are limited to the charges for carriage unless the parties have agreed to insert a higher figure in the consignment note. This will involve the payment of an additional sum of money to the carrier for accepting increased liability.

The limitations set out above do not apply if the carrier or his agents and servants have been guilty of wilful misconduct. In addition, the carrier is liable to pay interest on damages at 5 per cent from the day when the claim was first made in writing to the carrier or where no such claim was made from the day of commencement of legal proceedings.

Time Limit for Claims. Various situations are dealt with by Art. 30 as follows—

(*a*) WHERE THE CONSIGNEE HAS CHECKED THE GOODS BEFORE TAKING DELIVERY. No evidence will be admissible to prove loss or damage which should have been apparent. Where the damage would not have been apparent, evidence contradicting the checking is admissible provided the consignee has sent reservations in writing to the carrier within seven days (excluding Sundays and public holidays) of checking.

(*b*) WHERE THE CONSIGNEE HAS NOT CHECKED THE GOODS BEFORE TAKING DELIVERY. His acceptance of the goods and failure, if any, to make reservations in writing to the carrier within seven days as above is only *prima facie* evidence that no loss or damage occurred during carriage and evidence that it did is admissible.

(*c*) DELAY. No damages are payable for delay unless the consignee notified the carrier in writing within 21 days (excluding Sundays and public holidays) from the time at which the goods were placed at his disposal. As we have already seen, undue delay can give rise to presumption of loss.

(*d*) LOSS OF RIGHT TO SUE. The following rights of action are lost unless proceedings are commenced within one year from—

(i) *the date of delivery to the consignee*—in the case of partial loss, damage, or delay;

(ii) *within 30 days from the date when the goods should have been delivered*—in the case of total loss with an agreed time limit for delivery;

(iii) *within 60 days from the date when the carrier took over the goods*—in the case of a total loss without an agreed time limit for delivery;

(iv) *three months after the contract of marriage was made*—in all other cases.

In all the time limits given above the day from which the time is reckoned is excluded from the number of days fixed, the period starting to run from the next following day.

Involvement of Two or more Carriers. There are a number of provisions in the Convention which relate to this situation as follows—

(*a*) *Art. 35*, which requires that a second or subsequent carrier shall when he takes over the goods give a dated and signed receipt for them to the first carrier and shall enter his name and address on the second copy of the consignment note;

(*b*) *Art. 34*, which provides that second and subsequent carriers accepting the goods and the consignment note become parties to the original contract of carriage and are liable to the owner of the goods for the whole duration of the carriage;

(c) *Art. 36*, which provides that legal proceedings for loss, damage or delay are to be brought against the first or last carrier whether responsible or not, or the carrier who had the goods when the loss, damage or delay occurred. The Convention gives all the carriers involved a right to claim a *contribution* from others who were *jointly* responsible for the loss, damage or delay, or an indemnity from others who were wholly responsible for the loss, damage or delay.

Jurisdiction and Contracting Out. Under Art. 31 actions under the Convention may be brought in only in the courts of the country in which—

(a) the defendant normally resides, or has his main place of business; or

(b) the contract was made; or

(c) the place of destination was situated.

The parties may agree to refer the case to an arbitrator provided he is required to apply the Convention.

By Art. 41 the parties cannot exclude the Convention and any contract which tries to do so is void but only to the extent to which its terms are repugnant to those of the Convention, though under Art. 40 where there are two or more carriers they can vary the Convention as regards their right of contribution and indemnity.

CARRIAGE BY RAIL

Transport Charges and Facilities Generally. Sect. 43 of the Transport Act, 1962, lays down general provisions governing charges and facilities and greatly frees the railways from the onerous obligations which they formerly had.

(1) None of the Boards shall be regarded as common carriers by rail or inland waterway.

(2) All previous statutory charges schemes cease to have effect and the Boards shall have power to demand, take and recover such charges for their services and facilities, and to make the use of those services and facilities subject to such terms and conditions, as they think fit.

(3) The Boards are not subject to enactments which—

(a) impose a duty to afford reasonable services and facilities; and

(b) regulate liability for negligence in the carriage of goods; and

(c) authorise the revision of railway freight charges on complaint by competitors or traders.

(4) However, the Boards shall not carry passengers by rail on terms or conditions which—

(a) purport, whether directly or indirectly, to exclude or limit their liability in respect of the death of, or bodily injury to, any passenger other than a passenger travelling on a free pass; or (*b*) purport, whether directly or indirectly, to prescribe the time within which or the manner in which any such liability may be enforced; and any such terms or conditions shall be void and of no effect.

Carriage of Goods. As we have seen, the Transport Act, 1962, abolishes the Standard Terms and Conditions which were given the force of law by rules and orders made under previous enactments—in particular the Railways Act, 1921. Since the 1st September, 1962, the conditions of carriage by the railway should be settled by the contract made by the parties.

However, the terms of the contracts into which British Rail are now prepared to enter are contained in the Book of Rules of British Rail and are virtually identical with the former Standard Terms and Conditions for carriage at company's risk and owner's risk in force prior to the Transport Act, 1962.

Conditions of Carriage at the Board's Risk. The British Railways Board issues *General Conditions of Carriage* for the carriage of merchandise (other than dangerous goods and merchandise for which conditions are specially provided) when carried at the *Board's Risk*. There are also conditions of carriage by water, and others governing the carriage of livestock and coal. The following are some of the more important aspects of the General Conditions of Carriage at the Board's Risk.

CONSIGNMENT NOTE. Consignments must be addressed in accordance with the Board's requirements and must be accompanied by a consignment note bearing the required particulars. The Board must, if required, acknowledge on a form prepared by the consignor the receipt of the consignment.

WARRANTY. In the absence of written notice to the contrary at the time of delivery to the Board, all merchandise is warranted by the sender to be fit to be carried or stored as handed to the Board, and not to be merchandise included in the Board's List of Dangerous Goods.

LIABILITY FOR LOSS OR DAMAGE. The Board is liable for loss or misdelivery of or damage to goods during transit unless the Board can prove that the loss, misdelivery or damage arose from—(*a*) act of God; (*b*) any consequences of war, invasion, act of foreign enemy, civil war, rebellion, confiscation, requisition, or destruction under order of government or public authority; (*c*) seizure under legal process; (*d*) act or omission of the trader or his servants; (*e*) inherent liability to wastage in bulk or weight, latent or inherent defect, vice or natural deterioration of the goods; (*f*) casualty (including fire and explosion).

The Board is liable for loss arising from delay, detention or unreasonable deviation unless the Board can prove that it used all reasonable foresight and care in the carriage.

The Board incurs no liability of any kind where there has been fraud on the part of the trader.

The Board is not liable where the loss, damage or delay can be proved by the Board to have arisen from (a) insufficient or improper packing; (b) riots, civil commotions, strikes, lockouts, stoppage or restraint of labour from whatever cause, whether partial or general; or (c) the consignee not taking or accepting delivery within a reasonable time.

LIABILITY FOR DELAY. The Board accepts, subject to the Conditions, liability for loss proved by the trader to have been caused by delay to, or detention of, or unreasonable deviation in the carriage, unless the Board can prove lack of negligence on the part of itself or its servants or agents.

LIMITATION OF LIABILITY. The Board limits its liability in respect of any one consignment as follows—

(i) Where the loss is in respect of the whole consignment the liability is limited to a sum at the rate of £800 per ton on the gross weight of the consignment.

(ii) Where the loss is in respect of part of a consignment, a sum ascertained on the same basis *pro rata*.

(iii) Nevertheless, the Board will remain liable up to £10 in respect of any one consignment.

(iv) The Board is entitled to proof of the value of the whole consignment.

The Board is not liable for indirect or consequential damages or for the loss of a particular market whether held daily or at intervals.

TIME LIMIT FOR CLAIMS. In the event of a claim for loss from a package or from an unpacked consignment, for damage, deviation, misdelivery, delay or detention, the Board must be advised within three days and a claim must be made in writing within seven days after the termination of transit. In the case of non-delivery of the whole of any consignment, or of a separate package forming part of a consignment, the Board must be advised within twenty-eight days, and a claim must be made in writing within forty-two days after handing in the consignment. The Board, however, remains liable if the trader can prove that it was not reasonably possible to observe these time limits, and that the advice and claim was made within a reasonable time.

UNDELIVERED OR UNCLAIMED MERCHANDISE. Where the Board is unable to deliver merchandise to the consignee, or where goods to be called for are not collected within a reasonable time, the Board may sell the goods and tender the proceeds of the sale to the consignee after deducting proper charges and expenses. The Board must, however, obtain a reasonable price and where the name and address of the sender or consignee is known must give them reasonable notice that the goods will be sold unless they are collected or delivery instructions given.

GENERAL LIEN. Merchandise delivered to the Board is received and held subject: (a) to a lien for carriage and charges or expenses in connection with the merchandise; and (b) to a general lien for any moneys and charges due from the owners of such merchandise for any services rendered or accommodation provided in relation to the carriage or custody of merchandise. If the lien is not satisfied within a reasonable time of the owners being notified of its exercise, the goods may be sold and the proceeds applied to the satisfaction of the lien and other appropriate charges and expenses. The Board must account to the owners of the goods for any surplus.

The general lien shall not prejudice an unpaid seller's right of stoppage *in transitu*. (See page 157.)

END OF TRANSIT. The transit is deemed to end when the merchandise is tendered at the consignee's address; or if it is to be retained pending instructions, after one clear day's notice in writing has been given to the consignee, or, if his address is unknown, to the sender; or where the merchandise is to be called for, one clear day after reaching the place of consignment.

After termination of the transit, the Board will hold the merchandise as warehousemen subject to specified conditions.

CARRIAGE INVOLVING WATER TRANSPORT. Where goods are to be carried partly by land and partly by water, or wholly by water, they shall be conveyed subject to the terms and conditions applicable to carriage by water.

Goods carried at Owner's Risk. Where goods are carried at Owner's Risk, the Board will not be liable for loss, damage, deviation, misdelivery, delay or detention of or to the consignment or any part of it unless it can be proved to be due to the wilful default or misconduct of the Board or their servants. This exemption from liability does not apply to the loss of or non-delivery of the whole of a consignment or of a separate package if liability would otherwise arise under the General Conditions of Carriage.

The burden of proving wilful default rests on the plaintiff and the fact that the Railways Board cannot or will not give an explanation of the damage or loss is not in itself evidence of wilful default. (*H. C. Smith Ltd.* v. *Great Western Rail Co.*, [1922] 1 A.C. 178.) Wilful default implies an element of will as opposed to mere negligence or carelessness. Thus in *Hartstoke Fruiterers* v. *London, Midland and Scottish Rail. Co.*, [1942] 2 All E.R. 488, where railway employees at the station at which goods arrived forgot an instruction to inform the consignee by telephone with the consequence that the goods perished, it was held that the railway company was not liable since the employees were not guilty of wilful misconduct but only of negligence.

Misdelivery is, however, always regarded as misconduct and because delivery is generally a conscious and intentional act even though to the wrong person, misdelivery normally amounts to wilful misconduct.

DAMAGEABLE GOODS. The Board is not liable for loss of or damage to a consignment or any part of it unless it can be proved to have been due to the wilful misconduct of the Board or their servants, or that it would have been suffered if the goods had been properly protected by packing and the Board would have been liable under the General Conditions of Carriage or Conditions of Carriage by Water as the case may be.

INTERNATIONAL TRAFFIC. Some international traffic is carried by British Rail under the International Convention concerning the Carriage of Goods by Rail, 1961. (See also Carriage by Railway Act, 1972.)

Carriage of Passengers' Luggage. The Railways Board is not liable for loss or damage to luggage which passengers retain in the compartment during the journey. Such luggage is not regarded as being in the possession of railway employees, so that the Board is not a carrier of it.

With regard to luggage which is not retained by the passenger but handed into the care of a railway employee, the Board is liable as a private carrier for negligence or wilful default.

CARRIAGE BY INLAND WATERWAYS

The British Railways Board also issues a document governing carriage by water which covers much the same ground as the General Conditions of Carriage with appropriate additions or modifications applicable to water transport. The conditions contain a long list of eventualities giving immunity from liability and even where the Board accepts liability the amount is limited by the following rules: (i) liability for loss of or damage to merchandise is limited to an amount not exceeding £200 per package or unit, or the equivalent of that sum in other currency; (ii) liability is excluded if the nature or value of the merchandise is knowingly mis-stated by the sender; (iii) limits are set to liability for livestock, e.g. £100 for a horse, £25 for a pig, £5 for a dog, and so on. The Board reserves both a particular and a general lien for its charges on the same lines as for carriage by rail, and prescribes conditions governing the termination of transit and the time limits and conditions for the making of claims.

Apart from the special conditions of carriage by British Rail, other carriers by water such as bargemen and ferrymen are common carriers if they hold themselves out as willing to carry goods for the public. They are subject to the same liabilities as a common carrier by land and may similarly limit their liability by special contract.

A carrier by water also warrants that his craft is seaworthy, which in this case means that it is fit for the purpose for which it is used. He is also liable as an insurer for passengers' luggage except where it is retained by the passenger. (*Willoughby* v. *Horridge* (1852), 12 C.B. 742.)

PIPE-LINES

The control of the construction of pipe-lines and regulations relating to operation and maintenance are contained in the Pipe-Lines Act, 1962.

CARRIAGE BY SEA

Until the end of 1924, contracts of carriage of goods by sea were governed by the common law though certain statutory provisions applied, i.e. those of the Bills of Lading Act, 1855, and the Merchant

Shipping Act, 1894. Since 1925, contracts of carriage of goods by sea may be governed by the Hague Rules which were given statutory force by the Carriage of Goods by Sea Act, 1924. Thus, the starting-point is to give a brief outline of the common law relating to the carriage of goods by sea which, along with the Merchant Shipping Act, 1894 (as amended), governs contracts which are not subject to the Hague Rules.

The next section gives an outline of the Carriage of Goods by Sea Act, 1924, which incorporates the Hague Rules.

In the third section consideration is given to the relevant provisions of the Merchant Shipping Act, 1894, as amended by the Merchant Shipping (Liability of Shipowners and Others) Act, 1958. These Acts are independent of and additional to the provisions of the Carriage of Goods by Sea Act, 1924.

The fourth section deals with the two kinds of contracts of carriage of goods by sea (or affreightment), i.e. bills of lading and charter parties.

COMMON LAW POSITION

The liability of a common carrier at sea is the same as that of a carrier on land and he has the same defences, i.e. Act of God or of the Queen's enemies, fault or fraud of the consignor, inherent vice, and one other, namely *jettison*. This defence is available where the goods have been intentionally thrown overboard to preserve the safety of the ship and cargo. Liability in this case is governed by general average already dealt with in the Chapter on Insurance.

The common law carrier gives an absolute warranty of seaworthiness, independent of any diligence he may exercise, and the carrier is liable for loss except where the question of seaworthiness is irrelevant to the particular loss.

Nevertheless, carriers often limit their liability by means of excepted perils in the contract, among which are—Act of God; Act of the Queen's enemies; restraints of princes and rulers; perils of the seas; fire; barratry; piracy; robbery; theft; collisions and accidents. Most of these terms have been defined in connection with Insurance.

A carrier must not deviate, except in saving or attempting to save life, or in order to avoid imminent peril to the ship. He may not, at common law, deviate to save property, and if he has rescued all persons on board a ship and then puts her in tow, this would amount to a deviation. It is, therefore, not uncommon for the contract specifically to permit deviation on these two grounds, and often the contract provides for deviation in order to call at intermediate ports.

CARRIAGE OF GOODS BY SEA ACT, 1924

The Hague Rules were drafted at a conference of the International Law Association at the Hague in 1921, and were adopted at the International Conference at Brussels in 1922. The Carriage of Goods by

Sea Act, 1924, gives statutory force to the nine articles embodied in the Schedule.

The object of the Act was to give some protection to shipowners. The common law liability of shipowners for *seaworthiness* became so onerous that their contracts with shippers contained so many exception clauses as to prove unjust. The Hague Rules addressed themselves to this problem.

The Act applies only to ships sailing *from* ports in Great Britain and Northern Ireland to any other port whether in or outside Great Britain and Northern Ireland. It is concerned with *outbound traffic*.

The contracts of carriage covered are those covered by a bill of lading or similar document, even if issued under a charter party, and presumably this applies even where the bill of lading is not issued if the shipper is entitled to demand one. The rules are not applicable to charter parties as such.

Goods are defined in Article I of the Rules as including goods, wares, merchandises and articles of every kind whatsoever, except live animals and cargo which by the contract of carriage is stated as being carried on deck, and is so carried.

The carriage of goods covers the period from the time when the goods are loaded on, to the time when they are discharged from, the ship, including the loading and unloading operations.

Liability of Carrier under the Hague Rules. The carrier does not warrant the seaworthiness of the ship but he is bound before and at the beginning of the voyage to *exercise due diligence to make the ship seaworthy*, to properly man, equip and supply her, and to make the holds, refrigerating and cool chambers, and all other parts of the ship in which goods are carried, fit and safe for their reception, carriage and preservation. *He is only liable if he does not exercise due diligence.* However, whenever there is loss or damage due to unseaworthiness, the burden of proving the exercise of due diligence is on the carrier or other person claiming exemption under this section.

The carrier has a duty to *properly and carefully* load, handle, stow, carry, keep, care for and discharge the goods carried, but he is *not responsible for loss or damage arising or resulting from*—

1. Act, neglect or default of the master, mariner, pilot, or the servants of the carrier in the navigation or management of the ship;
2. Fire, unless caused by the actual privity or fault of the carrier;
3. Perils, dangers and accidents of the sea or other navigable waters;
4. Act of God;
5. Act of war or of public enemies, or arrest or restraint of princes, rulers, or people, or seizure under legal process;
6. Quarantine restrictions;
7. Act or omission of the shipper or owner of the goods, or his agent or representative;

8. Strikes or lockouts or stoppages of labour, whether partial or general;

9. Riots and civil commotions;

10. Saving or attempting to save life or property at sea;

11. Wastage in bulk or weight or any other loss or damage arising from inherent defect, quality or vice of the goods;

12. Insufficiency of packing, or of marks;

13. Latent defects not discoverable by due diligence;

14. Any other cause arising without the privity of the carrier and without actual fault or neglect of him or his servants or agents.

The burden of proof is on the person claiming the benefit of this exception that there was no such privity, fault or neglect on the part of himself, his servants or agents. It should be noted that stevedores are the servants or agents of the shipowner for this purpose. (*Leesh River Tea Co. Ltd.* v. *British India S.N. Co. Ltd.*, 1966.)[658]

Deviation. Art. IV (4) provides that any deviation in saving or attempting to save life or property at sea, or any reasonable deviation, shall not be deemed to be an infringement of these Rules or of the contract of carriage, and the carrier shall not be liable for any loss or damage resulting therefrom. What is a reasonable deviation is a question of fact bearing in mind the interests of all concerned, shipowner and cargo-owners alike.

Dangerous Goods. The carrier is given a right to land, destroy or render harmless any inflammable, explosive or dangerous goods which he has not knowingly consented to carry, and to recover the costs from the shipper. If he ships such goods with knowledge and consent and they endanger the ship, he may similarly dispose of them without liability except to general average.

Issue of Bill of Lading. After receiving the goods, the carrier or the master or agent of the carrier shall, on demand of the shipper, issue to the shipper a bill of lading. This must show among other things—

(*a*) The leading marks necessary for identification of the goods;

(*b*) Either the number of packages or pieces or the quantity or weight, as the case may be, as furnished in writing by the shipper;

(*c*) The apparent order and condition of the goods.

Such a bill of lading shall be *prima facie* evidence of the receipt by the carrier of the goods therein described and, although the shipper is deemed to have guaranteed to the carrier the accuracy of the marks, number, quantity and weight as furnished by him, the carrier may still be responsible under the contract of carriage to a person other than the shipper for any loss resulting from the supply of inaccurate particulars.

Limitation of Damages. Neither the carrier nor the ship shall in any event be, or become liable for, any loss or damage to or in connection with goods in an amount exceeding £100 per package or unit, unless the nature and value of such goods have been declared by the shipper before shipment and inserted in the bill of lading, when it becomes *prima facie* evidence but not conclusive. A higher maximum may be fixed by agreement, and no liability attaches to the carrier or ship in connection with goods whose value and nature has been knowingly mis-stated by the shipper in the bill of lading. The monetary limit applies to goods of all kinds. However, there is some ambiguity in the limit of £100, since Article IX of the Hague Rules provides that the monetary units mentioned in the Rules are to be taken to be gold value which would make the limit much higher if the rule applies to this figure. To meet the difficulty British shipowners and shippers who are members of the British Maritime Law Association made an agreement to observe a limit of £200, to extend the time limit for commencing actions from one to two years, and to bring actions only in the courts of the United Kingdom. Nevertheless, if gold value is in fact the correct interpretation, the £200 is probably too small a limit in view of the rapid rise in the value of gold since 1921.

No Contracting Out. An agreement to relieve the carrier from liability arising under the Rules is null and void, and a benefit of insurance or similar clause is deemed to be a clause relieving the carrier from liability. However, the carrier may surrender in whole or in part his rights and immunities, or increase his responsibilities under the Rules, if the variations are embodied in the bill of lading. Thus the parties can, by agreement, increase but not lessen the carrier's liabilities.

However, in contracts to which the rules do not apply, but where they are incorporated into the contract, the rules may be modified as the parties may agree.

The Clause Paramount. Every bill of lading or similar document of title issued in Great Britain or Northern Ireland, which contains or is evidence of any contract to which the Rules apply, shall contain an express statement that it is to have effect subject to the provisions of the said Rules as applied by the Act. All contracts which are subject to the Hague Rules are subject to the relevant sections of the Merchant Shipping Act, 1894, relating to the limitation of owners' liability.

MERCHANT SHIPPING ACT

The following provisions of the Merchant Shipping Act, 1894, should be noted—

(i) FIRE. The shipowner is not liable for loss or damage arising, without his actual fault or privity, from fire on board the ship.

(ii) VALUABLES. The shipowner is not liable for loss or damage by reason of robbery or embezzlement of gold, silver, diamonds, watches, jewels or precious stones on board ship, unless the true nature and value have been declared to the master of the ship in bills of lading or otherwise in writing.

(iii) LIMITATION OF DAMAGES. Limits were set to the shipowner's liability for loss of life or injury to persons, or for loss of or damage to goods on the ship, or for similar losses on other ships caused by improper navigation. The limits are now amended by the Merchant Shipping (Liability of Shipowners and Others) Act, 1958, and are as follows—

(a) *For damage to goods* an aggregate amount not exceeding 1,000 gold francs *for each ton* of the ship's tonnage; and

(b) *For loss of life or personal injury*, either *alone or together with* loss of or damage to vessels or goods, an aggregate not exceeding 3,100 gold francs *per ton* of tonnage. For this purpose the multiplier for all ships under 300 tons is reckoned as 300, so that a vessel of one ton would be regarded as of 300 tons for the purpose of liability. There is no such "platform" tonnage where damage is to goods. The owner of a ship may claim limited liability under the Act even though he is also the master. (*The Annie Hay*, 1968.)[659]

Where two or more liabilities are incurred on the same occasion, the claimants must share the statutory aggregate if it is not adequate for all claims. (*Mersey Docks and Harbour Board* v. *Hay*, 1923.)[660]

Where there are claimants for personal injuries or loss of life and claimants for damage to goods, the former may claim up to 2,100 gold francs per ton of tonnage, and rank proportionately with claimants for damage to goods as to the balance of 1,000 per ton.

The Department of Trade and Industry may change the maximum sums of 3,100 and 1,000 gold francs and may order by statutory instrument the English equivalents to the sums mentioned. By an order in 1972, they were declared to be £85·6826 and £27·6396 respectively.

Suppose, therefore, a ship's tonnage is 1,000 tons and claims are made for loss of life and personal injury amounting to £75,000 and for damage to goods amounting to £50,000. The sum available to claimants is £74 (approx.) multiplied by 1,000 which = £74,000. Of this sum £50,000 is available for personal claims and £24,000 for damage to goods. Both are inadequate. The personal claims will attract the whole of the £50,000 and will also share in the £24,000 in the ratio of 25,000:50,000 or 1:2. These shares are respectively £8,000 for personal claims and £16,000 for damage to goods. The result, therefore, is as follows—

(i) *Personal Claims*. Total claimed £75,000; Amount available £58,000; Each claimant receives 77⅓ per cent.

(ii) *Damage to Goods*. Total claimed £50,000; Amount available £18,000; Each claimant receives 36 per cent.

AFFREIGHTMENT

Contracts of affreightment may be of two kinds—

1. Bills of Lading. A bill of lading is a document normally issued and signed by the master of a ship. A bill of lading is not essential but it serves three functions—(i) it is a receipt for goods delivered to the carrier; (ii) it normally embodies the terms of the contract of carriage; (iii) it acts as a document of title to the goods.

2. Charter Parties. A charter party is a contract whereby the charterer takes over a ship for a period of time, or for a voyage or series of voyages.

(*a*) In a charter party by way of demise, the *charterer* becomes the carrier and the master and crew become his servants.

(*b*) In a charter party not by way of demise, the *ship owner* is the carrier and the master and the crew are his servants.

Bills of Lading. When goods are brought to a ship to be loaded, it is common for the mate to issue a document called the *mate's receipt* for the goods, and this is subsequently exchanged for a bill of lading signed by the master. Unlike the bill of lading, the mate's receipt is not a document of title, but is *prime facie* evidence that the holder is entitled to the bill of lading (if there is one) or to the delivery of the goods (if not).

Bills of lading are used where a ship carries cargoes belonging to different consignors, and a bill, normally giving details of the goods to be carried, is given to each consignor. The owner of the goods can transfer the title to them while in transit by endorsement and delivery. It should be noted, however, that, unlike the holder of a bill of exchange, the holder of a bill of lading takes subject to equities, and normally acquires no better title than had the person who transferred it to him.

The bill of lading acts as *prima facie* evidence that the carrier has received the goods set out in it, and if, as is common, it contains a statement that the goods were shipped "in good order and condition," this is conclusive in favour of the holder of the bill, except with regard to hidden defects. The bill of lading is conclusive evidence against the master who signs it, but not against the carrier. Bills of lading may take many forms and may contain a variety of provisions to cover special cases.

The bill of lading normally contains the terms of the contract of carriage; it is not the actual contract but is merely evidence of the terms included in it, and verbal evidence may be admitted to vary or supplement it. (*S.S. Ardennes (Cargo Owners)* v. *S.S. Ardennes (Owners)*, 1951.)[661] In the case of a bill of lading issued to a charterer under a charter party, the charter party contains the terms of the contract and the bill is just a receipt, unless the bill of lading was clearly by way of variation of the terms of the charter party in which case the terms of the bill of lading will prevail over those terms of the charter party *with which they are inconsistent.* Thus where a bill of lading was clearly intended to contain the terms of a new contract between charterer and shipowner but made no reference to arbitration, an arbitration clause in the charter party remained in force so that the charterer could not sue the shipowner by an action in the ordinary courts but was required to resort to arbitration. (*The President of India* v. *Metcalfe Shipping Co. Ltd.*, [1969] 2 Q.B. 123.)

A bill of lading transferred for valuable consideration *conveys the ownership* of the goods to the transferee. A bill of lading may, therefore, be mortgaged or pledged. Moreover, the transfer not only transfers the ownership of the goods, but acts as an assignment of the rights and liabilities under the original contract of carriage in respect of these particular goods.

Bills of lading are commonly executed in three parts, one of which the master keeps, and the other two are handed to the consignor who sends one to the consignee. Where copies of the bill are acquired by different purchasers, the first in time acquires the property in the goods; but since the carrier cannot know of these dealings, he is protected from liability if he delivers the goods to a person presenting one part, even if that person is not entitled to the goods, although such delivery in no way prejudices the title of the real owner.

Charter Parties. Where a *shipowner* makes a written agreement with a *charterer* to let him a ship, or part of a ship, for the carriage of goods, either for a specified period of time, or for a voyage or voyages, in return for a charge called *freight*, the agreement is called a *charter party*. To charter a ship by demise is almost like taking a lease of premises, and it is sometimes done by shipping companies or by governments. A more common form is where the charterer retains the right to have his goods carried, and the shipowner retains possession and control of the ship.

The charter party usually stipulates the name, nationality and class of the ship (e.g. steam or sail), its registration class at Lloyd's, its registered tonnage and carrying capacity, its position at the time the charter party was made, the date when it will be ready to load, and an undertaking that it will proceed to the port where loading is to take place. These stipulations may be either *conditions precedent* to the charter party, or *warranties*. In the former case their breach will amount to a repudiation of the contract, in the latter case a breach will give rise to an action for damages.

Examples of conditions precedent are: (i) the position of the ship when the charter party is made (*Behn* v. *Burness*, 1863);[183] (ii) a stipulation that the ship will be at a specified port ready to load at a specified date; and (iii) the tonnage and carrying capacity of the ship if the charterer intends to load the ship fully—but not if the charter party is for part only of the ship and its capacity is irrelevant.

The charterer must load a full cargo except where: (*a*) the shipowner has broken a condition precedent, or (*b*) the loading turns out to be illegal (*Avery* v. *Bowden*, 1855);[282] or (*c*) the contract is frustrated; but the charter party often stipulates conditions under which failure to load may be excused. The most common are labour disputes, riots and civil commotions, bad weather as specified, and accidents outside the charterer's control. If the shipowner fails to supply a ship without adequate excuse, then the charterer may claim damages. (*Watts, Watts & Co. Ltd.*, v. *Mitsui & Co. Ltd.*, 1917.)[662]

Lay Days and Demurrage. If the charter party allows a specified number of days for loading or uloading, these are known as *lay days*. In the absence of such provision the loading and unloading must be accomplished in a reasonable time. Where the period allowed for unloading is exceeded, extra days may be allowed, and the charterer pays a *demurrage charge* at a daily rate. *Demurrage* is payable either after a stipulated number of lay days, or if no stipulation is made, after a reasonable time has been allowed for the loading or unloading. Even if the charterer exceeds both the period allowed as lay days and demurrage days, the shipowner cannot sail off unless the charterer refuses to load or the contract has been frustrated.

Where the vessel is detained for a period in excess of the lay days and the demurrage provisions cover such delay, damages in excess of the demurrage payments cannot be claimed. (*The Suisse Case*, 1966.)[197]

THE CARRIAGE OF GOODS BY SEA ACT 1971

This Act at the time of writing has received the Royal Assent and will come into effect on a date to be appointed.

Under the Act, the United Kingdom is enabled to ratify a protocol signed by the United Kingdom and twenty other countries in Brussels in February, 1968, which amends the Hague Rules of 1924.

When the Act comes into force, i.e. when the protocol has been ratified by at least ten of the signatory nations, five of which must have registered under their particular flag at least one million tons of shipping, a shipowner's limit of liability per package or unit will be increased to 10,000 gold francs. Under the conversion formula provided this would at present equal £270·00 sterling. In addition, there is a weight limitation of 30 (gold) francs per kilogram (80p sterling per kilogram at present). The liability of the shipowner is based on the highest of the two figures. In consequence a person who ships a small and valuable package would in the event of damage or loss be paid on the package or unit basis and not on weight. The critical point comes at six and two-thirds tons weight. At that stage and beyond, the weight limitation becomes the higher and is available to the owner. As regards container traffic, the Act provides that the parties may at their option—

　　(*a*) enumerate in the bill of lading the number of packages in a container, in which case they will count as packages for the purpose, of liability, or

　　(*b*) not enumerate the packages, in which case the container will be regarded as a unit and will count in the weight limitation.

The Act also confers the benefit of limitation of liability for negligence and the shipowner's defences in the Hague Rules upon the shipowner's servants or agents: thus changing, in this regard, the rule laid down for example in *Adler* v. *Dickson*, 1955,[191] where it was held that servants and agents were not entitled to protection under the Hague Rules. This provision will prevent a shipper circumventing the Hague Rules by the device of suing a servant or agent of the shipowner in the knowledge that the shipowner will pay the damages, as was the case in *Adler* v. *Dickson*, 1955.[191] The limitation of liability of servants and agents does not extend to *intentional* or *reckless* damage caused by them.

The Act also provides that the Hague Rules as amended shall apply as a matter of law in all cases where the bill of lading is issued in a contracting state or where the carriage is from a port in a contracting state, and not only where it is issued in this country (which is the present law). Other contracts may voluntarily provide that the rules shall apply.

The Act makes it clear that the rules apply to coastal traffic, but do not apply where the parties do not issue or contemplate the issue of a bill of lading.

CARRIAGE BY AIR

The law of carriage by air is now governed by the following conventions and enactments—

(*b*) the original Warsaw Convention of 1929 governs international carriage comprised in a flight between two states, both of which have ratified the Convention of 1929 but only one of which or neither of which has ratified the amended Convention of 1955 (see below);

(*b*) the Warsaw Convention, as amended at the Hague in 1955, governs all cases of international carriage comprised in a flight between two states, both of which have ratified the amended Convention. The Convention as amended at the Hague was given the force of law by the Carriage by Air Act, 1961. This Act was brought into force by Order in Council on 1st June, 1967. The Order (S.I. 1967, No. 480) also applied the original Warsaw Convention of 1929 to cases of international carriage still governed by that convention. This was essential in view of the fact that the 1961 Act repealed the Carriage by Air Act, 1932, which had previously given the force of law to the 1929 Convention.

(*c*) all other cases of carriage by air are subject to the Non-International Carriage Rules of 1967.

Thus the starting-point is to consider the provisions of the original Warsaw Convention of 1929 and then to consider the amended Convention of 1955 and the non-international carriage rules.

THE ORIGINAL WARSAW CONVENTION OF 1929

The Convention applies to international carriage of persons, luggage or goods performed by aircraft for reward, and to gratuitous carriage by aircraft performed by an air transport undertaking. In *international carriage* both the place of departure and the place of destination are in states which are parties to the Convention, even if there is an agreed stopping place in a third state which is not a party to the Convention.

Carriage is also international where both the place of departure and destination are in the territory of the same state, if there is an agreed stopping place in the territory of another state, whether or not this other state is a party to the Convention. Thus a flight from Manchester to Gibraltar is non-international if it is direct, but is international if there is a scheduled stop in Paris.

Liability of Carrier for Goods. Every carrier of goods has the right to require the consignor to make out and hand over to him a document called an "air consignment note" (now called an "air way-bill" by S.I. 1967, No. 480—see above, p. 431); and every consignor has a right to require the carrier to accept this document. The waybill is made out in three original parts: one signed by the consignor and marked "for the carrier", a second signed by both the consignor and the carrier and marked "for the consignee" (and intended to accompany the goods); and the third is signed by the carrier and handed back to the consignor after the goods have been accepted. The carrier may require a separate air waybill when there is more than one package.

The *air consignment note* should contain the following particulars—

(*a*) the place and date of its execution;

(*b*) the place of departure and of destination;

(*c*) the agreed stopping places (which the carrier may alter under necessity);

(*d*) the name and address of the consignor;

(*e*) the name and address of the first carrier;

(*f*) the name and address of the consignee, if the case so requires;

(*g*) the nature of the goods;

(*h*) the number of the packages, the method of packing and the particular marks or numbers upon them;

(*i*) the weight, the quantity and the volume or dimensions of the goods;

(*j*) the apparent condition of the goods and of the packing;

(*k*) the freight, if it has been agreed upon, the date and place of payment, and the person who is to pay it;

(*l*) if the goods are sent for payment on delivery, the price of the goods, and, if the case so requires, the amount of the expenses incurred;

(*m*) the amount of the value declared in accordance with Art. 22 (2) (see p. 434);

(*n*) the number of parts of the air waybill;

(*o*) the documents handed to the carrier to accompany the air waybill;

(*p*) the time fixed for the completion of the carriage and a brief note of the route to be followed, if these matters have been agreed upon;

(*q*) a statement that the carriage is subject to the rules relating to liability established by the Convention. (Art. 8.)

Art. 9 provides that, if the carrier accepts goods without an air way-bill, or if the air waybill does not contain all the particulars set out in Art. 8 (*a*) to (*i*) inclusive and also in (*q*), then the carrier will not be able to avail himself of the provisions of the Convention which exclude or limit his liability. (*Westminster Bank Ltd.* v. *Imperial Airways Ltd.*, 1936,[663] and *Samuel Montague and Co. Ltd.* v. *Swiss Air Transport Ltd.*, 1966.)[663a] He is thus liable for all damage howsoever caused unless he can prove that it did not occur during the carriage by air. The provisions of Arts. 8 and 9 have been changed in the Amended Convention of 1955. (See p. 436.)

Liabilities of Carriers by Air.

1. LOSS OF OR DAMAGE TO GOODS. The carrier is liable for the loss of, for damage to, any registered luggage or any goods during the carriage by air, and this includes any period, during which the goods or luggage are in the charge of the carrier, whether in the aerodrome, or on board an aircraft, or, in the case of a landing outside an aerodrome, in any place whatsoever. (Art. 18.)

2. LIABILITY FOR DELAY. The carrier is liable for damage occasioned by delay in the carriage by air of passengers, luggage or goods. (Art. 19.) Delay arises after the agreed time for carriage has expired, or, if no such time is prescribed, after a reasonable time has passed without delivery.

Avoidance of Liability. The carrier can avoid liability as follows—

(i) If he proves that he and his agents have taken all necessary measures to avoid the damage, or that it was impossible for him or them to take such measures;

(ii) If, in the case of the carriage of goods or luggage, he proves that the damage was caused by negligent pilotage or negligence in the handling of the aircraft or in navigation, and that, in all other respects, he and his agents have taken all necessary measures to avoid the damage. (Art. 20.)

The carrier may in appropriate cases raise the defence of contributory negligence against the person whose goods are damaged. (Law Reform (Contributory Negligence) Act, 1945.)

Loss of Limit on Liability. Under Art. 25 the carrier is not entitled to avail himself of the provisions of the Convention which exclude or limit his liability in the following cases—

(*a*) if the damage is caused by wilful misconduct, or default equivalent to misconduct;

(*b*) if the damage is caused by the wilful misconduct, or default equivalent to misconduct, of his servants or agents acting within the scope of their employment.

The onus of proof under Art. 25 rests, it seems, on the plaintiff, though in view of the greater dangers attracting to carriage by air comparatively minor acts of misconduct if wilful may suffice. (*Horabin* v. *British Overseas Airways Corporation*, [1952] 2 All E.R. 1016.)

The provisions of Arts. 20 and 25 have been changed in the amended Convention of 1955 (see p. 436).

Deviation. The Convention does not contain provisions relating to deviation, and if a carrier deviates from the route he can nevertheless rely on the provisions in the Convention which limit his liability, though deviation could in some cases amount to wilful misconduct. These principles would seem to apply to carriage under the amended Convention of 1955 and to non-international carriage.

Delivery. The carrier is required to inform the consignee of the arrival of the goods at the destination. If the carrier fails to deliver the goods within seven days from the time of arrival of the aircraft, the consignee may begin legal proceedings for loss of the goods (Art. 13).

The consignor is liable to the carrier if he does not take all possible steps to ensure that the goods satisfy the customs regulations at the point of departure and destination (Art. 16).

Carrier's Lien. There is no provision in the Convention with regard to carriers' lien. Furthermore, there is no authority as to whether the concept of common law lien applies to carriers by air. Even if the common law applied, there would be no lien since carriers by air are private carriers. The matter is, therefore, one to be settled by special contract which may provide for a lien.

Stoppage *in Transitu.* This matter is not referred to as such in the Convention but Art. 12 provides that the consignor may require the carrier to stop the goods and not deliver them to the consignee so long as the goods are in the carrier's charge either at an aerodrome or in an aircraft. Art. 16 provides that the carrier may be liable to the consignee if, acting on the instructions of the consignor, he stops the goods without ascertaining that the consignor has not delivered the air waybill to some other person.

Limitation on Damages. In the carriage of registered luggage and goods, the liability of the carrier is limited to the sum of 250 francs per kilogram, unless the consignor has made, at the time when the package was handed over to the carrier, a special declaration of the value at delivery and has paid a supplementary sum if the case so requires. (*Westminster Bank Ltd.* v. *Imperial Airways Ltd.*, 1936.)[663] In that case, the carrier will be liable to pay a sum not exceeding the declared sum, unless he proves that the sum is greater than the actual value to the consignor at delivery. (Art. 22 (2).)

The franc is the French gold franc of 1924 and is converted into other currencies in round figures. Conversion into sterling is specifically mentioned as being at the current rate of exchange, either at the time of payment or judgment in the action. (Art. 22 (4).)

Any provision tending to relieve the carrier of liability or to fix a lower limit is null and void, but the nullity of such provision does not nullify the contract, which remains subject to the provisions of the Convention. (Art. 23.) The provisions of Art. 23 have been changed in the amended Convention of 1955 (see p. 436).

Passengers' Baggage. Apart from small hand luggage, the carrier must make out and deliver a baggage check in duplicate, retaining one part and handing the other to the passenger. This check should contain the following particulars—(*a*) the place and date of issue; (*b*) the place of departure and destination; (*c*) the name and address of the carrier or carriers; (*d*) the number of the passenger ticket; (*e*) a statement that delivery of the luggage will be made to the bearer of the baggage check; (*f*) the number and weight of the packages; (*g*) the amount of the value declared in accordance with Art. 22 (2); (*h*) a statement that the carriage is subject to the rules of the Convention relating to liability. *If the carrier does not deliver a baggage check,* of if it does not contain the details set out in (*d*), (*f*) and (*h*) above, he loses the benefit of the provisions of the Convention which exclude or limit his liability. (Art. 4.)

The provisions of Art. 4 have been changed in the amended Convention of 1955 (see p. 436).

The limitation on damage where the carrier takes charge of the baggage is governed by Art. 22 (2), (see p. 434).

With regard to objects which the passenger takes charge of himself, the liability of the carrier is limited to 5,000 francs per passenger. (Art. 22 (3).)

Complaints and Claims. In the case of damage to luggage or goods, the person entitled to delivery must complain to the carrier forthwith after the discovery of the damage, and, at the latest, within three days from the receipt of the luggage and seven days from the receipt of goods. In the event of delay, the complaint must be made at the latest within fourteen days from the date on which the luggage or goods have been placed at the carrier's disposal.

Every complaint must be made in writing upon the document of carriage or by separate notice in writing despatched within the times aforesaid. Failing complaint within these times, no action lies against the carrier, save in the case of fraud on his part. (Art. 26.)

The right to damages is extinguished if an action is not brought within two years reckoned from the date of arrival at the destination, or from the date on which the aircraft ought to have arrived, or from the date on which the carriage stopped. (Art. 29.)

The Carriage by Air Act, 1961, extends the provision of Art. 29 to cases where the carrier's servant or agent is sued personally.

Special Contracts. Art. 33 provides—

"Nothing contained in this Convention shall prevent the carrier either from refusing to enter into any contract of carriage or from making regulations which do not conflict with the provisions of this Convention."

There is no decided case in which this Article has been interpreted, but it would appear to give only a limited right to make a special contract. One of these is the right to refer disputes to arbitration under

Art. 32. Apart from this, the parties are not able to contract out of the provisions of the Convention but may add terms regarding matters not covered by the Convention, e.g. carriers' lien.

THE AMENDED CONVENTION OF 1955

The Warsaw Convention was amended at the Hague in 1955 and the Carriage by Air Act, 1961, was enacted to give effect to this amended Convention.

The Act was given the force of law by the Carriage by Air Acts (Application of Provisions) Order, 1967, on 1st June, 1967. The changes, apart from minor verbal alterations, are set out below.

The Air Waybill. Art. 8 of the Warsaw Convention is amended by Art. 8 of the 1961 Act which provides as follows—

"The air waybill shall contain:

(*a*) an indication of the places of departure and destination;

(*b*) if the place of departure and destination are within the territory of a single High Contracting Party, one or more agreed stopping places being within the territory of another State, an indication of at least one such stopping place;

(*c*) a notice to the consignor to the effect that if the carriage involves an ultimate destination or stop in a country other than the country of departure, the Warsaw Convention may be applicable, and that the Convention governs and in most cases limits the liability of carriers in respect of loss of or damage to cargo."

In addition Art. 9 of the Amended Convention modifies the stringent provisions of Art. 9 of the Warsaw Convention by providing as follows—

"If, with the consent of the carrier, cargo is loaded on board the aircraft without an air waybill having been made out, or if the air waybill does not include the notice required by Article 8, paragraph (*c*), the carrier shall not be entitled to avail himself of the provisions of Article 22, paragraph (2)."

The carrier may, therefore, rely on all the other provisions limiting his liability except Art. 22 (2) which limits his liability to 250 francs per kilogram. These provisions apply also to the "baggage check" issued in connection with passengers' baggage.

Carrier's Liability. Article 20 of the Warsaw Convention exempting the carrier from liability in respect of damage caused by negligent pilotage or negligence in handling or navigation is abolished. The only defence open to the carrier is now contained in Art. 20 of the 1955 Convention which provides as follows—

"The carrier is not liable if he proves that he and his agents have taken all necessary measures to avoid the damage or that it was impossible for him or them to take such measures."

Article 25 of the Warsaw Convention, under which the carrier was not entitled to avail himself of the provisions of the Convention which excluded or limited his liability where he was guilty of wilful misconduct, is replaced by Art. 25 of the 1955 Convention which provides as follows—

"The limits of liability specified in Article 22 shall not apply if it is proved that the damage resulted from an act or omission of the carrier, his servant or agents, done with intent to cause damage or recklessly and with knowledge that damage would probably result; provided that, in the case of such act or omission of a servant or agent, it is also proved that he was acting within the scope of his employment."

If an agent or servant of the carrier is sued personally he can rely on Art. 22 so long as he was acting within the scope of employment.

Article 23 of the Warsaw Convention is retained as Art. 23 (1) of the 1955 Convention, but a new provision is added as Art. 23 (2). Now Art. 23 reads as follows—

"(1) Any provision tending to relieve the carrier of liability or to fix a lower limit than that which is laid down in this Convention shall be null and void, but the nullity of any such provision does not involve the nullity of the whole contract, which shall remain subject to the provisions of this Convention.

(2) Paragraph (1) of this Article shall not apply to provisions governing loss or damage resulting from the inherent defect, quality or vice of the cargo carried."

Art. 23 (2) appears unnecessary in view of the provisions of Art. 20 (see p. 436).

Sect. 5 of the 1961 Act (not the amended Convention) provides that Art. 29 which places a limit of two years on actions brought against the carrier shall apply also to actions brought against the carrier's agents and servants in a personal capacity. Actions for a contribution between persons held jointly liable for damages (joint tortfeasors) must also, by Sect. 5, be brought within two years of the judgment against the person who is claiming the contribution.

Application of 1955 Convention. The Warsaw Convention did not apply to experimental and certain other flights in extraordinary circumstances beyond the scope of the air carrier's business. Art. 34 in the 1955 Convention contains a similar provision as follows—

"Articles 3 to 9 relating to documents of carriage shall not apply to carriage performed in extraordinary circumstances outside the normal scope of an air carrier's business."

RULES OF NON-INTERNATIONAL CARRIAGE

Every case of carriage by air which is not governed by the Warsaw Convention or the amended Convention of 1955 is subject to the

Non-International Carriage Rules of 1967. These rules are almost identical with the amended Convention though the following differences should be noted—

(*a*) the Rules do not include any provisions regarding the air waybill or baggage check. These documents may be issued if the parties wish, but no legal consequences flow from failure to issue them. Thus, the Rules have no provision comparable to Art. 8 of the original or amended Conventions;

(*b*) the Rules do not contain any provision relating to delay or stoppage *in transitu*;

(*c*) since the Rules govern non-international carriage, all disputes are determined by English Law and there are no provisions relating to jurisdiction;

(*d*) there is no provision in the Rules similar to that of Art. 34 of the 1955 Convention. Such a provision is unnecessary since Arts. 3 to 9 of the amended Convention do not appear in the Rules.

The Rules include the same maximum limit of 250 francs per kilogram and 5,000 francs per passenger for loss or damage to goods or passengers' baggage but fix a much higher limit for personal injury than does the amended Convention.

All other aspects of the amended Convention apply.

CARRIAGE BY AIR (SUPPLEMENTARY PROVISIONS) ACT, 1962

The Warsaw Convention lays down the basic liability of the carrier in regard to passengers and goods but it has never been clear whether the limitation of liability protects only the actual carrier, or whether it extends also to a sub-contracting carrier who contracts with the actual carrier for the work. The Guadalajara Convention which was signed in 1961 provides that both are covered. The Carriage by Air (Supplementary Provisions) Act, 1962, enables the United Kingdom to ratify the Guadalajara Convention. The Act came into force on 1st May, 1964, and has been extended by the Carriage by Air (Non-International Carriage) (United Kingdom) Order, 1964, to apply, with minor verbal alterations, to non-international carriage.

CHAPTER XII

SURETYSHIP AND GUARANTEE

Nature of a Guarantee. A guarantee is a collateral or accessory contract whereby the promisor (called the *surety*) undertakes to be answerable to the promisee (called the *creditor*) for the debt, default or miscarriage of a third person (called the *principal debtor* or *the principal*) who is, or is expected to have, a primary liability to the promisee.

The guarantee may be for one transaction, in which case it usually ends when the principal contract or liability is discharged; or it may be a guarantee extending to a series of transactions and called a continuing guarantee.

Distinctions. A guarantee may be distinguished from other similar contracts, e.g. contracts of insurance and contracts of indemnity.

(*a*) INSURANCE. It is possible to insure against losses arising from the failure of a third party to carry out an obligation, and this has the appearance of a guarantee since both contracts aim at protecting the creditor against loss. However, the following differences are important: (i) a contract of insurance is a contract *uberrimae fidei* (of utmost good faith) and a contract of guarantee is not; (ii) an insurer undertakes a direct obligation to the insured, whereas a guarantee is a mere collateral undertaking to be answerable if and when the principal debtor defaults.

(*b*) GUARANTEE AND INDEMNITY. In the case of a contract of guarantee, there is always a contract between the creditor and the principal debtor to which the guarantee is ancillary. The guarantor's liability arises on default. In the case of a contract of indemnity, the promisor makes himself directly responsible to the promisee by means of an independent promise. The distinction is not easy to make and is a question of fact. If G and P go into C's shop, and G, in order to get C to give credit to P, says: "Let him have the goods and if he does not pay you I will," this is a contract of guarantee. P has a primary liability; G becomes liable on default. If, however, G says: "Let P have the goods and I will see you paid," this is not a contract of guarantee but of indemnity. Indeed, G may have little hope, or even no intention, that P will pay. (*Mountstephen* v. *Lakeman*, 1871.)[53]

It is not necessary for the guarantor to undertake personal liability for payment, it is enough if he provides a security. (*Re Conley*, [1938] 2 All E.R. 127.) The guarantor must not have any financial interest in the contract, and for this reason persons receiving commission such as *del credere* agents (see p. 213) cannot become guarantors in respect of transactions in which they have a financial interest. They may, of course, give an indemnity. (*Sutton & Co.* v. *Grey*, 1894.)[664]

The difference is important because, as we have seen in the chapter on Contract, the Statute of Frauds, 1677, requires contracts of guarantee to be evidenced in writing, whereas contracts of indemnity may be made orally. What constitutes a memorandum in writing has already been discussed in the chapter on Contract (see p. 15).

Rights of indemnity may arise out of express or implied (or quasi) contracts or out of obligations imposed by law. Whenever M is compelled by law to pay to R money which P is ultimately liable to pay, and P is thereby discharged of his liability to R, then M may claim to be indemnified by P (see p. 95). Rights of indemnity are often incidents of contracts and apply as between the acceptor and indorsers of a bill of exchange, as between principal and agent, or as between master and servant. Most types of insurance are contracts of indemnity in the widest sense of the term.

Essentials of a Guarantee. A guarantee must have the elements of a valid contract.

(1) OFFER AND ACCEPTANCE. An offer of a guarantee may be so framed that it needs express or implied acceptance in its own right. But quite often a guarantee is offered so that a third person may obtain goods on credit or loans of money, and acceptance of the surety's offer takes place when the goods are supplied or the loans made.

(2) CONSENSUS AD IDEM. A guarantee may be void for mistake where the party signing the document was deceived into thinking it was something else. (*Carlisle and Cumberland Banking Co.* v. *Bragg*, 1911,[130] but see *Gallie* v. *Lee*, 1969[131] and *Saunders* v. *Anglia Building Society*, 1970),[131a] but not if he was merely mistaken as to its precise effect. (*Blay* v. *Pollard and Morris*, 1930.)[665]

Duress and undue influence of which the creditor is aware will destroy the validity of a guarantee procured by those means. (*Lancashire Loans Ltd.* v. *Black*, 1934.)[205]

(3) CAPACITY. A minor's guarantee is void and cannot be ratified on coming of age. If a minor who has just reached his majority acts as guarantor for a parent, the guarantee may be invalid unless the guarantor had independent advice. (*Lancashire Loans Ltd.* v. *Black*, 1934.)[205]

In the case of a minor's loans which are guaranteed by an adult, the guarantee is worthless to the creditor. Since the minor cannot default on a void contract, the guarantor cannot be liable. (*Coutts & Co.* v. *Browne-Lecky*, 1947.)[100]

(4) CONSIDERATION. A guarantee must either be made under seal or be supported by valuable consideration, which must move from the creditor but need not benefit the surety, although it may do so. Often the consideration is some benefit given to the principal debtor by the creditor at the request of the surety. Where the creditor agrees to refrain from suing the principal debtor, the guarantee will be effective if the forbearance is at the express or implied request of the surety, and if the creditor forbears for the stipulated time, or, if none is stipulated, for a reasonable time. A guarantee amounting to a fraudulent preference or given for an illegal consideration will not be enforced.

Sometimes all members of a group of companies may give cross-guarantees supported by floating charges and other securities with the intention, as part of a system of borrowing, that all the assets of the group should be available for all liabilities. This is a frequent commercial practice but is doubtful in law because it has not yet been established beyond doubt whether company A in guaranteeing the liabilities of company B must receive some benefit from the transaction. Company A will not normally do so, at least in monetary terms, and yet it is said that a company cannot exercise a gratuitous act even if within its powers unless that act is done for the benefit of and to promote the prosperity of the company. In *Charterbridge Corporation Ltd.* v. *Lloyds Bank Ltd.*, 1969,[666] the court took the view that inter-company guarantees were beneficial, but the matter was put in doubt by the decision of the Court of Appeal in *Introductions Ltd.* v. *National Provincial Bank*, 1969,[124] which states, in effect, that the exercise of an express power in the memorandum, e.g. to give guarantees, must be for the purposes of the company's *own business* and not for other purposes.

(5) WRITING. We have seen that a contract of guarantee must be evidenced in writing, but it is not necessary for the consideration to be set out in the writing used as evidence. (Mercantile Law Amendment Act, 1856.) While an oral guarantee cannot be enforced it is not void. Money paid under it cannot be recovered, and it may be used as a defence. (*Monnickendam* v. *Leanse*, 1923.)[61]

SURETY'S LIABILITY

The liability of the surety does not arise until the principal debtor has made default. The surety's guarantee must be strictly construed and the creditor cannot hold him liable for more than he agreed to undertake.

(i) If a surety has guaranteed advances up to £500, and £750 is lent, he is liable for £500 only.

(ii) If a surety has guaranteed payment of a bill of exchange to be drawn for £500 and it is drawn for £750, or any sum larger than £500, the surety is not liable at all.

(iii) If he has become a surety on consideration of the creditor's forbearance to sue the principal debtor, the conditions attaching to the forbearance must be strictly complied with by the creditor.

(iv) The surety is often liable for the interest on the principal sum when it is overdue and unpaid, e.g. where he has guaranteed payment of a bill of exchange. Overdue bills of exchange and promissory notes bear interest (see p. 95).

(v) If the creditor brings a fruitless action against the principal debtor without notice to the surety, the surety will not be liable for the costs of such action.

The liability of the surety arises when the principal debtor makes default, and thereafter the surety is debarred from setting-off adverse claims against the creditor. On such default, the surety is liable without the need for notice or a request for payment, and the creditor need not sue the principal debtor, or even request him to pay, unless the contract of suretyship otherwise provides.

If the surety has laid down conditions precedent to his liability, these conditions must be fulfilled exactly. Thus, if the guarantee is given on the undertaking of the creditor to forbear to sue the principal debtor for a period of three months, this undertaking must be carried out before liability can arise under the guarantee.

Some guarantees are limited to a single transaction; others are intended to cover a series of transactions spread over a period of time and are called *continuing guarantees*. The duration of a guarantee depends upon its terms and it is important to frame the guarantee carefully so that the precise scope and duration are beyond dispute.

A continuing guarantee is not discharged by the first advance up to the pecuniary limit. Thus, if X agrees to guarantee Y's overdraft up to £500 and Y overdraws up to £500, then reduces the overdraft to £300 and later overdraws to £500 again, X is still liable if the guarantee is a continuing one.

Fidelity Guarantees. A surety may guarantee that a person holding a particular office will faithfully discharge his duties to another person who would suffer loss if they are not so discharged. The surety is not liable for acts done outside the scope of the office or subsequently imposed by statute. The duration of such a guarantee may give rise to difficult problems.

The fidelity bond should stipulate its duration and state that it is to be determinable by the surety's death or by notice. The following examples illustrate how duration is determined—

(*a*) The surety ceases to be liable if the principal debtor is appointed to a fresh office which ends the original appointment, even if the duties attached to the new office are the same; the more so if the two offices are incompatible.

(*b*) The surety ceases to be liable where the office is changed from an "annual office" to one held "during pleasure," but not where the period of notice is varied unless this is a term of the contract of guarantee.

(*c*) The surety ceases to be liable when the duties of the principal debtor are materially altered, but if they are merely reduced in scope the liability continues. Changes in salary will not necessarily be relevant, although if the duration of the guarantee is for the period for which the principal debtor holds office, and he is re-appointed at a different salary, the surety's liability ends.

(*d*) *A continuing guarantee is revoked by a change in the constitution of a firm to whom a guarantee is given*, e.g. by the turning of a partnership into a company, or by the amalgamation or reconstruction of companies, *or by a similar change in the status of the principal debtor.*

SURETY'S RIGHTS AGAINST THE CREDITOR

Rights before Payment. The surety has certain rights against the creditor arising out of the contract of guarantee even before he has discharged the obligations of the principal debtor.

(i) If the guaranteed debt has become due, and even before he has been asked to pay, the surety may require the creditor to call on the principal debtor to meet his obligations, but the *creditor need not sue* the principal debtor before turning to the surety.

(ii) After the debt is due, the surety may pay the creditor and then *either* sue the principal debtor in the creditor's name (giving the creditor an indemnity for costs) *or* (if he obtains an assignment of the guaranteed debt) in his own name.

(iii) In the case of a fidelity guarantee—

(*a*) If a surety knows that an employee whose conduct is guaranteed has misconducted himself so as to make him liable to dismissal, the surety may compel the employer to dismiss him or forfeit the benefit of the guarantee;

(*b*) If the employer knows of misconduct which is unknown to the surety, and yet continues to employ the offending employee, the surety will not be liable for any subsequent misconduct by that employee. (*Phillips* v. *Foxall*, 1872.)[667]

(iv) If the creditor sues the surety for the guaranteed debt, the surety may avail himself of any set-off or counterclaim possessed by the principal debtor against the creditor.

Rights after Payment. The surety has the following rights after payment—

(i) If he has paid the creditor the amount due under the guarantee, he is entitled to be subrogated to all the creditor's rights in that connection, unless he has waived them.

(ii) The surety can claim (whether he knew of them or not when he became a surety) the benefit of all the securities received by the creditor from the principal debtor.

(iii) A surety for part of a debt who pays such part is entitled to a proportionate share in any security held by the creditor for the whole debt. If, however, *unknown to the surety*, the principal debtor gave security for another part of the debt *at a different time*, such security is not available to the surety.

(iv) If the guaranteed debt is secured by a mortgage executed by the principal debtor, the surety may, even though not originally aware of its existence, require the mortgage to be transferred to him on paying the debt.

(v) The surety is entitled to all the equities of the creditor both against the principal debtor himself and against all those claiming under him.

These rights may be expressly waived in the contract of guarantee, or *waived by implication* if the surety accepts an indemnity from the principal debtor instead of the rights he would otherwise have had.

THE SURETY'S RIGHTS AGAINST THE PRINCIPAL
DEBTOR

Indemnification. The principal debtor may give the surety an express right to an *indemnity* which becomes a debt due to the surety when he has paid the creditor.

In the absence of such express right, the surety possesses certain implied rights against a principal debtor who has made a request, actual or constructive, for the guarantee. Such a request gives the surety a right of indemnification, and the principal debtor is liable, even in the absence of further requests, for all payments made thereafter by the surety in respect of the guarantee.

It is a general principle of quasi-contract (see p. 95) that if G is compelled to make a payment which benefits P, and for which P is ultimately liable, G may recover this payment from P. Even in the absence of a previous request, this rule will often enable a surety to claim indemnification.

Rights before the Surety has paid the Guaranteed Debt. The following rights exist against the principal debtor—

(i) The surety, as soon as he becomes liable to pay the guaranteed debt to the creditor, and even though the creditor has not asked either him or the principal debtor to pay, is entitled to call upon the principal debtor to pay off the debt. He cannot, however, compel the principal debtor to make provision for payment of the debt before it is due.

(ii) If the principal debtor fails to pay the debt, the surety may obtain an order to compel him to do so. (*Tate* v. *Crewdson*, 1938.)[668]

(iii) Where the creditor and the principal debtor have by their acts and conduct relieved the surety of his liability, he may bring an action to obtain a declaration to this effect before payment falls due.

(iv) If the principal debtor makes an agreement with the surety to pay the guaranteed debt by a named day and fails to do so then, if the contract expressly provides, the surety may obtain damages from the principal debtor.

Rights after the Surety has paid the Guaranteed Debt. When the surety has paid money to the creditor under the guarantee, he becomes to that extent the creditor of the principal debtor.

(*a*) Every time the surety pays part of the guaranteed debt, he has an immediate right of action against the principal debtor, who may thus be liable to successive actions arising from the same guarantee. The surety cannot be compelled to pay the whole debt before suing the principal debtor for part, nor can he pay the whole before it is due in order to speed up his remedy.

(*b*) If the contract from which the liability of the principal debtor stems was *under seal*, the surety becomes a specialty creditor of the principal debtor and his right of action survives for the limitation period of twelve years. (Mercantile Law Amendment Act, 1856.)

(*c*) The indemnity to which the surety is entitled is the sum he has actually paid *with interest*, but if he has suffered damage beyond principal and interest, this too may be recovered. (*Fisher* v. *Fallows*, 1804.)[669]

(*d*) Where the surety defends an action: (i) with the authority of the principal debtor; or (ii) in reasonable defence of the latter's interests, the surety may recover the costs from the principal debtor. Nevertheless, if the surety has no good defence, he may make a compromise and recover such amount from the principal debtor.

THE RIGHTS AND LIABILITIES OF CO-SURETIES

Where one of several sureties has paid more than his share of the common liability, *he can obtain contribution* from his co-sureties. (*In re Snowdon, Ex parte Snowdon*, 1881.)[670] *The right exists—*

    (i) Whether the liability is several, or joint and several;

    (ii) Whether the liability arises under one instrument or more than one;

    (iii) Regardless of whether the claimant knew when he became a surety that there were other co-sureties.

The right is not contractual but equitable, and equity requires them to contribute in equal or rateable proportions where there is a common demand. The amount recoverable from each of the co-sureties depends on the number who are alive and solvent.

Contribution does not arise—

    (*a*) where the sureties are liable for equal portions of the same debt due from the same debtor under different contracts of guarantee;

    (*b*) where the co-surety became such at the request of the person claiming contribution;

    (*c*) where the co-sureties expressly contract each to be individually responsible for his own share;

    (*d*) where the contract and the surrounding circumstances seem to show that the parties were not intending to become co-sureties;

    (*e*) where the claimant has been guilty of fraudulent concealment.

The right to contribution after payment arises when a surety has paid more than his share of the common liability.

    (i) If there are three equal co-sureties for a total sum of £1,800, and S has paid £600, he has no right of contribution. The others are still liable for £600 each.

    (ii) If, however, S pays the £1,800, he may claim contribution of £600 from each of the other two, or, if one is insolvent, £900 from the remaining solvent co-surety.

(iii) If, for some reason, the creditor were to accept a payment of £450 from S in full settlement of the debt of £1,800, then S could claim £150 from each of the other co-sureties.

Where the co-sureties are not equally liable, they must contribute in proportion to their assumed liability. If an action is brought against a surety which he wishes to defend, he should obtain the consent of his co-sureties or be fully satisfied that the defence is a reasonable one to undertake; otherwise he will be unable to recover contribution in respect of his costs.

A surety who pays more than his proportion of the common liability can have assigned to him all the creditor's rights and securities in order to obtain contribution. He may even claim for this purpose the benefit of—

(*a*) securities given by his co-sureties to the creditor;

(*b*) securities taken by another co-surety as an indemnity against the common liability;

(*c*) any judgment obtained by the creditor against the principal debtor and his sureties.

Whatever is received from a counter-security obtained from the principal debtor must be brought into hotchpot. (*Steel* v. *Dixon*, 1881.)[671]

DISCHARGE OF GUARANTEE

1. Payment. The surety is discharged by payment.

(i) If the principal debtor pays the guaranteed debt, the surety is discharged unless the payment amounts to a fraudulent preference.

(ii) If the principal debtor clears the guaranteed debt by setting-off some debt due to him by the creditor, and the creditor attempts to sue the surety, the surety may avail himself of the set-off by way of defence.

(iii) If the surety pays the creditor the sum guaranteed, he is completely discharged.

2. Fraud. Fraud of which the creditor was aware releases the surety. A contract of guarantee is not *uberrimae fidei* (of utmost good faith) and is valid unless material facts have been *fraudulently concealed*. It is beside the point whether the fraudulent concealment was intended to benefit the guilty party or not.

3. Disclosure and Misrepresentation. The creditor need not, in the absence of enquiry, volunteer information or disclose to the surety such matters as the state of the debtor's credit or of any circumstances, other than those arising out of the guarantee, which would suggest that his position is very risky. (*Cooper* v. *National Provincial Bank Ltd.*, 1946.)[672]

Nevertheless, if the creditor procures a guarantee by a material misrepresentation, even if innocent, as distinct from concealment, the contract may be set aside. Indeed if a creditor, during the negotiations, makes a statement, believing it to be true, and later finds it to be false before the negotiations are completed, he must correct it.

4. Material Alteration. The sureties under a guarantee are released from liability if it undergoes material alteration, e.g. by deleting the names of one or more co-sureties, or by reducing their liability, or by sealing a simple contract to convert it into a deed. (*Ellesmere Brewery Co.* v. *Cooper*, 1896.)[673] It is the duty of the creditor to protect the guarantee from alteration while it is in his custody, and so even unauthorised alterations by a stranger will effectively discharge the sureties.

5. Failure of Consideration. Where the creditor fails to carry out the promise which is the foundation of the guarantee, or where a condition precedent to the acceptance of liability by the surety has not been carried out, the surety is released and the guarantee may be cancelled.

6. Variation in Terms of Contract. The creditor must not vary the terms of the contract made with the principal debtor without the agreement of the surety, and knowledge is not to be interpreted as consent. A material variation so made will discharge the surety from liability. (*National Bank of Nigeria Ltd.* v. *Awolesi*, 1965.)[674]

Nor may the creditor depart from the express terms of the contract of guarantee without the consent of the surety. Any alteration of the surety's obligations which are not manifestly of a minor or trivial character will release him from liability even if the alteration does him no injury. If a guarantee stipulates that three months' credit be given to the principal debtor, it will be invalidated if the creditor gives either two months or four. If a surety has made himself liable for money to be received by X, this liability only extends to money received by X personally. If a surety is liable for the default of X, this will not extend to the joint default of X and Y.

7. Giving Time for Payment. In the absence of consent, the surety will be discharged if the creditor and the principal debtor make a binding agreement, enforceable for valuable consideration, to give the debtor time for payment, of however short duration, provided time is actually given. It would be enough if the creditor agreed to the paying by instalments of an amount due in a single payment. However, many agreements expressly exclude this rule and allow the creditor to give time if he chooses.

If the creditor remains passive and merely refrains from pressing the principal debtor to pay, this is not giving time and the surety is not discharged; and this remains true even if the principal debtor later becomes insolvent.

Where there is a continuing guarantee and the contract is severable, the giving of time in respect of one part will not affect the liability of the surety in respect of earlier or later parts where the conditions of the guarantee have been strictly observed, and the surety will only be discharged from liability in respect of the part affected by the giving of time.

8. Interference with Securities. When the surety offers to pay the guaranteed debt to the creditor, the creditor must be able to hand over all the securities held for the debt exactly as they were received by him. If the creditor has in any way acted so as to impair their value, this will discharge the surety.

9. Discharge of Principal Debtor. Anything which discharges the liability of the principal debtor normally operates to discharge the surety also. However, a creditor's acceptance of a debtor's wrongful repudiation of a contract does not discharge a guarantor from liability under his guarantee, though the action against him is not to repay the debt but to pay damages for breach of contract. (*Moschi* v. *L.E.P. Air Services*, 1972.)[696]

10. Release of Co-surety. Where there are co-sureties and the creditor releases one unconditionally without the consent of the others, the remaining co-sureties are discharged. (*Smith* v. *Wood*, 1929.)[675] Giving a surety time to pay, or agreeing not to sue him, is not a release and does not relieve the others.

11. Revocation of Guarantee. A guarantee may be revoked by express agreement, by novation, i.e. the substitution of a new contract, by waiver, or by notice given in accordance with the terms of the agreement. Such notice leaves the guarantor with the liabilities already accrued but prevents future liabilities from arising. The creditor may revoke the guarantee by giving the surety an express release from future liability.

12. Death of Surety. This has the following effects.

(*a*) If a continuing guarantee provides for its termination by notice, then proper notice must be given and the creditor's knowledge of the surety's death does not terminate liability.

(*b*) Where the consideration for the guarantee is divisible, e.g. a guarantee of a running account with a banker, then in the absence of a contrary stipulation, the guarantee is revoked when the banker has notice of the surety's death. (*Bradbury* v. *Morgan*, 1862.)[41]

(*c*) If the consideration for the guarantee has been given all at once, then death does not operate as a revocation.

(*d*) Even when a guarantee is revoked by notice of the death of the surety, his estate remains liable for earlier transactions.

(*e*) The death of one co-surety, in the case of a joint and several continuing guarantee, does not in itself release the others.

The liability of a surety is determined by his mental disorder on the same principle as by his death. (*Bradford Old Bank* v. *Sutcliffe*, 1918.)[676]

CHAPTER XIII

ARBITRATION

ARBITRATION is a method of settling disputes and differences between two or more parties by referring them to a nominated person or persons who decide the issues after hearing both sides in a quasi-judicial manner. An arbitration is an *alternative* to a legal action and is not *in lieu* of one. (*Re Davstone Estates Ltd.*, 1969.)[239]

THE ARBITRATION AGREEMENT

An arbitration may arise out of an agreement between the parties or out of some statute or statutory instrument. An arbitration agreement may be—

(a) *A common law submission*, which may be made orally and is subject to common law rules; *or*

(b) *A reference*, which is governed by the Arbitration Act, 1950, and which consists of a "written agreement to submit present or future differences to arbitration, whether an arbitrator is named therein or not." (Sect. 32.)

Such a *reference* is the commonest form of arbitration and it is with this type that we shall be chiefly concerned. All references, unless otherwise stated, are to the Arbitration Act, 1950.

Although the agreement must be in writing, it need not be made in any particular form and may be in more than one document, or may consist of an exchange of letters, provided it is clear that all the parties concerned are agreed to a reference to arbitration on the same terms. In practice, an arbitration agreement usually consists of a single document, or of an *arbitration clause* written into a contract where a dispute may arise, e.g. a building contract or an insurance contract. An arbitration agreement which is contained in a single document need not be signed by all parties, provided that a party who has not signed can be shown to have agreed to the terms contained in it. (*Baker* v. *Yorkshire Fire and Life Assurance Co.*, 1892.)[677]

An arbitration agreement is a contract and cannot be revoked unilaterally. An arbitration agreement is not discharged by the death of any party thereto, either as respects the deceased or any other party, but is enforceable against the personal representatives of the deceased. Nor is the authority of an arbitrator revoked by the death of the party who appointed him. (Sect. 2.)

Where a party to a contract is a bankrupt and the contract contains an arbitration clause, if the trustee in bankruptcy adopts the contract he must also submit to the arbitration if the need arises. (Sect. 3 (1).)

Arbitrations and Valuations. It is essential to distinguish an arbitration (*Re Hopper*, 1867)[678] from a valuation. (*Re Carus-Wilson and Greene*, 1886.)[679]

(*a*) *An arbitration* has for its object the settling of a dispute or difference which already exists. The arbitrator adopts a quasi-judicial procedure, hears evidence, and determines the issues in the light of such hearing. His award can be enforced as a court judgment, and may in certain situations be remitted or set aside. He cannot be sued for negligence.

(*b*) *A valuation* has for its object the prevention of a dispute, and the valuer has to fix a value or a price to the subject-matter of the contract. The valuer does not hear evidence but is chosen for his skill and judgment on which he is expected to rely. The valuation must be enforced by action and not by court order, and a valuation once made cannot be remitted or set aside. If the valuer is negligent he can be sued.

The Subject-Matter of the Agreement. The difference between the parties must be an issue which is capable of being tried civilly. It may be a dispute which has already arisen, in which case the agreement will have reference to the elements of such dispute, or, more commonly, it may refer to possible disputes which may arise in the future, particularly out of contracts of a commercial nature. Arbitration clauses are of frequent occurrence in contracts of insurance, building contracts and contracts of partnership.

Certain types of dispute are outside the scope of arbitration, e.g. offences of a public nature, petitions for divorce, agreements void under the Gaming Acts, or those requiring the arbitrator to give a judgment *in rem* (*The Sylph*, 1867).[680]

The Scope of the Agreement. An agreement of reference to arbitration may contain any clauses the parties choose to insert but it must not attempt to oust the court's jurisdiction as this would be contrary to public policy. (*Re Davstone Estates Ltd.*, 1969.)[239] It is not uncommon, however, for agreements to make the award of the arbitrator a condition precedent to a right of action, and in these cases, in the absence of clear grounds for doing so, the court would be reluctant to set such an award aside.

The Arbitration Act, 1950, lays down that, *unless a contrary intention is expressed in the arbitration agreement, the following provisions are implied*—

(*a*) Reference shall be to a single arbitrator. (Sect. 6.)

(*b*) If the agreement provided for two arbitrators, they must appoint an umpire immediately after they are themselves appointed. (Sect. 8 (1).)

(*c*) If the arbitrators state in writing that they cannot agree, the umpire may enter on the reference in lieu of the arbitrators. (Sect. 8 (2).)

(*d*) The parties must submit to being examined on oath or affirmation before the arbitrator and must produce all documents and do all other things which the arbitrator or umpire may require. (Sect. 12 (1).)

(*e*) Witnesses shall be examined on oath or affirmation if required. (Sect. 12 (2).)

(*f*) The arbitrator or umpire *may make an interim award* where appropriate. (Sect. 14.)

(*g*) *The arbitrator has the same power as the High Court to order specific performance of a contract other than a contract relating to land or an interest in land.* (Sect. 15.) Thus his power to award specific performance is virtually non-existent.

(*h*) The award shall be final and binding on the parties. (Sect. 16.)

(*i*) The arbitrator or umpire has power to award costs and settle their amount. (Sect. 18.)

Most of these matters will be dealt with in detail later.

Enforcing the Agreement. A party may attempt to obstruct the arbitration or try in the alternative to bring an action at law.

(1) FAILURE TO PROCEED. Where a party fails to proceed with an arbitration there are remedies available to an aggrieved party.

(*a*) If the only obstacle to proceeding is the refusal of the defaulter to appoint or concur in appointing an arbitrator, the aggrieved party can remedy this defect either himself, or with the aid of the court, as we shall see when we discuss the appointment of arbitrators. The reference can then proceed *ex parte*, in the absence of the defaulter, provided he is given due notice.

(*b*) Alternatively, or in different circumstances, the aggrieved party may bring an action for breach of the agreement; but unless this induces the defaulting party to refer the matter, he would only obtain damages for breach and the basic dispute would remain unsettled.

(2) STAY OF PROCEEDINGS. If one party to the agreement commences legal proceedings in court against another in respect of matters agreed to be referred to arbitration, the latter may at any time after entering an appearance and before delivering any pleadings or taking steps in the action, apply to the court to stay the proceedings, and the court may grant such a stay. (*Hickman* v. *Kent or Romney Marsh Sheep Breeders Association*, 1915.)[521]

A stay may be granted in the following circumstances—

(i) Where there is a valid arbitration agreement covering the dispute; and

(ii) Where the person applying for the stay is a party to the agreement or some person claiming under him; and

(iii) Where the applicant has taken *no step in the proceedings* after appearance; and

(iv) Where the applicant is ready and willing to arbitrate; and

(v) There is no sufficient reason why the matter should not be referred to arbitration in accordance with the agreement. (Sect. 4.)

A stay may be refused if the above conditions are not met or if it appears that the arbitrator is unfit to arbitrate by reason of misconduct or bias, or where the point at issue is a point of law which, if it were remitted to the arbitrator would have to be sent back to the court for decision. A court will not stay proceedings to enable an arbitration to continue at the instance of a defendant who is making charges of fraud or professional dishonesty against the plaintiff. (*Radford* v. *Hair*, 1971.)[681]

ARBITRATORS

An arbitration may be referred to a single arbitrator, or to two arbitrators who are required to appoint an umpire, or to three arbitrators one of whom may or may not be an umpire. A judge of the Commercial Court may accept appointment as a sole arbitrator or as umpire with permission of the Lord Chief Justice. Appeals from a judge/arbitrator are to the Court of Appeal and not to the High Court. (Administration of Justice Act, 1970, Sect. 4 and Sch. 3.)

A Single Arbitrator. A reference may be to a single arbitrator where the parties make express provision for this in the arbitration agreement.

(*a*) If the agreement contains no other mode of reference, then reference shall be to a single arbitrator. (Sect. 6.)

(*b*) Where an arbitration agreement provides for two arbitrators, one to be appointed by each of the parties X and Y, then, unless a contrary intention is expressed, if Y fails to appoint an arbitrator either originally, or by way of substitution of an appointee who refuses to act, is incapable of acting, or who dies, X may adopt the following procedure—

(i) He should appoint his own arbitrator, Z;

(ii) He should serve on Y, the defaulting party, a notice to make his own appointment within seven clear days;

(iii) If no appointment is then made, X may *appoint* Z to be the sole arbitrator in the reference and his award shall be binding on the parties as if he had been appointed by consent (subject to the right of the High Court or a judge thereof to set aside the appointment).

(*c*) At any time after the appointment of an umpire, however appointed, the High Court may, on the application of any party to the reference and notwithstanding anything to the contrary in the arbitration agreement, order that the umpire shall enter upon the reference in lieu of the arbitrators as if he were the sole arbitrator. (Sect. 8 (3).)

(*d*) Where the authority of an arbitrator or arbitrators or umpire is revoked by leave of the High Court, or a sole arbitrator or all the arbitrators or an umpire who has entered on the reference is or are removed by the High Court, the High Court may, on the application of any party to the arbitration agreement, either—

(i) appoint a person to act as sole arbitrator in place of the person or persons so removed; or

(ii) order that the arbitration agreement shall cease to have effect with reference to the dispute referred. (Sect. 25 (2).)

Two Arbitrators. An arbitration agreement may provide for two arbitrators, one to be appointed by each party. In the absence of a contrary intention in the agreement, if either of the appointed arbitrators refuses to act, or is incapable of acting, or dies, the party who has appointed him may appoint a new arbitrator in his place, and if this is not done, the other party may, by using the procedure already outlined, have the issue referred to the single arbitrator already chosen. (Sect. 7.)

Where the agreement provides for two arbitrators, they are required to appoint an umpire immediately after they are themselves appointed. Then, if the arbitrators subsequently deliver to any party to the arbitration agreement, or to the umpire, a notice in writing stating that they cannot agree, the umpire may forthwith enter on the reference in lieu of the arbitrators. (Sect. 8.) The appointment of an arbitrator is not effective until he has been notified and has expressed his willingness to act, even though one or both of the parties has agreed upon a particular person(s). (*Tradax Export S.A.* v. *Volkswagenwerk A.G.* (1969), S.J. 978.)

Three Arbitrators. Where an arbitration agreement provides that the reference shall be to three arbitrators, one to be appointed by each party and the third to be appointed by the two appointed by the parties, this third party shall occupy the role of umpire. (Sect. 9 (1).)

Where, however, the arbitration agreement provides that the reference shall be to three arbitrators appointed otherwise than as provided in the last paragraph, the award of *any two* of these arbitrators shall be binding. (Sect. 9 (2).)

Authority Irrevocable. The authority of an arbitrator or umpire appointed by or by virtue of an arbitration agreement shall, unless a contrary intention is expressed in the agreement, be irrevocable except by leave of the High Court or a judge thereof. (Sect. 1.) An application under Sect. 1 to revoke the authority of an arbitrator will only succeed in very exceptional circumstances, e.g. misconduct on the part of the arbitrator. (*City Centre Properties* v. *Matthew Hall & Co.*, [1969] 1 W.L.R. 772.)

Appointment by Court. An arbitrator may be appointed by the court in the following cases—

(*a*) Where an arbitration agreement provides that the reference shall be to a single arbitrator, and all the parties do not, after differences have arisen, concur in the appointment of an arbitrator.

(*b*) Where the parties or two arbitrators are *at liberty to appoint* an umpire or third arbitrator and do not appoint him, or where two arbitrators are *required to appoint* an umpire and do not appoint him.

(*c*) Where an appointed arbitrator, umpire or third arbitrator refuses to act or is incapable of acting, or dies, and the arbitration agreement does not show any intention that the vacancy should not be supplied, and the parties or arbitrators, as the case may be, do not supply the vacancy.

Any party may serve the other parties or the arbitrators, as the case may be, with a written notice to appoint or concur in an appointment, and if the appointment is not made within seven clear days after the service of the notice, he may apply to the High Court, or a judge thereof, to appoint an arbitrator, umpire or third arbitrator who shall have the like powers to act in the reference and make an award as if he had been appointed by consent of all parties. (Sect. 10.) (*Tritonia Shipping Inc.* v. *South Nelson Forest Products Corpn.*, 1966.)[682]

Official Referee. Where an arbitration agreement provides that the reference shall be to an official referee (a permanent officer of the court appointed by the Lord Chancellor), any official referee to whom application is made shall, subject to any order of the High Court or a judge thereof as to transfer or otherwise, hear and determine the matters agreed to be referred. (Sect. 11.) Under the Courts Act, 1971 the office of Official Referee becomes that of a circuit judge.

CONDUCT OF ARBITRATION

When an arbitrator is called upon to arbitrate, he should acquaint himself with the nature of the dispute. The arbitrator, or the arbitrators by agreement among themselves, must fix the time and place for the hearing of the reference. Normally they will study the wishes of the parties so far as possible, but they have absolute discretion in the matter. One party should not be heard in the absence of the other or others, and the parties may appear in person or they may, if they wish, be legally represented by solicitor or counsel. The procedure of the hearing is analogous with a civil action in the High Court.

Where the reference is to two arbitrators and an umpire, the umpire has no power unless and until the two arbitrators fail to agree or fail to make an award within the prescribed time (if any). Nevertheless, since it is the umpire's duty, if he is called upon to act, to decide the dispute on the evidence, he usually attends the hearing to avoid going through the whole of the evidence again. In a commercial arbitration if the two arbitrators appointed by the parties fail to agree, they may, when the umpire takes over, cease to act judicially and act as advocates for their respective sides or give evidence before him.

An arbitrator may use his own expert knowledge in reaching a conclusion and is not debarred from consulting experts himself, though this is unwise without the consent of the parties. An arbitrator must not delegate his powers under the reference nor, where there are several arbitrators, may one delegate his powers to another.

The Conduct of the Hearing. The arbitrators, in hearing the case, must follow any directions given in the reference, but the normal procedure is that of the trial of a civil action in the High Court. The proceedings run as follows—

(*a*) The claimant puts his case himself or by counsel, and calls witnesses who are examined, cross-examined and re-examined if required.

(*b*) The respondent similarly presents his case and calls witnesses.

(*c*) The respondent sums up and the claimant replies.

(*d*) The arbitrator makes the award.

Powers. Sect. 12 of the Arbitration Act, 1950, makes provision for the following.

(1) The parties to the reference, and all persons claiming through them, must give evidence on oath or affirmation, must produce any relevant documents required by the arbitrator or umpire, and do such things with reference to the proceedings as he may require.

(2) The arbitrator or umpire may, if he thinks fit, examine witnesses on oath or affirmation.

(3) The arbitrator or umpire has power to take such oaths or affirmations.

(4) Any party to a reference may require a witness, wherever he may be in the United Kingdom, to appear before the arbitrator or umpire in order to give testimony or produce documents, but only if he could have been compelled to produce such documents on the trial of an action.

(5) The High Court or a judge thereof may also issue a writ of *habeas corpus ad testificandum* to bring a prisoner for examination before an arbitrator or umpire.

(6) Without prejudice to any powers of the arbitrator or umpire in this connection, the High Court (or a judge or master) has the same power in relation to a reference as to a High Court action to make orders in respect of: (*a*) security for costs; (*b*) discovery of documents and interrogatories; (*c*) the giving of evidence on affidavit; (*d*) examining witnesses on oath and requesting their examination out of jurisdiction; (*e*) the preservation, custody and sale of goods; (*f*) securing the amount in dispute in the reference; (*g*) the detention, preservation or inspection of any property or thing being the subject of the reference; (*h*) interim injunctions or the appointment of a receiver. (Sect. 12.)

Stating a Case. Where a reference involves a difficult point of law, the arbitrator may state a special case for decision by the High Court. The power is conferred by statute and cannot be taken away or restricted by the agreement.

An arbitrator or umpire may, and shall if so directed by the High Court, state: (*a*) any question of law arising in the course of the reference; or (*b*) an award or any part of an award, in the form of a special case for the decision of the High Court. (Sect. 21 (1).)

A special case with respect to an interim award or with respect to a question of law arising in the course of the reference may be stated, or may be directed by the High Court to be stated, notwithstanding that proceedings under the reference are still pending. (Sect. 21 (2).)

If the point at issue goes to the root of the matters in reference, the case may be stated early in the reference which may be suspended until the point has been cleared. In other circumstances it may be embodied in the award by giving alternative findings according to the outcome of the case.

A case may be stated either at the request of a party to the reference or on the initiative of the arbitrator or umpire.

THE AWARD

Time. If the parties prescribe a time limit, the award must be made within the limit prescribed, but further time may be allowed by the consent of all the parties to the reference, or by application to the court where the time for making the award has been exceeded. The court may extend the time for making an award even where a definite time has been stipulated in the agreement, and such extension will normally be for one month.

In the absence of a provision as to time, the award may be made at any time; but the High Court may, on the application of a party to the reference, remove an arbitrator or umpire who fails to use reasonable dispatch in entering on and proceeding with the reference and making an award, and the person so removed loses his right to remuneration. (Sect. 13.)

Form. The award must normally be in writing and it is customary to insert *recitals* before coming to the *operative part* of the award. Such recitals outline, *inter alia*, the basis of the agreement to arbitrate, the subject-matter, the circumstances of appointment and powers of the arbitrators and, where an umpire has taken over the reference, the circumstances in which this has occurred.

The *operative part* gives the decision of the arbitrator on the matters in dispute and may be made in such form as the arbitrator thinks fit. This is the essential part of the award and recitals are not necessary; indeed even where recitals conflict with the award they will not invalidate it, though such discrepancies are obviously undesirable as leading to difficulties of interpretation.

The Essentials of a Valid Award. The following points should be noted.

(1) Although not expressly required by the Act, *an award should be in writing* unless a contrary intention is expressed in the arbitration agreement, *and it should comply strictly with any special directions in the agreement* as to the time in which and the manner in which it is to be made.

(2) *The award must be certain in meaning and self-consistent as to its parts.* It should state clearly which parties are to be bound by it and what they are to perform. If sums are to be paid they should be specified or be readily ascertainable; if conditions are to be observed they should be clearly defined; and any periods of time should be stipulated or be ascertainable beyond doubt. An uncertain award will be remitted. (*Stonehewer* v. *Farrar*, 1845.)[683] An award will be bad for inconsistency. (*Ames* v. *Milward*, 1818.)[684]

(3) *The award must not go outside the scope, but must deal with all matters which form the subject of the reference.* (In re *Green* v. *Balfour*, 1890.)[685] If an award is made on matters falling both within and without the

scope of the agreement, the awards may be valid as to the former but not as to the latter, *if the parts are severable.* If severance is not possible, the whole award is bad. If the award does not cover all the matters referred, it will be bad (*Randall* v. *Randall*, 1805),[686] although the courts assume that all matters have been covered unless it appears on the face of the award that they have not. (*Re Duke of Beaufort and the Swansea Harbour Trustees*, 1860.)[687]

(4) Unless a contrary intention is expressed in the agreement, the arbitrator may, in appropriate cases, make an interim award; otherwise *the award when made must be final.* The arbitrator must not reserve questions to be subsequently decided either by himself or by someone to whom judicial authority is delegated. (*Tomlin* v. *Mayor of Fordwich*, 1836.)[688] An award may still be final notwithstanding that some *ministerial act not requiring discretion* remains to be carried out in order to implement it.

(5) *The award must be legal, capable of being performed* (*Lewis* v. *Rossiter*, 1875),[689] *and all directions necessary to its proper performance must be given.* Thus, if the parties are to give each other mutual releases, the nature of the documents and the method of preparation should be specified.

(6) *The award must be properly executed* in accordance with the terms of the arbitration agreement. In the absence of contrary instructions it should normally be signed by the arbitrator or umpire or, if there are two or more arbitrators by them all at the same time and place and in each other's presence. The signatures may, but need not, be witnessed and the award need not now be stamped.

When an arbitrator has made his award he is *functus officio*, he loses his powers and has no power to alter his award except to correct mere clerical errors. (*Sutherland* v. *Hannevig Brothers Ltd.*, 1921.)[690]

Sect. 20 of the Act of 1950 gives arbitrators discretion to decide whether an award should or should not carry interest. It does not give them power to decide what rate it should be, the interest being limited to that applicable to a judgment debt (currently $7\frac{1}{2}$ per cent). (*Timber Shipping Co. S.A.* v. *London and Overseas Freighters*, [1971] 2 All E.R. 599.)

Remitting and Setting Aside Awards. The court has power to remit awards.

(1) In all cases of reference to arbitration the High Court or a judge thereof may from time to time remit the matters referred, or any of them, to the reconsideration of the arbitrator or umpire.

(2) Where an award is remitted, the arbitrator or umpire shall, unless the order otherwise directs, make his award within three months after the date of the order. (Sect. 22.)

This enables errors to be corrected or further information to be obtained in order to reach a proper decision. It is appropriate—

(a) where the award has some obvious defect or error; or is ambiguous and uncertain;

(*b*) where the arbitrator or umpire has admitted making a mistake and wishes to correct it;

(*c*) where further evidence has come to light which could not have been discovered before the award was made and which is material to the case, but not evidence which was known at the time of the reference and ought then to have been produced;

(*d*) where there has been misconduct on the part of the arbitrator or umpire, e.g. where he has refused to state a special case, or delegated part of his authority, or heard evidence in the absence of the parties or one of them.

Application to remit must be made within six weeks of the award to a single judge of the Queen's Bench Division or to a Master in Chambers. On remission the arbitrator should, if necessary, hold a fresh hearing and may have to reconsider the whole reference. His powers revive unless part of the award is good and part bad, in which case he is *functus officio* as to the good part.

The setting aside of an award has more serious consequences since the parties are back where they started. Sect. 23 provides that—

(1) Where an arbitrator or umpire has misconducted himself or the proceedings, the High Court may remove him.

(2) Where an arbitrator or umpire has misconducted himself or the proceedings or an arbitration or award has been improperly procured, the High Court may set the award aside.

(3) Where an application is made to set aside an award, the High Court may order that any money made payable by the award shall be brought into court or otherwise secured pending determination of the application. (Sect. 23.)

Misconduct is a wide term. Some examples have already been given in connection with remission but it extends from bribery and corruption to errors as to the scope of the arbitrator's authority, errors of procedure and errors of law.

Enforcing the Award. An award on an arbitration agreement may, by leave of the High Court or a judge thereof, be enforced in the same manner as a judgment or order to the same effect, and where leave is so given, judgment may be entered in terms of the award. (Sect. 26.) It may also be enforced by an action at law, and indeed this is the only method of enforcing an oral submission.

Costs of the Award. Sect. 18 provides that, in the absence of contrary agreement, the costs of the reference and the award are in the discretion of the arbitrator or umpire, and such costs are taxable (assessable) in the High Court.

The arbitration agreement must not provide that each party shall pay his own costs in any event, unless the agreement is to submit to arbitration a dispute which has arisen before the making of the agreement. If no provision as to costs is made in the award, any party to the reference may apply to the arbitrator within fourteen days to amend his award by giving directions as to payment of the costs of the reference.

Remuneration of Arbitrator or Umpire. The parties may fix the arbitrator's remuneration in advance by agreement; otherwise he is entitled to a reasonable remuneration which he may fix and include in his award. Where two arbitrators disagree and the umpire takes over, he may include both his own and their fees in the award as part of the costs. If the remuneration is not included in the award, the party required to pay it may have the amount taxed. The arbitrator has a lien on the arbitration agreement and the award for his charges, and may detain them until his charges are paid.

Where an arbitrator or umpire refuses to deliver his award except on payment of the fees demanded by him, the High Court may, on application, order the award to be delivered to the applicant on payment into court of the fees demanded. These fees are then taxed (assessed) by the taxing officer who pays to the arbitrator such sum as is found reasonable and returns the balance (if any) to the applicant. (Sect. 19.) This rule does not apply where the fees have been fixed by agreement.

A taxation of fees may be reviewed in the same manner as a taxation of costs, and the arbitrator or umpire may appear and be heard on the matter. The arbitrator or umpire may also bring an action to recover the stated or a reasonable remuneration.

COMMON LAW SUBMISSIONS

Where an agreement to go to arbitration is made orally it is called a submission and is governed by the rules of the common law. The dispute must exist when the agreement is made and the submission is not complete until the arbitrator has been appointed. His authority may be revoked at any time before the publication of the award, subject only to an action for damages by the other party. An oral submission will be unenforceable if it concerns the transfer of land or an interest in land, and even during the submission it is open to a party to start an action which the court cannot stay.

The award when made is not enforceable as a judgment, as is the case with a reference, and an action may have to be brought if the other party does not carry out its terms.

STATUTORY ARBITRATIONS

Many statutes provide for the settlement of disputes by arbitration either on a voluntary or compulsory basis. Thus the Agricultural Holdings Act, 1948, provides for compulsory arbitration in certain cases and provision for voluntary arbitration is made in connection with building societies, companies, friendly societies, railways and many other institutions.

THE LAW OF CONTRACT

1. Vincent v. Premo Enterprises (Voucher Sales) Ltd. and Others, [1969] 2 All E.R. 941

The plaintiffs, Mr. Vincent and his sister Miss Vincent, owned a freehold house in Central Road, Yeovil. They let four rooms on the first floor to Darch & Willcox Ltd. who kept two of the rooms for themselves and sublet the other two rooms to the first defendants, Premo Enterprises. The tenancy of Darch & Willcox Ltd. was due to end on 25th March, 1967, whereupon the sub-tenancy of Premo Enterprises would also end. However, negotiations took place whereby Premo Enterprises were to take a tenancy of the whole floor direct from the plaintiffs.

The terms of the agreement were set out in two letters from which it appeared that Premo Enterprises were to take a tenancy of the whole first floor for five years from 25th March, 1967, at a rent of £250 per annum subject to the lease being prepared and signed.

On 25th March, 1967, Darch & Willcox Ltd. vacated their accommodation and moved into premises across the road, Mr. Willcox taking the key and saying to Premo's two girl employees that they could have the key whenever they required it. It was accepted by the court that the girls did not ask for the key until 1st May, 1967, which was regarded as the date when Premo's went into possession of the whole of the first floor.

The plaintiffs signed, sealed and delivered the lease and handed it to their solicitors. Premo's signed and sealed the counterpart on condition that the date when they took vacant possession should be agreed and that no rent should be payable in respect of the time before they took vacant possession, i.e. between 25th March, 1967, and 1st May, 1967. Before the solicitors exchanged the documents Premo's sought to withdraw from the transaction. The plaintiffs claimed that the lease was binding and sued in Yeovil County Court for rent from 25th March, 1967. Premo's said in defence that the deed had not been delivered but was an escrow and that the conditions had not been fulfilled. At the hearing in the County Court the plaintiffs agreed to give credit for the period 25th March, 1967, to 1st May, 1967, but the judge held that the lease was not binding on Premo's, being an escrow and that it was too late for the plaintiffs to say that the condition had been fulfilled at the hearing. He rejected the plaintiffs' claim and they appealed. *Held*—by the Court of Appeal—since the first defendants intended to be bound subject only to the date of possession being agreed, the deed was delivered as an escrow. However, it was not too late to fulfil the condition at the hearing and the deed was therefore binding on the first defendants.

"The question is whether this deed was 'delivered' at all, or whether it was delivered subject to a condition, i.e. as an 'escrow'. . . . The defendants did intend to be bound, but subject to the date of possession being agreed. That makes it, I think, an escrow. . . . This deed was signed, sealed and delivered by the first defendants, subject only to the condition that the date on which possession was given should be ascertained and the rent adjusted accordingly. The next question is whether the condition was fulfilled. I think it was fulfilled at the hearing before the county court when the date of possession was ascertained by the judge to be 1st May, 1967; and the plaintiffs agreed to adjust the rent accordingly. The judge thought it was too late. He did not think the condition could be fulfilled after the action was brought. I do not share his view. . . . I see nothing in this case to debar the plaintiffs from insisting on their legal rights. They did not know of this condition imposed by the defendants to their solicitors until the defence was pleaded; and they acted quite reasonably from that time onwards. The deed having been delivered, the condition having been fulfilled, the defendants are bound." (*per* Lord Denning, M.R.)

2. Wilson *v.* Wilson [1969] 3 All E.R. 945

In 1961 the defendant wished to buy a freehold property in Battersea but his income was not sufficient to qualify him for a building society loan. Accordingly his brother, the plaintiff, joined him in the application to the building society but paid no part of the purchase price, nor any of the costs and expenses, nor the mortgage repayments. The transfer of the property declared that the plaintiff and defendant were joint owners and the title was registered in their joint names as was the charge in favour of the building society.

In March, 1967, the plaintiff commenced an action claiming a half share in the property. The defendant alleged that it was never intended that he and his brother should be beneficial joint owners but that the property was held on trust by the defendant and his brother for the sole benefit of the defendant. The defendant asked, amongst other things, for rectification of the deed of transfer. *Held*—by Buckley, J.—that the court would order rectification of the deed by striking out that part of it which declared beneficial interests so as to show the true intention of the parties, i.e. that the beneficial ownership of the property was in the defendant alone. In the course of his judgement, Buckley, J., said " . . . where a deed is rectifiable (that is to say, ought to be rectified), the doctrine of estoppel by deed will not bind the parties to it . . ."

3. Carlill *v.* Carbolic Smoke Ball Co., [1893] 1 Q.B. 256

The defendants were proprietors of a medical preparation called "The Carbolic Smoke Ball." They inserted advertisements in various newspapers in which they offered to pay £100 to any person who contracted influenza after using the ball three times a day for two weeks. They added that they had deposited £1,000 at the Alliance Bank, Regent Street "to show our sincerity in the matter." The plaintiff, a lady, used the ball as advertised, and was attacked by influenza during the course of treatment, which in her case extended from 20th November, 1891, to 17th January, 1892. She now sued for £100 and the following matters arose out of the various defences raised by the company. (*a*) It was suggested that the offer was too vague since no time limit was stipulated in which the user was to contract influenza. The court said that it must surely have been the intention that the ball would protect its user during the period of its use, and since this covered the present case it was not necessary to go further. (*b*) The suggestion was made that the matter was an advertising "puff" and that there was no intention to create legal relations. Here the court took the view that the deposit of £1,000 at the bank was clear evidence of an intention to pay claims. (*c*) It was further suggested that this was an attempt to contract with the whole world and that this was impossible in English law. The court took the view that the advertisement was an offer to the whole world and that, by analogy with the reward cases, it was possible to make an offer of this kind. (*d*) The company also claimed that the plaintiff had not supplied any consideration, but the court took the view that using this inhalant three times a day for two weeks or more was sufficient consideration. It was not necessary to consider its adequacy. (*e*) Finally the defendants suggested that there had been no communication of acceptance but here the court, looking at the reward cases, stated that in contracts of this kind acceptance may be by conduct.

4. Pharmaceutical Society of Great Britain *v.* Boots Cash Chemists (Southern) Ltd., [1953] 1 Q.B. 401

The defendants' branch at Edgware was adapted to the "self service" system. Customers selected their purchases from shelves on which the goods were displayed and put them into a wire basket supplied by the defendants. They then took them to the cash desk where they paid the price. One section of shelves was set out with drugs which were included in the Poisons List referred to in Sect. 17 of the Pharmacy and Poisons Act, 1933, though they were not dangerous drugs and did not require a doctor's prescription. Sect. 18 of the Act requires that the sale of such drugs shall take place in the presence of a qualified pharmacist. Every sale of the drugs on the Poison List was supervised at the cash desk by a qualified pharmacist, who had authority to prevent customers from taking goods out of the shop if he thought fit. One of the duties of the society was to enforce the provisions of the Act, and the action was brought because the plaintiffs claimed that the defendants were infringing Sect. 18. *Held*—The display of goods in this way did not constitute an offer. The contract of sale was not made when a customer selected goods from the shelves, but when the company's servant at the cash desk accepted the offer to buy what had been chosen. There was, therefore, supervision in the sense required by the Act at the appropriate moment of time.

5. Spencer *v.* Harding (1870), L.R. 5 C.P. 561

The defendants had sent out a circular in the following terms: "We are instructed to offer to the wholesale trade for sale by tender the stock-in-trade of Messrs. Gilbeck and Co., amounting as per stock-book to £2,503 13s. 1d. and which will be sold at a discount in one lot. Payment to be made in cash. The stock may be viewed on the premises up to Thursday the 20th instant, on which day, at 12 o'clock noon precisely, the tenders will be received and opened at our offices." The plaintiffs suggested that the circular was an offer to sell the stock to the person who made the highest bid for cash, and that they had sent the highest bid which the defendants had refused to accept. *Held*—The circular was an invitation to treat and not an offer, and the defendants need not accept a tender unless they wished to do so. Willes, J., said of the circular: "It is a mere attempt to ascertain whether an offer can be obtained within such a margin as the sellers are willing to accept."

6. Partridge *v.* Crittenden, [1968] 2 All E.R. 421

Mr. Partridge inserted an advertisement in a publication called *Cage and Aviary Birds* containing the words "Bramblefinch cocks, bramblefinch hens, 25s. each." The advertisement appeared under the general heading "Classified Advertisements" and in no place was there any direct use of the words "offer for sale." A Mr. Thompson answered the advertisement enclosing a cheque for 25s. and asking that a "bramblefinch hen" be sent to him. Mr. Partridge sent one in a box, the bird wearing a closed ring.

Mr. Thompson opened the box in the presence of an R.S.P.C.A. inspector, Mr. Crittenden, and removed the ring without injury to the bird. Mr. Crittenden brought a prosecution against Mr. Partridge before the Chester magistrates alleging that Mr. Partridge had offered for sale a brambling contrary to Sect. 6 (1) of the Protection of Birds Act, 1954, the bird being other than a close-ringed specimen bred in captivity and being of a species which was resident in or visited the British Isles in a wild state.

The justices were satisfied that the bird had not been bred in captivity but had been caught and ringed. A close-ring meant a ring that was completely closed and incapable of being forced or broken except with the intention of damaging it; such a ring was forced over the claws of a bird when it was between three and ten days old, and at that time it was not possible to determine what the eventual girth of the leg would be so that the close-ring soon became difficult to remove. The ease with which the ring was removed in this case indicated that it had been put on at a much later stage and this, together with the fact that the bird had no perching sense, led the justices to convict Mr. Partridge.

He appealed to the Divisional Court of the Queen's Bench Division where the conviction was quashed. The Court accepted that the bird was a wild bird, but since Mr. Partridge had been charged with "offering for sale," the conviction could not stand. The advertisement constituted in law an invitation to treat, not an offer for sale, and the offence was not, therefore, established. There was of course a completed sale for which Mr. Partridge could have been successfully prosecuted but the prosecution in this case had relied on the offence of "offering for sale" and failed to establish such an offer.

7. Harvey *v.* Facey, [1893] A.C. 552

The plaintiffs sent the following telegram to the defendant: "Will you sell us Bumper Hall Pen? Telegraph lowest cash price." The defendant telegraphed in reply: "Lowest price for Bumper Hall Pen £900." The plaintiffs then telegraphed: "We agree to buy Bumper Hall Pen for £900 asked by you. Please send us your title deeds in order that we may get early possession." The defendant made no reply. The supreme Court of Jamaica granted the plaintiffs a decree of specific performance of the contract. On appeal the Judicial Committee of the Privy Council *held* that there was no contract. The second telegram was not an offer, but was in the nature of an invitation to treat at a minimum price of £900. The third telegram could not therefore be an acceptance resulting in a contract.

8. Clifton *v.* Palumbo, [1944] 2 All E.R. 497

The plaintiff who was the owner of a very large estate wrote to the defendant as follows: "I am prepared to offer you or your nominee my Lytham estate for £600,000. I also agree that a reasonable and sufficient time shall be granted to you for the examination and consideration of all the data and details necessary for the preparation of the Schedule of Completion." The defendant purported to accept this offer, but later the plaintiff thought the price too low and brought this action for a declaration that there was no binding contract between himself and the defendant. The defendant counterclaimed for specific performance. *Held*—The plaintiff's letter was an invitation to treat and not an offer, so that the defendant's purported acceptance did not give rise to a binding contract between the parties. Findlay, L.J. (following Lord Green, M.R.), said of the plaintiff's letter: 'It is quite possible for persons on a half-sheet of notepaper, in the most informal and unorthodox language, to contract to sell the most extensive and most complicated estate that can be imagined.

That is quite possible, but, having regard to the habits of the people in this country, it is very unlikely."

9. Bigg *v.* Boyd Gibbins Ltd., [1971] 2 All E.R. 183

The plaintiff and the defendants were negotiating for the sale of a freehold property called Shortgrove Hall at Newport, Essex. The following material correspondence passed between them—

(*a*) on 22nd *December*, 1969, *from the plaintiffs to the defendants.*

". . . As you are aware that I paid £25,000 for this property, your offer of £20,000 would appear to be at least a little optimistic. For a quick sale I would accept £26,000 so that my expenses may be covered. If you are not interested in this price, would you please let me know immediately as then I shall open negotiations with—(some other people)."

(*b*) on 8th *January*, 1970, *from the defendants to the plaintiffs.*

"re: Shortgrove Hall, Newport. Thank you for your letter of the 22nd December. I have just recently returned from my winter holiday and, turning this matter over in my mind now, would advise you that I accept your offer. Perhaps you will be good enough to contact—(a firm of solicitors) who will be handling this for us."

(*c*) on 13th *January*, 1970 *from the plaintiffs to the defendants.*

"Dear Mr. Gibbins, I thank you for your letter (i.e. the letter of 8th January, 1970) received this morning, accepting my price of £26,000 for the sale of Shortgrove Hall. I am putting the matter in the hands of my solicitors . . . . My wife and I are both pleased that you are purchasing the property . . ."

The plaintiffs alleged that this exchange of letters constituted an agreement for the sale of the property and brought an action for specific performance. *Held*—by the Court of Appeal—that although an agreement on price did not necessarily mean an agreement for sale and purchase and the word 'offer' did not always mean offer in the sense of offer for actual sale, but might be related to a particular term of the agreement whilst other negotiations in respect of the agreement continued, in the present case it was clear from the terms of the letters that the plaintiffs' first letter constituted an offer the acceptance of which by the defendants constituted a binding agreement; accordingly the plaintiffs were entitled to specific performance.

(*N.B.*: *Harvey* v. *Facey*[7] and *Clifton* v. *Palumbo*[8] were distinguished on the facts.)

10. Harris *v.* Nickerson (1873), L.R. 8 Q.B. 286

The defendant, an auctioneer, advertised in London newspapers that a sale of office furniture would be held at Bury St. Edmunds. A broker with a commission to buy furniture came from London to attend the sale. Several conditions were set out in the advertisement, one being: "The highest bidder to be the buyer." The lots described as office furniture were not put up for sale but were withdrawn, though the auction itself was held. The broker sued for loss of time in attending the sale. *Held*—He could not recover from the auctioneer. There was no offer since the lots were never put up for sale, and the advertisement was simply an invitation to treat.

11. Brogden *v.* Metropolitan Railway (1877), 2 App.Cas. 666

The plaintiff had been a supplier of coal to the Railway Company for a number of years, though there was no formal agreement between them.

Eventually the plaintiff suggested that there ought to be one, and the agents of the parties met and a draft agreement was drawn up by the Railway Company's agent and sent to the plaintiff. The plaintiff inserted several new clauses into the draft, and in particular filled in the name of an arbitrator to settle the parties' differences under the agreement should any arise. He then wrote the word "Approved" on the draft and returned it to the Railway Company's agent. There was no formal execution, the draft remaining in the agent's desk. However, coal was supplied according to the prices mentioned in the draft, though these were not the market prices, and prices were reviewed from time to time in accordance with the draft. The parties then had a disagreement and the plaintiff refused to supply coal to the Railway Company on the grounds that, since the Railway Company had not accepted the offer contained in the amended draft, there was no binding contract. *Held*—

(i) The draft was not a binding contract because the plaintiff had inserted new terms which the Railway Company had not accepted; but

(ii) the parties had indicated by their conduct that they had waived the execution of the formal document and agreed to act on the basis of the draft. There was, therefore, a binding contract arising out of conduct, and its terms were the terms of the draft.

12. Williams *v.* Carwardine (1833), 5 C. & P. 566

The defendant published a handbill by the terms of which he promised to pay the sum of £20 to any person who should give information, leading to the discovery of the murderer of Walter Carwardine. Two persons were tried for the murder at Hereford Assizes and were acquitted. Shortly afterwards the plaintiff, who was living with one Williams, was severely beaten by him and, believing that she was going to die and to ease her conscience, she gave information leading to the conviction of the man Williams for the murder. In an action to recover the reward the jury found that the plaintiff was not induced to give the information by the reward offered, but by motives of spite and revenge. *Held*—She was nevertheless entitled to the reward, for she had seen the handbill and had given information. Patteson, J., said: "We cannot go into the plaintiff's motives."

13. Winn *v.* Bull (1877), 7 Ch. D. 29

The defendant had entered into a written agreement with the plaintiff for the lease of a house, the term of the lease and the rent being agreed. However, the written agreement was expressly made "subject to the preparation and approval of a formal contract." It appeared that no other contract was made between the parties. The plaintiff now sued for specific performance of the agreement. *Held*—The written agreement provided a memorandum sufficient to satisfy Sect. 4 of the Statute of Frauds, 1677 (now Sect. 40 of the Law of Property Act, 1925), but there was no binding contract between the parties because, although certain covenants are normally implied into leases, it is also true that many and varied express covenants are often agreed between the parties. The words "subject to contract" indicated that the parties were still in a state of negotiation, and until they entered into a formal contract there was no agreement which the Court could enforce.

14. Filby *v.* Hounsell, [1896] 2 Ch. 737

Property had been offered for sale by auction but had not been sold. An offer was then made to buy the property, stating that if the offer was accepted the purchaser would sign a contract "on the auction particulars." This offer was accepted "subject to contract as agreed." *Held*—The parties were bound by a contract drafted on the auction particulars, although they had not signed a formal contract.

15. Chillingworth and another *v.* Esche, [1923] All E.R. Rep. 97

By a document, dated 10th July, 1922, Chillingworth and Cummings agreed to purchase the defendant's nursery gardens at Cheshunt, Herts., for £4,800 "subject to a proper contract to be prepared by the vendor's solicitors." The plaintiffs paid a deposit of £240. After the solicitors on both sides had agreed on the terms of a contract the plaintiffs refused, without reason, to go on and claimed a declaration that the document of 20th July, 1922, was not binding and that the deposit must be repaid. *Held*—by the Court of Appeal— that the document was nothing more than a conditional offer and a conditional acceptance and would only ripen into a binding agreement when a formal document was signed. Further, on the construction of the documents and in the circumstances, the plaintiffs were entitled to the repayment of the deposit. The plaintiffs' solicitors were not agents of their clients, so as to bind them, when they agreed with the defendant's solicitors on the terms of the contract.

16. Goding *v.* Frazer, [1966] 3 All E.R. 234

An estate agent had arranged, on behalf of a vendor, the sale of the latter's land "subject to contract." The agent accepted a deposit from the potential purchaser, but there was no mention of the capacity in which he received it, i.e. either as agent for the vendor or as stake-holder. At a later stage the purchaser withdrew and, the estate agent being insolvent, claimed the return of his deposit from the vendor. *Held*—when an estate agent receives a deposit on a subject-to-contract sale, he receives it as agent for the vendor, unless there is an agreement to the contrary, and the vendor remains liable for returning the said deposit. The purchaser succeeded in his claim.

16a. Burt v. *Claude Cousins & Co. Ltd., and Shaw* (1971), 115 S.J. 207

The plaintiff paid a ten per cent deposit of £2,075 to an estate agent in respect of the purchase price of an hotel "subject to contract." The sale fell through and the estate agent went into liquidation having put the deposit into the bank and used it. *Held*—by the Court of Appeal following *Goding* v. *Frazer*[16]—that the vendor Shaw was liable to repay the deposit although he had never received it. Lord Denning, M.R., dissented saying an estate agent in this situation is a stake-holder not an agent in respect of the deposit and that the vendor should not be liable to repay.

16b. Barrington v. *Lee, The Times,* 29th October, 1971

The plaintiff, who was intending to purchase a house, paid a deposit to an estate agent who took it in the agreed capacity of a stake-holder and not on behalf of the vendor. The sale did not go through but the agent failed to repay the deposit. The plaintiff obtained judgment against the agent but the agent did not pay. *Held*—by the Court of Appeal—that the plaintiff was not entitled to succeed in a fresh action against the vendor. *Per* Lord Denning, M.R., *Burt* v. *Claude Cousins & Co.*[16a] was wrongly decided. An estate agent receives a deposit as stake-holder not only when he agrees to act in this capacity but also where nothing is said by the parties as to his situation. Consequently, if he misappropriates the money the vendor is not liable to repay it.

N.B. Edmund Davies and Stephenson, L.JJ., would only *distinguish Burt* because the agent received *specifically* as a stake-holder.

17. Branca *v.* Cobarro, [1947] 2 All E.R. 101

The defendant agreed to sell to the plaintiff the lease and goodwill of a mushroom farm. The contract ended with the words "This is a provisional agreement until a full legalised agreement, drawn up by a solicitor and embodying all the conditions herewith stated is signed." The defendant alleged that the agreement was not binding on him but it was *held*—by the Court of Appeal —that the words "provisional" and "until" were not appropriate words to indicate conditional assent. They indicated that the parties intended a binding agreement which would remain in force until superseded by a more formal contract between the parties.

18. Tomlin *v.* Standard Telephones and Cables Ltd., [1969] 3 All E.R. 201

The plaintiff was a fitter employed to weld on board H.M. tele-communications ship *Alert.* In the course of his duties he strained his back and claimed against the defendants, his employers, for damages in respect of that accident. The plaintiff's solicitors and the employers' insurers negotiated an agreement that liability would be accepted on a 50 per cent basis. In this action the defendants alleged that they were not bound by the agreement entered into by their representatives the insurers, because it appeared that the letters constituting the agreement were headed "Without Prejudice." *Held*—by the Court of Appeal—that on a proper construction of the letters written by the defendants' representatives there was a definite and binding agreement to pay half the damages though the actual amount was left for further negotiation.

"A point that arises is that all the letters written by the agent of the insurance company bore the words 'Without Prejudice.' The point is taken that, by reason of those words, there could not be any binding agreement between the parties . . . *Walker* v. *Wilsher*, (1889), 23 Q.B.D. 335. . . . Lindley, L.J., said at p. 337 'What is the meaning of the words "without prejudice?" I think they mean without prejudice to the position of the writer of the letter if the terms he proposes are not accepted. If the terms proposed in the letter are accepted a complete contract is established and the letter, although written without prejudice, operates to alter the old state of things and to establish a new one.' That statement of Lindley, L.J., is of great authority and seems to me to apply exactly to the present case if in fact there was a binding agreement, or an agreement intended to be binding, reached between the parties; and, accordingly, it seems to me that not only was the court entitled to look at the letters although they were nearly all described as 'Without Prejudice,' but it is quite possible (and in fact the intention of the parties was) that there was a binding agreement contained in that correspondence." (*per* Danckwerts, L.J.)

19. Hillas & Co. Ltd. *v.* Arcos Ltd., [1932] All E.R. Rep. 494

The plaintiffs had entered into a contract with the defendants under which the defendants were to supply the plaintiffs with "22,000 standards of soft wood (Russian) of fair specification over the season 1930." The contract also contained an option allowing the plaintiffs to take up 100,000 standards as above during the season 1931. The parties managed to perform the contract throughout the 1930 season without any argument or serious difficulty in spite of the vague words used in connection with the specification of the wood. However, when the plaintiffs exercised their option for 100,000 standards during the season 1931, the defendants refused to supply the wood, saying that the specification was too vague to bind the parties, and the agreement was therefore inchoate as requiring a further agreement as to the precise specification. *Held*—by the House of Lords—that the option to supply 100,000 standards during the 1931 season was valid. There was a certain vagueness about the specification, but there was also a course of dealing between the parties which operated as a guide to the Court regarding the difficulties which this vagueness might produce. Since the parties had not experienced serious difficulty in carrying out the 1930 agreement, there was no reason to suppose that the option could not have been carried out without difficulty had the defendants been prepared to go on with it. Judgment was given for the plaintiffs.

20. Foley *v.* **Classique Coaches Ltd.,** [1934] 2 K.B. 1

F owned certain land, part of which he used for the business of supplying petrol. He also owned the adjoining land. The company wished to purchase the adjoining land for use as the headquarters of their charabanc business. F agreed to sell the land to the company on condition that the company would buy all their petrol from him. An agreement was made under which the company agreed to buy its petrol from F "at a price to be agreed by the parties in writing and from time to time." It was further agreed that any dispute arising under the agreement should be submitted "to arbitration in the usual way." The agreement was acted upon for three years. At this time the company felt it could get petrol at a better price, and the company's solicitor wrote to F repudiating the contract. *Held*—Although the parties had not agreed upon a price, there was a contract to supply petrol at a reasonable price and of reasonable quality, and although the agreement did not stipulate the future price, but left this to the further agreement of the parties, a method was provided by which the price could be ascertained without such agreement, i.e. by arbitration. An injunction was therefore granted requiring the company to take petrol from F as agreed.

A similar problem arose in *F. & Sykes (Wessex)* v. *Fine-Fare, The Times,* 17th November, 1966. In that case producers of broiler chickens agreed with certain retailers to supply between 30,000 and 80,000 chickens a week during the first year of the agreement and afterwards "such other figures as might be agreed." The agreement was to last for not less than five years, and it was agreed that any differences between the parties should be referred to arbitration. Eventually the retailers contended that the agreement was void for uncertainty. *Held*—by the Court of Appeal—it was not, because in default of the further agreement envisaged the number of chickens should be such reasonable number as might be decided by the arbitrator.

20a. Brown v. *Gould and Others, The Times,* April 30th, 1971

A lease contained an option to renew "at a rent to be fixed having regard to the market value of the premises at the time of exercising the option taking into account to the advantage of the tenant any increased value of such premises attributable to structural improvements made by the tenant." The landlords maintained that the option was void for uncertainty. *Held*—by Meggarry, J.—it was not. The parties had laid down a formula by which the rent might be ascertained. Although there was no machinery (e.g. arbitration) for resolving a dispute as to the application of the formula, the court could provide that machinery and determine the rent. The option was therefore valid and enforceable.

21. Scammell (G.) and Nephew Ltd. *v.* Ouston, [1941] A.C. 251

Ouston wished to acquire a new motor van for use in his furniture business. Discussions took place with the company's sales manager as a result of which the company sent a quotation for the supply of a suitable van. Eventually Ouston sent an official order making the following stipulation, "This order is given on the understanding that the balance of the purchase price can be had on hire-purchase terms over a period of two years." This was in accordance with the discussions between the sales manager and Ouston, which had taken place on the understanding that hire purchase would be available. The company seemed to be content with the arrangement and completed the van. Arrangements were made with a finance company to give hire-purchase facilities, but the actual terms were not agreed at that stage. The appellants also agreed to take Ouston's present van in part exchange, but later stated that they were not satisfied with its condition and asked him to sell it locally. He refused and after much correspondence he issued a writ against the appellants for damages for non-delivery of the van. The appellants' defence was that there was no contract until the hire-purchase terms had been ascertained. *Held*—The defence succeeded; it was not possible to construe a contract from the vague language used by the parties.

N.B. If there is a trade custom, business procedure or previous dealings between the parties, which assist the court in construing the vague parts of an agreement, then the agreement may be enforced. Here there was no such evidence.

22. The Moorcock (1889), 14 P.D. 64

The appellants in this case were in possession of a wharf and a jetty extending into the River Thames, and the respondent was the owner of the steamship *Moorcock*. In November, 1887, the appellants and the respondent agreed that the ship should be discharged and loaded at the wharf and for that purpose should be moored alongside the jetty. Both parties realised that when the tide was out the ship would rest on the river bed. In the event the *Moorcock* sustained damage when she ceased to be waterborne owing to the centre of the vessel settling on a ridge of hard ground beneath the mud. There was no evidence that the appellants had given any warranty that the place was safe for the ship to lie in, but it was *held*—by the Court of Appeal—that there was an implied warranty by the appellants to this effect, for breach of which they were liable in damages. "Now, an implied warranty, or as it is called, a covenant in law, as distinguished from an express contract or express warranty, really is in all cases founded on the presumed intention of the parties, and upon reason. The implication which the law draws from what must obviously have been the intention of the parties, the law draws with the object of giving efficacy to the transaction and preventing such a failure of consideration as cannot have been within the contemplation of either side; and I believe if one were to take all the cases, and there are many, of implied warranties or covenants in law, it will be found that in all of them the law is raising an implication from the presumed intention of the parties with the object of giving to the transaction such efficacy as both

parties must have intended that at all events it should have. In business transactions such as this, what the law desires to effect by the implication is to give
such business efficacy to the transaction as must have been intended at all events
by both parties who are business men; not to impose on one side all the perils
of the transaction, or to emancipate one side from all the chances of failure, but
to make each party promise in law as much, at all events, as it must have been
in the contemplation of both parties that he should be responsible for in respect
of those perils or chances." (*per* Bowen, L.J.)

23. Nicolene Ltd. *v.* Simmonds, [1953] 1 All E.R. 882

The plaintiffs alleged that there was a contract for the sale by them of 3,000
tons of steel reinforcing bars and that the defendant seller had broken his
contract. When the plaintiffs claimed damages the seller set up the defence
that, owing to one of the sentences in the letters which constituted the contract,
there was no contract at all. The material words were "We are in agreement
that the usual conditions of acceptance apply." In fact there were no usual
conditions of acceptance so that the words were meaningless but the seller
nevertheless suggested that the contract was unenforceable since it was not
complete. *Held*—by the Court of Appeal—that the contract was enforceable
and that the meaningless clause could be ignored. "In my opinion a distinction
must be drawn between a clause which is meaningless and a clause which is yet
to be agreed. A clause which is meaningless can often be ignored, whilst still
leaving the contract good; whereas a clause which has yet to be agreed may
mean that there is no contract at all, because the parties have not agreed on all
the essential terms. . . . In the present case there was nothing yet to be agreed.
There was nothing left to further negotiation. All that happened was that the
parties agreed that 'the usual conditions of acceptance apply'. That clause was
so vague and uncertain as to be incapable of any precise meaning. It is clearly
severable from the rest of the contract. It can be rejected without impairing
the sense or reasonableness of the contract as a whole, and it should be so rejected.
The contract should be held good and the clause ignored. The parties themselves treated the contract as subsisting. They regarded it as creating binding
obligations between them; and it would be most unfortunate if the law should
say otherwise. You would find defaulters all scanning their contracts to find
some meaningless clause on which to ride free." (*per* Denning L.J.)

24. Hyde *v.* Wrench (1840), 3 Beav. 334

The defendant offered to sell his farm for £1,000. The plaintiff's agent made
an offer of £950 and the defendant asked for a few days for consideration, after
which the defendant wrote saying he could not accept it, whereupon the
plaintiff wrote purporting to accept the offer of £1,000. The defendant did not
consider himself bound, and the plaintiff sued for specific performance.
Held—The plaintiff could not enforce this "acceptance" because his counter
offer of £950 was an implied rejection of the original offer to sell at £1,000.

24a Neale v. Merrett, [1930] W.N. 189

The defendant offered to sell land to the plaintiff for £280. The plaintiff
replied, purporting to accept the offer and enclosing £80, promising to pay
the balance by monthly instalments of £50 each. *Held*—The plaintiff could
not enforce the acceptance because it was not unqualified, since he had
introduced a system of deferred payment.

24b. *Northland Airlines Ltd.* v. *Dennis Ferranti Meters Ltd.* (1970), 114 Sol. J. 845

Ferranti offered to sell Northland an aircraft by a telegram in the following terms—

"Confirming sale to you—aircraft—£27,000 fob Winnipeg. Please remit £5,000 for account of—(a bank account was named)."

Northland replied by telegram as follows—

"This is to confirm your cable and my purchase—aircraft on terms set out in your cable. Price £27,000 delivered fob Winnipeg. £5,000 forwarded your bank in trust for your account pending delivery. Balance payable on delivery. Please confirm delivery to be made 30 days within this date." Ferranti did not regard this as an acceptance and disposed of the aircraft elsewhere. Northland sued for damages for breach of contract. *Held*—by the Court of Appeal—that the second telegram was not an acceptance because the deposit was not paid over outright as requested but left in trust pending delivery and Northland had inserted a delivery date whereas the offer did not mention one. These were new terms so that the second telegram was a counter offer and not an acceptance.

25. Stevenson v. McLean (1880), 5 Q.B.D. 346

The defendant offered to sell to the plaintiffs a quantity of iron "at 40s. nett cash per ton till Monday." On Monday the plaintiffs telegraphed asking whether the defendant would accept 40s. for delivery over two months, or if not what was the longest limit the defendant would give. The defendant received the telegram at 10.1 a.m. but did not reply, so the plaintiffs, by telegram sent at 1.34 p.m., accepted the defendant's original offer. The defendant had already sold the iron to a third party, and informed the plaintiffs of this by a telegram despatched at 1.25 p.m. arriving at 1.46 p.m. The plaintiffs had therefore accepted the offer before the defendant's revocation had been communicated to them. If, however, the plaintiffs' first telegram constituted a counter offer, then it would amount to a rejection of the defendant's original offer. *Held*—The plaintiffs' first telegram was not a counter offer, but a mere inquiry which did not amount to a rejection of the defendant's original offer, so that the offer was still open when the plaintiffs accepted it.

26. Trollope & Colls Ltd. v. Atomic Power Constructions Ltd., [1962] 3 All E.R. 1035

The plaintiffs were sub-contractors for the civil engineering aspects of the building of a new power station. The defendants were the main contractors, the Central Electricity Board being the employing authority. The plaintiffs had submitted a tender in 1959 in which they had said that the price for their part of the work would be nine million pounds. Part A of this tender contained a price adjustment clause allowing the plaintiffs to adjust the price tendered according to variations, if any, in the cost of labour and materials during the course of completing the work. Numerous changes were made in this part of the tender and in the price adjustment clause by the Central Electricity Board, but at a meeting of the parties on 11th April, 1960, the tender as amended was agreed by the plaintiffs. The plaintiffs had by this time already done a considerable amount of work on the site.

Later the plaintiffs regretted the agreement of 11th April, 1960, and claimed that they were free to terminate operations at any time and asked for a *quantum meruit* for their services up to 11th April, 1960. The Board claimed that a binding contract existed between themselves and the plaintiffs on the terms of the agreement of 11th April, 1960, and that this agreement, when made, operated retrospectively to cover the work done by the plaintiffs up to 11th April and subsequently. The plaintiffs then alleged that the agreement of 11th April could only operate for the future, and that work done up to 11th April, 1960, should be assessed by the Court on a *quantum meruit*, or alternatively be based on an implied contract on the terms of the tender of 1959 before amendments. *Held*—The agreement of 11th April, 1960, operated retrospectively so that the plaintiffs were entitled to payment for work done prior to 11th April only on the basis of the amended tender and were also bound to operate for the future on the same basis.

N.B. The action was one in which many parties were joined, and the Central Electricity Board was in fact one of the defendants.

27. Great Northern Railway *v.* Witham (1873), L.R. 9 C.P. 16

The company advertised for tenders for the supply for one year of such stores as they might think fit to order. The defendant submitted a tender in these words: "I undertake to supply the company for twelve months with such quantities of (certain specified goods) as the company may order from time to time." The company accepted the tender, and gave orders under it which the defendant carried out. Eventually the defendant refused to carry out an order made by the company under the tender, and this action was brought. *Held*—The defendant was in breach of contract. A tender of this type was a standing offer which was converted into a series of contracts as the company made an order. The defendant might revoke his offer for the remainder of the period covered by the tender, but must supply the goods already ordered by the company.

28. Powell *v.* Lee (1908), 99 L.T. 284

The defendants were managers of a school and wished to appoint a headmaster. Powell applied for the position and together with two other applicants was selected for the final choice of the managers. The managers passed a resolution appointing Powell but gave no instructions that this decision was to be communicated to him, although D (one of the managers) was instructed to inform one of the other candidates (Parker) that he had not been appointed. D, without authority, also informed Powell that he had been selected. The matter was then re-opened and Parker was properly appointed. Lee then informed the plaintiff that this appointment had been made. The plaintiff now sued the six managers for damages for breach of contract. *Held*—There was no contract because there was no authorised communication of the intention to contract by the managers.

29. Felthouse *v.* Bindley (1862), 11 C.B.(N.S.) 869

The plaintiff had been engaged in negotiations with his nephew John regarding the purchase of John's horse, and there had been some misunderstandings as to the price. Eventually the plaintiff wrote to his nephew as follows: "If I hear no more about him I consider the horse is mine at £30 15s." The nephew did not reply but, wishing to sell the horse to his uncle, he told the defendant, an auctioneer who was selling farm stock for him, not to sell the horse as it had already been sold. The auctioneer inadvertently put the horse up with the rest of the stock and sold it. The plaintiff now sued the auctioneer in conversion, the basis of the claim being that he had made a contract with his nephew and the property in the animal was vested in him (the uncle) at the time of the sale. *Held*—The plaintiff's action failed. Although the nephew intended to sell the horse to his uncle, he had not communicated that intention. There was, therefore, no contract between the parties, and the property in the horse was not vested in the plaintiff at the time of the auction sale.

30. Eliason *v.* Henshaw (1819), 4 Wheat. 225 (Supreme Court U.S.A.)

Eliason offered to buy flour from Henshaw. The offer was sent by a wagoner employed by Eliason, there being a stipulation that any reply to the offer should be sent by the wagoner who brought the offer. Henshaw sent his reply accepting the offer by post, his letter arriving some time after the wagoner had returned to Eliason's premises. Eliason, assuming that Henshaw was not interested in his offer, had purchased the flour he needed elsewhere. *Held*—There was no contract. Eliason had specified a mode of acceptance and his wishes must be respected, particularly since the wagoner had arrived before Henshaw's letter.

31. Manchester Diocesan Council for Education *v.* Commercial and General Investments Ltd., [1969] 3 All E.R. 1593

The plaintiffs, a corporate body, were the owners of a freehold property known as Hesketh Fletcher Senior Church of England School. The property was vested in the plaintiffs on a condition that it could be sold subject "to the approval of the purchase price" by the Secretary of State for Education and Science. Late in 1963 the plaintiffs decided to sell the property by tender, the conditions requiring that tenders be sent to the plaintiffs' surveyor by 27th August, 1964. Clause 4 of the form of tender stated "The person whose tender is accepted shall be the purchaser and shall be informed of the acceptance of his tender by letter sent to him by post addressed to the address given in the tender . . . ." The following events then occurred—

    (i) On 25th August, 1964, the defendants completed the form of tender and stated that they agreed to its conditions.

    (ii) On 26th August, 1964, the completed tender was sent to the plaintiffs' surveyor.

    (iii) On 1st September, 1964, the plaintiffs' surveyor informed the defendants' surveyor that he would recommend acceptance of the defendants' offer and would write again as soon as he had formal instructions.

    (iv) On 14th September, 1964, the defendants' surveyor replied saying that he looked forward to receiving formal acceptance and naming the solicitors who would act for the defendants.

    (v) On 15th September, 1964, the plaintiffs' solicitor acknowledged this letter by correspondence with the defendants' surveyor which also stated that the "sale has now been approved," and that instructions had been given to obtain the approval of the Secretary of State.

    (vi) On 18th November, 1964, the approval of the Secretary of State was obtained.

    (vii) On 23rd December, 1964, the plaintiffs' solicitors wrote to the defendants' solicitors stating that the contract was now binding on both parties.

    (viii) The defendants' solicitors replied to the effect that they did not agree that there was any binding contract.

    (ix) On 7th January, 1965, the plaintiffs' solicitors wrote to the defendants at the address given in the tender giving formal notice of acceptance.

The question in issue in this case was whether the offer contained in the tender lapsed before 7th January, 1965, by reason of lapse of time between 25th August, 1964, and 7th January, 1965. It was *held*—by Buckley, J.—

(i) that the letter of 15th September, 1964, looked at in the light of earlier correspondence, was communication to the defendants that their offer had been accepted. The failure to inform the defendants of the acceptance in the manner laid down in Clause 4 did not nullify acceptance of the offer since Clause 4 did not say that a letter addressed to the address given in the tender was the only mode of acceptance and acceptance by any other equally advantageous method was valid. (*Tinn* v. *Hoffman* (1873), 29 L.T. 271 applied.)

(ii) Alternatively, if the letter of 15th September, 1964, did not constitute an acceptance, the offer had not lapsed because the plaintiffs had not by any conduct refused the offer. In fact the letter of 15th September, 1964, showed a continuing intention to accept and there was no evidence of a change of mind before 7th January, 1965. Thus the offer was still open to be accepted on 7th January, 1965. (*Ramsgate Victoria Hotel Co.* v. *Montefiore*, 1866,[39] distinguished.)

32. Entores Ltd. v. Miles Far Eastern Corporation, [1955] 2 Q.B. 327

The plaintiffs, who conducted a business in London, made an offer to the defendants' agent in Amsterdam by means of a teleprinter service. The offer was accepted by a message received on the plaintiffs' teleprinter in London. Later the defendants were in breach of contract and the plaintiffs wished to sue them. The defendants had their place of business in New York and in order to commence an action the plaintiffs had to serve notice of writ on the defendants in New York. The Rules of Supreme Court allow service out of the jurisdiction when the contract was made within the jurisdiction. On this point the defendants argued that the contract was made in Holland when it was typed into the teleprinter there, stressing the rule relating to posting. *Held*—Where communication is instantaneous, as where the parties are face to face or speaking on the telephone, acceptance must be received by the offeror. The same rule applied to communications of this kind. Therefore the contract was made in London where the acceptance was received.

N.B. The suggestion was made that the doctrine of estoppel may operate in this sort of case so as to bind the offeror, e.g. suppose X telephones his acceptance to Y, and Y does not hear X's voice at the moment of acceptance, then Y should ask X to repeat the message, otherwise Y may be estopped from denying that he heard X's acceptance and will be bound in contract.

33. Household Fire Insurance Company v. Grant (1879), 4 Ex. D. 216

The defendant handed a written application for shares in the company to the company's agent in Glamorgan. The application stated that the defendant had paid to the company's bankers the sum of £5, being a deposit of one shilling per share on an application for one hundred shares, and also agreed to pay nineteen shillings per share within twelve months of the allotment. The agent sent the application to the company in London. The company secretary made out a letter of allotment in favour of the defendant and posted it to him in Swansea. The letter never arrived. Nevertheless the company entered the defendant's name on the share register and credited him with dividends amounting to five shillings. The company then went into liquidation and the liquidator sued for £94 15s., the balance due on the shares allotted. It was *held*—by the Court of Appeal—that the defendant was liable. Acceptance was complete when the letter of allotment was posted. Bramwell, L.J., in a dissenting judgment, regarded actual communication as essential. If the letter of acceptance does not arrive, an unknown liability is imposed on the offeror. If actual communication is required the *status quo* is preserved, i.e. the parties have not made a contract.

34. Re London and Northern Bank, ex parte Jones, [1900] 1 Ch. 220

Dr. Jones, who lived in Sheffield, applied for shares in the bank. He then sent a letter of revocation which was received by the bank at 8.30 a.m. on 27th October. The bank's letter of allotment was taken to the G.P.O. at St. Martins-le-Grand at 7 a.m. on 27th October, but was handed to a postman. Evidence showed that the letter did not go straight into the system. The allotment letter to Jones was delivered at 7.30 p.m. on 27th October, the postmark showing that it was posted at a branch office, not at the G.P.O. If the letter had been posted at 7.30 a.m., it would have gone to Sheffield on the 10 a.m. train. Evidence showed that it went by the 12 o'clock train. *Held*—The letter was not posted when it was handed to the postman. The evidence did not show with any clarity when the letter was posted, but, since the burden of proof was on the company, it was possible to say that they had not shown the letter of acceptance was posted before 8.30, or even before 9.30 a.m., when the bank's secretary opened the letter of revocation.

An additional point is that evidence given for the Post Office showed that, under the terms of the Post Office Guide, a town postman is not allowed to take letters in this way, and would be disciplined if he did. The position may be different in the country where the custom of taking letters in this way is perhaps better established.

35. Adams *v.* Lindsell (1818), 1 B. & A. 681

The defendants were wool dealers in business at St. Ives, Huntingdon. By letter dated 2nd September they offered to sell wool to the plaintiffs who were wool manufacturers at Bromsgrove, Worcestershire. The defendants' letter asked for a reply "in course of post" but was misdirected, being addressed to Bromsgrove, Leicestershire. The offer did not reach the plaintiffs until 7 p.m. on 5th September. The same evening the plaintiffs accepted the offer. This letter reached the defendants on 9th September. If the offer had not been misdirected, the defendants could have expected a reply on 7th September, and accordingly they sold the wool to a third party on 8th September. The plaintiffs now sued for breach of contract. *Held*—Where there is a misdirection of the offer, as in this case, the offer is made when it actually reaches the offeree, and not when it would have reached him in the ordinary course of post. The defendants' mistake must be taken against them and for the purposes of this contract the plaintiffs' letter was received "in course of post."

N.B. The position may be different if the fact of delay is obvious to the offeree so that he is put on notice that the offer has lapsed, e.g. A writes to B offering to sell him certain goods and saying that the offer is open until 30th June. If A misdirects the offer so that it does not reach B until 2nd July, it is doubtful whether B could accept it.

36. Byrne *v.* Van Tienhoven (1880), 5 C.P.D. 344

On 1st October the defendants in Cardiff posted a letter to the plaintiffs in New York offering to sell them tin-plate. On 8th October the defendants wrote revoking their offer. On 11th October the plaintiffs received the defendants' offer and immediately telegraphed their acceptance. On 15th October the plaintiffs confirmed their acceptance by letter. On 20th October the defendants' letter of revocation reached the plaintiffs who had by this time entered into a contract to resell the tin-plate. *Held*—(a) that revocation of an offer is not effective until it is communicated to the offeree, (b) the mere posting of a letter of revocation is not communication to the person to whom it is sent. The rule is not, therefore, the same as that for acceptance of an offer. Therefore the defendants were bound by a contract which came into being on 11th October.

37. Dunmore (Countess) *v.* Alexander (1830), 9 Sh (Ct. of Sess.) 190

In this case a letter accepting an offer of employment was followed by a further letter withdrawing the acceptance. Both letters were received by the offerer by the same post. *Held*—The acceptance was validly cancelled.

38. Dickinson *v.* Dodds (1876), 2 Ch.D. 463

The defendant offered to sell certain houses by letter stating, "This offer to be left over until Friday, 9 a.m." On Thursday afternoon the plaintiff was informed by a Mr. Berry that the defendant had been negotiating a sale of the property with one Allan. On Thursday evening the plaintiff left a letter of acceptance at the house where the defendant was staying. This letter was never delivered to the defendant. On Friday morning at 7 a.m. Berry, acting as the plaintiff's agent, handed the defendant a duplicate letter of acceptance explaining it to him. However, on the Thursday the defendant had entered into a contract to sell the property to Allan. *Held*—Since there was no consideration for the promise to keep the offer open, the defendant was free to revoke his offer at any time. Further Berry's communication of the dealings with Allan indicated that Dodds was no longer minded to sell the property to the plaintiff and was in effect a communication of Dodd's revocation. There was therefore no binding contract between the parties.

39. Ramsgate Victoria Hotel Co. *v.* Montefiore (1866), L.R. 1 Exch. 109

The defendant offered by letter dated 8th June, 1864, to take shares in the company. No reply was made by the company, but on 23rd November, 1864, they allotted shares to the defendant. The defendant refused to take up the shares. *Held*—His refusal was justified because his offer had lapsed by reason of the company's delay in notifying their acceptance.

40. Financings Ltd. *v.* Stimson, [1962] 3 All E.R. 386

On 16th March, 1961, the defendant saw a motor car on the premises of a dealer and signed a hire-purchase form provided by the plaintiffs (a finance company), this form being supplied by the dealer. The form was to the effect that the agreement was to become binding only when the finance company signed the form. It also carried a statement to the effect that the hirer (the defendant) acknowledged that before he signed the agreement he had examined the goods and had satisfied himself that they were in good order and condition, and that the goods were at the risk of the hirer from the time of purchase by the owner. On 18th March the defendant paid the first instalment and took possession of the car. However, on 20th March, the defendant being dissatisfied with the car, he returned it to the dealer though the finance company were not informed of this. On the night of 24th-25th March the car was stolen from the dealer's premises and was recovered badly damaged. On 25th March the finance company signed the agreement accepting the defendant's offer to hire the car. The defendant did not regard himself as bound and refused to pay the instalments. The finance company sold the car, and now sued for damages for the defendant's breach of the hire-purchase agreement. *Held*—The hire-purchase agreement was not binding on the defendant because—

   (i) he had revoked his offer by returning the car, and the dealer was the agent of the finance company to receive notice;

   (ii) there was an *implied* condition in the offer that the goods were in substantially the same condition when the offer was accepted as when it was made.

41. Bradbury *v.* Morgan (1862), 1 H. & C. 249

The defendants were the executors of J. M. Leigh who had entered into a guarantee of his brother's account with the plaintiffs for credit up to £100. The plaintiffs, not knowing of the death of J. M. Leigh, continued to supply goods on credit to the brother, H. J. Leigh. The defendants now refused to pay the plaintiffs in respect of such credit after the death of J. M. Leigh. *Held*— The plaintiffs succeeded, the offer remaining open until the plaintiffs had *knowledge* of the death of J. M. Leigh.

N.B. This was a continuing guarantee which is in the nature of a standing offer accepted piecemeal whenever further goods are advanced on credit. Where the guarantee is not of this nature, it may be irrevocable. Thus in *Lloyds* v. *Harper* (1880), 16 Ch. D. 290, the defendant, while living, guaranteed his son's dealings as a Lloyds underwriter in consideration of Lloyds admitting the son. It was *held* that, as Lloyds had admitted the son on the strength of the guarantee, the defendant's executors were still liable under it, because it was irrevocable and was not affected by the defendant's death. It continued to apply to defaults committed by the son after the father's death.

42. Re Cheshire Banking Co., Duff's Executors' Case (1886), 32 Ch. D. 301

In 1882 the Cheshire and Staffordshire Union Banking Companies amalgamated, and Duff received a circular asking whether he would exchange his shares in the S Bank for shares in the C Bank which took the S Bank over. Duff held 100 £20 shares on which £5 had been paid, but he did not reply to the circular and died shortly afterwards. The option was exercised on behalf of his executors, Muttlebury, Bridges and Watts, and a certificate was made out in their names and an entry made in the register in which they were entered as shareholders, described as "executors of William Duff, deceased." The executors objected to having the share certificate in their names, so the directors of the Cheshire Banking Co. cancelled the certificate and issued a fresh one in the name of William Duff. On 23rd October, 1884, the company went into voluntary liquidation, and on 26th October it was ordered that the winding up should be under supervision. *Held*—The liquidator acted rightly when he restored the executors' names to the register. The executors wished to enter into a new contract which had not previously existed. They could not make a dead man liable and so could only make themselves personally liable. Their names were improperly removed and must be restored. Although they had a right of indemnity against the estate, they were personally liable for the full amount outstanding on the shares, regardless as to whether the estate was adequate to indemnify them.

43. Balfour *v.* Balfour, [1919] 2 K.B. 571

The defendant was a civil servant stationed in Ceylon. In November, 1915, he came to England on leave with his wife, the plaintiff in the present action. In August, 1916, the defendant returned alone to Ceylon because his wife's doctor had advised her that her health would not stand up to a further period of service abroad. Later the husband wrote to his wife suggesting that they should remain apart, and in 1918 the plaintiff obtained a decree nisi. In this case the plaintiff alleged that before her husband sailed for Ceylon he had agreed, in consultation with her, that he would give her £30 per month as maintenance, and she now sued because of his failure to abide by the said agreement. The Court of Appeal *held* that there was no enforceable contract because the parties did not intend to create legal relations. The provision for a flat payment of £30 per month for an indefinite period with no attempt to take into account changes in the circumstances of the parties did not suggest a binding agreement. Duke, L.J., seems to have based his decision on the fact that the wife had not supplied any consideration.

44. Spellman *v.* Spellman, [1961] 2 All E.R. 498

The parties were husband and wife and relations between them were very strained and the husband promised to buy a car for his wife in an effort to bring about a reconciliation. In May, 1960, the husband had a car delivered to the matrimonial home, saying that he had bought it for his wife. The registration book was put in the name of the wife, though the husband's reasons for doing this were not clear, although it had something to do with insurance. Relations between the parties continued to be strained, and eventually the husband left the matrimonial home taking the car with him, the wife keeping the registration book. The car was the subject of a hire-purchase agreement under which the husband was liable for the instalments. The Court of Appeal *held* that the husband was entitled to the car and that the wife should transfer the log book to him. The points of interest raised by the case are as follows—

(i) The wife claimed that the husband had made her a gift of the car. This was rejected by the court because, under the hire-purchase agreement, the title in the car was in the hire-purchase company. Therefore the car was not the husband's to give.

(ii) The wife also claimed that there had been an equitable assignment of the car to her. This was rejected because, although no formalities are required for an equitable assignment, intention to assign must be shown and there was insufficient evidence of this. Danckwerts, L.J., held the view that, although the hire-purchase agreement prohibited assignment, this would not have been fatal in the face of intention to assign by the husband. Willmer, L.J., thought it would.

(iii) A further claim by the wife was that, when the husband put the registration book in her name, he had declared a trust over it for her and held it on trust. The court rejected this view stating that there was not sufficient evidence of declaration of trust.

(iv) The court applied the principle in *Balfour* v. *Balfour*[43] and held that there was no intention to create legal relations on the ground that domestic arrangements between spouses were not within the cognisance of the law.

45. Merritt *v.* Merritt, [1970] 2 All E.R. 760

After a husband had formed an attachment for another woman and had left his wife a meeting was held between the parties on 25th May, 1966, in the husband's car. The husband agreed to pay the wife £40 per month maintenance and also wrote out and signed a document stating that in consideration of the wife paying all charges in connection with the matrimonial home until the mortgage repayments had been completed, he would agree to transfer the property to her sole ownership. The wife took the document away with her and in the following months paid off the mortgage. The husband did not subsequently transfer the property to his wife and she claimed a declaration that she was the sole beneficial owner and asked for an order that her husband should transfer the property to her forthwith. The husband's defence was that the agreement was a family arrangement not intended to create legal relations. *Held*—by the Court of Appeal—

(i) that the agreement, having been made when the parties were not living together in amity, was enforceable. (*Balfour* v. *Balfour*, 1919[43], distinguished) and

(ii) the contention that there was no consideration to support the husband's promise could not be sustained. The payment of the balance of the mortgage was a detriment to the wife and the husband had received the benefit of being relieved of liability to the building society.

Accordingly the wife was entitled to the relief she claimed.

46. Gould *v.* Gould, [1969] 3 All E.R. 728

On 15th May, 1966, the appellant left his wife for the second time agreeing to pay her £15 per week as maintenance for herself and the two children of the marriage. The agreement was made orally and was subject to the qualification that the appellant would pay "as long as I can manage it." He kept to the agreement until October, 1967, when he began to fall behind with his payments. In February, 1968, he told the wife that he could not pay the full amount in the future. The wife then issued a writ claiming the balance outstanding for the period up to 17th February, 1968. She claimed 13 weeks at £15 per week but gave credit for payments made by the appellant in January and February of £60, making a total claim of £135. The appellant put in a defence denying that he had agreed to pay his wife maintenance as alleged or at all. The judge at Exeter County Court found the agreement proved and enforceable, there being an intention to create legal relations. The husband appealed to the Court of Appeal where it was *held* that it had not been within the contemplation of the parties to make a legally binding agreement. The uncertainty of the terms and the absence of any consideration from the wife such as an undertaking not to seek maintenance if the payments were kept up precluded that result.

Lord Denning, M.R., dissented and would have held the agreement to be legally binding, saying with regard to the uncertainty of the agreement: "I think a good meaning can be given to the husband's statement by implying a term that, if the husband found that he could not manage to keep up the payments, he could, on reasonable notice, determine the agreement. That is a perfectly intelligible term. If it were included in a written document, I have no doubt the court would enforce it. I should also do so when it is included in an oral agreement." On the matter of consideration he said: "There is ample consideration for such agreement. First, there is the consideration that neither is insisting on the matrimonial right to live together. Second, whilst the payments are being made, she cannot complain of wilful neglect to maintain. Third, the agreement means that she has no authority to pledge his credit at common law for necessaries." (See now page 196.)

47. Simpkins *v.* Pays, [1955] 3 All E.R. 10

The defendant and the defendant's granddaughter made an agreement with the plaintiff, who was a paying boarder, that they should submit in the defendant's name a weekly coupon, containing a forecast by each of them, to a Sunday newspaper fashion competition. On one occasion a forecast by the granddaughter was correct and the defendant received a prize of £750. The plaintiff sued for his share of that sum. The defence was that there was no intention to create legal relations but that the transaction was a friendly arrangement binding in honour only. *Held*—There was an intention to create legal relations. Far from being a friendly domestic arrangement, the evidence showed that it was a joint enterprise and that the parties expected to share any prize that was won.

48. Parker *v.* Clark, [1960], 1 All E.R. 93

The plaintiffs, Mr. & Mrs. Parker, were a middle-aged couple and lived in their own cottage in Sussex. The defendants, Mr. & Mrs. Clark, who were aged 77 and 78 respectively, lived in a large house in Torquay. Mrs. Parker was the niece of Mrs. Clark. In 1955 the plaintiffs visited the defendants and, as a result of certain conversations held at that time, Mrs. Clark wrote to Mrs. Parker suggesting that the plaintiffs should come to live in the defendants' house in Torquay, setting out detailed financial terms as to the sharing of expenses. Mrs. Clark also suggested that the plaintiffs' cottage might be sold and the proceeds invested, and that the defendants would leave the house in Torquay, and its major contents, to Mrs. Parker, her sister and her daughter. Mrs. Parker wrote accepting this offer and the cottage was sold. After the mortgage was paid off, £2,000 of the remaining money was lent to their daughter to enable her to buy a flat. The plaintiffs then moved into the defendants' house in Torquay. For a time all went well and Mr. Clark executed a will leaving the property as agreed. In 1957 differences between the parties arose, and after much unpleasantness Mr. Clark told the plaintiffs to go and they left in December, 1957. The plaintiffs claimed damages for breach of contract. *Held*—There was an intention to create legal relations arising from the circumstances. In view of the fact that the plaintiffs had sold their home and lent £2,000 to their daughter, it was obvious that, having "burned their boats," they must have relied on the agreement. The letter from Mrs. Clark was an offer sufficiently precise and detailed; it was not merely a statement of terms for a future agreement. Further it was a sufficient memorandum to satisfy Sect. 40 of the Law of Property Act, 1925. Finally, the fact that Mr. Clark had altered his will indicated that he regarded the agreement as binding.

The damages awarded were divided as follows—

(i) Damages of £1,200 plus costs, in favour of the parties jointly, based on the value per annum of living rent free in the house. (£300 multiplied by four because of the expectation of life of the defendants.)

(ii) Damages of £3,400 in favour of Mrs. Parker separately, in respect of the value to her of inheriting a share in the defendants' house on their death.

49. Jones *v.* **Padavatton**, [1969] 2 All E.R. 616

In 1962 the plaintiff, Mrs. Jones, who lived in Trinidad, made an offer to the defendant, Mrs. Padavatton, her daughter, to provide maintenance for her at the rate of £42 a month if she would leave her job in Washington in the United States and go to England and read for the Bar. Mrs. Padavatton was at that time divorced from her husband, having the custody of the child of that marriage. The agreement was an informal one and there was uncertainty as to its exact terms. Nevertheless the daughter came to England in November, 1962, bringing the child with her and began to read for the Bar, her fees and maintenance being paid for by Mrs. Jones. In 1964 it appeared that the daughter was experiencing some discomfort in England, occupying as she did one room in Acton for which she had to pay £6 17s. 6d. per week. At this stage Mrs. Jones offered to buy a large house in London to be occupied partly by the daughter and partly by tenants, the income from rents to go to the daughter in lieu of maintenance. Again there was no written agreement but the house was purchased for £6,000 and conveyed to Mrs. Jones. The daughter moved into the house in January, 1965, and tenants arrived, it still being uncertain what precisely was to happen to the surplus rent income (if any) and what rooms the daughter was to occupy. No money from the rents was received by Mrs. Jones and no accounts were submitted to her. In 1967 Mrs. Jones claimed possession of the house from her daughter, who had by that time married again, and the daughter counter-claimed for £1,655 18s. 9d. said to have been paid in connection with running the house. At the hearing the daughter still had one subject to pass in Part I of the Bar examinations and also the whole of Part II remained to be taken.

Held—by the Court of Appeal—

(i) that the arrangements were throughout family agreements depending upon the good faith of the parties in keeping the promises made and not intended to be rigid binding agreements. Furthermore, the arrangements were far too vague and uncertain to be enforceable as contracts. (*per* Danckwerts and Fenton Atkinson, L.JJ.)

(ii) that although the agreements to maintain while reading for the Bar might have been regarded as creating a legal obligation in the mother to pay (the terms being sufficiently stated and duration for a reasonable time being implied), the daughter could not claim anything in respect of that agreement which must be regarded as having terminated in 1967, five years being a reasonable time in which to complete studies for the Bar. The arrangements in relation to the home were very vague and must be regarded as made without contractual intent. (*per* Salmon, L.J.)

The mother was therefore entitled to possession of the house and had no liability under the maintenance agreement. The counter-claim by the daughter was left to be settled by the parties, Salmon, L.J., saying—"If this reference is pursued, it will involve an account being meticulously taken of all receipts and expenditure from December, 1964, until the date on which the daughter yields up possession. This will certainly result in a great waste of time and money, and can only exacerbate ill-feeling between the mother and the daughter. With a little goodwill and good sense on both sides, this could and should be avoided by reaching a reasonable compromise on the figures. I can but express the hope that this may be done, for it would clearly be to the mutual benefit of both parties."

50. **Buckpitt** *v.* **Oates,** [1968] 1 All E.R. 1145

The plaintiff and the defendant, both aged 17 years, were in the habit of riding together in each other's cars. Neither of them had insurance cover against injury to passengers (but see now Sched. 8 of the Road Traffic Act, 1972, p. 378). The defendant had a notice affixed to the facia panel of his car stating that any passenger travelled at his own risk, and it was found as a fact that the plaintiff was aware of this notice. On a drive from Paignton to Newton Abbot the defendant, at the plaintiff's request, carried him as a passenger in his (the defendant's) car. The car struck a wall due to the defendant's negligence and the plaintiff was injured. The plaintiff had paid 10s. towards the cost of the petrol (which in fact cost less). The plaintiff claimed damages for personal injuries and it was *held* dismissing the claim—

(i) there was no legal contract of carriage, the arrangement between the parties being one not intended to create a legal relationship;

(ii) the plaintiff had agreed to be carried at his own risk and, though a minor in law, could not enforce a right which he had voluntarily waived or abandoned. The defence of *volenti non fit injuria* succeeded.

John Stephenson, J., said "No man—and it seems to me, no infant—can enforce a right which he has voluntarily waived or abandoned . . . . Of course the court will always consider with great care whether a particular plaintiff had the means and the knowledge and experience to appreciate fully and freely the risk and what he was consenting to."

51. **Jones** *v.* **Vernon's Pools Ltd.,** [1938] 2 All E.R. 626

The plaintiff said that he had sent to the defendants a football coupon on which the penny points pool was all correct. Defendants denied having received it and relied on a clause printed on every coupon. The said clause provided that the transaction should not "give rise to any legal relationship . . . or be legally enforceable . . . but . . . binding in honour only." The court *held* that this clause was a bar to any action in a court of law.

N.B. This case was followed by the Court of Appeal in *Appleson* v. *Littlewood Ltd.,* [1939] 1 All E.R. 464, where the contract contained a similar clause.

52. **Rose and Frank Co.** *v.* **Crompton (J. R.) & Brothers Ltd.,** [1925] A.C. 445

In 1913 the plaintiffs, an American firm, entered into an agreement with the defendants, an English company, whereby the plaintiffs were appointed sole agents for the sale in the U.S.A. of paper tissues supplied by the defendants. The contract was for a period of three years with an option to extend that time. The agreement was extended to March, 1920, but in 1919 the defendants terminated it without notice. The defendants had received a number of orders for tissues before the termination of the contract, and they refused to execute them. The plaintiffs sued for breach of contract and for non-delivery of the goods actually ordered. The agreement of 1913 contained an "Honourable Pledge Clause" drafted as follows: "This arrangement is not entered into nor is this memorandum written as a formal or legal agreement and shall not be subject to legal jurisdiction in the courts of the United States of America or England . . ." It was *held* by the House of Lords that the 1913 agreement was not binding on the parties, but that in so far as the agreement had been acted upon by the defendants' acceptance of orders, the said orders were binding contracts of sale. Nevertheless the agreement was not binding for the future.

53. Mountstephen v. Lakeman (1871) L.R. 7 Q.B. 196

The defendant was chairman of the Brixham Local Board of Health. The plaintiff, who was a builder and contractor, was employed in 1866 by the board to construct certain main sewage works in the town. On 19th March, 1866, notice was given by the board to owners of certain homes to connect their house drains with the main sewer within twenty-one days. Before the expiration of the twenty-one days Robert Adams, the surveyor of the board, suggested to the plaintiff that he should make the connections. The plaintiff said he was willing to do the work if the board would see him paid. On the 5th April, 1866, i.e. before the expiration of the twenty-one days, the plaintiff commenced work on the connections. However, before work commenced it appeared that the plaintiff had had an interview with the defendant at which the following conversation took place—

Defendant—"What objection have you to making the connections?"
Plaintiff—"I have none, if you or the board will order the work or become responsible for the payment."
Defendant—"Go on Mountstephen and do the work and I will see you paid."

The plaintiff completed the connections in April and May, 1866, and sent an account to the Board on 5th December, 1866. The board disclaimed responsibility on the ground that they had never entered into any agreement with the plaintiff nor authorised any officer of the board to agree with him for the performance of the work in question. It was *held*—that Lakeman had undertaken a personal liability to pay the plaintiff and had not given a guarantee of the liability of a third party, i.e. the board. In consequence Lakeman had given an indemnity which did not need to be in writing under Sect. 4 of the Statute of Frauds, 1677. The plaintiff was therefore entitled to enforce the oral undertaking given by the defendant.

54. Carr v. Lynch, [1900] 1 Ch. 613

The defendant was lessor of the Warden Arms, Kentish Town, which was leased to Charles Smith. In September, 1898, the premises were assigned to Arthur Jayne for the residue of the term. On the expiration of the lease Jayne applied to the defendant to grant him a further lease, and the defendant consented on condition that Jayne paid him £50. When Jayne paid the money he produced a memorandum which he had prepared and the defendant signed it. The memorandum read as follows: "Dear Sir, In consideration of you having this day paid me the sum of £50, I hereby agree to grant you or your assigns a further lease of 24 years." Before the new lease was to commence Jayne assigned the lease to the plaintiff, Arthur Carr, but the defendant refused to grant the new lease to Carr. This action was for specific performance of the agreement for a lease, and the defence was that the memorandum did not satisfy the Statute of Frauds because it did not sufficiently identify the parties. *Held*—The plaintiff succeeded. The memorandum was sufficient because the defendant had admitted that Jayne had paid him £50 on the day in question and the person who had paid was the person to get the lease according to the document. Therefore Jayne was adequately identified, and Carr, being Jayne's assignee, was entitled to a lease.

55. G. Goldsmith (Sicklesmere) Ltd. *v.* Baxter, [1969] 3 All E.R. 733

By an agreement dated 9th April, 1968, the defendant agreed to purchase a piece of land, cottage and buildings known as "Shelley," Standstead, Suffolk from the plaintiff company. The memorandum of agreement was signed by a Mr. Brewster, one of the company's directors, "for and on behalf of Goldsmith Coaches (Sicklesmere) Limited." Mr. Brewster thought that this was the company's name and it did carry on business under that description. The property known as "Shelley" was described in the particulars of sale and the memorandum of agreement stated that the vendor company, described as Goldsmith Coaches (Sicklesmere), Ltd., was the beneficial owner of it. The defendant's solicitors were subsequently unable to trace a company called Goldsmith Coaches (Sicklesmere), Ltd. and the defendant refused to complete by conveying the property on the ground that since there was no vendor there was no contract. The company thereupon sued for specific performance. *Held*—by Stamp, J.—that specific performance would be granted. A contract was to be construed by reference to the surrounding circumstances or in the light of known facts. Accordingly it was clear that the name inserted in the memorandum of sale as being that of the vendor was merely an inaccurate description of the plaintiff company which was therefore a party to the contract and could easily be identified as such by reference to other characteristics. "Looking at the memorandum alone, and without regard to the surrounding circumstances, I find that the person—the persona ficta—said to be the vendor has the following characteristics: (i) it is named Goldsmith Coaches (Sicklesmere), Ltd.; (ii) its registered office is said to be at Sicklesmere; (iii) it has an agent called Brewster who claims to act for it; (iv) it is the beneficial owner of "Shelley."

"Then, applying the rule that a contract is to be construed by reference to the surrounding circumstances, or in the light of the known facts, I find first, that there is no limited company which in law has the name Goldsmith Coaches (Sicklesmere), Ltd., but that the plaintiff company is often known as "Goldsmith Coaches" and carries on business as a bus and coach contractor, and does so at Sicklesmere. Then I find, secondly, that the plaintiff company's registered office is at Sicklesmere, in the very place at which it carries on the bus and coach business. Thirdly, I find that the plaintiff company has an agent called Brewster; and, fourthly, that it is the beneficial owner of "Shelley." I find in addition that there is no other company having those characteristics. Applying this process, if it be permissible, I conclude beyond peradventure that Goldsmith Coaches (Sicklesmere), Ltd., is no more, nor less, than an inaccurate description of the plaintiff company, F. Goldsmith (Sicklesmere), Ltd. . . . In the absence of authority constraining me to do so—and none has been cited—I would find it impossible to hold that a company incorporated under the Companies Acts has no identity but by reference to its correct name, or that, unless an agent acts on its behalf by that name, or a name so nearly resembling it that it is obviously an error for that name, he acts for nobody. A limited company has in my judgment characteristics other than its name by reference to which it can be identified: for example, a particular business, and a particular place or places where it carries on business, particular shareholders, and particular directors."

56. Hawkins *v.* Price, [1947] Ch. 645

On 31st January, 1946, the plaintiff and defendant entered into a bargain for the sale of a freehold bungalow and land. The plaintiff paid a deposit of

£100, and the defendant signed a deposit receipt thus: "Received of H.H. the sum of £100 being deposit on bungalow named 'Oakdene,' Station Road, Stoke Mandeville, Bucks, sold for £1,000." The plaintiff now sued for specific performance of the agreement, and it was discovered that there was a term that vacant possession be given by 31st March, 1946. This term was not mentioned in the deposit receipt. Nevertheless the plaintiff claimed that the said receipt was a sufficient memorandum to satisfy Sect. 40 of the Law of Property Act, 1925. *Held*—It was not because—

(i) The deposit receipt did not contain reference to the fact that the sale was with vacant possession. Although it is not necessary that the memorandum should contain every term, it must at least contain all material terms. In the view of the court the question of vacant possession was material and not collateral.

(ii) The plaintiff suggested that since the term was solely for his benefit he could waive it. The court decided that the term was not solely for his benefit because, although it governed the date on which he could take possession, it also informed Mrs. Price of how long she might remain in possession.

(iii) It was difficult for the plaintiff to waive the term because he was suing for specific performance with vacant possession.

56*a*. *Scott* v. *Bradley*, [1971] 1 All E.R. 538

The plaintiff and defendant agreed that the defendant would sell her freehold property to the plaintiff for £5,000. The plaintiff agreed to pay half the defendant's legal costs but this was not recorded on the receipt. The plaintiff sought to enforce the contract and offered to pay half the defendant's legal costs of the sale. *Held*—by Plowman, J.—that on making this offer the plaintiff could enforce the contract.

57. Caton v. Caton (1867), L.R. 2 H.L. 127

A Mr. Caton and a Mrs. Henley proposed to marry, and decided to enter into a marriage settlement. A document was drafted as a basis for the marriage settlement and the names Caton and Henley appeared in it, but only for the purpose of showing what Mr. Caton was to do and what Mrs. Henley was to have under the agreement. The document was not signed by either of the parties. At the time when this action was brought a marriage settlement had to be evidenced in writing under the provisions of the Statute of Frauds, 1677, and this document was produced as a memorandum. *Held*—It was not a sufficient memorandum because, although the names of the parties appeared in the document, they did not appear as signatures intended to subscribe it.

58. Pearce v. Gardner, [1897] 1 Q.B. 688

The plaintiff brought this action to recover damages for breach of a contract by the defendant under the terms of which the defendant had agreed to sell the plaintiff certain gravel which was *in situ* on the land. At the trial the plaintiff put in evidence a letter signed by the defendant and commencing "Dear Sir." The letter did not contain the plaintiff's name. The plaintiff then put in evidence an envelope which had been used to post the letter, which showed the plaintiff's name and address. *Held*—The letter and the envelope together provided a memorandum sufficient to satisfy the Statute of Frauds.

N.B. Before documents can be connected so as to provide a memorandum, they must be *prima facie* connected as in the case of a letter and an envelope.

See *Williams* v. *Lake* (1860), 2 E. & E. 349. In this case the plaintiff put in evidence as a memorandum a letter similar to the one put forward in the above case. He was not able to produce an envelope, however, and the court *held* that the letter was not a memorandum sufficient to satisfy the Statute of Frauds.

59. Timmins *v.* Moreland Street Property Ltd., [1958] Ch. 110

The defendants agreed to buy certain property belonging to the plaintiff for £39,000 and gave him a cheque for £3,900 as a deposit, the cheque being made payable to his solicitors. The plaintiff made out a signed deposit receipt which stated that the sum of £3,900 was a deposit for the purchase of the property which was adequately described, and that the plaintiff agreed to sell for £39,000. Subsequently the defendants stopped the cheque and repudiated the contract. The plaintiff sued for breach of contract and the defendants pleaded absence of a memorandum under Sect. 40 of the Law of Property Act, 1925. The plaintiff claimed that a sufficient memorandum existed if the deposit receipt were read together with the cheque containing the defendants' signature. *Held*—The two documents could not be connected, because the cheque was made payable to the plaintiff's solicitors and there was no necessary connection between it and the deposit receipt.

60. Griffiths *v.* Young, [1970] 3 W.L.R. 246

Following an agreement concerning the sale of land by the defendant to the plaintiff the plaintiff's solicitor wrote to the defendant's solicitor stating a price "subject to contract." A telephone conversation between the solicitors followed and later there was a letter from the defendant's solicitor confirming the defendant's instructions to sell for an agreed price. *Held*—by the Court of Appeal—the letters constituted a sufficient memorandum and the phrase "subject to contract" did not render the first letter defective in view of later events.

61. Monnickendam *v.* Leanse (1923), 39 T.L.R. 445

The plaintiff orally agreed to buy a house from the defendant and paid a deposit of £200. Later the plaintiff refused to go on with the contract and pleaded lack of memorandum in writing, though the defendant was always willing to complete. The plaintiff now sued to recover the deposit. *Held*— He could not recover the deposit.

N.B. The case illustrates that the difficulties arising out of the absence of a memorandum in writing are procedural rather than substantive. The contract, though unenforceable, is not wholly without effect, for in the above case the contract was raised as a defence to an action for the deposit. It is essential of course that the vendor be prepared to complete the bargain; he cannot deny the enforceability of the contract and yet claim its existence as a defence to the action for recovery of the deposit.

62. Rawlinson *v.* Ames, [1925] 1 Ch. 96

The defendant orally agreed to take a lease of the plaintiff's flat. The plaintiff carried out alterations in the flat at the defendant's request and under her supervision. She then refused to take the lease and pleaded absence of memorandum required by the Statute of Frauds. The plaintiff claimed specific performance of the contract on the grounds that the alterations made in the flat were unequivocal acts of part performance. *Held*—The plaintiff succeeded. The alterations were not in themselves unequivocal in that the plaintiff might have been altering the flat for some other purpose, but the fact that the defendant supervised and approved of the alterations indicated that she was then minded to take the lease.

63. Broughton v. Snook, [1938] 1 Ch. 505

The plaintiff orally agreed to purchase an inn from X and gave an undertaking not to disturb the sitting tenant until the tenant's lease expired. Before the end of his term the tenant vacated the inn and let the plaintiff take possession without X's knowledge. The plaintiff thereupon effected substantial improvements. X died and his executors advertised the sale of the inn. The plaintiff claimed specific performance of the oral agreement. *Held*—Although the plaintiff had gone into possession, this did not constitute an act of part performance because it might have referred to an agreement with the tenant. However, the improvements he had made were unequivocal and constituted part performance. Specific performance was granted.

64. Daniels v. Trefusis, [1914] 1 Ch. 788

The defendant orally agreed to buy land from the plaintiff. In the course of negotiations the plaintiff's solicitors, in accordance with the agreement, gave notice to two weekly tenants of the plaintiff so that the defendant might have vacant possession on completion. The tenants gave up possession and then the defendant refused to complete the contract, pleading absence of memorandum in writing. The plaintiff now claimed specific performance of the contract on the grounds of part performance. *Held*—Notice to the tenants was an act of part performance, and their subsequent eviction was an unequivocal act referable only to the contract. It would be a fraud on the plaintiff for the defendant to plead absence of memorandum. Specific performance was granted.

65. Wakeham v. MacKenzie, [1968] 2 All E.R. 783

Some two years after his wife's death a widower aged 72 orally agreed with the plaintiff, a widow of 67, that if she would move into his house and look after him for the rest of his life she should have the house (of which he was the owner) together with the contents on his death. It was also agreed that the plaintiff should pay her own board and buy her own coal.

The plaintiff gave up her council flat and moved into the widower's house and looked after him as agreed, paying for her board and coal. He died in February, 1966, but did not leave the house or contents to her. The executor of the widower's estate contended that if there was a contract no action could be brought upon it at common law because there was no memorandum in writing as required by Sect. 40 of the Law of Property Act, 1925, which was accepted. However in respect of the plaintiff's claim for the equitable remedy of specific performance the adequacy of her acts of part performance was in question. On this matter Stamp, J., *held*—

> I conclude from *Kingswood Estate Co. Ltd.* v. *Anderson* first that it is not the law that the acts of part performance relied on must be not only referable to a contract such as that alleged, but referable to no other title, the doctrine to that effect laid down by Warrington, L.J., in *Chaproniere* v. *Lambert* having been exploded; and secondly that the true rule is that the operation of acts of part performance requires only that the acts in question be such as must be referred to some contract and may be referred to the alleged one; that they prove the existence of some contract and one consistent with the contract alleged.

His Lordship accordingly made an order for specific performance of the oral agreement on which the plaintiff relied.

66. Maddison *v.* Alderson (1883), 8 App. Cas. 467

The plaintiff had been employed as a housekeeper to Thomas Alderson for a number of years. At one period Alderson was pressed for money, and asked the plaintiff whether she would be willing to carry on working as housekeeper for the rest of his life without wages, in return for which he would leave her a life interest in a farm by his will. Alderson made a will in those terms but unfortunately it was not properly attested, and on his death it was declared void. The plaintiff brought this action against Alderson's executor who relied on absence of memorandum as required by the Statute of Frauds. The plaintiff claimed that the work she had carried out without payment constituted part performance, which entitled her to specific performance of the contract. *Held*— The fact that she had stayed in Alderson's service was not sufficient part performance. It did not even prove the existence of a contract since she might merely have wanted a home.

N.B. The acts of part performance relied upon in *Wakeham* v. *McKenzie*[65], i.e. the giving up of a home and sharing expenses, at least suggest the existence of a contract.

67. Congresbury Motors Ltd. *v.* Anglo-Belge Finance Co. Ltd., [1969] 3 All E.R. 545

In January, 1965, the plaintiffs borrowed £46,000 from the defendants, Anglo-Belge Finance Co. Ltd. to finance the purchase of a filling station and garage. Later they borrowed another £4,000 from the defendants who were registered moneylenders. In this action the plaintiffs were claiming—

(i) a declaration that their undertaking to repay the loans was unenforceable since there was not a sufficient note or memorandum of the transaction as required by Sect. 6 of the Moneylenders Act, 1927. The mortgage deed used to secure the loan which might have been regarded as a sufficient memorandum did not in fact show the date on which the loan was made;

(ii) an injunction to restrain the defendants from enforcing the mortgage, and

(iii) an order for the cancellation and delivery up of the mortgage deed.

In effect the plaintiffs were claiming to retain their garage without paying for it.

The defendants counterclaimed—

(i) for payment under the mortgage and alternatively;

(ii) for a declaration that the plaintiffs held the money in trust for them, and in the further alternative;

(iii) a declaration that they were entitled to a lien on the property for the money paid to the vendors of the property and,

(iv) an order for sale.

It was *held*—by Plowman, J., and subsequently by the Court of Appeal— that the plaintiffs' undertaking to repay the loan was unenforceable because there was not a sufficient note or memorandum under Sect. 6(2) of the Moneylenders Act, 1927, the date on which the loan was made having been omitted. However, the defendants' claim for a lien on the property succeeded. The money borrowed was actually used to acquire the property and in these circumstances the moneylenders became entitled to the lien on the property which the vendors would have had if the purchase price remained unpaid. In other words the moneylenders acquired by subrogation the usual lien of the unpaid seller of land. The claim that the property was held in trust for the moneylenders failed. This claim was based on the case of *Barclays Bank Ltd.* v. *Quistclose Investments Ltd.*, [1968] 3 All E.R. 651, where it was held that if money is lent for a specific purpose which is not carried out the money is held on trust for the lenders. However, the present case was distinguished because the purpose had not failed, the borrowers having actually purchased the filling station and garage.

N.B. Bankers, properly so called, are exempt from the Moneylenders Acts though they may be affected where they are on notice that the purpose of a bank loan is the repayment of another loan, which is illegal under the Acts. In such a case the loan made by the banker could not be recovered. (*Spector* v. *Ageda*, 1971).[68]

68. Spector *v.* Ageda (1971), 115 Sol. Jo. 426

The plaintiff was a solicitor acting for the defendant. The defendant was indebted to the plaintiff's brother who was a moneylender. The moneylender was not licensed under the relevant Acts and the plaintiff knew this. She also knew that the moneylending contract between the defendant and her brother did not show the rate of interest and also provided for compound interest, these being further illegalities under the relevant Acts. The plaintiff lent the defendant money on the security of certain property to enable him to repay the loan made by her brother. This second loan was not repaid and the plaintiff claimed possession of the mortgaged property. The Court had to decide whether the second loan was affected by the admitted illegality of the first. *Held*—by Megarry, J.—that it was. A loan knowingly made to discharge a loan which was wholly or partially illegal was itself illegal and could not be recovered.

69. Dunlop *v.* Selfridge, [1915] A.C. 847

The appellants were motor tyre manufacturers and sold tyres to Messrs. Dew & Co. who were motor accessory dealers. Under the terms of the contract Dew & Co. agreed not to sell the tyres below Dunlop's list price, and as Dunlop's agents, to obtain from other traders a similar undertaking. In return for this undertaking Dew & Co. were to receive special discounts some of which they could pass on to retailers who bought tyres. Selfridge & Co. accepted two orders from customers for Dunlop covers at a lower price. They obtained the covers through Dew & Co. and signed an agreement not to sell or offer the tyres below list price. It was further agreed that £5 per tyre so sold should be paid to Dunlop by way of liquidated damages. Selfridge's supplied one of the two tyres ordered below list price. They did not actually supply the other, but informed the customer that they could only supply it at list price. The appellants claimed an injunction and damages against the respondents for breach of the agreement made with Dew & Co., claiming that Dew & Co. were their agents in the matter. *Held*—There was no contract between the parties. Dunlop could not enforce the contract made between the respondents and Dew & Co. because they had not supplied consideration. Even if Dunlop were undisclosed principals, there was no consideration moving between them and the respondents. The discount received by Selfridge was part of that given by Dunlop to Dew & Co. Since Dew & Co. were not bound to give any part of their discount to retailers the discount received by Selfridge operated only as consideration between themselves and Dew & Co. and could not be claimed by Dunlop as consideration to support a promise not to sell below list price. (See now Restrictive Trade Practices Act, 1956, Sect. 25 and Resale Prices Act, 1964.)

70. Haigh v. Brooks (1839), 10 A. & E. 309

The defendant had guaranteed a debt of £10,000 which a firm named John Lees and Son owed to the plaintiffs. Subsequently the plaintiffs agreed to give up the document and release Brooks from liability on it if Brooks would undertake to pay at maturity certain bills of exchange which had already been accepted by John Lees and Son. The bills amounted to £9,666 13s. 7d. Brooks gave the required undertaking but failed to pay the bills when they matured, and the plaintiffs brought this action. The defence was that the plaintiffs had not supplied consideration for Brooks' promise to pay the bills because the guarantee from which he had been released was in any case unenforceable, since the memorandum evidencing the guarantee did not contain a statement of the consideration as required by the Statute of Frauds. (See now Mercantile Law Amendment Act, 1856, Sect. 3.) *Held*—Even if the guarantee was not binding, the surrender of it was sufficient consideration to support the defendant's promise to pay the bills. He had got what he had bargained for, i.e. his release from the guarantee, and it did not matter that the consideration was inadequate.

71. White v. Bluett (1853), 23 L.J.Ex. 36

This action was brought by White who was the executor of Bluett's father's estate. The plaintiff, White, alleged that Bluett had not paid a promissory note given to his father during his lifetime. Bluett admitted that he had given the note to his father, but said that his father had released him from it in return for a promise not to keep on complaining about the fact that he had been disinherited. *Held*—The defence failed and the defendant was liable on the note. The promise not to complain was not sufficient consideration to support his release from the note.

72. Chappell & Co. Ltd. v. Nestlé Co. Ltd., [1959] 2 All E.R. 701

The plaintiffs owned the copyright in a dance tune called "Rockin' Shoes," and the defendants were using records of this tune as part of an advertising scheme. A record company made the records for Nestlés who advertised them to the public for 1s. 6d. each but required in addition three wrappers from their 6d. bars of chocolate. When they received the wrappers they threw them away. The plaintiffs sued the defendants for infringement of copyright. It appeared that under the Copyright Act of 1956 a person recording musical works for *retail* sale need not get the permission of the holder of the copyright, but had merely to serve him with notice and pay 6¼ per cent of the retail selling price as royalty. The plaintiffs asserted that the defendants were not retailing the goods in the sense of the Act and must therefore get permission to use the musical work. The basis of the plaintiffs' case was that retailing meant selling entirely for money, and that as the defendants were selling for money plus wrappers, they needed the plaintiffs' consent. The defence was that the sale was for cash because the wrappers were not part of the consideration. *Held*—The plaintiffs succeeded because the wrappers were part of the consideration and the question of their adequacy did not arise.

73. Coggs *v.* Bernard (1703), 2 Ld. Ray. 909

The defendant had agreed to take several hogsheads of brandy, belonging to the plaintiff, from the cellar of one inn to another. One of the casks was broken and the brandy lost and the plaintiff alleged that this was due to the defendant's carelessness. The defendant denied liability on the grounds that there was no consideration to support the agreement to move the casks. *Held*—the plaintiff's claim succeeded. The court made an attempt to find consideration by saying that when the plaintiff entrusted the goods to the defendant this was sufficient consideration to oblige him to be careful with them. However, it is hard to see how such a "trusting" can amount to consideration for it was not a benefit to the defendant, nor was it a detriment to the plaintiff because he wished his goods to be carried. It does not appear to have been the price of any promise and the case seems to have been decided on the ground that once the relationship of bailor and bailee is established certain duties fall upon the bailee independently of any contract.

73a. *Gilchrist Watt and Sanderson Pty.* v. *York Products Pty.*, [1970] 1 W.L.R. 1262

Two cases of German clocks were bought by the respondents and shipped to Sydney. The shipowners arranged for the appellant stevedores to unload the ship. The goods were put in the appellants' shed but when the respondents came to collect them one case of clocks was missing. It was admitted that this was due to the appellants' negligence. *Held*—by the Privy Council —that the appellants were liable. Although there was no contract between the parties an obligation to take due care of the goods was created by delivery and voluntary assumption of possession under the sub-bailment.

74. Collins *v.* Godefroy (1831), 1 B. & Ad. 950

The plaintiff was subpoenaed to give evidence for the defendant in an action to which the defendant was a party. The plaintiff now sued for the sum of six guineas which he said the defendant had promised him for his attendance. *Held*—The plaintiff's action failed because there was no consideration for the promise. Lord Tenterden said: "if it be a duty imposed by law upon a party regularly subpoenaed to attend from time to time to give his evidence, then a promise to give him any remuneration for loss of time incurred in such attendance is a promise without consideration."

75. Vanbergen *v.* St Edmunds Properties Ltd., [1933] 2 K.B. 223

The plaintiff owed the defendants £208 and the defendants had issued a bankruptcy notice to be served on 7th July. On 6th July the plaintiff told the defendants' solicitors that he hoped to raise the money at Eastbourne, but that he could not do so until 8th July. The solicitors agreed to put off the service of the notice until noon on 8th July, in return for the plaintiff's promise to pay the money into an Eastbourne Bank by that time. The plaintiff paid the money in as directed on 7th July, but his letter advising the solicitors went astray. They thereupon served the bankruptcy notice. The plaintiff now sued for damages for breach of contract. *Held*—The action could not be sustained because the plaintiff was already bound to pay the sum of £208 long before 8th July and was not supplying consideration by paying it into the bank on 7th July. The solicitors were in order in serving the notice.

76. Stilk *v.* Myrick (1809), 2 Camp. 317

A sea-captain, being unable to find any substitutes for two sailors who had deserted, promised to divide the wages of the deserters among the rest of the crew if they would work the ship home shorthanded. *Held*—The promise was not enforceable because of absence of consideration. In sailing the ship home the crew had done no more than they were already bound to do. Their original contract obliged them to meet the normal emergencies of the voyage of which minor desertions were one. *cf. Hartley* v. *Ponsonby* (1857), 7 E. & B. 872, where a greater remuneration was promised to a seaman to work the ship home when the number of deserters was so great as to render the ship un-seaworthy. *Held*—This was a binding promise because the sailor had gone beyond his duty in agreeing to sail an unseaworthy ship. In fact the number of desertions was so great as to discharge the remaining seamen from their original contract, leaving them free to enter into a new bargain.

77. Ward *v.* Byham, [1956] 2 All E.R. 318

An unmarried mother sued to recover a maintenance allowance by the father of the child. The defence was that, under Sect. 42 of the National Assistance Act, 1948, the mother of an illegitimate child was bound to maintain it. However, it appeared that in return for the promise of an allowance the mother had promised—

    (*a*) to look after the child well and ensure that it was happy; and,
    (*b*) to allow it to decide whether it should live with her or the father.

Held—There was sufficient consideration to support the promise of an allowance because the promises given in (*a*) and (*b*) above were in excess of the statutory duty, which was merely to care for the child.

78. Shadwell *v.* Shadwell (1860), 9 C.B. (N.S.) 159

The plaintiff was engaged to marry a girl named Ellen Nichol. In 1838 he received a letter from his uncle, Charles Shadwell, in the following terms: "I am glad to hear of your intended marriage with Ellen Nicholl and, as I promised to assist you at starting, I am happy to tell you that I will pay you one hundred and fifty pounds yearly during my life and until your income derived from your profession of Chancery barrister shall amount to six hundred guineas, of which your own admission will be the only evidence that I shall receive or require." The plaintiff duly married Ellen Nicholl and his income never exceeded six hundred guineas during the eighteen years his uncle lived after the marriage. The uncle paid twelve annual sums and part of the thir-teenth but no more. On his death the plaintiff sued his uncle's executors for the balance of the eighteen instalments to which he suggested he was entitled. *Held*—The plaintiff succeeded even though he was already engaged to Ellen Nicholl when the promise was made. His marriage was sufficient consideration to support his uncle's promise, for, by marrying, the plaintiff had incurred responsibilities and changed his position in life. Further the uncle probably derived some benefit in that his desire to see his nephew settled had been satisfied.

79. Roscorla v. Thomas (1842), 3 Q.B. 234

The plaintiff bought a horse from the defendant and, after the sale had been completed, gave an undertaking that the horse was sound and free from vice. The horse was in fact a vicious horse, and the plaintiff sued on the express warranty which he alleged had been given to him. *Held*—If the warranty had been given at the time of sale it would have been supported by consideration and therefore actionable, but since it had been given after the sale had taken place, the consideration for the warranty was past, and no action could be brought upon it. Further, no warranty could be implied from the circumstances of the sale.

80. Re McArdle, [1951] Ch. 669

Certain children were entitled under their father's will to a house. However, their mother had a life interest in the property and during her lifetime one of the children and his wife came to live in the house with the mother. The wife carried out certain improvements to the property, and, after she had done so, the children signed a document addressed to her stating: "In consideration of your carrying out certain alterations and improvements to the property . . . at present occupied by you, the beneficiaries under the Will of William Edward McArdle hereby agree that the executors, the National Provincial Bank Ltd., . . . shall repay to you from the said estate when so distributed the sum of £488 in settlement of the amount spent on such improvements . . ." On the death of the testator's widow the children refused to authorise payment of the sum of £488, and this action was brought to decide the validity of the claim. *Held*— Since the improvements had been carried out before the document was executed, the consideration was past and the promise could not be enforced.

81. Re Casey's Patents, Stewart v. Casey, [1892] 1 Ch. 104

Patents were granted to Stewart and another in respect of an invention concerning appliances and vessels for transporting and storing inflammable liquids. Stewart entered into an arrangement with Casey whereby Casey was to introduce the patents. Casey spent two years "pushing" the invention and then the joint owners of the patent rights wrote to him as follows: "In consideration of your services as the practical manager in working both patents we hereby agree to give you one-third share of the patents." Casey also received the letters patent. Some time later Stewart died and his executors claimed the letters patent from Casey, suggesting that he had no interest in them because the consideration for the promise to give him a one-third share was past. *Held*—The previous request to render the services raised an implied promise to pay. The subsequent promise could be regarded as fixing the value of the services so that Casey was entitled to a one-third share of the patent rights.

82. Dungate v. Dungate, [1965] All E.R. 818

The plaintiff lent £500 with interest at 5 per cent to his brother George and George's business partner, a Mr. Elson. The loan was acknowledged in writing dated 12th October, 1953. The plaintiff also lent further sums of money to George in 1956 and 1957 although these loans were without interest.

George paid the interest of £25 per annum by quarterly instalments until 13th April, 1957. On 23rd February, 1962, George wrote to the plaintiff saying, among other things, "Keep a check on totals and amounts I owe you and we will have account now and then." The letter did not say how much was owed. George died on 30th May, 1963, and on 16th October, 1964, the plaintiff sued George's widow and administratrix of his estate for the repayment of the loans. The defendant pleaded that the plaintiff's claim was statute barred. *Held*—The defence failed and the claim was not statute barred because the letter of 23rd February, 1962, made it clear that George owed money to the plaintiff. Although no amount was stated it was sufficient acknowledgment of the plaintiff's claim to make time run again from 23rd February, 1962, and not from the date of the loans.

83. Tweddle *v.* Atkinson (1861), 1 B. & S. 393

William Tweddle the plaintiff was married to the daughter of William Guy. In order to provide for the couple, Guy promised the plaintiff's father to pay the plaintiff £200 if the plaintiff's father would pay the plaintiff £100. An agreement was accordingly drawn up containing the above mentioned promise, and giving William Tweddle the right to sue either promisor for the sums promised. Guy did not make the promised payment during his lifetime and the plaintiff now sued Guy's executor. *Held*—The plaintiff's action failed because he had not given any consideration to Guy in return for the promise to pay £200. The provision in the agreement allowing William Tweddle to sue was of no effect without consideration.

84. Dunlop *v.* New Garage & Motor Co. Ltd., [1915] A.C. 79

The facts of this case are somewhat similar to those of case 69 except that here the wholesalers obtained an undertaking from the respondents by means of a written agreement in which the wholesalers were clearly described as the agents of Dunlop. There was therefore a direct contractual relationship between the parties, and the appellants could enforce the agreement not to sell below the list price. The discounts to be received by the respondents in return for observing the price maintenance clause were offered to them by the wholesaler on behalf of Dunlop as their agent. Thus there was consideration moving between the appellants and the respondents. The case is also concerned with the distinction between liquidated damages and a penalty, because it was suggested that the sum of £5 per tyre was not recoverable because it was not a genuine pre-estimate of loss, but it was inserted to compel performance by the respondents. There is, of course, a presumption that where a single sum is payable on the occurrence of one or more or all of several events then the sum stipulated is a penalty because it is unlikely that all the events can attract the same loss. The contract in this case listed five events on the occurrence of which the sum of £5 was payable. Even so the House of Lords *held* that the presumption need not always apply, and that it did not apply in this case. Where precise estimation is difficult as it was here, then any contractual provision is likely to represent the parties' honest attempt to provide for breach, and the court will follow it.

Certain points of interest arise out of the two cases—

(i) In neither case did the court regard a re-sale price maintenance agreement as illegal because it was in restraint of trade.

(ii) *Dunlop* v. *Selfridge*[69] illustrates that restrictive covenants do not run with chattels though they may with land. (Compare *Tulk* v. *Moxhay*.)[88]

85. Les Affréteurs Réunis Société Anonyme *v.* Walford, [1919] A.C. 801

The respondent Walford was a broker and he had negotiated a charter party between the owners of a ship the S.S. *Flore* and a fuel oil company. One of the clauses in the charter party stated that the owners of the ship promised the charterers that they would pay the broker (Walford) a certain commission on a figure estimated to be the gross amount of hire. In an action for the commission it was *held*—Although Walford was not a party to the contract, which was between the owners and the charterers, there was nevertheless a trust created in his favour and the commission was recoverable.

N.B. The case was, with the agreement of the appellants, dealt with as if the charterers were co-plaintiffs though they had not in fact been joined.

86. Shamia v. Joory, [1958] 1 Q.B. 448

The defendant, an Iraqi merchant having a business in England, employed the plaintiff's brother as an agent in Baghdad. At the end of 1952 the defendant admitted that he owed his agent £1,300, and was requested, and agreed, to pay £500 of this as a gift to the plaintiff, who was the agent's brother and a student in England. The agent informed his brother of the defendant's promise. The plaintiff then wrote to confirm this promise, and the defendant sent a cheque which was not paid because it was not properly drawn. The defendant asked for the return of the cheque to correct it, but shortly afterwards repudiated all liability to the plaintiff having, by this time, reason to doubt the account presented by the plaintiff's brother. The plaintiff now sued to recover the sum of £500 as money had and received to his use (an action in quasi-contract) and Barry, J., *held*—He must succeed.

87. Smith and Snipes Hall Farm Ltd. v. River Douglas Catchment Board, [1949] 2 K.B. 500

In 1938 the defendants entered into an agreement with eleven persons owning land adjoining a certain stream, that, on the landowners paying some part of the cost, the defendants would improve the banks of the stream and maintain the said banks for all time. In 1940 one landowner sold her land to Smith, and in 1944 Smith leased the land to Snipes Hall Farm Ltd. In 1946, because of the defendants' negligence, the banks burst and the adjoining land was flooded. *Held*—The plaintiffs could enforce the covenant in the agreement of 1938 even though they were strangers to it. The covenants were for the benefit of the land and affected its use and value and could therefore be transferred with it.

88. Tulk v. Moxhay (1848), 2 Ph. 774

The plaintiff was the owner of several plots of land in Leicester Square and in 1808 he sold one of them to a person called Elms. Elms agreed, for himself, his heirs and assigns, "to keep the Square Garden open as a pleasure ground and uncovered with buildings." After a number of conveyances, the land was sold to the defendant who claimed a right to build on it. The plaintiff sued for an injunction preventing the development of the land. The defendant, whilst admitting that he purchased the land with notice of the covenant, claimed that he was not bound by it because he had not himself entered into it. *Held*—An injunction to restrain building would be granted because there was a jurisdiction in equity to prevent, by way of injunction, acts inconsistent with a restrictive covenant on land, so long as the land was acquired with notice of that covenant, and the defendant retains land which can benefit from the covenant.

N.B. Such notice may now be constructive where the covenant is registered under the Land Charges Act, 1925.

89. Beswick *v.* **Beswick,** [1967] 2 All E.R. 1197

A coal merchant agreed to sell the business to his nephew in return for a weekly consultancy fee of £6 10s. payable during his lifetime, and after his death an annuity of £5 per week was to be payable to his widow for her lifetime. After the agreement was signed the nephew took over the business and paid his uncle the sum of £6 10s. as agreed. The uncle died on 3rd November, 1963, and the nephew paid the widow one sum of £5 and then refused to pay her any more. On 30th June, 1964, the widow became the administratrix of her husband's estate, and on 15th July, 1964, she brought an action against the nephew for arrears of the weekly sums and for specific performance of the agreement for the future. She sued in her capacity as administratrix of the estate and also in her personal capacity. Her action failed at first instance and on appeal to the Court of Appeal, [1966] 3 All E.R. 1, it was decided amongst other things that—

    (i) specific performance could in a proper case be ordered of a contract to pay money;

    (ii) "property" in Sect. 56 (i) of the Law of Property Act, 1925, included a contractual claim not concerned with realty and that therefore a third party could sue on a contract to which he was a stranger. The widow's claim in her personal capacity was therefore good (*per* Denning, M.R., and Danckwerts, L.J.);

    (iii) the widow's claim as administratrix was good because she was not suing in her personal capacity but on behalf of her deceased husband who had been a party to the agreement;

    (iv) that no trust in her favour could be inferred.

There was a further appeal to the House of Lords, though not on the creation of a trust, and there it was *held* that the widow's claim as administratrix succeeded, and that specific performance of a contract to pay money could be granted in a proper case. However, having decided the appeal on these grounds their Lordships went on to say that the widow's personal claim would have failed because Sect. 56 of the Law of Property Act, 1925, was limited to cases involving realty. The 1925 Act was a consolidating not a codifying measure, so that if it contained words which were capable of more than one construction, effect should be given to the construction which did not alter the law. It was accepted that when the present provision was contained in the Real Property Act, 1845, it had applied only to realty. Although Sect. 205 (i) of the 1925 Act appeared to have extended the provision to personal property, including things in action, it was expressly qualified by the words: "unless the context otherwise requires," and it was felt that Parliament had not intended to sweep away the rule of privity by what was in effect a sidewind.

90. **Charnock** *v.* **Liverpool Corporation and Another,** [1968] 3 All E.R. 473

The plaintiff took his car, which had been damaged in an accident, to the second defendants' garage for repair. On 25th June there was a meeting at the garage between the plaintiff, an assessor employed by the plaintiff's insurance company, and the second defendants' service manager. It was agreed that the insurance company would pay the cost of the repairs, and on 25th June the insurance company sent a letter to the second defendants saying: "We confirm that it is in order for you to proceed with the repairs as per your estimate. Please forward your final account to this office."

The garage company took eight weeks to repair the car and were paid by the insurance company. The plaintiff was awarded damages against the garage company for unreasonable delay in repairing the car. The garage company appealed on the ground that there was no contract between them and the plaintiff and that their contract was with the insurance company. *Held*—by the Court of Appeal—that a reasonable time for effecting the repairs would have been five weeks. Furthermore, the plaintiff was entitled to sue because there were two contracts, one between the plaintiff and the garage company, the other between the insurance company and the garage company. Accordingly the plaintiff was entitled to claim damages for delay in effecting repairs.

91. Foakes *v.* Beer (1884), 9 App. Cas. 605

Mrs. Beer had obtained a judgment against Dr. Foakes for debt and costs. Dr. Foakes agreed to settle the judgment debt by paying £500 down and £150 per half-year until the whole was paid, and Mrs. Beer agreed not to take further action on the judgment. Dr. Foakes duly paid the amount of the judgment plus costs. However, judgment debts carry interest by statute, and while Dr. Foakes had been paying off the debt, interest amounting to £360 had been accruing on the diminishing balance. In this action Mrs. Beer claimed the £360. *Held*—She could do so. Her promise not to take further action on the judgment was not supported by any consideration moving from Dr. Foakes.

92. D. & C. Builders Ltd. *v.* Rees, [1965] 3 All E.R. 837

D. & C. Builders, a small company, did work for Rees for which he owed £482. 13s. 1d. There was at first no dispute as to the work done but Rees did not pay. In August and October, 1964, the plaintiffs wrote for the money and received no reply. On 13th November, 1964, the wife of Rees (who was then ill) telephoned the plaintiffs, complained about the work, and said, "My husband will offer you £300 in settlement. That is all you will get. It is to be in satisfaction." D. & C. Builders, being in desperate straits and faced with bankruptcy without the money, offered to take the £300 and allow a year to Rees to find the balance. Mrs. Rees replied: "No, we will never have enough money to pay the balance. £300 is better than nothing." The plaintiffs then said: "We have no choice but to accept." Mrs. Rees gave the defendants a cheque and insisted on a receipt "in completion of the account." The plaintiffs, being worried, brought an action for the balance. The defence was bad workmanship and also that there was a binding settlement. The question of settlement was tried as a preliminary issue and the judge, following *Goddard* v. *O'Brien*, [1880] 9 Q.B.D. 33, decided that a cheque for a smaller amount was a good discharge of the debt, this being the generally accepted view of the law since that date. On appeal it was *held* (*per* The Master of the Rolls, Lord Denning) that *Goddard* v. *O'Brien* was wrongly decided. A smaller sum in cash could be no settlement of a larger sum and "no sensible distinction could be drawn between the payment of a lesser sum by cash and the payment of it by cheque." In the present case there was no true accord. The debtor's wife had held the creditors to ransom, and there was no reason in law or equity why the plaintiffs should not enforce the full amount of the debt.

93. Good *v.* Cheesman (1831), 2 B. & Ad. 328

The defendant had accepted two bills of exchange of which the plaintiff was the drawer. After the bills became due and before this action was brought, the plaintiff suggested that the defendant meet his creditors with a view perhaps to an agreement. The meeting was duly held and the defendant entered into an agreement with his creditors whereby the defendant was to pay one third of his income to a trustee to be named by the creditors, and that this was to be the method by which the defendant's debts were to be paid. It was not clear from the evidence whether the plaintiff attended the meeting, though he certainly did not sign the agreement. There was, however, evidence that the agreement had been in his possession for some time and it was duly stamped before the trial. No trustee was in fact appointed, though the defendant was willing to go on with the agreement. *Held*—The agreement bound the plaintiff and the action on the bills could not be sustained. The consideration, though not supplied to the plaintiff direct, existed in the forbearance of the other creditors. Each was bound in consequence of the agreement of the rest.

The better view is that the basis of this decision is to be found not in the law of contract but in tort, in the sense that once an agreement of this kind has been made it would be a *fraud* on the other creditors for one of their number to sue the debtor separately.

94. Welby *v.* Drake (1825), 1 C. & P. 557

The plaintiff sued the defendant for the sum of £9 on a debt which had originally been for £18. The defendant's father had paid the plaintiff £9 and the plaintiff had agreed to take that sum in full discharge of the debt. *Held*—The payment of £9 by the defendant's father operated to discharge the debt of £18.

N.B. Here again the basis of the decision is that it would be a fraud on the third party to sue the original debtor. "If the father did pay the smaller sum in satisfaction of this debt, it is a bar to the plaintiff's now recovering against the son; because by suing the son, he commits a fraud on the father, whom he induced to advance his money on the faith of such advance being a discharge of his son from further liability." (*per* Lord Tenterden, C.J.)

95. Combe *v.* Combe, [1951] 2 K.B. 215

The parties were married in 1915 and separated in 1939. In February, 1943, the wife obtained a decree *nisi* of divorce, and a few days later the husband entered into an agreement under which he was to pay his wife £100 per annum, free of income tax. The decree was made absolute in August, 1943. The husband did not make the agreed payments and the wife did not apply to the court for maintenance but chose to rely on the alleged contract. She brought this action for arrears under that contract. Evidence showed that her income was between £700 and £800 per annum and the defendant's was £650 per annum. Byrne, J., at first instance, held that, although the wife had not supplied consideration, the agreement was nevertheless enforceable, following the decision in the High Trees case, as a promise made to be acted upon and in fact acted upon. *Held*—(i) That the *High Trees* decision was not intended to create new actions where none existed before, and that it had not abolished the requirement of consideration to support simple contracts. In such cases consideration was a cardinal necessity. (ii) In the words of Birkett, L.J., the doctrine was "a shield not a sword," i.e. a defence to an action, not a cause of action. (iii) The doctrine applied to the modification of existing agreements by subsequent promises and had no relevance to the formation of a contract.

(iv) It was not possible to find consideration in the fact that the wife forebore to claim maintenance from the court, since no such contractual undertaking by her could have been binding even if she had given it. Therefore this action by the wife must fail because the agreement was not supported by consideration.

96. Central London Property Trust Ltd. *v.* High Trees House Ltd., [1947] K.B. 130

In 1937 the plaintiffs granted to the defendants a lease of ninety-nine years of a new block of flats at a rent of £2,500 per annum. The lease was under seal. During the period of the war the flats were by no means fully let owing to the absence of people from the London area. The defendant company, which was a subsidiary of the plaintiff company, realised that it could not meet the rent out of the profits then being made on the flats, and in 1940 the parties entered into an agreement which reduced the rent to £1,250 per annum, this agreement being put into writing but not sealed. The defendants continued to pay the reduced rent from 1941 to the beginning of 1945, by which time the flats were fully let, and they continued to pay the reduced rent thereafter. In September, 1945, the receiver of the plaintiff company investigated the matter and asked for arrears of £7,916, suggesting that the liability created by the lease still existed, and that the agreement of 1940 was not supported by any consideration. The receiver then brought this friendly action to establish the legal position. He claimed £625, being the difference in rent for the two quarters ending 29th September and 25th December, 1945. *Held*—(i) A simple contract can in Equity vary a deed (i.e. the lease), though it had not done so here because the simple contract was not supported by consideration. (ii) As the agreement for the reduction of rent had been acted upon by the defendants, the plaintiffs were estopped in Equity from claiming the full rent from 1941 until early in 1945 when the flats were fully let. After that time they were entitled to do so because the second agreement was only operative during the continuance of the conditions which gave rise to it. To this extent the limited claim of the receiver succeeded.

N.B. The rule established by the case seems to be that where a person has indicated by a promise that he is not going to insist upon his strict rights, as a result of which the other party alters his position by acting on that promise, then the law, although it does not give a cause of action in damages if the promise is broken, will require it to be honoured to the extent of refusing to allow the promisor the right to act inconsistently with it, even though the promise is not supported by consideration. The doctrine has been called "equitable estoppel," "quasi-estoppel," and "promissory estoppel," in order to distinguish it from estoppel at common law. At common law estoppel arises when the defendant by his conduct suggests that certain existing facts are true. Here the estoppel was based on a promise not conduct, and the promise related to future conduct not to existing facts.

97. Durham Fancy Goods Ltd. *v.* Michael Jackson (Fancy Goods) Ltd., [1968] 2 All E.R. 987

On September 18th, 1967, the plaintiffs drew a bill of exchange on the first defendants in the following form "M. Jackson (Fancy Goods) Co." The bill was signed by Mr. Jackson who was the director and company secretary. The bill was dishonoured and the plaintiffs brought an action against Mr. Jackson contending that by signing the form of acceptance he had committed a criminal offence under Sect. 108 of the Companies Act, 1948, and had made himself personally liable on the bill because he should either have returned the bill with a request that it be readdressed to Michael Jackson (Fancy Goods) Ltd., and the form of acceptance changed, or he should have accepted it "M. Jackson (Fancy Goods) Ltd. p.p. Michael Jackson (Fancy Goods) Ltd., Michael Jackson." It was *held*—by Donaldson, J.—that the misdescription was in breach of Sect. 108 of the Companies Act, 1948, and that Mr. Jackson was personally liable, under the section, to pay the bill. However, since the error was really that of the plaintiffs they were estopped from enforcing Mr. Jackson's personal liability. The principle of equity upon which the promissory estoppel cases were based was applicable and barred the plaintiff's claim. That principle was formulated by Lord Cairns in *Hughes* v. *Metropolitan Railway Co.* (1877), 2 App. Cas. 439, p. 448, and although in his enunciation Lord Cairns assumed a pre-existing contractual relationship between the parties, that was not essential provided that there was a pre-existing legal relationship which could in certain circumstances give rise to liabilities and penalties. Such a relationship was created by Sect. 108.

N.B. A holder other than the plaintiffs might have been able to bring an action against Mr. Jackson under Sect. 108 since such a holder would not have been affected by the equity in that he would not have drawn the bill in an incorrect name.

Sect. 108 provides: "(1) every company . . . (*c*) shall have its name mentioned in legible characters . . . in all bills of exchange . . . purporting to be signed by or on behalf of the company . . . (4) If an officer of the company or any person on his behalf . . . (b) signs . . . on behalf of the company any bill of exchange . . . wherein its name is not mentioned in manner aforesaid . . . he shall be liable to a fine not exceeding 50 pounds, and shall further be personally liable to the holder of the bill of exchange . . . for the amount thereof unless it is duly paid by the company."

98. Ajayi *v.* Briscoe (Nigeria) Ltd., [1964] 3 All E.R. 556

The plaintiff claimed hire-purchase instalments due on Seddon Tipper lorries supplied to the defendant. The defendant claimed the equitable principle of promissory estoppel because, when the lorries could not be used by reason of servicing difficulties, the plaintiff had promised to service the vehicles and had also said, "we are agreeable to you withholding instalments due on Seddon Tippers as long as they are withdrawn from active service." The defendant could not establish that he had changed his position because of the promise. He was not using the lorries when they went for service and still did not use them after the plaintiffs had repaired them. He was not able to show that he had had to reorganise his business in any way, but in spite of this still did not pay the instalments. *Held*—by the Privy Council—that the plaintiff's action succeeded. The defence of promissory estoppel did not apply.

99. Mighell *v.* Sultan of Johore, [1894] 1 Q.B. 149

The Sultan, who was a foreign sovereign, was living in England as a private person under an assumed name. He made a promise of marriage to the plaintiff. *Held*—the promise was not actionable.

100. Coutts & Co. *v.* Browne-Lecky, [1947] K.B. 104

The first defendant, an infant, had been permitted to overdraw his account with the plaintiffs who were bankers. The overdraft was guaranteed by the second and third defendants who were adults. The overdraft was not repaid and the plaintiffs now sued the adult guarantors. *Held*—Since the loan to the infant was void under the Infants Relief Act, 1874, the infant could not be in default because he was not liable to repay the loan. Since the essence of a guarantee is that the guarantor is liable for the default or miscarriage of the principal debtor, it followed that the adult guarantors could not be liable. The action therefore failed.

N.B. Had the contract been one of indemnity the adult defendants would have been liable, because, under a contract of indemnity, the person giving the indemnity is in effect the principal debtor and his liability does not depend on the default of any other person. (*Yeoman Credit Ltd.* v. *Latter,* [1961] 1 W.L.R. 828.)

101. R. v. Wilson (1879), 5 Q.B.D. 28

Wilson was charged with, and convicted of, feloniously leaving England with intent to defraud his creditors. His conviction was quashed because his debts were void under the Infants' Relief Act, 1874, and in law he had no creditors.

102. Nash v. Inman, [1908] 2 K.B. 1

The plaintiff was a Savile Row tailor and the defendant was an infant undergraduate at Trinity College, Cambridge. The plaintiff sent his agent to Cambridge because he had heard that the defendant was spending money freely, and might be the sort of person who would be interested in high class clothing. As a result of the agent's visit, the plaintiff supplied the defendant with various articles of clothing to the value of £145 0s. 3d. during the period October, 1902, to June, 1903. The clothes included eleven fancy waistcoats. The plaintiff now sued the infant for the price of the clothes. Evidence showed that the plaintiff's father was in a good position, being an architect with a town and a country house, and it could be said that the clothes supplied were suitable to the defendant's position in life. However, his father proved that the defendant was amply supplied with such clothes when the plaintiff delivered the clothing now in question. *Held*—The plaintiff's claim failed because he had not established that the goods supplied were necessaries.

103. Elkington v. Amery, [1936] 2 All E.R. 86

The defendant was an infant and the son of a former cabinet minister. He purchased from the plaintiffs an engagement ring and an eternity ring, the court treating the latter as a wedding ring. He also purchased a lady's gold vanity bag. The Court of Appeal treated the two rings as being necessaries, but did not accept that the vanity bag was a necessary because there was no evidence to show that it was purchased in respect of the engagement.

104. Roberts v. Gray, [1913] 1 K.B. 520

The defendant wished to become a professional billiards player and entered into an agreement with the plaintiff, a leading professional, to go on a joint tour. The plaintiff went to some trouble in order to organise the tour, but a dispute arose between the parties and the defendant refused to go. The plaintiff now sued for damages of £6,000. *Held*—The contract was for the infant's benefit, being in effect for his instruction as a billiards player. Therefore the plaintiff could sustain an action for damages for breach of contract, and damages of £1,500 were awarded.

105. Chaplin *v.* **Leslie Frewin (Publishers)**, [1965] 3 All E.R. 764

The plaintiff, the infant son of a famous father, made a contract with the defendants under which they were to publish a book written for him and telling his life story. The plaintiff sought to avoid the contract on the ground that the book gave an inaccurate picture of his approach to life. *Held*— Amongst other things—that the contract was binding if it was for the infant's benefit. The time to determine that question was when the contract was made and at that time it was for the infant's benefit and could not be avoided.

N.B. In *Denmark Productions* v. *Boscobel Productions* (1967), 111 S.J. 715, Widgery, J., held that a contract by which an infant appoints managers and agents to look after his business affairs is, in modern conditions, necessary if he is to earn his living and rise to fame, and if it is for his benefit it will be upheld by analogy with a contract of service.

106. De Francesco *v.* **Barnum** (1890), 45 Ch.D. 430

Two infants bound themselves in contract to the plaintiff for seven years to be taught stage dancing. The infants agreed that they would not accept any engagements without his consent. They later accepted an engagement with Barnum and the plaintiff sued Barnum for interfering with the contractual relationship between himself and the infants, and also to enforce the apprenticeship deed against the infants and to obtain damages for its breach. The contract was, of course, for the infants' benefit and was *prima facie* binding on them. However, when the court considered the deed in greater detail, it emerged that there were certain onerous terms in it. For example the infants bound themselves not to marry during the apprenticeship; the payment was hardly generous, the plaintiff agreeing to pay them 9d. per night and 6d. for matinee appearances for the first three years, and 1s. per night and 6d. for matinee performances during the remainder of the apprenticeship. The plaintiff did not undertake to maintain them whilst they were unemployed and did not undertake to find them engagements. The infants could also be engaged in performances abroad at a fee of 5s. per week. Further the plaintiff could terminate the contract if he felt that the infants were not suitable for the career of dancer. It appeared from the contract that the infants were at the absolute disposal of the plaintiff. *Held*—The deed was an unreasonable one and was therefore unenforceable against the infants. Barnum could not, therefore, be held liable, since the tort of interference with a contractual relationship presupposes the existence of an enforceable contract.

107. Clements *v.* **L. & N.W. Railway**, [1894] 2 Q.B. 482

Clements became a porter with the railway company and agreed to join the company's insurance scheme and to forego his rights under the Employers Liability Act, 1880. He sustained an injury at work and claimed under the company's scheme. He now made a claim under the Act on the grounds that the contract was not for his benefit since it deprived him of an action under the Act. The company's scheme was on the whole a favourable one because it covered more injuries than the statute but the scale of compensation was lower. *Held*—The contract as a whole was for the infant's benefit and was binding on him. He had no claim under the Act.

108. Mercantile Union Guarantee Corporation *v.* **Ball,** [1937] 2 K.B. 498

The purchase on hire-purchase terms of a motor lorry by an infant carrying on business as a haulage contractor was *held* not to be a contract for necessaries, but a trading contract by which the infant could not be bound.

N.B. It would be possible for the owner to recover the lorry because a hire-purchase contract is a contract of bailment not a sale. Thus ownership does not pass when the goods are delivered.

109. Steinberg *v.* **Scala (Leeds) Ltd.,** [1923] 2 Ch. 452

The plaintiff, Miss Steinberg, purchased shares in the defendant company and paid certain sums of money on application, on allotment and on one call. Being unable to meet future calls, she repudiated the contract whilst still an infant and claimed—

    (*a*) Rectification of the Register of Members to remove her name therefrom, thus relieving her from liability on future calls; and

    (*b*) The recovery of the money already paid.

The company agreed to rectify the register and issue was joined on the claim to recover the money paid.

Held—The claim under (*b*) above failed because there had not been total failure of consideration. The shares had some value and gave some rights, even though the plaintiff had not received any dividends and the shares had always stood at a discount on the market.

110. Davies *v.* **Beynon-Harris** (1931), 47 T.L.R. 424

An infant took a lease of a flat a fortnight before attaining his majority. Three years later he was sued for arrears of rent and claimed that he could avoid the contract. *Held*—He was liable to pay the rent because the lease was voidable not void, and was now binding on him because he had not repudiated it during minority or within a reasonable time thereafter.

N.B. An infant cannot take a legal estate in land, Sect. 1 (6), Law of Property Act, 1925. This prevents him from taking a lease at law. However, he does obtain an equitable interest and must observe the covenants in the lease so long as he retains a beneficial interest in the property.

111. Goode *v.* **Harrison** (1821), 5 B. & Ald. 147

An infant partner, who took no steps to avoid a partnership contract upon attaining his majority, was *held* liable for the debts of the firm incurred after he came of age.

112. Coxhead *v.* **Mullis** (1878), 3 C.P.D. 439

Mullis whilst an infant offered to marry the plaintiff and she accepted him. After Mullis came of age he continued to recognise the engagement and wrote affectionate letters to the plaintiff and paid visits to her but made no fresh promise to marry her. In an action by the plaintiff for breach of promise it was *held* that the defence of infancy succeeded in view of Sect. 2 of the Infants Relief Act, 1874. Although ratification might have been enough at common law the section no longer allowed ratification to be effective.

113. Northcote *v.* **Doughty** (1879), 4 C.P.D. 385

The defendant offered marriage to the plaintiff and she agreed to accept him if he obtained his parents' consent. The defendant later wrote to the plaintiff saying that he had told his mother and father all about it and that their reaction was favourable. When he came of age he wrote to the plaintiff saying that he would now marry her as soon as he could. It was *held* that there was sufficient evidence from which the jury could infer a fresh promise to marry after age.

114. Pearce *v*. **Brain**, [1929] 2 K.B. 310

Pearce an infant, exchanged his motor-cycle for a motor-car belonging to Brain. The infant had little use out of the car, and had in fact driven it only a short distance when it broke down because of serious defects in the back axle. Pearce now sued to recover his motor-cycle, claiming that the consideration had wholly failed. *Held*—(*a*) That a contract for the exchange of goods, whilst not a sale of goods, is a contract for the supply of goods, and that if the goods are not necessaries, the contract is void if with an infant. (*b*) The car was not a necessary good and therefore the contract was void. (*c*) Even so the infant could only recover the motor-cycle in the same circumstances as he could recover money paid under a void contract, i.e. if the consideration had wholly failed. The court considered that the infant had received a benefit under the contract, albeit small, and that he could not recover the motor-cycle.

115. Corpe *v*. **Overton** (1833), 10 Bing. 252

An infant agreed to enter into a partnership and deposited £100 with the defendant as security for the due performance of the contract. The infant rescinded the contract before the partnership came into being. *Held*—He could recover the £100 because he had received no benefit, having never been a partner.

116. Stocks *v*. **Wilson**, [1913] 2 K.B. 235

An infant obtained furniture from the plaintiff by falsely stating that he was of full age. *Held*—The property in the furniture passed to the infant, under the Infants Relief Act, 1874. Even if he sold the property the infant could not be sued in conversion. The infant had sold part of the furniture to a third party for £30, and Lush, J., *held* that the plaintiff could recover this sum by applying the equitable principle of restitution.

N.B. Pearce v. *Brain*, 1929, (supra) supports *Stocks* v. *Wilson* because, if the property in the car had not passed to the infant, there would have been total failure of consideration, thus enabling him to recover his motor-cycle.

117. Leslie *v*. **Sheill**, [1914] 3 K.B. 607

Sheill an infant borrowed £400 from R. Leslie, Ltd., moneylenders, by fraudulently representing that he was of full age. The contract was void under Sect. 1 of the Infants Relief Act, 1874, and the plaintiffs sued for the return of the money, either as damages for the tort of deceit, or in quasi-contract as money had and received to the plaintiff's use. *Held*—Neither claim could succeed because they were attempts to circumvent the Act and the infant was entitled to retain the money advanced. With regard to the equitable doctrine of restitution, it was suggested that, since the money had been spent and could not be precisely traced, restitution was not possible; for to order restitution would mean that the infant would have to pay an equivalent sum out of his present or future resources, and this would be closer to enforcing a void contract than to granting equitable restitution. It was also suggested that *Stocks* v. *Wilson*, 1913, was wrongly decided in so far as Lush, J., granted restitution of the £30 which the infant had received by selling the property to a third party.

The court in this case suggested that "Restitution ends where repayment begins," i.e. unless the actual property passing under the contract can be recovered, the remedy of restitution does not lie to recover money or property received in its stead.

118. Burnard *v.* Haggis (1863), 14 C.B.N.S. 45

Burnard was an undergraduate and hired Haggis's mare for riding. Haggis warned Burnard that the mare was not to be used for "jumping or larking." Burnard allowed a friend to ride the mare and the latter put the mare at a fence, in consequence of which the mare was impaled on a stake and died. Haggis sued Burnard in trespass. *Held*—The infant was liable. Though the trespass actually happened because there had been a contract, yet the act of jumping the mare was just as distinct from the contract as if Burnard had run a knife into her and killed her. Therefore Burnard's infancy, which might have been a defence in contract, did not apply in this action which was, in fact, an action in pure tort.

119. Jenkin *v.* Pharmaceutical Society, [1921] 1 Ch. 392

The defendant society was incorporated by Royal Charter in 1843 for the purpose of advancing chemistry and pharmacy and promoting a uniform system of education of those who should practise the same, and also for the protection of those who carried on the business of chemists or druggists. *Held*— The expenditure of the funds of the society in the formation of an industrial committee, to attempt to regulate hours of work and wages and conditions of work between masters and employee members of the society, was *ultra vires* the charter, because it was a trade union activity which was not contemplated by the Charter of 1843. Further, the expenditure of money on an insurance scheme for members was also not within the powers given in the charter, for it amounted to converting the defendant society into an insurance company. The plaintiff, a member of the society, was entitled to an injunction to restrain the society from implementing the above schemes.

120. Ashbury Railway Carriage and Iron Co. *v.* Riche (1875), L.R. 7 H.L. 653

The company bought a concession for the construction of a railway system in Belgium, and entered into an agreement whereby Messrs. Riche were to construct a railway line. Messrs. Riche commenced the work, and the company paid over certain sums of money in connection with the contract. The company later ran into difficulties, and the shareholders wished the directors to take over the contract in a personal capacity, and indemnify the shareholders. The directors thereupon repudiated the contract on behalf of the company, and Messrs. Riche sued for breach of contract. The case turned on whether the company was engaged in an *ultra vires* activity in building a complete railway system, because if so, the contract it had made with Messrs. Riche would be *ultra vires* and void, and the claim against the company would fail. The objects clause of the company's memorandum stated that it was established—

"to make or sell or lend on hire railway carriages, wagons and all kinds of railway plant, fittings, machinery and rolling stock; to carry on the business of mechanical engineers and general contractors, to purchase and sell as merchants timber, coal, metal and other materials, and to buy and sell such materials on commission or as agents."

The House of Lords *held* that the purchase of the concession to build a complete railway system from Antwerp to Tournai was *ultra vires* and void because it was not within the objects of the company. The words empowering the company to carry on business of general contracting must be construed *ejusdem generis* with the preceding words, and must therefore be restricted to contracting in the field of plant, fittings and machinery only. The contract with Messrs. Riche was therefore void, and the directors were entitled to repudiate it. It was also stated that even if all the shareholders had assented to the contract, it would still have been void because there can be no ratification of an *ultra vires* contract.

121. Re Jon Beauforte, [1953] Ch. 131

The company was authorised by its memorandum to carry on the business of costumiers, tailors, drapers, haberdashers, milliners and the like. It decided to manufacture veneered wall panels, and for this purpose had a factory erected, and ordered and was supplied with veneers. It was clear that the contracts for the erection of the factory and supply of veneers were *ultra vires* and void, but one of the questions before the court was whether the liquidator of the company had been correct in disallowing a claim made by a supplier of coke. The supplier argued that the coke might have been used in connection with *intra vires* activities and that it was not self-evident that the coke was to be used for an *ultra vires* purpose. The court decided against him because the order for coke was given on headed paper describing the company as "veneered panel manufacturers." From this the coke supplier was deemed to know that the contract was *ultra vires*, because everyone is deemed to know the contents of the memorandum of association of a registered company, which is registered at the Companies' Registry in London, and can be inspected.

N.B. This doctrine of constructive notice of a company's objects is now well established and yet it is based on the assumption that, because inspection is possible, it should always be made before contracts are entered into. However, business would grind to a halt if this sort of inquiry were made every time a contract was made; it does not accord therefore, with normal business practice.

122. Deuchar *v.* The Gas Light and Coke Co., [1925] A.C. 691

The plaintiff was a shareholder in the defendant company and was also the secretary of a company which supplied the defendants with caustic soda. The plaintiff sought a declaration from the court that the manufacture of caustic soda and chlorine by the defendants, and the erection of a factory for the purpose, was *ultra vires* the company. He also asked for an injunction to restrain the defendants from manufacturing caustic soda and chlorine. Astbury, J., at first instance, had found that the activities were fairly incidental to the powers given in the objects clause, and the Court of Appeal affirmed this decision. On appeal to the House of Lords it appeared that the defendants derived their powers from a special Act of Parliament, the Gas Light and Coke Companies Act, 1868, which gave them power to make and supply gas and deal with and sell by-products. The Act authorised the conversion of the by-products into a marketable state. One of the residuals of gas-making was naphthalene which could be converted into beta-naphthol and profitably sold, conversion being by the use of caustic soda. The company had formerly purchased this from the company of which the plaintiff was secretary, but later erected a factory on their land and began to make it themselves, though they only made what they required for their own use and did not make caustic soda for resale. Chlorine was a by-product of the manufacture of caustic soda, and the chlorine, it was admitted, was converted into bleaching powder and sold. The House of Lords *held* that the manufacture of caustic soda was fairly incidental to the company's powers, and although the sale of the bleaching powder was not incidental, the matter was trivial and on the basis of the maxim *de minimis non curat lex* (the law does not concern itself with trifles) the court would not interfere.

123. Cotman v. Brougham, [1918] A.C. 514

The parties to this action were liquidators. Cotman was liquidator of the Essequibo Rubber Estates Ltd., and Brougham was liquidator of Anglo-Cuban Oil Co. It appeared that E underwrote the shares in A-C although the main clause of E's objects clause was to develop rubber estates abroad. However, a sub-clause allowed E to promote companies and deal in the shares of other companies and gave numerous other powers. The final clause of E's objects clause said in effect that each sub-clause should be considered as an independent main object. The E Company, not having paid for the shares which it had agreed to underwrite, was put on the list of contributories of A-C, and E's liquidator asked that his company be removed from that list because the contract to underwrite was *ultra vires* and void. *Held*—by the House of Lords— that it was not, and that the E Company was liable to pay for the shares underwritten. The final clause of E's objects clause meant that each object could be pursued alone, because the Registrar had accepted the memorandum in this form and had registered the company. All the judges of the House of Lords deplored the idea of companies being registered with an objects clause in this wide form, and thought that the matter ought to have been raised by mandamus by the Registrar refusing to register the company. However, since the certificate of incorporation had been issued, it was conclusive; and matters concerning the company's registration could not be gone into.

124. Introductions Ltd. v. National Provincial Bank Ltd., [1969] 1 All E.R. 887

Introductions Ltd. was incorporated in 1951 and the objects of the company were to promote and provide entertainment and accommodation for overseas visitors. This business was not successful and in November, 1960, the company embarked on a new business, pig farming. The company ran short of cash and arranged to borrow money from the defendants. The company executed certain debentures in favour of the bank for its indebtedness, which at the time of the winding up order in November, 1965, was £29,571.

The bank now wished to enforce its security under the debentures and recover the loan. The liquidators of the company claimed that the loan was *ultra vires* and void, and the bank did not dispute that it was aware that the company's business was that of pig breeding and had notice of the company's objects. However, one of the sub-clauses of the memorandum related to borrowing and the bank said it was entitled to lend money on the strength of the sub-clause alone as it formed one of the objects of the company. There was a proviso to the memorandum which clearly stated that all sub-clauses of the memorandum were to be treated as separate and independent objects. *Held*—by the Court of Appeal—that the loan was *ultra vires* and void. The bare power to borrow contained in the sub-clause could not legitimately stand alone. The company must have had in view purposes to which the money was to be applied, i.e. for the purposes of the objects of the company. This being so the sub-clause did not authorise the raising or borrowing of money for something which was not an object of the company. However if the bank had not known the purpose for which the money was required the loan would have been valid because the bank was not bound to inquire as to its purpose.

125. Bell Houses Ltd. *v.* City Wall Properties Ltd., [1966] 2 All E.R. 674

The plaintiff company claimed £20,000 as commission under an alleged contract with the defendant company for the introduction of the latter to a financier who would lend the defendant company £1,000,000 for property development. As a preliminary issue the defendant company alleged that the contract was *ultra vires* and could not be enforced against them.

The principal business of the plaintiff company was the development of housing estates, and therefore the occasional raising of finance formed a necessary part of its activities. In consequence the company had obtained valuable knowledge of various sources of finance and because of this the company was able to arrange finance for the defendants. The defendants contended that the plaintiff company, in arranging finance for an outside organisation, was, in effect, embarking on a new type of business, i.e. "mortgage broking," and since this was not expressly included in the objects, nor reasonably incidental thereto, it was *ultra vires*. One of the sub-clauses in the objects clause of the plaintiff company was as follows: "To carry on any other trade or business *whatsoever* which can *in the opinion of the board of directors* be *advantageously* carried on by (the company) in connection with, or as ancillary to, any of the above businesses or the general business of the (company)." *Held*— by the Court of Appeal—that the alleged contract was *intra vires* in particular because of the clause set out above. In the court's view the *bona fide* opinion of the board, in this case represented by the managing director who arranged the finance, that the contract could be advantageously carried on with the company's principal business, was enough no matter how unreasonable in the *objective* sense that opinion might seem to be.

126. Sharp Bros. and Knight *v.* Chant, [1917] 1 K.B. 771

Landlord and tenant agreed that the rent of a certain small house should be increased by the sum of 6d. per week. The tenant paid this increased rent for some time and it was then discovered that Rent Restriction legislation prevented the landlord from recovering any increase in rent he might make on certain properties of which the small house in question was one. *Held*—The tenant had paid the extra rent under a mistake of law, and could not sue for its return or deduct it from future payments of rent.

127. Solle *v.* Butcher, [1950] 1 K.B. 671

Butcher had agreed to lease a flat in Beckenham to Solle at a yearly rental of £250, the lease to run for seven years. Both parties had acted on the assumption that the flat which had been substantially reconstructed so as to be virtually a new flat, was no longer controlled by the Rent Restriction legislation then in force. If it were so controlled, the maximum rent payable would be £140 per annum. Nevertheless Butcher would have been entitled to increase that rent by charging 8 per cent of the cost of repairs and improvements which would bring the figure up to about £250 per annum, the rent actually charged, if he had served a statutory notice on Solle before the new lease was executed. No such notice was in fact served. Actually they both for a time mistakenly thought that the flat was decontrolled when this was not the case. Solle realised the mistake after some two years, and sought to recover the rent he had over-paid and to continue as tenant for the balance of the seven years as a statutory tenant at £140 per annum. Butcher counterclaimed for rescission of the lease in Equity. It was *held*—by a majority of the Court of Appeal—that the mistake was one of *fact* and not of law, i.e. the fact that the flat was still within the provisions of the Rent Acts, and this was a bilateral mistake as to quality which would not invalidate the contract at common law. However, on the counterclaim for rescission, it was *held* that in spite of the decision in *Seddon* v. *North Eastern Salt Co.* (1905)[171] and *Angel* v. *Jay* (1911),[172] the lease could be rescinded even though it had been executed. In order not to dispossess Solle, the court offered him the following alternatives—

(*a*) to surrender the lease entirely; or

(*b*) to remain in possession as a mere licensee until a new lease could be drawn up after Butcher had had time to serve the statutory notice which would allow him to add a sum for repairs to the £140 which would bring the lawful rent up to £250 per annum.

128. Cooper v. Phibbs (1867), L.R. 2 H.L. 149

Cooper agreed to take a lease of a fishery from Phibbs. Unknown to either party the fishery already belonged to Cooper who now brought this action to set aside the lease and for delivery up of the lease. *Held*—The agreement must be set aside on the grounds of common or identical bilateral mistake. However, since Equity has the power to give ancillary relief, Phibbs was given a lien on the fishery for the improvements he had made to it during the time he believed it to be his. This lien could be discharged by Cooper paying Phibbs the value of the improvements.

129. Foster v. Mackinnon (1869), L.R. 4 C.P. 704

The plaintiff was a person entitled to receive payment on a bill of exchange for £3,000; the defendant was an endorser of the bill and was *prima facie* liable on it. The evidence showed that the defendant was an old man of feeble sight, and that he had signed the bill under the mistaken impression that it was a guarantee. *Held*—The defendant was not negligent under the circumstances in signing the bill and his plea of mistake was successful so that he was not liable on it.

130. Carlisle and Cumberland Banking Co. v. Bragg, [1911] 1 K.B. 489

Two persons named Rigg and Bragg were drinking together. Rigg showed a paper to Bragg and said that it was a duplicate of an insurance document signed by Bragg on the previous day. Rigg asserted that the original document had become wet and blurred by rain, and asked Bragg to sign the duplicate, which Bragg did. Actually it was a continuing guarantee of Rigg's current account with the bank, and by forging the signature of a witness Rigg obtained an overdraft. The bank now sued Bragg on the guarantee. *Held*—Although Bragg was negligent in signing the document, he was able to plead mistake so that the guarantee was not enforceable against him.

N.B. The Court of Appeal, in *Muskham Finance Ltd.* v. *Howard*, [1963] 3 All E.R. 81 and *Gallie* v. *Lee*, (1969)[131] suggested that this decision should be reconsidered, implying that negligence in signing the document might estop the signer from pleading that the document was mistakenly signed. (See now *Saunders* v. *Anglia Building Society*, 1970.)[131a]

131. Gallie *v.* Lee and Another, (1969) 1 All E.R. 1062

The plaintiff, a widow aged 78 years, signed a document which Lee told her was a deed of gift of her house to her nephew. She did not read the document but believed what Lee had told her. In fact the document was an assignment of her leasehold interest in the house to Lee and Lee later mortgaged that interest to a building society. In an action by the plaintiff against Lee and the building society it was *held* at first instance—(i) that the assignment was void and did not confer a title on Lee, (ii) although the plaintiff had been negligent she was not estopped from denying the validity of the deed against the building society for she owed it no duty. The Court of Appeal, in allowing an appeal by the building society, *held* that the plea of *non est factum* was not available to the plaintiff. The transaction intended and carried out was the same, i.e. an assignment.

131a. Saunders *v. Anglia Building Society*, [1970] 3 All E.R. 961

This appeal to the House of Lords was brought by the executrix of Mrs. Gallie's estate. The House of Lords affirmed the decision of the Court of Appeal but took the opportunity to restate the law relating to the avoidance of documents on the ground of mistake as follows—

(*a*) the plea of *non est factum* will rarely be available to a person of full capacity who signs a document apparently having legal effect without troubling to read it;

(*b*) a mistake as to the identity of the person in whose favour the document is executed will not normally support a plea of *non est factum* though it may do if the court regards the mistake as fundamental (Lord Reid and Lord Hodson). Neither judge felt that the personality error made by Mrs. Gallie was sufficient to support the plea;

(*c*) the distinction taken in *Howatson* v. *Webb* [1908], 1 Ch. 1, that the mistake must be as to the class or character of the document and not merely as to its contents was regarded as illogical. A better test would be whether the document which was in fact signed was "fundamentally different," "radically different" or "totally different." This test is more flexible than the character/contents one and yet it still restricts the operation of the plea of *non est factum;*

(*d*) *Carlisle and Cumberland Banking Co.* v. *Bragg,* 1911,[130] was overruled. Henceforth carelessness on the part of a person signing a document will prevent him from raising the plea. In addition the person claiming to have taken proper care bears the burden of proving that he did.

132. Legal and General Assurance Society *v.* General Metal Agencies, [1969] 113 S.J. 876

Legal and General, who were the landlords of General Metal Agencies, served a statutory notice of termination of the tenancy. General Metal applied to the County Court for a new tenancy but Legal and General opposed the application on the grounds of persistent late payment of rent and it was dismissed. However, Legal and General subsequently sent by mistake a computerised demand for the next quarter's rent in advance over the signature of their general manager. General Metal sent a cheque for the rent and this was presented to the bank and paid. In this action Legal and General claimed possession of the premises and General Metal contended that Legal and

General, by demanding and accepting the next quarter's rent in advance, had by implication created a new tenancy. It was *held*—by Fisher, J.—

(i) that Legal and General were entitled to show that the demand was sent and the rent received by mistake. There was no intention to create a new tenancy and the defendants must be deemed to have known this. The use of a computer made no difference to the established common law principle;

(ii) that, in consequence, Legal and General were entitled to possession of the premises.

133. Higgins (W.) Ltd. *v.* Northampton Corporation, [1927] 1 Ch. 128

The plaintiff entered into a contract with the corporation for the erection of dwelling houses. The plaintiff made an arithmetical error in arriving at his price, having deducted a certain sum twice over. The corporation sealed the contract, assuming that the price arrived at by the plaintiff was correct. *Held*— The contract was binding on the parties. Rectification of such a contract was not possible because the power of the court to rectify agreements made under mistake is confined to common not unilateral mistake. Here, rectification would only have been granted if fraud or misrepresentation had been present.

134. Cundy *v.* Lindsay (1878), 3 App. Cas. 459

The respondents were linen manufacturers with a business in Belfast. A fraudulent person named Blenkarn wrote to the repondents from 37 Wood Street, Cheapside, ordering a quantity of handkerchiefs but signed his letter in such a way that it appeared to come from Messrs. Blenkiron, who were a well-known and solvent house doing business at 123 Wood Street. The respondents knew of the existence of Blenkiron but did not know the address. Accordingly the handkerchiefs were sent to 37 Wood Street. Blenkiron then sold them to the appellants, and was later convicted and sentenced for the fraud. The respondents sued the appellants in conversion claiming that the contract they had made with Blenkarn was void for mistake, and that the property had not passed to Blenkarn or to the appellants. *Held*—The respondents succeeded; there was an operative mistake as to the party with whom they were contracting.

135. King's Norton Metal Co. Ltd. *v.* Edridge, Merrett & Co. Ltd. (1897), 14 T.L.R. 98

The plaintiffs were metal manufacturers in Worcestershire, the defendants being metal manufacturers at Birmingham. In 1896 the plaintiffs received a letter from a firm called Hallam & Co., Soho Wire Works, Sheffield. The letter was written on headed paper, the heading depicting a large factory, and in one corner was a statement that the company had depots and agencies at Belfast, Lille, and Ghent. The letter requested a quotation for the supply of brass rivet wire, and a quotation was sent and later an order was received and the goods dispatched. These goods were never paid for. It later emerged that a person named Wallis had set up in business as Hallam & Co. and had fraudulently obtained the goods by the above methods. Wallis sold the goods to the defendants who bought *bona fide* and for value. The plaintiffs had previously done business with Wallis's firm, Hallam & Co., and had been paid by cheque signed Hallam & Co. The plaintiffs sued the defendants in conversion, regarding this as a better action than the one for fraud against Wallis. In order to sustain the action in conversion, the plaintiffs had to establish that the contract with Hallam & Co. was void for mistake, and that because of this the defendants had no title to the wire. *Held*—The plaintiffs' claim failed because the contract with Hallam & Co. was voidable for fraud but not void for mistake. The firm Hallam & Co. was a mere alias for Wallis, and since there was no other firm of Hallam & Co. with whom the plaintiffs had previously done business, they were really dealing with one person who from time to time used different names, i.e. Wallis or Hallam & Co. Although the contract was voidable for fraud, it had not been avoided when the goods were sold to the defendants; their title was good and they were not liable in conversion.

136. Phillips v. Brooks Ltd., [1919] 2 K.B. 243

A fraudulent person named North went into the plaintiff's jewellers shop and selected goods to the value of £3,000. He then asked whether he could take away one of the items (a ring) which he said he wanted for his wife's birthday. He said, no doubt to reassure the jeweller, that he was Sir George Bullough of St. James's Square. The plaintiff had heard of the name and, on referring to a directory and finding the address was correct, he allowed North to take away the ring in return for a cheque. Then North, using the name Firth, pledged the ring with the defendants who were pawnbrokers. They took the ring in good faith and advanced £350 upon it. North was subsequently convicted of obtaining the ring by false pretences, and this action was brought by the plaintiff who claimed that he was mistaken in his contract with North, and that since the contract was void the property had not passed. He, therefore, asked that the ring be returned to him or that he be paid £450, its value. *Held*—The contract between Phillips and North was not void for mistake and Brooks obtained a good title to the ring. The representation by North that he was Sir George Bullough only affected the taking away of the ring and the acceptance by Phillips of the cheque. By that time the sale had taken place and so far as the sale was concerned the identity of the purchaser was not important to Phillips.

136a. Lewis v. Averay, The Times, July 23, 1971

Mr. Lewis agreed to sell his car to a rogue who called on him after seeing an advertisement. Before the sale took place the rogue talked knowledgeably about the film world giving the impression that he was the actor Richard Green in the "Robin Hood" serial. He signed a dud cheque for £450 in the name of "R. A. Green" and was allowed to have the log book and drive the car away late the same night when he produced a film studio pass in the name of "Green". It was *held*—by the Court of Appeal—that Mr. Lewis had effectively contracted to sell the car to the rogue and could not recover it or damages from Mr. Averay, a student, who had bought it from the rogue for £200. The contract between Mr. Lewis and the rogue was voidable for fraud but not void for unilateral mistake.

137. Ingram and others v. Little, [1961] 1 Q.B. 31

The plaintiffs, three ladies, were the joint owners of a car. They wished to sell the car and advertised it for sale. A fraudulent person, introducing himself as Hutchinson, offered to buy it. He was taken for a drive in it and during conversation said that his home was at Caterham. Later the rogue offered £700 for the car but this was refused, though a subsequent offer of £717 was one which the plaintiffs were prepared to accept. At this point the rogue produced a cheque book and one of the plaintiffs, who was conducting the negotiations, said that the deal was off and that they would not accept a cheque. The rogue then said that he was P. G. M. Hutchinson, that he had business interests in

Guildford, and that he lived at Stanstead House, Stanstead Road, Caterham. One of the plaintiffs checked this information in a telephone directory and, on finding it to be accurate, allowed him to take the car in return for a cheque. The cheque was dishonoured, and in the meantime the rogue had sold the car to the defendants and had disappeared without trace. The plaintiffs sued for the return of the car, or for its value as damages in conversion, claiming that the contract between themselves and the rogue was void for mistake, and that the property had not passed. At the trial judgment was given for the plaintiffs, Slade, J., finding the contract void. His judgment was affirmed by the Court of Appeal, though Devlin, L.J., dissented, saying that the mistake made was as to the credit-worthiness of the rogue, not as to his identity since he was before the plaintiffs when the contract was made. A mistake as to the substance of the rogue would be a mistake as to quality and would not avoid the contract. Devlin, L.J., also suggested that legislation should provide for an apportionment of the loss incurred by two innocent parties who suffer as a result of the fraud of a third.

N.B. The distinctions drawn in some of these cases are fine ones. It is difficult to distinguish *Ingram* from *Phillips* and *Lewis*. The question for the court to answer in these cases is whether or not the offeror at the time of making the offer regarded the identity of the offeree as a matter of vital importance. The general rule seems to be that where the parties are face to face when the contract is made identity will not be vital and the contract voidable only. *Ingram* would appear to be the exceptional case.

138. Webster *v.* Cecil (1861), 30 Beav. 62

The parties had been negotiating for the sale of certain property. Later Cecil offered by letter to sell the property for £1,250. Webster was aware that this offer was probably a slip because he knew that Cecil had already refused an offer of £2,000, and in fact Cecil wished to offer the property at £2,250. Webster accepted the offer and sued for specific performance of the contract. The court refused to grant the decree.

139. Couturier *v.* Hastie (1856), 5 H.L.C. 673

Messrs. Hastie dispatched a cargo of corn from Salonica and sent the charter-party and bill of lading to their London agents so that the corn might be sold. The London agents employed Couturier to sell the corn and a person named Callander bought it. Unknown to the parties the cargo had become over-heated, and had been landed at the nearest port and sold, so that when the contract was made the corn was not really in existence. Callander repudiated the contract and Couturier was sued because he was a *del credere* agent, i.e. an agent who, for an extra commission, undertakes to indemnify his principal against losses arising out of the repudiation of the contract by any third party introduced by him. *Held*—The claim against Couturier failed because the contract presupposed that the goods were in existence when they were sold to Callander.

140. McRae *v.* The Commonwealth Disposals Commission, [1951] Argus L.R. 771

The defendants had invited tenders for the purchase of a tanker, said to be lying on the Jourmand Reef off Papua, together with the oil it was said to contain. The plaintiff submitted a tender of £285 which the defendants accepted. The plaintiff went to considerable trouble and expense to modify a ship which he owned for salvage work, and also bought equipment and engaged a crew. In fact there was no tanker anywhere near the latitude and longitude given by the defendants, and there was no such place as the Jourmand Reef. The plaintiff sued for damages for breach of contract. The High Court of Australia *held* that the plaintiff succeeded because the defendants had impliedly warranted that the goods existed. The court distinguished *Couturier* v. *Hastie* (1856)[139] on the ground that in that case the goods had existed but had perished whereas in the present case the goods had never existed at all.

N.B. The implied term solution is not too sound because when the court implies a term it generally does so on the ground that the parties would have included it had they addressed themselves to the matter. It is by no means certain in this case that the defendants would have agreed to such a term. However, there would now be a possible solution in tort if the plaintiff chose to sue in negligence because since the decision of the House of Lords in *Hedley Byrne* v. *Heller and Partners* (1963),[165] it would appear that there is a liability for careless misstatements resulting in monetary loss.

141. Cochrane *v.* Willis (1865), 1 Ch. App. 58

Cochrane was the trustee in bankruptcy of Joseph Willis who was the tenant for life of certain estates in Lancaster. Joseph Willis had been adjudicated bankrupt in Calcutta where he resided. The remainder of the estate was to go to Daniel Willis, the brother of Joseph, on the latter's death, with eventual remainder to Henry Willis, the son of Daniel. Joseph Willis had the right to cut the timber on the estates during his life interest, and the representative of Cochrane in England threatened to cut and sell it for the benefit of Joseph's creditors. Daniel and Henry wished to preserve the timber and so they agreed with Cochrane through his representatives to pay the value of the timber to Cochrane if he would refrain from cutting it. News then reached England that when the above agreement was made Joseph was dead, and therefore the life interest had vested in Daniel. In this action by the trustee to enforce the agreement it was *held* that Daniel was making a contract to preserve something which was already his and the Court found, applying the doctrine of *res sua*, that the agreement was void for an identical or common mistake.

142. Bell *v.* Lever Bros. Ltd., [1932] A.C. 161

Lever Bros. had a controlling interest in the Niger Company. Bell was the chairman, and a person called Snelling was the vice-chairman, of the Niger Company's Board. Both directors had service contracts which had some time to run. They became redundant as a result of amalgamations and Lever Bros. contracted to pay Bell £30,000 and Snelling £20,000 as compensation. These sums were paid over and then it was discovered that Bell and Snelling had committed breaches of duty during their term of office by making secret profits on a cocoa pooling scheme. They could, therefore, have been dismissed without compensation. Lever Bros. sought to set aside the payments on the ground of mistake. *Held*—The contract was not void because Lever Bros. had got what they bargained for, i.e. the cancellation of two service contracts which, though they might have been terminated, were actually in existence when the cancellation agreement was made. The mistake was as to the quality of the two directors and such mistakes do not avoid contracts.

N.B. The case also illustrates that the contract of service is not of utmost good faith. A servant is not bound to disclose his wrongdoing to his master, so that the silence of the two directors did not amount to a misrepresentation which could assist Lever Bros. in the setting aside of the agreement.

143. Leaf v. International Galleries, [1950] 2 K.B. 86

In 1944 the plaintiff bought from the defendants a drawing of Salisbury Cathedral for £85. The defendants said that the drawing was by Constable. Five years later the plaintiff tried to sell the drawing and was told that this was not so. He now sued for rescission of the contract. The decision in the county court was that rescission could not be granted because the representation was innocent and the contract had been executed. The appeal to the Court of Appeal was concerned with the question of the right to rescind; no claim for damages was made. The following points of interest emerged: (i) It was possible to restore the *status quo* by the mere exchange of the drawing and the purchase money so that rescission was not affected by inability to restore the previous position. (ii) The mistake made by the parties in assuming the drawing to be a Constable was a mistake as to quality and did not avoid the contract. (iii) The statement that the drawing was by Constable could have been treated as a warranty giving rise to a claim for damages, but it was not possible to award damages because the appeal was based on the plaintiff's right to rescind. (iv) The court, therefore, treated the statement as a representation and, finding it to be innocent, refused to rescind the contract because of the passage of time since the purchase. (v) Denning, L.J., criticised the rule in *Seddon* v. *North Eastern Salt Company*[171] and suggested that rescission was not always lost merely because the contract was executed. Evershed, M.R., whilst not suggesting that *Seddon* v. *North Eastern Salt Company* was good law, thought that it ought not to be lightly disregarded because it had stood as law since 1905.

Note the effect that the Misrepresentation Act, 1967, would have on certain parts of this decision. (See p. 41.)

144. Jones v. Clifford (1876), 3 Ch.D. 779

Clifford agreed to buy from Jones some freehold and leasehold land, thinking that Jones was the owner. Before Clifford actually completed the contract, he entered into an agreement with a sub-purchaser for the sale of the property. The sub-purchaser discovered, whilst searching the title, that Clifford was in fact the true owner of the property, having derived his title from a conveyance to one of his ancestors in 1781. Clifford, on learning this, refused to complete, and Jones now sued for specific performance. *Held*—Specific performance would not be granted because the contract was affected by an identical bilateral or common mistake. The court also ordered an investigation into the title.

145. Magee v. Pennine Insurance Co. Ltd., [1969] 2 All E.R. 891

In 1961 the plaintiff, a man of 58, acquired an Austin car. He also signed a proposal form for insurance in which he said that the car belonged to him. He was asked to give details of his driving licence and of all other persons who, to his present knowledge, would drive the car. He gave the necessary details to a Mr. Atkinson at the garage where he bought the car and it appeared that Mr. Atkinson did not write them down correctly on the proposal form. However, the details given were that the vehicle would be driven by the plaintiff as a provisional licence holder, his elder son, who had an annual licence, and his younger son John, aged 18, who was shown as a provisional licence holder. In fact the plaintiff had never held a licence, not even a provisional one. Thus, although the trial judge later found that the plaintiff was not fraudulent, a misrepresentation had been made and on the faith of it being true the defendants granted an insurance policy to the plaintiff. The plaintiff was also required by the defendants to sign the following declaration—

> "I do hereby declare that the Car described is and shall be kept in good condition and that the answers above given are in every respect true and correct and I hereby agree that this Declaration shall be the basis of the Contract of Insurance between the Company and myself."

This normally has the effect of making all the statements in the proposal form conditions of the contract. (See *Dawsons Ltd.* v. *Bonnin*, 1922.)[609]

The policy was renewed each year and the premiums paid, and in 1964 the car was replaced by another. The policy was renewed for the new car without anything further being said about the drivers or the ownership. At 4 a.m. on 25th April, 1965, John Magee was driving the new car when he ran into a shop window. The plate glass was smashed and the car was a complete wreck. The insurance company sent an engineer to look at the car and he pronounced it a write-off, whereupon the insurers offered to pay the plaintiff £385 and this offer was accepted by him. Afterwards the insurance company made further enquiries and on discovering that the statements in the proposal form of 1961 were untrue refused to pay. The plaintiff then sued the insurers and was given judgment for £385 in the County Court. The insurers appealed to the Court of Appeal where it was *held* in allowing the appeal—

(i) (*per* Lord Denning, M.R.) that although the acceptance by the plaintiff of the insurance company's offer constituted a contract of compromise that contract was made under circumstances of common mistake which rendered the contract voidable in equity. (*Solle* v. *Butcher*, 1950,[127] applied.)

(ii) (*per* Fenton Atkinson, L.J.—referring to the misapprehension as a mutual mistake) that on the basis of certain statements in *Bell* v. *Lever Bros.*, 1932,[142] the contract could be avoided at common law, where, as in this case, the misapprehension was on a fundamental matter.

N.B. Lord Denning, M.R. and Winn, L.J. did not take this view of the decision in *Bell* v. *Lever Bros.*, 1932.[142]

(iii) (*per* Winn, L.J., dissenting) that following *Bell* v. *Lever Bros.*, 1932,[142] the contract was binding on the insurers. No reference was made by Winn, L.J., to *Solle* v. *Butcher*, 1950.[127]

146. Grist *v.* Bailey, [1966] 2 All E.R. 875

In September, 1954, the defendant agreed to sell to the plaintiff a freehold dwelling house for £850 "subject to the existing tenancy." Both parties believed at that time that the property was occupied by a tenant who was protected by the Rent Acts. In fact both the tenant and her husband had died before the contract was made and since the rent had always been paid to the vendor's agent he was not aware of the true position. The house was occupied by the son of the former tenant, but he was not protected by the Rent Acts and gave up possession. The plaintiff sought specific performance of the contract of sale and the defendant asked for rescission. *Held*—by Goff, J.—applying the dictum of Denning, L.J., in *Solle* v. *Butcher*, 1950,[127]—there was a jurisdiction in Equity to set aside an agreement for common mistake of a fundamental fact. Had the defendant known the true state of affairs she would not have agreed to sell at such a low price. However, being a case of equitable relief it could be granted unconditionally or on terms, and a term offered by the defendant was imposed, i.e. that, if required, she would enter into a fresh contract with the plaintiff at a proper price for vacant possession.

147. Joscelyne v. Nissen, [1970] 2 W.L.R. 509

The plaintiff, Mr. Joscelyne, sought rectification of a written contract made on 18th June, 1964, under which he had made over his car hire business to his daughter, Mrs. Margaret Nissen. It had been expressly agreed that in return for the car hire business Mrs. Nissen would pay certain expenses including gas, electricity and coal bills but the agreement on these matters was not expressly incorporated in the written contract.

Mrs. Nissen failed to pay the bills and the plaintiff brought an action in the Edmonton County Court claiming amongst other things a declaration that Mrs. Nissen should pay the gas, electricity and coal bills and alternatively that the written agreement of 18th June, 1964, should be rectified to include a provision to that effect. The county court judge allowed the claim for rectification in view of his finding that there was no complete antecedent agreement between the parties on the issue of payment of the expenses. The Court of Appeal, after considering different expressions of judicial views upon what was required before a contractual instrument might be rectified by the court, *held* that the law did not require a complete antecedent concluded agreement, provided there was some outward expression of agreement between the contracting parties.

148. Frederick Rose (London) Ltd. v. William Pim & Co. Ltd., [1953] 2 Q.B. 450

The plaintiffs received an order from an Egyptian firm for feveroles (a type of horse bean). The plaintiffs did not know what was meant by feveroles and asked the defendants what they were and whether they could supply them. The defendants said that feveroles were horsebeans and that they could supply them, so the plaintiffs entered into a written agreement to buy horsebeans from the defendants which were then supplied to the Egyptian firm under the order. In fact there were three types of horsebeans: feves, feveroles and fevettes, and the plaintiffs had been supplied with feves, which were less valuable than feveroles. The plaintiffs were sued by the Egyptian firm and now wished to recover the damages they had had to pay from the defendants. In order to do so they had to obtain rectification of the written contract with the defendants in which the goods were described as "horsebeans." The word "horsebeans" had to be rectified to "feveroles," otherwise the defendants were not in breach.

Held—

(i) Rectification was not possible because the contract expressed what the parties had agreed to, i.e. to buy and sell horsebeans. Thus the supply of any of the three varieties would have amounted to fulfilment of the contract.

(ii) The plaintiffs might have rescinded for misrepresentation but they could not restore the *status quo*, having sold the beans.

(iii) The plaintiffs might have recovered damages for breach of warranty, but the statement that "feveroles are horsebeans and we can supply them" was oral, and warranties in a contract for the sale of goods of £10 and upwards had in 1953 to be evidenced in writing. (Sale of Goods Act, 1893, Sect. 4.) The plaintiff would now have a remedy under the Law Reform (Enforcement of Contracts) Act, 1954. (See p. 14.)

(iv) The defence of mistake was also raised, i.e. both buyer and seller thought that all horsebeans were feveroles. This was an identical bilateral or common mistake, but since it was not a case of *res extincta* or *res sua* it had no effect on the contract.

149. Henkel *v.* Pape (1870), L.R. 6 Ex. 7

The parties to this action had been negotiating for the sale of certain rifles. No contract was made but later the purchaser ordered three rifles by telegram. Owing to the telegraph clerk's negligence the message was transmitted as "the" rifles. From previous negotiations this was understood to mean fifty rifles and that number was dispatched. *Held*—there was no contract between the parties.

150. Wood *v.* Scarth (1858), 1 F. & F. 293

The plaintiff was suing for damages for breach of contract alleging that the defendant had entered into an agreement to grant the plaintiff a lease of a public house, but had refused to convey the property. It was shown in evidence that the defendant intended to offer the lease at a rent, and also to include a premium on taking up the lease of £500. The defendant had told his agent to make this clear to the plaintiff, but the agent had not mentioned it. After discussions with the agent the plaintiff wrote to the defendant proposing to take the lease "on the terms already agreed upon" to which the defendant replied accepting the proposal. There was a mutual or non-identical bilateral mistake. The defendant thought that he was agreeing to lease the premises for a rent plus a premium, and the plaintiff thought he was taking a lease for rental only because he did not know of the premium. The plaintiff had sued for specific performance in 1855, and the court in the exercise of its equitable jurisdiction had decided that specific performance could not be granted in view of the mistake, as to grant it would be unduly hard on the defendant. However, in this action the plaintiff sued at common law for damages, and damages were granted to him on the ground that in mutual or non-identical mistake the court may find the sense of the promise and regard a contract as having been made on these terms. Here it was quite reasonable for the plaintiff to suppose that there was no premium to be paid. Thus a contract came into being on the terms as understood by the plaintiff, and he was entitled to damages for breach of it.

151. Raffles *v.* Wichelaus (1864), 2 H. & C. 906

The defendants agreed to buy from the plaintiffs 125 bales of cotton to arrive "*ex Peerless* from Bombay." There were two ships called *Peerless* sailing from Bombay, one in October and one in December. The defendants thought they were buying the cotton on the ship sailing in October, and the plaintiffs meant to sell the cotton on the ship sailing in December. In fact the plaintiffs had no cotton on the ship sailing in October. The defendants refused to take delivery of the cotton when the second ship arrived and were now sued for breach of contract. *Held*—Since there was a mistake as to the subject matter of the contract there was in effect no contract between the parties.

152. Scriven Bros. & Co. *v.* Hindley & Co., [1913] 3 K.B. 564

An auctioneer was selling bales of tow and hemp. Hindley's agent bid £17 per ton for certain bales which had been put up for sale. The bid was about right for hemp but extravagant for tow. The auctioneer knew that the bales

were of tow but he accepted the bid. Hindley & Co. refused to take delivery of
the tow and were sued for breach of contract. *Held*—There was no contract
between the parties since there was no consensus; and there was no negligence
on the part of the agent in mistaking the lot offered, because the markings in
the catalogue were such that such a mistake might be made. In fact the ship
which had brought the tow normally brought hemp, and buyers were given to
assuming that all her cargo was hemp.

153. Tamplin *v.* James (1880), 15 Ch.D. 215

James purchased a public house at an auction sale. The property was
adequately described in the particulars of sale and by reference to a plan.
James thought he knew the property and did not bother to refer to the particulars. In fact a field which had been occupied by the publican, and which
James thought to be included in the sale, was held under a separate lease and
was not part of the lot offered. Tamplin sued for specific performance and
James raised this mistake as a defence. *Held*—Specific performance would be
granted. Although the parties were not at one on the question of the subject
matter, James had by his conduct raised an implication that he was prepared to
buy the property offered.

154. Edgington *v.* Fitzmaurice (1885), 29 Ch.D. 459

The plaintiff was induced to lend money to a company by representations
made by its directors that the money would be used to improve the company's
buildings and generally expand the business. In fact the directors intended to
use the money to pay off the company's existing debts as the creditors were
pressing hard for payment. When the plaintiff discovered that he had been
misled, he sued the directors for damages for fraud. The defence was that the
statement they had made was not a statement of a past or present fact but a
mere statement of intention which could not be the basis of an action for fraud.
Held—The directors were liable in deceit. Bowen, L.J., said: "There must be
a misstatement of an existing fact; but the state of a man's mind is as much a
fact as the state of his digestion. It is true that it is very difficult to prove what
the state of a man's mind at a particular time is, but if it can be ascertained, it
is as much a fact as anything else. A misrepresentation as to the state of a
man's mind is, therefore, a misstatement of fact."

155. Smith *v.* Land and House Property Corporation (1884), 28 Ch.D. 7

The plaintiffs put up for sale on 4th August, 1882, the Marine Hotel, Walton-
on-the-Naze, stating in the particulars that it was let to "Mr. Frederick Fleck
(a most desirable tenant) at a rental of £400 for an unexpired term of 27½
years." The directors of the defendant company sent the Secretary, Mr. Lewin,
to inspect the property and he reported that Fleck was not doing much business
and that the town seemed to be in the last stages of decay. The directors, on
receiving this report, directed Mr. Lewin to bid up to £5,000, and in fact he
bought the hotel for £4,700. Before completion Fleck became bankrupt and
the defendant company refused to complete the purchase, whereupon the
plaintiffs sued for specific performance. It was proved that on 1st May, 1882,
the March quarter's rent was wholly unpaid; that a distress was then threatened, and that Fleck paid £30 on 6th May, £40 on 13th June, and the remaining £30 shortly before the sale. No part of the June quarter's rent had
been paid. The chairman of the defendant company said that the hotel would

not have been purchased but for the statement in the particulars that Fleck was a most desirable tenant. *Held*—specific performance would not be granted. The description of Fleck as a most desirable tenant was not a mere expression of opinion, but contained an implied assertion that the vendors knew of no facts leading to the conclusion that he was not. The circumstances relating to the unpaid rent showed that Fleck was not a desirable tenant and there was a misrepresentation. Bowen, L.J., said—

> It is material to observe that it is often fallaciously assumed that a statement of opinion cannot involve the statement of a fact. In a case where the facts are equally well known to both parties, what one of them says to the other is frequently nothing but an expression of opinion. The statement of such opinion is in a sense a statement of a fact about the condition of the man's own mind, but only of an irrelevant fact, for it is of no consequence what the opinion is. But if the facts are not equally known to both sides, then a statement of opinion by the one who knows the facts best involves very often a statement of a material fact, for he impliedly states that he knows facts which justify his opinion.

156. Curtis *v.* Chemical Cleaning and Dyeing Co., [1951] 1 K.B. 805

The plaintiff took a wedding dress, with beads and sequins, to the defendant's shop for cleaning. She was asked to sign a receipt which contained the following clause: "The company is not liable for damage howsoever arising." The plaintiff asked what the effect of the document was, and the assistant told her that it exempted the company from liability in certain ways, and particularly that in her case she would have to take the risk of damage to beads and sequins. Thereupon the plaintiff signed the document without reading it. The dress was returned stained, and the plaintiff sued for damages. The company relied on the clause. *Held*—The company could not rely on the clause because the assistant had misrepresented the effect of the document so that the plaintiff was merely running the risk of damage to the beads and sequins.

156a. Mendelssohn v. Normand Ltd., [1969] 2 All E.R. 1215

The plaintiff left his car in the defendants' garage as he had done before. He was about to lock it as he had done on previous occasions when the attendant said that he could not do so. The plaintiff explained that there was a suitcase containing jewellery on the back seat and the attendant agreed to lock the car when he had moved it. He gave the plaintiff a ticket on the back of which was printed a statement that the proprietors would not "accept responsibility for any loss sustained . . . no variation of these conditions will bind the (proprietors) unless made in writing signed by their duly authorised manager." A conspicuous written notice at the reception desk exempted the defendants from loss or damage to the vehicle or its contents. When he returned the plaintiff found the car unlocked and the key in the ignition. It was later discovered that the suitcase had been stolen while the car was in the defendants' garage. In an action by the plaintiff for damages it was *held*—by the Court of Appeal—that—

(i) the notice at the reception desk was of no effect. It was not seen by a driver until he came to collect his car. The plaintiff had seen it before but had not read it;

(ii) the plaintiff must be taken to have agreed to the conditions on the ticket which were incorporated in the contract, but

(iii) the defendants could not rely on the ticket because—

   (a) the attendant had ostensible authority to promise to lock the car and thus to see that the contents were safe. This promise was repugnant to and took priority over the printed condition, and

   (b) the defendants through their employee agreed to keep the car locked but had left it unlocked so performing the contract in an entirely different way from the manner agreed. The defendants were therefore liable.

157. With v. O'Flanagan, [1936] Ch. 575

The defendant was a medical practitioner who wished to sell his practice. The plaintiff was interested and in January, 1934, the defendant represented to the plaintiff that the income from the practice was £2,000 a year. The contract was not signed until May, 1934, and in the meantime the defendant had been ill and the practice had been run by various other doctors as *locum tenentes*. In consequence the receipts fell to £5 per week, and no mention of this fact was made when the contract was entered into. The plaintiff now claimed rescission of the contract. *Held*—He could do so. The representation made in January was of a continuing nature and induced the contract made in May. The plaintiff had a right to be informed of a change in circumstances, and the defendant's silence amounted to a misrepresentation.

158. Tate v. Williamson (1866), 2 Ch. App. 55

An extravagant Oxford undergraduate who was being pressed for money by his creditors sought financial advice from Williamson who recommended the sale of the undergraduate's estate in Staffordshire. Williamson then offered to buy it himself for £7,000 without disclosing the existence of minerals under the land which made the undergraduate's interest worth at least £14,000. The offer was accepted and a conveyance executed but some years later the sale was set aside by the court at the instance of the undergraduate's heir. Williamson had been guilty of constructive fraud in that he had exploited to his own advantage the confidence placed in him.

159. Peek v. Gurney (1873), L.R. 6 H.L. 377

Peek purchased shares in a company on the faith of statements appearing in a prospectus issued by the respondents who were directors of the company. Certain of the statements were false and Peek sued the directors. It appeared that Peek was not an original allottee, but had purchased the shares on the market, though he had relied on the prospectus. *Held*—Peek's action failed because the statements in the prospectus were only intended to mislead the original allottees. Once the statements had induced the public to be original subscribers, their force was spent.

160. Gross v. Lewis Hillman Ltd. and Another, [1969] 3 All E.R. 1476

Mrs. Gross instructed property dealers Grace Rymer Investments to find a suitable shop for her to purchase as an investment. Lewis Hillman Ltd. owned a shop which they had leased and Henry James and Partners had been instructed to sell the shop. Lewis Hillman Ltd. was controlled by a Mr. Edward James who also controlled the firm of Henry James and Partners. Edward James had arranged to let the shop to a dormant wool company, H. G. Somers & Sons Ltd., whose shares had recently been bought by two brothers planning to set up a chain of wool shops. Henry James and Partners introduced the shop to Grace Rymer by two letters, the first of which said that the shop had been let to H. G. Somers & Sons Ltd. on a 21 years' full repairing and insuring lease of £800 p.a. exclusively for the sale of wool and hosiery and that the company had branches in Liverpool, Blackpool and Southport. Grace Rymer asked for tenants' references and in a second letter Henry James and Partners replied that H. G. Somers & Sons Ltd. was incorporated in 1928, had a paid up capital of £5,000 and enclosed a banker's reference relating to the letting of another shop to H. G. Somers & Sons Ltd. at a rent of £3,000 p.a.

Grace Rymer, believing as a result of the letters that H. G. Somers was a going concern, agreed to purchase the shop on its own behalf and recommended Mrs. Gross to purchase it offering to let her have the benefit of Grace Rymer's contract for a commission of 2¼% of the purchase price. Mrs. Gross purchased the shop and it was conveyed directly by Lewis Hillman Ltd. to whom she paid the purchase price at the request of Grace Rymer. Three months later H. G. Somers & Sons Ltd. became insolvent and went into liquidation. In an action by Mrs. Gross against Lewis Hillman Ltd. to rescind the conveyance and against both Lewis Hillman Ltd. and Henry James & Partners for damages for deceit on the ground of fraudulent misrepresentation Mrs. Gross relied upon the representations in the two letters relating to the status of H. G. Somers & Sons Ltd. *Held*—by the Court of Appeal—that although the letters if read together might have amounted to fraudulent misrepresentation the trial judge had acquitted Edward James of any intention to deceive and the court would not interfere with that finding, not having seen or heard James. Neither would the court order a new trial since even if there was a fraudulent misrepresentation Mrs. Gross could not rescind the contract on the strength of it. The right to rescind for misrepresentation was not an equity which ran with the land and any misrepresentation to Mrs. Gross was spent when her agents, Grace Rymer, bought the property on their own behalf prior to selling it to her. Had Grace Rymer remained her agents throughout the transaction the misrepresentations made to them as agents would have been in effect made to Mrs. Gross who could have then rescinded the contract.

161. Redgrave *v.* Hurd (1881), 20 Ch.D. 1

The plaintiff was a solicitor who wished to take a partner into the business. During negotiations between the plaintiff and Hurd the plaintiff stated that the income of the business was £300 a year. The papers which the plaintiff produced showed that the income was not quite £200 a year, and Hurd asked about the balance. Redgrave then produced further papers which he said showed how the balance was made up, but which only showed a very small amount of income making the total income up to about £200. Hurd did not examine these papers in any detail, but agreed to become a partner. Later Hurd discovered the true position and refused to complete the contract. The plaintiff sued for breach and Hurd raised the misrepresentation as a defence, and also counterclaimed for rescission of the contract. *Held*—Hurd had relied on Redgrave's statements regarding the income and the contract could be rescinded. It did not matter that Hurd had the means of discovering their untruth; he was entitled to rely on Redgrave's statement.

162. Smith *v.* Chadwick (1884), 9 App. Cas. 187

This action was brought by the plaintiff, who was a steel manufacturer, against Messrs. Chadwick, Adamson and Collier, who were accountants and promoters of a company called the Blochairn Iron Co. Ltd. The plaintiff claimed £5,750 as damages sustained through taking shares in the company which were not worth the price he had paid for them because of certain mis-representations in the prospectus issued by the defendants. The action was for fraud. Among the misrepresentations alleged by Smith was that the prospectus stated that a Mr. J. J. Grieves, M.P., was a director of the company, whereas he had withdrawn his consent the day before the prospectus was issued. It was *held* that the statement regarding Mr. Grieves was untrue but was not material to the plaintiff, because the evidence showed that he had never heard of Mr. Grieves. His action for damages failed.

163. Horsfall *v.* Thomas (1862), 1 H. & C. 90

Thomas asked Horsfall to make him a gun and agreed to pay for it by means of two bills of exchange. Horsfall made the gun, and at the third trial by Thomas the gun flew to pieces. Evidence showed that the breech was defective and that a plug of metal had been driven into the breech to conceal the defect. Horsfall sued on one of the bills and Thomas pleaded fraud. *Held*—Horsfall succeeded and the defence failed because it appeared that Thomas had never inspected the gun so that any attempt to conceal the defect could not have had any operation on his mind. Even if the plug had not been put into the breech the defendant's position would have been the same.

164. Derry *v.* Peek (1889), 14 App. Cas. 337

The Plymouth, Devonport and District Tramways Company had power under a special Act of Parliament to run trams by animal power, and with the consent of the Board of Trade by mechanical or steam power. Derry and the other appellants were directors of the company and issued a prospectus, inviting the public to apply for shares in it, stating that they had power to run trams by steam power, and claiming that considerable economies would result. The directors had assumed that the permission of the Board of Trade would be granted as a matter of course, but in the event the Board of Trade refused per-mission except for certain parts of the tramway. As a result the company was wound up and the directors were sued for fraud. The court *decided* that the directors were not fraudulent but honestly believed the statement in the pros-pectus to be true.

N.B. This case gave rise to the Directors' Liability Act, 1890, now Sect. 43 of the Companies Act, 1948, which makes directors liable to pay compensation for misrepresentation in a prospectus, subject to a number of defences.

165. Hedley Byrne & Co. Ltd. *v.* Heller & Partners Ltd., [1963] 2 All E.R. 575

The appellants were advertising agents and the respondents were merchant bankers. The appellants had a client called Easipower Ltd. who were customers of the respondents. The appellants had contracted to place orders for advertis-ing Easipower's products on television and in newspapers, and since this involved giving Easipower credit, they asked the respondents, who were Easipower's bankers, for a reference as to the creditworthiness of Easipower. The respondents said that Easipower Ltd. was respectably constituted and considered good, though they said that the statement was made without responsibility on their part. Relying on this reply, the appellants placed orders for advertising time and space for Easipower Ltd., and the appellants assumed personal responsibility for payment to the television and newspaper companies concerned. Easipower Ltd. went into liquidation, and the appellants lost over £17,000 on the advertising contracts. The appellants sued the respondents for the amount of the loss, alleging that the respondents had not informed themselves sufficiently about Easipower Ltd. before writing the statement, and were therefore liable in negligence. *Held*—In the present case the respondents' disclaimer was adequate to exclude the assumption by them of the legal duty of care, but, in the absence of the disclaimer, the circumstances would have given rise to a duty of care in spite of the absence of a contract or fiduciary relationship. The dissenting judgment of Denning, L.J., in *Candler* v. *Crane, Christmas*, 1951, 1 All E.R. 426 was approved, and the majority judgment in that case was disapproved.

166. Doyle *v.* Olby (Ironmongers) Ltd., and Others, [1969] 2 All E.R. 119

In 1963 the plaintiff wished to buy a business. He saw an advertisement in Dalton's Weekly and obtained particulars of an ironmonger's business in Epsom belonging to the first defendants. The price asked for the lease, the business and goodwill was £4,500 the stock to be taken at valuation. In 1964, after negotiations with various members of the Olby family the plaintiff purchased the business paying £4,500 covering goodwill and fixtures and fittings, and £5,000 for the stock. He also needed a longer lease and so surrendered the existing lease taking on a longer one at an increased rent. The owner of the shop who benefited from this transaction was another of the Olby family. In order to pay the money the plaintiff put up all the cash he had, i.e. £7,000 and borrowed £3,000 on mortgage. When he went into occupation he discovered that the defendants had made a number of false statements relating to the business. In particular the plaintiff discovered that half the trade was wholesale which could only be obtained by employing a traveller to go round to the customers. The plaintiff could not afford to employ a traveller and all the wholesale trade was lost. The second defendant had told the plaintiff in the course of negotiations that all the trade was over the counter.

The plaintiff was most dissatisfied and in May, 1964, he brought an action for damages for fraud and conspiracy against Olby (Ironmongers) Ltd. and several members of the Olby family who had been involved in the sale of the Epsom business. At the trial the judge awarded damages on a contractual basis as if the statement "the trade is all over the counter. There is no need to employ a traveller" had been a term of the contract. In consequence the judge accepted that the proper measure of foreseeable damage was, in accordance with *Hadley* v. *Baxendale*, 1854,[305] the reduction in the value of goodwill due to the misstatement. The goodwill was valued at £4,000 and since 50% of the turnover was wholesale, goodwill would have been reduced by 35% to 40% giving £1,500 as a round figure for damages.

In the Court of Appeal Lord Denning, M.R., said on this point: "On principle the distinction seems to be this: in contract, the defendant has made a promise and broken it. The object of damages is to put the plaintiff in as good a position, as far as money can do it, as if the promise had been performed. In fraud, the defendant has been guilty of a deliberate wrong by inducing the plaintiff to act to his detriment. The object of damages is to compensate the plaintiff for all the loss he has suffered, so far, again, as money can do it. In contract, the damages are limited to what may reasonably be supposed to have been in the contemplation of the parties. In fraud, they are not so limited.

The defendant is bound to make reparation for all the actual damage directly flowing from the fraudulent inducement. The person who has been defrauded is entitled to say: 'I would not have entered into this bargain at all but for your representation. Owing to your fraud, I have not only lost all the money I have paid you, but what is more, I have been put to a large amount of extra expense as well and suffered this or that extra damages.' All such damages can be recovered: and it does not lie in the mouth of the fraudulent person to say that they could not reasonably have been foreseen. For instance, in this very case the plaintiff has not only lost the money which he paid for the business, which he would never had done if there had been no fraud; he put all that money in and lost it; but also he has been put to expense and loss in trying to run a business which has turned out to be a disaster for him. He is entitled to damages for all his loss, subject, of course, to giving credit for any benefit that he has received. There is nothing to be taken off in mitigation: for there is nothing more that he could have done to reduce his loss. He did all that he could reasonably be expected to do."

Accordingly damages were assessed by the Court of Appeal at £5,500 being made up as follows—

Cost of acquiring business		£4,500
Cost of acquiring stock		5,000
		9,500

Less:	Cash received by Doyle when business sold in 1967	£3,500	
	Cash received on sale of stock	800	
	Value of living accommodation during the three years	2,500	
			7,000 (as a round figure)
	Loss		2,500
	Additional damages for strain and worry and interest on loans and bank overdraft		3,000
	Damages awarded		£5,500

167. Mafo v. Adams, [1969] 3 All E.R. 1404

In July, 1965, the plaintiff, a Nigerian, was granted a weekly tenancy in Richmond by the defendant, a West Indian. On 10th December, 1965, the defendant gave the plaintiff notice to quit though the plaintiff appeared to have been a good tenant. The plaintiff then claimed the benefit of the Rent Acts and refused to leave. On 15th February, 1966, the plaintiff was invited to see alternative accommodation at Norbury and saw a lady who posed as Mrs. Williams. The plaintiff arranged to move into the accommodation at Norbury and paid Mrs. Williams £6 10s. od. representing two weeks' rent in advance, though the cheque was never cashed. The plaintiff and his pregnant wife then left the Richmond tenancy but were unable to obtain entry to the Norbury accommodation. It later emerged that Mrs. Williams was in fact Adams' wife, from whom he was separated, and that he and she had combined in a piece of trickery to get the plaintiff out of the Richmond tenancy. The plaintiff was unable to resume the possession of the Richmond accommodation and subsequently suffered physical inconvenience but no financial damage although it appeared that the accommodation he found was unlikely to be as securely protected by the Rent Acts as the Richmond flat had been. On appeal by the landlord from an award to the tenant of £100 for breach of covenant of quiet enjoyment and £100 exemplary damages for deceit it was *held*—by the Court of Appeal—that—

(i) £100 was a proper figure for compensatory damages;

(ii) Lord Devlin's statements in *Rookes* v. *Barnard*, [1964] 1 All E.R. 367 at p. 411, that "Exemplary damages can properly be awarded whenever it is necessary to teach a wrongdoer that tort does not pay" might well have extended the number of cases in which exemplary damages could potentially be awarded. However, assuming that exemplary damages could be awarded in an action for deceit, the plaintiff was not entitled to them because there was no finding that the landlord had acted in such a way as to bring himself within Lord Devlin's statement. Exemplary damages are in the main to be awarded in cases where the defendant realises that he is breaking the law, and that damages may be awarded against him, but nevertheless makes what has been described as a cynical calculation of profit and loss and says that he will flout the powers of the court because on a purely cash basis he can show a profit. Where exemplary damages were claimed the court must be careful to see that the case for punishment was as well established as in other penal proceedings. The plaintiff was not therefore entitled to exemplary damages.

168. Car & Universal Finance Co. Ltd. *v.* Caldwell, [1963] 2 All E.R. 547

On 12th January, 1960, Mr. Caldwell sold a motor car to a firm called Dunn's Transport, receiving a cheque signed "for and on behalf of Dunn's Transport, W. Foster, F. Norris." Caldwell presented the cheque to the bank but it was dishonoured, and so he went to see the police and asked them to recover the car. He also saw officials of the Automobile Association and asked them to trace the car by their patrols. The car was found on 20th January, 1960, in the possession of a director of a firm of car dealers called Motobella & Co. Ltd. The company claimed to have bought it on 15th January from Norris and to have a good title. On 29th January, the defendant's solicitors demanded the car from Motobella and at the same time Norris was arrested and pleaded guilty to obtaining the car by false pretences. The defendant sued Motobella & Co. Ltd. for the return of the car and obtained judgment, but when he tried to repossess the car, a finance house, Car & Universal Finance Co. Ltd., claimed that it belonged to them. It appeared that Motobella had transferred the ownership to a finance house called G. & C. Finance on 15th January, 1960, and they had transferred it to the plaintiffs on 3rd August, 1960, the latter company taking the vehicle in good faith. In this action the plaintiffs claimed the car. It was *held* that Caldwell was entitled to it because, amongst other things, he had avoided the contract of sale to Norris when he asked the police to get the car back for him so that later sales of the car to Motobella and to G. & C. Finance did not pass the property.

N.B. This case is now of little practical importance since although it decides that a contract of sale induced by fraud can be rescinded without actually communicating with the fraudulent person, the third party can still keep the property by relying on Sect. 9 of the Factors Act, 1889, instead of Sect. 23 of the Sale of Goods Act, 1893. (See p. 151.)

169. Long *v.* Lloyd, [1958] 2 All E.R. 402

The plaintiff and the defendant were haulage contractors. The plaintiff was induced to buy the defendant's lorry by the defendant's misrepresentation as to condition and performance. The defendant advertised the lorry for sale at £850, the advertisement describing the vehicle as being in "exceptional condition." The plaintiff saw the lorry at the defendant's premises at Hampton Court on a Saturday. During a trial run on the following Monday the plaintiff found that the speedometer was not working, a spring was missing from the accelerator pedal, and it was difficult to engage top gear. The defendant said there was nothing wrong with the vehicle except what the plaintiff had found. He also said at this stage that the lorry would do 11 miles to the gallon.

The plaintiff purchased the lorry for £750, paying £375 down and agreeing to pay the balance at a later date. He then drove the lorry from Hampton Court to his place of business at Sevenoaks. On the following Wednesday, the plaintiff drove from Sevenoaks to Rochester to pick up a load, and during that journey the dynamo ceased to function, an oil seal was leaking badly, there was a crack in one of the road wheels, and he used 8 gallons of petrol on a journey of 40 miles. That evening the plaintiff told the defendant of the defects, and the defendant offered to pay half the cost of a reconstructed dynamo, but denied any knowledge of the other defects. The plaintiff accepted the offer and the dynamo was fitted straight away. On Thursday the lorry was driven by the plaintiff's brother to Middlesbrough, and it broke down on the Friday night. The plaintiff, on learning of this, asked the defendant for his money back, but the defendant would not give it to him. The lorry was subsequently examined and an expert said that it was not roadworthy. The plaintiff sued for rescission. *Held*—at first instance, by Glyn-Jones, J.—that the defendant's statements about the lorry were innocent and not fraudulent because the evidence showed that the lorry had been laid up for a month and it might therefore have deteriorated without the defendant's precise knowledge. The Court of Appeal affirmed this finding of fact and made the following additional points—

(i) The journey to Rochester was not affirmation because the plaintiff was merely testing the vehicle in a working capacity.

(ii) However, the acceptance by the plaintiff of the defendant's offer to pay half the cost of the reconstructed dynamo, and the subsequent journey to Middlesbrough, did amount to affirmation and rescission could not be granted to the plaintiff.

The Court was non-committal on the validity of the decision in *Seddon* v. *North Eastern Salt Co.* (1905)[171] and *Angel* v. *Jay* (1911)[172] which were relevant since the contract had been executed. However, it was said in the judgments that if the plaintiff's action was not barred by the decisions in these two cases, there was affirmation, and it was on the ground of affirmation that rescission was not granted. Presumably the Court would not treat the defendant's statements as warranties because he was not a dealer in lorries but merely a user.

N.B. Damages could now be obtained for negligent misrepresentation under the Misrepresentation Act, 1967, Sect. 2(i), for how could the seller say he had reasonable grounds for believing that the lorry was in first-class condition?

170. Clarke v. Dickson (1858), E.B. & E. 148

In 1853 the plaintiff was induced by the misrepresentation of the three defendants, Dickson, Williams and Gibbs, to invest money in what was in effect a partnership to work lead mines in Wales. In 1857 the partnership was in financial difficulty and with the plaintiff's assent it was converted into a limited company and the partnership capital was converted into shares.

Shortly afterwards the company commenced winding-up proceedings and the plaintiff, on discovery of the falsity of the representations, asked for rescission of the contract. *Held*—Rescission could not be granted because capital in a partnership is not the same as shares in a company. The firm was no longer in existence, having been replaced by the company, and it was not possible to restore the parties to their original positions.

N.B. It should be noted that in addition to the problem of restoration, third-party rights, i.e. creditors, had accrued on the winding up of the company and this is a further bar to rescission.

171. Seddon *v.* North Eastern Salt Co. Ltd., [1905] 1 Ch. 326

The plaintiff agreed to purchase certain company shares from the defendants. The shares were transferred to him in October, 1903. It emerged that the defendants had misled him as to certain losses made by the company, though there was no suggestion of fraud. The plaintiff retained the shares until January, 1904, and then asked for rescission of the contract. *Held*—The contract to take the shares had been executed and in the absence of fraud it could not be rescinded. (See now Sect. 1 (*b*) Misrepresentation Act, 1967.)

172. Angel *v.* Jay, [1911] 1 K.B. 666

The plaintiff agreed to take a lease of a dwelling house from the defendant, the lease to be for three years. During the negotiations the defendant innocently misrepresented that the drains were in good order when in fact they were not. The plaintiff was in possession for six months and then brought this action for rescission of the contract. *Held*—The contract to take the lease having been executed, it could not be rescinded. (See now Sect. 1 (*b*) Misrepresentation Act, 1967.)

173. Henderson & Co. *v.* Williams, [1895] 1 Q.B. 521

The plaintiffs were sugar merchants at Hull. The defendant was a warehouseman at Hull and Goole. On 3rd June, 1894, a fraudulent person named Fletcher, posing as the agent of one Robinson, negotiated a purchase of sugar from Messrs. Grey & Co., who were Liverpool merchants. The sugar was lying in the defendant's warehouse at Goole, and Messrs. Grey & Co. sent a telegram and later a letter advising the defendant that the sugar was to be held to the order of Fletcher, and the defendant entered the order in his books. Robinson was a reputable dealer and a customer of Messrs. Grey & Co., and of course Fletcher had no right to act on Robinson's behalf. Fletcher sold the goods to the plaintiffs who, before paying the price, got a statement from the defendant that the goods were held to the order of Fletcher. The defendant later discovered Fletcher's fraud and refused to release the sugar to the plaintiffs who now sued in conversion. *Held*—The defendant was estopped from denying Fletcher's title and was liable in damages based on the market price of the goods at the date of refusal to deliver. Further the true owners, Messrs. Grey & Co., could not set up their title to the sugar against that of the plaintiffs, since they had allowed Fletcher to hold himself out as the true owner.

174. Whittington *v.* Seale-Hayne (1900), 82 L.T. 49

The plaintiffs were breeders of prize poultry and they took a lease of the defendant's premises. The defendant misrepresented, though not fraudulently, that the premises were in a sanitary condition but in fact the water supply was poisoned, and this caused the illness of the plaintiff's manager. In addition, certain of their poultry died or became valueless for breeding purposes. The local authority required the plaintiffs to carry out certain work in order to render the premises sanitary, the plaintiffs having agreed in the lease to do such work if it became necessary. The plaintiffs now asked for rescission of the contract and for an indemnity against the following losses: Stock lost, £750; loss of profit on sales, £100; loss of breeding season, £500; removal of stores and rent, £75; medical expenses, £100. *Held*—The lease could be rescinded, but the plaintiffs' indemnity was restricted to the losses necessarily incurred by taking a lease of the premises, i.e. rent, rates and the cost of the repairs ordered by the local authority.

N.B. The reason for restricting the indemnity in this sort of case seems to be based on the fact that although Equity is prepared to rescind contracts for innocent misrepresentation, thus providing a remedy where the common law does not, Equity will not circumvent the law by making an indemnity (the object of which is to help restore the *status quo*) the equivalent of damages for fraud. (See now Sect. 2 (1) of the Misrepresentation Act, 1967, which might have provided a remedy of damages for negligent misrepresentation.)

175. Pym *v.* Campbell (1856), 6 E. & B. 370

An agreement for the sale of a patent was drawn up and signed. It was also agreed at the time that the written agreement was not to be binding unless a third party approved of the invention. In an action on the written agreement evidence was admitted to show that the third party had not approved and therefore the agreement was not effective.

176. Quickmaid Rental Services Ltd. *v.* Reece, (1970), *The Times*, 22nd April, 1970

In 1967 a salesman named Burbridge persuaded Mr. Reece to install on his service station premises in Ashton New Road, Manchester, a Quickmaid machine which supplied coffee, tea and other beverages to travellers who put coins into a slot. Mr. Reece was asked to sign two written agreements, one for the machine itself and the other for a canopy. The agreements were to last for five years. Mr. Reece paid £37 10s. down for the machine and was to pay monthly rentals thereafter. Before Mr. Reece agreed to or signed anything Mr. Burbridge made an important statement to him. He said that he would not install any other such machine in Ashton New Road. That stipulation induced Mr. Reece to sign the documents. Mr. Burbridge realised that any other machine would affect Mr. Reece's business considerably and later he made a memorandum saying he would not sell any more machines in that particular road.

However, in May, 1968, Mr. Reece discovered that the company, through another salesman, had, in January, 1968, installed a machine at premises further up the road. The second machine was in a more advantageous position in terms of custom. On discovering these facts Mr. Reece, who had had mechanical trouble with his machine, stopped his banker's order for the rental. The company thereupon sued Mr. Reece in the County Court for £73 15s., being the instalments from June to October, 1968. *Held*—by the Court of Appeal—that the company's claim failed. The proper way to approach the case was to regard it as a contract made partly in writing by the signed documents and partly by word of mouth, by what was said at the time.

The stipulation relating to other machines in the road was most important; it was a term which amounted to a condition. When it was broken it was broken in a manner which went to the root of the contract. It destroyed the profitable basis of the contract. Breach of that condition gave Mr. Reece the right to say he would no longer go on; nor on the evidence did he affirm the contract after discovering the breach. (*per* Lord Denning, M.R.) The appeal was dismissed.

177. Bannerman *v.* White (1861), 10 C.B.(N.S.) 844

The defendant was intending to buy hops from the plaintiff and he asked the plaintiff whether sulphur had been used in the cultivation of the hops, adding that if it had he would not even bother to ask the price. The plaintiff said that no sulphur had been used, though in fact it had. It was *held* that the plaintiff's assurance that sulphur had not been used was a term of the contract and the defendant was justified in raising the matter as a defence to an action for the price.

178. Oscar Chess Ltd. *v.* Williams, [1957] 1 W.L.R. 370

In May, 1955, Williams bought a car from the plaintiffs on hire-purchase terms. The plaintiffs took Williams' Morris car in part exchange. Williams described the car as a 1948 model and produced the registration book, which showed that the car was first registered in April, 1948, and that there had been several owners since that time. Williams was allowed £290 on the Morris. Eight months later the plaintiffs discovered that the Morris car was a 1939 model, there being no change in appearance in the model between 1939 and 1948. The allowance for a 1939 model was £175 and the plaintiffs sued for £115 damages for breach of warranty that the car was a 1948 model. Evidence showed that some fraudulent person had altered the registration book but he could not be traced, and that Williams honestly believed that the car was a 1948 model. *Held*—The contract might have been set aside in equity for misrepresentation but the delay of eight months defeated this remedy. The mistake was a mistake of quality which did not avoid the contract at common law and in order to obtain damages the plaintiffs must prove a breach of warranty. The court was unable to find that Williams was in a position to give such a warranty, and suggested that the plaintiffs should have taken the engine and chassis number and written to the manufacturers, so using their superior knowledge to protect themselves in the matter. The plaintiffs were not entitled to any redress. Morris, L.J., dissented, holding that the statement that the car was a 1948 model was a fundamental condition.

179. D'Mello *v.* Loughborough College of Technology, (1970), *The Times,* June 17th, 1970

In 1961 the college advertised a one-year postgraduate course in economics and administration in the oil industry. The plaintiff, who was then working for an oil company in India, saw the advertisement and wrote asking for further details. The college sent him a prospectus containing a syllabus of the course and a college calendar for 1961/62 and 1962/63 together with an application form. In due course the college accepted him for the course and in September, 1963, he joined four other students who had already begun their studies. All the other students completed the course but D'Mello gave up early in 1964 because he said that the course was different from the one in the prospectus and in particular did not have sufficient relevance to the oil industry. He now claimed damages for breach of contract. *Held*—by O'Connor, J.—that the prospectus was part of the contract but the plaintiff failed in that he had not shown that the college was in breach of it. It was a matter for the College authorities to decide as a matter of skill and judgment how to conduct the course and there was no evidence to show that they were in breach of their duty to the plaintiff in this regard.

180. De Lassalle *v.* Guildford, [1901] 2 K.B. 215

A person who was intending to take a lease of a house refused to execute the lease unless the lessor would first give him an assurance that the drains were in good condition. The lessor gave this undertaking and the lessee signed the lease, though the lessor's assurance regarding the drains was not incorporated in it. Even so *the lessor was held liable* when the drains were found to be out of order on the grounds that he was in breach of a collateral contract.

181. Shanklin Pier, Ltd. *v.* Detel Products, Ltd., [1951] 2 All E.R. 471

The plaintiffs owned a pier and made a contract with a firm to have the pier repainted with bituminous paint. A director of the defendant company went to Shanklin and persuaded the plaintiffs to use paint, called D.M.U., made by the defendant company. The director assured the plaintiffs that D.M.U. would have a life of at least seven to ten years. The plaintiffs then approached the contractors who were to do the work and the specification regarding the type of paint to be used was altered and D.M.U. substituted. The contractors applied D.M.U. to the pier but it was unsatisfactory and lasted about three months. The plaintiffs sued the defendants for breach of warranty that the paint would last at least seven to ten years. Judgment was given for the plaintiffs by McNair, J., who said "Counsel for the defendants submitted that in law a warranty could give rise to no enforceable course of action except between the same parties as the parties to the main contract in relation to which the warranty was given. In principle, this submission seems to me to be unsound. If, as is elementary, the consideration for the warranty in the usual case is the entering into of the main contract in relation to which the warranty is given, I see no reason why there may not be an enforceable warranty between A and B supported by the consideration that B should cause C to enter into a contract with A or that B should do some other act for the benefit of A."

182. Harling *v.* Eddy, [1951] 2 K.B. 739

The plaintiff purchased a heifer at an auction sale. The auction sale was subject to certain conditions which were printed in the catalogue issued to potential buyers. One of the conditions stated that no warranties were given regarding animals purchased unless such warranties appeared on the purchaser's account. When the heifer was brought into the ring, potential buyers showed little interest, and no bids were made until the auctioneer, with the authority of the owner, said: "There is nothing wrong with her. I will guarantee her in every respect and I will take her back if she is not what I say she is." The plaintiff thereupon purchased the animal, no warranties being given on the account. The heifer gave little milk and died of tuberculosis four months after purchase. The plaintiff sued for damages and the defence was the exemption clause in the auctioneer's catalogue. *Held*—The plaintiff succeeded. The following points arise out of the judgment in the Court of Appeal—

(*a*) A statement that an animal is sound in every respect would *prima facie* have been no more than a warranty, but the auctioneer's statement that he would take the animal back implied a right in the purchaser to reject the animal, thus making the statement a condition and not a warranty so that the exemption clause was not effective to exclude it. However, since the plaintiff had sued for breach of warranty, it was necessary also to treat the statement of the auctioneer as a warranty in which case it was possible to take the view that the statement was not incorporated into the original contract but was a collateral contract. This conclusion could be reached by bearing in mind the initial silence which greeted the entry of the animal into the ring; and the fact that the bidding only began when the statement had been made suggested that the defendants were not contracting on the auction particulars but on the auctioneer's statement. (*per* Evershed, M.R.)

(*b*) Denning, L.J., proceeded on the assumption that the statement was a warranty and held that, even so, the exemption clause did not exclude it because "the party who is liable in law cannot escape liability by simply putting up a printed notice or using a printed catalogue containing exempting conditions. He must go further and show affirmatively that it is a contractual document and accepted as such by the party affected."

183. Behn *v.* Burness (1863), 3 B. & S. 751

A ship, the *Martaban,* was chartered to carry coal from Newport to Hong Kong. The charterparty described the ship as "now in the port of Amsterdam" whereas in fact the ship was at Niewdiep about 62 miles from Amsterdam. She was late in arriving at Newport and the charterers refused to load her. *Held*— The charterers were justified in their refusal. In a charterparty the situation of the ship when the charter was made was a term of great commercial importance and must be treated as a condition.

184. Poussard *v.* Spiers and Pond (1876), 1 Q.B.D. 410

Madame Poussard had entered into an agreement to play a part in an opera, the first performance to take place on 28th November, 1874. On 23rd November Madame Poussard was taken ill and was unable to appear until 4th December. The defendants had hired a substitute, and discovered that the only way in which they could secure a substitute to take Madame Poussard's place was to offer that person the complete engagement. This they had done, and they refused the services of Madame Poussard when she presented herself on 4th December. The plaintiff now sued for breach of contract. *Held*—The failure of Madame Poussard to perform the contract as from the first night was a breach of condition, and the defendants were within their rights in regarding the contract as discharged.

185. Bettini *v.* Gye (1876), 1 Q.B.D. 183

The plaintiff was an opera singer. The defendant was the director of the Royal Italian Opera in London. The plaintiff had agreed to sing in Great Britain in theatres, halls and drawing rooms for a period of time commencing on 30th March, 1875, and to be in London for rehearsals six days before the engagement began. The plaintiff was taken ill and arrived on 28th March, 1875, but the defendant would not accept the plaintiff's services, treating the contract as discharged. *Held*—The rehearsal clause was subsidiary to the main purposes of the contract, and its breach constituted a breach of warranty only.

The defendant had no right to treat the contract as discharged and must compensate the plaintiff, but he had a counterclaim for any damage he had suffered by the plaintiffs' late arrival.

186. Chapelton v. Barry Urban District Council, [1940] 1 K.B. 532

The plaintiff Chapelton wished to hire deck chairs and went to a pile owned by the defendants, behind which was a notice stating: Hire of chairs 2d. per session of three hours." The plaintiff took two chairs, paid for them, and received two tickets which he put into his pocket after merely glancing at them. One of the chairs collapsed and he was injured. A notice on the back of the ticket provided that "The council will not be liable for any accident or damage arising from hire of chairs." The plaintiff sued for damages and the council sought to rely on the clause in the ticket. *Held*—The clause was not binding on Chapelton. The board by the chairs made no attempt to limit the liability, and it was unreasonable to communicate conditions by means of a mere receipt.

187. Thompson v. L.M.S. Railway, [1930] 1 K.B. 41

Thompson, who could not read, asked her niece to buy her an excursion ticket, on the front of which were printed the words, "Excursion. For conditions see back." On the back was a notice that the ticket was issued subject to the conditions in the company's timetables, which excluded liability for injury however caused. Thompson was injured and claimed damages. *Held*—Her action failed. She had constructive notice of the conditions which had, in the court's view, been properly communicated to the ordinary passenger.

N.B. The Transport Act, 1962, provides that the British Railways Board shall not carry passengers by rail on conditions which purport directly or indirectly to exclude the Board's liability for the death of, or bodily injury to passengers except those travelling on a free pass. Thus, on its own facts, this case is of historical interest only, though still relevant on the question of constructive notice.

188. Richardson Steamship Company Ltd. v. Rowntree, [1894] A.C. 217

Rowntree booked a passage on the appellants' ship travelling from Philadelphia to Liverpool. The ticket was folded so that no writing was visible until it was opened. A clause printed on the ticket limited the appellants' liability for injury or damage to passengers or their luggage to $100. The clause was printed in rather small type and was rendered less obvious by a red ink stamp on the ticket. *Held*—Rowntree was not bound by the clause as she did not know of its existence, and there was no constructive notice because the shipowner had not given reasonable notice of the condition.

189. L'Estrange v. Graucob (F.), [1934] 2 K.B. 394

The defendant sold to the plaintiff a slot machine, inserting in the order form the following clause: "Any express or implied condition, statement or warranty, statutory or otherwise, is hereby excluded." The plaintiff signed the order form but did not read the relevant clause, and she now sued in respect of the unsatisfactory nature of the machine supplied. *Held*—The clause was binding on her, although the defendants made no attempt to read the document to her nor call her attention to the clause.

190. Olley v. Marlborough Court Ltd., [1949] 1 K.B. 532

Husband and wife arrived at an hotel as guests and paid for a room in advance. They went up to the room allotted to them; on one of the walls was the following notice: "The proprietors will not hold themselves responsible for articles lost or stolen unless handed to the manageress for safe custody." The wife closed the self-locking door of the bedroom and took the key downstairs to the reception desk. A third party took the key and stole certain of the wife's furs. In the ensuing action the defendants sought to rely on the notice as a term of contract. *Held*—The contract was completed at the reception desk and no subsequent notice could affect the plaintiff's rights.

N.B. As was pointed out in *Spurling* v. *Bradshaw*, [1956] 1 W.L.R. 461, if the husband and wife had read the notice on a previous visit to the hotel it would have been binding on them.

190a. *Thornton* v. *Shoe Lane Parking Ltd.*, [1971] 1 All E.R. 686

The plaintiff suffered physical injuries when taking his car out of a multistorey car park and sued the proprietors for these injuries. They claimed that they were not liable by reason of an exclusion clause on the ticket issued to the plaintiff. The sequence of relevant events was as follows—

(*a*) the plaintiff drove up to the automatic barrier where there was a notice saying "All cars parked at owner's risk." This did not cover physical injury. Most people would think it referred to the car or its contents.

(*b*) An automatic device issued a ticket at the barrier. This referred to further conditions which were displayed inside the premises. These conditions exempted the defendants from a number of possible liabilities including physical injury. The plaintiff did not read these and had not used the park before.

Held—by the Court of Appeal—the terms of the offer were those contained in the notice at the ticket machine. The plaintiff was not bound by the conditions inside the premises to which the ticket referred because the ticket came too late in the transaction to incorporate them.

191. Adler v. Dickson, [1955] 1 Q.B. 158

The plaintiff was travelling as a first class passenger on the Peninsular and Orient Company's liner *Himalaya*. The ticket contained the following term: "Passengers are carried at passengers' risk . . . The company will not be responsible for any injury whatsoever to the person of any passenger arising from, or occasioned by, the negligence of the company's servants." The plaintiff fell from the gangway on to the wharf and was injured. Since the exemption clause exempted the company from liability, the plaintiff brought an action for negligence against the master and boatswain of the ship. *Held*—The plaintiff succeeded. The master and boatswain were not parties to the contract and could not claim the benefit of the exemption clause.

192. McCutcheon v. David MacBrayne, [1964] 1 All E.R. 430

McCutcheon wished to have his motor car transported from Islay to the Scottish mainland, and McCutcheon's agent made a contract of carriage on behalf of McCutcheon with the respondent company. The ship sank owing to the respondents' negligent navigation and the appellant sued for damages. The respondents contended that they were not liable because of certain exemption clauses displayed on a notice in the booking office and also contained in a "risk note" which was normally given to each customer, though one was not given to the appellant's agent in this case. However, on previous occasions when the parties had done business, "risk notes" containing exemptions had sometimes been given either to the appellant or his agent. The appellant and his agent knew that some conditions were attached to the respondents' contracts, but did not know specifically what they were. *Held*—by the House of Lords—allowing the appellant's appeal, that since this was an oral contract, the conditions relied on were not incorporated into it so as to exempt the respondents from liability in negligence. Lord Devlin was of opinion that previous dealings are relevant only if they prove actual and not constructive knowledge of the terms and also prove assent to them.

193. Akerib v. Booth, [1961] 1 All E.R. 380

The defendants were the owners of premises where they carried on business as packers and forwarders of goods. They made a contract with the plaintiff under which they agreed to pack the plaintiff's goods and also to lease to him six rooms in the premises to be used partly as an office and partly as a store by the plaintiff. Because of the defendants' negligence water escaped from a cistern on the top floor of the premises, and this damaged the plaintiff's goods and some office material in the rooms which he was leasing. The plaintiff sued for damages, and the defendants pleaded a paragraph in the schedule to the contract which said that the defendants were not in any circumstances to be responsible for damage caused by water to any goods whether in the possession of the defendants or not. The Court was concerned to decide the meaning and scope of these words. Taken as they stood and read in isolation, the words applied to all goods without any restriction. However, the plaintiff argued that if the words were read in the context of the whole contract, the *main* purpose of which was to cover the defendants in the process of packing, the words must be confined to goods which had been handed over to the defendants for this purpose. The Court of Appeal *held* that either interpretation was possible. However, since the words were ambiguous they must be construed against the defendants who had drafted the contract and put the term into it. The immunity must, therefore, be confined to goods handed over to the defendants for packing, and the plaintiff succeeded.

N.B. This is really an aspect of the *contra proferentem* rule which construes all ambiguous statements in written contracts against the draftsman and in favour of the other party.

194. Karsales (Harrow) Ltd. v. Wallis, [1956] 2 All E.R. 866

The defendant inspected a Buick car which a Mr. Stanton wished to sell him. The defendant found it to be in excellent condition and agreed to pay £600 for it, effecting the purchase through a finance company. The car was badly damaged before it was delivered to Wallis; the new tyres which were on the car when Wallis saw it had been replaced by old ones; the radio had been removed; the cylinder head was off; all the valves were burnt; and the engine had two broken pistons. Wallis would not agree to take delivery of the car but is was towed to his place of business and left there. The finance company originally involved assigned its rights under the agreement with Wallis to Karsales, and in this action Karsales were trying to recover the instalments due under the agreement. In so doing they relied on the following clause in the agreement assigned to them: "No condition or warranty that the vehicle is roadworthy, or as to its age condition or fitness for any purpose, is given by the owner or implied herein." The county court judge decided that the exemption clause was effective and ordered Wallis to pay. Wallis now appealed. The Court of Appeal held that Wallis was not liable because exemption clauses, no matter how widely expressed, only avail the party who includes them when he is carrying out his contract in its essential respects. Here there was a breach of a fundamental obligation amounting to non-performance. As Birkett, L.J., said: "A car that will not go is not a car at all."

195. Alexander *v.* Railway Executive, [1951] 2 All E.R. 442

Alexander was a magician who had been on a tour together with an assistant. He left three trunks at the parcels office at Launceston station, the trunks containing various properties which were used in an "escape illusion." The plaintiff paid 5d. for each trunk deposited and received a ticket for each one. He then left saying that he would send instructions for their dispatch. Some weeks after the deposit and before the plaintiff had sent instructions for the dispatch of the trunks, the plaintiff's assistant persuaded the clerk in the parcels office to give him access to the trunks, though he was not in possession of the ticket. The assistant took away several of the properties and was later convicted of larceny. The plaintiff sued the defendants for damages for breach of contract, and the defendants pleaded the following term which was contained in the ticket and which stated that the Railway Executive was "not liable for loss misdelivery or damage to any articles where the value was in excess of £5 unless at the time of the deposit the true value and nature of the goods was declared by the depositor and an extra charge paid." No such declaration or payment had been made. *Held*—The plaintiff succeeded because, although sufficient notice had been given constructively to the plaintiff of the term, the term did not protect the defendants because they were guilty of a breach of a fundamental obligation in allowing the trunks to be opened and things to be removed from them by an unauthorised person.

N.B. Devlin, J., said that a deliberate delivery to the wrong person did not fall within the meaning of "misdelivery," and this may be regarded as the real reason for the decision, as it involves the application of the *contra proferentem* rule.

196. Hunt and Winterbotham (West of England) Ltd. *v.* B.R.S. (Parcels) Ltd., [1962] 1 All E.R. 111

The defendants entered into a contract with the plaintiffs under the terms of which the defendants were to carry 15 parcels of woollen goods to Manchester. In fact only 12 parcels arrived and the plaintiffs now sued for damages for the value of the three parcels lost. The defendants pleaded an exemption clause excluding their liability for loss "however sustained." The plaintiffs based their claim on negligence and did not plead breach of a fundamental obligation. There was no evidence as to how the parcels had been lost, the defendants being unable to offer an explanation. In view of this the Court of Appeal gave judgment for the defendants saying that if they were negligent, the exemption clause would protect them. The plaintiffs had not alleged breach of a fundamental obligation and had produced no evidence to suggest that the defendants were in breach of a fundamental obligation which would have been essential if such a breach were alleged.

197. Suisse Atlantique Société D'Armament Maritime S.A. *v.* N.V. Rotterdamsche Kolen Centrale, [1966] 2 All E.R. 61

The plaintiffs were shipowners and the defendants chartered a ship from them for "two years' continuous voyages." Under the contract, demurrage of $1,000 per day had to be paid by the charterers to the owners if the ship was detained in port longer than the loading time permitted and specified by the contract. There were substantial delays and the demurrage was paid, but the shipowner's loss of freight was greater than the demurrage they had received and they claimed general damages over and above the demurrage. It was suggested for the owners that the delay was deliberate and enabled them to regard the contract as *repudiated* so that the demurrage provisions did not apply and they could recover their full loss. The owners further argued that because of the cases relating to fundamental breach and exemption clauses the demurrage clause could not cover a breach as serious as this. The House of Lords, after consideration of the fundamental breach cases. *Held*—that—

(*a*) a fundamental breach no longer automatically nullifies an exemption clause. The matter is one of construction of the contract.

(*b*) The demurrage clause was not so much an exemption clause as a provision for liquidated damages, but was wide enough to cover the breaches complained of.

(*c*) Even if the charterer's conduct had given the owners the right to treat the contract as repudiated, they had not done so and the contract including the demurrage clause remained in force.

197a. *Kenyon, Son and Craven Ltd.* v. *Baxter Hoare & Co. Ltd.*, [1971] 2 All E.R. 708

The defendants stored nuts for the plaintiffs. The contract included an exception clause under which the defendants were not liable for loss or damage unless due to their "wilful neglect." The nuts were seriously damaged by rats. The defendants' servant had made some effort to control the rats but had not, through ignorance, used appropriate measures. The plaintiffs sued for breach of the contract of bailment. *Held*—the defendants' neglect could not be said to be "wilful." They were not therefore guilty of a fundamental breach and could rely on the exception clause (*Suisse Case*[197] applied.) The plaintiffs' claim failed.

198. Harbutt's Plasticine Ltd. *v.* Wayne Tank and Pump Co. Ltd., [1970] 1 All E.R. 225

In 1961 the defendants agreed to install certain equipment in the plaintiff's factory for the purpose of storing, heating and dispensing wax for certain manufacturing processes. A clause of the contract provided that until the installation was taken over by the plaintiff the defendant would indemnify the plaintiffs for any damage caused by the negligence of the defendant's servants, but that the total liability should not exceed £2,330. Owing to the negligent switching on of the machine by the defendant's servants it became overheated, caught fire and destroyed the factory. *Held*—

(i) The defendants were liable for the full amount of loss (£146,581). There had been a fundamental breach of the contract and in the circumstances the exclusion clause limiting the damage to £2,330 did not apply.

(ii) To determine whether a breach of contract was fundamental not only the breach itself but also the events resulting from the breach must be considered. In this case the breaches by the defendants and the consequences of them were so fundamental as to bring the contract to an end.

(iii) Where the defendant had been guilty of such a fundamental breach that the contract was automatically at an end so that the innocent party had no chance of an election whether to continue or not, the guilty party could not rely on an exclusion or limitation clause when sued for damages for breach.

(iv) Where the innocent party with knowledge of a fundamental breach can and does treat the contract as continuing, and sues for damages, the application of an exclusion clause exempting the defendant from liability depends upon the relevant rules of construction of contracts.

(v) The proper measure of damages was the cost of building a new factory, even though the new factory was in many ways better than the old one. However, the money received by the plaintiffs from their insurance company should go in relief of the damages paid by the defendants and reduce them by the relevant amount.

198a. *Farnworth Finance Facilities Ltd.* v. *Attryde*, [1970] 2 All E.R. 774

Mr. Attryde bought a motor-cycle on hire purchase. The contract, which was not covered by the Hire Purchase Acts, contained a clause to the effect that the vehicle was supplied "subject to no conditions or warranties whatsoever express or implied." The machine had many faults and although Mr. Attryde always complained about them he did drive the machine for some 4,000 miles before deciding to repudiate the contract. He was then sued by the finance company who claimed that the exemption clause applied to exclude liability for defects. *Held*—by the Court of Appeal—that it did not. There was a rule of construction which provided that in general terms an exclusion clause was not effective to exclude a fundamental breach which was what had occurred in this case. The defects taken together amounted to a fundamental breach. Mr. Attryde had not affirmed the contract by using the machine. He had always complained about the defects and had indicated that he would only finally accept the machine if they were remedied. It should be noted that Lord Denning appears in his judgment to have tried to square the decision in both *Harbutt*[198] and *Suisse*[197] as follows—"We have in this case to apply the principles about fundamental breach, which were recently considered by this court in *Harbutt's Plasticine Ltd.* v. *Wayne Tank and Pump Co. Ltd.*[198] The first thing to do, is, no doubt, to construe the contract, remembering always the proposition of Pearson L.J. which was approved by the House of Lords in *Suisse Atlantique Société d'Armament Maritime S.A.* v. *N.V. Rotterdamsche Kolen Centrale:*[197] ". . . there is a rule of construction that normally an exception or exclusion clause or similar provision in a contract should be construed as not applying to a situation created by a fundamental breach of contract." That rule of construction applies here. It means that we must see if there was a fundamental breach of contract. If there was, then the exempting condition should not be construed as applying to it. We look, therefore, to the terms of the contract, express or implied (apart from the exception clauses) and see which of them were broken. If they were broken in a fundamental respect, the finance company cannot rely on the exception clauses."

199. Pollock & Co. *v.* Macrae, [1922] S.C. (H.L.) 192

The defendants entered into a contract to build and supply marine engines. The contract carried an exemption clause which was designed to protect the defendant from liability for defective materials and workmanship. The engines supplied under the contract had a great many defects and could not be used. *Held*—by the House of Lords—that on a true construction of the contract the exemption clause did not apply because it was repugnant to the main purpose of the contract. Lord Dunedin said: "Now, when there is such a congeries of defects as to destroy the workable character of the machine

I think this amounts to a total breach of contract, and that each defect cannot be taken by itself separately so as to apply the provisions of the conditions of guarantee and make it impossible to claim damages."

200. Thomas National Transport (Melbourne) Pty. Ltd. and Pay *v.* May and Baker (Australia) Pty. Ltd., [1966] 2 Lloyd's Rep. 347

The owners of certain packages made a contract with carriers under which the packages were to be carried from Melbourne to various places in Australia. The carriers employed a sub-contractor to collect the parcels and take them to the carriers' depot in Melbourne. When the sub-contractor arrived at the Melbourne depot it was locked and so he drove the lorry full of packages to his own house and left it in a garage there. There was a fire and some of the packages were destroyed. The owners sued the carriers who pleaded an exemption clause in the contract of carriage. *Held*—by the High Court of Australia—that the plaintiffs succeeded. There had been a fundamental breach of contract. The intention of the parties was that the goods would be taken to the carriers' depot and not to the sub-contractors' house, in which case the carriers could not rely on the clause. The decision in the *Suisse Case*[197] was applied.

201. Hutton *v.* Warren (1836), 150 E.R. 517

The plaintiff was the tenant of a farm and the defendant the landlord. At Michaelmas, 1833, the defendant gave the plaintiff notice to quit on the Lady Day following. The defendant insisted that the plaintiff should cultivate the land during the period of notice which he did. The plaintiff now asked for a fair allowance for seeds and labour of which he had no benefit having left the farm before harvest. It was proved that by custom a tenant was bound to farm for the whole of his tenancy and on quitting was entitled to a fair allowance for seeds and labour. *Held*—the plaintiff succeeded. "We are of opinion that this custom was, by implication, imported into the lease. It has long been settled, that, in commercial transactions, extrinsic evidence of custom and usage is admissable to annex incidents to written contracts, in matters with respect to which they are silent. The same rule has also been applied to contracts in other transactions of life, in which known usages have been established and prevailed; and this has been done upon the principle of presumption that, in such transactions, the parties did not mean to express in writing the whole of the contract by which they intended to be bound, but a contract with reference to those known usages." (*per* Parke, B.)

202. Lister *v.* Romford Ice and Cold Storage Co. Ltd., [1957] 1 All E.R. 125

The defendants' lorry driver negligently reversed the company's vehicle into another servant of the company (his father) who received damages from the company under the doctrine of vicarious liability. The defendants were insured against this liability and the insurance company paid the damages and, under the doctrine of subrogation, sued the lorry driver in the name of the company to recover what they had paid. It was unanimously *held* by the House of Lords that the lorry driver, as a servant of the company, owed them a duty to perform his work with reasonable care and skill, and that a servant who involves his master in vicarious liability by reason of negligence is liable in damages to the master for breach of contract. This liability arises out of an implied term in the contract of service to indemnify the master for loss caused

to him by the servant's negligence. The damages will in such a case amount
to a complete indemnity in respect of the amount which the employer has
been held vicariously liable to pay the injured plaintiff.

203. Cumming *v.* Ince (1847), 11 Q.B. 112

An old lady was induced to settle property on one of her relatives by the
threat of unlawful confinement in a private mental home. *Held*—The settlement could be set aside on the ground of duress, i.e. the threat of false
imprisonment.

204. Williams *v.* Bayley (1866), L.R. 1 H.L. 200

A father agreed to make a mortgage of property to a bank in consideration
of the return by the bank of certain promissory notes forged by his son. The
banker concerned had suggested in conversation with the father that the son
would be prosecuted if some agreement were not reached. The promise to
make the mortgage was held invalid because of undue influence which,
though not presumed in this case, had been proved.

205. Lancashire Loans Ltd. *v.* Black, [1934] 1 K.B. 380

A daughter married at eighteen and went to live with her husband. Her
mother was an extravagant woman and was in debt to a firm of moneylenders.
When the daughter became of age, her mother persuaded her to raise £2,000 on
property in which the daughter had an interest, and this was used to pay off
the mother's debts. Twelve months later mother and daughter signed a joint
and several promissory note of £775 at eighty-five per cent interest in favour of
the moneylenders, and the daughter created a further charge on her property
in order that the mother might borrow more money. The daughter did not
understand the nature of the transaction, and the only advice she received was
from a solicitor acting for the mother and the moneylenders. The moneylenders brought this action against the mother and daughter on the note. *Held*
—The daughter's defence that she was under undue influence of her mother
succeeded, in spite of the fact that she was of full age and married with her own
home.

206. Hodgson *v.* Marks, [1970] 3 All E.R. 513

Mrs. Hodgson, who was a widow of 83, owned a freehold house in which
she lived. In 1959 she took in a Mr. Evans as a lodger. She soon came to
trust Evans and allowed him to manage her financial affairs. In June, 1960,
she transferred the house to Evans, her sole reason for so doing being to prevent
her nephew from turning Evans out of the house. It was orally agreed between
Mrs. Hodgson and Evans that the house was to remain hers although held in
the name of Evans. Evans later made arrangements to sell the house without
the knowledge or consent of Mrs. Hodgson. The house was bought by Mr.
Marks and Mrs. Hodgson now asked for a declaration that he was bound to
transfer the property back to her. The following questions arose—

(*a*) whether Evans held the house in trust for Mrs. Hodgson. It was *held*
—by Ungoed-Thomas, J.,—that he did. The absence of written evidence
of the trust as required by Sect. 53 of the Law of Property Act, 1925, was
not a bar to Mrs. Hodgson's claim. The Act was not intended to assist a
fraud;

(*b*) whether Evans had exercised undue influence. It was *held* that he
had and that a presumption of undue influence was raised. Although the

parties were not in the established categories, Evans had a relationship of trust and confidence with Mrs. Hodgson of a kind which raised a presumption of undue influence.

However, Mrs. Hodgson lost the case because Mr. Marks was protected by Sect. 70 of the Land Registration Act, 1925, which gives rights to a purchaser of property for value in respect of interests in that property of which the purchaser is not aware. In this case Mr. Marks bought the house from Mr. Evans, the house being in the name of Evans and he had no reason to suppose that Mrs. Hodgson had any interest in it.

207. Allcard v. Skinner (1887), 36 Ch.D. 145

In 1868 the plaintiff joined a Protestant institution called the sisterhood of St. Mary at the Cross, promising to devote her property to the service of the poor. The defendant Miss Skinner was the Lady Superior of the Sisterhood. In 1871 the plaintiff ceased to be a novice and became a sister in the order, taking her vows of poverty, chastity and obedience. By this time she had left her home and was residing with the sisterhood. The plaintiff remained a sister until 1879 and, in compliance with the vow of poverty, she had by then given property to the value of about £7,000 to the defendant. The plaintiff left the order in 1879 and became a Roman Catholic. Of the property she had transferred, £1,671 remained in 1885 and the plaintiff sought to recover this sum, claiming that it had been transferred in circumstances of undue influence. *Held*—The gifts had been made under pressure of an unusually persuasive nature, particularly since the plaintiff was prevented from seeking outside advice under a rule of the sisterhood which said, "Let no sister seek the advice of any extern without the superior's leave." However, the plaintiff's claim was barred by her delay because, although the influence was removed in 1879, she did not bring her action until 1885.

208. Goodinson v. Goodinson, [1954] 2 All E.R. 255

A contract made between husband and wife, who had already separated, provided that the husband would pay his wife a weekly sum by way of maintenance in consideration that she would indemnify him against all debts incurred by her, would not pledge his credit, and would not take matrimonial proceedings against him in respect of maintenance. The wife now sued for arrears of maintenance under this agreement. The last promise was admittedly void since its object was to oust the jurisdiction of the courts, but it was *held* that this did not vitiate the rest of the contract; it was not the sole or even the main consideration, and the wife's action for arrears succeeded.

209. Dann v. Curzon (1911), 104 L.T. 66

An agreement was made for advertising a play by means of collusive criminal proceedings brought as a result of a pre-arranged disturbance at the theatre. The plaintiffs, who agreed to create the disturbance and did in fact do so, sued for the remuneration due to them under the agreement. *Held*—The action failed because it was an agreement to commit a criminal offence and was therefore against public policy.

210. Anderson Ltd. v. Daniel, [1924] 1 K.B. 138

Sellers of artificial fertilisers were required by statute to give purchasers an invoice stating the percentages of chemical substances contained in the fertiliser. Any seller who failed to give such an invoice was liable to a fine.

Here the sellers had delivered ten tons of artificial fertiliser without complying with the statute. *Held*—They could not recover the price. The purpose of the statute was to protect a section of the public, i.e. the purchasers of artificial manure, and the sellers had carried out the contract in an illegal way.

211. Shaw *v.* Groom, [1970] 1 All E.R. 702

Mrs. Groom was the tenant of a room in North London and Mrs. Shaw was her landlord. The tenancy was a controlled one and Mrs. Groom had occupied the room for some 20 years at a rent of 7/11d. per week plus 2/6d. for electricity. Mrs. Groom fell into arrears with her rent and Mrs. Shaw brought this action to recover the money owing to her. Unfortunately Mrs. Shaw had failed, during the tenancy, to comply with Sect. 4 of the Landlord and Tenant Act, 1962, which required that the tenant be provided with a rent book. Mrs. Groom now alleged that Mrs. Shaw could not recover the arrears of rent because her failure to provide a rent book was illegal performance of the contract. *Held*—by the Court of Appeal—that Mrs. Shaw succeeded. The intention of the legislature was not to preclude the landlord from recovering rent due or to impose on him any forfeiture beyond the fines stipulated in the Act of 1962. It was accepted that the requirement of a rent book was to protect a class of persons of whom Mrs. Groom was one. This did not, however, automatically prevent Mrs. Shaw's claim. The rule that an illegal contract cannot be enforced by the guilty party must be sensibly restricted in its operation. *Anderson Ltd.* v. *Daniel*[210] was distinguished.

212. Smith *v.* Mawhood (1845), 14 M. & W. 452

It was held in this case that a tobacconist could recover the price of tobacco sold by him even though he did not have a licence to sell it and had not painted his name on his place of business. Here the statutory penalty was £200, but the object of the statute was not to affect the contract of sale but to impose a fine on the offender for the purpose of revenue.

213. Brogden *v.* Marriott (1863), 3 Bing. (N.C.) 88

In this case the parties had agreed to buy and sell a horse, the price to be £200 if it transpired that the horse could trot at eighteen miles per hour within a month of purchase. If this speed was not attained the price was to be a shilling. The horse did not achieve this speed and the purchaser claimed it for a shilling. *Held*—There was no claim because the contract was in fact a wager.

214. Rourke *v.* Short (1856), 5 E. & B. 904

The two parties were making a contract for the sale of certain rags but could not agree on the price that had been paid on a previous sale between them. It was eventually agreed that if the seller's memory was correct the rags should be sold for six shillings per cwt. and if not the price should be three shillings per cwt. The seller's memory proved to be correct but the buyer would not take delivery of the rags. This action by the seller failed because the previous selling price was in fact the subject of a wager, the difference in the prices being a stake.

215. Pearce *v.* Brooks (1866), L.R. 1 Exch. 213

The plaintiffs hired a carriage to the defendant for a period of twelve months during which time the defendant was to pay the purchase price by instalments. The defendant was a prostitute and the carriage, which was of attractive design, was intended to assist her in obtaining clients. One of the plaintiffs knew that the defendant was a prostitute but he said that he did not know that she intended to use the carriage for purposes of prostitution. The evidence showed to the contrary. The jury found that the plaintiffs knew the purpose for which the carriage was to be used and thereupon the court *held* that the plaintiffs' claim for the sum due under the contract failed for illegality.

216. Foster *v.* **Driscoll,** [1929] 1 K.B. 470

Several persons entered into what was in effect a partnership contract to equip a ship and load it with six different varieties of whisky. The ship was then to be sent to the U.S.A. and the whisky was to be sold either in the U.S.A. or on its borders to persons who would then dispose of it in violation of the U.S.A.'s prohibition laws. This action was brought on a bill of exchange which had been accepted by members of the syndicate or partnership as a method of paying for the whisky. *Held*—The contract of partnership was void as against public policy because it had been formed to procure an act which was illegal by the law of a foreign but friendly country, and no action was possible in respect of any matter arising out of the scheme.

217. Regazzoni *v.* **K. C. Sethia Ltd.,** [1958] A.C. 301

The defendants agreed to sell and deliver jute bags to the plaintiff, both parties knowing and intending that the goods would be shipped from India to Genoa so that the plaintiff might then send them to South Africa. Both parties knew that the law of India prohibited the direct or indirect export of goods from India to South Africa, this law being directed at the policy of apartheid adopted by South Africa. The defendants did not deliver the jute bags as agreed and the plaintiff brought this action in an English court, the contract being governed by English law. *Held*—Although the contract was not illegal in English law, it could not be enforced because it had as its object the violation of the law of a foreign and friendly country in which part of the contract was to be carried out.

218. John *v.* **Mendoza,** [1939] 1 K.B. 141

The defendant owed the plaintiff £852 15s. 6d. The defendant was made bankrupt and the plaintiff was intending to prove for his debt in the bankruptcy. The defendant asked him not to do so, but to say that the £852 15s. 6d was a gift whereupon the defendant would pay the plaintiff in full regardless of the sum received by other creditors. In view of the defendant's promise the plaintiff withdrew his proof, but in the event all the other creditors were paid in full and the bankruptcy was annulled. The plaintiff now sued for the debt. *Held*—There was no claim, for the plaintiff abandoned all right to recover on failure to prove in the bankruptcy, and the defendant's promise to pay in full was unenforceable, being an agreement designed to defeat the bankruptcy laws.

21. Parkinson *v.* **The College of Ambulance Ltd. and Harrison,** [1925] 2 K.B. 1

The first defendants were a charitable institution and the second defendant was the secretary. Harrison fraudulently represented to the plaintiff, Colonel Parkinson, that the charity was in a position to obtain some honour (probably a knighthood) for him if he would make a suitable donation to the funds of the charity. The plaintiff paid over the sum of £3,000 and said he would pay more if the honour was granted. No honour of any kind was received by the plaintiff and he brought this action to recover the money he had donated to the College. *Held*—The agreement was contrary to public policy and illegal. No relief could be granted to the plaintiff.

220. Napier *v.* National Business Agency Ltd., [1951] 2 All E.R. 264

The defendants engaged the plaintiff to act as their secretary and accountant at a salary of £13 per week plus £6 per week for expenses. Both parties were aware that the plaintiff's expenses could never amount to £6 a week and in fact they never exceeded £1 per week. Income Tax was deducted on £13 per week, and £6 per week was paid without deduction of tax as reimbursement of expenses. The plaintiff, having been summarily dismissed, claimed payment of £13 as wages in lieu of notice. *Held*—The agreement was contrary to public policy and illegal. The plaintiff's action failed.

221. Alexander *v.* Rayson, [1936] 1 K.B. 169

The plaintiff was the lessee of certain flats in Piccadilly. He let one of the flats to Mrs. Rayson by granting her an underlease at £450 a year. Another agreement was made whereby Mrs. Rayson was to pay £750 a year for certain services provided by the plaintiff. The defendant paid both sums for a time, but later paid a quarter's rent under the underlease, i.e. £112 10s., refusing to pay for services on the ground that they had not been rendered. The plaintiff sued in respect of the sum owing for services. The defendant alleged, amongst other things, that the contract for services was illegal since it was designed to defraud the Westminster City Council, the latter having assessed the rateable value of the flat on the basis of a rental of £450 a year, which was the income under the lease shown to the assessment committee. *Held*—The agreement for services could not be enforced because it was illegal. In any case there was no consideration moving from the plaintiff in respect of the services, for it emerged that he was already bound to carry out the services under his own lease.

222. Edler *v.* Auerbach, [1950] 1 K.B. 359

The defendant leased premises to the plaintiff for use as offices. The lease was contrary to the provisions of the Defence Regulations of 1939, since the premises had previously been used as residential accommodation and should have been let as such. The local authority discovered the illegal use and would not allow it to continue. The plaintiff now sued for rescission of the lease together with rent paid under it. The defendant counterclaimed for rent due and for damage done to the premises, including the removal of a bath. *Held*—The landlord could not enforce the illegal lease but was entitled to damages for the plaintiff's failure to replace the bath.

223. Bowmakers Ltd. *v.* Barnet Instruments Ltd., [1944] 2 All E.R. 579

Bowmakers bought machine tools from a person named Smith. This contract was illegal because it contravened an Order made by the Minister of Supply under the Defence Regulations, Smith having no licence to sell machine tools. Bowmakers hired the machine tools to Barnet Instruments under hire-purchase agreements which were also illegal because Bowmakers did not have a licence to sell machine tools. Barnet Instruments failed to keep up the instalments, sold some of the machine tools and refused to give up the others. Bowmakers sued, not on the illegal hire-purchase contracts, but in conversion, and judgment was given for Bowmakers. The Court of Appeal declared the contracts illegal but, since Bowmakers were not suing under the contracts but as owners, their action succeeded. The wrongful sales by Barnet Instruments terminated the hire-purchase contracts.

N.B. Although the contract between Smith and Bowmakers was illegal, ownership passed to Bowmakers by reason of delivery. When goods are delivered the person receiving them has some evidence of title by reason of possession and need not necessarily plead a contract. Where, in an illegal situation, the goods have not been delivered there may be difficulty in establishing ownership without relying on the illegal contract. Nevertheless, ownership was established without delivery in *Belvoir Finance Co. Ltd.* v. *Stapleton*, [1970] 3 W.L.R. 530. In this case A (a dealer) sold certain cars to B (a finance company) which let them on hire purchase to C (a car hire firm). C did not pay the minimum deposit required by regulation to B; thus the hire-purchase contract was illegal. Later C's manager, S, sold the cars to innocent purchasers. C did not pay the hire-purchase instalments and B sued S in conversion, the company C having gone into liquidation. It was *held*— by the Court of Appeal—that B succeeded. They were the owners of the cars and S had converted their property. The decision is of interest since B (the finance company) had never taken delivery of the cars; they were sent direct from A to C as is usual in these transactions. Nevertheless B was accepted as owner although the only means of proving ownership open to B seems to have been the illegal hire-purchase contract with C. This was the only document which showed how B came to acquire ownership of the cars.

224. Fielding and Platt Ltd. *v.* Najjar, [1969] 2 All E.R. 150

The plaintiffs entered into an agreement with a Lebanese company to make and deliver an aluminium press. Payment was to be made by six promissory notes given at stated intervals by the defendant personally. The defendant, who was the managing director of the Lebanese company, told the plaintiffs that they ought to invoice the goods as part of a rolling mill, his intention being to deceive the Lebanese import authorities into believing that the import of the press was authorised whereas in fact it was not. The first promissory note was dishonoured and the plaintiffs stopped work on the press and cabled a message to the Lebanese company to that effect. The second promissory note was then dishonoured and the plaintiffs sued upon the notes. It was *held*— by the Court of Appeal—that—

(i) since the first note covered work in progress there was no defence based on failure of consideration;

(ii) any illegality in connection with the importing of the press was not part of the contract or agreed to by the plaintiffs;

(iii) the plaintiffs' claim was not, therefore, affected by illegality;

(iv) since the plaintiffs had repudiated the contract before the second note was dishonoured they had no claim for the amount of the note as such but could only sue for damages. The defendant was not liable on the second note.

225. Atkinson *v.* Denby (1862), 7 H. & N. 934

The plaintiff was in financial difficulties and offered to pay his creditors the sum of 5s. in the £ as a full settlement. All the creditors except the defendant agreed to this. The defendant said that he would agree only if the plaintiff paid him £50. Afraid that the scheme would not go through without the defendant's co-operation, the plaintiff made the payment. *Held*—He could recover it because he had been coerced into defrauding his creditors.

226. Hughes *v.* Liverpool Victoria Legal Friendly Society, [1916] 2 K.B. 482

John Henry Thomas, a grocer, had originally taken out five policies on customers who owed him money. It was agreed that Thomas had an insurable interest in the customers because they were his debtors. Thomas let the policies drop and an agent of the defendant company persuaded a Mrs. Hughes to take them up, assuring her that she had an insurable interest which she had not. She now brought this action to recover the premiums paid. *Held*— The contract was illegal but the plaintiff could recover the premiums. She had been induced to take up the policies by the fraud of the defendants' agent.

227. Kiriri Cotton Co. *v.* Dawani, [1960] A.C. 192

A tenant paid a premium to his landlord in order to get possession of a flat. The acceptance of the premium was an offence under Sect. 3 (2) of the Uganda Rent Restriction Ordinance, and the Ordinance did not provide for recovery of the premium. Both parties were ignorant of the Ordinance. In this action to recover the premium the Judicial Committee of the Privy Council *held* that the premium paid by the tenant must be recoverable because the object of the statute was to protect tenants.

228. Taylor *v.* Bowers (1876), 1 Q.B.D. 291

The plaintiff was under pressure from his creditors and in order to place some of his property out of their reach he assigned certain machinery to a person named Adcock. The plaintiff then called a meeting of his creditors and tried to get them to settle for less than the amount of their debts, representing his assets as not including the machinery. The creditors would not and did not agree to a settlement. The plaintiff now sued to recover his machinery from the defendants who had obtained it from Adcock. *Held*—The plaintiff succeeded because the illegal fraud on the creditors had not been carried out.

229. Kearley *v.* Thomson (1890), 24 Q.B.D. 742

The plaintiff had a friend who was bankrupt and wished to obtain his discharge. The defendant was likely to oppose the discharge and accordingly the plaintiff paid the defendant £40 in return for which the defendant promised to stay away from the public examination and not to oppose the discharge. The defendant did stay away from the public examination but before an application for discharge had been made the plaintiff brought his action claiming the £40. *Held*—The claim failed because the illegal scheme had been substantially effected.

230. Bigos *v.* Bousted, [1951] 1 All E.R. 92

The defendant was anxious to send his wife and daughter abroad for the sake of the daughter's health, but restrictions on currency were in force so that a long stay abroad was impossible. In August, 1947, the defendant, in contravention of the Exchange Control Act, 1947, made an agreement under which the plaintiff was to supply £150 of Italian money to be made available at Rapallo, the defendant undertaking to repay the plaintiff with English money in England. As security, the defendant deposited with the plaintiff a share certificate for 140 shares in a company. The wife and daughter went to Italy but were not supplied with currency, and had to return sooner than they would have done. The defendant, thereupon, asked for the return of his share certificate but the plaintiff refused to give it up. This action was brought by the plaintiff to recover the sum of £150 which she insisted she had lent to the defendant. He denied the loan, and counter-claimed for the return of his certificate. In the course of the action the plaintiff abandoned her claim, but the defendant proceeded with his counter-claim saying that, although the contract was illegal, it was still executory so that he might repent and ask the court's assistance. *Held*—The court would not assist him because the fact that the contract had not been carried out was due to frustration by the plaintiff and not the repentance of the defendant. In fact his repentance was really want of power to sin.

231. Fisher *v.* Bridges (1854), 188 E.R. 713

The plaintiff agreed to sell the defendant certain land which the defendant intended to use as a prize in a lottery. The use of land for lotteries was forbidden by statute but the land was conveyed and the purchase price all but £630 was paid. Later the defendant entered into a deed with the plaintiff under the terms of which he agreed to pay the £630 and the plaintiff now sued upon that deed. *Held*—No action lay on the deed. Jervis, C.J., said: "It is clear that the covenant was given for the payment of the purchase money. As it springs from, and is the creature of the illegal agreement, and as the law would not enforce the original illegal contract, so neither will it allow the parties to enforce a security for the purchase money which, by the original bargain, was tainted with illegality."

232. Southern Industrial Trust *v.* Brooke House Motors (1968), 112 S.J. 798

A customer wished to buy a car from the defendants who were dealers. The dealers and the customer inserted incorrect figures relating to price and deposit in the hire-purchase agreement so that it became illegal under statutory provisions then applying to such agreements. The car was then sold to the plaintiff finance company which was unaware of the true position. The finance company hired it out to the customer under the falsified hire-purchase agreement. The dealers had represented both to the customer and the finance company that the car was a 1962 model whereas in fact it was registered in 1958. When the customer discovered this he refused to pay any further instalments to the finance company and the company sued the dealers for breach of a warranty in the contract of sale to them, i.e. that the car was a 1962 model. It was *held*—by the Court of Appeal—that damages were recoverable notwithstanding the illegality of the hire-purchase agreement between the plaintiffs and the customer. The sale by the dealers to the finance company was collateral to that and was not tainted by the illegality in the other agreement.

233. Kaufman *v.* Gerson, [1904] 1 K.B. 591

The defendant's husband had misappropriated money entrusted to him by the plaintiff, his employer. The defendant made a contract in writing with the plaintiff under which she agreed to make good the loss, the plaintiff agreeing not to prosecute. The events took place in France and the agreement was governed by French law, which did not regard the element of coercion in the case as a vitiating element. Nevertheless, the action being brought on the contract in an English court, it was dismissed because it was contrary to public policy for an English court to enforce a contract obtained in this way.

234. Cowan *v.* Milbourn (1867), L.R. 2 Ex. 230

A person hired a hall to deliver blasphemous lectures and then was refused possession of it. His action claiming possession was refused on the grounds that no relief could be granted by the court where the purpose of the contract was illegal.

235. Berg *v.* Sadler and Moore, [1937] All E.R. 637

The plaintiff was a hairdresser and sold tobacco and cigarettes. He was a member of the Tobacco Trade Association, the Association having as its object the prevention of price cutting. Manufacturers would supply tobacco to traders who agreed not to sell at less than the fixed retail price. The plaintiff sold tobacco at cut prices and was put on the manufacturers' stop list which meant that he could not obtain supplies. The plaintiff made contact with a person named Reece who was a member of the Association and Reece agreed to obtain goods from manufacturers and hand them over to the plaintiff, in return for which Reece was to receive a commission from the plaintiff. One such transaction was carried out. On a later occasion the plaintiff's assistant and a representative of Reece went to defendant's premises to obtain a supply of cigarettes. The plaintiff's assistant handed over £72 19s. od. to Moore, who had some doubt about the matter and said he would send the goods direct to Reece's shop. Thereupon the plaintiff's assistant demanded the return of the money, Moore refused to give it back, and this action was brought to recover it. *Held*—This was an attempt by the plaintiff to obtain goods by false pretences and, since no action arises out of a base cause, the plaintiff's action failed.

236. Clay *v.* Yates (1856), 1 H. & B. 73

The plaintiff made an agreement with the defendant under which he was to print for the defendant 500 copies of a treatise to which a dedication was to be prefixed. The plaintiff began printing the book and later the dedication. The dedication was defamatory and the plaintiff omitted it from the book, and the defendant refused to pay for the book without the dedication. *Held*— The plaintiff was justified in refusing to print defamatory matter and was entitled to payment for so much of his work as was lawful.

237. Strongman Ltd. *v.* Sincock, [1955] 2 Q.B. 525

The defendant, who was an architect, employed the plaintiffs, who were builders, to modernise certain property. It was illegal at the time to carry out such work without the necessary licences. The defendant did get licences for part of the work, but the builders also did work for him which was £3,459 in excess of what was covered by licence. The defendant now refused to pay for the work, claiming that the contract was illegal. *Held*—The plaintiffs had acted in good faith but the contract, being illegal, could not be sued upon. However, they were entitled to damages up to the value of the unlicensed work on the basis of the defendant's breach of a collateral warranty that he would get the licences required.

238. Marles *v.* Trant (Philip) & Sons Ltd., [1954] 1 Q.B. 29

The defendants innocently sold wheat as spring wheat to the plaintiff. The wheat was in fact winter wheat but had been sold to the defendants as spring wheat. The contract with the plaintiff was not illegal as formed but was illegal as performed because the defendants did not comply with a statutory provision which required an invoice to be delivered with the goods. The plaintiff discovered that the seed was winter wheat and sued the defendants for breach of contract. *Held*—In spite of the illegality of the performance the plaintiff, could, being the innocent party, receive damages.

239. Re Davstone Estates Ltd., [1969] 2 All E.R. 849

The plaintiffs were landlords of a block of flats in St. Albans. The plaintiffs agreed with the tenants to keep the common parts of the block in good repair and the tenants agreed to pay £15 per year to the plaintiffs for this service. The tenants were also required to agree to a clause which provided that if the tenants' proportionate share of the actual cost of repairs incurred by the plaintiffs should exceed £15 in any year the tenants would pay the excess. A certificate by the plaintiffs' surveyor was to be conclusive as to the tenants' liability to pay any excess. The plaintiffs had to make good any structural defects as distinct from repairs and maintenance and the court was required as a matter of construction of the tenancy agreement to say whether any of these costs were recoverable from the tenants. In the course of his judgment, Ungoed-Thomas, J., said that the provision as to the finality of the plaintiffs' surveyor's certificate ousted the jurisdiction of the court and was void as contrary to public policy.

240. Horwood *v.* Millar's Timber Co., [1917] 1 K.B. 305

The plaintiff was a moneylender and he had lent money to a person named Bunyon who was employed as a clerk by the defendants. Bunyon owed £42 together with a sum of £31 as interest. Bunyon assigned to the plaintiff a policy of assurance on his life worth £100, and all the salary or wages due or to become due to him with the defendants or any other employer. The plaintiff attached certain conditions to the agreement and under these Bunyon agreed not to leave his job without the plaintiff's permission; to do nothing to get himself dismissed; not to borrow; not to sell, pledge or otherwise dispose of his property, and not to obtain credit. If Bunyon was in breach of any of the conditions the whole sum was immediately payable. The plaintiff now sued Bunyon's employers in respect of the salary assigned. *Held*—The contract was illegal, being against public policy, and it was therefore unenforceable. That part of the contract which dealt with the assignment of salary was not severable from the rest and so the action failed.

241. Denny's Trustee *v.* Denny, [1919] 1 K.B. 583

A young man with dissolute habits had fallen into the hands of moneylenders. A deed was entered into under the terms of which the son transferred all his property to the father, who agreed to pay all his debts and to make him a reasonable allowance. The deed provided that the son should not go within eighty miles of Piccadilly Circus without his father's consent, otherwise the annuity would be forfeited. The son became bankrupt and his trustee, wishing to set aside the deed and claim the property for the benefit of creditors, suggested that the deed constituted an illegal restraint. *Held*—The deed was good and could not be set aside; its purpose was to reform the son.

242. Neville *v.* Dominion of Canada News Co. Ltd., [1915] 3 K.B. 556

The plaintiff was a director of a land company engaged in property deals in Canada and the defendants were newspaper proprietors who owed the plaintiff a certain sum of money. Other newspapers had made adverse comments on certain of the plaintiff's land deals and had refused to accept his advertisements. The plaintiff agreed with the defendants to accept less than the sum owed to him, if the defendants would undertake not to comment unfavourably on his dealings. The defendants did publish such comment in spite of the agreement and the plaintiff sought to enforce the contract. *Held*—His action failed because the restraint was against public policy. It was the ordinary and proper business of a newspaper to comment on fraudulent schemes.

243. Wallis *v.* Day (1837), 2 M. & W. 273

The plaintiff was in business as a carrier and he sold that business to the defendant. The plaintiff agreed in return for a weekly salary of £2 3s. 10d. to serve the defendant as assistant for life and further agreed that except as assistant he would not for the rest of his life exercise the trade of carrier. This action was brought by the plaintiff to recover eighteen weeks' arrears of salary. The defence was that the contract was void as being an unlawful restraint of trade and that no part of it was enforceable. It was unnecessary to decide this point because the court *held* that the restraint was reasonable but Lord Abinger, dealing with the defence, said: "The defendants demurred on the ground that the covenant being in restraint of trade was illegal and therefore the whole contract was void. I cannot however accede to that conclusion. If a party enters into several covenants one of which cannot be enforced against him he is not therefore released from performing the others, and in the present case the defendants might have maintained an action against the plaintiff for not rendering them the services he covenanted to perform, there being nothing illegal in that part of the contract."

244. Hermann *v.* Charlesworth, [1905] 2 K.B. 123

C agreed that he would introduce gentlemen to Miss Hermann with a view to marriage. She agreed to make an immediate payment of £52 and a payment of £250 on the day of the marriage. He introduced her to several gentlemen and corresponded with others on her behalf but no marriage took place. Miss Hermann now sued for the return of the £52 and succeeded. Although the claim succeeded at common law on the ground of total failure of consideration, Sir Richard Henn-Collins said in the course of his judgment that he could have granted the return of the money by the use of Equity even after a marriage had taken place.

245. Kenyon *v.* Darwin Cotton Manufacturing Co., [1936] 2 K.B. 193

The plaintiff was employed by the defendants and joined a scheme under which the employees were to finance the company by taking up shares in it. Payment for the shares was to be made by deductions from wages and the employees signed documents agreeing to take the shares and authorising a sum of money to be deducted from their wages. This second document was illegal under the Truck Act, 1831. The plaintiff now sued to recover that part of her wages which had been applied in paying for shares, and the defendants counter-claimed for the amount due on the shares. The plaintiff succeeded because her action was a statutory one under the Truck Act of 1831. The defendants claimed that the agreement to take the shares was legal and should be severed from the part of the agreement dealing with the method of payment. *Held*—There could be no severance because that would leave a contract in which the employees agreed to pay for the shares not out of their wages but out of their assets generally, and this was an agreement which they did not intend to make.

246. Nordenfelt *v.* Maxim Nordenfelt Guns and Ammunition Co., [1894] A.C. 535

Nordenfelt was a manufacturer of machine guns and other military weapons. He sold the business to a company, giving certain undertakings which restricted his business activities. This company was amalgamated with another company and Nordenfelt was employed by the new concern as managing director. In his contract Nordenfelt agreed that for twenty-five years he would not manufacture guns or ammunition in any part of the world, and would not compete with the company in any way. *Held*—The covenant regarding the business sold was valid and enforceable, even though it was world-wide, because the business connection was world-wide and it was possible in the circumstances to sever this undertaking from the rest of the agreement. However, the further undertaking not to compete in any way with the company was unreasonable and void.

247. Morris & Co. *v.* Saxelby, [1916] 1 A.C. 688

On leaving school Saxelby entered the drawing office of a company engaged in the manufacture of lifting machinery, pulley blocks and travelling cranes. The company had its head office and works in Loughborough and branch offices in eight large cities. Eventually Saxelby became head of one of the company's departments at a salary of £3 17s. 6d. a week. He had entered into a covenant not to engage in a similar business in the United Kingdom for a period of seven years from the date of leaving the company's service. In this action the company sought to enforce that covenant and it was *held*—by the House of Lords—that it was unreasonably wide, having regard to Saxelby's interests because it would "deprive him for a lengthened period of employing, in any part of the United Kingdom, that mechanical and technical skill and knowledge which, as I have said, his own industry, observation, and intelligence have enabled him to acquire in the very specialized business of the appellants, thus forcing him to begin life afresh, as it were, and depriving him of the means of supporting himself and his family." (*per* Lord Atkinson.)

Furthermore, their Lordships were unanimously of the opinion that the covenant was wider than was necessary to protect those interests which the company was entitled to protect, being aimed at securing the appellants against all competition from Saxelby.

248. Esso Petroleum Co. Ltd. *v.* Harper's Garage (Stourport) Ltd., [1967] 1 All E.R. 699

The defendant company owned two garages with attached filling stations, the Mustow Green Garage, Mustow Green, near Kidderminster, and the Corner Garage at Stourport-on-Severn. Each garage was tied to the plaintiff oil company, the one at Mustow Green by a solus supply agreement only with a tie clause binding the dealer to take the products of the plaintiff company at its scheduled prices from time to time. There was also a price-maintenance clause which was no longer enforceable and a "continuity clause" under which the defendants, if they sold the garage, had to persuade the buyer to enter into another solus agreement with Esso. The defendants also agreed to keep the garage open at all reasonable hours and to give preference to the plaintiff company's oils. The agreement was to remain in force for four years and five months from 1st July, 1963, being the unexpired residue of the ten-year tie of a previous owner. At the Corner Garage there was a similar solus agreement for twenty-one years and a mortgage under which the plaintiffs lent Harpers £7,000 to assist them in buying the garage and improving it. The mortgage contained a tie covenant and forbade redemption for twenty-one years. In August, 1964, Harpers offered to pay off the loan but Esso refused to accept it. Harpers then turned over all four pumps at the Corner

Garage to V.I.P. and later also sold V.I.P. at Mustow Green. The plaintiff company now asked for an injunction to restrain the defendants from buying or selling fuels other than Esso at the two garages during the subsistance of the agreements. *Held*—by the House of Lords—that the rule of public policy against unreasonable restraints of trade applied to the solus agreements and the mortgage. The shorter period of four years and five months was reasonable so that that tie was valid but the other tie for twenty-one years in the solus agreement and the mortgage was invalid, so that the injunction asked for by the plaintiffs could not be granted.

248a. Cleveland Petroleum Co. Ltd. v. *Dartstone Ltd.*, [1969] 1 All E.R. 201

The owner of a garage and filling station at Crawley in Sussex leased the property to Cleveland and they in turn granted an underlease to the County Oak Service Station Ltd. The underlease contained a covenant under which all motor fuels sold were to be those of Cleveland. There was power to assign in the underlease and a number of assignments took place so that eventually Dartstone Ltd. became the lessee, having agreed to observe the covenants in the underlease. They then challenged the covenant regarding motor fuels and Cleveland asked for an injunction to enforce it. The injunction was granted. Dealing in the Court of Appeal with *Harper's Case*[248] Lord Denning, M.R., said " . . . it seems plain to me that in three at least of the speeches of their lordships a distinction is taken between a man who is *already* in possession of the land before he ties himself to an oil company and a man who is *out* of possession and is let into it by an oil company. If an owner in possession ties himself for more than five years to take all his supplies from one company, that is an unreasonable restraint of trade and is invalid. But if a man, who is out of possession, is let into possession by the oil company on the terms that he is to tie himself to that company, such a tie is good."

249. Rother v. Colchester Corporation, [1969] 2 All E.R. 600

The Corporation as landlords covenanted with Mr. Rother as tenant of a hardware shop on an estate in Colchester that they would not let any other shop on the estate for the purpose of a general hardware merchant and ironmonger. They let a shop to the local Co-operative Society as a food hall, the lease stating that they were not to sell any commodity or item which might cause the landlord to commit a breach of any of his covenants for the benefit of tenants of adjacent shops. The premises were used by the Society mainly as a food hall but items usually sold by hardware merchants were on display for sale. In this action by Mr. Rother for breach of the covenant it was *held*—by Megarry, J.—that a covenant not to let premises for a particular purpose could not be enlarged into a covenant not to permit the premises to be used for that purpose. A restrictive covenant must be construed strictly so as not to create a wider obligation than is imputed by the actual words.

250. George Silverman Ltd. v. Silverman, (1969), *The Times*, 3rd July, 1969

Mr. David Silverman, a young dress designer, and his father held shares in George Silverman Ltd. a company by which David Silverman was employed. They sold their shares to Cope Allman International Ltd. as part of a package deal under which that company acquired the ownership and goodwill of George Silverman Ltd. and the services of David Silverman under a contract of employment. The contract of employment provided that if David Silverman left the service of George Silverman he would not for a period of two years thereafter have any interest, either on his own account or as shareholder, director, servant, advisor, or agent of any person, firm, or company in any business similar to or competing with the business carried on by George Silverman Ltd. in any part of the United Kingdom or Eire. He was later found guilty of possessing cannabis and discharged by the company. The company then asked for an injunction to restrain him from competing with its business according to the terms of the restraint. *Held*—by the Court of Appeal —an injunction could be granted restraining David Silverman. Although the restraint appeared in a contract of service and might in other circumstances have been too wide, David and his father had been paid £90,000 for their shares with a further £20,000 which they would get in the future. The restraint had to be looked at as if it was between vendor and purchaser of a business. The Cope Allman company was entitled to protect its investment in George Silverman Ltd. for the two-year period of the restraint.

251. Attwood *v.* Lamont, [1920] 3 K.B. 571

Attwood carried on business as a draper, tailor and general outfitter in a shop at Kidderminster. The business was organised into different departments, each with a manager. Lamont was appointed as head cutter and manager of the tailoring department, and in his contract of service he agreed that he would not at any time, whether on his own account or on behalf of anybody else, carry on the trades of tailor, dressmaker, general draper, milliner, hatter, haberdasher, gentlemen's, ladies', or children's outfitter at any place within ten miles of Kidderminster. Some time later Lamont asked Attwood to release him from the covenant or to make him a partner, but Attwood refused to do this. Lamont left his employment and set up in business at Worcester, which was outside the ten-mile limit. However, he did do business with Attwood's customers and took orders in Kidderminster. Attwood now asked for an injunction to restrain Lamont in respect of his tailoring activities, claiming that that part of the covenant was severable, though admitting the covenant as a whole was too wide. *Held*—The part of the agreement concerning tailoring was not severable; and even if severable was invalid because it was a covenant against competition. Lamont was a rival largely because of his skill and not because of trade connection.

252. Fitch *v.* Dewes, [1921] 2 A.C. 158

A solicitor at Tamworth employed a person who was successively his articled clerk and managing clerk. In his contract of service, the clerk agreed, if he left the solicitor's employment, never to practise as a solicitor within seven miles of Tamworth Town Hall. *Held*—The agreement was good because during his service the clerk had become acquainted with the details of his employer's clients, and could be restrained even for life from using that knowledge to the detriment of his employer.

253. G. W. Plowman and Son *v.* Ash, [1964] 2 All E.R. 10

The plaintiffs, who were corn merchants, asked for an interlocutory injunction to restrain a former salesman from soliciting orders from customers or former customers in breach of an undertaking in his contract of service that he would not "canvass or solicit for himself or any other person or persons any farmer or market gardener who shall at any time during the employment of the employee hereunder have been a customer of the employers." *Held*— by the Court of Appeal—Since there was an implied limitation in the clause relating to the goods which were the subject of the employment, an interlocutory injunction should be granted. A covenant in restraint of trade regarding solicitation in a contract of service may be good provided its duration is reasonable, even though it covers customers whom the employee did not know and persons who were but have ceased to be customers and it is unlimited as to area.

253*a*. *Home Counties Dairies Ltd.* v. *Skilton*, [1970] 1 All E.R. 1227

Skilton, a milk roundsman employed by the plaintiffs, agreed, amongst other things, not "to serve or sell milk or dairy produce" to persons who within six months before leaving his employment were customers of his employers. Skilton left his employment with the plaintiffs in order to work as a roundsman for Westcott Dairies. He then took the same milk round as he had worked when he was with the plaintiffs. *Held*—by the Court of Appeal—This was a flagrant breach of agreement. The words "dairy produce" were not too wide. On a proper construction they must be restricted to things normally dealt in by a milkman on his round. "A further point was taken that the customer restriction would apply to anyone who had been a customer within the last six months of the employment and had during that period ceased so to be, and it was said that the employer could have no legitimate interest in such persons. I think this point is met in the judgment in *G. W. Plowman & Sons Ltd.* v. *Ash*, 1964,[253] where it was said that a customer might have left temporarily and that his return was not beyond hope and was therefore a matter of legitimate interest to the employer." (*per* Harman, J.L.)

254. Gledhow Autoparts *v.* Delaney, [1965] 3 All E.R. 288

The defendant, a commercial traveller, was employed by a company under a contract of service which provided that for three years from the termination of his employment he would not "solicit or seek to obtain orders . . . from any person firm or company situate or carrying on business within the districts in which the traveller had operated during the course of this agreement or during any periods of employment with" the company.

The defendant sold parts for the lighting systems of cars and was required to call at garages in various districts in Southern England. However, there were many garages in this area which were not, and never had been, the plaintiff's customers, and on which the defendant did not call. After leaving his employment the defendant continued to solicit orders on his own account from garages in the districts in which he had worked for the company. An injunction to restrain him from so doing was granted at first instance. The traveller appealed to the Court of Appeal where it was *held* that the injunction should not have been granted. The condition was invalid as being in unreasonable restraint of trade. Where an employer imposes a restraint which is to last three years and which extends to many persons, firms or companies which are not customers, and on whom the employee does not call, the restraint is wider than is reasonably necessary for the protection of the employer's business.

N.B. According to Sellers and Diplock, L.JJ., the restraint would have been reasonable if it had included—

(*a*) Actual customers.
(*b*) Persons on whom the traveller had called in the course of his work, even though they were not his employer's customers.

255. Scorer *v.* Seymour Jones, [1966] All E.R. 347

Under a contract dated 2nd June, 1964, between an estate agent and one of his unqualified employees who was the estate agent's clerk and negotiator, the employee agreed that he would not, for three years after leaving his employment, carry on or be employed or interested in the business of an auctioneer, surveyor or estate agent within five miles of the employer's premises at Kingsbridge and Dartmouth. The employee was the manager of the branch office at Kingsbridge and there were recurring customers at this branch. The employee was unsatisfactory and was dismissed in November, 1964; thereafter he practised on his own account as an estate agent in Salcombe within five miles of Kingsbridge, but outside a five-mile radius of Dartmouth. The employer Scorer asked for an injunction restraining his former employee Seymour Jones from practising within five miles of the Kingsbridge office. The injunction was granted at Kingsbridge County Court, and on appeal by the employee against the granting of an injunction it was *held*—by the Court of Appeal—that the injunction was rightly granted because the employer had many recurring clients and the restraint on practising within five miles of the Kingsbridge office was reasonable. Further, the restriction on practising within five miles of the Dartmouth office was not a reasonable restraint but was severable. *Per* Sellers, L.J., in considering whether the restriction was contrary to the public interest, it was proper to take into account the fact that the employee was unqualified and not controlled by professional rules.

256. Printers and Finishers *v.* Holloway (No. 2). [1964] 3 All E.R. 731

The plaintiffs brought an action against Holloway, their former works manager, and others, including Vita-Tex Ltd., into whose employment Holloway had subsequently entered, claiming injunctions against Holloway and other defendants based, as regards Holloway, on an alleged breach of an implied term in his contract of service with the plaintiffs that he should not disclose or make improper use of confidential information relating to the plaintiff's trade secrets. Holloway's contract did not contain an express covenant relating to non-disclosure of trade secrets. The plaintiffs were flock-printers and had built up their own fund of "know-how" in this field. The action against Vita-Tex arose because Holloway had, on one occasion, taken a Mr. James, who was an employee of Vita-Tex Ltd., round the plaintiff's factory. Mr. James's visit took place in the evening and followed a chance meeting between himself and Holloway. However, the plant was working and James did see a number of processes. It also appeared that Holloway had, during his employment made copies of certain of the plaintiff's documentary material and had taken these copies away with him when he left their employ. The plaintiffs sought an injunction to prevent the use of disclosure of the material contained in the copies of documents made by Holloway.

Held—by Cross, J.—

(*a*) the plaintiffs were entitled to an injunction against Holloway so far as the documentary material was concerned, although there was no express term in his contract regarding non-disclosure of trade secrets;

(*b*) no injunction would be granted restraining Holloway from putting at the disposal of Vita-Tex Ltd. his memory of particular features of the plaintiffs' plant and processes. He was under no express contract not to do so and the Court would not extend its equitable jurisdiction to restrain breach of confidence in this instance. Holloway's knowledge of the plaintiffs' trade secrets was not readily separable from his general knowledge of flock printing;

(*c*) an injunction would be granted restraining Vita-Tex Ltd. from making use of the information acquired by James on his visit.

257. Robb *v.* Green, [1895] 2 Q.B. 315

The plaintiff was a dealer in live game and eggs. The major part of his business consisted of procuring the eggs, and the hatching, rearing and sale of game birds. For the purpose of carrying on this business, the plaintiff occupied game farms at Liphook in Hampshire, and at Elstead near Godalming. His customers were numerous and for the most part were country gentlemen and their gamekeepers. The plaintiff kept a list of these customers in his order book. The defendant, who was for three years the plaintiff's manager, copied these names and addresses, and after leaving the plaintiff's employ set up in a similar business on his own and sent circulars both to the plaintiff's customers and their gamekeepers inviting them to do business with him. The plaintiff sought damages and an injunction. *Held*—by the Court of Appeal (affirming the judgment of Hawkins, J.)—Although there was no express term in the defendant's contract to restrain him from such activities, it was an implied term of the contract of service that the defendant would observe good faith towards his master during the existence of the confidential relationship between them. The defendant's conduct was a breach of that contract in respect of which the plaintiff was entitled to damages of £150 and an injunction.

258. Sanders *v.* Parry, [1967] 2 All E.R. 803

In January, 1964, the defendant was engaged by the plaintiff solicitor as assistant solicitor. The defendant had been told by the plaintiff that he was to undertake the legal work of an important client, Mr. Tully. The defendant took up his employment on 16th March, 1964. During August or September, 1964, the defendant and Tully agreed that the defendant would set up in practice on his account whereupon Tully would transfer all his legal business from the plaintiff to the defendant and this was done. In an action for damages for breach of an implied term of the contract that the defendant would serve the plaintiff faithfully, the defendant admitted the term but said that he was not in breach of it because the agreement between him and Tully had been initiated by Tully and he had merely accepted an offer which Tully had made. *Held*—That even if the agreement had not been initiated by the defendant, he had, in accepting the offer during the substance of his agreement with the plaintiff, acted contrary to the interests of the plaintiff and was in breach of the implied term of fidelity.

259. Hivac Ltd. *v.* Park Royal Scientific Instruments Ltd., [1946] 1 All E.R. 350

The plaintiffs were manufacturers of midget valves used in deaf aids, the work requiring a high degree of skill. The defendants were newcomers to the trade and concerned themselves mainly with the assembly of hearing aids. The plaintiffs' employees worked a five and a half day week, having Sunday free. Five such employees worked on Sundays for the defendants, assisting in the assembly of midget valves. The plaintiffs asked for an injunction to restrain their employees from carrying out such work. *Held*—In the special circumstances of the case an injunction would be granted, not because of any specific contractual restraint but because the conduct of the particular employees constituted a breach of the duty of fidelity which every servant owes to his master.

260. Commercial Plastics *v.* Vincent, [1964] 3 All E.R. 546

The plaintiffs employed Vincent, a plastics technologist, to co-ordinate research and development in the production of their P.V.C. (Poly-vinyl-chloride) calendered sheeting, which was made up into adhesive tape. Vincent's contract forbade him to seek employment with any of the plaintiffs' competitors in the P.V.C. calendering field for one year after leaving their employment. Vincent had access to secret material, including certain mixing specifications recorded in code and, although he could not remember these, he could probably remember, in relation to any matter concerning adhesive tape, what was the problem and what was the solution, what experiments were made and whether the results were positive or negative. Vincent left his employment with the plaintiffs and proposed to take up employment with a competitor. The plaintiffs asked for an injunction to restrain Vincent from breaking the restraining term in his contract with them. *Held*—by the Court of Appeal—An injunction could not be granted. Although what Vincent could remember was sufficiently definite to be capable of protection by an appropriate condition or covenant, the term in the agreement was excessive. It was world-wide in scope, although the plaintiffs did not, on the facts of the case, require protection outside the United Kingdom. Furthermore, the term extended to the plaintiff's competitors in the whole field of P.V.C. whereas they required protection, so far as Vincent was concerned, only in relation to calendered sheeting for adhesive tape.

261. Kores Manufacturing Co. Ltd. *v.* Kolok Manufacturing Co. Ltd., [1959] Ch. 108

The two companies occupied adjoining premises in Tottenham and both manufactured carbon papers, typewriter ribbons and the like. They made an agreement in which each company agreed that it would not, without the written consent of the other, "at any time employ any person who during the past five years shall have been a servant of yours." The plaintiffs' chief chemist sought employment with the defendants, and the plaintiffs were not prepared to consent to this and asked for an injunction to enforce the agreement. *Held*—by the Court of Appeal—

(*a*) A contract in restraint of trade cannot be enforced unless—

    (i) it is reasonable as between the parties, *and*
    (ii) it is consistent with the interests of the public.

(*b*) The mere fact that the parties are dealing on equal terms does not prevent the court from holding that the restraint is unreasonable in the interests of those parties.

(*c*) The restraint in this case was grossly in excess of what was required to protect the parties and accordingly was unreasonable in the interests of the parties.

(*d*) The agreement therefore failed to satisfy the first of the two conditions set out in (*a*) above and was void and unenforceable.

262. General Billposting Co. Ltd. *v.* Atkinson [1909], A.C. 118

Atkinson was manager to a Newcastle billposting company for a number of years upon terms that he should hold office subject to termination at twelve months' notice by either party, and with a restriction on his right to trade after termination of his employment. The restriction on trade was that he should not, whilst in the employment of the company or within two years afterwards, carry on a similar business within a certain radius of Newcastle without the company's permission. In 1906 Atkinson was dismissed without notice and he successfully sued the company for wrongful dismissal. Having recovered damages he began to trade as a billposter on his own account within the prohibited area. The General Billposting Co. Ltd., having taken over the company with which Atkinson was employed, brought an action for an injunction and for damages for breach of contract. *Held*—by the House of Lords —Atkinson was entitled to treat the dismissal as a repudiation of the contract and to sue for damages for breach of contract, and was no longer bound by the restriction on trade.

263. Bromley *v.* Smith, [1919] 2 K.B. 235

The plaintiff was a baker at Clacton and it was his practice to send carts containing bread on various rounds to visit boarding houses and shops. In 1895 the plaintiff required an assistant to undertake what was known as the town round and by means of an advertisement he came into communication with the defendant, a young man of eighteen years, who lived some miles away at a place called Great Baddow. The defendant had since the age of twelve been engaged in the bakery trade. On 18th November, 1895, the plaintiff and defendant entered into an agreement under which the defendant agreed that he would not at any time within the space of three years after the date of leaving the plaintiff's service engage or be engaged in the business of miller, baker, hay, straw or corn dealer, or restaurant keeper, or in the manufacture of flour meal. Eventually the defendant terminated his employment by giving notice to the plaintiff and then in partnership with a man named Green he took over premises in Clacton, three miles from the plaintiff's premises, and commenced business as a baker and confectioner. Both before and after he left the plaintiff's employment the defendant, on his own admission, canvassed the plaintiff's customers and some of these customers gave their custom to the defendant. At the time of the agreement the plaintiff did not carry on any business other than that of a baker and confectioner but he was contemplating an extension of his business and was considering opening a restaurant. *Held*— by Channell, J.—the restraint must coincide with what is necessary for the protection of the existing business of the employer and the restriction relating to the business of restaurant keeper went further than was necessary. However, the restraint was severable because each of the prohibited trades was stated separately and those restraints relating to the business of baker or confectioner were enforceable. Furthermore, the contract as severed was enforceable, even though the defendant was an infant when he made it. It was a contract for his benefit even though it contained restraints. "A contract which contains only terms on which an infant can reasonably expect employment must, I think, be for his benefit."

264. Bull *v.* Pitney-Bowes, [1956] 3 All E.R. 384

The plaintiff was employed by the defendant and it was a term of that employment that the plaintiff should belong to a non-contributory pension scheme. It was also provided that any retired member of the pension scheme who took employment in any activity in competition with, or detrimental to, the defendant's interests would forfeit his rights under the pension scheme unless he discontinued the activity when required to do so. The plaintiff retired and took up employment with one of the defendant's competitors. He was requested to discontinue this activity but refused to do so, and he sued his former employer and the committee and custodian trustee of the pension fund for declarations that the forfeiture provision was void and that he was entitled to a pension. *Held*—by Thesiger, J.—that the declarations should be made; the forfeiture clause was void as an unreasonable restraint of trade.

265. Initial Services *v.* Putterill, [1967] 3 All E.R. 145

The first defendant was employed by the plaintiff launderers as their sales manager but he resigned and took a number of the plaintiff's documents which he handed to reporters of the *Daily Mail*, who were the second defendants. He also gave the reporters of the same newspaper information about the company's affairs. The newspaper published articles alleging a liaison system between launderers to keep up their prices, and that the plaintiffs had increased their prices after the imposition of the Selective Employment Tax ostensibly to offset that tax, when in fact they were getting substantial extra profit. On the plaintiff's action for breach of an implied term of the defendant's contract of service that he would not disclose to strangers confidential information obtained by him in the course of his employment, the defendant pleaded that the plaintiffs had agreements which ought to have been registered under the Restrictive Trade Practices Act, 1956, that they ought to have been referred to the Monopolies Commission, and that they had issued misleading circulars about their reasons for raising their prices. *Held*—

    (i) The servant was under no obligation not to disclose information which ought, in the public interest, to be disclosed to a person having a proper interest to receive it;
    (ii) it was at least arguable that the information supplied by the defendant was in the above category;
    (iii) the allegations in the defence could not be said to be so invalid that they ought to be struck out.

There was argument on the question as to whether the press was the proper authority for the receipt of confidential information but this doubt was not enough to invalidate the defence at this stage.

266. Lyne-Pirkis *v.* Jones, [1969] 3 All E.R. 738

The plaintiff and the defendant were medical practitioners in practice at Godalming. A clause in the partnership deed stated that if any partner retired he should not "for a period of five years immediately following such retirement . . . engage in practice as a medical practitioner whether alone or jointly with any other person within a radius of 10 miles of the Market House in Godalming." The defendant terminated the partnership and the plaintiff asked for an injunction to prevent him from practising within the stated area. The patients of the partnership all lived within a radius of five miles. *Held*—by the Court of Appeal—that the covenant was not enforceable. It was wider than was reasonably necessary to restrict competition because it used the phrase "medical practitioner" which could include medical consultant and was not limited to general practice. In these circumstances there was no need for the court to decide whether a radius of 10 miles was too wide, though Russell, L.J., thought it was.

267. Pharmaceutical Society of Great Britain *v.* Dickson, [1968] 2 All E.R. 686

The Society passed a resolution to the effect that the opening of new pharmacies should be restricted and be limited to certain specified services, and that the range of services in existing pharmacies should not be extended except as approved by the Society's council. The purpose of the resolution was clearly to stop the development of new fields of trading in conjunction with pharmacy. Mr. Dickson, who was a member of the Society and retail director of Boots Pure Drug Company Ltd., brought this action on the grounds that the proposed new rule was *ultra vires* as an unreasonable restraint of trade. A declaration that the resolution was *ultra vires* was made and the Society appealed to the House of Lords where the appeal was dismissed, the following points emerging from the judgment.

(i) Where a professional association passes a resolution regulating the conduct of its members the validity of the resolution is a matter for the courts even if binding in honour only, since failure to observe it is likely to be construed as misconduct and thus become a ground for disciplinary action.

(ii) A resolution by a professional association regulating the conduct of its members is *ultra vires* if it is not sufficiently related to the main objects of the association. The objects of the society in this case did not cover the resolution, being "to maintain the honour and safeguard and promote the interests of the members in the exercise of the profession of pharmacy."

(iii) A resolution by a professional association regulating the conduct of its members will be void if it is in unreasonable restraint of trade.

268. Re Chocolate and Sugar Confectionery Reference, [1967] 3 All E.R. 261

The Restrictive Practices Court was asked to make an order exempting chocolate, sugar confectionery, and related types of goods from the general ban on resale price maintenance. The case for the suppliers, i.e. virtually all of the major manufacturers, was that without resale price maintenance there would be a major shift in trade from confectionery shops to supermarkets as a result of price cutting. This would lead to a loss of sales since chocolate and similar goods were often bought on impulse from small outlets. This would in turn lead to loss of variety and higher prices in the long run.

That price cutting by supermarkets would take place was accepted by the Court but the consequences were not regarded as inevitably those put forward by the suppliers. A normal shopper would not, for example, travel more than a short distance to buy a bar of chocolate for say, one new penny less than the recommended price. Some shops would go out of business, probably to the extent of 10 per cent of outlets, but in the view of the Court this reduction would not cause the public significant inconvenience. Accordingly the Court ruled that the suppliers had not established their case and that resale price maintenance for chocolate and sweets was unlawful.

A significant feature of the case was the acceptance by the Court of evidence of economic principles and statistics. It marks the first real sign of co-operation between lawyers and economists; the arguments were economic and statistical rather than legal.

269. Moore & Co. *v.* Landauer & Co., [1921] 2 K.B. 519

The plaintiffs entered into a contract to sell the defendants a certain quantity of Australian canned fruit, the goods to be packed in cases containing 30 tins each. The goods were to be shipped "per S.S. *Toromeo*." The ship was delayed by strikes at Melbourne and in South Africa, and was very late in arriving at London. When the goods were discharged about one half of the consignment was packed in cases containing 24 tins only, instead of 30, and the buyers refused to accept them. *Held*—Although the method of packing made no difference to the market value of the goods, the sale was by description under Sect. 13 of the Sale of Goods Act, 1893, and the description had not been complied with. Consequently the buyers were entitled to reject the whole consignment by virtue of the provisions of Sect. 30 (3) of the Sale of Goods Act.

270. Cutter *v.* Powell (1795), 6 Term Rep. 320

The defendant was the master of a ship called the *Governor Parry* and the plaintiff was the second mate on that ship. The ship sailed from Jamaica on 2nd August, 1793, and Cutter sailed in her and carried out all his duties as second mate. However, he died on 20th September, 1793, i.e. before the ship completed her voyage to Liverpool on 9th October, 1793. The contract under which Cutter rendered the services was worded as follows—

"Ten days after the ship Governor Parry my self master arrives at Liverpool I promise to pay to Mr. T. Cutter the sum of 30 guineas provided he proceeds, continues and does his duty as second mate in the said ship from hence to the port of Liverpool. Signed at Kingston, 31st July, 1793."

Cutter's widow now sued to recover a proportionate part of his wages, but Lord Kenyon, C.J., held that the contract was entire and there could be no claim on a *quantum meruit* for partial performance.

N.B. The Merchant Shipping Act, 1970, now provides for the payment of wages for partial performance in such cases, and the Law Reform (Frustrated Contracts) Act, 1943, would also have assisted the widow to recover, because the sailor had conferred a benefit on the master of the ship prior to his death, which would now frustrate the contract, giving the widow the right to sue the master for the benefit of Cutter's work up to the time of his death.

271. Sumpter *v.* Hedges, [1898] 1 Q.B. 673

The plaintiff entered into a contract with the defendant under the terms of which the plaintiff was to erect some buildings for the defendant on the defendant's land for a price of £565. The plaintiff did partially erect the buildings up to the value of £333, and the defendant paid him a part of that figure. The plaintiff then told the defendant that he could not finish the job because he had run out of funds. The defendant then completed the work by using material belonging to the plaintiff which had been left on the site. The plaintiff now sued for work done and materials supplied, and the Court gave him judgment for materials supplied, but would not grant him a sum of money by way of *quantum meruit* for the value of the work done prior to his abandonment of the job. The reason was given that, before the plaintiff could sue successfully on a *quantum meruit*, he would have to show that the defendant had voluntarily accepted the work done, and this implied that the defendant must be in a position to refuse the benefit of the work as where a buyer of goods refuses to take delivery. This was not the case here; the defendant had no option but to accept the work done, so his acceptance could not be presumed from conduct. There being no other evidence of the defendant's acceptance of the work, the plaintiff's claim for the work done failed.

272. De Barnardy *v.* Harding (1853), 8 Exch. 822

The plaintiff agreed to act as the defendant's agent for the purpose of preparing and issuing certain advertisements and notices designed to encourage the sale of tickets to see the funeral procession of the Duke of Wellington. The plaintiff was to be paid a commission of 10 per cent upon the proceeds of the tickets actually sold. The plaintiff duly issued the advertisements and notices, but before he began to sell the tickets, the defendant withdrew the plaintiff's authority to sell them and in consequence the plaintiff did not sell any tickets and was prevented from earning his commission. The plaintiff now sued upon a *quantum meruit* and his action succeeded.

273. Hoenig *v.* Isaacs, [1952] 2 All E.R. 176

The defendant employed the plaintiff who was an interior decorator and furniture designer to decorate a one room flat owned by the defendant. The plaintiff was also to provide furniture, including a fitted bookcase, a wardrobe and a bedstead, for the total sum of £750. The terms of the contract regarding payment were as follows—"Net cash as the work proceeds and the balance on completion." The defendant made two payments to the plaintiff of £150 each, one payment on the 12th April and the other on the 19th April. The plaintiff claimed that he had completed the work on 28th August, and asked for the balance, i.e. £450. The defendant asserted that the work done was bad and faulty, but sent the plaintiff a sum of £100 and moved into the flat and used the furniture. The plaintiff now sued for the balance of £350, the defence being that the plaintiff had not performed his contract, or in the alternative that he had done so negligently, unskilfully and in an unworkmanlike manner.

The Official Referee assessed the work that had been done, and found that generally it was properly done except that the wardrobe door required replacing and that a bookshelf was too short and this meant that the bookcase would have to be remade. The defendant claimed that the contract was entire and that it must be completely performed before the plaintiff could recover. The Official Referee was of opinion that there had been substantial performance, and that the defendant was liable for £750 less the cost of putting right the above mentioned defects, the cost of this being assessed at £55 18s. 2d. The Court accordingly gave the plaintiff judgment for the sum of £294 1s. 10d.

274. Narbeth *v.* James (the Lady Tahilla), [1967] 1 Lloyds' Rep. 591

The plaintiff sold his motor-yacht to the defendant in April, 1960, for a price of £8,000. The defendant paid £5,000 and it was agreed that the balance be met at the defendant's option in one of three ways—(i) by allowing the plaintiff free use of the yacht for one month during each of the years 1962, 1963 and 1964, subject to the plaintiff giving the defendant three months' notice of the month in which he required the yacht; (ii) by paying the plaintiff £1,000 for any year in which the yacht was not available for use under method (i); (iii) by payment in cash if the vessel was disposed of by the defendant. In April, 1960, the defendant secured the balance due from him by executing a mortgage in favour of the plaintiff. In 1966 the plaintiff sued the defendant for the whole balance with interest under the mortgage. The defendant denied liability and contended that the yacht was made available for the plaintiff in 1962, 1963 and 1964, but the plaintiff had not given notice of the month he required her. *Held*—By Brandon, J.,—that the plaintiff was entitled to the £3,000 plus interest. As a general proposition where A had an option to perform a contract in more than one way and the obligations of B depended on which way A chose and could only be effectively performed by B if he had notice beforehand, then A would be under an implied obligation to give B proper notice. Thus in the present case in order to give business efficacy to the contract it was necessary to imply a term that the defendant would give the plaintiff reasonable prior notice whether or not he was choosing method (i) in respect of any of the three relevant years. No notice had been given, therefore the mortgage remained undischarged and the plaintiff was entitled to the judgment.

275. Bowes v. Shand (1877), 2 App. Cas. 455

The action was brought for damages for non-acceptance of 600 tons (or 8,200 bags) of Madras rice. The sold note stated that the rice was to be shipped during "the months of March and/or April 1874." 8,150 bags were put on board ship on or before February 28th, 1874, and the remaining 50 bags on March 2nd, 1874. The defendants refused to take delivery because the rice was not shipped in accordance with the terms of the contract. *Held*—The bulk of the cargo was shipped in February and therefore the rice did not answer the description in the contract and the defendants were not bound to accept it.

276. Chas. Rickards Ltd. v. Oppenheim, [1950] 1 K.B. 616

The defendant ordered a Rolls-Royce chassis from the plaintiffs, the chassis being delivered in July, 1947. The plaintiffs found a coach builder prepared to make a body within six or at the most seven months. The specification for the body was agreed in August, 1947, so that the work should have been completed in March, 1948. The work was not completed by then but the defendant still pressed for delivery. On 29th June, 1948, the defendant wrote to the coach-builders saying that he would not accept delivery after 25th July, 1948. The body was not ready by then and the defendant bought another car. The body was completed in October, 1948, but the defendant refused to accept delivery and counter-claimed for the value of the chassis which he had purchased. *Held*—Time was of the essence of the original contract, but the defendant had waived the question of time by continuing to press for delivery after the due date. However, by his letter of 29th June he had again made time of the essence, and had given reasonable notice in the matter. Judgment was given for the defendant on the claim and counter-claim.

277. Elmdore Ltd. v. Keech (1969), 113 S.J. 871

The plaintiffs agreed to print an advertisement in their plastic telephone directory cover which they said would be distributed within 120 days. The covers were distributed 11 days late. It was *held*—by the Court of Appeal—that since this was a mercantile contract the general rule that time was of the essence applied unless the circumstances showed otherwise. There were no special circumstances on the facts of the case and the plaintiffs' action for the price must be dismissed.

278. Deeley v. Lloyds Bank Ltd., [1912] A.C. 756

A customer of the bank had mortgaged his property to the bank to secure an overdraft limited to £2,500. He then mortgaged the same property to the appellant for £3,500, subject to the bank's mortgage. It is the normal practice of bankers, on receiving notice of a second mortgage, to rule off the customer's account, and not to allow any further withdrawals, since these will rank after the second mortgage. In this case the bank did not open a new account but continued the old current account. The customer thereafter paid in moneys which at a particular date, if they had been appropriated in accordance with the rule in *Clayton's* case, would have extinguished the bank's mortgage. Even so the customer still owed the bank money, and they sold the property for a price which was enough to satisfy the bank's debt but not that of the appellant. *Held*—The evidence did not exclude the rule in *Clayton's* case, which applied, so that the bank's mortgage had been paid off and the appellant, as second mortgagee, was entitled to the proceeds of the sale.

279. Hochster *v.* De la Tour (1853), 2 E. & B. 678

The defendant agreed in April, 1852, to engage the plaintiff as a courier for European travel, his duties to commence on 1st June, 1852. On 11th May, 1852, the defendant wrote to the plaintiff saying that he no longer required his services. The plaintiff commenced an action for breach of contract on 22nd May, 1852, and the defence was that there was no cause of action until the date due for performance, i.e. 1st June, 1852. *Held*—The defendant's express repudiation constituted an actionable breach of contract.

279a. Gorse v. *Durham County Council*, [1971] 1 W.L.R. 775

The plaintiffs were school teachers employed by the defendants. Their contracts allowed suspension for misconduct without loss of salary if there was reinstatement. On the instructions of their union the plaintiffs refused to serve school meals whereupon the education office excluded them from the school and withheld their salaries. They were later reinstated and sued for the salary withheld. Cusack, J. *held* that supervising meals was a normal part of a teacher's duties and refusal was an express repudiation of the contract. However, since the defendants had not accepted the repudiation but had reinstated the plaintiffs they must be regarded as having been suspended and were entitled under the terms of their contracts to the salary withheld.

280. Omnium D'Entreprises and Others *v.* Sutherland, [1919] 1 K.B. 618

The defendant was the owner of a steamship and agreed to let her to the plaintiff for a period of time and to pay the second plaintiffs a commission on the hire payable under the agreement. The defendant later sold the ship to a purchaser, free of all liability under his agreement with the plaintiffs. *Held*— The sale by the defendant was a repudiation of the agreement and the plaintiffs were entitled to damages for breach of the contract.

281. Maredelanto Compania Naviera S.A. *v.* Bergbau-Handel GmbH The Mihalis Angelos, [1970] 3 All E.R. 125

The vessel Mihalis Angelos, which was owned by Maredelanto, was chartered by Bergbau-Handel under a charterparty dated 25th May, 1965. The charterparty provided—

    (i) that the vessel should be ready to load about 1st July, 1965; and
    (ii) that if it was not ready to load on or before 20th July, 1965, the charterers should have the option of cancelling the contract.

The purpose of the charterparty was for the charterers to load mineral ore (apatite) in Haiphong in North Vietnam and transport it to Hamburg or other port in Europe. Sometime before 12th July, 1965, the railway which was to bring the ore to Haiphong was allegedly destroyed by American bombing. However, the Mihalis Angelos was in Hong Kong on 23rd July and could not have reached Haiphong before 27th July. Instead of waiting until 20th July when they could have cancelled the contract legitimately, the charterers decided to repudiate it on 17th July on the grounds of *force majeure* because they thought the railway had been destroyed so that the apatite ore could not be transported to Haiphong, thus rendering the charterparty useless to them. The shipowners did not accept that *force majeure* applied and they sued for £4,000 being damages for loss of the charter. At first instance Mocatta, J., *held* that the charterers were not entitled to repudiate on 17th July. The situation was not necessarily one of *force majeure* at that time. They were therefore in breach on 17th July and the owners were entitled to sue at that time. In addition they were entitled to damages of £4,000 and it did not matter that they would have been unable to perform the contract at the due date, i.e. 20th July. In the Court of Appeal, however, it was decided that the owners were only entitled to nominal damages. The fact that the owners could not have performed the contract on 20th July was a contingency which had to be taken into account.

282. Avery *v.* Bowden (1855), 5 E. & B. 714

The defendant chartered the plaintiff's ship and agreed to load her with a cargo at Odessa within forty-five days. The ship went to Odessa and remained there for most of the forty-five day period. The defendant told the captain of the ship that he did not propose to load a cargo and that he would do well to leave, but the captain stayed on at Odessa, hoping that the defendant would change his mind. Before the end of the forty-five day period the Crimean War broke out so that performance of the contract would have been illegal. *Held*— The plaintiff might have treated the defendant's refusal to load a cargo as an anticipatory breach of contract but his agent, the captain, had waived that right by staying on at Odessa, and now the contract had been discharged by something which was beyond the control of either party.

283. White and Carter (Councils) Ltd. *v.* McGregor, [1961] 2 W.L.R. 17

The respondent was a garage proprietor on Clydebank and on 26th June, 1957, his sales manager, without specific authority, entered into a contract with the appellants whereby the appellants agreed to advertise the respondent's business on litter bins which they supplied to local authorities. The contract was to last for three years from the date of the first advertisement display. Payment was to be by instalments annually in advance, the first instalment being due seven days after the first display. The contract contained a clause that, on failure to pay an instalment or other breach of contract, the whole sum of £196 4s. became due. The respondent was quick to repudiate the contract for on 26th June, 1957, he wrote to the appellants asking them to cancel the agreement, and at this stage the appellants had not taken any steps towards carrying it out. The appellants refused to cancel the agreement and prepared the advertisement plates which they exhibited on litter bins in November, 1957, and continued to display them during the following three years. Eventually the appellants demanded payment, the respondent refused to pay, and the appellants brought an action against him for the sum due under the contract. *Held*—The appellants were entitled to recover the contract price since, although the respondent had repudiated the contract, the appellants were not obliged to accept the repudiation. The contract survived and the appellants had now completed it.

N.B. Although the respondent's agent had no actual authority, he had made a similar contract with the appellants in 1954, and it was not disputed that he had apparent authority to bind his principal.

284. Allen *v.* Robles (Compagnie Parisienne de Guarantie Third Party), [1969] 3 All E.R. 154

The defendant, Mr. Robles, drove his car in a negligent fashion and ran into the plaintiff's house. In an action at Nottingham Assizes the judge awarded the plaintiff damages against Mr. Robles and the question arose as to whether Mr. Robles could claim on his insurance policy with the French insurance company which was joined as third party in this action. Mr. Robles was in breach of his contract of insurance because that contract provided that he must notify the insurance company of any claim made against him within five days of the claim. This he had not done. In fact he failed to inform the insurance company of the claim by the plaintiff until two months after he knew it had been made. On the other hand the insurance company did not repudiate their liability until some four months after Mr. Robles informed them of the claim. It was *held*—by the Court of Appeal—that the insurance company had not lost its right to repudiate the contract. The delay was not so long as to indicate that they had accepted liability and it had in no way changed the circumstances of the case. It had not, for example, increased Mr. Allen's loss or altered Mr. Robles' liability. There was thus no prejudice to those concerned.

285. Total Oil Great Britain Ltd. *v.* Thompson Garages (Biggin Hill) Ltd., *The Times*, October 8, 1971

The plaintiffs leased a garage to the defendants for fourteen years on terms that the defendants would purchase all their fuel supplies from the plaintiffs and that payment was on delivery. Later the plaintiffs changed the method of payment to a banker's draft sent to the plaintiffs depot *before* delivery. This was a repudiation of the contract by the plaintiffs which was accepted by the defendants who went elsewhere for their fuel. The plaintiffs claimed, amongst other things, an injunction restraining the defendants from selling fuels other than those obtained from the plaintiffs. The plaintiffs also agreed to revert to the "cash on delivery" system of payment. *Held*—by the Court of Appeal— that an injunction would be granted. A lease which conveys an interest in land does not come to an end like an ordinary contract by repudiation and acceptance of repudiation, and so was still in existence in the present case. The plaintiffs could insist upon the enforcement of the tie since they were now prepared to adhere to the terms of supply and payment.

N.B. The Court referred to *Cricklewood Property and Investment Trust Ltd.* v. *Leighton's Investment Trust Ltd.*, 1945[295] and stated, following Lord Russell and Lord Goddard, that the better view was that a lease cannot come to an end by frustration.

286. Davis Contractors Ltd., *v.* Fareham U.D.C., [1956] A.C. 696

In July, 1946, the plaintiff contracted with the defendants to build seventy-eight houses for £92,425 within a period of eight months. Owing to lack of adequate supplies of labour and building materials, it took the plaintiffs twenty-two months to complete the work. There was no provision in the contract regarding such eventualities. The extra expense incurred by the plaintiffs was £17,651, and they claimed that the original contract with the council was frustrated and that they were entitled to recover the total cost on a *quantum meruit*. *Held*—Events had made the contract more onerous to the plaintiffs but had not frustrated the contract. The eventuality should have been provided for. The only claim the plaintiffs had was for the sum agreed in the contract; *quantum meruit* was not available in the absence of frustration.

287. Re Shipton, Anderson & Co. and Harrison Bros.' Arbitration, [1915] 3 K.B. 676

A contract was made for the sale of wheat lying in a warehouse in Liverpool. Before the seller could deliver the wheat, and before the property in it had passed to the buyer, the Government requisitioned the wheat under certain emergency powers available in time of war. *Held*—Delivery being impossible by reason of lawful requisition by the Government, the seller was excused from performance of the contract.

288. Storey v. Fulham Steel Works (1907), 24 T.L.R. 89

The plaintiff was employed by the defendants as manager for a period of five years. After he had been working for two years he became ill, and had to have special treatment and a period of convalescence. Six months later he was recovered, but in the meantime the defendant had terminated his employment. The plaintiff how sued for breach of contract, and the defendants pleaded that the plaintiff's period of ill-health operated to discharge the contract. *Held*—The plaintiff's illness and absence from duty did not go to the root of the contract, and was not so serious as to allow the termination of the agreement.

289. Taylor v. Caldwell (1863), 3 B. & S. 826

The defendant agreed to let the plaintiff have the use of a music hall for the purpose of holding four concerts. Before the first concert was due to be held the hall was destroyed by fire, and the plaintiff now sued for damages because of the defendant's breach of contract in not having the premises ready for him. *Held*—The contract was impossible of performance and the defendant was not liable.

290. Krell v. Henry, [1903] 2 K.B. 740

The plaintiff owned a room overlooking the proposed route of the Coronation procession of Edward VII, and had let it to the defendant for the purpose of viewing the procession. The procession did not take place because of the King's illness and the plaintiff now sued for the agreed fee. *Held*—The fact that the procession had been cancelled discharged the parties from their obligations, since it was no longer possible to achieve the real purpose of the agreement.

291. Herne Bay Steamboat Co. v. Hutton, [1903] 2 K.B. 683

The plaintiffs agreed to hire a steamboat to the defendant for two days, in order that the defendant might take paying passengers to see the naval review at Spithead on the occasion of Edward VII's Coronation. An official announcement was made cancelling the review, but the fleet was assembled and the boat might have been used for the intended cruise. The defendant did not use the boat, and the plaintiffs employed her on ordinary business. This action was brought to recover the fee of £200 which the defendant had promised to pay for the hire of the boat. *Held*—The contract was not discharged, as the review of the fleet by the sovereign was not the foundation of the contract. The plaintiffs were awarded the difference between £200 and the profits derived from the use of the ship for ordinary business on the two days in question.

292. Joseph Constantine Steamship Line Ltd. *v.* Imperial Smelting Corporation Ltd., [1942] A.C. 154

The respondents chartered a steamship to proceed to Port Pirie, Australia, to load a cargo. On the day before the ship was due to load her cargo, and whilst she was lying in the roads off Port Pirie, there was an explosion in one of her boilers. She was therefore unable to perform the charter as agreed, although she could have done so after rather extensive repairs. The respondents claimed damages for breach of contract. *Held*—The explosion frustrated the contract and the appellants were not liable. The cause of the explosion was unknown, and negligence could not be proved against the appellants; otherwise they would have been liable on the ground that the frustrating event would have been self-induced.

293. Jackson *v.* Union Marine Insurance Co. (1874), L.R. 10 C.P. 125

The plaintiff was the owner of a ship which had been chartered to go with all possible dispatch from Liverpool to Newport, and there load a cargo of iron rails for San Francisco. The plaintiff had entered into a contract of insurance with the defendants, in order that he might protect himself against the failure of the ship to carry out the charter. The vessel was stranded in Caernarvon Bay whilst on its way to Newport. It was not re-floated for over a month, and could not be fully repaired for some time. The charterers hired another ship and the plaintiff now claimed on the policy of insurance. The insurance company suggested that since the plaintiff might claim against the charterer for breach of contract there was no loss, and the court had to decide whether such a claim was possible. *Held*—The delay consequent upon the stranding of the vessel put an end, in the commercial sense, to the venture, so that the charterer was released from his obligations and was free to hire another ship. Therefore, the plaintiff had no claim against the charterer and could claim the loss of the charter from the defendants.

294. Maritime National Fish Ltd. *v.* Ocean Trawlers Ltd., [1935] A.C. 524

The respondents were the owners and the appellants the charterers of a steam trawler, the *St. Cuthbert*. The *St. Cuthbert* was fitted with, and could only operate with, an otter trawl. When the charter party was renewed on 25th October, 1932, both parties knew that it was illegal to operate with an otter trawl without a licence from the Minister. The appellants operated five trawlers and applied for five licences. The Minister granted only three and said that the appellants could choose the names of three trawlers for the licences. The appellants chose three but deliberately excluded the *St. Cuthbert* though they could have included it. They were now sued by the owners for the charter fee, and their defence was that the charter party was frustrated because it would have been illegal to fish with the *St. Cuthbert*. It was *held* that the contract was not frustrated, in the sense that the frustrating event was self-induced by the appellants and that therefore they were liable for the hire.

295. Cricklewood Property and Investment Trust Ltd. *v.* Leighton's Investment Trust Ltd., [1945] A.C. 221

In May, 1936, a building lease was granted between the parties for 99 years, but before any building had been erected war broke out in 1939 and government restrictions on building materials and labour meant that the lessees could not erect the buildings as they intended, these buildings being in fact shops. Leighton's sued originally for rent due under the lease and Cricklewood, the builders, said the lease was frustrated. The House of Lords *held* that the doctrine of frustration did not apply because the interruption from 1939 to 1945 was not sufficient in duration to frustrate the lease, and so they did not deal specifically with the general position regarding frustration of leases, basing their judgment on the question of the degree of interruption. In so far as they did deal with the general position this was *obiter*, but Lord Simon thought that there could be cases in which a lease would be frustrated, and the example that he quoted was a building lease where the land was declared a permanent open space before building took place; here he thought that the fundamental purpose of the transaction would be defeated. Lord Wright took much the same view on the same example. Lord Russell thought frustration could not apply to a lease of real property, and Lord Goddard, C.J., took the same view. Lord Porter expressed no opinion with regard to leases generally and so this case does not finally solve the problem.

296. Hillingdon Estates Co. *v.* Stonefield Estates Ltd., [1952] Ch. 627

By a contract dated 13th January, 1938, the vendors, Stonefield, and the plaintiffs, Hillingdon, who were the purchasers, agreed to buy and sell a freehold. The purchasers were to take a conveyance on 31st January, 1939, and the use of the land was to be for building an estate only. The completion was delayed by the outbreak of war and on 11th October, 1948, the contract was still not completed by a conveyance, and at that time the Middlesex County Council compulsorily purchased the land, leaving the *owners* with the compensation which would, of course, be less than the market value in 1948. The plaintiffs said that the contract was discharged. They did not ask for rescission but for a declaratory judgment to this effect and the defendants claimed specific performance. It was *held* that the plaintiffs failed and the defendants succeeded and specific performance was granted, the plaintiffs' claim being refused. It would appear therefore that the doctrine of frustration does not apply to a contract for the sale of land once a legal or equitable estate has passed.

297. Chandler *v.* Webster, [1904] 1 K.B. 493

The defendant agreed to let the plaintiff have a room for the purpose of viewing the Coronation procession on 26th June, 1902, for £141 15s. The contract provided that the money be payable immediately. The procession did not take place because of the illness of the King and the plaintiff, who had paid £100 on account, left the balance unpaid. The plaintiff sued to recover the £100 and the defendant counter-claimed for £41 15s. It was *held*—by the Court of Appeal—that the plaintiff's action failed and the defendant's counter-claim succeeded because the obligation to pay the rent had fallen due before the frustrating event.

298. The Fibrosa Case, [1942] 2 All E.R. 122

An English company (Fairburn) agreed to sell to a Polish firm (Fibrosa), machinery for £4,800, one-third to be paid with the order. Delivery of the machinery was to be made within three or four months of the settlement of final details at a place called Gdynia in Poland. Only £1,000 was paid with the order and on 3rd September, 1939, Britain declared war on Germany. On 23rd September, Gdynia was occupied by the Germans, the machinery was not delivered and the Polish company sued for the return of the £1,000. It was *held*—by Mr. Justice Tucker and the Court of Appeal—that the contract was frustrated under the rule in *Chandler* v. *Webster* (1904)[297] and that the action failed. The House of Lords, however, *held* that the money was recoverable, not because the contract was void *ab initio*, but in quasi contract on the grounds that there had been a total failure of consideration. Lord Simon said that under the law relating to the formation of contracts, a promise to do something provides consideration (thus a promise supports a promise), but under the law relating to failure of consideration, the promise is not enough, the performance of the promise is looked to. Here the money was paid to secure performance and there was no performance.

299. Lovell *v.* Lovell, [1970] 1 W.L.R. 1451

In the course of an action based on a claim for money lent fourteen years before the issue of a writ, the plaintiff served interrogatories on the defendant. This is allowed as part of civil procedure in order to ascertain facts material to the claim. Two of the questions were—"On (a certain date) did you owe (the plaintiff) £2,300?" and "If not £2,300 did you owe her any sum and if so, what sum?" *Held*—by the Court of Appeal—the questions need not be answered. To allow interrogatories of this kind would mean that no one could ever rely on the Limitation Act since he would be forced to give an acknowledgment of the debt on which an action could subsequently be brought.

300. Lynn *v.* Bamber, [1930] 2 K.B. 72

In 1921 the plaintiff purchased some plum trees from the defendant, and was given a warranty that the trees were "Purple Pershores." In 1928 the plaintiff discovered that the trees were not "Purple Pershores" and sued for damages. The defendant pleaded that the claim was barred by the Statutes of Limitation. *Held*—The defendant's fraudulent misrepresentation and fraudulent concealment of the breach of warranty provided a good answer to this plea, so that the plaintiff could recover.

301. Wilson *v.* United Counties Bank, [1920] A.C. 102

A business man left his business affairs in the hands of the bank whilst he went to serve in the war of 1914–18. The bank mismanaged his affairs, and he was eventually adjudicated bankrupt. The trader and his trustee brought this action against the bank for breach of their contractual duty. Damages of £45,000 were awarded for loss of estate, and of £7,500 for the injury caused to the trader's credit and business reputation. With regard to the damages the court *held* that the £45,000 belonged to the trustee for the benefit of creditors, and the £7,500 went to the trader personally.

302. Sunley & Co. Ltd. *v.* Cunard White Star Ltd., [1940] 1 K.B. 740

The defendants agreed to carry a machine, belonging to the plaintiffs, to Guernsey, but because of delays for which the defendants were responsible, the machine was delivered a week late. The plaintiffs were not able to show that they had an immediate use for the machine, and could not prove loss of profit. However, it was *held* that, to compensate the plaintiffs for the defendant's breach of contract, they should recover £20 as one week's depreciation of the machine, and the sum of £10 as interest on the capital cost.

303. Chaplin v. Hicks, [1911] 2 K.B. 786

The defendant organised a beauty contest inviting the readers of certain newspapers to select fifty girls from whom the defendant would select twelve. The twelve successful entrants were to be offered theatrical engagements. The plaintiff was one of the fifty girls selected by the newspaper readers, but the defendant did not invite her to the final selection. She now claimed damages for breach of contract, and the defendant pleaded that, even if he had invited her to the final selection, it was by no means certain that she would have been one of the successful twelve, and therefore, the damages should be nominal. *Held*—Although it was difficult to assess damages, yet the plaintiff was entitled to an assessment, whereupon the jury awarded her £100.

304. Beach v. Reed Corrugated Cases Ltd., [1956] 2 All E.R. 652

This was an action brought by the plaintiff for wrongful dismissal by the defendants. The plaintiff was the managing director of the company and he had a fifteen-year contract from 21st December, 1950, at a salary of £5,000 per annum. His contract was terminated in August, 1954, when he was fifty-four years old and the sum of money that he might have earned would have been £55,000, but the general damages awarded to him were £18,000 after the court had taken into account income tax, including tax on his private investments.

N.B. The same principle has been applied to damages recoverable in tort for loss of earnings (*B.T.C. v. Gourley*, [1956] A.C. 185).

305. Hadley v. Baxendale (1854), 9 Exch. 341

The plaintiff was a miller at Gloucester. The driving shaft of the mill being broken, the plaintiff engaged the defendant, a carrier, to take it to the makers at Greenwich so that they might use it in making a new one. The defendant delayed delivery of the shaft beyond a reasonable time, so that the mill was idle for much longer than should have been necessary. The plaintiff now sued in respect of loss of profits during the period of additional delay. The court decided that there were only two possible grounds on which the plaintiff could succeed—(i) That in the usual course of things the work of the mill would cease altogether for want of the shaft. This the court rejected because, to take only one reasonable possibility, the plaintiff might have had a spare. (ii) That the special circumstances were fully explained, so that the defendant was made aware of the possible loss. The evidence showed that there had been no such explanation. In fact the only information given to the defendant was that the article to be carried was the broken shaft of a mill, and that the plaintiff was the miller of that mill. *Held*—That the plaintiff's claim failed, the damage being too remote.

However, loss of profits for non-delivery or delayed delivery are recoverable if foreseeable as a consequence of the breach. Thus in *Victoria Laundry Ltd.* v. *Newman Industries Ltd.*, [1949] 1 All E.R. 997, the defendants agreed to deliver a new boiler to the plaintiffs by a certain date but failed to do so with the result that the plaintiffs lost (*a*) normal business profits during the period of delay, and (*b*) profits from dyeing contracts which were offered to them during the period. It was *held* that (*a*) but not (*b*) were recoverable as damages.

In *Czarnikow Ltd.* v. *Koufos*, [1967] 3 All E.R. 686, shipowners carrying sugar from Constanza to Basrah delayed delivery at Basrah for nine days during which time the market in sugar there fell and the charterers lost more than £4,000. It was *held* that they could recover that sum from the shipowners because the very existence of a "market" for goods implied that prices might fluctuate and a fall in sugar prices was reasonably foreseeable by the shipowners.

306. Horne v. Midland Railway Co. (1873), L.R. 8 C.P. 131

The plaintiff had entered into a contract to sell 4,595 pairs of boots to the French Army at a price above the market price. The defendants were responsible for a delay in the delivery of the boots, and the purchasers refused to accept delivery, regarding time as the essence of the contract. The plaintiff's claim for damages was based on the contract price namely 4s. per pair, but it was *held* that he could only recover the market price of 2s. 9d. per pair unless he could show that the defendants were aware of the exceptional profit involved, and that they had undertaken to be liable for its loss.

307. Pinnock Brothers v. Lewis and Peat Ltd., [1923] 1 K.B. 690

The plaintiffs bought from the defendants some East African Copra Cake which, to the defendants' knowledge, was to be used for feeding cattle. The cake was adulterated with castor oil and was poisonous. The plaintiffs resold the cake to other dealers, who in turn sold it to farmers, who used it for feeding cattle. Cattle fed on the cake died, and claims were made by the various buyers against their sellers, the whole liability resting eventually on the plaintiffs. In this action the plaintiffs sued for the damages and costs which they had been required to pay. Two major defences were raised, the first being an exemption clause saying that the goods were not warranted free from defects, and the other that the damage was too remote. The court dismissed the exemption clause and *held* that, when a substance is quite different from that contracted for, it cannot merely be defective. Further the damage was not too remote, since it was in the implied contemplation of the defendants that the cake would at some time be fed to cattle.

308. Charter v. Sullivan, [1957] 2 Q.B. 117

The plaintiffs who were motor dealers agreed to sell a Hillman Minx car to the defendant for £773 17s. 0d. which was the retail price fixed by the manufacturers. The defendant refused to complete the purchase and the plaintiffs re-sold the car a few days later to another purchaser at the same price. The plaintiffs sued for breach of contract, the measure of damages claimed being £97 15s. 0d., the profit the plaintiffs would have made on the sale to the defendant if it had gone through. Evidence showed that the plaintiffs could have sold the second purchaser another Hillman Minx which would have been ordered from the manufacturers' stock had the defendant taken the first Hillman Minx as agreed. The plaintiffs' sales manager said in his evidence, "We can sell all the Hillman Minx cars we can get." This evidence was accepted by the trial judge. The plaintiffs were really suggesting that, but for the defendant's refusal to complete, they would have sold two cars and not one and in so doing would have made two lots of profit. *Held*—Sect. 50 (3) of the Sale of Goods Act, 1893, did not apply here because the language of the sub-section postulates that in the case to which it applies there will or may be a difference between the contract price and the market or current price which cannot be the case where the goods are, as here, saleable only at a fixed retail price.

Having discarded Sect. 50 (3), the Court of Appeal applied Sect. 50 (2) which provides that damages should be the loss directly and naturally resulting in the ordinary course of events from the buyer's breach of contract. This was in the view of the court nominal damages of 40s. only, because, as the plaintiffs' sales manager said, the plaintiffs could always find a purchaser for every Hillman Minx car they could get from the manufacturers and so the plaintiffs must have sold the same number of cars and made the same number of fixed profits as they would have sold and made if the defendant had duly carried out his promise.

309. Thompson (W. L.) Ltd. *v.* Robinson (Gunmakers) Ltd., [1955] Ch. 177

On March 4th, 1954, the defendants agreed in writing with the plaintiffs who were motor car dealers to purchase from them a Standard Vanguard car. On March 5th, 1954, the defendants said they were not prepared to take delivery. The plaintiffs returned the car to their suppliers who did not ask for any compensation. The plaintiffs now sued for damages for breach of contract. The selling price of a Standard Vanguard was fixed by the manufacturers and the plaintiffs' profit would have been £61 1s. 9d. When the agreement was made there was not sufficient demand for Vanguards in the locality as would absorb all such cars available for sale in the area, but evidence did not show that there was no available market in the widest sense, i.e. in the sense of the country as a whole. *Held*—The plaintiffs were entitled to compensation for loss of their bargain, i.e. the profit they would have made being £61 1s. 9d. because they had sold one car less than they would have sold. Even if the "available market" concept as used in Sect. 50 (3) of the Sale of Goods Act, 1893, meant taking in the whole of the country, it would not be just to apply Sect. 50 (3) in this case, and therefore Sect. 50 (3) was no defence to the plaintiffs' claim. Sect. 50 (3) need not be applied if the court thinks it would be unjust in the circumstances.

310. Luker *v.* Chapman (1970), 114 S.J. 788

The plaintiff lost his right leg below the knee as a result of a traffic accident in which his motor cycle was in collision with the defendant's sports car. The accident was partly caused by the defendant's negligence. After the accident the plaintiff was unable to continue with his employment as a telephone engineer and refused a clerical job, taking up teacher training instead. *Held*—by Browne, J.—that the plaintiff was required to mitigate damages and should have accepted the clerical job. The defendant was not liable for the loss of income involved in the period of teacher training.

311. Ford Motor Co. (England) Ltd. *v.* Armstrong (1915), 31 T.L.R. 267

The defendant was a retailer who received supplies from the plaintiffs. As part of his agreement with the plaintiffs the defendant had undertaken—

    (i) not to sell any of the plaintiffs' cars or spares below list price;
    (ii) not to sell Ford cars to other dealers in the motor trade;
    (iii) not to exhibit any car supplied by the company without their permission.

The defendant also agreed to pay £250 for every breach of the agreement as being the agreed damage which the manufacturer will "sustain." The defendant was in breach of the agreement and the plaintiffs sued. It was *held*—by the Court of Appeal—that the sum of £250 was in the nature of a penalty and not liquidated damages. The same sum was payable for different kinds of breach which were not likely to produce the same loss. Furthermore its size suggested that it was not a genuine pre-estimate of loss.

312. Cellulose Acetate Silk Co. Ltd. v. Widnes Foundry Ltd., [1933] A.C. 20

The Widnes Foundry entered into a contract to erect a plant for the Silk Co. by a certain date. It was also agreed that the Widnes Foundry would pay the Silk Co. £20 per week for every week they took in erecting the plant beyond the agreed date. In the event the erection was completed thirty weeks late, and the Silk Co. claimed for their actual loss which was £5,850. *Held*—The Widnes Foundry were only liable to pay £20 per week as agreed.

313. Craven-Ellis v. Canons Ltd., [1936] 2 K.B. 403

The plaintiff was employed as managing director by the company under a deed which provided for remuneration. The Articles provided that directors must have qualification shares, and must obtain these within two months of appointment. The plaintiff and other directors never obtained the required number of shares so that the deed was invalid. However, the plaintiff had rendered services, and he now sued on a *quantum meruit* for a reasonable sum by way of remuneration. *Held*—He succeeded on a *quantum meruit*, there being no valid contract.

314. Gilbert and Partners v. Knight, [1968] 2 All E.R. 248

The respondent Knight, agreed, in August, 1965, to pay Gilbert, who was a member of the appellant firm of surveyors, a fee of £30 to supervise specified building work estimated to cost £600. In May, 1966, when the builder started work, the respondent ordered some additional work which brought the cost to £2,238. Gilbert supervised this additional work but made no request for an additional payment until the work was completed. He then rendered an account for £135 being the agreed £30 plus a scale fee of 100 guineas for supervising the additional work. The respondent paid only the agreed £30 and would not pay more. Gilbert and Partners' action against Knight was dismissed and they appealed. It was *held*—by the Court of Appeal—dismissing the appeal, that the firm was entitled to £30 only. No *quantum meruit* claim lay for supervising the additional work unless a new contract to pay for that work had been made because the parties never discharged the original contract for one lump-sum fee of £30.

315. Metropolitan Electric Supply Co. v. Ginder, [1901] 2 Ch. 799

The defendant entered into a contract with the plaintiffs in which he agreed to take all the electricity he required from them. The plaintiffs sued for an injunction to prevent the defendant from obtaining energy elsewhere. *Held*—The plaintiffs succeeded since the agreement was in essence an undertaking not to take supplies of electricity from elsewhere, and could be enforced by injunction.

316. Whitwood Chemical Co. v. Hardman, [1891] 2 Ch. 416

The defendant entered into a contract of service with the plaintiffs and agreed to give the whole of his time to them. In fact he occasionally worked for others, and the plaintiffs tried to enforce the undertaking in the service contract by injunction. *Held*—An injunction could not be granted because there was no express negative stipulation. The defendant had merely stated what he would do, and not what he would not do, and to read into the undertaking an agreement not to work for anyone else required the court to imply a negative stipulation from a positive one. No such implication could be made.

317. Warner Brothers Pictures Incorporated *v.* Nelson, [1937] 1 K.B. 209

The defendant, the film actress Bette Davis, had entered into a contract in which she agreed to act exclusively for the plaintiffs for twelve months. She was anxious to obtain more money and so she left America, and entered into a contract with a person in England. The plaintiffs now asked for an injunction restraining the defendant from carrying out the English contract. *Held*—An injunction would be granted. The contract contained a negative stipulation not to work for anyone else, and this could be enforced. However, since the contract was an American one, the court limited the operation of the injunction to the area of the court's jurisdiction, and although the contract stipulated that the defendant would not work in any other occupation, the injunction was confined to work on stage or screen.

318. Ryan *v.* Mutual Tontine Westminster Chambers Association, [1893] 1 Ch. 116

The defendants leased a residential flat to the plaintiff and also agreed to employ a porter who would be resident on the premises. The porter was to clean the flats and deliver parcels, take in articles for safe custody, and take charge of keys. The defendants appointed a porter but the man concerned was also a chef at a club in Westminster and was absent from the flats each day from 11 a.m. to 3 p.m., carrying out his duties as a chef. While he was away his duties were carried out in a most indifferent fashion by a number of boys and a charlady. These persons were not resident. The plaintiff now sued for breach of contract and asked for specific performance of the promise to appoint a full time porter. *Held*—Specific performance could not be granted because the court could not supervise the day-to-day performance of such an obligation. The plaintiff's remedy was an action for damages.

319. Page One Records Ltd. *v.* Britton, [1967] 3 All E.R. 822

By a written contract made in 1966 the defendants, a group of four musicians ("The Troggs"), appointed the plaintiffs to manage their professional careers for five years, they being persons of no business experience who were unlikely to survive as a "pop" group without the services of a manager. The contract was world-wide. The plaintiffs agreed to use all their resources of knowledge and experience to advance the defendants' careers, and the contract further provided that the defendants would not engage any other person to act as manager or agent for them, and that they would not act themselves in such capacity. The plaintiffs were to receive twenty per cent of all moneys earned by the defendants during the period of the contract. The Troggs became an established group, earning as much as £400 per night. In 1967 the defendants signified their intention to repudiate the management contract, but the court held that there had been no breaches of duty by the plaintiffs to justify the repudiation. In fact the plaintiffs had supported the group in the fullest measure and were to a large extent responsible for the success of the group. The plaintiffs sued for damages for breach of contract and applied also for an interlocutory injunction restraining the defendants until trial from engaging any person, firm or corporation, other than the plaintiffs, as their manager. *Held*—by Stamp, J.—that the injunction must be refused because—

(i) The defendants had no business experience and had to have a manager. If an injunction was granted it would *compel* not merely *encourage* the defendants to carry out their contract with the plaintiffs. *Warner Bros.* v. *Nelson*, 1937,[317] was distinguishable because Bette Davis was a person of intelligence, capacity and means and if she had chosen not to act at all, rather than for Warner Bros., she would have been able to employ herself both usefully and remuneratively in other spheres of activity. Other similarly remunerative employment was not available to the "Troggs."

(ii) The injunction, if granted, would also have the effect of enforcing a contract for personal services of a fiduciary nature, because the plaintiffs were managers and it would be necessary for them to see, and be friendly with, the defendants for a further four years. In *Warner Bros.* v. *Nelson*, 1937,[317] the obligation of the plaintiffs was largely to pay money to Miss Davis; they were not involved in the much more intimate relationship of managing her career.

320. Brook's Wharf and Bull Wharf Ltd. *v.* Goodman Bros., [1936] 3 All E.R. 696

The plaintiff company had agreed to store in its warehouse goods imported by the defendant. The defendants were liable by Act of Parliament to pay customs duties but the Act also allowed the authorities to recover these duties from the warehouseman. The goods were stolen before the defendants had paid the customs duties and they refused to do so. The authorities claimed the duties from the plaintiffs who paid them. *Held*—by the Court of Appeal— that the plaintiffs could recover the sums paid by way of duty from the defendants in quasi-contract.

321. Metropolitan Police District Receiver *v.* Croydon Corporation, [1957] 1 All E.R. 78

A policeman had recovered damages for an accident resulting from the defendants' negligence. The injuries were received while the policeman was on duty and while he was unfit his wages were paid by the Police Receiver who was required by Act of Parliament to make these payments. In this action the Receiver was seeking to recover the amount paid in wages on the ground that the defendants would have had to pay more damages to the policeman if he had not received his pay. *Held*—by the Court of Appeal—that the action failed. The defendants were not under a common and legal obligation to pay the policeman's wages so that quasi-contract did not apply.

322. Rowland *v.* Divall, [1923] 2 K.B. 500

In April, 1922, the defendant bought an "Albert" motor car from a man who had stolen it from the true owner. One month later the plaintiff, a dealer, purchased the car from the defendant for £334, repainted it, and sold it for £400 to Colonel Railsdon. In September, 1922, the police seized the car from Colonel Railsdon and the plaintiff repaid him the £400. The plaintiff now sued the defendant for £334 on the grounds that there had been a total failure of consideration since the plaintiff had not obtained a title to the car. *Held*— The defendant was in breach of Sect. 12 of the Sale of Goods Act, 1893, which implies conditions and warranties into a sale of goods relating to the seller's right to sell, and there had been a total failure of consideration in spite of the fact that the car had been used by the plaintiff and his purchaser. The plaintiff contracted for the property in the car and not the mere right to possess it. Since he had not obtained the property, he was entitled to recover the sum of £334 and no deductions should be made for the period of user.

N.B. Although the court purported to deal with this case as a breach of Sect. 12 (1) of the Act, it would appear that in fact they operated on common law principles and gave complete restitution of the purchase price because of total failure of consideration arising out of the seller's lack of title. The condition under Sect. 12 (1) had by reason of the plaintiff's use of the car and the passage of time become a warranty when the action was brought and if the court had been awarding damages for breach of warranty it would have had to reduce the sum of £334 by a sum representing the value to the plaintiff of the use of the vehicle which he had had.

323. Cox v. Prentice (1815), 3 M. & S. 344

The defendant wished to sell a bar of silver to Cox but before the sale the bar was weighed by an assay master. Cox paid £88 for the bar on the basis of the weight ascribed to it by the assay master. It was later discovered that the weight was less than that certified by the assay master who had made a mistake in the weighing. *Held*—Cox could recover the excess from Prentice since the money had been paid under a mistake of fact.

SOME FUNDAMENTAL CONCEPTS

324. Durham Brothers v. Robertson, [1898] 1 Q.B. 765

This action was brought to recover the sum of £1,080 said to be due from the defendant to Smith & Co. under a building contract. The plaintiffs alleged that the sum had been assigned to them in writing and that proper notice of the assignment had been given to the defendant. The alleged assignment was a letter dated 19th August, 1895, written by Smith & Co. to the plaintiffs as follows—"Re Building Contract of Middle Class Dwellings situate on the west side South Lambeth Road, S.W.—In consideration of money advanced from time to time we charge the sum of £1,080, which will become due from John Robertson Esq., on completion of the above buildings as security for the above advances and we hereby assign our interest in the above-mentioned sum until the money with added interest be paid." *Held*— The assignment was not a legal one because it was not absolute, being expressed to be by way of charge and conditional upon repayment of the loans in respect of which it was made. However, it was a good equitable assignment, though not enforceable in this action, because Smith & Co. had not been joined in the action which is essential in Equity in order that the rule regarding privity of contract is not infringed.

324a. Hughes v. Pump House Hotel Co., [1902] 2 K.B. 190.

The plaintiff, who was a building contractor, assigned all his interest in a building scheme at the hotel to Lloyds Bank in consideration for keeping his account, the assignment ensuring that sums of money would be credited to the account. The bank was to receive the money for work done and could give valid receipts and control all accounting. A notice in writing of the assignment had been given to the hotel company. *Held*—by the Court of Appeal—this was not a mere assignment by way of charge; it was an absolute assignment of the whole debt due or to become due and was therefore enforceable.

325. Ballett *v.* Mingay, [1943] K.B. 281

The appellant was an infant and he borrowed from the respondent an amplifier and a microphone. When the respondent demanded the return of the articles, the appellant failed to do so, having lent them to another. The infant was sued in detinue. It was suggested that in this action the respondent was seeking to make the appellant liable in tort for an act which was really a breach of contract and for which, as an infant, he could not be liable. *Held*—The infant was properly sued in tort because his action in parting with possession of the articles was not allowed by the contract of bailment and was therefore outside the terms of the contract.

326. South Staffordshire Water Co. *v.* Sharman, [1896] 2 Q.B. 44

The plaintiffs sued the defendant in detinue, claiming possession of two gold rings found by the defendant in the Minster Pool at Lichfield. The plaintiffs were owners of the pool and the defendant was a labourer employed by them to clean it. It was in the course of cleaning the pool that the defendant came across the rings. He refused to hand them to his employers, but gave them to the police for enquiries to be made to find the true owners. No owner was found and the police returned the rings to the defendant, who retained them. *Held*—The rings must be given over to the plaintiffs. The plaintiffs were freeholders of the pool, and had the right to forbid anyone coming on the land; they had a right to clean the pool out in any way they chose. They possessed and exercised a practical control over the pool and they had a right to its contents.

327. The Winkfield, [1902] P. 42

This was an Admiralty action arising because a ship called the *Mexican* was negligently struck and sunk by a ship called the *Winkfield*. The *Mexican* was carrying mail from South Africa to England during the Boer War. The Postmaster General made, among other things, a claim for damages in respect of the estimated value of parcels and letters for which no claim had been made or instructions received from the senders. The Postmaster General undertook to distribute the amount recovered when the senders were found. An objection was made that the Postmaster General represented the Crown and was not liable to the senders (see now Crown Proceedings Act, 1947). *Held*—As a bailee in possession the Postmaster General could recover damages for the loss of the goods irrespective of whether or not he was liable to the bailors.

328. Ashby *v.* Tolhurst, [1937] 2 All E.R. 837

The plaintiff drove his car on to a piece of land at Southend owned by the defendants. He paid 1s. to an attendant who was the defendant's servant and was given a ticket. He left the car with the doors locked. When he returned his car had gone, the attendant having allowed a thief, who said he was a friend of the plaintiff, to drive it away. The ticket was called a "car-park ticket" and contained the words "The proprietors do not take any responsibility for the safe custody of any cars or articles therein, nor for any damage to the cars or articles however caused nor for any injuries to any persons, all cars being left in all respects entirely at their owner's risk. Owners are requested to show ticket when required." *Held*—

(i) The relationship between the parties was that of licensor and licensee, not that of bailor and bailee because there was in no sense a transfer of possession. There was, therefore, no obligation upon the defendants towards the plaintiff in respect of the car.

(ii) If there was a contract of bailment, the servant delivered possession of the car quite honestly under a mistake and the conditions on the tickets were wide enough to protect the defendants.

(iii) There could not be implied into the contract a term that the car should not be handed over without production of the ticket.

N.B. Where the plaintiff hands over the key, the court may find a transfer of possession and a bailment, but the delivery of the key is not conclusive.

329. Ultzen v. Nicols, [1894] 1 Q.B. 92

A waiter took a customer's overcoat, without being asked to do so, and hung it on a peg behind the customer. The coat was stolen and it was *held* that the restaurant keeper was a bailee of the coat and that there was negligence in supervision on the part of the bailee.

N.B. In this case the servant seems to have been regarded as taking possession, but it is unlikely that a bailment will arise if a customer merely hangs his coat on a stand or other device provided by the establishment.

330. Deyong v. Shenburn, [1946] 1 All E.R. 226

An allegation that an actor who left his clothes in a dressing room had constituted the theatre owners bailees of the clothes was not sustained.

331. Newman v. Bourne & Hollingsworth (1915), 31 T.L.R. 209

The plaintiff went into the defendants' shop on a Saturday in order to buy a coat. While trying on coats she took off a diamond brooch and put it on a show case. She left the shop having forgotten the brooch, an assistant found it and handed it to the shopwalker who put it in his desk. By the firm's rules the brooch ought to have been taken to their lost property office. The brooch could not be found on the following Monday. *Held*—There was evidence to support the trial judge's finding that the firm had become bailees and had not exercised proper care.

332. Neuwirth v. Over Darwen Industrial Co-operative Society (1894) 70 T.L.R. 374

A concert hall was hired for an evening performance. No mention was made of rehearsal but the orchestra rehearsed in the hall during the afternoon without opposition from the proprietors or the keeper of the hall. After the rehearsal Neuwirth left his double-bass fiddle in an ante-room in such a position that when the hall keeper came to turn on the gas in the ante-room he could not do so without first moving the instrument. The fiddle fell and was badly damaged. *Held*—There was no contract of bailment between the parties. The care of musical instruments was outside the scope of the hall keeper's authority and there was no evidence that he had been guilty of negligence in the course of his employment.

333. Elvin and Powell Ltd. *v.* Plummer Roddis Ltd. (1933), 50 T.L.R. 158

A fraudulent person ordered a consignment of goods from the plaintiffs in the name of the defendants. He then telephoned the defendants in the plaintiff's name, saying that the goods had been dispatched to them in error and that they would be collected. The fraudulent person then himself collected the goods from the defendants and absconded with them. The plaintiffs now sued the defendants for conversion. *Held*—As involuntary bailees of goods, the defendants had acted reasonably in returning them, as they believed, to the plaintiffs, by a trustworthy messenger. They had not committed conversion.

334. Donoghue (or M'Alister) *v.* Stevenson, [1932] A.C. 562

The appellant's friend purchased a bottle of ginger beer from a retailer in Paisley and gave it to her. The respondents were the manufacturers of the ginger beer. The appellant consumed some of the ginger beer and her friend was replenishing the glass, when, according to the appellant, the decomposed remains of a snail came out of the bottle. The bottle was made of dark glass so that the snail could not be seen until most of the contents had been consumed. The appellant became ill and served a writ on the manufacturers claiming damages. The question before the House of Lords was whether the facts outlined above constituted a cause of action in negligence. The House of Lords *held* by a majority of three to two that they did. It was stated that a manufacturer of products, which are sold in such a form that they are likely to reach the ultimate consumer in the form in which they left the manufacturer with no possibility of intermediate examination, owes a duty to the consumer to take reasonable care to prevent injury. This rule has been broadened in subsequent cases so that the manufacturer is liable more often where defective chattels cause injury. The following important points also arise out of the case.

(i) It was in this case that the House of Lords formulated the test that the duty of care in negligence is based on the foresight of the reasonable man.

(ii) Lord Macmillan's remark that the categories of negligence are never closed suggests that the tort of negligence is capable of further expansion.

(iii) The duty of care with regard to chattels as laid down in the case relates to chattels not dangerous in themselves. The duty of care in respect of chattels dangerous in themselves, e.g. explosives, is much higher.

(iv) The appellant had no cause of action against the retailer in contract because her friend bought the bottle, so that there was no privity of contract between the retailer and the appellant. Therefore terms relating to fitness for purpose and merchantable quality, implied into such contracts by the Sale of Goods Act, 1893, did not apply here.

335. Hyman *v.* Nye (1881), 6 Q.B.D. 685

The plaintiff hired a landau with a pair of horses and a driver for a drive from Brighton to Shoreham and back. The plaintiff was involved in an accident owing to a broken bolt which caused the carriage to upset so that the plaintiff was thrown out of it. *Held*—The trial judge's direction to the jury that the plaintiff must prove negligence was wrong. There was an implied warranty that the carriage was as fit for the purpose for which it was hired as skill and care could make it.

336. Reed *v.* Dean, [1949] 1 K.B. 188

The plaintiffs hired a motor launch called the *Golden Age* from the defendant for a family holiday on the Thames. The plaintiffs set sail at about 7 p.m. on

22nd June, 1946, and at about 9 p.m., when they were near Sonning, they discovered that a liquid in the bilge by the engine was on fire. They attempted to extinguish the fire but were unable to do so, the fire-fighting equipment with which the launch was supplied being out of order. The plaintiffs had to abandon the launch and suffered personal injuries and loss of belongings. The plaintiffs admitted to a fireman after the accident that they might have spilt some petrol when the tank was refilled. *Held*—The plaintiffs succeeded because there was an implied undertaking by the defendant that the launch was as fit for the purpose for which it was hired as reasonable care and skill could make it. Further, as the launch had caught fire due to an unexplained cause, there was a presumption that it was not fit for this purpose. The defendant's failure to provide proper fire-fighting equipment was a breach of the implied warranty of fitness.

337. Houghland *v.* R. Low (Luxury Coaches), Ltd., [1962] 2 All E.R. 159

The defendants supplied a coach for the purposes of an old people's outing to Southampton. On returning the passengers put their luggage into the boot of the coach. During a stop for tea the coach was found to be defective and another one was sent for and the luggage was transferred from the first coach to the relief coach. The removal of the luggage from the first coach was not supervised, but the restacking of the luggage into the new coach was supervised by one of the defendants' employees. When the passengers arrived home a suitcase belonging to the plaintiff was missing and he brought an action against the defendants for its loss. It was *held*—by the Court of Appeal —that whether the action was for negligence or in detinue, the defendants were liable unless they could show that they had not been negligent. On the facts they had failed to prove this and were therefore liable. It was in this case that Ormerod, L.J., made some observations on bailments in general. The County Court Judge had found that the bailment was gratuitous and that the defendants were liable only for gross negligence. Dealing with this question Ormerod, L.J., said "For my part I have always found some difficulty in understanding just what was gross negligence, because it appears to me that the standard of care required in a case of bailment or any other type of case is the standard demanded by the circumstances of the particular case. It seems to me to try and put bailment, for instance, into a water-tight compartment, such as gratuitous bailment on the one hand and bailment for reward on the other, is to overlook the fact that there might well be an infinite variety of cases which might come into one or other category."

338. Global Dress Co. *v.* W. H. Boase & Co., [1966] 2 Ll. Rep. 72

B & Co. were master porters and had custody of thirty cases of goods belonging to G & Co. at a Liverpool dock shed. One case was stolen and G & Co. brought an action for damages against B & Co. B & Co. offered evidence of their system of safeguarding the goods and the County Court Judge at first instance found the system to be as good as any other in the Liverpool Docks, but notwithstanding this he found B & Co. liable. On appeal to the Court of Appeal it was *held* that if B & Co. could not affirmatively prove that their watchman was not negligent it was of no avail to show that they had an impeccable system, and the appeal should be dismissed. Thus the onus of proving that their servant was not negligent lay upon B & Co.

339. **Doorman** *v.* **Jenkins** (1834), 2 Ad. & El. 256

The plaintiff left the sum of £32 10s. with the defendant, who was a coffee-house keeper, for safe custody and without any reward. The defendant put the money in with his own in a cash box which he kept in the taproom. The taproom was open to the public on a Sunday but the rest of the house was not and the cash was, in fact, stolen on a Sunday. Lord Denman *held* that the loss of the defendant's own money was not enough to prove reasonable care and the court found for the plaintiff.

340. **Brabant** *v.* **King**, [1895] A.C. 632

This action was brought against the government of Queensland for damage to certain explosives belonging to the plaintiff which the government as bailees for reward had stored in sheds situated near the water's edge on Brisbane River. The water rose to an exceptional height and the store was flooded. The question of inevitable accident was raised and also the degree of negligence required. The Privy Council *held* that because of the nature of the site the bailees were required to place the goods at such a level as would in all probability ensure their absolute immunity from flood water, and the defendants were held liable. The Privy Council went on to say that in a case of a deposit for reward the bailees were "under a legal obligation to exercise the same degree of care, towards the preservation of the goods entrusted to them from injury, which might reasonably be expected from a skilled storekeeper, acquainted with the risks to be apprehended from the character either of the storehouse or of its locality; and the obligations included, not only the duty of taking all reasonable precautions to obviate these risks but the duty of taking all proper measures for the protection of the goods when such risks were imminent or had actually occurred." Counsel for the government suggested that a bailee was not liable for damage caused by the defects in his warehouse where these defects were known to the bailor, in this case the proximity of the warehouse to the Brisbane River. The Privy Council dismissed this argument on the grounds that it was a dangerous one, not supported by any authority. They said that the bailor could rely on the skill of the bailee in this matter. It will be seen from this decision that a bailee for reward is liable even in the case of uncommon or unexpected danger, unless he uses efforts which are in proportion to the emergency to ward off that danger.

341. **Wilson** *v.* **Brett** (1843), 11 M. & W. 113

Wilson was in process of selling his horse and Brett volunteered to ride the horse in order to show it off to a likely purchaser. Brett rode the horse on to wet and slippery turf and the horse fell and was injured. Brett pleaded that he was not negligent but the court *held* that he had not used the skill he professed to possess when he volunteered to ride the horse and that he was liable.

342. **Saunders** (**Mayfair**) **Furs** *v.* **Davies** (1965), 109 S.J. 922

The plaintiffs delivered a valuable fur coat to a shop belonging to the defendants on sale-or-return terms. The defendants displayed it in their shop window and at 2.30 one morning the coat was stolen in a smash-and-grab raid. *Held*—That in all the circumstances and because of the valuable nature of the property, the defendants had taken an unreasonable risk and were negligent in leaving the coat on display in the window all night.

343. **Coldman** *v.* **Hill,** [1919] 1 K.B. 443

The defendant was a bailee of cows belonging to the plaintiff. Two of these cows were stolen through no fault of the defendant, though he failed to notify the plaintiff and did not inform the police or take any steps to find the cows. The plaintiff now sued him for negligence and it was *held*—by the Court of Appeal—that it was up to the defendant to prove that even if notice had been given, the cows would not have been recovered. In the circumstances of this case that burden had not been discharged and the defendant was liable.

344. **Cheshire** *v.* **Bailey,** [1905] 1 K.B. 237

In this case jewellery had been deposited in a carriage by the hirer and was stolen by thieves. It transpired that the coachman, who was the servant of the person who let out the carriage, was in league with the thieves, but it was *held* that the owner of the carriage was not liable for the loss because the dishonesty of his servant was beyond the scope of employment.

345. **Morris** *v.* **C. W. Martin & Sons Ltd.,** [1965] 2 All E.R. 725

The plaintiff sent a mink stole to a furrier for the purpose of cleaning. The furrier later told the plaintiff by telephone that he did not clean furs himself but intended to send the stole to the defendants, one of the biggest cleaners of fur in the country. The plaintiff knew of Martin & Sons and agreed that the stole be sent to them. Martin & Sons did work only for the fur trade and had issued to the furrier printed conditions which provided that goods belonging to customers were at customer's risk when on the premises of Martin & Sons, and that they should not be responsible for loss or damage however caused, though they would compensate for loss or damage to the goods during the cleaning process by reason of their negligence, but not by reason of any other cause. The furrier knew of these conditions when he handed the stole to the defendants and the defendants knew that it belonged to a customer of the furrier but they did not know that it was Morris. While in the possession of Martin & Sons the fur was stolen by a youth named Morrisey who had been employed by them for a few weeks only, though they had no grounds to suspect that he was dishonest. The plaintiff sued the defendants for conversion or negligence but the County Court Judge felt bound by *Cheshire* v. *Bailey*, [1905],[344] and held that the act of Morrisey, who had removed the stole by wrapping it round his body, was beyond the scope of his employment. In the Court of Appeal it was *held* that *Cheshire* v. *Bailey*, [1905],[344] had been impliedly overruled by *Lloyd* v. *Grace, Smith & Co.*, [1912],[475] (where it was held that a solicitor was liable for the criminal frauds of his managing clerk so long as the clerk was acting in the apparent scope of his authority). The defendants, as sub-bailees, were liable to the plaintiff, and on the matter of the exemption clause the Court of Appeal said that the terms of such a clause must be strictly construed, and since they referred only to goods "belonging to customers" this could be taken to mean goods belonging to the furrier and not to the furrier's customer, and because of this ambiguity the clause was inapplicable.

N.B. The above decision applies only to bailees for reward and only in circumstances where the servant is entrusted with, or put in charge of, the bailor's goods by his master. The mere fact that the servant's employment gave him the opportunity to steal the bailor's goods is not enough.

346. Davies *v.* Collins, [1945] 1 All E.R. 247

An American Army officer sent his uniform to the defendant to be cleaned. It was accepted on the following conditions—"Whilst every care is exercised in cleaning and dyeing garments, all orders are accepted at owner's risk entirely and we are unable to hold ourselves responsible for damage." The defendant did not clean the uniform but sub-contracted the work to another firm of cleaners. In the event the uniform was lost and the defendant was *held* liable in damages. The Court of Appeal took the view that the limitation clause operated to exclude the right to sub-contract because it used the words "every care is exercised," which postulated personal service.

347. Edwards *v.* Newland, [1950] 2 All E.R. 1072

The defendant agreed to store the plaintiff's furniture for reward. Later, without the plaintiff's knowledge, the defendant made arrangements with another company to store the plaintiff's furniture. The third party's warehouse was damaged by a bomb and they asked the defendant to remove the furniture but this was not done immediately because there was a dispute about charges. Eventually the plaintiff removed his furniture but some pieces were missing. *Held*—The plaintiff could recover from the defendant because he had departed from the terms of the contract of bailment by sub-contracting. However, the defendant was not entitled to damages against the third party because the latter, though a bailee, had not, in the circumstances, been negligent.

348. Learoyd Bros. & Co. *v.* Pope & Sons, [1966] 2 Ll. Rep. 142

The plaintiffs entered into an agreement with a carrier for the transport of their goods. The carrier sub-contracted the work to the defendants, who were also a firm of carriers, though the plaintiffs had no notice of this arrangement. The lorry was stolen while the defendants' driver was in the wharf office upon arrival at London Docks, and the carrier with whom the plaintiffs had contracted paid some of the plaintiffs' loss and the plaintiffs now sued the defendants for the balance. *Held*—That the defendants were bailees to the plaintiffs, notwithstanding the absence of any contract between them, and that the defendants' driver was negligent in leaving the lorry unattended and therefore the defendants were liable for the plaintiffs' loss.

349. Rogers Sons & Co. *v.* Lambert & Co., [1891] 1 Q.B. 318

The plaintiffs had purchased copper from the defendants but did not take delivery of it and left it with the defendants as warehousemen. The plaintiffs then resold the copper to a third person. Sometime later the plaintiffs asked for delivery of the copper from the defendants but the defendants refused to deliver on the grounds that the plaintiffs no longer had a title to it. *Held*—This was no defence to an action of detinue. The defendants must show that they were defending the action on behalf of, and with, the authority of the true owner.

350. Robins & Co. *v.* Gray, [1895] 2 Q.B. 501

The plaintiffs dealt in sewing machines and employed a traveller to sell the machines on commission. The plaintiffs' traveller put up at the defendant's inn in April, 1894, and stayed there until the end of July, 1894. During this time the plaintiffs sent the traveller machines to sell in the neighbourhood. At the end of July, the traveller owed the defendant £4 for board and lodging, and he failed to pay. The defendant detained certain of the goods sent by the plaintiffs to their traveller, claiming he had a lien on them for the amount of the debt due to him although the defendant knew that the goods were the property of the plaintiffs. *Held*—The defendant was entitled to a lien on the plaintiffs' property for the traveller's debt.

351. Caldwell *v.* Sumpters, *The Times*, July 7th, 1971.

The defendants, who were a firm of solicitors, were holding the title deeds to property recently sold by a former client, Mrs. Caldwell, who had not paid their charges. They voluntarily released the deeds to another firm which had been instructed to take their place to complete the sale, stating that they did so on the understanding that the deeds would be held to their order until Mrs. Caldwell had paid. The second firm of solicitors kept the deeds and refused to accept that understanding. *Held*—by Megarry, J.—Sumpters' lien was lost when they voluntarily parted with possession of the deeds and could not be retained by a one-sided reservation of the kind made. If the agreement of the second firm of solicitors had been obtained the lien would have been preserved as it would also if Sumpters had lost possession by trickery or other wrongdoing. The second firm was under no obligation to accept the reservation or to return the deeds.

N.B. The decision of Megarry, J., was reversed by the Court of Appeal (*Caldwell* v. *Sumpters, The Times*, December 20th, 1971), the Court holding that Sumpters' lien was not lost when they parted with the deeds since—

(*a*) possession was given up on the clear and express understanding that the deeds were to be held to Sumpters' order; and

(*b*) solicitors as officers of the court could not be allowed to take advantage of this sort of situation even out of regard for any duty owed to a client.

352. Larner *v.* Fawcett, [1950] 2 All E.R. 727

The defendant owned a racehorse and made an agreement with a Mr. Davis under which it was agreed that Davis would train and race the filly and receive half of any prize money she might win. Davis, unknown to the defendant, agreed to let Larner have the animal to train. Larner did so, and when his charges had reached £125, he discovered that Fawcett was the true owner. Larner, being unable to recover the cost of training and feeding the filly from Davis, who had no funds, now applied to the court for an order for sale. Fawcett was brought in as defendant. *Held*—by the Court of Appeal—that Larner had a common law lien for his charges, and although such a lien does not carry with it a power of sale, the power given in the Rules of the Supreme Court to make an order for sale was appropriate here, particularly since the filly was eating her head off. Fawcett had not made any attempt to get his property back but had clothed Davis with all the indicia of ownership. An order for sale would therefore be made unless Fawcett paid into court the amount of Larner's charges by a given date.

353. Walsh *v.* Lonsdale (1882), 21 Ch.D. 9

The defendant agreed in writing to grant a seven-years lease of a mill to the plaintiff at a rent payable one year in advance. The plaintiff entered into possession without any formal lease having been granted, and he paid his rent quarterly and not in advance. Subsequently the defendant demanded a year's rent in advance, and as the plaintiff refused to pay, the defendant distrained on his property. At common law the plaintiff was a tenant from year to year because no formal lease had been granted, and as such his rent was not payable in advance. The plaintiff argued that the legal remedy of distress was not available to the defendant. *Held*—As the agreement was one of which the court could grant specific performance, and as Equity regarded as done that which ought to be done, the plaintiff held on the same terms as if a lease had been granted. Therefore the distress was valid.

354. Knightsbridge Estates Trust Ltd. *v.* Byrne, [1939] Ch. 441

The plaintiffs were the owners of a large freehold estate close to Knightsbridge. This estate was mortgaged to a friendly society for a sum of money, which, together with interest, was to be repaid over a period of forty years in eighty half-yearly instalments. The company wished to redeem the mortgage before the expiration of the term, because it was possible for them to borrow elsewhere at a lower rate of interest. *Held*—The company was not entitled to redeem the mortgage before the end of the forty years because, in the circumstances, the postponement of the right was not unreasonable, since the parties were men of business and equal in bargaining power. A postponement of the right of redemption is not by itself a clog on the equity of redemption; much depends upon the circumstances. Further, the postponement did not offend the rule against perpetuities which did not apply to mortgages.

355. Noakes *v.* Rice, [1902] A.C. 24

The appellants were a brewery company and the respondent wished to become the purchaser of a public house owned by the company. The respondent borrowed money from the company in order to effect the purchase, and agreed that the company should have the exclusive right to supply the premises with malt liquors during the period of the mortgage and afterwards, whether any money was or was not owed. The respondent subsequently gave notice to the company that he was prepared to pay off the money secured by the mortgage, if the company would release him from the above-mentioned contract. This was refused and the respondent asked the court for relief. *Held*—The covenant was invalid as a clog on the equity of redemption in so far as it purported to tie the public house after payment of the principal money and interest due on the security.

356. Kreglinger *v.* New Patagonia Meat and Cold Storage Co., [1914] A.C. 25

The appellants were a firm of merchants and wool brokers. The respondents carried on the business of preserving and canning meat, and of boiling down carcasses of sheep and other animals. The appellants advanced money to the respondents, the loan being secured by a charge over all the respondents' property. The appellants agreed not to demand repayment for five years, but the respondents could repay the debt at an earlier period on giving notice. The agreement also contained a provision that the respondents should not sell sheepskins to anyone but the appellants for five years from the date of the agreement, so long as the appellants were willing to purchase the same at an agreed price. The loan was paid off before the expiration of the five years. *Held*—The option of purchasing the sheepskins was not terminated on repayment, but continued for the period of five years. The option was a collateral contract which was not a mortgage and in no way affected the right to redeem the property.

357. Cityland and Property (Holdings) Ltd. *v.* Dabrah, [1967] 2 All E.R. 639

A first mortgage of £2,900 was granted by the seller of property to a purchaser and was expressed to be repayable in the sum of £4,553 for which the property was charged. The £4,553 was to be repaid over six years by equal monthly instalments and there was no mention in the mortgage of any interest. The whole of the balance of the £4,553 became payable if the borrower defaulted and for this reason Goff, J., *held* that the premium amounting to £1,653 was an unreasonable collateral advantage and therefore void under the principle in *Kreglinger's Case,* 1914.[356] The Judge having disallowed the premium was prepared to allow interest at seven per cent on a day-to-day basis which he thought to be somewhat more than market rates, but in fact it was far below market rates. The premium was an interest computation of nine-and-a-half per cent, non-reducing over six years and if it had been expressed as such in the mortgage it would appear that the court could not have set it aside since the court can only set aside unreasonable collateral advantages. However, in regard to interest rates, it appears that "equity does not reform mortgage transactions because they are unreasonable," (Greene, M.R., in *Knightsbridge Estates Trust Ltd.* v. *Byrne,* 1939.)[354] But this case was not cited to Goff, J. It would seem that for the future, interest in mortgages should be expressed as such and not disguised as premium.

358. White *v.* City of London Brewery Co. (1889), 42 Ch.D. 237

The plaintiff had a lease of a public house in Canning Town, and he mortgaged it to the defendants to secure a loan of £900 with interest. One year later, no interest having been paid since the date of the mortgage, the defendants entered into possession of the public house. They later let the premises on a tenancy determinable at three months' notice under which the tenant was to take all his beer from the defendants. Eventually the lease was sold by the defendants, and the plaintiff asked the defendants to account and pay him what should be found due. *Held*—The defendants must account to the plaintiff for the increased rent they might have received if they had let the public-house without the restrictive condition regarding the sale of the defendants' beer since a "free house" would produce more rent than a "tied house."

359. Cuckmere Brick Co. *v.* Mutual Finance, [1971] 2 All E.R. 633

The plaintiffs charged land with planning permission for 100 flats to the defendants for £50,000. Later planning permission was granted to build 35 houses. The defendants' power of sale under the charge became exercisable because the plaintiffs had not commenced building by the agreed date. The defendants advertised the land referring only to the planning permission for the houses but not to that for the flats. The plaintiffs informed the defendants of this omission but the defendants refused to postpone the sale. The price received was £44,000, and the plaintiffs sued for damages. *Held*—by the Court of Appeal—that the plaintiffs succeeded. A mortgagee was not a trustee of the power of sale for the mortgagor and, where there was a conflict of interests, he was entitled to give preference to his own over those of the mortgagor, in particular in deciding on the timing of the sale. In exercising the power of sale, however, the mortgagee was not merely under a duty to act in good faith, i.e. honestly and without reckless disregard for the mortgagor's interest, but also to take reasonable care to obtain whatever was the true market value of the mortgaged property at the time when he chose to sell it. (*Kennedy* v. *De Trafford*, [1897] A.C. 180, further explained.) The case was remitted for an enquiry as to the value of the property as a basis for an award of damages to the plaintiff.

360. McCarthy & Stone Ltd. *v.* Julian S. Hodge & Co. Ltd., [1971] 2 All E.R. 973

Cityfields Properties Ltd., who were property developers, purchased land and negotiated with a bank (Hodge & Co.) for finance to pay for it. The bank knew that the development was to be carried out by McCarthy & Stone who had agreed to purchase the property. Cityfields then entered into a formal contract to sell the land to McCarthy. The bank then agreed to grant City-fields an overdraft to pay for the land and secured this loan with an equitable mortgage which included a power of attorney allowing the bank to execute a legal charge in its favour if necessary. This equitable mortgage was registered by the bank in 1964, and in 1965 McCarthy registered their contract to buy the land as an estate contract Class C (iv) under the Land Charges Act, 1925. In June, 1967, the bank created a legal charge in favour of itself under the power of attorney. In October, 1967, Cityfields went into compulsory liquidation and McCarthy claimed the legal estate in the property free of the bank's charge. *Held*—by Foster, J.—McCarthy was entitled to the legal estate free of the charge in favour of the bank. McCarthy's equitable interest in the agreement to buy the land was known to the bank when they entered into an equitable mortgage with Cityfields. Of the two equitable interests the first in time (McCarthy's) had priority. The fact that the bank had later created a legal charge did not affect this position.

361. Koppel *v.* Koppel, [1966] 2 All E.R. 187

Mr. Koppel, who was estranged from his wife, invited a Mrs. Wide to come to his house and look after his children on a permanent basis. Mrs. Wide agreed to do so provided that Mr. Koppel transferred the contents of his house to her to compensate for giving up her own home and disposing of her furniture. The transfer was recorded in writing. Later Mrs. Koppel sought to levy execution on the contents of the house for her unpaid maintenance which amounted to £114. In proceedings resulting from Mrs. Wide's claim to the property, the Registrar of the County Court held that the written transfer of the property to Mrs. Wide was void as an unregistered Bill of Sale. *Held*— By the Court of Appeal—That the contents of the house were not in Mr. Koppel's "possession or apparent possession" within Section 8 of the Bills of Sale Act, 1878, because—

(i) Mr. Koppel had transferred possession to Mrs. Wide under the document which was an absolute Bill of Sale;
(ii) the grantor of the Bill, Mr. Koppel, had therefore neither possession nor apparent possession. He did not have apparent possession because Mrs. Wide was living in the house with him and both had apparent possession of the property, not merely Mr. Koppel;
(iii) Mrs. Wide was therefore entitled to the property.

362. Davies *v.* Rees (1866), L.R. Q.B.D. 408

This action was for trespass to goods seized by the defendant under a bill of sale which had been granted by the plaintiff, the original grantor having assigned the bill to the defendant, Rees. The plaintiff claimed that the bill was void under Sect. 9 of the Bills of Sale Act, 1882, because it was not in the form required by the schedule to that Act. The defendant counter-claimed for the amount of the loan plus interest at 58 per cent, as agreed by the plaintiff in the Bill of Sale. *Held*—The Bill not being in the form required by the Act was void in respect of the assignment of the personal chattels and the plaintiff's claim for damages for trespass succeeded. Further, the covenant by the plaintiff to repay the loan with interest was also void, and the defendant's counter-claim failed.

SALE OF GOODS

363. **Howell** *v.* **Coupland** (1876), 1 Q.B.D. 258

In March, 1892, the defendant agreed to sell to the plaintiff 200 tons of potatoes to be grown on the defendant's land at Whaplode. The potatoes were to be delivered in the following September and October. The defendant accordingly sowed enough seed potatoes on his land at Whaplode to meet the requirements of the contract in the ordinary course of events. Before the time for the performance of the contract arrived, a large portion of the crop was destroyed by disease without any fault on the defendant's part. The plaintiff now sued for damages for non-delivery. *Held*—The contract was for the sale of a specific crop. There was no warranty that the crop would exist at the time of performance and the defendant was excused from performance, the contract being frustrated. The decision in *Taylor* v. *Caldwell* (1863)[289] was applied.

N.B. A transaction of the type set out above may, according to the circumstances, be treated in four ways viz., (i) as a sale of specific goods, the destruction of which frustrates the contract; (ii) as a contingent sale under Sect. 5 (2) so that if the crop does not come into existence the contract does not operate and neither party is bound; (iii) as a sale where the seller is regarded as warranting the eventual existence of the crop and is liable for non-delivery if it fails; (iv) as a sale of a mere chance so that the buyer risks the failure of the crop and must still pay the price.

364. **Barrow Lane and Ballard Ltd.** *v.* **Phillip Phillips & Co. Ltd.**, [1929] 1 K.B. 574

The plaintiffs bought 700 bags of Chinese Ground Nuts, marked E.C.P. and known as "Lot 7 of Chinese Ground Nuts in shell now lying at National Wharves in London." The plaintiffs later re-sold the ground nuts to the defendants. Because of fraudulent abstraction by the wharfingers, there were only 591 bags left when the contract with the defendants was made, but the defendants obtained 150 bags from the warehouse before the discrepancy was discovered. The wharfingers subsequently went into liquidation, and the defendants were unable to obtain any further consignments. The defendants had made payment by means of two bills of exchange, which they now dishonoured, and the plaintiffs sued on the bills, or alternatively for the price of goods sold and delivered. The defendants denied liability, saying that there was an express or implied condition that there were 700 bags lying at the wharf and available for the defendants. The defendants had also tendered £180 for the 150 bags they had received and the plaintiffs had rejected it. This money had been paid into court. *Held*—Where there is a contract for the sale of specific goods and at the date of the contract some but not all of the goods have ceased to exist without the knowledge of either seller or buyer, the case falls within Sect. 6 of the Sale of Goods Act, 1893, and the contract if not severable is void. The plaintiffs therefore failed in their claim, but were entitled to the money tendered for the 150 bags received by the defendants.

N.B. This case leaves open the question of when stolen goods can be regarded as perished. The groundnuts were likely to have been sold after the theft and consumed. If the subject matter is a durable product, e.g. a car, it is likely to be in existence for some time after theft and the position of the parties left uncertain.

365. Myers (G. H.) & Co. *v.* Brent Cross Service Co., [1934] 1 K.B. 46

The plaintiffs gave instructions to the defendants, who were motor engineers, to repair a car belonging to the plaintiffs. The defendants were authorised to replace such parts as in their opinion needed replacement. In order to repair the car it was necessary for the defendants to supply and fit six re-metalled connecting rods, five of which were obtained from the manufacturers of the car, and one from the manufacturers' authorised agent. The car had run for 1,500 miles after the repair when one of the connecting rods supplied and fitted by the defendants broke whilst the car was in motion, causing extensive damage to the engine. The plaintiffs now sued for damages. Evidence showed that there was no faulty workmanship by the defendants and that they had used reasonable skill and care throughout; neither could they have discovered the flaw in the connecting rod. *Held*—Although the contract was not one of sale of goods, but was a contract for work and labour, the liability of a contractor supplying goods in the ordinary course of doing work of this nature was not less than the liability of a seller of goods. There was an implied warranty as to fitness and merchantable quality similar to that in the Sale of Goods Act, 1893, for breach of which the plaintiffs could claim damages.

366. London Jewellers Ltd. *v.* Attenborough, [1934] 2 K.B. 206

A fraudulent person named Waller told the plaintiffs that he could sell jewellery to a well-known actress and the plaintiffs gave him certain items of jewellery for that purpose. Waller signed a note in respect of each article and the note described the goods as being "on appro" or on approval. Waller was also entitled to the difference between the selling price and the price marked on the note. Waller pledged the goods, using women agents, and the defendants, who were pawnbrokers, received the goods *bona fide*. Waller was later arrested and charged with larceny while a bailee, and the plaintiffs sued the defendants in detinue and conversion. *Held*—The defendants had a good title and were not liable. When Waller pledged the goods he signified that he adopted the transaction and had approved them. The property therefore passed to him at that moment and he was able to give the defendants a good title.

367. Wallis, Son & Wells *v.* Pratt & Haynes, [1911] A.C. 394

The appellants and the respondents were corn and seed merchants. The appellants purchased from the respondents 27½ quarters of seed by sample at 40s. per quarter. Since it was impossible to see precisely what sort of seed it was from the sample, the respondents added a description "Common English Sainfoin" (which is a kind of clover). The sold note contained the following clause: "The sellers give no warranty express or implied as to the growth, description or any other matters; and they shall not be held to guarantee or warrant the fitness for any purpose of any grain, seed, flour, cake, or other article sold by them, or its freedom from injurious quality, or from latent defect."

When the seed grew up it was found to be "Giant Sainfoin" and not "Common English," and as Giant Sainfoin is of inferior quality to Common English, the appellants brought this action for damages under Sect. 13 of the Sale of Goods Act, 1893, alleging that the goods did not answer the description. The respondents' defence was the exemption clause. *Held*—The sample being inadequate as a means of identification, the appellants had relied on the description and the respondents were in breach of Sect. 13. The exemption clause failed because it was effective only to exclude implied warranties. Although the appellants' acceptance of the goods had, from the point of view of remedies, converted the implied condition under Sect. 13 into a warranty, it was not converted for other purposes and retained its original status as a condition. It was not, therefore, excluded by the exemption clause.

368. Niblett Ltd. *v.* Confectioners' Materials Co. Ltd., [1921] 3 K.B. 387

The defendants agreed to sell to the plaintiffs 3,000 cases of condensed milk to be shipped from New York to London. 1,000 cases bore labels with the word "Nissly" on them. This came to the notice of the Nestlé Company and they suggested that this was an infringement of their registered trade mark. The plaintiffs admitted this and gave an undertaking not to sell the milk under the title of "Nissly." They tried to dispose of the goods in various ways but eventually discovered that the only way to deal with the goods was to take off the labels and sell the milk without mark or label, thus incurring loss. *Held*—by the Court of Appeal—that the sellers were in breach of the implied condition set out in Sect. 12 (1) of the Sale of Goods Act. A person who can sell goods only by infringing a trade mark has no right to sell, even though he may be the owner of the goods. Banks and Atkin, L.JJ., found that the sellers were also in breach of Sect. 14 (2), since the goods were not merchantable under the "Nissly" mark. Atkin, L.J., also found the sellers to be in breach of the warranty under Sect. 12 (2) because the buyer had not enjoyed quiet possession of the goods.

369. Beale *v.* Taylor, [1967] 1 W.L.R. 1193

The defendant advertised a car for sale as being a 1961 Triumph Herald 1200 and he believed this description to be correct. The plaintiff answered the advertisement and later visited the defendant to inspect the car. During his inspection he noticed, on the rear of the car, a metal disc with the figure 1200 on it. The plaintiff purchased the car, paying the agreed price. However, he later discovered that the car was made up of the rear of a 1961 Triumph Herald 1200 welded to the front of an earlier Triumph Herald 948. The welding was unsatisfactory and the car was unroadworthy. *Held*—By the Court of Appeal—that the plaintiff's claim for damages for breach of the condition implied in the contract by Section 13 of the Sale of Goods Act, 1893, succeeded. The plaintiff had relied on the advertisement and on the metal disc on the rear and the sale was one by description even though the plaintiff had seen and inspected the vehicle.

370. Varley *v.* Whipp, [1900] 1 Q.B. 513

The plaintiff, who was not a dealer, told the defendant that he had a piece of farming equipment called a self-binder for sale. The plaintiff also said that the machine had been used for one season only and had cut 50 to 60 acres. The defendant agreed to buy the machine although he had not seen it. When the machine was delivered, the defendant discovered that it was rather old and had been mended. He wrote to the plaintiff repudiating the contract and returned the machine. The plaintiff now sued to recover £21, the price of the machine. *Held*—The plaintiff's action failed, for in a contract of sale of specific goods or ascertained goods where the buyer has not seen the goods but relies on a description, the contract is a sale by description under Sect. 13 of the Sale of Goods Act, and there is an implied condition that the goods shall correspond with the description.

371. Munro (Robert A.) & Co. Ltd. *v.* Meyer, [1930] 2 K.B. 312

The plaintiffs agreed to supply the defendants with 1,500 tons of meat and bone meal of a specified quality, delivery to be made by instalments. The contract provided that each delivery or shipment should be treated as a separate contract, and that failure to give or to take any delivery or shipment should not cancel the contract with regard to future deliveries or shipments. It further provided that the goods were to be taken with all faults and defects, damaged or inferior. After half the deliveries had been made, the buyers discovered that not all of the meal delivered had been in accordance with the contract, but that some of it was a mixture of meat and bone meal and cocoa husks, though the sellers who had themselves purchased the meal were not aware that it had been adulterated with cocoa husks. The defendants repudiated the contract and the plaintiffs sued for money owing under the agreement. The defendants counter-claimed for damages in respect of the inferior quality of the meal. *Held*—On the counter-claim—that the sale was a sale by description under Sect. 13 of the Sale of Goods Act, and since all of the goods did not comply with the description, the defendant was not bound to take delivery of goods then delivered, and was also entitled to damages in respect of the inferior quality of the meal. Wright, J., was of the opinion that the exemption clause in the contract only applied once goods which answered the trade description were delivered, and could not exclude the operation of Sect. 13 here, because the goods delivered did not all correspond with the description.

372. Ashington Piggeries Ltd. *v.* Christopher Hill Ltd., [1971] 1 All E.R. 847

Ashington Piggeries, who were breeders of animals, contracted with Hill for the supply of food for mink. The food was a form of herring meal to be made up according to a formula supplied by the breeders and agreed by the suppliers. Hill obtained the food from a firm named Norsildmel who were also involved in this action. Unknown to the parties the food supplied contained a poison harmful to most animals and seriously dangerous to mink, and many of the mink who ate it died. The presence of the poison (D.M.N.A.) was the result of treating the herring with a preservative, sodium nitrate, which was poisonous to mink.

Hill sued Ashington for the price of the feed and Ashington counter-claimed for the loss of the mink. Hill also claimed an indemnity against Norsildmel. The case eventually reached the House of Lords where it was *held*—

(i) the suppliers were not liable for breach of Sect. 13 of the 1893 Act. The substance had been described as "herring meal" and this was not a misdescription even though what was supplied was herring meal plus

D.M.N.A. (*Pinnock Bros.* v. *Lewis and Peat*, 1923,[307] distinguished on the grounds that the adulteration in that case was much greater. Lord Dilhorne dissented regarding *Pinnock Bros.* as applicable and rendering the suppliers liable under Sect. 13.)

(ii) The suppliers were liable under Sect. 14 (1) since the goods were not fit for the purpose. Although the breeders had supplied the formula they had relied on the supplier's skill and judgment to exercise discretion and obtain at least non-poisonous food. Furthermore, the suppliers were, in general terms, in business to supply animal foods and it did not matter that they had not sold this particular brand of food before (this decision was unanimous).

(iii) The suppliers were also liable under Sect. 14 (2). The section was capable of application even in a situation in which the seller was selling a particular article for the first time. (Lords Hodson and Diplock dissented. The suppliers could not be regarded as dealing in goods of the particular kind supplied, which was vital to liability under Sect. 14 (2), though not under Sect. 14 (i) where the sole requirement was that it must be in the course of the seller's business to supply goods of that *class*.)

(iv) The suppliers were entitled to be indemnified by Norsildmel, the defence of remoteness of damage being unacceptable in view of the fact that feeding to mink was a possibility contemplated by both Norsildmel and Hill.

372a. *Kendall (Henry) & Sons* v. *William Lillico & Sons Ltd.*, [1969] 2 A.C. 31

Brazilian ground nut extraction was sold in order that it could be made into feeding stuff for cattle and poultry. It was held by the House of Lords that there was a breach of Sect. 14 (1) because the feed proved fatal to turkeys, though it was not dangerous to cattle.

373. Nichol *v.* Godts (1854), 10 Ex. 191

The plaintiff agreed to sell to the defendant certain oil described as "foreign refined rape oil." The plaintiff supplied a sample of oil and the sold note said that the oil was "warranted only equal to samples." The defendant refused to accept the oil in question, alleging that it was a mixture of rape and hemp oil which was inferior. However, the oil actually delivered did correspond with the samples. *Held*—The defendant was not obliged to take the oil. He was entitled to oil answering the description of "foreign refined rape oil." and the statement in the sold note referred only to the quality of the oil and did not absolve the plaintiff from supplying oil corresponding to the description.

374. Priest *v.* Last, [1903] 2 K.B. 148

The plaintiff, a draper who had no special knowledge of hot water bottles, bought such a bottle from the defendant who was a chemist. It was in the ordinary course of the defendant's business to sell hot water bottles and the plaintiff asked him whether the indiarubber bottle he was shown would stand boiling water. He was told that it would not, but that it would stand hot water. The plaintiff did not state the purpose for which the bottle was required. In the event the bottle was filled with hot water and used by the plaintiff's wife for bodily application to relieve cramp. On the fifth time of using, the bottle burst and the wife was severely scalded. Evidence showed that the bottle was not fit for use as a hot water bottle. *Held*—The plaintiff was entitled to recover for the defendant's breach of Sect. 14 (1) of the Sale of Goods Act, 1893. The circumstances showed that the plaintiff had relied on the defendant's skill and judgment, and although he had not mentioned the purpose for which he required the bottle, he had in fact used it for the usual and obvious purpose.

375. Grant *v.* Australian Knitting Mills Ltd., [1936] A.C. 85

This was an appeal from the High Court of Australia to the Privy Council in England by a Dr. Grant of Adelaide, South Australia. Dr. Grant bought a pair of long woollen underpants from a retailer, the respondents being the manufacturers. The underpants contained an excess of sulphite which was a chemical used in their manufacture. This chemical should have been eliminated before the product was finished, but a quantity was left in the underpants purchased by Dr. Grant. After wearing the pants for a day or two, a rash, which turned out to be dermatitis, appeared on the appellant's ankles and soon became generalised, compelling the appellant to spend many months in hospital. He sued the retailers and the manufacturers for damages. *Held*— (i) The retailers were in breach of Sect. 14 (1) and (2) of the South Australian Sale of Goods Act, 1895 (which is in the same terms as the English Act of 1893). They were liable under Sect. 14 (1) because the appellant had made known the purpose for which the goods were required, and had relied on the retailer's skill and judgment, and the article was not fit for the purpose. They were liable under Sect. 14 (2) because the sale was by description. Even though the goods were displayed before the appellant on the counter, the article was not sold as a specific thing but as a thing corresponding to a description i.e. woollen underwear, and the article could not be merchantable in this case because it was not fit for the purpose. (ii) The manufacturers were liable in negligence, following *Donoghue* v. *Stevenson*.[334] This was a latent defect which could not have been discovered by a reasonable examination. It should also be noted that the appellant had a perfectly normal skin. (Compare *Griffiths* v. *Peter Conway Ltd.*, 1939—*ante* Case No. 379.)

376. Wren *v.* Holt, [1903] 1 K.B. 610

The plaintiff was a builder's labourer at Blackburn, and the defendant was the tenant of a beerhouse in the same town. The beerhouse was a tied house so that the defendant was obliged to sell beer brewed by a firm called Richard Holden Limited. The plaintiff was a regular customer and knew that the beerhouse was a tied house, and that only one type of beer was supplied. The plaintiff became ill and it was established that his illness was caused by arsenical poisoning due to the beer supplied to him. He now sued the tenant. *Held*— There was no claim under Sect. 14 (1) because the plaintiff could not have relied on the defendant's skill and judgment in selecting his stock, because he was bound to supply Holden's beer. However, Sect. 14 (2) applied, and since the beer was not of merchantable quality, the plaintiff was entitled to recover damages.

376a. *Manchester Liners Ltd.* v. *Rea* [1922] 2 A.C. 74

The defendants supplied coal to the owners of a ship called the *Manchester Importer*. The coal was not suitable for that particular vessel and the sellers were *held*—by the House of Lords—to be in breach of Sect. 14 (1), even though the buyers suspected that the sellers might not have suitable coal owing to a rail strike. Thus a mere suspicion (as distinct from certainty) that only goods of a certain kind can be sold is not enough.

N.B. Griffiths v. *Peter Conway Ltd.*, 1939,[379] was distinguished. The defendants had undertaken to supply coal for a particular class of ship and knew ships differed as to type and fuel requirements. There were no normal or standard ships. There are normal human beings who would not have been affected by the coat supplied in *Griffiths* case. See also *Ashington Piggeries*,[372] where it was regarded as essential to show that the herring meal was toxic to most animals and not just to mink.

377. Frost *v.* Aylesbury Dairy Co. Ltd., [1905] 1 K.B. 608

The defendants, whose business was the selling of milk, supplied milk to the plaintiff's household. The account book supplied to him contained several statements regarding the precautions taken by the defendants to keep their milk free from germs. This action was brought by the plaintiff for damage sustained by him on the death of his wife by typhoid fever contracted from the milk supplied by the defendants. *Held*—The plaintiff succeeded because the circumstances showed that he had relied on the defendants' skill and judgment to select and supply milk free from germs. He was, therefore, entitled to the benefit of Sect. 14 (1) of the Sale of Goods Act, 1893, because the milk was not fit for human consumption. It was not a defence that no skill or judgment would have enabled the sellers to find out the defect.

378. Geddling *v.* Marsh, [1920] 1 K.B. 668

The defendants were manufacturers of mineral waters and they supplied the same to the plaintiff who kept a small general store. The bottles were returnable when empty. One of the bottles was defective, and whilst the plaintiff was putting it back carefully into a crate, it burst and injured her. *Held*— Even though the bottles were returnable, they were supplied under a contract of sale within Sect. 14 of the Sale of Goods Act, 1893. The fact that the bottles were only bailed to the plaintiff was immaterial. There was an implied warranty of fitness for the purpose for which they were supplied, and the defendant was liable in damages.

N.B. Bray, J., was careful to point out that his decision was an interpretation of Sect. 14 of the Sale of Goods Act only. It does not decide that the liability of a bailor is the same as that of a vendor.

379. Griffiths *v.* Peter Conway Ltd., [1939] 1 All E.R. 685

The defendants, who were retail tailors, supplied the plaintiff with a Harris tweed coat which was made to order for her. The plaintiff wore the coat for a short time and then developed dermatitis. She brought this action for damages alleging that the defendants were in breach of Sect. 14 (1) of the Sale of Goods Act, 1893, because the coat was not fit for the purpose for which it was bought. Evidence showed that the plaintiff had an abnormally sensitive skin and that the coat would not have affected the skin of a normal person. *Held*—The plaintiff failed because Sect. 14 (1) did not apply. The defendants did not know of the plaintiff's abnormality and could not be expected to assume that it existed.

380. Baldry *v.* Marshall, [1925] 1 K.B. 260

The plaintiff was the owner of a Talbot racing car and was anxious to change it for a touring car because his wife refused to ride in the Talbot. The plaintiff wrote to the defendants asking for details of the Bugatti car for which they were agents. The plaintiff knew nothing of the Bugatti range, but asked for a car that would be comfortable and suitable for touring purposes. The defendants' manager said that a Bugatti would be suitable. The plaintiff later inspected a Bugatti chassis and agreed to buy it when a body had been put on it. When the car was delivered it was to all intents and purposes a racing car and not suitable for touring. The plaintiff returned the car, but he had paid £1,000 under the contract and now sued for its return on the grounds that the defendants were in breach of Sect. 14 (1) of the Sale of Goods Act, the car not being fit for the purpose. The defendants alleged that Sect. 14 (1) did not apply since the car was sold under its trade name. *Held*—The plaintiff had relied on the skill and judgment of the defendants and it was in the course of their business to supply cars. Therefore, there was a breach of Sect. 14 (1) even though the car was sold under a trade name.

N.B. In this case the plaintiff had accepted a manufacturer's guarantee in which was contained the following clause: "The foregoing guarantee is accepted instead of and expressly excludes any other guarantee statutory or otherwise." The court found that the sellers were in breach of the implied condition of fitness in Sect. 14 (1), and since the exemption clause excluded only warranties, it did not affect the plaintiff's rights in this case.

381. Wilson *v.* Rickett, Cockerell & Co. Ltd., [1954] 1 Q.B. 598

The plaintiff, a housewife, ordered from the defendants, who were coal merchants, a ton of "Coalite." The Coalite was delivered and when part of it was put on a fire in an open grate, it exploded causing damage to the plaintiff's house. In this action the plaintiff claimed damages for breach of Sect. 14 of the Sale of Goods Act, 1893. The county court judge found that the explosion was not due to the Coalite but to something else, possibly a piece of coal with explosive embedded in it, which had got mixed with the Coalite in transit and had not come from the manufacturers of the Coalite. Therefore, he held that Sect. 14 (1) applied only to the Coalite and dismissed the action since the Coalite itself was fit for the purpose. The Court of Appeal, however, in allowing the appeal, pointed out that fuel of this kind is not sold by the lump but by the bag, and a bag containing explosive material is, as a unit, not fit for burning. The explosive matter was "goods supplied under the contract" for the purposes of Sect. 14, and clearly Sect. 14 (2) applied, because the goods supplied were not of merchantable quality. Damages were awarded to the plaintiff. Regarding the applicability of Sect. 14 (1), the Court of Appeal did not think this applied since the sale was under a trade name, and the plaintiff had not relied on the defendants' skill and judgment in selecting a fuel.

382. Thornett and Fehr *v.* Beers and Son, [1919] 1 K.B. 486

The plaintiffs were dealers in glue and the defendants, being interested in purchasing glue, sent a representative to the plaintiffs' factory to discuss the matter. The representative was given a sample of the glue but the defendants said that it was not large enough to ascertain the quality. It was therefore arranged that the defendants should send a representative to the plaintiffs' factory at Nottingham to inspect the glue. The plaintiffs gave instructions that every facility was to be given to the defendants' representative to carry out the examination. In the event, the representative who went to the factory discussed the quality of the glue but did not have the casks opened, although the plaintiffs would have allowed this. If the casks had been opened, the defects which the defendants later complained of would have been revealed. The defendants bought some of the glue at an agreed price, and on finding it not of suitable quality, refused to pay for it. The plaintiffs now sued for the agreed price and the defendants counter-claimed that there was a breach of Sect. 14 (2) because the goods were not of merchantable quality. *Held*—There was no implied condition of merchantable quality under Sect. 14 (2) because the provision in the section relating to examination applied.

N.B. This was not a sale by sample because, since the sample was too small, the defendants did not rely on it but relied instead on the inspection carried out by their representative.

383. B. S. Brown & Son Ltd. *v.* Craiks Ltd., [1970] 1 All E.R. 823

Brown & Son ordered a quantity of cloth from Craiks who were manufacturers. Brown's wanted it for making dresses but did not make this purpose known to Craiks who thought the cloth was wanted for industrial use. The price paid by Brown's was 36·25p per yard which was higher than the normal price for industrial cloth but not substantially so. The cloth was not suitable for making dresses and Brown's cancelled the contract and claimed damages. Both parties were left with substantial quantities of cloth but Craiks had managed to sell some of their stock for 30p per yard. Having failed in the lower court to establish a claim under Sect. 14 (1) since they had not made the purpose known to Craiks', Brown's now sued for damages under Sect. 14(2). *Held*—by the House of Lords—that the claim failed. The cloth was still commercially saleable for industrial purposes though at a slightly lower price. It was not a necessary requirement of merchantability that there should be no difference between purchase and resale price. If the difference was substantial however, it might indicate that the goods were not of merchantable quality. The difference in this case was not so material as to justify any such inference.

384. Godley *v.* Perry, [1960] 1 All E.R. 36

The first defendant Perry was a newsagent who also sold toys, and in particular displayed plastic toy catapults in his window. The plaintiff, who was a boy aged six, bought one for 6d. While using it to fire a stone, the catapult broke, and the plaintiff was struck in the eye, either by a piece of the catapult or the stone, and as a result he lost his left eye. The chemist's report given in evidence was that the catapults were made from cheap material unsuitable for the purpose and likely to fracture, and that the moulding of the plastic was poor, the catapults containing internal voids. Perry had purchased the catapults from a wholesaler with whom he had dealt for some time, and this sale was by sample, the defendant's wife examining the sample catapult by pulling the elastic. The wholesaler's supplier was another whosesaler who had imported the catapults from Hong Kong. This sale was also by sample and the sample catapult was again tested by pulling the elastic. In this action the plaintiff alleged that the first defendant was in breach of the conditions implied by Sect. 14 (1) and (2) of the Sale of Goods Act. The first defendant brought in his supplier as third party, alleging against him a breach of the conditions implied by Sect. 15 (2) (*c*), and the third party brought in his supplier as fourth party, alleging breach of Sect. 15 (2) (*c*) against him. *Held*—

    (i) The first defendant was in breach of Sect. 14 (1) and (2) because—

        (*a*) The catapult was not reasonably fit for the purpose for which it was required. The plaintiff relied on the seller's skill or judgment, this being readily inferred where the customer was of tender years. (Sect. 14 (1).)

        (*b*) The catapult, even though sold over the counter, was bought by description and was not merchantable. (Sect. 14 (2).)

(ii) The third and fourth parties were both in breach of Sect. 15 (2) (c) because the catapult had a defect which rendered it unmerchantable, and this defect was not apparent on reasonable examination of the sample. The test applied, i.e. the pulling of the elastic, was all that could be expected of a potential purchaser. The third and fourth parties had done business before, and the third party was entitled to regard without suspicion any sample shown to him and to rely on the fourth party's skill in selecting his goods.

385. Champanhac & Co. Ltd. *v.* Waller & Co. Ltd., [1948] 2 All E.R. 724

In 1947 the plaintiffs' agent, a Mr. Marks, visited the defendants' premises and was offered a quantity of government surplus balloons. Marks was shown a sample of material of which the balloons were made and he examined it, tested it, and found it strong and merchantable. Marks thereupon orally agreed to buy 200 at 30s. each. The defendants drew up a letter and gave it to Marks, the material terms of the contract being stated in the letter. The letter stated that the goods sold were "as sample taken away" and "it is distinctly understood that these are government surplus goods and we sell them to you with all faults and imperfections." Marks had been given to understand that the balloons might be dirty and he thought that this was the imperfection envisaged by the letter. When the balloons were delivered they were perished and unmerchantable, and the plaintiffs brought this action. *Held*—The sale was by sample and the words "with all faults and imperfections" meant that if the bulk corresponded with the sample as to type and quality, the bulk would be accepted with whatever faults and imperfections it had. In fact the fabric of the balloons did not correspond with the sample so that the defendants were in breach of the implied conditions under Sects. 15 (2) (a) and 15 (2) (c) of the Sale of Goods Act. However, since the plaintiffs had not rejected the goods, the condition had become a warranty and the defendants were liable in damages only and were not bound to take them back.

386. Clarke *v.* Army and Navy Co-operative Society Ltd., [1903] 1 K.B. 155

The defendants sold to the plaintiff a tin of chlorinated lime for use as disinfectant. The defendants knew that other tins from the consignment had caused injury to persons opening them because the tins were badly constructed. No warning was given to the plaintiff when the goods were purchased and she was injured when in the course of opening the tin, lime flew into her eyes. In this action by the plaintiff for damages, the defendants raised a rule of the society that "No warranties are given with the goods sold by the Society except on the written authority of one of the managing directors or the assistant manager." *Held*—Regardless of whether the rule was effective or not to exclude liability under Sect. 14 (1) that the goods were fit for the purpose, a seller of goods, which have a dangerous quality which the seller knows and the buyer does not, has a duty independent of any warranty to warn the buyer of that dangerous quality. Therefore, the defendants were liable for their negligent act in not warning the plaintiff that the tins were dangerous.

387. Fisher *v.* Harrods (1966), 110 S.J. 133

The defendants bought a jewellery cleaner from a manufacturer without making enquiries as to its safety in use. It contained substances which were injurious to the eyes but no indication or warning of this was given either on the bottle or in any other way. A bottle of the cleaner sold by the defendants injured the plaintiff when the contents exploded, damaging her eyes. She now claimed damages from the defendants and it was *held* that they had been negligent in the circumstances of the case by failing to make enquiries of the manufacturer; failing to have the cleaner analysed; and selling it without a warning.

388. Daniels *v.* R. White and Sons Ltd., [1938] 4 All E.R. 258

The plaintiffs, who were husband and wife, sued the first defendants, who were manufacturers of mineral waters, in negligence. The plaintiffs had been injured because a bottle of the first defendants' lemonade, which they had purchased from a public house in Battersea, contained carbolic acid. Evidence showed that the manufacturer took all possible care to see that no injurious matter got into the lemonade, and that the husband when he bought the lemonade from the public house asked for it by mentioning the manufacturers' name. It was *held* that the manufacturers were not liable in negligence because the duty was not one to ensure that the goods were in perfect condition but only to take reasonable care to see that no injury was caused to the eventual consumer. This duty had been fulfilled. The second defendant, who was the landlady of the Battersea public house from which the goods were purchased, was held liable under Sect. 14 (2) of the Sale of Goods Act, 1893, because the goods were not of merchantable quality. The landlady was not liable under Sect. 14 (1) since the goods were asked for by the manufacturers' name.

389. Andrews *v.* Hopkinson, [1957] 1 Q.B. 229

The plaintiff purchased from the defendant, who was a second-hand car dealer at Doncaster, a 1934 saloon car for £120. The defendant's manager said during negotiations with the plaintiff, "It's a good little bus. I would stake my life on it. You will have no trouble with it." The plaintiff bought the car on hire purchase, the defendant selling the car to a finance company and the finance company hiring it to the plaintiff. A week after the car was purchased, the plaintiff was involved in a collision with a lorry because of the car's defective steering which evidence showed could have been discovered by a competent mechanic. In this action by the plaintiff for breach of warranty it was *held* that the words used by the defendant's sales manager amounted to a warranty, and the plaintiff could enforce the warranty *even though he did not purchase the car from the defendant* but merely hired it from the finance company. The warranty was a contract between the plaintiff and defendant collateral to the hire-purchase transaction. The defendants were also sued in the tort of negligence and found liable. The point of this case in Sale of Goods is that, where there is an exemption clause in the actual contract of sale which prevents the buyer relying on the implied terms of the Sale of Goods Act, he may nevertheless sue upon a collateral undertaking of the sort given in this case, i.e. any express warranties the seller may give during the course of sale.

N.B. See now Sect. 16 of the Hire-Purchase Act, 1965. (p. 178.)

390. Underwood Ltd. *v.* Burgh Castle Brick & Cement Syndicate, [1922] 1 K.B. 343

The plaintiffs agreed to sell a condensing engine to the defendants. At the time the contract was made the engine was at the plaintiffs' premises in Millwall and was fixed to a bed of concrete by bolts. It was necessary to detach the engine before it could be delivered. The engine was damaged in the course of preparing it for dispatch, and when it was delivered the defendants refused to accept it. The plaintiffs argued that the property had passed when the contract was made, so that the defendants must accept their own goods. *Held*—The property had not passed to the defendants because the goods were not in a deliverable state when the contract was made. The engine was at that time a fixture and not in the true sense of the word a movable chattel.

390*a*. *Phillip Head & Sons Ltd.* v. *Showfronts Ltd.* (1969), 113 S.J. 978

The plaintiffs agreed with the defendants to sell and lay carpet. The carpet was delivered to the defendants' premises but it was stolen before it was laid. It was *held* that the carpet was not in a deliverable state and therefore the property and risk had not passed to the defendants. Two grounds were mentioned—(i) that the carpet was in a heavy bundle and could not easily be moved; (ii) that the carpet had to be laid as part of "delivery."

N.B. This case was brought under Sect. 18 Rule 5 (1), which also contains the words "in a deliverable state."

391. Poole *v.* Smith's Car Sales (Balham) Ltd., [1962] 2 All E.R. 482

In August, 1960, the plaintiff, a car dealer, supplied two second-hand cars to the defendants who were also car dealers. The cars were supplied on "sale or return" terms whilst the plaintiff went on holiday, the agreement being that the defendants would return the cars if they were not sold in that time. One car was sold and paid for on September 21st, 1960, but the other car, a 1956 Vauxhall Wyvern, had not been sold or returned by the end of October, 1960. The plaintiff tried to get it returned by making telephone calls but finally he wrote a letter to the defendants, dated November 7th, in which he said that, if the car was not returned by November 10th, 1960, it would be deemed sold to the defendants. The car was not returned until about November 24th, and was then in a bad condition, having been used by the defendants' employees for their own purposes. The plaintiff rejected the car and sued for its price, i.e. £325, which was the sale or return value agreed in August, 1960. *Held*—The contract was one of delivery "on a sale or return" and therefore fell within Sect. 18, Rule 4. The property had passed to the defendants because it had not been returned within a reasonable amount of time and the court was particularly concerned with the depreciation of a 1956 car between September and October when the market was declining. The defendants must pay the contract price as agreed.

392. Weiner *v.* Harris, [1910] 1 K.B. 285

The plaintiff was a jeweller and he entrusted certain goods to one Fisher who was a traveller in the jewellery trade. The terms of the agreement were that Fisher had the goods on "sale or return" and that they were to remain the property of the plaintiff until sold or paid for. The defendant was a moneylender and he advanced money to Fisher on the security of the goods. The plaintiff now sued to recover the goods from the moneylender. *Held*—The defendant had a good title in spite of the terms of the contract between the plaintiff and Fisher. Fisher was a mercantile agent for the purposes of Sect. 1 of the Factors Act, 1889, and therefore had power to pledge the goods under Sect. 2 of the Factors Act, 1889.

393. Laurie and Morewood *v.* Dudin & Sons, [1926] 1 K.B. 223

On February 2nd, 1925, Messrs. Alcock and Sons sold to John Wilkes & Sons 200 quarters of maize from 618 quarters belonging to Alcock and Sons and lying in the defendants' warehouse. Wilkes & Sons were given a delivery note which they sent to the defendants who were therefore on notice of the sale. On February 18th, Wilkes & Sons sold the 200 quarters of maize to the plaintiffs and gave them a delivery note which the plaintiffs sent to the defendants on February 19th. On both occasions when they received delivery notes the defendants merely made entries in their books and no attempt was made to appropriate the goods to the contract. Wilkes & Sons failed to pay Alcock and Sons for the maize and Alcock and Sons instructed the defendants to withhold delivery. The plaintiffs now sued the defendants in detinue, claiming that the property in the maize had passed to them. *Held*—The plaintiffs' action failed. The maize did not belong to them because there had been no appropriation of the goods and therefore the property in the maize had not passed either to Wilkes & Sons or to the plaintiffs.

394. Gibraltar Packers Ltd. *v.* Basic Economy and Development Corporation Ltd., [1966] 1 Ll. Rep. 615

The plaintiffs agreed to buy goods from the defendants upon terms that the defendants would repurchase some items if not sold by the plaintiffs. The plaintiffs later called upon the defendants to repurchase certain named items and the defendants refused for reasons which need not be dealt with. The plaintiffs now sued for the price of the named items, alleging that the property in them had passed to the defendants. *Held*—By Megaw, J.—that the goods to be purchased became ascertained when the plaintiffs called upon the defendants to repurchase them and the property in them passed to the defendants at the same date. The plaintiffs were therefore entitled to recover the price from the defendants and not merely damages for breach of contract.

395. Wait and James *v.* Midland Bank (1926), 31 Comm. Cas. 172

The sellers sold 1,250 quarters of wheat on credit from a larger cargo lying in a warehouse. The buyers were given delivery orders which were acceptable to the warehouseman for purposes of delivery when required. The buyers did not ask for delivery but pledged the delivery orders to a bank as security. At this time no severance of the buyers' wheat had taken place. Later the sellers sold and delivered the remainder of the wheat leaving the buyers' share of the cargo in the warehouse. It was *held*—by Roche, J.—that the second sale had the effect of passing the property in the remaining wheat to the first buyers and the bank's security was good against the 1,250 quarters left.

N.B. Roche, J., appears to have assumed that ascertainment was enough to pass the property. There had been no unconditional appropriation.

396. Pignataro *v.* Gilroy & Son, [1919] 1 K.B. 459

By a contract made on February 12th, 1918, the defendants sold to the plaintiff 140 bags of rice, the plaintiff to take delivery within 14 days. The rice was unascertained when the contract was made. On February 27th, the plaintiff sent a cheque for the rice and asked for a delivery order. On February 28th the defendants sent a delivery order for 125 bags which were lying at a place called Chambers' Wharf. A letter accompanying the delivery order said that the remaining 15 bags were at the defendants' place of business at 50 Long Acre, and requested the plaintiff to collect them there. The plaintiff did not send for the 15 bags until March 25th when it was found that they had been stolen without negligence on the part of the defendants. *Held*—The goods were at the plaintiff's risk. He had not dissented from the appropriation made by the defendants, and his assent to it must therefore be implied.

397. Healey *v.* Howlett & Sons, [1917] 1 K.B. 337

Howlett & Sons were fish dealers in Ireland and they supplied fish to English customers. They had an agent at Holyhead, all fish being sent to the agent who selected parcels of fish for dispatch to customers in England. The plaintiff was a fish salesman in London and he ordered 20 boxes of mackerel from the defendants. The defendants dispatched 122 boxes of mackerel to their agent in Holyhead to fulfil the plaintiff's order and others. The agent selected 20 boxes for dispatch to the plaintiff, but because of delays in getting the fish to Holyhead, the fish was found to be bad on arrival in London. The delay in getting the fish to Holyhead was not the defendants' fault. The plaintiff refused to pay the defendants and the defendants sued in the City of London Court for the full price on the ground that the dispatch of 122 boxes of fish to their agent was sufficient appropriation to pass the property to Healey in respect of his 20 boxes. Healey now appealed from the decision of the City of London Court. *Held*—There was no appropriation until the agent at Holyhead earmarked the 20 boxes for the appellant. The fish had deteriorated before arrival at Holyhead and was at the respondents' risk when it did deteriorate. The appellant was therefore not liable to pay for the fish.

398. National Coal Board *v.* Gamble, [1958] 3 All E.R. 203

The Coal Board supplied coal to a buyer at a colliery by loading from a hopper into the buyer's lorry. The lorry was then driven to a weighbridge so that the weight of the coal could be ascertained and a weight-ticket, as required by statute, issued. The court held that the property did not pass until the coal had been weighed and the ticket given to and accepted by the buyer. The court was also of opinion that under the system in operation at the colliery any coal in excess of the buyer's requirement could have been unloaded before the weight-ticket was issued and accepted. It would seem, therefore, that the court was assuming that although appropriation took place when the coal was loaded on to the lorry, it was not unconditional until it was weighed and the weight-ticket accepted by the buyer.

399. Sterns Ltd. *v.* Vickers Ltd., [1923] 1 K.B. 78

On January 3rd, 1920, the Admiralty sold to Vickers Ltd., 120,000 gallons of white spirit out of a larger quantity of 200,000 gallons then lying at Thames Haven in Tank No. 78. The tank belonged to a storage company called London and Thames Haven Oil Wharves Company. Vickers Ltd. sold the spirit to Sterns Ltd., who did not take delivery for some months. When they did take delivery, the specific gravity of the spirit had changed by deterioration over time. Sterns Ltd. claimed damages for breach of warranty against the sellers. *Held*—Whether or not the property in the oil had passed at the time of sale (the goods being unascertained), the oil was at the plaintiffs' risk from the time of sale and the defendants were not liable for breach of warranty.

400. Head *v.* Tattersall (1870), L.R. 7 Ex. 7

Tattersall sold a horse to Head warranting that it had hunted with the Bicester Hounds, and giving Head the right to return the horse by a certain date if it did not comply with the warranty. Head discovered that the horse had not hunted with the Bicester Hounds and returned it to Tattersall within the time stipulated. However, whilst the horse was in Head's possession, it was injured, though without negligence on his part. *Held*—In the circumstances it was possible to take the view that the property had passed but not the risk, and Tattersall was obliged to accept the injured horse.

401. Demby, Hamilton & Co., Ltd. *v.* Barden, [1949] 1 All E.R. 435

The plaintiffs were sellers of apple juice and on November 8th, 1945, they entered into a contract with the defendants who were wine merchants. Under the contract the plaintiffs were to supply and the defendants were to buy 30 tons of apple juice to be delivered by lorry in weekly instalments, the contract to be completed by the end of February, 1946. The plaintiffs crushed a quantity of apples and put the juice into casks, but the property did not pass at that stage since the casks were not specifically appropriated to the contract. 20½ tons of apple juice were delivered and at that stage the buyers said that they could not take the other instalments until further notice. The last delivery was made on April 4th, 1946. The plaintiffs repeatedly asked for delivery instructions and on November 7th, 1946, they informed the defendants that the contents of the remaining casks had gone putrid and had been thrown away. The plaintiffs now sued for the price of the goods sold and delivered, and for damages in respect of the apple juice which had been thrown away. *Held*—Under the proviso to Sect. 20 of the Sale of Goods Act the goods were at the buyer's risk because he was responsible for the delay. If the sellers could have sold the remainder of the apple juice elsewhere, the loss might have fallen on them, but their contract with the defendants obliged the plaintiffs to hold the goods available for delivery as and when required by the defendants. The plaintiffs' action for the price of the goods sold and for damages succeeded.

402. Eastern Distributors Ltd. *v.* Goldring, [1957] 2 Q.B. 600

A person named Murphy was the owner of a Bedford van and wished to buy a Chrysler car from one Coker who was a car dealer. Murphy could not find the money to pay the hire-purchase deposit on the Chrysler. Coker suggested that Murphy authorise him to sell the van to a Finance Company and get an agreement from the Finance Company under which they agreed to sell the van to Murphy on hire-purchase terms and then Murphy could apply the proceeds of the sale of his van in putting down deposits on the van and the Chrysler.

Murphy gave Coker authority, but limited it to selling the van and arranging the hire purchase of the van and the Chrysler. Under the authority given to him Coker was bound to effect *both* transactions and not one only. Murphy then signed the necessary documents leaving Coker to fill them in. In the proposal form for the hire purchase of the van Coker described himself as owner of the vehicle and without authority from Murphy sold the van to the plaintiffs, who were the finance company, as if it was his own. The plaintiffs then hired it out to Murphy and sent him a copy of the agreement. The hire purchase of the Chrysler was not carried out and later Coker told Murphy that the whole deal had fallen through, and was cancelled. Murphy then sold the van which he believed to be his own to Goldring, who bought in good faith and without knowledge of Murphy's previous dealings. Murphy made no payments under the hire-purchase agreement, and the plaintiffs terminated it and claimed the van or its value from the defendant. *Held*—by the Court of Appeal—

(i) That Coker had no actual authority to sell the van separately to the plaintiffs but only as part of a double transaction. However, Murphy, by providing Coker with documents which enabled him to represent himself to the plaintiffs as entitled to the van, had clothed Coker with apparent authority to sell and was prevented by Sect. 21 (1) of the Sale of Goods Act from denying that authority. The plaintiffs had obtained a good title and Murphy had no title to give Goldring.

(ii) Sect. 25 (1) of the Sale of Goods Act did not make the sale to Goldring valid, because Murphy was, after the hire-purchase agreement, not in possession as a seller but as a bailee by virtue of the agreement.

N.B. If Goldring was a private purchaser he would now obtain a good title under Sect. 27 (2) of the Hire-Purchase Act, 1964.

402*a*. *Pacific Motor Auctions Party Ltd.* v. *Motor Credits (Hire Finance) Ltd.,* [1965] A.C. 867

A Ltd., who were dealers, sold cars to B Ltd. (the plaintiffs) under a "display agreement" whereby A Ltd. remained in possession of the vehicles which were displayed in their showrooms. A Ltd. were paid 90 per cent. of the price and authorised to sell the cars as agents for B Ltd. At a later date A Ltd. got into financial difficulties and B Ltd. revoked the authority to sell the cars. Nevertheless A Ltd. sold some of them to the defendants who purchased *bona fide* and for value. The defendants were aware of the display agreement and could not have assumed A Ltd. were owners though they did think A Ltd. had authority to sell. On appeal from the Australian High Court the Privy Council decided that the defendants were protected by Sect. 25 (1) of the New South Wales Sale of Goods Act (which is identical with the English Act). The words "continues . . . in possession" referred to a continuity of physical possession regardless of a change in legal title under which possession is retained. Unless there is an actual transfer of physical possession the seller is able to pass a good title under Sect. 25 (1).

402*b*. *Worcester Finance* v. *Cooden Engineering Co.,* [1971] e All E.R. 708

In June, 1966, the defendants sold a car to a dealer called Griffiths (who turned out to be a fraud). Griffiths, who paid by cheque, then purported to sell the car to Worcester Finance as part of a hire-purchase transaction under which a Mr. Millerick was to hire it with a view to purchase. Mr. Millerick never took possession and Griffiths kept the car. In due course the cheque by which Griffiths paid the defendants was dishonoured and the defendants took possession of the car. Worcester Finance claimed to be owners of the vehicle and claimed damages from Cooden in conversion. *Held*—by the Court of Appeal—that—

(*a*) Griffiths had continued in possession of the car within Sect. 25 (1) of the Sale of Goods Act, 1893, after the sale to Worcester Finance, "possession" meaning physical possession and continuing even though Griffiths might have become a trespasser as against Worcester Finance; and

(*b*) that when Cooden retook possession of the vehicle from Griffiths there was a "disposition" by Griffiths which vested the title in Cooden free from Worcester Finance's rights, Cooden having acted in good faith and without notice of the sale to Worcester Finance.

N.B. Eastern Distributors v. *Goldring*[402] was not followed; *Pacific Motor Auctions Party Ltd.* v. *Motor Credits (Hire Finance) Ltd.*[402a] was applied.

403. Clayton v. Le Roy, [1911] 2 K.B. 1031

In 1902 Mrs. Clayton, the plaintiff's wife, bought a gold watch from the defendant for £100 and gave it to her husband. In 1908 the watch was stolen from Major Clayton whilst he was on the Riviera and shortly afterwards the watch was pawned with a firm of pawnbrokers. In 1909 the watch was sold as an unredeemed pledge by public auction at the auctioneer's auction rooms, No. 38, Gracechurch Street in the City of London. The watch was bought at the auction by a *bona fide* purchaser for £26 and eventually came into the hands of a Mr. Bennett who bought it for £44. In May, 1910, Mr. Bennett brought the watch to the defendant for examination in order to find out if it was a genuine gold watch. Mrs. Clayton had told the defendant that the watch had been stolen and now the defendant recognised it, and wrote to Bennett telling him that the watch was stolen and asking him how much he wanted for it. Bennett said he would let the true owner have it back, the price being what Bennett gave for it. The defendant then wrote to Mrs. Clayton telling her he had found the stolen watch and of Bennett's proposals. The Claytons instructed their solicitor to act and he went to the defendant's shop and demanded the return of the watch. The defendant refused to give it up and this action was commenced. It was held by Scrutton, J., after inspecting the auctioneer's sale rooms, that the defence of sale in market overt failed. The city auction rooms were not a shop, and because passers-by could not see the sale taking place, the sale was not open in the sense required by the custom. The ground floor windows of the premises were ordinary office windows, and nothing could be seen from the street of what took place on the ground floor. The first floor also had office windows only and, although the sales of jewellery were advertised, a passer-by could not see them actually taking place. Because of this decision on the defence of market overt, the purchaser at the auction did not get a good title, the goods being stolen, and Bennett had derived his title from the original purchaser. The plaintiff was therefore entitled to the watch and had no need to pay Bennett anything.

404. Galbraith & Grant Ltd. v. Block, [1922] 2 K.B. 155

The plaintiffs were wine merchants and they sued the defendants for £16 2s. 11d. being the price of a case of champagne delivered to the defendant who was a licensed victualler. The defendant admitted the contract but said that the champagne had never been delivered to him. Evidence showed that the defendant asked the plaintiffs to deliver the goods and they employed a carrier who delivered them to the defendant's premises and obtained a receipt signed in the defendant's name by a person on the defendant's premises who seemed to the carrier to have authority to receive them. In fact the person to whom the goods were delivered had no authority to receive them and did not hand them over to the defendant. It was *held* that, where a vendor has been told to deliver goods at the buyer's premises, he fulfils his obligation if he delivers them to those premises and without negligence gives them over to a person apparently having authority to receive them. The trial judge had not taken sufficient evidence on the care taken by the carriers so that it was not possible to say whether they were negligent or not, and the case was sent back for a new trial on this point.

405. Shipton Anderson & Co. Ltd. v. Weil Bros., [1912] 1 K.B. 574

By a contract dated September 5th, 1910, the plaintiffs sold to the defendants a cargo of wheat, the actual weight of the wheat to be as per the bill of lading.

but to be 4,500 tons, 2 per cent more or less. The plaintiffs also reserved to themselves the right to ship a further 8 per cent of wheat of the contract quality if they wished. The plaintiffs exercised the option and shipped 4,950 tons 55 lbs, which was 55 lbs over the maximum allowed by the contract. The cost of the extra 55 lbs was 4s. on a total bill of £40,000, and in any case the plaintiffs never demanded the 4s. The defendants rejected the whole consignment on the ground of the 55 lbs excess, and the plaintiffs sold the rejected cargo and now claimed the difference between the price obtained and the contract price, as damages. *Held*—The plaintiffs succeeded, since the excess of 55 lbs was so trifling as not to amount to a breach of contract.

406. Maple Flock Co. Ltd. *v.* Universal Furniture Products (Wembley) Ltd., [1934] 1 K.B. 148

The plaintiffs agreed to sell to the defendants 100 tons of black linsey flock at £15 2s. 6d. per ton to be delivered three loads a week, 1½ tons per load, as required. The plaintiffs guaranteed that the flock should not contain more than 30 parts of chlorine to 100,000 parts of flock. The sixteenth delivery contained 250 parts of chlorine to 100,000 parts of flock. The buyers repudiated the contract and refused to take further deliveries. The sellers sued for breach of contract. Evidence showed that the first fifteen deliveries were as per contract, and the plaintiffs' plant and equipment was good so that there was little chance of subsequent deliveries being affected. *Held*—The matter was covered by Sect. 31 (2) of the Sale of Goods Act and the main tests to be applied in cases falling under that section were—(i) The ratio quantitatively which the breach bears to the contract as a whole, and (ii) The degree of probability or improbability that such a breach will be repeated.

In this case a delivery of 1½ tons was defective out of a contract to supply 100 tons and there was little chance of the breach being repeated. The buyers were not, therefore, entitled to repudiate the contract and were liable for breach. They could have recovered damages in respect of the defects in the 16th delivery but did not claim any because the delivery had been used in the manufacture of bedding and furniture before the sample was tested and found defective.

N.B. In Munro (Robert A.) & Co., Ltd. v. *Meyer*, 1930,[371] where the contract was for the sale of 1,500 tons of bone meal and 611 tons were found to be defective, it was held that the buyers were entitled to repudiate the contract.

407. Broome *v.* Pardess Co-operative Society, [1939] 3 All E.R. 603

The plaintiffs were London fruit brokers and they agreed to sell the defendants' oranges in London. The terms of the contract were that the plaintiffs were to pay the defendants 7s. 6d. per case in any event. The plaintiffs were then to charge commission on the oranges sold and deduct this commission and the 7s. 6d. per case from any sum received on sale of the oranges, sending the balance to the defendants. The weather during a particular growing season was very wet and a consignment of oranges, though saleable when dispatched by the defendants from Palestine, was unsaleable when it arrived in London. The plaintiffs were unable to sell the oranges and suffered loss because they were bound by their contract to pay the defendants the agreed 7s. 6d. per case. The plaintiffs sued for damages, asking the court to imply a term into the contract that the goods be in such condition as to be saleable in the London market. The defence was that the contract was complete in itself and no other terms should be implied. *Held*—The implied term asked for by the plaintiffs would be implied into the contract and damages would be awarded to them.

N.B. The contract was not one for the sale of goods but was an agency contract. Nevertheless it is thought to apply to contracts of sale of goods where the goods reach the buyer in an unmerchantable state.

408. Kendall *v.* Marshall, Stevens & Co. (1883), 11 Q.B.D. 356

This was an action to recover damages for conversion of 55 bales of waste cotton. The plaintiff was the liquidator of one Leoffer, trading as Higginbottom & Co. The defendants were shipping agents and carriers, and the second defendants were Peter Ward & Son of Bolton, who sold the bales of cotton. It appeared that on November 9th, 1880, Ward & Son sold the cotton to Leoffer and on November 12th Leoffer asked the vendors to send the goods to Marshall, Stevens & Co. at Garston. He also informed Marshall, Stevens & Co. that they were to ship the goods as soon as possible to Durend & Co. at Rouen, France. The actual transit of the goods was therefore from Bolton to Rouen. On November 13th, the goods were sent by the vendors to Marshall, Stevens & Co. and they arrived at Garston on November 15th. The railway company's advice note which accompanied the goods gave Marshall, Stevens & Co. notice that unless the goods were collected by a certain time, the company would hold them as warehousemen at owner's risk and not as common carriers. On November 18th, Leoffer filed a petition for the liquidation of his estate, and on November 22nd, Ward & Son telegraphed Marshall, Stevens & Co. to stop the goods. This was done and they were returned to Bolton on November 24th. The liquidator sued in conversion to recover the value of the goods for the benefit of the estate. *Held*—The right to stop the goods expired when they arrived at Garston *and* when the railway company's notice had expired, which it had in this case. Once the railway company held the goods as warehousemen the goods were in the constructive possession of the buyer, Leoffer, and the defendants were liable in conversion.

409. Leask *v.* Scott Bros. (1877), 2 Q.B.D. 376

Green & Co., who were merchants, were indebted to the plaintiff, who was a broker, and asked him for a further advance of £2,000. The plaintiff agreed to make the further advance but wanted some security. Green & Co. gave him a bill of lading which they had received from the defendants for goods shipped to Green & Co. Two days later Green & Co. became insolvent and the defendants stopped the goods in transit. The jury found that the plaintiff took the bill of lading honestly and fairly and that he gave valuable consideration on the understanding that he was being given a security. *Held*—The plaintiff was entitled to the goods as against the defendants.

410. R. V. Ward Ltd. *v.* Bignall, [1967] 2 W.L.R. 1050

The defendant bought a Ford Zodiac and a Vanguard from the plaintiffs for a total price of £850, paying a deposit of £25 and leaving both cars with the plaintiffs until payment of the balance. The defendant refused to pay the balance, alleging that he had been misled as to the date of manufacture of the Vanguard, although he did offer to take the Zodiac but his offer was refused. Eventually the plaintiffs resold the Vanguard for £350 and brought an action against the defendant, claiming £497 10s., being the balance of the total purchase price less £350 with the addition of £22 10s. for expenses incurred in advertising in order to resell the cars. *Held*—By the Court of Appeal—that when an unpaid seller exercised his right to resell the whole or part of the goods under Sect. 48 (3) of the Sale of Goods Act, 1893, he could no longer perform his contract which must therefore be regarded as rescinded. Accordingly the plaintiffs' proper claim was for damages for non-acceptance. Sellers, L.J., said ". . . the plaintiffs cannot recover the price of the Zodiac, which is in the circumstances their property. They can, however, recover any loss which they have sustained by the buyer's default. The parties have sensibly agreed that the value of the Zodiac in May, 1965, was £450. The total contract price was £850, against which the plaintiffs have received £25 in cash and £350 in respect of the Vanguard, and have to give credit for £450 for the Zodiac. To the loss of £25 must be added the sum for advertising, which was admittedly reasonably incurred—£22 10s. 0d. The plaintiffs loss was, therefore, £47 10s. 0d.

I would allow the appeal and enter judgment for £47 10s. 0d. in favour of the plaintiffs . . ."

411. Hall *v.* Pim, [1928] All E.R. Rep. 763

Hall bought from Pim an unascertained cargo of Australian wheat at 51s. 9d. per quarter. The contract provided that notice of appropriation to the contract of a specific cargo in a specific ship should be given to the buyer within a specified time. An arbitration clause in the contract gave rights to persons to whom the goods might be re-sold. Both parties knew when the contract was made that the buyer might re-sell the cargo before delivery, but the buyer gave no express notice of intention to re-sell. The market rose after Hall bought the wheat, and he re-sold it to one Williams at 56s. 9d. per quarter, and Williams in turn sold the cargo when the market rose further. Pim gave Hall notice of appropriation of a specific cargo and Hall gave notice to Williams and the other sub-buyer. The market then fell, and when the ship arrived with the cargo, it was not delivered up to Hall because Pim, wishing to take advantage of the rising market and regretting his earlier sale to Hall, had re-sold the goods to other buyers at 59s. 11½d. per quarter. Hall sued for breach of contract, which was admitted by Pim, but Pim said that the damages should be the difference between the price ruling on the day of the contract was made, i.e. 51s. 9d., and the market price at the date of failure to deliver, i.e. 53s. 9d., and should not include loss of profit on re-sale to Williams. *Held*—The loss of profit on the re-sale was recoverable because such damages must reasonably be supposed to have been in the contemplation of the parties when the contract was made.

412. Slater *v.* Hoyle and Smith Ltd., [1920] 2 K.B. 11

The plaintiffs, who were manufacturers of cotton cloth, sued for damages for the refusal of the defendants to accept 1,375 pieces of unbleached cotton cloth, being the balance of 3,000 pieces which the defendants agreed to purchase from the plaintiffs. The defence was that the 1,625 pieces delivered and paid for were unmerchantable, and the defendants counter-claimed for damages in respect of this. The defendants had contracted to sell *bleached* cloth to other persons, and had bleached and sold 691 pieces of the cloth bought from the plaintiffs for this purpose. The plaintiffs took the view that the defendants should not recover on their counter-claim damages for 1,625 pieces of cloth as unmerchantable but, 1,625 less the 691 pieces actually sold. *Held*—The sub-contract should not be taken into account and the defendants should recover on their counter-claim for the reduced value of the 1,625 pieces of cloth delivered to them. The sub-contracts were not known to the plaintiffs, and a sub-sale cannot be relied upon in mitigation of damages unless the sub-sale is of the identical article bought. Here what was bought was unbleached cloth and what was sold was bleached.

413. McManus *v.* Fortescue, [1903] 2 K.B. 1

The defendants were auctioneers and offered for sale certain property on the terms of a printed catalogue and conditions of sale. Condition No. 2 was as follows—

"Each lot will be offered subject to a reserve price, and the vendors reserve the right of bidding up to such reserve price. The highest bidder for each lot shall be the purchaser. If any dispute arise concerning a bidding, the lot in question shall be put up again and re-sold, or the auctioneer may determine the dispute."

The lot in question was a corrugated iron building for which the plaintiff made a bid of £85. This was the highest bid and the auctioneer knocked the lot down to the plaintiff. Before the memorandum of sale was made and signed by the auctioneer, he opened a sealed envelope containing the reserve price and discovered that it was £200. The auctioneer then withdrew the lot and would not sign the memorandum of sale or accept the plaintiff's deposit. The plaintiff now sued the auctioneer for breach of his duty to sign the memorandum of sale. *Held*—When the hammer falls on a bid at an auction sale of property subject to a reserve, the auctioneer agrees on behalf of the vendor to sell at the amount of the last bid *provided* that such bid is equal to the reserve that has been made. The plaintiff's action failed.

414. Aruna Mills *v.* Dhanrajmal Gobindram, [1968] 1 All E.R. 113

A contract for sale of cotton provided for a variation in price if the prevailing rate of exchange should vary between the contract date and the date when the price was payable. The sellers, in breach of contract, failed to ship the cotton until 27th June, 1966, although the last permitted date for shipment was 31st May, 1966. The rupee was devalued on 6th June, 1966, and the buyers paid the additional price on receipt of the shipping documents which were received *after* 6th June, 1966. They now sued to recover that additional price by way of damages for late shipment, alleging that if the goods had been shipped on or before 31st May, 1966, they would have received the shipping documents and made payment on or before 5th June, 1966, i.e. before devaluation. *Held*—by Donaldson, J.—that the loss flowing from the devaluation was not too remote, for the parties had contemplated it as likely to result from late shipment. The case was remitted to the arbitrators to decide whether, as a matter of fact, if shipment had been made on or before 31st May, 1966, the documents would in the ordinary course of events have been tendered and the price paid before 5th June, 1966.

HIRE PURCHASE AND CREDIT SALES

415. Helby *v.* Matthews, [1895] A.C. 471

Helby was a trader having a place of business in Baker Street, London. By an agreement made on December 23rd, 1892, Helby agreed to let a piano on hire purchase to one, Charles Brewster. The agreement provided that:

"If Brewster punctually paid the full sum of £18 18s. od. by 10s. 6d. at signing and by 35 monthly instalments of 10s. 6d. each, the piano would become 'the sole and absolute property of the hirer.' " Brewster was also given the right to terminate the agreement and return the piano if he wished to do so. Four months after the making of the agreement Brewster, without Helby's permission, pledged the piano with the respondents and the question of their title arose. *Held*—by the House of Lords—that Helby could recover it from the pawn-brokers and need not repay the money which the respondents had lent to Brewster. The respondents were not protected by Sect. 9 of the Factors Act, 1889, because Brewster was not a person who had "bought or agreed to buy" the piano; he was a mere hirer and could buy or not as he pleased.

416. Bridge *v.* Campbell Discount Co. Ltd., [1962] 1 All E.R. 385

A contract of hire purchase of a Bedford Dormobile provided that if the hirer exercised his option to determine, or if the agreement was terminated by his breach, i.e. failure to pay instalments, two-thirds of the total hire-purchase price would be payable to the owner. After paying the deposit and one instalment the hirer wrote to the owners saying: "Owing to unforeseen personal circumstances I shall be unable to pay any more payments on the Bedford." The owner repossessed the vehicle and sued for £206 3s. 4d. under the clause. The Court of Appeal held that the hirer was exercising his option to determine the contract, the 'fee' for which was £206 3s. 4d., under the clause. Since this sum was never intended as damages it was not subject to the rules regarding penalties. The House of Lords reversed this decision, *holding* that from the general tone of the letter the hirer was in breach of the contract and was not exercising his option. On this view the sum of £206 3s. 4d. could be regarded as liquidated damages and was subject to the rules regarding penalties. Accordingly the sum was irrecoverable because it was in the nature of a penalty. The £206 3s. 4d. depreciation was not a genuine pre-estimate of the owner's loss.

417. Brown *v.* Sheen and Richmond Car Sales Ltd.. [1950] 1 All E.R. 1102

The defendants advertised a motor car as being in perfect condition, and when the plaintiff went to discuss purchase with the defendants, their sales manager told him that it was in perfect condition and was "good for thousands of trouble free miles." The car was sold to a finance company and they hired the car out to Brown. The car gave trouble and Brown was compelled to have repairs done to it at a cost of between £60 and £70 so as to put the car into a proper roadworthy condition. The plaintiff now sued the defendants for breach of warranty. *Held*—The plaintiff succeeded. The defendants had given a warranty as to the condition of the car which had induced Brown to make the hire-purchase agreement. This warranty had been broken and the defendants must pay the plaintiff £66 damages, because he had paid more for the car than it was worth and was induced to buy it by the defendants' warranty.

N.B. See now Sect. 16 of the Hire-Purchase Act, 1965. (p. 178.)

418. Herschtal *v.* Stewart and Arden Ltd., [1940] 1 K.B. 155

The plaintiff was a director of a company known as Utility Products Ltd. The defendants, who were motor engineers and distributors, supplied the Utility Products Ltd. with a second-hand car. The car was sold to a finance company, S. and A. Services Ltd., who hired it out to Utility Products Ltd.

The defendants knew that the car was intended mainly for the plaintiff's use. The day after the car was delivered the plaintiff drove it only a few miles when the wheel came off and the plaintiff managed to get the car to the kerb and stop it but he suffered from nervous shock. Evidence showed that the threads of the wheel nuts were stripped and therefore the wheel had not been tightened properly. *Held*—The defendants were liable in negligence. They owed a duty to customers to take reasonable care to see that the car was in roadworthy condition.

419. Lowe *v.* Lombank Ltd., [1960] All E.R. 611

On June 8th, 1958, the plaintiff, a sixty-five-year-old widow, agreed to purchase a second-hand car from a dealer for £200. The dealer sold the car to the defendants who hired it to the plaintiff, the total price being £223. The plaintiff never saw the car but acted on the dealer's statement that the car was in perfect, or almost perfect condition. The hire-purchase agreement had an exclusion clause which said that Mrs. Lowe (as hirer) had not made known to the owners expressly or by implication the particular purpose for which the goods were required and that she acknowledged that the goods were fit for the purpose for which they were in fact required and were of merchantable quality. Mrs. Lowe never read the agreement but she did sign it. The car, when delivered, was completely unroadworthy, the engine, steering and brakes being all defective. The plaintiff sued the finance company for damages for breach of Sect. 8 of the Hire-Purchase Act, 1938, because the car was not fit for driving and she had by implication made known to the defendants that she required it for driving. *Held*—by the Court of Appeal— that the plaintiff did by implication make known to the defendants within Sect. 8 of the Hire-Purchase Act, 1938, that she required the car as a means of transport as what else could she want it for? The exclusion clause in the agreement was no defence because no one had explained the clause to Mrs. Lowe or made its effect clear to her. Damages of £160 were awarded.

420. Handley *v.* Marston (1962), 106 S.J. 327

A second-hand 1951 Vanguard car was let out under a hire-purchase agreement after a four-minute trial run during which the hirer did not drive the car. The hire-purchase agreement contained a clause excluding liability for breach of warranty or condition as to its fitness for the purpose. The car was in a deplorable state of repair having defective steering, defective brakes, excessive oil leakage and badly worn tyres. The handbrake would not operate and the footbrake would not work until the driver's foot was almost on the floor. The owner, when sued by the hirer for £60 for the cost of repairing the car, raised the exclusion clause in the agreement as a defence. *Held*—by the Court of Appeal—that the clause was effective to exclude liability. There was no fundamental breach of contract because, although the car was unroadworthy and unsafe and in a deplorable condition, yet it could still function as a car.

421. Barker *v.* Bell (Ness, Third Party), [1971] 2 All E.R. 867.

A man called Hudson had a Morris Mini on hire purchase from Auto Finances (Hallamshire) Ltd. He sold it to Mr. Ness, who was not a dealer in cars, after telling him that the car had formerly been on hire purchase but that the last instalment had been paid. Hudson produced a receipt for £6 across which was written "Final Payment." This receipt was in fact from Bowmakers

Ltd. and had no connection with the hire arrangements with Auto Finances, though Mr. Ness had no way of knowing this. Mr. Ness resold the vehicle and eventually the car was purchased by a dealer, Mr. Barker. The vehicle was repossessed by Auto Finances from Mr. Barker who then sued the dealer from whom he bought the car, Mr. Bell. Mr. Bell brought in Mr. Ness as third party. It was *held*—by the Court of Appeal—that Mr. Ness had obtained a good title from Hudson and that in consequence Barker and Bell had good titles even though they were dealers. Mr. Ness was a *bona fide* purchaser without notice of a hire-purchase agreement as required by Sect. 27 (2) of the Act. "Notice" meant notice of a relevant existing agreement. A hire-purchase agreement which had supposedly been paid off was irrelevant for this purpose.

AGENCY

422. Comber *v.* Anderson (1808), 1 Camp. 523

A merchant instructed his agent, an insurance broker, to insure a cargo of corn, but gave no specific instructions as to the type of policy or with whom it was to be effected. The broker effected a policy with a company which used an exception clause excluding liability for the loss of cargo by the stranding of the ship. There were private underwriters who did not insist on such a clause. The ship carrying the cargo was stranded and there was a loss for which the merchant could not recover under the insurance. The question arose as to whether the agent was liable as having no authority to make such a policy. *Held*—Since the agent was given a discretion, authority to make the sort of policy he had made was implied. There was no suggestion of fraud and the agent was free to elect as between insurers.

423. Australia and New Zealand Bank *v.* Ateliers de Constructions Electriques de Charleroi, [1966] 2 W.L.R. 1216

The Belgian company sued the Australian bank for conversion of cheques drawn payable to the company and indorsed and paid by the company's Australian agent into his own account at the bank. The agent had no express authority to pay the company's cheques into his own account though if he had been paid cash he would have had authority to receive the money. The company had no bank account in Australia and they knew that their agent there had previously paid large sums into his own account, at the bank under other contracts. The company had given no instructions and had made no enquiry as to their agent's methods of receiving money and making remittances and had made no complaint about the method on discovering what it was, until the Australian agent could not, because of liquidation, pay over £55,540 18s. 7d. of the company's money. *Held*—By the Privy Council—That in all the circumstances authority could be implied in the agent and the company's action failed.

424. Watteau *v.* Fenwick, [1893] 1 Q.B. 346

For some time prior to 1888 the Victoria Hotel, Stockton-on-Tees, had been owned by a Mr. Humble. In 1888 he sold the hotel to the defendants but remained in the hotel as manager, his name remaining on the door and the licence continuing in his name. The defendants had forbidden Humble to buy cigars on credit, but he bought a supply from the plaintiff who gave credit to Humble personally since he did not know of the existence of the defendants. When the plaintiff discovered what the true situation was, he brought this action against the defendants for the price of the cigars. *Held*— The cigars were articles which would usually be supplied to and dealt in at such an establishment, and Humble was acting within the scope of his *usual authority* as the manager of such a house. The defendants were bound by the contract made by Humble and could not set up secret instructions to him as a defence to the plaintiff's action.

425. Dodsley *v.* **Varley** (1840), 12 A. & E. 632

The defendant's agent W occasionally employed B to purchase wool on behalf of the defendant. B's previous purchases from the plaintiff had always been ratified by the defendant. In June, 1839, the defendant wrote to B saying that he did not wish B to make any further purchases for him. In July, 1839, B bought wool from the plaintiff which the defendant refused to pay for and the plaintiff now sued for the price. *Held*—The plaintiff succeeded. B was the defendant's agent by *apparent authority*, and although there was some doubt as to whether the revocation of authority was notified to the plaintiff, the jury found as a fact that the plaintiff did not have such notice when he sold the wool.

426. Povey *v.* **Taylor** (1966), 116 New L.J. 1656

The defendants ran an agency for pop artists and from time to time they had leaflets printed by the plaintiffs. The defendants let a room on their premises to X who also ran an entertainment agency. X placed orders with the plaintiffs for leaflets and the defendants were aware that he had done so and, in fact, advertised their own agency in one of X's leaflets. The plaintiffs sent a number of invoices on behalf of X's leaflets to the defendants who did not challenge them. X disappeared owing the plaintiff £75 for work done to his order and in this action the plaintiffs sought to recover that sum from the defendants. The defendants denied liability, saying that X was not their agent and had no authority to order leaflets on their behalf. *Held*—by the Court of Appeal—the defendants were aware that the plaintiffs were printing leaflets to X's order and had not challenged invoices sent by the plaintiffs. In the circumstances it was reasonable for the plaintiffs to assume that X was ordering the leaflets with the authority of the defendants and the defendants were therefore estopped from denying that X had such authority.

427. Great Northern Railway Co. *v.* **Swaffield** (1874), L.R. 9 Ex. 132

The defendant sent an unattended horse by the plaintiffs' trains from King's Cross to Sandy, Bedfordshire. The horse arrived at Sandy at 10.8 p.m. but there was no one to meet it. The officials at Sandy station did not know the defendant or his address and accordingly the station master directed that the horse be put into a livery stable near to the station. Shortly afterwards the defendant's servant arrived to collect the horse and was told that it was in the livery stable and that he could have it for a charge of 6d. He refused to pay, as did the defendant when informed of the situation. The dispute over the charges went on and the horse was eventually delivered to the defendant four months later, the plaintiffs having paid £17 for stable charges. They now sued to recover this sum of money. *Held*—They could recover it.

428. Springer *v.* **Great Western Railway Co.,** [1921] 1 K.B. 257

The defendants agreed to carry tomatoes for the plaintiff from Jersey to Covent Garden market. The ship was late in arriving at Weymouth, and when it did arrive the defendants' employees were on strike. When the cargo was unloaded by casual labour some of the tomatoes were good and some were bad. However, the defendants' traffic agent decided to sell the whole consignment locally because he felt that they could not be taken to Covent Garden in time to arrive in a saleable condition. He did not communicate with any of the consignees, the plaintiff being one. The plaintiff claimed damages in conversion based on the market price of the goods at Covent Garden, and since the strike had caused shortages, this price was high. The defendants claimed that in the circumstances they must be considered as having a right to sell. The plaintiff said that if he had been informed of the position he could have got lorries to transport the goods to London. *Held*—The plaintiff was entitled to damages because the defendants were not in the position as agents of necessity so long as they could communicate with the owner and get his instructions.

429. Prager v. Blatspiel, Stamp and Heacock Ltd., [1924] 1 K.B. 566

The plaintiff was a fur dealer in Bucharest and the defendants were fur dealers in London. Between 1915 and 1916 the plaintiff asked the defendants to buy certain skins for him and to have them dressed and delivered to Bucharest as soon as possible. Skins to the value of £1,900 were bought by the defendants, but they were unable to deliver them to the plaintiff because of the occupation of Rumania by the Germans at the end of 1916. During 1917 and 1918, when the market in skins was rising rapidly, the defendants sold the skins. When hostilities ceased the plaintiff wrote to the defendants asking for delivery of the skins, but was informed that they had been sold. He now sued in conversion. The defendants contended that they were agents of necessity. *Held*—They were not, and were liable for conversion. The furs, being dressed, could have been stored until the end of hostilities and the plaintiff was entitled to damages.

430. Sachs v. Miklos, [1948] 2 K.B. 23

In 1940 the plaintiff made an arrangement with the defendant under which she was to store the plaintiff's dining room furniture in a room in her boarding house. In 1944 the boarding house was damaged by enemy action and the plaintiff found it necessary to use the storage room for her boarders. The plaintiff had ceased to visit the defendant in 1941 but she obtained an address from his bank and wrote to him asking him to remove the furniture. She received no reply and wrote again saying that unless she was instructed to the contrary she would sell the furniture. No reply was received to this letter and, after further attempts to get in touch with the plaintiff by telephone, the defendant sold the furniture in July, 1944, by auction. The furniture realised £13. The plaintiff later heard of the sale and now sued Mrs. Miklos and the auctioneer in detinue and for conversion, claiming £115, the current value of the furniture. *Held*—The defendants were not agents of necessity and were liable. In this sort of action damages are usually awarded on the value of the goods at the date of judgment, but in this case a new trial was ordered in the county court to decide whether the plaintiff ever received the letters, because, if he did, damages would be assessed as at the date of receipt.

N.B. A somewhat similar case is *Munro* v. *Willmott*, [1949] 1 K.B. 295, where the owner of a motor car parked it in the yard of an inn with the landlord's consent. She left the district and the car was by then causing an obstruction to other garage users. The landlord, being unable to communicate with the owner, sold the car but was held liable in conversion.

431. Binstead v. Buck (1777), 2 Wm. Bl. 1117

The plaintiff lost his pointer dog and one year later found it on the defendant's property. The defendant said that it had strayed there and refused to give up the dog unless the plaintiff paid him £1 per week for the twenty weeks it had been in the defendant's possession. *Held*—The plaintiff was entitled to recover the animal and, although the point was not fully considered by the court, it appears that the defendant was not entitled to any compensation for the cost of keeping the dog.

432. Nicholson v. Chapman (1793), 2 Hy. Bl. 254

Certain timber which was stacked on the bank of a river accidentally slipped into the water and was carried downstream where the defendant took it into his care. The owner, having discovered its whereabouts, now claimed it back, but the defendant would not release it until he was paid £6 10s. 4d. for looking after it. *Held*—The defendant was liable in conversion and had no right to compensation for the cost of looking after the timber.

N.B. A finder of livestock which has done damage to his property may detain it, subject to notice to the owner and police, for compensation supported by a right of sale. (Animals Act, 1971.)

433. Keighley, Maxsted & Co. v. Durant, [1901] A.C. 240

The appellants were corn merchants at Hull and the respondent was a corn merchant in London. On May 11th, Durant offered wheat by telegram to a corn merchant in Wakefield by the name of Roberts. The offer was to sell 500 tons of White Wheat at 46s. per quarter and 500 tons of Red Wheat at 45s. per quarter. Roberts discussed the offer with the appellants' manager, a Mr. Wright, and Wright told Roberts that if Roberts could get the White Wheat for 45s. 3d. and the Red for 44s. 3d., Roberts and Keighley, Maxsted and Co. would buy it on joint account. Roberts could not get the price but later on, after apparently abandoning the joint account purchase, Roberts bought the wheat for 45s. 6d. White, and 44s. 6d. Red. Roberts informed Wright of this and Wright said that it was too dear but to go ahead. It was a question whether this statement could be treated by the court as a ratification. Roberts refused to take delivery of the wheat and Durant re-sold it at a loss and now sued Roberts and the appellants as joint purchasers. *Held*—The appellants were not liable. Where a man makes a contract purporting to act on his own behalf, but having an undisclosed intention to give the benefit of the contract to a third party, the contract cannot be ratified by that third party so as to make him able to sue or liable to be sued on the contract.

434. Kelner v. Baxter (1866), L.R. 2 C.P. 174

The plaintiff carried on a business as a wine merchant and licensed victualler in Gravesend. In 1865 the plaintiff and the defendants started a project for forming an hotel company to take over the plaintiff's premises and stock. Before the company was incorporated the defendants, purporting to be agents of the company, entered into an agreement with the plaintiff under which it was agreed that the defendants would buy the plaintiff's stock on behalf of the proposed company. The company was formed after this agreement was made but having been in business for a time it was wound up. The plaintiff now sued the defendants for the value of the stock. *Held*—The defendants were personally liable. Erle, C.J., said that if the company had been in existence, the defendants would have agreed as agents of the company, but since the company did not exist, the contract was inoperative unless it was a contract between the plaintiff and the defendants. If there is no existent principal such a contract binds the persons professing to be agents. The company might have been held to have ratified the contract because the stock was sold over the Hotel bars, but Willes, J., said on this point that a ratification must be made by a person who can be ascertained when the act was done which is to be ratified, i.e. by a person *then in existence.*

435. Newborne *v.* Sensolid (Great Britain) Ltd., [1954] 1 Q.B. 45

The plaintiff was the promoter and prospective director of a limited company, Leopold Newborne (London) Ltd., which had not been registered. The company was to be a provision company. The plaintiff made a contract to sell tinned ham to the defendants, the contract being made on the company's notepaper and signed "Leopold Newborne (London) Ltd., Leopold Newborne." The defendants failed to accept the goods and the plaintiff brought this action for breach of contract, the market price of ham having fallen. When the action began the company was the plaintiff, but the plaintiff's solicitors discovered that it was not incorporated when the contract was made and substituted the plaintiff in the action. The defendants alleged that they did not contract with the plaintiff but with a non-existent company. *Held*—At the date of making the contract the company was non-existent, and the contract purported to be made by a non-existent company and was therefore a nullity. The plaintiff could not adopt it or sue upon it as his own contract. The plaintiff had not purported to contract as agent or principal; he had merely put a non-existent company's signature to the contract. The only effect of his own signature was to show who had put the company's signature on.

436. Greenwood *v.* Martins Bank Ltd., [1933] A.C. 51

The appellant, who was a dairy man in Blackpool, opened with the respondents a joint account in the name of himself and his wife. Cheques drawn on this account were to bear the signatures of them both. Later on the appellant opened a further account with the respondents in his own name, though the wife kept the pass books and cheque books in respect of both accounts. In October, 1929, Greenwood asked his wife to give him a cheque, saying he wanted to draw £20 from his own account. His wife then told him that there was no money in the bank, and that she had used it to help her sister who was involved in legal proceedings over property. He asked her who had forged his signature but she would not say. However, she did ask him not to inform the respondents of the forgeries until her sister's case was over. Greenwood complied with this request until June 5th, 1930, when he discovered that there were no legal proceedings instituted by his wife's sister and that his wife had been deceiving him. He told his wife that he intended to go to the bank and reveal her forgeries, but before he actually made the visit she shot herself. Greenwood now claimed £410 6s. od. from the Bank on the grounds that this sum had been paid out of his own account and the joint account by means of forged cheques. The Bank pleaded ratification, adoption or estoppel. *Held*—There could be no ratification or adoption in this sort of case, but the essential elements of estoppel were present. The appellant's failure to inform the Bank was a representation that the cheques were good. The Bank had suffered a detriment because, if Greenwood had told the Bank when his wife first confessed to forgery, they might have brought an action against her. Under the law *existing at that time* they could not bring such an action after her death. The Bank had, therefore, a legal right to debit Greenwood's account with the amount of the forged cheques.

437. Bolton Partners v. Lambert (1889), 41 Ch.D. 295

The plaintiffs claimed specific performance of an agreement under which the defendant was to take a lease of the plaintiffs' premises. Preliminary negotiations had taken place between Lambert and a Mr. Scratchley, who was a director of the plaintiff company. As a result of these negotiations, the defendant wrote to the plaintiffs on December 8th, 1886, offering to take the lease. On December 9th, Scratchley wrote to Lambert to say that the offer would be placed before the Board, and on December 13th, Scratchley wrote again to say that the Board had accepted the offer. On January 13th, 1887, the defendant wrote to the plaintiffs alleging that he had been misled as to the value of certain plant and machinery on the premises, and stated that he withdrew all offers made to the plaintiffs in any way. Evidence showed that Scratchley had no authority to bind the company when he wrote the letters of December 9th and 13th. The matter had not been put before the Board but merely a works committee which had no authority to bind the company. The Board did ratify Scratchley's acts but not until after January 13th, 1887. *Held*—The acceptance by Scratchley would have constituted a contract in all respects except for his lack of authority. However, once that authority was given, it was thrown back to the time when the act was done by Scratchley and prevented the defendant from withdrawing his offer because it was then no longer an offer but a binding contract.

438. Grover and Grover Ltd. v. Mathews, [1910] 2 K.B. 401

The plaintiffs claimed to be entitled to recover for total loss under a policy of fire insurance on their pianoforte factory at New Southgate effected with the defendant and other underwriters at Lloyds. The plaintiffs took out a Lloyd's policy in March, 1908, for twelve months from March 26th, 1908. This policy was effected through a Mr. Brows who was the manager of the London and Provincial Bank at New Southgate. Brows had dealt with a broker named Dott. In March, 1909, Brows wrote to Dott asking him whether a renewal notice would be sent for the plaintiffs' policy. At the time he wrote the letter Brows had moved to another bank and had no instructions from the plaintiffs to insure. Nevertheless Dott prepared a slip to insure the plaintiffs' factory for a further twelve months from March 26th, 1909. The slip was initialed by the defendants' representative, but Brows did not tell the plaintiffs at the time that he had effected the insurance. When he did inform them there was an argument about the amount of the premium which lasted from March 19th until March 26th, when Brows wrote to the plaintiffs saying he could not get the rate reduced. On the afternoon of March 27th, the factory was destroyed by fire, and later the same day the directors of the plaintiff company tendered a cheque for the premium and reported the fire. The underwriters would not accept liability. *Held*—There could be no retrospective ratification in this case. The rule that a principal could ratify an insurance even after the loss was known was anomalous. Such a right existed only in connection with marine insurance and it was not desirable to extend it.

439. Walter v. James (1871), L.R. 6 Exch. 124

One Southall, who was acting for the defendant, induced the plaintiff to accept £60 in full discharge of a liability the defendant had to the plaintiff on a bill. Before the money was handed over, James withdrew Southall's authority, but Southall nevertheless paid Walter. When Walter discovered that the payment had been made without authority, he agreed to return the money to Southall. Walter then sued James for the money, and at that stage James purported to ratify Southall's act of payment, hoping to prevent Walter from succeeding on the grounds that the money had already been paid by his agent and that Walter had handed it back voluntarily. *Held*—Ratification was not possible here because, if it was allowed, the plaintiff would lose his action and would suffer undue hardship.

440. Watson *v.* Davies, [1931] 1 Ch. 455

The plaintiff sued on behalf of the Board of Management of an Institution for the Blind and asked for specific performance of a contract to sell premises called Colet House situated at Rhyl and owned by the defendant. The following facts emerged from the evidence. Preliminary negotiations had taken place between the plaintiff and a Mr. Bannister, one of the directors of the Institution, regarding the purchase of Colet House but nothing was settled at that stage. On January 7th, 1930, the defendant wrote to Bannister stating a price of £6,500 for Colet House, plus fittings, and adding that a Miners' Welfare Committee was also interested. The Board of the Institution for the Blind met on January 9th, 1930, and authorised certain members of the Board to accept the defendant's offer if they thought Colet House suitable for a home for the blind. On January 11th, 1930, twelve members of the Board went with the plaintiff and Mr. Bannister to inspect the premises. They agreed to buy "subject to the ratification of the full Board." A meeting of the full Board was called for January 14th to ratify the agreement. On the morning of January 14th, the defendant, having received a better offer from the Miners' Welfare Committee, sent a telegram to Mr. Bannister saying: "Colet House, Rhyl. Please treat all negotiations between us as cancelled. Property not for sale. R. L. Davies." This telegram was before the Board of the Institution for the Blind when it met on the afternoon of the January 14th. The Board nevertheless ratified the acts of the deputation of January 11th, and purported to accept the offer made at that time by Davies. *Held*—The ratification was ineffective. An acceptance by an agent subject to ratification by his principal is legally a nullity until ratification, and, being a conditional acceptance, is not binding on the other party. Since the defendant had revoked the offer before ratification took place, he was not bound to the plaintiffs.

441. Warehousing and Forwarding Company of East Africa Ltd. *v.* Jafferali and Sons Ltd., [1963] 3 W.L.R. 489

The respondents were trying to lease a warehouse to the appellants. The appellants' branch manager seemed to have entered into an agreement for a lease but his acts were subject to the ratification of the appellants' general manager. Whether the respondents knew this or not, they certainly knew that the branch manager did not have a general authority to bind the appellants. Before ratification the offer to lease the warehouse was withdrawn. *Held*—Following *Watson v. Davies*[440] the branch manager's acceptance was conditional and no contract came into being before ratification. Until then the offer could be revoked. The Privy Council also suggested (*obiter*) that, even when the agent's acceptance is not made expressly "subject to ratification" but the third party is on notice that the agent's authority is limited, neither the agent's principal nor the third party is bound until ratification. The decision throws doubt on the case of *Bolton Partners* v. *Lambert.*[437]

442. De Bussche v. Alt (1878), 8 Ch.D. 286

The plaintiff was the registered owner of a steamer called the *Columbine.* The steamer was mortgaged and the mortgagees were pressing for their money. The plaintiff, therefore, sent the steamer to Gilman and Co., merchants carrying on business in China, for sale in that country. Gilman and Co. had authority to sell for not less than 90,000 dollars cash. They also had authority to appoint sub-agents, and employed Alt, who had a business in Japan, to try to sell the ship in Japan. The plaintiff was informed that Alt had been employed. Alt later informed Gilman and Co. that he did not think he could sell and offered to take the vessel over himself for 90,000 dollars cash, but before he made this offer Alt had already negotiated a sale to a Japanese prince for 160,000 dollars. The ship was assigned to Alt and he carried out the sale to the prince early in 1869. In April, 1873, the plaintiff brought this action for an account and payment of profits made by the defendant as his agent for the sale of the vessel. The following defences were raised—

(i) That there was no privity of contract between the plaintiff and defendant and this was a bar to the plaintiff's claim;

(ii) If there was a contractual relationship, it terminated before the sale of the *Columbine* to the Prince;

(iii) If there was the relationship of principal and agent when the *Columbine* was sold, the plaintiff had lost his right to sue by his acquiescence from 1869 to 1873.

Held—(i) Since Gilman and Co. had authority to appoint a sub-agent, and since Alt was not merely appointed to assist Gilman and Co. but as a substitute for them, there was privity of contract between the plaintiff and the defendant.

(ii) Once Gilman and Co. had appointed Alt, the appointment could only be terminated by the plaintiff and there was no evidence that he had terminated Alt's appointment. Therefore Alt sold the ship to the Japanese prince as the plaintiff's agent.

(iii) Evidence showed that the plaintiff had had difficulty in obtaining possession of the material facts of the case, and he was not therefore prevented from pursuing his claim by virtue of acquiescence, laches or estoppel, having brought the action as soon as he could.

443. Keppel v. Wheeler, [1927] 1 K.B. 577

The plaintiff sued the defendants, who were estate agents at Walham Green, for damages for breach of duty whilst acting as his agents. The plaintiff had instructed the defendants to sell a block of flats of which he was the owner. The flats were valued at £7,000 but the plaintiff was desirous of a quick sale, and when the defendants introduced a purchaser, E, who was prepared to offer £6,150, the plaintiff instructed the defendants to go ahead, and an agreement to sell "subject to contract" was made. This agreement was not, of course, binding on the parties. Before contracts were exchanged, another purchaser, D, offered to pay £6,750 but the defendants told him that the flats were sold, and instead of communicating with the plaintiff they put D in touch with E. Contracts were exchanged between the plaintiff and E at a price of £6,150, and later between E and D for £6,950 which was the price eventually agreed between E and D. The plaintiff heard of the transaction between E and D and sued the defendants. *Held*—The defendants were under a duty to tell the plaintiff of D's offer because at the time he was not bound to E. The defendants were therefore liable in damages. The measure of damages was the difference between the two offers i.e. £600, but the defendants were entitled to commission on the offer of £6,150 and also on the damages, and since the agreement provided for 1½ per cent commission which had already been paid on the £6,150, the plaintiff recovered £591.

444. McPherson *v.* Watt (1877), 3 App. Cas. 254

The respondent was a Scottish solicitor advising certain trustees. The trustees wished to sell the trust property and were about to advertise it when the respondent promised to find a purchaser. The respondent's brother made an offer for the trust property which the trustees accepted. The sale to the brother was a mere sham because the intention was that the respondent would get the property via the brother, and they had an arrangement to this effect. The trustees were ignorant of the arrangement, and when they discovered the true state of affairs, they brought this action to set aside the sale. *Held*—The sale could be set aside, and it was immaterial that the contract was a fair one.

445. Anglo-African Merchants Ltd. *v.* Bayley, [1969] 2 All E.R. 421

The plaintiff instructed a broker to effect the insurance of a quantity of government surplus army leather jerkins. The broker negotiated insurance with the defendant who was an underwriter at Lloyds. Some of the insured property was stolen and the plaintiffs claimed under the policy. It appeared that the broker had, without telling the plaintiffs, taken instructions from the underwriter to obtain a report from an assessor as to the value of the property stolen. The broker gave the report to the underwriter but would not give the plaintiffs a copy. *Held* (on this point)—by Megaw, J.,—that the broker was in breach of his duty as an agent. Even if what he had done was a customary practice, it would not be upheld since it contradicted the rule that an agent should not serve two principals in the same transaction unless he has obtained the informed consent of both.

446. Reiger *v.* Campbell-Stuart, [1939] 3 All E.R. 235

The plaintiff was anxious to buy property suitable for conversion into flats and she asked the defendant to look for suitable properties. During his search and whilst the plaintiff's agent, the defendant found a leasehold house selling at £2,000, but instead of informing the plaintiff, he arranged that his brother-in-law should buy it for £2,000, after which the defendant then purported to buy it from his brother-in-law for £4,500. This transaction was a sham. The defendant then offered to sell the house, which was by now his own property, to the plaintiff for £5,000, having told her that he had paid £4,000 for it. When the defendant told the plaintiff that the property was his own and began to sell it as a principal, the agency relationship between plaintiff and defendant was brought to an end; and when the plaintiff eventually bought the house from the defendant for £5,000 the defendant was not her agent. The plaintiff later discovered what had really happened and claimed the profit made by the defendant. *Held*—She could do so. Although the agency had been terminated before the sale, the defendant was, even as an ex-agent, bound to act honestly and faithfully and must therefore account for the profits he had made on the deal.

447. Bertram, Armstrong & Co. *v.* Godfrey (1830), 1 Knapp 381

Godfrey was a broker and Bertram gave him instructions to sell certain stock when the market price reached £85 per unit of stock. Godfrey did not sell when the price reached £85, but held on to the stock, and later sold it at less than £85. Bertram now sued to recover the difference. There was no agreement or usage in the profession of broker which allowed Godfrey to use his discretion and wait for the price to rise further, and it was *held* that by doing so he had in effect bought the stock himself when the price reached £85, and must now account to Bertram for the price plus interest. However, Bertram must also account to Godfrey for the dividends he had received when he did not know that the price had reached £85 and still thought the stock was his.

448. Bexwell *v.* Christie (1776), Cowp. 395

An auctioneer at a sale expressed to be "without reserve" was given secret instructions by the owner not to sell certain articles below a certain price. The auctioneer did in fact sell the goods and was now sued for breach of the agency agreement. *Held*—Since the instructions were unlawful, as a fraud on those attending the sale, the auctioneer was not bound to follow them so that he was not liable for breach of the agreement.

449. Andrews *v.* Ramsay & Co., [1903] 2 K.B. 635

The plaintiff was a builder and the defendants were auctioneers and estate agents. The plaintiff instructed the defendants to find a purchaser for certain property belonging to the plaintiff, the price to be £2,500 and the agreed commission £50. A month later the defendants wrote to the plaintiff saying that a person named Clutterbuck had made an offer of £1,900 for the property, but the plaintiff would not sell. Later Clutterbuck offered £2,100 and as the defendants said they could not get more, the plaintiff agreed to sell. Clutterbuck paid the defendants a deposit of £100 and the defendants paid £50 to the plaintiff and retained £50 as commission. After the sale had been completed the plaintiff discovered that the defendants had received a commission of £20 from Clutterbuck. The plaintiff recovered the £20 in the county court and now sought to recover the £50 commission because of the defendants' breach of duty whilst acting as agents. *Held*—He could do so. Where an agent takes a secret commission, the principal can recover that commission and also any commission which he himself has paid to the agent.

450. Salford Corporation *v.* Lever, [1891] 1 Q.B. 168

The defendant was a coal supplier and had at various times supplied coal to the corporation. The negotiations regarding these sales were conducted by the corporation's gas manager, a Mr. Hunter. Evidence showed that Hunter induced Lever to put up the price of his coal by 1s. per ton and to pay this over to Hunter by saying that unless Lever agreed to do this, he would buy coal for the corporation elsewhere. At the time of the action the excess paid by the corporation to Lever was £2,329 and they sought to recover that sum from Lever. Lever's defence was that the corporation had already recovered the money from Hunter. *Held*—Lever was guilty of fraud, and his fraud was wholly independent of that of Hunter and therefore both were liable to pay to the corporation the sums obtained by their separate frauds.

451. Shipway *v.* Broadwood, [1899] 1 Q.B. 369

The defendant wished to buy a pair of horses and asked a veterinary named Pinkett to find him a pair. Pinkett suggested that the defendant should buy a pair of horses which were being sold by a Worcester horse dealer. The defendant agreed to buy them if Pinkett passed them as sound. Pinkett gave the defendant a certificate of soundness and the horses were delivered to the defendant who sent a cheque to the dealer. On delivery the horses were found to be unsound, and the defendant returned them and stopped the cheque. The dealer now sued on the cheque, and the defence was that there had been total failure of consideration and that the plaintiff had warranted the horses sound. The plaintiff succeeded at first instance, the judge finding that no warranty had been given and that the defendant had simply agreed to buy if Pinkett certified the horses sound, as he had done. Evidence showed that Pinkett had received a commission from Shipway, but the judge gave no ruling as to the effect of this on Pinkett's judgment. It was *held*—by the Court of Appeal—that no such ruling was necessary. It was possible to find for the defendant merely on the evidence that a commission had been paid. It was not necessary to inquire whether Pinkett had been biased by receiving it.

452. Turnbull *v.* Garden (1869), 20 L.T. 218

An agent who was employed without payment to buy clothing for the principal's son received certain discounts from the seller. The agent tried to charge his principal the full price. *Held*—the principal was only required to pay the agent the sum charged by the seller of his son's outfit. The agent could not make a secret profit out of the transaction.

453. Hippisley *v.* Knee Bros., [1905] 1 K.B. 1

The plaintiff employed Knee Bros., who were auctioneers, to sell certain pictures on commission. Knee Bros. arranged for printing and advertising and debited the principal with the full cost although they had received from the printer a discount of 10 per cent. in accordance with normal trade practice. Hippisley claimed the discount and would not pay the defendants their commission. *Held*—by the Court of Appeal—that the discount could be recovered but the commission was payable. Although the defendants had acted honestly they were in breach of their obligations as agents in respect of the extra profit. Since they had not perpetrated any fraud on the principal they were entitled to commission.

454. Crouch & Lees *v.* Haridas, [1971] 3 All E.R. 172

The plaintiffs, who were estate agents though not retained by the landlords, gave the defendant particulars of a flat provided he agreed to pay them 10 per cent. of a year's rent if he took a lease of it. *Held*—by the Court of Appeal— that the plaintiffs had demanded payment of a sum of money in consideration of supplying particulars of a flat within Sect. 1 (1) (*b*) of the Accommodation Agents Act, 1953, which forbade such conduct. The agreement was illegal and unenforceable and it did not matter that no part of the commission had been demanded or paid.

455. Rimmer *v.* Knowles (1874), 30 L.T. 496

The plaintiff was a surveyor and the defendant asked him to sell an estate for an agreed commission of £50 if the plaintiff obtained a price of £2,000. The defendant then raised the price to £3,000 and, although the plaintiff could not get an outright purchaser, he did make a contract with a builder who was prepared to take a lease for 999 years for £150 per annum, with an option to purchase during the first 20 years of the lease. The plaintiff now sued for his commission, but the county court judge refused this on the grounds that he had not substantially performed the contract. On appeal it was *held* that there had been substantial performance and the plaintiff was able to recover his commission.

456. Coles *v.* Enoch, [1939] 3 All E.R. 327

The defendant was the owner of a shop in Victoria Street, London. The plaintiff was the proprietor of certain pin-table arcades in the North of England and was desirous of finding a site in London. In December, 1937, the plaintiff had a conversation with the defendant regarding the purchase of the Victoria Street premises. The plaintiff said that if he could not raise the money to buy the premises, he would turn agent and find a purchaser for the defendant on commission terms. The defendant agreed and the plaintiff later spoke to a Mr. Adickes regarding the purchase of the premises by his firm. This conversation was overheard by a person named Wilkie who was in the offices of the firm at the time. Wilkie asked Adickes about the premises but was merely told that they were in the neighbourhood of Victoria. Wilkie then found the premises himself and, having read the notice on the empty shop window, got in touch with the defendant and took a lease at £1,000 per annum. The plaintiff now sued for his commission. *Held*—He failed. His action was not the direct cause of Wilkie taking the shop. Adickes was the plaintiff's sub-agent for the purposes of the conversation with Wilkie and the fact that he deliberately withheld the actual address meant that Wilkie really found the premises for himself.

456a. *Rolfe & Co.* v. *George* (1968), 113 S.J. 244

The plaintiffs undertook to sell a grocery business for the defendant. In the event a third party introduced a potential purchaser to the defendant but the plaintiffs were asked to be present at the negotiations, which they were. *Held*—The plaintiffs must by reason of their presence at, and involvement in, the negotiations have been the efficient cause of the sale or produced the sale and were entitled to commission.

457. Luxor (Eastbourne) Ltd. *v.* Cooper, [1941] A.C. 108

The appellants wished to raise money and decided to dispose of certain cinemas which they owned. The respondent was appointed agent for the purpose of sale, and commission was to be payable on its completion. The respondent did introduce a company, the London and Southern Super Cinemas Ltd., who were at all times ready, willing, and able to buy for the figure of £185,000 asked by the appellants, but no contract was made. The appellants then decided to raise the money they required by a sale of shares and would not proceed with the sale of the cinemas. The respondent sued for his commission claiming that, although his agreement stated that commission was payable on completion of the sale, the court should imply a term to the effect that the vendor would not refuse to go on with the sale. *Held*—No such term could be implied. The appellants were not liable for breach of contract and the respondent's claim failed.

458. Christie, Owen & Davies Ltd. *v.* Stockton, [1953] 2 All E.R. 1149

The defendant instructed the plaintiffs to sell a London restaurant business for him and agreed to pay them commission on any completed transaction. The agreement also provided that "should the owner withdraw after having accepted an offer to purchase by a person able and willing to enter into a formal contract" the plaintiffs should be entitled to commission. The plaintiffs introduced a Mr. Hannay as a possible purchaser and the defendant met him and they agreed orally on a sale "subject to contract." The defendant's solicitors sent a draft contract to Mr. Hannay's solicitors and, both firms of solicitors having agreed it, Mr. Hannay signed his part and paid a deposit to his solicitors. The defendant then refused to sign his part and would not go on with the transaction. The plaintiffs claimed commission in accordance with the agreement. *Held*—They failed. The word *offer* meant an offer capable of being turned into a contract by mere acceptance. An offer "subject to contract" was not such an offer. Further, it was not possible to say that at the time of the oral agreement Mr. Hannay was in the legal sense willing to buy, because the words "subject to contract" indicated that the matter was still in negotiation.

459. Drewery and Drewery *v.* **Ware Lane,** [1960] 3 All E.R. 529

The defendant owned a leasehold house and there were 78 years of the lease to run. He instructed the plaintiffs to sell it at £2,250 and they got an offer from S of £2,160 which the defendant agreed to accept. The defendant then signed a *letter of authority* in which he agreed to the plaintiffs' commission "if and when (*a*) a prospective purchaser signs your 'purchaser's agreement'; and (*b*) I sign your 'vendor's agreement.'" The defendant also signed the vendor's agreement. On the same day S signed the purchaser's agreement. Both agreements were expressed to be "subject to contract." S delayed in completion, being anxious to buy the freehold of the property but prepared to buy the lease. The defendant sold the house to another purchaser and the agents sued for their commission on the deal with S. *Held*—They were entitled to commission. S was at all times a prospective purchaser and the conditions as to signing the agreement had been fulfilled.

460. Peter Long and Partners *v.* **Burns,** [1956] 3 All E.R. 207

The defendant instructed the plaintiffs to sell her garage business. She agreed that she would not sell except to a person introduced by the plaintiffs. She also agreed to pay commission upon the plaintiffs introducing "a person ready, willing and able to enter into a binding contract to purchase" the business. The plaintiffs found a possible purchaser who signed a contract of sale, but afterwards avoided the contract because of the plaintiffs' innocent misrepresentation as to the extent of a road-widening scheme. It appeared that the purchaser had seen work going on down the road from the garage, and had asked the plaintiffs about its effect on the garage. The plaintiffs, acting on the defendant's statement but without checking it, told the purchaser that the scheme would take two or three feet off the frontage, whereas in fact it took in the whole site. The defendant and the purchaser, having mutually agreed to call the contract off, the plaintiffs now sued for their commission. *Held*—The contract which the purchaser signed was not a "binding contract" but a voidable one, and the plaintiffs were not entitled to their commission.

460a. *Blake & Co.* v. *Sohn,* [1969] 3 All E.R. 123

The plaintiffs, who were estate agents, introduced to the defendants a potential purchaser of an hotel and adjoining land. A written agreement was made and signed but the defendants were not able to give a good title to the adjoining land. They had an easement over it and felt they could establish squatters' rights. This was not good enough for the defendant who obtained rescission of the contract. *Held*—by Nield, J.—that neither the commission agreement nor the failure of the defendants to make out a title gave the plaintiffs any cause of action for commission. There was no implied promise by a vendor that the title to land could be made out and the contract being voidable, no binding agreement had been achieved by the plaintiffs.

461. Scheggia *v.* Gradwell, [1963] 3 All E.R. 114

The appellant Scheggia was the proprietor of a leasehold café and snack bar off Finchley Road, and the respondent Gradwell was in business as an estate agent. Scheggia was anxious to sell the business and he signed an agreement with Gradwell, the form used providing by clause 5(*a*) that the vendor would pay the agency commission "if within three months any person introduced by the agents enters into a legally binding contract to purchase the business and the property." The agents introduced a purchaser, a Mr. Yik Ping Chung, and he signed an agreement to buy the business. The contract required the purchaser to submit suitable references for the landlord's approval. The references produced by Chung were not thought satisfactory by the landlord and the sale went off. The county court judge held that the agents were entitled to their commission of £172 in accordance with the agreement. The appellant appealed. *Held*—by the Court of Appeal—that the agents were entitled to their commission because the event in Clause 5(*a*) of the agreement had happened. Lord Denning dissented and thought that the agents were not entitled to their commission since the purchaser they introduced ought to be able to purchase, this being implicit in an agreement such as this.

462. Wilkinson *v.* Brown, [1966] 1 All E.R. 509

Mrs. Brown engaged the plaintiffs, who were estate agents, to sell her fruit and vegetable business. She agreed to make them agents for two months and to pay them commission in the event of their introducing "a person prepared to enter into a contract to purchase." The plaintiffs introduced a Mr. Norton and it was agreed that the right price for this leasehold property and business was £2,500 with stock at valuation. Negotiations proceeded with Mr. Norton for the period of two months and although he was interested in buying the property there were always one or two matters unsettled during the period of the agency. In the first place Mr. Norton had to sell his present property, and secondly, there were financial arrangements to make with money-lenders. There were also difficulties in obtaining the landlord's consent to the assignment of the leasehold business premises because Mr. Norton's references were not, at first, satisfactory to the landlord. The period of the agency expired without Mr. Norton entering into a contract, and shortly afterwards the defendant sold the property to someone else; the plaintiffs now sued for their commission of £250. *Held*—By the Court of Appeal—that their action failed. Mr. Norton could not be said to have been "prepared" to enter into a contract to purchase at any time during the period of the agency, his willingness to buy was always conditional on matters never resolved. Commenting on the decision in *Scheggia* v. *Gradwell*, 1963,[461] Salmon, L.J., said, "in my judgment, however, the scope of that decision ought not to be extended." In his view the decision in *Scheggia's Case* turned on the use of the words "any person" in the contract. The Court of Appeal in *Scheggia's Case* would not imply into the contract that the words "any person" meant a person ready, willing, and able, to buy. Having reached that position the prospective vendor in *Scheggia's Case* was making himself liable to pay commission to the estate agent in consideration of his obtaining anyone's signature on a contract even though that person was not in a position to complete. Although *Scheggia's Case* may have to be applied in a case in which the contract is couched in the same language as the language used in *Scheggia's Case*, or language indistinguishable from it, the method of construction applied in *Scheggia's Case* ought not to be extended."

463. Christoforides *v.* Terry, [1924] A.C. 566

The appellant employed a Mr. Thomson who was a broker on the Cotton Exchanges of Liverpool and New York. Thomson was to make transactions on these exchanges for the appellant. The terms of the agreement were that if at any time the indebtedness of either party to the other should exceed £1,000, the party in credit should be entitled to call upon the other party for the payment of that sum. In November, 1920, the market in cotton fell and the appellant owed Thomson a large sum of money, which Thomson called for under the terms of the agreement but which was not paid. Thomson closed the account, as he was entitled to do, and sold the appellant's cotton, which he held at the time, at a loss of £6,385 13s. 1d. Thomson called for an indemnity for this loss but the appellant did not pay it. Thomson got into financial difficulties and assigned his property for the benefit of his creditors, Terry being the trustee of the assignment. In this action Terry tried to recover the indemnity for the benefit of Thomson's creditors. *Held*—Terry succeeded. Thomson, as agent, was entitled to the indemnity now being claimed on his behalf.

464. Davison *v.* Fernandes (1889), 6 T.L.R. 73

The plaintiff was a stockbroker and the defendant was the holder of stock which he wished to sell. He asked the plaintiff for a price *ex* (or without) *dividend* but the plaintiff negligently quoted a price which was *cum* (or with) *dividend*. The defendant, thinking that the price was *ex dividend*, authorised the plaintiff to sell, because if the price had really been *ex dividend* it would have been a good one. The broker sold the shares and when the plaintiff discovered the error he repudiated the contract. In accordance with the custom of the Stock Exchange, the plaintiff had to pay certain sums of money to the purchaser of the shares by way of compensation for losses incurred by the defendant's repudiation and the plaintiff now sought to recover those sums by way of an indemnity. *Held*—He could not do so as his negligence in giving the wrong price barred any claim to an indemnity.

465. Dickinson *v.* Lilwal (1815), 4 Camp. 279

An agent was given authority to sell the goods of a principal who was in the Irish provision trade. By a custom of the trade the authority of an agent expired with the day on which it was given. *Held*—A contract made by the agent some days after he had been appointed was not binding on the principal.

466. Stevenson & Sons *v.* Aktiengesellschaft für Cartonnagen Industrie, [1918] A.C. 239

The plaintiffs were an English company and the defendants were a German company carrying on business at Dresden. By an agreement in writing dated November 22nd, 1906, the plaintiffs became (i) sole agents of the defendants for Great Britain and the Colonies for the sale of the defendants' machines which were used for fixing metal edges and studs to cardboard boxes, and (ii) partners in the business of manufacturing in England and selling here and in the Colonies the metal edges and studs. The plaintiffs asked for a declaratory judgment confirming that the agency and partnership were terminated by the outbreak of war on August 4th, 1914, and what the financial position of the partners was in consequence. *Held*—(i) That a contract of agency between a foreign principal and a British Agent resident in their respective countries, under which the agent is to sell the principal's goods in Britain and the Colonies, is terminated by the outbreak of war between the two countries. (ii) A partnership between a British partner and a foreign partner which involves the carrying on of a business in this country is dissolved by the outbreak of war between the respective countries of the partners.

467. Drew *v.* Nunn (1879), 4 Q.B.D. 661

The plaintiff was a tradesman and brought this action to recover from the defendant the price of boots and shoes supplied to the defendant's wife between April, 1876, and June, 1877. Evidence showed that the plaintiff began to supply goods on credit to the defendant's wife in 1872 and the defendant was present when some of the goods were ordered and had paid for certain of them by cheque. In 1873 the defendant fell ill and made arrangements for his income to be paid to his wife, directing his bankers to honour cheques drawn by her and to allow her to deal with his securities. In December, 1873, the defendant became insane and was placed in an asylum until April, 1877, when he recovered his reason. Whilst the defendant was in the asylum the plaintiff sold the above-mentioned goods to the defendant's wife on credit without knowing of the defendant's insanity. When sued for the price the defendant claimed that his insanity revoked his wife's authority so that he was not liable. The Court of Appeal *held* that he was liable for the price of the goods supplied. Brett, L.J., dealing with the death of the principal, said, "Although it is not necessary to decide the question today, I should think that the same rule would apply in the case of the principal's death as of his insanity, and that if representations made by a person during his life were acted upon after his death by an innocent party without knowledge of his death, the principal's estate would be bound."

N.B. Drew v. *Nunn* was approved and followed in a more recent Canadian case—*Re Parks, Canada Permanent Trust Co.* v. *Parks*, [1957] 8 D.L.R. (2d) 155.

468. Yonge *v.* Toynbee, [1910] 1 K.B. 215

The plaintiff alleged that the defendant had written and published a letter which was a libel on her and proceeded to bring an action against him. The defendant instructed a firm of solicitors, W and Sons, to act for him in the matter. Before the action commenced the defendant was certified as being of unsound mind. However, W and Sons, not knowing of this, entered an appearance in the action for the defendant after his insanity and also delivered a defence. Various other interlocutory proceedings took place but the action was not in fact tried, and the plaintiff's solicitors asked that all proceedings be struck out, and that W and Sons, who had acted for the defendant after his insanity, should be personally liable to pay the plaintiff's costs because they had acted without authority. *Held*—by the Court of Appeal—that W and Sons had impliedly warranted that they had authority to act when they had not, and that they were personally liable for the plaintiff's costs.

469. Chappell *v.* **Bray** (1860), 30 L.J. (Ex.) 24

The defendant was part owner of a ship, and on January 23rd, 1860, he authorised the plaintiff along with the other part owner to make a contract with the shipbuilder to cut the ship in two and lengthen her. On January 24th, 1860, the plaintiff made the contract with a shipbuilder and work commenced almost immediately on the job. On January 26th, 1860, the defendant wrote to the plaintiff saying he would not be answerable for the cost of the work on the ship. *Held*—The defendant could not revoke the agency after it had been acted upon by both agent and shipbuilder.

470. Clarkson, Booker Ltd. *v.* **Andjel,** [1964] 2 All E.R. 260

The plaintiff company carried on the business of travel agents and supplied the defendant with airline tickets from Athens to London to the value of £728 7s. 6d. The defendant contracted as if he were a principal. Later the plaintiffs received a letter from a company called Peters & Milner Ltd., which said that the debt was due by Peters & Milner Ltd., and was not a personal debt of the defendant. The plaintiffs replied that when the defendant had booked the flights in question he had not made it clear that anyone else was responsible for payment. In the same letter the plaintiffs requested a settlement. There was further correspondence between the plaintiffs and the defendant and the plaintiffs and Peters & Milner Ltd., in which the plaintiffs made it clear that they regarded both the defendant and Peters & Milner Ltd. as liable, but eventually the plaintiffs issued a writ against Peters & Milner Ltd. Two months later the plaintiffs were informed that Peters & Milner Ltd. was insolvent and they discontinued their action against that company and commenced the present proceedings against the defendant. His defence was, that since the plaintiffs had made a claim against the undisclosed principal, they had lost their right to sue him. *Held*—By the Court of Appeal—in order to constitute an election the decision to commence proceedings must be taken with full knowledge of all relevant facts and must be a truly unequivocal act. In this case the plaintiffs had never withdrawn their claim against the defendant and there had, therefore, been no unequivocal election.

471. Said *v.* **Butt,** [1920] 3 K.B. 497

The plaintiff was a wealthy Russian gentleman and the defendant was the managing director of a theatre. The plaintiff had put on a light opera at the theatre but takings had been poor, mainly because of a railway strike. After much argument the defendant gave the plaintiff notice to take the light opera off, and it was taken off on October 18th, 1919. On December 23rd, 1919, a new play was to begin at the theatre and the plaintiff wanted tickets but had been refused. He asked a friend to get the tickets for him but not to reveal whom they were for. The tickets were obtained but by the defendant's orders the plaintiff was refused admission. He now sued the defendant for maliciously procuring the theatre company to break its contract with him. *Held*—There was no such contract. The tickets had been bought for the plaintiff as an undisclosed principal, and since the identity of the principal was of importance to the proprietors of the theatre company, the plaintiff could not intervene and claim the contract as his. The defendant was not therefore liable in tort for procuring a breach of contract.

472. Starkey *v.* **Bank of England,** [1903] A.C. 114

Starkey was a member of a firm of stockbrokers in London. In December, 1897, two trustees, Frederick and Edgar Oliver, held stock in trust for others and were registered as holders of the stock in the respondents' books. Starkey received authority to sell the stock under a power of attorney purporting to be signed by both trustees, but in fact the signature of Edgar Oliver was forged. Starkey's firm sold the stock and sent the proceeds to Frederick Oliver who paid them into his private account. Frederick Oliver died 18 months later. On discovering what had happened, Edgar Oliver brought an action against the Bank for replacement of the stock, and the Bank brought in Starkey as liable to indemnify them. *Held*—by the House of Lords—that Edgar Oliver succeeded against the Bank, and they in turn succeeded against Starkey for an indemnity, because Starkey had impliedly warranted his authority to the Bank.

473. Brady *v.* Todd (1861), 9 C.B.N.S. 592

Todd was a tradesman living in London who also had a farm in Essex. The farm was managed by his bailiff, Grieg. Todd gave Grieg authority to sell a horse, and in the course of selling it to the plaintiff, Grieg warranted it quiet to ride and quiet in harness. The plaintiff sued for breach of warranty when he discovered that the horse was not quiet. It appeared that Todd had not given Grieg any authority to give warranties of any kind. *Held*—The servant of a private owner instructed to sell, as in this case, has no authority to give warranties unless he has his master's permission to give them. However, the servant of a *horse dealer* would be able to give such warranties.

474. Hill *v.* Harris, [1956] 2 All E.R. 358

The defendant's estate agent told the plaintiff that certain premises which he was interested in sub-leasing could be used for a confectionery and tobacco business when in fact the use of the premises was limited in the head lease to the trade of boot and shoe making. The plaintiff took a sub-lease and the freeholder prevented his use of the premises for his confectionery and tobacco business. The plaintiff sought to recover damages from the defendant for breach of what was described as a "warranty" given by the estate agent. *Held*—By the Court of Appeal—that the estate agent had no express authority to give the warranty and no authority could be implied.

475. Lloyd *v.* Grace, Smith & Co., [1912] A.C. 716

The respondent, Smith, was a Liverpool solicitor and the appellant, Lloyd, was a widow who owned two properties at Ellesmere Port and had also lent money on mortgage. She was dissatisfied with the income from these investments and so she went to see the respondent's managing clerk, Sandles, for advice. He advised her to sell the properties and call in the mortgages and re-invest the proceeds. He got her to sign two deeds which, unknown to her, transferred the properties and the mortgages to him. Sandles then mortgaged the properties, and transferred the other mortgages for value and paid a private debt with the proceeds. *Held*—The firm was responsible, because a principal is liable for his agent's frauds if the agent is acting within the scope of his authority, whether the fraud is for the benefit of the principal or, as here, for the sole benefit of the agent.

476. Armstrong *v.* Strain, [1952] 1 K.B. 232

The plaintiffs purchased a bungalow from Strain and during the negotiations Strain's agent made certain statements about the property and in particular that it was in nice condition. The property was subject to subsidence of the clay foundations, and had been underpinned several times, but the agent was aware of one underpinning only. After the plaintiffs had purchased the bungalow, large cracks appeared in the walls and the plaintiffs sued Strain and the agent for fraudulent misrepresentation. *Held*—They were unable to prove fraud because the ingredients of deceit were split, Strain having knowledge of the defects but not having made the statement, and the agent having made the statement without full knowledge of the defects. Devlin, J., at first instance suggested that Strain might have been liable if the evidence had shown that he had deliberately kept his agents in ignorance of the defects in the expectation and hope that they would mislead the plaintiff, but the evidence did not establish this. Regarding an action for breach of warranty, Devlin, J., held that no warranty could arise out of the rather casual conversations which preceded the sale. Regarding liability of the agent in negligence, there was no duty of care in respect of careless misstatements of this sort, following *Candler* v. *Crane, Christmas,* [1951] 2 K.B. 164.

N.B. In *Hedley Byrne* v. *Heller and Partners*[165] in 1963, the House of Lords decided that there was a duty of care in respect of careless misstatements of this kind, and this decision may provide a remedy in negligence in a situation like that in *Armstrong* v. *Strain.* (See also Misrepresentation Act, 1967.)

477. Wells *v.* Smith, [1914] 3 K.B. 722

The plaintiff was the owner of a furnished house and put it into the hands of agents, B and Co., for the purpose of letting. A Mrs. Pridgeon wished to take it, and she gave the defendant's name as a referee. The agents wrote to the defendant and he gave her a favourable reference. Mrs. Pridgeon took the house but was an immoral woman and was visited at the house by men for immoral purposes. She did not regularly pay the rent or keep the place in good order. It appeared that B and Co. knew that Mrs. Pridgeon was not a respectable woman and so did the defendant. The plaintiff now sued for damages for loss of rent and damage to her furniture. The defence was that the agent's knowledge of Mrs. Pridgeon's character must be imputed to the plaintiff so that when she let the house to Mrs. Pridgeon, the plaintiff knew in effect of her character and the defendant's reference could not have misled her. *Held*—The fact that the plaintiff's agent knew of the untruth of the defendant's statement could not be imputed to the plaintiff and she could therefore recover damages from the defendant because she had relied on his statement which was fraudulent.

478. Dresser *v.* Norwood (1864), 17 C.B. (N.S.) 466

The plaintiff placed timber into the possession of his agent, Holderness, so that Holderness could sell it in his own name. The defendants bought the timber from Holderness through their agent, Chaplin, believing Holderness to be the owner of the timber. When the plaintiff sued for the price of the timber the defendants sought to set-off against the plaintiff's claim the sum of £600 due to them from Holderness. This set-off would have been possible if the plaintiff had been an undisclosed principal, i.e. if the defendants could show they did not know they were dealing with an agent. However, it appeared that Chaplin knew that the timber did not belong to Holderness and knew he was a *del credere* agent acting for various principals. *Held*—The knowledge of Chaplin must be imputed to his employers, the defendants, so they were not entitled to set-off the money Holderness owed them.

479. Lowther v. Harris, [1927] 1 K.B. 393

The plaintiff wished to sell certain antiques and he arranged with a Mr. Prior that Prior should find purchasers. Prior was an antique dealer in a small way of business. Among the articles to be sold were certain tapestries called the Aubusson and the Leopard tapestries. To facilitate the sale of the articles, the plaintiff took a house near to Prior's shop and stored the antiques in the house. Prior lived in a flat on the top floor of the house, and used a sitting room on the floor below. People who were taken to view the antiques were not in general told that Prior was an agent. Prior claimed that he could sell the Aubusson tapestry for £525 to a purchaser who did not in fact exist, and the plaintiff allowed him to take it away and Prior later sold it to the defendant for £250. Prior also sold the Leopard tapestry to the defendant but was never given authority to sell or remove that tapestry. The plaintiff now sued the defendant for damages for detinue or conversion. *Held*—Prior's authority was limited and he was not acting for other principals; yet he could still be a mercantile agent and was one in this case. He was in possession of the Aubusson tapestry with the consent of the plaintiff and gave a good title to the defendant under the Factors Act, 1889. Regarding the Leopard tapestry Prior was never in possession of it with the plaintiff's consent, did not give a good title and the plaintiff could recover its value.

480. Staffordshire Motor Guarantee Ltd. v. British Wagon Co. Ltd., [1934] 2 K.B. 305

A Mr. Heap, who was a dealer in motor cars at Stoke-on-Trent, made an agreement with the defendants under which he sold to them a motor lorry, of which he was the owner, and they let it out to him on hire. Later Heap, representing himself as still the owner, sold the lorry to a Mr. Pettitt, the lorry being taken on hire purchase and sold to the plaintiffs who hired it out to Pettitt. Heap allowed his payments to fall in arrear and the defendants repossessed the lorry and now refused to deliver it up to the plaintiffs. The plaintiffs sued for damages for detention of the lorry and for its return. *Held*— Heap was not in possession as a mercantile agent for the purpose of the Factors Act, 1889, Sect. 2 (1). He was merely a bailee and the sale by him to the plaintiffs was not rendered valid by the Act.

481. Kendrick v. Sotheby & Co. (1967), 117 New L.J. 408

The plaintiff bought a statuette which he later left with X to arrange for a photograph of the statuette to be taken and signed by the sculptor's widow. X handed the statuette to the defendants, who were auctioneers, with instructions to sell it. The defendants gave him an advance. *Held*—The plaintiff was the true owner. The defendants had been unable to establish a defence under the Factors Act, 1889, that X was a mercantile agent and were ordered to deliver the statuette to the plaintiff. X was ordered to repay the advance paid by the defendants and also to pay all the costs.

482. Pearson v. Rose and Young Ltd., [1951] 1 K.B. 275

The plaintiff was the owner of a motor car and entrusted it for the purpose of sale to a Mr. Hunt who was the managing director of a firm of car dealers. It was admitted that Mr. Hunt was a mercantile agent. There was at the time a system whereby purchasers of new cars agreed not to sell them for a certain period of time and, in order to convince Hunt that this car could be sold without being in breach of a covenant not to sell, the plaintiff showed Hunt the registration book as proof of the date of its first registration. Hunt, who had formed the intention to defraud the plaintiff, then asked him to give Mrs. Hunt a lift to a local hospital, thus diverting the plaintiff's attention from the registration book. The plaintiff left without it and forgot it, but later the same day Hunt sold the car to a person named Little, who then sold to one Marshall, who then sold to the defendants. The plaintiff now sued the three purchasers in conversion and they claimed a good title under Sect. 2 (1) of the Factors Act, 1889. *Held*—The plaintiff consented to Hunt's possession of the car as a mercantile agent, but did not consent to his possession of the registration book as a mercantile agent. The sale of a car without its registration book was not a sale "in the ordinary course of business" for the purposes of Sect. 2 (1). Further, the consent required to pass a good title here was consent to possession of the car and the registration book. The plaintiff succeeded, as the defendants had not obtained a good title.

N.B. The point was made in the case that if the mercantile agent had obtained the car by false pretences, e.g. by giving a worthless cheque, or by larceny by a trick, e.g. by coming to view the car and representing himself to be another reputable dealer (as in *Cundy* v. *Lindsay*, 1878),[134] he would nevertheless be in possession of the car "with the consent of the owner" for the purposes of Sect. 2 (1) of the Factors Act, 1889. (See now Theft Act, 1968.)

483. Stadium Finance Ltd. *v.* Robbins, [1962] 2 All E.R. 633

The defendant wishing to sell his Jaguar car left it with a car dealer, Palmer, with a view to sale. Palmer was to inform him if inquiries were made. The defendant did not leave the ignition key but by accident left the registration book in the glove compartment which was locked. Palmer obtained a key, opened the glove compartment and took possession of the registration book. Palmer sold the car to one of his salesmen, Grossman, who bought it on hire purchase, the deal being financed by the plaintiffs. Grossman defaulted on his payments and the plaintiffs sought to take possession of the car. However, the defendant, having discovered what had happened, had already retaken possession of the car. The question of title now arose. *Held*—The car was "goods" for the purposes of Sect. 2 (1) even without the ignition key. However, the sale of the car by a mercantile agent who had not been put into possession of the registration book or key was not a sale in the "ordinary course of business" for the purposes of Sect. 2 (1). Further, since Palmer was not given the registration book or key by the defendant, he was not in possession of the vehicle with the "consent" of the owner for the purposes of Sect. 2 (1).

484. George *v.* Revis (1966), 111 S.J. 51

The plaintiff offered his car for sale and X, a fraudulent person, agreed to buy it subject to a satisfactory engineer's report. The plaintiff allowed X to drive the car away in order to obtain an engineers' report but he did not allow X to take the registration book. However, X managed to steal the registration book before leaving with the car. Later X sold the car to the defendant, who was an innocent purchaser. The plaintiff now claimed damages for conversion of the car and it was held—by Megaw, J.—that since X did not obtain possession of the registration book with the plaintiff's consent and since the book was of great importance in the sale of a car, the defendant did not acquire a title under the Factors Act, 1889, and was liable in damages.

PARTNERSHIP

485. Reid v. Hollinshead (1825), 4 B. & C. 867

The plaintiff, who was a London merchant, wrote to a firm called Davison & Co., who were Liverpool brokers, asking them to buy 1,000 bales of cotton for him and to take a third interest in the proceeds of the sale of the cotton instead of a commission. Davison & Co. agreed and purchased the cotton. In subsequent letters the relationship between the plaintiff and Davison & Co. was referred to as a joint account; a joint venture; a joint concern; a joint speculation; a joint purchase; and a joint cotton adventure. Davison & Co. also insured the cotton and warehoused it, and pledged the cotton as security for a loan to the defendant. The plaintiff now sued the defendant for conversion of the cotton alleging that Davison & Co. had no authority to pledge it. *Held*—The defendant had a good title as against the plaintiff because Davison & Co. must be deemed partners of the plaintiff and in the circumstances they had authority to bind the plaintiff by the pledge.

486. Keith Spicer Ltd. v. Mansell, [1970] 1 All E.R. 462

The defendant and a Mr. Bishop having lost their jobs decided to go into business together and to form a limited company. Before incorporation of the company Mr. Bishop ordered goods from the plaintiffs which were intended for the use of the company. In addition Mr. Mansell and Mr. Bishop opened a bank account in the name of the proposed company but without the word "limited." The company was not formed and Mr. Bishop went bankrupt before any payment had been made to the plaintiffs in respect of the goods they had supplied. The plaintiffs sued Mr. Mansell on the basis that he was a partner with Mr. Bishop and was therefore liable to pay for the goods. *Held*— by the Court of Appeal—that Mr. Mansell was not liable. There was no partnership under Sect. 1 (1) of the 1890 Act. The defendant and Mr. Bishop were not carrying on a business together in partnership. They were preparing to carry on business as a company as soon as they could. This negatived the suggestion that they were partners.

487. Cox v. Hickman (1860), 8 H.L.C. 268

The Stanton Iron Company carrying on business as a partnership near to Derby was in financial difficulties and the partners assigned the business to trustees who were also creditors of the firm. The trustees were to manage the business in the name of the firm until the firm's debts were paid. The deed was entered into for the benefit of creditors and with their consent. Under the deed the creditors had power to appoint new trustees, to alter the trust instrument, and to direct that the company be discontinued. The business was carried on and an agent of the trustees accepted a bill of exchange as follows; "Per pro Stanton Iron Co." Hickman, who was the drawer of the bill, brought this action against Cox, who was a creditor of Stanton Iron Company and a retired trustee, for the amount of the bill, since the firm could not pay. The plaintiff was really suggesting that the arrangement which the creditors of the firm had entered into made them partners in the Stanton Iron Company. *Held*—It did not.

488. Holme v. Hammond (1871), L.R. 7 Ex. 218

By articles of partnership dated July, 1868, Thomas Fisher, William Fisher and George Smith agreed to carry on the business of auctioneers for seven years under the name of Fisher & Co. If any of the partners died during the seven years, the survivors were to carry on the firm and pay to the personal representatives of the deceased partner the share of profits he would have had if living. Thomas Fisher died in August, 1869, and after his death the surviving partners carried on the business. Thomas Fisher's personal representatives never interfered in the business but did claim the share of profit to which he would have been entitled. Sums of money were paid to the personal representatives from time to time amounting in all to about £625. After the death of Thomas Fisher, the plaintiff employed the firm to sell the machinery of a mill, and they did sell it and received the proceeds but did not pay them over to the plaintiff. This action was brought against William Fisher and the personal representatives of Thomas Fisher—a Mr. Hammond and a Mr. Gaskill. *Held*—The representatives of Thomas Fisher were not liable as partners even though they had received a share of the profits, because other than that there was no evidence of partnership between the representatives and the surviving partners of Fisher & Co.

489. Cox *v.* Coulson, [1916] 2 K.B. 177

The defendant was the lessee of a theatre and he made an agreement with a Mr. Mill, who was the manager of a travelling company of players, to present a play called "In Time of War." The arrangement was that the defendant was to provide the theatre and pay for the lighting and advertising and receive 60 per cent. of the *gross* takings. Mill paid the players and provided the scenery for the play and got 40 per cent. of the *gross* takings. The plaintiff purchased a 9d. seat in the dress circle to see the play and during the performance she was shot by a defective cartridge which should have been blank. She now sued the defendant as the person liable. One aspect of the defendant's liability was whether the servant who discharged the pistol was the defendant's servant for whose conduct the defendant would be vicariously liable. It was held that the actor was not the defendant's servant but was employed solely by Mill. On the question whether the defendant was liable as a partner of Mill, the court decided that the sharing of gross returns did not give rise to a partnership under Sect. 2 (2) of the Partnership Act, 1890. The defendant might have been liable as an occupier of premises and the Court of Appeal ordered a new trial to ascertain whether the defendant exercised proper supervision over the loading of the firearms used in the play.

N.B. There may be a partnership where the partners share gross returns if the agreement so provides.

490. Walker *v.* Hirsch (1884), 27 Ch.D. 460

The plaintiff made an agreement with the defendant firm of tea merchants under which the plaintiff was to receive £180 per annum plus an eighth share of the net profits. He was also to bear an eighth share of any losses. The plaintiff also agreed to advance £1,500 to the business. The agreement was at four months' notice on either side. The plaintiff had previously been the defendants' clerk, and after the agreement he continued his duties as before and was never introduced to the firm's customers. The defendants gave the plaintiff notice, being dissatisfied with his services, and he brought this action, claiming to be a partner and asking for an order to wind up the firm. *Held*—He was not a partner but a servant, and as such was not entitled to the order claimed; but in refusing the order the court did require the defendants to pay into court for the plaintiff the sum of £1,500 which the firm had received from him.

491. Dungate v. Lee, [1967] 1 All E.R. 241

The plaintiff and the defendant agreed to set up a bookmaking business at Newhaven, contributing £500 each to it. The defendant was to attend full-time at the betting office and draw £10 per week, and the plaintiff was to give part-time assistance and draw nothing. The rest of the profits were to be shared equally. The lease of the premises and certain other contracts were to be in the name of the defendant only and one betting licence was to be obtained, also in the defendant's name. The plaintiff did not obtain a bookmaker's permit. There was no agreement, before business commenced, between the plaintiff and the defendant precisely what each should do although the defendant was, and the plaintiff was not, to deal with clients over the counter. In the event the plaintiff never did deal with clients over the counter though he did handle credit betting by telephone, which may have amounted to acting as a book-maker. There was disagreement between the parties and eventually the plaintiff gave the defendant notice terminating the partnership and issued a writ claiming a declaration of dissolution and a winding up. In his defence the defendant pleaded that the partnership was contrary to the Betting and Gaming Act, 1960, which required a book-maker to have a permit which the plaintiff had never had. In the course of his judgment, Buckley, J., said "A contract of partnership is illegal if the purpose for which the partnership is intended to be formed is illegal or if, although that purpose is one which could be attained by legal means, it is the intention of the parties that it shall be attained in any illegal way. There is, of course, nothing illegal about the carrying on of a betting office business with due regard to the Betting and Gaming Act, 1960, nor anything illegal about forming a partnership to carry on such a business with due regard to the requirements of the Act of 1960. I have no doubt that a great number of such partnerships exists. The question is whether a partnership formed to carry on a betting office business with the intention that only one partner shall obtain a bookmaker's permit offends against the Act of 1960 . . . ." The Judge went on to *hold* that the Act did not require every partner in a book-maker's business to have a permit and that as there was nothing illegal in what was agreed before business commenced there was a partnership and the plaintiff was entitled to the relief sought.

492. Jay's Ltd. v. Jacobi, [1933] All E.R. Rep. 690

The plaintiffs were ladies' costumiers in Regent Street, London, and ran a high class business. They asked for an injunction to restrain the defendants from carrying on a business in Brighton under the name of "Jays." The defendant, Mrs. Fay Jacobi, had for some fifteen years prior to 1931 been in the employ of a company known as "Lafayettes (Brighton) Ltd.," also ladies' outfitters, and she was always known to the customers as Miss Jay. Her contract with Lafayettes terminated when the company was liquidated in 1931 and so Miss Jacobi took a partner, a Miss Limburg, and they set up in business in Hove under the firm name of "Jays." It was agreed that the defendants had acted innocently in the matter. *Held*—Mrs. Jacobi had acquired the name "Jay" by reputation, and had a right to trade under that name. She and Miss Limburg could not be restrained from trading under that name, even though there might occasionally be confusion, although this was doubtful since the two businesses catered for different kinds of customers.

493. **Pilling** *v.* **Pilling** (1865), 3 De G. J. & Sm. 162

A father took his two sons into partnership with him. The articles provided that the business was to be carried on with the father's capital which should remain his, and that the partners should share profits and losses in thirds. Each son was to have, in addition to a third share of the profits, £150 per annum out of the father's share of profit, and repairs and expenses were to be paid out of profits. It was also agreed that the father should have £4 per cent. on his capital per annum and that depreciation of the mill and machinery was to be deducted before the profit was calculated. The partnership existed for ten years and no depreciation was charged on the mill and machinery. £150 per annum was paid to the sons but it was charged against the profits of the business and not against the father's share. Each partner was credited with interest on capital, not merely the father, and the profit was divided in thirds. *Held*—This mode of dealing evidenced a new agreement, and in the action brought by one partner for an account as to his interest, the mill and machinery were deemed to be partnership property even though the articles said that the capital brought in by the father was to remain his.

494. **Miles** *v.* **Clark,** [1953] 1 All E.R. 779

The defendant wished to start a photography business and he took a lease of premises for the purpose. He was not a skilled photographer and employed other persons to do photography. The business made a considerable loss, but after some negotiations, the plaintiff, who was a successful free-lance photographer, decided to join in with the defendant. The plaintiff brought in his business connection which was considerable. The agreement made between the plaintiff and the defendant merely provided that the profits be shared equally, and the plaintiff was to draw £125 per month on account of his share in the business. The business prospered, but the plaintiff and the defendant quarrelled and the business had to be wound up. In this action the court was being asked to decide the ownership of the assets, and the plaintiff, Miles, was claiming a share in all the assets of the business. *Held*—There was no agreement except as to the division of profits and so the stock-in-trade of the firm, and other consumable items such as films, must be considered as part of the partnership assets, even though they were brought in by Clark. However, the lease and other plant and equipment should be treated as belonging to the partner who brought them in, i.e. Clark. The personal goodwill belonged to the person who brought it in, so Miles retained the value of his connection and Clark retained the value of his.

495. **Waterer** *v.* **Waterer** (1873), L.R. 15 Eq. 402

A nurseryman on his death left his real property to his three sons F, M, and J as tenants in common. The nursery business was operated on part of this land. The sons carried on the business and bought more land out of the money left by their father. This new land was also employed in the business. F and J bought M's share of the land and the business and paid (i) out of money in their father's estate, and (ii) out of money borrowed on the security of the land. F died intestate, and the question arose as to whether his share in the real property was a share in the partnership property or not, because this would affect the inheritance of it since partnership land is personalty and not realty. *Held*—Both the land left by will and the land later purchased was partnership property and was converted into personalty.

496. Davis v. Davis, [1894] 1 Ch. 393

A testator, who was a fan maker, left freehold business premises and other property to his two sons, George and Charles, in equal shares as tenants in common. The sons carried on the business, though without any articles or real agreement. They borrowed money on a mortgage of certain property left to them, and used the money to expand the workshops. Charles died intestate and letters of administration were granted to his widow. The question whether the additional property was partnership land or not arose. *Held*—The Partnership Act, 1890, Sect. 20 (3), applied, and the additional property acquired to expand the workshops was not partnership land and so on the death of Charles his share did not descend as personalty but as realty.

497. Law v. Law, [1905] 1 Ch. 140

Two brothers, William Law and James Law, were partners in a woollen manufacturers' business at Halifax. William lived in London and did not take a very active part in the business, and James offered to buy William's share for £10,000. After the sale William discovered that certain partnership assets, i.e. money lent on mortgage, had not been disclosed to him by James. William brought an action against James for misrepresentation. *Held*—There was a duty of disclosure in this sort of case and the action was settled by the payment of £3,550 to William, which he accepted in discharge of all claims between him and his brother.

498. Bentley v. Craven (1853), 18 Beav. 75

The plaintiff carried on business in partnership with the defendants, Craven, Prest and Younge, as sugar refiners at Southampton. Craven was the firm's buyer and because of this he was able to buy sugar at great advantage as to price. He bought supplies of sugar cheaply and sold it to the firm at the market price. The other partners did not realise that he was selling on his own account and Bentley, when he found out, brought this action, claiming for the firm the profit of £853 17s. 3d. made by Craven. *Held*—The firm was entitled to it.

499. Pathirana v. Pathirana, [1966] 3 W.L.R. 666

Robert and Ariya Pathirana were partners in selling petrol at a service station in Ceylon. Robert gave notice determining the partnership but before the date of termination he obtained new agreements with the Caltex Company supplying the petrol, giving himself the sole agency for its sale. He continued to trade on the same premises under his own name. Ariya discovered the new agreements and claimed a share of the profits. *Held*—By the Privy Council—that Ariya was entitled to such a share because—

(i) Robert had continued to carry on the business on the premises using Ariya's share of the capital and profits without accounting for them, and Ariya was accordingly entitled under Sect. 42 (1) of the Partnership Act, 1890, to a share of the profits made since the dissolution;

(ii) that Sect. 29 of the Partnership Act, 1890, which provided for the accountability of a partner deriving any benefit from the use by him of partnership property without the consent of other partners, also applied.

500. Aas v. Benham, [1891] 2 Ch. 244

The defendant was a member of a firm of shipbrokers, the firm dealing with the chartering of vessels. The defendant gave considerable assistance in the formation of a company whose object was the building of ships. The information and experience he had obtained as a shipbroker greatly assisted him in the work of promoting the company. He also used the firm's notepaper from time to time in correspondence on the subject of the promotion of the company. The defendant was paid for his promotion services and was made a director of the company at its formation, being paid a salary. He also threatened to go into business as a ship owner, using the firm name. The other partners in the firm of shipbrokers brought this action to obtain an injunction to restrain the defendant from using the firm's name, and also to claim an account of his salary and promotion fees in connection with the new company. *Held*—The defendant must be restrained from using the firm name in the business of ship owner. However, there could be no account of salary and fees as requested by the plaintiffs, because the business of the company which the defendant had assisted in promoting was beyond the scope of and did not compete with the partnership business. The mere use of the firm's notepaper was not itself enough to show that the defendant regarded his company promotion activities as within the scope of the firm's business.

501. Fawcett *v.* Whitehouse (1829), 1 Russ. & M. 132

Messrs. Knight & Co. were lessees for a long term of land and other property at Varteg in Monmouth, and they carried on business as ironmasters. They wished to get rid of the lease and the business, and Whitehouse agreed to find others to take over the business as partners with him. He obtained the interest of a Mr. Fawcett and a Mr. Shand, and later the three of them, Whitehouse, Fawcett and Shand, formed a partnership to take over the lease and the business. It later emerged that Whitehouse had received a bribe of £12,000 from Knight & Co. for his part in procuring Fawcett and Shand to enter into these engagements. *Held*—Whitehouse must account for two-thirds of the £12,000 to the firm since he held it as a trustee for his fellow-partners.

502. Re Garwood's Trusts, Garwood *v.* Paynter, [1903] 1 Ch. 236

Three partners carried on a colliery business, and the partnership articles provided that they should share profits equally. No provision was made for the payment of salaries to the partners. One of the partners, J. T. Garwood, separated from his wife and in February, 1889, he made a settlement in connection with the separation under which he charged his share in the partnership business and assets with payment to the trustees of the settlement of £10,000, and he also agreed to pay to the trustees two-thirds of his annual share of the profits. After the settlement had been made, the management of the business became much more complex and took much more of the partners' time. They therefore agreed to pay themselves salaries, thus reducing the share of the profit accruing to J. T. Garwood, and reducing also the amount of money going to his wife. The wife objected to the payment of salaries. *Held*—It having been proved that the partners acted *bona fide* in the matter and did genuinely work for their salaries, the payment of such salaries was part of the management or administration of the business within Sect. 31 (1) of the Partnership Act and was binding on the assignees under the settlement, namely the trustees of the settlement made on J. T. Garwood's separation.

503. Mann *v.* D'Arcy, [1968] 2 All E.R. 172

D'Arcy and Co. carried on business as a partnership dealing with produce. One of the partners agreed on behalf of the partnership to enter into a joint venture with Mann for the purchase and re-sale of a part cargo of potatoes. The venture was to be under the practical management of D'Arcy and Co. and profits and liabilities were to be shared between the firm and Mann. D'Arcy and Co. failed to share with Mann the profit made on the sale of the potatoes and he sued the firm. *Held*—by Megarry, J.—that in the circumstances the venture was "in the usual way business of the kind carried on by" D'Arcy and Co. within the meaning of Sect. 5 of the Partnership Act, 1890. In consequence the partner concerned had implied authority to bind the firm to the venture and Mann was entitled to his share.

504. Wegg-Prosser *v*. Evans, [1895] 1 Q.B. 108

The plaintiff was the owner of a farm and he leased it to one Thomas Williams. The defendant and a Mr. Thomas *jointly* guaranteed the payment of rent by Williams. Williams failed to pay a half-year's rent and Thomas gave the plaintiff a cheque for it. The cheque was dishonoured and the plaintiff sued Thomas on it and obtained judgment. The judgment was never satisfied. The plaintiff now sued the defendant on the guarantee and the defence was that the judgment against Thomas on the cheque discharged the defendant from liability under the guarantee. *Held*—The cause of action on the guarantee was not the same as that in the action on the cheque and had not been lost when the plaintiff sued to judgment on the cheque.

505. Hamlyn *v*. Houston & Co., [1903] 1 K.B. 81

The plaintiff was a merchant carrying on a business in London buying grain. The defendant firm ran a similar business also in London. There were two partners in the defendant firm, Houston and Strong, and it appeared that Houston bribed the plaintiff's clerk to give information to the defendants which enabled them to compete more favourably with the plaintiff. *Held*—Both partners were liable in damages to the plaintiff on the grounds that Houston's tortious act was within the general scope of his authority as a partner.

506. Arbuckle *v*. Taylor (1815), 3 Dow 160

One partner of a firm instituted a criminal prosecution against the plaintiff for alleged theft of certain of the partnership property. The plaintiff now sued for malicious prosecution and wrongful imprisonment and the question of the liability of the other partners arose. *Held*—The partner instituting the proceedings was alone liable. It was not within the general scope of the firm's activities to institute criminal proceedings, and the other partners were not liable simply because the property alleged to have been stolen was partnership property.

507. Plumer *v*. Gregory (1874), L.R. 18 Eq. 621

This action by the plaintiff, a Mrs. Plumer, was brought against a firm of solicitors, Gregory & Co., alleging that money entrusted to two former members of the firm had been misapplied by them. The firm had three partners, Jonas and William Gregory, and Thomas Clark. The money was entrusted to Jonas and William Gregory for investment but the money was never invested and was misappropriated. This state of affairs was discovered after the death of the two partners concerned, though the business had been carried on by Mr. Clark who had not been involved in the misappropriation. *Held*—The plaintiff's action succeeded. Where a client has entrusted a firm of solicitors with money for the purposes of investment the client can, if the money is misappropriated, sue all or any of the members of the firm, their liability being both joint and several.

508. Cleather *v.* Twisden (1884), 28 Ch.D. 340

The plaintiffs were the trustees of the will of Colonel Cleather. The colonel had during his lifetime employed a firm of solicitors, the partners being Twisden, Parker and Kelley. The trustees continued to employ the same firm, and deposited three New Zealand Bonds, which were negotiable securities, with Parker for safe keeping. The bonds were paid off whilst they were in Parker's custody and he absconded with the proceeds. The trustees now sued Twisden, Kelley being dead. The trustees' claim was that the firm now represented by Twisden was liable to make good the loss to the trustees arising out of Parker's default. The defence was that the other partners knew nothing about the deposit of the bonds, although Parker had referred to his possession of them to third parties on the firm's notepaper. Even so the defendant suggested that the bonds were handed to Parker not as a partner but in his personal capacity. *Held*—Though the case was very near the line, the defendant was not liable because it is not the business of solicitors to keep negotiable securities for their clients. If one partner does take such securities into his custody and deals improperly with them, the other partners are not liable unless evidence shows, which it did not in this case, that the partners authorised the holding of such securities, or wilfully ignored the fact that they were so held.

509. Tower Cabinet Co. Ltd. *v.* Ingram, [1949] 2 K.B. 397

In January, 1946, Ingram and a person named Christmas began to carry on business in partnership as household furnishers under the name of "Merry's" at Silver Street, Edmonton. The partnership lasted until April, 1947, when it was dissolved by mutual agreement. Ingram gave notice of the dissolution to the firm's bankers, and arranged with Christmas to notify those dealing with the firm that Ingram was no longer connected with it. There was no advertisement to this effect in the *London Gazette*. After the dissolution of the partnership, Christmas continued to run "Merry's" and had new notepaper printed on which Ingram's name did not appear. In January, 1948, Christmas was approached by the plaintiffs' representative and eventually ordered furniture from the plaintiffs who had not had previous dealings with "Merry's." The order was confirmed on notepaper which had been in use before the dissolution and which bore Ingram's name as well as that of Christmas. Ingram had no knowledge of this and it was contrary to the arrangement between him and Christmas. The company obtained a judgment for the price of the goods against "Merry's" and now applied for leave to issue execution against Ingram as a former member of the firm. *Held*—Ingram had not knowingly allowed himself to be represented as a partner in "Merry's" within Sect. 14 of the Partnership Act, 1890. Further the plaintiffs did not know Ingram as a partner before the dissolution, therefore Sect. 36 (3) applied, and Ingram was not liable for debts contracted after the partnership was dissolved.

510. Floydd *v.* Cheney, [1970] 1 All E.R. 446

Mr. Floydd was in practice as an architect and in 1963 he employed Mr. Cheney as an assistant with a view to partnership, though at a later stage Cheney entered into an agreement which made him an associate but expressly negatived partnership. In 1968 there were further discussions as to partnership and although no agreement was made an insertion was put in the Journal of the Royal Institute of British Architects to the effect that Cheney had become a full partner. While Floydd was away on holiday Cheney made copies of various drawings and papers belonging to the firm and refused to return them. Floydd then sought, among other things, an injunction to prevent Cheney from making copies of documents and to compel him to return all originals and copies alleging that such acts were in breach of his duty of good faith as a partner. *Held*—by Megarry, J.—

(i) there was probably no partnership in spite of the holding out. It did not appear that a partnership agreement had superseded the initial master and servant relationship;

(ii) nevertheless Floydd was entitled to the injunction because Cheney's acts were in breach of his duty of good faith as a servant. It was not necessary to establish a partnership.

511. Thompson *v.* Percival (1834), 5 B. & Ad. 925

James and Charles Percival were in partnership, but Charles later retired from the firm. A notice was placed in the *London Gazette* regarding the dissolution and saying also that James would carry on the business and receive and pay the debts of the firm. The plaintiffs, who were creditors of the firm, applied to James for the sum due to them for goods sold to the firm and were told that Charles had retired and that James alone was responsible for payment. The plaintiffs thereupon drew a bill for the amount of the sum due to them on James Percival alone. *Held*—This amounted to an implied discharge of Charles Percival by the plaintiffs.

512. Firth *v.* Armslake (1964), 108 S.J. 198

In 1948 two medical practitioners, Dr. Firth and Dr. Armslake, entered into a partnership which was to be for their joint lives under a written partnership deed. In 1958 they agreed with another doctor that all three would go into partnership, sharing profits and losses equally. It was also agreed that they would obtain a lease of the premises where Dr. Firth and Dr. Armslake had their joint surgery, make a clinic there and equip it at their joint expense. In 1959 a lease was granted to the three doctors who were described as the lessees who would carry on the business of medical practitioners in partnership. Dr. Armslake instructed solicitors to draft a deed of partnership which it was agreed would be signed. In the event the deed was not signed because Dr. Firth objected to the seniority and holiday provisions in it. However, from May, 1959, all three doctors had their surgeries at the clinic and also practised at their respective private addresses. In October, 1959, Dr. Firth and the other doctor wrote to Dr. Armslake saying that since agreement could not be reached on the issues mentioned above the partnership ought to be dissolved as from 30th November, 1959. In proceedings for dissolution of the partnership, it was *held*—by Plowman, J.—that the effect of the partnership between the three doctors was to supersede the partnership between Dr. Firth and Dr. Armslake. However, where there was no express agreement about the duration of a partnership, Sect. 26 of the Partnership Act, 1890, applied, rendering the partnership a partnership at will which could be dissolved by notice of any partner. Therefore the partnership between the three doctors was dissolved on 30th November, 1959.

513. Re Yenidji Tobacco Co. Ltd., [1916] 2 Ch. 426

In 1914 Weinberg and Rothman amalgamated their cigarette and tobacco businesses, forming a private limited company in which they were the only shareholders and directors. They had equal voting powers, one director was to form a quorum, and disputes were to be referred to arbitration. Up to June, 1915, things went well, but differences then arose, one of which was a dispute on the appointment of a manager which was submitted to arbitration, the costs of which were over £1,000 of which Rothman was to pay two-thirds which he never did. Disputes continued, although the firm continued to make substantial profits. Rothman brought an action against Weinberg for fraudulent misrepresentation, and the directors were so hostile that they refused to speak to each other, and communicated, even at directors' meetings, by means of notes passed through the agency of the secretary. Weinberg presented a petition for winding up, alleging that complete deadlock had arisen, that the substratum of the company had gone, and that it was just and equitable that an order be made. *Held*—by the Court of Appeal—affirming the decision of Astbury, J., that the position amounted to deadlock and it was "just and equitable" that the company be wound up. Points made were that a private company is analogous to a partnership, and in a case of partnership there would be grounds for dissolution. Although there was provision for disputes to be settled by arbitration, it was not envisaged that the parties, who were at loggerheads, should be continually using such an expensive procedure. When one person is suing another, who is tantamount to a partner, for fraud, they cannot be expected to work together. The fact that the company was making larger profits was accountable by the growth in the tobacco trade generally, and was no bar to the making of a winding-up order.

514. Troughton *v.* Hunter (1854), 18 Beav. 470

In an action to dissolve a partnership the plaintiff asked the court to order the defendant to concur in procuring the insertion of a notice of dissolution in the *London Gazette*. It appeared that by the practice of the *London Gazette* no advertisement of the dissolution of a partnership was inserted unless signed by both partners. *Held*—The court would make such an order requiring the defendant to do all acts necessary to procure notice of the dissolution of the firm.

515. Re Bourne, [1906] 1 Ch. 113

W. T. Bourne and G. Grove carried on business in partnership under the name of Bourne and Grove. Grove died and at the time the firm was indebted to its bankers, Messrs. Bernick & Co., to the amount of £6,476 9s. 6d. Bourne continued the business in the firm name and continued the bank account. He deposited the title deeds of certain real estate forming part of the partnership assets to secure the overdraft and later died insolvent, the bank overdraft being £4,463 12s. 4d. The partnership articles gave the personal representatives of a partner who died whilst a member of the firm the right to his capital plus interest at 5 per cent. The executors of Grove alleged in this case that they had a lien on the partnership assets, including the realty mortgaged by Bourne, for £3,000, the value of Grove's capital. They alleged that Bourne had no authority to mortgage the realty. The bank claimed that its equitable mortgage took priority over the executors' lien. *Held*—In the absence of evidence to the contrary, the bank was entitled to assume that the dealings with the account by Bourne were for the purpose of winding up the partnership, and the mortgage was a valid security and took priority over the lien of Grove's executors.

516. Garner *v.* Murray, [1904] 1 Ch. 57

A firm had three partners, the plaintiff Garner, and the defendants Murray and Wilkins. Articles of partnership had been drawn up but the deed had never been executed. The partnership was carried on, the terms being that capital was to be provided by the partners in unequal shares but the net profits were to be divided equally. Later the partnership was dissolved and a receiver was appointed. The plaintiff had originally contributed £2,500 of which £1,300 had been repaid, leaving a balance of £1,200 due to him and £314 3s. 4d. was due to the defendant Murray. Wilkins was indebted to the firm in the sum of £263 3s. 1d. which in his financial position was taken as irrecoverable. After payment of all debts and liabilities due from the firm there was a fund in court to the credit of the firm amounting to £764 9s. 4d. which was not enough to meet the deficiency of capital. The question before the court was how the fund of £764 9s. 4d. was to be distributed in the circumstances, having regard to Sect. 44 of the Partnership Act, 1890. *Held*—The true principle of division of assets under Sect. 44 was for each partner to be treated as liable to contribute an equal third of the deficiency (i.e. the proportion in which the partners shared profits) and then apply the assets in paying each partner rateably what was due to him in respect of capital. Thus, solvent partners must make up all deficiency so far as is necessary to pay creditors' and partners' advances, but if there is only a loss of capital, as in this case, the one of the partners is unable to contribute his share of the loss, the solvent partners are not bound to contribute for him.

517. Manley *v.* Sartori, [1927] 1 Ch. 157

At his death on October 19th, 1913, Charles Calder was carrying on the business of timber merchants in partnership with his son James Calder. Charles Calder left part of his share in the business to the plaintiff, Manley, and the business was continued by James Calder, Manley and Sartori, the last two being also the trustees of the will of Charles Calder. This state of affairs lasted until James Calder died in 1919, Manley then becoming the surviving partner. The court made an order that the partnership had been dissolved by the death of James Calder and directed Manley to wind up the partnership business. In the course of the winding up, the question of the rights of the partners in respect of profits earned since the death of James Calder arose. Manley had been actively engaged in the supervision and general management of the business during that time. *Held*—Before the parties concerned were entitled to share in the profits earned since the death of James Calder by the use of the assets of the firm, an inquiry must be made to see what extra sum should be paid to Manley for his part in the management during that time, since some of the profit made must be attributed to his skilful management of the firm.

REGISTERED COMPANIES

518. Salomon *v.* Salomon & Co., [1897] A.C. 22

Salomon carried on business as a leather merchant and boot manufacturer. In 1892 he formed a limited company to take over the business. The memorandum of association was signed by Salomon, his wife, daughter and four sons. Each subscribed for one share. The company paid £30,000 to Salomon for the business and the mode of payment was to give Salomon £10,000 in debentures, secured by a floating charge, and 20,000 shares of £1 each. The company fell on hard times and a liquidator was appointed. The debts of the unsecured creditors amounted to nearly £8,000 and the company's assets were approximately £6,000. The unsecured creditors claimed all the remaining assets on the ground that the company was a mere alias or agent for Salomon. *Held*—The company was a separate and distinct person. The debentures were perfectly valid and therefore Salomon was entitled to the remaining assets in part payment of the secured debentures held by him.

519. Ewing *v.* Buttercup Margarine Company Ltd., [1917] 2 Ch. 1

The plaintiff had since 1904 been carrying on a business dealing in margarine and tea, and had upwards of 150 shops of his own selling 50 tons of margarine a week in all. The plaintiff's concern was called "The Buttercup Dairy Co." The plaintiff's shops were situated in Scotland and in the North of England, but he was planning to expand his business into the South of England. The defendant company was registered in November, 1916, and as soon as the plaintiff heard about it, he complained to the management of the concern, and later brought this action for an injunction to prevent the defendant company from trading in that name. It appeared that although the defendants were in the business of selling margarine, they were wholesalers, whereas the plaintiff was a retailer, and the defendants put this forward as a defence suggesting that there would be no confusion. Another defence was that the company would operate only around London and there would be no confusion with a Northern concern. *Held*—by the Court of Appeal—that an injunction would be granted to the plaintiff restraining the defendant company from trading in that name. Although the defendants were at the moment wholesalers, the objects clause of the memorandum did give power to retail which they might exercise in future. Further the plaintiff intended to open up branches in the South of England where there would be confusion.

520. Re Parent Tyre Co. Ltd., [1923] 2 Ch. 222

In this case the company was petitioning the court to confirm a special resolution altering its objects under the provisions of Sect. 8 of the Companies Act, 1908. The company was incorporated to manufacture rubber tyres and parts of vehicles and to invest in companies which manufactured such goods. It wished to change to the business of finance, banking and underwriting. The company had not traded since 1912 but had made a business of investing within the limits allowed by the memorandum. *Held*—by Lawrence, J.—that the alteration would be upheld under the provisions of the Companies Act, 1908 (now Companies Act, 1948, Sect. 5) because it would enable the company to carry on a business which could be conveniently or advantageously combined with its existing business. The company was the best judge of what was convenient or advantageous.

N.B. An alteration would not be allowed under Sect. 5 of the 1948 Act if the proposed new objects conflict with the original ones. (*Re Cyclists Touring Club*, [1907] 1 Ch. 269.) Here it was held that a company formed for the protection of cyclists could not alter its objects "to assist and protect the pastime of touring by the use of all vehicles" because the interests of pedal cyclists and other vehicle users often conflicted, and the company could not serve both masters properly.

521. Hickman v. Kent or Romney Marsh Sheepbreeders' Association, [1915] 1 Ch. 881

The defendant company was incorporated under the Companies Acts in 1895. The objects of the company were to encourage and retain as pure the sheep known as Kent or Romney Marsh and the establishment of a flock book listing recognised sires and ewes to be bred from. The articles provided for disputes between the company and the members to be referred to arbitration. This action was brought in the Chancery Division by the plaintiff because the Association had refused to register certain of his sheep in the flock book and he asked for damages. The company had also tried to expel him and he asked for an injunction to prevent this. *Held*—The company was entitled to have the action stayed. The articles amounted to a contract between the company and the plaintiff to refer disputes to arbitration.

522. Rayfield v. Hands, [1958] 2 All E.R. 194

The articles of a private company provided by Article 11 that "every member who intends to transfer shares shall inform the directors who will take the said shares . . . at a fair price." The plaintiff held 725 full-paid shares of £1 each and he asked the directors to buy them but they refused. *Held*— The directors were bound to take the shares. Having regard to Sect. 20 (1) of the Companies Act, 1948, the provisions of Article 11 constituted a binding contract between the directors as members and the plaintiff as a member in respect of his rights as a member. The word "will" in the article did not import an option in the directors. Vaisey, J., did say that the conclusion he had reached in this case may not apply to all companies, but it did apply to a private company because such a company is an intimate concern closely analogous with a partnership.

523. Eley v. Positive Government Security Life Assurance Co. (1876), 1 Ex.D. 88

The articles contained a clause appointing the plaintiff as solicitor of the company. The plaintiff was not appointed by a resolution of the directors or by any instrument under the seal of the company, but he did act as solicitor for some time. The company ceased to employ him and he brought an action for breach of contract. *Held*—The action failed because there was no contract between the company and Eley under the articles. He was an outsider in his capacity as a solicitor and, even if he had also been a member, he could not have enforced the articles since they gave him rights in his capacity as solicitor only.

524. Dafen Tinplate Co. Ltd. v. Llanelly Steel Co., (1907) Ltd., [1920] 2 Ch. 124

The principal shareholders of the defendant company were other steel companies and it was hoped that the member companies would buy their steel bars from the defendants, though there was no contract to this effect. In the main the member companies did buy their steel bars from the defendants, but the plaintiff company began in 1912 to get its steel from a concern called the Bynea Company in which the plaintiffs had an interest. The defendant company then sought to alter its articles to expel the plaintiff company. The alteration provided that the defendant company could by ordinary resolution require any member to sell his shares to the other members at a fair price to be fixed by the directors. The plaintiff sought a declaration that the alteration was void. *Held*—The plaintiff was entitled to such a declaration. The power taken by the articles was a bare power of expulsion and could be used to expel a member who was not acting to the detriment of the company. Therefore, whatever its merits in the circumstances of this case, it could not be allowed.

525. Sidebottom *v.* Kershaw, Leese & Co., [1920] 1 Ch. 154

The defendant company altered its articles to empower the directors to require any member who carried on a business competing with that of the company to sell his shares at a fair price to persons nominated by the directors. The plaintiff was a member of the defendant company, and ran mills in competition with it, and this action was brought to test the validity of the alteration in articles. The Vice-Chancellor of the Court of the County Palatine found for the plaintiff, regarding the alteration as a bare power of expropriation, though there was no dispute that the price fixed for the purchase of the shares was fair. In the Court of Appeal it was *held* that the evidence showed that the plaintiff might cause the defendant company loss by information which he received as a member, and as the power was restricted to expulsion for competing, the alteration was for the benefit of the company as a whole and was valid.

526. Baily *v.* British Equitable Assurance Co. (1904), 1 Ch. 373

Baily made a contract of life assurance with the company on the terms that the entire profits of the Life Department were to be divided among the policy holders without deduction. The company proposed to alter its articles so as to provide that 5 per cent of the profits of the Life Department should be carried to a reserve fund. The plaintiff on behalf of himself and other policy holders asked for a declaration that the company could not make the alteration. *Held*—by the Court of Appeal—that the alteration would be a breach of contract between Baily and the company, and the company could not alter its articles so as to affect this contract.

N.B. The difficulty in this section of company law is the nature of the remedy which the court can give in such a case as this one. In *Baily's* case the judgment indicates that the court would have granted an injunction to prevent alteration but the court was only giving a declaratory judgment and the plaintiff did not actually obtain an injunction. The better view seems to be that a company is free to alter its articles and cannot be restrained by injunction from doing so. However, it must, having made the alteration, face the normal consequences of breaking its contract, i.e. an action for damages.

527. Southern Foundries (1926) Ltd. *v.* Shirlaw, [1940] A.C. 701

The appellant company was incorporated in 1926 as a private company, and was engaged in the business of iron founders. The respondent, Shirlaw, became a director of the company in 1929 under a provision in the articles. In 1933 he became managing director under a separate contract, the appointment to be for ten years, and containing restraints under which Shirlaw agreed that he would not, for a period of three years after leaving the employment of the appellants, engage in foundry work within 100 miles of Croydon. In 1935 there was a merger between the appellant company and ten other concerns, and the group was called Federated Industries. The members of the group agreed that they should make certain alterations in their articles regarding directors; the articles of each member were altered, and in their new form gave Federated Industries power to remove any director of the company, and also stipulated that a managing director should cease to hold office if he ceased to be a director. In 1937 Shirlaw was removed from office as a director, under the provision in the articles, by an instrument in writing, signed by two directors and the secretary of Federated Industries. This meant that Shirlaw could no longer be managing director of Southern Foundries, and since his contract had still some time to run, he brought this action for wrongful dismissal. The trial judge found for Shirlaw and awarded him £12,000 damages, and the Court of Appeal affirmed that decision. The company now appealed to the House of Lords where it was *held*, by a majority, that Shirlaw's contract as managing director contained an implied term that the article making him a director would not be altered. Since it had been altered, there was a breach of contract and the company was liable for it. Lord Wright took the view that since there was no privity of contract between Shirlaw and Federated Industries, it was difficult to see how they could dismiss him. Lord Romer, dissenting, did not think a term against alteration of the articles could be implied and thought that Shirlaw took the risk of alteration. Lord Porter lent support in this case to *Punt* v. *Symons*, 1903, and said that a company could not be prevented by injunction from altering its articles but that the only remedy for an alteration which had caused a breach of contract was damages.

528. Royal British Bank *v.* Turquand (1855), 5 E. & B. 248

A company issued a bond under its common seal signed by two directors. The registered deed of settlement (which corresponded to the articles of a modern company) provided that the directors might borrow on bond such sums as they should be authorised by a general or ordinary resolution of the company to do. The directors issued the bond without obtaining the necessary resolution. *Held*—The bond was binding on the company because the lender was entitled to assume that a resolution authorising the borrowing had been passed.

529. Piercy *v.* Mills (S.) & Co., [1920] 1 Ch. 77

Mr. Shercliff and Mr. King were the two directors of the company of which Piercy had been appointed temporary manager at a remuneration. The directors considered him unsuitable, but unfortunately for them he held 2,146 of the 4,252 issued shares. Piercy wished to become a director and, after consulting some law books, he sent a notice to the directors requiring them to call a meeting to consider a certain resolution which, while not entirely consistent, would, if passed, enable him and his nominees to control the board. To circumvent this, Shercliff and King decided to issue enough further shares to retain control of the voting power and they met and issued 300 preference shares, 100 each to themselves, and 100 to a Mr. Neal. They admitted that the shares were issued solely to retain control of the business and by this manoeuvre the plaintiff's resolutions were defeated. However, Piercy acquired still more shares and the directors countered this by a further issue. *Held*—The power to issue shares given to the directors is to raise capital for the company. It is a fiduciary power to be exercised *bona fide* for the general advantage of the company and they were not entitled to use the device of issuing shares merely to retain control, or to defeat the wishes of the existing majority of shareholders. The allotments of shares were invalid and ought to be declared void.

530. Overend, Gurney & Co. Ltd. *v.* Gibb (1872), L.R. 5 H.L. 480

This action was brought by a company which was in liquidation against the directors of the company, seeking to make them liable for loss sustained by reason of the directors having purchased a bill broking and money dealing business which turned out to be a losing concern. The directors were authorised by the company's memorandum and articles to purchase the business. The main claim of the plaintiff company was that the directors had acted negligently in making the purchase. *Held*—They had been imprudent in buying the business but even so they were not liable. The imprudence must be so great and manifest as to amount to gross negligence, and the evidence in this case did not show the great degree of negligence required to make the directors personally liable.

N.B. This case and other similar cases were decided in the days of non-technical directors. In modern times, directors often have expertise in a particular branch of the company's activities and it is doubtful whether the duty of care they owe to the company is as low as that found in the earlier cases involving non-technical directors.

531. Percival *v.* Wright, [1902] 2 Ch. 421

The plaintiffs wished to sell shares in the company and wrote to the secretary asking if he knew of anyone willing to buy. After negotiations, the chairman of the board of directors arranged the purchase of 253 shares, eighty-five for himself and eighty-four for each of his fellow directors at a price based on the plaintiffs' valuation of £12 10s. per share. The transfers were approved by the board and the transaction completed. The plaintiffs subsequently discovered that prior to and during the negotiations for the sale, a Mr. Holden was also negotiating with the board for the purchase of the company for resale to a new company, and was offering various prices for shares, all of which exceeded £12 10s. per share. No firm offer was ever made, and the negotiations ultimately proved abortive, and the court was not satisfied that the board ever intended to sell. The plaintiff brought the action against the three directors, asking for the sale to be set aside for non-disclosure. *Held*—The directors are not trustees for the individual shareholders and may purchase their shares without disclosing pending negotiations for the sale of the company. A contrary view would mean that they could not buy or sell shares without disclosing negotiations, a premature disclosure of which might well be against the best interests of the company. There was no unfair dealing since the shareholders in fact approached the directors and named their own price.

532. Gluckstein *v.* Barnes, [1900] A.C. 240

In 1893 the National Hall Co. Ltd. owned a place of entertainment called the Olympia Company which was being wound up. A syndicate was formed to raise funds to buy Olympia and resell it, either to a company registered under the Companies Acts for the purpose, or to another purchaser. If a company was formed, the appellant Gluckstein and three other persons Lyons, Hart, and Hartley, who were members of the syndicate, had agreed to become its first directors and to promote it. In the event a company was formed, called the Olympia Company Ltd., and the promoters issued a prospectus stating that the syndicate which was promoting the company had purchased Olympia for £140,000 and was selling it to the company for £180,000, thus properly disclosing a profit of £40,000. What they did not disclose was the fact that they had purchased certain mortgage debentures in the old Olympia Company for less than their face value, and that these mortgage debentures were to be redeemed at their face value out of the proceeds of the issue of shares. This meant that the syndicate made a further £20,000 on the promotion. The company afterwards went into liquidation, Barnes being the liquidator, and he sought to recover the £20,000 as an undisclosed secret profit. *Held*—The profit of £20,000 should have been disclosed and the appellant was bound to pay over to the liquidator his share of it. The fact that the promoters had disclosed this profit to themselves in their capacity as directors was not enough.

533. Lee *v.* Neuchatel Asphalte Co. (1887), 41 Ch.D. 1

The plaintiff brought this action on behalf of himself and all the other ordinary shareholders of the defendant company to restrain it from paying a dividend of 9s. per share to the preference shareholders out of the alleged profits for the year ended December 31st, 1885. The company was formed to take over a concession to mine asphalte for twenty years, and this concession was renewed for a further twenty years. In 1885 the accounts showed a surplus and the company proposed to pay most of this over to the preference shareholders without allowing for the fact that the concession was running out. *Held*—Where the capital, in the sense of assets, of a company is of a wasting nature there is no obligation by law or statute to create a fund out of revenue to recoup the wasting nature of the capital. The division among the shareholders of the surplus profits of such wasting property, after retaining enough to pay the company's creditors, is not a return of capital and is not prohibited.

534. Verner *v.* General Commercial Investment Trust, [1894] 2 Ch. 268

This action was brought by the plaintiff on behalf of himself and all the stockholders of the defendant company against the company and its directors for an injunction to restrain the defendants from declaring or distributing any dividend for the financial year ending February 28th, 1894. The objects of the company were to invest its capital in stocks, funds, shares and securities of various kinds, the income from these investments being applied in the payment of dividend. In 1894 the surplus over expenditure was £23,000, but the value of the investments had depreciated by £250,000. *Held*—The plaintiff's claim failed and the company could declare a dividend. Where a limited company has sunk its capital in any trade or business authorised by its memorandum, and part of such capital is lost, the company is not bound, in the absence of any special provisions in the memorandum or articles, to make good the loss out of the excess of receipts over expenditure before declaring a dividend. However, where the income of the company arises from the turning over of circulating capital, no dividend can be paid unless the circulating capital is kept up to its original value; otherwise there will be a payment of dividend out of capital. Thus, if in the above case the company's business had consisted of buying and selling investments, the investments would not have been fixed capital, and any loss on them would have to be taken into account before payment of dividend.

535. Ammonia Soda Co. *v.* Chamberlain, [1918] 1 Ch. 226

This action was brought by the plaintiff company to recover from Mr. Chamberlain and another former director of the company sums amounting to

£12,468 16s. 4d. paid as dividends on the company's preference shares, on the ground that they had been paid out of capital. The two directors had made a revaluation of the land which formed the greater part of the company's assets and had increased its value by over £20,000. This sum was used to cancel a loss standing in the Profit and Loss Account. In this way unrealised capital profits were used to write off trading losses. Later on the directors paid dividends out of subsequent profits and the plaintiffs claimed that the directors had paid these dividends out of capital since they had not wiped out the earlier trading losses except by the device of revaluing the capital assets. *Held*— The directors were not liable because there had not been a payment of dividend out of capital. There was no objection in law to such a revaluation and the payment of an appreciation in value out as a dividend, provided that the directors acted *bona fide* as the evidence showed they did in this case.

536. Foster *v.* New Trinidad Lake Asphalt Co. Ltd., [1901] 1 Ch. 208

In 1897 the defendant company purchased the property of an American company. Among the assets taken over were promissory notes for 100,000 dollars in favour of the American company. These notes were not thought to have any value because they were not at the time of purchase of the assets likely to be paid. However, they were suddenly paid off with arrears of interest and the directors proposed to regard this as an unexpected profit and pay it out as dividend. The present proceedings were brought on behalf of the debenture holders and by one of the stockholders to restrain the division of the fund without looking at the position of the company's assets as a whole. *Held*—an injunction must be granted to restrain the division of the fund. A realised accretion to the estimated value of one item of the capital assets cannot be deemed to be profit divisible among the shareholders unless the whole position is looked at and the actual value of the assets taken over be reviewed. If there was a genuine capital appreciation, this might be paid out.

537. Dimbula Valley (Ceylon) Tea Co. Ltd. *v.* Laurie, [1961] 1 All E.R. 769

The share capital of the company, incorporated in 1896, was divided into ordinary and preference shares and the preference shares had the following rights—(1) to a cumulative preferential dividend of 6 per cent; (2) the right on winding up to priority in repayment of capital and arrears of dividend; (3) to participate in surplus assets rateably with other shareholders. Directors were empowered to place profits to reserves, but the original articles made no provisions for capitalisation of these reserves. In 1946 the company adopted new articles which included a capitalisation article. Certain questions arose concerning rights on winding up, and particularly whether the company had power to allot shares credited as full-paid up exclusively to ordinary shareholders by way of capitalisation of reserves resulting from the revaluation of capital assets. *Held*—

(i) The preference shareholders would be entitled to participate rateably with ordinary shareholders in the assets of the company after paying the company's debts, arrears of preference dividend, after returning members' credited and paid-up capital, and after providing for the costs of the liquidation.

In other words they were entitled to participate in the distribution of *all* surplus assets even though certain of those assets consisted of ploughed back profits which could have been distributed as dividend to ordinary shareholders.

(ii) A reserve fund resulting from a revaluation of unrealised fixed assets, made in good faith by competent valuers and not likely to be liable to short-term fluctuations, might be capitalised or, if the company's regulations permitted, might be distributed as dividend. As the surplus could in fact have been distributed to the ordinary shareholders in this case in the form of dividends, and would have gone exclusively to the ordinary shareholders, the capitalisation, though exclusively for their benefit, did not infringe the rights of preference shareholders and was valid.

538. Stapley v. Read Bros. Ltd., [1924] 2 Ch. 1

Up to and including 1906 the balance sheets of the company showed an item of £140,000 for goodwill. From time to time amounts were written off and a reserve fund was built up out of profits until the item goodwill was finally eliminated from the accounts in 1918 by writing the balance of it off against a reserve account. Further financial adjustments were made to the company's capital structure, including the issue of £40,000 worth of bonus shares, but in 1923 preference dividends were three years in arrear, and the directors in their report pointed out that the company had retained in the business £180,000 which could have been paid out as dividends, and proposed to write back to a reserve £40,000 which was a conservative estimate of the value of the goodwill, thus enabling the arrears of dividend to be paid off. This was beneficial to the company since the arrears were injuring its financial standing. Doubts were raised as to the legality of the procedure. *Held*—by Russell, J.—that although goodwill had been written off against a reserve fund, the company still owned the asset whatever it might be worth. If £40,000 was a fair estimate of its value, this sum could have been distributed as profits. The facts of the situation were independent of the form in which the accounts were kept. The shareholders never bound themselves to give up their claims to these profits, and they could be written back to profit account since there was no prejudice to creditors.

539. Weeks v. Propert (1873), L.R. 8 C.P. 427

The defendants were the directors of a railway company and they issued a prospectus inviting persons to lend money to the company on the security of debentures. Weeks was a trustee of certain funds and he lent £500 of the trust money to the company, obtaining a debenture. The company had, unknown to Weeks, already exceeded its borrowing powers so that it was not possible to sue the company, the loan being *ultra vires*. *Held*—The plaintiff succeeded in this action against the directors. The latter were in breach of warranty that the company had power to borrow, which could be implied from the prospectus.

540. Re Kingston Cotton Mill Co., [1896] 2 Ch. 279

The directors of a company were enabled to pay dividends out of capital because the stock in trade of the company was overstated for several years. The auditors had not required the production of the stock records but had accepted the certificate of the company's manager regarding the value of the stock. *Held*—The auditors were not liable. It was stated that an auditor is "a watchdog not a bloodhound." He can assume that the company's servants are honest and can rely upon statements they make unless there are suspicious circumstances which would give reason for distrust.

N.B. The rule laid down in the above case has been modified by subsequent cases. For example in *Re City Equitable Fire Insurance Co. Ltd.*, [1930] 2 Ch. 293, the chairman of the company committed frauds by purporting to buy Treasury Bonds just before the end of the accounting period and selling them just after the audit. By this method a debt due to the company from a firm in which the chairman had an interest was considerably reduced on the balance sheet by increasing the gilt-edged securities shown as assets. The auditors were held liable for trusting the chairman. They should have asked for the production of the Treasury Bonds. Again in *Westminster Road Construction and Engineering Company Ltd.* (1932) unreported, a company paid dividend out of profits which were overstated by reason of the overvaluation of work in progress. This figure was supplied by the manager and secretary and it was held that the auditor was liable to repay the money paid out as dividend because he had accepted the certificate given by them without making proper enquiries which would have revealed that the valuation was inflated.

541. Re Thomas Gerrard & Son Ltd., [1967] 2 All E.R. 525

The managing director of the company had falsified its accounts in three ways—

(i) he had included non-existent stock in the half-yearly stock returns;
(ii) he had altered dates on invoices for purchases so that goods bought in one period did not appear in the accounts until the following period;
(iii) he had destroyed copy invoices for goods sold thus making it look as if money received in one period had been received in the preceding period.

The auditors accepted the managing director's assurances that the documents and invoices were correct. The result was that tax was paid on, and a dividend declared out of, non-existent profits. *Held*—By Pennycuick, J.— that the auditors were guilty of misfeasance. Their suspicions should have been aroused by the altered invoices. They were not entitled to rely on the explanation of the managing director, however honest they believed him to be. They must compensate the company for tax paid, which was a direct result of their breach of duty, and for the payment of dividends, which, although an indirect result of their breach, was not too remote because it was the natural and probable consequence of their breach. On the basis of expert evidence the standard of care and skill to be expected from an auditor may be higher today than it was in 1896 when the decision in *Re Kingston Cotton Mill Co.*,[540] was made.

NEGOTIABLE INSTRUMENTS

542. Goodwin v. Robarts (1875), L.R. 10 Exch. 337

In 1873 the Russian Government raised loans by means of bonds through Messrs. Rothschilds who were London bankers. Rothschilds issued a document of title called scrip to purchasers, the scrip to be exchanged in due course for bonds. In February, 1874, the plaintiff purchased £500 worth of scrip and left it in the hands of his broker who was to await the plaintiff's instructions. The broker pledged the scrip with the defendants as security for a loan of £800 on 27th February, 1874. In April he was declared a defaulter on the Stock Exchange, was made bankrupt, and absconded, not having repaid the loan of £800. The defendants, in ignorance of the plaintiff's claim, sold the scrip for £471 5s. If the scrip could be considered negotiable, then the defendants were entitled as against the plaintiff, for a major characteristic of such an instrument is that it passes from one party to another free of previous defects in title. It was proved that it was a custom of merchants all over Europe to treat such scrip as negotiable, and so the court was prepared to recognise it as negotiable by the common law of England.

543. Crouch v. Credit Foncier of England (1873), L.R. 8 Q.B. 374

The defendants were a limited company registered under an Act of 1862. In May, 1869, they sold to a person named Macken a document under the seal of the company, and signed by two directors and the secretary. The document was called a debenture. In July, 1869, the bond was stolen from Macken, and in October, 1871, this bond came up for payment under a system whereby certain bonds were drawn for payment at intervals of time. The plaintiff had purchased the bond from a person named Stanley who had since absconded. The defendants having notice of the theft refused to pay the plaintiff on the bond, and he brought this action claiming that he was the lawful bearer of the bond, and that the instrument had been treated by merchants as negotiable, so that he could acquire a good title even from a thief. *Held*—It was impossible to add to the common law of England by recent custom of merchants. This custom must have been recent, since the document was a company debenture bond, and companies of this kind had only been in existence since 1844. The custom could not, therefore, have been part of the Law Merchant. The plaintiff's claim failed, the court holding that the instrument was not negotiable at law or by statute.

N.B. Company Bearer Debentures are now negotiable under the provisions of the Companies Act, 1948.

544. Barclays Bank Ltd. v. The Astley Industrial Trust Ltd., [1970] 1 All E.R. 719

Mabons Garage Ltd. were motor dealers who banked with the plaintiffs and arranged hire-purchase transactions with the defendants. In November, 1964, the plaintiffs gave Mabons a temporary overdraft up to £2,000 and on the 18th November when the account was £1,910 overdrawn cheques for £2,673 drawn by Mabons were presented for payment. The bank manager agreed to pay them only after receiving an assurance from the directors of Mabons that cheques for £2,850 in favour of Mabons and drawn by the defendants would be paid into the account the next day. On 19th November when Mabons overdraft stood at £4,673 two further cheques for £345 drawn by Mabons were presented for payment and the bank manager refused to pay these until he had received the defendants' cheques for £2,850. On the 20th November the defendants stopped their cheques which it appeared they had been induced to draw by the fraud of Mabons' directors. In an action by the bank claiming to be holders in due course of the cheques the defendants alleged that the bank had not taken them for value. *Held*—by Milmo, J.—that the bank was a holder in due course since—

(a) a banker who takes a cheque as agent for collection can also be a holder in due course under Sect. 2 of the Cheques Act, 1957;

(b) the bank was a holder in due course. They were holders because they had a lien on the cheques and were entitled to hold them pending payment of the overdraft. The value was the overdraft of £4,673. An antecedent debt would support a bill of exchange.

The bank was entitled to recover the amount of the cheques from the defendants.

Regarding the decision in *Westminster Bank Ltd.* v. *Zang*, 1965,[587] Milmo, J., said "I should mention that *Westminster Bank Ltd.* v. *Zang* was strongly relied upon by the defendants, but I do not consider that it established their contentions. The facts were materially different from those in the present case and in particular there was no question of the bank having a lien such as there admittedly was in the present case."

N.B. The bank appears to have obtained the benefit of the antecedent overdraft by virtue of their bankers lien.

545. Halesowen Presswork and Assemblies Ltd. *v.* Westminster Bank Ltd., [1970] 3 All E.R. 473

The company opened a No. 2 account with the bank at a time when its No. 1 account was overdrawn by £11,879. It was agreed between the company and the bank that there should be no dealings on the No. 1 account for four months. Later the company paid a cheque for some £8,000 into the No. 2 account. This cheque was cleared and credited. Meantime the company had gone into liquidation and the bank sought to set off the money in the No. 2 account against the overdraft in the No. 1 account and prove in the liquidation for the balance. The liquidator claimed that the two accounts did not represent mutual dealings and could not be set off. He claimed the £8,000 contending that the bank should claim for the £11,879 in the liquidation. *Held*—by the Court of Appeal—

 (i) there could be no contracting out of Sect. 31 of the Bankruptcy Act, 1914 (extended to company liquidation by Sect. 317 of the Companies Act, 1948); but

 (ii) it was possible for an agreement between the parties to provide that certain dealings between them should not be regarded as mutual. The agreement not to operate the No. 1 account suggested that there was no mutuality between that account and the No. 2 account at least for four months, and since the four months' period had not expired when the liquidation commenced, there could be no setoff by the bank.

 (iii) as regards banker's lien, this did not avail the bank. Such a lien was not a true lien. It would be better to consider the rights of a banker in terms of set-off, and not regard all securities, including moneys paid in, as available to discharge debts owed to the bank by a customer. (The Lords reversed the decision [1972] 1 All E.R. 641, deeming this agreement to end on winding up.)

546. Arab Bank Ltd. *v.* Ross, [1952] 2 Q.B. 216

The plaintiffs claimed to be holders in due course of two promissory notes made by Ross and payable to "Fathi and Faysal Nabulsy Company," a firm of which the two men named were the only partners. Ross alleged that he had been induced to make the notes by the fraud of the payees, and attempted unsuccessfully to show that the plaintiffs had knowledge of this fraud and had not taken the notes in good faith. The plaintiffs claimed to be holders in due course, but the point was taken that the indorsement on the notes was simply "Fathi and Faysal Nabulsy" with the omission of the word "Company." *Held*—By the Court of Appeal—that an indorsement could be valid to pass the property without being regular on the face of it. Regularity is different from validity. The Arab Bank were not holders in due course, because the indorsement was not regular, but were holders for value. Although the indorsers were in fact the only two partners, the word Company did not imply this, and therefore the indorsement was not manifestly regular by reference only to the instrument. The circumstances under which an indorsement gives rise to doubt is a practical matter and is best answered by the practice of bankers. This practice insists that the indorsement shall correspond exactly with the payee as named.

547. Oliver *v.* Davis and Another, [1949] 2 K.B. 727

On July 18th, 1947, the plaintiff lent £350 to William Davis and received from him a cheque for £400, post-dated to August 8th, 1947. This was presented on August 19th, 1947, and Davis was not able to meet it. Davis persuaded a Miss Marjorie Woodcock (he was "engaged" to her sister although he was married) to draw a cheque for £400 in favour of the plaintiff, and an envelope containing this cheque, but without any covering letter, was left at the plaintiff's house.

The plaintiff was away at the time and returned on August 22nd when he received Miss Woodcock's cheque but did not know who had sent it. Miss Woodcock, however, had discovered that Davis was a rogue and she informed the plaintiff within an hour or two of his receiving the cheque why she had sent it and also that she had stopped payment of it. On August 23rd, the plaintiff presented Davis's cheque which was dishonoured and later presented Miss Woodcock's cheque which was returned marked, "Stopped by order of the drawer." In an action by the plaintiff against Miss Woodcock, suing her on the cheque, the plaintiff relied, *inter alia*, on Sect. 27 (1) (*b*) of the Bills of Exchange Act, 1882. Miss Woodcock contended that there was no consideration for the cheque. *Held*—An antecedent debt or liability within the meaning of Sect. 27 (1) (*b*) was a debt or liability due from the maker or negotiator of the instrument and not from a third party. The plaintiff, therefore, could not rely on Sect. 27 (1) (*b*) but must show consideration sufficient to satisfy a simple contract under Sect. 27 (1) (*a*). This he could not do because he had not given her any promise, express or implied, to forbear in respect of any remedy he might have against Davis, nor had he changed his position for the worse in regard to his claim on Davis's cheque. There was no evidence of any consideration and the plaintiff's action failed.

548. Bavins *v.* London and South Western Bank Ltd., [1900] 1 Q.B. 270

In the course of this action, the Court of Appeal had to deal with an instrument given to the plaintiffs by the Great Northern Railway Co. for work done. The instrument read as follows: "The Great Northern Railway Company No. 1 Accountants drawing account London, 7th July, 1898. The Union Bank of London Limited . . . . Pay to J. Bavins Jnr. and Sims the sum of Sixty-nine Pounds Seven Shillings. Provided the receipt form at the foot hereof is duly signed, stamped, and dated. £69 7s." *Held*—That the instrument was not a cheque within the definition given by the Bills of Exchange Act, 1882, because it was not an unconditional order. The bank was not to pay the instrument unless the receipt was signed.

549. Nathan *v.* Ogdens Ltd. (1905), 94 L.T. 126

In the course of this action the Court of Appeal was dealing with an instrument on the face of which were printed the words "The receipt at the back hereof must be signed, which signature will be taken as an indorsement of the cheque." *Held*—The order to pay was unconditional and therefore the cheque was valid. The words could be taken as addressed to the payee and not to the bank.

N.B. It may now be settled that it is not a condition that a banker must obtain the payee's signature, on a receipt form, on a cheque before paying out. If the condition is regarded as addressed to the payee, the instrument is unconditional. However, bankers usually obtain an indemnity from customers having receipt forms on their cheques. This indemnity protects the bank if it incorrectly treats an instrument requiring a receipt as a cheque.

550. Penrose *v.* Martyr (1858), E.B. & E. 499

A limited company was described on a bill of exchange as "The Saltash Watermens' Steam Packet Company, Saltash." The bill was drawn on the company and was accepted by the secretary in the following form—"Accepted. John Martyr, Secy. to the sd. Coy." The bill when presented for payment was dishonoured by the company. *Held*—The secretary was personally liable because the company's correct name did not appear on the bill. "The intention of the enactment plainly was to prevent persons from being deceived into the belief that they had a security with the unlimited liability of common law when they had but the security of a Company Limited." *per* Crompton, J.

551. Stacey & Co. Ltd. *v.* Wallis (1912), 28 T.L.R. 209

A bill was drawn on a company as "J. & T. H. Wallis Ltd." and accepted by three persons in the following form—"James Wallis, Thomas Wallis, Henry Bowles, Secty." *Held*—The correct name of the company was mentioned in the bill as required by the Companies Act. The name appeared on the face of the bill as drawee and in these circumstances it did not matter that it did not appear on the acceptance. Furthermore the abbreviation "Ltd." could be used for the word "Limited." The persons who had signed the acceptance were not liable on the bill.

552. Childs *v.* Monins and Bowles (1821), 2 Brod. and B. 460

The defendants were the executors of Thomas Taylor, and as such executors made a promissory note as follows: "Ringwould, December 28th, 1816, as executors to the late Thomas Taylor, of Ringwould, we severally and jointly promise to pay to Mr. Nathaniel Childs the sum of £200 on demand, together with lawful interest for the same. J. Monins, Phineas Bowles, executors." *Held*—The executors were personally liable. The words "on demand" implied that the executors had assets to satisfy the note. If they had meant to limit their liability, they should have added the words "out of the estate of Thomas Taylor." Burrough, J., said, "The insertion of the words 'as executors' cannot alter the case if, on the whole instrument, the parties appear liable."

553. Vinden *v.* Hughes, [1950] 1 K.B. 795

A clerk persuaded the plaintiff, his employer, to draw cheques in favour of his actual customers by saying the employer owed money to them which he did not. The clerk then forged the customers' indorsements and kept the proceeds. *Held*—These were existing payees and therefore order cheques and the defendants had no title.

This case was followed in *North & South Wales Bank* v. *Macbeth*, [1908] A.C. 137. It may be that the principle in *Vagliano's Case*[554] can never apply to a cheque, since the drawer of a cheque usually intends the payee to receive payment.

554. Bank of England *v.* Vagliano Bros., [1891] A.C. 107

Glyka, a clerk of Vagliano Bros., forged the signatures of Vucina and Petriai and Co. as drawer and payees of bills drawn on Vagliano Bros. The bills were accepted by Vagliano, since he knew the parties concerned and had done business with them. Glyka got possession of the bills and then forged indorsements in favour of fictitious persons whereby he was able to cash them with the Bank of England. Glyka was arrested and acknowledged the forgeries but the Bank had debited Vagliano Bros. account with the sums paid out. Vagliano now sued the Bank for repayment. *Held*—by the House of Lords on appeal— Fictitious does not mean "imaginary" but "feigned" or "counterfeit." The bills were fictitious from beginning to end and all the persons were feigned or counterfeit persons put forward as real persons, and were not less fictitious because real persons did correspond to the names used. Since bills drawn payable to a fictitious payee can be treated as payable to bearer, the Bank of England was in order in paying them and Vagliano Bros. failed in their action.

555. Clutton *v.* Attenborough & Son (1879), A.C. 90

A clerk persuaded his employer to draw cheques in favour of one Brett by telling the employer that Brett had done work for the firm. The employer had never heard of Brett. The clerk then forged the indorsements. *Held*—Brett was a non-existing payee. Therefore the cheques were bearer cheques and the indorsee received a good title to them.

556. Orbit Mining and Trading Co. Ltd. *v.* Westminster Bank, [1962] 3 All E.R. 565

The plaintiff company had an account with the Midland Bank, and cheques drawn on this account had to be signed by two directors. One of these directors, A, was often abroad and had been in the habit of signing cheque forms in blank before going abroad, assuming that the other director authorised to sign, B, would use the cheques only for trading purposes.

B added his signature to three cheque forms and inserted the word "cash" between the printed words "Pay" and "or order" and passed the cheques for collection to the Westminster Bank Ltd., where he had a private account. The Westminster Bank collected the sums due on the cheques and B used the money for his private purposes. The Westminster Bank did not know that B was connected with the plaintiff company and his signature on the cheques was, in any case, illegible. Each cheque form was crossed generally and was stamped "for and on behalf of" the company under which appeared the signatures of A and B. *Held*—The three instruments in this case were not cheques, but were documents issued by a customer of a banker intended to enable a person to obtain payment from that banker within Sect. 4 (2) of the Cheques Act, 1957, and since the bank had acted without negligence it was entitled to the protection of the Act in respect of the collection of an instrument to which the customer had no title.

557. Hamilton Finance Co. Ltd. *v.* Coverley Westray Walbaum and Tosetti Ltd. and Portland Finance Co. Ltd., [1969] 1 Lloyd's Rep. 53

An action was brought upon five 90-day bills of exchange which were not stamped until after they had been returned unpaid to the plaintiffs. After a long review of relevant statutes and judicial decisions, Mocatta, J., made the following points of interest in a number of areas of law relating to bills of exchange. (*N.B.* his remarks were *obiter*.)—

(i) The due date of payment of the first bill was Saturday 1st January, 1966. It was received from the plaintiffs by Martins Bank, St. James's Street, on Friday, 31st December, and sent on the same day to Martins Bank, Lombard Street, for collection. It was not received by the paying bank until 4th January, 1966. It was not, therefore, presented on its due date as required by Sect. 45 of the 1882 Act.

(ii) The plaintiffs relied on Sect. 46 (1) claiming postal delays over the New Year. Since there was no evidence to show whether the bill had been sent to Lombard Street by post or messenger, Mocatta, J., felt unable to accept this submission.

(iii) The second bill was due for payment on Saturday, 1st January, 1966. This bill was received by the paying bank on Friday, 31st December, 1965, and returned dishonoured by post the same day. It was not presented on 1st January, 1966, because the bank felt sure it would not be paid. Mocatta, J., said it was clear that Sect. 45 had not been complied with.

(iv) As regards notice of dishonour, Mocatta, J., decided that the two addresses involved, i.e. Upper Brook Street, W.1., and Seething Lane, E.C.3., were "in the same place." The plaintiffs having received notice of dishonour on 20th January gave notice to the first defendants by letter dated 21st January. This letter arrived on Monday, 24th January, and it was held that the notice was not given in time.

(v) As regards the fourth bill, the plaintiffs were told on Tuesday, 15th February, by their bank that it had been dishonoured. They wrote a letter informing the first defendants the same day to be sent by registered post. This letter was not received by the first defendants until Thursday, 17th February, at 9 a.m. The plaintiffs contended that this was due to postal delays but had no evidence of posting on 15th February. Mocatta, J., did not feel able to find that the letter had been sent off in time to reach the first defendants on 16th February which it should have been to comply with Sect. 49.

(vi) The plaintiffs were informed on 5th February that the fifth bill had been dishonoured. They wrote to the first defendants on 4th February informing them of the dishonour. This letter was received at noon on Monday, 7th February. The office of the first defendants was not open on Saturday. The fact that the letter was not received until noon on Monday 7th February indicated some postal delay, but being satisfied that the letter was posted on the 4th February, the judge decided that notice of dishonour had been given so as to comply with Sect. 49.

558. Cornelius *v.* Banque Franco-Serbe, [1942] 1 K.B. 29

A bill was drawn on a bank in Amsterdam and was received by the plaintiff in England. Soon afterwards Amsterdam was occupied by German forces. *Held*—Presentation for payment was excused by Sect. 46 (2) (*a*).

559. Williamson *v.* Rider, [1962] 2 All E.R. 268

R signed a document in these terms "In consideration of the loan of £100 from W., I, R, agree to repay W the sum of £100 on, or before, 31st December, 1956." *Held*—This was not a promissory note because the option to pay at an earlier date created an uncertainty or contingency in the time of payment.

560. Jones (R.E.) Ltd. *v.* Waring and Gillow, [1926] A.C. 670

A fraudulent person named Bodenham was indebted to Waring and Gillow in the sum of £5,000 which he could not pay. He went to the plaintiffs and said that he was an agent for International Motors and that Jones Ltd. could be sole agents of International Motors' new car the Roma, but they would have to take 500 cars and pay a deposit of £5,000. The plaintiffs were interested in the deal but did not wish to pay Bodenham or International Motors because they did not know these parties. Bodenham then said that Waring and Gillow were the real backers and asked the plaintiffs to make out a cheque for £5,000 to them, which the plaintiffs did. Waring and Gillow received payment of the cheque and when the fraud was discovered the plaintiffs sought to recover their money from Waring and Gillow. The House of Lords *held* that the plaintiffs succeeded because the money was paid under a mistake of fact and that the original payee of a bill of exchange is not a holder in due course.

561. Lloyds Bank *v.* Cooke, [1907] 1 K.B. 794

The plaintiffs as the payees of a promissory note sued the defendant as the maker of the note. Defendant had signed his name on a blank stamped paper and given it to X with authority to fill it up as a promissory note for a certain sum payable to the plaintiffs and to deliver it to the plaintiffs as security for an advance. X filled it in for more than the loan to the defendant and kept the balance. *Held*—Defendant estopped from denying validity of note as between himself and the plaintiffs, and the plaintiffs succeeded against him for the full value of the note.

562. Wilson and Meeson *v.* Pickering, [1946] K.B. 422

A partner in the firm of W & M signed on behalf of the firm a blank crossed cheque marked "not negotiable." The cheque had the words "client's account" stamped below the signature since the firm had two accounts at the bank one being a client's account and the other a general account. The cheque was handed to a Mrs. Paice, an employee, who had instructions to fill it up for £2 and make it payable to the Commissioners of Inland Revenue. Mrs. Paice, who owed money to Mrs. Pickering, the respondent, filled in the cheque for £54 and inserted Mrs. Pickering's name as payee. She obtained payment through her bank and it was admitted that she acted in good faith. The appellants sued her for the amount of the cheque as money had and received, or as damages for conversion. *Held*—The instrument was not negotiable and the principle of estoppel in respect of blank instruments applied only to negotiable instruments.

563. Hibernian Bank *v.* Gysin and Hanson, [1939] 1 All E.R. 166

A bill of exchange was drawn by the Irish Casing Co. on the defendants in the terms "Payable to the order of the Irish Casing Co. only—not negotiable." The defendants accepted the bill and the Casing Co. indorsed it to the plaintiffs who presented it for payment and it was dishonoured because the defendants were owed a greater sum of money by the Casing Co. and wished to set off. *Held*—The bill was not a negotiable instrument and the defendants were not liable to anyone but the Casing Co. The words "to order" did not negative the crossing "not negotiable" and the latter covered the whole legal position of the bill.

564. Raphael and Another *v.* Bank of England (1855), 17 C.B. 161

The plaintiff, St. Paul, was a money-changer in Paris, and Raphael was his London correspondent. In November, 1852, some Bank of England notes were stolen in Liverpool, and the Bank immediately stopped payment and advertised the loss by circulating handbills in Liverpool, London and Paris. Evidence showed that St. Paul probably received a notice in April, 1853. St. Paul gave French money in exchange for a stolen £500 note in June, 1854, to a person who presented it, after first inspecting his passport and requiring him to write his name and address on the note. St. Paul did not, however, look at his file of stolen or lost notes. The plaintiffs sued the Bank of England for £500 with interest. *Held*—The plaintiffs gave value, took the note *bona fide*, and had no knowledge of the loss when they changed the note. They therefore had a good title. St. Paul could have found out that the note had been stolen, and his neglect might have amounted to negligence, but this is not enough. Notice means not merely express notice but knowledge or the means of knowledge to which the party wilfully shuts his eyes—a suspicion and means of knowledge wilfully disregarded.

565. In Re Keever, A Bankrupt; Ex Parte the Trustee of the Property of the Bankrupt *v.* The Midland Bank Ltd., [1966] 3 W.L.R. 779

The Midland Bank Ltd. received from Mrs. Keever, on 15th November, 1962, for collection a cheque for £3,000, which it credited to her private account, this account being overdrawn by £352 5s. 11d. There was also a £1,000 debit balance on a loan account. The proceeds of the cheque were received by the Midland Bank on 16th November, but the Midland Bank was not aware that a receiving order had been made against Mrs. Keever on that day. Mrs. Keever had committed an act of bankruptcy on 5th October, 1962. The trustee in bankruptcy claimed the £3,000 as the property of Mrs. Keever, the bankrupt. The Midland Bank claimed to offset the £3,000 against the two debit balances.

The court decided in favour of the Midland Bank. This transaction was one of the protected "transactions" covered by the Bankruptcy Act, 1914, S. 45 (1) (*d*). The delivery of the cheque to the Midland Bank amounted to a "contract, dealing or transaction" within the meaning of the section, since the Midland Bank had a lien on the cheque and the amount to which the cheque referred, though, in fact, that lien was not yet exercised.

Further, on 15th November, the Midland Bank had become a holder in due course, as it had taken the cheque in good faith, without notice of any defect in the title of the previous holder, and could, therefore, rely on the protection of the Bills of Exchange Act, 1882, S. 38 (2).

566. Callow *v.* Lawrence (1814), 3 M. & W. 95

A drew a bill on Lawrence payable "to A or order." He indorsed it to B and B then indorsed it to D. The bill was dishonoured, A paid the amount to D, and D struck out his own and B's indorsements and returned the bill to A. A then transferred the bill to Callow. *Held*—Callow could recover against the acceptor Lawrence.

567. Jenkins *v.* Jenkins, [1928] 2 K.B. 501

In 1912 Joseph Elliott appointed the plaintiff executor of his will. In 1923 the plaintiff and the defendant and two others signed a promissory note whereby they jointly and severally promised to pay Joseph Elliott £100. In March, 1924, Joseph Elliott died, the debt being unpaid. In May, 1924, probate of the will was granted to the plaintiff. In 1927 the plaintiff commenced an action as executor against the defendant on the promissory note. *Held*—The plaintiff failed because the debt he sought to recover had been discharged. At common law the appointment of the plaintiff as executor released the debt, and even if the debt would have subsisted in equity, it was deemed to be discharged at probate.

568. Scholfield *v.* Earl of Londesborough, [1896] A.C. 514

Sanders drew a bill of exchange on the Earl of Londesborough for £500. The bill bore a stamp value 40s. which would cover an amount of £4,000. Sanders craftily left room to alter the bill by inserting the appropriate figure "3" and the words "three thousand" in spaces conveniently left for the purpose, thus making it a bill for £3,500. Sanders then indorsed the bill to Scott from whom Scholfield acquired it in good faith and for value. The plaintiff sued for £3,500; the defendant paid £500 into court and admitted no further liability. The plaintiff alleged that the defendant was negligent in accepting a £500 bill on a form bearing a stamp worth £2. *Held*—by the House of Lords —The plaintiff failed. The acceptor of a bill has no duty to take precautions against subsequent alteration. The acceptor is under an obligation to sign a bill, and if he were to return it on the grounds that it might be capable of alteration, great inconvenience would ensue. Nor is it consistent with the general spirit of the law to hold innocent persons responsible for not taking measures to prevent the commission of a crime which they may have no reason to anticipate.

N.B. The relationship of banker and customer does impose a duty as to cheques. Cf. *London Joint Stock Bank Ltd.* v. *Macmillan and Arthur*, [1918] A.C. 777.[569]

569. London Joint Stock Bank Ltd. *v.* Macmillan and Arthur, [1918] A.C. 777

Macmillan and Arthur were customers of the bank and entrusted their clerk with the duty of filling in cheques for signature. The clerk presented a cheque to a partner for signature, drawn in favour of the firm or bearer, and made out for £2 os. od. in figures but with no sum written in words. The clerk then easily altered the figures to £120 os. od. and wrote "one hundred and twenty pounds" in words, presenting the cheque to the bank and obtaining £120 in cash. The firm contended that the bank could only debit them with £2; the bank alleged negligence on the part of the firm. *Held*—by the House of Lords—that the relationship of banker and customer imposes a special duty of care on the customer in drawing cheques. A cheque is a mandate to the banker to pay according to the tenor. The customer must exercise reasonable care to prevent the banker being misled. If he draws a cheque in a manner which facilitates fraud, he is guilty of a breach of duty as between himself and the banker, and he will be responsible to the banker for any loss sustained by the banker as a natural and direct consequence of this breach of duty. If the cheque is drawn in such a way as to facilitate or almost to invite an increase in the amount by forgery if the cheque should get into the hands of a dishonest person, forgery is not a remote but a very natural consequence of such negligence. The bank could, therefore, debit Macmillan and Arthur with the full £120 os. od.

Cf. *Scholfield* v. *Earl of Londesborough*, [1896] A.C. 514.[568]

570. Gardner *v.* Walsh (1855), 5 E. & B. 83

This was an action against the defendant and Elizabeth Burton and Alice Clarke on a promissory note now overdue. The defendant agreed to be jointly and severally liable to pay to the plaintiff or his order the sum of £500. Evidence showed that Elizabeth Burton was indebted to the plaintiff and she agreed to get two sureties, the defendant and Alice Clarke to join her in a joint and several promissory note to the plaintiff. Burton and Walsh signed the note together and gave it to the plaintiff. The plaintiff got Alice Clarke to sign it although the defendant did not know there was to be another party. In this action on the note Walsh alleged that the note was avoided by virtue of a material alteration after issue, namely the addition of another party without Walsh's knowledge. *Held*—The addition of Clarke's name was a material alteration and if made after the note was issued would avoid it.

571. Eagleshill Ltd. *v.* J. Needham Builders Ltd., [1972] 1 All E.R. 417

The plaintiffs were holders for value of a bill of exchange for £7,660 drawn by the defendants on Fir View Furniture Co. Ltd. Fir View had accepted the bill but had then gone into liquidation. Both the plaintiffs and the defendants knew that the bill would be dishonoured if presented for payment. On 30th December, 1970, the plaintiffs sent a notice of dishonour to the defendants which arrived first post on 31st December, 1970. The bill was presented for payment on the 31st December and was dishonoured. The defendants would not accept liability alleging that the notice was invalid. *Held*—by the Court of Appeal—that the defendants were not liable. A notice of dishonour must follow and not precede the dishonour. (Sects 55 (1) (*a*) and 48 of the 1882 Act.) Even a person who knew a bill would be dishonoured was entitled to proper notice. A notice sent before the due date and received before presentation was invalid.

572. McDonald (Gerald) & Co. *v.* Nash & Co., [1924] A.C. 625

In May, 1920, the appellants sold to Archer & Co. 19,000 cases of tinned soup at 10s. per case for cash against delivery orders. Archer & Co., not being able to find the money, made an arrangement with the appellants and the respondents whereby McDonald & Co. drew seven bills of exchange for £1,000 and one for £117 6s. 4d. on Archer & Co. and these were to be indorsed by Nash & Co. The bills were to be payable six months after date to the appellants' order, and the appellants then agreed to hand over the delivery orders to Archer & Co. The bills were accepted by Archer & Co. and duly indorsed by Nash & Co. who left room above their signature for the insertion of the name of any person to whom McDonald & Co. would direct payment. On receipt of these bills, McDonald & Co. handed over the delivery orders. One bill for £1,000 was discharged and the appellants, before the others became due, indorsed their own names as payees immediately above Nash's signature of indorsement. The bills were dishonoured by Archer & Co. on presentation for payment, and the respondents, who were given notice of dishonour, denied liability. *Held*—by the House of Lords—Nash & Co. had by their indorsement intended to make themselves liable to McDonald & Co. on the bills. Although the bills were lacking in a material particular, McDonald & Co. not having indorsed the bills above the signature of Nash & Co., nevertheless McDonald & Co. had implied authority to fill in their own name as payees over the name of Nash & Co., and when this was done, the bills became enforceable retrospectively.

573. N.V. Ledebeter v. Hibbert, [1947] K.B. 964

Where a bill payable in 1940 was not paid until 1945, because the holder was in enemy-occupied territory so that payment would have been a criminal offence, this was not a case of breach of duty to pay so that no damages could be awarded.

574. Burnett v. Westminster Bank, [1965] 3 All E.R. 81

P had for a number of years had accounts at the X branch and the Y branch of the defendant bank. The bank then began to issue him with cheque books with a notice on the cover to this effect "the cheques in this book will be applied to the account for which they have been prepared." In the course of a transaction P used an X branch cheque but altered it as payable at Y branch and later stopped payment by giving notice to Y branch. The cheque was electronically sorted by a computer which was not equipped to read the alteration and the cheque went to X branch, which paid it. P sued the bank for the amount of the cheque. *Held*—The bank should not have debited P's account with the cheque and he succeeded.

N.B. P seems to have succeeded largely because he was an *existing* customer and the notice was on the cover. The court did say that if such a cheque book was in fact issued to a customer on opening an account, he might be bound by it, and any customer would have been bound by a notice printed on each cheque.

575. Tournier v. National Provincial and Union Bank of England, [1924] 1 K.B. 461

Tournier banked with the defendants and, being overdrawn by £9 6s. 8d., signed an agreement to pay this off at the rate of £1 a week, disclosing the name and address of his employers, Kenyon & Co., with whom he had a three months' contract as a traveller. The agreement to repay was not observed and the bank also discovered, through another banker, that Tournier had indorsed a cheque for £45 over to a bookmaker. The manager of the bank thereupon telephoned Kenyon & Co. to find out Tournier's private address and told them that Tournier was betting heavily. Kenyon & Co., as a result of this conversation, refused to renew Tournier's contract of employment. Tournier sued the bank for slander and for breach of an implied contract not to disclose the state of his account or his transactions. Judgment was entered for the defendants but the Court of Appeal allowed Tournier's appeal and ordered a new trial. Bankes, L.J., laid down four qualifications to the duty of non-disclosure: (*a*) Where the disclosure is under compulsion of law; (*b*) Where there is a duty to the public to disclose; (*c*) Where the interests of the bank require disclosure: (*d*) where the disclosure is made by the express or implied consent of the customer. Atkin, L.J., said: "I do not desire to express a final opinion on the practice of bankers to give one another information as to the affairs of their respective customers, except to say it appears to me that if it is justified it must be upon the basis of an implied consent of the customer."

576. Sunderland v. Barclays Bank Ltd. (1938), *The Times*, November 25th

Mrs. Sunderland had drawn a cheque in favour of her dressmaker on an account containing insufficient funds. The cheque was returned because the bank knew she indulged in gambling and thought it unwise to grant her an overdraft. Mrs. Sunderland complained to her husband and the manager of the bank informed him, over the 'phone, of the wife's transactions with bookmakers. Mrs. Sunderland regarded this as a breach of the bank's duty of secrecy, but in fact the husband's telephone conversation was a continuation of one of her own in which she requested the bank to give an explanation to the husband concerning the return of the cheque. The bank pleaded implied authority to disclose. du Parcq, L.J., gave judgment for the defendants and affirmed the criteria relating to disclosure laid down in *Tournier* v. *National Provincial and Union Bank of England*, 1924.[575] However, each case must depend on its own facts. The relationship of husband and wife was a special one. The demand by Dr. Sunderland for an explanation required an account of why the bank had done what it had done. It might be said that the disclosure was with the implied consent of the customer and the interests of the bank required disclosure. Since the husband had taken over conduct of the matter, the manager was justified in thinking that the wife did not object to the offer of an explanation. If judgment had been for the plaintiff, the damages were assessed at forty shillings—nominal damages.

577. Slingsby v. District Bank, [1931] All E.R. Rep. 147

The executors of an estate drew a cheque payable to John Prust & Co. but left a space between the payee's name and the printed words "or order." A fraudulent solicitor named Cumberbirch wrote "per Cumberbirch and Potts" after the payee's name. He then indorsed the cheque and received payment. *Held*—There was no negligence on the part of the executors; it was not a usual precaution to draw lines before or after the name of the payee and the executors were entitled to recover the amount of the cheque from the bank.

N.B. If the precaution of filling in the gap after the payee's name is more usual now than in 1931, then a present-day court may not follow Slingsby because the question of what is usual is purely one of evidence.

578. Gibbons v. Westminster Bank Ltd., [1939] 2 K.B. 882

The plaintiff drew a cheque for rent which she gave to her landlords and which was dishonoured in error. The bank had credited to another account funds paid in by the plaintiff sufficient to meet the cheque. The bank offered her £1 1s. od. in full satisfaction of her complaint, but the jury found that she did not accept this. As a result of the bank's action the plaintiff's landlords insisted thereafter that she pay her rent in cash. However, she did not claim special damage and was not allowed to amend her statement of claim during the trial. *Held*—The plaintiff was entitled to nominal damages of forty shillings. A trader is entitled to recover substantial damages for wrongful dishonour without pleading or proving actual damage, but a person who is not a trader is not entitled to recover substantial damages for the wrongful dishonour of a cheque, unless the damage he has suffered is alleged and proved as special damage.

579. Davidson v. Barclays Bank Ltd., [1940] 1 All E.R. 316

Davidson was both a cash and credit bookmaker who drew a cheque for £2 15s. 8d. on his account. The bank had previously paid a cheque for £7 15s. 9d. which Davidson had stopped by letter, and this wrongful payment made it appear that Davidson had not funds to meet the cheque for £2 15s. 8d.

which was therefore returned marked "Not sufficient" across its face. The plaintiff alleged libel in that the bank held him out to be a person who had drawn a cheque on an account without sufficient funds to meet it, and gave the impression that the plaintiff and his firm were unsafe to do business with or to deal with on credit. The bank pleaded that the words were published only to the payee to whom they owed an explanation as to why the cheque had not been met; that the words were published in the honest though mistaken belief that they were true; and that the occasion was privileged. *Held*— The bank had no duty to publish. There was no common interest requiring such a communication. The bank made a mistake in returning the cheque and this was the reason for the need for explanation. It was self-created. The case is essentially different from one where the bank might make an error in replying to a specific request for a reference, since then the occasion of privilege is already constituted. Judgment was given for the plaintiff for £250.

580. Curtice v. London, City & Midland Bank Ltd., [1908] 1 K.B. 293

The plaintiff drew a cheque for £63 in favour of a Mr. Jones to pay for some horses. When the horses were not delivered he stopped the cheque by a telegram to the bank which was delivered into the bank's letter box at 6.15 p.m. The telegram was not noticed on the next day and the bank paid the cheque, only to find on the following day both the telegram which had been overlooked and a written confirmation of countermand which had been posted. The plaintiff was notified that the countermand was received too late to be effective, and he retorted by drawing a cheque on the bank for the whole of his funds, including the £63, which the bank naturally enough dishonoured. The plaintiff brought an action for money had and received. The county court gave judgment for the plaintiff; the Divisional Court dismissed the bank's appeal; but it was *held*—by the Court of Appeal—that there had been no effective countermand of payment and the bank were not liable for money had and received. They might have been held liable in negligence, but the damages would not then have been the same. Cozens-Hardy, M.R., said: "There is no such thing as a constructive countermand in a commercial transaction of this kind."

581. Brewer v. Westminster Bank, [1952] 2 All E.R. 650

Cheques drawn on an estate account required the signature of each of the two executors. One executor drew over £3,000 by forging the signature of his co-executor. The latter brought an action for a declaratory judgment to the effect that the account should not have been debited. The declaration was refused by the court on the grounds that a joint contractor could not sue on a joint contract unless the other joint contractor could sue also, which in this case he could not. The decision has been criticised and in fact settlement was made, the bank paying the plaintiff the full amount claimed, and costs. (See now *Jackson* v. *White and Midland Bank Ltd.*, [1967] 2 Lloyd's Rep. 68, p. 328.)

582. Woods v. Martins Bank Ltd., [1958] 3 All E.R. 166

The plaintiff claimed, amongst other things, damages against the defendant bank and Mr. Joseph Johnson, the manager of the defendants' Quayside branch at Newcastle upon Tyne, and the case is reported only on the liability of the bank. The bank had advertised investment advice, saying "the very best advice is available through our managers," and as a result of a request for financial advice by the plaintiff, who was a customer, the manager arranged for the plaintiff to invest £14,800 in a private company called Brocks Refrigeration, although, to the manager's knowledge, the company had considerable overdraft and was in need of funds. The whole of this sum was eventually lost. The bank's defence was that the giving of financial advice was not part of a banker's business, relying on earlier decisions that had suggested this, and that they were not therefore vicariously liable for the negligence of their manager, since he was not acting within the scope of his employment. *Held*—By Salmon, J.—(i) The limits of a banker's business could not be laid down as a matter of law. In this case the advertisement showed that the giving of financial advice was part of the business and therefore the bank was vicariously liable for the act of its servant, the manager. (ii) The duty to give proper and not negligent advice extended to potential customers as well as existing customers.

583. Schioler *v.* Westminster Bank Ltd., [1970] 3 All E.R. 177

Mrs. Schioler was Danish, residing in England but domiciled in Denmark. She opened an account in 1962 with a bank in Guernsey. Dividends were forwarded in sterling to the Guernsey branch by a Malaysian company and Mrs. Schioler's account was credited without deduction of U.K. income tax to which she was not liable unless the dividends were sent to a branch in the United Kingdom. In 1969 the Malaysian company converted its shares from sterling into Malaysian dollars. They also sent the 1967 dividend voucher and warrant to the Guernsey branch expressed in Malaysian dollars. The Guernsey branch lacked the facilities to realise the warrant so it was sent to the bank's stock officer in England for realisation. The dividends thus became liable to U.K. income tax. In this action by the plaintiff for breach of a contractual duty by the bank it was *held*—by Mocatta, J.—that in the absence of special arrangements bankers could not in discharge of their contractual duties in crediting an account with a dividend be obliged to consider the tax implications to the customer or consult him before acting in accordance with their ordinary practice.

584. Lloyds Bank Ltd. *v.* E. B. Savory & Co., [1933] A.C. 201

Two clerks, Perkins and Smith, stole bearer cheques from Savory & Co., their employers, who were stockbrokers, and paid them into branches of Lloyds Bank—Perkins into an account at Wallington, and Smith into his wife's account at Redhill and subsequently at Weybridge. The clerks paid in the cheques at other branches, using the "branch credit" system, with the result that the branches in which the accounts were kept did not receive particulars of the cheques. Neither bank made inquiries concerning the employers of Smith and Perkins. The frauds were discovered and Savory & Co. brought an action against the bank for conversion. The bank pleaded Sect. 82 of the Bills of Exchange Act, and denied negligence, since the "branch credit" system was in common use by bankers. At first instance judgment was given for the bank, but this was reversed on appeal and the bank then appealed to the House of Lords. *Held*—The appeal should be dismissed as the bank had not been able to rebut the charge of negligence. With regard to the defence under Sect. 82, the court held that, although the branch credit system had been in use for forty years, it had "an inherent and obvious defect which no reasonable banker could fail to observe." Lord Wright said: "Where a new customer is employed in some position which involves his handling, and having the opportunity of stealing, his employer's cheques, the bankers fail in taking adequate precautions if they do not ask the name of his employers. . . . Otherwise they cannot guard against the danger known to them of his paying in cheques stolen from his employers." This is not the ordinary practice of bankers but that does not acquit them of negligence. Such inquiries should be made on the opening of an account even though they could turn out to be useless if the customer changed his employment immediately afterwards.

585. Lumsden & Co. *v.* London Trustee Savings Bank, [1971] 1 Lloyd's Rep. 114

Stockbrokers employed a temporary accountant called Mr. Blake. Blake opened an account with the bank in the fictitious name of "Brown" and managed to divert to that account a sum of £5,451 paid out by his employer ostensibly to other stockbrokers. When opening the account he gave the bank the name and address of a spurious referee and subsequently made up and submitted his own reference. The bank made no check on "Brown's" business address nor did they obtain independent confirmation of his identity. The bank manager did ask for the address of the spurious referee's own bankers but drew no adverse conclusions when this information was not given to him. The stockbrokers claimed the value of the cheques from the bank. *Held*—by Donaldson, J.—that the bank was guilty of negligence and was not protected by Sect. 4 (1) of the Cheques Act, 1957. However, the stockbrokers could only recover 90 per cent of the damages which would otherwise have been awarded because they had drawn their cheques in a negligent fashion, often omitting the initials of the payee; and this had facilitated Blake's fraud.

N.B. This is the first reported case in which damages for conversion have been reduced by apportionment under the Law Reform (Contributory Negligence) Act, 1945.

586. Marfani & Co. *v.* Midland Bank, [1967] 3 All E.R. 967

The managing director of the plaintiff company signed a cheque for £3,000 drawn by the office manager Kureshy payable to Eliaszade and gave it to Kureshy for despatch. However, Kureshy opened an account with the cheque at the Midland Bank by falsely representing that he was Eliaszade and that he was about to set up a restaurant business. The bank asked for references and Kureshy gave the names of two satisfactory customers of the bank, and one of these references indicated, while on a visit to the bank, that Kureshy, whom he knew as Eliaszade, would be a satisfactory customer. The second referee did not reply to the bank's inquiry. Kureshy then drew a cheque for £2,950 on the account and absconded. It appeared that the bank did not ask to see Kureshy's passport and his spelling of Eliaszade was inconsistent with the spelling on the cheque. Further the bank officials did not notice the similarity in handwriting between the cheque and the indorsement. The plaintiff company sued the bank for conversion and it was held that the bank had not fallen short of the standard of ordinary practice of careful bankers and was protected by Sect. 4 of the Cheques Act, 1957.

587. Westminster Bank Ltd. *v.* Zang, [1965] 1 All E.R. 1023

Mr. Zang, having lost heavily at seven-card rummy, drew a cheque for £1,000 payable to "J. Tilley or order," receiving from Mr. Tilley £1,000 in cash to pay part of his gambling debts. The £1,000 cash belonged to Tilley's Autos Ltd., a company of which Mr. Tilley was managing director. Tilley took Zang's cheque to his bank, asking them to credit the account of the company, which was overdrawn. Tilley did not indorse the cheque before paying it in. The cheque was dishonoured and the bank returned it to Tilley so that he could sue Zang. The action was commenced but discontinued and the cheque was returned to the bank who sued Zang as holder in due course or holder for value of the cheque. The bank failed in its claim. The reasons given in the Court of Appeal were—

(i) as the payee (Tilley) had asked the bank to credit the cheque to the account of a third party (Tilley's Autos), the cheque had not been received for collection within the meaning of Section 2, and as the cheque was not indorsed the bank were not "holders" (*per* Cenning, M.R.);

(ii) the cheque had been received for collection but the bank had not given value, so that Sect. 2 did not apply (*per* Salmon, L.J.);

(iii) the cheque had been received for collection but the bank in returning the cheque to Tilley lost their lien and consequently the protection of Sect. 2 (*per* Danckwerts, L.J.)

In the House of Lords their Lordships unanimously held that the cheque had been received for collection, but the bank had not given value.

The company's account was overdrawn, but it was hard to see how, by crediting the cheque to the account and reducing the overdraft, the bank gave value for it, because in fact interest had been charged on the original amount of the overdraft unreduced by the cheque. There was no agreement express or implied to honour the cheques of Tilley's Autos before they had been cleared, and consideration could not, therefore, be established in this way.

BANKRUPTCY

588. Re Phillips, Ex parte Barton, [1900] 2 Q.B. 329

Edward Thomas Phillips and Arthur Henry Marsh were in partnership in the business of cab proprietors and livery stable keepers. During the course of the partnership, the partners assigned the partnership assets to trustees for the benefit of trade creditors, the deed being duly registered under the Deeds of Arrangement Act, 1887. The trade creditors of the firm were paid in full under the provisions of the deed, but a separate creditor of E. T. Phillips, a Joseph Brown, obtained judgment against Phillips and presented a bankruptcy petition, alleging as the act of bankruptcy that Phillips had made a conveyance or assignment of his property to a trustee (jointly with his partner in trade) for the benefit of creditors generally. The Registrar of the Cheltenham county court made a receiving order against Phillips as a result of the petition. The debtor now appealed against the order. *Held*—The Registrar was in error in holding that the deed of assignment was for the benefit of creditors generally since it was merely for the benefit of trade creditors. However, Wright and Darling, JJ., thought it was a fraudulent preference under what is now Sect. 1 (1) (*c*) of the Bankruptcy Act, 1914, and also a fraudulent conveyance under Sect. 1 (1) (*b*) of the same Act.

589. Sharp *v.* Jackson, [1899] A.C. 419

Mr. Prance, who was a trustee of certain funds and was a partner in the firm of New, Prance and Garrard, had committed breaches of trust by paying trust funds into the firm's general banking account instead of investing them.

Without any pressure from his co-trustees or the beneficiaries, and two days before a receiving order was made against him, he conveyed an estate of land by deed on trust to make good the breaches of trust he had committed. Prance's trustee in bankruptcy brought this action to have the deed declared void as a fraudulent preference. *Held*—It was not a fraudulent preference because the object of the bankrupt in executing it was not to prefer some creditors to others but to shield himself from the consequences of his breaches of trust.

590. Re Dalton, [1962] 2 All E.R. 499

Dalton was a grocer and sold a business, the proceeds being paid into the hands of his solicitors. The solicitors paid a number of creditors without knowing that Dalton was insolvent, though they did have knowledge of an act of bankruptcy that had taken place within three months during which the trustee in bankruptcy could claim "relation back." In this action the trustee claimed reimbursement of £4,114 19s. 6d. from the solicitors, this sum being the total amount of the payments the solicitors had made. The act of bankruptcy was a seizure of Dalton's goods, and it was disputed in the case as to whether this was an act of bankruptcy. The sheriff's officer, a bailiff, had taken what is called "walking possession," i.e. he had marked certain goods and departed. He had also agreed that the goods could be sold if they were replaced. *Held*—by Russell and Cross, JJ. in the Divisional Court of the Chancery Division—that the "walking possession" agreement was an act of bankruptcy within Sect. 1 (1) (e) of the Bankruptcy Act, 1914, the goods of the debtor having been seized in execution and not redeemed within 21 days. However, although the solicitors were not protected by Sect. 45 because they knew of an available act of bankruptcy, they were protected by Sect. 46 because the payments were made in the ordinary course of business and were *bona fide* within the meaning of Sect. 46 and without knowledge of the presentation of a bankruptcy petition.

591. Crook v. Morley, [1891] A.C. 316

A debtor sent a circular letter to his creditors which read: "Being unable to meet my engagements as they fall due, I invite your attendance at the Guildhall Tavern on Wednesday next at 3 p.m., when I will submit a statement of my position for your consideration and decision." *Held*—That this was an act of bankruptcy because the statement was such that a reasonable man would infer that the writer intended to suspend payment.

592. Re A Debtor, Ex parte Customs and Excise Commissioners v. Debtor, [1950] Ch. 282

The debtor was an infant who carried on business with her mother as wholesalers in cosmetics, the articles dealt in being subject to purchase tax. The debtor and her mother failed to account for purchase tax which they collected and the tax became a debt due to the Crown by virtue of Sect. 31 (2) of the Finance (No. 2) Act, 1940. The Crown obtained judgment and presented a bankruptcy petition against the infant and her mother. A receiving order was made against the mother but the court refused to make an order against the infant on the grounds that because she was an infant it had no jurisdiction to do so. *Held*—The Bankruptcy Act, 1914, applied to an infant if the debt was enforceable and the court had jurisdiction to make a receiving order against the infant.

593. Re A. & M. (Debtors), [1926] 1 Ch. 274

Two infant debtors presented a petition against themselves. An adjudication order was made but was annulled after their status was discovered by the official receiver because no debt was enforceable against them.

594. Re Wigzell, Ex parte Hart, [1921] 2 K.B. 835

A receiving order was made against the debtor, Wigzell, in the Edmonton county court on October 8th, 1919. The court suspended the advertisement of the order pending an appeal by Wigzell to the Divisional Court. The appeal was dismissed. During the time in which Wigzell was waiting for his appeal to be heard, he paid moneys into his account at Barclays Bank, Stoke Newington, and also drew money out. The bank acted *bona fide* in the matter and had no notice of the receiving order. The trustee, Hart, claimed to be entitled to the moneys paid out by the bank during this period and asked that the bank repay these sums to him. *Held*—They must do so. The bank was not protected by Sect. 45 of the Bankruptcy Act, 1914. The bank relied on the decision in *Re Thellusson, Ex parte Abdy*, 1919.[596] However, the court, in considering the above case, understood it to mean that the court will not allow its officer, the trustee, to do what is not honest whereas in this case the court could not see any dishonesty in the trustee enforcing his claim. They would not therefore, exercise their discretion in favour of the bank.

595. Re Condon, Ex parte James (1874), 9 Ch. App. 609

A creditor for a debt of over £50 levied execution on the goods of a baker and the sheriff sold the goods and handed the proceeds to the creditor. At the same time other creditors of the trader were taking bankruptcy proceedings against the trader who was eventually adjudicated bankrupt. The execution creditor handed over the proceeds of his execution to the trustee in bankruptcy, thinking that he was required to do so by law. However, it transpired that in the circumstances the execution was not affected by the bankruptcy. The creditor sought to recover the proceeds of the execution from the trustee, but the latter suggested that it was not recoverable, being money paid under a mistake of law. *Held*—Though this was a voluntary payment made under a mistake of law, yet the trustee, being an officer of the court, was bound to repay the money to the person properly entitled to it.

596. Re Thellusson, Ex parte Abdy, [1919] 2 K.B. 735

The appellant, a Mr. Abdy, became acquainted with the debtor in October, 1918. In November, 1918, the debtor asked the appellant if he would lend him a sum of money to enable him to discharge a pressing debt. The appellant did not realise when he lent the money that, on the day before the loan was made, a receiving order had been made against the debtor. The appellant would not have lent the money if he had known this. The Official Receiver, as trustee in bankruptcy, came into possession of the money lent to the bankrupt and the appellent asked for its return. *Held*—The court would in this case compel its officer, the trustee in bankruptcy, to pursue a line of conduct which an honest man, actuated by motives of morality and justice, would pursue even though not compellable by legal process. The money must be paid back to the appellant.

597. Re L. G. Clarke, [1966] 3 All E.R. 622

Mr. Clarke assented to an arrangement in the form of a deed of assignment of property which was to be realised and the sums received paid to creditors.

Mr. Clarke's assent was given on the understanding that the judgment debtor was the sole owner of two hotels, whereas in fact the judgment debtor and his wife were jointly interested in the property. After Mr. Clarke had discovered this he allowed the trustee to sell one of the hotels and accepted the purchase money, the judgment debtor's wife joining in the conveyance. Mr. Clarke then presented a bankruptcy petition against the judgment creditor and his wife and sought to withdraw his assent to the arrangement. *Held*—By the Divisional Court—that as the purchaser had paid for the hotel it was too late for Mr. Clarke to withdraw. The judgment debtor's wife had joined in the conveyance and was willing to execute a supplementary deed of assignment. In the circumstances the judgment debt could no longer be relied upon.

598. Re Croom, England *v.* **Provincial Assets Co.,** [1891] 1 Ch. 695

On 4th May, 1888, Henry Lance Croom, a trader, filed a petition in bankruptcy in the Poole county court and a receiving order was made on the same day. Later his creditors agreed to a scheme of arrangement which was approved by the court of July 16th, 1888. There was no express stipulation in the deed of arrangement regarding after-acquired property. In September, 1889, Charles Croom, the uncle of H. L. Croom, died, and H. L. Croom received £306 under his will. *Held*—A scheme of arrangement operates only to convey to the trustee property to which the debtor is entitled up to the date of the approval of the scheme by the court. It does not, in the absence of an express provision to that effect, include property coming to the debtor after that date.

599. Cohen *v.* **Mitchell** (1890), 25 Q.B.D. 262

Arthur Cohen, an undischarged bankrupt, was carrying on a business without leave or knowledge of his trustee in bankruptcy. Cohen commenced an action against one, Foale, for wrongful conversion of certain agricultural machines required by Cohen in the course of carrying on this business. After the action commenced, Cohen assigned the benefit of the action to Hyman Cohen in consideration of advances of money. Hyman Cohen knew he was dealing with a bankrupt but acted *bona fide* in making the advances and taking the assignment. Arthur Cohen recovered damages against Foale, and Hyman Cohen gave notice that he claimed the damages under the assignment. The defendant also claimed the money as trustee of Arthur Cohen. *Held*—Until the trustee in bankruptcy intervenes, all transactions by the bankrupt after his bankruptcy with any person dealing with him *bona fide* and for value in respect of his after-acquired property, whether with or without knowledge of the bankruptcy, are valid against the trustee. Therefore the plaintiff was entitled to the damages recovered by the bankrupt against Foale.

600. Hill *v.* Settle, [1917] 1 Ch. 319

Hill, who was adjudicated bankrupt on December 19th, 1908, never obtained his discharge. In 1913 he entered into partnership with Settle to carry on the profession of physicians and surgeons. On October 26th, 1915, the Official Receiver, as trustee in bankruptcy, served the following notice on Settle—

Re John Robert Hill. As Official Receiver and trustee of the estate of John Robert Hill, described as of 456, Attercliffe Road, Sheffield, surgeon, I beg to give you notice that I require payment to be made by you to me of all moneys which may now and hereafter be and become due from you to the bankrupt on the ground that he has not obtained his discharge in the proceedings.

On March 13th, 1916, Hill issued a writ against Settle for moneys owed by Settle to Hill under the partnership agreement. Settle asked that the action be stayed until the Official Receiver be joined as a party, since any proceeds of the action would be the after-acquired property of Hill and the trustee would be entitled to them. *Held*—The action must be stayed. Although the notice of October, 1915, was in general terms, and did not specify with particularity the debts which might become due from the defendant to the bankrupt, it unmistakably manifested the trustee's intention and constituted a valid intervention by the trustee under Sect. 47 (1) of the Bankruptcy Act, 1914. It was, therefore, effective to vest in the trustee the after-acquired property represented by the action against Settle.

601. Re Ginger, [1897] 2 Q.B. 461

A dairy farmer assigned his farm stock and furniture as security for a debt, using a bill of sale. He retained possession of the property assigned. Later the farmer was adjudicated bankrupt and the grantee under the bill claimed the property. *Held*—On the facts of the case the farmer was the reputed owner of the farm stock and it passed to his trustee in bankruptcy for distribution among the farmer's creditors.

N.B. The furniture was not subject to the reputed ownership rule because it was not used by the farmer in his trade or business.

602. Lamb *v.* Wright & Co., [1924] 1 K.B. 857

The plaintiff delivered a car to one, Pinchin, on hire purchase. The agreement provided that if Pinchin failed to pay the instalments, or if a receiving order was made against him, the plaintiff could take possession; and that no alteration should be made to the car without the consent of the plaintiff. The car was constructed to be used for pleasure purposes. Pinchin used the car mainly for pleasure purposes but also to some extent for business purposes as grocer and fruiterer. The plaintiff assumed that the car was being employed for pleasure purposes and the car was never altered in any way to make it convenient for use in business. Pinchin paid two instalments and then a receiving order was made against him. He was later adjudicated bankrupt, and a trustee was appointed. The defendants took possession of the vehicle for the benefit of creditors and the trustee ratified their act. The question before the court was whether the car was within the reputed ownership of Pinchin and could therefore be taken. *Held*—In order that the goods might be in the possession, order or disposition of the bankrupt in his trade or business within the meaning of Sect. 38, they must be not merely visibly employed in his trade or business, but acquired and used for the purposes of the business. Sect. 38 did not apply, and the plaintiff was entitled to recover possession.

603. Re Seymour, The Trustee *v.* Barclays Bank Ltd., [1937] 3 All E.R. 499

Early in 1936 Seymour had accounts at each of two branches of Barclays Bank. One of the accounts had not been used since October, 1935, and had an overdraft secured by a guarantee. On March 17th, 1936, a petition in bankruptcy was presented against Seymour. The bank, it was admitted, was at all material times ignorant of the petition and the act of bankruptcy on which it was founded. The manager of the branch at which Seymour had an overdraft had been pressing Seymour and the guarantor to pay it off. Whilst awaiting the result of the petition, Seymour tried to obtain an overdraft at the other branch but the manager there would not grant it until the overdraft at the first branch was paid off. On May 5th, 1936, before the hearing of the petition, Seymour obtained an advance from a moneylender and paid off the overdraft at the first branch and the guarantee was returned to the guarantor. Seymour then obtained an overdraft at the second branch. A receiving order was made against Seymour on 27th July, 1936, and the trustee claimed that his title related back to March 17th, 1936, and claimed the money paid in discharge of the first overdraft. *Held*—The bank was protected by the Bankruptcy Act, 1914, Sect. 45, and the trustee was not entitled to recover the money claimed. Such a transaction was not contrary to the bankruptcy legislation.

604. Columbine v. Penhall (1853), 1 Sm. & Giff. 228

A solicitor, who was in financial difficulties, married his mistress on the eve of his bankruptcy and conveyed the whole of his real and personal estate to trustees for his wife. One of the questions before the court was as to the validity of this settlement as against the solicitor's creditors. *Held*—The consideration of marriage will not support a settlement made on the eve of bankruptcy, if there is a clear intention to put the settled property beyond the reach of creditors and to make the marriage part of the scheme to defeat them.

605. Re Butterworth, Ex parte Russell (1882), 19 Ch.D. 588

Charles Butterworth, a baker, wished to purchase a grocery business which he intended to carry on along with the baker's business. Before purchasing the grocery business and being solvent at the time, he made a voluntary settlement of the bulk of his property for the benefit of his wife and children. He then bought the grocery business and ran it for six months. He lost money on it and sold it for what he had given for it but carried on the baker's business for three years after the execution of the settlement. He was by then in financial difficulties and filed a petition against himself. The debts which he owed at the time of the settlement had all been paid. Russell, as trustee, claimed that the settlement was void. *Held*—In the circumstances it was. Although Butterworth was solvent when he made the settlement, he clearly made it with the intention of putting his property out of the reach of his creditors in case the new undertaking should fail. The settlement was, therefore, void as against the trustee.

606. Re Hooley, Ex parte United Ordnance and Engineering Co. Ltd., [1899] 2 Q.B. 579

Hooley's trustee disclaimed certain unpaid shares which Hooley held in the company, the shares being of low value. Hooley owed £25,000 under the contract to take the shares. The court assessed the damages payable to the company on the basis of the company's indebtedness. It appeared that the gross amount owed by the company was £16,169. The court deducted from this the cash in hand of £4,000 and directors' fees owing of £1,669, leaving a balance of £10,500. *Held*—This was the measure of damages which the company could prove for in the bankruptcy.

INSURANCE

607. London Assurance v. Mansel (1879), 11 Ch.D. 363

Mansel completed a proposal for a life assurance of £10,000 with London Assurance. He was asked on the form if he had made a proposal on his life at any other office, and whether it was accepted at the ordinary or an increased premium, or declined. His reply was: "Insured now in two offices for £16,000 at ordinary rates. Policies effected last year." He signed a declaration that the particulars were true and formed the basis of the contract. He paid the premium and received a certificate of assurance. London Assurance then discovered that, although the statement was true so far as it went, Mansel had tried to increase a policy he held for £6,000 and the company had refused his request, and other proposals to other companies had been declined. London Assurance therefore refused to go on with the assurance and returned the cheque for the premium to Mansel, who sent it back to the company. The plaintiffs now asked for a declaration that the contract was void because the defendant had failed in his duty of disclosure. *Held*—The defendant had a duty to disclose and the contract was void. In cases of insurance to conceal anything material is a fraud, and to conceal anything which may influence the rate of premium vitiates the policy, even if the proposer does not know it would have that effect.

608. Roselodge Ltd. *v.* Castle, [1966] 2 Lloyd's Rep. 113

The plaintiffs, who were diamond merchants, claimed under an indemnity policy after a director of the company had been robbed of £300,000 worth of diamonds. It appeared that when taking out the policy with the defendant underwriter the diamond merchants had not disclosed that their Sales Manager had been convicted eight years before in the United States for smuggling diamonds into that country. The diamond merchants thought that fact to be immaterial. *Held*—The Sales Manager's conviction was a material fact which should have been disclosed and the claim under the policy failed.

609. Dawsons Ltd. *v.* Bonnin, [1922] 2 A.C. 413

Dawsons Ltd. insured their motor lorry against loss by fire with Bonnin and others, and signed a proposal form which contained the following as Condition 4: "Material misstatement or concealment of any circumstance by the insured material to assessing the premium herein, or in connection with any claim, shall render the policy void." The policy also contained a clause saying that the "proposal shall be the basis of the contract and shall be held as incorporated therein." Actually the proposal form was filled up by an insurance agent, and although he stated the proposer's address correctly as 46 Cadogan Street, Glasgow, he also stated that the vehicle would usually be garaged there, although there was no garage accommodation in the Cadogan Street address and the lorry was garaged elsewhere. Dawsons' secretary, who signed the proposal, overlooked this slip made by the agent. The lorry was destroyed by fire and Dawsons claimed under the policy. *Held*—on appeal, by the House of Lords—The statement was not material within the meaning of Condition 4. However, the basis clause was an independent provision, and since the statement, though not material, was untrue, the policy was void. Viscount Cave said: "The meaning and effect of the basis clause, taken by itself, is that any untrue statement in the proposal, or any breach of its promissory clauses, shall avoid the policy, and if that be the contract of the parties, the question of materiality has not to be considered."

610. Newsholme Bros. *v.* Road Transport and General Insurance Co., [1929] 2 K.B. 356

Newsholme Bros. wished to insure a motor-bus and Willey, an agent of the insurance company, filled in the proposal form and handed it to A. Newsholme, a partner in the firm, who signed it without reading it. Newsholme had given Willey correct oral answers to the questions, but the latter, whether in error or intentionally in order to earn a commission he would not otherwise have got, put down three incorrect answers. The proposal contained a warranty that the answers were true and should be the basis of the contract. A policy was issued and a premium paid. An accident occurred, the plaintiffs claimed indemnity and the company denied liability. *Held*—The agent was not authorised by the company to fill in the proposal and must be regarded as the agent of the proposer. Knowledge of the untruth of the answers by the agent was not, therefore, notice to the company. The written contract alone could be looked at, and therefore the company was not liable. Scrutton, L.J., said: "I have great difficulty in understanding how a man who has signed, without reading it, a document which he knows to be a proposal of insurance, and which contains statements in fact untrue, and a promise that they are true and the basis of the contract, can escape from the consequences of his negligence by saying that the person he asked to fill it up for him is the agent of the person to whom the proposal is addressed."

610a. *O'Connor v. B. D. B. Kirby & Co. (A Firm)*, [1971] 2 W.L.R. 1233

The plaintiff consulted the defendants, who were insurance brokers, with regard to insuring his car. The brokers filled in the proposal form incorrectly saying that the car was garaged at night, whereas it was parked in the road outside the plaintiff's house. The plaintiff had read the proposal form and signed it. Some time later the plaintiff's car was damaged while parked in the road and the insurance company repudiated liability. *Held*—by the Court of Appeal—that it was the proposer's duty to see that the information given in the proposal form was correct. There was no negligence on the part of the defendants who could reasonably rely on the plaintiff to correct errors on the form.

611. Mutual Life Insurance Company of New York *v.* Ontario Metal Products Co. Ltd., [1925] A.C. 344

The managing director of the respondent company, F. J. Schuch, took out a life policy with the appellants when he was aged 44 and apparently in good health. In the application for the policy, Schuch was asked to give details of illnesses, diseases or surgical operations since childhood, and the physicians consulted in the preceding five years. He failed to mention that on several occasions during that time he had obtained from his own doctor a tonic when he was feeling overworked or run down. Schuch died less than 18 months after the issue of the policy from a disease (cancer) which was not present when he made his proposal. The interest under the policy became vested in the respondent company and when they tried to enforce it the appellants claimed to avoid it on the grounds of non-disclosure. *Held*—by the Judicial Committee of the Privy Council—The omission was not material and the policy was enforceable.

612. Re Universal Non-Tariff Fire Insurance Co., Forbes & Co.'s Claim (1875), L.R. 19 Eq. 485

Forbes & Co. entered into a fire policy through one, William Donald, who was an agent of the insurance company. Donald inspected the premises before the policy was made. One of the conditions of the policy was that any material misdescription of any of the property insured should render the policy void. The policy stated that the property was built of brick and slate but when a fire occurred, it was discovered that part of the building was roofed with tarred felt. The insurance company went into liquidation and Forbes & Co. claimed £1,350 under the policy. The liquidator of the insurance company resisted the claim on the grounds of misdescription and that Donald was not the agent of the company. Evidence showed that Donald was truly the agent of the company and it was *held* that the misdescription did not render the policy void because (i) it was not material; and (ii) even if material, the knowledge of Donald was imputed to the insurance company.

613. Ionides *v.* Pender (1874), L.R. 9 Q.B. 531

A cargo of goods worth £8,000 was shipped to Russia and, because the adventure was expected to be very profitable, was insured for £20,000. The ship was lost in suspicious circumstances in mid-ocean in fair weather without any known cause. *Held*—An insurance of profits must be taken to imply possible profits. Where the assured does not disclose to the underwriters the fact that the goods are largely overvalued, it is a question for the jury whether the concealment is material in the light of the reasonable practice of underwriters. The jury were in this case justified in finding that the overvaluation was a material fact which ought to have been disclosed, and the claim under the policy failed.

614. Looker *v.* Law Union and Rock Insurance Co. Ltd., [1928] 1 K.B. 554

Looker made a proposal to insure his life which the company accepted, conditions being that he remained in good health until the first premium was paid and that no risk should attach until then. Looker became ill with pneumonia but he did not notify the company and sent off a cheque for the first premium three days before he died of the disease. The company then accepted the proposal and promised to send a policy. *Held*—Looker's executors could not claim under the policy. Looker had a duty to inform the insurance company of the change in risk arising from his illness, and this duty existed independently of the company's stipulation that he should do so.

615. Farr *v.* Motor Traders' Mutual Insurance Society, [1920] 3 K.B. 669

The plaintiff was the owner of two taxicabs and insured them with the defendants in February, 1918, for one year against accidental damage. In the proposal form the plaintiff, in answering a question, said that each of the cabs was to be driven for one shift in every 24 hours. The policy provided that all statements in the proposal form were to be the basis of the contract. In August, 1918, while one of the cabs was being repaired, the other cab was driven for two shifts in 24 hours for a short time, and then went back to the original pattern of one shift in 24 hours. In November, 1918, the cab that had been driven in two shifts in August was damaged in an accident, being driven for one shift in 24 hours when this accident occurred. In an action on the policy, the defendants contended that the policy was avoided because the vehicle had for a short time been used for two shifts in a day. *Held*—The statement was not a warranty but merely described the sort of risk involved, i.e. that the cab would be covered only if an accident occurred whilst it was being used for one shift in 24 hours. Since this is what had happened, the plaintiff could recover.

616. Harris v. Poland, [1941] 1 K.B. 462

The plaintiff, who lived in a flat at 4, Chartfield Avenue, London, took out in January, 1939, at Lloyd's comprehensive insurance policy against fire, burglary and housebreaking. There was an attempted burglary at her flat during the summer and, being nervous concerning the safety of her jewellery, worth £500, she hid it, together with £100 in banknotes, under the coalite on the fire in her sitting-room on an occasion when she would be out all day. She wrapped the money and jewellery in a newspaper and mixed it with newspaper already there. Returning home late in the afternoon and feeling cold, the plaintiff lighted the fire and only remembered the hiding of the notes and valuables next morning when the notes and most of the jewellery were completely destroyed. She claimed under her policy which insured her "from loss or damage caused by fire." The underwriters did not allege negligence or that the loss was the result of her own act, but alleged that the loss was not covered because the fire was where it was intended to be and had not broken bounds, and although it was a loss which might be covered by an all risks policy, it was not a loss by fire within the meaning of the policy. It was claimed that there must be ignition where no ignition ought to be in order to create liability. Atkinson, J., applied three rules of construction. (1) Construction depends on the meaning of the words and not the intention of the parties; (2) the court has no right to imply terms into a written contract; (3) the policy must be construed most strongly against the underwriters who prepared it. *Held*—The fire came within the terms of the policy and the plaintiff was awarded £460 and costs.

617. Elliott v. Grey, [1960] 1 Q.B. 367

On February 7th, 1959, the appellant's car, which was parked outside his house in Belloc Avenue, South Shields, was run into by another motor car. This attracted the attention of the police and it appeared that the appellant's car had broken down on December 20th, 1958, and could not be driven, so he placed it outside his house and left it there until February 7th when the accident occurred. He had jacked up the car and removed the battery and, since he did not intend to drive the car until it was repaired, had terminated his insurance cover. On the very day, February 7th, he had turned his attention to the car and had unjacked it and done some work on it, although at the time in question the engine would still not work, nor had the appellant any intention of driving or removing it. He was charged with unlawfully using on the road a motor car without the statutory insurance cover. The South Shields justices convicted him and the matter came before the Queen's Bench Division by way of a case stated. *Held*—To "use a motor vehicle on the road" means to "have the use of a motor vehicle on the road," and, as the car could be moved, the appellant had the use of it, even if it could not be driven, and there might be a risk to third parties.

618. Monk v. Warbey and Others, [1935] 1 K.B. 75

Albert Warbey, the owner of a Morris car which was properly insured in accordance with the provisions of the Road Traffic Act, 1930, while he himself or members of his family were driving, was not covered if some other person were allowed to drive. He lent the car out of kindness of heart to Knowles, one of the defendants, in the expectation that the car would be driven by another defendant, Frank May. An accident occurred owing to the admitted negligence of Frank May, and Monk, who was injured, brought the action not only against Knowles and May, but also against Warbey. Warbey was clearly in breach of Sect. 35 of the Road Traffic Act, 1930. *Held*—A person damaged as a result of a breach of statute has a right to recover damages from the person who has broken the provisions of the statute, unless it can be established by looking at the whole of the Act that it was not the intention that he should have such a right. The statute was not designed to limit civil remedies and the plaintiff was entitled to damages on the grounds that (i) Warbey had committed a breach of a statutory duty; and (ii) the damage resulting to the plaintiff was not too remote.

619. Digby *v.* **General Accident Fire and Life Assurance Corporation,** [1943] A.C. 121

Under a motor policy taken out by Merle Oberon, the actress, the insurers agreed to indemnify her against claims by "any person", and the policy covered persons driving with her consent. Her car was involved in an accident, owing to her chauffeur's negligence, and she was injured. Miss Oberon then recovered damages against her chauffeur and the question of the payment of an indemnity to the chauffeur arose. *Held*—By the House of Lords—that an indemnity was payable because—

(*a*) the policy covered claims by "any person" thus including a claim by Miss Oberon herself;

(*b*) as the chauffeur was driving with Miss Oberon's consent he was covered against the risk of accident and could claim an indemnity from the insurers under the Road Traffic legislation then in force.

N.B. The relevant provision is now Sect. 148 (4), Road Traffic Act, 1972.

620. Tattersall *v.* **Drysdale,** [1935] 2 K.B. 174

A comprehensive motor policy was issued covering a specified vehicle and extending cover to the insured while driving other cars. The insured drove another vehicle after having sold the specified car. *Held*—That when he sold the specified vehicle the policy ceased to have effect.

621. Boss *v.* **Kingston,** [1963] 1 All E.R. 177

In this case the prosecution alleged that the defendant was guilty of driving an uninsured motor cycle. It appeared that the defendant had owned a Triumph motor-cycle and had taken out a policy which covered his legal liability to third parties while riding the Triumph and also purported to cover him while riding other motor-cycles not owned or hired by him. The policy in this case seemed to be an insurance of the defendant personally rather than of the Triumph motor-cycle, though it did require him to keep the Triumph in good condition and give the insurers access to it. The defendant sold the Triumph and while riding a motor-cycle belonging to a friend was prosecuted for using an uninsured vehicle. *Held*—As a matter of construction the insurance was effective only while the defendant retained the Triumph, because the conditions regarding maintenance and access could not be complied with after sale. Therefore the defendant was guilty of the offence with which he was charged.

622. D. H. R. Moody (Chemists) *v.* **Iron Trades Mutual Insurance Co.,** *The Times,* November 11th, 1970

A motor car which was lent by a member of Clacton-on-Sea Urban District Council to take French guests from Valence (with which Clacton was twinned) to Heathrow Airport was involved in an accident when it was being driven back by Mr. Ramsden, the Clerk to the Council. The car was covered by an insurance policy covering only use for "social, domestic and pleasure purposes and use for the business of the insured." The defendant insurance company repudiated liability on the ground that the car was being used otherwise than in accordance with the terms of the policy. *Held*—by Wrangham, J.—that at the material time the car was being used for "social purposes" within the terms of the policy. The activities of an individual could be divided into those which he pursued because he had to in order to earn a living, which would be business, and those which he pursued of his own free will, such as social or domestic pleasures. The activities of a local authority could also be so divided into those duties that they were compelled by statute or convention to carry out, and voluntary activities which might be, and probably were, of a social character. There was no reason why the council's activities in trying to arrange contact with Valence should not be regarded as social. Cars being used in the course of those activities were being used for a social purpose. There remained the defence argument that at the time of the accident the car was being used by Mr. Ramsden, the clerk to enable him to carry out his council duties, in other words for a business purpose. But the car had not been lent to Mr. Ramsden but to the local authority for it was the social duty of the local authority to convey their visitors to the airport. And the fact that the actual driver of a car was fulfilling his duty to his employer by driving it, did not prevent its use from being for a social purpose.

623. Stuart *v.* Freeman, [1903] 1 K.B. 47

The plaintiff had taken an assignment of a policy on another person's life. The policy was for a year, the premium being payable quarterly and the first of such premiums having been paid at the date of the policy. The policy provided that if at the time of the death of the assured any quarterly premium should be more than 30 days in arrear, the policy should be of no effect. The life assured died during the year—after one of the dates laid down for payment of a quarterly premium, but before the 30 days of grace had expired. The premium was paid by the plaintiff after the death of the assured but within the days of grace. The plaintiff now sued to recover the amount of the policy. *Held*—The policy was prevented from lapsing by the plaintiff's payment and he was entitled to recover.

624. James Morrison & Co. Ltd. *v.* Shaw, Savill and Albion Co. Ltd., [1916] 2 K.B. 783

The plaintiff shipped wool in the *Tokomaru* from New Zealand to London, the ship being empowered to stop at certain ports. The usual route was round Cape Horn to Montevideo or La Plata or Rio de Janeiro, and then to Madeira or Teneriffe and then direct to London. The defendants later accepted a consignment of frozen meat and when the ship reached Teneriffe, the master was instructed to land at Havre. The course from Teneriffe to London or Havre was the same for a considerable distance, after which the courses diverged. By deviating to Havre the voyage was lengthened by some 54 miles. In the event the ship was torpedoed and sunk some eight miles from Havre, and the plaintiffs claimed the value of the wool on the ground of deviation, the defendants relying on an exception clause releasing them of liability for acts of the King's enemies. *Held*—There was deviation but the ship owner could not prove that the ship would have been lost in the absence of deviation. Since the defendants had broken their contract of carriage, they had lost the benefit of the exception clause. It was held that, in determining what was an intermediate port, account must be taken of the size and class of ship, the nature of the voyage, the usual and customary course, the natural or usual ports of call, and the nature and position of the ports in question. Havre did not satisfy these criteria. Deviation is the same in contracts of insurance as in contracts of carriage by sea.

625. Slattery *v.* Mance, [1962] 1 Q.B. 676

The plaintiff brought an action claiming £4,500 under a Lloyd's policy for the loss by fire of his vessel, the *Treworval Light*. The defendant disclaimed liability on the ground that, although the vessel was lost by fire, the plaintiff wilfully caused or connived at the destruction of the vessel. The defendant argued that the onus of proof was on the plaintiff to prove that the fire was caused other than by his own act. Salmon, J., said in the course of his judgment: "On the law as it now stands, when a plaintiff claims for loss under a policy of marine insurance, asserting that the loss was caused by perils of the sea, the onus is on him to prove that the loss was accidental." In the case of fire the onus of proof is different and it is for the defendant to prove that, on the balance of probability, the plaintiff destroyed the ship.

626. Cleaver *v.* Mutual Reserve Fund Life Association, [1892] 1 Q.B. 147

James Maybrick insured his life for £2,000 with the defendants on October 3rd, 1888, and died on May 11th, 1889, being murdered by his wife, Florence Maybrick, who was convicted in August, 1889, although sentence of death was commuted to penal servitude for life. The policy moneys were to be payable to the wife, if living at the time of Maybrick's death. Before her trial Mrs. Maybrick assigned the policy by deed to the plaintiff, Cleaver. James Maybrick had appointed as his executors, Thomas and Michael Maybrick, also plaintiffs in the action. The insurers refused to pay the £2,000. *Held*—The contract of insurance was made between the husband on the one side and the defendants on the other. The husband died by the criminal act of the wife. Upon his death the right to sue went to his executors. The rule of public policy prevents the wife or anyone claiming through her from recovering and reaping the fruits of her crime. The executors were suing for the estate of the husband and would hold it as trustees for the estate, available for the deceased's creditors or his children (if any). Children are not shut out since they claim through the father and not the mother. Therefore the insurers must pay the money to T. and M. Maybrick as executors.

626a. *Gray v. Barr, Prudential Assurance Co. (Third Party)*, [1970] 2 All E.R. 702

Mr. Barr went to seek his wife at the house of Mr. Gray, her paramour, carrying a loaded shotgun to frighten him. Barr threatened Gray, there was a scuffle during which Barr fell and the gun went off accidentally killing Gray. Barr was tried and acquitted of murder and manslaughter. Gray's administrators brought an action against Barr for damages and Barr joined the Assurance Company in order to claim an indemnity from them under an accident insurance policy which he had taken out with them. *Held*—by Geoffrey Lane, J., on the matter of the insurance claim—on the grounds of public policy a person who is guilty of another's death by deliberate, intentional and unlawful violence or threats of violence, may not avail

himself of an insurance indemnity however unintentional the death itself
may be.

626b. *Re Giles,* [1971] 3 W.L.R. 640

A woman who had killed her husband pleaded not guilty to murder but
guilty to manslaughter on the ground of diminished responsibility. Her
plea was accepted and she was sent to Broadmoor. *Held*—by Pennycuick,
V.C.—that she could not benefit under her husband's will or intestacy.
The principle of public policy demands that a criminal should not benefit
from his crime. This rule is not dependent on the degree of moral culpability
in the criminal.

627. Beresford *v.* Royal Insurance Co. Ltd., [1938] A.C. 588

Major Rowlandson took out a policy on his life with the Royal Insurance
Co. in 1925. The policy provided that—

> If the life assured shall die by his own hand whether sane or insane within one
> year from the commencement of the insurance the policy shall be void as against
> any person claiming the amount hereby assured or any part thereof.

Major Rowlandson paid the premiums regularly until August 3rd, 1934. At
about 2.57 p.m. on that day he shot himself being in debt to the extent of
£60,000. It was found as a fact by the jury that Major Rowlandson was sane
at the time of his death. *Held*—by the House of Lords—that the condition in
the policy implied an undertaking by the insurance company to pay if the
assured died by his own hand sane or insane after the expiry of one year from
the commencement of the policy. However, it was contrary to public policy
that either a person who had committed a crime, or his personal representatives,
should be allowed to benefit from that crime. Therefore the policy was
unenforceable.

628. Trim Joint District School Board of Management *v.* Kelly, [1914] A.C. 667

Kelly was a dependant of an assistant master at an industrial school. Whilst
the master was engaged in the performance of his duties, two of the pupils
of the school attacked and killed him. The boys were unruly and badly
disposed towards the master. Kelly claimed compensation from the managers
of the school on the grounds that the assistant master met his death by accident
in the course of his employment. *Held*—by the Judicial Committee of the
Privy Council—that although the master was murdered, his death was nevertheless caused by an accident and, being in the course of his employment,
compensation was recoverable under the relevant industrial legislation.

629. Miller *v.* Law Accident Insurance Co., [1903] 1 K.B. 712

A cargo of cattle was insured from Liverpool to Buenos Aires, the risks
insured against including "arrests, restraints, and detainments of all princes
and people." The policy, however, also contained a warranty against "capture, seizure, or detention." When the cattle arrived at Buenos Aires, they were
found to be suffering from foot-and-mouth disease, and in pursuance of a
general government decree, the Argentine officials forbade the landing of the
cattle. The assured gave notice of abandonment and claimed under the policy
for total or partial loss. *Held*—The action of the Argentine Government
amounted to an exercise of force bringing the case within the word "restraint"
in the risk insured against. However, the warranty, being designed to exclude

the risk, removed the liability from the underwriters which they would otherwise have had and the plaintiff failed in his claim.

630. Leyland Shipping Co. Ltd. *v.* Norwich Fire Insurance Society Ltd., [1918] A.C. 350

A ship sailing from South America to Havre was torpedoed by a German
submarine, but, although badly damaged, was towed into Havre by tugs.
While there she alternately grounded and floated with the ebb and flow of
the tides so that she ultimately sank and became a total loss. The ship was
insured against perils of the sea but war risks were excepted. *Held*—The
proximate cause of the loss was the torpedoing. The exception clause applied
and the underwriters were not liable.

631. Hamilton, Fraser & Co. *v.* Pandorf & Co. (1877), 12 App. Cas. 518

Pandorf & Co. shipped a cargo of rice on conditions excepting the ship
owners from liability for "dangers and accidents of the seas." While the ship
was at sea, rats gnawed a hole in a pipe with the result that sea water entered
the ship and damaged the rice. Pandorf & Co. sued for damages; the appellants relied on the exception clause. *Held*—by the House of Lords—that there
was no negligence and the shipowners could claim the protection of the clause.
If the rats had gnawed the rice, this would have been a risk unconnected with
the sea but connected with the storage of rice whether on land or sea. Where
rats make a hole, or where one of the crew leaves a port-hole open, through
which the sea enters and injures the cargo, the sea is the immediate cause of
the mischief.

632. Verelst's Administratrix *v.* Motor Union Insurance Co. Ltd., [1925] 2 K.B. 137

The plaintiff was the administratrix of a lady who had been killed in a
motor accident in India. The policy of insurance covered the death of the
insured by an accident of the type in question but it contained the following
condition: "In case of any accident, injury, damage, or loss . . . the insured,
or the insured's representative for the time being, shall give notice . . . in
writing to the head office of the company of such accident, injury, damage, or
loss as soon as possible after it has come to knowledge of the insured, or of the
insured's representatives for the time being." The accident which killed the
insured took place on January 14th, 1923, and the plaintiff heard of the death
within a month afterwards but she only discovered the existence of the policy
in January, 1924. She then gave notice to the insurance company as soon as
possible, but the insurance company denied liability on the ground that notice
had not been given as soon as possible within the meaning of the condition in
the policy. The dispute was submitted to arbitration and the arbitrator
found for the plaintiff. On appeal it was *held* that, taking into account all the
circumstances, the plaintiff had given notice as soon as she possibly could and
the arbitrator's decision was right.

633. Cassel *v.* Lancashire & Yorkshire Accident Insurance Co. Ltd. (1885), 1 T.L.R. 495

The plaintiff had an accident while paddling a canoe but did not feel the
effects until some months later. He had an accident policy with the defendants
which required notice of an accident within 14 days together with medical
certificates describing the injuries received. He did not notify the accident

until he felt the effects and it was *held* that he was not entitled to recover because of the delay and non-compliance with the terms of the policy.

634. Provincial Insurance Co. *v.* Morgan and Foxon, [1933] A.C. 240

In a proposal form for insurance of a lorry against damage and third party claims, the proposal form asked the proposer to state the purposes in full for which the vehicle would be used, and the nature of the goods to be carried. His answers were: Delivery of Coal; and Coal; respectively. He agreed that the answers in the proposal should form the "basis" of the contract. The lorry did carry on one occasion both coal and timber, but it collided with a car while loaded with coal only. *Held*—The questions and answers were a mere description of the risk covered. The lorry was only carrying coal when the accident occurred and was, therefore, covered. The term "purposes in full" did not mean "exclusive purposes." The clause, being drafted by the insurers, was construed in favour of the insured, using the *contra proferentem* rule.

635. Elcock *v.* Thomson, [1949] 2 K.B. 755

In 1940 a mansion at Easthampstead Park, near Wokingham, was insured against fire. The value was agreed at £106,850. The mansion was damaged by fire in 1947 when it was found that the true value of the premises was £18,000 before the fire, and the actual value was £12,600 after the fire, i.e. the depreciation in value was 30 per cent. *Held*—In assessing the claim this percentage of depreciation should be applied to the agreed value and the insured was entitled to 30 per cent of £106,850, namely £32,055.

636. Rodoconachi *v.* Elliott (1874), L.R. 9 C.P. 518

In a transit of goods from Shanghai to London, part of the journey was by land through France, and the goods arrived in Paris in September, 1870, just when the Germans were surrounding the town. The goods were immobilised and could not be forwarded, and on October 7th, the goods being insured, the assured gave the insurers notice of abandonment and claimed for constructive total loss. The insurance included, *inter alia*, cover for restraint of princes. *Held*—This was a case of constructive total loss by restraint of princes and, as the assured had lost all control over his goods for an indefinite time, he had a right to abandon them and throw the risk on the underwriter. It was not a mere temporary retardation of the voyage, but a breaking up of the whole adventure.

637. Overseas Commodities Ltd. *v.* G. W. Style, [1958] 1 Lloyd's Rep. 546

Tinned goods were insured against all risks including the blowing of the tins and inherent vice or hidden defect. There was a warranty that all the tins should bear a code mark showing the date of manufacture. The tins suffered loss by blowing, rusting or leakage and the court *held* that the cause of loss came within the category of inherent vice or hidden defect. However, many of the tins did not bear the code mark required under the warranty and, although this was not material to the loss, the insurers were not liable.

638. Quebec Marine Insurance Co. *v.* Commercial Bank of Canada (1870), L.R. 3 P.C. 234

A ship was insured for a voyage partly on inland waters and partly by sea. When the policy was effected and at the beginning of the voyage, the ship had a cracked boiler which made her unfit for a voyage in salt water and, indeed, on entering salt water she had to put back to port for repairs. Shortly after setting off again she became stranded in a hurricane with a broken rudder and was lost. The insurers denied liability on the ground that the ship was unseaworthy at the beginning of the voyage. *Held*—by the Judicial Committee of the Privy Council—that it was immaterial that the ship had been repaired and the original defect had been remedied when the loss occurred. The ship was unseaworthy at the commencement of the insurance and this discharged the insurers from liability.

639. Thomas *v.* Tyne and Wear Steamship Freight Insurance Association, [1917] 1 K.B. 938

A ship, which was insured under a time policy, put to sea in an unseaworthy state. Her crew was inadequate; this the assured knew: the ship's hull was damaged; this the assured did not know. The ship was lost because of the defects in her hull. *Held*—In the case of a time policy, the assured cannot recover for loss caused by his own fault. Where a ship is sent to sea and is unseaworthy in two respects, one known to the assured and one unknown, the insurer is only protected if the loss arises from the former or known cause. In this case, therefore, the assured could recover.

640. Lees *v.* Motor Insurers Bureau, [1952] 2 All E.R. 511

By an agreement between the Ministry of Transport and the Motor Insurers Bureau, the bureau undertook to satisfy any judgment not satisfied within seven days in respect of "any liability which is required to be covered by a policy of insurance . . . under Part II of the Road Traffic Act, 1930." An employer had a policy which "excluded liability in respect of death arising out of and in the course of his employment of a person in the employment of the insured." One employee killed another by the negligent driving of a lorry, and the latter's widow obtained judgment against the lorry driver which was unsatisfied. She claimed on the Motor Insurers Bureau under the agreement. *Held*—The Road Traffic Act, 1930, did not require cover for liability of the type set out in the exclusion clause, and therefore the bureau was not liable.

641. Prudential Staff Union *v.* Hall, [1947] K.B. 685

The plaintiff in this case was a union of the employees of an insurance company. The employees concerned were agents and collectors and often held sums of money on behalf of the company. The union took out a policy with Lloyd's underwriters to cover loss by its members of such moneys by burglary and housebreaking. The policy described the union as "the assured" and under the provisions of the policy the underwriters agreed to pay the union in respect of losses occurring by reason of the perils mentioned above. The union received 3s. from each member in respect of the premium, and paid 2s. 6d. per member to the insurers. Claims were made at various times and were met by the insurers but on one occasion, when the union made a claim in respect of loss by burglary of moneys held by two of its members, one of the underwriters, Hall, refused to pay the claim, pleading that the union had no cause of action, having no insurable interest. *Held*—The union had no insurable interest in the moneys insured, since liability for losses of money was in the members themselves and not the union. Nor did such an interest arise out of the union's general concern for the welfare of its members. However, the union was entitled to recover the money because the underwriters had contracted to pay the union, and the union was in the position of trustee for the members concerned in respect of the money received.

N.B. The Life Assurance Act of 1774 did not render the contract void since, for the purposes of the policy, moneys were "goods" within that Act, and insurances on goods were excepted from it.

642. Castellain *v.* Preston (1883), 11 Q.B.D. 380

In March, 1878, the defendants insured their premises against fire and in July, 1878, they agreed to sell the premises for £3,100, took a deposit, and arranged for the contract to be completed on a day within two years to be named by them. A fire damaged the premises in August and the insurers paid the defendants £330, not knowing of the sale. The purchasers completed the sale in December, 1879, and paid the balance of the price to the defendants. The insurers claimed (*a*) a refund of the £330 on the ground that, because of the sale, the defendants had suffered no loss; and (*b*) the right to be subrogated to the rights of the defendants to the proceeds of the sale up to £330. *Held*—by the Court of Appeal—that the insurers be given judgment for £330. Brett, L.J., made the following points: (i) a contract of marine or fire insurance is a contract of indemnity and the assured shall be fully, but never more than fully, indemnified; (ii) as between the underwriter and the assured, the underwriter is entitled to the advantage of every right of the assured, whether in contract or tort, or any other right legal or equitable, by exercising or acquiring that by which the loss insured against can or has been diminished.

643. A. Tomlinson (Hauliers) Ltd. *v.* Hepburn, [1966] A.C. 451

The plaintiffs, who were carriers, were required by their contract with tobacco owners to "insure and keep insured with a full comprehensive cover against loss of goods in transit or otherwise." The plaintiffs insured the tobacco owners' goods with the defendant, who was an underwriter, the policy being a Lloyd's Goods in Transit Policy. The policy provided for insurance for the goods "in transit. . . . including loading and unloading" and also for "all risks of loss or damage however arising." The plaintiffs' vehicles carried tobacco to the owners' depot but arrived after working hours so that the lorries were left in the depot but not unloaded. The same evening the lorries and tobacco were stolen without negligence on the part of the plaintiffs. The plaintiffs claimed on the policy and the defence was that the goods were "off risk" because the transit had ended; that the policy covered the carriers in respect of their negligence, if any, but did not cover the owners' proprietary interest; that the carriers had no insurable interest outside of their own charges. *Held*—By the House of Lords—that as transit was defined as including loading and unloading, the goods were on risk until unloading was completed; that this was a policy on goods and was not solely concerned with the bailees' negligence; that the carriers had an insurable interest in the tobacco, the value of which was recoverable under the policy, though the bailees must account to the bailor for his share of the loss after deducting what was owing to them.

644. Macaura *v.* Northern Assurance Co. Ltd., [1925] A.C. 619

Macaura agreed to sell timber to a company for £42,000 which was paid for by allotting him 42,000 fully-paid shares in the company of £1 each. No other shares were issued. He also financed the company and was an unsecured creditor for £19,000, its other debts being trifling. He insured the timber against fire and on February 23rd, 1922, most of the timber was destroyed by fire. Macaura claimed under his policies, but he was *held* not to have an insurable interest. Macaura could only be insuring either as a creditor or as a shareholder of the company, and neither a simple creditor nor a shareholder has any insurable interest in a *particular* asset which the company holds.

645. North British & Mercantile Insurance Co. *v*. London, Liverpool & Globe Insurance Co. (1877), 5 Ch.D. 569

Wharfingers insured grain and seed stored with them against loss or damage by fire. The policy was subject to the following condition: "If at any time of any loss or damage by fire happening to any property hereby insured there be any other subsisting insurance or insurances, whether effected by the insured or by any other person, covering the same property, the company shall not be liable to pay or contribute more than its rateable proportion of such loss or damage." The grain and seed in question were also insured by the merchant who had an interest in it. The merchant's policy, however, also covered grain stored elsewhere. The policy contained a similar clause to the one set out above. While both policies were subsisting, a fire destroyed the grain stored with the wharfingers. The wharfingers were paid in full by their own insurers, and this action was brought by the insurers concerned to determine the liability of the insurers *inter se*. *Held*—The merchant's insurers were not liable to contribute. The condition as to double insurance only applied to a case where the same property was the subject matter of the contract and the interests were the same. Here the merchant's policy covered other goods in addition to those destroyed, and the merchant's interest was that of owners, while that of the wharfingers was that of bailee.

646. Darrell *v*. Tibbitts (1880), 5 Q.B.D. 560

The defendant leased certain premises, taking a covenant from the tenant to repair them if the premises should be damaged by gas. The defendant also insured the premises under a fire policy. The premises were damaged by an explosion of gas caused by the negligence of the local authority. The defendant obtained payment of £750 from the insurer; the tenant, who was obliged to repair and did so, recovered damages against the local authority. In this action the insurer sought to recover from the defendant the money paid under the policy. *Held*—Since the policy was a contract of indemnity, the insurer could recover the £750, otherwise the landlord would have received, in effect, £1,500 for damage amounting to £750.

647. Goole & Hull Steam Towing Co. *v*. Ocean Marine Insurance Co., [1928] 1 K.B. 589

The defendants were the insurers of the plaintiffs' ship against the usual marine risks. The steamer, which was valued at £4,000, was in collision with another vessel. The plaintiffs paid for the repair of the ship and then sued the owners of the other vessel. The action was settled by payment to the plaintiffs of £2,500, which sum represented half the actual damage. The plaintiffs now sued the insurers to recover the balance of the loss, i.e. £2,500, claiming that they were entitled to that sum in full since they had insured the ship for £4,000. *Held*—The defendants need only pay £1,500, as representing the difference between the value of the policy, £4,000, and the £2,500 which the plaintiffs had already recovered from the owners of the other vessel.

648. Phoenix Assurance Co. *v.* Spooner, [1905] 2 K.B. 753

The defendant took out a fire policy with the plaintiff company in respect of her buildings. While the policy was in force, the Plymouth Corporation served her with a notice to acquire the buildings under the Lands Clauses Consolidation Act, 1845. Before the corporation had taken any further steps under the notice, the buildings were destroyed by fire. The plaintiffs paid to the defendant the agreed sum representing the loss she had incurred. When the corporation actually came to take over the property, the price they were to pay was agreed between them and the defendant, and was reduced by the amount which the defendant had received from the insurance company, the corporation agreeing to indemnify the defendant against any claim which the insurance company might make against her. *Held*—The insurance contract was one of indemnity, and when the plaintiffs paid the agreed amount under the policy, they became entitled to all the rights of the defendant. These included the right to be paid by the corporation the full value of the property as it existed at the date of service of the notice to acquire. The defendant had no right to deprive the plaintiffs of that right by compromising with the corporation. Therefore the plaintiffs were entitled to recover from the defendant the amount paid to her under the policy.

N.B. Under the agreement with the corporation, the defendant would be able to claim an indemnity in respect of the money paid back to the insurers.

649. Morley *v.* Moore, [1936] 2 K.B. 359

Moore, a motorist, negligently damaged the car of Morley, another motorist, in a collision. Moore and Morley were both insured with companies who had a "knock for knock" agreement whereby Moore's insurer paid for Moore's damage and Morley's insurer paid for Morley's. Morley's insurer paid Morley £28 2s. 8d. The actual damage was £33 2s. 8d. but under the policy Morley was to bear the first £5 of any claim. Since the object of the "knock for knock" agreement was to obviate litigation, Morley's insurers strongly dissuaded him from pursuing action against Moore. However, Morley persisted and claimed £33 2s. 8d. Moore admitted liability but only for £5, since Morley had already received the balance under his insurance. *Held*—Morley could recover the full amount. Although his insurance company did not want him to sue, they could not prevent him from so doing. Nor could Moore refuse to pay the £28 2s. 8d. on the grounds that Morley's insurers had paid it. He had no rights to the benefits of Morley's insurance. Morley would be liable to refund the £28 2s. 8d. to the insurance company. They had said they did not desire this in the hope that he would not sue. If they chose to make Morley a gift of this sum, that was their affair. It in no way impaired his legal right to claim it from Moore.

CARRIAGE OF GOODS

650. Jackson *v.* Rogers (1683), 2 Show. 327

The plaintiff brought a parcel of goods to the defendant who was a common carrier of goods from London to Lymington. The defendant refused to carry the goods, though he had room for them. The plaintiff brought this action against the carrier, and Jeffries, C.J., *held* that the action was maintainable by common custom of England, in much the same way as an innkeeper is liable for refusing accommodation to a traveller.

651. Baxendale *v.* Eastern Counties Railway Co. (1858), 4 C.B. (N.S.) 63

The plaintiffs brought an action to recover alleged overcharges in respect of goods sent by the plaintiffs from London to Norwich and from Norwich to London by the defendants' railway. The main complaint of the plaintiffs was that where a number of parcels weighing less than 1 cwt. were addressed to one individual a lower rate was charged than if parcels of the same description were directed to different individuals. The plaintiffs sent parcels of less than 1 cwt. to different individuals and were charged the higher rate. They contended that the defendants, as common carriers, could not differentiate between customers in regard to charges, the defendants having a monopoly of railway services between London and Norwich. *Held*—The extra charges made were reasonable in the circumstances, because parcels addressed to different consignees caused more trouble to the defendants; and further there was no common law obligation on a carrier to charge equal rates of carriage to all his customers.

652. Edwards *v.* Sherratt (1801), 1 East 604

The defendant was a common carrier by water from Wolverhampton to Birmingham and then on to Radford. The plaintiff delivered corn to the defendant at Wolverhampton, asking him to take it to Birmingham, but not revealing to the defendant that the reason he wanted it taken away was because rioters had destroyed a corn mill at Wolverhampton and threatened the cargo. The rioters seized the cargo from the defendant 40 miles from Wolverhampton. The question of liability arose, and this depended on whether the defendant was a common carrier. *Held*—He was not, because he took the goods in circumstances where he might have refused them because of the riotous state of the area. The defendant, not being a common carrier, was not answerable for the loss of the corn.

653. Hales *v.* London & North Western Railway Co. (1863), 4 B. & S. 66

On Wednesday, August 7th, 1861, the defendants received a regalia from the plaintiff to be carried from London to Seaham Harbour, near Sunderland. The plaintiff had entered into a contract to supply it for a festival at Seaham Harbour on Saturday, August 10th. The ordinary practice of the defendants, where goods did not make a truck load, was to send the goods to Newcastle, and then deliver to Sunderland by private carrier who made the journey on Tuesdays and Thursdays. As the goods were not a truck load, they were sent to Newcastle, arriving there on Friday, August 9th. They could have been sent straight away to Sunderland by train, but instead the defendants held them over until Tuesday, August 13th, when the private carrier took the goods to Seaham, arriving on Wednesday, August 14th. The plaintiff was not informed of the defendants' method of delivery, nor did the plaintiff inform the defendants that the goods had to be at Seaham by August 10th. The plaintiff now sued for damages for loss of hire of the goods, and for his expenses in inquiring for them. *Held*—A carrier need not carry by the shortest route, if that is not his usual route, and the defendants were not liable merely for sending the goods to Newcastle. However, the delay at Newcastle was unreasonable, given the facilities available to the defendants, and they were liable to pay the plaintiff's expenses in inquiring for the goods, but not the loss of the hiring fee.

654. Harris v. Packwood (1810), 3 Taunt. 264

The defendants were common carriers. The plaintiffs sued because a consignment of silk, delivered to the plaintiffs in London, did not arrive at Coventry. There was no evidence as to how the silk was lost. The silk was valued at £126. The defence was that the carrier had given notice to all silk traders who used his waggon, including the plaintiff, that he would not be accountable for any package over the value of £20 unless the value was declared and insurance paid. The necessary insurance was not paid in this case. *Held*—The plaintiff could not recover since he had not paid the insurance, even though the price he agreed to pay for the carriage was, because of the superior value of the goods, higher than the ordinary charge made. Further, the carrier need not prove that the loss happened by way of an accident against which the law makes him an insurer, nor was he bound to show that he used reasonable care. Moreover, a carrier is entitled to make a higher charge for the greater risk attending the carriage of valuable goods, but the charge must be reasonable.

655. Nugent v. Smith (1876), 1 C.P.D. 423

The defendant was a common carrier by sea from London to Aberdeen and the plaintiff sent the defendant a mare to be carried to Aberdeen where it was to be hired. In the course of the voyage the ship ran into violent weather, the mare became frightened, and in struggling she was injured and died. Her death was partly due to her own struggles and partly due to the violence of the storm. There was no negligence on the part of the defendant's servants. The plaintiff sued for damages. *Held*—The defendant was not liable because the storm was a violent act of nature for which he was not responsible. "The Act of God is merely a short way of expressing the proposition that a common carrier is not liable for any accident as to which he can show that it is due to natural causes directly and exclusively, without human intervention, and that it could not have been prevented by any amount of foresight and pains and care reasonably to have been expected of him. In this case the defendant has made this out."

656. Heugh v. London & North Western Railway Co. (1870), L.R. 5 Ex. 51

The plaintiffs delivered to the defendants as carriers a bale of cotton to be carried from Manchester to London and to be delivered in London to the Southwark India Rubber Co. The consignees refused to accept the goods and the defendants took them back to their own premises and advised the plaintiffs of the circumstances. They told the plaintiffs that from then on the goods would be at the plaintiffs' risk and would be delivered to the person producing the advice note sent to the plaintiffs. One, Frederick Nurse, a former employee of the consignees, fraudulently obtained the advice note and presented it to the defendants who delivered the goods to him. The plaintiffs sued in conversion, regarding the carriers as liable for misdelivery. *Held*—Upon the goods being refused, the defendants' duty as a carrier was at an end and they became involuntary bailees. Since they had acted with reasonable care in the matter, they were not liable.

657. Skinner *v.* Upshaw (1702), 2 Ld. Raym. 752

The plaintiff sued the defendant, who was a common carrier, for the return of the plaintiff's goods handed over to the defendant for carriage. The defence was that the defendant had offered to deliver the goods to the plaintiff if the plaintiff would pay his charges. The plaintiff refused and the defendant retained the goods. *Held*—by Holt, C.J.—that a carrier may retain the goods for his hire. Verdict for the defendant.

658. Leesh River Tea Co. Ltd. *v.* British India S.N. Co. Ltd., [1966] 3 W.L.R. 642

Tea was shipped from Calcutta to Rotterdam under bills of lading which incorporated the Hague Rules. The ship was carrying other goods in the same hold as the tea and these goods were unloaded at an intermediate port. During the unloading stevedores stole the cover plate of a storm valve though the officers and crew of the ship were not negligent in their supervision of the stevedores. During the remainder of the voyage to Rotterdam sea-water entered the ship and damaged the tea. *Held*—The carriers were not liable because the damage was the result of "any other cause" and there was no fault on the part of the carrier's servants. The stevedores would normally have been the agents of the carrier and rendered him liable for their wrongful act but, in this case, they were acting outside their authority when they stole the storm-valve cover.

659. *The Annie Hay.* Coldwell-Horsfall *v.* West Country Yacht Charterers Ltd., [1968] 1 All E.R. 657

A motor launch, the *Annie Hay*, collided with another vessel, the *Rosewarne*, in Falmouth harbour. The plaintiff owned the *Annie Hay* and was, at the time of the collision, her master and navigator. It was admitted that the collision was caused largely by the negligence of the plaintiff and that he could limit his liability under the Merchant Shipping Acts to £188 (1,000 gold francs at the date of the hearing being assessed at about £24 per ton), although the actual claim against him was for £2,716, if the Act applied to an owner who was also master of the ship. *Held*—by Brandon, J.—that as a matter of construction of Sect. 3 (2) of the Merchant Shipping (Liability of Shipowners and Others) Act, 1958, the Act did apply to owner/masters and the plaintiff was entitled to limit his liability to £188. The case is of importance to owners of small boats who are often masters of their own vessels.

660. Mersey Docks & Harbour Board *v.* Hay, The Countess, [1923] A.C. 345

The steamship *Countess*, belonging to Hay & Sons, burst through the dock gates of a dock belonging to the appellant Board, and did damage to the dock to the extent of £10,014. The *Countess* fell into the Mersey and drifted up river causing more damage. The Board took the vessel into their possession because she was a danger to the port, and effected repairs at a cost of £1,048. The question of compensation arose, and the court decided that the Board was only entitled to share rateably in the limited statutory fund. The *Countess* was 558·83 tons, and the statutory amount of her liability at £8 per ton was £4,468 4s. 9d. under the Merchant Shipping Act, 1894. However, the appellants were entitled to £1,048 in addition for the repairs carried out.

661. S.S. Ardennes (Cargo Owner) *v.* S.S. Ardennes (Owners), [1951] 1 K.B. 55

A shipper in Cartagena, Spain, shipped three thousand cases of mandarines to London on November 22nd, 1947. He relied on the promise of the shipowner's agent that the ship would proceed direct to London and this led him to believe that the ship would arrive in London by November 30th. This was important for two reasons: (i) The import duty on the goods would go up on December 1st; (ii) The sooner they arrived, the better prices they would fetch. These facts were known to all persons handling these goods and the shipper had stressed the importance of their arrival by November 30th. The bill of lading contained a clause allowing the shipowner to proceed to the port of destination "by any route, and whether directly or indirectly to such port, and in so doing to carry the goods beyond their port of destination." The ship did not go direct to London but went first to Antwerp, arriving there on November 30th. She did not reach London until December 4th when the shipper had to pay the higher import duty and accept a lower price for the goods than he could have obtained earlier. The shipper claimed damages for breach of contract. The ship owner relied, *inter alia*, on the clause in the bill of lading and contended that evidence of any other contract was inadmissible. *Held*—The bill of lading was not in itself the contract between the shipowner and the shipper and evidence was admissible of the contract made before the bill was signed and containing a different term. The shipper had not waived his claim by taking delivery and paying the freight. He was, therefore, in the circumstances, entitled to damages representing the increased import duty, and also the extra amount which the oranges would have realised had they arrived in time to be sold in Covent Garden Market on December 2nd.

662. Watts, Watts & Co. Ltd. *v.* Mitsui & Co. Ltd., [1917] A.C. 227

In June, 1914, the charterers chartered a vessel from shipowners to go to Mariopol on the Sea of Azov to take on board a cargo of sulphate of ammonia and carry it to Japan. The charterparty excepted "arrests and restraints of princes." On August 4th, 1914, war broke out between Great Britain and Germany and the shipowners refused to provide a ship in accordance with the charterparty on the ground that, if they did so, it would be seized by the King's enemies. They feared that the Dardenelles might be closed and that if the ship arrived at Mariopol it would not be able to leave for Japan. As a result of the refusal to supply a ship, the charterers had to repudiate their contract with their sellers and pay them £4,500. The charterers brought an action against the shipowners for damages for breach of the charter. *Held*—The mere apprehension of seizure was not enough to justify the failure to supply the ship. A restraint of princes must be an existing fact. This does not mean that a ship must continue a useless voyage until physical force is actually used, but the reasonable apprehension of a prudent man and the futility of doing what will turn out to be useless may help to define the area of an existing restraint. Judgment was given for the charterers and the damages were the value of the cargo at the port of destination at the date on which it would have arrived, had a ship been supplied, less the price which would have been payable by the charterers to their sellers for the goods, together with the cost of insuring them against marine and war perils during the voyage.

663. Westminster Bank Ltd. *v.* Imperial Airways Ltd., [1936] 2 All E.R. 890

The plaintiffs delivered to the defendants bar gold valued at £9,138 to be transported from London to Paris. The gold was placed in a strong room at Croydon airport, but next day the room was found open and the gold was stolen. The consignment note had on the back the following statement—

Carriage by Air: The general conditions of carriage of goods are applicable to both internal and international carriage. These general conditions are based upon the Convention of Warsaw of October 12, 1929, in so far as concerns international carriage within the meaning of the said convention.

Westminster Bank sought to recover the value of the gold and many points were raised for decision. It was *held*—

(i) The carriage had commenced (Art. 18 of the Convention);

(ii) The statement on the consignment note should have been that the carriage is *subject to* the rules relating to liability established by this Convention. To say that the conditions were *based upon* the convention is not enough. The requirement of the Act is a simple, clear statement and there is a statutory duty to incorporate it without variation.

(iii) Although the Bank had declared the value of the gold at £9,000 and had paid a higher rate than for other types of merchandise, it was a rate appropriate to gold bars and the valuation was needed to calculate the *ad valorem* rate. The payment of this higher rate was not, however, the payment of a supplementary sum since this should be something over and above the normal rate *for that type of merchandise*. If, therefore, the statement on the consignment note had complied with the Act, the liability of Imperial Airways would have been subject to the limits of the Convention.

663a. Samuel Montague and Co. Ltd. v. Swiss Air Transport Co. Ltd., [1966] 1 All E.R. 814

In this case the Court of Appeal *held* that the insertion after the words required by Art. 8 (9) of the additional words "unless such carriage is not 'international carriage' as defined by the Convention" did not contravene the provisions of Art. 9, since the parties to a contract of carriage by air must be deemed to know what constitutes "international carriage" under the Convention.

SURETYSHIP

664. Sutton & Co. *v.* Grey, [1894] 1 Q.B. 285

Sutton & Co., who were stockbrokers, made an agreement with the defendant, Grey, under which Grey would have half the commission earned by Sutton & Co. from clients whom Grey introduced. Grey agreed to pay to Sutton & Co. half of any loss sustained by them as a result of their dealings with clients introduced by Grey. *Held*—The contract was not one of guarantee, because of Grey's interest in half the commission, though it was an indemnity.

665. Blay *v.* Pollard and Morris, [1930] 1 K.B. 628

Morris signed an agreement for the dissolution of a partnership between himself and Pollard. The agreement contained a term whereby Morris agreed to indemnify Pollard against certain partnership liabilities. There had been a previous oral agreement which made no mention of the indemnity. Morris read the written document but was not versed in the ways of business and did not truly understand it. However, he did sign it. He now sought to avoid the agreement on the grounds of mistake. *Held*—The agreement was binding upon him because he was mistaken as to the effect of the agreement, not as to its nature.

666. Charterbridge Corporation Ltd. *v.* Lloyds Bank Ltd., [1969] 2 All E.R. 1185

A property developer by the name of Pomeroy owned several companies through which various developments were carried out. These companies formed a group in that each one was owned by Pomeroy. The main company in the group, P. Ltd., was not the holding company of the other companies in the group but did co-ordinate their activities providing, amongst other things, finance and administration services. One of the companies in the group, Pomeroy Developments (Castleford) Ltd., held a long building lease of a piece of land at Castleford and this company gave a guarantee to Lloyds Bank in respect of a large overdraft owed to the bank by P. Ltd., the guarantee being secured by giving to the bank a first legal charge on the land at Castleford. The first paragraph of the objects clause of the memorandum of Pomeroy Developments (Castleford) Ltd., gave *express* power to enter into guarantees of obligations incurred by anyone who had an undertaking in which Pomeroy Developments (Castleford) Ltd., was concerned or interested.

The Charterbridge Corporation, which was not within the group, had entered into an agreement to buy the land at Castleford from Pomeroy Developments (Castleford) Ltd. but did not wish to take the land subject to the charge in favour of Lloyds Bank and now sought to show that it was *ultra vires* and void. Charterbridge relied in the main on the decision in *Re Lee Behrens & Co. Ltd.*, [1932] 2 Ch. 46, contending that the guarantee, and therefore the charge securing it, was *ultra vires* unless created for the benefit of Pomeroy Developments (Castleford) Ltd. and for the purposes of its business. Since the guarantee was given for the benefit of P. Ltd. and the group of companies as a whole, the interests of Pomeroy Developments (Castleford) Ltd. were not the primary consideration. In addition these facts were known to the bank and therefore the guarantee and charge were void. *Held*—by Pennycuick, J.—that in considering whether the exercise of an *express* power in the memorandum of a company is *ultra vires* it is irrelevant to ask whether it is for the benefit of and to promote the prosperity of the company. Where a company is carrying out the purposes expressed in its memorandum and acts within the scope of an express power the act is *intra vires*. (*Re Lee Behrens & Co. Ltd.*, [1932] 2 Ch. 46, distinguished.) However, if that view of the law was wrong the guarantee and charge were in any case valid because they were clearly made for the benefit of Pomeroy Developments (Castleford) Ltd. It would have been disastrous for that company if P. Ltd. had collapsed. Regarding benefit to the company the judge said—"The proper test, I think . . . must be whether an intelligent and honest man in the position of a director of the company concerned, could, in the whole of the existing circumstances, have reasonably believed that the transactions were for the benefit of the company."

N.B. Pennycuick, J., gave his judgment before the decision of the Court of Appeal in *Introductions Ltd.* v. *National Provincial Bank*, 1969.[124] The decision of the Court of Appeal in that case says in effect that an exercise of an express power in the memorandum must be for the purposes of the company's *own business* and not for other purposes.

667. Phillips *v.* Foxall (1872), L.R. 7 Q.B. 666

On June 8th, 1869, the defendant guaranteed to be answerable for any loss not exceeding £50 which the plaintiff, who was a tea merchant, might sustain through any breach of duty by one, Smith, who was her van driver and collector of money. Smith did embezzle certain sums of money and the plaintiff now sued upon the guarantee. Evidence showed that, after the giving of the guarantee by the defendant and before November 12th, 1869, Smith embezzled £57 and that the plaintiff became aware of this on or about November 20th, 1869. Without informing the defendant, the plaintiff agreed with Smith that he should continue in her employ and should pay off the £57 at the rate of £3 per month. Smith continued in the plaintiff's service until April 4th, 1871, and paid off during that time £48 towards the £57 he owed the plaintiff. However, he did embezzle further sums of money after November 20th, 1869, the defendant still guaranteeing Smith from that date until April 4th, 1871, without knowledge of Smith's dishonesty. In respect of the sums received and embezzled by Smith before November 12th, 1869, the defendant had paid into court the sum of £10 which was sufficient to cover the loss to the plaintiff up to that time. With regard to the balance of the plaintiff's claim, the defendant pleaded the non-disclosure of Smith's dishonesty. *Held*—The plaintiff's claim failed. The defendant was discharged from liability in respect of the loss caused to the plaintiff by the dishonesty of Smith after November 20th, 1869. The plaintiff should have told the defendant that she had condoned Smith's dishonesty and thus given the defendant a chance to revoke his guarantee if he wished.

668. Tate *v.* Crewdson, [1938] Ch. 869

Lloyds Bank lent £25,000 to Tate and Crewdson, and Tate was also a surety for the whole amount of the loan. The borrowers and the plaintiff as surety agreed jointly and severally to repay the loan on demand and interest meanwhile half-yearly. The borrowers later made a supplementary agreement between themselves that the money should be deemed lent one-half to each of them, and that each should be liable to pay his half and the interest on it. The agreement further provided that neither the plaintiff nor the defendant should be at liberty to compel the other to repay his half for ten years from the date of the agreement so long as the interest owing thereon should be paid within 30 days of its becoming due. The defendant failed on three occasions to pay the half-year's interest within 30 days and the plaintiff asked the court for an order that if he, Tate, paid off his half of the principal, the defendant be required to do so as well. At the time of the issue of the writ there was no interest payable by the defendant which was more than thirty days overdue. The following defences were raised—

(i) Neither party could compel the other to pay unless interest was in arrear for more than thirty days;
(ii) The plaintiff had no right to compel the defendant to pay a debt to another (the Bank) because there was no demand from the Bank for it.

Held—(i) The defendant's non-payment on three occasions brought the period of ten years in the agreement to an end. (ii) The plaintiff was a person entitled to an indemnity and such a person may enforce his right whether any demand has or has not been made on the person whose debt he has guaranteed. Moreover it did not matter that Tate had not paid the money to the bank.

669. Fisher v. Fallows (1804), 5 Esp. 171

The plaintiff became bail for the defendant thus guaranteeing that he would be present at his trial. The plaintiff incurred expense in sending for the defendant in order to ensure that he was present and now sued for an indemnity. *Held*—The action succeeded. Should a surety sustain damage other than the principal and interest which he has agreed to pay under the guarantee, then he is entitled to recover such damage from the person guaranteed.

670. In re Snowdon, Ex parte Snowdon (1881), 17 Ch.D. 44

In December, 1876, T. Snowdon, the appellant, and J. Hall executed a bond whereby they became jointly and severally liable to the National Provincial Bank as sureties for R. Hall. The bond contained a provision that the sureties should not be called upon to pay more than a principal sum of £1,000 plus interest, commission and other charges. In June, 1879, R. Hall became bankrupt and there was due to the bank the principal sum of £1,000 plus some interest. J. Hall, on application by the Bank, paid them £541 2s. 1d., being half the principal and half the interest. T. Snowdon refused to pay J. Hall half the amount he had paid to the bank and J. Hall presented a bankruptcy petition against T. Snowdon, alleging an unpaid debt of £270 11s. 0½d. Snowdon opposed the petition on the ground that the petitioner as surety could only recover against his co-surety the excess paid by him beyond his share of the loan. Nevertheless an adjudication order was eventually made against T. Snowdon. From the making of this order T. Snowdon appealed. There was no evidence to show that the bank had called upon Snowdon to pay his share of the debt and interest. *Held*—by the Court of Appeal—that there could be no bankruptcy. T. Snowdon did not owe the money to J. Hall because a surety can only sue his co-surety for contribution if he has paid the whole of the principal debt, or a part in satisfaction of the whole debt, or more than his share of the principal debt.

671. Steel v. Dixon (1881), 17 Ch.D. 825

In October, 1878, T. A. Steel and W. Chater, plaintiffs, and G. W. Dixon and F. Gurney, defendants, signed a joint and several promissory note for £800 as the sureties of one, Robinson, to a bank. The principal debtor defaulted and the four sureties had to pay £200 each on the note. Before Dixon and Gurney signed the note, Robinson had promised to give them security, and on February 20th, 1879, Robinson executed a deed assigning to Dixon and Gurney a leasehold house and the furniture in it. The affairs of Robinson were put into the hands of a trustee and the defendants realised the property being ultimately left with a balance of £400 after clearing their own payments and expenses. The plaintiffs claimed to participate in the benefit of the security. *Held*—A surety who has obtained a security from the principal debtor is bound to bring into hotchpot for the benefit of his co-sureties any sum he obtains from that source even though he agreed to become a surety only because he was to have that security, and even though the co-sureties were ignorant of the agreement for a security when they entered into the contract of suretyship.

N.B. The rule as to hotchpot works as follows. Suppose A guarantees three-quarters of a debt of £100 and B guarantees one-quarter. If B takes a counter-security from the principal debtor which when sold realises £50, then this £50 is available to A and B in proportion to their liabilities and A is entitled to £37·50 and B to £12·50.

672. Cooper *v.* National Provincial Bank Ltd., [1946] K.B. 1

The plaintiff was a customer of the defendant bank and gave two guarantees in respect of a Mrs. Rolf who was also a customer of the bank. The plaintiff brought this action to have the guarantees set aside because when he made the contract the bank failed to disclose (1) that Mrs. Rolf's husband was an undischarged bankrupt; (2) that he had his wife's authority to draw on her account; (3) that the account was irregularly operated in that cheques had been drawn and then orders had been given not to pay them. The bank had disclosed that the account was overdrawn. The bank counter-claimed for £1,386 2s. 7d. being the sum due under the two guarantees and suggested that they had no obligation in law to disclose the matters mentioned above. *Held*—The plaintiff failed and the bank succeeded. A person giving a guarantee to a bank is not entitled to disclosure without inquiry of all the circumstances of the dealings between the principal debtor and the bank. Such matters may very well be material but need not be disclosed voluntarily as the contract is not *uberrimae fidei* as is the case with contracts of insurance.

673. Ellesmere Brewery Co. *v.* Cooper, [1896] 1 Q.B. 75

This action was against Cooper and four other defendants who had signed a fidelity bond as sureties for Cooper, the latter being an agent and traveller for the plaintiffs. The bond provided that the five defendants were jointly and severally liable to the plaintiffs in the sum of £150 in total and that if Cooper duly accounted for all moneys received by him for the plaintiffs, and otherwise performed his duties as agent, the bond should be void. Further the liability of Nunnerley and Emberton, two of the defendants, should be limited to £50 each and that of Pay and Bromfield, two other of the defendants, to £25 each. The effect of the bond as drawn up was that the principal and the sureties were jointly and severally liable in the sum of £150 but that liability could not be enforced against any of the sureties beyond the limit specified by each of them. Nunnerley was the last to sign and he signed as follows: "Walter Nunnerley, twenty-five pounds only." The witness to the execution of each of the signatures was a Mr. Bruce, the plaintiffs' manager. There was no evidence that Nunnerley tried to limit his liability by bad faith. The probability was that Cooper had stated erroneously that Nunnerley would be surety for £50, whereas Nunnerley only intended to be surety for £25. Cooper received £48 for his employers, the brewery, and failed to account for it. The question was whether the other sureties were liable at all in view of the limitation put in by Nunnerley. *Held*—The addition of the words by Nunnerley reducing the amount of his liability was a material alteration and the bond was void against all the defendants, including himself, with the exception of Cooper against whom it was enforceable.

674. National Bank of Nigeria Ltd. *v.* Awolesi, [1965] 2 Lloyd's Rep. 389

The bank allowed a man named Taiwo to overdraw his account at its Shagamu branch to a sum of £10,096 16s. 9d. T's uncle Awolesi agreed, "in consideration of the bank continuing the existing account," to guarantee T's debt to the amount of £10,500. The bank opened a new account (No. 2 account) for T and this was done without the knowledge or consent of A. T paid considerable sums of money into the No. 2 account but eventually he was in credit on that account only to the extent of £2 19s. 4d. The bank then tried to enforce the guarantee in respect of the money owed by T. *Held*— The action failed because A was discharged by the alteration of the terms of the principal debt to which he had not assented. By opening a No. 2 account the bank had made it possible for T to make payments into the bank without releasing A from his liability under the guarantee.

675. Smith *v.* Wood, [1929] 1 Ch. 14

The defendant guaranteed an overdraft of £5,000 which was granted by the Manchester and County Bank to Smith Bros. (Burnley) Ltd., who were builders. The bank had already lent £34,000 to the company and required an independent surety before they would advance the £5,000. Wood agreed to give the guarantee, and the plaintiffs, twelve members of the Smith family, deposited with the defendant the title deeds to certain property and also certain insurance policies to secure payment to the defendant of the £5,000 should he have to pay that sum to the bank. A memorandum charging the deeds and policies was entered into by them. One of the depositors, Mrs. Caroline Smith, was allowed by the defendant to take back the title deeds she had deposited in order to raise money to fit out her son who was going to South Africa. The company went into liquidation and the bank called on the defendant to fulfil his guarantee. He announced his intention of realising the deposited securities other than the deeds already released, and the plaintiffs brought this action claiming a declaration that the securities deposited by them had been released from liability since Mrs. Caroline Smith's deeds had been released. *Held*—The plaintiffs had not agreed to the release of Mrs. Caroline Smith's security and were therefore relieved of all liability under the memorandum of charge.

676. Bradford Old Bank *v.* Sutcliffe, [1918] 2 K.B. 833

In 1894 the plaintiffs agreed to grant a company, Samuel Sutcliffe & Sons, Ltd., a fixed loan of £3,600 and to allow an overdraft of £2,500. The company agreed to deposit with the bank debentures worth £6,100 and the directors gave a guarantee to protect the bank against any loss which might arise on realisation of the debentures, and to pay on demand all sums owing by the company not exceeding £6,100. In 1898 Frank Sutcliffe was found insane and the plaintiffs had notice of this in 1899. The company continued to bank with the plaintiffs until 1907 when the plaintiffs amalgamated with another bank and took the name of the United Counties Bank. The new company bought all the debts of the Bradford Old Bank and the benefit of all its securities and guarantees. The debt for £6,100 continued to be registered in the name of the plaintiffs. In 1912 the plaintiffs demanded payment from the company of the amount owing and started an action to enforce the debentures, realising some money by this means. In 1915 the plaintiffs commenced an action on the guarantee against the defendant as the committee of Frank Sutcliffe who was one of the guarantors for the balance. The following defences were raised amongst others—

(i) The amalgamation of the plaintiffs with the new bank had discharged the surety. *Held*—It had not. In the case of amalgamation, a transfer of an *existing and ascertained* debt does not discharge the surety.

(ii) The plaintiffs' claim was barred by the Statute of Limitations. *Held*—It was not because no cause of action arose against the surety until a demand had been made, and no demand was made by the plaintiffs until 1912.

(iii) The lunacy of Frank Sutcliffe had terminated his liability. *Held*—Where there is a continuing guarantee of an overdraft, notice to the bank of the fact of the guarantor's lunacy determines his liability for sums becoming due after, although not for sums accrued due before, the date of such notice.

ARBITRATION

677. Baker *v.* Yorkshire Fire and Life Assurance Co., [1892] 1 Q.B. 144

Baker brought an action to recover money alleged to be due under a fire policy made with the defendants. The policy contained a condition that any differences arising between the company and the assured under the policy as to the amount of loss and so on should be referred to arbitration. The defendants had obtained an order staying proceedings under Sect. 4 of the Arbitration Act, 1889 (since repealed), and the plaintiff appealed, alleging that he was not bound by the conditions because he had not signed the policy. *Held*—It was not necessary that there should be a written submission signed by the parties and the order staying the proceedings was rightly made. By bringing the action the assured recognised the policy and had affirmed it with all its terms. He was therefore bound by the arbitration clause.

678. Re Hopper (1867), L.R. 2 Q.B. 367

By an agreement for a lease it was provided that, if the premises leased should be sold during the term, the tenant, a Mr. Wrightson, should give up the premises, and Wrightson and John Hopper (the landlord) should each appoint a valuer to estimate the compensation to be paid to Wrightson, and, if the valuers disagreed, they were given power to appoint an umpire whose decision was to be final. The premises were sold during the term, and Wrightson gave them up and arbitrators were appointed. The arbitrators named an umpire and several meetings were held, witnesses were called, and attorneys attended. After the last meeting Wrightson, who was an innkeeper, invited the two arbitrators, the umpire and his own attorney to dinner at his inn. They all dined together but in the absence of Hopper or his representatives. Matters relating to the arbitration were mentioned, but in a joking manner, the umpire eventually becoming completely intoxicated. An award favourable to Wrightson was made and this action was brought to set it aside, the defence being that, *inter alia*, this was a mere valuation over which the court had no jurisdiction.

Held—

(i) It was an arbitration and the court had jurisdiction.

(ii) Although the conduct of the umpire was very objectionable, the court would not set aside the award as there was nothing to show that Wrightson had intended to corrupt or influence the umpire, or that there was such corruption or influence.

679. Re Carus-Wilson and Greene (1886), 18 Q.B.D. 7

By the conditions of sale of certain land sold by the Rev. W. Carus-Wilson to B. B. Greene, the timber on the land was to be taken by the purchaser at a valuation. It was provided that the vendor and purchaser should each appoint a valuer, and that the valuers "should appoint an umpire who should make the valuation in the event of their disagreement." The appointments were made and, as the valuers could not agree, the umpire made the valuation. In this action, the Rev. W. Carus-Wilson asked the court to set aside the valuation of the umpire claiming that, since it was in the nature of an arbitration, the court had jurisdiction. *Held*—In the circumstances the umpire was not an arbitrator and his valuation was not in the nature of an arbitration award. The court had no power to set it aside.

680. The Sylph (1867), L.R. 2 A. & E. 24

A marine diver, Ellis Jevons, while engaged in diving in the Mersey, was caught and injured by the paddle wheel of the ferry boat, *Sylph*. His action against the owners of the *Sylph* was, by agreement of the parties, referred to arbitration. The arbitrator awarded Jevons £410, but the defendants never paid this sum. Jevons now instituted an action *in rem* against the ship and the defence was that the petition should be dismissed because Jevons, by agreeing to arbitration, abandoned his right to institute any suit or bring any action upon the same subject in any court. *Held*—An arbitration agreement could not debar a person from bringing an action *in rem* and Jevons could obtain his damages by bringing an action against the ship in the Admiralty Court.

681. Radford v. Hair, [1971] 2 W.L.R. 1101

The plaintiff had been in partnership with the defendants as surveyors and estate agents under a deed which contained an arbitration clause. The partnership was dissolved and the plaintiff sued in the ordinary courts for accounts and other relief. The defendants alleged professional misconduct by the plaintiff in relation to the partnership including misrepresentation as to his interest in a company which was a client. The defendants asked for a stay of proceedings in view of the arbitration clause. *Held*—by Pennycuick, V.C.— a stay would not be granted. The allegations of the defendants were tantamount to charges of fraud and the plaintiff was entitled to have them heard by the Court.

682. Tritonia Shipping Inc. v. South Nelson Forest Products Corpn., [1966] 1 Lloyd's Rep. 114

A ship called the *Tanais* was chartered for a voyage between Canada and Italy. A clause in the charterparty provided for disputes to be settled by arbitration in London. A dispute arose and the owners of the *Tanais* asked the charterers to agree on an arbitrator but the charterers would not concur in an appointment. *Held*—Arbitration was the proper method of settling the dispute and the court would appoint an arbitrator.

683. Stonehewer v. Farrar (1845), 6 Q.B. 730

The plaintiff, Martha Stonehewer, conducted a bleaching and dyeing business and the defendant polluted the water supply obtained from an adjacent stream by discharging into the stream quantities of lime. The dispute was submitted to arbitration and the arbitrator said the defendant must filter the effluent from his premises "by the ordinary and most approved process of filtering." The action was brought to set aside the award on the grounds of uncertainty. *Held*—The description of the action the defendant must take referred only to the "ordinary and most approved process." It was, therefore, uncertain and the award was bad and unenforceable.

684. Ames *v.* **Milward** (1818), 8 Taunt. 637

The plaintiffs were distillers at Birmingham and the defendant was a maltster at the same place. The defendant had dealings with one, William Bate, in 1815 and 1816, supplying him with quantities of malt on credit and taking a warrant of attorney by way of security. The plaintiffs inquired through their traveller as to Bate's creditworthiness, and the defendant said, "He pays me very well," and asserted that the plaintiffs could trust Bate with malt. Actually Bate owed the defendant money which was not in fact paid, and the defendant subjected Bate's goods to execution, although the execution was set aside because of a previous act of bankruptcy. The plaintiffs lost money by supplying Bate with goods on credit and the case came to arbitration. The arbitrator acquitted the defendant of collusion with Bate, and of fraud at the time of the misrepresentation, but nevertheless felt compelled by decided cases to award £50 18s. od. in favour of the plaintiffs. *Held*—The award should be set aside. Park, J., said in judgment: "The conclusion to which the arbitrator has come is quite absurd. He says, I think he is innocent, and then awards against him."

685. Re Green & Co. and Balfour, Williamson & Co. (1890), 63 L.T. 97

Green & Co. agreed to buy from Balfour, Williamson & Co. 1,000 cases of tinned salmon at 32s. per case, quality guaranteed good. The contract provided that disputes as to quality should be referred to arbitration. Green & Co. objected that certain of the salmon tendered was not equal to contract quality and proposed arbitration. Both sides appointed arbitrators who made the following award—"That the buyers accept the salmon and that the sellers make an allowance to the buyers of 1s. 6d. per case." This action was brought to have the award set aside and the matter referred back to the arbitrators because they had exceeded their jurisdiction, had attempted to deal with the right of the buyers to reject the goods, and had not confined themselves to matters of quality only. *Held*—The arbitrators had exceeded their authority and the award was bad. The matter must be referred back to them.

686. Randall *v.* **Randall** (1805), 7 East 81

Arbitrators were required by the parties to determine by May 12th "all actions and controversies, etc. depending between them; and also of and concerning the value to be put on the hop-poles and potatoes in certain land and the workmanship done thereto and taxes and rates paid in respect thereof by the defendant; and also concerning the rent to be paid annually by the plaintiff to the defendant for the land, together with costs, etc." The arbitrators found the value of the hop-poles and potatoes and the other items, but they made no award concerning the rent. *Held*—Upon a reference of all actions and controversies, and also two distinct matters of difference, if the arbitrator omits to decide one of such distinct matters, that vitiates the whole award. Le Blanc, J., said: "The contract of the parties is in effect this; one says that he will submit to the arbitrators to ascertain what he is to pay for the hop-poles etc. upon condition that it shall also be referred to them to decide what rent is to be paid for certain land. He may fairly have said that unless both those matters of reference were referred, he would not refer either of them singly. If then the arbitrators omit to decide one of them, the condition fails on which the reference was agreed to."

687. Re Duke of Beaufort and the Swansea Harbour Trustees (1860), 29 L.J.C.P. 241

The trustees of Swansea harbour required certain land belonging to the Duke of Beaufort and served him with the required notices of their intention to take it under compulsory purchase. The Duke gave notice of his desire to settle the amount of compensation payable by arbitration under the Lands Clauses Consolidation Act, 1845. The Duke claimed £7,046 5s. od. for the land taken and £1,424 for severance damage, i.e. the depreciation to his remaining land by the loss of this piece. The arbitrator awarded £5,627 for the purchase of the land without specifically referring in his award to severance damage. The Duke now sought to set the award aside as not dealing with all matters forming the subject of the reference. *Held*—The award was final and good, and the arbitrator by his silence had negatived any right to compensation for severance damage. The award must be read as having been made on all matters of difference. The court assumes that the award was made on all matters submitted to the arbitrator unless it appears on the face of it that it was not so made.

688. Tomlin v. Mayor Fordwich (1836), 5 Ad. & E. 147

The defendant agreed to grant and the plaintiff agreed to take a lease for a specified term of premises belonging to the defendant and covenanted that all questions between them should be submitted to an arbitrator, that they would perform his award, the penalty on default being £500 as liquidated damages. The arbitrator awarded that the defendant should, within a time named, put the premises in good and tenantable repair to the satisfaction of one, James Moyes; and on a later day named execute a lease to the plaintiff containing a covenant by the plaintiff to keep in repair, and that the plaintiff should accept a lease on those terms and execute a counterpart. The plaintiff claimed £500 on the grounds that the defendant had not put the premises in good and tenantable repair to the satisfaction of Moyes; nor had the defendant executed a lease. *Held*—The award was bad as to the delegation to Moyes and that part was not separable from the rest of the award. The award was not final. It ordered that repairs be performed not in a specified way, but to the satisfaction of a third party. This is delegation of the power of the arbitrators and therefore bad. Lord Denman, C.J., said, "We cannot detach the part in question. I always find difficulty in separating the good part of an award from the bad. The arbitrator probably frames one part with a view to the other; and each may be varied by the view which he takes of the whole. But here the award is clearly bad."

689. Lewis v. Rossiter (1875), 44 L.J. Ex. 136

A claim made by the plaintiff against the defendant for breaches of covenant to repair a mill and premises, leased by the plaintiff to the defendant, was submitted to arbitration. The arbitrator awarded damages to be paid by the defendant to the plaintiff for failure to keep the mill in repair as agreed. The arbitrator also ordered that the defendant should forthwith repair the weir and the eastern bank of the river, on the banks of which the mill stood, so that water would be diverted to the mill in the way it had been when the lease was granted. An attempt was made to set aside the award because the land on the eastern bank of the river was not the land of the plaintiff or the defendant, and the defendant had no right to go on it to effect repairs. *Held*—The first part of the award was good but the second part was bad, since an arbitrator had no power to order a trespass. However the first part of the award was severable and enforceable.

690. **Sutherland & Co.** *v.* **Hannevig Bros. Ltd.,** [1921] 1 K.B. 336

By a charterparty made between Sutherland & Co. and the owners, the latter chartered the *S.S. Steady* to Sutherland & Co. who re-chartered it to Hannevig Bros. Disputes arose at the end of the charter period as to who should make certain payments. The owners claimed against Sutherland & Co. who in turn claimed against Hannevig Bros. The matter was submitted to arbitration. In the arbitration between Sutherlands and Hannevigs, the arbitrator awarded that Hannevigs should pay certain sums and then went on to order that the costs of the arbitration between Sutherlands and Hannevigs and also the costs of the arbitration between Sutherlands and the owners be paid by Hannevig Bros. His award was not clear as to the extent of the costs payable in the latter arbitration and Sutherlands wrote to the arbitrator asking him to define the nature of the costs they could claim. The arbitrator admitted that he had made an error in his award of costs and altered his award so as to make it clear and explicit that Sutherland & Co. were to have all the costs of their arbitration with the owners. Hannevig Bros. refused to pay costs under the amended award and asked that it be set aside. *Held*—The original award was in the language intended by the arbitrator and did not contain words which he had meant to omit or omit words which he had intended to insert. The fact was that he had failed to convey his proper meaning and this was not an "accidental slip or omission" entitling him to amend his award and the amended award must be set aside.

RECENT CASES

691. Snelling *v.* John G. Snelling Ltd. [1972] 1 All E.R. 79

The plaintiff and the second and third defendants were brothers and co-directors of John G. Snelling Ltd. Prior to 1967 the company had been financed by loans from each of them. In 1968 additional finance was required and a finance company agreed to provide it and the brothers agreed with the finance company not to reduce their loans to John G. Snelling Ltd. until the loan from the finance company had been repaid. The brothers also made a separate agreement between themselves that if any of them voluntarily resigned before the loan from the finance company was repaid, the money due to him from John G. Snelling Ltd. should be forfeited. The company John G. Snelling Ltd. was not a party to this agreement. The plaintiff resigned voluntarily and sued the company for the return of his loan. His brothers were joined as co-defendants and counter-claimed for a declaration that the loans to the plaintiff had been forfeited. It was *held*—by Ormrod, J.—

(i) that the agreement between the brothers was intended to affect the legal rights of them all and was intended to create legal relations even though made by members of a family;

(ii) that the company could not rely directly on the agreement between the brothers since it was not a party to it;

(iii) that although the company could not rely on the agreement, the plaintiff brothers could enforce it being parties;

(iv) that their appropriate remedy was either to apply for an injunction before the plaintiff issued a writ or (as had happened) after issue of the writ to apply for a stay of proceedings under Sect. 41 of the Supreme Court of Judicature (Consolidation) Act, 1925;

(v) that since all the parties were before the court and also that the reality of the matter was that the plaintiff's case failed, the proper order to make was one dismissing the plaintiff's claim and not one which merely stopped his action.

(Note: this case does not affect the basic rule of privity but shows an additional method of avoiding the operation of the rule. It could, for example, have been used in cases such as *Adler* v. *Dickson*, 1955,[191] since if A makes a contract with B under which B attempts to exclude the liability of his servants, it may be possible to enforce that clause because B could apply to the court which could stay any action by A against B's servants and in fact dismiss A's claim under Sect. 41 of the 1925 Act. The only qualifications would seem to be that the promise not to sue should be clear and unambiguous (per Ormrod, J.).)

692. Gosling *v.* Anderson, *The Times*, 6th February 1972.

Miss Gosling, a retired schoolmistress, entered into negotiations for the purchase of one of three flats in a house at Minehead owned by Mrs. Anderson. Mr. Tidbury, who was Mrs. Anderson's agent in the negotiations, represented to Miss Gosling by letter that planning permission for a garage to go with the flat had been given. Mrs. Anderson knew that this was not so. The purchase of the flat went through on the basis of a contract and a conveyance showing a parking area but not referring to planning permission which was later refused. Miss Gosling now sought damages for misrepresentation under Sect. 2(1) of the Misrepresentation Act, 1967. *Held*—the facts revealed an innocent misrepresentation by Mr. Tidbury made without reasonable grounds for believing it to be true. Mrs. Anderson was liable for the acts of her agent and must pay damages under the Act of 1967. The Court ordered an enquiry as to damages before the local county court judge.

(Note the effect of this case and the Misrepresentation Act, 1967 on *Armstrong v. Strain*, 1952.[380] Before the 1967 Act where both agent and principal were innocent of actual fraud there was no cause of action in damages. Now there need not be any question of fraud. Where the statement is made negligently the agent may be made liable for his own negligence and the principal is liable also under the doctrine of vicarious liability.)

693. Hill *v.* C. A. Parsons & Co. Ltd. [1971] 3 All E.R. 1318.

The defendant company had given in to the demands of a militant trade union called Data that certain of their employees should belong to that union. The plaintiff, who was a chartered engineer aged 63 with 35 years' service in the company, refused to join the union and the defendants gave him one month's notice terminating his employment. The plaintiff thereupon commenced an action for an injunction restraining the company from implementing the notice. The Court of Appeal granted an injunction to prevent dismissal. The following are matters of particular interest arising from the judgments—

(i) Lord Denning, M.R. and Sachs, L.J. were influenced to some extent by the fact that by the time a period of six months' notice (which they regarded as reasonable in this case) had elapsed, Part II of the Industrial Relations Act, 1971 would be in force so that the plaintiff could under that Act seek an order allowing him to remain at work or alternatively obtain compensation for dismissal much in excess of the damages he would be likely to obtain at common law.

(ii) Nevertheless both Lord Denning, M.R. and Sachs, L.J. did not rely on the coming into force of the 1971 Act but based their judgments in part at least on the need to bring the law into line with 'the realities of the day'.

(iii) Lord Denning, M.R. in particular referred to the principle *ubi jus ibi remedium* (where there is a right there is a remedy) and treated the plaintiff's right to damages as inadequate, concluding that that principle enabled the court 'to step over the trip-wires of previous cases and bring the law into accord with the needs of today'.

694. Karak Rubber Co. Ltd. *v.* Burden (No. 2), [1972] 1 All E.R. 1210.

A take-over transaction involved the purchase by a director of the company's issued share capital. The director used the company's assets to finance the purchase of the shares by borrowing money from a third party to buy them and repaying the third party by a cheque for £99,504 drawn on the company's account at Barclays Bank. The cheque was paid by the bank which was held liable to repay Karak for breach of their contractual duty because—

(*a*) although a bank was obliged to pay on demand a cheque which was in proper form and backed by adequate funds, it did not follow that a paying bank was under an absolute unqualified duty to pay without enquiry; it was, on the contrary, under a contractual duty to exercise such care and skill as would be exercised by a reasonable banker and that care and skill included, in appropriate circumstances, a duty to enquire before paying;

(*b*) in exercising its duty of care the paying bank was bound to make such enquiries as might, in given circumstances, be appropriate and practical, where it had, or a reasonable banker would have, grounds for believing that the authorised signatories were misusing their authority for the purpose of defrauding their principal or otherwise defeating his true intentions;

(c) the circumstances in which the Karak cheque came to be tendered to Barclays were so unusual and out of the ordinary course of banking business, the sum involved was so large, and the ground so solid for suspecting that someone was using Karak money to finance the take-over transaction, that a reasonable banker, in the interests of his customer, would have made further enquiries before inviting or allowing the customer's signatories to pay over £99,504 of the customer's money.

The bank was also liable as a constructive trustee. Although, in order to establish liability as a constructive trustee on the part of a third party who has assisted a trustee as his agent in a breach of trust, it was necessary to show that the third party had assisted with knowledge of a dishonest and fraudulent design on the part of the trustee, it was not necessary to show that the third party had actual knowledge; it was sufficient to show constructive knowledge, i.e. that the third party had knowledge of circumstances which would have indicated to an honest, reasonable man that such a design was being committed or would have put him on enquiry whether it was being committed.

695. Stone *v.* **Reliance Mutual Insurance Society Ltd.,** *The Times*, 15th March 1972

The plaintiff signed a proposal form for burglary insurance. The form contained a clause stating "I further declare in so far as any part of this proposal is not written by me the person who has written the same has done so by my instructions and as my agent for that purpose. I agree that the above proposal and this declaration shall be the basis of the contract of insurance between the society and myself."

The defendant's district inspector put questions to the plaintiff and wrote down the answers and later asked the plaintiff's wife to sign the completed forms which she did without reading them. During the currency of the policy a burglary took place and the plaintiff made a claim on the defendants. They repudiated liability on the ground that the following questions had been answered incorrectly—

Ques. 5: 'State policy numbers of insurances held by you and whether lapsed or in force'. Answer—'None'.

Ques. 6: 'Give particulars of any claims you have made in respect of any risks hereby proposed to be insured'. Answer—'None'.

It appeared that the plaintiff had taken out another policy with the defendants which had lapsed and had not disclosed a claim made under the earlier policy in respect of a loss by fire. *Held*—by the Court of Appeal distinguishing *Newsholme*[610]—that the plaintiff's claim succeeded. The mistakes were those of the district inspector because in spite of the agency clause it was obviously the defendant's practice to rely on the answers the district inspector arrived at with the proposer and—

(i) the inspector must have known that there had been an earlier policy which had lapsed for he only called on those whose policies had lapsed;

(ii) the inspector might have forgotten or never known about the fire. Thus there was no misrepresentation or non-disclosure to defeat the policy.

696. Moschi *v.* **L.E.P. Air Services,** [1972] 2 All E.R. 393

L.E.P., who were forwarding agents, agreed to give up their lien over the goods of a firm called Rolloswin Investments, who were importers, in return for repayment of £40,000 in seven weekly instalments. Mr. Moschi guaranteed that Rolloswin would make the payments. Rolloswin defaulted after making payments totalling £10,000. L.E.P. treated this as a repudiation of the agreement and sued Mr. Moschi for the full amount less what had been paid. *Held—* by the House of Lords—Mr. Moschi was not discharged from his obligations. He had guaranteed performance by Rolloswin and when they defaulted Mr. Moschi was also in breach of his own contract of guarantee. He was thus liable not in debt to pay the remaining instalments, but for damages for breach of contract. The measure of damages was assessed at the total sum guaranteed less payments made by Rolloswin.

INDEX TO STATUTES

Accommodation Agents Act, 1953
Sect. 1 (1) (b) 623
Administration of Justice Act, 1965
Sect. 20 340
Sect. 21 339
Administration of Justice Act, 1969
Sect. 22 95
Administration of Justice Act, 1970 109
Sect. 4 452
Sect. 29 340
Sect. 36 109
Sch. 3 452
Advertisements (Hire Purchase) Act,
1957 . . . . . 185, 189
Sect. 1 (1) 186
(2) 186
Sect. 2 187
Agricultural Holdings Act, 1948 . 459
Animals Act, 1971 616
Arbitration Act, 1889
Sect. 4 699
Arbitration Act, 1950
Sect. 1 453
Sect. 2 449
Sect. 3 (1) 449
Sect. 4 451
Sect. 6 . . . . . 450, 452
Sect. 7 453
Sect. 8 453
(1) 450
(2) 450
(3) 452
Sect. 9 (1) 453
(2) 453
Sect. 10 454
Sect. 11 454
Sect. 12 455
(1) 450
(2) 451
Sect. 13 450
Sect. 14 451
Sect. 15 451
Sect. 16 451
Sect. 18 . . . . 451, 458
Sect. 19 459
Sect. 21 (1) 455
(2) 455
Sect. 22 457
Sect. 23 458
Sect. 25 (2) 452
Sect. 26 458
Sect. 32 449
Auctions (Bidding Agreements) Act,
1927 165
Auctions (Bidding Agreements) Act,
1969 165
Sect. 3 165

Bankers' Books Evidence Act, 1879
Sect. 7 325

Banking and Financial Dealings
Act, 1971 . . . . 299, 304
Bankruptcy Act, 1914 . . 337, 670
Sect. 1 337
(b) 362, 363
(1) (b) 669
(c) 669
(e) 670
Sect. 7 342
Sect. 12 343
Sect. 14 343
Sect. 15 (2) 345
Sect. 16 . 342, 344, 346, 357, 359
Sect. 21 . . . . . 347, 359
Sect. 25 345
Sect. 26 (2) 366, 367
(3) 367
Sect. 29 347
Sect. 31 . . . . . 354, 655
Sect. 32 346
Sect. 33 355
(4) 356
Sect. 34 355
Sect. 35 355
(2) 356
Sect. 37 351
Sect. 38 . . . 359, 360, 673
Sect. 40 352
Sect. 42 . . 338, 357, 363, 364
Sect. 43 364
Sect. 44 . . . . . 361, 362
Sect. 45, 351, 352, 362, 670, 671, 672
(1) (d) 661
Sect. 46 . . . . 351, 352, 670
Sect. 47 360
(1) 360, 673
Sect. 54 364
Sect. 66 356
Sect. 74 343
Sect. 93 351
Sect. 108 343
Sect. 129 367
Sect. 167 353
Bankruptcy Act, 1926 . . . 337
Sect. 3 368
Sect. 4 352
Betting and Gaming Act, 1960 . 636
Betting and Loans (Infants) Act,
1892 . . . . . . 28, 31
Bills of Exchange Act, 1882
99, 286, 291, 656
Sect. 2 . . . . 291, 292, 309
Sect. 3 287
(2) 293
(4) 296
Sect. 4 (1) 290
Sect. 6 296
Sect. 7 (3) 300
Sect. 8 (1) 306
(5) 305

Bills of Exchange Act, 1882 (*contd.*)—

Sect. 9 (1)	301
(2)	301
(3)	301
Sect. 10	303
(1) (*b*)	324
Sect. 11	303
Sect. 12	304
Sect. 13 (1)	304
(2)	303
Sect. 14	
(1)	304
(2)	304
(3)	304
(4)	304
Sect. 16	293
Sect. 17	296
Sect. 18 (1)	296
(2)	296
Sect. 19 (2)	297
Sect. 20	296
(1)	306
(2)	306
Sect. 21	305
(1)	305
Sect. 22 28,	292
Sect. 23	294
(2)	224
Sect. 25	294
Sect. 26	294
(2)	206
Sect. 27 . . . 20, 106,	292
(1) (*a*)	656
(1) (*b*)	656
(2)	291
(3)	291
Sect. 28 (1)	298
(2)	298
Sect. 29 (1) . . . 292,	301
(2)	310
(3)	310
Sect. 30	310
Sect. 31 307,	336
Sect. 32	308
Sect. 33	308
Sect. 34	308
Sect. 35	308
Sect. 36	307
Sect. 38	
(1)	311
(2) 311,	661
(3) 310,	311
Sect. 39	298
Sect. 40 299,	310
Sect. 41	310
(1)	299
(2)	299
(3)	299
Sect. 42	310
Sect. 43	310
Sect. 44	310
(2)	297
(3)	297
Sect. 45 . . 301, 310,	659
(1)	301

Bills of Exchange Act, 1882 (*contd.*)—

(2)	301
(*a*)	659
(3)	302
(4)	302
(5)	302
(6)	302
(8)	302
Sect. 46 305,	310
(1)	302
(2)	302
Sect. 47 310,	314
Sect. 48 . . . 310, 314,	663
Sect. 49 310,	659
(12)	315
Sect. 50 310,	316
Sect. 51 310,	316
Sect. 52 . . . 301, 310,	318
Sect. 54 (1)	318
(2) . . . 295, 318,	319
Sect. 55 (1)	319
(*a*)	663
(2) 295,	319
Sect. 57	319
Sect. 58 309,	323
Sect. 59 . . . 330, 331,	332
(1)	311
(2)	311
(3)	311
Sect. 60 . . 330, 331, 332,	333
Sect. 61	312
Sect. 62	312
Sect. 63 (1)	312
(2)	312
(3)	313
Sect. 64 (1)	313
(2)	313
Sect. 65 194,	300
Sect. 66 194,	300
Sect. 67	194
Sect. 68	194
(1)	303
(3)	303
(5)	303
(7)	303
Sect. 69	320
Sect. 70	320
Sect. 71	319
Sect. 72 (1)	321
(2)	321
(3)	321
(4)	321
(5)	321
Sect. 73	323
Sect. 74 . . . 301, 324,	326
Sect. 75	326
Sect. 76 (1)	329
(2)	329
Sect. 77 329,	330
Sect. 78	330
Sect. 79 330,	331
Sect. 80	333
Sect. 81	331
Sect. 82 334,	667
Sect. 83 (1)	321

Bills of Exchange Act, 1882 (*contd.*)—
   (2) 322
   (3) 322
   (4) 322
  Sect. 85 322
  Sect. 86 323
  Sect. 87 323
  Sect. 88 323
  Sect. 89 (4) 322
  Sect. 95 332
Bills of Lading Act, 1855 . . . 422
Bills of Sale Acts, 1878–1882
  112–117, 126, 127, 169, 188, 361, 364
  Sect. 8 . . . . . . 127, 589
  Sect. 9 590
Building Societies Act, 1962
  Sect. 36 109

Carriers Act, 1830 . . 408, 411, 413
  Sect. 1 412
  Sect. 2 412
  Sect. 4 412
  Sect. 8 412
Carriage by Air Act, 1932 . . . 431
Carriage by Air Act, 1961
    431, 435, 436, 437
Carriage by Air (Supplementary
  Provisions) Act, 1962 . . . 438
Carriage of Goods by Railway Act,
  1972 422
Carriage of Goods by Road Act,
  1965 413
Carriage of Goods by Sea Act,
  1924 . . . . . 423, 424
Carriage of Goods by Sea Act,
  1971 430
Cheques Act, 1957
  Sect. 1 . . . . . 333, 336
  Sect. 2 . . . 335, 336, 654, 669
  Sect. 3 336
  Sect. 4 . . . 332, 334, 335, 336
   (1) 334, 668
   (2) 301, 334, 658
   (3) 334
Companies Act, 1908
  Sect. 8 645
Companies Act, 1948
    32, 93, 99, 236, 341, 654
  Sect. 5 . . . . . 238, 645
  Sect. 10 240
  Sect. 17 237
  Sect. 18 237
  Sect. 20 (1) 646
  Sect. 22 240
  Sect. 28 272
  Sect. 32 . . . . . 33, 127
  Sect. 38 251
  Sect. 43 . . 41, 45, 252, 254, 524
  Sect. 47 250
  Sect. 53 253
  Sect. 57 251
  Sect. 61 268
  Sect. 64 240
  Sect. 65 268

Companies Act, 1948 (*contd.*)—
  Sect. 66 (1) 269
  Sect. 86 274
  Sect. 87 273
  Sect. 92 270
  Sect. 95 272
  Sect. 104 . . . . 271, 273
  Sect. 107 (2) 238
  Sect. 108 501
   (4) 294
  Sect. 110 . . . . 273, 274
  Sect. 111 273
  Sect. 117 . . . . 242, 258
  Sect. 124 275
  Sect. 126 276
  Sect. 127 276
  Sect. 128 276
  Sect. 130 258
  Sect. 131 258
  Sect. 132 259
  Sect. 134 (*c*) 259
  Sect. 136 260
  Sect. 137 260
  Sect. 141 260
  Sect. 143 260
  Sect. 145 . . . . 259, 273
  Sect. 146 273
  Sect. 147 (1) . . . 261, 262
   (2) 261
   (3) 261
  Sect. 148 (1) . . . 261, 262
   (2) 261
  Sect. 149 (1) . . . 261, 262
  Sect. 150 (1) . . . 261, 262
   (2) 261, 262
  Sect. 154 (5) 263
  Sect. 157 (1) 246
  Sect. 159 . . . . 276, 278
  Sect. 161 216
  Sect. 163 249
  Sect. 176 242
  Sect. 177 242
  Sect. 181 (1) 192
  Sect. 184 243
  Sect. 187 . . . . 243, 347
  Sect. 195 245
  Sect. 196 . . 249, 265, 266
  Sect. 199 244
  Sect. 212 (1) (a) 284
  Sect. 222 279
  Sect. 278 280
  Sect. 294 280
  Sect. 299 281
  Sect. 300 281
  Sect. 311 281
  Sect. 317 655
  Sect. 319 284
   (4) 283, 284
  Sect. 340 281
  Sect. 429 215
  Sect. 434 215
  Sect. 454 (1) 266
  Sect. 455 (1) 251
  Schedule 4 . . . . 53, 251
  Part I 275

Companies Act, 1948 (*contd.*)—
Part II 275
Schedule 8 . . . . 262, 266
Companies Act, 1967 236
Sect. 2 236
Sect. 3 (1) 262, 263
(3) . . . 241, 262, 263, 274
(4) 262, 263, 264
(5) 263, 264
(6) 263
Sect. 4 (1) 262, 263
(2) 263
(3) 241, 263, 274
(4) 264
(5) 264
(8) 263
Sect. 5 (1) 262, 264
(2) 264
Sect. 6 . . 243, 249, 262, 265, 266
(1) 264
(2) 265
(3) 265
(4) 266
(6) 265
(7) 265
Sect. 7 . . . 249, 262, 265, 266
(3) 266
Sect. 8 . . . 249, 262, 265, 266
(4) 266
Sect. 9 . . . . . 262, 266
Sect. 10 266
Sect. 11 (1) 266
(2) 266
Sect. 12 266
Sect. 14 277
Sect. 15 246
Sect. 16 246
(1) 246
(*b*) 246
(*c*) 247
(*d*) 247
(*e*) 247
(*f*) 247
Sect. 17 . . . . . 246, 247
Sect. 18 . . . . . 246, 247
Sect. 19 . . . . . 246, 247
Sect. 20 . . . . . 246, 247
Sect. 21 . . . . . 246, 249
Sect. 22 . . . . . 246, 249
Sect. 23 . . . . . 246, 249
Sect. 24 249
Sect. 25 245
Sect. 26 . . 243, 245, 274, 275
Sect. 27 . . . 245, 272, 274
(1) (*b*) 274
Sect. 28 . . 245, 246, 272, 274
Sect. 29 . . . 245, 272, 274
(2) 274
Sect. 30 245
Sect. 31 . . . 246, 272, 274
Sect. 32 246
Sect. 33 . . . . . 241, 274
Sect. 34 . . . . 241, 274, 275
Sect. 43 239
Sect. 44 239

Companies Act, 1967 (*contd.*)—
Sect. 46 . . . . . . 237, 238
Sect. 47 276
Sect. 51 260
Sect. 119 216
Sect. 120 236
Sect. 121 234
Schedule 1 . . . . . 262, 266
Schedule 2 . . . . . 262, 266
Consular Relations Act, 1968 . . 27
Consumer Protection Act, 1971 . 139
Contracts of Employment Act,
1963 . . . . 72, 77
Copyright Act, 1956 491
Corporate Bodies Contracts Act,
1960 . . . . . . 33, 127
Criminal Law Act, 1967 . . . 148
Sect. 13 58
Sect. 14 58
Crown Proceedings Act, 1947 . . 579

Debtors Act, 1869
Sect. 11 347
Deeds of Arrangement Act, 1914
337, 357, 669
Sect. 24 357
Diplomatic Immunities (Common-
wealth Countries and Republic
of Ireland) Act, 1952 . . . 27
Diplomatic Privileges Act, 1708 . 26
Diplomatic Privileges Act, 1964 . 27
Diplomatic Privileges Act, 1971 . 27
Directors' Liability Act, 1890 . . 527
Disposal of Uncollected Goods Act,
1952 . . . . . 105, 148

Employers' Liability Act, 1880 . 503
Employers' Liability (Compulsory
Insurance) Act, 1969 . . . 376
Exchange Control Act, 1947 . . 547

Factors Act, 1889
121, 147, 211, 632, 633
Sect. 1 601
(1) 211
Sect. 2 . . . . . 144, 601
(1) . . . 151, 212, 632, 533
(4) 262
Sect. 6 213
Sect. 8 . . . . 127, 149, 160
Sect. 9
150, 151, 168, 183, 185, 527, 611
Sect. 10 145
Family Law Reform Act, 1969
Sect. 1 (1) 27
(2) 27
Sect. 9 27
Schedule 3 86
Finance (No. 2) Act, 1940 . . 670
Finance Act, 1968 . . . . .
Sects 35–38 21
Finance Act, 1971
Sects 29–335 81
Fire Prevention (Metropolis) Act,
1774 392
Sect. 83 404

Gaming Act, 1845 398
Gas Light and Coke Companies Act,
  1868 507

Hire Purchase Act, 1938 . 171, 172
  Sect. 8 612
Hire Purchase Act, 1954 . . 171
Hire Purchase Act, 1964 . . 178
  Sect. 10 (1) 178
  (2) 178
  (3) 178
  Sect. 27 . . . . 184, 185
  (2) 184, 605, 613
  (3) 184
  (4) 184
  (6) 185
  Sect. 28 185
  Sect. 29 (1) 185
  (2) 184
  Sect. 30 186
  Sect. 31 186
  Sect. 32 187
  Part III 150, 151, 184
Hire Purchase Act, 1965
  53, 124, 125, 127, 168, 184, 189, 190
  Sect. 1 . . . . . 182, 183
  Sect. 2 171
  (3) 171
  Sect. 3 171
  Sect. 4 . . . . . 171, 182
  Sect 5 (1) 172, 183
  Sect. 6 (2) 172, 183
  (3) 172
  Sect. 7 (1) (a) . . . 172, 183
  (b) 172
  (2) 173
  Sect. 8 . . . 172, 173, 183
  Sect. 9 . . . . 172, 183
  (4) 174
  (5) 174
  Sect. 10 . . . . 173, 183
  (1) 173
  Sect. 11 (1) . . . 173, 183
  (2) 173
  (4) 174
  Sect. 12 (1) 183
  (a) 174
  (b) 174
  (2) 174
  (3) 178
  Sect. 13 (2) . . . 174, 183
  (3) 175
  (5) 175
  (9) 175
  Sect. 14 (1) . . 175, 179, 183
  (2) 174, 175
  (3) 175
  Sect. 15 . . . . 176, 183
  Sect. 16. . . 178, 183, 600, 611
  Sect. 17 (1) . . 178, 179, 183
  (2) 179
  (3) 179
  (4) 179
  (5) 179

Hire Purchase Act, 1965 (*contd.*)—
  Sect. 18 (3) . . . 179, 180, 183
  (4) 179
  Sect. 19 (1) 180, 183
  (2) 180
  Sect. 20 (1) 183
  (2) 183
  (3) 182, 183
  (4) 182
  Sect. 21 (1) 177, 183
  (2) 177
  Sect. 22 . . . . . 182, 183
  Sect. 23 182
  Sect. 24 (1) 177
  (2) 177
  Sect. 25 . . . . . 180, 181
  Sect. 27 183
  (1) 176
  (2) 183
  Sect. 28 176
  (2) 176
  (3) 176
  (4) 176
  Sect. 29 (3) 183
  Sect. 31 183
  Sect. 32 177
  Sect. 33 180
  Sect. 34 (2) 180
  Sect. 35 181
  Sect. 41 181
  Sect. 45 (3) 183
  Sect. 53 (1) 360
  Sect. 54 . . . . . 150, 183
  Sect. 58 (1) 174, 182
  (2) 180

Infants' Relief Act, 1874
  28, 31, 192, 341, 502
  Sect. (1) 28, 505
  Sect. (2) . . 19, 30, 196, 504
Innkeepers Act, 1878 . . 105, 148
International Organisations Act,
  1968 27

Judicature Acts, 1873–75 . . . 98
Judicature Act, 1925
  Sect. 47 307

Land Charges Act, 1925
  111, 357, 496, 589
Landlord and Tenant Act, 1709 . 356
Landlord and Tenant Act, 1962
  Sect. 4 543
Land Registration Act, 1925
  Sect. 70 542
Lands Clauses Consolidation Act,
  1845 . . . . . . 688, 702
Law of Property Act, 1925 . 127, 286
  Sect. 1 (6) 504
  Sect. 40
  14, 121, 466, 481, 486, 487, 488
  Sect. 41 80
  Sect. 47 404
  Sect. 53 . . . . . 107, 541
  Sect. 56 (1) 22, 497

Law of Property Act, 1925 (*contd.*)—
   Sect. 87 107
   Sect. 109 . . . . . 109, 110
   Sect. 136 . . . . . 98, 99
   Sect. 172 . . . 338, 362, 363
   Sect. 205 (1) . . . 21, 497
Law Reform (Contributory Negli-
   gence) Act, 1945 . . 433, 668
Law Reform (Enforcement of Con-
   tracts) Act, 1954 . 14, 123, 518
Law Reform (Frustrated Contracts)
   Act, 1943 . . 84, 85, 86, 562
Law Reform (Husband and Wife)
   Act, 1962 376
Law Reform (Married Women and
   Tortfeasors) Act, 1935 32, 226, 341
Law Reform (Miscellaneous Pro-
   visions) Act, 1934 . . . 95
   Sect. 1 226
Law Reform (Miscellaneous Provi-
   sions) Act, 1970
   Sect. 1 . . . . . . 88, 90
Life Assurance Act, 1774 397, 398, 686
   Sect. 1 397
Limitation Act, 1939 3, 20, 81, 86, 323
   Sect. 23 19
   Sect. 26 42
Limited Partnership Act, 1907 . . 234

Marine Insurance Act, 1906 . . 369
   Sect. 1 379
   Sect. 2 379
   Sect. 3 . . . . . 379, 387
   Sect. 4 400
   (2) 400
   Sect. 5 399
   Sect. 6 399
   Sect. 8 399
   Sect. 9 (2) 402
   Sect. 14 (1) 399
   (2) 399
   Sect. 16 (1) 394
   Sect. 18 (1) 373
   (2) 373
   (3) 373
   Sect. 19 374
   Sect. 20 374
   Sect. 21 372
   Sect. 22 370
   Sect. 24 (2) 370
   Sect. 25 382
   Sect. 26 380
   Sect. 27 379
   Sect. 29 (1) 380
   Sect. 31 (2) 384
   Sect. 32 400
   Sect. 33 395
   Sect. 42 (1) 383
   Sect. 45 383
   Sect. 46 384
   Sect. 47 384
   Sect. 49 384
   Sect. 50 404
   Sect. 51 404
   Sect. 53 (1) 372

Marine Insurance Act, 1906 (*contd.*)—
   Sect. 55 389
   Sect. 56 394
   Sect. 60 395
   Sect. 61 395
   Sect. 62 395
   Sect. 63 (1) 395
   Sect. 65 (1) 393
   Sect. 66 (1) 393
   (2) 393
   (3) 393
   (4) 393
   Sect. 68 394
   Sect. 69 394
   Sect. 77 394
   Sect. 86 500
   Schedule 1
     Rule 15 380
     Rule 17 380
Married Women's Property Act, 1882
   Sect. 11 21
Married Women (Restraint upon
   Anticipation) Act, 1949 . 32
Matrimonial Proceedings and Pro-
   perty Act, 1970
   Sect. 4 364
   Sect. 23 364
   Sect. 41 196
Mental Health Act, 1959
   Part VIII 34
Mercantile Law Amendment Act,
   1856 . . . . . 15, 445
   Sect. 3 491
Merchandise Marks Acts . . . 165
Merchant Shipping Act, 1894 423, 426
   Sect. 1 25
   Sect. 24 127
Merchant Shipping Act, 1970 . . 562
Merchant Shipping (Liability of
   Shipowners and others) Act,
   1958 . . . 423, 427, 691
   Sect. 3 (2) 691
Misrepresentation Act, 1967
   46, 47, 48, 129, 142, 170, 178, 183,
         210, 516, 631
   Sect. 1 (*a*) 43
      (*b*) . . . 43, 48, 529
   Sect. 2 (1) 42, 44, 45, 48, 128, 129,
        252, 253, 528, 530
   (2) . . 42, 43, 45, 48, 128
   Sect. 3 . . . 50, 129, 140
   Sect. 4 . . . 142, 155
Moneylenders Acts,
   1900–27 . . . 168, 189, 490
   Sect. 6 . . . . . 17, 489
   (2) 489
Monopolies and Mergers Act, 1965 76
Monopolies and Restrictive Practices
   Act, 1948 76

National Assistance Act, 1948
   Sect. 42 493
National Debt Act, 1972 . . . 286
New South Wales Sale of Goods Act,
   Sect. 25 (1) 605

Partnership Act, 1890 214
  Sect. 1 (1) 214, 634
    (2) 214
  Sect. 2 (1) 214
    (2) 214, 635
    (3) 215
  Sect. 3 . . . . . 215, 356
  Sect. 4 217
  Sect. 5 . . . . . 223, 640
  Sect. 6 224
  Sect. 7 225
  Sect. 8 223
  Sect. 9 225
  Sect. 11 225
  Sect. 12 226
  Sect. 13 226
  Sect. 14 . . . . . 215, 641
    (1) 226
    (2) 226
  Sect. 17 (1) 226
    (2) 226
    (3) 227
  Sect. 18 227
  Sect. 19 218
  Sect. 20 (1) 218
    (2) 219
    (3) 638
  Sect. 21 219
  Sect. 22 219
  Sect. 23 220
  Sect. 24 (1) 220, 221
    (2) 221, 225
    (3) 220
    (4) 220
    (5) 221
    (6) 221
    (7) 221
    (8) 218, 221
    (9) 221
  Sect. 25 221
  Sect. 26 642
  Sect. 27 228
  Sect. 28 221
  Sect. 29 638
    (1) 222
    (2) 222
  Sect. 30 222
  Sect. 31 (1) 222, 639
    (2) 222
  Sect. 32 228
  Sect. 33 (1) 228
    (2) 228
  Sect. 34 228
  Sect. 35 229
  Sect. 36 (1) 227
    (2) 227
    (3) 227, 641
  Sect. 37 229
  Sect. 38 . . . . . 229, 233
  Sect. 39 229
  Sect. 40 230
  Sect. 41 232
  Sect. 42 (1) 234, 638
    (2) 232

Partnership Act, 1890 (*contd.*)—
  Sect. 44 644
    (a) 231
    (b) 231
  Sect. 91 (1) 224
Pawnbrokers Acts, 1872 and 1960
      117, 118, 148
Pharmacy and Poisons Act, 1933
  Sect. 17 463
  Sect. 18 463
Pipe-Lines Act, 1962. 422
Policies of Assurance Act, 1867 100, 404
Powers of Attorney Act, 1971 . . 205
Prevention of Corruption Act, 1894 199
Protection of Birds Act, 1954
  Sect. 6 (1) 464
Public Bodies Corrupt Practices
  Act, 1889 200

Real Property Act, 1845 . . . 497
Registration of Business Names Act,
  1916 . . . . . 217, 238
Resale Prices Act, 1964 21, 71, 72, 491
  Sect. 1 (1) 72
    (2) 72
    (3) 72
    (4) 72
  Sect. 2 (1) 72
    (3) 73
    (4) 73
  Sect. 3 (1) 73
    (2) 73
  Sect. 4 (1) 73
    (2) 73
    (3) 73
    (4) 73
  Sect. 5 . . . . . . 74, 75
    (1) 73
    (2) 74
  Sect. 6 74
    (1) 75
    (2) 74
    (3) 75
    (4) 75
  Sect. 7 (1) 75
    (2) 75
    (3) 75
    (4) 75
  Sect. 13 76
Restrictive Trade Practices Act,
  1956 . . 56, 67, 70, 76, 560
  Sect. 1 67
  Sect. 2 68
  Sect. 6 68
    (3) 68
  Sect. 7 68
  Sect. 11 (3) 68
  Sect. 12 69
  Sect. 14 69
  Sect. 25 . . . . 21, 71, 491
  Part I 70
Restrictive Trade Practices Act,
  1968 . . . . . . 67, 70
  Sect. 1 70
  Sect. 2 70

Restrictive Trade Practices Act, 1968
(*contd.*)—
Sect. 4 70
Sect. 5 70
Sect. 6 . . . . . . 70, 71
Sect. 7 71
Sect. 10 71
Road Traffic Act, 1930 . . 678, 685
Sect. 35 679
Road Traffic Act, 1972 . . . 378
Sect. 143 377
Sect. 148 (4) . . . 377, 689
Schedule 8 483
Sale of Goods Act, 1893 . 53, 105, 121,
128, 179, 183, 187, 293, 581, 591
Sect. 1 (1) 121, 124
(2) 29, 35, 126
(3) 121
Sect. 4 . . . . . 123, 518
(*b*) 144
Sect. 5 (2) 590
Sect. 6 . . . 85, 122, 123, 591
Sect. 7 . . . . 85, 123
Sect. 8 126
Sect. 9 126
Sect. 10 (1) 130
Sect. 11 142
(1) . . . . . .
(*a*) 130
(*b*) 129
(*c*) . . . 141, 142, 183
Sect. 12 . . . . 141, 577
(1) . . 130, 131, 578, 592
(2) . . . 131, 132, 592
(3) . . . 131, 132, 178
Sect. 13 129, 132, 133, 141, 562, 592,
593, 594
Sect. 14 . 134, 135, 141, 596, 597
(1) 133, 134, 141, 594, 595, 596
(2) 132, 134, 135, 137, 141, 592, 597,
598, 600
(3) 136
Sect. 15 (1) 136, 141
(2) 135
(*a*) 136, 599
(*b*) 136
(*c*) . . . 136, 598, 599
Sect. 16 145
Sect. 17 . . . . . 143, 144
Sect. 18 . . . . . 142, 143
Rule 1 . . . . . 142, 143
Rule 2 . . . . . 143, 144
Rule 3 . . . . . 143, 144
Rule 4 . . . . . 144, 601
Rule 5 (1) 145
(2) 146
Sect. 19 (1) 144
(3) 145
Sect. 20 . . . . 146, 604
Sect. 21 84
(1) . . . 147, 148, 605
(2) 147, 148
Sect. 23 . . . . 149, 151, 527
Sect. 25 (1) 124, 127, 149, 160, 605
(2) . . . 145, 150, 168, 183

Sale of Goods Act, 1893 (*contd.*)—
Sect. 27 152
Sect. 28 152
Sect. 29 (1) 152
(2) 130
(3) 152, 153
(4) 153
Sect. 30 (1) 153
(2) 153
(3) 153, 562
Sect. 31 (1) 153
(2) . . . 141, 153, 607
Sect. 32 (1) 154
(2) 154, 166
(3) 154, 166
Sect. 33 . . . . 146, 154
Sect. 34 . . . . 154, 155
(1) 154
(2) 154
Sect. 35 . 141, 142, 143, 154, 155
Sect. 36 . . . . 155, 162
Sect. 37 . . . . 155, 160
Sect. 38 (1) 156
(2) 156
Sect. 39 (1) . . . 155, 156
(2) 155
(3) 152
Sect. 41 (*a*) 156
(*b*) 156
(*c*) 156
Sect. 42 156
Sect. 43 157
Sect. 44 157
Sect. 45 (1) 157
(2) 158
(3) 158
(4) 158
(5) 158
(6) 158
(7) 158
Sect. 46 (1) 159
(2) 159
Sect. 47 . . . . 145, 158
Sect. 48 (1) 157
(2) 160
(3) . . 130, 159, 160, 609
(4) 159, 160
Sect. 49 (1) 160
(2) 160
Sect. 50 (1) 160
(2) 160, 574
(3) . . . 160, 573, 574
Sect. 51 (1) 162
(2) 163
(3) 163
Sect. 52 164
Sect. 53 (1) 163
(3) 164
Sect. 55 139
Sect. 58 (1) 164
(2) 164, 165
(3) 165
(4) 164

Sale of Goods Act, 1893 *(contd.)*—
Sect. 61 147
  (4) 127
Sect. 62 84, 121, 127, 128, 129, 152
  (3) 156
Part IV 155
South Australian Sale of Goods Act,
1895
Sect. 14 (1) 595
  (2) 595
Stamp Act, 1891 81
Statute of Frauds, 1677 14, 370, 439, 487
Sect. 4 . . . . . 466, 484, 486
Stock Transfer Act, 1963 . 99, 256
Suicide Act, 1961 385

Theft Act, 1968 149
Sect. 28 . . . . . 149, 218
Third Party (Rights Against Insurers)
Act, 1930 . . . 378, 391, 405
Trade Descriptions Act, 1968–72
45, 139, 165, 166
Sect. 35 166
Trading Stamps Act, 1964 . . . 276
Transport Act, 1962 . 411, 419, 534
Sect. 43 . . . . 407, 418, 419
Treasury Bills Act, 1877 . . . 286
Truck Act, 1831 551

Unsolicited Goods and Services Act,
1971 . . . . 8, 101

INDEX TO CASES

NOTE. The number of the case in the Appendix is printed in **bold type;** the page on which the case is cited is printed in ordinary type.

Aas v. Benham, **500,** 222
Adams v. Lindsell, **35,** 9
Adler v. Dickson, **191,** 50, 138, 430, 431
Affréteurs (Les) Réunis Société Anonyme v. Walford, **85,** 21
Ajayi v. Briscoe, **98,** 25
Akerib v. Booth, **193,** 50, 52
Alexander v. Railway Executive, **195,** 51, 52, 410
Alexander v. Rayson, **221,** 58
Allcard v. Skinner, **207,** 55
Allen v. Robles (Compagnie Parisienne de Garantie, Third Party), **284,** 82, 391
Allison v. Bristol Marine Insurance Co. Ltd., 143
Ames v. Milward, **684,** 456
Ammonia Soda Co. v. Chamberlain, **535,** 267, 268
Anderson v. Daniel, **210,** 56, 543
Andrews v. Hopkinson, **389,** 140, 170, 177, 178
Andrews v. Ramsay & Co., **449,** 199
Angel v. Jay, **172,** 43, 510, 528
Anglia Television Ltd. v. Reed, 87
Anglo-African Merchants Ltd. v. Bayley, **445,** 198, 371
Annie Hay, The, **659,** 427
Appleson v. Littlewood Ltd., 483
Arab Bank Ltd. v. Barclays Bank Ltd., 25
Arab Bank Ltd. v. Ross, **546,** 291, 309
Arbuckle v. Taylor, **506,** 225
Ardennes (S.S.) (Cargo Owners) v. Ardennes (S.S.) (Owners), **661,** 428
Armstrong v. Strain, **476,** 210, 631
Aruna Mills v. Dhanrajmal Gobindram, **414,** 88, 167
Ashbury Railway Carriage and Iron Co. v. Riche, **120,** 32, 195, 209, 238
Ashby v. Tolhurst, **328,** 101
Ashington Piggeries Ltd. v. Christopher Hill Ltd., **372,** 133, 135, 596
Astley Industrial Trust Ltd. v. Grimley, 169
Atkinson v. Denby, **225,** 59
Attwood v. Lamont, **251,** 64
Australia and New Zealand Bank v. Ateliers de Constructions Electriques de Charleroi, **423,** 192
Avery v. Bowden, **282,** 82, 429

Baily v. British Equitable Assurance Co., **526,** 240
Baker v. Yorkshire Fire and Life Assurance Co., **677,** 449
Baldry v. Marshall, **380,** 134, 140
Balfour v. Balfour, **43,** 12, 479, 480

Ballett v. Mingay, **325,** 100
Bank of England v. Vagliano Bros., **554,** 300, 657
Bannerman v. White, **177,** 47
Barclays Bank Ltd. v. Astley Industrial Trust Ltd., **544,** 291, 292, 336
Barclays Bank Ltd. v. Quistclose Investments Ltd., 490
Barker v. Bell, **421,** 184
Barrington v. Lee, **16b,** 6, 202
Barrow, Lane & Ballard Ltd. v. Phillip Phillips & Co., **364,** 123
Bartlett v. Sydney Marcus Ltd., 135
Bavins v. London & S.W. Bank, **548,** 293
Baxendale v. Bennett, 305
Baxendale v. Eastern Counties Railway Co., **651,** 407
Beach v. Reed Corrugated Cases Ltd., **304,** 88
Beale v. Taylor, **369,** 132
Beauforte (Jon), Re, **121,** 32, 238, 240
Behn v. Burness, **183,** 49, 429
Bell v. Lever Bros. Ltd., **142,** 38, 54, 517
Bell Houses Ltd. v. City Wall Properties Ltd., **125,** 33, 238
Belvoir Finance v. Cole, 211, 546
Bentinck Ltd. v. Cromwell Engineering Co., 181
Bentley v. Craven, **498,** 222
Beresford v. Royal Insurance Co. Ltd., **627,** 385
Berg v. Sadler and Moore, **235,** 60
Bertram, Armstrong & Co. v. Godfrey, **447,** 199
Beswick v. Beswick, **89,** 22
Bettini v. Gye, **185,** 49, 79
Bevan v. Bevan, 26
Bexwell v. Christie, **448,** 199
Biddle v. Bond, 200
Bigg v. Boyd Gibbins Ltd., **9,** 5
Bigos v. Bousted, **230,** 59
Binstead v. Buck, **431,** 194
Birkin v. Wing, 34
Blake & Co. v. Sohn, **460a,** 203
Blay v. Pollard and Morris, **665,** 440
Bolton Partners v. Lambert, **437,** 195, 620
Borthwick (Thomas) (Glasgow) Ltd. v. Bunge & Co., 130
Boss v. Kingston, **621,** 378
Bourne, Re, **515,** 229
Bowes v. Shand, **275,** 79, 130, 167
Bowmakers Ltd. v. Barnet Instruments Ltd., **223,** 59
Brabant v. King, **340,** 102
Bradbury v. Morgan, **41,** 11, 448
Bradford Old Bank v. Sutcliffe, **676,** 448

Brady v. Todd, **473**, 209
Branca v. Cobarro, **17**, 6
Brekkes Ltd. v. Cattel, 71
Brewer v. Westminster Bank, **581**, 328
Bridge v. Campbell Discount & Co. Ltd., **416**, 171
British Transport Commission v. Gourley, 572
Brogden v. Marriott, **213**, 57
Brogden v. Metropolitan Railway, **11**, 5
Bromley v. Smith, **263**, 66
Brook's Wharf and Bull Wharf Ltd. v. Goodman Bros., **320**, 95
Broome v. Pardess Co-operative Society, **407**, 154
Broughton v. Snook, **63**, 16
Brown v. Gould, **20a**, 6
Brown v. Sheen & Richmond Car Sales Ltd., **417**, 177
Brown (B.S.) & Son Ltd., v. Craiks Ltd., **383**, 135
Buckpitt v. Oates, **50**, 13
Bull v. Pitney-Bowes, **264**, 66
Burnard v. Haggis, **118**, 31
Burnett v. Westminster Bank, **574**, 324, 327
Burt v. Claud Cousins & Co. Ltd., **16a**, 6, 202, 467, 468
Butterworth, Re, **605**, 362
Byrne v. Van Tienhoven, **36**, 9, 10

Caldwell v. Sumpters, **351**, 105, 586
Cammell Laird & Co. Ltd. v. Manganese Bronze & Brass Co. Ltd., 124
Callow v. Lawrence, **566**, 311
Candler v. Crane, Christmas, **525**, 631
Car & Universal Finance Co. v. Caldwell, **168**, 42, 149, 151
Carlill v. Carbolic Smoke Ball Co., **3**, 4, 8, 12, 19, 56
Carlisle and Cumberland Banking Co. v. Bragg, **130**, 36, 440, 511
Carl-Zeiss Stiftung v. Herbert Smith & Co. (No. 2), 200
Carr v. Lynch, **54**, 15
Carter (John) Ltd., v. H. Hanson Haulage (Leeds) Ltd., 413
Carus-Wilson and Green, Re, **679**, 450
Casey's Patents, Stewart v. Casey, Re, **81**, 20
Cassel v. Lancashire and Yorkshire Accident Insurance Co. Ltd., **633**, 391
Cassell & Co. Ltd. v. Broome, 91
Castellain v. Preston, **642**, 398
Caton v. Caton, **57**, 15
Cellulose Acetate Silk Co. Ltd. v. Widnes Foundry Ltd., **312**, 92
Central London Property Trust Ltd. v. High Trees House Ltd., **96**, 24
Central Newbury Car Auctions Ltd. v. Unity Finance Ltd., 184
Champanhac & Co. Ltd. v. Waller & Co. Ltd., **385**, 136

Chandler v. Webster, **297**, 84, 571
Chapelton v. Barry U.D.C., **186**, 50
Chaplin v. Hicks, **303**, 88
Chaplin v. Leslie Frewin (Publishers), **105**, 29
Chappell v. Bray, **469**, 205
Chappell v. Nestle, **72**, 19
Chaproniere v. Lambert, 16, 17, 488
Charnock v. Liverpool Corporation, **90**, 22
Charter v. Sullivan, **308**, 89, 161
Charterbridge Corporation Ltd. v. Lloyds Bank Ltd., **666**, 441
Cheshire v. Bailey, **344**, 103, 584
Cheshire Banking Co., Duff's Executors' Case, Re, **42**, 11
Childs v. Monins and Bowles, **552**, 294
Chillingworth v. Esche, **15**, 6, 202
Chocolate and Sugar Confectionery Reference, Re, **268**, 76
Christie, Owen and Davies Ltd. v. Stockton, **458**, 202
Christoforides v. Terry, **463**, 203
City Centre Properties v. Matthew Hall & Co., 453
City Equitable Fire Insurance Co. Ltd., Re, 652
Cityland and Property (Holdings) Ltd. v. Dabrah, **357**, 108
Clarke, Re, **597**, 357
Clarke v. Army & Navy Co-operative Society Ltd., **386**, 137
Clarke v. Dickson, **170**, 42
Clarkson Booker Ltd. v. Andjel, **470**, 208
Clay v. Yates, **236**, 60
Clayton v. Le Roy, **403**, 148
Clayton's Case, 81, 565
Cleather v. Twisden, **508**, 225
Cleaver v. Mutual Reserves Fund Life Association, **626**, 385
Clements v. L. and N.W. Railway Co., **107**, 29
Cleveland Petroleum Co. Ltd. v. Dartstone Ltd., **248a**, 62
Clifton v. Palumbo, **8**, 5, 465
Clutton v. Attenborough, **555**, 300
Cochrane v. Willis, **141**, 38
Coggs v. Bernard, **73**, 19, 102
Cohen, Re, 360
Cohen v. Mitchell, **599**, 360
Coldman v. Hill, **343**, 103
Coles v. Enoch, **456**, 202
Collins v. Godefroy, **74**, 19
Columbine v. Penhall, **604**, 362
Combe v. Combe, **95**, 24
Comber v. Anderson, **422**, 192
Comet Radiovision Services v. Farnell-Tandberg, 72
Commercial Plastics v. Vincent, **260**, 66
Condon, Ex Parte James, Re, **595**, 352
Congresbury Motors Ltd. v. Anglo-Belge Finance Co. Ltd., **67**, 17
Conley, Re, 439
Consolidated Tea and Lands Company v. Oliver's Wharf, 406

Constantine (Joseph) Steamship Line Ltd. *v.* Imperial Smelting Corporation Ltd., **292**, 83

Cooper *v.* National Provincial Bank Ltd., **672**, 446

Cooper *v.* Phibbs, **128**, 36, 38, 96

Cornelius *v.* Banque Franco-Serbe, **558**, 302

Corpe *v.* Overton, **115**, 31

Cotman *v.* Brougham, **123**, 33, 238

Coutts & Co. *v.* Browne-Lccky, **100**, 28, 29, 440

Coutourier *v.* Hastie, **139**, 37, 515

Cowan *v.* Milbourn, **234**, 60

Cox *v.* Coulson, **489**, 214

Cox *v.* Hickman, **487**, 214

Cox *v.* Prentice, **323**, 96

Coxhead *v.* Mullis, **112**, 30

Craig Dec'd, *Re*, 55

Craven-Ellis *v.* Canons Ltd., **313**, 92

Cricklewood Property and Investment Trust Ltd. *v.* Leightons Investment Trust Ltd., **295**, 83, 567

Crook *v.* Morley, **591**, 339

Croom, England *v.* Provincial Assets Co., *Re*, **598**, 358

Crouch *v.* Credit Foncier of England, **543**, 286

Crouch and Lees *v.* Haridas, **454**, 201

Cuckmere Brick Co. *v.* Mutual Finance, **359**, 110

Cumming *v.* Ince, **203**, 54

Cundy *v.* Lindsay, **134**, 36, 147, 149, 151, 633

Currie *v.* Misa, 17, 18

Curtice *v.* London, City and Midland Bank Ltd., **580**, 326

Curtis *v.* Chemical Cleaning and Dyeing Co., **156**, 40, 50, 140

Cutter *v.* Powell, **270**, 78

Cyclists Touring Club, *Re*, 645

Czarnikow *v.* Koufos, 573

D. & C. Builders Ltd. *v.* Rees, **92**, 23, 25

Dafen Tinplate Co. *v.* Llanelly Steel Co. Ltd., **524**, 240

Dalton, *Re*, **590**, 339, 352

Daniels *v.* Trefusis, **64**, 16

Daniels *v* White and Sons, **388**, 137

Dann *v.* Curzon, **209**, 55, 58

Darlington (Peter) Partners Ltd. *v.* Gosho Co. Ltd., 136

Darrell *v.* Tibbitts, **646**, 96, 403

Davidson *v.* Barclays Bank Ltd., **579**, 325

Davies *v.* Benyon-Harris, **110**, 30

Davies *v.* Collins, **346**, 103

Davies *v.* Rees, **362**, 115

Davis Contractors Ltd. *v.* Fareham U.D.C., **286**, 83, 92

Davis *v.* Davis, **496**, 219

Davison *v.* Fernandes, **464**, 203

Davstone Estates Ltd., *Re*, **239**, 60, 449, 450

Dawsons Ltd. *v.* Bonnin, **609**, 371, 374, 517

Dearle *v.* Hall, 112

De Barnardy *v.* Harding, **272**, 79

Debtor, A, *Re*, (No. 5 of 1967), 353

Debtor, A, *Re* (No. 12 of 1968), 345

Debtor, A, *Re*, (No. 12 of 1970), 343

Debtors, A. and M., *Re*, **593**, 347

Debtor, A, *Ex Parte* Customs and Excise Commissioners *v.* The Debtor, *Re*, **592**, 341

De Bussche *v.* Alt, **442**, 197

Decro-wall International S.A. *v.* Practitioners in Marketing, 82

Deeley *v.* Lloyds Bank Ltd., **278**, 81

De Francesco *v.* Barnum, **106**, 29

De Lassalle *v.* Guildford, **180**, 48, 129

De Mattos *v.* Benjamin, 198

Demby Hamilton & Co. Ltd. *v.* Barden, **401**, 146

Denmark Productions *v.* Boscobel Productions, 503

Denny's Trustee *v.* Denny, **241**, 61

Derry *v.* Peek, **164**, 41

Deuchar *v.* Gas, Light and Coke Co., **122**, 32

Deyong *v.* Shenburn, **330**, 101

Dickinson *v.* Dodds, **38**, 10

Dickinson *v.* Lilwal, **465**, 203

Digby *v.* General Accident Fire and Life Assurance Corporation, **619**, 377

Dimbula Valley (Ceylon) Tea Co. Ltd. *v.* Laurie, **537**, 268

Dixons Ltd. *v.* J. L. Cooper Ltd., 89

D'Mello *v.* Loughborough College of Technology, **179**, 47

Donoghue *v.* Stevenson, **334**, 102, 137, 139, 170

Dodsley *v.* Varley, **425**, 193

Doorman *v.* Jenkins, **339**, 102

Doyle *v.* Olby (Ironmongers) Ltd., **166**, 41

Dresser *v.* Norwood, **478**, 211

Drew *v.* Nunn, **467**, 203, 204, 628

Drewery and Drewery *v.* Ware Lane, **459**, 202

Drury *v.* Victor Buckland Ltd., 169

Du Jardin *v.* Beadman Bros., 151

Duke of Beaufort and the Swansea Harbour Trustees, *Re*, **687**, 457

Dungate *v.* Dungate, **82**, 20, 86

Dungate *v.* Lee, **491**, 216

Dunlop *v.* New Garage and Motor Co. Ltd., **84**, 20, 92, 125

Dunlop *v.* Selfridge, **69**, 18, 20, 125, 131, 147, 495

Dunmore (Countess) *v.* Alexander, **37**, 9

Durham Bros. *v.* Robertson, **324**, 98

Durham Fancy Goods Ltd. *v.* Michael Jackson (Fancy Goods) Ltd., **97**, 24, 294

Eagleshill Ltd. *v.* J. Needham Builders Ltd., **571**, 315

Eardley *v.* Brood, 219

Eastern Distributors v. Goldring, **402**, 147, 150, 172, 605
Eastwood v. Kenyon, 18
Edgington v. Fitzmaurice, **154**, 39
Elder v. Auerbach, **222**, 59
Edwards v. Newland, **347**, 103
Edwards v. Sherratt, **652**, 407
Elcock v. Thomson, **635**, 393
Electrical Installations at Exeter Hospital Agreement, *Re*, 68
Eley v. Positive Life Assurance Co., **523**, 240
Eliason v. Henshaw, **30**, 8
Elkington v. Amery, **103**, 29
Ellesmere Brewery Co. v. Cooper, **673**, 447
Elliott v. Grey, **617**, 377
Elmdore Ltd. v. Keech, **277**, 80
Elvin and Powell Ltd. v. Plummer Roddis Ltd., **333**, 101
Empire Meat Co. Ltd. v. Patrick, 65
Entores Ltd. v. Miles Far East Corporation, **32**, 8, 9
Eshun v. Moorgate Mercantile Co., 181
Esso Petroleum Co. Ltd. v. Harper's Garage (Stourport) Ltd., **248**, 62, 553
Ewing v. Buttercup Margarine Co. Ltd., **519**, 237

Farnworth Finance Facilities v. Attryde, **198a**, 52
Farr v. Motor Traders' Mutual Insurance Society, **615**, 374
Farrell v. Federated Employers Insurance Association, 391, 405
Fawcett v. Whitehouse, **501**, 222
Felthouse v. Brindley, **29**, 8
Fender v. Mildmay, 57
Ferrier, *Re*, 144
Fibrosa Case, The, **298**, 84
Fielding and Platt Ltd. v. Najjar, **224**, 59
Filby v. Hounsell, **14**, 5
F. C. Finance Ltd. v. Francis, 181
Financings Ltd. v. Stimson, **40**, 10
Firth v. Armslake, **512**, 228
Fisher v. Bridges, **231**, 59
Fisher v. Fallows, **669**, 445
Fisher v. Harrods, **387**, 137
Fitch v. Dewes, **252**, 64
Flemyng v. Hector, 33
Floydd v. Cheney, **510**, 226
Foakes v. Beer, **91**, 23
Foley v. Classique Coaches Ltd., **20**, 6, 62
Fomento (Sterling Area) Ltd. v. Selsdon Fountain Pen Co. Ltd., 277
Ford Motor Co. (England) Ltd. v. Armstrong, **311**, 92
Foster v. Driscoll, **216**, 58, 216
Foster v. Mackinnon, **129**, 36, 294
Foster v. New Trinidad Lake Asphalte Co. Ltd., **536**, 267
Frebold v. Circle Products Ltd., 166
Frost v. Aylesbury Dairy Co. Ltd., **377**, 133, 134

Galbraith and Grant Ltd. v. Block, **404**, 152
Gallie v. Lee, **131**, 36, 440, 510
Galvanized Tank Manufacturers' Association's Agreement, *Re*, 70
Gardner v. Walsh, **570**, 313
Garner v. Murray, **516**, 231
Garwood's Trusts, Garwood v. Paynter, *Re*, **502**, 223
Geddling v. Marsh, **378**, 133
General Bill Posting Co. Ltd. v. Atkinson, **262**, 66
George v. Revis, **484**, 212
Gerard (Thomas) & Sons Ltd., *Re*, **541**, 278
Gibbons v. Westminster Bank Ltd., **578**, 325
Gibraltar Packers Ltd. v. Basic Economy and Development Corporation Ltd., **394**, 145
Gilbert and Partners v. Knight, **314**, 93
Gilchrist Watt and Sanderson Pty v. York Products Pty, **73a**, 19
Giles, *Re*, **626b**
Gilford Motor Co. Ltd. v. Horne, 64
Ginger, *Re*, **601**, 360, 361
Gledhow Autoparts v. Delaney, **254**, 65
Global Dress Co. v. Boase & Co., **338**, 102
Gluckstein v. Barnes, **532**, 254
Goddard v. O'Brien, 498
Goding v. Frazer, **16**, 6, 202, 467
Godley v. Perry, **384**, 136
Goldsmith (F.) (Sicklesmere) Ltd. v. Baxter, **55**, 15
Good v. Cheeseman, **93**, 24
Goode v. Harrison, **111**, 30
Goodinson v. Goodinson, **208**, 55, 61
Goodwin v. Robarts, **542**, 286
Goole and Hull Steam Towing Co. v. Ocean Marine Insurance Co., **647**, 403
Gore v. Gibson, 34
Gorse v. Durham County Council, **279a**, 81
Gosling v. Anderson, **692**, 42
Gould v. Gould, **46**, 12
Grant v. Australian Knitting Mills Ltd., **375**, 133, 137
Gray v. Barr, **626a**, 385
Great Northern Railway v. Swaffield, **427**, 194
Great Northern Railway v. Witham, **27**, 8
Green v. Balfour, *Re*, **685**, 456
Greenwood v. Martins Bank Ltd., **436**, 195, 295, 327
Griffiths v. Peter Conway Ltd., **379**, 133, 595
Griffiths v. Young, **60**, 16
Grist v. Bailey, **146**, 38
Gross v. Lewis Hillman Ltd., **160**, 40, 42
Grover and Grover v. Matthews, **438**, 195, 400

Hadley *v.* Baxendale, **305**, 88, 411, 525
Haigh *v.* Brooks, **70**, 19, 24
Hain Steamship Co. *v.* Tate and Lyle Ltd., 408
Hales *v.* London & N.W. Railway Co., **653**, 408
Halesowen Presswork *v.* Westminster Bank Ltd., **545**, 291, 354
Hall (R.H.) Ltd. *v.* W. H. Pim & Co. Ltd., **411**, 163
Hamilton Finance Co. Ltd. *v.* Coverley and Others, **557**, 301, 302, 316
Hamilton, Fraser & Co. *v.* Pandorf & Co., **631**, 389
Hamlyn *v.* Houston & Co., **505**, 225
Handley *v.* Marston, **420**, 180
Harbutt's Plasticine Ltd. *v.* Wayne Tank & Pump Co. Ltd., **198**, 51, 52, 88, 539
Hardwick Game Farm *v.* Suffolk Agricultural & Poultry Producers Association Ltd., 133
Hare *v.* Nichol, 80
Hargreaves Transport Ltd. *v.* Lynch, 77
Harling *v.* Eddy, **182**, 49, 140
Harris *v.* Nickerson, **10**, 5
Harris *v.* Packwood, **654**, 408
Harris *v.* Poland, **616**, 375
Hartley *v.* Hymans, 130
Hartley *v.* Ponsonby, 493
Hartstoke Fruiterers *v.* London, Midland and Scottish Rail Co., 421
Harvey *v.* Facey, **7**, 5, 465
Hawkins *v.* Price, **56**, 15
Head (Phillip) & Sons Ltd. *v.* Showfronts Ltd., **390a**, 143
Head *v.* Tattersall, **400**, 146
Healey *v.* Howlett & Sons, **397**, 146
Hedley Byrne *v.* Heller & Partners, **165**, 41, 45, 48, 129, 140, 170, 178, 210, 253, 277, 325, 328, 515, 631
Helby *v.* Matthews, **415**, 168, 169
Henderson *v.* Williams, **173**, 45, 147
Henkel *v.* Pape, **149**, 39
Hermann *v.* Charlesworth, **244**, 61
Herne Bay Steamboat Co. *v.* Hutton, **291**, 83
Herschtal *v.* Stewart and Ardern Ltd., **418**, 178
Heugh *v.* London & North Western Railway Co., **656**, 410
Hibernian Bank *v.* Gysin and Hanson, **563**, 307
Hickman *v.* Kent or Romney Marsh Sheep-breeders Association, **521**, 239, 451
Higgins *v.* Northampton Corporation, **133**, 36, 38
Hill *v.* Harris, **474**, 209
Hill *v.* Parsons, **693**, 94
Hill *v.* Settle, **600**, 360
Hillas *v.* Arcos, **19**, 6
Hillingdon Estates Co. *v.* Stonefields Estates Ltd., **296**, 83
Hippisley *v.* Knee, **453**, 200

Hivac Ltd. *v.* Park Royal Scientific Instruments Ltd., **259**, 65
Hochster *v.* De la Tour, **279**, 181
Hodgson *v.* Marks, **206**, 55
Hoenig *v.* Isaacs, **273**, 79
Holme *v.* Hammond, **488**, 214
Home Counties Dairies Ltd. *v.* Skilton, **253a**, 65
Hooley, *Ex Parte* United Ordnance & Engineering Co., *Re*, **606**, 365
Hopper, *Re*, **678**, 450
Horabin *v.* British Overseas Airways Corporation, 433
Horne *v.* Midland Railway Co., **306**, 88
Horsefall *v.* Thomas, **163**, 41
Horwood *v.* Millar's Timber Co., **240**, 61
Houghland *v.* R. Low (Luxury Coaches) Ltd., **337**, 102, 407
Household Fire Insurance Co. *v.* Grant, **33**, 9, 250
Howatson *v.* Webb, 511
Howell *v.* Coupland, **363**, 122
Hughes (C. W. and A. L.) *Re*, 283
Hughes *v.* Liverpool Victoria Legal Friendly Society, **226**, 59, 391
Hughes *v.* Metropolitan Railway, 24, 501
Hughes *v.* Pump House Hotel Co., **324a**, 98
Humble *v.* Hunter, 208
Hunt and Winterbottom (West of England) Ltd. *v.* B.R.S. Parcels Ltd., **196**, 51
Hutton *v.* Warren, **201**, 53, 136
Hyde *v.* Wrench, **24**, 7
Hyman *v.* Nye, **335**, 102

Imperial Loan Co. *v.* Stone, 34
Ingram *v.* Little, **137**, 37, 143, 147, 514
Initial Services *v.* Putterill, **265**, 66
Introductions Ltd. *v.* National Provincial Bank Ltd., **124**, 33, 441, 694
Ionides *v.* Pender, **613**, 373

Jackson *v.* Rogers, **650**, 407
Jackson *v.* Union Marine Insurance Co. Ltd., **293**, 83
Jackson *v.* White and Midland Bank Ltd., 328
James *v.* Commonwealth, 145
Jay's Ltd. *v.* Jacobi, **492**, 218
Jenkin *v.* Pharmaceutical Society, **119**, 32
Jenkins *v.* Jenkins, **567**, 312
John *v.* Mendoza, **218**, 58
Jones *v.* Bellgrove Properties Ltd., 86
Jones *v.* Clifford, **144**, 38
Jones *v.* Padavatton, **49**, 13
Jones *v.* Vernon's Pools Ltd., **51**, 13
Jones *v.* Waring & Gillow, **560**, 306
Joscelyne *v.* Nissen, **147**, 38

Karak Rubber Co. Ltd. *v.* Burden (No. 2) **694**, 324
Karflex Ltd. *v.* Poole, 131, 169, 179
Karsales (Harrow) Ltd. *v.* Wallis, **194**, 51, 52, 140, 180

Kaufman v. Gerson, **233**, 60
Kaye (P. & M.) Ltd. v. Hosier & Dickinson Ltd., 79
Kearley v. Thomson, **229**, 59
Keever, Re, **565**, 311, 351
Keighley, Maxsted v. Durant, **433**, 195, 208
Kelly v. Cornhill Insurance Co., 377
Kelner v. Baxter, **434**, 195, 208
Kendall v. Lillico, **372a**, 133, 134
Kendall v. Marshall Stevens & Co., **408**, 158
Kendrick v. Sotheby & Co., **481**, 211
Kennedy v. De Trafford, 109, 589
Kenyon v. Darwin Cotton Mfg. Co., **245**, 61
Kenyon, Son & Craven Ltd. v. Baxter Hoare & Co. Ltd., **197a**, 51, 254
Keppel v. Wheeler, **444**, 198
Kings Norton Metal Co. Ltd. v. Edridge, Merrett & Co. Ltd., **135**, 37
Kingston Cotton Mill Co., Re, **540**, 277, 653
Kingswood Estate Co. Ltd. v. Anderson, 17, 488
Kiriri Cotton Co. v. Dawani, **227**, 59, 96
Knightsbridge Estates Trust Ltd. v. Byrne, **354**, 108, 588
Koppel v. Koppel, **361**, 115
Kores Mfg. Co. Ltd. v. Kolok Mfg. Co. Ltd., **261**, 66, 67
Kreglinger v. New Patagonia Meat and Cold Storage Co., **356**, 108, 588
Krell v. Henry, **290**, 83

Lacis v. Cashmarts, 143
Lamb v. Wright & Co., **602**, 361
Lancashire Loans Ltd. v. Black, **205**, 55, 440
Larner v. Fawcett, **352**, 105, 194
Laurie & Morewood v. John Dudin & Sons, **393**, 145
Law v. Law, **497**, 221
Leaf v. International Galleries, **143**, 38, 42
Learoyd Bros. v. Pope, **348**, 103, 197
Leask v. Scott Bros., **409**, 158
Ledebeter (N.V.) v. Hibbert, **573**, 319
Lee v. Griffin, 124
Lee v. Neuchatel Asphalte Co. Ltd., **533**, 267
Lee Behrens & Co. Ltd., Re, 694
Lees v. Motor Insurers' Bureau, **640**, 397
Leesh River Tea Co. Ltd. v. British India S.N. Co. Ltd., **658**, 425
Legal and General Assurance Society Ltd. v. General Metal Agencies Ltd., **132**, 36
Leslie (R.) Ltd. v. Sheill, **117**, 31
L'Estrange v. Graucob, **189**, 50, 139
Lewis v. Averay, **136a**, 37, 42, 514
Lewis v. Rossiter, **689**, 457
Leyland Shipping Co. Ltd. v. Norwich Union Fire Insurance Society Ltd., **630**, 389

Lister v. Romford Ice and Cold Storage Co. Ltd., **202**, 53
Lloyd v. Grace Smith & Co., **475**, 210, 584
Lloyds v. Harper, 478
Lloyds Bank v. Cooke, **561**, 301
Lloyds Bank Ltd. v. E. B. Savory & Co., **584**, 335
London and Northern Bank, Ex Parte Jones, Re, **34**, 9
London and River Plate Bank v. Bank of Liverpool, 312
London Assurance v. Mansel, **607**, 371, 373
London Jewellers Ltd. v. Attenborough, **366**, 125, 144, 150
London Joint Stock Bank v. Macmillan and Arthur, **596**, 313, 325, 327, 662
Long v. Lloyd, **169**, 42
Long (Peter) and Partners v. Burns, **460**, 203
Longbottom & Co. Ltd. v. Bass Walker & Co. Ltd., 141
Looker v. Law Union and Rock Insurance Co. Ltd., **614**, 373
Lovell v. Lovell, **299**, 86
Lowe v. Lombank Ltd., **419**, 180
Lowther v. Harris, **479**, 211
Luker v. Chapman, **310**, 89
Lumsden & Co. v. London Trustee Savings Bank, **585**, 335
Luxor (Eastbourne) Ltd. v. Cooper, **457**, 202
Lyne-Pirkis v. Jones, **266**, 67
Lynn v. Bamber, **300**, 86

M. & S. Drapers v. Reynolds, 64
McArdle, Re, **80**, 20
McCarthy & Stone Ltd. v. Julian S. Hodge & Co. Ltd., **360**, 112
McCutcheon v. David MacBrayne, **192**, 50
McDonald & Co. v. Nash & Co., **572**, 319
McManus v. Fortescue, **413**, 165
McPherson v. Watt, **444**, 198
McRae v. Commonwealth Disposals Commission, **140**, 37, 123
Macaura v. Northern Assurance Co. Ltd., **644**, 398
Maddison v. Alderson, **66**, 17
Mafo v. Adams, **167**, 41, 91
Magee v. Pennine Insurance Co. Ltd., **145**, 38
Malas (Hamzeh) v. British Imex Industries, 22
Manchester Diocesan Council for Education v. Commercial and General Investments Ltd., **31**, 8, 10
Manchester Liners Ltd. v. Rea, **367a**, 133
Manley v. Sartori, **517**, 232
Mann v. D'Arcy, **503**, 223
Maple Flock Co. Ltd. v. Universal Furniture Products (Wembley) Ltd., **406**, 154

Marcel (Furriers) Ltd. *v.* Tapper, 124

Marfani & Co. *v.* Midland Bank, **586**, 335

Maritime National Fish Ltd. *v.* Ocean Trawlers Ltd., **294**, 83

Marles *v.* Trant (Philip) & Sons Ltd., **238**, 60

Marshall *v.* Green, 15

Matthews *v.* Baxter, 35

Medicaments Reference (No. 2), *Re*, 74

Mellenger *v.* New Brunswick Development Corporation, 27

Mendelssohn *v.* Normand Ltd., **156a**, 50, 52

Mercantile Bank of India Ltd. *v.* Central Bank of India Ltd., 147

Mercantile Credit Co. Ltd. *v.* Cross, 180

Mercantile Union Guarantee Corporation Ltd. *v.* Ball, **108**, 29

Merritt *v.* Merritt, **45**, 12

Mersey Docks and Harbour Board *v.* Hay, **660**, 427

Metropolitan Electric Supply Co. *v.* Ginder, **315**, 93

Metropolitan Police District Receiver *v.* Croydon Corporation, **321**, 95

Mighell *v.* Sultan of Johore, **99**, 26

The Mihalis Angelos, **281**, 82

Miles *v.* Clark, **494**, 219

Miller *v.* Law Accident Insurance Co. Ltd., **629**, 387

Mills, *Re*, 366

Mirabita *v.* Imperial Ottoman Bank, 167

Monk *v.* Warbey, **618**, 387

Monnickendam *v.* Leanse, **61**, 16, 441

Montague (Samuel) & Co. Ltd. *v.* Swiss Air Transport Ltd., **663a**, 433

Moody, (D.H.R.), (Chemists) *v.* Iron Trades Mutual Insurance Co., **622**, 379

Moorcock, The, **22**, 7, 53

Moore *v.* D.E.R. Ltd., 89

Moore & Co. *v.* Landauer & Co., **269**, 78, 132, 153

Morley *v.* Moore, **649**, 403

Morris *v.* C. W. Martin & Sons Ltd., **345**, 103

Morris & Co. *v.* Saxelby, **247**, 62, 63, 64

Morrison (James) and Co. Ltd., *v.* Shaw, Savill and Albion Co. Ltd., **624**, 383

Moschi *v.* L.E.P. Air Services, **696**, 448

Mountstephen *v.* Lakeman, **53**, 14, 439

Munro (Robert A.) & Co. Ltd., *v.* Meyer, **371**, 133, 154, 607

Munro *v.* Willmott, 615

Murray *v.* Legal and General Assurance Society, 405

Muskham Finance Ltd. *v.* Howard, 510

Mutual Life Insurance Company of New York *v.* Ontario Metal Products Co. Ltd., **611**, 373

Myers & Co. Ltd., *v.* Brent Cross Service Co., **365**, 123

Nanka Bruce *v.* Commonwealth Trust Ltd., 144

Napier *v.* National Business Agency Ltd., **220**, 58

Narbeth *v.* James, The Lady Tahilla, **274**, 79

Nash *v.* Inman, **102**, 29

Nathan *v.* Ogdens Ltd., **549**, 293

National Bank of Nigeria Ltd. *v.* Awolesi, **674**, 447

National Coal Board *v.* Gamble, **398**, 146

Neale *v.* Merrett, **24a**, 7

Neuwirth *v.* Over Darwen Industrial Co-operative Society, **332**, 101

Neville *v.* Dominion of Canada News Co. Ltd., **242**, 61

Newborne *v.* Sensolid (Great Britain) Ltd., **435**, 195

Newsholme Brothers *v.* Road Transport and General Insurance Co., **610**, 371

Newman *v.* Bourne and Hollingsworth, **331**, 101

Nichol *v.* Godts, **373**, 133

Nicholson *v.* Chapman, **432**, 194

Nicolene *v.* Simmonds, **23**, 7

Niblett *v.* Confectioners' Materials Co. Ltd., **368**, 131, 135

Noakes *v.* Rice, **355**, 108

Nordenfelt *v.* Maxim Nordenfelt Guns and Ammunition Co., **246**, 62, 63, 64

North and South Wales Bank *v.* Macbeth, 657

North British and Mercantile Insurance Co. *v.* London, Liverpool and Globe Insurance Co., **645**, 401

North Central Wagon Finance Co. Ltd. *v.* Brailsford, 128

Northcote *v.* Doughty, **113**, 30

Northland Airlines Ltd. *v.* Dennis Ferranti Meters Ltd., **24b**, 7

North Western Salt Co. Ltd. *v.* Electrolytic Alkali Co. Ltd., 67

Nugent *v.* Smith, **655**, 409

O'Connor *v.* B.D.B. Kirby & Co., **610a**, 371

Oliver *v.* Davis and Another, **547**, 292

Olley *v.* Marlborough Court Ltd., **190**, 50

Omnium D'Enterprises *v.* Sutherland, **280**, 82

Orbit Mining and Trading Co. Ltd. *v.* Westminster Bank, **556**, 301

Oscar Chess Ltd. *v.* Williams, **178**, 47

Overend & Gurney *v.* Gibb, **530**, 244

Overseas Commodities Ltd. *v.* G. W. Style, **637**, 395

Oxford Printing Ltd. *v.* Letraset Ltd., 73

Pacific Motor Auctions *v.* Motor Credits Ltd., **402a**, 150, 605

Page One Records Ltd. *v.* Britton, **319**, 94

Pagnan (R.) & Fratelli *v.* Corbisa Industrial Agropacuaria, 163

Panorama Developments (Guildford) *v.* Fodelis Furnishing Fabrics, 193

Parent Tyre Co. Ltd., *Re*, **520**, 238

Parker *v.* Clark, **48**, 13

Parker *v.* Staniland, 14

Parkinson *v.* The College of Ambulance Ltd. and Harrison, **219**, 58

Parks, Canada Permanent Trust Co. *v.* Parks, *Re*, 628

Partridge *v.* Crittenden, **6**, 4

Pathirana *v.* Pathirana, **499**, 222, 232

Payne *v.* Cave, 5

Pearce *v.* Brain, **114**, 31, 505

Pearce *v.* Brooks, **215**, 57

Pearce *v.* Gardener, **58**, 16

Pearson *v.* Rose & Young Ltd., **482**, 212

Peek *v.* Gurney, **159**, 40

Penrose *v.* Martyr, **550**, 294

Percival *v.* Wright, **531**, 245

Pharmaceutical Society of Great Britain *v.* Boots Cash Chemists Ltd., **4**, 4

Pharmaceutical Society of Great Britain *v.* Dickson, **267**, 67

Phillips, *Ex Parte* Barton, *Re*, **588**, 337

Phillips *v.* Brooks, **136**, 37, 42, 149, 151, 514

Phillips *v.* Foxhall, **667**, 443

Phoenix Assurance Co. *v.* Spooner, **648**, 403

Piercy *v.* Mills, **529**, 244

Pignataro *v.* Gilroy and Son, **396**, 145

Pillans *v.* Van Mierop, 18

Pilling *v.* Pilling, **493**

Pinnel's Case, 23

Pinnock Bros. *v.* Lewis and Peat Ltd., **307**, 88, 164, 594

Plant *v.* Bourne, 15

Plant Engineers (Sales) *v.* Davies, 206

Plowman (G.W.) & Son *v.* Ash, **253**, 65, 555

Plumer *v.* Gregory, **507**, 225

Pollock & Co. *v.* Macrae, **199**, 52

Poole *v.* Smith's Car Sales (Balham) Ltd., **391**, 144

Porter *v.* Freudenberg, 25

Poussard *v.* Spiers and Pond, **184**, 49, 79, 83

Povey *v.* Taylor, **426**, 193

Powell *v.* Lee, **28**, 8

Prager *v.* Blatspiel Stamp and Heacock Ltd., **429**, 194

President of India (The) *v.* Metcalfe Shipping Co. Ltd., 166, 428

Priest *v.* Last, **374**, 133

Printers and Finishers *v.* Holloway (No. 2), **256**, 65, 66

Provincial Insurance Co. *v.* Morgan and Foxon, **634**, 392

Prudential Staff Union *v.* Hall, **641**, 397, 398

Punt *v.* Symons, 648

Pym *v.* Campbell, **175**, 46

Quebec Marine Insurance Co. *v.* Commercial Bank of Canada, **638**, 396

Quickmaid Rental Services *v.* Reece, **176**, 46

R. *v.* Bonner, 219

R. *v.* Hartley, 347

R. *v.* Pentonville Prison Governor, *Ex Parte* Teja, 27

R. *v.* Wilson, **101**, 29

Radford *v.* Hair, **681**, 452

Raffles *v.* Wichelhaus, **151**, 39

Rampgill Mill Ltd., *Re*, 283

Ramsgate Victoria Hotel Co. *v.* Montefiore, **39**, 10, 475

Randall *v.* Randall, **686**, 457

Rann *v.* Hughes, 18

Raphael *v.* Bank of England, **564**, 309

Rawlinson *v.* Ames, **62**, 16

Rayfield *v.* Hands, **522**, 240

Redgrave *v.* Hurd, **161**, 40

Reed *v.* Dean, **336**, 102

Regazzoni *v.* K. C. Sethia Ltd., **217**, 58

Reid *v.* Hollingshead, **485**, 214

Reiger *v.* Campbell-Stuart, **446**, 198

Richardson Steam Ship Co. Ltd. *v.* Rowntree, **188**, 50

Rickards (Charles) Ltd. *v.* Oppenheim, **276**, 79, 130

Rimmer *v.* Knowles, **455**, 201

Robb *v.* Green, **257**, 65

Roberts and Cooper Ltd., *Re*, 285

Roberts *v.* Gray, **104**, 29

Robins *v.* Gray, **350**, 104

Robinson *v.* Graves, 124

Rodoconachi *v.* Elliott, **636**, 395

Rogers, Sons & Co. *v.* Lambert & Co., **349**, 103

Rolfe & Co. *v.* George, **456a**, 202

Rolls Razor *v.* Cox, 354

Rookes *v.* Barnard, 90, 91, 527

Roscorla *v.* Thomas, **79**, 20

Rose and Frank Co. *v.* Crompton and Brothers Ltd., **52**, 13

Rose *v.* Pim, **148**, 38

Roselodge Ltd. *v.* Castle, **608**, 371, 373

Rother *v.* Colchester Corporation, **249**, 62

Rourke *v.* Short, **214**, 57

Rowland *v.* Divall, **322**, 96, 125, 131

Royal British Bank *v.* Turquand, **528**, 240

Ryan *v.* Mutual Tontine Westminster Chambers Association, **318**, 94

Sachs *v.* Miklos, **430**, 194

Said *v.* Butt, **471**, 208

Salford Corporation *v.* Lever, **450**, 199

Salomon *v.* Salomon & Co., **518**, 236

Sanders *v.* Parry, **258**, 65

Sanders (Mayfair) Furs *v.* Davies, **342**, 102

Saunders *v.* Anglia Building Society, **131a**, 36, 440, 510

Scammell *v.* Ouston, **21**, 6, 7

Scaramanga *v.* Stamp, 384
Scheggia *v.* Gradwell, **461,** 203, 626, 627
Schioler *v.* Westminster Bank, **583,** 328
Scholfield *v.* Earl of Londesborough, **586,** 313, 662
Schweppes Ltd's. Agreement No. 2, *Re,* 68
Scorer *v.* Seymour Jones, **255,** 65
Scott *v.* Bradley, **56a,** 15
Scriven Brothers & Co. *v.* Hindley & Co., **152,** 39
Seddon *v.* North Eastern Salt Co., **171,** 43, 510, 516, 528
Seymour, *Re,* **603,** 361
Shadwell *v.* Shadwell, **78,** 20
Shamia *v.* Joory, **86,** 21, 96
Shanklin Pier Ltd. *v.* Detel Products Ltd., **181,** 48, 138, 139
Sharp *v.* Jackson, **589,** 338, 361
Sharp Bros. and Knight *v.* Chant, **126,** 35, 96
Shaw *v.* Groom, **211,** 56
Shaw *v.* Shaw, 90
Shephard *v.* Cartwright, 191
Shipton, Anderson & Co. and Harrison Brothers' Arbitration, **287,** 83
Shipton Anderson & Co. Ltd. *v.* Weil Bros., **405,** 153
Shipway *v.* Broadwood, **451,** 199
Sidebottom *v.* Kershaw, Leese & Co. Ltd., **525,** 240
Silverman (George) Ltd. *v.* Silverman, **250,** 63
Simpkins *v.* Pays, **47,** 13
Skinner *v.* Upshaw, **657,** 410
Slater *v.* Hoyle and Smith, **412,** 164
Slattery *v.* Mance, **625,** 385, 387
Slingsby (C.H.) *v.* District Bank, **577,** 325
Smart Bros. *v.* Pratt, 180
Smith *v.* Chadwick, **162,** 41
Smith *v.* Land and House Property Co., **155,** 39
Smith *v.* Mawhood, **212,** 56
Smith *v.* Morgan, 6
Smith (H.C.) Ltd., *v.* Great Western Rail Co., 421
Smith and Snipes Hall Farm Ltd. *v.* River Douglas Catchment Board, **87,** 21
Smith *v.* Union Bank of London, 330
Smith *v.* Wood, **675,** 448
Snelling *v.* John G. Snelling Ltd., **691,** 22
Snowdon, *Ex Parte* Snowdon, *Re,* **670,** 445
Solle *v.* Butcher, **127,** 35, 38, 96, 517
Southern Foundries *v.* Shirlaw, **527,** 240
Southern Industrial Trust *v.* Brooke House Motors, **232,** 60
South Staffordshire Water Co. *v.* Sharman, **326,** 100
Spanish Prospecting Co. Ltd., *Re,* 267
Spector *v.* Ageda, **68,** 17, 60, 490
Spellman *v.* Spellman, **44,** 12
Spencer *v.* Harding, **5,** 4
Spicer (Keith) *v.* Mansell, **486,** 214

Springer *v.* Great Western Railway, **428,** 194
Spurling *v.* Bradshaw, 535
Stacey *v.* Wallis, **551,** 294
Stadium Finance *v.* Robbins, **483,** 212
Staffs Motor Guarantee Co. *v.* British Wagon Co., **480,** 211
Stapley *v.* Read Bros., **538,** 268
Starkey *v.* Bank of England, **472,** 209
Steel *v.* Dixon, **671,** 446
Steinberg *v.* Scala, **109,** 30, 31, 240
Sterns Ltd. *v.* Vickers Ltd., **399,** 146
Stevenson & Sons Ltd. *v.* A. G. für Cartonnagen Industrie, **466,** 203, 228
Stevenson *v.* McLean, **25,** 7, 10
Stilk *v.* Myrick, **76,** 19
Stocks *v.* Wilson, **116,** 31, 505
Stone *v.* Reliance Mutual Insurance Society Ltd., **695,** 371
Stonehewer *v.* Farrar, **683,** 456
Storey *v.* Fulham Steel Works, **288,** 83
Strange (S.W.) Ltd. *v.* Mann, 64
Stromdale and Ball Ltd. *v.* Burden, 2
Strongman Ltd. *v.* Sincock, **237,** 60
Stuart *v.* Freeman, **623,** 381
Suisse Atlantique Société D'Armament Maritime S.A. *v.* N.V. Rotterdamsche Kolen Centrale, **197,** 51, 52, 103, 140, 180, 430, 538, 539, 540
Sumpter *v.* Hedges, **271,** 79
Sunderland *v.* Barclays Bank Ltd., **576,** 325
Sunley (B.) & Co. Ltd. *v.* Cunard White Star Ltd., **302,** 87
Sutherland *v.* Hannevig Brothers Ltd., **690,** 457
Sutton & Co. *v.* Grey, **664,** 439
Sykes (F. & S.) (Wessex) *v.* Fine-Fare, 469
Sylph, The, **680,** 450

Tamplin *v.* James, **153,** 39
Tate *v.* Crewdson, **668,** 444
Tate *v.* Williamson, **158,** 40
Tattersall *v.* Drysdale, **620,** 378
Taylor *v.* Bowers, **228,** 59
Taylor *v.* Caldwell, **289,** 83, 590
Teheran-Europe Co. *v.* S. T. Belton (Tractors), 207
Teh Hu, The, 88
Thellusson, *Ex Parte* Abdy, *Re,* **596,** 352, 671
Thomas *v.* Tyne and Wear Freight Insurance Association, **639,** 396
Thomas National Transport (Melbourne) Pty Ltd. and Pay *v.* May and Baker (Australia) Ltd., **200,** 52
Thompson *v.* L.M.S. Railway, **187,** 50
Thompson *v.* Percival, **511,** 227
Thompson (W. L.) Ltd. *v.* Robinson (Gunmakers) Ltd., **309,** 89, 161
Thornett & Fehr *v.* Beers & Son, **382,** 135
Thornton *v.* Shoe Lane Parking Ltd., **190a,** 50

Timber Shipping Co. S.A. *v.* London and Overseas Freighters, 457

Timmins *v.* Moreland Street Property Ltd., **59,** 16

Tinn *v.* Hoffman, 9, 475

Tomlin *v.* Mayor of Fordwich, **688,** 457

Tomlin *v.* Standard Telephone and Cables Ltd., **18,** 6

A. Tomlinson (Hauliers) Ltd. *v.* Hepburn, **643,** 398

Tool Metal Manufacturing Co. Ltd. *v.* Tungsten Electric Co. Ltd., 24

Total Oil Great Britain Ltd. *v.* Thompson Garages (Biggin Hill) Ltd., **285,** 82, 84

Tournier *v.* National Provincial and Union Bank of England, **575,** 324, 665

Tower Cabinet Co. Ltd. *v.* Ingram, **509,** 226

Tradax Export S.A. *v.* Volkswagonwerk A.G., 453

Trim Joint District School Board of Management *v.* Kelly, **628,** 386

Tritonia Shipping Inc. *v.* South Nelson Forest Products Corpn., **682,** 454

Trollope and Colls Ltd. *v.* Atomic Power Constructions Ltd., **26,** 7

Troughton *v.* Hunter, **514,** 229

Tulk *v.* Moxhay, **88,** 21, 495

Turnbull *v.* Garden, **452,** 200

Tweddle *v.* Atkinson, **83,** 20, 22

Twycross *v.* Grant, 254

Ultzen *v.* Nichols, **329,** 101

Underwood Ltd. *v.* Burgh Castle Brick & Cement Syndicate, **390,** 143

Universal Non-Tariff Fire Insurance Co., Forbes & Co.'s Claim, *Re*, **612,** 373, 374

Vanbergen *v.* St. Edmunds Properties Ltd., **75,** 19

Van Lynn Developments *v.* Pelias Construction Co., 98

Varley *v.* Whipp, **370,** 133

Verelst's Administratrix *v.* Motor Union Insurance Co. Ltd., **632,** 391

Verner *v.* General and Commercial Investment Trust, **534,** 267

Victoria Laundry Ltd. *v.* Newman Industries Ltd., 572

Vincent *v.* Premo Enterprises (Voucher Sales) Ltd., **1,** 2

Vinden *v.* Hughes, **553,** 300

Wakeham *v.* Mackenzie, **65,** 17, 489

Wait and James *v.* Midland Bank, **395,** 145

Walker *v.* Hirsch, **490,** 215

Walker *v.* Wilsher, 468

Wallis *v.* Day, **243,** 61

Wallis, Son & Wells *v.* Pratt & Haynes, **367,** 129, 140

Walsh *v.* Londsdale, **353,** 108

Walter *v.* James, **439,** 196

Ward (R. V.) Ltd. *v.* Bignall, **410,** 159

Ward *v.* Byham, **77,** 19

Warehousing and Forwarding Co. of East Africa *v.* Jafferali & Sons, **441,** 196

Warlow *v.* Harrison, 5, 165

Warner Bros. Pictures Inc. *v.* Nelson, **317,** 93, 94, 577

Waterer *v.* Waterer, **495,** 219

Watts, Watts & Co. Ltd. *v.* Mitsui & Co. Ltd., **662,** 429

Watson *v.* Davies, **440,** 196, 619

Watteau *v.* Fenwick, **424,** 193

Webster *v.* Cecil, **138,** 37

Weeks *v.* Propert, **539,** 270

Wegg-Prosser *v.* Evans, **504,** 225

Weiner *v.* Harris, **392,** 144

Welby *v.* Drake, **94,** 24

Wells *v.* Smith, **477,** 211

Wenlock (Baroness) *v.* River Dee Co., 32

Westminster Bank Ltd. *v.* Imperial Airways Ltd., **663,** 433

Westminster Bank Ltd. *v.* Zang, **587,** 336, 434, 655

Westminster Road Construction and Engineering Co. Ltd., 653

West of England and South Wales District Bank, *Re*, 32

Whaite *v.* Lancashire and Yorkshire Railway Co., 412

White *v.* Bluett, **71,** 19

White *v.* City of London Brewery Co., **358,** 109

White and Carter (Councils) Ltd. *v.* McGregor, **283,** 82, 161

Whittington *v.* Seal-Hayne, **174,** 45, 128

Whitwood Chemical Co. *v.* Hardman, **316,** 93, 94

Wigzell, *Ex Parte* Hart, *Re*, **594,** 352

Wilkie *v.* London Passenger Transport Board, 5

Wilkinson *v.* Brown, **462,** 203

Williams *v.* Bayley, **204,** 54

Williams *v.* Carwardine, **12,** 5

Williams *v.* Lake, 487

Williamson *v.* Rider, **559,** 303

Willoughby *v.* Horridge, 422

Wilson *v.* Brett, **341,** 102

Wilson *v.* United Counties Bank, **301,** 87

Wilson *v.* Wilson, **2,** 3

Wilson and Meeson *v.* Pickering, **562,** 306

Wilson *v.* Rickett, Cockerell & Co. Ltd., **381,** 134

Winkfield, The, **327,** 101

Winn *v.* Bull, **13,** 5

With *v.* O'Flanagan, **157,** 40

Wood *v.* Scarth, **150,** 39

Woods *v.* Martins Bank, **582,** 328

Worcester Finance *v.* Cooden Engineering Co., **402b,** 150

Wren *v.* Holt, **376,** 133

Yenidji Tobacco Co. Ltd., **513,** 229

Yeoman Credit Ltd. *v.* Latter, 502

Yonge *v.* Toynbee, **468,** 204, 209

GENERAL INDEX

ACCORD AND SATISFACTION, 22–5
ADVERTISEMENTS—
  hire-purchase, 185–7
  offers, 12
AGENCY, 191–213 (*see also* AGENTS)
  creation of, 192–6
  definition of, 191
  necessity, of, 193–4, 196
  principal's liability for agent's war-
    ranties, frauds, etc., 209–10
  ratification, 194–6
  termination of, 203–5
  undisclosed principal, 20, 207–8
  wife of, 196
AGENTS (*see also* AGENCY)—
  authority of,
    actual, 192
    apparent, 193
    to receive payment, 210
  capacity, 191–2
  del credere, 14, 213
  duties of, 197–200
  factors, 211–13
  liabilty to third parties, 206–11
  notice to, 210–11
  rights against principal, 200–3
ALIENS, 25–6, 341
ARBITRATION, 449–59 (*see also* ARBITRA-
    TORS)
  agreement, 449–52
    enforcement of, 451–2
    scope of, 450–1
    subject-matter of, 450
  award, 456–9
    costs of, 458
    enforcement of, 458
    essentials of, 456–7
    form of, 456
    remitting and setting aside of, 457–8
    time of, 456
  common law submissions, 459
  compared with valuation, 450
  conduct of, 454–6
  definition of, 449
  official referee, 454
  stating a case, 455
  statutory arbitrations, 459
ARBITRATORS (*see also* ARBITRATION)—
  appointment by court, 453–4
  authority irrevocable, 453
  powers of, 455
  remuneration of, 459
  single, 452
  three, 453
  two, 453
  umpires, 453
ARTICLES OF ASSOCIATION, 239–40
ASSIGNMENT—
  contractual rights, of, 98–100

ASSIGNMENT (*contd.*)—
  insurance of, 403–5
  invalid, 361–4
  partner's share in partnership, of 222–3
ASSURANCE (*see also* INSURANCE)—
  meaning of, 369
AUCTION SALES, 164–5
AVERAGE, 402

BAILMENT, 100–4
  bailee,
    delegation by, 103
    estoppel of, 103
    lien, 103
    obligations of, 102
  bailor,
    obligations of, 101–2
  definition, 100
  finders, 101
  involuntary recipients, 101
  licence,
    distinguished, 101
  possession, 100
BANKER AND CUSTOMER, 324–8
BANKRUPTCY, 337–68
  acts of, 337–40
  adjudication order, 345–7
    annulment of, 347
    effect of, 346
    insured, of, 405
  capacity, 341–2
  committee of inspection, 348
  composition, 344, 357–9
  creditors, 353–7
    deferred, 356–7
    landlord, 355–6
    preferential, 354–5
    proof of debts, 354
    secured, 353–4
  debtor's property, 359–64
    after-acquired, 360
    invalid assignments, 361–4
    reputed ownership, 360–1
  discharge, 366–8
  disclaimer, 364–6
  fraudulent conveyances, 362–3
  fraudulent preferences, 361–2
  invalid assignments, 361–4
  meetings of creditors, 344–5
  official receiver, 347–8
  partners, of, 233–4
  petition, 340–1
  public examination, 345
  receiving order, 342–3
  relation back, doctrine of, 351–2
  scheme of arrangement, 344, 357–9
  small bankruptcies, 367
  special manager, 348
  statement of affairs, 343–4

BANKRUPTCY (*contd.*)—
subsequent bankruptcies, 368
trustee, 348–51
BARRATRY, 387
BILLS OF EXCHANGE, 286–323
acceptance, 296–300
honour, for, 300
presentment for, 299
types of, 297–8
advantages of, 287–8
alterations to, 313
bills in a set, 319–20
characteristics of, 286
conflict of laws, 321
damages on dishonour, 319
delivery, 305–6
discharge of, 311–13
dishonour, 313–18
drawee of, 295–6
drawer of, 292–3
forgery, 294–5
holder in due course, 291–2, 309–10
holders, 291, 309–11
indorsement, valid, 307
liabilities of parties, 318–19
life cycle of, 288–9
lost instrument, 320–1
nature of, 287
negotiability, 305–9
negotiation, 307
noting of, 290, 316–18
order, 293
payment, 300–3
due date, 304–5
payee, 300
presentation for, 301–3
sum certain, 300
time of, 303–5
protesting of, 290, 316–18
signature, 293–4
transferor by delivery, 309
types of, 286–87
BILLS OF LADING, 425, 427, 428–9
BILLS OF SALE, 112–17
definition, 113
personal chattels, 113–14
rights and liabilities of parties, 116
schedule to, 114
seizure, statutory causes of, 116–17
statutory requirements of, 114–15
void, 115–16

CAPACITY—
agency, 191–2, 208
bankruptcy, 341–2
contract, 25–35
guarantee, 440
sale of goods, 126
CARRIAGE BY AIR, 431–8
air waybill, 436
amended Convention of 1955, 436
application of 1955 Convention, 437
avoidance of liability, 433
Carriage by Air (Supplementary
Provisions) Act, 1962, 438

CARRIAGE BY AIR (*contd.*)—
carrier's liability, 436
carrier's lien, 434
complaints and claims, 435
delivery, 434
deviation, 434
liability of carriers by air, 433
liability of carrier for goods, 432
limitation on damages, 434
loss of limit on liability, 433
passengers' luggage, 435
rules on non-international carriage, 437
special contracts, 435
stoppage in transitu, 434
Warsaw Convention, 1929, 431–6
CARRIAGE BY INLAND WATERWAY—
British Waterways Board, 422
conditions of carriage, 422
CARRIAGE BY RAIL, 418–22
carriage at Board's risk, 419
carriage at owner's risk, 421
carriage of goods, 419
carriage of passengers' luggage, 422
transport charges and facilities, 418
CARRIAGE BY ROAD, 406–18
Carriers Act, 1830, 411–13
carrier's lien, 410
common carriers, 406
common carriers, duties and liabilities
at common law, 407
delivery, 409
goods specified, 412
measure of damages, 411
private carriers, 407, 413
variation of common law duties and
liabilities, 411
CARRIAGE BY SEA, 422–31
affreightment, 427–30
bills of lading, 427, 428–9
charterparties, 428, 429
lay days and demurrage, 430
Carriage of Goods by Sea Act, 1924,
423
bill of lading, issue of, 425
contracting out, 426
damages, limitation of, 425
dangerous goods, 425
deviation, 425
liability of carrier under Hague
Rules, 426
the clause paramount, 426
Carriage of Goods by Sea Act, 1971,
430
common law position, 423
Merchant Shipping Act, 1894, 426–7
CARRIAGE OF GOODS BY ROAD,
INTERNATIONAL, 413–18
carrier liability, 414
consignment note, 413
dangerous goods, 416
delay, 415
deviation, 416
involvement of two or more carriers,
417
jurisdiction and contracting out, 418

CARRIAGE OF GOODS BY ROAD (*contd.*)
  limitation of damages, 416
  presumption of loss, 415
  time limit for claims, 417
CAVEAT EMPTOR, 53
CHAMPERTY, 58
CHARTER PARTIES, 428, 429
  CHEQUES, 323–36 (*see also* BILLS OF
    EXCHANGE)
  banker and customer, 324–8
  crossed—
    account payee, 331–2
    banker's duties, 330
    crossing procedure, 329–30
    effect of crossing on holder, 331
    nature of crossing, 328–9
    protection for banker, 332
  Cheques Act, 333–6
  definition of, 323
C.I.F. CONTRACTS, 166–7
CLAYTON'S CASE, 81
COMMITTEE OF INSPECTION, 348
COMPANIES (*see* REGISTERED COMPANIES)
COMPENSATION BY DIRECTORS, 41, 252
CONDITIONAL SALE, 182
CONFIRMATORY AGENT, 207
CONSIDERATION, 17–25
CONTRACT, 1–95
  acceptance, 5
  accord and satisfaction, 22
  appropriation of payments, 81
  breach—
    damages for, 87
    injunction, 93
    quantum meruit, 92
    refusal of further performance, 94
    remedies for, 87–95
    rescission, 94
    specific performance, 93
  capacity, 25
    aliens, 25
    corporations, 32
    diplomats, 26
    drunkards, 34
    foreign sovereigns, 26
    married women, 32
    minors, 27
    persons with mental disorder, 34
    unincorporated bodies, 33
  classification of, 1
  conditions, 49
  consideration, 17
  deeds, 2
  definition of, 1
  discharge, 76–87
    by agreement, 76
    by breach, 81
    by lapse of time, 86
    by operation of law, 86
    by performance, 78
    by subsequent impossibility, 83
  duress in, 54
  essentials of, 1
  exemption clauses, 49
  formalities, 13

CONTRACT (*contd.*)—
  fraud, 41
  frustration, 83
  fundamental breach, 51
  illegal, 55
  innocent misrepresentations, 41
  instantaneous communications, 8
  intention to create legal relations, 11
  invitation to treat, 4
  memorandum of, 14
  misrepresentation, 39
  mistake, 35
  negligent misrepresentation, 41
  offer, 4
  offer and acceptance, 4
  option, 9
  part performance, 16
  privity of, 20
  post, use of, 8
  reality of consent, 35
  record, of, 3
  rectification, 38
  representations, 39
  rescission, 42
  restraint of trade, in, 62
  revocation, 9
  simple, 3
  specialty, 2
  specific performance, 93
  tender, 80
  terms, 45, 52
  uberrimae fidei, 53
  undue influence, 54
  warranties, 49
  writing required, 13
CONTRIBUTION—
  co-sureties, 445
  insurance, 401
CORPORATIONS—
  capacity in contract, 32
CREDIT SALE (*see* HIRE-PURCHASE)

DAMAGES, 87
DE MINIMIS NON CURAT LEX, 153
DEL CREDERE AGENT, 14, 213
DEVIATION, 383, 434
DIPLOMATS, 26
DISCLAIMER, 364–6
DISCLOSURE, 53, 370, 446
DRUNKARDS, 34
DURESS AND UNDUE INFLUENCE, 54, 440

ESCROW, 2
ESTOPPEL—
  deed, in, 3
  minors, 31
  partnership, in, 217
  promissory, 20
EX-SHIP CONTRACTS, 167
EX-STORE CONTRACTS, 167
EX-WORKS CONTRACTS, 167

FACTORS, 147, 184, 211–13
FIDELITY GUARANTEES, 442

F.O.B. CONTRACTS, 166
FORGERY, 257, 294
FRAUDULENT CONVEYANCES, 338, 362
FRAUDULENT PREFERENCES, 338, 361
FRUSTRATION OF CONTRACT, 83

GAMING, 57
GARNER *v.* MURRAY, 231
GENERAL AVERAGE LOSS, 393
GRACE, DAYS OF, 304, 382
GUARANTEE (*see* SURETYSHIP)
GUARANTEE AND INDEMNITY DISTIN-
    GUISHED, 14

HADLEY *v.* BAXENDALE, 88, 411
HAGUE RULES, 424
HIRE-PURCHASE, 168–90
    advertisements, 185
    agreement, 315–19, 390, 392–6
    common law of, 169–71
    contrasted with sale, 121–2
    credit sale, 183
    Crowther Report, 187
    dealer's liability, 177
    default of hirer, 180
    definition of, 168
    disposition, 185
    documents—
        legibility of, 177
        position of signature, 173
        statutory copies, 172
        supply of, 176
    exclusion clauses, 180
    execution distress and bankruptcy,
        182
    guarantees and indemnities, 182
    Hire-Purchase Acts, 171
        general requirements, 171
    implied terms, 178
    motor vehicles, 184
    owner's right to recover possession,
        180
    parties, 168
    penalties, 187
    right of cancellation, 173
    right of determination, 176
    warranties and conditions, 178

ILLEGAL CONTRACTS, 55
IMMORAL CONTRACTS, 57
INCHMAREE CLAUSE, 388
INDEMNITY, CONTRACT OF, 439
INJUNCTION, 93
INSURABLE INTEREST, 397
INSURANCE, 369–405 (*see also* INSURANCE,
    FIRE; INSURANCE, LIFE; INSURANCE,
    MARINE)
    agent, by, 371
    assignment of, 403
    average, 402
    bailee, by, 398
    bankruptcy of assured, 405
    claims, 391
        notice of, 391

INSURANCE (*contd.*)—
    contract of, 370
    contribution, 401
    cover notes, 371
    disclosure, extent of, 371
    double, 400
    grace, days of, 382
    insurable interest, 397
    liability insurance, 376
    motor vehicle insurance, 377
        knock for knock agreement, 403
        Motor Insurers' Bureau, 396
    nature of, 369
    personal accident insurance, 324, 375,
        386
    policy, 374–80
        duration of, 380
        renewal of, 381
    premium, 390
    proposal, 370
    re-insurance, 402
    risk, 384
    subrogation, 402
    uberrimae fidei, 373
    wagering policies, 400
INSURANCE, FIRE (*see also* INSURANCE)
    assignment, 404
    claims, 392
    contribution clause, 401
    insurable interest, 398
    policy, 375
    reinstatement, 392
    risk, 386
    subrogation, 402
INSURANCE, LIFE (*see also* INSURANCE)
    assignment, 404
    claims, 392
    continuing character, 381
    insurable interest, 397
    policy, 375
    risk, 384
    subrogation, 403
INSURANCE, MARINE (*see also* INSURANCE)
    arrests, restraints, etc., 387
    assignment, 404
    claims, 393
    collision or running down clause, 389
    double insurance, 400
    effecting, 372
    Inchmaree clause, 388
    insurable interest, 399
    losses—
        abandonment, 395
        constructive total, 394
        general average, 393
        partial, 394
        particular average, 393
        successive, 394
        total, 394
    policies—
        mixed, 382
        time, 382
        types of, 379
        voyage, 383
P.P.I., policy, 400

INSURANCE, MARINE (*contd.*)—
proximate cause, 389
risks—
nature of, 386
war, 387
subrogation, 402
voyage policies, 383
change of voyage, 383
deviation, 383
excuses for deviation, 384
warranties, 395
INTEREST, RECOVERY OF, 95

JETTISONS, 387

LIEN—
active, 410
agent's, 200
banker's, 106
common carrier's, 410
equitable, 106
general, 104, 410, 420
hire-purchase, in, 176
maritime, 105
particular, 104, 410
partner's, 229
possessory, 104
railways, 420
unpaid seller's, 156
LIMITATION OF ACTIONS, 3, 42, 66, 86
LLOYD'S, 370, 372

MAINTENANCE, 58
MARITIME PERILS, 386
MARKET OVERT, 148
MARRIED WOMEN—
bankruptcy of, 341
capacity in contract, 32
MATERIAL ALTERATIONS, 313, 447
MEMORANDUM IN WRITING, 14
MEMORANDUM OF ASSOCIATION, 231
MERGER, 3, 86
MINORS, 27–31
bankruptcy, 341
ratification of contracts, 39
valid contracts, 29
void contracts, 28
voidable contracts, 29
MISREPRESENTATION, 39, 128
MISTAKE, 35
MORTGAGES OF CHOSES IN ACTION, 120
MORTGAGES OF LAND, 106–12
equitable, 107
legal, 106
mortgage rights of, 109
MORTGAGES OF LAND (*contd.*)—
mortgagor, rights of, 108
priorities, 111
MOTOR INSURERS' BUREAU, 396
MOTOR VEHICLES ON HIRE-PURCHASE, 184

NECESSITY, AGENCY OF, 193–4, 196

NEGOTIABLE INSTRUMENTS, 286–336 (*see also* BILLS OF EXCHANGE, PROMISSORY NOTES AND CHEQUES)

OFFICIAL RECEIVER, 347
OFFICIAL REFEREE, 454

PART-PERFORMANCE, DOCTRINE OF, 16
PARTICULAR AVERAGE LOSS, 393
PARTNERS (*see also* PARTNERSHIP)
assignment of share, 222
bankruptcy of, 233
capacity of, 216
duties of, 221
indemnity, 221
number of, 215
relations with each other, 218
relations with third parties, 223
changes in constitution, 226
partners' powers, 223
partners' liabilities, 225
salaried, 215
transmission of share, 223
PARTNERSHIP, 214–35 (*see also* PARTNERS)
agreement, 216
breach of, 223
rescission of, 232
variation of, 218
capital, 220
compared with other associations, 214
dissolution of, 227
method, 227
partner's insolvency on, 231
powers on, 229
profits after winding up, 232
treatment of assets on, 230
firm name, 217
limited, 234
management of, 221
nature of, 214
objects of, 218
property, 218
profits, 220
registration of business names, 217
PASSING OFF, 218
PAWNBROKERS, 118
PAWNS, 117
PIPELINES, 422
PIRATES, 387
PLEDGES, 117
POWERS OF ATTORNEY, 205
PRIVITY OF CONTRACT, 20
PROMISSORY NOTES, 321–3 (*see also* BILLS OF EXCHANGE)
definition, 321
joint and several, 322
liability of maker, 323
payment on demand, 322
presentment for payment, 323
PUBLIC POLICY—
contracts contrary to, 57

QUANTUM MERUIT, 92
QUASI-CONTRACT, 95–7

RATIFICATION, 34, 194
RECEIPTS, 80
RECTIFICATION, 38
REGISTERED COMPANIES, 224-77
  accounts, 261
  alteration of share capital, 268
  articles of association, 239
  auditors, 276
  borrowing powers, 269
  brokerage, 253
  classification, 236
  compared with partnerships, 236
  debentures, 270
  defunct, 281
  directors, 242
  dividends and profits, 266
  incorporation, 253
  meetings, 258
  membership, 240
  memorandum of association, 237
  name, 237
  nominee holdings, 241
  promoters, 254
  prospectus, 251
  proxies, 260
  public and private companies, 272
  registers, 272, 273
  resolutions, 258
  share capital, 249
    alteration of, 247
    calls, 255
    forfeiture of shares, 255
    forged transfers, 257
    issue of shares, 250
    mortgages, 257
    share certificates, 255
    share warrants, 255
    stock, 250
    transfer and transmission of shares, 256
    types of shares, 249
  statutory books and returns, 273
  underwriting, 253
  winding-up—
    compulsory, 278
    under supervision, 281
    voluntary, 280
REGISTRATION OF BUSINESS NAMES, 217
RELATION BACK, 351
REMOTENESS OF DAMAGE, 87
REPUTED OWNERSHIP, 360
RES PERIT DOMINO, 146
RESALE PRICE MAINTENANCE, 71
RESTRICTIVE TRADE PRACTICES, 67

SALE OF GOODS, 121-167
  acceptance, 154
  anticipatory breach, 161
  auction sales, 164
  breach of condition and warranty, 123-4, 128, 163
  breach of condition treated as breach of warranty, 141
  buyer's remedies, 162
  buyer's right to examine goods, 154

SALE OF GOODS (*contd.*)—
  capacity of parties, 126
  conditions and warranties, 128
  consideration, 126
  damages, measure of, 160, 163
  definition of, 121
  delivery, 152
  existence of goods, 122
  export sales, 166
  formalities, 127
  goods, 121
  implied terms—
    exclusion of, 139
    quality and fitness, 133
    sale by description, 132
    sale by sample, 136
    time, 130
    title, 130
  manufacturer, liability of, 137
  market overt, 148
  negligence, manufacturer's liability for, 137
  performance of contract, 152
  price, 126
  property in goods, transfer of, 143
  resale, right of, 159
  sales contrasted with—
    barter, 124
    contracts for work and materials, 124
  seller's liability for dangerous goods, 137
  seller's lien, 156
  seller's remedies, 155
    personal remedies, 160
    real remedies, 155
  specific performance, 164
  stoppage *in transitu*, 157
  title, seller's right to give, 159
  title, transfer of, 146
SEAWORTHINESS, 396
SECRET PROFITS, 199
SECURITIES, 104, 446
SPECIAL MANAGER, 348
SPECIFIC PERFORMANCE, 93, 164
STOPPAGE IN TRANSITU, 157, 434
SUBROGATION, 402
SURETYSHIP, 439-48
  co-sureties, rights and liabilities of, 445
  fidelity bond, 442
  guarantee—
    discharge of, 446
    distinguished from insurance and indemnity, 439
    essentials of, 440
    nature of, 439
  surety—
    liability of, 441
    rights against creditor, 443
    rights against principal debtor, 444

TENDER—
  contract, for, 7
  money, of, 70

Thieves, 387

Uberrimae fidei, 53, 373, 439
Ultra Vires Contracts, 32
Undisclosed Principal, 207
Unincorporated Bodies, 33
Unsound Mind, 34, 204, 341, 448

Valuations, 450

Wagering, 56, 400
Warranties, 49, 128, 395
Warsaw Convention, 431–6
Wife, Agency of, 196